Biographical Dictionary of American Sports

BASEBALL

Biographical Dictionary of American Sports

BASEBALL

Edited by David L. Porter

GREENWOOD PRESS

New York • Westport, Connecticut • London

Library of Congress Cataloging-in-Publication Data

Biographical dictionary of American sports.

Bibliography: p.
Includes index.
1. Baseball—United States—Biography—Dictionaries.
2. Baseball—United States—History.   I. Porter, David
L., 1941–
GV865.A1b55   1987   796.357′092′2   [B]   86–12091
ISBN 0–313–23771–9 (lib. bdg. : alk. paper)

Library of Congress Catalog Card Number: 86–12091
ISBN: 0–313–23771–9

First published in 1987

Greenwood Press, Inc.
88 Post Road West, Westport, Connecticut 06881

Printed in the United States of America

The paper used in this book complies with the
Permanent Paper Standard issued by the National
Information Standards Organization (Z39.48–1984).

10 9 8 7 6 5 4 3 2 1

Contents

Preface

Sports have played a dynamic role in American life and history. Until the early 1970s, however, historians devoted relatively little space in scholarly works to American sport history and underplayed the significant impact of sports on the nation's development.[1] Several sports histories have been published since then,[2] but there still is a need for a scholarly, comprehensive biographical dictionary of notable American athletic figures. Sports encyclopedias typically concentrate on statistical achievements rather than comprehensive biographical background data, while sports biographical works usually treat a very select group of America's greatest athletic figures.[3]

This biographical dictionary, which consists of several companion volumes, provides comprehensive biographical information on over 2,000 of the nation's most extraordinary sports figures. The editor originally contemplated a one-volume biographical reference work covering 500 notable American sports figures. After compiling a list of around 4,000 worthy athletic subjects, however, the editor expanded the project to several companion volumes covering over 500 sports figures each. Biographical essays range from about 200 to 900 words depending on the relative importance of the sports figure. Subjects excelled as players, managers, coaches, officials, club executives, league administrators, rules developers, broadcasters, writers, and/or promoters. All subjects performed since the Revolutionary War, with a vast majority from the twentieth century. Most athletic subjects are either deceased or retired, but a considerable number remain active participants as of December 1986.

The companion volumes are classified by sport and list biographical entries in alphabetical order. Since baseball and football have played especially large roles in the development of American sport, the first two volumes are devoted exclusively to them. This volume covers baseball figures, while the second will encompass football subjects. The third and fourth cover distinguished persons from other team sports and prominent competitors in dual and individual sports. Major outdoors sports figures from auto racing, golf, harness and thoroughbred racing, lacrosse, skiing, soccer, tennis, and track and field will be featured in the third volume. Volume four will highlight major indoor sports persons from basketball, bowling, boxing, gymnastics, ice hockey, figure and speed skating, swimming and diving, weightlifting, and wrestling. In addition, a few other sports figures who do not fall into the categories mentioned above, including broadcasters, writers, and promoters, will be treated in either the third or fourth volume. Sports played both indoors and outdoors and subjects excelling in at least two sports will be covered in the volume deemed most appropriate by the editor.

Three general criteria determined the selection of athletic figures. First, the sports figure either must have been born or spent his or her childhood years in the United States. The editor made a few exceptions if the subject lived most of his or her adult life in the United States and had a crucial impact on the development of a particular American sport. Second, the person must have made exceptional accomplishments in at least one sport. Memberships in national Halls of Fame, notable statistical achievements and records, major awards earned, and championship teams performed for served as principal measurement standards. Third, the athletic figure must have made a significant impact on his or her sport. Essays describe the accomplishments and achievements of the subject and often assess his or her importance in the development of American sport.

The selection of baseball personalities for this volume proved very challenging. Before making final choices, the editor thoroughly researched baseball encyclopedias, daguerreotypes, the Hall of Fame, and history books.[4] The baseball figures selected for this volume usually met several of the criteria listed below:

1. Excelled as a player, manager, coach, umpire, and/or administrator;

2. Election to the National Baseball Hall of Fame in Cooperstown, NY;

3. A lifetime batting average near or above .300, with at least 2,000 hits or 300 home runs.

4. At least 175 major league wins as a pitcher and/or an outstanding win-loss percentage and excellent earned run average;

5. Demonstration of remarkable fielding and/or running abilities; and

6. Having a major impact on the development of professional baseball.

Society for American Baseball Research members helped the editor immeasurably in the selection of subject entries. John Thorn and James Smith III provided invaluable assistance on nineteenth century personalities, while John Holway helped on Negro league figures.[5] In several instances, contributing authors suggested subjects worthy of inclusion. Of course, the editor assumes ultimate responsibility for any significant baseball figure inadvertently excluded from this volume. Several promising active major league players still in the earlier part of their professional baseball careers are not included.

Over one-hundred contributors, mostly participants in either the Society for American Baseball Research or the North American Society for Sport History, submitted biographical entries for this volume. The authors are primarily university or college professors, many of whom teach courses in American sport history and are authorities on baseball history. Other professions frequently represented include public and private school teachers, writers, publishers, editors, journalists, librarians, consultants, and government employees. Each essay is signed.

Entries usually cite the baseball subject's (1) full given name; (2) date and place of birth and, where applicable, date and place of death; (3) parental background, if known; (4) formal education, if known; (5) wife and children, if applicable and known; and (6) major personal characteristics. Authors typically searched with diligence and persistence for these often elusive data; in several instances, however, all of the above information was not ascertainable.

Each essay highlights the subject's baseball career through December, 1986, and usually includes (1) entrance into professional baseball; (2) positions played; (3) teams played for with respective leagues; (4) lifetime batting, fielding, and/or pitching records and achievements; (5) notable individual records set, awards won, and All-Star and World Series appearances; and (6) personal impact on the sport. Professional baseball major leagues represented include the National Association (1871–1875), National League (1876–   ), American Association (1882–1891), Union Association (1884), Players League (1890), American League (1901–   ), Federal League (1914–1915), Negro National League (1920–1931, 1933–1948), Eastern Colored League (1923–1928), and Negro American League (1933–1950). Negro league entries typically contain fewer biographical data and statistical records because of the relative paucity of accurate information. Entries on the managers describe (1) teams guided, with inclusive dates; (2) major statistical achievements; (3) career win-loss records and percentages; (4) premier players developed; and (5) coaching philosophy, strategy, and innovations. Sketches of umpires, league officials, and club executives concentrate on positions held, notable accomplishments, and impact on baseball development.

The *Biographical Dictionary of American Sports* contains several additional features. First, bibliographies list pertinent sources by and about the sports figure. Several authors benefited from interviews or correspondence with the subject, or with relatives or acquaintances. Other contributors researched primary sources at the National Baseball Hall of Fame in Cooperstown, NY, *The Sporting News* in St. Louis, baseball club offices, city newspapers, and libraries throughout the United States. Second, cross-references are provided. When subjects treated in separate entries are referred to in a profile, they are asterisked at first mention; for example, Willie Mays.* When a person profiled in another volume of *Biographical Dictionary of American Sports* is mentioned, an abbreviation follows the asterisked name to indicate the appropriate volume: (FB) for Football, (OS) for Outdoor Sports, and (IS) for Indoor Sports. Third, the Appendixes list (1) all entries by main category; (2) players by main position played; (3) entries by place of birth; (4) Negro league baseball figures; (5) major and Negro leagues since 1871; and (6) National Baseball Hall of Fame members.

Several individuals contributed very generously to this project at various times. Paul MacFarlane of *The Sporting News* helped in the formative stages, while Tom Heitz of the National Baseball Hall of Fame Library and W. Lloyd Johnson of the Society for American Baseball Research answered queries made by numerous authors. Many unnamed baseball subjects, relatives, and acquaintances kindly furnished valuable personal data and reminiscences for contributors. The editor deeply appreciates the enormous amount of time, energy, and effort expended by all authors in searching for sometimes rather inaccessible information. Alan Asnen, Terry Baxter, Gaymon Bennett, Lowell Blaisdell, William Borst, John DiMeglio, John Evers, James Harper, Merl Kleinknecht, Douglas Martin, Frank Olmsted, Frank Phelps, Duane Smith, Luther Spoehr, and A. D. Suehsdorf contributed ten or more baseball entries. The editor is especially grateful to John L. Evers, Albert Figone, Leonard Frey, Frank Phelps, Duane Smith, and Luther Spoehr, who kindly agreed to write several essays when last minute cancellations occurred. William Penn College, notably librarians Marion Rains, Ed Goedeken, and Jim Hollis, made the atmosphere very conducive for working on this project. The editor also benefited from personal visits to the National Baseball Hall of Fame, Chicago Historical Society, and other repositories in the northeastern and midwestern United States. Mary Sive, Cynthia Harris, and Neil Kraner of Greenwood Press gave adept guidance and made many valuable suggestions in the planning and writing of this volume. Above all, the editor deeply appreciates the many sacrifices that his wife Marilyn and children Kevin and Andrea made throughout this project.

NOTES

1. Two notable exceptions were Foster Rhea Dulles, *A History of Recreation: America Learns to Play* (New York, 1965), and Herbert Manchester, *Four Centuries of Sport in America: 1490–1890* (New York, 1968).

2. These sport histories include John Rickards Betts, *America's Sporting Heritage: 1850–1950* (Reading, MA, 1974); Wells Twombly, *200 Years of Sport in America: A Pageant of a Nation at Play* (New York, 1976); John A. Lucas and Ronald A. Smith, *Saga of American Sport* (Philadelphia, 1978); William J. Baker, *Sports in the Western World* (Totowa, NJ, 1982); and Benjamin G. Rader, *American Sports: From the Age of Folk Games to the Age of Spectators* (Englewood Cliffs, NJ, 1983).

3. Notable sports encyclopedias include Frank G. Menke, *The Encyclopedia of Sports*, 5th rev. ed. (New York, 1975), and Roger L. Treat, *Encyclopedia of Sports*, 4th rev.

ed. (Cranbury, NJ, 1969). Two notable sport biographical works are Ralph Hickok, *Who Was Who in American Sports* (New York, 1971), and *The Lincoln Library of Sports Champions*, 14 vols. (Columbus, OH, 1974).

4. Sources consulted included Joseph L. Reichler, ed., *The Baseball Encyclopedia*, 6th ed. (New York, 1985); Paul MacFarlane, ed., *TSN Daguerreotypes of Great Stars of Baseball* (St. Louis, 1981); Gene Karst and Martin J. Jones, Jr., *Who's Who in Professional Baseball* (New Rochelle, NY, 1973); Martin Appel and Burt Goldblatt, *Baseball's Best: The Hall of Fame Gallery* (New York, 1977); Lowell Reidenbaugh, *Cooperstown: Where Baseball's Legends Live Forever* (St. Louis, 1983); and Robert Smith, *Baseball's Hall of Fame*, rev. ed. (New York, 1973). For the history of baseball, see Harold Seymour, *Baseball: The Early Years* (New York, 1960), and *Baseball:The Golden Age* (New York, 1971); David Quentin Voigt, *American Baseball: From Gentleman's Sport to the Commissioner System* (Norman, OK, 1966), *American Baseball: From the Commissioners to Continental Expansion* (Norman, OK, 1970), and *American Baseball: From Postwar Expansion to the Electronic Age* (University Park, PA, 1983); and Lawrence Ritter and Donald Honig, *The Image of Their Greatness: An Illustrated History of Baseball from 1900 to the Present* (New York, 1979).

5. John Holway, *Voices from the Great Black Baseball Leagues* (New York, 1975), Robert W. Peterson, *Only the Ball Was White* (Englewood Cliffs, NJ, 1970), James A. Riley, *The All-Time All-Stars of Black Baseball* (Cocoa, FL, 1983), and Donn Rogosin, *Invisible Men: Life in Baseball's Negro Leagues* (New York, 1983) also provided valuable information on Negro league figures.

David L. Porter

Abbreviations

LEAGUES AND ASSOCIATIONS

AA	American Association
AL	American League
AlL	Alaskan League
AML	Arkansas-Missouri League
ANL	American Negro League
ApL	Appalachian League
ArTL	Arizona-Texas League
AtA	Atlantic Association
AtL	Atlantic League
BeL	Bethlehem Steel League
BGL	Blue Grass League
BL	Border League
BRL	Blue Ridge League
BSL	Bi-State League
BStL	Big State League
CA	Central Association
CaL	California League
CAL	Canadian-American League
CaSL	California State League
CbL	Cumberland League
CdL	Colorado League
CIL	Central Insterstate League
CL	Central League
ClL	Colonial League
CmA	Commercial Association

CnL	Canadian League
CNL	Cuban National League
CntL	Continental League
CPL	Central Pennsylvania League
CrL	Carolina League
CRL	Cocoa Rookie League
CSL	Cotton States League
CtL	Connecticut League
CtSL	Connecticut State League
CUL	Cuban League
CUWL	Cuban Winter League
CWL	California Winter League
DL	Dakota League
ECL	Eastern Colored League
EDL	East Dixie League
EIL	Eastern Interstate League
EL	Eastern League
ESL	Eastern Shore League
ETL	East Texas League
EvL	Evangeline League
EWL	East-West League
FECL	Florida East Coast League
FIL	Florida International League
FL	Federal League
FlL	Florida League
FSL	Florida State League
GAL	Georgia-Alabama League
GCL	Gulf Coast League
GCRL	Gulf Coast Rookie League
GFL	Georgia-Florida League
GML	Green Mountain League
GSL	Georgia State League
HRL	Hudson River League
IA	International Association
IdSL	Idaho State League
IIL	Illinois-Iowa League
IL	International League
IlML	Illinois-Missouri League

IoSL	Iowa State League
IOL	Iron and Oil League
ISDL	Iowa and South Dakota League
ISL	Interstate League
KL	Kitty League
KSL	Kansas State League
KOML	Kansas-Oklahoma-Missouri League
MAL	Middle Atlantic League
MasL	Massachusetts League
MEL	Mexican League
MISL	Michigan State League
MiVL	Mississippi Valley League
ML	Midwest League
MnL	Manila League
MOL	Michigan-Ontario League
MOVL	Mississippi-Ohio Valley League
MVL	Missouri Valley League
MSL	Middle States League
MtL	Montana League
MtnSL	Mountain State League
MtSL	Montana State League
MWL	Minnesota-Wisconsin League
NA	National Association
NAL	Negro American League
NatL	North Atlantic League
NCAA	National Collegiate Athletic Association
NCL	North Carolina League
NCSL	North Carolina State League
NEAL	Northeast Arkansas League
NECSL	Northeastern Connecticut State League
NEL	New England League
NeL	Northeastern League
NeSL	Nebraska State League
NL	National League
NNL	Negro National League
NoA	Northern Association
NoL	Northern League
NSL	Negro Southern League

NTL	North Texas League
NWL	Northwestern League
NYPL	New York-Pennsylvania League
NYSL	New York State League
OIL	Ohio-Indiana League
OKSL	Oklahoma State League
OPL	Ohio-Pennsylvania League
OSL	Ohio State League
PCL	Pacific Coast League
PiL	Piedmont League
PL	Players' League
PNL	Pacific Northwest League
PoL	Pony League
POML	Pennsylvania-Ohio-Maryland League
PrL	Pioneer League
PRWL	Puerto Rican Winter League
PSA	Pennsylvania State Association
PSL	Pennsylvania State League
PuL	Puerto Rico League
RAL	Rookie Appalachian League
RRV	Red River Valley League
SA	Southern Association
SAL	South Atlantic League
SDA	South Dakota League
SEL	Southeastern League
SIL	Southwest International League
SL	Southern League
SML	Southern Michigan League
SNEL	South New England League
SpL	Sophomore League
SSL	Sooner State League
SWL	Southwestern League
3IL	Three I League
TL	Texas League
TOL	Texas-Oklahoma League
TSL	Tri-State League
UA	Union Association
UIL	Utah-Idaho League

USL	United States League
VL	Virginia League
WA	Western Association
WCaL	Western Canadian League
WCL	West Carolinas League
WeIL	Western International League
WIL	Wisconsin Illinois League
WL	Western League
WSL	Wisconsin State League
WTL	Western Tri-State League

CROSS-REFERENCES TO FORTHCOMING VOLUMES OF BIOGRAPHICAL DICTIONARY

FB	Football Volume
IS	Indoor Sports Volume
OS	Outdoor Sports Volume

FREQUENTLY CITED REFERENCE SOURCES

CB	*Current Biography*
DAB	*Dictionary of American Biography*
NYT	*New York Times*
SEP	*Saturday Evening Post*
SI	*Sports Illustrated*
TSN	*The Sporting News*
WWA	*Who's Who in America*

BASEBALL TERMS

ERA	Earned Run Average
HRs	Home Runs
MVP	Most Valuable Player
RBIs	Runs Batted In

Biographical Dictionary of American Sports

BASEBALL

A

AARON, Henry Louis "Hank" (b. 5 February 1934, Mobile, AL), player and executive, is the son of Herbert and Estelle (Pritchett) Aaron. His father worked as a rivet bucker in a shipbuilding company. His brother Tommy played major league baseball with Hank for three years in Milwaukee and four years in Atlanta and then coached with the Braves until his death. Other siblings include Sarah, Herbert, Jr., Gloria, Alfred, and Alfreda.

Aaron attended Central High School and graduated from Josephine Allen Institute in 1951. He played end and halfback with the football team, but the institute fielded no baseball team. At age 16 he began playing semi-professional baseball with the Mobile Black Bears. He performed one year with the Indianapolis Clowns (NNL) before signing with the Milwaukee Braves in 1952. After playing in Eau Claire, WI, and Jacksonville, FL (SAL), as a shortstop, he joined the Braves in 1954 and was converted to an outfielder.

During his twenty-three-year major league career, he established twelve major league career records. His best known, the home run record of 755, surpassed Babe Ruth's* 714. Other career records included most games played (3,298), most times at bat (12,364), most total bases (6,856), most extra-base hits (1,477), and most RBIs (3,771). His career records for games played and most at bats have been broken. He ranks second in runs scored (2,174) and eighth in doubles and sixth in putouts and chances among out-fielders. Aaron, who had a major league lifetime batting average of .305 and a lifetime slugging percentage of .555, set more major league career records than any other player.

As a major leaguer, Aaron played first, second, and third base, gained recognition as a great outfielder, and won a Gold Glove for defensive excellence in 1958. Besides playing in 24 All-Star games, he appeared in World Series against the New York Yankees in 1957 and 1958 and batted .364 in these Series (fourth highest). He was selected as the Major League Most Valuable Player in 1957 and *The Sporting News* Player of the Year in 1956 and 1963.

Aaron led the NL four times in home runs (1957, 1963, 1966, 1967), RBIs (1957, 1960, 1963, 1966) and slugging percentage (1957, 1959, 1962, 1971); twice in hits (1956, 1959), twice in batting average (.328, 1956; .355, 1959), and three times in runs scored (1957, 1963, 1967). He slugged 30 home runs and scored 100 runs on fifteen occasions, both major league records.

In 1969, Atlanta Braves fans named Aaron the Greatest Player Ever. He played his final two years with the Milwaukee Brewers (AL) in 1975 and 1976 and returned to the Braves as corporate vice-president in charge of player development in 1976. In January, 1982, Aaron was inducted into the National Baseball Hall of Fame and missed unanimous selection by only nine votes (406 of 415 votes). Willie Mays* alone received more votes, while only Ty Cobb* gained a higher percentage of the total vote.

Aaron married Barbara Lucas on October 3, 1953, and had five children, Gail, Hank Jr., Larry, Dorinda, and Ceci. After a 1971 divorce, Aaron married Billy Suber Williams on November 12, 1973. As director of player development, he has built the Atlanta Braves farm system into one of the most productive in baseball. He sponsors the Hank Aaron Scholarship Program and is involved with the Cystic Fibrosis Foundation, Sickle Cell Anemia Research Program, Salvation Army, and Boy Scouts.

BIBLIOGRAPHY: Henry Aaron and Furman Bisher, *Henry Aaron* (New York, 1974); Atlanta Braves publications and media files; Stanley Baldwin, *Bad Henry* (Radnor, PA, 1974); Robert T. Bowen, interview with Henry Aaron, January 17, 1985; Milton Shapiro, *The Henry Aaron Story* (New York, 1961).

Robert T. Bowen

ADAMS, Charles Benjamin "Babe" (b. 18 May 1882, Tipton, IN; d. 27 July 1968, Silver Spring, MD), player and sportswriter, was the son of a farmer of English descent. After moving to Mt. Moriah, MO, he attended school there for eight years. Since his family was poor, he was "adopted" by a local farmer Lee Sarver, who encouraged his baseball ambitions. In 1905 he won 30 games as a pitcher for Parsons, KS (MVL). He pitched the first half of the 1906 season with the St. Louis Cardinals (NL) and then hurled for Denver (WL) in late 1906 and 1907. After a brief stay with the Pittsburgh Pirates (NL) in late 1907, he pitched for Louisville (AA) the next year.

Adams performed for the Pirates from 1909 through 1926 but spent 1917 with St. Joseph, MO, and Hutchinson, KS, (WL), and most of 1918 with Kansas City (AA). The highlight of his major league career came in 1909, when he won 12 of 15 decisions in the regular season and triumphed in all three complete-game starts for the Pirates against the Detroit Tigers in the World Series. Besides hurling a shutout in the decisive seventh game, he allowed only 5 runs and 18 hits in the three games. The right-hander won 22 decisions in 1911, 21 in 1913, 18 in 1910, and 17 in 1919 and 1920. After the 1926 season, he left the Pirates, allegedly because Fred Clarke* shared the management with William McKechnie.* Adams spent the 1927 season with Johnstown, PA, (MAL), and Springfield, MO (WA), before retiring from baseball.

Control proved crucial to his success. During nineteen major league seasons, he walked only 430 batters and struck out 1,036 in 2,995.1 innings. In 1920 he walked only 18 batters in 263 innings. Adams averaged less than one walk a game in 1909, 1919, 1920, and 1922 and holds the major league record for the longest game pitched without surrendering a base on balls (21 innings against the New York Giants on July 17, 1914). He twelve times compiled ERAs under 3.00, highlighted by a sparkling 1.98 ERA in 1919. Forty-seven of his 194 wins were shutouts, including an NL-leading 7 in 1911 and 8 in 1920. He completed 206 of his 355 starts, losing 140 games and posting a 2.76 ERA. The 5 foot, 11 1/2 inch, 185 pounder possessed a good fastball but depended on his curveball as his most intimidating pitch.

After leaving baseball, Adams farmed at Mt. Moriah, became a sportswriter, and went overseas during World War II and the Korean War. He married Blanch Wright Adams on March 2, 1909, and moved with her to Silver Spring, MD, in 1958. Although remembered mainly for his 1909 World Series heroics and overshadowed by great contemporaries like Christy Mathewson,* Adams enjoyed a long, noteworthy career that embraced both the dead and live ball eras.

BIBLIOGRAPHY: Harry Grayson, *They Played the Game* (New York, 1945); Frederick G. Lieb, *The Pittsburgh Pirates* (New York, 1948).

Luther W. Spoehr

ADCOCK, Joseph Wilber "Joe" (b. 30 October 1927, Coushatta, LA), player and manager, grew up in rural northwest Louisiana Adcock began playing baseball seriously upon entering Louisiana State University in 1944. After attending L.S.U. from 1944 to 1947, he left school to play professional baseball. He played first base for Columbia, SC (SL), in 1947–1948 and for Tulsa (TL) in 1949 and joined the Cincinnati Reds (NL) in 1950.

Adcock, traded to the Boston Braves (NL) after the 1952 season, played on the original Milwaukee Braves when the franchise moved in 1953. Milwaukee's regular first baseman from 1953 through 1962, he developed into one of baseball's hardest hitters. On July 31, 1954, he hit four home runs and a double against the Brooklyn Dodgers, setting a major league record with 18 total bases in one game. With his homer the previous day, Adcock tied the record for most HRs (5) in two consecutive games. The 6 foot, 4 inch, 210 pound slugger became the first player to hit a ball into the center field bleachers at the Polo Grounds and the only one to slug a ball over the left field grandstands at Ebbets Field.

At Milwaukee, Adcock teamed with Henry Aaron* and Eddie Mathews* to form one of the NL's most dangerous trios. Adcock considered the Braves' pennant and World Series victory over the New York Yankees in 1957 his greatest baseball thrill. Although repeating as pennant winners in 1958, the Braves lost the World Series to the Yankees. Adcock's best seasons included 1954 (.308 batting average), 1956 (38 HRs, 103 RBIs), and 1961 (35 HRs, 108 RBIs). In 1960 he played in both All-Star games.

Adcock spent four mediocre AL seasons with the Cleveland Indians (1963) and the California (Los Angeles) Angels (1964–1966). In 1,959 career games, Adcock slugged 336 home runs, knocked in 1,122 runs, batted .277, and compiled a .485 slugging average. After managing Cleveland (AL) to eighth place in 1967 and Seattle (PCL) in 1968, he left baseball. He now lives on a thoroughbred horse farm in Coushatta, LA.

BIBLIOGRAPHY: Atlanta *Journal Constitution*, December 18, 1983; Allison Danzig and Joe Reichler, *The History of Baseball* (Englewood Cliffs, NJ, 1959); Gene Karst and Martin J. Jones, Jr., *Who's Who in Professional Baseball* (New Rochelle, NY, 1973); Paul MacFarlane, ed., *TSN Daguerreotypes of Great Stars of Baseball* (St. Louis, 1981).
                                                                           Clark Nardinelli

ALEXANDER, Grover Cleveland "Pete," "Old Pete", "Old Low-and-Away" (b. 26 February 1887, Elba, NE; d. 4 November 1950, St. Paul, NE), player, was the sixth of eight surviving children of farmer William and Margaret (Cootey) Alexander. After completing St. Paul High School, he became a telephone lineman and entered professional baseball as a pitcher in 1909 with Galesburg, IL (IlML). The following year he won 29 games, including 15 shutouts, for Syracuse, NY (NYSL), and was acquired by the Philadelphia Phillies (NL) for less than $1,000.

During his spectacular rookie season (1911), he recorded 28 wins, 7 shutouts (4 consecutive), 31 complete games, 367 innings pitched, 227 strikeouts, and a 2.57 ERA. His victories included a twelve-inning, one-hit, 1–0 shutout over the legendary Cy Young.*

Until he left the Phillies in 1918, Alexander peformed better each year. In 1915 he won 31 games, 9 of them consecutively. His 12 shutouts included 4 one-hitters (3 within 31 days) and 3 two-hitters. Besides pitching a league-leading 36 complete games, he hurled 376 innings and struck out 241 batters. Only eight pitchers in baseball history have surpassed his 1.22 ERA.

In 1916 Pete established career highs for victories (33), innings pitched (388), complete games (38), and shutouts (16). He shut out the Cincinnati Reds five times and all other opposing clubs at least once, allowed only 50 walks, and compiled a 1.55 ERA. In 1917 he won at least 30 games for the third straight year.

Fearing that Alexander would soon be lost to the U.S. Army, the Phils traded him to the Chicago Cubs (NL) with his longtime battery mate, "Reindeer Bill" Killefer. In seven years, Alexander had won 32 percent of Philadelphia's victories.

After pitching three games for the Cubs in the spring of 1918 and marrying Aimee Marie Arrants on May 31, he was shipped to France with a field artillery unit, the 342nd Battalion of the 89th Division. He returned from the war with sergeant's stripes and a hearing loss from gunfire, and began suffering from epileptic seizures. His longtime dependency on alcohol was aggravated.

In eight years with the Cubs, Alexander pitched impressively, but not at the phenomenal level he achieved in Philadelphia. Although increasingly eccentric from alcohol and epilepsy, he still won 128 games, or a quarter of Chicago's total, before being waived at age 39 to the St. Louis Cardinals (NL) in 1926.

"Old Pete," as he now was known, contributed 200 innings and nine victories to the Cardinals' pennant drive and easily won the second and sixth games of the World Series against the New York Yankees. Perhaps the best-remembered event of his splendid baseball career, however, came when he relieved Jesse Haines* in the seventh inning of the seventh game with two out and the bases full. Debate continues whether Alexander was sober or hung over when summoned from the bullpen. Nevertheless, he struck out Tony Lazzeri* on four knee-high curves to end the inning and set down the Yankees in the eighth and ninth inning to assure the Cardinals' championship.

"Old Low-and-Away" won 21 games in 1927 (thereby earning his peak contract of $17,500) and 16 in 1928, but his skills began fading. Traded back to the Phillies (NL), he was released in 1930 without earning the 374th victory that would have moved him ahead of Christy Mathewson.* He finished the 1930 season with Dallas (TL).

Alexander's superb major league statistics rank him among baseball's best pitchers: 373 wins and 208 losses (.642), 5,189.1 innings pitched, 2,199 strikeouts, and an average of only 1.65 bases on balls per nine-inning game. Aside from victories, he also tied Mathewson in complete games (439) and consecutive 30-win seasons (3). He holds the NL record for season shutouts (16), ranks second in lifetime shutouts (90), and twice won two games in one day. In three World Series, he won three games and lost two. An excellent fielder, he ranks third on the lifetime list for assists (1,419), fifth for total chances (1,633), and eighth for fielding average (.985).

Alexander's later life proved sad and humiliating. He pitched until age 51 for semi-pro and independent clubs, notably the bearded House of David. He was divorced by Aimee, remarried her, and was divorced again without having children.

Although 6 feet, 1 inch and a well-built 185 pounds, Alexander appeared unathletic. His manner seemed lackadaisical and his gait shambling, and his uniform never seemed to fit. Yet on the mound he performed with grace, economy, and perfect coordination. The right-hander's motion was easy, with barely a windup and scarcely a stride. He pitched quickly, his games often lasting only ninety minutes.

In a tough era, he treated rookies generously and bore his uncontrollable physical torments quietly. He was elected to the National Baseball Hall of Fame in 1938 and saw his Phillies in the 1950 World Series a month before he died.

BIBLIOGRAPHY: Grover Cleveland Alexander file, National Baseball Hall of Fame Library, Cooperstown, NY; Lee Allen and Tom Meany, *Kings of the Diamond* (New York, 1965); Bob Broeg, "Incredible Alex—The Mound Master," *TSN*, June 14, 1969, pp. 28–29; Paul F. Doherty, "Cy Young's Final Fling," *Baseball Research Journal*, 8 (1979), pp. 6–9; Stanley Fleming, "Complete Games by Pitchers," *Baseball Research Journal* 6 (1976), pp. 96–98; Leonard Gettelson, "Iron Man Pitching Peformances," *Baseball Research Journal* 7 (1977), pp. 19–23; Grand Island (NE) *Daily Independent*, November 4, 1950; Donald Honig, *October Heroes* (New York, 1979); Gordon Hurlburt, "Alexander's Shutout Record in 1916," *Baseball Research Journal* 11 (1982), pp. 13–15; Allen Lewis, *The Philadelphia Phillies* (Virginia Beach, VA, 1981); Frederick G. Lieb, *Baseball as I Have Known It* (New York, 1977); Tom Meany, *Baseball's Greatest Players* (New York, 1953); Lawrence S. Ritter, *The Glory of Their Times* (New York, 1966); Harold Seymour, *Baseball: The Golden Age* (New York, 1971); *Spalding's Official Base Ball Record, 1910* (New York, 1910). A. D. Suehsdorf, telephone interview with Mrs. Ruby Alexander, November, 1983.

A. D. Suehsdorf

ALLEN, Newton Henry "Newt" (b. 19 May 1903, Austin, TX), player, proved a slick fielding, switch-hitting second baseman from 1922 through 1944. The 5 foot, 7 1/2 inch, 170 pounder attended Western Baptist College for two and one-half years and has two sons from a marriage that terminated when he still played baseball. Aside from playing in 1931 with the St. Louis Stars, Allen spent his entire career with the Negro league Kansas City Monarchs. During winters he played baseball in CA, Cuba, Mexico, Puerto Rico, and Venezuela and toured the Far East in 1935–1936 with the Monarchs.

Noted for his pivot ability on double plays, he keystoned some outstanding infields on ten championship teams (NNL: 1923–1925, 1929, 1931; and NAL: 1937, 1939–1942). The 1924–1925 unit included Lemuel Hawkins (1B), Allen (2B), Newt Joseph (3B), and Dobie Moore (SS). The 1924 team won the first interleague Black World Series, while the 1925 team lost the repeat match. The 1929 Monarchs touted Dink Mothel (1B), Allen (2B), Joseph (3B), and Hallie Harding (SS), whereas the 1931 Stars featured George Giles (1B), Allen (2B), Dewey Creacy (3B), and Willie Wells* (SS). Kansas City infields of the late 1930s and early 1940s boasted John "Buck" O'Neil (1B), Allen and later Bonnie Serrell (2B), Rainey Bibbs and Allen (3B), and Ted Strong and then Jessie Williams (SS). The 1942 team won the revived Black World Series by sweeping the Washington Grays.

Allen's World Series appearances produced batting averages of .282 in

1924, .259 in 1925, and .267 in 1942 for an aggregate .272 mark, with 22
hits and 9 doubles in 81 at bats. He appeared in four East-West (Negro
league) All-Star games, starting the 1936 through 1938 and 1941 contests.

Ranked among the top second basemen from the old Negro leagues, Allen
usually held down the number two spot in the batting order. He hit .301
against white major league pitching in the off-season. Scanty Negro league
figures place his lifetime batting average in the .280s. He proved an aggressive
and intimidating performer whether defending or running the bases. After
retiring from baseball, Allen participated in Kansas City politics for the
Democratic party. He currently resides at a rest home in Cincinnati.

BIBLIOGRAPHY: Janet Bruce, *The Kansas City Monarchs: Champions of Black Baseball*
(Lawrence, KS, 1985), Chicago *Defender*, October, 1924, October, 1925; John Holway, *Voices from the Great Black Baseball Leagues* (New York, 1975); Robert W. Peterson,
Only the Ball Was White (Englewood Cliffs, NJ, 1970); Philadelphia *Afro-American*,
and *Independent Tribune*, September, October, 1942; Pittsburgh *Courier*, October,
1924; James A. Riley, *The All-Time All-Stars of Black Baseball* (Cocoa, FL, 1983).
                                                                    Merl F. Kleinknecht

ALLEN, Richard Anthony "Richie," "Dick" (b. 8 March 1942, Wampum,
PA), player and coach, became a leading power hitter of the 1960s and 1970s.
Allen entered professional baseball as an infielder at Elmira, NY (NYPL) in
1960. He played for Twin Falls (PrL) in 1961, Williamsport, PA (EL) in
1962, and Arkansas (IL) in 1963 before joining the Philadelphia Phillies (NL)
in late 1963. The NL Rookie of the Year in 1964, he hit .318, made 201
hits, scored 125 runs, and batted in 91 runs. Adversely, he struck out 138
times, a then NL record, and was considered a defensive liability at third
base. Through 1967, he hit over .300 each season. Allen's team proved quite
dependent on his batting and suffered badly during his slumps and frequent
injuries. After Allen played first base during the 1969 season, the Phillies
grew tired of him and his personality conflicts and traded him. He spent
single seasons with the St. Louis Cardinals (NL) and Los Angeles Dodgers
(NL) without achieving his earlier distinction.

After the 1971 season, Allen was traded to the Chicago White Sox (AL).
In spacious Comiskey Park a power hitter of Allen's character seemed unlikely
to flourish. But Allen enjoyed his finest seasons there, hitting over .300 for
three consecutive years. Remarkably, he led the AL in home runs with 37
in 1972 and 32 in 1974. In 1972 he drove in 113 runs and was chosen AL
Most Valuable Player. By this time he had become a competent fielder at
first base and had pioneered wearing a batting helmet in the field.

Before the 1975 season, Allen returned to the Phillies (NL). After hitting
.233 and .268 the next two seasons, he signed as a free agent with the Oakland
Athletics (AL). In 1977 he hit only .240 in 54 games and retired from baseball.
Allen alienated managements by avoiding spring training, which he found

unnecessary because of his strong physique, and by leaving teams before the end of seasons. During fifteen seasons, he batted .292 in 1,749 games, hit 351 home runs, and batted in 1,119 runs. Although never on a pennant winner, he played on the Phillies' 1976 divisional champions. He made two hits in nine times at bat as the Reds swept the series in three games.

Allen married Barbara Moore on February 18, 1962. Following his baseball career, he became a gentleman farmer and an owner of racehorses. In 1986 the White Sox appointed Allen a minor league batting instructor.

BIBLIOGRAPHY: *TSN Baseball Register, 1966* (*St. Louis, MO, 1966*) *p. 6; TSN Official Baseball Guide, 1961–1978* (St. Louis, MO, 1961–1978); *Who's Who in Baseball, 1977* 62nd ed. (New York, 1964–1977).

George W. Hilton

ALSTON, Walter Emmons "Smoky" (b. 1 December 1911, Venice, OH; d. 1 October 1984, Oxford, OH), player and manager, was the son of farmer and automobile worker Emmons and Lenora (Neanover) Alston. He graduated in 1929 from Milford Township High School, Darrtown, OH, and in 1935 from nearby Miami University, Oxford, OH, where his all-around athletic abilities qualified him for its Hall of Fame. Alston, who immediately joined the St. Louis Cardinals (NL) farm system, married Lela Alexander of Darrtown on May 10, 1930, and had one child.

As a slugging first baseman, Alston spent thirteen years in the minors, from 1935 to 1947. His clubs included Greenwood (EDL), Huntington, WV (MAL), Rochester, NY (IL), Houston (TL), Columbus (SAL), Springfield (MAL), Trenton (ISL), Nashua, NH (NEL), and Pueblo (WL). He won various league home run crowns four times, RBI titles twice, hit above .300 seven times, and once hit .350. Despite these impressive statistics he batted only once in the major leagues because stars Rip Collins, Jim Bottomley,* and Johnny Mize* played first base for the Cardinals. During the off-seasons, he taught and coached football and basketball at New Madison (OH) and Lewistown (OH) high schools. Branch Rickey,* who established the Cardinals' farm chain, regarded Alston as a fine managerial prospect and in 1940 made him a playing manager. Alston managed in the minor leagues for twelve seasons, at Portsmouth, OH and Springfield, OH (MAL), Trenton, NJ (ISL), Nashua, NH (NEL), Pueblo, CO (WL), St. Paul, MN (AA), and Montreal (IL), winning three pennants and finishing second three times. Rickey took over the Brooklyn Dodgers (NL) and in 1946 brought Alston in their system.

When Brooklyn fired Chuck Dressen after the 1953 season, Alston became the Dodgers' manager. The Dodgers had refused to give Dressen, who had won two consecutive NL championships, a multiyear contract. Alston managed the Dodgers for twenty-three seasons through 1976 and never asked for a multiyear contract. During that time, Alston's Dodgers won seven NL pennants (1955, 1956, 1959, 1963, 1965, 1966, 1974). In 1959 the Dodgers tied the Milwaukee Braves for first place, winning the playoff series in two straight games. In 1962 the Dodgers tied the San Francisco Giants and lost the playoff, two games to one. Alston was noted for quiet leadership and for meeting problems directly. During his tenure, the Dodgers won four world championships (1955, 1959, 1963, 1965). His outstanding players included Jim Gilliam, Maury Wills,* Sandy Koufax,* Roy Campanella,* Don Newcombe,* Duke Snider,* Sal Maglie, Pee Wee Reese,* Don Drysdale,* Steve Garvey,* Carl Furillo, and Jackie Robinson,* while his coaching staff included Leo Durocher,* Chuck Dressen, and Tommy Lasorda. Alston was named Major League Manager of the Year by *The Sporting News* in 1955, 1959, and 1963, and in 1983 was elected to the National Baseball Hall of Fame.

After retiring, Alston resided in Darrtown, served as an adviser and coach for the Dodgers, hunted avidly, rode horseback and trail bikes, and pursued furniture building and woodworking.

BIBLIOGRAPHY: Walter Alston, with Si Burick, *Alston and the Dodgers* (New York, 1966); Walter Alston, and Don Weiskopf, *Complete Baseball Handbook 1972* (Boston, 1972); Joseph L. Reichler, ed., *The Baseball Encyclopedia*, 6th ed. (New York, 1985), p. 616.

John E. DiMeglio

ANDERSON, George Lee "Sparky" (b. 22 February 1934, Bridgewater, SD), player and manager, is one of five children of Leroy and Shirley Anderson of Riverside, CA. Leroy, a house painter, moved his family to Los Angeles in 1942 to seek employment in the emerging defense industry. Young George learned to love baseball by playing with his father, a pitcher, and an uncle, a former minor league catcher. Rod Dedeaux, the enormously successful baseball coach at the nearby University of Southern California, nurtured Anderson's interest by making him team batboy. Anderson played baseball at Dorsey High School, from which he graduated in 1953, and spent his first professional season at Santa Barbara (CaL). On October 3, 1953, Anderson married Carol Valle, his high school sweetheart, whom he had known since fifth grade. The couple has three children, George Jr., Shirley, and Albert, and resides in Thousand Oaks, CA.

Anderson, one of the most successful major league managers ever, proved a fiery if marginally talented player for one major league and ten minor league seasons from 1953 to 1963. His early clubs included Pueblo, CO (WL) in 1954, Fort Worth (TL) in 1955, Montreal (IL) in 1956 and 1958 and Los Angeles (PCL) in 1957. After being named Most Valuable Player of the Montreal Royals (IL), the 5 foot, 9 inch, 168 pound Anderson earned his only big league job with the 1959 Philadelphia Phillies (NL). In 152 games as the Phillies' second baseman, he batted only .218 with 34 RBIs and was assigned to Toronto (IL) the next season. He played with Toronto through the 1963 season. Anderson realized that his limited physical skills would not take him back to the majors and consequently concentrated on learning managerial skills. Former major league manager Charley Dressen, who valued Anderson's competitiveness, fighting spirit, and alertness, encouraged him. "Little Man," he told him, "you ain't never missed a sign. Someday you'll be a manager."

He spent five years as a minor league manager, at Toronto in 1964, Rock Hill, SC (WCL) in 1965, St. Petersburg, FL (FSL), in 1966, Modesto, CA (CaL), in 1967, and Asheville, NC (SL), in 1968 and served as a coach for the San Diego Padres (NL) in 1969. In 1970 Anderson was named manager of the Cincinnati Reds (NL). From 1970 to 1978 he guided the decade's most dominant team, winning NL pennants in 1970, 1972, and 1973 and World Series titles in 1975 over the Boston Red Sox and in 1976 over the New York Yankees. The 1976 team, led by Pete Rose,* Joe Morgan,* and Johnny Bench,* ranks with the 1927 and 1961 Yankees among the three greatest teams of all time. No NL team since the 1921–1922 New York Giants had won two successive World Series. Anderson twice was named NL Manager of the Year and piloted the Reds longer than any other manager.

Despite his great success at Cincinnati, Anderson was released following the 1978 season. After being hired in 1979 by the Detroit Tigers (AL), Anderson through 1984 guided his talented young club to better records each year. In 1983 the Tigers won 92 games to finish in second place. After making Anderson the only manager to win 100 games in a season in both leagues, the Tigers in 1984 defeated San Diego in the World Series. Through the 1986 season, Anderson has compiled a 1,513–1,122 (.574) mark.

Anderson, respected for his hard work, honesty, and loyalty, has never forgotten his humble beginnings. His autobiography, *The Main Spark*, gratefully acknowledges the people who helped him attain his present position of prominence.

BIBLIOGRAPHY: Sparky Anderson and Si Burick, *The Main Spark: Sparky Anderson and the Cincinnati Reds* (Garden City, NY, 1978); Anthony Cotton, "Platoon, For-r-r-d Harch!" *SI* 52 (July 21, 1980), pp. 44ff; *CB* (1977), pp. 23–26; Ron Fimrite, "Sparky and George," *SI* 60 (June 11, 1984), pp. 70–74ff; Roger Kahn, "The Cincinnati Kid," *Time* 109 (April 11, 1977), p. 78.

Allen E. Hye

ANSON, Adrian Constantine "Cap," "Pop" (b. 17 April 1852, Marshalltown, IA; d. 18 April 1922, Chicago, IL), player and manager, was the son of Henry and Jeannette Rice Anson, both of English descent. His father, a transplanted New Yorker who founded Marshalltown, IA, homesteaded and operated a hotel there. Anson, a mediocre student, attended Marshalltown public schools, Notre Dame University, and the University of Iowa. In 1867 he played second base on the state championship Marshalltown baseball team.

From 1871 to 1875, Anson played professional baseball in the NA and received a salary of $800 to $1,800. In 1871 he played third base for the Rockford Forest City team (NA) and led his club with a .352 batting average. Because Rockford disbanded, in 1872 he joined the Philadelphia Athletics (NA) and hit a composite .352 average the next four seasons. When the NL was formed, the Chicago White Stockings secretly signed him for $2,000. When the Athletics offered him $2,500, Anson unsuccessfully sought to be released from the Chicago contract. In 1876 Anson married Virginia Fiegal of Philadelphia. They had seven children, Grace, Adrian H., Adele, Adrian, Jr., Dorothy, John, and Virginia.

Anson played with Chicago (NL) from 1876 to 1897, setting a major league longevity record. The 6 foot, 1 inch, 220 pound Anson compiled a .334 lifetime batting average and was the first NL player to surpass 3,000 hits. Anson hit a career-high .399 in 1881, exceeded the .300 mark in twenty of twenty-two seasons, and won batting titles in 1879, 1881, and 1888. A power hitter in a dead ball era, he drove in over 1,700 runs, hit 96 home runs, and led the NL in RBIs four times and in doubles twice. Anson, an inconsistent fielder, led first basemen in fielding twice and in errors three times, making 674 miscues.

The premier nineteenth-century manager, "Cap" piloted the White Stockings from 1879 to 1897. Ranked high among all-time managers, he won nearly 1,300 games for a .575 career win-loss percentage. In his first eight years at the helm, Anson directed Chicago to five NL pennants (1880–1882, 1885–1886). Chicago played St. Louis (AA) in the 1885–1886 post-season championships. In 1888 he signed a ten-year contract giving him control over field operations and 130 shares of club stock.

Anson, who popularized baseball, managed many exceptional players, including Larry Corcoran,* Jim McCormick,* Clark Griffith,* Michael Kelly,* Ed Williamson, and Bill Lange.* A strong disciplinarian, he did not allow his players to drink alcoholic beverages, smoke cigarettes or cigars, or use drugs. He was a strict taskmaster, expecting aggressive, team-oriented behavior. The innovative Anson utilized spring training, invented signals, devised the hit-and-run play, encouraged base stealing, developed coaching boxes, and rotated pitchers. He participated on American All-Star teams visiting England in 1874 and touring the world in 1888–1889.

Anson played an instrumental role in barring black players from organized baseball. He nearly cancelled games with Toledo and Newark because those clubs had black players, and he persuaded the New York Giants not to promote outstanding Negro pitcher George Stovey. From 1891 to 1897 Anson feuded with Chicago president James Hart over club policies and saw his team experience several losing seasons. Dismissed as manager in early 1898, he briefly piloted the New York Giants (NL) and returned to Chicago.

In *A Ball Player's Career* (1900), he described his professional baseball days and goodwill tours. Anson established billiard and bowling businesses in Chicago and organized a semi-professional baseball team, but these enterprises foundered financially. From 1905 to 1907, he served as city clerk of Chicago. Despite touring the vaudeville circuit to earn additional income, he went bankrupt and saw his home foreclosed. The NL attempted to establish a pension fund for Anson, but he rejected any assistance. Anson, who had hoped to become baseball's first commissioner in 1920, managed Chicago's Dixmoor Club at the time of his death. In 1939 he was elected to the National Baseball Hall of Fame. Anson's hitting and managerial skills, innovative leadership, and aggressive style helped transform a sandlot sport into the national pastime.

BIBLIOGRAPHY: Adrian C. Anson, *A Ball Player's Career* (Chicago, 1900); Arthur Bartlett, *Baseball and Mr. Spalding* (New York, 1951); "Baseball's Grand Old Man," *Literary Digest* 73 (May 6, 1922), pp. 62–65; Chicago *Tribune*, 1876–1898, April 18, 1922; *DAB* 1 (1928), pp. 311–312; Peter Levine, *A. G. Spalding and the Rise of Baseball* (New York, 1985); George S. May, "Major League Baseball Players from Iowa," *The Palimpsest* 36 (April, 1955), pp. 133–165; *NYT*, 1876–1898, April 18, 1922; David L. Porter, "Cap Anson of Marshalltown: Baseball's First Superstar," *The Palimpsest* 61 (July/August, 1980), pp. 98–107; Albert G. Spalding, *America's National Game* (New York, 1911); Roger H. Van Bolt, " 'Cap' Anson's First Contract," *The Annals of Iowa* 31 (April, 1953), pp. 617–625.

David L. Porter

APARICIO, Luis Ernesto, Jr., "Little Looie" (b. 29 April 1934, Maracaibo, Venezuela), player, manager, and executive, is the son of Luis E. Aparicio, Sr., and attended Maracaibo public schools. His father, an oil company tractor driver and an outstanding professional baseball player, was the first Venezuelan ever offered a major league contract and taught young Luis diamond skills. The good-natured 5 foot, 9 inch, 155 pound son left high school after his sophomore year to join a Caracas amateur baseball team. After batting .350 for Venezuela in the Latin American World Series, he played shortstop for the Barquisimeto Cardenales. In 1953 Aparicio began his pro career by replacing his father as shortstop with the Maracaibo Gavilanes. Chicago White Sox (AL) scout Luman Harris soon signed the excellent fielder for $6,000.

Aparicio played shortsop in 1954 with Waterloo, IA (3IL), and in 1955 with Memphis (SA), leading the SA in stolen bases and fielding. The right-handed throwing Aparicio, who married Sonia Llorente on October 1, 1956, and has five children, replaced Venezuelan Chico Carrasquel as starting Chicago White Sox shortstop in 1956. Besides thrilling fans with his fielding and base running, he batted .266 and stole 21 bases as AL Rookie of the Year. From 1956 to 1964, he established a major league record by leading the AL nine straight seasons in stolen bases. In 1959 his career-high 56 stolen bases helped the White Sox dethrone the New York Yankees as AL champions. He pilfered 160 bases from 1959 to 1961 to become the first major leaguer since Ty Cobb* to record at least 50 for three consecutive campaigns.

Aparicio tied a major league record by leading AL shortstops eight consecutive seasons in fielding (1959–1966) and broke one by pacing AL shortstops six straight years in assists (1956–1961). His AL records included most years (5) leading shortstops in games played (1956–1960) and highest fielding percentage by a shortstop in a season (.9826) in 1963. In tandem with second baseman Nelson Fox,* he topped AL shortstops in double plays (117) in 1960. Chicago president Bill Veeck* commented, "Luis always makes plays that can't be made." The Gold Glove was awarded to Aparicio as the best AL fielding shortstop from 1958 to 1962 and in 1964, 1966, 1968, and 1970. *The Sporting News* made him its All-Star team shortstop in 1964, 1966, 1968, 1970, and 1972.

In January, 1963, the White Sox traded the right-handed batter to the Baltimore Orioles (AL). Aparicio hit .276 to help the Orioles win the 1966 AL pennant and sweep the Los Angeles Dodgers in the World Series. He returned in November, 1967, to the White Sox, where he enjoyed his best hitting seasons with .280 in 1969 and a career-high .313 in 1970. He was traded in December, 1970, to the Boston Red Sox (AL) and finished his career there in 1973. The Maracaibo resident also co-owned a baseball club and managed several winters in Venezuela. During his eighteen-year major league career, he appeared in 2,599 games (AL record for shortstops), made 2,677 hits, scored 1,335 runs, stole 506 bases (10th best), and batted .262 lifetime. The eight-time AL All Star was selected from 1958 through 1962 and in 1969 and 1970. In World Series competition, he batted .308 in 1959 and .250 in 1966 against Los Angeles. Besides reviving base stealing, he demonstrated what smaller players could accomplish and that base running and fielding could rival home runs for excitement among fans. In 1984 he was elected to the National Baseball Hall of Fame.

BIBLIOGRAPHY: Ed Linn, "How Luis Aparicio Steals the Limelight," *Sport* 33 (June, 1962), pp. 62–70; "Luis Aparicio," *The Lincoln Library of Sports Champions*, vol. 1 (Columbus, 1974); Harold Rosenthal, "Luis Aparicio, SS," *Sport* 28 (November, 1959), pp. 20–21, 64–65; "Sharpest Shortstop," *Newsweek* 53 (June 29, 1959), pp. 86–87; Leonard Shecter, "The Case Against Aparicio," *Sport* 35 (June, 1963), pp. 42–44, 78–79; *TSN Baseball Register, 1967, 1973* (St. Louis, 1967, 1973); George Vecsey, "Luis Aparicio: New Life at 36," *Sport* 50 (December, 1970), pp. 42–45, 84–85; *Who's Who in Baseball*, 59th ed. (1974), p. 4; *WWA*, 38th ed. (1974–1975): p. 81.

David L. Porter

APPLING, Lucius Benjamin "Luke," "Old Aches and Pains" (b. 2 April 1907, High Point, NC), player, coach, and manager, grew up in a family of seven children in High Point and attended Fulton High School in Atlanta, GA. Active in all sports, he played football and baseball for Fulton and was

selected All-City shortstop. Appling participated in the same sports for Og-
lethorpe College, once hitting four home runs in a single game. At the end
of his sophomore year in 1930, he signed professionally with Atlanta (SA).
Although making 42 errors that year, the 5 foot, 10 inch, 180 pound Appling
was called the SA's best shortstop and batted .326. Following that season,
the Chicago White Sox (AL) paid Atlanta $20,000 for his contract. Appling
substituted for two years and from 1933 to 1949 held the regular shortstop
position there. He hit over .300 his first nine of ten full seasons and achieved
that level sixteen times. A weak fielder initially, he improved greatly under
instruction from Lew Fonseca and Jimmy Dykes.* The right-handed Appling
led the AL three times in chances and seven times in assists.

Appling's hitting made him famous. His lifetime record includes 2,749
hits, 1,302 walks, only 528 strikeouts, and a .310 batting average. Although
remembered for his homer off Warren Spahn* in a 1983 Old-timers game
at age 74, he hit only 45 round trippers in his career. But he proved a superb
contact hitter, whom Dykes called the league's most dangerous batter with
two strikes. Allegedly he once hit fourteen consecutive foul balls into the
stands to get even with an owner who would not give him two extra game
passes. He led the AL in hitting twice, batting .388 in 1936 and .328 in
1943. His 1936 mark, a personal high, led both leagues. Appling also made
204 hits in 1936, the only time he reached that level. Although the White
Sox did not reach the World Series during Appling's active career, he made
the All-Star team several times and in 1964 was elected to the National
Baseball Hall of Fame.

"Old Aches and Pains" often complained of having bad ankles, pink eye,
the flu, and a perpetual sore back, and suffered a broken finger and a broken
leg. Nevertheless, Appling usually led the White Sox in games played and,
at age 42, still batted .301. For many years he held the AL record for total
games played at shortstop. Even military service failed to hurt Appling's
game. He missed all 1944 games and all but 17 contests in 1945, yet still hit
.362.

Luke, one of the most popular players, subsequently was offered many
coaching jobs. He managed Memphis (SA) from 1951 to 1953 and was chosen
1952 minor league Manager of the Year. Appling also piloted Richmond (IL)
in 1954–1955, Memphis (SA) in 1959, and Indianapolis (AA) in 1962. He
coached for the Detroit Tigers (AL) in 1960, Cleveland Indians (AL) in 1960
and 1961, Baltimore Orioles (AL) in 1963, and Kansas City Athletics (AL)
from 1964 to 1967. In 1967, he managed Kansas City to a 10–30 record.
Appling scouted for the Oakland Athletics (AL) in 1968 and 1969, coached
for the White Sox in 1971 and 1972, Minnesota Twins (AL) in 1973, and
Atlanta Braves (NL) in 1974 before retiring. In 1932 he married Faye Dodd;
they had two daughters and one son. In recent years, Appling has resided
in the Atlanta area.

BIBLIOGRAPHY: Lee Allen, *The American League Story* (New York, 1962); Martin Appel and Burt Goldblatt, *Baseball's Best: The Hall of Fame Gallery* (New York, 1977); Warren Brown, *The Chicago White Sox* (New York, 1952); Richard Lindberg, *Who's on Third?* (South Bend, IN, 1983); David Neft, Richard Cohen, and Jordan Deutsch, *The Sports Encyclopedia: Baseball*, 5th ed. (New York, 1982); *Newsweek* 30 (September 22, 1947), pp. 79–80; *NYT*, 1933–1974, December 28, 1936, March 29, 1938, November 28, 1943; Lowell Reidenbaugh, *Cooperstown: Where Baseball's Legends Live Forever* (St. Louis, 1983).

Thomas L. Karnes

ASHBURN, Don Richie "Whitey," "Put-Put" (b. 19 March 1927, Tilden, NE), player and broadcaster, is the son of blacksmith Neil and Genevieve Ashburn. Nicknamed "Whitey" and "Put-Put," he attended Norfolk Junior College in Nebraska. On November 6, 1949, he married Nebraskan Herberta Cox; they have four daughters and two sons.

In 1945 began his career as a catcher with Utica, NY (EL), but manager Eddie Sawyer shifted him to the outfield. After a year in military service and another year at Utica, he excelled from 1948 to 1959 as center fielder for the Philadelphia Phillies (NL). An alert player and a clutch performer, he made a perfect throw to nail the Brooklyn Dodgers' Cal Abrams at home plate to enable the 1950 Phils to win the NL pennant on the season's final day. After being traded to the Chicago Cubs (NL) in 1960, Ashburn was sold to the New York Mets (NY) for the 1962 season. He joined the Phillies' television-radio broadcasting team in 1963 and combined perceptive commentary with a wry sense of humor.

With a career .308 batting average and 2,574 hits, Ashburn won NL batting titles in 1955 and 1958 and four times led the NL in singles to tie the league record. Ashburn also led the NL in walks three times and tied for the lead once and paced the league three times in hits, twice in triples, and once in stolen bases. In 1948 he hit safely in 23 consecutive games to set an NL rookie record. Defensively, he established records by leading the NL in outfield putouts and total chances accepted nine years, in most years with 500 or more putouts by an outfielder (four), and in most years with 400 or more putouts by an outfielder (nine). Three times he paced the NL in outfield assists, and once led and twice tied for the lead in double plays involving an outfielder. A durable player, he appeared in 731 consecutive games and averaged 146 games his fifteen seasons. In three All-Star games, he batted an extraordinary .556.

A serious, hustling player with a superb knowledge of the strike zone, Ashburn excelled as a defensive outfielder and an intelligent hitter and remains a perennial candidate for election to the National Baseball Hall of Fame. Besides his television career, Ashburn wrote the introduction to Allen Lewis' *The Philadelphia Phillies: A Pictorial History* (1981) and compiled the *Phillies Trivia Book.*

BIBLIOGRAPHY: Joe Archibald, *The Richie Ashburn Story* (New York, 1960); Frank Bilovsky and Rich Westcott, *The Phillies Encyclopedia* (West Point, NY, 1983); Mary G. Bonner, *Baseball Rookies Who Made Good* (New York, 1964); Allen Lewis, *The Philadelphia Phillies: A Pictorial History* (Virginia Beach, VA, 1981); Allen Lewis, and Larry Shenk, *This Date in Philadelphia Phillies History* (Briarcliff Manor, NY, 1979); Frederick G. Lieb and Stan Baumgartner, *The Philadelphia Phillies* (New York, 1953).

Ralph S. Graber

ASHFORD, Emmett Littleton (b. 23 November 1914, Los Angeles, CA; d. 1 March 1980, Marina Del Ray, CA), umpire, became the first black major league umpire and a racial pioneer in sports officiating. Abandoned at an early age by their father, Ashford and an older brother grew up with their mother, an ambitious, achievement-oriented woman who worked as a secretary for the *California Eagle*, a black newspaper. He attended Los Angeles public schools and served as the first black student body president and newspaper editor at Jefferson High School. An excellent student, he matriculated at Los Angeles City College. Ashford received a Bachelor of Science degree from Chapman College, where he played baseball and was sports editor of the college newspaper.

Ashford began umpiring sandlot and recreation league games during a brief career as a semi-pro player. After serving in the U.S. Navy (1944–1947), he took a civil service job with the U.S. Post Office in Los Angeles. Ashford devoted an increasing amount of time to umpiring high school, junior college, and college games. In 1951 he became the first black umpire in professional baseball on the recommendation of major league scout Rosey Gilhousen. During fifteen years in the minor leagues, he umpired in the SIL (Class C), 1951–1952; ArTL (Class C), 1952; WeIL (Class A), 1953; and PCL (Class AAA), 1954–1965; and served as PCL umpire-in-chief 1963–1965. In the off-season Ashford became the first black to referee high school, junior college, and small college football and basketball in California. He also umpired during the winter in the Dominican Republic (1958–1959, 1964).

In 1966 Ashford reached the major leagues as a member of the AL staff. He umpired the 1967 All-Star Game and the 1970 World Series and conducted umpiring clinics in Canada, Europe, and Korea. After retiring in 1970, Ashford umpired Pacific-10 Conference college games, served as commissioner and umpire-in-chief of the pro-amateur AIL, and worked until his death as the West Coast public relations representative for Commissioner Bowie Kuhn.*

Ashford's major league career proved controversial apart from the racial slurs and hostilities directed toward the first black umpire. Some umpires resented his popularity with the fans and the press. He was criticized for his flamboyance, symbolized by wearing cufflinks and using exaggerated motions to make calls. He was also charged with being a "clown" who sacrificed accuracy for attention. Others believed that he was promoted to the majors only because of pressures from civil rights groups and government officials.

The criticisms were misplaced. Although his skills had deteriorated by the time he reached the majors at age 51, he proved a thoroughly competent arbiter. His style and popularity violated the traditionally conservative demeanor of umpires but helped initiate the modern era of sports officials with personality and recognition. Political pressures aided his promotion, but his long overdue elevation to the majors had been delayed by racist attitudes.

A pioneer of racial integration in sport, the courageous, determined Ashford used wit and charm to overcome the obstacles of racism on and off the field. Ashford may be of greater historical importance than Jackie Robinson* because he represents the advancement of blacks in baseball to a role other than that of hired performer.

BIBLIOGRAPHY: "Ashford Arrives," *Ebony* 21 (June, 1966), pp. 65–70; "Emmett Ashford: Ultra Ump," *Look* 30 (October 4, 1966), pp. 92–95; Larry R. Gerlach, *The Men in Blue: Conversations with Umpires* (New York, 1980); Los Angeles *Sentinel*, March 6, 1980; Los Angeles *Times*, March 2, 4, and 7, 1980; *NYT*, June 13, 1954, September 16, 1965, December 4, 1970, and March 4, 1980; Art Rust, Jr., *Get That Nigger off the Field!* (New York, 1976).

Larry R. Gerlach

AVERILL, Howard Earl "Rock," "The Earl of Snohomish" (b. 21 May 1902, Snohomish, WA; d. 16 August 1983, Everett, WA), player, was the son of logger Joseph and area pioneer Annie (Maddox) Averill. After attending Snohomish public schools, Averill played with the Snohomish Pilchuckers town team and then semi-professionally with teams in Bellingham, WA, and Butte, MT. In 1926 he began his professional career with the San Francisco Seals (PCL). He married Gladys Loette Hyatt on May 15, 1922, and had four sons, Howard, Bernard, Earl, and Lester. Young Earl played major league baseball from 1956 through 1963.

Nicknamed "Rock," Averill excelled for San Francisco three seasons before the Cleveland Indians (AL) purchased him. The first Hall of Famer to homer his first time at bat, the left-handed slugger hit 238 home runs over thirteen seasons. After playing for Cleveland from 1929 to 1939, he was traded to the Detroit Tigers (AL). He spent 1940 with the Tigers, participating in his only World Series. He concluded his major league career in 1941 with the Boston Braves (NL), retiring prematurely because of a back injury suffered in 1937.

One of the game's great outfielders, Averill compiled a lifetime .318 batting average and achieved a career high of .378 in 1936. At various times the center fielder led the AL in games (1934), hits (1936), at bats (1931), triples (1936), and putouts (1929, 1934). During his ten peak years, "Rock" averaged

189 hits, 37 doubles, 12 triples, 23 home runs, 115 runs scored, 108 RBIs, and a .534 slugging percentage. He played in 673 straight games from 1931 through 1935, one of the longest such records.

The batter who broke Dizzy Dean's* toe with a line drive in the 1937 All-Star Game, Averill became the only outfielder selected for the first six All-Star games. He made *The Sporting News* Major League All-Star team in 1931, 1932, 1934, and 1936. Averill toured in 1931 with the Babe Ruth All-Stars and in 1934 played on the All-Star team visiting the Orient. In a 1930 doubleheader against Washington, "The Earl of Snohomish" hit four home runs, nearly missed on two other long flies, and drove in eleven runs.

Averill, who stood 5 feet, 9 inches, and weighed 172 pounds, saw his Number 3 uniform retired by the Indians. Bob Feller* and Lou Boudreau* remain the only other Indians so honored. In 1975 Averill belatedly was elected to the National Baseball Hall of Fame.

BIBLIOGRAPHY: Russ Dille, "I Remember Earl Averill," *Sports Collectors Digest* 10 (October 14, 1983), pp. 144, 146; John Eichmann, "Perennial American League Centerfielder," *Sports Scoop* 1 (March-July, 1973); Steve Mitchell, "DeWitt Nominates Earl Averill," *Sports Scoop* 2 (March, 1974), p. 35.; Lowell Reidenbaugh, *Cooperstown: Where Baseball's Legends Live Forever* (St. Louis, 1983); Doug Simpson, "The Earl of Snohomish," *Baseball Research Journal* 11 (1982), pp. 151–161.

                                                              Douglas G. Simpson

B

BAKER, John Franklin "Home Run" (b. 13 March 1886, Trappe, MD; d. 28 June 1963, Trappe, MD), player, manager, and executive, was the son of Franklin Adams Baker, a farmer, and Mary Catherine (Rust) Baker. After grade school, Baker began playing baseball in local leagues and later failed in a tryout with the Baltimore Orioles. In 1908 he signed professionally with Reading, PA (TSL).

In late 1908 the Phildelphia Athletics (AL) acquired his contract. The 5-foot 11-inch, 175 pound Baker quickly became a regular third baseman. In his 1909 debut Baker hit a home run in the first inning with the bases loaded. In the dead ball era, he led the AL in home runs from 1911 through 1914. Nicknamed "Home Run," he hit two round trippers in the 1911 World Series against the New York Giants. Despite his nickname, Baker never hit more than twelve home runs in a single season and slugged only 96 lifetime, ranking behind scores of later home run sluggers.

With the Athletics for seven years, Baker played under renowned manager Connie Mack.* The Philadelphia club made the World Series four times during the span (1910, 1911, 1913, and 1914), winning the world championship twice. In 1914 Baker played with Stuffy McInnis,* Eddie Collins,* and Jack Barry in the Athletics' famous "$100,000 infield." Baker was sold to the New York Yankees (AL) for $37,500 in 1915, when Mack trimmed his team's budget by selling his high-paid stars. After playing semi-pro ball in Upland, PA, in 1915, Baker played for the New York Yankees (AL) until 1922. In 1920 he temporarily retired following the death of his first wife, Ottilie Rosa Tschantre, whom he had married in 1909. They had two daughters. He rejoined the Yankees for the 1921 and 1922 seasons, participating in World Series both times. In 1919 Baker hit 10 home runs, placing second in the AL behind Boston Red Sox pitcher Babe Ruth.* A year later, Ruth hit 54 home runs and rewrote all previous power standards.

A left-handed batter who threw right-handed, Baker holds the fifth highest career batting average in World Series history. Using a 52 ounce bat, he compiled a .307 career batting average. Baker's speed declined, causing him to retire after the 1922 season. That year he married Margaret E. Mitchell and subsequently had two children.

After retiring as a player, Baker served in 1924 and 1925 as a manager of Easton, MD (ESL), and later was president of that club for a year. During retirement he managed several Maryland farms, raised and trained hunting dogs, fished, and hunted. In 1955 he was chosen for the National Baseball Hall of Fame. Baker's power focused attention on the home run, preparing the baseball world for later sluggers who revolutionized the national sport. One must speculate what Baker might have done with a lighter bat and a livelier ball.

BIBLIOGRAPHY: *DAB*, Suppl. 7 (1961–1965), pp. 27–28; *NYT*, June 29, 1963; Joseph L. Reichler, ed., *The Baseball Encyclopedia* (New York 1985); Lowell Reidenbaugh, *Cooperstown: Where Baseball's Legends Live Forever* (St. Louis, 1983); Lawrence S. Ritter, *The Glory of Their Times* (New York, 1966).

Stephen D. Bodayla

BANCROFT, David James "Dave," "Beauty" (b. 20 April 1891, Sioux City, IA; d. 9 October 1972, Superior, WI), player, coach, and manager, was the son of Milwaukee Railroad news vendor and truck farmer Frank and Ella (Gearhart) Bancroft. The youngest of three children, he had a brother, Robert, and a sister, Annis Jane (Garretson). Bancroft attended Hopkins Grade School and Sioux City Central High School (1908–1910), playing baseball there and on community sandlots. After moving to Superior, WI, he married Edna H. Gisin in November 1910; they had no children. In 1909 he began his professional baseball career with a brief stint at Duluth-MN (MWL). After being released, he joined Superior (MWL) as the regular shortstop the same season. The light-hitting Bancroft starred defensively there through 1911 and at Portland, OR (PCL), from 1912 to 1914.

In the NL, he played shortstop with the Philadelphia Phillies (1915–1920), New York Giants (1920–1923, 1930), Boston Braves (1924–1927), and Brooklyn Dodgers (1928–1929). The scrappy 5 foot, 9 1/2 inch, 160 pound Bancroft made 2,004 hits, including 320 doubles, and compiled a career .279 batting average. A leadoff batter, the switch-hitting Bancroft crowded the plate and walked 827 times. Nicknamed "Beauty," he batted over .300 five seasons, stretched many singles into extra-base hits, scored 1,048 runs, and knocked in 591 runs. Defensively, Bancroft possessed quick hands, moved gracefully in either direction, and excelled at fielding bad-hop ground balls, cutting off outfield throws, and picking runners off base. He made only 660 errors in 12,000 fielding chances for a lifetime .944 mark. Sportswriter Frank Graham called Bancroft "the greatest shortstop the Giants ever had and one of the greatest that ever lived," while the Philadelphia Sports Writers Association in 1954 named him the Phillies' "all-time outstanding shortstop."

As a rookie in 1915, Bancroft hit .254 for Philadelphia and sparked the Phillies to their first NL pennant. Although he batted .294 in the World Series, the Phillies lost to the Boston Red Sox. New York Giants manager John McGraw,* who considered Bancroft baseball's best shortstop, acquired him in a June, 1920, trade and made him team captain. Later that month, Bancroft made six singles in a game against Philadelphia. An energetic, competitive, inspirational, intuitive leader, he helped the Giants win the 1921–1923 NL pennants and two World Series titles. Bancroft threw out three New York Yankee runners attempting to take extra bases in the 1921 World Series and in 1922 handled 984 chances defensively and led shortstops in double plays.

From 1924 to 1927, Bancroft piloted the Boston Braves (NL). Although batting over .300 twice, he lacked talented players and managed the club to four second division finishes. Bancroft coached with the New York Giants (1930–1932) and had hoped to pilot the club when McGraw retired. He managed the Minneapolis Millers (AA) in 1933, Sioux City Cowboys (WL) in 1936, and St. Cloud Rox (NoL) in 1947. Bancroft worked as warehouse supervisor for Lakehead Pipe Line Company until his 1956 retirement. His honors included election to the National Baseball Hall of Fame (1971), Iowa Sports Hall of Fame (1954), Superior Athletic Hall of Fame (1964), Sioux City Athletic Hall of Fame (1965), and Duluth Sports Hall of Fame (1971).

BIBLIOGRAPHY: Martin Appel and Burt Goldblatt, *Baseball's Best: The Hall of Fame Gallery* (New York, 1977); Des Moines *Register*, March 28, 1954, October 11, 1972; Frank Graham, *The New York Giants* (New York, 1952); Harold Kaese, *The Boston Braves* (New York, 1948); Frederick G. Lieb and Stan Baumgartner, *The Philadelphia Phillies* (New York, 1953); George S. May, "Major League Baseball Players from Iowa," *The Palimpsest* 36 (April, 1955), pp. 133–165; *NYT*, November 13, 1923, October 15, 1927, October 10, 1972; David L. Porter, correspondence with Frank Garretson, July 13, 1984, David L. Porter Collection, Oskaloosa, IA; David L. Porter, correspondence with David Mook, July 11, 1984; Joseph L. Reichler, ed., *The Baseball Encyclopedia*, 6th ed (New York, 1985), pp. 617, 696; Lowell Reidenbaugh, *Cooperstown: Where Baseball's Legends Live Forever* (St. Louis, 1983); Sioux City *Journal*, November 26, 1926; Robert Smith, *Baseball's Hall of Fame* (New York, 1973); Superior *Evening Telegram*, July 30, 1927, January 23, 1954, October 10, 1972.

David L. Porter

BANKS, Ernest "Ernie," "Mr. Cub" (b. 31 January 1931, Dallas, TX), player and coach, is the son of laborer Eddie and Essie Banks and had seven brothers and four sisters. At Booker T. Washington High School in Dallas, Banks starred in football, basketball, track, and baseball. During the summer, he played for the Detroit Colts, a Negro baseball team. Following graduation in 1950, Banks joined the Kansas City Monarchs (NAL). After serving in the U.S. Army (1951–1952), Banks rejoined the Monarchs until the Chicago Cubs (NL) purchased him in 1953.

Banks, a shortstop–first baseman, played for the Cubs from 1953 to 1971. Although the Cubs finished pennantless, Banks starred in contrast. In 2,528 games, he batted 9,421 times, scored 1,305 runs, made 2,583 hits, 407 doubles, 90 triples, 512 home runs (eleventh place on the all-time list), knocked in 1,636 runs, and compiled .274 batting and .986 fielding averages. Banks, who leads the Cubs in nine of eleven modern all-time offensive departments, holds the NL record with 5 grand slam home runs in 1955. He slugged 12 career grand slams.

Besides establishing a major league season record for home runs by a shortstop (47), Banks hit over 40 home runs in five different seasons and led the NL in 1958 and 1960. He hit at least two home runs in one game forty-two times and three in one game four times. In 1958 and 1959 he led the NL in RBIs with 129 and 143, respectively.

An outstanding defensive player, Banks in 1969 led NL first basemen with a .997 fielding mark. Ten years earlier, he had set the single season major league record for fielding percentage as a shortstop (.985), making the fewest errors (12) at that position. A team player and an inspirational leader, Banks in 1969 was voted the "Greatest Cub Ever" and "Chicagoan of the Year" and later was the first black enshrined in the Texas Hall of Fame. Banks, the NL's Most Valuable Player two consecutive seasons (1958–1959), made several All-Star teams (1955–1962, 1965, 1967, and 1969).

Married to Eloyce Johnson in 1958, Banks has three children, twin sons Joey and Jerry and daughter Jan Elizabeth. Since retirement, Banks has served as a coach and Director of Group Sales and Community Relations for the Cubs. In 1982 he became Vice-President of Associated Film Promotions in Los Angeles. The co-author of the book "Mr.Cub," Banks in 1977 was elected to the National Baseball Hall of Fame and became the eighth player so honored in the first year of eligibility.

BIBLIOGRAPHY: Ernie Banks and Jim Enright, "Mr. Cub" (Chicago, 1971); Jim Enright, Chicago Cubs (New York, 1975); TSN Official Baseball Register 1973, (St. Louis, 1973).

John L. Evers

BARLICK, Albert Joseph "Al" (b. 2 April 1915, Springfield, IL), umpire, is the son of coal miner John and Louise (Gorence) Barlick. His attendance at Converse High School, Springfield, was cut short by financial necessity. He worked as a loader (helping his father) at bituminous coal mine Peabody No. 59 in Springfield until a labor strike shut it down. Barlick began umpiring in 1935 in a local municipal league. In August, 1936, he entered organized baseball as umpire in the Class D NEAL. Barlick's ability, efficiency, and hard work earned him rapid promotion to the PiL in 1937 and 1938, the EL in 1939, and the IL in 1939 and 1940.

During September, 1940, Barlick joined the NL umpires as a replacement for the ailing Bill Klem.* With a strong performance and Klem's endorsement, Barlick become a regular NL umpire in 1941 and remained one until retirement after the 1971 season. Interruptions included World War II service in the U.S. Coast Guard from October, 1943, to November, 1945; medical leave during the 1956 and 1957 seasons because of heart strain; and "resignation" for five days in 1960 due to a misunderstanding with NL officials. During his active career, he umpired in seven World Series and seven All-Star games. Since retirement, he has served as an NL consultant.

The burly 5 foot, 11 inch, 185 pound Barlick frequently was called the loudest, most colorful, and best umpire in baseball. Unique vigorous "out" gestures and booming "stee-ruck-huh" calls identified him unmistakably. Barlick's total commitment, unerring accuracy, and complete control of the game made him a truly great arbiter. When *The Sporting News* writers' poll in 1961 voted Barlick the best NL umpire, he protested his displeasure of the results as a slur on his peers by persons not competent to judge the arbiters' professionalism. He accepted an Umpire of the Year award in 1970, however, because the balloting had been conducted among umpires. A lifetime Springfield, IL, resident, Barlick married Jennie Marie Leffel of Springfield in February, 1941, and has two daughters, Marlene and Kathleen.

BIBLIOGRAPHY: Albert J. Barlick, "Voice of the Umpires," *TSN*, October 26, 1974; Harold Parrott, "Al Barlick, 25, Youngest Umpire . . . ," *TSN*, October 17, 1940; Frank V. Phelps, correspondence with Albert J. Barlick, October 19, 1985, Frank V. Phelps Collection, King of Prussia, PA; J. G. Taylor Spink, comp., *TSN Baseball Register, 1958* (St. Louis, 1958), p. 301; *TSN*, November 6, 1957, August 2, 1961, October 15, 1966, December 25, 1971; Brad Willson, "Veteran Al Barlick Honored as Umpire of Year," *TSN*, February 20, 1971; Herbert Warren Wind, "How an Umpire Gets That Way," *SEP*, 226 (August 8, 1953), pp. 25, 119–122.

Frank V. Phelps

BARNARD, Ernest Sargent "Barny" (b. 17 July 1874, West Columbia, WV; d. 27 March 1931, Rochester, MN), executive, was the son of minister Elias Barnard, who moved his family to several West Virginia towns before settling in Delaware, OH. He attended Otterbein Academy and College, graduating in 1895, and coached the football and baseball teams there the next three years. After moving to Columbus, OH, he became secretary of that city's Builders Exchange and also coached the Ohio Medical University football team. Nicknamed "Barny," he became sports editor in 1900 of the Columbus *Dispatch*.

In 1903 Cleveland Indians owner Charles Somers* hired Barnard as the club's traveling secretary. After the 1908 season, he was elevated to vice-president and general manager and introduced uniform numbers. When James C. Dunn purchased the team in 1916, he initially took Barnard's responsibilities away. Dunn reappointed Barnard to his former position as general manager after two years. His 1920 club won Cleveland's first AL pennant and defeated Brooklyn in the World Series.

Upon Dunn's death in 1922, Barnard assumed the presidency of the Indians. His clubs generally finished in the middle of the AL standings and challenged for the pennant only in 1926, when they finished a close second to the New York Yankees. In the mid–1920s, Barnard played an increasingly important role as mediator and peacemaker in the bitter disputes between baseball commissioner Judge Kenesaw Mountain Landis* and AL president Ban Johnson.*

The AL owners in 1927 ousted Johnson, the league's founder and president since 1900. Barnard was named AL president after satisfying Dunn's widow by selling the Indians to a group of Cleveland businessmen headed by Alva Bradley. As AL president, he acted as an administrator and left the public spotlight to the commissioner. He applied modern management principles to the AL office in Chicago, running it with an even disposition and a sense of order. In 1930 the AL owners reelected him to a five-year term.

He entered the Mayo Clinic in March 1931 and died there only a few hours before Johnson. He was survived by his widow, the former Josephine Flick of Cleveland, whom he had married in 1918. His quiet, efficient administrative approach and his concern for good public relations contributed to baseball's image of respectability in the 1920s.

BIBLIOGRAPHY: Lee Allen, *The American League Story* (New York, 1962); Franklin Lewis, *The Cleveland Indians* (New York, 1949); Eugene C. Murdock, *Ban Johnson* (Westport, CT, 1982); Harold Seymour, *Baseball: The Golden Age* (New York, 1971); J. G. Taylor Spink, *Judge Landis and Twenty-five Years of Baseball* (New York, 1947).

William E. Akin

BARNES, Roscoe Conkling "Ross" (b. 8 May 1850, Mt. Morris, NY; d. 8 February 1915, Chicago, IL), player, was a hard-hitting infielder for five consecutive NA and NL pennant winners from 1872 to 1876. Barnes hit over .400 for the Boston Red Stockings (NA) in 1872 and 1873 and for the Chicago White Stockings (NL) in 1876, won the batting championship in 1873, 1875, and 1876, and hit for power. His lifetime .379 batting average led the NA, while his NL career mark was .319. His career .351 average paced all infielders until Rogers Hornsby* fifty years later.

The right-handed hitting Barnes exploited one of the scoring rules. Through the 1876 season, any batted ball hit in fair territory was considered fair even if it subsequently went foul. Barnes mastered this type of hitting and proved virtually impossible to defend against. Before the 1877 season, the rule was changed to the present requirement. Although NL averages increased from 1876 to 1877, Barnes found the change disastrous and hit only .269 in his last three major league seasons. He suffered a serious illness which caused him to miss many games in 1877. When Chicago refused to pay his full salary, Barnes became the first star to go to court for redress of contractual grievances. The court ruled in favor of the owners, setting a pattern until the 1970s.

Although only 5 feet, 8 inches tall and weighing 145 pounds, he compensated for his small stature by being a fast runner and an above average fielder. Primarly a second baseman, he led that position in fielding percentage in 1876. He apparently exhibited considerable fielding range, leading shortstops in 1879 in chances per game as a Cincinnati Red (NL).

BIBLIOGRAPHY: Warren Brown, *The Chicago Cubs* (New York, 1946); Joseph L. Reichler, ed. *The Baseball Encyclopedia*, 6th ed (New York, 1985), pp. 48, 699; George Wright, *Record of the Boston Base Ball Club Since Its Organization* (Boston, 1874).

Gordon B. McKinney

BARROW, Edward Grant "Ed," "Cousin Ed" (b. 10 May 1868, Springfield, IL; d. 15 December 1953, Port Chester, NY), manager and executive, was the eldest of four sons of farmer and grain dealer John and Effie Ann (Vinson-Heller) Barrow. His name was synonymous with the success of the New York Yankees (AL) between 1921 and 1945. During his tenure as general manager, the Yankees won fourteen AL pennants and ten World Series and captured five fall classics without losing a game. Barrow organized and developed the farm system that established the Yankees as the all-time kings of baseball. Baseball peers respected his genius at evaluating talent and his administrative ability. The forceful, straightforward Barrow possessed an explosive temper, once challenging Babe Ruth* to a fight, and he exercised strict discipline as manager and executive.

Barrow moved with his family to Des Moines, IA, in 1877 and quit school at age 16 to clerk for the Des Moines *Daily News*. He soon joined the Des Moines *Blade*, became advertising manager of the Des Moines *Leader*, and managed a semi-pro baseball team. In 1890 he moved to Pittsburgh, where he became assistant manager of the Staley Hotel and entered into partnership with Harry Stevens. Stevens operated scorecard concessions at the Pittsburgh Pirates' Exposition Park. Four years later, he began his professional baseball career as manager, general manager, and one-third owner of the Wheeling, WV, club of the newly organized ISL. When the ISL dissolved in midseason, the partners shifted the winning club to the IOL. Barrow in 1895 acquired the Paterson, NJ, franchise in the newly formed AtL, discovered and developed Honus Wagner,* and served as president of the circuit between 1896 and 1900. In 1900 he purchased a part interest in Toronto (EL) and became its manager. Two years later, he piloted Toronto to the EL championship. Detroit (AL) signed Barrow as manager in 1903, but he resigned in 1904 following a dispute with the general manager. Barrow managed Indianapolis (AA) in 1905 and 1906 and guided Toronto (EL) to a pennant in 1907. He then left baseball and spent the next three years managing a Toronto hotel.

After his wife died in 1910, Barrow returned to baseball as Montreal (EL) manager. He married Frances Taylor in 1912 and had one daughter, Audrey. From 1910 to 1918 Barrow served as EL president and renamed it the IL. He fought the attempted inroads of the FL, thus gaining the respect of AL president Ban Johnson.* In 1918 the Boston Red Sox (AL) named Barrow field manager upon Johnson's recommendation. Barrow immediately led Boston to the AL pennant and World Series title over the Chicago Cubs in six games. That same season, he began converting pitcher Babe Ruth* into an outfielder. In January, 1920, the powerful Ruth was sold to the New York Yankees. At the close of that season, Barrow became New York's secretary and general manager. Barrow's five seasons as a major league manager resulted in 310 victories in 630 games. At the time, he was the only front office executive ever to win a pennant and World Series title. The Yankees won their initial pennant in 1921 in Barrow's first year with the club and then repeated in 1922 and 1923. After the Yankees experienced disappointing seasons in 1924 and 1925, Barrow's rebuilding program produced successive AL pennants.

With the help of a farm system built by Barrow and his assistant, George Weiss,* New York developed the most consistent pennant-winning organization in major league history. The Yankees captured AL pennants in 1932 and from 1936 through 1939. When Yankees owner Colonel Jacob Ruppert* died in 1939, Barrow became club president. He held that position until January 1945 when a syndicate of Leland MacPhail, Sr.,* Dan Topping,* and Del Webb bought the Yankees. From 1941 through 1943, New York captured additional AL pennants. Barrow served as chairman of the board from 1945 until his retirement and was enshrined in the National Baseball Hall of Fame in September, 1953.

BIBLIOGRAPHY: "Ed Barrow: Founder of the Yankee Dynasty," *Yankee Magazine* (April 12, 1984); Edward G. Barrow with James Kahn, "My Baseball Story," *Collier's*, 125 (May 20-June 24, 1950); *DAB*, Supp. 5 (1951–1955), pp. 40–41; Dan Daniel, "From Peanuts to Pennants: The Story of Edward G. Barrow," New York *World Telegram*, February, 1933; James M. Kahn, *My Fifty Years in Baseball* (New York, 1951); Frederick G. Lieb, *The Boston Red Sox* (New York 1947); Paul MacFarlane, ed., *TSN Daguerreotypes of Great Stars of Baseball* (St. Louis, 1971); Tom Meany, *The Yankee Story* (New York, 1960); *NYT*, December 16, 1953, pp. 1, 54; Lowell Reidenbaugh, *Cooperstown: Where Baseball's Legends Live Forever* (St. Louis, 1983).

                                                          Donald J. Proctor and John L. Evers

BARTELL, Richard William "Dick," "Rowdy Richard" (b. 22 November 1907, Chicago, IL), player, coach, and manager, was the only child of Harry and Emma (Greakel) Bartell. His father worked as an accountant, real estate agent, and county supervisor, and as a semi-pro baseman once made an unassisted triple play. The Bartells moved to California during his infancy. He graduated from Alameda High School in 1926 and was offered athletic scholarships by three colleges, but signed instead with the Pittsburgh Pirates

(NL). He married Olive Loretta Jensen on October 24, 1928, and had two children. On August 1, 1981, he married Anise Walton.

In 1927 he began his pro career by batting .280 as a shortstop for Bridgeport, CT (EL). His eighteen-year major league career began in 1927 with one game for the Pirates. By 1929 he had replaced Glenn Wright* as regular shortstop. After hitting .320 in 1930, he was traded to the Philadelphia Phillies (NL). Four years later, after having played in the first All-Star Game, he was traded to the New York Giants (NL) for four players and cash. In 1939 the Giants sent Bartell to the Chicago Cubs (NL) in a six-player deal. A year later Chicago traded him to the Detroit Tigers (AL). He returned to the Giants (NL) in 1941 for three wartime seasons, served in the U.S. Navy in 1944–1945, and ended his career with five games for the Giants in 1946. In three World Series (1936–1937, 1940), he hit .294.

A lifetime .284 hitter, Bartell batted over .300 in six seasons and usually hit first or second in the order. Besides being a good bunter, he hit well behind the runner and seldom struck out. He slashed 442 doubles, ranking fifty-second on the all-time list. In 1933 he equalled the major league record for most doubles in one game with four. At shortstop, he frequently led the NL in double plays, putouts, assists, and total chances per game. Ironically, he once played a ten-inning game without a single fielding chance. A lively, aggressive player, he was nicknamed "Rowdy Richard."

He managed at Sacramento (PCL) in 1947, Kansas City (AA) in 1948, and Montgomery-Knoxville (SAL) in 1956, and coached for the Tigers from 1949 to 1952 and Cincinnati Reds (NL) in 1954 and 1955. Between 1957 and 1972 he worked as a sales representative for a dairy products company and owned a liquor store. He has remained active in the Association of Professional Baseball Players.

BIBLIOGRAPHY: Richard M. Cohen, David S. Neft, and Jordan A. Deutsch, *The World Series* (New York, 1979); F. C. Lane, "A Human Dynamo at Short," *Baseball Magazine* 52 (January, 1934), pp. 347–348; Allen Lewis, *The Philadelphia Phillies* (Virginia Beach, VA, 1981); Jim McMartin, "Two Measures of Fielding Ability," *Baseball Research Journal* 12 (1983), pp. 56–61; A. D. Suehsdorf, interviews with Richard Bartell, October 15, 1983, March 9, 1984; Joseph L. Reichler, ed., *The Baseball Encyclopedia*, 6th ed. (New York, 1985), p. 702.

David L. Porter

BEAUMONT, Clarence Howeth "Ginger" (b. 23 July 1876, Rochester, WI; d. 10 April 1956, Burlington, WI), player, was a one-time NL batting champion and star center fielder for the Pittsburgh Pirates (NL) from 1899 to 1906. The first player to bat in a World Series game (1903), he was nicknamed "Ginger" for his red hair. Older players harassed him for his "sissified" name of Clarence. The son of Thomas and Mary (Jones) Beaumont, he attended Rochester (WI) Academy and later Beloit College for one year and played semi-professional baseball in Wausau, WI. Connie Mack,* manager of the Milwaukee club (WL), signed him in 1898. After batting .354 for Milwaukee in 24 games, the hard-hitting, speedy Beaumont was purchased by Pittsburgh (NL) for the 1899 season. He remained with the Pirates until December, 1906, when he was traded to the Boston Nationals (NL) with Claude Ritchey for Ed Abbaticchio. He played with Boston from 1907 to 1909 and with the Chicago Cubs (NL) in 1910, his last major league season. Following the 1911 year with St. Paul (AA), Beaumont retired from baseball. He married Norma Olive Vaughan in November 1901 and had two daughters and a son.

Beaumont joined Pittsburgh two years before manager Fred Clarke* assembled the great 1901–1903 pennant-winning Pirate clubs. Although overshadowed by Hall of Famers Clarke and Honus Wagner,* he contributed substantially to his team's success. In 1902 he led the NL in batting (.357) and hits (194). The next season he batted .341 and paced the NL in at bats (613), runs (137), and hits (209). Beaumont led the NL in hits again in 1904, the first player ever to top a major league in hits three consecutive seasons. At Boston in 1907, he also led the NL in hits. During twelve major league campaigns, he collected 1,760 hits and compiled a .311 batting average.

The stocky 5 foot, 8 inch, 190 pound Beaumont possessed good speed. Besides stealing over 30 bases three times, he pilfered 254 bases in his career. Expert at punching the ball through the infield and beating out slow rollers, on July 22, 1899, he made six infield hits in six at bats and scored six times. On the fourth hit, Beaumont recalled, "The third baseman stood ten feet from the plate and I still beat out a bunt." A weak fielder initially, Beaumont improved quickly and nearly led the NL centerfielders in 1902 with a .972 mark.

BIBLIOGRAPHY: William Connelly, "The Greatest Baseball Team in All History," *Baseball Magazine* 12 (May, 1914), pp. 33–42, 96; MacLean Kennedy, *The Great Teams of Baseball* (St. Louis, 1928); Frederick G. Lieb, *The Pittsburgh Pirates* (New York, 1948); Paul MacFarlane, ed., *TSN Daguerreotypes of Great Stars of Baseball* (St. Louis, 1981); Eugene C. Murdock, correspondence and phone interviews with Mrs. Enoch Squires, Spring, 1984, Eugene C. Murdock Collection, Williamstown, WV; Alfred H. Spink, *The National Game: A History of Baseball* (St. Louis, 1911); *TSN*, April 18, 1956.

                                                        Eugene C. Murdock

BECKLEY, Jacob Peter "Jake," "Old Eagle Eye" (b. 4 August 1867, Hannibal, MO; d. 25 June 1918, Kansas City, MO), player, manager, and umpire, ranked among the game's most notable performers around the turn of the century. In twenty major league seasons, the 5 foot, 10 inch, 200 pound Beckley batted above .300 thirteen times. Beckley began his professional career with Leavenworth, KS, and Lincoln, NB (WL), in 1886 and 1887 and played 34 games in his third minor league season with St. Louis (WA). The left-handed first baseman then joined Pittsburgh (NL) as a 20-year-old in June, 1888, and in 71 games batted .343, one point less than NL batting champion Cap Anson.*

After eight seasons with Pittsburgh (NL) and one with Pittsburgh (PL) (1890), Beckley was traded to New York (NL) in 1896. Beckley then played for Cincinnati (NL) from 1897 through 1903 and for St. Louis (NL) from 1904 through 1907. Despite being a weak thrower, Beckley tied for the NL lead in fielding percentage (1889) and led the NL (1898–1899) in that category. He paced the circuit in putouts six seasons (1892, 1894–1895, 1900, 1902, 1904) and batted above .300 six consecutive campaigns (1899–1904). Beckley's major league records include most games played (2,386), most putouts (23,709), and most chances accepted (25,505) at first base. By leading the NL in putouts six seasons, Beckley tied Frank McCormick* for the major league record. On September 27, 1898, he made 21 putouts at first base in one game. Beckley also paced the NL with 2,265 games played, 22,438 putouts, and 23,687 chances accepted at first base. On September 26, 1897, Beckley slugged three home runs in a game at St. Louis and became the last major leaguer to perform that feat until 1922. Twice he hit three triples in one game.

Beckley, credited with developing an unusual hidden-ball trick, concealed the baseball under one corner of the bag, extracted it, and then tagged out the runner. Beckley's lifetime major league statistics included 2,931 hits (tied for 21st on the all-time list with Rogers Hornsby*), 1,600 runs scored (32nd), 1,575 RBIs in (22nd), 475 doubles (37th), and 244 triples (4th). In 2,386 games, he hit 88 home runs, stole 315 bases, and compiled a .308 batting average. Beckley played 2,377 games at first base, topping Lou Gehrig's* 2,136 and Charlie Grimm's* 2,129 contests.

Beckley completed his baseball career as player-manager with Kansas City (AA), in 1908 and 1909, Bartlesville, OK (WA), and Topeka (WL) in 1910, and Hannibal, MO (CA), in 1911. He managed a semi-pro tream in Kansas City (1912) and last appeared in baseball as an umpire in the FL (1913). The National Baseball Hall of Fame enshrined him in 1971.

BIBLIOGRAPHY: Paul MacFarlane, ed., *TSN Daguerreotypes of Great Stars of Baseball* (St. Louis, 1971); Lowell Reidenbaugh, *Cooperstown: Where Baseball's Legends Live Forever* (St. Louis, 1983); *TSN Official Baseball Record Book, 1985* (St. Louis, 1985).

John L. Evers

BECKWITH, John (b. 1902, Louisville, KY), player and manager, first played baseball as a child in Sunday School leagues in Chicago and began his professional career in 1919 with the Chicago Giants. Upon signing with Rube Foster's* Chicago American Giants in 1921, the 230 pound right-handed pull hitter already had become one of the game's most versatile players. He caught, played any infield or outfield position, and even pitched in a pinch, but achieved his greatest fame as one of the most intimidating power hitters in black baseball. Pitcher Willie Foster* called him one of the toughest hitters he ever faced. As a 19-year-old, he became the first player ever to hit a ball over the left field fence in Cincinnati's Redland Field. In 1921 he batted .419 for the second best mark in the NNL. He hit for both power and average. For the Baltimore Black Sox (ANL), he batted .452 and clubbed 40 home runs in 1924 and hit .419; and finished second in home runs in 1925. With the Harrisburg Giants in 1927, he batted .338 and finished second in ANL home runs, reputedly hitting 72. After slugging 54 home runs the next year for the Homestead Grays, he batted .443 in 1929 to finish second in ANL standings. The next year he led the ANL in hitting with a remarkable .546. His .408 lifetime average in league play was supplemented by his .337 average in exhibitions with major leaguers. He left the American Giants in 1924, perhaps because of his combative personality, and spent the remainder of his career with various eastern teams, including the Baltimore Black Sox, Homestead Grays, Harrisburg Giants, Lincoln Giants, and New York Black Yankees.

BIBLIOGRAPHY: John Holway, *Voices from the Great Black Baseball Leagues* (New York, 1975); Robert W. Peterson, *Only the Ball was White* (Englewood Cliffs, NJ, 1970); James A. Riley, *The All-Time All-Stars of Black Baseball* (Cocoa, FL, 1983).

Gerald E. Brennan

BELL, David Gus "Buddy" (b. 27 August 1951, Pittsburgh, PA), player and announcer, is the son of Gus Bell, former major leaguer with the Pittsburgh Pirates, Cincinnati Reds, New York Mets, and Milwaukee Braves (NL), and Joyce (Sutherland) Bell. Bell grew up in Cincinnati, where he graduated from Archbishop Moeller High School in 1969 and played baseball, basketball, and football. Upon his father's advice, he dropped football after two years. Bell studied during the off-seasons at Xavier University in Cincinnati and at Miami University in Oxford, OH. On February 6, 1971, Bell married his childhood sweetheart, Gloria Jean Eysoldt. The couple has four children and resides in Cincinnati. As the son of a major leaguer, Bell grew up around baseball players and frequently visited his father's clubhouse. Although never pushed by his family to pursue baseball, he nurtured the dream of playing for the hometown Reds. To his disappointment, the Reds did not select him in the 1969 free agent draft. Bell, an infielder, was not chosen until the sixteenth round by the cross-state Cleveland Indians (AL).

Bell's association with the Indians proved very rewarding. After only three minor league seasons with Sarasota, FL (GCL), Sumter, SC (WCL), and Wichita, KS (AA), he made the 1972 Cleveland roster. Bell's strong spring hitting and successful conversion from third base to the outfield helped him.

He made only three errors his first year and hit well enough to finish high in the balloting for AL Rookie of the Year. When an opening developed at third base, Bell returned to the infield in 1973 and has remained there. In seven years with Cleveland, he batted .274 with 64 home runs. Bell, an extremely popular player, exhibited hard play and selfless regard for the team.

On December 8, 1978, Bell was traded to the Texas Rangers (AL) and proved a consistent bright spot for a generally mediocre team. Besides batting .295 his seven years with the Rangers, Bell led the AL in game-winning RBIs (16) in 1979 and sacrifice flies (10) in 1981. Bell also excelled defensively, winning a Gold Glove every season. At least once, he has led the AL third baseman in total chances, assists, putouts, and double plays. He has appeared in five All-Star games (1973, 1980–1982, and 1984). In 1985 the Rangers traded Bell to the Cincinnati Reds (NL). Through the 1986 season, he had batted .282 with 2,273 hits, 392 doubles, 177 home runs, and 993 RBIs. In the winter of 1985–1986, Bell announced Xavier University basketball games.

BIBLIOGRAPHY: Jim Kaplan, "For Whom the Bell Tolls . . . ," *SI* 58 (April 18, 1983), pp. 66ff; Russell Schneider, "Bell Tolls Knell of Tribe Outfield Competition," *TSN* April 8, 1972; Russell Schneider, "Buddy's Friendly Gesture Booms Indians' Battle Cry," *TSN*, April 30, 1977, p. 15; Russell Schneider, "Pressure on Bell in '73—Shift to Tribe Hot Corner," *TSN*, January 13, 1973.

                                                                    Allen E. Hye

BELL, James Thomas "Cool Papa" (b. 17 May 1903, Starkville, MS), player and manager, is the son of a farmer and the great-grandson of an Oklahoma Indian. In 1920 he joined his older brothers in St. Louis, MO, there being no high school and few job opportunities in Starkville. He attended high school for two years, worked in a packing plant, and pitched for the semi-pro Compton Hill Cubs. In 1922 he signed his first professional contract for $90 per month with the St. Louis Stars (NNL). From 1922 to 1931 Bell played for the Stars and initially performed as a left-handed pitcher. His knuckler and screwball complemented his curveball, which he threw with three different motions. His calm demeanor impressed other players and manager Bill Gatewood so much that he thereafter was nicknamed "Cool Papa." Besides being an effective pitcher, Bell also proved extremely fast and a good right-handed hitter. In 1924 Gatewood installed him in the outfield and made him into a switch-hitter.

After the 1931 season the NNL disbanded. In 1932 the 6 foot, 145 pound Bell played briefly for the Detroit Wolves, the Homestead Grays' farm club. When the Wolves folded, he joined the Kansas City Monarchs. From 1933 to 1936, Bell roamed center field for the Pittsburgh Crawfords (NNL) nine that included manager Oscar Charleston,* Satchel Paige,* Judy Johnson,* Josh Gibson,* Jimmie Crutchfield,* and Ted Page. In 1937 the dictator of the Dominican Republic Rafael Trujillo, lured Bell, Paige, and other Craw-fords south to play for the Trujillo All-Stars. Bell played in Mexico from 1938 to 1941, earning $450 per month and enjoying life in an integrated society. In 1940 Bell batted a career-high .437 and led the MEL in every offensive category.

Two years later, Bell returned to the United States to play for the Chicago American Giants (NAL) and briefly for the Memphis Red Sox. The 1943–1946 summer seasons were spent with the Homestead Grays (NNL) and the 1947 campaign with the Detroit Senators. Bell concluded his baseball career from 1948 to 1950 as player-manager for the Kansas City Stars, the Monarchs' farm club. After declining an offer in 1951 from the St. Louis Browns (AL), Bell worked as a custodian and then as night security officer at St. Louis City Hall until retiring in 1970. He resides with his wife Clarabelle near the site of old Busch Stadium.

"Cool Papa" became one of the greatest hitters and outfielders and perhaps the fastest player of all time. In 1933 he stole 175 bases in about 200 games. Even during his forties, he ranked among the league leaders in stolen bases. Bell, considered faster than Ty Cobb* and even Jesse Owens* (OS), once circled the bases in twelve seconds flat to easily beat the major league record. He routinely scored from second base on ground balls and scored from first on a bunt in 1948 against Bob Lemon's* All Stars. Paul Waner* and Bill Veeck* included the outstanding hitting Bell on their all-time outfield. Ac-cording to available records for his twenty-nine summer and twenty-one winter seasons, Bell batted over .400 several campaigns and compiled an estimated .340-.350 lifetime average. In 54 recorded games against white major leaguers, he batted .391. In recognition of a truly outstanding career hidden from a majority of fans by segregation, Bell in 1974 was inducted into the National Baseball Hall of Fame.

BIBLIOGRAPHY: Martin Appel and Burt Goldblatt, *Baseball's Best: The Hall of Fame Gallery* (New York, 1977); James Bell and John Holway, "How to Score from First on a Sacrifice," *American Heritage* 21 (August, 1970), 30–36; William Brashler, *Josh Gibson: A Life in the Negro Leagues* (New York, 1978); Anthony J. Connor, *Voices from Cooperstown* (New York, 1982); John Holway, *Voices from the Great Black Baseball Leagues* (New York, 1975); Donald Honig, *Baseball When the Grass Was Real* (New York, 1975); Robert W. Peterson, *Only the Ball Was White* (Englewood Cliffs, NJ, 1970).

                                                                Douglas D. Martin

BENCH, Johnny Lee (b. 7 December 1947, Oklahoma City, OK), player and announcer, grew up in Binger, OK, where his father Ted, a truck driver, had moved his family when Johnny was age five. Bench earned All-State honors in baseball and basketball at Binger High School, from which he graduated as class valedictorian in 1965. Rejecting several college scholarship offers, he signed a bonus contract with the Cincinnati Reds (NL). After three minor league seasons with Tampa (FSL) in 1965, Peninsula, VA (CrL) in 1966, and Buffalo (IL) in 1967, Bench joined the Reds late in the 1967 season. In 1968 the catcher batted .275 in 154 games and was named NL Rookie of the Year. Two years later, Bench led the NL with 45 homers and 148 RBIs. For leading the Reds to the NL pennant, Bench was named NL Most Valuable Player. He won the MVP award again in 1972, when he led the NL with 125 RBIs and 40 home runs.

With Bench as starting catcher throughout the 1970s, the Reds won six NL Western Division titles, four NL pennants, and world championships in 1975 and 1976. Bench was selected MVP of the 1976 World Series, which the Reds won in a four-game sweep of the New York Yankees to become the first NL team in over fifty years to win consecutive World Series. During the 1970–1979 decade, Bench led the major leagues with 1,013 RBIs and the NL three times in RBIs. His lifetime 389 home runs surpassed that of all other major league catchers. During his career, he drove in 1,376 runs and compiled a .267 batting average. In 2,158 games, he made 2,048 hits, 381 doubles, 1,091 runs, and 1,278 strikeouts. Additionally, he was recognized as an outstanding, durable defensive catcher. He caught over 120 games in each of his first ten major league seasons and won ten consecutive Gold Gloves for outstanding defense behind the plate.

Bench retired as an active player after the 1983 season to concentrate on various business and professional interests. Having once undergone minor cancer surgery, he headed the Athletes' Division of the American Cancer Society. Bench frequently competed in celebrity golf tournaments to raise money for charitable organizations. He ranks along with Hall of Famers Bill Dickey,* Mickey Cochrane,* and Yogi Berra* as one of the greatest offensive and defensive catchers in baseball history. In 1986 ABC hired Bench as a baseball commentator.

BIBLIOGRAPHY: Johnny Bench and William Brashler, *Catch You Later* (New York, 1979); George Vecsey, "Johnny Bench: The Man Behind the Mask," *Sport* 54 (October, 1972), pp. 101–112.

Fred M. Shelley

BENDER, Charles Albert "Chief" (b. 5 May 1883, Crow Wing County, MN; d. 22 May 1954, Philadelphia, PA), player, coach, manager, and scout, grew up at White Earth (Indian) Reservation, MN. He was the son of Albertus Bliss Bender, a farmer of German-American descent, and Mary Razor (Indian name: Pay shaw de o quay) of half Ojibwa (Chippewa) parentage. Bender attended Lincoln Institution, a school for Indians and whites at Philadelphia, from ages eight to twelve and then returned briefly to White Earth. At Carlisle Indian School (PA) from 1898 to 1901, he played baseball and football. In 1902 he attended Dickinson College. As "Charles Albert," he pitched that summer for Harrisburg (PA) Athletic Club and was discovered there by Philadelphia Athletics (AL) scout Jesse Frisinger.

Resembling a full blooded Indian, the swarthy, rangy Bender reported the next spring to Philadelphia and immediately was nicknamed "Chief." From 1903 through 1914, the 6 foot, 2 inch, 185 pound right-hander won 191 games for the Athletics. In his best season (1910), he compiled a 23–5 won-lost record and a 1.58 ERA and hurled a no-hit game. He won six and lost four in five World Series and posted two victories each in the 1911 and 1913 fall classics. Bender, who lacked abundant stamina, was used by manager Connie Mack* principally in "must win" games and proved an effective stopper. His winning percentages led the AL in 1910, and 1914. Twice Bender won more than 20 games in a season. The cool, relaxed Bender exhibited excellent control and curves and utilized his hard fastball as his best pitch. A career .212 batter, he occasionally pinch-hit and played outfield or first base.

Bender joined the FL in 1915, compiling a 4–16 mark with Baltimore. He recorded 7–7 and 8–2 seasons in 1916 and 1917 with the Philadelphia Phillies (NL), giving him 210 career wins, 127 losses, 1,711 strikeouts, and a 2.45 ERA. After working in a shipyard during 1918, he managed Richmond, VA (VL), in 1919 and pitched 29 victories against only 2 defeats (which he called his finest baseball achievement).

Subsequently he pitched and managed at New Haven, CT (EL), in 1920–21, Reading, PA (IL) in 1922, and Johnstown, PA (MAL), in 1927; coached at Chicago (AL) in 1925–1926, New York (NL) in 1931, and the U.S. Naval Academy in 1928; and managed at the independent House of David during the 1930s, Erie, PA (CL), in 1932, Wilmington, DE (ISL), in 1940, Newport News, VA (VL), in 1941, and Savannah (SAL) in 1946. For the Athletics, he scouted in 1945 and 1947 through 1950. He then coached there through 1953, the year he was elected to the National Baseball Hall of Fame.

Bender married Marie Clements of Detroit in 1904; they had no children. The gentle, intelligent, and versatile hurler engaged in the watchmaking, jewelry, and clothing businesses; painted landscapes in oils; and proved an excellent marksman, trapshooter, golfer, and billiard player.

BIBLIOGRAPHY: Charles A. Bender, "Record of Graduates and Returned Students, United States Indian School, Carlisle, Pennsylvania", ca. 1908–1909; Charles A. Bender file, National Baseball Hall of Fame Library, Cooperstown, NY; Paul MacFarlane, ed., *TSN Daguerreotypes of Great Stars of Baseball* (St. Louis, 1981), pp. 23–24; Philadelphia *Press*, September 12, 1909; Joseph L. Reichler, ed., *The Baseball Encyclopedia*, 6th ed. (New York, 1985), p. 1588; J. G. Taylor Spink, *TSN*, December 24, 1942, December 30, 1953; Robert Tholkes, "Chief Bender—The Early Years," *Baseball Research Journal* 12 (1983), pp. 8–13; *TSN*, June 2, 1954.

Frank V. Phelps

BERGER, Walter Antone "Wally" (b. 10 October 1905, Chicago, IL), player and manager, learned to play baseball on San Francisco sandlots. He played third base for a Mission High School team that included Joe Cronin* at second base. Berger began organized baseball in 1927 as an outfielder at Pocatello, ID, where he led the UIL in putouts, batted .385, and hit 24 home runs before moving up to the PCL. He played for Los Angeles from 1927 to 1929, hitting .365 his first year, .327 in 1928, and .355 in 1929. In 1929 he belted 40 home runs and produced 166 RBIs. Berger remains among the all-time leading sluggers in minor league history. From 1930 to 1939 Berger starred for the Boston Braves (NL). He set the club season record with 38 home runs and 169 extra bases on long hits his rookie season when he batted .310 and drove home 119 runs. Berger's homers as a rookie remained the NL standard until bested by Frank Robinson* in 1956. In his next three seasons, Berger compiled .323, .307, and .313 batting marks. He played in three consecutive major league All-Star games from 1933 through 1935 and was named to *The Sporting News* Major League All-Star team in 1933. Although his batting average dropped below .300 after 1933, the 6 foot, 2 inch, 205 pound outfielder remained a productive power hitter. He hit 34 home runs in 1934 and 1935, leading the NL the latter year. His 130 RBIs in 1935 paced the NL and set a Boston Braves record.

In 1937 the Braves traded Berger to the New York Giants (NL). After spending one year there, he played for the Cincinnati Reds until being released in 1940. He played 20 games for the Philadelphia Phillies (NL) before being sent to Indianapolis. In 1941 Berger finished his playing career as a first baseman–outfielder for Los Angeles (PCL). Berger, who had married Bertha Wilson in October, 1929, and then Martha Subzhak in April 1942, managed Manchester, NH (NEL) in 1949. Among his era's premier sluggers and run producers, he played in 1,350 games, amassed 1,550 hits, 299 doubles, 242 home runs, and 898 RBIs, compiled a .522 slugging percentage, and hit .300 in five of eleven major league seasons. Berger, now retired, lives in Manhattan Beach, CA.

BIBLIOGRAPHY: Walter Berger file, National Baseball Hall of Fame Library, Cooperstown, NY; Paul MacFarlane, ed., *TSN Daguerreotypes of Great Stars of Baseball* (St. Louis, 1971); National Association of Professional Baseball Leagues, *The Story of Minor League Baseball* (Columbus, 1952); Lowell Reidenbaugh, "Memories . . . The Fifteen Surviving Members of the First All-Star Game Remember the Big Event," *TSN 1983 All-Star Special* (St. Louis, 1983), pp. 3–8.

Douglas D. Martin

BERRA, Lawrence Peter "Yogi" (b. 12 May 1925, St. Louis, MO), player, manager, and coach, is the son of shoe factory worker Peter and Pauline (Longsoni) Berra, both of Italian origin. In 1932 the Berra family moved to the famed Italian "Hill" section of St. Louis, where Yogi attended the Wade

Grammar School. Boyhood friend Jack Maguire nicknamed him "Yogi" after seeing a movie about India. Berra, who left school at age 14, worked in a coalyard, drove a soft-drink truck, and toiled as a tack-puller in the shoe factory. At age 17, Berra tried out with Joe Garagiola* (OS) for the St. Louis Cardinals (NL). Despite being the best athlete in South St. Louis and a star for the YMCA Stags, Yogi failed to impress Cardinals' executive Branch Rickey.* The Cardinals offered $500 to Garagiola, who showed more discipline at the plate. The New York Yankees (AL) eventually signed Berra for $500.

After spending 1943 with Norfolk, VA (Pil), Berra joined the U.S. Navy. He was stationed on a rocket launcher off the coast of Normandy Beach for fifteen days following the D-Day attack. After being discharged in 1946, Berra hit .314 for the Newark Bears (IL). With the New York Yankees that same year, Berra wore number 35 while alternating between left field and home plate. Yankee great Bill Dickey* helped make Berra a more accurate thrower and one of the sport's best catchers.

In 1951, 1954, and 1955, Berra was named the AL's Most Valuable Player. A notorious bad-ball hitter, he hit with power (30 homers in 1952 and 1956) and batting average (.322 in 1950). Berra hit 313 home runs, the most by an AL catcher. He played with the Yankees from 1946 to 1964 and appeared in four games for the New York Mets (NL) in 1965, hitting .285 in 2,120 career games, slugging 358 homers, and knocking in 1,430 runs. A participant in fourteen World Series, he played on ten championship teams.

Berra holds many fielding records, including playing in 148 consecutive games without an error. During that streak from 1957 to 1959, he accepted 950 chances, also a major league mark. He made an unassisted double play against the St. Louis Browns in 1947 to tie an AL record. His World Series records include most games (75) and most hits (71). The first player to pinch-hit a home run in the World Series in 1947, in 1956 he joined a handful of players hitting grandslams in the fall classic.

In his first full season as manager of the Yankees, Berra guided the team to the 1964 pennant and a near World Series triumph. Player discontent, most notably the Phil Linz harmonica incident, prompted the Yankees to fire him. He coached the New York Mets (NL) from 1965 to 1972 and managed them to the pennant the next season. The 1973 Mets nearly defeated Oakland in the World Series. From the middle of 1975 through 1983, Berra coached for the Yankees. After being named Yankees' manager in December, 1983, he guided New York to a 87–75 record in 1984. The Yankees removed Berra as manager after a lackluster 6–10 start in 1985. The Houston Astros (NL) signed Berra as a coach in November, 1985. His career managerial record through 1985 remained 484–444 for a .522 percentage. In 1972 he was elected to the National Baseball Hall of Fame.

He on January 21, 1949, married Carmine Short, a former waitress for Musial and Biggies in St. Louis. They have three sons, including former major league shortstop Dale. A shy, affable New York man with a penchant for comic books, Berra has made many malapropisms. While giving gratitude at a benefit, Berra commented, "I want to thank all those who made this evening necessary." After experiencing difficulty playing left field in Yankee Stadium, Berra remarked, "It gets late early out there!"

BIBLIOGRAPHY: Maury Allen, *Baseball's 100* (New York, 1959); Bob Broeg, *Superstars of Baseball* (St. Louis, 1971); Bob Burnes, "My Favorite Yankee," *TSN Baseball Register 1958* (St. Louis, 1958); Arthur Daley, *Sports of the Times* (New York, 1959); Ed Fitzgerald, *The Autobiography of a Professional Baseball Player* (New York, 1961); Joe Garagiola and Dave Anderson, "Yogi of the Yankees," *Reader's Digest* 85 (July, 1964), pp. 110–113; William Gleason, "Is Lollar Better Than Berra?" *SEP* 229 (June 15, 1957), pp. 36ff.; Gene Karst and Martin J. Jones, Jr., *Who's Who in Professional Baseball* (New York, 1973); Paul MacFarlane, ed., *TSN Daguerreotypes of Great Stars of Baseball* (St. Louis, 1981); Richard Marazzi and Len Fiorito, *Aaron to Zuverink* (New York, 1982); Tom Meany, "Muscle Men," in Ben Epstein, *Magnificent Yankees* (New York, 1957); Tom Meany and Tom Holmes, *Baseball's Best* (New York, 1964); Jim Ogle, "Why the Yankees Fired Berra," *Look* 28 (December 29, 1964), pp. 30ff; Harry T. Paxton, "Everything Happens to Me," *SEP* 272 (April 29, 1950), pp. 32–33ff; Phil Pepe, *The Wit and Wisdom of Yogi Berra* (New York, 1974); Joe Reichler, "Mr. Backstop," in *Baseball Stars of 1955* (New York, 1955); *WWA*, 41st ed. (1980–1981), p. 278.

William A. Borst

BLUE, Vida Rochelle, Jr. (b. 28 July 1949, Mansfield, LA), player, is the son of Vida Rochelle Meschach Abednego and Sallie (Henderson) Blue. His father, an iron foundry worker, died during Vida's senior year at Desoto High School. Blue, who led his school to district championships in both football and baseball that year, declined many football scholarship offers to sign with the Kansas City Athletics (AL) partly to help support his family.

The A's selected Blue in the second round of the free agent draft in 1967 and signed him for a bonus reportedly between $28,000 and $50,000. He pitched for Burlington, IA (ML), in 1968 and for Birmingham, AL (SL), in 1969. Blue started the 1970 season with Iowa (AA), where he compiled the league's best winning percentage and strikeout record. He finished with the Oakland A's (AL), hurling one- and no-hitters in his two decisions.

The 6 foot, 190 pound left-handed fastballer pitched regularly for the Oakland A's from 1971 to 1977. In 1971 he compiled a 24–8 record, leading the AL in shutouts with 8 and in ERA with 1.82. He won both the Cy Young* and AL Most Valuable Player awards and was named AL Pitcher of the Year by *The Sporting News*. Blue experienced a losing season in 1972, when he did not start pitching until May 24 because of a salary dispute with owner Charles O. Finley.* He posted winning records the next four years, winning 20 in 1973 and 22 in 1975. Blue appeared in five championship series from 1971 to 1975, posting a 1–2 record, and pitched in three World

Series without recording a win. A six-time All Star, he won twice and became the only pitcher to win for each league.

In 1978 Blue was traded to the San Francisco Giants (NL) for seven players and $390,000. He initially was paid $205,000, but the Giants in 1979 gave him a new pact reportedly worth $750,000 per year. With the best won-lost record on the Giants' staff, he was named 1978 NL Pitcher of the Year by *The Sporting News*. The Giants traded him in 1982 to the Kansas City Royals (AL), where he pitched until being released on August 5, 1983.

Blue, known primarily for his moving fastball, compiled a 209–161 record with a 3.26 ERA, 2,175 strikeouts, and 35 shutouts. During Blue's first full season in the majors, attendance at Oakland and other AL cities increased markedly for his appearances. He similarly affected Giants' attendance in 1978.

Blue, who is single and lives in Oakland, worked in public relations for Pakon Industries in nearby Union City, CA, in 1984. He played winter ball in 1984 for Ponce and Arecibo (PuL), compiled an 8–8 mark in 1985 and a 10–10 record in 1986 with the San Francisco Giants. In January 1987 the Oakland A's (AL) signed Blue as a free agent.

BIBLIOGRAPHY: "Baseball's Amazing Vida Blue," *Ebony* 26 (September, 1971), pp. 95–99; Roy Blount, "Humming a Rhapsody in Blue," *SI* 35 (July 12, 1971), pp. 22–27; Vida Blue, "Next Year Is Going to Be Different," *Ebony* 27 (October, 1972), pp. 132–138; *CB* (1972), pp. 39–41; Jack Hicks, "Unwinding with Vida Blue," *Sport* 68 (June, 1979), pp. 70–76; Larry Keith, "These Giants Are Jolly Blue," *SI* 48 (May 29, 1978), pp. 22–23; Joseph L. Reichler, ed., *The Baseball Encyclopedia*, 6th ed. (New York, 1985), pp. 1598–1599; Barry Siegel, ed., *TSN Official Baseball Register, 1984* (St. Louis, 1984); *TSN*, October 17, 1983, p. 24, January 21, 1985, pp. 35, 45; Wells Twombly, "How to Throw the Ultimate Fast Ball," *NYT Magazine* (July 25, 1971), pp. 22–24; *WWA*, 42nd ed. (1982–1983), p. 306.

Gaymon L. Bennett

BOND, Thomas Henry "Tommy" (b. 2 April 1856, Granard, Ireland; d. 24 January 1941, Boston, MA), player and manager, became a successful right-handed pitcher in professional baseball's early years and one of the sport's first immigrant ballplayers. In 1874 Bond began his ten-year career with the Brooklyn Atlantics (NA). Pitching his team's entire 55 games, Bond led the NA with 32 losses. During his first NL season with Hartford, Bond in 1876 blossomed into one of baseball's premier pitchers. His 31 victories represented the NL's third best, while his 1.68 ERA came out fourth best. The small 5 foot, 7 inch, 160 pound Bond led the NL in strikeout average, earning his reputation as a "cannon ball" thrower.

From 1877 to 1880, Bond excelled as the chief pitcher for the highly successful Boston Red Stockings (NL). Besides hurling over 490 innings annually, Bond consistently ranked among NL leaders in strikeouts and ERA. From 1877 to 1879, he won 40 or more games and led the NL in shutouts. Despite using a more natural underhand motion, Bond apparently developed a sore arm. He continued pitching in 1881, 1882, and 1884, but lost most of his effectiveness. In the twilight of his career, Bond sought to remain in the game as a manager. He directed the Worcester (NL) team during the 1882 season but was released after his weak team won only 5 of 27 games. Unlike many contemporary players, Bond made a successful transition to a second career. After briefly working in the leather business and coaching the Harvard varsity nine, he was employed for thirty-five years in the Boston city tax assessor's office.

BIBLIOGRAPHY: Harold Kaese, *The Boston Braves* (New York, 1948); Joseph L. Reichler, ed., *The Baseball Encyclopedia*, 6th ed. (New York, 1985), pp. 733, 1,601; *NYT*, January 26, 1941.

                                                                                                          Gordon B. McKinney

BONDS, Bobby Lee (b. 15 March 1946, Riverside, CA), player and coach, is the son of a building contractor. After attending Riverside public schools and graduating from Riverside Polytechnic High School in 1964, he married Patricia Howard. His son Barry plays major league baseball with the Pittsburgh Pirates (NL). Bonds played Little League ball at age seven and starred in baseball, football, basketball, and track at Riverside Polytechnic. Named Southern California Schoolboy Athlete of the Year in 1964, Bonds signed with the San Francisco Giants (NL) and began his seventeen year playing career with Lexington, NC (WCL). He spent 1966 with Fresno (CaL), 1967 with Waterbury, CT (EL), and early 1968 with the Giants' top farm club in Phoenix (PCL). On June 25, 1968, he hit a grand slam home run in the seventh inning of his first major league game.

In his first full major league season, Bonds in 1969 shared the NL lead in runs scored with Pete Rose* at 120, became only the fourth player in baseball history to hit 30 home runs and steal 30 bases in the same season, and established an NL record with 187 strikeouts. He led in strikeouts again in 1970 and 1973, including a major league record (189) in 1970. In 1973 Bonds paced in runs scored (131) and total bases (341). The much traveled outfielder played in the AL with the New York Yankees (1975), California Angels (1976–1977), Chicago White Sox (1978), Texas Rangers (1978), and Cleveland Indians (1979), then returned to the NL, joining the St. Louis Cardinals (1980). The Chicago Cubs (NL) purchased him in June, 1981, from the Rangers' minor league system for his final major league playing season. After being released at the season's end, he played with the Columbus Clippers (IL) from May through June 1982. In January 1984, he joined the Cleveland Indians (AL) as batting and baserunning coach.

With one of the best combinations of speed and power in baseball history, Bonds established then records for most home runs by a leadoff batter lifetime (35) and single season (11 in 1973). The only player to hit 30 home runs and steal 30 bases in one season in both major leagues, he accomplished this feat five times. Bonds made *The Sporting News* All-Star team five consecutive years (1973–1977) and appeared in three All-Star games, one of a limited number to represent both leagues. He retired with a lifetime .268 batting average, 302 doubles, 332 home runs, 1,258 runs scored, 1,024 RBIs, and 461 stolen bases.

BIBLIOGRAPHY: Gene Karst and Martin J. Jones, Jr., *Who's Who in Professional Baseball* (New Rochelle, NY, 1973); David Klein, *Stars of the Major Leagues* (New York, 1974); Joseph L. Reichler, ed., *The Baseball Encyclopedia*, 6th ed. (New York, 1985), p. 733; *TSN Official Baseball Guide, 1983* (St. Louis, 1983).

Alan R. Asnen

BOTTOMLEY, James LeRoy "Jim," "Sunny Jim" (b. 23 April 1900, Oglesby, IL; d. 11 December 1959, St. Louis, MO), player, manager, and scout, was nicknamed "Sunny Jim" because of his ever-present smile and good humor. The 6 foot, 175 pound Bottomley broke into professional baseball with Sioux City, IA (WL), in 1920 and came to the St. Louis Cardinals (NL) in 1922 after minor league seasons at Mitchell, SD (SDA), Houston (TL), and Syracuse (IL). Bottomley played sixteen seasons at first base for the Cardinals (1922–1932), NL Cincinnati Reds (1933–1935), and AL St. Louis Browns (1936–1937). On September 16, 1924, he enjoyed one of the greatest batting days in major league history against the Brooklyn Dodgers. He drove in 12 runs with 2 home runs, 1 double, and 3 singles to power the Cardinals to a 17–3 victory. In 1928 he slugged 31 home runs to tie Hack Wilson* for the NL lead and led the NL in triples (20) and RBIs (136) to win the Most Valuable Player Award.

Bottomley's lifetime .310 batting average included a career-high .371 mark for the 1923 season. He made 2,313 hits with 465 doubles, 151 triples, 219 home runs, 1,177 runs scored, and 1,422 RBIs. In 1931 he participated in the closest batting championship race in baseball history. Bottomley finished third with a .3482 average, placing behind teammate Chick Hafey* (3.489) and the New York Giants' Bill Terry* (.3486). With left-hander Bottomley at first base, the Cardinals won NL pennants in 1926, 1928, 1930, and 1931 and captured the World Series in 1926 and 1931. After the 1932 season, Bottomley was traded to the Cincinnati Reds (NL). In 1936 he joined the St. Louis Browns (AL) and managed them to a 21–58 record from July 22, 1937 to the end of that season. After completing his major league career, Bottomley piloted Syracuse (IL) in 1938. In 1957 he scouted for the Chicago Cubs (NL) and managed Pulaski, VA (ApL). Bottomley, who married Betty Brawner on February 4, 1933, had no children. He was elected to the National Baseball Hall of Fame in 1974.

BIBLIOGRAPHY: Jim Bottomley file, National Baseball Hall of Fame Library, Cooperstown, NY; Gene Karst and Martin J. Jones, Jr., *Who's Who in Professional Baseball* (New Rochelle, NY, 1973); Joseph L. Reichler, ed., *The Baseball Encyclopedia*, 6th ed.

(New York, 1985), p. 738; Joseph L. Reichler, *The Great All-Time Baseball Record Book* (New York, 1981).

Horace R. Givens

BOUDREAU, Louis, Jr. "Lou" (b. 17 July 1917, Harvey, IL), baseball and basketball player, manager, and announcer, is the son of Louis, Sr., a machinist and semi-pro baseball player, and Birdie (Henry) Boudreau. He graduated from Thornton High School in Harvey and the University of Illinois in 1939. Boudreau married Della De Ruiter in June, 1938, and has four children. One son plays professional baseball, while one daughter married former Detroit pitcher Dennis McLain.* Boudreau quickly demonstrated fine leadership and athletic ability. He captained his high school basketball team as a sophomore, made All-State three years, and in 1933 helped his team win the state championship. He also starred at third base for Thornton. At the University of Illinois, he played third base and captained the basketball team as a junior.

In 1938 he played 60 games for Cedar Rapids (3IL) and one contest with Cleveland (AL). After dividing the 1939 season between Buffalo (IL) and Cleveland, he played shortstop for the Indians from 1940 through 1950. In 1942 24-year-old Boudreau became manager, making him the youngest to manage a full season in the majors. In 1944 he led the AL in batting with a .327 mark. He managed the Indians through 1950, the Boston Red Sox (AL) from 1952 through 1954, and the Kansas City Athletics (AL) from 1955 through 1957. He became a sports broadcaster in Chicago in 1958 and in May, 1960, replaced Charlie Grimm* as manager of the Cubs. Grimm took his place in the broadcasting booth, but in 1961 Boudreau returned permanently to broadcasting. As a major league manager, Boudreau compiled 1,162 wins and 1,224 losses for a .487 mark.

He proved extremely popular with the fans. In 1947 public outcry prevented Bill Veeck* from trading Boudreau to the St. Louis Browns. The next year Boudreau won the AL Most Valuable Player and *The Sporting News* Player of the Year awards. In the 1948 playoff game for the AL title, Boudreau hit two homers and two singles and walked once to spark his club to an 8–3 victory over Boston. In the World Series, he led the Indians with bat and glove to the championship.

He compiled a career .295 batting average and led the AL shortstops in fielding eight seasons. In 1,646 games, he made 1,779 hits, 385 doubles, 68 home runs, 861 runs, 789 RBIs, and 51 stolen bases. He not only recorded the best lifetime fielding percentage of any shortstop to that time, but also devised a successful shift against Boston pull hitter Ted Williams.* All four infielders were stationed to the right of second base, with the second baseman in short right field. Two outfielders played to the right of center. Only the left fielder remained on the left side of the diamond, twenty feet back of the normal shortstop spot. Williams usually tried to overpower that defense but in 1946 once hit to left field for an inside-the-park homer. The round tripper not only won the game, but clinched the AL pennant for Boston.

In 1941 and 1942 Boudreau coached freshman baseball and basketball at the University of Illinois. The author of *Good Infield Play* (1949), he played professional basketball with Hammond (National Basketball League) in 1940 and 1941. Of his numerous honors, Boudreau particularly cherishes his 1970 election to the National Baseball Hall of Fame.

BIBLIOGRAPHY: Lee Allen and Tom Meany, *Kings of the Diamond* (New York, 1965); Martin Appel and Burt Goldblatt, *Baseball's Best* (New York, 1977); Bill Dean, "The Best Fielders of the Century," *The National Pastime*, (Fall, 1982), 3–4; Lou Boudreau with Ed Fitzgerald, *Player-Manager* (Boston, 1949); Daniel Okrent and Harris Lewine, eds., *The Ultimate Baseball Book* (Boston, 1979).

Emil H. Rothe

BOWA, Lawrence Robert "Larry" (b. 6 December 1945, Sacramento, CA), player and manager, is the son of former minor league infielder-manager Paul Bowa and the nephew of former minor league infielder Frank Bowa. After graduating from McClatchy High School in Sacramento, he attended Sacramento City College. Bowa began his professional baseball career in 1966 in Spartanburg, SC (WCL), and San Diego (PCL). He also played with Bakersfield, CA (CaL), in 1967, Reading, PA (EL), in 1967 and 1968, and Eugene, OR (PCL) in 1969. As a National Leaguer, he performed for the Philadelphia Phillies (1970–1981), Chicago Cubs (1982–1985), and New York Mets (1985). In January 1982, he was traded with infielder Ryne Sandberg for shortstop Ivan DeJesus. After being released by the Cubs in August, 1985, Bowa joined the New York Mets for the rest of that season.

The 5 foot, 10 inch, 155 pound switch-hitter led NL shortstops in fielding percentage a record six times (1971–1972, 1976, 1978–1979, 1983) and set an NL record for most games by a shortstop (2,222). The winner of Gold Glove awards (1972 and 1978), he set major league records for the highest career fielding percentage by a shortstop with .980 and for a season with .991 in 1979. Bowa also established season NL records for fewest errors (6) in 1979 and for total chances (843) in 1971. As a batter, he enjoyed his finest performances with a .305 mark in 1975 and a .294 average in 1978 and made *The Sporting News* NL All-Star teams both seasons. He led the NL in at bats (650) in 1971, triples (13) in 1972, and singles (153) in 1978. Besides playing in five All-Star games, Bowa batted .375 and stole three bases against the Kansas City Royals in the 1980 World Series. Bowa also appeared in post-season playoffs in 1976, 1977, 1978, 1981, and 1984. During his career, Bowa compiled a career .260 batting average in 2,248 games, made 2,191 hits, scored 987 runs, and stole 318 bases. Bowa managed the Las Vegas Stars to the PCL championship with an 80–62 record in 1986 and was named to replace Steve Boros as manager of the San Diego Padres (NL) in October 1986. The Seminole, FL, resident is married to the former Sheena Gibson and has one child, Victoria.

BIBLIOGRAPHY: *Chicago Cubs Press Guide 1984*; *TSN Baseball Register, 1984* (St. Louis, 1984); *Who's Who in Baseball 1984*, 69th ed., (New York, 1984).

Brian R. Kelleher

BOYER, Kenton Lloyd "Ken" (b. 20 May 1931, Liberty, MO; d. 7 September 1982, Ballwin, MO), player, coach, and manager, was the son of marble-cutter Chester and Mabel (Means) Boyer. All six Boyer brothers played professional baseball. Cloyd pitched for the St. Louis Cardinals (NL), while Cletis enjoyed his best years as the New York Yankees' (AL) third baseman. St. Louis Cardinals' scout Runt Marr, who had inked Cloyd four years earlier, signed Ken in 1949 after his graduation from Alba (MO) High School. Boyer, who played for Buford Cooper's Alba Aces, agreed to the contract and a $6,000 bonus to help pay for his father's medical bills.

During his first season at Lebanon, PA (NatL), he pitched and sported a lofty .455 batting average. Boyer moved swiftly through the St. Louis minor league system, hitting .306 as a third baseman for Omaha (WL) in 1951. Before Boyer could report to Houston (TL), however, he was drafted into the U.S. Army in 1951. Discharged as a corporal in 1953, he hit .319 for Houston the following season.

The Cardinals liked his progress so much that they traded regular third baseman Ray Jablonski to the Cincinnati Reds after the 1954 season. Boyer, an unabashed success his rookie season, hit .264 and fielded his position with skill. In 1956 he raised his batting average to .306, the first of five times he exceeded the .300 level in his fifteen-year career. Boyer slumped to .265 in 1957 partly because he feuded with general manager Frank Lane. Lane wanted him to assert himself more defensively so the club would draw more fans.

In 1957 Boyer moved to center field in an unselfish attempt to allow the Cardinals to use rookie Eddie Kasko at third. The outfield gave the thick-legged, deceptively fast Boyer more room to display his fielding ability. He led the NL outfielders with a .996 fielding average.

In 1964 Boyer enjoyed his greatest year, hitting .295, knocking in 119 runs, slugging 24 home runs, and winning the NL's Most Valuable Player award. His grand slam off New York Yankees hurler Al Downing in the fourth game of the World Series sparked the Cardinals, who won the classic in seven games.

A bad back in 1965 hampered Boyer, whose batting average slipped to .260. The Cardinals traded him after the 1965 season to the New York Mets (NL) for Al Jackson and Charley Smith. In July 1967, New York traded him to the Chicago White Sox (AL). Boyer finished his active career with the Los Angeles Dodgers (NL) in 1969.

In 2,034 career games, Boyer scored 1,104 runs, made 2,143 hits, slugged 282 homers, knocked in 1,141 runs, and compiled a .287 average. Boyer won five Gold Glove awards (1958–1961, 1963) and led the NL five consecutive years in double plays (1956–1960), tying a record. *The Sporting News* All Star in 1956 and 1961 through 1964, Boyer hit .222 in the 1964 World Series.

After managing Arkansas (TL) in 1970, Boyer coached the next two seasons for the Cardinals. A good organization man, he managed Sarasota, FL (GCL), in 1973 and Tulsa OK (AA) in 1974. In 1977 he advanced to Rochester, NY (IL) but was not chosen to succeed Red Schoendienst* as Cardinals manager. The team instead selected Vern Rapp, a strict disciplinarian. When Rapp was fired during the 1978 season, Boyer became Cardinals manager and compiled a 166–191 record through June 8, 1980. Boyer was scheduled to manage the Cardinals franchise at Louisville (AA) in 1982, when it was discovered that he had inoperable lung cancer. He married Kathleen Oliver on April 11, 1952, and had two daughters and two sons.

BIBLIOGRAPHY: *CB* 43 (1982), p. 44; Gene Karst and Martin J. Jones, Jr., *Who's Who in Professional Baseball* (New York, 1973); Paul MacFarlane, ed., *TSN Daguerreotypes of Great Stars of Baseball* (St. Louis, 1981); Richard Marazzi and Len Fiorito, *Aaron to Zuverink* (New York, 1982); *Newsweek* 100 (September 20, 1982), p. 86; *NYT*, September 8, 1982; *TSN*, September 20, 1982.

William A. Borst

BREADON, Sam (b. 26 July 1876, New York, NY; d. 10 May 1949, St. Louis, MO), owner, combined with Branch Rickey* to bring the St. Louis Cardinals to NL prominence from the 1920s through the 1940s after the franchise had struggled through the first two decades of the century. Breadon's twenty-seven years with the Cardinals saw the development of the NL's first successful farm system, the emergence of the famed Gas House Gang, and NL pennant wins in 1926, 1928, 1930–1931, 1934, 1942–1944, and 1946.

The son of William and Jane (Wilson) Breadon, he attended public schools in New York City (whose accent he never lost). He earned $125 a month as a bank clerk in 1902, then moved west to St. Louis and entered the newly developing automobile business. He started as a $90 a month mechanic and eventually became a partner of socially prominent Marion Lambert in a successful auto sales venture. Breadon first bought into the Cardinals organization with four shares of stock at $50 a share. (He eventually controlled about 80 percent of the club's stock.) Encouraged by civic leader James Jones, he contributed about $7,000 to help buy out Cardinals owner Helene Britton in 1917. Rickey was lured away from the crosstown Browns as club president. In 1920 the Cardinals syndicate moved Breadon into the presidency and made Rickey vice-president and general manager. Breadon's first move involved arranging with Browns owner Philip Ball for a lease on Sportsman's Park in 1921. (The Cardinals continued as tenants until they bought out the Browns in the early 1950s.) In the Cardinals' first NL pennant years in 1926 and 1928, Breadon and Rickey began their history of controversial, generally successful trades and sales. The Cardinals sent their formidable player-manager Rogers Hornsby* to the New York Giants for Frank Frisch,* who led the Redbirds to four NL pennants. In 1938 and 1940 Breadon and Rickey traded Dizzy Dean* and Joe Medwick* of the legendary Gas House Gang when both stars had passed their prime. During the 1940s, Mort and Walker Cooper, Johnny Mize,* and less famous players were sold for very high prices with the fulfilled expectations of youthful replacements from the farm system. Before selling the franchise to Fred Saigh and Postmaster General Robert Hannegan in November 1947, Breadon had seen the Cardinals win nine NL pennants and six World Series under his ownership.

Breadon was considered a hard, fair bargainer by his players, with whom he maintained a formal but genial relationship. With his first wife Josephine (married in 1905) and second wife Rachael (married in 1912), he had two daughters. From 1947 until his death from cancer in 1949, he worked with Hampton Village real estate development in St. Louis.

BIBLIOGRAPHY: Bob Broeg, *Redbirds: A Century of Cardinal Baseball* (St. Louis, 1981); *WWA*, 24th ed. (1950–1951), p. 310.

Leonard Frey

BRESNAHAN, Roger Philip "The Duke of Tralee" (b. 11 June 1879, Toledo, OH; d. 4 December 1944 Toledo, OH), player, coach, and manager, grew up in Toledo, where his family had settled after leaving Tralee, County Kerry, Ireland. As a stocky, powerful teenager playing on the city's sandlots, he quickly impressed local scouts. After a brief stint with Lima, OH (OSL), the right-handed pitcher signed with Washington (NL) late in 1897. He made his major league debut as a pitcher in August of that year and, in his first appearance, shut out St. Louis 3–0 on six hits. In the final month of the 1897 season, he made six more pitching appearances and compiled a perfect 4–0 record.

When Bresnahan held out for more money prior to the 1898 season, Washington released him. He drifted back to the minor leagues, playing briefly for Toledo (ISL) in 1898 and Minneapolis (WL) in 1899. After appearing in two games in 1900 for Chicago (NL), he signed with John McGraw's* Baltimore Orioles (AL) in 1901. In the middle of the 1902 season, McGraw became manager of the New York Giants (NL) and persuaded Bresnahan and Oriole teammates Frank Bowerman, Joe McGinnity,* and John Cronin to jump to the Giants to help rebuild the struggling franchise.

Bresnahan spent the next six seasons with McGraw's Giants, who rose from the cellar in 1902 to finish second in 1903 and first in 1904 and 1905. Despite his bulky 5 foot, 9 inch, 200 pound frame, he played center field in 1903 and 1904 and frequently hit in the leadoff position. In 1903 he enjoyed his best season offensively, getting 142 hits (including 42 for extra bases), stealing 34 bases, and batting .350. Bresnahan, who worked as a detective in the off-season, became the Giants' regular catcher in 1905 and quickly developed innovative catching techniques, game strategies, and natural leadership qualities. As the batterymate for Giant pitchers Christy Mathewson,* McGinnity, Red Ames, Dummy Taylor, and Hooks Wiltse, he won the nickname "The Duke of Tralee." In the 1905 World Series, he hit .313 and caught Mathewson's three shutouts over Connie Mack's* Philadelphia Athletics. Disregarding the taunts of players and fans, he began using shin guards in 1907 and paved the way for their rapid adoption throughout baseball. In 1908 he caught in 139 games and led NL batters with 83 walks.

In a three-way deal in December 1908, the Giants traded Bresnahan to the St. Louis Cardinals (NL). He served as player-manager there from 1909 through 1912, but the Cardinals hired Miller Huggins* as manager in 1913. After a long salary dispute with Bresnahan, the Cardinals sold him to the Chicago Cubs (NL) in June. From 1913 through 1915, Bresnahan shared the Cubs' catching duties with Jimmy Archer. As player-manager in 1915, he guided Chicago to a fourth place finish. From 1916 through 1923, he managed Toledo (AA) and briefly held a controlling interest in the club.

Bresnahan coached for the New York Giants (NL) from 1925 to 1928 and helped develop young southpaw Carl Hubbell.* In 1931 he joined the Detroit Tigers (AL) coaching staff and stayed two seasons before retiring from the game. After returning to Toledo, he worked as turnkey of the city's municipal workhouse and later as a brewing company salesman. In the November 1944 general election, he ran unsuccessfully for county commissioner on the Democratic ticket. Bresnahan, who suffered from a chronic heart ailment, died one month later.

Bresnahan served pro baseball for one-third of a century as a player, coach, manager, and owner, appearing in 1,430 major league games and compiling a lifetime .279 batting average. Best known for his defensive skills and hard-nosed competitiveness, he played an instrumental role in the development of the modern-day catcher's position. Bresnahan, whom McGraw and Branch Rickey* considered the best catcher they had ever seen, was inducted into the National Baseball Hall of Fame in 1945.

BIBLIOGRAPHY: Chicago *Daily Tribune*, Demember 5, 1944; Cappy Gagnon, "The Debut of Roger Bresnahan," *Baseball Research Journal* 8 (1979), pp. 41–42; Irving A. Leitner, *Baseball: Diamond in the Rough* (New York, 1972); Paul MacFarlane, ed., *TSN Daguerreotypes of Great Stars of Baseball* (St. Louis, 1981); New York *Herald Tribune*, December 5, 1944; Joseph L. Reichler, ed., *Official Baseball Encyclopedia*, 6th ed. (New

York, 1985); pp. 619, 747–748; David Quentin Voigt, *American Baseball*, vol. 2 (Norman, OK 1970).

Raymond D. Kush

BRETT, George Howard (b. 15 May 1953, Glendale, WV), player, is the youngest son of accountant Jack and bookkeeper Ethel Brett. His brother Kenneth pitched in the major leagues, while brothers John and Robert played minor league baseball. The Bretts moved in 1955 to Hermosa Beach, CA, where George starred in football and baseball at El Segundo High School. An easygoing bachelor, Brett attended El Camino Junior College (CA) and Longview Community College (MO).

The Kansas City Royals (AL) drafted him as a shortstop in 1971 and assigned him to Billings, MT, where he hit .291 and made the All-PrL team. In 1972 he led the CaL in sacrifice hits and assists for third basemen at San Jose. At Omaha in 1973, he batted .284, knocked in 117 runs, and made the AA All-Star team as third baseman. The 6 foot, 185 pound Brett, who bats left-handed and throws right-handed, joined the Kansas City Royals (AL) in late 1973 and started at third base in 1974. Batting instructor Charlie Lau made Brett, who had never hit .300 in the minor leagues, a consistent spray line drive hitter, while Hal McRae* taught him to run the bases aggressively. In 1975 Brett batted .308, paced the AL with 195 hits and 13 triples, and led third basemen in nearly all offensive categories. In 1976 Brett again led the AL in triples, tying a major league mark for accomplishing the feat two consecutive seasons. He established a major league record for most consecutive games (6) with three or more hits from May 8 through 13, 1976.

As a major leaguer, the sandy-haired Brett compiled a .314 batting average through the 1986 season. He has made 2,095 hits, including 428 doubles, 112 triples, and 209 home runs, and knocked in 1,050 runs. Besides exceeding the .300 mark in nine of thirteen full seasons, Brett won AL batting titles with .333 in 1976 and .390 in 1980. He also paced the AL in hits, triples (1975, 1976, 1979), and slugging percentage three times (1980, 1983, 1985), and once each in doubles (1979) and total bases (1976). The only player besides Ty Cobb* to win three AL titles in hits and triples, in 1979 he became one of only five players to slug at least 20 doubles, 20 triples, and 20 home runs the same season. Brett hit for the cycle on May 28, 1979, and slugged three home runs in the same game on July 22, 1979, and April 20, 1983. Defensively, Brett possesses good hands and range at third base and often makes errors because of inconsistent throws. Through 1986, Brett has batted .304 in nine All-Star games (1976–1979, 1981–1985) and .340 in six AL Championship Series (1976–1978, 1980, 1984–1985).

In 1980 Brett enjoyed among the finest batting performances of the modern era. From May to the All-Star break, he raised his batting average from .247 to .337. Brett then hit in 37 consecutive games from mid-July to mid-August to reach the .400 mark and finished the season with a sparkling .390. Besides recording the highest major league batting average since 1941, he tied John McGraw* for the highest hitting percentage by a third baseman. In 117 games, Brett compiled a .664 slugging percentage and a .461 on-base percentage and knocked in 118 runs to become the first player in thirty years to drive in over one run per game played. Brett slugged 24 home runs and struck out only 22 times. He hit two home runs in the AL playoffs, helping the Royals defeat the New York Yankees. Although Brett batted .375 and made four extra-base hits in the World Series, the Royals lost to the Philadelphia Phillies. An AL MVP, he won the AL Silver Bat, Joe Cronin,* and Fred Hutchinson awards and was named *The Sporting News*, *Sport*, and Associated Press Major League Player of the Year. The highly competitive, enthusiastic Brett negotiated a multiyear contract for $1 million per season.

In 1985 Brett paced the Royals to their second AL pennant and first World Series title and finished second in the MVP balloting. During the regular season, he finished first in slugging percentage (.585), second in batting average (.335) and on-base percentage (.436), and fifth in RBIs (112), doubles (38), and runs scored (108), and belted a career-high 30 home runs. Five Brett home runs came in the final six victories that gave Kansas City its Western Division title. The AL playoff MVP, Brett batted .348 overall and hit two homers, one double, and one single and knocked in three runs in game three against Toronto. In the World Series, he batted .370 against the St. Louis Cardinals.

At Yankee Stadium in July 1983, Brett hit a controversial ninth inning home run, temporarily giving the Royals the lead. After the New York Yankees appealed, however, the umpire disallowed the home run because of pine tar on the hitting surface of Brett's bat. AL president Leland MacPhail, Jr.* later reinstated Brett's home run. In 1986 Brett made his 2,000th major league hit and was named to the AL All-Star team for the eleventh consecutive time.

BIBLIOGRAPHY: *CB* (1981), pp. 33–36; *TSN Baseball Register, 1985* (St. Louis, 1985); Gib Twyman, *Born to Hit: The George Brett Story* (New York, 1982)

David L. Porter

BRIDGES, Thomas Jefferson Davis "Tommy" (b. 28 December 1906, Gordonsville, TN; d. 19 April 1968, Nashville, TN), player, coach, and scout, was the elder of two children of Dr. Joe Gill and Florence (Davis) Bridges. He graduated from Gordonsville elementary and high schools and attended the University of Tennessee. He married Carolyn Jellicorse on March 21, 1930, had one daughter, and later wed Iona Veda Kidwell on May 17, 1950. The Bridges family included several generations of doctors and expected Tommy to carry on the tradition. In 1929, however, after four years at Tennessee, he left without a degree to play professional baseball.

He was signed by Detroit Tiger (AL) scout Billy Doyle, who had seen him pitch for the Vols, and joined Wheeling, WV (MAL), in midseason. At Evansville, IN (3IL), the following year, he struck out 189 batters in 20 games and was promoted to the Tigers. In his first major league appearance, in relief against the New York Yankees, he retired Babe Ruth* on a grounder and struck out Lou Gehrig.*

In 1932 Bridges shut out the Washington Senators 12–0, coming within one out of a perfect game before yielding a pinch hit single to Dave Harris. He hurled two other one-hitters and 33 career shutouts. He teamed with Eldon Auker in 1936 to win the biggest double shutout of all time (14–0, 12–0) against the St. Louis Browns. The slender 5 foot, 10 1/2 inch, 155 pounder was quiet in demeanor; even his frequent laughter was silent. Besides demonstrating good speed, he gained fame for a sharp-breaking, down-and-out curve, the best thrown by any right-hander in the league. Less well recognized was his occasional spitter. Despite his personal control, Bridges was plagued by wildness on the mound. He issued more than 100 walks in each of six seasons and averaged .42 walks per inning.

During a sixteen-year career with the Tigers, Bridges won 194 games and lost 138 for a .584 percentage and a 3.57 ERA. From 1934 to 1936 he won 66 games and twice led the AL in strikeouts. He also pitched in the 1934, 1935, 1940, and 1945 World Series, winning four of five decisions. In his second triumph over the Chicago Cubs in 1935, he entered the ninth inning of the sixth game with the score tied. The Cubs' Stan Hack* led off with a triple, only to be stranded when Bridges retired the side on ten pitched balls.

Tommy served in the U.S. Army for two years and rejoined the Tigers for the 1946 season. He pitched for Portland (PCL) from 1947 to 1949 and San Francisco (PCL) and Seattle (PCL) in 1950 and coached and scouted for the Cincinnati Reds (NL) in 1951. He scouted for the Tigers (AL) from 1958 through 1960 and New York Mets (1963 to 1968) and worked for a Detroit tire company. Aside from baseball, he enjoyed hunting, fishing, and golf.

BIBLIOGRAPHY: Clifford Bloodgood, "Tom Bridges of the Tigers," *Baseball Magazine* 50 (April, 1933) pp. 507–508; Detroit *Free Press*, August 31, September 7, 1941, February 10, 1957; Donald Honig, *Baseball When the Grass Was Real* (New York, 1975); Frederick G. Lieb, *The Detroit Tigers* (New York, 1946); Ronald G. Liebman, "The Most Lopsided Shutouts," *Baseball Research Journal* 7 (1976) p. 53; Thomas Bridges file, National Baseball Hall of Fame Library, Cooperstown, NY; Joseph L. Reichler, ed., *The Baseball Encyclopedia*, 6th ed. (New York, 1985), pp. 1,612–1,613.

A. D. Suehsdorf

BRIGGS, Walter Owen "Spike" (b. 27 February 1877, Ypsilanti, MI; d. 17 January 1952, Miami Beach, FL), club owner and president, was a son of locomotive engineer Rodney Davis and Ada (Warner) Briggs. He played first base and caught for the John S. Newberry Public School in Detroit but left school at age 14 to become a car checker for the Michigan Central Railroad. He advanced to car department foreman before leaving the company eleven years later. Subsequently, he worked as a cement plant foreman, shipping clerk, and auto body trimmer before joining B. F. Everitt Company, Detroit car body makers, in 1904 as vice-president. In 1906 he became company president. Three years later he organized the Briggs Manufacturing Company and merged B. F. Everitt with it. The new company rapidly became a major supplier of automotive bodies for the Ford and later Chrysler motor companies, making Briggs a multimillionaire.

A rabid lifetime baseball fan, Briggs acquired ownership of the Detroit Tigers (AL) in stages. At the invitation of club president Frank Navin,* he bought a 25 percent interest from the William Yawkey estate in 1920 and another 25 percent after part-owner John Kelsey died. He purchased the balance following Navin's death in late 1935. Briggs drew no salary, turned all profits into team operations, and spent his own money lavishly on the Tigers. Reputedly, he put over $5 million into the remodeling of Briggs Stadium (formerly Navin Field). He provided liberal salaries for his players and advanced huge sums for the acquisition of Mickey Cochrane,* Al Simmons,* Freddy Hutchinson, and prize rookie Dick Wakefield. In 1941 *The Sporting News* named Briggs baseball Executive of the Year for his acumen in operating the Tigers, salary generosity, faith in baseball, and sportsmanship. During his sole ownership, the Tigers won AL pennants in 1940 and 1945 and the World Series in 1945.

Briggs married Jane Cameron in 1904 and had five children: Grace Mary (Mrs. William D. Robinson), Elizabeth Jane (Mrs. Charles T. Fisher, Jr.), Walter Owen II "Spike," Susan Ann (Mrs. Everell Fisher), and Jane Cameron (Mrs. Philip A. Hart, Jr.). Briggs died of a kidney infection at his Miami Beach winter home. The energetic, willful Briggs became a major industrialist by expanding his automotive body company, promoting land developments in Florida and Arizona, and engaging in other diverse business enterprises. He remained undeterred by a paralysis of the legs, which confined him to a wheelchair during his final dozen years. He donated money frequently (often anonymously) for the civic betterment of Detroit and its people. His other sports interests included ownership of a racing stable and a 236-foot yacht. Son "Spike" succeeded him as president of the Tigers and served until 1956, when control of the Detroit club passed from the Briggs family to an eleven-man syndicate.

BIBLIOGRAPHY: Frederick G. Lieb, *The Detroit Tigers* (New York, 1946); *National Cyclopedia of American Biography* 51 (New York, 1969), p. 524; *The New England Historical and Genealogical Register*, vol. 110 (Boston, January 1956), p. 65; *NYT*, January 18, 1952, July 4, 1970; *TSN*, November 28, December 5, 1935, July 30, 1942, January 23, 1952, February 23, 1955, July 18, 1970; *Who Was Who in America* 3 (1951–1960), pp. 103–104.

Frank V. Phelps

BROCK, Louis Clark "Lou" (b. 18 June 1939, El Dorado, AR), player, is
the son of Maud and Paralee Brock and the seventh of nine children. When
Maud deserted the family shortly after Louis' birth, Paralee moved to Col-
liston, LA, just below the Arkansas border and performed domestic and farm
work to support the family. Brock attended all-black schools in Mer Rouge,
LA, and from 1954 to 1957 starred on the Union High School baseball and
basketball teams. In 1957 he received a scholarship to Southern University
at Baton Rouge. Although hitting a paltry .186 as a freshman, he impressed
big league scouts with a .645 batting average his sophomore year. In 1959
he played in the Pan American games at Chicago. Brock married college
sweetheart Katie Hay in December 1960, and has two children, Wanda and
Louis, Jr.

After accepting a $30,000 bonus with the Chicago Cubs (NL) in 1961, he
led the NoL the same year with 268 total bases, 181 hits, 117 runs, 33
doubles, and a .361 batting average at St. Cloud, MN(NoL). In September
1961, he was called up by the Cubs (NL). After two mediocre seasons in
Chicago, Brock was sent on June 15, 1964, to St. Louis (NL) for Ernie
Broglio and Bobby Shantz. Although initially outraged, Cardinals fans
quickly admired their new left fielder. The 5 foot, 11 1/2 inch, 170 pound
Brock hit .348 and pilfered 33 bases the remainder of 1964, sparking the
Redbirds to their first NL pennant since 1946. His career comprised fifteen
more seasons, all with St. Louis.

From 1965 through 1969, Brock averaged 100 runs, 190 hits, and 61 stolen
bases per year. He dominated the 1967 and 1968 World Series, hitting .414
and .464 and setting World Series records with seven stolen bases in each.
Although leading NL outfielders in errors seven times and striking out over
1,700, times, Brock compensated with his hitting and revolutionary daring
on the basepaths. From 1970 through 1976, Brock collected 1,295 hits, swiped
478 bases, and averaged .306 at the plate.

On September 10, 1974, Brock broke Maury Wills'* single-season major
league theft record of 104 on his way to 118. Longtime teammate Tim
McCarver attributed Brock's success to his intimidation of infielders. In 1977
Brock surpassed Ty Cobb's* career stolen base record of 892. Brock hoped
in 1978 to join boyhood hero Stan Musial* in the 3,000 hit club, but a dismal
.221 season left him 100 hits short. At age 40 in 1979, Brock rebounded to
hit .304 in his last campaign and made his 3,000th hit on August 13 against
the Cubs' Dennis Lamp. Brock's nineteen-year major league career included
3,023 hits, 1,610 runs, a record 938 stolen bases, 486 doubles, 141 triples,
and 149 home runs. He stole 50 or more bases twelve consecutive seasons,
another major league record.

Brock played healthy or injured, always with enthusiasm and determination. He demonstrated that speed could be a viable alternative to power,
making the stolen bases as exciting as the home run. Former Redbird skipper
Red Schoendienst* commented in Brock's book, *Stealing is My Game*: "He

just loves to play ball. If you could play as well as him, wouldn't you?" Brock is very dedicated to the St. Louis community and has been involved with the Lou Brock Boys' Club since 1965. His civic awards include the B'nai B'rith Brotherhood Award, St. Louis Jaycees' Man of the Year, and the Roberto Clemente Award. Brock is engaged in the florist business in St. Louis and has several other commercial interests there. In 1985 he was elected to the National Baseball Hall of Fame.

BIBLIOGRAPHY: Louis Brock and Franz Schulze, *Stealing Is My Game* (Englewood Cliffs, NJ, 1976); Bob Broeg, *Redbirds: A Century of Cardinal Baseball* (St. Louis, 1981); *CB* (1975), pp. 43–45; Nila Gilcrest, "Katie Brock: In Every Way an All-Star," *TSN*, July 1, 1972, p. 15; Bill Guzman, *Munson, Garvey, Brock, and Carew* (New York, 1976); Rich Koster, "Tim McCarver: Twenty Years Behind the Mask," *Baseball Digest* 38 (December, 1979); Neal Russo, "At Age 32, Base Thief Brock Plots More, Bigger Heists," *TSN*, January 1, 1972, p. 33; Neal Russo, "Brock Still a Jet Fast Thief on 33rd Birthday," *TSN*, July 1, 1972, pp. 15, 20.

Frank J. Olmsted

BROUTHERS, Dennis Joseph "Dan," "Big Dan" (b. 8 May 1858, Sylvan Lake, NY; d. 2 August 1932, East Orange, NJ), player, coach, and scout, was reared in Wappingers Falls, N.Y. and attended school there to age 16. He began semi-professional ball in his late teens with the Wappingers Falls Actives, playing five years for various semi-pro and independent clubs, with brief stops in 1879–1880 at Troy, NY (NL). From 1881 to 1885 Brouthers played for Buffalo and twice (1882, 1883) led the NL in batting. The hard-hitting first baseman proved the mightiest of the team's renowned "big four," which also included Hardy Richardson, Jack Rowe, and Deacon White.* In December 1884, he married Mary Ellen Croak of Wappingers Falls. They had four children, Leo A., Allison, Margaret, and Lillian M.

Sold as a group in late 1885 to Detroit (NL), the big four helped the Wolverines capture their first pennant in 1887. Brouthers spent three seasons in Detroit (1886–1888) and then played three years for Boston teams in three major leagues (NL, 1889; PL, 1890; AA, 1891). At Boston, he twice won his league's batting championship (1889, 1891) and twice helped his club win the pennants (1890, 1891).

Brouthers spent the remainder of his major league career in the NL. At Brooklyn in 1892 he won his fifth batting title. After joining Baltimore in 1894, he helped the Orioles with their first pennant and formed a lifelong friendship with teammate John McGraw.* Except for two games played in 1904 for McGraw's New York Giants, Brouthers finished his major league career with Louisville in 1895 and Philadelphia in 1896.

Brouthers played minor league ball in the EL from 1896 to 1899 with Springfield, MA, Toronto, and Rochester, NY, leading the EL in batting in 1897. He returned to the ball field intermittently after 1899, performing in 1904–1905 for Poughkeepsie, NY (HRL).

Brouthers remained active in baseball as a coach and scout (finding future Giants players Fred Merkle, Larry Doyle,* and Buck Herzog), and briefly owned a minor league club in Newburgh, NY. He worked many years until his death for McGraw's Giants as night watchman, press box chief, and stadium attendant. Mary Allen, his wife of over forty-seven years, died just two weeks after him and was survived by two daughters and two sons.

Christened Dennis but called "Dan" or "Big Dan," the 6 foot, 2 inch, 207 pound Brouthers was physically large for his day. He batted and threw left-handed, and reputedly possessed the sharpest batting eye in baseball. (He allegedly originated the familiar advice to hitters to "keep your eye on the ball.") As a major leaguer, he struck out less than once every seven games. From 1882 to 1892, he ranked among the top six batters in his league. His .343 lifetime batting average ranks fourth highest among his contemporaries and ninth highest of all time. In 1,673 games, he compiled 2,304 hits, 461 doubles, 106 home runs, 1,523 runs, 1056 RBIs, and 235 stolen bases.

The premier power hitter of his era, Brouthers led his league seven times in slugging average (1881–1886, 1891), four times in total bases, three times in doubles, twice in home runs, and once in triples. His .520 lifetime slugging average surpassed that of the next best nineteenth century slugger by 15 points. Brouthers was elected to the National Baseball Hall of Fame in 1945. In 1971 his home town of Wappingers Falls erected a monument to him at a Little League park by renaming it Brouthers Field.

BIBLIOGRAPHY: "Big Dan's Bat," *TSN*, February 5, 1898; Sam Crane, "Dan Brouthers," New York *Journal*, December 11, 1911; Paul MacFarlane, ed., *TSN Daguerreotypes of Great Stars of Baseball* (St. Louis, 1981), p. 33; Tom Meany, "McGraw Praises Brouthers," New York *World Telegram*, August 4, 1932; Newark *Star Eagle*, August 3, 1932; *NYT*, August 3, 1932; Poughkeepsie (NY) *Evening Star*, August 3, 1932; Joseph L. Reichler, ed., *The Baseball Encyclopedia*, 6th ed. (New York, 1985), p. 754; "Two Old Timers Talk Things Over," New York *World Telegram*, June 2, 1931; *Wappingers Falls Past and Present 1871–1971* (Wappingers Falls, NY, 1971), pp. 47–49; Will Whitman, "Dan Brouthers Noted Batsman," Canton (NY) *Advertiser*, August 20, 1932.

Frederick Ivor-Campbell

BROWN, Mordecai Peter Centennial "Three Finger," "Miner" (b. 19 October 1876, Nyesville, IN; d. 14 February 1948, Terre Haute, IN), player and manager, grew up in rural Indiana. Nicknamed "Three Finger" and "Miner," he played third base for the Coxville, IN, semi-professional team, composed mostly of miners. In 1901 he pitched for Terre Haute (3IL), winning 23 games and losing 8. The following year saw him at Omaha (WL), where his record was 27 wins, 15 losses.

During his major league career, he pitched for the St. Louis Cardinals

(1903), Chicago Cubs (1904–1912, 1916), and Cincinnati Reds (1913) of the NL, and St. Louis, Brooklyn, and Chicago of the FL (1914–1915). Brown, whose career ERA was a near-record 2.06, threw 57 career shutouts and won 239 games and lost 129 for a .649 winning percentage. His outstanding pitching helped Chicago capture NL championships from 1906 to 1908 and in 1910. He won five World Series games, including two in relief, fielded superbly, and handled 108 chances without an error in 1908. He shared with Christy Mathewson* several World Series fielding records for pitchers. During a remarkable 1911 season, Brown won 16 of 27 starts, completed 21 games, and led the NL with 26 relief appearances and 13 saves.

After his major league career, Brown pitched for Columbus (IL) in 1917–1918 and was player-manager for Terre Haute (3IL) in 1919–1920. The Terre Haute resident managed a semi-professional team and operated a filling station until he retired in 1945. In 1949 he was elected to the National Baseball Hall of Fame.

As a youth, "Three Finger" Brown caught his hand in a feed cutter and lost the top joint of his index finger and the use of his little finger. When his injured hand was still in a cast, he broke the other two fingers, which became permanently misshapen. With his crippled hand, Brown threw a natural sinker ball.

BIBLIOGRAPHY: Warren Brown, *The Chicago Cubs* (New York, 1946); Ralph Hickok, *Who Was Who in American Sports* (New York, 1971); Gene Karst and Martin J. Jones, Jr., *Who's Who in Professional Baseball* (New Rochelle, NY, 1973); *Macmillan Baseball Encyclopedia* (New York, 1969); *NYT*, February 15, 1948; Lowell Reidenbaugh, *Cooperstown Where Baseball's Legends Live Forever* (St. Louis, 1983).

John E. Findling

BROWN, Robert William "Bobby" (b. 25 October 1924, Seattle, WA), player and executive, is the son of William Christopher Brown, an executive with Schenley Distillery, and Myrtle Katherine (Berg) Brown. Brown, whose father started him playing baseball "before I can remember," attended Columbia High School in San Francisco from 1940 through 1942. After studying at Stanford University in 1942–1943 and the University of California at Los Angeles in 1943–1944, he enrolled in Tulane University's School of Medicine in 1944 and graduated in 1950. He since has been named to the Athletic Halls of Fame at both Stanford and Tulane.

Brown, whose sole competitive athletic interest was baseball, threw right-handed, batted left-handed, and found hitting his strong suit. He signed for a substantial bonus with the New York Yankees (AL) in 1946 and played that season with their Newark (IL) farm team, where he roomed with Yogi Berra.* (Berra once finished a comic book, turned to Brown, who was putting down a medical text, and asked, "How'd yours come out?") In 1946 Brown was named Outstanding New Jersey Athlete. Brown appeared briefly with the Yankees in 1946 and made the permanent team roster in 1947, leading the AL in pinch hits (9). Platooned at third base, he played against right-handed pitchers and never appeared in more than 113 games or accumulated over 363 at bats in a season. The 6 foot, 1 inch, 180 pound Brown batted .279 lifetime and hit with some power, as 98 of his 452 major league hits went for extra bases. In 548 games, he slugged 62 doubles, 14 triples, and 22 home runs, scored 233 runs, knocked in 237 runs, and walked 214 times. In four World Series (1947, 1949–1951), he batted .439 and made 8 extra-base hits among his 17 total hits. Brown was drafted into the U.S. Army during the 1952 season and missed the entire 1953 campaign. After appearing in 28 games in 1954, he retired to begin his medical internship.

From 1958 to 1984 Brown practiced cardiology in Fort Worth, TX. He lived there with his wife, Sara Kathryn (French) Brown, whom he had married in October 16, 1951. By 1984 Brown commented that he "wanted to either decrease my patient load or get into a different type of medicine." In 1984 he was offered the AL presidency, "an offer too tempting to turn down." By combining professional baseball and specialized medicine, Brown has already enjoyed an unorthodox career. The AL presidency gives him a third unconventional challenge.

BIBLIOGRAPHY: Joseph L. Reichler, ed., *The Baseball Encyclopedia*, 6th ed. (New York, 1985), p. 754; Luther W. Spoehr, correspondence with Robert W. Brown, 1985.

Luther W. Spoehr

BROWN, Willard Jesse (b. 26 June 1915, Shreveport, LA), player, starred from 1935 through 1956 in the NAL, MEL, PRWL, and TL. Brown and Hank Thompson were the major leagues' first black teammates with the 1947 St. Louis Browns (AL), but rejection by team members and prevailing attitudes in this border city gave Brown little opportunity to display his talents. Before being released, he batted .179 in 21 games.

He played professionally with the Kansas City Monarchs (NAL) from 1935 through 1951, except for 1940 in Mexico, 1943–1945 in the U.S. Army, 1950 with Ottawa (BL), and his stint with the Browns. After playing in the Dominican Republic in 1952, Brown performed in the TL with Dallas, Houston, Austin, San Antonio, and Tulsa from 1953 through 1956 and completed his career at Topeka (WL).

Available statistics indicate a .351 average with 8 home runs, 61 RBIs, and 13 stolen bases on a 70-game MEL tour in 1940. From 1946 through 1948, he posted .348, .336, and .374 batting averages for the Monarchs and paced the NAL with 18 home runs in 66 1948 contests. In two Negro World Series competitions, Brown hit .304 with three homers and 14 RBIs in 11 games. His 10 RBIs in the 1946 classic led all batters. He batted .309 in 588 games over five consecutive minor league seasons with 95 home runs and

437 RBIs. His best season in organized baseball came in 1954 with 35 home runs, 120 RBIs, and a .314 batting average for Dallas and Houston (TL).

Brown's winter league accolades included setting the Puerto Rican single season record with 27 home runs (1947–1948) and 97 RBIs (1949–1950). From 1946–1947 through 1949–1950 there, he claimed three home run crowns, four RBI titles, and three batting championships. The 5 foot, 11 inch, 200 pound right-hander possessed great speed and proved an excellent outfielder with a strong arm. Brown played on five NAL championship teams with Kansas City (1937, 1939, 1941–1942, 1946). The 1942 club swept the powerful Washington Grays in the Negro World Series, as Brown hit .412 in four games. He performed for two TL titlists, Dallas in 1953 and Houston the following year. Brown appeared in six Negro league All-Star games from 1936 through 1949.

BIBLIOGRAPHY: Baltimore *Afro-American*, September 20, 1947; Chicago *Defender*, September 28, October 5, 1946; Kansas City *Call*, September 20, 27, 1946; *Mexican League Individual Batting* (1940); National Baseball Hall of Fame, *Negro Players Reports*, No. 4 (April 1, 1972); *Negro American League Statistics* 1948; Newark (NJ) *News*, *September 18, 24, 30, 1946;* Newark (NJ) *Star Ledger*, September 30, 1946; New Jersey *Afro-American*, September 21, 28, October 5, 1946; Robert W. Peterson, *Only the Ball Was White* (Englewood Cliffs, NJ, 1970); Philadelphia *Afro-American*, September 19, 1942; Philadelphia *Tribune*, September 19, 1942; James A. Riley, *The All-Time All-Stars of Black Baseball* (Cocoa, FL, 1983); Pepe Seda, *Don Q Baseball Cues* (Ponce, PR, 1970); *TSN Official Baseball Guide, 1951, 1954–1957* (St. Louis, 1951, 1954–1957); Jules Tygiel, *Baseball's Great Experiment* (New York, 1983).

Merl F. Kleinknecht

BROWNING, Louis R. "Pete," "Old Pete," "The Gladiator" (b. 17 June 1861, Louisville, KY; d. 10 September 1905, Louisville, KY), player, received minimal education at home. Nicknamed "Old Pete" or "The Gladiator," he played principally with Louisville (AA). One of baseball's most colorful players, the superstitious Browning invariably touched third base on his way to the dugout (believing it made him a better hitter), refused to cross puddles, and referred to his eyes as "lamps." The notoriously loquacious Browning fully enjoyed his stardom and often introduced himself as a "champion batter."

Partially deaf, Browning suffered from mastoiditis or an infection of the middle ear. This painful affliction may have caused his excessive drinking. Browning's club once left him behind when he was too intoxicated to find the train. "I can't hit the ball," Pete tragically commented, "until I hit the bottle." A writer observed, "Pete is a queer character. In spite of his faults he has the qualities of a popular favorite."

Baseball has seen few better natural hitters. During his career from 1882 to 1894, Browning compiled the tenth highest batting average (.343 to .355, depending on the source consulted) in major league baseball history. Browning, it was noted, loved to hit. A three-time batting champion (AA, 1882 and 1885; PL, 1890), Browning hit an incredible .402 in 1887 when walks counted as hits. Tip O'Neill hit above .400 that year, with Browning placing second. After a .382 rookie season, he only twice hit below .300. "Browning," famed pitcher Charles Radbourne* declared, "is the most wicked hitter in the business," while another pitcher commented, "He can hit the ball any-where." During his career, the powerful Browning slugged 299 doubles, 89 triples, and 47 home runs among his 1,654 hits.

In May 1887, a reporter described his all-around baseball skills: "His work in center field has been capital, and some of his difficult catches have not been equalled on the local grounds [Louisville]. He is playing the best game of his life, and that is saying a great deal. The reason is clear—Pete is abstaining from drink." Although he disliked sliding, Browning ran the bases well and stole 103 bases in 1887. Primarily an outfielder, he also played the infield early in his career and even pitched. Since Pete insisted on bats made to his specifications, John Hillerich made him a special one known later as the Louisville Slugger. Browning's success generated demands from other players for made-to-order bats, enabling the Hillerich & Bradsby firm to launch a successful business.

Browning, contemporaries said, knew and thought only of baseball. After a game, his temper was "reckoned by the number of hits" he made. A longtime Louisville favorite, Pete jumped to Cleveland (PL) in 1890 because "they ain't treated me right here since 1886." The Louisville club retorted, "He was treated much better than he deserved." The feud failed to trouble Browning, whose .387 average won the PL batting title. After Browning's last major league appearance (three games in 1894), he played several seasons in the minors and retired. Returning to Louisville, he tried several careers unsuccessfully. An only slightly exaggerated tribute from 1890 noted, "Browning is the greatest hitter the world has ever produced."

BIBLIOGRAPHY: Louis R. Browning file, National Baseball Hall of Fame Library, Cooperstown, NY; Louisville *Times*, September 11, 1905; Joseph Reichler, *The Great All-Time Baseball Record Book* (New York, 1981); Joseph Reichler, ed., *The Baseball Encyclopedia*, 6th ed. (New York, 1985); Harold Seymour, *Baseball: The Early Years* (New York, 1960); Robert Smith, *Pioneers of Baseball* (Boston, 1978); *Spalding's Base Ball Guide, 1882–1893* (New York, 1882–1893); *Sporting Life*, September 16, 1905.

Duane A. Smith

BUCKNER, William Joseph "Bill" (b. 14 December 1949, Vallejo, CA), player, starred in football and baseball at Napa (CA) High School, and was elected to the Northern California Football Hall of Fame. After graduating from Napa High School in 1968, he subsequently attended the University of Southern California and Arizona State University. His brothers Robert and James both played minor league baseball. The Los Angeles Dodgers

(NL) selected Buckner in the second round of the June, 1968, draft and assigned him to Ogden, UT (PrL), where he won the batting championship with a .344 average. In 1969 Buckner hit .307 for Albuquerque (TL) and .315 for Spokane (PCL). Buckner's .335 batting average in 1970 at Spokane ranked him third in the PCL.

After brief appearances with the Los Angeles Dodgers in 1969 and 1970, Buckner hit .277 his rookie 1971 season there. Although playing some games at first base, he was used primarily as an outfielder with the Dodgers. Buckner helped the Dodgers with the 1974 NL pennant by batting .314 and then hit .250 in the World Series against the Oakland Athletics. In April, 1975, Buckner suffered a severely sprained left ankle while sliding into second base. This led to an operation in September, 1975, to remove a tendon. Bone chips were removed later from his left ankle during another operation, causing him to become a first baseman. Buckner was traded in January, 1977, to the Chicago Cubs (NL) and remained there until being sent to the Boston Red Sox (AL) in May, 1984.

An extremely competitive player, the left-hander has emerged as an excellent contact hitter and rarely walks or strikes out. The 6 foot, 185 pound Buckner hits to all fields and is an excellent student of pitchers, batting over .300 seven times. He led the NL with a .324 batting average in 1980 and 35 doubles in 1981 and tied for the NL lead with 38 doubles in 1983. In 1982 Buckner became the first Cub since Billy Williams* in 1970 to surpass 200 hits. Besides making 201 hits, he established career highs in runs (93) and walks (36) and knocked in 105 runs. Buckner also established a major league record for most assists by a first baseman (159), but broke the mark the next year with 161 assists and in 1985 with 184 assists. In 1985 Buckner batted .299 and ranked second in the AL in doubles (46) and third in hits (201), and tied for sixth in RBIs (110). Buckner's games played (162), at bats (673), doubles, and RBIs established career highs, while his hits tied a career peak. The next year, Buckner batted .269, tied for third in doubles (39), slugged 18 home runs, and knocked in 102 runs in helping the Red Sox win the AL pennant. Buckner, who suffered from a strained achilles tendon and had two bad legs, batted .214 in the AL Championship Series against the California Angels. He hit only .188 in the World Series against the New York Mets and made an error that let in the winning run in game six. Through the 1986 season, Buckner batted .292 in 2,176 career games, and recorded 1,008 runs scored, 2,464 hits, 462 doubles, 46 triples, 164 home runs, 1,072 RBIs, and 175 stolen bases. He is married to Jody Schenck and has two children, Brittany and Kristen Ashley.

BIBLIOGRAPHY: *Boston Red Sox 1985 Media Guide*; William Buckner file, National Baseball Hall of Fame Library, Cooperstown, NY; Jim Kaplan, "He's off in a Zone of His Own," *SI* 57 (September 13, 1982), pp. 48–51; Louis Kraft, "Bill Buckner: The Odyssey of a Major League Survivor," *Baseball Digest* 44 (May, 1985), pp. 25–28; Dick Miller, "Bill Buckner: Profile of a Contact Hitter," *Baseball Digest* 38 (August,

1979), pp. 20–24; David S. Neft and Richard M. Cohen, *The Sports Encyclopedia*, 6th ed. (New York, 1985); Joseph L.Reichler, ed., *The Baseball Encyclopedia*, 6th ed. (New York, 1985), pp. 761–762.

Robert J. Brown

BUFFINTON, Charles G. "Charlie" (b. 14 June 1861, Fall River, MA; d. 23 September 1907, Fall River, MA), player and manager, was the son of John and Phoebe Buffinton. He married Alice Thornley and had three children. One of baseball's premier pitchers in the 1880s, Buffinton achieved early fame in only his second season. He helped pitch Boston (NL) to the 1883 pennant with a 24–13 record and 34 complete games. From 1882 to 1892 the 6 foot, 1 inch, 180 pound pitcher won 231 games, lost 151, notched at least 20 victories seven times, and compiled a 2.96 ERA. In his superlative 1884 season, he won 47 of 63 decisions for Boston, pitched 8 shutouts, and walked only 76. He also struck out 417 batters, including 8 consecutively against Cleveland, and won 13 games in a row. Besides pitching 587 innings, he registered 63 complete games. On August 9 he lost a no-hit game 2–1 on errors.

A sore arm limited Buffinton's effectiveness in 1886, causing Boston to release him. Overcoming this physical problem, he enjoyed three successful seasons for Philadelphia (NL). In 1890 he jumped to the PL, where he pitched for and managed Philadelphia. In his last outstanding year, 1891, he compiled a 28–9 record for Boston (AA). Occasionally he played outfield and first base, registering a .245 lifetime batting average.

Contemporary sportswriters credited Buffinton with originating the drop ball and the hard overhand curve. In 1885 one commented, "There isn't a ball tosser in the country today who has more deceptive curves." Another remarked that his "perplexing curve . . . explodes in the dirt and gives catchers a workout." Every inch a gentleman, Buffinton exhibited outstanding character in an age when professional baseball still fielded rowdy elements. The Boston *Globe* eulogized him as a modest workman and a phenomenal ballplayer who helped to lay "the foundation of our great sport."

Among the highest paid players of the 1880s with a $2,800 salary, Buffinton benefited from the struggle between the rival PL and NL. Without warning, clubs slashed payrolls from 30 to 40 percent. Buffinton, who objected strongly to this mid-year cut, refused to report in 1893. He never played major league baseball again and returned to Fall River to become a successful businessman.

BIBLIOGRAPHY: Charles Buffinton file, National Baseball Hall of Fame Library, Cooperstown, NY; *Herald News* (Fall River, MA), June 18, 1979; Joseph L. Reichler, *The Great All-Time Baseball Record Book* (New York, 1981); Joseph L. Reichler, ed., *The Baseball Encyclopedia*, 6th ed., (New York, 1981), pp. 762, 1621; Harold Seymour, *Baseball: The Early Years* (New York, 1960); *Spalding's Base Ball Guide, 1885–1893* (New York, 1885–1893).

Duane A. Smith

BULKELEY, Morgan Gardner (b. 26 December 1837, East Haddam, CT; d. 6 November 1922, Hartford, CT), executive, was the son of Eliphalet and Lydia S. (Morgan) Bulkeley, descendants of *Mayflower* settlers. His father, an attorney and Connecticut State Senator and Representative, served as president of the Aetna Life Insurance Company. After attending East Haddam elementary school, Morgan moved with his family in 1846 to Hartford and continued his education through high school until age 15. He joined his uncle's dry goods business in Brooklyn, NY, in 1852 as an errand boy and became a partner there within seven years. During the Civil War, he enlisted in the 13th New York Volunteers and fought in the Virginia peninsular campaign. Upon his father's death in 1872, Bulkeley returned to Hartford, founded the US Bank there, and was its president for seven years.

Bulkeley, who played amateur baseball, served in 1874 and 1875 as president of the professional Hartford Dark Blues (NA). When the NL was formed in February, 1876, the distinguished banker was elected unanimously as its first president and agreed to serve one year. The initial NL season progressed reasonably well, as Bulkeley enhanced baseball's image by reducing gambling and drinking at games. A figurehead president, Bulkeley faced several awkward problems. NL attendance lagged, partly because Chicago captured the pennant easily. The New York Mutuals and Philadelphia Athletics, expecting to lose money, refused to make their last western trip. Bulkeley did not attend the December, 1876, NL meeting, at which owners expelled those two clubs and elected William Hulbert* as president. For over thirty years, Bulkeley also was connected with the National Trotting Association.

Bulkeley presided over the Aetna Life Insurance Company from 1879 until his death, establishing two subsidiary companies. Under his management, Aetna became one of the soundest institutions in the industry, with $200 million in assets and 1,500 paid employees. He married Fannie Briggs (Houghton) on February 11, 1885, in San Francisco, and had two sons and one daughter. The Republican was elected as Hartford City Councilman (1875), Alderman (1876), Hartford Mayor (1880–1888), Connecticut Governor (1889–1893), and U.S. Senator (1905–1911) and was a delegate to the Republican national convention in 1888 and 1896. He was awarded an honorary Master of Arts degree by Yale University in 1889 and Doctor of Laws degree by Trinity College in 1917. Upon his death, NL club owners praised him for "invaluable aid " as "a founder of the national game." In 1937 he was elected to the National Baseball Hall of Fame as a pioneer and executive.

BIBLIOGRAPHY: *Appleton's Cyclopaedia of American Biography* 1 (New York 1887), p. 444; *Biographical Dictionary of the American Congress* (Washington, D.C., 1961), p. 623; *DAB* 3 (New York, 1929), pp. 248–249; Eddie Gold, "Hall Would Be Home for Hulbert," *Baseball Historical Review* (1981), pp. 89–91; *National Cyclopaedia of American Biography* 10 (New York 1900), p. 345; Lowell Reidenbaugh, *Cooperstown: Where*

Baseball's Legends Live Forever (St. Louis, 1983); Harold Seymour, *Baseball: The Early Years* (New York, 1960); Robert Smith, *Baseball's Hall of Fame* (New York, 1973); *Who Was Who in America* 1 (1897–1942), p. 163.

David L. Porter

BUNNING, James Paul David "Jim" (b. 23 October 1931, Southgate, KY), player and manager, played baseball at Xavier University in Cincinnati. The 6 foot, 3 inch, 185 pound right-hander spent six years in the minor leagues at Richmond, IN (OIL) in 1950, Davenport, IA (3IL) in 1951, Williamsport, PA (EL) in 1952, Buffalo (IL) in 1953, and Little Rock, AR (SA) in 1954 and 1955. He joined the Detroit Tigers (AL) in 1955 and 1956. After posting a 5–1 record in 1956, he enjoyed his best season of his seventeen-year career in 1957 with a 20–8 record and an AL-leading 267.1 innings pitched. Although having an uneven record from 1958 through 1963, he posted 17 and 19 wins in 1961 and 1962, respectively, and led the AL in strikeouts with 201 in both 1959 and 1960. After winning 118 games and losing 87 for the Tigers, he was traded in December, 1963 to the Philadelphia Phillies (NL). He enjoyed three remarkable 19-win seasons and led the staff in innings pitched. After a 17–15 season in 1967, he spent the next campaign with the Pittsburgh Pirates (NL). He was traded to the Los Angeles Dodgers (NL) for part of the 1969 season and finished his career with losing campaigns for Philadelphia (NL) in 1970 and 1971. As an NL pitcher, he recorded well over 200 strikeouts in four consecutive seasons from 1964 through 1967. In 1967 he led the NL with 253 strikeouts and 302 1/3 innings pitched. Overall, he won 224 and lost 184 games for a .549 percentage and a 3.27 ERA and hurled over 100 victories in both leagues. He pitched no-hitters in each league and tossed a perfect game against the New York Mets in 1964. In eight All-Star game appearances, he compiled and impressive 1.13 ERA. His 2,855 strikeouts and only 1,000 walks rank him among the best control pitchers and strikeout artists in baseball history. Bunning never played on a pennant-winning club, but his 17–11 record in 1961 helped the Tigers to a 101–61 season record and second place finish. Subsequently he managed Phillies' farm teams in 1972 and 1973 and then worked as a stockbroker, agent for major league players, and politician. He served as Ronald Reagan's local campaign manager in Campbell County, KY, in 1980. In 1982 he was elected to the Kentucky State Senate, defeating a sixteen-year incumbent. His campaign promised better representation of a badly depressed and underrepresented northern Kentucky region. In 1984 he won the Republican nomination for governor but lost in the general election. In 1986 he was elected to the U.S. House of Representatives from the Fourth Kentucky congressional district. He and his wife, Mary Theis, whom he married in January, 1952, have nine children. Since 1974 he has become a respected part of the business and political community in Cincinnati and northern Kentucky. Bunning's transition to a successful post-playing career is illustrated by his determination to gain his degree from Xavier, as he skipped spring training trips to finish a Bachelor of Science degree in economics in 1953.

BIBLIOGRAPHY: Stan Grosshandler, "These Players Excelled in Both Major Leagues!" *Baseball Digest*, 42 (November, 1983), pp. 29–32; Gene Karst and Martin J. Jones, Jr., *Who's Who in Professional Baseball* (New Rochelle, NY, 1973); Edward Kiersh, *Where Have You Gone, Vince DiMaggio?* (New York, 1983).

Douglas A. Noverr

BURDETTE, Selva Lewis, Jr. "Lew" (b. 22 November 1926, Nitro, WV), player, coach, and scout, excelled as a right-handed pitcher for the Milwaukee Braves (NL). Nitro High School, from which he graduated did not have a baseball team. Burdette pitched for the local America Vicose Plant and earned a baseball scholarship to the University of Richmond. After signing with the New York Yankees (AL), Burdette in 1947 pitched for Norfolk, VA (Pil), and Amsterdam, NY (CAL). At Quincy, IL, in 1948, he led the 3IL in victories with 16. Burdette pitched for Kansas City, MO (AA), in 1949 and 1950 and made two appearances for the New York Yankees in late 1950. The following season, he compiled a 14–12 mark for San Francisco (PCL) before being traded with $50,000 cash to the Boston Braves (NL) for veteran pitcher Johnny Sain.

Over the next thirteen years, Burdette combined with Warren Spahn* as one of the most successful righty-lefty pitching duos in baseball. Between 1953 and 1961, he won at least 13 games every season. His best campaigns included 19 wins in 1956 and 1960, 20 in 1958, and an NL leading 21 in 1959. Burdette, who eight times recorded at least 15 triumphs, won 179 total games in Boston and Milwaukee Braves uniforms. In the 1957 World Series, Burdette started and won the second, fifth, and seventh games against the New York Yankees. He allowed only two earned runs in 27 innings for a 0.67 ERA. He established a World Series mark by pitching two shutouts and tied records with three wins and three complete games in a seven-game series. His fortunes were reversed in the 1958 World Series when he won one contest and lost two, and allowed 17 runs in his three starts, as the Yankees defeated the Braves. The 5 home runs he allowed also tied a series mark.

Burdette paced the NL in ERA (2.70) in 1956 and shared the lead in shutouts (4) in 1959. He also led the NL once each in pitching percentage (1958), games started (1959), complete games (1960), and innings pitched (1961). He tossed a 1–0 no-hit victory against the Philadelphia Phillies on August 18, 1960, and on two separate occasions homered twice in the same game. The Braves in 1963 traded Burdette to St. Louis (NL), where he pitched until May, 1964. Burdette's other major league clubs included the Chicago Cubs (NL) in 1964 and 1965, Philadelphia Phillies (NL) in 1965, and California Angels (AL) in 1966 and 1967. His playing career ended in 1967 with Seattle (PCL). In 626 major league games Burdette recorded 203 wins, 144 losses (.585), 158 complete games, 33 shutouts, and a 3.66 ERA. He struck out 1,074 batters and employed numerous pitches, including, according to many NL hitters, an extremely effective spitball.

Burdette married Mary Ann Shelton on June 30, 1949, and has three children, Lewis, Madge, and Mary Lou. After retiring, Burdette scouted the southeastern area for the Central Scouting Bureau in 1968 and coached for the Atlanta Braves (NL) in 1972. He also worked as vice-president of a real estate firm in Sarasota, FL, and as public relations specialist for a cable television company in Athens, GA.

BIBLIOGRAPHY: Gene Karst and Martin J. Jones, Jr., *Who's Who in Professional Baseball* (New Rochelle, NY, 1973); Paul MacFarlane, ed., *TSN Daguerreotypes of Great Stars of Baseball* (St. Louis, 1981); Joseph L. Reichler, ed., *The Baseball Encyclopedia*, 6th ed. (New York, 1985), p. 1,622.

Jack R. Stanton

BURKETT, Jesse Cail "The Crab" (b. 4 December 1868, or 12 February 1870, Wheeling, WV; d. 27 May 1953, Worcester, MA), player, manager, owner, coach, and scout, spent his youth fishing and swimming along the upper Ohio River. Burkett, whose early life is obscure, never knew his precise birthdate. He entered professional baseball as a pitcher in 1888, winning 27 games for Scranton (CL). The following season, the 5 foot, 8 inch, 155 pound left-hander posted an unbelievable 39–6 mark with Worcester (AtA) and earned $125 per month. He purchased a house in Worcester and made it his permanent residence. In 1890 Burkett married Nellie McGrath of Worcester.

Indianapolis held Burkett's contract in 1890, but when the franchise folded that spring the New York Giants (NL) signed him. He compiled a 3–10 log with a 5.56 ERA and fielded only .824, but batted .309 in 101 games. In 1891 he was sold to the Cleveland Spiders (NL) who assigned him to Lincoln, NE (WA). A .349 batting average earned him a promotion in August to Cleveland. In his inauspicious first full big league season, 1892, he hit .275 and committed 28 errors in left field. A speedy runner, he stole 36 bases and scored 119 runs, and often coupled fine bunting with speed to leg out infield hits.

At Cleveland, Burkett teamed with stars Cy Young,* Cupid Childs,* George Cuppy, and Patsy Tebeau. Nicknamed "Crab" because of a cranky disposition, Burkett, who did not drink or smoke, often fought with umpires, managers, and fans. Off the field, the gentle Burkett took a special interest in children.

Burkett rarely showed power, but hit solid line drives. In 1893 he improved his batting average nearly 75 points, to .348, scored 145 runs, and made a NL-leading 42 errors in the outfield. After hitting .358 in 1894, he compiled a record three .400 seasons. He paced Cleveland in 1895 with a NL-high .423 batting average on 235 hits and pilfered a career-high 47 bases. Burkett led the NL the next season with a .410 average. In 1899 Burkett, Cy Young, and others were transferred to St. Louis by Frank Robison, who owned the Spiders and Cardinals. During three seasons in St. Louis, he hit .402, .363, and .382. From 1893 through 1901, Burkett batted a remarkable .382 and made 1,911 hits.

In 1902 Burkett jumped to the St. Louis Browns (AL) and saw his hitting slide. After batting .273 with the 1904 Browns, he was traded to the Boston Red Sox (AL) for rookie outfielder George Stone. After Burkett led AL outfielders in errors and hit only .257 in 1905, the Red Sox released him. His brilliant major league career included 2,872 hits, 314 doubles, 185 triples, 1,713 runs, 952 RBIs, 392 stolen bases, and a .342 batting average.

In 1906 Burkett bought the Worcester (NEL) franchise and served as its owner, field manager, and outfielder through the 1913 season, hitting .325 in 483 games. From 1906 through 1909, Worcester finished first four times under Burkett's leadership. In 1916 he returned to the field as manager and utility player with Lawrence, MA, Hartford, CT, and Lowell, MA (EL). From 1917 to 1920, he coached baseball at Holy Cross College and scouted for the New York Giants (NL). After coaching for John McGraw's* New York Giants in 1921 and 1922, Burkett again managed the Worcester club for the next two seasons. He ended his managerial career with Lewiston, ME (NEL) in 1928 and 1929 and Lowell (NEL) in 1933.

Burkett, who enjoyed reunions with old baseball friends and never lost his love of the game, retired to his Worcester home and later suffered from hardening of the arteries. In 1946 Burkett was elected to the National Baseball Hall of Fame.

BIBLIOGRAPHY: Martin Appel and Burt Goldblatt, *Baseball's Best: The Hall of Fame Gallery* (New York, 1977); Bob Broeg, *Redbirds: A Century of Cardinals' Baseball* (St. Louis, 1981); John Lardner, "The Snake Pit and the Letter," *Newsweek* (June 15, 1953), p. 91; *NYT*, May 28, 1953, p. 23; Lowell Reidenbaugh, *Cooperstown: Where Baseball's Legends Live Forever* (New York, 1983).

Frank J. Olmsted

BURNS, George Henry "Tioga George," "The Tioga Kid," "General George" (b. 31 January 1893, Niles, OH; d. 7 January 1978, Kirkland, WA), player and manager, grew up in Tioga, PA. Nicknamed "Tioga George" and "The Tioga Kid" to help distinguish him from his contemporary, George Joseph Burns* (NL outfielder), the 6 foot, 1 1/2 inch, 185 pound, right-hander spent his entire major league career in the AL. Burns quit Philadelphia Central High School at age 16 to pursue a professional baseball career. In 1913 the first baseman signed his first legitimate pro contract with Quincy, IL (CA), for $150 per month. Before playing a single game, however, he was sold to Burlington, IA (CA), with a $90 a month contract. In 1913 he also performed for Ottumwa, IA (CA), at $300 per month and Sioux City, IA (WL), before the Detroit Tigers (AL) bought his contract.

He began a sixteen-year major league career with Detroit in 1914 and played first base for the Tigers through the 1917 season. On March 8, 1918, he was sold to the New York Yankees (AL). The Yankees, however, immediately sent him to the Philadelphia A's (AL) for Ping Bodie. In 1918 he batted a spectacular .358 and led the AL with 178 hits. After marrying Marian R. Harris in April, 1919, he had four daughters and became a devoted family man. On May 29, 1920, he was sold for cash to the Cleveland Indians (AL). Cleveland survived a tight AL pennant race to capture its first championship, as Burns played a supporting role. Burns batted .300 splitting first base duties with Wheeler "Doc" Johnston in the 1920 World series against Brooklyn, and then hit .361 as part-time first baseman in 1921.

Burns, Joe Harris, and Elmer Smith were traded to Boston (AL) for Stuffy McInnis* on December 24, 1921. The highlight of his Red Sox career came on his unassisted triple play against Cleveland on September 14, 1923. On January 7, 1924, Boston traded Burns to Cleveland in a multi-player deal for William Wambsganss of unassisted triple play fame. During this Cleveland stint, "General George" enjoyed his best seasons with .310, .336, .358, and .319 batting averages. In 1926 he captured the AL Most Valuable Player Award and led the AL in hits and doubles. Babe Ruth* did not receive a single vote for the trophy, although he joined Burns on the All-AL team. Burns' 216 hits included 64 doubles, a record not broken until 1931 and still among the best season totals ever.

In September, 1928, Burns was released unconditionally by the Indians and signed by the New York Yankees (AL). New York once again sold him to Philadelphia (AL) on June 19, 1929. He concluded his major league career after making unsuccessful pinch hit appearances in the 1929 World Series against Chicago. In 1,866 major league games, Burns batted .307 and garnered 2,018 hits, 444 doubles, 72 triples, 72 home runs, 901 runs, 948 RBIs, and 153 stolen bases. He played in the PCL with Missions, CA (1930–1931), Los Angeles (1931), Seattle (1932–1934), and Portland (1934). After managing Seattle (1932–1934) and Portland (1934–1935), he settled in the Seattle area to manage apartments. In 1947 he became a deputy sheriff of King County (Seattle), WA, and held that position until retiring to Kirkland, WA.

BIBLIOGRAPHY: George H. Burns file, National Baseball Hall of Fame Library, Cooperstown, NY; Paul MacFarlane, ed., *TSN Daguerreotypes of Great Stars of Baseball* (St. Louis, 1968), pp. 27–28; Joseph L. Reichler, ed., *The Baseball Encyclopedia*, 6th ed. (New York, 1985), p. 767.

David B. Merrell

BURNS, George Joseph (b. 24 November 1889, Utica, NY; d. 15 August 1966, Gloversville, NY), player, manager, and coach, was the son of cigarmaker John Burns and participated in sandlot and amateur baseball. Burns began his professional career as a catcher for the Utica Harps (NYSL) in 1909. Two years later, he became an outfielder and was sold for $4,000 to the New York Giants (NL). Burns played with the Giants for ten years and developed into one of the era's best outfielders and hitters. During his first two years (1911–1912), he played little because manager John McGraw* wanted to groom him carefully. Burns became the regular left fielder in 1913 and married Mary Baker on October 7, 1914. The right-handed, 5 foot, 7 inch, 160 pound outfielder exhibited excellent speed and possessed a strong arm. Defensively, he wore a special long-billed cap with blue sunglasses attached, which helped him master the Polo Grounds sunfield. Burns, who moved to center field in 1920 and combined with Irish Meusel* and Ross Youngs* to give McGraw the NL's best outfield, also became the Giants' leadoff hitter. Besides setting a then NL record of 459 consecutive games in the outfield, he led the NL in at bats and stolen bases twice, and in walks and runs scored five times. He appeared in three World Series, batting .333 in the 1921 classic and leading the Giants with eleven hits. Burns made four hits in one game and delivered the game-winning safety in game four. In 1918 McGraw rated Burns next to Christy Mathewson* as the greatest player he had managed.

After the 1921 season, McGraw reluctantly traded Burns to the Cincinnati Reds (NL) to acquire third baseman Heinie Groh.* Burns enjoyed two solid seasons with the Reds, but declined at the plate in 1924 and was released. He then joined the Philadelphia Phillies (NL) in 1925, hitting .292 in 88 games in his last major league season. Overall, Burns recorded 2,077 hits in 1,853 games and averaged 169 hits per season as a regular. Lifetime, he batted .287, scored 1,188 runs, knocked in 611 runs, collected 872 walks, and stole 383 bases. Between 1926 and 1930, Burns served as player-manager for various minor league teams, including Newark (IL) in 1926, Williamsport, PA (NYPL) in 1927 and 1928, Hanover, PA (BRL) in 1928, Springfield, MA (EL) in 1929, and San Antonio (TL) in 1930. With the exception of his last minor league season, he hit at least .295 between 1926 and 1930. In 1931 he returned to the New York Giants (NL) as a coach. Burns lived in Gloversville, NY, where he operated his father's pool hall and became payroll clerk in a tannery. He retired in 1957 and resided in Gloversville until his death. Burns was survived by his second wife, Pauline Rezek, whom he married on October 18, 1952, and by two stepchildren.

BIBLIOGRAPHY: George Joseph Burns file, National Baseball Hall of Fame Library, Cooperstown, NY; Frank Graham, *McGraw of the Giants* (New York, 1944); Paul MacFarlane, ed., *TSN Daguerreotypes of Great Stars of Baseball* (St. Louis, 1971); *NYT*,

December 7, 31, 1921, August 16, 1966; Richard A. Puff, "Silent George Burns: A Star in the Sunfield," *Baseball Research Journal* 12 (1983), pp. 119–125.

Douglas D. Martin

BUSCH, August Adolphus, Jr. "Gussie" (b. 28 March 1899, St. Louis, MO), corporation executive and owner, is the son of Anheuser and Alice (Zisemann) Busch and attended Fremont Public School and Smith Academy. Married four times and the father of eleven children, Busch wedded former secretary Margaret M. Snyder in 1981. Frequently compared to his dynamic grandfather Adolphus, Anheuser-Bush co-founder in 1865, young Gussie worked from vat scrubber to chief executive officer by 1946. His vigorous expansion program made the firm the national leader in 1953 and the world's largest brewery by his 1975 retirement.

Busch's lifestyle resembled "a Rhineland baron of old, devoted to hounds, horses, and magnificent entertainments" on his "Grant's Farm" estate in St. Louis County. Responsive to civic causes, Busch purchased the St. Louis Cardinals (NL) baseball club in February, 1953, for $3.75 million as a "sporting venture," to block the team's departure for Milwaukee. Although only marginally interested in baseball beforehand, Busch helped pioneer the now commonplace corporate executive's entry into big-time sports. With explosive energy, Busch spent $7 million on new players and farm system development and purchased and refurbished old Sportsman's Park. Subsequently he piloted the drive to construct Busch Memorial Stadium in downtown St. Louis (1966), the last major sports complex to be built solely with private funds. Busch's efforts produced Cardinal NL pennants in 1964, 1967, 1968, 1982, and 1985 and three world championships.

Imbued with relentless drive, Busch frequently participated in spring training drills. His motto, "Work hard—love your work," fired his denunciation of inflationary player salaries when the Cardinal payroll in 1969 exceeded $1 million. Holdouts by top left-handed pitchers Steve Carlton* and Jerry Reuss forced their departures because Busch regarded their attitude and outfielder Curt Flood's* court challenge to baseball's reserve clause as crass ingratitude. Busch stormed "I'm fed up. I can't understand what's happening here, or on our campuses in our great country." His gravelly voice and table-pounding vehemence demanded adamant owner resistance to the 1972 and 1981 strikes.

When inducted into Missouri's Sports Hall of Fame in his retirement year, Busch listed his lifelong dedications: (1) his wife and family, (2) the brewery, and (3) St. Louis. The city owed much to the "Big Eagle," especially for his retention of the Cardinals, only the best known of his many generosities to his community.

BIBLIOGRAPHY: *CB* (1973) *pp. 69–71*; "Gussie vs. the Cards," *Newsweek* 79 (June 19, 1972), p. 61; Leonard Koppett, "Busch, Beer, and Baseball," *NYT Magazine* (April 11, 1965), p. 32; William Leggett, "A Bird in Hand and a Burning Busch," *SI* 32

(March 23, 1970), pp. 18–23; Roy Malone, William H. Kester, and Bob Broeg, "Gussie Busch," St. Louis *Post-Dispatch*, August 25–29, 1975; Harold H. Martin, "The Cardinals Strike It Rich," *SEP* 225 (June 27, 1953), p. 22; *WWA*, 42nd ed. (1982–1983), p. 466.

William J. Miller

C

CAMPANELLA, Roy (b. 19 November 1921, Philadelphia, PA), player, is one of five children of fruit and vegetable market owner John and Ida Campanella. He married Ruthe Willis in 1941 and had six children, including sons David, Tony, and Roy, Jr., and daughters Joyce, Beverly, and Depayton (Princess). He was legally separated from Ruthe in early 1960. Following her death, he married Mrs. Roxie Doles on May 5, 1964. From 1937 to 1945 he caught for the Baltimore Elite Giants (NNL) and appeared in the 1941, 1944 and 1945 All-Star games.

Campanella was the second black player approached to play professional baseball in the twentieth century. Brooklyn Dodger (NL) president Branch Rickey* met with Campanella in October, 1945, after Chuck Dressen made the arrangements. The 5 foot, 9 1/2 inch, 205 pound catcher began in the minor leagues in 1946 with Nashua, NH (NEL), and played for the Montreal Royals (IL) in 1947 and St. Paul Saints (AA) in 1948 before joining the parent Brooklyn Dodgers (NL) in May, 1948. At Nashua, manager Walter Alston* was indisposed one day and asked Campanella to serve as acting manager. Campanella thus became the first black to serve in that capacity in the white minor leagues.

Campanella caught for the Brooklyn Dodgers for ten years (1948 to 1957) and, at his retirement, had slugged more career home runs (242) and more single season home runs (41 in 1953) than any other major league catcher. He also became the only catcher to play at least 100 games for nine consecutive seasons (1949–1957) and would have appeared in that many games his rookie season if he had not spent the first month in the minor leagues. His 142 RBIs during 1953 established a then record for catchers.

In 1,215 major league games, he batted .276, made 1,161 hits, including 178 doubles, and knocked in 856 runs. Campanella holds the NL record for most consecutive years leading in chances accepted by a catcher (6) and tied the NL record for most years leading catchers in putouts (6). The NL Most Valuable Player in 1951, 1953, and 1955, he was selected as catcher on *The*

Sporting News Major League All-Star teams in 1949, 1951, 1953, and 1955 and as the publication's Outstanding NL Player in 1953. Campanella, who appeared in the 1949, 1952–1953, 1955, and 1956 World Series, was named in 1969 to the National Baseball Hall of Fame.

A tragic automobile accident after the 1957 season left him substantially paralyzed and terminated his playing career. Campanella's extraordinary courage in attempting to recover from this paralysis led to the book *It's Good to Be Alive*, which subsequently became a made-for-television movie. Campanella currently works with former teammate and roommate Don Newcombe* for the Los Angeles NL Baseball Club in the field of community services.

BIBLIOGRAPHY: *Brooklyn Dodger Yearbooks*, 1949–1957; Roy Campanella, *It's Good to Be Alive* (New York, 1959); Harvey Frommer, *Rickey and Robinson* (New York, 1972); Hall of Fame Plaque of Roy Campanella, Cooperstown, NY, 1969; Roger Kahn, *The Boys of Summer* (New York, 1972); Murray Polner, *Branch Rickey: A Biography* (New York, 1982); Gene Schoor, *Roy Campanella: Man of Courage* (New York, 1959); Dick Young, *Roy Campanella* (New York, 1952).

Ronald L. Gabriel

CAREW, Rodney Cline "Rod" (b. 1 October 1945, Gatun, Panama), player, is the son of construction worker Eric and Olga Carew and has a brother, Eric, and three sisters, Sheridan, Diana, and Dorinne. Carew married Marilynn Levy, a white Jewish native of North Minneapolis, in October 1970, and has three daughters, Charryse, Stephanie, and Michelle. Carew was born on a train transporting his mother from Gatun to Gamboa and was delivered by Dr. Rodney Cline, for whom he was named. At age 11 he was hospitalized for six months with rheumatic fever. Carew then began playing Little League baseball and was taught by his uncle, Joe French. Within two years Carew hit so well that he played with 17-year-olds. His family moved to Washington Heights near the Polo Grounds in New York City, but his father did not join them. Carew attended George Washington High School, worked in a grocery store, and played sandlot baseball with the Cavaliers on weekends.

Herbert Stein, a teammate's father, persuaded the Minnesota Twins (AL) to give Carew a tryout. In 1964 Carew signed with the Twins for a $5,000 bonus, played second base for Melbourne, FL, and led the CRL in triples (3). After batting .325 at Melbourne, he hit .303 with Orlando (FSL) in 1965 and was the first black player there. Although batting only .242 with Wilson, NC (CrL), in 1966, he was helped considerably by coach Vern Morgan.

In 1967 Carew joined the Minnesota Twins, batted .292, and won AL Rookie of the Year honors. The 6 foot, 182 pound Carew, who bats left and throws right-handed, played with Minnesota (1967–1978) as a second baseman and later first baseman. He was traded to the California Angels (AL) for four players in February, 1979, and played first base there. Carew won seven AL batting titles (1969, 1972–1975, 1977–1978) with averages of .332, .318, .350, .364, .359, .388, and .333. The AL Most Valuable Player in 1977, he performed in the All-Star games in 1967–1969, 1971–1978, and 1983–1984. He was selected for the 1970, 1979, and 1982 squads but withdrew his name because of injuries. In All-Star games, he has made ten hits and compiled a .244 batting average. Although never in a World Series, Carew played in four Championship series (1967, 1970, 1979, 1982) and made eleven hits for a .220 batting average. *The Sporting News* named him Major League Player of the Year (1977) and to its All-Star team (1967–1969, 1972, 1977–1978).

Carew's best season came in 1977, when he achieved career personal highs in at bats (616), batting average (.388), hits (239), triples (16), and runs (128) to lead the AL; that year he also hit 38 doubles, had 100 RBIs and tied his best home run output (14). His manager, Gene Mauch, commented: "He's got everything—intelligence, strength, confidence, speed afoot, and hand-eye coordination. Many ballplayers are pleasant to manage, but managing Rodney is a privilege."

In 2,469 career major league games, Carew compiled 9,315 at bats, 1,424 runs scored, 3,053 hits, 445 doubles, 112 triples, 92 home runs, 1,015 RBIs, 353 stolen bases, and a .328 batting average. On August 4, 1985, against the Minnesota Twins, Carew became the sixteenth major leaguer to make 3,000 career hits. He hit at least .300 for fifteen consecutive seasons from 1969 to 1983 and led the AL in hits with 203 (1973), 218 (1974), and 239 (1977). He also made 200 hits in 1976 and led the AL in triples in 1973 (11) and 1977 (16) and in runs scored in 1977 (128). In 1969 Carew tied major league records by stealing home seven times and pilfering three bases in one inning. Defensively, Carew made 13,510 career putouts, 3,709 assists, 260 errors, and a .985 lifetime fielding percentage and led the AL in errors in 1968, 1974, and 1984. Following the 1985 season, the Angels released Carew.

BIBLIOGRAPHY: Rod Carew with Frank Pace and Armin Keteylon, *Rod Carew's Art and Science of Hitting* (New York, 1986); *CB* (1978), pp. 63–66; Zander Hollander, ed., *Complete Handbook of Baseball, 1984*, (New York, 1984), pp. 63–66; *TSN Baseball Register, 1986* (St. Louis, 1986); *Who's Who in Baseball*, 71st ed. (New York, 1986), pp. 23–24; Jack Zanger, "It's Easier to Hustle in the Big Leagues," *Sport* 44 (November, 1967), pp. 60–61, 72, 74.

                                                                Kevin R. Porter

CAREY, Max George "Scoops" (b. Maximillian Carnarius 11 January 1890, Terre Haute, IN; d. 30 May 1976, Miami Beach, FL), player, coach and manager, was one of four sons of contractor Frank August Ernst Carnarius and Catherine Augusta (Astroth) Carnarius, both of German descent. In 1903 Carey's Lutheran parents enrolled him in a six-year, preministerial program at Concordia College in Fort Wayne, IN. After graduating in 1909, he spent the 1909–1910 academic year at Concordia Seminary in St. Louis.

Carey played amateur baseball in college and in 1909 signed (as Max Carey) with South Bend (CL) as a shortstop, third baseman, and outfielder, and became a switch-hitter. He joined the Pittsburgh Pirates (NL) late in the 1910 season. Carey's lifetime .285 batting average featured a career-high .343 in the 1925 regular season and .458 for the victorious Pirates in the 1925 World Series against the Washington Senators. Best known as a base stealer, he led the NL ten times between 1913 and 1925, establishing a career NL record of 738 thefts (since broken by Lou Brock*). He stole 51 bases in 53 attempts in 1922, 61 bases in 1913, and 63 in 1916. Against the New York Giants in an 18-inning game in 1922, he made six hits in six official at bats, added three walks and three stolen bases (including home), and made several spectacular catches. Carey, whose nickname, "Scoops," derived from his outstanding defensive ability, led NL outfielders in putouts nine times and established an NL career record of 6,363 putouts (eventually broken by Willie Mays*).

Carey was waived by the Pirates in 1926 after a dispute with management and played with the Brooklyn Dodgers (NL) until his 1929 retirement. In 2,476 games covering twenty years, he compiled 2,665 hits, 419 doubles, 159 triples, 69 home runs, 1,545 runs, 800 RBIs, and 1,040 walks. He coached with the Pirates in 1930 and managed the Dodgers in 1932–1933 to a 146–161 win-loss record (.476) and one third place finish.

Carey married Aurelia Behrens on June 22, 1913, and had two sons. He invested in the early 1920s in Florida real estate, but lost money in the 1929 stock market crash. After retiring as a player, he worked at business ventures and scouted for the Baltimore Orioles (AL) in 1955. He also managed Miami (FECL) in 1940, Cordele, GA (GFL) in 1955, and Louisville (AA) in 1956. He left baseball in 1957 and worked as a racing official in Miami Beach. He was elected to the National Baseball Hall of Fame in 1961 and died in 1976 after a long illness. The long-legged, slender 6 foot, 165 pound Carey, a swift, daring baserunner and outfielder, easily made the transition to the lively ball era and demonstrated that speed could generate as much excitement as home runs.

BIBLIOGRAPHY: Frederick G. Lieb, *The Pittsburgh Pirates* (New York, 1948); Lowell Reidenbaugh, *Cooperstown: Where Baseball's Legends Live Forever* (St. Louis, 1983).

Luther W. Spoehr

CARLTON, Steven Norman "Steve," "Lefty," "Ichabod" (b. 22 December 1944, Miami, FL), player, is the son of Joseph and Anne (Powers) Carlton. Joseph Carlton, a chicken farmer, later became a maintenance worker for Pan American Airways. Steve loved the Everglades and acquired the nickname "Ichabod" for his tall, lean physique. He played baseball throughout his youth, beginning in the North Miami Little League. Carlton attended North Miami High School from 1959 to 1963, winning eight of ten decisions his senior year. He played American Legion ball in Miami and attended Miami-Dade Community College. On the advice of Carlton's Legion coach, St. Louis Cardinals (NL) scout Chase Riddle signed Steve on October 6, 1963, for a $5,000 bonus.

In 1964 Carlton compiled a 15–6 composite mark for Rock Hill, SC (WCL), Winnipeg (NoL), and Tulsa (TL). He married Beverly Ann Brooks in 1965 and has two sons, Steven and Scott. After pitching 15 games for St. Louis in 1965, he returned to the Cardinals (NL) in late 1966. He won 27 composite games for the 1967–1968 Redbirds, appearing in both World Series. In 1969 Carlton sparkled with a 17–11 record and 2.17 ERA. On September 15, 1969, he broke the major league record by striking out 19 Mets in a 4–3 loss in New York. Carlton led the NL with 19 defeats in 1970, but rebounded with a 20–9 season the next year. His ratio of strikeouts and hits to innings pitched actually was better in 1970 than in 1971.

Carlton requested a $60,000 contract for 1972, but the Redbirds offered him only $55,000. Cardinals General Manager Bing Devine traded the 6 foot, 4 inch, 220 pound left-hander to Philadelphia (NL) for a right-hander Rick Wise. Carlton pitched with the Phillies until 1986, making St. Louis regret the transaction. From 1972 through 1983, Carlton compiled a 37–12 edge over the Cardinals and registered his 100th and 300th victories against them.

The 1972 Phillies proved to be a terrible team with the exception of the spectacular Carlton. Philadelphia triumphed in only 59 games, with Carlton winning 27, or 46 percent. He led the NL in wins, ERA (1.97), innings pitched (346), and strikeouts (310), won 15 straight contests, and earned his first Cy Young Award. The press closely followed Carlton, predicting 30 wins for him in 1973. After Carlton struggled through a 13–20 year in 1973 and mediocre 1974 and 1975 seasons, the press began criticizing his interest in meditation and Eastern philosophies. Carlton began refusing interviews, a policy he continued until the middle of the 1986 season.

From 1976 to 1982, Carlton was the dominant NL pitcher with 137 wins. His slider, fastball, and curve, coupled with tremendous concentration and self-confidence, powered him to four 20-victory seasons with three Cy Young awards. Carlton finished the 1983 campaign with a 15–16 record, but his 275 strikeouts paced the NL for the fifth time. On September 24, 1983, he became the sixteenth pitcher to win 300 games. By the end of the 1986 season, he had amassed 4,040 strikeouts. In 1985 Carlton suffered a strained pitching shoulder and was placed on the disabled list for the first time in his major league career.

Carlton, a ten-time All-Star, appeared in the 1980 and 1983 World Series. Besides receiving the American Legion Graduate Award in 1971, he was named *The Sporting News* Pitcher of the Year in 1972, 1977, 1980, and 1982, and won a Gold Glove in 1981. He finished the 1986 season with a 323–229 career record and a 3.11 ERA, hurling 55 shutouts and 5,055 innings. Carlton has compiled 20 or more victories six seasons and won in double figures eighteen consecutive campaigns. A master of physical conditioning, Carlton regularly engages in Kung Fu workouts to stay in shape. After Carlton had struggled for two seasons with a shoulder injury and control problems, the Phillies released him in June, 1986. In July, 1986, the San Francisco Giants (NL) signed Carlton. In 1986 Carlton compiled a combined 5–11 mark with Philadelphia and San Francisco. He completed the season with the Chicago White Sox (AL), posting a 4–3 record.

BIBLIOGRAPHY: Kansas City *Star*, September 25, 1983; John Kuenster, "Phils' Steve Carlton in Pursuit of His Third Cy Young Award," *Baseball Digest* 39 (November, 1980), pp. 17–19; John Kuenster, "Steve Carlton: He's Disciplined, Durable, and Still Competitive," *Baseball Digest*, 42 (November, 1983), pp. 13–15; Allen Lewis, "Carlton Earns Legion Graduate Award," *TSN*, June 24, 1972, p. 23; Allen Lewis, "Super Steve Is Thinking Thirty," *TSN*, April 14, 1973, p. 3; Bus Saidt, "Steve Carlton: Silent, but Deadly," *Baseball Magazine*, 144 (April, 1980), pp. 42, 49, 52, 92–93; St. Louis *Globe-Democrat*, September 23, 1983; Martha Ward, *Steve Carlton Star Southpaw* (New York, 1975).

Frank J. Olmsted

CARPENTER, Robert R.M., Jr., "Bob" (b. 31 August 1915, New Castle DE), executive, is the son of Du Pont Chemical Company Vice President Robert R.M. Carpenter, Sr., and Margaretta (Du Pont) Carpenter, a member of the Du Pont family. His education included the Tower Hill School in Wilmington, DE and three years at Duke University. From 1944 to 1946, he served in the U.S. Army. He and his wife, Mary Kaye, who were married in June, 1938, have two children, Robert R.M. III ("Ruly") and Mary Kaye. A sports enthusiast, Carpenter played end on the Duke University football team and dabbled in sports ownership as an employee in the public relations department of Du Pont. At the urging of Connie Mack* in the late 1930s, he bought the Wilmington Blue Rocks (IL). He also briefly owned a professional franchise in the American Basketball League.

    In 1943 he persuaded his father to buy him the ailing Philadelphia Phillies (NL) franchise for $400,000. The previous owner, William Cox, had been banned from baseball for gambling activities. The Carpenters controlled 80 percent of the Phillies stock. The Phillies, one of the weakest franchises in baseball, had suffered financially for many years and had sold numerous quality players, including Grover Cleveland Alexander,* Chuck Klein,* and Bucky Walters,* to pay their bills. Carpenter created a modern franchise by hiring excellent advisers, including seasoned general manager Herb Pennock.* To develop a minor league system, Carpenter spent over $1 million on bonus players. By the late 1940s, the Phillies fielded a respectable team. Carpenter developed talent including Richie Ashburn,* Robin Roberts,*

Curt Simmons, and Willie Jones. The Phillies, under the skillful direction of Eddie Sawyer, finished third in 1949, won the 1950 NL pennant, and lost the World Series in four games to the New York Yankees.

Carpenter, serving as his own general manager after Pennock's death in 1948, could not build on the success of the 1950 Whiz Kids. The team drifted toward mediocrity by the mid–1950s, despite the hiring of Roy Hamey as general manager in 1954. Hamey's administration failed largely because the Phillies belatedly scouted black and Latin American talent and were the last NL team to have a black on their roster.

After Hamey resigned in 1959, Carpenter hired successful Milwaukee Braves executive John Quinn as general manager. Quinn and Carpenter rebuilt the Phillies as a contending ball club by dismantling the Whiz Kids. Through shrewd trades and a revamped farm system, the Phillies totally remodeled. After four straight cellar finishes (1958–1961), the Phillies again gained respectability and from 1962 to 1967 finished above .500 each year. In 1964, however, the Phillies suffered a terrible collapse, losing a 6 1/2 game lead with only 12 games left. Nevertheless, the 92–70 record and the 1964 squad marked the club's best record since the 1950 pennant winners.

When the team declined in the late 1960s, Carpenter gradually turned over direction of the ball club to his son, Ruly. After being trained in every aspect of baseball administration, Ruly became Phillies president in 1973 and retained his father as chairman of the board. Under Ruly's direction, the Phillies ranked among the dominant NL powers, captured three consecutive Eastern Division titles (1976–1978), and secured the club's first World Series victory in 1980 over the Kansas City Royals. In 1981 the Carpenters announced their intention to sell the team because of the impact that high player salaries were having on the financial structure of baseball. A financial group led by club vice-president Bill Giles and including the Taft Broadcasting System and a consortium of local investors, purchased a controlling interest from the Carpenters for $30 million. The sale ended a thirty-eight-year era during which the Phillies became one of the healthiest major league franchises.

BIBLIOGRAPHY: Frank Bilovsky and Rich Westcott, *The Phillies Encyclopedia* (Philadelphia, 1984).

John P. Rossi

CARTER, Gary Edmund (b. 8 April 1954, Culver City, CA), player, excelled as a scholar-athlete at Sunnyhills High School in Fullerton, CA, and captained the school's baseball, basketball, and football teams for two years. Selected in the third round of the 1972 free-agent draft, Carter rejected countless college scholarship offers to sign with the Montreal Expos (NL). Since his mother died of leukemia when he was 12 years old, he has remained close to his father James, an aircraft parts inspector. Carter, completely devoted to his wife, high school sweetheart Sandy Lahm, and two daughters Christina and Kimberly, is a talkative, gung-ho athlete, and applies the all-out approach to everything he does on the diamond.

After beginning his professional baseball career with Cocoa, FL (FECL), and West Palm Beach, FL (FSL), Carter moved to Quebec City (EL) and Peninsula, VA (IL) during the 1973 season. He played for Memphis (IL) in 1974 and finished the season with Montreal. Used primarily as an outfielder for the Expos, Carter was named NL Rookie of the Year in 1975. He won the regular catching job in 1977, as special tutoring by Norm Sherry improved his performance greatly.

Carter hit three home runs in one game on April 20, 1977, and on September 2, 1985, and tied a New York Mets record by slugging 13 home runs in September, 1985. His .294 batting average (1984), 106 RBIs (1984), and 32 home runs (1985) rank as career highs. In 1978 Carter established a major league record for fewest passed balls (1). He led NL catchers in total chances (1977–1982), putouts (1977–1980, 1982), assists (1977, 1979–1980, 1982), and double plays (1978–1979, 1983). In 1980 and 1983 he paced NL catchers in fielding. Named to the All-Star team (1975, 1979–1986), Carter was voted the game's Most Valuable Player in 1981 and 1984. His two home runs in the 1981 classic tied a record for most homers in one game. The next year he led All-Star balloting with nearly 3 million votes. He was named the catcher on *The Sporting News* All-Star fielding team (1980–1982) and Silver Slugger team (1981–1982).

In 1981 Carter batted .421 in the Eastern Division playoffs and .438 in the NL Championship Series (the Expos' first), as Montreal lost to the Los Angeles Dodgers in five games.

Through the 1986 season, Carter has played in 1,689 major league games, batted 6,063 times, scored 847 runs, made 1,646 hits, 287 doubles, 26 triples, and 271 home runs, knocked in 999 runs, and compiled a .271 batting average. Carter, named Montreal Player of the Year four times, has hit more home runs than any other player in Expos history. In December 1984, he was traded to the New York Mets for four players. During 1986, Carter batted .255, slugged 24 home runs, and knocked in 105 runs to help lead the New York Mets to the NL pennant. Although hitting only .148 in the NL Championship Series against the Houston Astros, Carter excelled in the 1986 World Series. He batted .276, made 8 hits, slugged 2 home runs, and knocked in 9 runs to help the Mets defeat the Boston Red Sox.

BIBLIOGRAPHY: Ron Fimrite, "His Enthusiasm Is Catching," *SI*, 58 (August 4 1983), pp. 52–55, 58, 61; Mark Ribowsky, "The Selling of Gary Carter," *Sport* 72 (August, 1981), 49–54; *TSN Official Baseball Register* (St. Louis, 1984).

John L. Evers

CARTWRIGHT, Alexander Joy, Jr. (b. 17 April 1820, New York, NY; d. 12 July 1892, Honolulu, HA), the "Father of Modern Baseball," was the son of sea captain and marine surveyor Alexander Joy and Ester Rebecca (Burlock) Cartwright. Cartwright attended school in New York City until 1836, when he left midway through the tenth grade to help support the family. From a lowly clerk, he advanced rapidly in the financial world. In 1842 he married Eliza Ann Gerrits Van Wie of Albany, NY. They had four children, Dewitt, Bruce, Kathleen Lee, and Alexander Joy Cartwright III.

A large, well-built man, Cartwright earned friends and continued success with his jovial, gregarious nature. In 1842 he joined a group of young bankers, lawyers, and merchants who regularly played baseball at Madison Square. At Cartwright's suggestion, in September, 1845, the Knickerbocker Base Ball Club became a permanent organization and established a constitution and by-laws. Cartwright and other officers divided club members into various teams for their biweekly games. In 1846 they began playing match games with other newly organized clubs. From 1846 through the 1870s, the Knickerbockers played at the Elysian Fields in Hoboken, NJ. According to Albert Spalding,* "The organization of the Knickerbockers began the most important era in the history of the game."

Cartwright's rules, although overlooked for nearly a century, transformed baseball into a mature sport. His major innovations included rules establishing nine-member teams with unalterable batting order, nine inning games, and ninety feet between bases, and prohibiting throwing the ball at a runner to put him out. These rules, drawn up and published in 1846, were adopted by many baseball clubs.

Cartwright remained an active Knickerbockers player and officer until 1849, when he joined the gold rush. He taught baseball to fellow travelers, saloon keepers, soldiers, miners, and Indians across the Great Plains and along the Santa Fe and Oregon trails. In August, 1849, he and former Knickerbocker Frank Turk introduced baseball in San Francisco. Cartwright then sailed for China, but illness forced him to make Honolulu his permanent home.

Success followed Cartwright to Hawaii, where his business became the prestigious Cartwright and Company. He became friend, adviser, and diplomatic envoy of the royal family. As one of Hawaii's leading citizens, he founded a bank, a hospital, the Honolulu fire and transportation departments, and the Masonic Lodge.

In 1852 Cartwright established Hawaii's first baseball field in Makiki Park. He organized teams and taught the game extensively, remaining an active player and an avid fan throughout his life. Consequently, baseball was played throughout the Hawaiian Islands before it was known in half of the United States. His family, which joined him in 1851, shared his enthusiasm for the sport. They read his diary and Knickerbocker Rules and played with the Knickerbocker baseball that he had brought from New York.

Despite Cartwright's popularity in Honolulu, Americans forgot him until plans were announced to celebrate in 1939 the centennial of Abner Doubleday's "invention of baseball." Bruce Cartwright then wrote the Centennial Committee about his grandfather's life and contribution to baseball. Consequently, Cartwright was inducted into the National Baseball Hall of Fame in 1938. In 1939 a replica of his Cooperstown plaque was placed in Honolulu City Hall, and Makiki Park was renamed Cartwright Park. A street and a baseball tournament also were named in his honor. Cartwright's innovative rules established him as the "Father of Modern Baseball," while his organization of the Knickerbocker Club and teaching of baseball across the United States and the Pacific sparked the growth and popularity of the game.

BIBLIOGRAPHY: Martin Appel and Bert Goldblatt, *Baseball's Best* (New York, 1977); Seymour R. Church, *Base Ball* (Princeton, NJ, 1902); Robert W. Henderson, *Ball, Bat, and Bishop* (New York, 1947); National Baseball Hall of Fame *Yearbook* (Cooperstown, NY, 1982), p. 69; Harold Peterson, *The Man Who Invented Baseball* (New York, 1969); Albert G. Spalding, *America's National Game* (New York, 1911).

Mary Lou LeCompte

CARUTHERS, Robert Lee "Bob," "Parisian Bob") (b. 5 January 1864, Memphis, TN; d. 5 August 1911, Peoria, IL), player and umpire, batted .282 in ten major league seasons and compiled one of the highest winning percentages for pitchers (.692). The 5 foot, 7 inch, 150 pound switch-hitter threw right-handed. He learned to play baseball in Chicago, where he moved in 1876 with his father, James P. Caruthers, a lawyer and former Tennessee state's attorney and Memphis judge, and his mother, the former Miss McNeil of Kentucky. After playing for two amateur clubs in Chicago (North End Club, 1882; Lake Views, 1883) and two professional WL clubs (Grand Rapids, 1883; Minneapolis, 1884), Caruthers joined the major league St. Louis Browns (AA) in September, 1884.

He helped the Browns win three consecutive pennants (1885–1887), leading AA pitchers with 40 wins in 1885 and in winning percentage in 1885 (.755) and 1887 (.763). He also ranked fourth among the AA's batters in 1886 (.334) and fifth in 1887 (.357). In slugging he placed second in 1886 (.527), a fraction of a point below AA leading Dave Orr,* and third in 1887 (.547). From 1888 through 1891, Caruthers played for Brooklyn (AA, NL). In 1889 his AA-leading 40 wins, .784 winning percentage, and 7 shutouts helped bring Brooklyn its first AA pennant. When Brooklyn moved the next year to the NL and again won the championship, Caruthers won 23 games as a pitcher, and played half his games in the outfield.

Used mainly as an outfielder, Caruthers concluded his major league career with St. Louis (1892), Chicago, and Cincinnati (1893) in the NL. After returning to the minors, he played outfield with Grand Rapids (WL) in 1894, Jackson (WA) in 1895 and Burlington, IA (WA) in 1896. Following his playing days, Caruthers umpired in the WL and 3IL. During the 1911 season, he suffered a nervous breakdown and died a few weeks later.

Caruthers, remembered primarily as a pitcher, won 218 major league games, lost only 97, registered six successive seasons of more than 20 victories, and compiled a 2.83 ERA. Among nineteenth century pitchers, his .692 major league winning percentage ranks him second behind Al Spalding* (.787). In 2,828 2/3 innings, he struck out 900 batters and hurled 25 shutouts. Caruthers pitched in early World Series with St. Louis (1885–1887) and Brooklyn (1889), winning seven games, losing eight, and tying one. Twice defeating Chicago in 1886, he hurled a ten-inning 4–3 win in the final game to give St. Louis the AA's only World Series victory over an NL champion.

BIBLIOGRAPHY: Henry Chadwick Scrapbooks, Albert Spalding Collection, New York Public Library, vols. 6, 7; Paul MacFarlane, ed., *TSN Daguerreotypes of Great Stars of Baseball* (St. Louis, 1981); Hy Turkin and S. C. Thompson, ed. *The Official Encyclopedia of Baseball*, jubilee ed. (New York, 1951), pp. 499–502; Joseph L. Reichler, ed., *The Baseball Encyclopedia*, 6th ed. (New York, 1985); pp. 785–786, 1,638; *Sporting Life*, August 12, 1911.

Frederick Ivor-Campbell

CASH, Norman Dalton "Norm," "Stormin' Norman") (b. 10 November 1934, Justiceburg, TX; d. 12 October 1986, Charlevoix, MI), player and announcer, attended San Angelo Junior College and starred in both baseball and football at Sul Ross State College. Upon graduation, he signed with the Chicago White Sox (AL) and spent the 1955 and 1956 seasons at Waterloo, IA (3IL), 1957 in military service, and part of 1958 at Indianapolis (AA). After one season as a part-time White Sox player, appearing in the 1959 World Series, Cash was traded to the Cleveland Indians (AL). As the 1960 season began, he was traded to the Detroit Tigers (NL).

A 6-foot, 190 pound first baseman, "Stormin' Norman" played the next fifteen years with the Tigers. In his second season with the Tigers (1961), Cash batted .361 to pace the AL. No major league ballplayer attained a higher seasonal average during the 1960s. In 1961 he led the AL in hits (193) and finished second in walks (124) and slugging average (.662). He hit 41 home runs—the most ever recorded by a Tiger left-handed hitter—and batted in 132 runs. Cash played in both 1961 All-Star games and the 1966, 1971, and 1972 contests. Despite mediocre mobility, in 1964 and 1967 he led AL first baseman in fielding percentage. In 1965 and 1971, he made the highest percentage of home runs to at bats in the AL.

Cash never again approached his 1961 statistics, but he became a Tigers mainstay until his retirement in 1974. Cash, who wed Myrta Harper in 1954, later married Dorothy Makoski in 1973. An integral part of the Tigers'1968 world champions, he batted a team-high .385 against the St.Louis Cardinals in the seven-game World Series. At retirement, he ranked among the top ten Tiger players in games (2,018), at bats (6,593), runs (1,028), hits (1,793), doubles (241), RBIs (1,087), and total bases (3,233). A lifetime .271 hitter, Cash ranked second to Hall of Famer Al Kaline* in club home runs and hit 377 career homers.

Well liked by his teammates, fans, and the press, the personable Cash remained in the Detroit area after his active career and served as a color commentator for Tiger games on cable television. Cash drowned while boating in Lake Michigan.

BIBLIOGRAPHY: Joseph L. Reichler, ed., *The Baseball Encyclopedia*, 6th ed. (New York, 1985), p. 787; Fred Smith, *995 Tigers* (Detroit, 1981).

Sheldon L. Appleton

CAVARETTA, Philip Joseph "Phil" (b. 19 July 1916, Chicago, IL), player, coach, and manager, is of Italian descent and attended Lane Tech High School for four years. The 5 foot, 11 1/2 inch, 175 pound Cavaretta married Lorayne Clares in 1936 and has three daughters. A brilliant high school player, Cavaretta turned professional in 1934 and played that year for Peoria, IL (CL), and Reading, PA (NYPL). At the season's end, he joined the Chicago Cubs (NL) and spent twenty years through 1953 there. He played 1954 and early 1955 with the Chicago White Sox (AL) and spent a season playing part-time with Buffalo (IL). Cavaretta played first base primarily and sometimes as an outfielder.

Cavaretta starred with the Cubs. As a 19-year-old regular, he hit a home run on September 25, 1935, to clinch an NL pennant tie for the Chicagoans and kept alive their 21-game winning streak. Cavaretta led the NL in total hits in 1944, batting (.355) in 1945, and pinch hits in 1951. In 1945 he was named NL Most Valuable Player. He batted .500 in three All-Star games and .317 in three World Series, appearing in seventeen games. A batting star for the losing 1938 and 1945 Cubs, he hit .462 and .423, respectively. While managing the Cubs, he won a game with a bases-loaded pinch home run on July 29, 1951, to duplicate a feat accomplished by Rogers Hornsby* twenty years earlier. Lifetime, he batted .293 with 1,977 hits, 347 doubles, 99 triples, 95 home runs, 990 runs scored, and 920 RBIs and performed capably defensively.

Cavaretta managed the Cubs to a 169–213 record (1951–1953) and served as Detroit Tigers (AL) coach (1961–1963) and scout (1964). Cavaretta managed many years in the minor leagues, including stints with Buffalo (IL) from 1956 to 1958; Lancaster, PA (EL), in 1960; Salinas, (CaL), in 1965 Reno (CaL) in 1966 and 1967, and Waterbury CT (EL) in 1968; and Birmingham (SL) from 1970 to 1972. He ended his association with baseball by serving as New York Mets (NL) minor league batting instructor (1973–1977) and Mets batting instructor (1978). Since then Cavaretta has lived in retirement at Palm Harbor, FL.

BIBLIOGRAPHY: Warren Brown, *The Chicago Cubs* (New York, 1946); *TSN*, August 22, 1935, May 31, 1945, January 4, 1948, July 25, 1970.

Lowell L. Blaisdell

CEPEDA, Orlando Manuel "The Baby Bull," "Cha-Cha" (b. 17 September 1937, Ponce, Puerto Rico), player, is the son of Peruchio Cepeda, Puerto Rico's most outstanding home run hitter. His father was nicknamed "The Bull," while Orlando became "The Baby Bull" and "Cha-Cha." After attending schools in Puerto Rico, he was signed in 1955 at age 17 by the New York Giants (NL). After a brief stint at Salem, VA (ApL), the 6 foot, 2 inch, 205 pound first baseman–outfielder batted .393 for Kokomo, IN, to lead the MOVL. In 1956 at St. Cloud, MN, the right-handed hitting and fielding Cepeda led the NoL with a .355 average. After hitting .309 with 25 homers for Minneapolis (AA), he batted .312 with 25 homers in 1958 for the San Francisco Giants and was named Rookie of the Year. Cepeda hit the first major league home run on the West Coast against the Los Angeles Dodgers in the opening game on April 15, 1958.

During his seventeen-year career, Cepeda played for San Francisco, the St. Louis Cardinals, and the Atlanta Braves in the NL and the Boston Red Sox and Kansas City Royals in the AL. He compiled a career .297 batting average with 2,351 hits, 417 doubles, 27 triples, and 379 home runs, scored 1,131 runs, drove in 1,365 runs, and stole 142 bases. He led the NL in homers with 46 and RBIs with 142 in 1961. Cepeda paced the NL with 111 RBIs in 1967 at St. Louis and was selected as the NL's Most Valuable Player. He played in two World Series with San Francisco and one with St. Louis, batting only .171 in nineteen games.

Cepeda played for San Francisco from 1958 to 1965 and was traded to St. Louis before the 1966 season. One of baseball's most misunderstood players, he experienced a stormy stay in San Francisco and held out each spring for more money. He clashed continually with managers Alvin Dark* and Herman Franks, who regarded him as lazy and indifferent. Fans irked him, once causing him to bean a San Francisco spectator. In 1965 he hurt his right knee and missed most of the season because of surgery. Although performing well with St. Louis, Cepeda was plagued by the knee injury the rest of his career.

After being traded to Atlanta (NL) in 1969, he limped through half of the 1971 season and was forced to have surgery on his right knee. The Braves traded Cepeda in 1972 to Boston (AL) where he was designated hitter. In 1974 he was traded to Kansas City (AL) and the next year became one of baseball's first players arrested on drug charges. Federal agents found 160 pounds of marijuana in his car trunk at the San Juan airport. Cepeda, who was convicted of drug smuggling, was sentenced to five years in prison and served ten months of that sentence. Subsequently, he operated a baseball school for children in San Juan.

BIBLIOGRAPHY: Orlando Cepeda and Bob Markers, *High and Inside: The Orlando Cepeda Story* (New York, 1983); Zander Hollander, ed., *The Complete Handbook of Baseball, 1972* (New York, 1972); Gene Karst and Martin J. Jones, Jr., *Who's Who in Professional Baseball* (New Rochelle, NY, 1973); Edward Kiersch, "Orlando Cepeda," in *Where Have You Gone Vince DiMaggio?* (New York, 1983), pp. 275–281; Joseph L. Reichler, ed., *The Baseball Encyclopedia*, 6th ed. (New York, 1985), pp. 790, 791.

James K. Skipper, Jr.

CHADWICK, Henry (b. 5 October 1824, Exeter, Devon, England; d. 20 April 1908, Brooklyn, NY), early promoter, shaper, chronicler, and conscience of baseball, was known as the "Father of Baseball" and later as "Father Chadwick." The son of English journalist James Chadwick, editor of the Exeter *Western Times*, he emigrated in 1837 with his parents to the United States. (His elder brother Edwin remained in England, where he gained international recognition as a pioneer in public health and sanitation.) The Chadwicks arrived a few days before Henry's thirteenth birthday and settled in Brooklyn, where Henry resided until his death. He began his journalistic career as a contributor to Brooklyn's *Long Island Star* in 1844. On August 19, 1848, he married Jane Botts, a native of Virginia.

Although Chadwick had played baseball around 1847 or 1848, he did not see his first match between skilled players until nearly a decade later and quickly recognized baseball's potential for becoming America's national game. Over the next fifty years, Chadwick wrote voluminously about baseball in newspapers, magazines, pamphlets, and books. He reported its games, chronicled its development, taught its skills, recommended changes in its rules, and battled the drinking and gambling that threatened its integrity.

Chadwick covered baseball for more than twenty newspapers and magazines, most notably the Brooklyn *Eagle* (1856–1894 on the staff, freelance thereafter) and the New York *Clipper* (1857–1888). He originated the annual baseball guide in 1860 with *Beadle's Dime Base Ball Player*, and edited *DeWitt's Guide* from 1869 to 1880 and *Spalding's Base Ball Guide* from 1881 to 1908. He wrote the first hardcover book devoted entirely to baseball (*The Game of Base Ball*, 1868) and numerous books and pamphlets on hitting, fielding, and base running, baseball jargon for British journalists, and other topics.

Chadwick influenced baseball's development unofficially through his writing and officially as a rules committee member of the National Association of Base Ball Players (1858–1870) and the NL. To improve record keeping, he perfected the box score and devised the system for scoring games essentially still used today. Chadwick saw himself as a guardian of baseball's image and well-being, inveighing against drinking and rowdiness by players and fans, and opposing disruptive influences like the outlaw PL of 1890. His opposition to gambling enabled baseball officials to stand firm against the persistent threats by gamblers to corrupt players and reduce baseball to a betting medium.

Though baseball dominated Chadwick's adult life, he pursued other interests. A songwriter and music teacher before becoming a baseball enthusiast, he continued to write music and play the piano. He also followed other sports and games, writing instructional guides on cricket, football, handball, and chess. He took particular delight in his family, which included his wife, two daughters, and numerous grandchildren and great-grandchildren.

In 1894 the NL elected Chadwick an honorary member, and in 1896 it granted him a lifetime pension of $600 per year. In 1904 Chadwick was awarded the only medal given to a journalist by the St. Louis World's Fair. In 1938 he was elected to the National Baseball Hall of Fame.

BIBLIOGRAPHY: Brooklyn *Eagle*, April 20, 1908; Henry Chadwick, Scorebooks, Scrapbooks, Diaries, Albert Spalding Collection, New York Public Library; Henry Chadwick file, National Baseball Hall of Fame Library, Cooperstown, NY; *DAB* 3 (1928), p. 587; *NYT*, April 21, 1908; Thomas S. Rice, "Henry Chadwick," *TSN*, May 21, 1936; Allen E. Sanders, "Henry Chadwick, the 'Father of Baseball,' " source unidentified; Harold Seymour, *Baseball: The Early Years* (New York, 1960); Albert G. Spalding, *America's National Game* (New York, 1911); *Sporting Life*, April 25, May 2, 1908.

Frederick Ivor-Campbell

CHANCE, Frank Leroy "Husk," "The Peerless Leader" (b. 9 September 1877, Fresno, CA; d. 15 September 1924, Los Angeles, CA), player and manager, played for the University of California in 1894–1895 and for an independent (probably semi-pro) team. Chance continued with baseball while studying dentistry at Washington College in Irvington, CA, where he was discovered in 1898 by Bill Lange,* former Chicago Colts outfielder. Upon Lange's recommendation, the Chicago Cubs (NL) signed Chance. He caught with Chicago until 1902, when manager Frank Selee* moved him permanently to first base. The good all-around player remained with Cubs from 1898 to 1912. Besides compiling a career .297 batting average, he led the NL in runs (103) in 1906 and in stolen bases in 1903 (67) and 1906 (57). In 20 World Series games, he hit .310 and stole 10 bases. He played very little after 1912 because of chronic headaches caused by several beanings. During his career, Chance made 1,274 hits, 199 doubles, 80 triples, 798 runs, 596 RBIs, and 405 stolen bases.

During the 1905 season, new Cubs owner Charlie W. Murphy appointed Chance player-manager. In nearly eight years as mentor, Chance directed his team to four NL pennants and 100-game victory seasons and two world championships. In 1912 Chance quarreled bitterly with Murphy over the amount of money the owner was willing to pay to obtain quality players. When Murphy refused to spend more, Chance resigned in protest at the season's end. That winter Chance underwent surgery for his headaches, which were attributed to blood clots. After managing the New York Yankees (AL) in 1913 and 1914 to seventh place finishes, Chance operated an orange grove in California. In 1916 and 1917 he was part-owner and manager of Los Angeles (PCL). He managed the Boston Red Sox (AL) to last place in 1923 and would have piloted the Chicago White Sox (AL) the following year had he remained healthy. In eleven seasons as a major league manager, he compiled 932 wins and 640 losses for the seventh best percentage (.593).

A member of the Cubs' famed Joe Tinker* to John Evers* to Chance double play combination, he was elected with his teammates to the National Baseball Hall of Fame in 1946. The origins of his nickname "Husk" are obscure, but Chicago baseball writer Charlie Dryden nicknamed him "Peerless Leader" for the championships the Cubs won under his direction.

BIBLIOGRAPHY: Warren Brown, *The Chicago Cubs* (New York, 1946); Ralph Hickok, *Who Was Who in American Sports* (New York, 1971); Gene Karst and Martin J. Jones, Jr., *Who's Who in Professional Baseball* (New Rochelle, NY, 1973); *Macmillan Baseball Encyclopedia* (New York, 1969); *NYT*, September 16, 1924; Lowell Reidenbaugh, *Cooperstown: Where Baseball's Legends Live Forever* (St. Louis, 1983).

John E. Findling

CHANDLER, Albert Benjamin "Happy" (b. 18 April 1898, Corydon, KY), commissioner, is the son of a handyman-farmer Joseph and Callie Chandler. An impoverished, hard-working, ambitious youth, he completed high school and enrolled at Transylvania College in 1917 with "a red sweater on my back, a $5 bill in my pocket, and a song in my heart." Chandler, a sports enthusiast, played and coached football and participated in baseball in the RRVL and the BGL. After earning his law degree from the University of Kentucky, he began practicing law in Versailles, KY, and coached high school baseball there. Chandler married Mildred Watkins in 1925 and had four children.

The outgoing Chandler entered public life as a Democrat in 1928. He served as governor of Kentucky from 1935 to 1939 and 1955 to 1959 and as U.S. Senator from 1939 to 1945. An energetic campaigner, he proved a shrewd and colorful politician. In 1945 Leland McPhail, Sr.* promoted Chandler's selection as baseball commissioner, a position vacant since the death in 1944 of the stern Judge Kenesaw Mountain Landis.* Chandler became the goodwill ambassador baseball needed, but proved less pliant than sportswriters and baseball owners assumed he would be. He served as commissioner when Jackie Robinson* integrated organized baseball. Although scholars debate the commissioner's role in the controversies that surrounded Robinson's initial years with the Brooklyn Dodgers (NL), Chandler acted with fair-mindedness and spoke in favor of integration when anything less might have denied Robinson his opportunity.

Chandler acted decisively on the key issues of players' rights and the outlaw MEL, which in 1946 lured baseball stars with sizeable financial offers. He imposed a five-year ban from organized baseball on eighteen jumpers, an edict which frightened magnates by nearly bringing a court ruling on the reserve clause. He also suspended Brooklyn Dodgers manager Leo Durocher* for the 1947 season for "an accumulation of unpleasant incidents . . . detrimental to baseball." In other instances, Chandler helped the players' association secure the radio and television revenue to bolster the new pension plan and supported a $5,000 minimum salary for major leaguers.

A clique of owners revolted against Chandler for arbitrarily jeopardizing the reserve clause and ordering investigations of the alleged gambling activities of one or two owners. Securing only nine of the twelve votes necessary for reelection, Chandler resigned in 1951 to resume an active role in Kentucky politics. An elder statesman in both sports and politics, Chandler in 1982 was elected to the National Baseball Hall of Fame. Upon this occasion, second baseman Joe Morgan* wired Chandler: "The Hall of Fame was made for people like you."

BIBLIOGRAPHY: Terry L. Birdwhistell, "A. B. 'Happy' Chandler," in Fred J. Hood, ed., *Kentucky: Its History and Heritage* (St. Louis, 1978), pp. 208–220; Albert B. Chandler Collection and Albert B. Chandler Oral History Project, Margaret I. King Library, University of Kentucky, Lexington, KY; A. B. "Happy" Chandler with John Underwood, "How I Jumped from Clean Politics to Dirty Baseball," *SI* 34 (April 26, 1971), pp. 73–86, and (May 3, 1971), pp. 52–58; *CB* (1956), pp. 106–108; Daniel M. Daniel, "Senator Chandler Eminently Fitted for Vital Job as Baseball Commissioner," *Baseball Magazine* 75 (July, 1945), pp. 255–257, 284–285; John Drebinger, "A Commissioner's Reign Ends," *Baseball Digest* 10 (May, 1951), pp. 399–400, 431–432; Milton Gross, "The Truth About Happy Chandler," *Sport* 6 (April, 1959), pp. 53–62; Lexington (KY) *Herald*, June 24, 1983; J. B. Shannon, " 'Happy' Chandler: A Kentucky Epic," in J. T. Salter, ed., *The American Politician* (Chapel Hill, NC, 1938), pp. 175–191; Jules Tygiel, *Baseball's Great Experiment: Jackie Robinson and His Legacy* (New York, 1983).

Lloyd J. Graybar

CHANDLER, Spurgeon Ferdinand "Spud" (b. 12 September 1907, Commerce, GA), player and scout, graduated from Carnesville (GA) High School in 1928 and excelled in football, baseball, and track at the University of Georgia, where he received a Bachelor of Science degree in 1932. That same year Chandler began his professional baseball career with Springfield, MA (EL), and Binghamton, NY (NYPL). The 6 foot, 181 pound, right-handed pitcher hurled for Binghamton and Newark (IL) in 1933. Chandler divided the 1934 season among Newark and Syracuse, NY (IL), and Minneapolis

(AA). In 1935 he pitched with Oakland (PCL) and Portland (PCL) and returned to Newark for 1936 and part of 1937.

Chandler joined New York (AL) in 1937 and spent his entire eleven-year major league career with the Yankees. He recorded a 7–4 won-lost record in 1937 and followed with 14–5, 3–0, 8–7, 10–4, and 16–5 marks. In 1943 he won 20, lost only 4, and led the AL with an .833 pitching percentage. His 1.64 ERA paced the majors, marking only the fourth time in AL history that a pitcher captured both laurels at once. Chandler topped the AL with 20 complete games, his 20 victories tying Dizzy Trout of Detroit for the AL lead. After serving in the military for much of the 1944 and 1945 seasons, Chandler won 20 and lost only 8 in 1946. His 2.46 ERA led the AL in 1947, when he posted a 9–5 record in his last major league season.

In 33 1/3 innings spanning four World Series (1941–1943, 1947), Chandler won two games, lost two decisions, and recorded a 1.62 ERA. The Yankees captured world championships in 1941, 1943, and 1947. His two victories in 1943 sparked the Yankees' World Series triumph over St. Louis (NL) in five games. Chandler in 1942 was credited with the win as the AL All-Stars defeated the NL 3–1. In 211 career major league games, Chandler won 109 decisions and lost 43 for a .717 percentage. He pitched 1,485 innings, allowed 1,327 hits, and struck out 614 batters, compiling a 2.84 ERA and 26 career shutouts. An exceptional batting pitcher, Chandler collected 110 hits in 548 plate appearances for a .201 average. On July 26, 1940, against the Chicago White Sox (AL), he slugged two home runs in one game, including a grand slam off Pete Appleton. Chandler, who later scouted for the Yankees, married Frances Willard on October 19, 1939.

BIBLIOGRAPHY: Gene Karst and Martin J. Jones, Jr., *Who's Who in Professional Baseball* (New Rochelle, NY, 1973); Joseph L. Reichler, ed., *The Baseball Encyclopedia*, 6th ed. (New York, 1985), p. 1,642; Frank Stevens, *Baseball's Forgotten Heroes* (Netcong, NJ, 1984).

                                                                    John L. Evers

CHAPMAN, William Benjamin "Ben" (b. 25 December 1908, Nashville, TN), player, manager, and coach, is the son of Harry C. "Tub" and Effie Chapman. His father, a minor league pitcher, left professional baseball after an arm injury and worked in the Birmingham, AL, steel mills. Chapman became an outstanding athlete at Phillips High School, participating in baseball, football, basketball, and track. The New York Yankees (AL) signed the 6 foot, 190 pound right-hander as a shortstop in 1928 and sent him to Asheville, NC (SAL). After hitting .336 and stealing 30 bases in 1928 there, he batted .336 and pilfered 26 bases the next year as a third baseman for St. Paul (AA). The New York Yankees started Chapman, who batted .316 his rookie year, at third base, then at second base in 1930. In 1931 he moved to the outfield and combined his hitting ability with a strong arm and speed.

New York used him at all three outfield positions before making him the regular center fielder in 1934.

The speedster led the AL in stolen bases in 1931 (61), 1932 (38), and 1933 (27) and tied for the AL lead in 1937 (35). Chapman's 13 triples in 1934 also topped the AL. In the 1932 World Series, he batted .294 to help the Yankees defeat the Chicago Cubs (NL). Chapman, selected for the All-Star team in 1933, 1934, and 1935, was traded to the Washington Senators (AL) in 1936. Subsequently, he played with the Boston Red Sox (AL) in 1937 and 1938, Cleveland Indians (AL) in 1939 and 1940, and Washington Senators (AL) and Chicago White Sox (AL) in 1941. He briefly returned to the major leagues as a pitcher and outfielder with the Brooklyn Dodgers (NL) in 1944 and 1945 and with the Philadelphia Phillies (NL) in 1945 and 1946. Chapman batted .302 lifetime and stole 287 career bases, including 14 thefts of home plate. In 1,716 major league games, he garnered 1,958 hits, 407 doubles, 107 triples, 90 home runs, 1,144 runs scored, and 977 RBIs. During 25 pitching appearances, he won 8 games and lost 6 in 141.1 innings for a 4.39 ERA.

Chapman also managed several clubs, beginning with Richmond, VA (Pil), in 1942 and 1944. He piloted the Philadelphia Phillies (NL) to four second division finishes from 1945 to 1948 and a 197–277 (.416) overall mark. Chapman's other managerial assignments included Gadsden, AL (SEL), in 1949, Danville, VA (CrL), in 1950, Tampa (FIL) in 1951 and 1953, and Toronto (IL) in late 1953. Chapman, who served as a coach with the Cincinnati Reds (NL) in 1952, married Ola Sanford on October 7, 1935, and has one son, William, Jr.

BIBLIOGRAPHY: Brooklyn *Eagle*, June 14, 1931; Ben Chapman file, National Baseball Hall of Fame Library, Cooperstown, NY; Mark Gallagher, *Fifty Years of Yankee All Stars* (New York, 1984); Paul MacFarlane, ed., *TSN Daguerreotypes of Great Stars of Baseball* (St. Louis, 1981); *NYT*, 1930–1948; New York *World Telegram*, 1928–1948; Murray Palmer, *Branch Rickey* (New York, 1982); Joseph L. Reichler, ed., *The Baseball Encyclopedia*, 6th ed. (New York, 1985), p. 794; Jackie Robinson, *I Never Had It Made* (Greenwich, CT, 1972); St. Louis *Star*, July 29, 1931; Jules Tygiel, *Baseball's Great Experiment* (New York, 1983).

Robert J. Brown

CHARLESTON, Oscar McKinley "The Black Ruth" (b. 12 October 1896, Indianapolis, IN; d. 6 October 1954, Philadelphia, PA), player and manager, ranked among the greatest Negro baseball players and was the son of jockey and construction worker Tom and Mary (Jeannette) Charleston. After attending school in Indianapolis until his sophomore year, he enlisted in the U.S. Army at age 15 and was shipped to the Philippines. He played his first baseball there with the Negro 24th Infantry and by 1914 became the only black player in the MnL. In 1915 the 6 foot, 1 inch, 180 pound Charleston returned to Indianapolis and starred immediately as a center fielder for the

ABCs, leading them to a championship the following year. His incredible speed, including clocking 23 seconds in the 220 yard dash with the Army track team, enabled him to play shallow, just behind second base. He caught short liners and bloop flies there, chased down long flies, and demonstrated a powerful throwing arm. According to Elwood "Bingo" De Moss,* "Oscar was the only player I've ever seen who could turn twice while chasing a fly and then take it over his shoulder. He had an uncanny knowledge of judging fly balls." His unparalleled speed and ability to detect flaws in a pitcher's motion became obvious assets on the basepaths. Above all, the "Black Babe Ruth" demonstrated natural fastball hitting ability by hitting to every part of the ballpark with enormous power. Hitting and speed, coupled with a swinging bunt, made Charleston a consistent offensive threat.

He joined Rube Foster's* Chicago American Giants as an outfielder in 1919, but returned to the ABCs (NNL) two years later. In 1921 the left-handed slugger batted .430, stole 35 bases, and led the NNL in doubles, triples, and home runs. The next season, he hit .399 and again paced the NNL in home runs. During the 1920s, he also played with the St. Louis Giants, Harrisburg Hilldales (ECL), and Philadelphia Hilldales (ANL). With Harrisburg, he led the ECL in batting in 1924 and in doubles and home runs the latter year. After the ECL broke up, he led the ANL by batting .396 for Philadelphia. In 1930 he joined Cum Posey's* great Homestead Grays, featuring "Double Duty" Radcliffe, Ted Page, Smoky Joe Williams,* and Josh Gibson.* With other Grays stars, he jumped to the Pittsburgh Crawfords (NNL) in 1932. Owner Gus Greenlee* outbid Posey for Charleston's services and enabled him to play at Greenlee Field, the nation's only black-owned stadium. By this time, Charleston had moved from outfield to first base. His great speed diminished, but he became player-manager of his teams from the late 1920s onward. Charleston starred with the Crawfords until 1936, batting .363 and .450 his first two seasons although well past his prime as a player. Through 1954 he managed various teams, including the Toledo Crawfords, Indianapolis Crawfords, and Philadelphia Stars. In 1954 Charleston led the Indianapolis Clowns to a Negro World Championship, his first as a manager.

Charleston's legendary feats included a lifetime .376 league average, a .326 mark against white major leaguers, and a .361 average for nine CUWL seasons. As a CUWL rookie, he averaged .405. He reputedly hit four homers in a single exhibition game against the St. Louis Cardinals in 1921 and occasionally played all nine positions in a game to display his versatility. From 1933 to 1935, he started the first three Negro All-Star games. When Branch Rickey* searched for an appropriate black player to sign with the Brooklyn Dodgers (NL), Charleston scouted the Negro leagues for him. Charleston, who died of a heart attack, was survived by his wife Jane; he had no children. In 1976 Charleston was elected to the National Baseball Hall of Fame as perhaps the greatest all around player in Negro league history.

BIBLIOGRAPHY: Chicago *Defender*, October 23, 1954; John Holway, *Voices from the Great Black Baseball Leagues* (New York, 1975); Robert W. Peterson, *Only the Ball Was White* (Englewood Cliffs, NJ, 1970); Pittsburgh *Courier*, October 16, 1954; James A. Riley, *The All-Time All-Stars of Black Baseball* (Cocoa, FL, 1983).

Gerald E. Brennan

CHASE, Harold Harris "Hal," "Prince Hal" (b. 13 February 1883, Los Gatos, CA; d. 18 May 1947, Colusa, CA), player and manager, generally was rated the greatest fielding first baseman in major league history. Chase starred for Santa Clara University in 1903 and for Los Angeles (PCL) in 1904 before the New York Highlanders (AL) purchased his contract for a reported $2,700.

Chase's career with the Highlanders (predecessor of the Yankees) from 1905 to 1913 was marked by his brilliant fielding and controversial behavior. Nicknamed "Prince Hal" by fans, he ranged far from first base to cut off grounders and scoop up bunt hits and developed into a respectable batter excelling at the hit-and-run play. His reputation for discontentment and dishonesty, however, also grew. He defied organized baseball by playing winter ball in the outlawed CaL under a false name for awhile. Amid rumors questioning his honesty, he left New York in midseason 1908 to play in California. Despite new accusations by Chase's manager, George Stallings, that he tried to throw a game, New York owner Frank Farrell exonerated him and appointed him playing manager late in the 1910 season. He managed New York to a sixth place finish in 1911 with 76 wins and 76 losses.

Chase's stardom and fan appeal may have shielded him from punishment by baseball authorities. When manager Frank Chance* reported Chase for throwing baseball games in 1913, New York traded the first baseman to the Chicago White Sox (AL). Unhappy there, after 58 games in 1914 he jumped to Buffalo (FL) for the 1914 and 1915 campaigns and led the FL with 17 home runs in 1915. After the FL collapsed, Chase played with the Cincinnati Reds from 1916 to 1918 and led the NL with a .339 batting average and 184 hits in 1916. Manager Christy Mathewson* suspended him in 1918 for crookedness, when an investigation produced fourteen allegations of misconduct. Chase escaped punishment and was traded to the New York Giants (NL) in 1919, his last major league season. In 1,917 games, he made 2,158 hits, 322 doubles, 124 triples, 57 home runs, 980 runs, 941 RBIs, 363 stolen bases, and .291 batting and .391 slugging averages.

The most damaging evidence against Chase surfaced in 1920. A teammate from the 1918 Reds testified that he and Chase bribed a Cincinnati pitcher and gambled $500 on the outcome. The fix failed, but Chase's check survived to record his involvement. Chase was also indicted in the Chicago Black Sox scandal, but avoided testifying and later privately admitted to having prior knowledge of the fixed World Series of 1919. Chase was accused of attempted bribery of a PCL player in 1920 and was barred from that and three other California leagues. Chase, whose private life was marred by two divorces, apparently spent his remaining years as player and manager for teams in Arizona and Mexico. Although portrayed by one historian as the "archetype of all crooked ball players" and by an earlier sportswriter as the player with a "corkscrew brain," Chase died without ever admitting any wrongdoing.

BIBLIOGRAPHY: Eliot Asinof, *Eight Men Out* (New York, 1963); Robert C. Hoie, "The Hal Chase Case," *Baseball Historical Review* (1981), pp. 34–41; Frederick G. Lieb, *Baseball as I Have Known It* (New York, 1977); *NYT*, 1905–1920, May 19, 1947; Harold Seymour, *Baseball: The Golden Age* (New York, 1971).

Joseph E. King

CHESBRO, John Dwight "Jack," "Happy Jack" (b. 5 June 1874, North Adams, MA; d. 6 November 1931, Conway, MA), player and coach, became one of the few pitchers to lead both current major leagues in won-lost percentage with .677 and .824 for the Pittsburgh Pirates (NL) in 1901 and 1902 and .774 for New York (AL) in 1904. The 5 foot, 9 inch, 180 pound right-hander exhibited great endurance in his most outstanding season (1904). Chesbro's 41 victories remain the modern era and AL record, while his 51 starts and 48 complete games rank second, and his 454.2 innings stands third. As a youth, Chesbro played with the Houghtonville Nine and several other western Massachusetts sandlot teams. In 1894 he began working for the state mental hospital in Middletown, NY, and was nicknamed "Happy Jack" because of his pleasant disposition. Although working with patients, he maintained principal interest in the hospital baseball team and learned about pitching from coach Pat McGreehy.

Chesbro began his minor league career in 1895 with Albany (NYSL). After the Albany club disbanded, he joined Johnstown, NY, and compiled a 7–10 combined season record. After the NYSL folded on July 6, 1895, he then logged a 3–0 mark for Springfield, MA (EL). In 1896 he married Mabel Shuttleworth and played for Roanoke, VA (VL), until it failed on August 20. Chesbro spent the rest of 1896 as a semi-pro in Cooperstown, NY, becoming perhaps the only Hall of Famer to pitch there regularly. He performed for Richmond, VA (AtL) in 1897 and 1898 and boasted a 17–4 mark through July, 1899, when he was sold to the Pittsburgh Pirates (NL) for $1,500. After appearing in 19 games for Pittsburgh in 1899, he was involved in one of the most complex deals ever made. The Louisville Colonels (NL) were about to be abolished and conducted a dispersal sale, in which fourteen players, including Honus Wagner,* Deacon Phillippe,* Rube Waddell,* and

Fred Clarke* moved to Pittsburgh for Chesbro and five others. The players traded to Louisville then rejoined Pittsburgh when the two clubs merged, and participated on the second place Pirates team in 1900.

Chesbro enjoyed his first 20-win season and led the NL with a .677 won-lost percentage as the Pirates captured their initial NL pennant in 1901. The next season Chesbro led the Pirates to another pennant with an NL-leading 28 victories and 8 shutouts (including three consecutive shutouts twice). Besides losing only 6 decisions, Chesbro compiled a 12-game winning streak from May 16 to July 24. During the 1902 season, he began throwing his famous spitball for Pirates manager-outfielder Clarke.* Chesbro seized an opportunity to earn more money by jumping with pitcher Jesse Tannehill* to manager Clark Griffith's* New York Highlanders for their first AL season in 1903. Chesbro logged a 21–15 mark for the fourth place Highlanders, while the Pirates won their third straight NL pennant and lost their first World Series.

Chesbro's 1904 season was the finest any pitcher has enjoyed in this century, as he completed each of his first 30 starts and 48 of 51 overall. On August 10 he was knocked out for the first time in a 5–1 loss to the Chicago White Sox. Chicago also knocked him out again on September 30 in three innings. Counting four relief appearances, Chesbro's innings totaled a remarkable 454.2. Besides striking out 239 batters and allowing only 338 hits, Chesbro recorded a 14-game winning streak from May 14 through July 4. Unfortunately, this great season ended on an unhappy note for Chesbro and the New York team. Chesbro won his 41st game on Friday, October 7, putting New York one-half game ahead of Jimmy Collins'* Boston Red Sox. Since Saturday's doubleheader was moved to Boston to avoid a conflict with a Columbia University football game, manager Griffith wanted Chesbro to stay in New York and rest for the season's final games on Monday, October 10. Owner Frank Farrell, however, persuaded Chesbro to journey to Boston, where he was knocked out for only the third time in a 13–2 loss. The Boston Red Sox also won the second game 1–0, putting New York 1 1/2 games behind. Chesbro started the first game in New York on October 10 against Boston's Bill Dinneen. Both pitchers were deadlocked 2–2 when Boston's Lou Criger reached base. With two men out and Criger on third base, Chesbro worked the count to no balls and two strikes on Fred Parent. Chesbro's next pitch, a powerful spitball, was a wild pitch and allowed Criger to score the winning run. Many writers claimed that catcher Jack Kleinow should have been charged with the passed ball, but the damage was done. Although New York won the second game 1–0, Boston captured the AL pennant.

Chesbro pitched 1,407 innings from 1903 through 1906, but an ankle injury in 1907 slowed him considerably. He lost four games in nine appearances in 1909, was sold to Boston for the waiver price, and lost his only decision there, falling short of 200 career victories. After leaving major league baseball, he built a chicken farm in Conway, MA, coached baseball at Amherst College, and played semi-pro baseball. In 1912 he launched an unsuccessful comeback with the New York Highlanders and then could not even make his town team. At Conway, he operated a sawmill and lumber yard and raised chickens. Griffith persuaded him to join the Washington Senators (AL) as a coach in 1924, but financial problems caused his release on Memorial Day. Chesbro was named to the National Baseball Hall of Fame in 1946 with 198 career victories. In 392 major league games, he lost only 132 games, completed 261 of 332 starts, struck out 1,265 and walked only 690 batters in 2,897 innings, hurled 35 shutouts, and compiled a 2.68 ERA. Chesbro led his league three times in winning percentage; twice in wins, appearances, and games started; and once each in complete games, innings, and shutouts.

BIBLIOGRAPHY: John Chesbro file, National Baseball Hall of Fame Library, Cooperstown, NY; Harry Grayson, *They Played the Game* (New York, 1945); Lowell Reidenbaugh, *Cooperstown: Where Baseball's Legends Live Forever* (St. Louis, 1983).

David B. Merrell

CHILDS, Clarence Algernon "Cupid," "Paca" (b. 14 August 1868, Calvert County, MD; d. 8 November 1912, Baltimore, MD), player, came from a large family in the rural Chesapeake backwaters. He entered professional baseball as a teenager in the NCL and played with Petersburg, VA (VL), in 1886 and Shamokin, PA (CPL), in 1887. In 1888 Childs, who threw right-handed but batted from the left side, made his major league debut as a second baseman in two games for Philadelphia (NL). He finished the 1888 season with Kalamazoo, MI (TSL), and the following year played for Syracuse, NY (IL).

In 1890 Childs remained in Syracuse, which became a major league franchise in the wobbly AA. After hitting .345 and leading the AA with 33 doubles, he joined the Cleveland Spiders (NL) the next year. In eight seasons with Cleveland (1891–1898), he built a reputation as a durable second baseman and a consistent hitter and averaged nearly .320 in that span. In 1892 he led all second sackers with a .946 fielding percentage, and scored an NL-leading 136 runs. At Cleveland, he averaged over 750 chances at second base each season and in 1896 led the NL with 369 putouts and 496 assists.

Before the 1899 season, Cleveland's owners Frank and Stanley Robison transferred the Spiders' best players to St. Louis (NL), which they had recently acquired in auction. Consequently, Childs, player-manager Patsy Tebeau, Cy Young,* Bobby Wallace,* and five other Cleveland players were sent to St. Louis. After playing there one season, Childs joined Chicago (NL) and in 1900 again led the NL with 759 total chances at second base. He was released by Chicago in early July, 1901, and finished the season with Toledo (WA). He divided the following season between Jersey City (EL) and Syracuse (NYSL), spent 1903 with Montgomery, AL (SA), and closed his career with Scranton (NYSL) in 1904.

Upon leaving pro baseball, Childs returned to Baltimore and became moderately well-to-do in the real estate business. A series of unsuccessful deals, however, brought him a sizeable financial loss, after which he became a local coalyard operator. Following a lengthy illness, he was hospitalized in October, 1912, and died early the next month. Former teammates contributed liberally to a fund established to defray his medical expenses and provided his wife and 8-year-old daughter a modest sum on which to live.

At the peak of his career in the mid–1890s, the stocky 5 foot, 8 inch, 185 pound infielder—nicknamed "Paca" and "Cupid"—was considered the NL's quickest second baseman and one of its heaviest hitters. At Cleveland, Childs and long time shortstop Eddie McKean* formed one of the game's most respected keystone combinations. He appeared in 1,467 major league games, playing all but 14 at second base. In his major league career, Childs collected 1,727 hits, scored 1,218 runs, and posted a .306 batting average.

BIBLIOGRAPHY: Baltimore *Sun*, November 9, 1912; Chicago *Daily Tribune*, November 9, 1912; Paul MacFarlane, ed. *TSN Daguerreotypes of Great Stars of Baseball* (St. Louis, 1981); Joseph L. Reichler, ed., *The Baseball Encyclopedia*, 6th ed. (New York, 1985), p. 796; David Quentin Voigt, *American Baseball*, vol. 1 (Norman, OK, 1966).

Raymond D. Kush

CICOTTE, Edward Victor "Eddie" (b. 19 June 1884, Detroit, MI; d. 5 May 1969, Detroit, MI), player, figured prominently in baseball's greatest scandal by helping throw the 1919 World Series to the Cincinnati Reds. Cicotte began a three-year minor league pitching apprenticeship in 1905. Due to his Detroit origins, he spent a brief stint in 1905 with the Tigers (AL). Finding his size unimpressive, Detroit let Atlanta (SAL) have him. After pitching well there, the Michigan native spent 1906 with Des Moines, IA (WL), and 1907 with Lincoln, NE (WL), and enjoyed very successful seasons.

Cicotte reached the major leagues in 1908 and performed reasonably well for four and one-half years with the Boston Red Sox (AL). Sold in mid–1912 to the Chicago White Sox (AL), he gradually advanced to great success over the next eight and one-half seasons. Had he not been expelled from baseball by Commissioner Kenesaw Mountain Landis* after the 1920 season, Cicotte surely would have been selected to the National Baseball Hall of Fame. A contemporary of outstanding pitchers Grover Cleveland Alexander* and Walter Johnson,* Cicotte led AL hurlers twice in winning percentage, innings pitched, and total wins, and once in ERA. He won 28 games in 1917 and 29 games in a 140-game schedule in 1919, helping the White Sox to two AL pennants and one world championship. During his career, he won 208 games, lost only 149 times, struck out 2,897 batters in 3,224 1/3 innings, and compiled an impressive 2.37 ERA.

A pitching artist, the 5 foot, 9 inch, 175 pound Cicotte finessed hitters via the first complete mastery of the knuckleball and through his superb control. Reputedly a trick-pitch magician, he utilized the spitball and its spinoffs, the shine, and emery balls. Babe Ruth,* the game's premier slugger, never slammed a home run off him, and commented, "That froggie can pitch!"

Cicotte ruined an otherwise admirable career by joining seven other "Black" Sox to lose the 1919 World Series deliberately. In return for pitching ineptly in two games, he received $10,000 from gamblers. His motives included worry over a large, unpaid farm mortgage and resentment toward the team's owner, Charles A. Comiskey.* In 1918 Comiskey paid Cicotte only $7,000, a much lower salary than was paid to some pitchers with less skill. After public disclosure of the scandal in 1920, Cicotte expressed remorse for his deed. Thereafter Cicotte lived inconspicuously in the Detroit area, worked many years for the Ford Motor Company, and also enjoyed modest success as a strawberry grower. His use of a pseudonym protected his wife and three children from adverse publicity.

BIBLIOGRAPHY: Eliot Asinof, *Eight Men Out* (New York, 1963); Frederick G. Lieb, *Baseball as I Have Known It* (New York, 1977); Victor Luhr, *The Great Baseball Mystery* (New York, 1966); *NYT*, May 9, 1969; *TSN*, May 24, 1969; Bill Veeck, *The Hustler's Handbook* (New York, 1965).

                                                      Lowell L. Blaisdell

CLARKE, Fred Clifford "Cap" (b. 3 October 1872, Winterset, IA; d. 14 August 1960, Winfield, KS), player, manager, and executive, was the son of farmer William D. and Lucy (Cutler) Clarke and brother of major league outfielder Joshua Clarke. The Clarkes moved to Winfield KS when Fred was age two, but returned to Iowa near Des Moines five years later. Fred attended Dickenson, IA, public shools, delivered newspapers under Des Moines circulation manager Edward Barrow,* and played baseball for the Des Moines Stars and Mascots. A left fielder, Clarke joined the Carroll, IA, semi-pro club in 1891 and began his professional career the next year with Hastings, NE (NSL). After splitting 1893 between St. Joseph, MO (WA), and Montgomery, AL (SL), he hit .311 in 1894 for Savannah (SL). He married Annette Gray in October, 1898, and had two daughters, Helen Donahoe (1900) and Muriel Sullivan (1904).

In 1894 Clarke joined the Louisville Colonels (NL) for a $100 guarantee and $175 a month if he remained with the team. Using a light bat, Clarke auspiciously debuted with a record four singles and one triple in five times at the plate. The 5 foot, 10 inch, right-handed Clarke batted .315 lifetime, made 2,708 hits, and scored 1,626 runs in 2,245 games for the Louisville Colonels (1894–1899) and Pittsburgh Pirates (1900–1915). Although only 165 pounds, he slugged 359 doubles, 223 triples, and 67 home runs and knocked in 1,015 runs. Clarke batted over .300 eleven seasons, including five consecutively, and surpassed the .350 mark in 1895, 1897, and 1903. He hit safely in 31 consecutive games in 1895 and batted a career-high .406 in 1897 for Louisville, finishing second to Willie Keeler.* Besides stealing over 30 bases seven seasons and pilfering 506 career bases, Clarke led the NL in doubles (32) and slugging percentage (.532) in 1903 and in walks (80) in 1909. Defensively, he handled nearly 5,000 chances and led NL left fielders in percentage nine times. Twice tying major league records, Clarke made four assists in an August, 1910, game and ten putouts in an April, 1911, contest. He often made spectacular catches with somersault dives.

Clarke piloted Louisville (1897–1899) and Pittsburgh (1900–1915), ranking high among major league managers with 1,602 victories and recording an impressive .576 win-loss percentage. An energetic, aggressive, inspirational leader, he stressed physical conditioning, practice, dedication, and desire. In 1897 Louisville appointed 24-year-old Clarke as baseball's first "boy manager." Although not faring well initially, Clarke's club improved dramatically when it merged with Pittsburgh in 1900. Outstanding batters Clarke, Honus Wagner,* and Ginger Beaumont,* along with excellent pitchers Deacon Phillippe,* Jesse Tannehill,* Sam Leever,* Jack Chesbro,* Vic Willis,* and Albert Leifield, transformed Pittsburgh from a perennial second division team to a premier club. Under Clarke's adept guidance, the Pirates captured pennants from 1901 to 1903 and in 1909, placed second five times, and finished in the second division only twice. From 1901 through 1913, the New York Giants and the Chicago Cubs were the only other teams to win NL pennants. Clarke helped the Pirates take the 1903 pennant by hitting .351, but his club lost to the Boston Red Sox in the first modern World Series. In 1909 he sparked the Pirates to their first World Series title by slugging two home runs against the Detroit Tigers. His World Series records included five sacrifice hits and four walks in one game. As Pittsburgh manager, Clarke earned only $3,600 annually. After retiring as manager, he raised wheat and livestock on a profitable 1,320 acre ranch near Winfield, KS. Clarke, who served briefly in the mid–1920s as Pirates coach and vice-president and later presided over non-professional baseball leagues, was elected to the National Baseball Hall of Fame (1951), Iowa Sports Hall of Fame (1951), and Kansas Sports Hall of Fame.

BIBLIOGRAPHY: Martin Appel and Burt Goldblatt, *Baseball's Best: The Hall of Fame Gallery* (New York, 1977); Des Moines (IA) *Register*, April 15, 1951, August 15, 1960; Frederick Lieb, *The Pittsburgh Pirates* (New York, 1948); George S. May, "Major League Baseball Players from Iowa," *The Palimpsest* 36 (April, 1955), pp. 133–165; Tom Meany, *Baseball's Greatest Teams* (New York, 1949); *NYT*, August 15, 1960; David L. Porter, correspondence with Mrs. Neal (Clarke) Sullivan, June 27, 1984; Joseph L. Reichler, ed., *The Baseball Encyclopedia*, 6th ed. (New York, 1985), pp. 621, 802–803; Lowell Reidenbaugh, *Cooperstown: Where Baseball's Legends Live Forever* (St.

Louis, 1983); Robert Smith, *Baseball's Hall of Fame* (New York, 1973); Winfield (KS) *Daily Courier*, August 15, 1960.

David L. Porter

CLARKSON, John Gibson (b. 1 July 1861, Cambridge, MA; d. 4 February 1909, Cambridge, MA), player, was one of five sons of wealthy manufacturer Thomas G. Clarkson and the brother of ball players Arthur "Dad" and Walter Clarkson. Clarkson, who married Ella Bar in March, 1886, and was inducted in 1963 into the National Baseball Hall of Fame, attended Webster Grammar School and Comer's Business School in Cambridge. In a whirlwind twelve-year major league career, Clarkson won 326 games (tenth on the all-time list), lost 177 decisions, compiled a .648 winning percentage, completed 485 starts, and recorded a lifetime 2.81 ERA. He led the NL in wins, appearances, starts, complete games, innings, and strikeouts in 1885, 1887, and 1889; in shutouts in 1885 and 1889; in strikeouts in 1886; and in ERA in 1889.

A pitcher for Adrian "Cap" Anson's* Chicago White Sox (NL) from 1884 to 1887, Clarkson led the team to pennants in 1885 and 1886. After winning 53 of the club's 87 victories in 1885, he performed similarly in 1886. Clarkson was traded to the Boston Beaneaters (NL) in 1888 and maintained his incredible form there. He won 49 of Boston's 83 victories in 1889 and combined with Charles "Kid" Nichols* to win or save 69 of Boston's 87 victories in 1891. A superlative fielder, Clarkson led the NL in assists and total fielding chances in 1885 and 1889 and recorded an amazing eight putouts in one game on his twenty-fourth birthday. On July 27, 1885, he pitched a no-run, no-hit game to beat the Providence Grays 6–0.

Anson praised Clarkson as "one of the greatest of pitchers," but observed that the handsome, high-strung young hurler needed continual ego boosting. Anson claimed that Clarkson "pitched on praise" and stated, "He won't pitch if scolded." Although quiet, Clarkson was not inhibited. He once threw a lemon instead of a regular baseball to prove that it was too dark to continue play. Peers regarded him as a calculating, scientific player who studied and pitched to each batter's individual weaknesses. With his long, cradling fingers and deep-set, dark eyes, he dominated NL batters partly by sheer intimidation. In 1884 he relied on his will power and superbly controlled curveball to strike out seven consecutive batters.

Clarkson began his career with Worcester, MA (NEL) in 1882, played with Saginaw, MI (NWL), in 1883, and was sold in early 1884 to Chicago. In 1888 Chicago owners made national headlines by selling Clarkson and battery mate Mike "King" Kelly* to Boston for a record $10,000 each. Four years later, Boston traded Clarkson to second place Cleveland (NL). Although performing well that season, Clarkson exhibited declining skills thereafter. He retired after the 1894 season and purchased a Cambridge cigar store, which he operated until his death from complications of pneumonia.

BIBLIOGRAPHY: Glenn Dickey, *The History of National League Baseball* (New York, 1979); Harold Kaese, *The Boston Braves* (New York, 1948); *NYT*, August 6, 1963; Paul MacFarlane, ed. *TSN Daguerreotypes of Great Stars of Baseball* (St. Louis, 1981); Joseph L. Reichler, ed., *The Baseball Encyclopedia*, 6th ed. (New York, 1985), p. 1,648.
                                                                    Alan R. Asnen

CLEMENTE, Roberto "Bob" (b. Clemente y Walker, 18 August 1934, Carolina, Puerto Rico; d. 31 December 1972 near Carolina, Puerto Rico), player, was the son of sugar mill worker and sugar cane cutter Melchor and Luisa (Walker) Clemente. The youngest of seven children, he adopted his island's passion for year-round baseball. By age 14 he competed against Negro league and major league professionals in exhibition matches. He first played professionally for the Santurce Crabbers in winter ball during 1952–1953, impressing major league talent hounds Branch Rickey* and Al Campanis. After another season with the Crabbers, he signed a $10,000 bonus with the Brooklyn Dodgers (NL) and spent the 1954 season with the Dodgers' Montreal (IL) farm team. Despite the organization's best efforts to hide him from rival scouts, he was drafted by the Pittsburgh Pirates (NL) at the end of the 1954 season. He joined the Pirates in 1955 and spent his entire major league career with Pittsburgh.

During the 1960s, the 5 foot, 11 inch, 185 pound Clemente became baseball's best all-around right fielder, winning NL batting titles in 1961, 1964, 1965, and 1967. He paced the NL in hits (1967) and triples (1969), tied for the lead in hits (1964), and topped NL outfielders in assists four times (1959–1960 and 1966–1967). In his career, he batted above .300 thirteen times en route to becoming the eleventh major leaguer to reach the 3,000 hit mark. Although lacking the home run power of Willie Mays* or Hank Aaron,* he proved a fearsome hitter, especially in clutch situations. In 2,433 games, he batted .317 with 440 doubles, 166 triples, 240 home runs, 1,416 runs scored, 1,305 RBIs, and 1,230 strikeouts. In the field, he mastered the Forbes Field and Three Rivers Stadium caroms and possessed an awe-inspiring throwing arm. He led the Pirates to world championships in 1960 and 1971. His all-around talents earned him the NL Most Valuable Player Award in 1966. Clemente hit safely in every game of his two World Series appearances, capturing the Babe Ruth* Award for his efforts in the 1971 fall classic.

Clemente's accomplishments dramatized the arrival of more Latin American ballplayers, including Tony Oliva from Cuba, Juan Marichal* from the Dominican Republic, and Orlando Cepeda* from his own Puerto Rico. Although Mexicans and Cubans had preceded him, Clemente became the first Latin superstar. He was sensitive to and outspoken about the discrimination encountered by Latin players on account of race and language, telling one reporter in 1965: "The Latin player doesn't get the recognition he deserves. Neither does the Negro unless he does something really spectacular." Clemente's belief that writers ignored Latin and black accomplishments was underscored by his low ranking in the 1960 MVP voting and low finish in the selection of the 1960s Player of the Decade. Spending his career in Pittsburgh no doubt contributed to a lack of publicity, only partially rectified by attention given Clemente's outstanding performance in the 1971 Series. Throughout his career, Clemente was plagued by headaches, muscle pulls, stomach pains, and especially back problems, which had been aggravated by a 1956 auto accident. However, critics labeled him a hypochondriac and suggested that he missed too many games.

Clemente became a folk hero in Puerto Rico. He married Vera Cristina Zabala on November 14, 1964, and insisted that all his children, Roberto, Luis Roberto, and Enrique Roberto, be born on his native island. In 1970 some 300,000 Puerto Ricans signed a salutory telegram as part of a "Roberto Clemente Night" in Pittsburgh. He participated in various Puerto Rican community projects, especially the creation of the "Sports City" complex to help underprivileged children improve their athletic skills. In December 1972, he helped organize relief efforts for victims of a Nicaraguan earthquake. He died when a plane carrying relief supplies to that country crashed shortly after takeoff. The widespread grief in Puerto Rico caused the governor's inaugural ceremonies to be canceled out of respect. Clemente's premature death prompted the National Baseball Hall of Fame Committee to waive its five-year rule. Clemente was voted into the shrine (the first Latin American to be so honored) eleven weeks after his funeral.

BIBLIOGRAPHY: Myron Cohen, "Aches and Pains and Three Batting Titles," *SI* 24 (March 7, 1966), pp. 30–34; Edward Grossman, "Pride of the Pirates," *Commentary*, 57 (January, 1974), pp. 72–76; Arnold Hano, *Roberto Clemente: Batting King* (New York, 1974); Roger Kahn, "Golden Triumphs, Tarnished Dreams," *SI* 45 (August 30, 1976), pp. 32–36, 62; Paul MacFarlane, ed., *TSN Daguerreotypes of Great Stars of Baseball* (St. Louis, 1981), p. 55; "Old Aches and Pains," *Time* 89 (May 26, 1967), p. 56; "Viva Roberto," *Ebony* 22 (September, 1967), pp. 38–41; Kal Wagenheim, *Clemente* (New York, 1973).

                                                                        James W. Harper

COBB, Tyrus Raymond "Ty," "The Georgia Peach" (b. 18 December 1886, The Narrows, Banks County, GA; d. 17 July 1961, Atlanta, GA), player and manager, was the eldest of three children born to William Herschel and Amanda (Chitwood) Cobb. Cobb grew up in Royston, GA., under the dominant influence of his father, variously a school teacher and principal, mayor, publisher of the Royston *Record*, state senator, and county school commissioner. "The Professor" stressed academics and urged Ty to become a doctor or lawyer, but Cobb preferred balls and bats to books.

Cobb, who batted left-handed but threw right-handed, made his professional debut in 1904 at age 17 with Augusta, GA (SAL). Released after two games, he played with a semi-pro team in Anniston, AL, before rejoining Augusta at the end of the season. He started the 1905 season with Augusta, but in August joined the Detroit Tigers. He retired twenty-four years later holding forty-three major league regular season career records. As a measure of Cobb's greatness, many of those career marks remained as of 1986 among the best in history: first in runs (2,245) and batting average (.367); second in hits (4,191), triples (297), and stolen bases (892); and fourth in games (3,034), at bats (11,429) doubles (724), and RBIs (1,961).

Cobb epitomized "scientific" baseball, which featured aggressive base running and precision batting to counter the overpowering pitching of the dead ball era. He was above average as an outfielder and was peerless on offense. No one ever ran the bases with more daring and guile than Cobb, who perfected the hook slide or "fade away." With a split grip (hands apart) on the bat, the 6 foot, 1 inch, 175 pound Cobb won nine consecutive AL batting titles from 1907 to 1915 and added three more from 1917 to 1919. After his first year with Detroit, he hit at least .320 for twenty-three consecutive years, capped by brilliant .401, .410, and .420 marks. His best season was 1911, when he led the AL in every offensive category except home runs and set personal career highs in hits (248), runs (147), RBIs (144), batting average (.420), and slugging percentage (.621). As a measure of his overall dominance, Cobb led the AL twelve times in batting average, eight times in slugging percentage, seven times in hits, six times in stolen bases, five times in runs scored, four times in triples and RBIs, and three times in doubles. He had at least 200 hits for nine seasons, and stole a career-high 96 bases in 1915.

Cobb, whose prime came during the dead ball era hit only 118 career home runs. But he once led the AL in homers and home run percentage (1909), became at age 38 the first modern player to hit five home runs in two games (1925), and had a .513 career slugging percentage. As player-manager of the Tigers from 1921 to 1926, he proved superb as a strategist but poor at handling players. Under his leadership the team finished no higher than second place (1923) and posted an overall .519 winning percentage with 479 wins and 444 losses. Unable to give up the game, Cobb played for Connie Mack's* Philadelphia A's in 1927 and 1928 and hit .357 and .323 there before retiring at age 41.

Cobb's brilliance was due more to a careful mastery of skills combined with a maniacal will to succeed than to native talent. His unrelenting quest to be the best featured an aggressive style of play simultaneously admired and abhorred by teammates, opponents, and fans alike. Cobb exhibited in extreme form all the aggressive, extroverted human characteristics—bravery, egotism, unyieldingness, hypersensitivity. He also proved to have a dyspeptic personality, being obstinate, obsessive, paranoid, vituperative, and racist. As a result, he engaged in numerous verbal and physical assaults on and off the field. Some of the ugliest encounters involved blacks, as Cobb, by lineage and upbringing an ardent defender of the Old South, could not abide the lack of "proper" deference shown by northern blacks. No misanthrope, however, he made countless private acts of generosity and charitable contributions, including $100,000 each for a hospital in Royston and a Georgia college scholarship fund.

Retirement for Cobb proved traumatic and tragic. A millionaire thanks to wise investments, he never found anything more meaningful to fill thirty-three years than playing golf and balancing bank accounts. Without baseball his life lacked meaning. He experienced two divorces (from Charlie Marion Lombard, whom he married in 1908, and from Frances Fairburn Cass, whom he married in 1949) and the alienation of his five children, Tyrus, Jr., Shirley, Roswell Herschel, Beverly, and James Howell. Increasingly critical of modern baseball and its players, he spent the last years of his life fighting the ravages of cancer and loneliness with drugs and alcohol.

The irascible personality that made Cobb's personal life so miserable also drove him to levels of unparalleled athletic achievement. The affliction was congenital, for Cobb admitted that he had been "a bad boy with a vying disposition." Two traumatic experiences in his late teens set his temperament for life. The first was a burning desire to win approval from a stern and distant father, who sent him off to professional baseball with the admonition, "Don't come home a failure." The effort to please became an obsession the next year, when his mother, ostensibly by accident, killed his father with a shotgun. The second incident was the unmercifully cruel hazing given by the Tigers to the cocky, young southern rookie in 1906. From then on Cobb battled the world en route to baseball glory.

When the intitial balloting was held in 1936 for election to the National Baseball Hall of Fame, Cobb received the most votes (222) and came within four ballots of unanimity. One of baseball's greatest performers, he was surely the game's greatest competitor. As contemporary great George Sisler* explained, "The greatness of Ty Cobb was something that had to be seen and to see him was to remember him forever."

BIBLIOGRAPHY: Charles C. Alexander, *Ty Cobb* (New York, 1984); Ty Cobb, *Busting 'Em and Other Stories* (New York, 1914); Ty Cobb, "They Don't Play Baseball Any More," *Life* 32 (March 17, 1952), pp. 136ff., and (March 24, 1952), pp. 63ff.; Ty Cobb with Al Stumpf, *My Life in Baseball* (Garden City, NY, 1961); *CB* (1951), pp. 111–113; John D. McCallum, *Ty Cobb* (New York, 1975); *NYT*, July 18, 1961; Joseph L. Reichler, ed., *The Baseball Encyclopedia*, 6th ed. (New York, 1985), p. 808; Al Stumpf, "Ty Cobb's Wild Ten-Month Fight to Live," *True* 14 (December, 1961), pp. 38ff.

Larry R. Gerlach

COCHRANE, Gordon Stanley "Mickey," "Black Mike" (b. 6 April 1903, Bridgewater, MA; d. 28 June 1962, Lake Forest, IL), player, coach, manager, executive, and scout, was the son of Scotch-Irish immigrants John and Sarah (Campbell) Cochrane. His father worked as a coachman and caretaker for a wealthy Boston family and later became part-owner of a local movie theater. Cochrane graduated from Bridgewater High School in 1921 and participated in all sports there. He later became one of the finest all-around athletes ever to attend Boston University (1921–1924), excelling in baseball, football, track, basketball, and boxing. Cochrane especially starred as a halfback in football and captained the 1923 squad. In 1921 against Tufts University, Cochrane dropkicked a 53 yard field goal, which remains a Terriers record.

Cochrane began playing professional baseball with Dover, DE (ESL), in 1923 and used the name "Frank King" to protect his amateur status. In 1924 his contract was sold to Portland, OR (PCL). After batting .333 in 1924, Cochrane was purchased by Connie Mack's* Philadelphia Athletics (AL) for a reported $50,000 and five players. Cochrane became the A's regular catcher in 1925, compiling a .331 batting average in 134 games. With intensive coaching from veteran Ralph "Cy" Perkins, he improved his catching and caught 100 or more games eleven successive seasons (1925–1935).

Cochrane excelled as a hitter (once slugging three home runs in one game), catcher, base runner, and team leader. Mack considered him the greatest single factor in winning AL pennants for the 1929–1931 Athletics, a team that included stars Al Simmons,* Jimmie Foxx,* and Lefty Grove.* In 1928 Cochrane was named AL Most Valuable Player. He helped the Athletics win the 1929 and 1930 World Series, but performed poorly in the 1931 classic, lost to the St. Louis Cardinals.

In December, 1933, the Detroit Tigers (AL) bought Cochrane from Philadelphia for $100,000 and catcher John Pasek and appointed him manager. Cochrane's Tigers in 1934 won the first AL pennant for Detroit since 1909 but lost the World Series to the Cardinals. The Tigers won their second consecutive AL pennant in 1935 and captured the world championship in seven games over the Chicago Cubs. Detroit finished second to the New York Yankees in 1936 and 1937. On May 25, 1937, Cochrane suffered a severe head injury when hit with a ball pitched by Irving "Bump" Hadley of the Yankees. His skull was fractured in three places, abruptly ending his exciting, productive, colorful playing career. Confined to the bench, Cochrane did not give the Tigers the leadership they desired and was released as field manager in August, 1938.

In thirteen seasons, Cochrane led two teams to five AL pennants and compiled a lifetime .320 batting average (.357 in 1930). In 1932 he slugged 23 home runs and knocked in 112 runs. In 1,482 career games, Cochrane made 1,652 hits, 1,041 runs, 333 doubles, 64 triples, 119 home runs, 832 RBIs, and 64 stolen bases. In 31 World Series games, he batted .245, collected 27 hits, 17 runs, 4 doubles, and 2 home runs, and batted in 6 runs. As a manager for five seasons, Cochrane won 413 of 712 games for a .582 percentage.

During World War II, Cochrane served as an officer in the U.S. Navy's fitness program, operated the athletic program at Great Lakes Naval Training

Station, and coached their baseball team. Cochrane and his wife, the former Mary Hohr, had two daughters and a son, Gordon Jr., who died in World War II. Following the war, Cochrane represented a trucking line and operated a dude ranch in Wyoming. He returned to baseball in 1950 as a coach and general manager of the Philadelphia Athletics (AL) and scouted for the New York Yankees (AL) in 1955 and for Detroit (AL) in 1960. In 1961 he was named vice-president of the Tigers and remained in that position until his death. He was elected to the National Baseball Hall of Fame in 1947.

BIBLIOGRAPHY: Bob Broeg, *Super Stars of Baseball* (St. Louis, 1971); Gene Karst and Martin J. Jones, Jr., *Who's Who in Professional Baseball* (New Rochelle, NY, 1973); Paul MacFarlane, ed., *TSN Daguerreotypes of Great Stars of Baseball* (St. Louis, 1971).

John L. Evers

COLAVITO, Rocco Domenico "Rocky" (b. 10 August 1933, Bronx, NY), player, coach and scout, is the son of Rocco and Angelina (Spofadino) Colavito, both of Italian descent. The youngest of five children, Colavito attended Public School No. 4 and Theodore Roosevelt High School in New York City. At age 16 he began playing semi-pro baseball and signed in 1951 for a $3,000 bonus as a pitcher-outfielder with the Cleveland Indians. In 1951 Colavito slugged 23 home runs and knocked in 111 runs for Daytona Beach, FL (FSL). The next year he played for Cedar Rapids, IA (3IL), and Spartanburg, SC (TSL). At Reading, PA, in 1953, he led the Class A EL with 28 homers and 121 RBIs. He played in 1954 and 1955 with Indianapolis, pacing the AA in 1954 with 38 home runs and 116 RBIs. After starting the 1956 season with San Diego (PCL), he was summoned by Cleveland.

The 6 foot, 3 inch, 190 pound, rifle-armed outfielder became one of the most popular and productive Indians players. In 1956 he slugged 21 home runs and then slumped in batting average the next year. He hit 41 homers, drove in 113 runs, batted .303, and topped the AL in slugging percentage (.620) in 1958. The next year his 42 circuit clouts, including four home runs on June 10 against Baltimore, tied for the AL lead. A controversial post-season trade sent Colavito to the Detroit Tigers for AL batting champ Harvey Kuenn.* Between 1960 and 1963, Colavito provided considerable power for the Detroit Tigers. In 1964 he slugged 34 home runs and drove in 102 runs for the Kansas City A's (AL). After Cleveland purchased Colavito in 1965, he responded with 26 homers and led the AL with 108 RBIs and 93 walks. He also set an AL record for outfielders by recording 234 consecutive errorless games from September 6, 1964, to June 15, 1966. In 1966 he belted 30 home runs, but his overall offensive production slipped significantly. He joined the Chicago White Sox (AL) in June, 1967, and finished his playing career in 1968 with the Los Angeles Dodgers (NL) and New York Yankees (AL).

In fourteen seasons, Colavito hit 374 home runs and surpassed 100 RBIs six times. For his career, he compiled 1,159 RBIs, 1,730 hits, 283 doubles, and 951 walks, and batted .266 as a major leaguer. He also pitched in two games, compiling a 1–0 record and an 0.00 ERA in 5 2/3 innings. He made *The Sporting News* All-Star team in 1961 and played in eight All-Star games from 1959 through 1966. After scouting for the New York Yankees in 1969 and 1973, he coached for the Cleveland Indians (1976–1978) and Kansas City Royals (1982–1983). Married in October, 1954, to Carmen Perroti, Colavito has three children and owns a mushroom farm in Temple, PA.

BIBLIOGRAPHY: Rocky Colavito file, National Baseball Hall of Fame Library, Cooperstown, NY; Rocky Colavito, "Secrets of a Home Run Hitter," *Official Baseball Annual* (New York, 1963); Hy Goldberg, "Colavito: Can He Save the Indians?" *Dell Sports* (July, 1965), pp. 36–37, 76–77; Paul MacFarlane, ed., *TSN Daguerreotypes of Great Stars of Baseball* (St. Louis, 1981); *Time* 74 (August 24, 1959), pp. 50–55, 92; (September 6, 1968), pp. 77.

Douglas D. Martin

COLLINS, Edward Trowbridge Sr. "Eddie," "Cocky" (b. 2 May 1887, Millerton, NY; d. 25 March 1951, Boston, MA), baseball and football player, manager, and executive, was the son of railroad freight agent John Rossman and Mary Meade (Trowbridge) Collins. He graduated from Irving School in Tarrytown, NY, in 1903. Collins began playing baseball at an early age, but considered football his favorite game. A varsity quarterback at Columbia University, he graduated from there in 1907. After playing semi-pro baseball, Collins was signed by the Philadelphia Athletics (AL). He played twenty games with the A's during the 1906 and 1907 seasons and four games with Newark (EL) in 1907, using the name "Sullivan" to retain his collegiate eligibility. In 1908 Collins became a regular second baseman for Philadelphia and helped lead Connie Mack's* A's to four AL pennants (1910–1911, 1913–1914) and three world championships (1910–1911, 1913).

The 5 foot 9 inch, 170 pound second baseman threw right-handed, batted left-handed, and starred in the famous $100,000 infield, which included Stuffy McInnis,* Jack Barry, and Frank "Home Run" Baker.* In 1914 Collins was named the AL Most Valuable Player, but was sold to the Chicago White Sox (AL) following the A's loss to the Boston Braves in the World Series. Collins remained with Chicago for twelve years, managing the White Sox two seasons. He played on the world championship 1917 club and in 1919 was one of the Chicago players making an honest effort to beat the Cincinnati Reds (NL) in the World Series. Eight teammates were accused of trying to fix the classic, known as the "Black Sox" scandal. In 1920 Collins achieved a career-high .369 batting average. With Collins as player-manager (1925–1926), the White Sox finished fifth both seasons and won 160 of 307 games. Chicago released him after the 1926 season. Collins returned to Philadelphia as player-coach and made his last appearance during the 1930 season.

Collins, who holds the record for longest service as an active AL player

(25 years), led the AL in runs scored three times (1912–1914) and stolen bases four times (1910, 1919, 1923–1924). He twice stole six bases in one game, a major league record. His 81 thefts in 1910 and 222 hits in 1920 remain club records. Collins made at least five hits in one game five times and set the all-time World Series record for most stolen bases (14), since equalled by Lou Brock.* He retains major league records by second basemen for most years (21), most games (2,650), most putouts (6,526), most assists (7,630), most chances accepted (14,591), and most years leading the AL in fielding average (9).

Collins ranks high on the all-time major league lists in several categories. He compiled a .333 lifetime batting average (22nd) and batted over .300 seventeen times (3rd), including nine consecutive times. In 2,826 games (10th), he batted 9,949 times (15th), scored 1,818 runs (11th), and collected 3,311 hits (8th). His hits included 2,641 singles (3rd), 437 doubles (56th), and 187 triples (12th). He amassed 4,259 total bases (31st), received 1,503 bases on balls (11th), knocked in 1,299 runs (52nd), and compiled a .414 slugging average. Collins stole 743 bases (3rd), including 17 steals of home (9th). In six World Series, he played in 34 games, batted 128 times, scored 20 runs, collected 42 hits, including 7 doubles and 2 triples, recorded 11 RBIs, and compiled a .328 batting average.

After coaching with Philadelphia (AL) in 1931 and 1932, Collins the following season became vice-president, treasurer, and business manager for Boston (AL). He served in this capacity until his death, helping build the Red Sox into consistent AL pennant contenders. Collins, who in 1939 was elected to the National Baseball Hall of Fame, married Mabel Doane on November 3, 1910, and had two sons, Edward, Jr., and Paul. Edward, Jr., played baseball for the Philadelphia A's (AL) between 1939 and 1942.

BIBLIOGRAPHY: Bob Broeg, *Super Stars of Baseball* (St. Louis, 1971); Paul MacFarlane, ed., *TSN Daguerreotypes of Great Stars of Baseball* (St. Louis, 1971); Lowell Reidenbaugh, *Cooperstown: Where Baseball's Legends Live Forever* (St. Louis, 1983); *TSN Official Baseball Record Book, 1985* (St. Louis, 1985).

                                                                    John L. Evers

COLLINS, James Joseph "Jimmy" (b. 16 January 1870 or 1873, Niagara Falls, NY; d. 6 March 1943, Buffalo, NY), player and manager, was the son of policeman Anthony Collins and Alice (O'Hara) Collins. Collins moved to Buffalo at age two, graduated from St. Joseph's Collegiate Institute there, and worked for the Lackawanna Railroad. He married Sarah Edwina Murphy on July 4, 1907, and had two daughters. Collins began his professional career as a third baseman and then as an outfielder with Buffalo (EL), batting .286 in 1893 and .352 in 1894. Boston (NL) purchased Collins and loaned him for one year to Louisville (NL) where he was shifted back to third base. After returning to Boston (NL) in 1896, he soon became recognized as the premier third baseman of his era. An innovative third baseman, Collins played far off the bag and rushed in on batters when bunts were anticipated. Managers Connie Mack* and John McGraw* both picked Collins as best third baseman on their all-time nines. Although only 5 feet, 7 1/2 inches and 160 pounds, Collins led the NL in home runs in 1898 with 15. From 1896 to 1900 with Boston, he batted .296, .346, .328, .277, and .304. In 1899 he handled 629 chances at third base.

Collins jumped to Boston (AL) in 1901 as player-manager at a $5,500 salary and 10 percent of the profits over $25,000. His Boston team finished second in 1901 and third in 1902 but won the AL pennant in 1903 and defeated Pittsburgh five games to three in the first modern World Series. Collins was dismissed as manager in 1906, when his team plunged to a 44–92 record. His overall record as Boston manager comprised 464 wins and 389 losses for a .544 percentage. In July, 1907, he was traded to the Philadelphia Athletics (AL) and closed out his major league career there the following season. During fourteen major league seasons, he batted .294, made 1,997 hits, 352 doubles, 1,055 runs and 982 RBIs, and fielded .929.

Collins managed Minneapolis (AA) in 1910 and Providence (EL) in 1911. He was employed by the city of Buffalo for many years and was working as a street inspector when he died. For twenty-two years he directed the Buffalo Municipal League, one of the nation's most extensive amateur baseball programs. Collins earned as much as $18,000 as a player-manager and held much real estate in the Buffalo area, but lost most of his wealth in the Depression. In 1945 he was elected to the National Baseball Hall of Fame.

BIBLIOGRAPHY: Lee Allen, *American League Story* (New York, 1961); Buffalo *Courier-Express*, March 6, 7, 1943; Buffalo *Evening News*, March 7, 1943; Paul MacFarlane, ed., *TSN Daguerreotypes of Great Stars of Baseball* (St. Louis, 1981); Lowell Reidenbaugh, *Cooperstown: Where Baseball's Legends Live Forever* (St. Louis, 1983); Harold Seymour, *Baseball: The Early Years* (New York, 1960).

Joseph M. Overfield

COMBS, Earle Bryan "The Kentucky Colonel," "The Gentleman from Kentucky" (b. 14 May 1899, Pebworth, KY; d. 21 July 1976, Richmond, KY), player and coach, was of Scotch-German ancestry and one of six children of hill farmer James J. and Nannie (Brandenburg) Combs of Owsley County, KY. To become a school teacher, Combs attended Eastern Kentucky State Normal School in Richmond. A talented athlete, he competed on the college basketball and track squads and played shortstop and outfield for the baseball nine. In his last season before graduation in 1921, he batted .591.

To pay for his education, Combs taught between college terms at one-room schools. He soon discovered that he could earn more than twice as much playing semi-pro baseball. In 1921, his second of two summers in the semi-pros, he hit .444 for Harlan, KY, and was signed by the Louisville

Colonels. Combs immediately starred for the Colonels (AA), batting .344 in 1922. His .380 average the following year ranked second highest in a league in which Al Simmons* and Bill Terry* also played. The New York Yankees (AL), outbidding several teams, acquired Combs for $50,000 plus two players. The previous year, Combs had married Ruth McCollum of Levi, KY; they had three sons.

Combs held out in spring training in 1924, vowing to return to teaching if he were not paid the share of the purchase price promised him by the Louisville front office. The highly principled Combs insisted: "I am not a dumb animal to be brow beaten, cowed, lashed, coerced, or goaded into anything I do not think is right. I am a human being and I intend to stay one whether I play with the New York Yankees or not."

The dispute was settled to Combs' satisfaction. He soon replaced veteran center fielder Whitey Witt, but a leg injury cut short his season. Although not a polished minor league fielder, Combs developed into an accomplished ballhawk for the Yankees. Limited only by a somewhat weak throwing arm, he possessed ideal range to play between Bob Meusel* and Babe Ruth* and became "the keystone in baseball's greatest outfield."

When Combs joined the Yankees, manager Miller Huggins* already had begun rebuilding the club into what would become by 1927 perhaps the greatest team ever. In that memorable year, Combs peaked with a .356 batting average and led the AL in times at bat (648), hits (231), and triples (23). As leadoff batter, Combs often reached base to set the stage for Ruth, Lou Gehrig,* and other sluggers in the middle of the lineup. The speedy 6 foot, 185 pounder, Combs often drove balls into the outfield gaps and stretched singles into doubles. For eight consecutive years, he scored over 100 runs and hit over 30 doubles. Three times he led the AL in triples. From 1924 to 1934, Combs' average dipped slightly under .300 only twice.

Combs had slowed down by 1934 and moved to left field, but still hit over .300. A fractured skull, suffered when he crashed into the left field wall in St. Louis in August, 1934, ended his career as a regular and prompted his decision to retire following the 1935 campaign. Although his feats were often overshadowed by those of his more colorful teammates, Combs gained recognition as the era's best leadoff man. Nicknamed "The Kentucky Colonel" and "The Gentleman from Kentucky," he hit .350 in four World Series and compiled a lifetime .325 average. In 1,454 games, he made 1,866 hits, 309 doubles, 154 triples, 1,186 runs, and 629 RBIs.

Combs remained with the Yankees as a coach until 1944, helping polish the skills of Joe DiMaggio.* Subsequently, Combs coached with the St.Louis Browns (AL) in 1947, Boston Red Sox (AL) from 1948 to 1952, and Philadelphia Phillies (NL) in 1954. Combs, who settled on his 400 acre farm near Richmond, KY, participated in various business and civic projects. He served with pride as a member and then chairman of the Board of Regents of Eastern

Kentucky University, his alma mater. Remembering his own youth, he anonymously paid the fees of several EKU students.

Elected to the National Baseball Hall of Fame in 1970, Combs said it was "the last thing I ever expected. I thought the Hall of Fame was for superstars, not just average players like I was." Those who saw him perform knew otherwise. "His value to a club was appreciated by the fans," wrote John Kieran* in the *New York Times* near the end of Combs' playing career. "But not to the extent it was appreciated by the managers. Miller Huggins had two personal favorites: Lou Gehrig and Earle Combs."

BIBLIOGRAPHY: Dave Anderson et al., *The Yankees: The Four Fabulous Eras of Baseball's Most Famous Team* (New York, 1981); Earle Combs Scrapbook and Correspondence, Eastern Kentucky University Archives, Richmond, KY; Knoxville (TN) *News-Sentinel*, April 26, 1964; Louisville *Courier-Journal*, March 24, 1922, February 9, 1924, April 27, 1944, April 7, 1953; John Mosedale, *The Greatest of All: The 1927 New York Yankees* (New York, 1974); *NYT*, July 26, 1976; "One of Baseball's Best," *The Berea Alumnus* (September-October, 1983), pp. 5, 6, 14; "Recognition Dinner: Earle B. Combs," Souvenir Program, Eastern Kentucky University, March 10, 1970; Richmond (KY) *Daily Register*, July 22, 1976; Ira L. Smith, *Baseball's Famous Outfielders* (New York, 1954); John J. Ward, "The Greatest Lead-Off Man in the American League," *Baseball Magazine* 40 (December, 1927), pp. 317, 324.

Lloyd J. Graybar

COMISKEY, Charles Albert "Charlie," "Old Roman," "Commy" (b. 15 August 1859, Chicago, IL; d. 26 October 1931, Eagle River, WI), player, manager, and owner, was the son of Irish immigrants, Chicago politician John and Annie (Kearns) Comiskey. Comiskey grew up in Chicago and briefly attended St. Mary's College in Dodge City, KS. In 1876 he began playing semi-professional baseball. Three years later, Ted Sullivan hired the center fielder to play for the Dubuque Rabbits (NWL). In 1882 Comiskey joined the St. Louis Browns (AA) and was converted to a first baseman. He served as player-manager in 1883 and from 1885 to 1894, winning AA titles from 1885 through 1888 with the Browns. One of the highest-paid players, Comiskey earned $6,000 in 1889. In 1890 he jumped to the Chicago Pirates (PL), a cooperative organization not recognizing the reserve clause. After the PL venture failed, Comiskey in 1891 rejoined the Browns. He moved in 1892 to Cincinnati when the AA merged with the NL. In 1,390 career games, he made 1,531 hits and batted .264. His 11-year managerial career included 824 wins and 533 losses for a .603 mark (3rd best).

Comiskey, who retired after the 1894 season, purchased the Sioux City, IA, franchise (WL) and quickly moved it to St. Paul. In 1900 league president Ban Johnson* renamed the loop the American League and shifted its clubs into larger cities. Comiskey's team moved to the South Side of Chicago, one-half mile from the old PL grounds, and named his club the White Stockings.

The AL proclaimed itself a major league in 1901 and quickly gained public acceptance by recruiting outstanding players.

Renamed the White Sox in 1902, Comiskey's club scored a great box office success and fared pretty well on the diamond. The 1906 White Sox, nicknamed the "Hitless Wonders" for their lack of batting prowess, won the AL pennant and defeated the powerful Chicago Cubs in the city's only crosstown World Series. In 1910 Comiskey opened a modern fire-resistant park at Thirty-fourth and Shields, site of the old Brotherhood Park. The ballpark, only the third built of cement and steel, seated about 30,000 spectators. In 1917 the White Sox won their second AL pennant and defeated the New York Giants in the World Series. After a disappointing 1918 campaign shortened by World War I, the White Sox in 1919 returned to first place on the feats of Eddie Collins,* Eddie Cicotte,* Ray Schalk,* Lefty Williams, and Shoeless Joe Jackson.* Although heavily favored in the World Series, the White Sox lost to the Cincinnati Reds five games to three. In September 1920, newspapers revealed that eight men had fixed the outcome of the Series. Jackson, Cicotte, and Williams confessed their involvement to the grand jury. The miserly Comiskey had paid the corrupted players poorly for several years. A court acquitted the players in 1921 after the confessions were lost, but Commissioner Kenesaw Mountain Landis* barred them permanently from organized baseball. When Jackson sued for back pay in 1924, Comiskey's attorney conveniently produced the missing documents. Comiskey never rebuilt a formidable club after the Black Sox Scandal, as the White Sox finished in the first division only once during the rest of his life. Son J. Louis, the sole child of his marriage to Nan Kelley in 1882, inherited the team when Charles died in 1931.

Comiskey founded and owned the White Sox for over thirty years. Experts blamed him in large part for the 1919 scandal because his tight-fisted management took advantage of the less sophisticated players. In 1939 he was voted into the National Baseball Hall of Fame.

BIBLIOGRAPHY: Adrian Anson, *A Ball Player's Career* (Chicago, 1900); Eliot Asinof, *Eight Men Out: The Black Sox and the 1919 World Series* (New York, 1963); Gustav Axelson, *"Commy": The Life Story of Charles A. Comiskey* (Chicago, 1919); Chicago *Tribune*, 1900–1920, October 26, 1931; Dave Condon, *The Go-Go Chicago White Sox* (New York, 1960); Richard Lindberg, *Who's on Third? The Chicago White Sox Story* (South Bend, IN, 1983); Eugene C. Murdock, *Ban Johnson, Czar of Baseball* (Westport, CT, 1982); *National Cyclopedia of American Biography* 24 (New York, 1935), p. 173; *NYT*, 1883–1921, October 26, 1931; Joseph L. Reichler, ed., *The Baseball Encyclopedia*, 6th ed. (New York, 1985); pp. 622, 815–816; Steven A. Riess, *Touching Base: Professional Baseball and American Culture in the Progressive Era* (Westport, CT, 1980); Harold Seymour, *Baseball: The Golden Age*, vol. 2 (New York, 1971); *TSN*, 1900–1931; David Q. Voigt, *American Baseball: From the Commissioners to Continental Expansion*, vol. 2 (Norman, OK, 1970).

                                                                    Steven A. Riess

CONLAN, John Bertrand "Jocko" (b. 6 December 1899, Chicago, IL), baseball player and umpire and boxing referee, is the son of Chicago policeman Audley and Mary Ann Conlan. He attended All Saints Parochial School and enrolled two years at De La Salle High School in Chicago. In 1912 and 1913, he served as batboy at Comiskey Park for the Chicago White Sox (AL). After playing in the Chicago semi-pro (ML), he entered professional baseball with Tulsa (WL). He was traded to Wichita (WL) and played outfield there in 1920, 1922, and 1923, but was suspended in 1921. The fast, 5 foot, 7 1/2 inch, 165 pound center fielder enjoyed six good seasons in the IL, three at Rochester, NY, and three at Newark, NJ. A knee injury cost him an opportunity in 1926 with the Cincinnati Reds (NL). After spending 1930 with Toledo (AA) and the next two years with Montreal (IL), he quit baseball. The injury-ridden Chicago White Sox, however, lured him out of retirement in 1934. A left-handed batter, he hit .249 in 63 games in 1934 and .286 in 65 games in 1935 for the White Sox.

Between games of a July 1935 doubleheader between Chicago and the St. Louis Browns (AL), umpire Red Ormsby suffered heat prostration and could not continue. Conlan, sidelined by a sprained thumb, volunteered to substitute for Ormsby in the second game and the next day and performed impressively and efficiently. Consequently, Conlan officiated in the NYPL during 1936 and 1937 and in the AA in 1938, 1939, and 1940. He advanced to the NL in 1941 and quickly established his authority, ejecting twenty-six players and managers during the season. Conlan remained an active NL umpire through the 1967 season, umpiring in six World Series, six All-Star games, and four pennant-deciding NL playoffs. Besides being the only big league arbiter of his time who made all his signals with his left hand, he was the only NL umpire to wear an outside chest protector.

In 1925, before umpiring baseball, he had become a licensed New York State boxing referee. He married Ruth Anderson in January 1926, and has two children, John (an Arizona state senator), and Ruth (Mrs. Page Watson). Conlan, whose brother Joe had a pitching trial with Brooklyn (NL) in 1920, was elected to the National Baseball Hall of Fame in 1974.

BIBLIOGRAPHY: Martin Appel and Burt Goldblatt, *Baseball's Best: The Hall of Fame Gallery* (New York, 1977); John B. Conlan file, National Baseball Hall of Fame Library, Cooperstown, NY; Paul Green, "Jocko Conlan," *Sports Collectors Digest* 10 (October 28, 1983), pp. 52–60; Sam Levy, "Jocko Conlan, New National League Umpire...," *TSN*, February 20, 1941; J. G. Taylor Spink, comp., *TSN Baseball Register, 1958* (St. Louis, 1958) p. 303; *TSN*, January 12, 1949, July 4, 1951; United States Census, 1900, Illinois, City of Chicago, Enumeration District 117, Sheet 12.

Frank V. Phelps

CONNOLLY, Thomas Henry, Sr. "Tom," "Tommy" (b. 31 December 1870, Manchester, England; d. 28 April 1961, Natick, MA), umpire, was the dean of AL arbiters. Connolly had at least one younger sister and one younger brother, both of whom were born in England. His brother Francis umpired professionally in the AA. Connolly played cricket in England as a youth, but never saw a baseball game there. The Connollys migrated to the United States in 1885 and settled in Natick, MA, where Tom became batboy for a local baseball team. Although he never played baseball, he assiduously studied the rule book and eventually became the nation's leading authority on baseball rules. NL arbiter Tim Hurst discovered Connolly officiating for a YMCA club in Natick and secured him a professional umpiring job in the NEL. Connoly officiated in the NEL from 1894 to 1897 and joined the NL in 1898. In 1900 he quit because NL president Nicholas Young* failed to back his rulings.

AL president Ban Johnson* hired Connolly in 1901 for the league's inaugural season. In April, 1901, Connolly umpired the Cleveland-Chicago contest behind home plate at Comiskey Park in the first AL game ever played. He also officiated at the first AL contests at Shibe Park in Philadelphia, Fenway Park in Boston, and Yankee Stadium in New York City. Besides calling the first World Series in 1903 between the Boston Pilgrims and Pittsburgh Pirates, he officiated in seven subsequent fall classics. Connolly ranked with Bill Klem,* Billy Evans,* Tim Hurst, and Silk O'Loughlin among the finest all-time major league umpires. The slim, quiet, subdued Connolly, who once described an umpire as "one with poise and without rabbit ears," did not try to please the crowd or engage in theatrical gestures. He lacked the color of Klem, but commanded great respect from players for his fairness.

Although ejecting ten players his first season, Connolly once went ten full seasons without ousting a protester. Teams usually did not become too demonstrative in objecting to Connolly's calls. Detroit Tigers star Ty Cobb* once remarked, "You can go just so far with Tommy. Once you see his neck get red it's time to lay off." During an AL pennant race, Connolly once aroused the ire of Detroit fans by calling Cobb out for crossing home plate while at bat. Cobb had hit the third pitch of an intentional walk for a triple, which would have scored a runner from second base. Connolly another time retorted to irate Cleveland Indians manager Tris Speaker,* "You're out of the game, of course. And if you don't change your thinking, you'll be out of baseball."

In June, 1931, new AL president William H. Harridge* appointed Connolly as the first AL umpire-in-chief. Nearly every AL club owner and manager had complained about the poor quality of umpiring that season. Headquartered in Chicago, he supervised AL umpires, scouted the minor leagues for umpiring talent, and advised Harridge on playing rules. Connolly retired as AL umpire-in-chief in January, 1954, at age 83 and was replaced by Cal Hubbard* (FB). Connolly, who the previous year had become the first umpire elected to the National Baseball Hall of Fame, had married Margaret L. Davin in 1902, with whom he had eight children. Four sons,

Thomas, Jr., Edward, Francis, and Arthur, and three daughters, Margaret, Helen, and Mrs. Richard Kilroy, survived him. His wife had died in 1943 after five years of illness.

BIBLIOGRAPHY: Lee Allen, *The Hot Stove League* (New York, 1955); Martin Appel and Burt Goldblatt, *Baseball's Best: The Hall of Fame Gallery* (New York, 1977); *NYT*, June 3, 1931; January 14, February 11, 1954; April 29, 1961; David L. Porter, correspondence with Frank V. Phelps, March 30, 1986, David L. Porter Collection, Oskaloosa, IA; David L. Porter, telephone conversation with Frank V. Phelps, April 3, 1986; Lowell Reidenbaugh, *Cooperstown: Where Baseball's Legends Live Forever* (St. Louis, 1983); Robert Smith, *Baseball's Hall of Fame* (New York, 1973); *TSN*, August 5, 1943; May 10, 1961.

David L. Porter

CONNOR, Roger (b. 1 July 1857, Waterbury, CT; d. 4 January 1931, Waterbury, CT), player, manager, and owner, was the son of immigrants from County Kerry, Ireland, and the brother of major league player Joseph Connor. Connor graduated from Waterbury schools, married a local woman and had one adopted daughter. He entered organized baseball in 1876 as a left-handed-throwing third baseman with the Waterbury Monitors (EL) and played there for two years. From 1878 to 1879, he became a power hitter for the Holyoke, MA (EL) squad. Rival Springfield, MA (EL) manager Bob Ferguson became mentor in 1880 of Troy, NY (NL) and signed Connor.

Connor played with Troy through the 1882 season, shifting to first base when a shoulder injury restricted his mobility. He transferred to the New York Gothams (renamed "Giants" in 1885) in 1883, when the Troy franchise was moved to New York City. Connor remained with the Giants through 1889, joined New York (PL) in 1890, and returned to the Giants in 1891. After being traded to Philadelphia (NL) in 1892, he again returned to the Giants in 1893. Still a solid performer, Connor was traded to St. Louis (NL) in the midseason of 1894 and played through the 1897 season.

The 6 foot, 3 inch, 220 pound Connor compiled a .318 batting average over eighteen major league seasons, hit over .300 eleven times, and paced the NL in 1885 with a .371 batting average. Connor, affectionately called "Dear Old Roger" by the Giants fans, led the NL in triples twice and ranked fifth in career triples with 233. The most productive home run hitter of the dead ball era, Connor slugged more round trippers (136) than any pre–twentieth century player. His career achievements included 442 doubles, 1,621 runs scored, and 1,077 RBIs.

An effective base runner for a big man, Connor stole 227 bases. He mastered a crowd-pleasing "come-up slide," sliding into a base feet first and bouncing to his feet instantly. Although not a superior fielding first baseman, he dug low throws out of the dirt, presented a large target, and led the NL in fielding twice.

Connor cut a dashing figure with his broad handlebar mustache and his confident bearing and personality. He organized the Giants' chapter of the Brotherhood of Professional Base Ball Players in 1885 and played for the New York entry (PL) in 1890. Connor managed unsuccessfully with St. Louis in 46 games in 1896 and two years later purchased the Waterbury club. Connor served as pilot and first baseman there through 1902, retiring as an active player at age 45. For many years he served as school maintenance inspector in Waterbury. In 1976 Connor belatedly was elected to the National Baseball Hall of Fame.

BIBLIOGRAPHY: Martin Appel and Burt Goldblatt, *Baseball's Best: The Hall of Fame Gallery* (New York, 1977); Lowell Reidenbaugh, *Cooperstown: When Baseball's Legends Live Forever* (St. Louis, 1983).

Fred Stein

COOMBS, John Wesley "Jack," "Colby Jack," "Iron Man" (b. 18 November 1882, LeGrande, IA; d. 15 April 1957, Palestine, TX), player, coach, and manager, was the son of an Iowa farmer. He moved to Maine with his parents at the age of four. Coombs grew up on a farm and attended Colburn Classic High School in Waterville, ME, where he learned to pitch. He studied chemistry at Colby College and starred on the baseball team there. In 1906 he signed with Connie Mack's* Philadelphia Athletics (AL) for the then fabulous sum of $2,400. He planned to use his baseball earnings to become a chemist, but instead made baseball a career. Coombs never played minor league baseball. After blanking the Washington Senators in his major league debut, Coombs a month later pitched an entire 24-inning game to defeat the Boston Red Sox. By pitching 42 innings in a ten-day period, he hurt his arm and finished the season with a 10–10 record. From 1907 to 1909 he compiled a mediocre 25–25 record.

Relying heavily on an improved curve ball developed with Mack's assistance, in 1910 he won 31 of 40 decisions and pitched 13 shutouts to head the star-studded staff that included Eddie Plank* and Chief Bender.* Mack discovered that Coombs' breaking pitches became more effective when his arm was tired. In the 1910 World Series against the Chicago Cubs, Coombs won three games in five days and improved as the Series progressed. He and Christy Mathewson* were considered among the games' greatest pitchers. In 1911 Coombs, nicknamed "Iron Man," led the Athletics with 28 victories and greatly helped his club overcome a seemingly insurmountable Detroit Tigers lead. During a crucial game with Detroit, a Coombs fastball broke the wrist of rookie first baseman Del Gainor. Gainor, a potential superstar, never regained full use of his wrist and never fulfilled his promise. In the third game of the 1911 World Series, Coombs bested Mathewson on a home run by Frank Baker.*

In 1912 Coombs won 21 and lost 10, but his club finished 15 games behind Boston. Although Coombs was a teetotaler, his teammates drank excessively, causing the Athletics' poor performance. During spring training in San Antonio in 1913, he was stricken with typhoid fever that settled in his spine and nearly caused his death. The next two seasons, he pitched only a few innings. Having lost both velocity and control, he no longer compared with Mathewson. After being released by the Athletics, he won 43 and lost 43 for the Brooklyn Dodgers (NL). Coombs, a popular figure in Philadelphia, managed the NL Phillies for part of the 1919 season to only 18 victories in 62 decisions. Manager Hugh Jennings,* a close friend, hired Coombs in 1920 to coach Detroit Tigers' (AL) pitchers. During fourteen seasons, he won 159 games, lost 110 decisions for a .591 percentage, compiled a 2.78 ERA, and struck out 1,052 batters in 2,320 innings.

Coombs retired from professional baseball after the 1920 season. He coached at Princeton and Duke universities, where he developed several major league players. Coombs and his wife Mary, who had no children, enjoyed campus life. He encouraged his players to visit him at his home in the evenings to talk baseball. The highly knowledgeable Coombs wrote a baseball textbook still used by coaches. Coombs maintained that the players of his era performed better than those he coached.

BIBLIOGRAPHY: Jack Coombs, "My Greatest Diamond Thrill," *TSN*, November 2, 1944; "Mack's Great Expectations," *Literary Digest* 36 (March 8, 1913), pp. 543–546; Connie Mack, *My Sixty-Six Years in the Big Leagues* (Philadelphia, 1950); Anthony J. Papalas, interview with Bo Farley, November 12, 1983, Greenville, NC.

Anthony J. Papalas

COOPER, Arley Wilbur (b. 24 February 1892, Bearsville, WV; d. 7 August 1973, Encino, CA), player and manager, began his professional baseball career in 1911 as a pitcher with Marion, OH (OSL), and posted a 17–11 mark there. In 1912 the lanky 5 foot, 11 inch, 165 pound southpaw compiled a 16–9 record with Columbus (AA) before joining the Pittsburgh Pirates (NL) late in the season. Cooper made an impressive debut with the Bucs, hurling an 8–0 shutout against St. Louis in his first major league game and compiling a 3–0 record with a 1.66 ERA in six mound appearances. The following season he was used primarily in relief and posted a modest 5–3 record in 30 games. When Pirates manager Fred Clarke* put him into the starting rotation in 1914, he responded with 19 complete games, a 2.13 ERA, and a 16–15 record.

After posting a dismal 5–16 mark in 1915, Cooper rebounded in 1916 with 16 complete games, a 1.87 ERA, and a 12–11 record that included seven shutout losses. In the middle of the season he married Edith Warden. For the next eight campaigns (1917–1924), Cooper ranked among the NL's most durable, successful left-handed pitchers, averaging over 35 starts, 295 innings, 26 complete games, and 20 wins per season. Following the 1924 campaign, he figured in one of the period's biggest trades. Pirates owner Barney Dreyfuss* traded Cooper, infielder Rabbit Maranville,* and first baseman Charlie Grimm* to the Chicago Cubs (NL) for pitcher Vic Aldridge, infielder George Grantham, and rookie first baseman Al Niehaus.

In 1925 Cooper started 26 games, completed 13 contests, and posted a 12–14 record for the last place Cubs. After a 2–1 start in 1926, Chicago sold him for the waiver price to the Detroit Tigers (AL) in early June. He went winless for the Tigers in four decisions and finished the season with Toledo (AA). Cooper pitched in the minor leagues at Oakland (PCL) in 1927–1928, Shreveport (TL) in 1929, and Shreveport and San Antonio (TL) in 1930. He retired from professional baseball after managing McKeesport, PA (PSA), in 1935, Jeannette, PA (EL), in 1936, and Greensburg, PA (PSA), in 1937.

Cooper compiled a lifetime 216–178 major league win-loss mark (.548 winning percentage) and hurled 36 career shutouts, including eight 1–0 complete game wins. He struck out 1,252 batters in 3,480 innings and recorded a 2.89 ERA. Twice he led the NL in games started (1921 and 1923) and complete games (1919 and 1922). Cooper also paced the NL with 327 innings pitched (1921), 22 victories (1921), and 19 losses (1923). A better than average right-handed batter, Cooper made 293 career hits and led all major league pitchers with a .346 batting average (36 hits in 104 at bats) in 1924. With 202 victories during his thirteen years with Pittsburgh, he remains the Pirates' all-time winningest pitcher.

BIBLIOGRAPHY: Morris Eckhouse and Carl Mastrocola, *This Date in Pittsburgh Pirate History* (New York, 1980); Charlie Grimm with Ed Prell, *Baseball, I Love You!* (Chicago, 1968); Paul MacFarlane, ed., *TSN Daguerreotypes of Great Stars of Baseball* (St. Louis, 1981); Joseph L. Reichler, ed., *The Baseball Encyclopedia*, 6th ed. (New York, 1985), p. 1,660; *TSN*, August 25, 1973.

Raymond D. Kush

COOPER, Cecil Celester (b. 20 December 1949, Brenham, TX), player, is the youngest of thirteen children. Cooper's mother died when he was 10, while his father worked as an itinerant laborer. Two of Cooper's older brothers, John and Sylvester, played baseball with the barnstorming Indianapolis Clowns. Cooper grew up with his eldest sister, Helen, in Independence, TX (population 300), about seventy miles northwest of Houston. Cooper attended all-black Packard High School until his senior year, when he transferred to the integrated Brenham High School. He played for two state high school championship baseball teams and later attended Blinn Junior College and Prairie View A and M College. The 6 foot, 2 inch, 190 pound

Cooper was selected by the Boston Red Sox (AL) in the sixth round of the June, 1968, free agent draft.

Cooper spent nearly six seasons in the Red Sox minor league system with Jamestown, NY (NYPL), Greenville, SC (WCL), Danville, IL (ML), Winston-Salem (CrL), and Pawtucket, RI (IL). He joined Boston during the 1971 season, but started both the 1972 (Louisville, AA) and 1973 (Pawtucket) seasons in the minors before being recalled. In 1974 Cooper became a regular first baseman with the Red Sox.

Cooper became a star after being traded to the Milwaukee Brewers (AL) on December 6, 1976, for first baseman George Scott and outfielder Bernie Carbo. Cooper already had shown flashes of brilliance, compiling a .327 batting average in the minor leagues and a .283 average with the Red Sox. But he blossomed as a fielder and hitter with the Brewers. After the trade, Cooper batted over .300 seven straight seasons. Cooper also won the Gold Glove Award twice and led AL first basemen in chances with 1,068 in 1981 and 1,550 in 1983, and in double plays from 1980 through 1983. He was named the first baseman on *The Sporting News* AL All-Star team from 1979 to 1982. In Cooper's finest season, 1980, he led the majors with 122 RBIs and the AL with 355 total bases. He placed second in the majors with 219 hits and a .352 batting average. From 1979 to 1983, Cooper compiled more hits (942) and RBIs (535) than any other baseball player. His .320 batting average over that span trailed only George Brett* and Rod Carew.* The four-time All-Star played in World Series with the 1975 Red Sox and 1982 Brewers, setting a record in the 1982 series with ten assists by a first baseman. Through the 1986 season, Cooper has a lifetime .300 batting average, 2,130 hits, 402 doubles, 235 home runs, 987 runs scored, and 1,089 RBIs. He won the 1983 Roberto Clemente* Award for humanitarianism and participates in Athletes for Youth, an organization that offers recreation and counseling to Milwaukee youth. Cooper and his wife, Octavia, who married in February 1983, have one daughter, Kelly.

BIBLIOGRAPHY: Anthony Cotton, "No Condolences, Please," *SI* 53 (September 22, 1980), p. 60; Rom Fimrite, "'I'm the Lou Gehrig of My Time,'" *SI* 59 (September 22, 1983), pp. 52–54; *Milwaukee Brewers Press Guide*, 1984; *NYT*, June 27, 1982; *TSN Baseball Register, 1986* (St. Louis, 1986).

Eric C. Schneider

CORCORAN, Lawrence J. "Larry" (b. 10 August 1859, Brooklyn, NY; d. 14 October 1891, Newark, NJ), player and umpire, ranked among the sport's great early pitchers. Besides winning 170 games for Cap Anson's* Chicago White Stockings (NL) between 1880 and 1884, he became the first major leaguer to pitch three no hitters. The diminutive right-hander began his career in 1877 with the Mutuals of Brooklyn and moved upstate to pitch for the Livingstons of Geneseo. He turned professional with Buffalo's first organized team, an independent with no league affiliation. After two years with Springfield, MA (IA, 1878; NA, 1879) he was acquired by the White Stockings. In his first season (1880), he won 43 games, hurled 536 innings, compiled a 1.95 ERA, scored his first no-hitter, and led the NL with 268 strikeouts. He paced the league with 31 victories in 1881 and with a .675 winning percentage and another 1.95 ERA in 1882.

Known for his speed, Corcoran alternated with slow balling Fred Gold-smith through three championship seasons. He also exhibited an effective, troublesome curve and good control and proved a plucky fielder who was adept at holding runners on base. When not pitching, Corcoran played short-stop or the outfield. Lifetime, he batted a meager .223, but his 287 hits included 47 doubles, 15 triples, and 2 home runs. He also tallied 192 runs in 1,289 times at bat. During a 1884 game with Buffalo, Corcoran tried to relieve the pain of an inflamed right index finger by pitching alternately with his right and left hands. After being hit hard for four innings, he was removed from the box. He was sent to shortstop, where he played the remainder of the game, and made three hits, including two triples. Eleven days later, the sufficiently recovered Corcoran blanked Providence for his third no-hitter.

His effectiveness was destroyed by a sore arm. From 1885 until the close of his career in 1887, he won 7 and lost 6 for Chicago, New York, and Indianapolis (NL), and batted .185 in 21 games as an outfielder and shortstop with Washington (NL). In eight seasons, Corcoran completed 257 of 269 starts, struck out 1,103 batters in 2,392.1 innings, hurled 23 shutouts, reg-istered 177 wins and 90 losses, and recorded a 2.36 ERA. His .663 winning percentage ranks as the eighth highest of all time.

He struggled through several minor league seasons, trying to regain his touch, and umpired in the AtL in 1890. He died from kidney disease, leaving his wife Gertrude and four children. His brother lost one complete game as a pitcher for the Chicago White Stockings in 1884.

BIBLIOGRAPHY: Lawrence Corcoran file, National Baseball Hall of Fame Library, Cooperstown, NY; Al Kermisch, "From a Researcher's Notebook," *Baseball Research Journal* 11 (1984), p. 66; Newark *Evening News*, October 15, 1891; Joseph Overfield, "Christo Von Buffalo: Was He the First Baseball Cartoonist?" *Baseball Research Journal* 10 (1981) pp. 147–150; Joseph L. Reichler, ed., *The Baseball Encyclopedia*, 6th ed. (New York, 1985), pp. 824, 1,660; Harold Seymour, *Baseball: The Early Years* (New York, 1960); *Sporting Life*, July 22, 1885, p. 5; David Quentin Voigt, *American Baseball*, vol. 1 (University Park, PA, 1983).

A. D. Suehsdorf

CORCORAN, Thomas William "Tommy" (b. 4 January 1869, New Ha-ven, CT; d. 25 June 1960, Plainfield, CT), player and umpire, was the second of five children of laborer Peter J. and Mary (McNally) Corcoran. He married Dasie M. Sykes in 1898 and Gladys May Dawley on December 5, 1925, and had four children by the first marriage and three by the second. An active amateur and semi-pro player around New Haven, Corcoran was recruited in 1886 as a pitcher and infielder for a Little Rock, AR, semi-pro team and turned professional the following year with Lynn, MA (NEL). He first played shortstop full-time at Wilkes Barre (CL) in 1888 and returned to New Haven for a successful 1889 season with the city's AA team. His excellent fielding earned him a position with Ned Hanlon's* Pittsburgh franchise of the ill-fated PL in 1890. After the Brotherhood's collapse, Corcoran joined Philadelphia (AA) and led the AA in putouts (300) and fielding average (.911). When Philadelphia did not survive the merger of the AA with the NL, Corcoran signed with the Brooklyn Bridegrooms (NL), for whom he played five seasons and achieved (1894) his top career batting mark of .300. His best seasons came from 1893 through 1897, when Corcoran averaged .286 and slugged 15 home runs.

In 1897 Cincinnati (NL) acquired him for two players and cash. For the next ten years he excelled as the Reds' shortstop and team captain. He led the NL in fielding average in 1904 (.936) and 1905 (.952), in assists in 1898 (561) and 1905 (531), and in double plays in 1902 (49) and 1905 (67). In 1903 against St. Louis, he set the major league record for assists by a shortstop in a nine-inning game (14). The New York Giants (NL) signed the 38-year-old veteran in 1907 as bench strength behind rookie second baseman Larry Doyle.* Released later in the year, he became playing manager at Uniontown, PA (POML), and in 1908 managed New Bedford, MA (NEL).

Over an eighteen-year major league career, Corcoran compiled modest averages at bat (.257) and afield (.927). "My work didn't show in the statistics," he told interviewers. Nevertheless, his overall record is impressive: 2,201 games (2,073 at shortstop, 8th on the all-time list), 2,264 hits, 1,188 runs, 155 triples (47th all-time), 387 stolen bases, and 1,135 RBIs. Initially a barehanded fielder, he ranks fourth in total chances (12,612), fifth in putouts (4,550) and assists (7,106), and seventh in average chances per game (6.1).

A wide-ranging shortstop with a strong and accurate arm who never earned more than $4,600 a year, Corcoran also proved an excellent sign stealer. At Philadelphia, he once uncovered an electric signaling device buried in the third base coaching box. His keystone partners included Yank Robinson at Pittsburgh, Monte Ward* and Tido Daly at Brooklyn, and Bid McPhee* and Miller Huggins* at Cincinnati. After retirement as a player, he umpired in the CtL (1912), NYSL (1913–1914), FL (1915), and IL (1919). In later years he lived on his 160 acre farm at Voluntown, CT, where he was an occasional fox hunter and amateur field-dog trainer.

BIBLIOGRAPHY: Lee Allen, *The Cincinnati Reds* (New York, 1948); Cincinnati (OH) *Enquirer*, January 30, 1960; Thomas W. Corcoran file, National Baseball Hall of Fame Library, Cooperstown, NY; Hartford (CT) *Courant*, June 27, 1960; Paul MacFarlane, ed., *TSN Daguerreotypes of Great Stars of Baseball* (St. Louis, 1981); Norwich (CT) *Bulletin*, April 15, 1956; January 5, 1957; January 4, 1958; January 3, 26, 1960; *NYT*,

January 3, 1960; Joseph L. Reichler, ed., *The Baseball Encyclopedia*, 6th ed. (New York, 1985); p. 824; *Spalding's Baseball Guide*, 1890–1900 (New York, 1890–1900); *Sporting Life*, July 14, 1906.

A. D. Suehsdorf and Duane A. Smith

COVELESKI, Stanley Anthony "Stan" (b. Stanislaus Kowalewski, 13 July 1889, Shamokin, PA; d. 20 March 1984, South Bend, IN), player, was born of Polish immigrant parents. Coveleski, the youngest of five boys, left St. Stanislaus Elementary School after the fourth grade and began working in the coal mines. For an eleven hour, six day week, the 12-year-old Coveleski earned $3.75. Coveleski's introduction to baseball proved quite unusual, considering his eventual success. He suspended a can from a tree limb with a piece of string, gave it a swing, and tried to hit it with a rock. His uncanny accuracy attracted the attention of some local baseball people. After pitching only five amateur baseball games, he signed his first professional contract in 1908 with Shamokin, PA (AtL).

In 1912 he received his first major league experience when the Philadelphia Athletics (AL) promoted him late in the season. He passed this test with a 2–1 record in three starts and remains one of the few players to pitch a shutout in his first major league appearance. His next major league opportunity came with Cleveland (AL) in 1916. During a nine-year stay there, he compiled a 172–123 record for a .583 winning percentage. The 5 foot, 11 inch, 166 pound Coveleski enjoyed four consecutive 20-win seasons, including the 1920 World Series championship campaign. In the 1920 World Series against the Brooklyn Dodgers, he won three games, allowed only fifteen hits, walked two batters, allowed two runs, pitched three complete games and compiled a brilliant 0.67 ERA.

Cleveland traded Coveleski to the Washington Senators (AL) before the 1925 season, believing that he already had seen his best years. In 1925 his record included a 20–5 mark, an AL-leading .800 winning percentage and a 2.84 ERA. He also made a second, less successful, World Series appearance, losing two games to the Pittsburgh Pirates. After helping the New York Yankees (AL) late in the 1928 season with a 5–1 record in twelve appearances, Coveleski retired his aged, sore right arm to a service station business in South Bend. He was elected to the Cleveland Indians Hall of Fame in 1966, the National Baseball Hall of Fame in 1969, and the Polish-American Hall of Fame in 1976.

Nearly sixty years after his retirement from baseball, his record still remains impressive. He compiled a 215–142 career mark for a .602 winning percentage and a 2.88 lifetime ERA, won 20 or more games five times, triumphed in 13 consecutive games in 1925, hurled 38 career shutouts, and pitched a 19-inning complete-game victory against New York. In 3,092.2 innings pitched, he struck out 981 batters and walked 802. He led the AL in shutouts (9) in 1917, hits surrendered (286) in 1919, strikeouts (133) in

1920, ERA in 1923 (2.76) and 1925 (2.84), and winning percentage (.800) in 1925. He and his brother Harry combined for a 296–197 record, placing them among the best in that category. Coveleski, an introverted figure known for his loyalty to team and family, gained plaudits for his control and ranked among the best spitball pitchers. He and sixteen other hurlers were allowed to continue using the spitball after the pitch was banned in 1920.

BIBLIOGRAPHY: Cleveland *Plain Dealer*, 1916–1925, March 21, 23, 1984; Stanley Coveleski file, National Baseball Hall of Fame Library, Cooperstown, NY; Gene Karst and Martin J. Jones, Jr., *Who's Who in Professional Baseball* (New Rochelle, NY, 1973); *NYT*, July 27, 29, 1969; Joseph L. Reichler, ed., *The Baseball Encyclopedia*, 6th ed., (New York, 1985), pp. 1,662–1,663; Joseph L. Reichler, *The Great All-Time Record Book* (New York, 1981).

John E. Neville

CRAMER, Roger Maxwell "Doc," "Flit" (b. 22 July 1906, Beach Haven, NJ), player and coach, is the son of butcher John Roger and Eva Jean (Spraigue) Cramer and attended Manahawkin (NJ) Grade School and Barnegat High School. He married Helen Letts of Manahawkin on December 25, 1927, and has two children, Elaine and Joan. A left-handed hitter and right-handed throwing outfielder, the 6 foot, 2 inch, 185 pound Cramer played in the AL from 1929 through 1948. Nicknamed "Doc," he led the AL in at bats seven times, a major league record, and in singles five times. Frequently ranking among AL leaders in hits, in 1940 he tied Barney McCosky and Rip Radcliff for most hits with 200. He was named to the AL All-Star team on five occasions.

In July, 1928, former Philadelphia Athletics catcher Cy Perkins discovered Cramer, then pitching for a semi-pro team in Beach Haven, and persuaded Athletics manager Connie Mack* to sign him. The blue-eyed youngster debuted as an infield-pitcher in 1929 at Martinsburg, WV (BRL), hitting .404 to win the batting championship. Cramer joined the Athletics in late 1929 and remained there through 1935, learning the game's finer points from Hall of Famer Eddie Collins.* Subsequently, Cramer played with the AL's Boston Red Sox (1936–1940), Washington Senators (1941), and Detroit Tigers (1942–1948). The outfielder starred in the 1945 World Series and helped the Tigers defeat the Chicago Cubs four games to three. Cramer made eleven hits (all singles) for a .379 batting average, scored seven runs, and drove in four tallies.

During his twenty-year major league career, Cramer batted .296, made 2,705 hits, 396 doubles, and 109 triples, scored 1,357 runs, and knocked in 842 tallies. Cramer twice recorded six hits in six consecutive times at bat (on June 20, 1932, at Comiskey Park in Chicago and on July 13, 1935, at Shibe Park in Philadelphia) to tie a major league record, and made a single, double, triple, and home run in a June 10, 1934, contest. An outstanding, agile fielder, Cramer was considered one of the fastest "big men" during his career. He led AL outfielders in putouts in 1936 and 1938 and in fielding in 1945, made 5,412 career putouts to rank eighth on the all-time list, and ranks thirty-second in all-time at bats. Cramer coached for the Tigers (1948), Seattle of the PCL (1950), and the AL Chicago White Sox (1951–1953). An avid hunter, Cramer worked as a carpenter in Manahawkin and resides there.

BIBLIOGRAPHY: Donald Honig, *Baseball: When the Grass Was Real* (New York, 1975); Harold (Speed) Johnson, *Who's Who in Major League Baseball* (Chicago, 1933); Stanley Kuminski, "Singles Are Important Too," *Baseball Research Journal* 3 (1974), pp. 60–63; Paul MacFarlane, ed., *TSN Daguerreotypes of Great Stars of Baseball* (St. Louis, 1968), pp. 47–48.

B. Randolph Linthurst

CRAVATH, Clifford Clarence "Gavvy," "Cactus" (b. 23 March 1881, Escondido, CA; d. 23 May 1963, Laguna Beach, CA), player and manager, was nicknamed "Gavvy" and "Cactus." In 1903 he married Californian Myrtle Wilson, with whom he had two daughters. They also brought up a nephew, Jeff Cravath, who coached the University of Southern California football team in the post–World War II years. An outfielder, Cravath played for Los Angeles (PCL) from 1903 through 1907. After being sold to the Boston Red Sox (AL) in 1908, he hit only .256 with one homer in 94 games. The Red Sox sold him in 1909 to the Chicago White Sox (AL), who soon dealt him to the Washington Senators (AL). After being released in 1911 to Minneapolis (AA) he hit 29 homers. The Philadelphia Phillies (NL) purchased his contract in 1912 for $9,000.

At Baker Bowl, Gavvy quickly led the home run hitters of the dead ball era. His 24 homers in 1915 set the major league mark for this century until Babe Ruth* hit 29 in 1919 for the Boston Red Sox. Cravath's slugging helped the Phillies win their first NL pennant in 1915; the same year he led the NL in RBIs and runs scored. In the fifth game of the 1915 World Series, Cravath made an unforgettable play. During the first inning with the bases loaded, none out and the count on Cravath three balls and two strikes, manager Pat Moran gave the slugger the bunt sign. The Red Sox converted the bunt into a double play, denying the Phillies a big inning.

In 1919 the Phillies fell into the cellar at midseason. Cravath reluctantly replaced Jack Coombs* as manager and continued through the 1920 season as player-manager. His two cellar-dwelling teams won only 40 percent of their games. He served as player-manager of Salt Lake City (PCL) in 1921 and as a pinch hitter for Minneapolis (AA) in 1922. Subsequently, he prospered in real estate in Laguna Beach, CA, and became justice of the peace and court judge.

A practical joker known for his modesty and geniality, the muscular right-handed hitter led the NL in homers five times (1913–1915, 1917–1919) and tied for the lead once, hit to all fields with power, and excelled as the outstanding slugger of the pre-Ruthian era. During an eleven-year major league career, he made 1,134 hits, smashed 232 doubles, 83 triples, and 119 homers, batted in 719 runs, and hit .287. His 128 RBIs in 1913 proved remarkable for his era.

BIBLIOGRAPHY: Frank Bilovsky and Rich Westcott, *The Phillies Encyclopedia* (West Point, NY, 1983); Allen Lewis, *The Philadelphia Phillies: A Pictorial History* (Virginia Beach, VA, 1981); Allen Lewis and Larry Shenk, *This Date in Philadelphia Phillies History* (Briarcliff Manor, NY, 1979); Frederick G. Lieb and Stan Baumgartner, *The Philadelphia Phillies* (New York, 1953); Tom Meany, *Baseball's Greatest Teams* (New York, 1949); *NYT*, May 24, 1963; Ira Smith, *Baseball's Famous Outfielders* (New York, 1954); *TSN*, June 8, 1963.

Ralph S. Graber

CRAWFORD, Samuel Earl "Sam," "Wahoo Sam" (b. 18 April 1880, Wahoo, NE; d. 15 June 1968, Hollywood, CA), player and umpire, ended his schooling after five grades and learned the barbering trade. After playing much semi-pro baseball around Nebraska, Crawford in 1899 joined Chatham, Ontario (CnL). A muscular 6 foot, 190 pounder who batted and threw left-handed, Crawford quickly advanced to Columbus-Grand Rapids (WL) and to Cincinnati (NL). Two years later (1901), he batted .330 and led the major leagues with 16 home runs. In 1903 the established NL star jumped his Cincinnati contract and signed with the Detroit Tigers in the new AL for a salary of $3,500.

After batting .335 his first season at Detroit, Crawford slumped for three years. Under the fiery rookie manager Hughey Jennings* and alongside the brilliant young Ty Cobb* in the Detroit outfield, Crawford in 1907 hit .323 to help the Tigers win the AL championship. Detroit repeated in 1908 and 1909, as Crawford continued to hit well above .300. In 1908 he led the AL with seven home runs, making him the only player to top both major leagues in round trippers. In the Tigers' three straight World Series losses, however, he averaged only .243.

Although Detroit won no more pennants during Crawford's years there, "Wahoo Sam" remained a strong, durable performer. In 1911 he batted a career-high .378 (to Cobb's league-leading .420). Although not fast, Crawford proved a clever base runner, stealing 41 bases in 1912. Crawford disliked the suspicious, easily riled Cobb, who was convinced that Crawford resented his spectacular achievements and bigger salaries. When Crawford left the Tigers in 1917, he still felt considerable bitterness toward Cobb. During nineteen seasons, Crawford compiled a lifetime .309 batting average, made 2,964 base hits, drove home 1,525 runs, and smashed 457 doubles, 97 home runs, and an unsurpassable 312 triples.

Crawford returned to California, where for several years he had made his off-season home, and played four seasons for Los Angeles in the strong PCL. Although considerably slower, he still hit .360, .332, and .318 before retiring as a player in 1921. During the late 1930s, he umpired for a few years in the PCL. Crawford held various jobs outside baseball, handled his money wisely, and provided comfortably for his wife Mary, whom he married when he was age 62, and son Samuel, Jr.

Despite their earlier enmity, Cobb always admired Crawford's ballplaying talents and for years campaigned to get him into the National Baseball Hall of Fame. In 1957 the Baseball Writers Association Veterans Committee voted Crawford into membership.

BIBLIOGRAPHY: Charles C. Alexander, *Ty Cobb* (New York, 1984); Frederick G. Lieb, *The Detroit Tigers* (New York, 1946); Paul MacFarlane, ed., *TSN Daguerreotypes of Great Stars of Baseball* (St. Louis, 1981); Lawrence Ritter, *The Glory of Their Times* (New York, 1966); *TSN*, June 29, 1968.

                                                                                    Charles C. Alexander

CREIGHTON, James "Jim" (b. 15 April 1841, Brooklyn, NY; d. 18 October 1862, Brooklyn, NY), player, was the son of James and Jane Creighton. Creighton grew up in King's County, NY, where he earned nationwide fame pitching for hometown teams. As baseball's popularity soared, he became America's earliest diamond hero and the first martyr. After his death, some clubs adopted his name. He revolutionized the game by pitching aggressively and throwing with speed and spin. Before Creighton developed his under-hand snap with the Niagaras of Brooklyn, pitchers tossed the ball easily to the batter.

After joining the Niagaras in 1858 as a second baseman, Creighton began pitching the following year. The Star Club, a high-ranked junior team, then lured him into their organization. On September 3, 1859, he beat the big-time Excelsiors 17–12, but lost 15–12 to the formidable Atlantics because of team fielding lapses. Creighton joined the Excelsiors the next year, making that well-traveled club nearly invincible with his innovative pitching strategy. After the Excelsiors visited Beantown, Lowell of Boston moundsman and captain James D'Wolff Lovett commented: "Creighton had a great influence upon my success as a pitcher. I noted him very carefully and found that his speed was not due to mere physical strength, but that this later was supplemented by a very long arm and a peculiar wrist movement, very quick and snappy." Henry Chadwick* praised Creighton's "head work" or intelligent style, while conservatives deemed his controversial form illegal.

A marvelous hitter, Creighton established an unbeatable record by completing one entire season without being put out. A hitting feat against the Unions of Morisania ended Creighton's career and life at age 21. John Chapman, who attended the game, reported: "He did it hitting a home run. When he crossed the rubber he turned to George Flanley and said 'I must have snapped my belt,' and George said 'I guess not.' It turned out that he suffered a fatal injury. Nothing could be done for him, and baseball met with a severe loss." After a few days of internal hemorrhaging, he died.

BIBLIOGRAPHY: Henry Chadwick, *The American Game of Baseball* (New York, 1868); James Creighton file, National Baseball Hall of Fame Library, Cooperstown, NY; James D'Wolf Lovett, *Old Boston Boys and the Games They Played* (Boston, 1906); Preston D. Orem, *Baseball 1845–1881* (Altadena, CA, 1961); Albert Spalding, *America's National Game* (New York, 1911).

Mark D. Rucker

CRONIN, Joseph Edward "Joe" (b. 12 October 1906, San Francisco, CA; d. 7 September 1984, Osterville, MA), player, manager, and executive, was the son of teamster Jerry and homemaker Mary (Caroline) Cronin and graduated in 1924 from Sacred Heart High School in San Francisco. He married Mildred Robertson on September 27, 1934, and had four children, Thomas, Michael, Maureen, and Kevin. Cronin, who exhibited high morality, strong Christian faith, honesty, fairness, and an excellent memory, fully appreciated the psychology and history of baseball. The extremely modest Cronin believed that baseball did more for him than he contributed to it and was the first ballplayer to rise through the ranks to become AL president. A jovial, friendly person, Cronin admired and exhibited loyalty, dedication, determination, and ability.

After being signed by the Pittsburgh Pirates (NL) in 1924, he played second base and shortstop the next year for Johnstown, PA (MAL). In 1926 he performed for New Haven, CT (EL), and appeared briefly for Pittsburgh. Cronin spent 1927 as a bench reserve for Pittsburgh and early 1928 with Kansas City (AA). On July 28, 1928, the Washington Senators (AL) bought his contract and used him that season as backup for Bobby Reeves. From 1929 to 1934, he started there at shortstop and managed the club the final two years. His 1933 team won the AL pennant but lost the World Series to the New York Giants four games to one. In the fall of 1934, the Boston Red Sox (AL) paid a record $250,000 and traded one player for his services. At Boston, he played shortstop from 1935 to 1945 and managed from 1935 to 1947. His 1946 club won the AL pennant but lost the World Series to the St. Louis Cardinals four games to three. Named the All-Time Washington Senators shortstop, he received the AL Most Valuable Player Award in 1930 and was selected as *The Sporting News* shortstop from 1930 to 1934 and in 1938 and 1939. Cronin led AL shortstops three times each in putouts and assists, twice in fielding percentage and doubles and once in triples. With Boston in 1943, Cronin set an AL record by slugging five pinch hit home runs. Besides batting a career .300 mark for Boston, he hit for the cycle on August 2, 1940, becoming the sixth Red Sox player to do so.

During his twenty-year major league career, he appeared in 2,124 games for three teams. In 7,579 times at bat, he made 1,482 singles, 515 doubles, 118 triples, 170 homers, received 1,059 walks, batted in 1,424 runs, scored 1,233 times, and compiled a .301 batting average. Afield he averaged .953, made 4,302 putouts, and handled 6,052 assists. The successful manager guided Washington to a 165–139 record and Boston to a 1,071–916 mark. During his fifteen managerial seasons, he finished with 1,236 wins and 1,055 losses for a .540 mark. Cronin, who holds the Red Sox record for managerial longevity and most victories, was elected in 1956 to the National Baseball Hall of Fame. In 1982 Boston fans selected him as second-team manager of their all-time "dream team."

Cronin served as Red Sox vice-president, treasurer, and general manager from 1948 to 1959, as AL president from 1959 to 1973, and as chairman of the AL board from 1973 to 1984. In addition, he became a director of the National Baseball Hall of Fame in 1959, chairman of its Veterans Committee in 1970, and president of the Baseball Players Association of America in 1977. His impact upon baseball included helping to incorporate the Reorganization Agreement into the AL constitution and adding new teams to the AL. Red Sox owner Thomas Yawkey* took a paternal, benevolent attitude toward his team personnel and staff, while manager Cronin ideally complemented his owner's admired personal philosophy and deservedly was acclaimed as Yawkey's devoted, loyal standard-bearer.

BIBLIOGRAPHY: *Boston Red Sox Media Guide, 1984*; Ellery H. Clark, Jr., *Boston Red Sox: 75th Anniversary History* (Hicksville, NY, 1975); Ellery H. Clark, Jr., Red Sox Analytical Letter Collection, correspondence with Joe Cronin, Dom DiMaggio, and Bob Doerr; Ellery H. Clark, Jr., *Red Sox Fever* (Hicksville, NY, 1979); Ellery H. Clark, Jr., *Red Sox Forever* (Hicksville, NY, 1977); Ellery H. Clark, Jr., Red Sox Interviews, Joe Cronin, June, July, August, 1983; Mrs. Cronin, August, 1983; Joseph L. Reichler, ed., *The Baseball Encyclopedia*, 6th ed. (New York, 1985), p. 875.

                                                                              Ellery H. Clark, Jr.

CROSLEY, Powel, Jr. (b. 18 September 1886, Cincinnati, OH; d. 28 March 1961, Cincinnati, OH), executive, was the son of attorney and real estate developer Powel Sr. and Charlotte (Utz) Crosley. The tall, restless Crosley was more interested in gadgetry than scholarship and graduated from the Ohio Military Institute in 1905. He attended the University of Cincinnati and pitched for its baseball team, but dropped out of college to engage in advertising, sales, and peddling novelties. Earlier he even had chauffeured to learn more about cars, his first and most enduring enthusiasm. He married Gwendolyn Aiken of Cincinnati in 1910 and had two children. Following her death in 1939, he was married three more times: to Marrianne Richards in 1943 (divorced 1944), to Eva Brokaw in 1952 (died 1955), and to Charlotte K. Wilson in 1956 (divorced 1960).

After early failures in automobile manufacturing, the innovative Crosley bought into a growing auto accessories company during World War I. He acquired control and expanded his business interests to include production of radio and broadcasting equipment and other mass market appliances, the most successful being the Shelvador refrigerator.

In 1934 Leland MacPhail, Sr.,* who was operating the bankrupt Cincinnati Reds (NL) for a local bank, interested Crosley in purchasing a share of the team and becoming the club's president. Crosley claimed that civic pride motivated him to acquire an interest in and then control of the Reds in 1936, but his ownership of the popular, profitable radio station WLW probably figured in his decision as well. Utilizing his business expertise, he promised Reds fans a "new deal." In 1935 he received permission to introduce major league night games. The first night game was played on May 24, matching the Philadelphia Phillies and the Reds. It was witnessed by over 20,000 fans, perhaps ten times more than would have turned out for an afternoon game. Drawing barely 200,000 fans in 1934 and finishing in last place since 1931, the Reds progressed during Crosley's regime. Under general managers MacPhail and Warren Giles,* the Reds made the first division by 1938 and in 1939–1940 won consecutive NL pennants. In the 1940 World Series, Crosley's club triumphed over the Detroit Tigers.

During Crosley's lifetime, the Reds never again achieved the same success. The Reds' modest farm system did not have the top caliber players to replace such aging stars from the 1939–1940 champions as catcher Ernie Lombardi* and pitcher Bucky Walters.* By 1945 the Reds returned to the second division and remained there until 1956.

After World War II, Crosley contracted his business interests. In 1945 he sold his appliance company and radio stations to the Aviation Corporation (AVCO). He hoped to manufacture a four-cylinder compact car for the postwar market, but sales lagged. In 1952 Crosley sold his auto business to the General Tire and Rubber Company. He spent more time at his island retreats off the Georgia coast and Lake Ontario than with the Reds. Nevertheless, he placed astute baseball men in control of the club. Under new general manager Gabe Paul,* the Cincinnati farm system in the mid–1950s became more productive. With young sluggers Wally Post and Frank Robinson* joining established star Ted Kluszewski,* the Reds in 1956 tied the NL home run record.

Crosley died before the Reds won their next NL pennant in 1961, but remained a good owner throughout his control of the club. He let experienced baseball men handle club operations, made the team profitable, and kept the Reds in Cincinnati. Rejecting opportunities to move his franchise to Los Angeles and New York, Crosley insisted that the Reds remain in Cincinnati and be controlled after his death by a family-directed foundation. Profits from the Reds went to charities. Crosley's baseball philosophy essentially remained unchanged: "I do . . . not want to see Cincinnati, the birthplace of major league baseball, become a minor league town. While Cincinnati is the smallest city in the big leagues, the love of baseball is deep rooted."

BIBLIOGRAPHY: Lee Allen, *The Cincinnati Reds* (New York, 1948); William H. Beezley, "Crosley, Powel, Jr.," *DAB*, Supp. 7 (1961–1965), pp. 154–155; Powel Crosley, Jr., interview, October 4, 1938, Cincinnati Baseball Club Press Releases, February 5, 1934 and November 6, 1936, all in the files of National Baseball Hall of Fame Library, Cooperstown, NY; Forrest Davis, "The Crosley Touch—And Go!" *SEP* 222 (September 30, 1939), pp. 18, 51–57; Lloyd J. Graybar, interview with Pat Harmon, November 28, 1983; "Love's Labor Lost," *Time* 60 (July 28, 1952), p. 70; *NYT*, February 5, 1934, July 1, September 19, 1936, July 19, October 26, November 3, 1960, March 29, 30, 1961; Gabe Paul to author, November 29, 1983; Gerard Piel, "Powel Crosley, Jr.," *Life* 22 (February 17, 1947), pp. 47–48, 50–54; Joe Rice, *Cincinnati's Powel Crosley Jr.: Industrialist, Pioneer Radio Builder* (Covington, KY, 1976); *TSN*, April 5, 1961.

Lloyd J. Graybar

CROSS, Lafayette Napoleon "Lave" (b. 11 May 1867, Milwaukee, WI; d. 4 September 1927, Toledo, OH), player and manager, was the son of Czechoslavakian immigrants and brother of less successful big league players Amos and Frank Cross. He played amateur ball in the Cleveland area before becoming a professional with Sandusky, OH in 1884. His big league career began at Louisville (AA) in 1887. He moved to the Philadelphia (AA) club in 1889, jumped to Philadelphia (PL) in 1890, then returned to the AA squad in 1891, the AA's last year. He remained in Philadelphia with the NL team through the 1897 season. In the next three years, he saw action with Cleveland, Brooklyn, and St. Louis, all of the NL. In 1901 Connie Mack* lured him to join the Philadelphia entry in the newly formed AL, where he remained through 1905. Cross moved to Washington (AL) in 1906 and ended his twenty-one year career in 1907 following an ankle injury.

One of the game's most versatile, durable, and popular stars, Cross played 2,275 big league games, appearing in every position except pitcher: 1,721 at third base, 324 as catcher, 119 as outfielder, 65 at shortstop, 60 at second, and 7 at first. With a lifetime .292 batting average, a .382 slugging average, 2,644 hits, 411 doubles, 135 triples, and 47 home runs, Cross holds an honored place in the history of the game. He once hit for the cycle and holds the record for most assists in a game by a second baseman (15 in 12 innings). He is tied for third in most assists by a third baseman, with 10 in 10 innings. He played third base with a catcher's mitt, a then legal ploy that enabled him to knock down many a hard drive and throw out the runner. He managed Cleveland (NL) briefly (1899), winning 8 and losing 30 for a .211 percentage. Cross played without distinction in one World Series (1905) as a third baseman.

BIBLIOGRAPHY: Joseph L. Reichler, *The Great All-Time Baseball Record Book* (New York, 1981); Joseph L. Reichler, ed., *The Baseball Encyclopedia*, 6th ed. (New York, 1985), pp. 836–837.

Robert G. Weaver

CRUTCHFIELD, John William "Jimmie" (b. 25 March 1910, Ardmore, MO), player, is the son of John H. and Carrie (Cooper) Crutchfield and attended elementary school in Ardmore and two years of high school in Moberly, MO. Crutchfield began his Negro league professional career in 1930 as an outfielder with the Birmingham Black Barons (NNL) and started the 1931 season with the Indianapolis ABC's (NNL). During that season he was acquired by the Pittsburgh Crawfords (NNL) and played there throughout the 1936 season. Crutchfield later performed for the Newark Eagles (NNL), and Cleveland Buckeyes (NAL), with a brief stint in 1943 in the U.S. Army.

Known as "The Black Lloyd Waner*" because of his ability to play hit and run, Crutchfield compiled a lifetime .325 batting average while displaying enthusiasm, hustle, and sportsmanship. His tenure with the Pittsburgh Crawfords is best remembered. Crutchfield was playing for the Indianapolis ABC's against the Crawfords in 1931, when Pittsburgh offered him $50 to stay. Crutchfield strengthened the Crawfords team, playing with legendary black stars Josh Gibson,* Satchel Paige,* Judy Johnson,* and "Cool Papa" Bell.* Crutchfield's most noteworthy honors included selection to four East-West All-Star games. As a member of the Pittsburgh Crawfords in 1934, 1935, and 1936, Crutchfield was selected as the starting right fielder. In 1941, while playing for the Chicago American Giants, he was named to the squad as an outfielder and played left field.

Crutchfield later served as a resource person for Robert W. Peterson's *Only the Ball Was White* and for Craig Davidson's Negro leagues film, *The Sun Was Always Shining Someplace*. Upon retiring from baseball, Crutchfield worked twenty-six years for the U.S. Postal Service. He married Julia Robertson Marshall in 1947 and resides in Chicago.

BIBLIOGRAPHY: Robert W. Peterson, *Only the Ball Was White* (Englewood Cliffs, NJ, 1970); Robert L. Ruck, *Sandlot Seasons: Sport in Black Pittsburgh* (Urbana, IL, 1986); William A. Sutton, correspondence with Jeff Kernan, William A. Sutton Collection, Columbus, OH.

William A. Sutton

CUMMINGS, William Arthur "Candy" (b. 17 October 1848, Ware, MA; d. 16 May 1924, Toledo, OH), player and executive, was an effective right-handed pitcher in amateur club baseball, the NA, and the NL. At age 17 he started playing baseball in New York City. His slight 5 foot, 9 inch, 120 pound frame accounted for his nickname. Between 1866 and 1871 Cummings played for several independent teams in the New York City area. He pitched primarily for the Excelsior Club of Brooklyn in 1866 and 1867 and for the Star of Brooklyn the next four seasons. During that period, Cummings allegedly invented the curveball. Henry Chadwick* occasionally supported the Cummings claim, but reported seeing curveball pitchers in the 1850s.

In 1871 Chadwick named Cummings the leading U.S. amateur pitcher. Cummings turned professional in 1872, joining the New York Mutuals (NA). In the NA, he pitched for the Lord Baltimores in 1873, Philadelphias in 1874, and Hartfords in 1875. Cummings starred in the NA, winning 33, 28, 28, and 35 games. In 1875 he hurled six shutouts and compiled an impressive 1.73 ERA. His NL career was limited to the 1876 and 1877 seasons, reflecting the heavy pitching loads of previous years. He won 16 and lost 8 for Hartford in 1876 and compiled a 5–14 in his final season with Cincinnati.

Unable to accept that his powers were declining, Cummings became president of the rival IA. This loose confederation of independent teams failed quickly and ended Cummings' connection with organized baseball. He settled in Athol, MA, where he owned a paint and wallpaper store until just before his death. In 1939 he was elected to the National Baseball Hall of Fame.

BIBLIOGRAPHY: Paul MacFarlane, ed., *TSN Hall of Fame Fact Book* (St. Louis, 1982); Joseph L. Reichler, ed., *The Baseball Encyclopedia*, 6th ed. (New York, 1985), pp. 52, 1,669; Lowell Reidenbaugh, *Cooperstown: Where Baseball's Legends Live Forever* (St. Louis, 1983).

Gordon B. McKinney

Cuyler, Hazen Shirley "Kiki" (b. 30 August 1899, Harrisville, MI; d. 11 February 1950, Ann Arbor, MI), player, coach, and manager, was the son of George and Anna Cuyler. His father, a Coast Guardsman and probate judge, played semi-pro baseball in Canada in the late 1800s. Hazen, who first played baseball at age nine, starred in high school baseball, track, basketball, and football. He also pitched and played outfield for several semi-pro organizations in northeastern Michigan and served a two-year U.S. Army stint. He married Bertha Kelly on January 8, 1919, and had two children, Harold and Kelly. While Cuyler was employed for Buick Motors in Flint, the Bay City, MI (MOL), club signed him in 1921 and sold his contract to the Pittsburgh Pirates (NL). He played outfield for Charleston, SC (SAL), in 1922 and Nashville (SA) in 1923. The latter year, he earned Most Valuable Player honors by averaging .340 at the plate and leading the SA in six categories.

For the Pittsburgh Pirates in 1924, he posted one of baseball's greatest rookie seasons with a .354 batting average. In 1925 he enjoyed an even better season with a .357 batting average, led the NL in triples (26) and runs scored (144), and drove in the run that won the World Series against the Washington Senators. Besides batting over .300 eight other seasons, he paced the NL in runs scored (113) in 1926 and doubles (42) in 1934. In August, 1927, Pirate manager Donie Bush benched Cuyler following a disagreement. Cuyler stayed there through the World Series but then was traded to the Chicago Cubs (NL). During seven years there, he averaged .325, helped the club capture NL pennants in 1929 and 1932, and batted .360, in 1929 and .355 in 1930. Cuyler joined the Cincinnati Reds (NL) in mid–1935 and ended his playing career with the Brooklyn Dodgers (NL) in 1938. In eighteen major league seasons, he batted .321 with 2,299 hits, 394 doubles, 157 triples, 127 home runs, 1,305 runs scored, and 1,065 RBIs.

Cuyler managed Chattanooga (SA) to first, fourth, and third place finishes from 1939 through 1941. After coaching for the Chicago Cubs (NL) from 1941 through 1943, he managed Atlanta (SA) in 1944. The Crackers made the SA playoffs in 1945 and won the SA championship the next year under Cuyler's tutelage. After two disappointing seasons, however, Cuyler joined Joe McCarthy's* Boston Red Sox as a coach in 1949. The quiet Cuyler, who neither drank nor smoked, excelled as a powerful line drive hitter, fleet runner, and talented outfielder with an outstanding arm. He led the NL four times in stolen bases between 1926 and 1930 and finished second two other times. His base-stealing career ended, however, after two leg injuries in the early 1930s. For many years, Cuyler toured the off-season with his All-Star basketball team. Cuyler died of a heart attack while fishing near Glennie, MI, and was elected in 1968 to the National Baseball Hall of Fame.

BIBLIOGRAPHY: *Alcona (MI) County Herald*, February 17, 1950; Hazen Cuyler Scrapbook Collection, Alcona County Library, Harrisville, MI; Joseph L. Reichler, ed., *The Baseball Encyclopedia*, 6th ed. (New York, 1985), pp. 843–844; *TSN*, February, 1950.

Gerald E. Brennan

D

DAHLEN, William Frederick "Bill," "Bad Bill" (b. 5 January 1871, Nel-
liston, NY; d. 5 December 1950, Brooklyn, NY), player and manager, came
from upstate New York and was the son of a masonry contractor. He attended
the local elementary school and graduated from Fort Plain (NY) High School.
For the next two years, he attended Clinton Liberal Institute and played on
its baseball team.

In 1890 the 5 foot, 9 inch, 170 pound infielder entered professional baseball
with Cobleskill, NY (NYSL). The right-handed hitting Dahlen joined Cap
Anson's* Chicago (NL) club the following year and played there for eight
seasons. He later played for Brooklyn (1899–1903), New York (1904–1907),
and Boston (1908–1909) in the NL. From 1910 through 1913, Dahlen managed the Brooklyn Superbas (Dodgers). He guided the team to two sixth and
two seventh place finishes, compiling 251 wins against 355 losses.

As a regular shortstop, Dahlen played for championship teams with Brooklyn in 1899 and 1900, and with the New York Giants in 1904 and 1905. His
clever base running and aggressive fielding earned the respect of opposing
NL players and managers. Dahlen led NL shortstops in fielding average
twice and in assists four times, and compiled 7,500 assists. His 972 errors
remains a major league record.

A .274 lifetime hitter, he made 2,482 hits, 416 doubles, 163 triples, and
84 home runs, drove in 1,233 runs, and stole 555 bases. In 1894 he belted
a career-high 15 home runs and set a major league record by hitting safely
in 42 consecutive games from June 20 to August 7. After being held hitless
on August 7, he began another streak by hitting in 28 straight games. This
mark was surpassed three years later by Willie Keeler,* who hit in 44 consecutive games.

Married to Jeanette Hoglund in December 1903, Dahlen had a daughter
and later worked for the Brooklyn Post Office and as an attendant at Yankee
Stadium. The steady, durable Dahlen spanned baseball's developing years
from the nineteenth century into its modern era and shares the major league
record with his twenty years at shortstop.

BIBLIOGRAPHY: Arthur R. Ahrens, "The Daily Dahlen of 1894," *Baseball Research Journal* 4 (1975), pp. 57–60; Warren Brown, *The Chicago Cubs* (NY, 1946); Gene Karst and Martin J. Jones, Jr., *Who's Who in Professional Baseball* (New Rochelle, NY, 1973); *NYT*, December 6, 1950; *TSN*, December 11, 1950.

Joseph Lawler

DANDRIDGE, Raymond "Hooks", "Ray" (b. 1913, Richmond, VA), player, manager, and scout, is the son of a textile worker and was a Golden Gloves boxer and football quarterback. The Detroit Stars (NNL) signed him as they barnstormed north during spring training in 1933. Dandridge, a sandlot ballplayer, impressed Detroit manager "Candy Jim" Taylor, who played him at shortstop. Dandridge performed the next season for the Newark, NJ Dodgers, who moved him to third base, and the Newark Eagles (NNL).

During his sixteen-year Negro league career, Dandridge was its premier third baseman. He played in the late 1930s in the Eagles' "million dollar infield," which supposedly would have been worth $1 million if they were white. The 5 foot 7 inch, bowlegged Dandridge also played for the New York Cubans (NNL) and winter ball in Venezuela, Cuba, Puerto Rico, and Mexico. In 1944 manager Cum Posey* ranked Dandridge among the greatest players in the Negro leagues. "There never was a smoother-functioning master at third base than Dandridge," Posey remarked, "and he can hit that apple, too."

Dandridge played for Vera Cruz in Mexico during the 1940s but returned to the United States to manage and play for the New York Cubans in 1949. He was sold that year to the Minneapolis Millers, the New York Giants' AA farm club. Dandridge told the Giants he was 29 years old, although he was actually 36 at the time. In 1949 he was selected the AA Rookie of the Year. The next season, he hit .311 and was named the AA Most Valuable Player for the champion Millers. Although Sal Maglie and Monte Irvin* urged the Giants (NL) to bring Dandridge up, New York did not comply, perhaps because of his age, informal quotas, and Dandridge's popularity in Minneapolis. In 1953 Dandridge played for Oakland (PCL), but hurt his arm and was released. When his arm recovered, he played in 1955 with Bismarck, ND, and then retired. He returned to Newark, where he tended bar and scouted for the Giants.

Considered by many the best third baseman never to make the major leagues, Dandridge regretted that he was not given the opportunity. "The only thing I ever wanted to do was hit in the major leagues . . . I just wanted to put my left foot in there. I just would have liked to have been up there for one day, even if it was only to get a cup of coffee."

BIBLIOGRAPHY: Robert W. Peterson, *Only the Ball Was White* (New York, 1970); Donn Rogosin, *Invisible Men: Life in Baseball's Negro Leagues* (New York, 1983); Jules Tygiel, *Baseball's Great Experiment: Jackie Robinson and His Legacy* (New York, 1983).

Robert L. Ruck

DARK, Alvin Ralph "Blackie," "Cap," "The Swamp Fox" (b. 7 January

1922, Comanche, OK), player and manager, was the third of four children of an itinerant oil rigger. He attended Louisiana State University in 1941 and 1942 and made both the 1942 and 1943 All-American football teams, the latter as a U.S. Marines ROTC student at Southwestern Louisiana Institute. Dark married Adrienne Vyra Managan in October, 1946, and had four children. In 1970 he married Jacolyn Rockwood and adopted her two children.

After World War II military service, Dark entered professional baseball in 1946 with the Boston Braves (NL) organization. In 1947 he played shortstop and batted .303 for Milwaukee (AA). The 1948 Baseball Writers Association of America NL Rookie of the Year, Dark tied an NL record with a 23-game hitting streak for the Braves. Traded with roommate and keystone partner Eddie Stanky to the New York Giants (NL) in 1950, Dark the next year was named team captain by manager Leo Durocher* and led the NL with 41 doubles. Dark made three All-Star teams, was voted *The Sporting News* All-Star shortstop in 1954, and played in three World Series. Besides batting a solid combined .415 in the 1951 and 1954 series, he tied a record for the most singles (7) in a four-game series (1954). His popularity as a player peaked with the Giants' victory over the Cleveland Indians in 1954. Dark rode in the lead car of the tickertape parade through Manhattan with Willie Mays,* who credited him as one of the greatest influences in his career. Dark's most memorable day came on October 3, 1951, when he led off the ninth inning and scored the first run in the playoff game rally against the Brooklyn Dodgers. The classic game ended with Bobby Thomson's famed "shot heard 'round the world." As a manager Dark utilized innovative strategy, including having a new relief pitcher intentionally walk the first batter faced and having pitchers take batting practice instead of shagging flies in the outfield. Dark played with the St. Louis Cardinals (1956–1958), Chicago Cubs (1958–1959), and Philadelphia Phillies and Milwaukee Braves (1960) of the NL, compiling a .289 career batting average. In 1,828 games, he made 2,089 hits, 358 doubles, 126 home runs, 1,064 runs scored, and 757 RBIs.

Nicknamed "Blackie" and "Cap" as a player, Dark was called "The Swamp Fox" as San Francisco Giants manager because of his southern Louisiana childhood and his tactic of watering down the dirt area around first base to slow down Maury Wills* and other NL base stealers. Dark piloted the Giants from 1961 to 1964, capturing the 1962 NL pennant. He managed the Kansas City Athletics (AL) in 1966 and 1967 after a year's absence from baseball because of alleged racial remarks. From 1968 to 1971, Dark piloted the

Cleveland Indians (AL) and assumed many of general manager Gabe Paul's* functions. An arrogant, stormy player and manager, Dark joined Charley Finley's* Oakland Athletics (AL) as pilot in 1974 as a softspoken "reborn Christian." Players, whom he characterized as an "incredibly talented bunch of backbiters," constantly chastised him for his apparent lack of aggressiveness. Nonetheless, he guided the A's to the 1974 and 1975 World Series, becoming only the third mentor to manage AL and NL teams to the fall classic. His managerial career ended in 1977 after one season leading the San Diego Padres (NL) because of "irreconcilable differences" with team owner Ray Kroc. As a manager thirteen seasons, Dark compiled a 994–954 mark (.510). His autobiography, *When in Doubt, Fire the Manager* (written with John Underwood), was published in 1980.

BIBLIOGRAPHY: Anthony J. Connor, *Baseball for the Love of It* (New York, 1982); Alvin Dark and John Underwood, *When in Doubt, Fire the Manager* (New York, 1980); Glenn Dickey, *The History of American League Baseball* (New York, 1980); Glenn Dickey, *The History of National League Baseball* (New York, 1979); Charles Einstein, *Willie Mays* (New York, 1963); Charles Einstein, *Willie's Time* (New York, 1979); Joseph L. Reichler, ed., *The Baseball Encyclopedia*, 6th ed. (New York, 1985), pp. 623, 848; John Thorn, *The Relief Pitcher* (New York, 1979).

Alan R. Asnen

DAUBERT, Jacob Ellsworth, Jr., "Jake" (b. 14 May 1885, Shamokin, PA; d. 9 October 1924, Cincinnati, OH), player, came from the Pennsylvania anthracite region, where his father Jacob, Sr., and two brothers worked as coal miners. Daubert attended an elementary school in Shamokin before moving with his family to nearby Llewellyn, PA, around 1896. At age 11 he began working as a breaker boy, separating slate and other impurities from coal. As a teenager, Daubert followed his brothers into baseball by pitching for local teams. With the Lykens, PA semi-pro club, the 5 foot, 10 inch, 160 pound left-hander occasionally filled in at first base. He showed great ability there and eventually abandoned pitching altogether.

In 1907 Daubert entered professional baseball with Kane, PA (ISL), and Marion OH (OPL). The Cleveland Indians (AL) drafted Daubert the following year, but he failed to make the team. He was sent to Nashville (SA) and spent the next two seasons polishing his batting skills. After hitting .314 for Memphis (SA) in 1909, he was sold to the Brooklyn Dodgers (NL). As a rookie in 1910, Daubert won the first base job and remained there for Brooklyn until 1918. In his first major league season, Daubert batted .264, hit 15 triples, and displayed outstanding defense.

Beginning in 1911, Daubert became the NL's finest all-around first baseman, hit over .300 in each of the next six seasons, and played brilliantly on defense. In 1913 and 1914 he won consecutive batting championships with .350 and .329 averages, respectively. During this stretch, he led all first basemen in assists once (1915) and in fielding average twice (1912, 1916). In 1913 Daubert received the Chalmers Award as the NL's Most Valuable Player. Five years later, he paced the NL in triples (15).

Daubert played a key role in Brooklyn's first pennant-winning season in 1916, directing play defensively as team captain and performing with his accustomed reliability at first base. In the World Series, however, he hit only .176 as the Dodgers lost to the Boston Red Sox, four games to one.

A salary dispute with Dodgers' owner Charles Ebbets* led to Daubert's trade to the Cincinnati Reds (NL) in March, 1919. Appointed captain of his new team, he helped the Reds capture their first pennant and defeat the Chicago White Sox in the World Series that fall. In 1922 the 37-year-old veteran enjoyed an outstanding season and attained personal highs in nearly every offensive and defensive category. In 156 games for Cincinnati, Daubert made 205 hits, scored 114 runs, hit 12 home runs, and batted .336. Besides hitting a league-leading 22 triples, he also paced the NL in putouts and double plays and tied for the lead in fielding average. Late in the 1924 season, Daubert became ill and was ordered back to his Schuylkill Haven, PA home to rest. Within the next month, he died from complications following an appendectomy.

Daubert, a regular his entire fifteen-year major league career, batted .303 with 2,326 hits in 2,014 games. Daubert compiled 250 doubles, 165 triples 56 home runs, 1,117 runs scored, 722 RBIs, and 251 stolen bases. He surpassed the .300 mark ten times and set the NL career record for sacrifice hits with 392. His four sacrifice hits in one 1914 game remain a major league record.

Daubert, who married Gertrude Viola Acaley in September, 1903, and had a son and a daughter, owned and operated a coal and ice business in Schuylkill Haven in the off-season. A talent for business and leadership led to his election as a vice-president of the Baseball Players' Fraternity, an early successful players' union. Daubert displayed consistency at bat and in the field, earning the respect of teammates and opponents alike. Considered by many the equal of the more colorful Hal Chase* at first base, the well-spoken, modest Daubert ranked among the most popular players of his time.

BIBLIOGRAPHY: Jake Daubert file, National Baseball Hall of Fame Library, Cooperstown, NY; Frank Graham, *The Brooklyn Dodgers: An Informal History* (New York, 1945); Gene Karst and Martin J. Jones, Jr., *Who's Who in Professional Baseball* (New Rochelle, NY, 1973); F. C. Lane, "Jake Daubert—A Self-Made Success," *Baseball Magazine* 12 (February, 1914), pp. 33–48; *New York World*, October 10, 1924; *NYT*, October 11, 1924.

                                                                              Joseph Lawler

DAUSS, George August "Hooks," "Hookie" (b. 22 September 1889, Indianapolis, IN; d. 27 July 1963, St. Louis, MO), player, was one of three sons of machinist John and Annie Dauss. He attended a local elementary school and spent one year at Manual Training High School in Indianapolis.

On May 29, 1915, he married Olie M. Speake. He joined South Bend, IN(CL), in 1909, but his manager thought him undersized and never pitched him in an official game. After shutting out Duluth (MWL) in an exhibition game, however, he was promptly signed by that club. He advanced to St. Paul (AA) in 1911 and was acquired by the Detroit Tigers (AL) late in 1912.

Dauss became one of six Tigers to spend their entire major league career with Detroit, the largest contingent of one-team players in either circuit. In fifteen seasons, he won 221 games and lost 183 to pace all pitchers in Tigers history. The club's mediocre record, however, obscured his impressive performance. Detroit won no pennants and finished better than fourth in only five of his years. Nonetheless, he achieved ten winning seasons and scored more than 15 victories seven times. His best pitching years were 1915 (24 wins) and 1919 and 1923 (21 each). His career ERA was 3.32, while his .547 winning percentage exceeded the Tigers' team record of .514.

A stocky right-hander, Dauss threw a serviceable fastball. He was nicknamed "Hooks" or "Hookie" because of a tantalizing curve ranking among the AL's best. He combined good control with a placid, friendly nature, leading some to believe he lacked aggressiveness on the mound. He led the AL in hit batsmen in 1914 (19), 1916 (16), and 1921 (15), however, and ranks tenth highest on the lifetime list with 121. A capable fielder, he made 1,128 assists to place thirteenth among pitchers. After a heart condition forced his retirement in 1927, he operated a farm in Missouri and worked for Pinkerton's National Detective Agency in St. Louis.

BIBLIOGRAPHY: George Dauss file, National Baseball Hall of Fame Library, Cooperstown, NY; Detroit *Free Press*, March 29, 1924; Ted DiTullio, "The One-Team Players," *Baseball Research Journal* 7 (1978), pp. 33–35; Raymond Gonzalez, "Pitchers Giving Up Home Runs," *Baseball Research Journal* 10 (1981), pp. 24–25; Alex J. Haas, "Batters Hit by Pitchers," *Baseball Historical Review* (1981), pp. 84–86; Indianapolis *News*, July 28, 1963; Indianapolis *Star*, July 27, 1963; Gene Karst and Martin L. Jones, *Who's Who in Professional Baseball* (New Rochelle, NY, 1973); Frederick G. Lieb, *The Detroit Tigers* (New York, 1946); Joseph L. Reichler, ed., *Baseball Encyclopedia*, 6th ed. (New York, 1985), p. 1674.

A. D. Suehsdorf

DAVIS, George Stacey (b. 23 August 1870, Cohoes, NY; d. 17 October 1940, Philadelphia, PA), player, manager, and scout, was the son of Wales native Abram Davis and English-born Sarah (Healy) Davis. He began his baseball career in 1889 with an Albany, NY, independent minor league team. He joined Cleveland (NL) in 1890 as an infielder and outfielder. In 1893 he was traded to New York (NL) and played shortstop for the Giants through the 1901 season. Davis managed the Giants in 1895 and 1900–1901, producing 108 wins and 139 losses (.437). In 1902 Davis jumped to the Chicago White Stockings (AL) and then returned to the Giants in 1903, violating the recent "peace treaty" between the two leagues. AL president Ban Johnson* and

Chicago owner Charles Comiskey* obtained a court injunction (defeating Davis' attorney John Montgomery Ward*) that kept Davis out of all but four games in 1903 and forced him to return to Chicago in 1904. With Chicago through 1909, he helped the White Stockings' "hitless wonders" win the 1906 World Series by batting .308 in three games. He served as player-manager of Des Moines (WL) in 1910 and then retired.

The 5 foot, 9 inch, 180 pound right-hander proved a stylish-fielding short-stop and a dangerous, intelligent switch-hitter, batting .297 in 2,377 games. His 2,688 hits included 454 doubles, 166 triples, and 73 home runs. He also stole 615 bases, scored 1,544 runs, drove in 1,435 tallies, and led the NL with 134 RBI's in 1897. He made six hits in six times at bat on August 15, 1895, slugged three triples in an April 23, 1894, contest, and hit two doubles, one triple, and one home run on May 18, 1906. Davis scouted for the New York Yankees (AL) in 1915 and for the St. Louis Browns (AL) in 1917, but little is known of his post-baseball career. He evidently sold automobiles for a time, and he married Jane Holden Davis. A steady, solid performer on the field and, briefly, an object of controversy off it, Davis both enjoyed the benefits of his sport's popularity and was frustrated by its economic consolidation.

BIBLIOGRAPHY: Lee Lowenfish, "The Later Years of John M. Ward," *The National Pastime* 2 (Fall, 1982), pp. 66–69; Joseph L. Reichler, ed., *The Baseball Encyclopedia*, 6th ed. (New York, 1985), pp. 851–852.

Luther W. Spoehr

DAVIS, Herman Thomas "Tommy" (b. 21 March 1939, Brooklyn, NY), player, grew up in Brooklyn, graduated in 1956 from Boys High, and lettered in baseball, basketball, and track there. During his senior year, he captained the basketball team, was selected for the All-City basketball team, and was chosen as the school's best athlete. After signing his first professional baseball contract with the Brooklyn Dodgers (NL), Davis hit .325 in 43 games as an outfielder for Hornell, NY (Pol), in 1956. During the next three minor league seasons, he hit above .300 and played first, second, and third base and the outfield. His minor league assignments included Kokomo, IN (ML), in 1957 and Victoria, TX (TL), and Montreal (IL) in 1958. In 1957 with Kokomo, he led the ML in batting average (.357), at bats (518), runs scored (115), and hits (185). At Spokane, WA, in 1959, he led PCL in batting average (.345), hits (211), at bats (612), and games played (153).

Davis hit .276 in his first full season with the Los Angeles Dodgers (NL) in 1960. With the Dodgers, the 6 foot, 2 inch, 200 pound right-hander played mainly as an outfielder and occasionally at third and first base. He led the NL in 1962 with a .346 batting average, 153 RBIs, and 230 hits, and also belted 27 home runs and scored 120 runs. In 1963 he again paced the NL with a .326 batting average to help the Dodgers win the NL pennant and batted .400 in the World Series sweep of the New York Yankees. Davis tied World Series records for most triples in a game and four-game series (2), most putouts by an outfielder in an inning (3), and most putouts by a left fielder in a game (6). He broke an ankle sliding into second base on May 1, 1965, and never regained his former speed. In 1966 he batted .313 to help the Dodgers capture another NL pennant and hit .250 in the World Series sweep by Baltimore.

Davis tied a major league record for most clubs belonged to (10). From 1967 to 1976, his clubs included the New York Mets (NL) in 1967, Chicago White Sox (AL) in 1968, Seattle Pilots (AL) from October 15, 1968, to August 31, 1969, Houston Astros (NL) from August 31, 1969, to June 22, 1970, Oakland Athletics (AL) from June 22 to September 16, 1970, and March 29, 1971, to July 6, 1972, Chicago Cubs (NL) from September 16 to December 22, 1970, and July 6 to August 18, 1972, Baltimore Orioles (AL) from August 18, 1972 to June 2, 1976, California Angels (AL) from June 2 to September 20, 1976, and Kansas City Royals (AL) for the remainder of the 1976 season. At Baltimore, Davis became the prototype of the designated hitter and set the standard for offensive output with his .289 batting average. His eighteen-year major league career produced a .294 batting average, 2,121 hits, 1,052 RBIs, 811 runs scored, 272 doubles, 153 home runs, and 136 stolen bases. Davis married Shirley Johnson on February 6, 1957, and has four children Lauren, Leslie, Carlyn, and Herman Thomas III.

BIBLIOGRAPHY: Bob Cottrol, "T. Davis, dh, Alive and Loved in Baltimore," *Black Sports* 4 (August, 1974), pp. 26–27, 54–55, 98; Tommy Davis file, National Baseball Hall of Fame Library, Cooperstown, NY; Paul MacFarlane, ed., *TSN Daguerreotypes of Great Stars of Baseball* (St. Louis, 1981); David S. Neft and Richard M. Cohen, *The Sports Encyclopedia: Baseball*, 6th ed. (New York, 1985); Joseph L. Reichler, ed., *The Baseball Encyclopedia*, 6th ed. (New York, 1985); p. 854; *TSN Official Baseball Record Book, 1985* (St. Louis, 1985).

Robert J. Brown

DAVIS, William Henry "Willie" (b. 15 April 1940, Mineral Springs, AR), player, moved to Los Angeles as a youth. An outstanding athlete at Theodore Roosevelt High School, he was selected All-City in baseball, basketball, and track. Davis, whose 25 foot, 5 inch broad jump established an All-City track record, batted right-handed and pitched for the school baseball team. After graduating in 1958, he signed with the Los Angeles Dodgers (NL). To make the greatest use of Davis' speed, Dodgers scout Kenny Myers converted him to an outfielder and left-handed batter. He began the 1959 season by playing seven games with Green Bay, WI (3IL), and then was assigned to Reno, NV (CaL), where he won the batting title with a .365 average and led the league in runs scored (135), hits (187), doubles (40), triples (16), and outfield putouts (302). These accomplishments earned Davis selection to the All-Star team and Rookie of the Year and Most Valuable Player honors. At Spokane, WA, in 1960, Davis won the PCL batting championship with a .346 average and paced the PCL in runs scored (126), hits (216), triples (26), and stolen bases (30). In 1960 Davis was named to the PCL and Class AAA All-Star teams and selected as *The Sporting News* Minor League Player of the Year.

Davis joined the Los Angeles Dodgers in late 1960, batting a career-high .318. He played his first full season with the Dodgers in 1961 and remained there until traded to the Montreal Expos (NL) in December 1973. The Texas Rangers (AL) acquired him in a December 1974 trade. He was sent in June 1975 to the St. Louis Cardinals (NL) and swapped to the San Diego Padres (NL) that October. After spending the 1976 season with the Padres, Davis played Japanese baseball for two years. He returned to the United States and played his final major league season with the California Angels (AL) in 1979.

Considered among baseball's fastest players, the 5 foot, 11 inch, 180 pound center fielder covered a wide area with his speed while making great defensive plays. Nevertheless, he led NL outfielders in errors (15) in 1962 and tied for most miscues (12) in 1974. During the 1966 World Series against the Baltimore Orioles, he made three errors in the fifth inning of game two. This established records for most errors by an outfielder in an inning and a game. Davis led NL outfielders in putouts with 400 in 1964 and 404 in 1971 and won Gold Glove awards in 1972 and 1973. His daring base running made him a constant threat to steal or take extra bases. Davis hit inside-the-park home runs four times and stole a career-high 42 bases in 1964. During the 1965 World Series against the Minnesota Twins, he tied Honus Wagner's* fall classic record by stealing three bases in one game. Davis also appeared in the 1963 World Series against the New York Yankees, but only compiled a .167 composite batting average in three fall classics.

As a batter, Davis established a Dodgers record by hitting in 31 consecutive games in 1969 and surpassed .300 averages from 1969 through 1971. Davis, who led the NL in triples in 1962 (10) and 1970 (16), was elected to the NL All-Star team in 1971 and 1973 and chosen as an outfielder on *The Sporting News* 1971 All-Star team. Dodgers manager Walter Alston* selected Davis as club captain in 1973. His major league career produced a .279 batting average, 2,561 hits, 1,053 RBIs, 1,217 runs scored, 395 doubles, 138 triples, 182 home runs, and 398 stolen bases.

BIBLIOGRAPHY: Willie Davis file, National Baseball Hall of Fame Library, Cooperstown, NY; *Los Angeles Dodgers 1985 Media Guide*; *Los Angeles Dodgers Yearbook, 1962*; Rich Marazzi and Len Fiorito, *Aaron to Zipfel* (New York, 1985); Joseph L. Reichler, ed., *Baseball Encyclopedia*, 6th ed. (New York, 1985), pp. 854–855; Joseph L. Reichler, ed., *The Baseball Trade Register* (New York, 1984); Gene Schoor, *The Complete Dodgers Record Book* (New York, 1984); *TSN Official World Series Records,1985* (St. Louis, 1985); Richard Wittingham, *The Los Angeles Dodgers: An Illustrated History* (New York, 1982).

Robert J. Brown

DAWSON, Andre Fernando "Hawk" (b. 7 or 10 July 1954, Miami FL), player, grew up and resides in Miami. The 6 foot, 3 inch, 190 pound Dawson played baseball at Southwest Miami High School and three years at Florida A&M University. The nephew of Theodore Taylor, an outfielder in the Pittsburgh Pirates organization from 1967 to 1969, he married Vanessa Turner on December 16, 1978.

The Montreal Expos (NL) selected Dawson, a center fielder, as the 251st player chosen in the 1975 free agent draft. Dawson played only 186 minor league games before joining the Expos. In 1975 he played 72 games at Lethbridge, Alberta (PrL), hitting .330 with 13 home runs and 50 RBIs. Dawson started the 1976 season with Quebec City (EL), batting .357 in 40 games, and was promoted to Denver (AA). In his first month at Denver, Dawson hit 14 home runs with 28 RBIs and finished the season with a .350 batting average. After the playoffs, the Expos purchased his contract.

Dawson started slowly in the majors. During the remainder of the 1976 season, he hit only .235 in 24 games. Dawson began the 1977 season as part-time outfielder and struggled at the plate until June, when manager Dick Williams* made him the permanent center fielder. Dawson then batted .282, knocked in 65 runs, stole 21 bases, and won the NL Rookie of the Year Award.

Since his rookie season, Dawson has developed into an All-Star center fielder and won Gold Glove awards from 1980 through 1983. He twice (1981 and 1983) finished runner-up in the voting for NL Most Valuable Player and was named *The Sporting News* NL Player of the Year in 1981. Major league players voted Dawson the best all-around player in a *New York Times* 1983 poll. Dawson deserves these plaudits. On July 30, 1978, he hit two homers in the third inning to tie a major league record. In 1978 and 1979 Dawson batted only .253 and .275, with 25 home runs each year. From 1980 to 1983, he hit .302 and averaged 24 home runs, 87 RBIs, and 31 stolen bases. During the same period, "Hawk" averaged 398 putouts and under 8 errors per season. He led the NL in both putouts and chances from 1981 through 1983. Since Dawson has experienced corrective surgery on both knees, recurring problems may limit his stellar career. In a disappointing 1984 season, he batted .248, hit 17 home runs, and compiled 86 RBIs. Dawson belted 3 homers, including 2 in a 12-run fifth inning, and tied a club record with 8 RBIs to help the Expos defeat the Chicago Cubs 17–15 on September 24, 1985. No other major leaguer has slugged 2 homers in the same inning twice. His 23 homers in 1985 included 7 in a five-game stretch in late September. His career through 1985 included a .279 batting average, 1,434 hits, 263 doubles, 65 triples, 205 home runs, and 760 RBIs.

BIBLIOGRAPHY: "Andre Dawson: Baseball's First 40–40 Man," *Sport* 73 (April, 1982), p. 49; *Montreal Expos Press Guide 1984*; *NYT*, July 4, 1983; *TSN Baseball Register 1985* (St. Louis, 1985).

                                                                      Eric C. Schneider

DAY, Leon (b. 30 October 1916, Alexandria, VA), player, performed as an infielder, outfielder, and right-handed pitcher in the Negro and minor leagues. The son of glass factory gas producer Ellis and Hattie (Lee) Day, he grew up in Baltimore's Mount Winan's district. He quit school in the tenth grade and participated in sandlot baseball with the local athletic club. In 1934 Day played second base for the semi-pro Silver Moons and switched to the Baltimore Black Sox (NNL) in midseason. The diminutive 5 foot, 7 inch, 145 pound Day jumped in 1935 to the Brooklyn Eagles (NNL), where manager "Candy Jim" Taylor converted him to a pitcher. He pitched in his first Negro East-West All-Star Game in Chicago, striking out three batters. In 1937 he moved with the Eagles to Newark. The soft-spoken Day played with Newark (NNL) from 1937 through 1946, but missed the 1938 season due to a monetary dispute and the 1944 and 1945 seasons because of U.S. Army service. Day married Helene Johnson on July 17, 1939; they had no children. Using a no-windup delivery, Day possessed a sharp curve and a good fastball and frequently struck out batters. He whiffed five of seven batters he faced and was credited with the win in the 1942 East-West All-Star Game. In seven All-Star games, he struck out a record 14 hitters. On opening day in 1946, Day hurled a no-hitter against the Philadelphia Stars. In 1946 he led the NNL in strikeouts, compiled a 9–4 record, and pitched in two Negro World Series games against the Kansas City Monarchs.

Day performed well in the winter leagues. An excellent hitter, he played in Puerto Rico in 1935–1936, 1940–1941, and 1941–1942 and hit .307, .330, and an NNL-leading .351 those three years. In Cuba in 1937–1938 he won seven and lost three. After the 1943 season, Day entered the U.S. Army and participated in the Normandy landings. He played baseball in the service, twice defeating Ewell "The Whip" Blackwell of the Cincinnati Reds (NL) in 1945.

Day played with the Mexico City Reds in 1947 and 1948 and briefly in the CUL in 1947–1948. He returned to the NNL in 1949, helping the Baltimore Elite Giants win the pennant. In 1950 and 1951, he played semi-pro ball with the Winnipeg Buffalos. Entering organized baseball, he played 14 games with Toronto (IL) in 1951. With Scranton (EL) the following season, he compiled a 13–9 record, batted .314, and led pitchers in fielding. He completed his career by playing semi-pro ball with Edmonton, Winnipeg, and Brandon, Manitoba, from 1953 to 1955.

Day later worked for the Tragfer Bakery Company, Revere Brass and Cooper, and Liberty Security Company as a security guard. In Newark, he was employed with Conmar Zipper Company, as a substitute mail carrier, and as a bartender at former Negro leaguer Len Pearson's lounge. After his first wife died, Day married his present wife, Geraldine, in November, 1980. A great pitcher and second baseman, the quiet gentleman helped pioneer the integration of minor league baseball. Considered the equal of Leroy "Satchel" Paige* by National Baseball Hall of Famer Monford Irvin,* Day exhibited skills establishing the excellence of Negro league play.

BIBLIOGRAPHY: Terry A. Baxter, correspondence with L. Robert Davids, 1984, Terry A. Baxter Collection, Lee's Summit, MO; Terry A. Baxter, correspondence with Leon Day, 1984, Terry A. Baxter Collection, Lee's Summit, MO; Terry A. Baxter, correspondence with Jorge Figueroda, 1984, Cuban League Statistics, Terry A. Baxter Collection, Lee's Summit, MO; Terry A. Baxter, correspondence with Cliff Kachline, 1984, Terry A. Baxter Collection, Lee's Summit, MO; Terry A. Baxter, telephone interview with Monte Irvin, 1984; John Holway, "One Day at a Time," *Baseball Research Journal* 12 (1983), pp. 137–143; Robert W. Peterson, *Only the Ball Was White* (Englewood Cliffs, NJ, 1970); James A. Riley, *The All-Time Stars of Black Baseball* (Cocoa, FL, 1983); Donn Rogosin, *Invisible Men: Life in Baseball's Negro Leagues* (New York, 1983); Jules Tygiel, *Baseball's Great Experiment: Jackie Robinson and His Legacy* (New York, 1983).

Terry A. Baxter

DEAN, Jay Hanna "Dizzy" (b. 16 January 1911, Lucas, AR; d. 17 July 1974, Reno, NV), player and broadcaster, was the son of itinerant farm workers Albert and Alma (Nelson) Dean and the younger brother of major league pitcher Paul. Dean, who attended public school only through the second grade, married Patricia Nash on June 6, 1931. They had no children. One of sport's most colorful personalities, Dean was nicknamed "Dizzy" because of his eccentric behavior. Dean began his professional career in 1930 with St. Joseph, MO (WL), where he won 17 and lost 8. The same year he won 8 of 10 decisions with Houston (TL) and pitched a three-hit, full game victory for the St. Louis Cardinals (NL). His strengths included a high, hard pitch, a fast curve (which he called his "crooky"), and control. After posting a 26–10 record and striking out 303 in 304 innings at Houston in 1931, he joined the Cardinals in 1932. Dean became the staff mainstay until injured in the 1937 All-Star Game. After being hit on the toe by an Earl Averill* line drive, Dean aggravated his arm by returning to activity too soon and lost his pitching effectiveness.

From 1932 through 1936, Dean won 120 games and lost 65 and struck out 962 in 1,530 innings. During that span, he enjoyed spectacular 30–7 and 28–12 seasons and led the NL in strikeouts four times and in innings pitched three times. In 1937, the year of his critical injury, he won 13 of 23 decisions and compiled excellent statistics. From 1938 until his release in mid-May, 1941, however, Dean won only 16 games, lost 8, and struck out merely 68 in 226 innings. In 1947 he pitched four innings for the St. Louis Browns (AL) as a promotional stunt, surrendering only three hits and one walk and allowing no runs.

With a lifetime record of 150 wins and 83 losses, Dean compiled a 3.03 ERA, struck out 1,155, and walked only 458 batters in 1,966 1/3 innings. Dean won two games over the Detroit Tigers in the 1934 World Series and also appeared in the 1938 fall classic. In the Gashouse Gang's 1934 World Series, Dean bragged considerably, played a tuba, and squeezed the tail of an oversized toy tiger. In the final game, Dean pitched the Cardinals to an 11–0 rout. Dean struck out 17 Chicago Cubs in 1933, at the time an NL record. With Pepper Martin,* Dean played numerous practical jokes in dugouts and hotels around the circuit. He was elected to the National Baseball Hall of Fame in 1953.

As a radio and television announcer, Dean provoked controversy with his peculiar wording ("purply passed" and "slud"), repeated use of "ain't," and constant mispronunciation of players' names ("Scarn" for Skowron, "Slooter" for Slaughter*, "Stingle" for Stengel*). Despite all criticisms, Dean remained very popular with his audiences. From the 1940s to 1965, Dean's version of the "Wabash Cannonball" was heard on the airwaves of St. Louis Cardinals and New York Yankees Broadcasts and CBS and NBC Game of the Week telecasts.

BIBLIOGRAPHY: Allen Churchill, "Close-up of the Undizzy Mr. Dean," *NYT* (April 22, 1951), pp. 15ff; Ted Shane, "His Dizziness—Jerome Herman Dean," *Reader's Digest* 59 (August, 1951), pp. 98–103; Curt Smith, *America's Dizzy Dean* (St. Louis, 1978).

John E. DiMeglio

DELAHANTY, Edward James "Ed," "Big Ed" (b. 30 October 1867, Cleveland, OH; d. 2 July 1903, Niagara Falls, NY), player, joined Frank, James, Joseph, and Thomas to form the largest brother combination in major league baseball. In 1888 he started his major league career with Philadelphia (NL) and later starred there in one of the greatest outfields in baseball history. Between 1891 and 1895, Delahanty teamed with Billy Hamilton* and Sam Thompson* to form one of the few all National Baseball Hall of Fame outfields.

Although renowned as a hitter, Delahanty exhibited considerable speed and proved a fine fielder. The 6 foot, 1 inch, 170 pound Delahanty stole 456 bases under the liberal scoring rules that prevailed before 1900. His ability to steal 29 bases at age 33 under modern rules confirmed his speed and base running skills. The swift Delahanty hit 183 triples, for sixteenth place on the all-time list. Despite playing with the fleet Hamilton in the same outfield, Delahanty performed at center field in 1891 and 1892. Although not playing center field in 1896, Delahanty led NL outfielders in chances per game.

In his sixteen-year career, he compiled a .345 batting average to rank fourth best in major league history. Delahanty knocked in 1,464 runs and made 2,591 hits, including 521 doubles, 183 triples, and 100 home runs. He twice hit at least .400 for a season and led the NL with a .408 mark in 1899. When he paced the AL in hitting in 1902 with a .376 average, he became the first player to lead both modern major leagues in batting. Besides his two batting titles, Delahanty led his league in doubles and slugging percentage five times, RBIs three times, and hits, triples, and home runs once. Conscious of his value as a star, Delahanty jumped to Cleveland (PL) in 1890 and Washington (AL) in 1902 to gain pay increases. He died while still an active player by falling off a bridge at Niagara Falls and being swept over the falls. Delahanty was elected to the National Baseball Hall of Fame in 1945.

BIBLIOGRAPHY: Paul MacFarlane, ed., *TSN Hall of Fame Fact Book* (St Louis, 1983); Joseph L. Reichler, ed., *The Baseball Encyclopedia*, 6th ed. (New York, 1985), pp. 858–859.

                                                                    Gordon B. McKinney

DE MOSS, Elwood "Bingo" (b. 5 September 1889, Topeka, KS; d. 26 January 1965, Chicago, IL), player and manager, began his baseball career with the Topeka Giants. Although originally a shortstop, he switched to second base after pitching a game and injuring his throwing arm. By 1915 he was considered the best second baseman in black baseball—perhaps the best ever. Being an adept gloveman, he retained his preeminent position until the mid–1920s. His speed gave him unusually wide range afield. De Moss, whose impeccable defensive skills served as a model for later second basemen, excelled in all phases of baseball. He proved a fine spray hitter who hit line drives to right field and could pull the ball if the situation warranted. An excellent bunter and a skilled hit-and run artist, he almost always made contact at the plate as second-place hitter in the lineup and rarely struck out. His speed made him a threat on the basepaths, while his enthusiasm on the bench contributed as much to his team as his ability on the field. De Moss played for various teams but enjoyed his most productive years with C. I. Taylor's* Indianapolis ABCs and Rube Foster's* Chicago American Giants. His 1911 Indianapolis club captured the championship. As team captain, he helped the American Giants win four titles (1917, 1920–1922) and batted .303 in 1921. His hustle and team play were suited to Foster's aggressive managerial style. After his playing days ended in 1930, he managed in the Negro leagues through 1945, utilizing the skills he had learned from Taylor and Foster with the Detroit Stars, Cleveland Giants, and Chicago Brown Bombers.

BIBLIOGRAPHY: John Holway, *Voices from the Great Black Baseball Leagues* (New York, 1975); Robert W. Peterson, *Only the Ball Was White* (Englewood Cliffs, NJ, 1970); James A. Riley, *All-Time All-Stars of Black Baseball* (Cocoa, FL, 1983).

                                                                    Gerald E. Brennan

DERRINGER, Paul "Duke," "Oom Paul" (b. 17 October 1907, Springfield, KY), player, is the son of tobacco farmer and business man Samuel P. Derringer and caught for the Springfield High School baseball team. He volunteered to pitch in a game that his team was losing, struck out eight batters the final few innings, and was converted to a pitcher. Derringer's performance for the Coalwood, WV, mining baseball team in 1926 impressed St. Louis Cardinals (NL) scout Jack Ryan, who signed him. The 6 foot, 4 inch, 210 pound, right-handed Derringer pitched two seasons each at Danville, IL (3IL) and Rochester, NY (IL). Derringer won 25 games at Danville and 40 decisions at Rochester, leading the Red Wings to two pennants (1929–1930).

Derringer became a starting pitcher for the defending NL champion St. Louis Cardinals in 1931, compiling an 18–8 mark and becoming the first rookie to lead the NL in winning percentage (.692). After helping the Cardinals win the pennant, Derringer suffered two losses to the Philadelphia Athletics in the World Series. He was traded to Cincinnati (NL) for Leo Durocher* and hurled for the Reds from 1933 through 1942. Derringer captured 22 victories, the NL's third best, for a sixth place club in 1935. Although suspended briefly by manager Chuck Dressen in 1936 for failing to slide into home plate in a game with the New York Giants, Derringer still paced the NL in games started (37). From 1938 through 1940, Derringer won 21, 25, and 20 contests to enjoy the peak years of his career. In 1939 he lost only seven decisions and led the NL with a .781 winning percentage. Derringer paced the NL in complete games (26) in 1938, pitched one-hit games against the Cardinals and Chicago Cubs in 1940, and appeared on the NL All-Star team in 1935 and 1939 through 1941. In 1939 and 1940, he helped Cincinnati take consecutive NL pennants. Derringer lost a 2–1 heartbreaker in the first game of the 1939 World Series, but returned to win two games and lead the Reds to the world championship against the Detroit Tigers in 1940. In the seventh game, Derringer hurled a 2–1 complete-game victory. After being traded to the Cubs in 1943, Derringer won 16 games in 1945 to help Chicago capture the NL pennant in his last major league season. In 1946 he recorded 9 victories for Indianapolis (AA).

Derringer, whose three different major league clubs made World Series appearances, ranks second on the all-time Cincinnati club list with 171 victories and first with 150 losses. In his fifteen major league seasons, Derringer pitched in 579 games, struck out 1,507 batters, and walked 761 hitters. He ranks high on the all-time major league lists for pitchers in numerous statistical categories. Derringer compiled 223 victories (55th), 212 losses (24th), and 251 complete games, pitched 3,645 innings (46th), allowed 1,652 runs, captured 10 1–0 complete game victories (7th), and had a 3.46 lifetime ERA. These impressive accomplishments were made by a pitcher who had been told in 1927 by Boston manager Lee Fohl, "Kid, you'll never be a big league pitcher. Your curve ball isn't good enough."

Derringer married three times, including to Eloise Brownback on October 17, 1937, and Mary Jane Stein on September 3, 1944. Following his retirement from baseball, Derringer was employed as a salesman for a plastics company.

BIBLIOGRAPHY: Paul Derringer file, National Baseball Hall of Fame Library, Cooperstown, NY; Paul MacFarlane, ed., *TSN Daguerreotypes of Great Stars of Baseball* (St. Louis, 1971); Gene Karst and Martin J. Jones, Jr., *Who's Who in Professional Baseball* (New Rochelle, NY, 1973); *TSN*, May 7, 1936, September 26, 1940; *TSN Official Baseball Record Book, 1985* (St. Louis, 1985).

David S. Matz and John L. Evers

DICKEY, William Malcolm "Bill" (b. 6 June 1907, Bastrop, LA), player, coach, and manager, is one of the seven children of railroader John and Laura Dickey. The family moved to Little Rock, AR, which he made his primary home ever since. After attending grammar school in Kensett, AR, the Scotch-Irish youngster starred for Searcy High School and spent one year at Little Rock Junior College. After playing one year of semi-pro ball, Dickey signed his first professional contract in 1925 at age 17 and caught the next few seasons with minor league teams at Little Rock (SA), Muskogee, OK (WA), Jackson, MS (CSL), Minneapolis (AA), and Buffalo (IL). In 1932 he married Violet Ann Arnold; he has one daughter, Vicki.

Dickey was promoted to the New York Yankees (AL) at the end of 1928, became regular catcher the next year, and caught over 100 games for a record thirteen consecutive years. With powerful Yankees teams, the tall, slender (6 foot, 1 1/2 inch, 185 pound) backstop compiled a .313 lifetime batting average over seventeen seasons. One of the better clutch hitters, he batted over .300 eleven times, drove in at least 100 runs on four occasions, and slugged 202 career home runs. Dickey, who tied a major league record by slugging grand slam homers in two consecutive games in August, 1937, made *The Sporting News* Major League All-Star team in 1932–1933, 1936, 1938–1939, and 1941. The great left-handed hitting catcher's top batting mark (.362) came in 1936. The following season, he drove in 133 runs and belted 29 homers. In 1,789 career games, he compiled 1,969 hits, 343 doubles, and 1,209 RBIs. A fine defensive catcher and thrower, he proved a masterful handler of pitchers. During his tenure, the Yankees played in eight World Series and lost only to the St. Louis Cardinals in 1942. He also appeared in seven All-Star contests. Although not a fast runner, Dickey demonstrated extreme agility.

Along with Mickey Cochrane,* Gabby Hartnett,* Yogi Berra,* Roy Campanella,* and Johnny Bench,* Dickey ranks among the best catchers in major league history. Many experts place him first. The quiet-spoken gentleman took control of the game on the field. In a rare display of anger, he fractured the jaw of Washington outfielder Carl Reynolds following a play at the plate in 1932. A fine and a thirty-day suspension followed.

After spending 1944 and 1945 in the U.S. Navy, Dickey finished his playing career in 1946. During that year, he succeeded Joe McCarthy* as Yankee manager, compiled a 57–48 record (.543), and left the position in September. After managing at Little Rock (SA) in 1947, he returned to New

York as a coach under Casey Stengel.* He coached for the Yankees through 1957 and scouted for them in 1959. During this period, he imparted his baseball knowledge to great Yankee backstop Berra.

Dickey, a close friend of Lou Gehrig* on and off the field, was the first Yankee to learn of his fatal illness. He has remained an avid hunter, fisherman, and golfer and until 1972 was a successful investment salesman in Little Rock. Dickey was elected to the National Baseball Hall of Fame in 1954. His younger brother George Willard ("Skeets") Dickey caught six seasons for Boston and Chicago (AL).

BIBLIOGRAPHY: Martin Appel and Burt Goldblatt, *Baseball's Hall of Fame Gallery* (New York, 1977); Violet Arnold (Mrs. Bill Dickey), "I Married a Ballplayer," *SEP* 240 (May 28, 1949), pp. 34ff.; Bill Dickey, ed. by Harry T. Paxton, "World Series Fever: I've Had It," *SEP* 222 (Oct. 6, 1951), p. 31; Stanley Frank, "Iron Man in a Mask," *SEP* 211 (June 17, 1939), pp. 17ff.; Frank Graham, *Baseball Extra* (New York, 1954), pp. 151–166; Gene Karst and Martin J. Jones, Jr., *Who's Who in Professional Baseball* (New Rochelle, NY, 1973); *NYT*, 1928–1943, 1946, 1949–1957; Joseph L. Reichler, ed., *The Baseball Encyclopedia*, 6th rev. ed. (New York, 1985) p. 866; Ken Smith, "Bill Dickey," in Christy Walsh, ed., *Baseball's Greatest Lineup* (New York, 1952), pp. 133–145.

Frank P. Bowles

DIHIGO, Martin (b. 25 May 1905, Mantanzas, Cuba; d. 20 May 1971, Cienfuegos, Cuba), player and manager, was considered the most versatile Negro league performer. The 6 foot, 1 inch, 190 pound right-hander, who excelled as a batter and pitcher and at all defensive positions except catcher, played summers in the U.S. Negro leagues through 1936. In 1923 the youthful Dihigo made his initial American appearance as a second baseman, first baseman, and pitcher for the touring Cuban Stars. After performing with the Cuban Stars (ECL) through 1927, he played with the Homestead Grays in 1928, Hilldale (ANL) in 1929, Darby Daisies in the early 1930s, and New York Cubans (NNL) in 1935 and 1936.

The casual, popular, humorous Dihigo starred offensively in the U.S. Negro leagues, hitting .307 in 1925 and .331 in 1927 for the Cuban Stars. He paced the ECL in home runs in 1926 and shared the ECL lead in homers the next year (18). At Hilldale in 1929, he captured the ANL batting crown with a superlative .386 mark. Dihigo enjoyed his best American season in 1935, batting .372 and managing the New York Cubans to the second half NNL title. For the East squad in the 1935 All-Star Game, Dihigo started in center field, batted third in the lineup, and finished as the losing relief pitcher. The Cubans lost a seven-game playoff for the 1935 NNL title to the formidable Pittsburgh Crawfords. Defensively, Dihigo possessed an extremely powerful throwing arm, wide range, and considerable speed. According to Manager Cum Posey,* Dihigo's "gifts afield have not been approached by any man—black or white."

Right-handed Dihigo excelled mainly as a pitcher in Latin America. Throughout his career, Dihigo performed winters in the Cuban leagues. Besides enjoying outstanding 11–2, 14–10, 11–5, and 14–2 seasons, he compiled an impressive 115–60 lifetime CUL mark. Dihigo twice hit over .400 there, once making five hits in the final season game to edge teammates Willie Wells* for the batting title. Dihigo starred summers in the MEL from 1937 to the 1950s, recording an impressive 119–57 overall pitching slate. In 1938 he finished at 18–2 with a 0.90 ERA and led the MEL with a .387 batting average. His MEL statistics four years later included a 22–7 pitching mark, league leadership in strikeouts and ERA, and a .319 batting average. Dihigo hurled the first MEL no-hitter and also tossed no-hitters in Venezuela and Puerto Rico.

In 1945 Dihigo played one full season with the Homestead Grays (NNL) and helped them to first and second half U.S. NNL titles. The Cuban and Mexican Baseball Hall of Fame member served as Cuban Minister of Sports at the time of his death, and in 1977 became the first Cuban elected to the National Baseball Hall of Fame. New York Giants (NL) manager John McGraw* lauded Dihigo as the greatest natural baseball player he had ever seen, while Negro leaguer Walter Leonard* called him "the greatest all-around player" and "the best ball player of all time, black or white."

BIBLIOGRAPHY: Paul MacFarlane, ed., *TSN Hall of Fame Fact Book* (St. Louis, 1983); Robert W. Peterson, *Only the Ball Was White* (Englewood Cliffs, NJ, 1970); Lowell Reidenbaugh, *Cooperstown: Where Baseball's Legends Live Forever* (St. Louis, 1983); James A. Riley, *The All-Time All-Stars of Black Baseball* (Cocoa, FL, 1983).

David L. Porter

DIMAGGIO, Joseph Paul "Joe," "Joltin' Joe," "The Yankee Clipper" (b. DeMaggio, 25 November 1914, Martinez, CA), player, was the second youngest of nine children of fisherman Joseph and Rosalie (Mercurio) DiMaggio and the brother of major league center fielders Dominic and Vincent. A San Francisco sportswriter misspelled the original family name, DeMaggio, but the outstanding success of the trio of sons led the family to accept the new spelling. DiMaggio attended San Francisco public schools through the eleventh grade. He was married and divorced twice (Dorothy Arnold, 1939–1947; Marilyn Monroe, 1954), and had one son.

At age 17, DiMaggio played three games at shortstop for the San Francisco Seals (PCL). During the next three seasons, he played outfield for the same team and hit .340, .341, and .398. In 1933 he hit safely in 61 consecutive games for San Francisco. DiMaggio spent his entire major league career (1936 to 1951) with the New York Yankees (AL). As a rookie in 1936, he hit .323, slugged 29 home runs, tied for the AL lead in triples with 15, and paced the AL's outfielders with 22 assists. From 1943 through 1945, DiMaggio served in the military.

Noted as a class ballplayer with a powerful arm, DiMaggio gracefully covered center field in vast Yankee Stadium. Many baseball authorities regard DiMaggio as the all-time greatest center fielder. The large Yankee Stadium dimensions notably affected the pull hitter's lifetime statistics, but DiMaggio still ranked among the sport's best. At Yankee Stadium, DiMaggio hit .315 and slugged one home run in every 22.7 at bats. By contrast, he hit .333 and slugged one home run in every 16.2 at bats on the road. Before enlisting in the military, "the Yankee Clipper" averaged .339 at the plate and hit a home run every 18.2 at bats. In his post-military career, DiMaggio compiled a .304 career average and slugged a home run every 20 at bats. If World War II had not occurred, DiMaggio probably would have enjoyed a significantly better career. Numerous injuries and ailments, including a very painful heel bone spur, also shortened his career.

DiMaggio compiled a .325 career batting average, winning AL batting titles with .381 in 1939 and .352 in 1940. During his career, he also hit 361 home runs (including AL titles, with 46 in 1937 and 39 in 1948), and won two RBI crowns. His 2,214 lifetime hits included 881 for extra bases. In 1941 he set an all-time major league record by hitting safely in 56 consecutive games. Averaging .408 during this span, DiMaggio made 91 hits in 223 at bats.

The team's quiet leader and "Big Guy" for thirteen seasons, DiMaggio led the Yankees to ten AL pennants and eight world championships. Although unable to play the first two months of the 1949 season because of a disabling heel injury, DiMaggio in late June hit four home runs and made a game-saving catch to help the Yankees sweep the Boston Red Sox in a three-game series at Fenway Park. DiMaggio's effort helped the Yankees win the 1949 AL pennant by a single game over the Red Sox.

Besides being the AL's Most Valuable Player in 1939, 1941, and 1947, DiMaggio was selected as *The Sporting News* All-Star center fielder eight times, received the most votes at all positions from 1937 through 1941, and was named their 1939 Major League Player of the Year. Despite these achievements, DiMaggio was not elected to the National Baseball Hall of Fame until his second year of eligibility (1955).

DiMaggio hosted a post-game telecast his first year of retirement, served as spring training coach and executive vice-president for the AL Oakland Athletics (1968–1989), represented a major New York bank, partly owned DiMaggio's Restaurant at San Francisco's Fisherman's Wharf, and served on the board of directors of the AL Baltimore Orioles (1980). To a younger generation, DiMaggio's television appearances in commercials made him familiar as "Mr. Coffee."

BIBLIOGRAPHY: Maury Allen, *Where Have You Gone, Joe DiMaggio?* (New York, 1975); Dave Anderson, "The Longest Hitting Streak in History," *SI* 15 (July 17, 1961), pp. 36–38ff.; George DeGregorio, *Joe DiMaggio: An Informal Biography* (New York,

1981); Christopher Lehmann-Haupt, *Me and DiMaggio* (New York, 1986); Jack B. Moore, *Joe DiMaggio: A Bio-Bibliography* (Westport, CT, 1986); Al Silverman, *Joe DiMaggio: The Golden Year 1941* (Englewood Cliffs, NJ, 1969); James Stewart-Gordon, "Unforgettable Joe DiMaggio," *Reader's Digest* 109 (August, 1976), pp. 173–176ff.; Gay Talese, "Silent Season of a Hero," *Esquire* 66 (July, 1966), pp. 40–43.

John E. DiMeglio

DIXON, Herbert Albert "Rap" (b. 15 September 1903, Kingston, GA; d. 20 July 1944, Detroit, MI), player, performed as an outfielder for numerous Negro league teams and was the eldest of five children of steelworker John and Rose (Goodwin) Dixon. Young "Rap," whose nickname was derived from Virginia's Rappahannock River and denoted his southern origin, began his baseball career with the semi-pro Steelton, PA, Keystone Giants. After completing two years at Steelton High School, he turned professional in 1922 with the Harrisburg, PA, Giants (ECL). When the ECL dissolved and the Harrisburg team disbanded in 1928, Dixon joined the Baltimore Black Sox (ANL). The next season, he made fourteen straight hits in games against the powerful Homestead Grays and helped Baltimore become the ANL champions. In 1930, in the first game ever played by black teams at Yankee Stadium, Dixon hit three home runs into the right field stands.

After a stint with the Chicago American Giants (NNL) in 1931, he batted .343 and hit 15 home runs for the Pittsburgh Crawfords (1934) and played with the Philadelphia Stars (1933–1934). In the first Negro All-Star Game at Comiskey Park, Chicago, in 1933, Dixon played right field for the East team. Batting second, he made one hit, stole a base, scored twice, and made no errors afield. Dixon helped the Stars win the NNL championship in 1934 and then joined an elite group of black stars invited to play winter ball in the strong PuL. Dixon played the next season with the Brooklyn Eagles and ended his playing career in 1936 with the Homestead Grays. He also managed the Baltimore Black Sox. After retiring from baseball, he was employed at the Steelton plant of the Bethlehem Steel Company. He was married to Rose Yarbrough in 1932 and had no children.

Negro leaguers surviving from Dixon's time assess his skills consistently. A lean 6 footer who threw right-handed and batted left-handed, Dixon proved an intelligent hitter with good power and excelled with men on base in close games. He is credited with a .340 career batting average and hit .362 in 13 exhibitions against major league pitching between 1926 and 1931. A swift runner afield and on the bases, he possessed a strong, accurate throwing arm. One contemporary described him as having "a Clemente arm." Although fellow players considered him "temperamental," he ranks among the Negro leagues' legitimate candidates for the National Baseball Hall of Fame.

BIBLIOGRAPHY: Herbert Dixon file, National Baseball Hall of Fame Library, Cooperstown, NY, biographical material; John Holway, *Voices from the Great Black Baseball Leagues* (New York, 1975); Robert W. Peterson, *Only the Ball Was White* (Englewood

Cliffs, NJ, 1970); James A. Riley, *The All-Time All-Stars of Black Baseball* (Cocoa, FL, 1983); Donn Rogosin, *Invisible Men: Life in Baseball's Negro Leagues* (New York, 1983); Art Rust, Jr., *Get That Nigger off the Field!* (New York, 1976); A. D. Suehsdorf, telephone interview interviews with: Leon Day, May 10, 1984; Paul Dixon, October 4 & 5, and December 30, 1983; Monte Irvin, August 29, 1983; William "Judy" Johnson, September 21, 1983; Walter "Buck" Leonard, September 21, 1983; Ted Page, October 3, 1983; Norman C. "Tweed" Webb, December 18, 1983.

A. D. Suehsdorf

DOBY, Lawrence Eugene "Larry" (b. 13 December 1923, Camden, SC), player, coach, and manager, is the son of David and Etta Doby. His father, a semi-pro baseball player, died when Larry was eight years old. He and his mother then moved to Paterson, NJ, where she worked as a domestic. Doby, a four-sport letterman at Paterson East Side High School, entered Long Island University in 1940 on a basketball scholarship. He soon transferred to Virginia Union University in Richmond and left school in 1943, when drafted to join the U.S. Navy. Stationed at the Great Lakes Naval Training School, Doby became aware of racial discrimination because the base had segregated white and black baseball teams. Doby starred on the latter and was signed to a professional contract by the NNL Newark Eagles. He married Helen F. Curvey on August 10, 1946 and has one daughter, Christine Lynn, born in 1949.

In 1946 Doby helped lead the Newark Eagles to a Negro World Series championship and started in the East-West (Negro leagues) All-Star Game. The following year, he led the NNL in batting average and home runs when Bill Veeck* of the Cleveland Indians (AL) paid Newark $15,000 for him. Doby joined the Indians and on July 4, 1947, became the first black to play in the AL. An AL player through 1959, Doby hit well and possessed excellent power and speed. Under the tutelage of Hall of Famer Tris Speaker,* he became a premier center fielder and often climbed fences to catch balls.

Doby's 1950 performance earned him Cleveland Baseball Man of the Year honors and a position on the Baseball Writers Association of America All-Star team. In 1952 he became the first black to win a major league home run crown, pacing the AL with 32 homers and 104 runs scored. He topped the AL with 32 home runs and 126 RBIs in 1954. Doby played in six major league All-Star games from 1949 through 1954 and was selected as starting center fielder in 1950. He posted a .300 batting average in 10 at bats and slugged a pinch-hit home run in the 1954 contest.

Doby, a member of the Indians 1948 world championship and 1954 AL championship teams, played there through 1955 and rejoined them for the 1958 season. He spent 1956 and 1957 with the Chicago White Sox (AL) and split the 1959 season between them and the Detroit Tigers (AL). A lifetime .283 batter, he slugged 243 doubles and 253 home runs and drove in 969 runs. Doby played in 1960 with San Diego (PCL) and spent his final professional season in 1962 in Japan. Since 1969 he has served in various capacities with the Montreal Expos (NL), Cleveland Indians (AL), and Chicago White Sox (AL). He managed Chicago the last half of the 1978 season to 37 wins and 50 losses.

BIBLIOGRAPHY: Leon Hardwick and Effa Manley, *Negro Baseball* (Chicago, 1976); Paul MacFarlane, ed., *TSN Daguerreotyupes of Great Stars of Baseball* (St. Louis, 1981); Art Rust, Jr., *Get That Nigger off the Field!* (New York, 1976); *TSN Official Baseball Guide, 1979* (St. Louis, 1979); Jules Tygiel, *Baseball's Great Experiment* (New York, 1983); A. S. "Doc" Young, *Great Negro Baseball Stars* (New York, 1953).

Merl F. Kleinknecht

DOERR, Robert Pershing "Bobby" (b. 7 April 1918, Los Angeles, CA), player, coach, and scout, is the son of telephone company supervisor Harold and Frances (Herrnberger) Doerr. A 1935 graduate of Fremont High School in Los Angeles, he married Monica Terpin on October 24, 1938, and had one son. Doerr began his professional baseball career with Hollywood (PCL) in 1934 and 1935 and San Diego (PCL) in 1936. Doerr played second base for the Boston Red Sox (AL) from 1937 through 1951, except for military service in 1945, and served as team captain during the post–World War II period. A .980 career fielder, Doerr once held the AL record for consecutive chances without an error by a second baseman (414), led AL second basemen in double plays five times, fielding percentage six times, putouts four times, and assists three times, and set a World Series record for assists by a second baseman (31). Recent sophisticated performance measures (fielding effectiveness and leader index ratings) show Doerr as the best fielding second baseman of the 1940s.

A straightaway hitter upon joining the Red Sox, he was converted to a pull hitter by the Boston brass to take advantage of the Fenway Park wall. The new stroke paid dividends at Fenway, where Doerr compiled a .315 career batting average, with 145 home runs in 3,554 at bats. On the road, however, Doerr frequently hit many long flyouts and batted only .261 with 78 home runs in 3,539 trips. Notable performance contrasts included 1942 (.342 in Fenway, .243 away), 1944 (.351 home, .286 away), and 1950 (.344 home, .238 away). In thirteen full seasons, Doerr hit below .300 only three times in Boston, with one of those being .299, and above .300 only twice on the road. Doerr batted .288 during his career, with 2,042 hits, 381 doubles, 89 triples, 223 home runs, 1,094 runs scored, and 1,247 RBIs. In his lone World Series (1946), he batted .409 with 9 hits in 22 at bats against the St. Louis Cardinals.

A competitive, honest, quiet leader, Doerr twice made the only hits off Bob Feller* in one-hit games. He scouted for the Red Sox from 1957 to 1966 and coached with Boston from 1967 to 1969. The expansionist Toronto Blue Jays (AL) lured him out of retirement in 1977 to coach hitting, and he has been with them since. *The Sporting News* named him the AL's Most Valuable Player in 1944, while Boston fans voted him the all-time Red Sox second baseman in 1969. An avid outdoorsman and fisherman, Doerr chose Junction City, OR as his retirement site. In 1986 the Veterans Committee elected him to the National Baseball Hall of Fame.

BIBLIOGRAPHY: Ellery H. Clark, Jr., *Boston Red Sox: 75th Anniversary Edition* (Hicksville, NY, 1975); John DiMeglio, interviews and correspondence with Bobby Doerr, 1984, John DiMeglio Collection, Mankato, MN; Frederick G. Lieb, *The Boston Red Sox* (New York, 1947).

John E. DiMeglio

DONLIN, Michael Joseph "Mike," "Turkey Mike" (b. 30 May 1878, Peoria, IL; d. 24 September 1933, Hollywood, CA), player, manager, and scout, was the sixth child of railroad conductor John and Maggie (Cayton) Donlin. He attended elementary school in Erie, PA, and worked as a machinist before entering professional baseball with Los Angeles (CaL) in 1897. He married actress and vaudeville star Mabel Hite on April 10, 1906. After her death, he wed vaudevillian Rita Ross on October 20, 1914. Donlin had no children through either marriage.

Originally a wild-throwing minor league pitcher, the versatile Donlin became a star major league outfielder and occasionally played first base and shortstop. In his twelve checkered seasons with six teams, he played more than 100 games only five times. A broken ankle shelved him for most of the 1906 season. He sat out 1907 because New York Giants manager John McGraw* would not meet his salary demands, and spent 1909, 1910, and 1913 performing on the vaudeville circuit.

Yet for his 1,050 games, including 431 with the Giants, he ranked among the best. He led the NL in only one statistic (124 runs in 1905), but proved a strong, consistent left-handed batter. Donlin topped .300 in all but two seasons and compiled a .333 lifetime average. During his career, the 5 foot, 9 inch, 170 pound Donlin made 1,287 hits, 670 runs, 175 doubles, 98 triples, and 51 home runs, batted in 543 runs, and stole 213 bases.

"Turkey Mike" was a flamboyant personality on and off the field. A strutting walk earned him his nickname, while his pugnacity made him a particular favorite of McGraw during his five seasons in New York. "Oh, you Mabel's Mike!" Giants fans used to yell after a rollicking play. But aggression combined with hard drinking often got him into serious trouble. He was arrested several times and missed most of the 1902 season with Cincinnati (NL) after a six-month jail sentence for assault.

Donlin's close association with McGraw began in 1900. He had started his sophomore season with the St. Louis Cardinals (NL), who had acquired him from the Santa Cruz, CA Sandcrabs (CaL) when McGraw quit Baltimore's NL Orioles to be the Cards' third baseman. When McGraw agreed to manage the new AL Orioles in 1901, Donlin joined him in Baltimore. He hit .341 and batted six for six one day against Detroit before moving to Cincinnati (NL) in 1902. Two years later, McGraw, now piloting the Giants, bought him from the Reds for cash.

With immortal Christy Mathewson,* "Turkey Mike" became the most popular of the 1905 Giants by hitting .356 in 150 games and performing well in the famous five-shutout World Series. He played only one complete season (1908) thereafter. In 1911 the Giants sold the 33-year-old Donlin to Boston (NL). The Braves traded him to Pittsburgh (NL), for whom he played 77 games in 1912. He then ignored a waiver claim by the Philadelphia Phillies (NL) and returned to vaudeville (and 36 games for Jersey City of the IL) before finishing his career with the Giants as a utility player in 1914.

He briefly managed Memphis (SA) in 1917 and the following year scouted the Pacific Coast for the Boston Braves. Thereafter he concentrated on the stage and movies. Although never the actor he fancied himself, he received respectable reviews and numerous small parts in both silent films and talkies.

BIBLIOGRAPHY: Baltimore *Evening Sun*, April 12, 1962; Detroit *Free Press*, November 30, 1947; Christy Mathewson, *Pitching in a Pinch* (Briarcliff Manor, NY, 1977); Michael Donlin file, National Baseball Hall of Fame Library, Cooperstown, NY, biographical materials; New York *Sun*, September 25, 1933; *NYT*, September 25, 1933; "Post-Playing Careers," *Baseball Research Journal* 9 (1980), pp. 1–5; Joseph L. Reichler, ed., *The Baseball Encyclopedia*, 6th ed. (New York, 1985), p. 872; Harold Seymour, *Baseball: The Early Years* (New York, 1960); Harold Seymour, *Baseball: The Golden Years* (New York, 1971); *Sporting Life*, February 16, 1907; *TSN*, January 25, 1945.

                                                                    A. D. Suehsdorf

DONOVAN, Patrick Joseph "Patsy" (b. 16 March 1865, County Cork, Ireland; d. 25 December 1953, Lawrence, MA), player and manager, was the son of an immigrant and American Civil War veteran. His father, Gerald, had returned to Ireland to take a wife. At age three, "Patsy" was brought by his parents from Ireland to Massachussetts. Donovan played outfield for Lawrence-Salem (NEL) in 1886 and 1887, and London (IL) in 1888 and 1889. He began his major league career with the Boston Nationals (NL) in 1890 as an outfielder for manager Frank Selee,* but an injury cut his rookie year short. He enjoyed his best years with the NL Pittsburgh Pirates (1893–1899), hitting over .300 six times and learning the finer points of the game from his manager, Connie Mack* (1894–1896). Due to a disputed play at second base involving Donovan, Mack was ejected from a game for the only time in his career. A good outfielder, a speedy base runner, and a scrappy, intelligent player, Donovan in 1900 led the NL with 45 stolen bases as a St. Louis Cardinal. His career 518 stolen bases, 2,249 hits, 1,318 RBIs, and .300 batting average revealed his impressive combination of speed and power.

He managed the Pittsburgh Pirates (1897, 1899) and St. Louis Cardinals

(1901–1903). After a contractual dispute with St. Louis, the National Commission permitted Donovan in 1904 to become player-manager of the Washington Senators (AL). Legal questions forced him to miss spring training. Besides batting only .229, he managed a last place club. Although his playing career was virtually over, he continued to manage. Donovan managed the Brooklyn Dodgers (NL) to second division finishes from 1906 through 1908, but achieved a good record against the New York Giants. He became one of John McGraw's* most hated rivals and always saved his premier pitcher, Nap Rucker, for the Giants. Donovan ended his major league managing career with the Boston Red Sox (AL) in 1910 and 1911. He never managed a team above fourth place, but lacked good personnel and left Boston the year before it acquired the players making it the dominant AL team. As a minor league manager, he greatly influenced Hall of Famer Joe McCarthy.* McCarthy considered Donovan one of the nation's finest baseball minds. Despite his solid achievements as player and manager, Donovan was best remembered as the "discoverer" of Babe Ruth.* He scouted Ruth in Baltimore and recommended that the Red Sox purchase his contract. His minor league managerial assignments included Buffalo (IL) from 1915 through 1917, Syracuse (IL) in 1918, Newark (IL) in 1919, Jersey City (IL) in 1921 and from 1924 through 1926, Springfield, MA (EL) in 1923, Providence (EL) in 1927, and Attleboro, MA (NEL) in 1928.

BIBLIOGRAPHY: Malcolm Bingay, *Of Me I Sing* (New York, 1949); Detroit Baseball Club Letterbooks, vols. 3–4, Ernie Harwell Collection, Detroit Public Library; Detroit *News*, December 10, 1923; G. H. Fleming, *The Unforgettable Season* (New York, 1981); Frederick G. Lieb, *The Detroit Tigers* (New York, 1946); *TSN*, January 6, 1954.

Anthony J. Papalas

DONOVAN, William Edward "Wild Bill" (b. 13 October 1876, Lawrence, MA; d. 9 December 1923, Forsyth, NY), player and manager, was the younger brother of Patrick "Patsy" Donovan.* He grew up in Philadelphia and played his first baseball at Fairmount Park. Donovan began his major league career as a pitcher with the Washington Senators (NL) in 1898 and the following year joined the Brooklyn Dodgers (NL), winning 25 games in 1901. In 1903 he jumped to the Detroit Tigers (AL) and played there until 1912, becoming one of the city's most popular athletes. The large, handsome, good-natured Donovan packed Bennett Park to capacity every time he faced Rube Waddell.* When Detroit trained in Augusta, GA, in the spring of 1905, he admired a teenage oufielder playing for the Augusta Tourists and brought Tyrus Cobb* to the attention of Detroit manager William Armour.

Although easygoing, Donovan became one of the game's best scrappers. During spring training in 1907, he broke up a fight between Charlie Schmidt and Cobb and saved the "Georgia Peach" from serious injury. Donovan's most memorable achievement came in a 17-inning 9–9 game against the

Philadelphia Athletics at the end of the 1907 season. Donovan surrendered most of the runs in the first few innings, but then became nearly unhittable. In a late inning fracas, he knocked out Monte Cross with one punch. Donovan stayed in the game because the police mistakenly arrested Detroit first baseman Claude Rossman. At Windsor, Canada, across the Detroit River, Donovan met and married the beautiful daughter of a saloon keeper. The fashionable, graceful Mrs. Donovan was often photographed in the Detroit newspapers. Donovan, who lived beyond his means, constantly asked part-owner and general manager Frank Navin* for salary advances. A teetotaler, he mainly needed the money to keep his wife in the latest fashions. Donovan beat up and nearly killed a Detroit mobster, Bill Constantine, who pursued his wife. The Donovans' highly publicized stormy marriage ended in divorce without any children.

Donovan pitched well in the 1907, 1908, and 1909 World Series, but bad fortune and a weak infield prevented him from winning more than one game. In two 1907 World Series games against the Chicago Cubs, he struck out 16 batters. A passed ball by Charlie Schmidt in the ninth inning led to an unearned run and a 12-inning tie game. In the second game of the 1908 World Series against the Cubs, he pitched a shutout for seven innings. A questionable eighth-inning call by one umpire, however, led to a six-run outburst. Donovan allowed only two runs in game five, but the Cubs shut out Detroit. He won the second game of the 1909 World Series against the Pittsburgh Pirates, but the primarily warm weather pitcher lost the crucial seventh game on a cold day. Donovan, who experienced arm trouble the last five years of his career, achieved a 186–139 mark (.572) and a 2.69 ERA.

From 1915 to 1917 he managed the New York Yankees (AL) to losing records. Navin, an admirer who kept Donovan's picture on his office wall, sent promising first baseman Wally Pipp to help rescue Donovan's New York club. Donovan suffered the managerial fate of his brother Patsy, leaving a mediocre team on the verge of becoming a superpower. Donovan managed the Philadelphia Phillies (NL) to an eighth place finish in 1921, and also piloted Providence (IL) in 1913 and 1914, Jersey City, (IL) in 1919 and 1920, and New Haven, CT (EL) in 1922–1923. He died in an automobile-train crash near Forsyth, NY.

BIBLIOGRAPHY: Malcolm Bingay, *Of Me I Sing* (New York, 1949); Detroit Baseball Club Letterbooks, vols. 3–4, Ernie Harwell Collection, Detroit Public Library; Detroit *News*, December 10, 1923; G. H. Fleming, *The Unforgettable Season* (New York, 1981); Frederick G. Lieb, *The Detroit Tigers* (New York, 1946); TSN, January 6, 1954.

Anthony J. Papalas

DOYLE, Lawrence Joseph "Larry," "Laughing Larry" (b. 31 July 1886, Caseyville, IL; d. 1 March 1974, Saranac Lake, NY), player, starred for over twelve years for the New York Giants (NL) and captained the team. In 1911 he was named the NL's Most Valuable Player (Chalmers Award) and led the NL in triples with 25. His best hitting performance came in 1915, when he paced the NL in hits (189), singles (139), doubles (40), and batting average (.320). A lifetime .290 batter, he stole home 17 times, made 1,887 hits, scored 960 runs, knocked in 793 runs, and pilfered 297 bases.

After Doyle began his playing career with Mattoon, IL (KL), in 1906 and Springfield, IL (3IL), in 1907, the New York Giants purchased his contract that June. Nervously anticipating his first appearance at the Polo Grounds, he took the wrong ferry across the Hudson River and arrived late for the game. Although Doyle had played only third base, manager John McGraw* started him that day at second base. In a close game against the World Series champion Chicago Cubs, in the ninth inning Doyle misplayed a fielding chance that led to the winning run. A furious McGraw summoned Doyle to his office the next day. The infielder expected to be released, but McGraw instead delivered encouragement.

The scrappy Doyle calmed down, reassuming the personality that earned him the nickname "Laughing Larry," and helped the Giants win the 1911–1913 NL pennants. During 1911 Doyle commented, "It's great to be young and a Giant." In that World Series, Doyle scored the well-documented "phantom" run on a fall-away slide at home plate to win the fifth game and delay the Philadelphia Athletics' ultimate victory. After the game, umpire Bill Klem* stated that any appeal on the Athletics' part would have resulted in an out call as Doyle had never touched the plate. Doyle shared with Eddie Collins* the record for the most lifetime World Series errors (8). In late 1916 the Giants traded Doyle to the Chicago Cubs (NL). He played in Chicago through 1917, rejoined the Giants for the 1918 season, and retired from baseball in 1920.

BIBLIOGRAPHY: Gene Karst and Martin J. Jones, Jr., *Who's Who in Professional Baseball* (New Rochelle, NY , 1973); Frederick G. Lieb, *Baseball As I Have Known It* (New York, 1977); *NYT*, March 2, 1974; Joseph L. Reichler, ed., *The Baseball Encyclopedia*, 6th ed. (New York, 1985), p. 878.

Alan R. Asnen

DREYFUSS, Barney (b. 23 February 1865, Freiburg, Germany; d. 5 February 1932, New York, NY), executive, was one of at least three children of Samuel Dreyfuss, an American of German-Jewish extraction, and Fanny (Goldsmith) Dreyfuss. He was educated at the Karlsruhe Gymnasium in Germany and worked for a year in a Karlsruhe bank. In 1881 he moved to Paducah, KY, reportedly to avoid military conscription. Although initially employed as a laborer by the Bernheim Brothers distillery, he became a company official within six years. At Paducah Dreyfuss operated a semi-professional baseball team from 1884 through 1888. In 1888 he moved to Louisville with the Bernheim company and the next year purchased an interest in the Louisville Colonels (NL). After buying out his associates for a reported $50,000 in 1899, he merged his team the following year with the Pittsburgh Pirates and brought Honus Wagner,* Deacon Phillippe,* Fred Clarke,* and other stars with him. With the legal aid of associate Harry Pulliam,* he bought out William Kerr's interest in 1901 and became sole owner.

Dreyfuss' Pirates won NL pennants in 1901, 1902, 1903, 1909, 1925, and 1927 and world championships in 1909 and 1925. In Dreyfuss' thirty-two years as team owner, the Pirates finished in the second division only four times. In 1930 he put his son Samuel in charge of daily operations, but resumed his active role when the latter died in February, 1931. As owner, Dreyfuss was a "benevolent despot." He gave his share of the 1903 World Series receipts to his players, although Pittsburgh had lost to Boston. Dreyfuss remained generous with Wagner and other players providing faithful service, but treated sternly those who crossed him or failed to measure up to his puritanical standards. He reportedly did not acquire Tris Speaker* after seeing the latter smoking a cigarette. After moving the Pirates into new, modern Forbes Field in 1909, he refused to allow advertising on its fences.

Dreyfuss' baseball team remained his principal business, as he guided it successfully through wars with the AL and FL. A major force within organized baseball, he proved instrumental in setting up the World Series and abolishing the three-man commission that ruled baseball until the Chicago "Black Sox" scandal of 1919–1920. After 1902 he chaired the committee coordinating NL and AL schedules. Dreyfuss fought losing battles against the lively ball and the growing use of farm systems. He preferred to scout players personally in independent leagues, keeping detailed records in his famous "dope book." An archetype of the entrepreneurs dominating the game in the first third of the twentieth century, Dreyfuss helped make baseball the national pastime through the teams he fielded, the economic sagacity he displayed in the front office, and the high standards of integrity he helped the game to meet. Dreyfuss, who married Florence Wolf of Louisville on October 16, 1894, and had two children, never lost his German accent. Throughout his career, he was active in Pittsburgh's community affairs.

BIBLIOGRAPHY: Frederick G. Lieb, *The Pittsburgh Pirates* (New York, 1948); *National Cyclopaedia of American Biography* 30 (New York, 1943), pp. 271–272.

                                                                    Luther W. Spoehr

DRYSDALE, Donald Scott "Don," "Big D" (b. 23 July 1936, Van Nuys, CA), player and announcer, is the son of Scott and Verna (Ley) Drysdale. His father, a former minor league pitcher, coached him in American Legion baseball and refused to allow him to pitch until age 16. During his senior year, however, he won 10 of 11 pitching decisions for Van Nuys High School. The Brooklyn Dodgers (NL) signed the 6 foot, 5 inch, 210 pound right-hander to a $4,000 bonus and assigned him to Bakersfield, CA (CaL), in 1954 and Montreal (IL) in 1955.

Drysdale occasionally started for Brooklyn (NL) in 1956 and defeated the Philadelphia Phillies 6–1 in his first outing. The "Big D" moved with the club in 1958 to Los Angeles, where he experienced four frustrating years pitching in the makeshift Coliseum ballpark. In 1959, however, he registered an NL-leading 242 strikeouts, played in both All-Star games, and won Most Valuable Player honors in one. He topped the NL in strikeouts again in 1960 with 246. Through 1966 he teamed with left-hander Sandy Koufax,* forming one of baseball's most effective pitching combinations.

His finest season came in the new Dodger Stadium in 1962, when his 314 innings pitched, 25 wins, and 232 strikeouts led both leagues. Besides pitching in the All-Star Game, he won the Cy Young* Award and *The Sporting News* Major League Pitcher of the Year honor. Drysdale, who enjoyed another 20-plus season in 1965 with a 23–12 record, the next year won a one-year $155,000 contract—highest on the Dodgers. He performed in five World Series, pitching a three-hit shutout in 1963 to help the Dodgers sweep the New York Yankees in four games, and made nine All-Star teams. In May and June, 1968, he established major league records for most consecutive shutout games (6) and most shutout innings (58), erasing Walter Johnson's* 55-year-old record of 56. His five shutouts in May tied the NL record. A good hitter, the right-hander twice tied the NL record for home runs by a pitcher with 7 (1958 and 1965) and finished his career with 29 round trippers.

The extremely competitive Drysdale threw a sidearm pitch, described as "all spikes, elbows, and fingernails," that intimidated right-handed hitters and tended to knock batters down. Although always a gentleman off the field, he hit a major league record 154 batsmen in fourteen seasons. In 1962 he developed a half-way overhand motion, increasing his effectiveness against left-handed batters. He retired from the Dodgers in 1969 with a lifetime record of 3,432 1/3 innings pitched, 209 wins, 166 losses, 2,486 strikeouts, 49 shutouts, and a 2.95 ERA, and was inducted into the National Baseball Hall of Fame in 1984.

Drysdale directly entered sports broadcasting, announcing games for the Montreal Expos, Texas Rangers, California Angels, and Chicago White Sox. Since 1978 he has served as an ABC sports commentator. He married Ginger Dubberly in September, 1958, has one daughter, and lives in Rancho Mirage, CA.

BIBLIOGRAPHY: *CB* (1965), pp. 132–134; "Departure of Big D," *Time* (August 22, 1969), pp. 59–60; Huston Horn, "Ex-Bad Boy's Big Year," *SI* (20 August, 1962), pp. 24–29; Paul MacFarlane, ed., *TSN Daguerreotypes of Great Stars of Baseball* (St. Louis, 1981); Joseph L. Reichler, ed., *The Baseball Encyclopedia*, 6th ed. (New York, 1985) p. 1, 694; Lowell Reidenbaugh, "Five for the Hall," *TSN* (August 6, 1984), pp. 2–3, 24; Milton J. Shapiro, *The Don Drysdale Story* (New York, 1964); *WWA* 42nd ed., (1982–83), p. 880.

Gaymon L. Bennett

DUFFY, Hugh (b. 26 November 1866, River Point, RI; d. 19 October 1954, Allston, MA), player, manager, executive, and owner, married Nora Moore in October, 1895, and was inducted into the National Baseball Hall of Fame in 1945. In a sixty-eight-year career, longer than that of Connie Mack,* Duffy participated in every aspect of baseball. The last of twenty-nine players active in each of baseball's major leagues, Duffy became the only player batting at least .300 in all four. In 1894 he enjoyed one of the best offensive seasons in baseball history. Duffy led the NL in hits (236), doubles (50), home runs (18), RBIs (145), and slugging percentage (.679), and established the all-time single-season major league record with a superb .438 batting average. He ended a seventeen-year playing career in 1906 with a .328 lifetime batting average and 599 stolen bases. In 1,736 games, he made 2,314 hits, 324 doubles, 116 triples, 103 home runs, 1,553 runs, 1,299 RBIs, and a .450 slugging percentage.

Called by Fred Tenney* the "right-handed Mel Ott"* because of his similar batting stance, Duffy ranked as his era's premier hitter and led the major leagues in home runs in the 1890s with 80. As a youth, he worked in Connecticut and Rhode Island cloth factories and played with amateur baseball clubs on weekends. The short, rather stocky Duffy began his professional career as a catcher with Hartford, CT (EL), in 1886 and Springfield, MA (EL), in 1887. That same year he played outfield for Salem/Lowell, MA (NEL), and was scouted by Adrian "Cap" Anson's* Chicago White Stockings (NL). Although Duffy signed with Chicago in 1888, Anson benched him until July because of his 5 foot, 7 inch stature. The single-minded, sharp-tongued Duffy jumped to the PL in 1890 and started in right field for Charles Comiskey's* Chicago club. He batted a solid .326, stole 79 bases, and led the league in runs, total bases, and at bats. After the PL folded, Duffy joined the Boston Reds (AA) in 1891. This team, which included infielders Dan Brouthers* and Charles "Duke" Farrell and pitchers Charley Buffinton,* "Gentleman" George Haddock, and Clark Griffith,* ranks among the greatest all-time ball clubs.

When the AA disbanded, the NL absorbed four of its franchises and its better players. Duffy joined manager Frank Selee's* championship-bound Boston Beaneaters and experienced his eight most productive seasons there, despite his troublesome temper and tongue. Named team captain by Selee in 1896, he earned the wrath of teammates because of his strict discipline. Duffy, who rarely drank or swore and whose actual authority as captain was limited, was criticized by other players for his self-assumed leadership role, standoffish nature, and anti-player sentiments. The undaunted Duffy joined

Comiskey, Griffith, and Connie Mack* in forming the AL. Duffy scouted and helped purchase the site where Fenway Park was built and convinced Braves stars Jimmy Collins* and Chick Stahl to jump to the new Boston AL franchise. In 1901 he became Mack's player-manager with the Milwaukee Brewers (AL). After the Brewers folded and became the St. Louis Browns, Duffy managed Milwaukee (WL) in 1902 and 1903 and served as player-manager of the Philadelphia Phillies (NL) from 1904 to 1906.

Duffy managed and owned Providence, RI (EL), from 1907 to 1909 and piloted the Chicago White Sox (AL) in 1910 and 1911 and Milwaukee (AA) in 1912. In 1913 he became manager and president of Portland, ME (NEL). After spending four seasons there, he scouted for the Boston Braves (NL) from 1917 to 1919. He managed Toronto (IL) in 1920 and the Boston Red Sox (AL) in 1921 and 1922 and scouted for the latter from 1924 until his death. During the 1920s and 1930s, Duffy coached baseball at Harvard University and Boston College. As a major league manager for eight seasons, Duffy compiled a 535–671 mark (.444) and never finished higher than fourth place.

BIBLIOGRAPHY: Harold Kaese, *The Boston Braves* (New York, 1948); Gene Karst and Martin J. Jones, Jr., *Who's Who in Professional Baseball* (New Rochelle, NY, 1973); Frederick G. Lieb, *The Boston Red Sox* (New York, 1947); Paul MacFarlane, ed., *TSN Daguerreotypes of Great Stars of Baseball* (St. Louis, 1981); *NYT*, October 20, 1954; Joseph L. Reichler, ed., *The Baseball Encyclopedia*, 6th ed. (New York, 1985) pp. 625, 881; *Time*, 64 (November 1, 1954), p.87.

Alan R. Asnen

DUROCHER, Leo Ernest "The Lip" (b. 27 July 1905, West Springfield, MA), player, manager, coach, and announcer, is the son of railroad engineer George and Clara (Provost) Durocher, both of French descent. Durocher attended Main Street and Park Avenue Schools in West Springfield, but left high school to work as a mechanic for the Wico Electric Company, Gilbert and Barker, and the Boston and Albany Railroad and to play for a local semi-pro team. Durocher's professional career began as a shortstop with the New York Yankees (AL) organization at Hartford, CT (EL), in 1925, Atlanta (SA) in 1926, and St. Paul (AA) in 1927. Manager Miller Huggins* liked Durocher's heady play with the Yankees in 1928 and 1929, but the latter's antics and weak bat led to his departure when Huggins died.

The remainder of Durocher's seventeen-year major league career, mostly as a shortstop, came in the NL from 1930 to 1933 with the Cincinnati Reds, from 1933 to 1937 with the St. Louis Cardinals, and from 1938 to 1946 with the Brooklyn Dodgers. The 5 foot, 10 inch, 175 pound Durocher, a smart, aggressive player, was recognized by 1934 as the best fielding shortstop in baseball. His hitting, however, proved erratic. Although hitting .333 in two All-Star games (1936 and 1938), he batted only .247 lifetime. In 1,637 games,

Durocher numbered 1,320 hits, 210 doubles, 575 runs scored, 567 RBIs, and 31 stolen bases. His leadership abilities were developed as captain of both the Cardinals "Gas House Gang" in 1935 and the Dodgers in 1938. In 1939 he became player-manager of the Dodgers and began an NL managing career lasting twenty-four years.

Durocher, among his era's most successful, controversial managers, favored scrappy players and the running game, played hunches, harassed umpires, and fought with owners and fans. He piloted the Brooklyn Dodgers (1939–1946), New York Giants (1948–1955), Chicago Cubs (1966–1972), and Houston Astros (1972–1973). He won three NL pennants (1941, 1951, 1954), guided the Giants to a sweep of the favored Cleveland Indians in the 1954 World Series, and quickly molded a last place Cubs team into a contender. In 1939, 1951, and 1954, he was named NL Manager of the Year. With four NL teams, he amassed a 2,010–1,710 won-lost record for a lifetime .540 winning percentage. Durocher's private life also proved controversial. Fond of gracious living, Durocher made friends in show business. He has been married four times (to Ruby Hartles, 1930; Grace Dozier, 1934; actress Laraine Day, 1947; and Lynne Walker Goldblatt) and has two adopted children, Christopher and Michele. In 1947 Commissioner Albert B. "Happy" Chandler* found Durocher's association with gamblers and other activities sufficient grounds for suspending him from baseball for twelve months, the harshest action ever taken against a major league pilot. During the 1955–1966 hiatus from managing, Durocher worked as an NBC television announcer (1956–1960) and coached third base for the NL Los Angeles Dodgers (1961–1964). Now retired, he lives in Palm Springs, CA, and has co-authored *Nice Guys Finish Last* (1975).

BIBLIOGRAPHY: Gerald Astor, "Return of the Lip," *Look* 30 (May 17, 1966), pp. 89–94; *CB* (1940), pp. 266–267, (1950), pp. 128–130, (1953), pp. 150–153; Anthony J. Connor, *Voices from Cooperstown* (New York, 1982); John Devaney, "Durocher and His Cubs: How Tensions Can Build a Winner," *Sport*, 48 (September, 1969), pp. 81–87; Leo Durocher, *Nice Guys Finish Last* (New York, 1975); Peter Golenbock, *Bums: An Oral History of the Brooklyn Dodgers* (New York, 1984); Roger Kahn, "They Ain't Getting No Maiden," *SEP* 139 (June 18, 1966), pp. 97–101; Harold Parrott, The Lords of Baseball (New York, 1976); Harold Rosenthal, *Baseball's Best Managers* (New York, 1961).

Douglas D. Martin

DYKES, James Joseph "Jimmy" (b. 10 November 1896, Philadelphia, PA; d. 15 June 1976, Philadelphia, PA), player, coach, and manager, was the son of an engineer at Bryn Mawr College and manager of a local team. Encouraged by his father, he starred on the Philadelphia sandlots and was signed by the Philadelphia Athletics (AL) in 1917. After a year with Gettysburg, PA (BRL), he joined the Athletics. Although a poor hitter, he proved

a natural fielder with a strong arm. Under the tutelage of Eddie Collins,*
Dykes became a respectable batsman. Dykes married Mary McMonagles in
1920 and had three children, James, Jr., Charlie, and Mary. During his
fourteen-year tenure with the Athletics, he enjoyed a close father-son-rela-
tionship with manager Connie Mack.*

The feisty, garrulous Dykes won the admiration of Detroit Tigers star
Tyrus Cobb* for his aggressiveness. In 1925 Cobb offered the Athletics
$50,000, then a considerable sum, for Dykes, but Mack declined. Dykes
became an integral part of the great 1929, 1930, and 1931 Philadelphia championship teams, batting well and playing before immense crowds. Dykes,
whose lifetime batting average was .280, made 2,256 hits, 453 doubles, and
109 home runs, scored 1,108 runs, and drove in 1,071 runs in 2,282 games.
During the Depression, the financially strapped Mack broke up his team. In
1933 he sold Dykes, Mule Haas, and Al Simmons* to the Chicago White
Sox (AL) for $150,000. Although age 37, Dykes proved the key player in
the deal and subsequently enjoyed four solid seasons with the White Sox.
He attributed his long career to good conditioning, enhanced by much golf
and bowling. The good-natured, nonstop conversationalist enjoyed enormous
popularity with the players, press, and fans. As a manager, however, he did
not have championship material and never finished higher than third place.

After he completed his managerial tenure with the White Sox (1934–1946),
the New York Yankees (AL) in 1946 and 1948 seriously considered making
Dykes their manager. In 1948 Dykes declined an opportunity to manage the
AL Cleveland Indians (a team that won the World Series) and returned to
the Athletics as a coach. He became their manager in 1951, but was fired
by Earle Mack after three lackluster seasons. Later he managed the AL
Baltimore Orioles (1954), NL Cincinnati Reds (1958), AL Detroit Tigers
(1959–1960), and AL Cleveland Indians (1960–1961). As a manager, he won
1,407 games while losing 1,538 contests. Winning without good players,
Dykes contended, was like trying to steal first base. An old-fashioned manager who did not believe in the platoon system, he considered the players
of his day more dedicated and skilled than those he managed. Dykes also
coached with Cincinnati (1955–1958), the NL Pittsburgh Pirates (1959), NL
Milwaukee Braves (1962), and AL Kansas City Athletics (1963–1964). Dykes
retired to Philadelphia in the mid–1960s to enjoy the role of baseball's elder
statesman. His autobiography, *You Can't Steal First*, includes charming anecdotes and stories about the stars of the 1920s. After his first wife died in the
early 1970s, he married Mildred Boyle.

BIBLIOGRAPHY: Jimmie Dykes and Charles O. Dexter, *You Can't Steal First* (New
York, 1967); Connie Mack, *My Sixty-six Years in the Big Leagues* (Philadelphia, 1950);
NYT, January 16, 1976; "Sox Retain Dykes," *TSN*, July 27, 1944.

Anthony J. Papalas

E

EBBETS, Charles Hercules "Charlie" (b. 29 October 1859, New York NY; d. 18 April 1925, New York, NY), owner, attended New York public schools and graduated with high honors. A trained draftsman and architect, he designed many New York buildings. He published novels, which he sold door to door, and later sold tickets to baseball games with the same entrepreneurial zest. He also served on the Brooklyn City Council for four years and in the state assembly one year.

Ebbets, who epitomized the generation of owner-sportsmen dominating the game at the turn of the century, became a minor stockholder of the Brooklyn (NL) club in 1890. He soon developed a fondness for marketing the game and making it a family sport. Ebbets assumed control of the club in 1898, although it is not clear when he became the principal owner. By 1902 he fully controlled the club's activities.

Ebbets, who managed Brooklyn to a 38–68 record and a tenth place finish in 1898, made little impact on the game with his field experience. His enterpreneurial outlook made him one of the more imaginative early leaders of American baseball. He is credited with originating the rain check, proposing that the worst teams should draft first, and espousing that World Series dates should be fixed to a permanent schedule. During World War I, his teams played charity matches for the benefit of widows and orphans. Ebbets also used these games successfully as a device to challenge laws that prohibited Sunday play.

In perhaps his most important contribution, Ebbets in 1912 sold 50 percent of the stock in the Dodgers to build a spacious new park for the team in Flatbush. Ebbets Field symbolized civic pride and community development centered around a sports franchise and became a model emulated thereafter in American sports history.

Ebbets married twice, his first wife being Minnie F. A. Ebbets. They had four children, one son and three daughters, but the marriage ended in divorce around 1920. Ebbets grew attached to Mrs. Grace Slade, who in 1922 became his second wife. His estate, which consisted principally of his ownership of the Dodgers, was valued at $1.25 million when he died of heart failure.

BIBLIOGRAPHY: Richard C. Crepeau, *Baseball: America's Diamond Mind 1919–1941* (Orlando, FL, 1980); Joseph Durso, *Casey: The Life and Legend of Charles Dillon Stengel* (Englewood Cliffs, NJ, 1967); Richard Goldstein, *Spartan Seasons: How Baseball Survived the Second World War* (New York, 1980); Gene Karst and Martin J. Jones, Jr., *Who's Who in Professional Baseball* (New Rochelle, NY 1973); *NYT*, January 11, May 10, 1922, April 19, 1925.

Charles R. Middleton

ECKERT, William Dole "Spike" (b. 20 January 1909, Freeport, IL; d. 16 April 1971, Freeport, Grand Bahamas), executive, was the son of Frank Lloyd and Harriet Julia (Rudy) Eckert. After his graduation from high school in Madison, IN, he attended the U.S. Military Academy at West Point (1926–1930). He married Catherine Douglas Givens on June 15, 1940; they had a son, William, and a daughter, Catherine. He also earned a Master's degree in business administration from the Harvard School of Business in 1940. Eckert enjoyed a distinguished career in the US Army Air Corps, serving as commander of the 452nd Bomber Group in Europe in World War II. He earned several awards, including the Distinguished Flying Cross and Distinguished Service Medal, and retired as Comptroller of the Air Force in 1961.

An organization man with executive ability, he was chosen Commissioner of Baseball on November 15, 1965. His selection surprised the baseball world because he had not sought the position. The 5 foot, 8 inch, 160 pound Eckert, was an affable man known for his moderation. He proved completely ineffectual as commissioner and became "a striking symbol of baseball's blandness and resistance to change" in the mid–1960s. From the outset, Eckert's real skill as an administrator could not mask his lack of ideas on how to promote the sport.

In 1968 he incurred the ire of the public by not cancelling league games after the assassinations of Robert Kennedy and Martin Luther King. More important, perhaps, he did not deal forcefully with the league presidents and thereby proved that the Commissioner's Office did not control the game. When the threat of a player's strike emerged in early 1969, therefore, the owners acted. Eckert was removed from office on February 3, 1969, although his contract had three years left. Two years later he died on the tennis court of a heart attack.

BIBLIOGRAPHY: Gene Karst and Martin J. Jones, Jr., *Who's Who in Professional Baseball* (New Rochelle, NY, 1973); *Newsweek*, 66 (November 29, 1965), p. 62 and 72 (December 16, 1968), pp. 71–72; *NYT*, April 17, 1971; *SI*, 24 (April 4, 1966), pp. 40–42ff., and 29 (December 16, 1968) pp. 24–25; *WWA*, 35th ed. (1968–1969), p. 655.

Charles R. Middleton

ELLIOTT, Robert Irving "Bob," "Mr. Team" (b. 26 November 1916, San Francisco, CA; d. 4 May 1966, San Diego, CA), player and manager, grew up in El Centro, CA. The son of a plaster plant superintendent, Elliott attended Harding Grammar School, Wilson Junior High, Union High School, and El Centro Junior College before signing with the Pittsburgh Pirates (NL). In 1938 he married Iva Reah Skipper, whom he had known since junior high school days; they had two daughters. After outstanding minor league seasons at Savannah (SAL), Knoxville (SA), Louisville (AA), and Toronto (IL), the 6 foot, 185 pound, right-handed Elliott played with the Pirates from 1939 through 1946. He participated in the 1941, 1942, 1944, and 1948 All-Star games. An outstanding clutch hitter, Elliott drove in over 100 runs from 1943 through 1945. He moved from the outfield to third base to help his team and developed into a wide-ranging fielder. From 1942 through 1944, he led NL third basemen in assists and errors.

After being traded to the Boston Braves (NL) in 1947, Elliott batted .317, slugged 22 home runs, made 113 RBIs, and led the NL in fielding. He became the first third baseman ever chosen the NL Most Valuable Player. In 1948 Elliott helped lead the Braves' drive to the NL pennant. Nicknamed "Mr. Team," Elliott paced the Braves in RBIs (100), runs scored (99), home runs (23), and walks (an NL-leading 131), and struck out only 57 times. Although the Braves lost the World Series, Elliott batted .333 and hit two consecutive home runs against Bob Feller* of the Cleveland Indians in the fifth game.

On September 4, 1949, Elliott belted three home runs in one game. He left the Braves after the 1951 campaign and played the next two seasons with the New York Giants (NL), St. Louis Browns (AL), and Chicago White Sox (AL). From 1939 through 1953, he made 2,061 major league hits, knocked in 1,195 runs, slugged 383 doubles and 170 home runs, and compiled a career .289 batting average. Elliott managed San Diego and Sacramento (PCL) from 1955 through 1959, piloted the last place Kansas City Athletics (AL) in 1960, and coached for the Los Angeles Angels (AL) in 1961.

BIBLIOGRAPHY: Joseph L. Reichler, ed., *The Baseball Encyclopedia*, 6th ed. (New York, 1985), pp. 625, 893; Frank Waldman, *Famous American Athletes of Today*, 11th series (Boston, 1949).

Sheldon L. Appleton

ENNIS, Delmer "Del" (b. 8 June 1925, Philadelphia, PA) player, grew up in the Olney section of Philadelphia. His father worked for the famous John B.Stetson Hat Company of Philadelphia. After graduation from Olney High School in 1943, Ennis signed with the Philadelphia Phillies (NL) and played with Trenton (ISL). He enjoyed a superb season there, hitting .346 with 18 home runs and 93 RBIs. In the U.S. Navy (1944–1945), he honed his baseball skills playing against Billy Herman,* Johnny Vander Meer, and other major leaguers. In April, 1946, he was discharged from the Navy and joined the Phillies roster. Although expecting assignment to the minors again, he played outfield in 141 games for Philadelphia and won *The Sporting News* Rookie of the Year Award. The 6 foot, 195 pound right-hander batted .313 with 17 home runs, the latter a club rookie record for eighteen years.

After a sluggish sophomore year, Ennis in 1948 belted 30 homers, batted .290, and knocked in 95 runs. From 1948 to 1950, he ranked among the top NL sluggers and as the best Phillies power hitter since Chuck Klein.* During that stretch, Ennis averaged 29 homers and 111 RBIs and hit over .300. In 1950 he helped Philadelphia win the NL pennant and became the first Phillie since Klein to lead the NL in RBIs with 126, a total no club member matched until Greg Luzinski drove in 130 runs in 1977. Ennis set another Phillies record that year by driving in 41 runs in one month (August). After an off season in 1951, he enjoyed five straight excellent power years and again averaged over 25 home runs and drove in over 100 runs per season. On the Phillies all-time list, Ennis ranks second in homers, third in RBIs, extra-base hits, and total bases, and fourth in doubles. His career 259 home runs remained a club mark until broken by Mike Schmidt* in 1980. The remarkably durable Ennis missed only 64 games in eleven years with Philadelphia.

In 1956 Ennis was traded to the St. Louis Cardinals (NL) for Rip Repulski and Bobby Morgan. After driving in 105 runs in 1957, he faded rapidly, was traded to the Cincinnati Reds (NL) in 1958, and finished his career briefly with the Chicago White Sox (AL) in 1959. An average defensive left fielder, he compiled a .284 lifetime batting average, 358 doubles, 288 home runs, and 1,284 RBIs.

Ennis married Lenore Clear in February 1947. He now lives in suburban Philadelphia with his second wife, Elizabeth, and has six grown children. For around three decades, he owned and managed a popular bowling alley, Del Ennis Lanes, in Huntington Valley, PA.

BIBLIOGRAPHY: Stan Baumgartner and Fred Lieb, *The Philadelphia Phillies* (Philadelphia, 1953); Frank Bilovsky and Rich Westcott, *The Phillies Encyclopedia* (Philadelphia, 1984).

John P. Rossi

EVANS, William George "Billy" (b. 10 February 1884, Chicago, IL; d. 23 January 1956, Miami, FL), baseball umpire and executive, football executive, and sportswriter, spent his childhood in Youngstown, OH, and attended Cornell University to study law in 1901. Upon his father's death in 1902, he left school to write for the Youngstown *Vindicator*. A year later, Evans substituted as the umpire at a local game he was covering. He spent two years as sports editor of the *Vindicator* and as part-time arbitrator and then became an umpire in the Class C OPL. In 1906 22-year-old Evans joined the AL umpire crew, thus becoming the youngest major league arbiter and the only one promoted directly from Class C ball. As an umpire, he worked six World Series and encouraged using four arbiters for fall classic games. On-field fights frequently occurred then, but Evans substituted diplomacy for belligerency. An impeccable dresser, he was lauded for fairness and high integrity and provided an excellent model for future umpires. Besides being an AL umpire from 1906 to 1927, Evans continued his writing career. He contributed articles to *Collier's* and *The Sporting News*, helped compile *Knotty Problems of Baseball*, authored *Umpiring from the Inside*, served as sports editor for the Newspaper Enterprise Association, and wrote the widely syndicated "Billy Evans Says" column.

Upon retiring as an umpire, he became general manager of the Cleveland Indians (AL) in 1927. During Evans' nine-year tenure, the Indians signed stars Bob Feller,* Tommy Henrich, Wes Ferrell,* and Hal Trosky* and improved in the standings. From 1936 to 1940, he served as farm director for the Boston Red Sox (AL). Evans persuaded Boston to purchase the Louisville (AA) franchise to obtain shortstop Pee Wee Reese,* but resigned when the Red Sox sold Reese to the Brooklyn Dodgers (NL). In 1941 he served as general manager of the Cleveland Rams (National Football League). As president of the Class AA SA from 1942 to 1946, he increased baseball attendance from 700,000 to over 2 million spectators per year. Evans, general manager of the Detroit Tigers (AL) from 1947 to 1951, was elected in 1973 to the National Baseball Hall of Fame.

BIBLIOGRAPHY: Martin Appel and Burt Goldblatt, *Baseball's Best: The Hall of Fame Gallery* (New York, 1977); James M. Kahn, *The Umpire Story* (New York, 1953); Lowell Reidenbaugh, *Cooperstown: Where Baseball's Legends Live Forever* (St. Louis, 1983).

Dan E. Krueckeberg

EVERS, John Joseph "Johnny," "The Trojan," "The Crab" (b. 21 July 1881, Troy, NY; d. 28 March 1947, Albany NY), player, coach, manager, and scout, was the son of Troy government clerk John J. and Ellen (Keating) Evers and graduated in 1898 from St. Joseph's Christian Brothers Teachers School. Evers married Helen Fitzgibbons and had two children, Helen and John, Jr. Evers, who threw right-handed and batted left-handed, began playing professional baseball in 1902 with his hometown team (NYSL) and joined the Chicago Cubs (NL) that same season. He played second base for the Cubs through 1913 and helped lead them to four NL pennants (1906–1908, 1910) and two world championships (1907–1908). A .270 career hitter, Evers paced the Cubs with a .300 batting average in 1908 and finished fourth among NL hitters in 1912 with a .341 average. The speedy Evers stole 324 career bases and ranks fourth on the all-time list with 21 thefts of home. In 20 World Series games, he batted 76 times, made 24 hits, and compiled a .316 batting average.

Evers, although small of stature, proved a smart, aggressive, driving, scrappy, trigger-tongued, determined player. With Joe Tinker* and Frank Chance,* he was the pivot man in baseball's most celebrated double-play combination. A participant in the famous play making the 1908 pennant race a tie, Evers observed that Fred Merkle had not touched second base on a game-winning hit. He called for the ball and forced Merkle out at second. In a replay to decide the NL pennant, the Cubs defeated the New York Giants.

After joining the Boston Braves (NL) in 1914, Evers participated on the "miracle team" which rose from the cellar in July to a world championship in October. At Boston, he teamed with "Rabbit" Maranville* to take the World Series from the powerful Philadelphia Athletics in four games. After batting .438 in the World Series, Evers was voted the NL's Most Valuable Player. In 1917 he completed his eighteen-year playing career. In 1,783 games, he made 1,658 hits, scored 919 runs, walked 778 times, and batted .270.

Evers managed the Cubs in 1913 and 1921 and piloted the Chicago White Sox (AL) in 1924, guiding his teams to 196 victories in 406 games. He also served as a major league coach (NL New York Giants, 1920; AL Chicago White Sox, 1922–1923); assistant manager (NL Boston Braves, 1929–1932); and scout (NL Boston Braves, 1933–1934). Evers managed Albany (IL) in 1935 and served as vice-president and general manager of Albany (EL) in 1939. Subsequently, Evers operated a sporting goods store and was superintendent of Bleeker Stadium, a municipal sports complex in Albany. The co-author of *Touching Second*, he was elected to the National Baseball Hall of Fame in 1946.

BIBLIOGRAPHY: Jim Enright, *Chicago Cubs* (New York, 1975); Paul MacFarlane, ed., *TSN Daguerreotypes of Great Stars of Baseball* (St. Louis, 1971); Lowell Reidenbaugh, *Cooperstown: Where Baseball's Legends Live Forever* (St. Louis, 1983).

John L. Evers

EWING, William Buckingham "Buck" (b. 17 or 27 October 1859, Hoaglands, OH; d. 20 October 1906, Cincinnati, OH), player and manager, was one of the finest all-around athletic performers of his day. Although basically a catcher, the 5 foot, 10 inch, 188 pound Ewing played many games at all other positions. Ewing was credited by some historians as the first catcher to crouch behind the plate. Ewing, who batted and threw right-handed, began his baseball career at age 19 with the Mohawk Browns and Buckeyes (1878–1880), independent teams in Cincinnati. After joining Rochester, NY (NA), Ewing in 1880 signed with Troy, NY (NL), and remained there until 1883. In 1883 he became a charter member of the New York team (NL) and stayed with the Giants through 1889. Ewing hit at least .300 in eleven of his eighteen major league seasons and compiled a .303 career batting average. He owned a remarkable arm, enabling him to throw out runners without rising from his squat position behind the plate. A brilliant field leader, Ewing stole 53 bases once, and seven times exceeded the 30 mark. He led the NL in home runs (1883), triples (1884), putouts and assists (1889), and in nine different seasons recorded 100 or more base hits. The captain of New York's first NL champions (1888 and 1889), Ewing participated in 15 post-season games against St. Louis and Brooklyn (AA), collecting 18 hits and a .290 batting average.

Ewing in 1890 joined many others in moving to the newly formed PL as player-manager of the New York entry. When the PL collapsed after one season, Ewing returned to the Giants for two seasons. In 1893 he was traded to Cleveland (NL) for George Davis.* Following his release in 1894, he signed as player-manager of the NL Cincinnati Red Stockings (1895–1897). He managed through 1899 and piloted the Giants part of the 1900 season. His clubs won 489 games, lost 395, finished third three times, and placed fourth once, sixth once, and eighth twice. In 1,315 major league games, Ewing collected 1,625 hits, 250 doubles, 178 triples, 70 home runs, and 732 RBIs. Upon retiring from baseball, Ewing was considered wealthy because of his land holdings in the West. He married Anna Lawson McCaig on December 12, 1889, and had two children. The Cincinnati resident, who died of diabetes and paralysis, was elected to the National Baseball Hall of Fame in 1939.

BIBLIOGRAPHY: *National Baseball Hall of Fame and Museum Brochure* (Cooperstown, NY, 1974); Lowell Reidenbaugh, *Cooperstown: Where Baseball's Legends Live Forever* (St. Louis, 1983); Paul MacFarlane, ed., *TSN Daguerreotypes of Great Stars of Baseball* (St. Louis, 1971).

                                                                John L. Evers

F

FABER, Urban Clarence "Red" (b. 6 September 1888, Cascade, IA; d. 25 September 1976, Chicago, IL), player, was the son of a hotel manager and grew up in Cascade. Nicknamed "Red," he attended a Wisconsin boarding school and spent two years at St. Joseph's College in Dubuque, IA. A fine college pitcher, he was signed by the Pittsburgh Pirates (NL) and assigned to Dubuque (3IL) for the 1910 season. Faber, who began experimenting with the spitball, worked 334 innings, struck out 200, and pitched a perfect game. He played the next year at Minneapolis (AA) and Pueblo CO (WL), and then two at Des Moines, where he led the WL in strikeouts.

Following the 1913 season, the Chicago White Sox (AL) purchased him for $35,000 and took him on the world tour against the New York Giants. To replace the absent Christy Mathewson,* the Giants "borrowed" Faber. Red won his first "major league" game in Hong Kong and beat his own team three more times before losing in London. John McGraw* tried to purchase Faber, but the White Sox refused the offer. From 1914 to 1933, Faber hurled for the White Sox.

The 6 foot, 2 inch, 185 pound Faber possessed a good fastball, but increasingly used his spitball to force batters to drive the ball into the ground. Faber once threw only 67 pitches in an entire game, and three times retired the side on three pitches. The right-hander compiled a career record of 254 wins and 212 losses, completed 274 games in 484 starts, and had a 3.15 ERA. Four times, he won at least 20 games in one season.

In 1915 he compiled 24 victories, second only to Walter Johnson,* and recorded a 2.55 ERA. In 1921 he led the AL with 32 complete games in 39 starts and recorded 25 victories. When the White Sox defeated the Giants in the 1917 World Series, Faber took three of four decisions. An unfortunate injury prevented him from playing in the 1919 World Series. In the midst of the Black Sox scandal of that Series, Faber remained one of the "clean" players. The spitball was outlawed in 1920, but Faber and a few others were permitted to continue to use it. The last legal AL spitball hurler, he was elected in 1964 to the National Baseball Hall of Fame. After the 1933 season, Faber operated a bowling alley, coached for the White Sox for three seasons (1946–1948), and worked as a surveyor. Faber, who had one son by his second wife, Fran, spent his retirement in the Chicago area.

BIBLIOGRAPHY: Lee Allen, *The American League Story* (New York, 1962); Martin Appel and Burt Goldblatt, *Baseball's Best: The Hall of Fame Gallery* (New York, 1977); Warren Brown, *The Chicago White Sox* (New York, 1952); Frank Graham, *McGraw of the Giants* (New York, 1944); Richard Lindberg, *Who's on Third?* (South Bend, IN, 1983); John J. McGraw, *My Thirty Years in Baseball* (repr. New York, 1974); George S. May, "Major League Baseball Players from Iowa," *The Palimpsest* 36 (April, 1955), pp. 133–164; David Neft, Richard Cohen, and Jordan Deutsch, *The Sports Encyclopedia: Baseball*, 5th ed. (New York, 1982); *NYT*, 1913–1934, February 18, 1934; Lowell Reidenbaugh, *Cooperstown: Where Baseball's Legends Live Forever* (St. Louis, 1983).

Thomas L. Karnes

FACE, Elroy Leon "Roy," "The Baron of the Bullpen" (b. 20 February 1928, Stephentown, NY), player, is the second of four children of Joe Face, a woodchopper, carpenter, farmer, and millhand, and Bessie Face. As a youth, he survived rickets and five bouts with pneumonia and suffered a weakened heart from excessive sulfa treatments for strep throat. He attended Averill Park High School in Averill Park, NY, for two years and played baseball there before serving in the U.S. Army from February, 1946, to July, 1947. After signing with the Philadelphia Phillies (NL), Face pitched for Bradford, PA (Pol), in 1949–1950. The Brooklyn Dodgers (NL) drafted him, after which he hurled for Pueblo, CO (WL), and Fort Worth (TL). He was drafted by Pittsburgh (NL) in 1952 and spent the 1953 season with the Pirates.

Face mastered the forkball in 1954 with New Orleans (SA) and returned to the Pirates in 1955. Between May 30, 1958, and September 11, 1959, he pitched in 98 games without a defeat. He won five straight contests at the end of 1958 and captured 17 consecutive games in 1959, finishing the year at 18–1. In Pittsburgh's 1960 World Series victory over the New York Yankees, he recorded three saves. His 802 appearances with Pittsburgh tied Walter Johnson's* record for pitching appearances with one team. He was traded to the Detroit Tigers (AL) in 1968 and the next year joined the Montreal Expos (NL), who released him on August 15, 1969.

The 5 foot, 8 inch, 145 pound right-hander, wrote Myron Cope, was "fearless . . . with a build like Frank Sinatra's and the impassive features of Buster Keaton." He won 104 major league games and lost 95, with 877 strikeouts and a 3.48 ERA. His .947 winning percentage in 1958 remains a major league record. He led the NL in pitching appearances in 1956 and 1960, in saves in 1958, 1961, and 1962, and in losses by a relief pitcher in 1956, 1961, and 1963. His 848 total appearances rank eighth, 96 relief wins fifth, and 193 saves sixth in major league history.

After leaving baseball, he pursued carpentry work full-time. He married Jeanne Kuran Face on July 15, 1953, and has three children. The "Baron of the Bullpen," he became premier reliever in the late 1950s and early 1960s and was a forkballing prototype for future split-fingered relief specialists.

BIBLIOGRAPHY: Myron Cope, "The Luck of Roy Face," *Sport* 29 (April, 1960), pp. 34–35, 85–87; Dick Groat and Bill Surface, *The World Champion Pittsburgh Pirates* (New York, 1961); Abby Mendelson, "Face to Face with ElRoy," *Baseball Quarterly* (Winter, 1977). pp. 23–27.

Luther W. Spoehr

FEENEY, Charles "Chub" (b. 31 August 1921, Orange, NJ), executive and administrator, is the son of Thaddeus and Mary (Stoneham) Feeney and nephew of Horace Stoneham.* He graduated from Dartmouth College and Fordham Law School. He has five children from a marriage that ended in divorce. After spending three years in the US Navy, Feeney was admitted in 1949 to the New York Bar Association. After joining the New York Giants' (NL) front office staff at the end of World War II, Feeney was elected vice-president of the franchise in 1946 and became general manager after the team moved to San Francisco in 1958.

With the forced retirement of General William Eckert* in 1969, Feeney became a leading candidate for major league baseball's Commissioner after John McHale* withdrew from consideration. The Cleveland Indian ownership, however, allegedly held some animosity toward Feeney because of a feared predisposition against its manager, Alvin Dark.* Feeney actually had interceded previously on Dark's behalf at the end of the 1964 season, keeping the stormy manager from being fired by the Giants' owner Stoneham. Team owners became deadlocked between Feeney and New York Yankees executive Mike Burke. This impasse produced the nomination and ultimate selection of Bowie Kuhn* as Commissioner.

NL owners, meanwhile, selected Feeney as their president in 1970 when Warren Giles* retired. Like his baseball mentors, the Stonehams, Feeney kept an extraordinarily low profile as league president. His face appeared before the cameras only during post-season play, while his name appeared in the papers only in conjunction with the assessment of fines and union negotiations. Feeney retired as NL President following the 1986 season.

BIBLIOGRAPHY: Alan R. Asnen, correspondence with Katy Feeney, September 6, 1984, Alan R. Ansen Collection, Columbia, SC; Charles Einstein, *Willie Mays* (New York 1963); Charles Einstein, *Willie's Time* (New York, 1979); Gene Karst and Martin J. Jones, Jr., *Who's Who in Professional Baseball* (New Rochelle, NY, 1973).

Alan R. Asnen

FELLER, Robert William Andrew "Bob," "Rapid Robert" (b. 3 November 1918, Van Meter, IA), player, was of German-French descent and grew up on a farm west of Des Moines. By performing farm chores, Feller developed strong muscles and broad shoulders. The 6 foot, 190 pounder graduated in 1937 from Van Meter High School. Feller developed a very close relationship with his father, William, who trained him to be a pitcher from his preteen years. By the time Feller pitched high school and local amateur baseball, he already had earned a regional reputation with his blinding fastball. In early 1936 he pitched five no-hitters for Van Meter High.

Feller, who exhibited rare ability, won games for the Cleveland Indians (AL) in 1936 before finishing high school. His experience illustrated how breaking the rules in professional sports paid rich dividends. Feller's discovery usually is credited to Indians general manager Cy Slapnicka and Iowa scout John McMahon. Feller, however, exhibited such natural talent that many scouts perceived his potential. In order to enlist him, Cleveland violated the prevailing regulations forbidding the signing of pre-college amateurs. The Indians "covered up" Feller for a few months via bookkeeping legerdemain, unveiling him as a pitcher in July, 1936. Commissioner Kenesaw Mountain Landis* could have made Feller a free agent for this offense, but his parents insisted that he wanted to pitch for Cleveland. The Fellers, grateful to the Indians for their solicitude when Bob briefly experienced a sore arm, declined a free agent fortune.

Feller enjoyed a spectacular career despite losing almost four peak years to World War II military service. As Navy chief specialist on the great battleship *Alabama*, Feller won five campaign ribbons and eight battle stars in Pacific theater combat. He married Virginia Winther in January, 1943, and has three sons.

Feller combined a phenomenal fastball with a great curve. Before World War II especially, he fanned numerous batters when strikeouts were more difficult to achieve. Feller reached his one-game peak on October 6, 1938 by striking out eighteen Detroit Tigers. In 1946 he fanned 348 batters, a near season record then and still the fifth highest total. Feller still ranks among the first twenty in career strikeouts. At Washington, DC, soon after World War II, his fastball was measured at 98.6 miles per hour.

Feller's pitching feats remain indelible. Despite military service, he led the AL in various pitching categories thirty-one times. Six times he won 20 or more games and paced in victories each time. His career high in victories came in 1940. Feller led the AL thrice in total games pitched and complete games, five times in innings pitched and shutouts, seven times in strikeouts, and once in winning percentage. He pitched three no-hit games, exceeded only by Nolan Ryan's* five and Sandy Koufax's* four, and a record twelve one-hitters. Feller, however, never won a World Series game. In the 1948 World Series, he lost two games to the Boston Braves. His controversial

1–0 loss resulted partly from an umpire's dubious call on an attempted pickoff play. In the 1954 fall classic, Feller did not pitch in Cleveland's four consecutive losses to the New York Giants.

Feller's career ended in 1956 with 266 wins, 162 losses, 2,581 strikeouts, and a sparkling .621 winning percentage. In 1962 he was elected to the National Baseball Hall of Fame. If World War II had not intervened, Feller probably would have ranked among the very greatest pitchers, with perhaps 100 more victories and another 1,000 strikeouts. Feller enjoyed touring minor league ballparks and visiting sports memorabilia shows and was employed in insurance after his retirement.

BIBLIOGRAPHY: Anthony J. Connor, *Baseball for the Love of It* (New York, 1982); Bob Feller, *Strikeout Story* (New York, 1947); Lowell Reidenbaugh, *Cooperstown: Where Baseball's Legends Live Forever* (St. Louis, 1983); *SEP* 165 (January 27, 1962), pp. 49–52; *TSN*, December 15, 1954, May 16, 1983.

Lowell L. Blaisdell

FERRELL, Richard Benjamin "Rick" (b. 12 October 1905, Durham, NC), player, coach, scout, and executive, grew up on a farm at Guilford, NC. He was one of six sons of Rufus Benjamin Ferrell, a Southern Railway locomotive engineer who raised dairy cattle, and Alice (Carpenter) Ferrell. His brother Wesley* played in the major leagues, while brother Marvin pitched in the minors and George played the outfield for twenty minor league seasons. Rick graduated from Guilford High School and attended Guilford College for three years (1924–1926). After rejecting an offer from the St. Louis Cardinals (NL), Ferrell signed with the Detroit Tigers (AL) and played at Kinston, NC (VL), in 1926 and at Columbus (AA) from 1926 through 1928. In 1928 he was selected as AA All-Star catcher. He complained to Judge Kenesaw Mountain Landis* when his name was omitted from draft lists that fall. Upholding the complaint, the judge declared him a free agent. He signed with the St. Louis Browns (AL) for a $25,000 bonus, bypassing a similar offer from the New York Giants (NL).

The cool, even-tempered Ferrell stayed with the Browns until mid–1933, when he was traded to the Boston Red Sox (AL). During the 1934 season, Boston acquired his brother Wes. For several years, Rick caught whenever Wes pitched. Both were traded to the Washington Senators (AL) in mid–1937, Rick remaining there until being dealt back to the Browns in early 1941. A March, 1944 trade returned Rick to the Senators, where he finished his catching career in 1947 as a player-coach. He continued coaching with Washington through 1949, then coached Detroit from 1950 through 1953. For Detroit, he scouted from 1954 through 1958 and served as general manager in 1960 and 1961, as vice-president from 1962 through 1975, and as a consultant thereafter.

In eighteen AL seasons, the 5 foot, 10 inch, 160 pound, right-handed Ferrell batted .280 (above average for a catcher) with 734 RBIs spanning

1,884 games. Ferrell's 1,692 hits included 324 doubles and 28 home runs. He struck out only 277 times in over 6,000 times at bat. Behind the plate, the fair-skinned North Carolinian set an AL record for most games caught (1,805). For nine consecutive years (1930–1938), he caught over 100 games per season. The smart, excellent receiver and expert handler of pitchers was elected to six consecutive AL All-Star teams from 1933 through 1938. In his youth, he proved a good lightweight boxer before entering professional baseball. Ferrell married Ruthe Virginia Wilson of Greenville, TN, in 1941. She predeceased him in 1968 and also was survived by two daughters and two sons. In 1984 Ferrell was elected to the National Baseball Hall of Fame.

BIBLIOGRAPHY: Bob Broeg, "Ferrell's a Blue-Ribbon Battery," *TSN*, January 29, 1977; Paul Green, *Forgotten Fields* (Waupaca, WI, 1984); Harold (Speed) Johnson, *Who's Who in Major League Base Ball* (Chicago, 1933); Paul MacFarlane, ed., *TSN Daguerreotypes of Great Stars of Baseball* (St. Louis, 1981); Joseph L. Reichler, ed., *The Baseball Encyclopedia*, 6th ed. (New York, 1985), p. 908; J. G. Taylor Spink, comp., *TSN Baseball Register, 1950* (St. Louis, 1950); *TSN*, December 12, 1951, July 23, 1952, March 18, 1968.

Frank V. Phelps

FERRELL, Wesley Cheek "Wes" (b. 2 February 1908, Greensboro, NC; d. 9 December 1976, Sarasota, FL), player and manager, grew up on a 150 acre dairy farm at Guilford, NC. He was the son of railroad locomotive engineer Rufus Benjamin Ferrell and Alice (Carpenter) Ferrell, graduated from Guilford High School, and attended a military school in Oak Ridge, TN. Rick Ferrell,* an older brother, also played major league baseball. During 1927 Wes pitched briefly for a semi-pro team at East Douglas, MA. After signing with Cleveland (AL), he pitched one inning there in 1927. Ferrell won 20 games and lost 8 for Terre Haute, IN (3IL) in 1928 before finishing 0–2 with Cleveland. During his first four full seasons (1929–1932) with the Indians, the handsome, blond, 6 foot, 2 inch, 195 pound right-hander uniquely won over 20 games each year. His other impressive marks included a 13-game winning streak in 1931 and a no-hit game against the St. Louis Browns on April 29, 1931. In 1933 he hurt his pitching arm and compiled a mediocre 11–12 record. After holding out the next spring, he was traded in May, 1934, to the Boston Red Sox (AL).

Although his blazing fastball had disappeared, Ferrell regained effectiveness as a curve and "junk stuff" hurler. With brother Rick as catcher, Wes achieved 14–5, 25–14, and 20–15 records from 1934 through 1936. After the Ferrells were traded to Washington (AL) in mid–1937, Wes finished 14–19 and was released in August, 1938. He signed with the New York Yankees (AL) and registered a composite 15–10 mark for the 1938 season. He pitched briefly for the Yankees in 1939 and toiled for the Brooklyn Dodgers (NL) in 1940 and Boston Braves (NL) in 1941. His fifteen-year major league totals included 193 wins, 128 losses, and a 4.04 ERA. Ferrell led the AL four times in complete games, three times in innings pitched and hits surrendered, twice in games started, and once in wins and walks. From 1941 through 1949, he was a manager-outfielder for southeastern minor league teams: Leaksville, VA (BSL), in 1941, Lynchburg, VA (VL), in 1942, Greensboro, NC (CrL), in 1945, Lynchburg, (Pil) in 1946, Marion, NC (WCL), in 1948, and Greensboro again and Tampa (FIL) in 1949. Out of organized baseball for fourteen years, he returned to manage Rock Hill, SC (WCL), in 1963 and Shelby, NC (WCL), in 1965.

The great major league hitting pitcher batted .280, slugged .446 and set home run by pitcher records: 38 career home runs and 9 for a single season (1931). He pinch-hit frequently and played 13 games in the 1933 Cleveland outfield. He also won batting championships in the VL with .361 (31 homers) in 1942 and in the WCL with .425 (.767 slugging percentage and 24 homers) at age 40 in 1948.

A fierce competitor, Ferrell often stormed and raged when he lost. He engaged in frequent salary disputes and periodic hot controversies with baseball authorities. In 1932 Cleveland manager Roger Peckinpaugh fined him $1,500 for refusing to leave the mound. Four years later, Boston manager Joe Cronin* fined him $1,000 for taking himself off the mound. In the minors, he drew a one-year suspension for punching an umpire and a sixty-day suspension for taking his team off the field. Ferrell married Lois Johnston in 1940 and had one son, Wesley Cheek, Jr., and one daughter, Mrs. Gwenlo F. Williard. In his later years, Ferrell became a gentleman farmer.

BIBLIOGRAPHY: Bob Broeg, "Ferrell Was a Blue-Chip Redneck," *TSN*, January 22, 1977; Wes Ferrell file, National Baseball Hall of Fame Library, Cooperstown, NY; Donald Honig, *Baseball When the Grass Was Real* (New York, 1975); Paul MacFarlane, ed., *TSN Daguerreotypes of Great Stars of Baseball* (St. Louis, 1981); Joseph L. Reichler, ed., *The Baseball Encyclopedia*, 6th ed. (New York, 1985), pp. 909, 1,714; *TSN*, November 12, 1942, December 14, 1944, July 23, 1952, December 25, 1976.

Frank V. Phelps

FINGERS, Roland Glenn "Rollie" (b. 25 August 1946, Steubenville, OH), player, is the son of George and Edna (Stafford) Fingers. Fingers, whose father and brother, Gordon, played minor league baseball, attended Chaffey Junior College in California. He signed with the Kansas City Athletics (AL) on Christmas Eve, 1964, and pitched for Leesburg, FL (FSL), in 1965, Modesto, CA (CaL), in 1966, and Birmingham, AL (SL), in 1967 and 1968.

From 1969 to 1976, the 6 foot, 4 inch, 190 pound right-hander pitched for the Oakland A's (AL) and teamed with Mudcat Grant, Blue Moon Odom, Catfish Hunter,* and Vida Blue.* He learned much from reliever Grant and developed into a dependable relief pitcher. Besides consistently ranking among leaders in saves, he also led the AL in total games with 76 in 1974 and 75 in 1975 and finished 59 games in relief the latter season. With the A's, Fingers pitched in five Championship Series and established an AL record for the most series saves. He compiled a 2–2 mark in three World Series and made 6 saves in 16 appearances (both league bests) for a 1.35 ERA. Fingers, whose performance in 1974 won him the World Series Most Valuable Player Award, was named to seven All-Star teams—twice from Oakland.

In 1977 Fingers joined the San Diego Padres and led the NL with 78 appearances, 69 games finished in relief, and 35 saves. He was named both Rolaids Relief Man of the Year and *The Sporting News* Fireman of the Year. In 1978 he tied the then NL record for most saves with 37 and again collected the top relief awards. After being traded to Milwaukee (AL) in 1980, Fingers propelled the Brewers to the AL playoff in 1981 with a 6–3 record, a league-leading 28 saves, and a 1.04 ERA. With an incredible strikeout-to-walk ratio of almost 5 to 1, he won or saved 55 percent of the Brewers wins and received both the AL MVP and Cy Young awards. He earned his $750,000 salary in 1982 by pitching well for the Brewers until September, when an arm problem kept him out of the playoffs and World Series. Although missing the 1983 season, he returned in 1984 with his trademark handlebar mustache to record 23 saves and a 1.96 ERA on a team that won only 67 games. In 944 games, he compiled a 114–118 mark, surrendered 1,474 hits in 1,701 innings, and recorded a 2.90 ERA. The Milwaukee Brewers released Fingers in November 1985.

By throwing 80 percent of his pitches where he wants them, Fingers compiled 1,299 strikeouts compared to only 492 bases on balls. His remarkable control and durability helped him establish baseball's all-time record for saves (341) and saves plus wins (455). Fingers and his former wife Jill have three children. During the off-season, he resided in the San Diego suburb of La Mesa.

BIBLIOGRAPHY: Dave Anderson, "Rollie Fingers Is Trying to Pitch," *NYT Biographical Service*, March 13, 1983, pp. 300–301; Melissa Ludtke Lincoln, "Rollie's Rolling Again," *SI*, 49 (September 11, 1978), pp. 81–82; Lawrence Linderman, "Sport Interview: Rollie Fingers," *Sport* 73 (May 1982), pp. 16–21; Joseph L. Reichler, ed., *The Baseball Encyclopedia*, 6th ed. (New York, 1985), pp. 1,176–1,717; Barry Siegel, ed., *TSN Official Baseball Register*, 1984 (St. Louis, 1984); *TSN*, October 15, 1984, p. 38; *WWA*, 42nd ed. (1982–1983), p. 1,041.

Gaymon L. Bennett

FINLEY, Charles O. "Charley" (b. 22 February 1918, Ensley, AL), owner, is the son of Burmah and Oscar Finley, a Birmingham, AL steel worker. He attended Emerson High School and graduated from Horace Mann High School in Gary, IN, in 1936. After attending Gary Junior College and Indiana University, he married Shirley McCartney in May, 1941; they had seven children. The enterprising Finley worked numerous odd jobs to augment his working-class family's meager savings, but still maintained an active interest in sports. Before moving north during the Depression, he had served as batboy for the 1931 Birmingham, AL Barons (SL). As a high school student, he played baseball and boxed in the Gary Golden Gloves tournament. In college, he worked nights at the U.S. Steel plant and spent days and weekends playing first base in several semi-pro leagues in Indiana. After World War II, Finley became a salesman for the Travelers Insurance Company and earned a fortune from his commission on the sale of a group insurance policy for the American College of Surgeons in 1952.

With his combined insurance, manufacturing, and real estate interests, Finley pursued his lifelong dream of owning a major league baseball franchise. During the 1950s, he attempted to purchase the Detroit Tigers, the Chicago White Sox, and the faltering Philadelphia Athletics and sought to create an expansion franchise in Los Angeles prior to the Brooklyn Dodgers' move west. In 1960 he purchased 52 percent of the Kansas City Athletics' (AL) stock and acquired the remainder the next two years. Finley, primarily a businessman regardless of his love for baseball, saw his losing team's dwindling profit margin, and after abortive attempts to shift his club to Louisville and Dallas, he moved the franchise to Oakland in 1968. The team encountered immediate success on the field and at the box office, finishing above .500 that first season in California. Finley's Athletics ultimately earned profits in nineteen of twenty seasons.

Finley assembled key young players who formed the first genuine baseball dynasty since the decline of the New York Yankees earlier in the 1960s. The very popular team was embroiled in turmoil, achieving notoriety because of constant feuding between Finley and his players and managers and because of the attention paid by the media to the owner's headline-making stunts and personality. Oakland finished second in the first two years of divisional play (1969, 1970), won its first divisional title in 1971, and captured its first AL pennant in 1972. The A's won AL pennants in 1973 and 1974 and a division title in 1975, but succumbed to Finley's refusal to coexist with free agency and declined considerably by the end of the decade. Finley hired ten managers, two of them twice, in fourteen seasons. Billy Martin,* the last mentor, brought the team in 1980 from seventh to second place. In 1979 the team drew sparse crowds (often under 1,000 paid customers) and had the worst attendance and win-loss records in baseball. Martin's demeanor and baseball knowledge brought renewed team success and rejuvenated popular interest in the Athletics. After being rumored to sell the franchise to interested parties in Denver, Memphis, and New Orleans, Finley sold the team to a local group headed by Walter J. Haas in 1981 and left baseball gracefully. After attempting to acquire the Chicago Cubs in 1981, he drew up plans the next year with Bill Veeck* for an international league with teams from U.S. minor league cities, Latin America, and Japan.

Finley also owned the California Golden Seals (National Hockey League) and the Memphis Pros/Tams (American Basketball Association). During twenty stormy years filled with interviews, press conferences, and the most media coverage ever devoted to one sports team owner, Finley changed the structure and nature of the baseball business almost single-handedly. He expedited general free agency for players with his firings of Ken Harrelson and Mike Andrews and engaged in contract disputes with Jim "Catfish" Hunter* and other star players. Volatile relationships with his players and managers led to much fan dissent and constant disputes with Commissioner Bowie Kuhn,* who often levied substantial fines on Finley. His players, protesting Finley's personal conservatism and reflecting the temper of the times, popularized facial hair in American baseball. Besides his persistent publicity stunts to increase ticket sales, Finley was partly responsible for initiating night World Series and All-Star games, brightly colored player uniforms, the designated hitter rule, and the increased use of special pro-motional dates and gifts. Several ideas not adopted by professional baseball included the use of yellow or orange baseballs, designated runner, interleague play, regional reorganization of the leagues, and early entry into the National Baseball Hall of Fame. No longer involved with professional baseball, Finley still operates his thirty-year-old insurance business, Charles O. Finley Cor-poration, and serves as president of a Canadian firm, Century Energy Corporation.

BIBLIOGRAPHY: Tom Clark, *Champagne and Baloney* (New York, 1976); Alvin Dark and John Underwood, *When in Doubt, Fire the Manager* (New York, 1980); Glenn Dickey, *The History of American League Baseball* (New York, 1980); *TSN*, May 28, 1984.

Alan R. Asnen

FISK, Carlton Ernest "Pudge" (b. 26 December 1948, Bellows Falls, VT), player, probably is best remembered for his game-winning home run with the Boston Red Sox (AL) at Fenway Park in the twelfth inning of the sixth game in the 1975 World Series against the Cincinnati Reds. Fisk, who at-tended the University of New Hampshire on a basketball scholarship, played for Waterloo, IA (ML), Pittsfield, MA, and Pawtucket, RI (EL), and Louis-ville (IL), during his minor league career in the Red Sox farm system. After brief trials with the Red Sox in 1969 and 1971, Fisk became the regular Boston catcher in 1972 and won the AL's Rookie of the Year Award. Al-though he has caught over 1,600 games, Fisk remains surprisingly quick afoot and has 115 career stolen bases through the 1986 season. Fisk also led the AL in triples (9) his rookie season. He appeared in nine All-Star games (1972–1973, 1976–1978, 1980–1982, 1985) for the AL and batted .240 in the 1975 World Series.

Fisk remained with Boston through the 1980 season before joining the

Chicago White Sox (AL) through the free agency route. In 1984 a season-long groin injury hampered Fisk's effectiveness, causing his batting average to drop nearly 60 points to .231 and his RBIs to plummet to one-half (43) of those of 1983. Consequently, many observers believed that his full-time playing days as a catcher were nearly over. Before the 1985 season, Fisk had turned 37 years old. Due to a winter-long weight training program, however, Fisk hit a career-high 37 home runs to set a single-season record for AL catchers, placed second in the AL in homers, and knocked in a career-high 107 runs. Hitting for a high batting average has remained a problem. Although impossible to quantify, Fisk's successful career has featured his leadership and ability to handle pitchers. Through 1986, he batted .271, made 1,767 hits, including 316 doubles, 42 triples, and 281 home runs, and knocked in 977 runs.

BIBLIOGRAPHY: Gene Karst and Martin J. Jones, Jr., *Who's Who in Professional Baseball* (New Rochelle, NY, 1973); George Vecsey, "Commanding Fisk Is a Red Sox Bastion," *NYT Biographical Service*, May, 1980, pp. 677–678.

William J. Serow

FITZSIMMONS, Frederick Landis "Freddie," "Fat Freddie" (b. 28 July 1901, Mishawaka, IN; d. 18 November 1979, Yucca Valley, CA), player, manager, and executive, pitched for the New York Giants (1925–1937) and Brooklyn Dodgers (1937–1943) of the NL. During his nineteen-year career, the 5 foot, 11 inch, right-handed Fitzsimmons compiled a 217–146 won-lost record with a 3.51 ERA and 29 shutouts. The control pitcher struck out 870 and walked 846 batters in 3,223 2/3 innings. Fitzsimmons' best year occurred in 1928, when he posted a 20–9 mark and hurled four relief victories. He led the NL in winning percentage (.889) in 1940 with a 16–2 record. From 1928 to 1937, Fitzsimmons and Carl Hubbell* combined for 325 victories and provided the Giants with a potent right-lefty duo. Fitzsimmons, who played in three World Series, was shutout 4–0 by the Washington Senators in game two of the 1933 classic. He suffered two defeats, including a four-hit 2–1 hard luck loss in game three, to the New York Yankees in the 1936 Series. In the 1941 Series, Fitzsimmons pitched for the Dodgers against the Yankees. After holding the Yankees scoreless for seven innings, he was hit in the knee by a line drive and forced to leave the game. The Yankees eventually won both the game and the Series, while Fitzsimmons never fully recovered. After the 1941 Series, he won only three more games the next two seasons and retired.

Fitzsimmons, who curiously never appeared in an All-Star game, batted a respectable .200 lifetime and hit 14 career home runs. On May 10, 1931, he hit a grand slam off Cubs pitcher Pat Malone. Fitzsimmons managed the Philadelphia Phillies (NL) three years (1943–1945), guiding them to one seventh place and two last place finishes. He also served as coach for the

NL Boston Braves (1942), New York Giants (1949–1955), NL Chicago Cubs (1957–1959, 1966), AL Kansas City Athletics (1960), and PCL Salt Lake City (1961) and as general manager of the Brooklyn Dodgers of the National Football League.

Of Irish ancestry, Fitzsimmons met his wife, Helen Burger, in 1924 in Indianapolis as a minor league player there. He had one daughter, Helen, born in 1930. Fitzsimmons' wife described him as having "bright blue eyes and a smile that warms you all over." Fitzsimmons regarded "mental discipline—the willingness to bear down and go all-out on every play" as a good ballplayer's chief asset.

BIBLIOGRAPHY: Craig Carter, ed., *TSN Official World Series Records* (St. Louis, 1983); Freddie Fitzsimmons, "Did the Best Teams Get in the Series?" *SEP* 228 (October 1, 1955), pp. 25, 110–112; Mrs. Freddie Fitzsimmons, "I Married Baseball," *Coronet* 38 (September, 1955), pp. 96–100; Tot Holmes, *Dodgers Blue Book* (Los Angeles, 1983); Joseph L. Reichler, ed., *The Baseball Encyclopedia*, 6th ed. (New York, 1985) p. 1,720; Larry Wigge, ed., *TSN Official Baseball Guide, 1980* (St. Louis, 1980).

Jack P. Lipton

FLICK, Elmer Harrison (b. 11 January 1876, Bedford, OH; d. 9 January 1971, Bedford, OH), player, was the son of Zachary Taylor and Mary (Caine) Flick. His father, a farmer, also conducted a threshing business. Flick attended Bedford High School, where he starred as a catcher on the baseball team. He married Mary Ella Gates in 1900 and had five daughters. Flick's introduction to semi-pro baseball was worthy of fiction, coming when he was at the station to give the Bedford team a send-off. Since the train was about to leave and only eight players were present, someone asked 15-year-old Flick to join. Flick jumped at the opportunity, even though he was barefoot.

Flick entered organized baseball as an outfielder with Youngstown, OH (ISL), in 1896 and spent the next season with Dayton (ISL). In the spring of 1898, he reported to Philadelphia (NL) with a bat that had been fashioned on a lathe. One writer described him as "one of the most promising youngsters the Phillies had ever had." Philadelphia boasted a veteran outfield, but Flick replaced the injured Sam Thompson* on April 26. He made two hits that day and remained a major leaguer for the next thirteen years. In four full years with Philadelphia, he averaged .345 at the plate and hit a career-high .378 in 1900. On May 11, 1902, he was sold to Cleveland of the fledgling AL. The speedster led the AL in stolen bases in 1904 and 1906 and in triples three years (1905–1907). In 1905 he topped the AL with a .306 batting average, the lowest leading mark up to then. His thirteen-year lifetime average stood nine points higher than that, at .315. After physical problems restricted his play the last three years at Cleveland (1908–1910), he closed out his career with Toledo (AA) in 1911 and 1912. In 1,484 major league games, Flick made 1,767 hits, 268 doubles, and 170 triples, scored 950 runs, and stole 334 bases.

Some of the best trades are those not made. Flick became involved in one such trade. After the 1907 season the Detroit Tigers offered Ty Cobb* for Flick. Despite Cobb's three great years, Detroit feared that his aggressive base running would shorten his career. Cleveland rejected the offer! Cobb played twenty-one more seasons in the majors, set numerous career records, and entered the National Baseball Hall of Fame with the first five players named in 1936. Flick lasted only three more years and 99 games in the majors.

When his baseball days ended, Flick became a builder in northern Ohio. Always an outdoorsman and horse fancier, he owned and ran trotters. A summer high school league and Bedford's ball park are named for Flick, who never lost interest in young people and baseball. In 1963 the Veterans Committee voted Flick into the National Baseball Hall of Fame.

BIBLIOGRAPHY: Lee Allen and Tom Meany, *Kings of the Diamond* (New York, 1956); Martin Appel and Burt Goldblatt, *Baseball's Best: The Hall of Fame Gallery* (New York, 1977); Paul MacFarlane, ed., *TSN Hall of Fame Fact Book* (St. Louis, 1983); Daniel Okrent and Harris Lewine, eds., *The Ulitmate Baseball Book* (Boston, 1979).

Emil H. Rothe

FLOOD, Curtis Charles "Curt" (b. 18 January 1938, Houston, TX), player and broadcaster, is the youngest child of hospital menials Herman and Laura Flood. The Floods moved with their six children to Oakland, CA, in 1940 in search of work. Flood experienced a typical, bleak ghetto upbringing in a world where sports offered one of the few ways out. The exceptionally fast Flood was developed by Oakland talent guru George Powels, whose list of young athletes included Frank Robinson,* Billy Martin,* and Vada Pinson* in baseball and Ollie Matson* (FB), John Brodie* (FB), and Bill Russell* (IS) in other sports. A superior center fielder and a versatile hitter, Flood starred at McClymonds and Oakland Technical high schools and was signed by the Cincinnati Reds (NL) upon graduation in 1956. The young ballplayer spent two years on southern minor league teams, Thomasville, NC (CrL), in 1956 and Savannah (SAL) in 1957, before being traded to the St. Louis Cardinals (NL) in 1957.

The 5 foot, 9 inch 165 pound Flood emerged as one of baseball's stars during the 1960s. From 1961 through 1969, he averaged .302, finished fourth in batting average in 1967, placed fifth in batting average in 1968, and tied for the NL lead in hits in 1964. Flood also replaced Willie Mays* in the minds of many as the game's premier defensive center fielder. He earned consecutive Gold Gloves from 1963 through 1969 and set major league records for consecutive chances and games by an outfielder without an error. A 1968 *Sports Illustrated* cover story proclaimed Flood "baseball's best centerfielder." His skills helped the Cardinals capture NL pennants in 1964, 1967, and 1968 and world championships in 1964 and 1967, when he served as team co-captain.

Flood made baseball and legal history in 1969 by declining a trade from St. Louis to the Philadelphia Phillies (NL). On December 24, 1969, he wrote Commissioner Bowie Kuhn,* "I do not feel I am a piece of property to be bought and sold irrespective of my wishes." Forsaking a $100,000 contract for 1970, he secured the moral and financial support of Marvin Miller* and the Major League Players Association and the legal counsel of former U.S. Supreme Court Justice Arthur Goldberg to challenge baseball's reserve clause in the federal courts. The U. S. Supreme Court rejected his plea in Flood v. Kuhn on June 18, 1972, in a 5–3 decision, but its ruling was narrowly construed and hinted that legislation or the collective bargaining process between owners and players could overturn the reserve system. Moreover, Flood's suit probably influenced the owners to agree to an arbitration system, which eventually terminated the reserve clause in December, 1972. Flood attempted a comeback with the Washington Senators (AL) in 1971, but advancing age and the pressure of off-the-field battles had eroded his skills. He retired at the end of the 1971 season and became a portrait painter and bar owner on the island of Minorca. In 1,759 career games, he batted .293 with 1,861 hits, 271 doubles, 44 triples, 85 home runs, 851 runs scored, 636 RBIs, and 88 stolen bases.

Flood's autobiography, *The Way It Is*, written with the assistance of journalist Richard Carter, occupies a major position in baseball literature, following the paths of candor paved by Jim Brosnan's *The Long Season* and *Pennant Race* and Jim Bouton's *Ball Four*. Flood confirmed their stories of player insecurity and tight-fisted owners, and amplified athletes' sexual exploits. But his book, above all, portrayed the residue of racism encountered at all levels of professional play. Besides its inside look at the game, *The Way It Is* frankly revealed a sensitive, introspective athlete whose public accomplishments and trials overshadowed a troubled personal life. Flood's February 1959 marriage to Beverly Collins ended in divorce, with his wife assuming guardianship of the four children. The murder of a close friend and the tragic imprisonment of his talented elder brother, Carl, further marred Flood's private life. *The Way It Is* depicted the story of a man seeking his own identity as it chronicled the life of a famous athlete.

During the late 1970s and in the 1980s, Flood appeared often in "where are they now pieces" that noted his pioneering role in the advent of free agency and observed that he had failed to profit from his fight. He secured a few commercial endorsements and found employment in the Oakland area as a broadcaster for Charles Finley's* A's, as a painter, and as head of the Oakland Little League.

BIBLIOGRAPHY: "Baseball's Forgotten Man," *Newsweek* 93 (April 2, 1979), p. 18; Curt Flood (with Richard Carter), *The Way It Is* (New York, 1970); William Leggett, "Not Just a Flood, but a Deluge," *SI* 29 (August 19, 1968), pp. 18–21; Lee Lowenfish and Tony Lupien, *The Imperfect Diamond* (New York, 1980); Richard Reeves, "The Last Angry Man," *Esquire* 89 (March 1, 1978), pp. 41–48; Jules Tygiel, *Baseball's Great Experiment* (New York, 1983); David Quentin Voigt, *American Baseball*, vol. 3 (University Park, PA, 1983); "What Ever Happened to Curt Flood?" *Ebony* 36 (March, 1981), pp. 55–56.

James W. Harper

FORD, Edward Charles "Whitey," "The Chairman of the Board" (b. 21 October 1928, New York, NY), player, coach, scout, and announcer, is the son of James and Edith Ford and graduated from Manhattan High School of Aviation in New York City. His father was employed as a bartender and meat market worker, while his mother worked at a grocery store and as a bookkeeper. After playing high school baseball, Ford performed as a pitcher and first baseman for the "Thirty-Fourth Avenue Boys" amateur club in the Queens-Nassau League. A New York Yankees (AL) scout urged Ford to concentrate on pitching and signed him in October 1946 to a Yankees contract and $7,000 bonus, outbidding both the Boston Red Sox (AL) and Brooklyn Dodgers (NL). The left-handed pitcher began his minor league career by posting a 13–4 record at Butler, PA (MAL), in 1947. After compiling a 16–8 mark at Norfolk, VA (Pil), in 1948, he boasted a 16–5 slate and a league-leading 1.61 ERA at Binghamton, NY (EL), the following year. Ford opened the 1950 season at Kansas City, MO (AA), with an impressive 6–3 record before joining the New York Yankees.

As an AL rookie, he triumphed in nine consecutive games and assembled a 9–1 record and a 2.81 ERA to help propel the Yankees to the 1950 pennant. He won the World Series clincher 5–2 against the Philadelphia Phillies. The U.S. Army then drafted Ford and assigned him the next two years to the Signal Corps at Fort Monmouth, NJ. Ford returned to the Yankee lineup in 1953 and posted an impressive 18–6 record in another AL pennant-winning season. By 1955, the 5 foot, 10 inch, 178 pounder was considered the Yankees' premier starter and consummate "money pitcher" by winning the most important games. In 1964 the Yankees named him the first active pitcher-coach in major league history. He retired in May 1967 because of a circulatory problem in his left arm and a bone spur in his elbow. Thereafter, he remained with the Yankees as a scout and minor league pitching coach (1967), first base coach (1968), television commentator for Yankees home games (1969), and full-time pitching coach in 1974. Since then, Ford has pursued various business interests and maintained his visibility as one of the Yankees' all-time great pitchers.

Ford's sixteen-year major league career with the Yankees featured nu-

merous records and remarkable achievements. In 498 games, he compiled a
236–106 mark and a major league record for the second best lifetime percentage (.690) by a pitcher with 200 or more decisions. He struck out 1,956
batters in 3,170 1/3 innings while recording a 2.75 ERA, the second best
lifetime ERA by a left-handed hurler with at least 200 victories. He hurled
consecutive one-hitters in September 1955 and struck out 6 batters in a
row twice. In a 14-inning game on April 22, 1959, Ford defeated Washington
1–0 and struck out 15 Senators. Two years later, he won the Cy Young*
Award as best pitcher and triumphed in 14 consecutive games, including 8
during June.

Ford led the AL in winning percentage with 19–6 (.760) in 1956, 25–4
(.862) in 1961, and 24–7 (.774) in 1963. He paced the AL in victories in 1955
(18), 1961, (25), and 1963 (24), in ERA in 1956 (2.47) and 1958 (2.01), in
innings pitched in 1961 (283) and 1963 (269 1/3), and in games started in
1961 (39) and 1963 (37). Besides having 45 career shutouts, he paced the AL
in that category in 1958 (7) and shared the lead in 1960 (4). Ford's pitching
prowess was reflected in his being named to the AL All-Star team from 1954
through 1956, 1958 through 1961, and in 1964. World Series records are
replete with Ford's pitching accomplishments. He holds the fall classic records for most series (11), games pitched (22), games started (22), opening
games started (8), innings pitched (146), victories (10), losses (8), strikeouts
(94), bases on balls (34), and consecutive scoreless innings (33.2). His World
Series performances include a .556 winning percentage, 2.71 ERA, and three
shutouts. Ford's brilliant career resulted in his induction into the National
Baseball Hall of Fame in 1974. Ford married Joan Foran on April 14, 1951,
and has three children, Sally Ann, Edward, and Thomas.

BIBLIOGRAPHY: Jim Brosnan, *Great Baseball Pitchers* (New York, 1965); Whitey Ford,
Mickey Mantle, and Joseph Durso, *Whitey and Mickey: An Autobiography of the Yankee
Years* (New York, 1977); Whitey Ford file, National Baseball Hall of Fame Library,
Cooperstown, NY; Mark Gallagher, *Fifty Years of Yankee All Stars* (New York, 1984);
Joseph Gies and Robert H. Shoemaker, *Stars of the Series: A Complete History of the
World Series* (New York, 1965); Al Hirshberg, *The Greatest American Leaguers* (New
York, 1970); Paul MacFarlane, ed., *TSN Daguerreotypes of Great Stars of Baseball* (St.
Louis, 1981); Joseph L. Reichler, ed., *The Baseball Encyclopedia*, 6th ed. (New York,
1985), p. 1,723; Milton J. Shapiro, *Baseball's Greatest Pitchers* (New York, 1969); Milton
J. Shapiro, *The Whitey Ford Story* (New York, 1962).

                                                                       Louis J. Andolino

FOSTER, Andrew "Rube" (b. 17 September 1879, Calvert, TX; d. 9 December 1930, Kankakee IL), player, manager, and executive, was "the Father
of Black Baseball." The son of Sarah and minister Andrew Foster, he attended
the Negro school in Calvert through the eighth grade and began pitching for
the Fort Worth Yellow Jackets by 1897. In 1902 Foster joined Frank Leland's
Giants in Chicago, but jumped later that year to the Otsego, MI, white semi-

pro team and then to E. B. Lamar's Philadelphia Cuban X-Giants. The next year the X-Giants played the Philadelphia Giants for the "colored championship of the world," as Foster pitched four of the five X-Giant victories. In 1904 he joined the Philadelphia Giants team he had defeated, leading them to the pennant and beating the X-Giants in the playoff.

He rejoined the Leland Giants in 1907 after a salary dispute, but left again in 1910 and took the entire team with him. The next year he entered a partnership with John Schorling, a white tavern owner and son-in-law of Charles Comiskey.* Schorling had leased the old White Sox grounds and erected a new grandstand, and wanted Foster to provide a black team to play there. They agreed to split the profits evenly and closed the deal with a handshake, thus forming the Chicago American Giants.

Foster's Giants became the "most consistently superior" team in Negro baseball between 1911 and 1915 and remained a power into the 1920s. Foster attracted black stars, including Christobel Torrienti, John Beckwith,* and Bingo De Moss.* Foster's playing days had ended except for an occasional stint at first base, but he employed his vast knowledge as the Giants' manager. He also dominated Chicago baseball, controlling the bookings of many white semi-pro teams and the American Giants.

Faced with declining attendance and feuding with East Coast baseball magnate Nat Strong, Foster began agitating in 1919 in the Chicago *Defender* for the creation of a Negro Association modeled after the white major leagues. On February 13, 1920, six Midwest owners met with Foster in the Kansas City YMCA to arrange details. Foster was elected temporary president, upon which he presented the gathering with a league charter already written and incorporated in six states! A constitution was drawn up literally overnight, after which Foster was formally elected president and treasurer of the new NNL. Foster cited many reasons for the new league. The NNL would "create a profession that would equal the earning capacity of any other profession" for black players. Economic advantages for the owners included pennant races, a possible Negro World Series, and an end to player raids. Detractors claimed that Foster extended his own power over black baseball and became a virtual dictator, but the formation of the NNL saved the Negro game.

Besides administering the NNL, Foster continued operating the American Giants as manager and owner. His work day often began at 8:30 A.M and stretched through midnight. He drew no salary for his NNL work and kept 5 percent of the gate of every NNL game, but contributed part of that to NNL expenses and often to players and clubs in financial straits. Foster's Giants won the first three NNL pennants from 1920 through 1922. In 1925 other owners grumbled about the extent of Foster's influence, but gave him a unanimous vote of confidence when he offered to resign. In 1926, perhaps because of his grueling schedule, Foster suffered a nervous breakdown and was committed to the state asylum at Kankakee, IL. After his death four years later, crowds lined up for three days to view his casket in an unparalleled outpouring of grief. Foster's wife, Sara, whom he had married in 1908, survived him. Due to the lack of a written contract, however, neither she nor her two children collected any money from the American Giants. In 1981 Foster was elected to the National Baseball Hall of Fame.

Foster dominated black baseball before Jackie Robinson.* One of the great right-handed pitchers of the black era, he survived on wiles and raw skill. As a manager, he believed that games were won or lost in an inning or two and that every opportunity must be seized upon. Foster expected his players to bunt proficiently and execute the hit-and-run on command. His teams dominated games although opponents frequently batted for much higher averages. The stern disciplinarian called games when on the bench, pitching, and hitting. Foster's players became the best paid in Negro baseball. With the advent of the NNL, player salaries throughout the league rose to an average of $2,000 per year. In 1923 Foster's lowest paid player earned $175 a month, a fine wage then. His teams resembled white major leaguers by traveling on Pullman coach and received regular bonuses, often as high as $3,000. He had planned to make further innovations, including playing big league teams on their off-days in Chicago and adding a white player to the American Giants' roster.

Foster's main contribution remained his belief in black baseball. "Foster had a chance to leave Negro baseball," Dave Malarcher recalls, "and go into white semipro baseball . . . when he was pitching . . . He refused because he knew that all we had to do was to keep on developing Negro baseball, keep it up to the high standards and the time would come when the white leagues would have to admit us."

BIBLIOGRAPHY: William Brashler, *Josh Gibson: A Life in the Negro Leagues* (New York, 1978); Janet Bruce, *The Kansas City Monarchs: Champions of Black Baseball* (Lawrence, KS, 1985); Chicago *American*, July 24, 1955; Chicago *Defender*, November 29, December 13, December 20, 1919; December 13, December 20, December 27, 1930; Chicago *Tribune*, July 4, 1955; John Preston Davis, *The American Negro Reference Book* (Englewood Cliffs, NJ, 1966); John Holway, *Rube Foster: The Father of Black Baseball*, (Alexandria, VA, 1981); John Holway, *Voices from the Great Black Baseball Leagues* (New York, 1975); Rayford W. Logan and Michael R. Winston, *Dictionary of American Negro Biography* (New York, 1982); Robert W. Peterson, *Only the Ball Was White* (Englewood Cliffs, NJ, 1970); James A. Riley, *The All-Time All-Stars of Black Baseball* (Cocoa, FL, 1983); Donn Rogosin, *Invisible Men: Life in Baseball's Negro Leagues* (New York, 1983); A. S. Young, *Great Negro Baseball Stars* (Chicago, 1953).

                                                                    Gerald E. Brennan

FOSTER, George Arthur "The Destroyer" (b. 1 December 1948 or 1949, Tuscaloosa, AL), player, was a teammate of Dave Kingman in Little League, graduated with scholastic honors from Leuzinger High School in Lawndale, CA, and lettered in football, basketball, and baseball there. After a lengthy bachelorhood, Foster married and has one daughter. Foster signed with the San Francisco Giants (NL) in 1968 and made the All-Star teams at Medford, OR (NWL), and Fresno (CaL). He joined the Giants in late 1969, was sent down to Phoenix (PCL) in 1970, and had another brief trial with the parent club. After being traded to the Cincinnati Reds (NL) in 1971, he experienced two mediocre seasons there and was shipped to their Indianapolis (AA) farm in 1973.

Foster remained with the Reds in 1974 as a part-time player and then reached stardom in 1975, slugging 23 home runs with a .300 batting average. In 1976 his .306 batting average, 29 home runs, and league-leading 121 RBIs placed him second to teammate Joe Morgan* in the Most Valuable Player voting. *The Sporting News*, however, named Foster its NL Player of the Year. In the 1976 World Series, he hit .167 with four RBIs in four games and set a fall classic record for most putouts (8) by a left fielder in one game. Nicknamed "The Destroyer," Foster in 1977 became only the tenth player in major league history to hit 50 or more home runs in a single season. Foster, whose 52 home runs included three in one game, on August 3 slugged one round tripper that an engineer estimated might have traveled 720 feet had it not struck the stands. He set a major league record that year for most home runs by a right-handed hitter on the road with 31. His 52 homers, 149 RBIs, and 388 total bases that season established Cincinnati club records. He was named the NL's Most Valuable Player that year and repeated as *The Sporting News* NL Player of the Year. In 1978 he tied a major league record by winning the NL's RBI title for the third straight season and belted 40 homers to again lead the NL. After Riverfront Stadium opened in 1970, Foster hit three of the eight balls slugged into the upper deck in the first decade.

In 1982 Foster was traded to the New York Mets (NL) and signed a multiyear, multimillion dollar contract, giving him the highest single salary in major league baseball history through 1984. His five seasons as a Met, however, produced disappointing results. Despite missing very few games, Foster averaged only 20 home runs a year and batted .257. Before the Mets signing, Foster enjoyed a .289 career batting average. After slumping to a .227 batting average in 1986, he was released by the Mets in mid-season. He batted .216 for the Chicago White Sox (AL) before being waived in September 1986. Foster batted .274 lifetime, made 1,925 hits, slugged 348 home runs, scored 986 runs, and knocked in 1,239 tallies. A very quiet, honest individual with dry wit, Foster holds deep religious convictions and makes his Bible a constant companion.

BIBLIOGRAPHY: Malka Drucker with George Foster, *The George Foster Story* (New York, 1979); Joe Jares, "Shouting over a Quiet Man," *SI* 45 (July 19, 1976), pp. 74ff.
                                                              John E. DiMeglio

FOSTER, Willie "Bill" (b. 1904, Calvert?, TX; d. 1981), player and manager, was the half-brother of Rube Foster* and moved with his mother, Sarah, to Mississippi when he was still an infant. He grew up with his maternal grandparents after Sarah's death around 1908 and attended the elementary school at Alcorn College. Around 1918 he journeyed to Chicago to work in the stockyards and approach half-brother Rube about playing for the American Giants. When Rube refused, Willie returned to Mississippi. In 1923 the tall left-hander signed as a pitcher with the Memphis Red Sox. Rube, however, reacted furiously and ordered Memphis owner Bubbles Lewis to send Willie to the Chicago American Giants (NNL). This action poisoned the relationship of the two brothers permanently. Pitcher Willie deliberately resisted Rube's coaching until the latter's nervous breakdown forced him off the bench. Then Willie began applying everything his half-brother had taught him. In 1926 he won 29 games, including 26 in a row. For the next ten years, Willie ranked as the top left-hander in the Negro leagues and may have surpassed even Satchel Paige.* As a young pitcher, Foster relied mainly on his blinding speed. Upon maturing, he added a fast-breaking curve, a change-up, and an early version of the slider to his repertoire, and delivered all his pitches with the same motion. At the end of the 1926 season, the American Giants needed to win the final two games to edge Kansas City for the NNL pennant. Foster pitched both ends of a doubleheader and won both games. He completed three contests during the ensuing Negro World Series against the Bacharach Giants (ECL), winning two decisions and compiling a 1.27 ERA. He repeated in 1927 with two more complete game victories and a 3.00 ERA. A participant in Negro All-Star games in 1933 and 1934, he played with the American Giants except for short stints with the Kansas City Monarchs and the Homestead Grays in 1931. He served as player-manager of the American Giants in 1931, but resigned as pilot, believing that he could not perform both roles simultaneously. In 1933 he pitched the American Giants to another pennant and hurled a complete game for a victory against the East All Stars. Foster, whose baseball career ended with the Yakima Browns in 1938, became Dean of Men and coach at Alcorn College (Mississippi) in 1960 and held the latter position until shortly before his death.

BIBLIOGRAPHY: John Holway, *Rube Foster: The Father of Black Baseball* (Alexandria, VA, 1981); John Holway, *Voices from the Great Black Baseball Leagues* (New York, 1975); Robert W. Peterson, *Only the Ball Was White* (Englewood Cliffs, NJ, 1970); James A. Riley, *The All-Time All-Stars of Black Baseball* (Cocoa, FL, 1983); Donn Rogosin, *Invisible Men: Life in Baseball's Negro Leagues* (New York, 1983).

                                                                                    Gerald E. Brennan

FOURNIER, John Frank "Jack," "Jacques" (b. 28 September 1892, Au Sable, MI; d. 5 September 1973, Tacoma, WA), player, manager, coach, and scout, attended Aberdeen (WA) High School for two years. A good boxer and wrestler as a youngster, he grew into a 6 foot, 195 pounder, batted left, and threw right-handed. Although beginning his baseball career as a catcher for Aberdeen-Seattle, WA (NWL), in 1908, he switched to first base in 1910. With Moose Jaw in 1911, he led the WCaL in batting average (.377), runs, hits, doubles, and triples. He started 1912 with the Chicago White Sox (AL), but finished the season with Montreal (IL).

From 1913 to 1917, he played first base for the White Sox, and he led the AL in slugging percentage in 1915. After being replaced by Chick Gandil in 1917, Fournier played the next two seasons for Los Angeles (PCL). During the war-shortened 1918 season, he briefly replaced the New York Yankees' (AL) Wally Pipp. Fournier batted .350 in 27 games before the National Commission ruled that his contract belonged to the White Sox. Chicago returned him to Los Angeles, where he stayed until the St. Louis Cardinals (NL) bought his contract in 1920. He performed well in his three years with the Cardinals, batting .317 and slugging .472. After Jim Bottomley* joined the Cardinals in 1922, Branch Rickey* traded Fournier to the Brooklyn Dodgers (NL).

On June 19, 1923, Fournier made six hits in six at bats for Brooklyn. Manager Wilbert Robinson,* record holder with seven for seven, ordered an unsuccessful steal with Fournier at the plate to end the game. In 1924 Fournier led the NL in home runs (27) and assists by a first baseman and finished second in RBIs and walks. Although batting .350 in 1925, Fournier publicly complained about the foul language Brooklyn fans directed at him. He belted three home runs in one game in 1926 but was replaced by Floyd Herman.* Fournier, a top-notch bench jockey and spring training absentee, finished his major league career in 1927 with the Boston Braves (NL). In fifteen seasons, he played 1,530 games, batted .313, made 1,631 hits, 252 doubles, 113 triples, and 136 home runs, scored 821 runs, knocked in 859 runs, and slugged .483. He managed Johnstown, PA (MAL), in 1937 and Toledo (AA) in 1943 and coached at the University of California, Los Angeles (1934–1938). Fournier scouted for the AL St. Louis Browns (1938–1942, 1944–1947), NL Chicago Cubs (1950–1957), AL Detroit Tigers (1960), and NL Cincinnati Reds (1961–1962). He married Helen L. Commings on November 27, 1913.

BIBLIOGRAPHY: *The Baseball Encyclopedia* (Toronto, 1969); Frank Graham, *The Brooklyn Dodgers* (New York, 1945); Joe Marcin, ed., *TSN Official Baseball Guide, 1974* (St. Louis, 1974); Ira Smith, *Baseball's Famous First Basemen* (New York, 1956).

                                                                      Steven P. Savage

FOUTZ, David Luther "Dave," "Scissors," "Hunkidori Boy" (b. 7 September 1856, Carroll County, MD; d. 5 March 1897, Waverly, MD), player and manager, was the son of Miriam and Solomon Foutz. He married Minnie Glocke. Leadville, CO, knew Foutz as the "Hunkidori Boy," while NL fans nicknamed him "Scissors." Foutz compiled the second highest winning percentage (.690) of any major league pitcher, winning 147 and losing only 66 decisions. He started 216 games and finished 202 (also appearing in 35 as a relief pitcher) with a 2.84 ERA. According to an 1887 reporter, Foutz made an "enviable reputation in the baseball world." Besides pitching, he played 915 games at first base and in the outfield and one game at shortstop. During his career, he hit .277 for St. Louis and Brooklyn (AA) and Brooklyn (NL). From 1893 to 1896, Foutz served as player, captain, and manager for the Brooklyn team.

The 6 foot, 2 inch, 167 pound "gentlemanly, earnest" Foutz traveled frequently before reaching the majors. He played for Baltimore in 1877, but found no openings as a pitcher and journeyed to America's best-known silver mining town, Leadville, CO. Foutz gained his first fame there by starring in 1882 for the champion Leadville Blues. Since the Leadville club succeeded beyond expectations, Foutz became the toast of the city and state. At Bay City, MI, he became one of the NWL's best pitchers.

In July, 1884, the owner of the St. Louis team (AA) purchased the entire Bay City franchise just to secure him, commenting that he "is a bewilder and make no mistake." The right-hander responded brilliantly by winning 99 games and helping to pitch St. Louis to three consecutive championships (1885–1887). In 1886 his 41–16 record led the AA, while his 504 innings pitched and 11 shutouts marked career highs. A solid team player, Foutz appeared in 45 other games and batted .280. Although winning only 25 games the next year, he batted a spectacular .357 in 102 games.

The premier St. Louis (AA) club, meanwhile, possessed several high-salaried stars. Owner Christian Von der Ahe* converted some of that fame to cash. To the astonishment of the baseball world, Foutz and star pitcher Robert Caruthers* were sold in November, 1887, to Brooklyn (AA) for $13,500. The *New York Times* predicted that these acquisitions would "add greatly to the playing strength of Brooklyn." The prediction proved accurate because a championship nine soon graced the City of Churches.

Although pitching only occasionally and playing primarily first base, Foutz was an important factor in Brooklyn's win in 1889, driving in 113 runs and averaging .277 for the NL champions the following season. Foutz, renowned for pitching and hitting, proved a good right fielder and first baseman and stole 263 bases during his career. A power hitter, he slugged 186 doubles, 91 triples, and 32 home runs among his 1,254 career hits.

As manager, he never succeeded in piloting his team to the first division. Commenting on the 1896 season, *Spalding's Base Ball Guide* noted that the record was the poorest of the past ten years, and "no club disappointed its patrons as much as the Brooklyns." Ill health forced Foutz to retire at the end of the 1896 season. He applied for an umpiring position but died before the next season started.

BIBLIOGRAPHY: David L. Foutz file, National Baseball Hall of Fame Library, Cooperstown, NY; Leadville (CO) *Daily Herald*, 1882, July 27, 29, 1884; *NYT*, November 30, 1887, March 6, 1897; Joseph Reichler, ed., *The Baseball Encyclopedia*, 6th ed., (New York, 1985), pp. 922–923, 1,725–1,726; Harold Seymour, *Baseball: The Early Years* (New York, 1960); Duane A. Smith, "Baseball Champions of Colorado," *Journal of Sport History* 4 (Spring, 1977), pp. 51–71; *Spalding's Base Ball Guide*, 1883–1897; *The Sun* (Baltimore), March 6, 1897; David Quentin Voigt, *American Baseball* (Norman, OK, 1966).

Duane A. Smith

FOWLER, John W. "Bud" (b. John W. Jackson, 16 March 1858, Fort Plain, NY; d. 26 February 1913, Frankfort, NY), player, was the first black professional baseball player and the son of barber John and Mary (Lansing) Jackson. He grew up in Cooperstown, NY and first played professionally on a white team in New Castle, PA, in the early 1870s. He could play any position, like most players of his era, but excelled as a second baseman. Over a thirty-year span, Fowler played in virtually every section of the United States, including eastern cities, midwestern crossroads towns, pioneer villages, western settlements, and southern communities during several winters. Near the end of his career, Fowler claimed to have performed on teams in twenty-two states and Guelph, Canada.

Between 1878 and 1895, he played in white organized leagues with Lynn, MA, and Binghamton, NY (IA); Keokuk IA and Topeka KS (WL); Pueblo (CdL); Montpelier, VT (NeL); Crawfordsville, IN, Terre Haute, IN, and Galesburg, IL, (CIL); Greenville, MI, Adrian, MI, and Lansing, MI (MISL); Sterling, IL, Galesburg, IL, and Burlington, IA (3IL); and Lincoln and Kearney, NE (NeSL). Fowler also played with the Cuban Giants, the era's best all-black team, and formed black barnstorming clubs. The 1895 Page Fence Giants of Adrian, MI, the best-known of these barnstormers, traveled in their own railroad car and paraded to the ballpark on bicycles. His most colorful barnstorming team, the All-American Black Tourists, formed in 1903, also traveled by rail and offered to play ball in full-dress suits, opera hats, and silk umbrellas.

At his peak, Fowler consistently batted over .300, pitched, and was ranked among the best second basemen. The color line, however, barred him from the major leagues. During the off-season, he sometimes worked as a barber. Fowler, who never married, died of pernicious anemia at the home of a sister following a long illness.

BIBLIOGRAPHY: Robert W. Peterson, correspondence with Ocania Chalk, Merl Kleinknecht, Jerry Malloy, and Raymond J. Nemec, Robert W. Peterson Collection,

Ramsey, NJ.; Robert W. Peterson, *Only the Ball Was White* (Englewood Cliffs, NJ, 1970); Sol White, *History of Colored Base Ball* (Philadelphia, 1970).

Robert W. Peterson

FOX, Jacob Nelson "Nellie" (b. 25 December 1927, St. Thomas, PA; d. 1 December 1975, Baltimore, MD), player and coach, was the son of carpenter Jacob and Mae Fox. Nicknamed "Nellie," he enjoyed soccer and baseball as a youth. After leaving school at age 16, Fox signed a professional contract with manager Connie Mack* of the Philadelphia Athletics (AL) in 1944. He married Joanne Statler in June, 1947, and had two daughters, Bonnie and Tracy. Fox spent the 1944–1948 seasons in the minor leagues at Lancaster, PA (ISL), Jamestown, NY (Pol), and Lincoln (WL) appearing briefly with Philadelphia in 1947 and 1948 and making the Athletics roster in 1949. After being traded to the Chicago White Sox (AL) in October 1949, Fox became the premier AL second baseman. He played there from 1950 through 1963 and spent his final two seasons with Houston (NL).

The 5 foot, 10 inch, 160 pound Fox used a short, thick bat, controlled swing, and sharp batting eye to set major league records for most years, leading the league in singles (8) and having fewest strikeouts (11). In 1958 he played 98 consecutive games without striking out. He led the AL in hits four times (1952, 1954, 1957–1958), batted over .300 six seasons, proved a good bunter, and compiled a .288 career batting average. In 2,367 games, he made 2,663 hits, scored 1,279 runs, and struck out only 216 times. Despite his size and the physical dangers of second base play, Fox played in 798 consecutive games (1955–1960) to set the record for second basemen. Only Eddie Collins* and Joe Morgan* surpassed Fox' 2,295 games at second base.

As a fielder, Fox holds major league records for most years leading second basemen in putouts (10) and total chances (9) as well as AL records for career double plays (1,619) and years leading in double plays (5). He paced the AL in fielding percentage six times and won four Gold Glove awards. Fox was selected for 15 All-Star games, batting .368 and making an AL record 14 hits. His hits won the 1954 game and the first 1959 game. The heart of the "Go-Go" White Sox teams of the 1950s, Fox led Chicago to the 1959 AL pennant and was chosen AL Most Valuable Player. He hit .375 against the Los Angeles Dodgers in his only World Series appearance. Fox' trademarks included his bottle bat, large chaw of tobacco, and energetic, enthusiastic play. His buoyant personality made him extremely popular in Chicago, with his uniform number (2) being one of only two retired by the White Sox. He served as coach for Houston (NL) in 1966 and 1967 and for the Washington Senators (AL) in 1968 and owned a bowling alley in Pennsylvania after his playing career. He died of lymph cancer in 1975.

BIBLIOGRAPHY: David Condon, *The Go-Go Chicago White Sox* (Chicago, 1960); William B. Furlong, "He Ain't Big But He's All Fire," *SEP* 227 (May 14, 1955), pp. 30, 139, 142; Roger Kahn, "Little Nellie's a Man Now," *Sport* 25 (April, 1958), pp. 52–61;

Rich Lindberg, *Who's on Third?* (Chicago, 1983); Edgar Munzel, "Fiery Fox," *TSN*, (September 2, 1959), pp. 1, 6; *NYT*, December 2, 1975; Bob Vanderberg, *Sox* (Chicago, 1982).

Phillip P. Erwin

FOXX, James Emory "Jimmie," "Double X," "The Beast" (b. 22 October 1907, Sudlersville, MD; d. 21 July 1967, Miami, FL), player, coach, and manager, was the son of farmer Samuel Dell and Margaret (Smith) Foxx and exhibited right-hand batting power at Sudlersville High School and in semi-pro games. Frank "Home Run" Baker,* then managing Easton, MD (ESL), discovered Foxx in 1924, converted him from an infielder to a catcher, and sold him to the Philadelphia A's (AL) for 1925 spring delivery. After the 16-year-old batted .296 in 76 games for Easton, however, Philadelphia manager Connie Mack* brought him up to sit on the Athletics bench for the balance of 1924. Foxx was inserted in 10 games in early 1925 and then optioned to Providence, RI (IL), where he hit .327. Mack used him sparingly at first, but increasingly through 1926 and 1927. Foxx started in 1928 and batted .328 in 118 games as a first baseman, third baseman, and catcher. For the rest of his career, he performed at first base with average ability and occasionally played other positions.

For seven more seasons and three World Series (1929–1931), Foxx starred for the Athletics and averaged 41 homers per season with his straddle stance. His 58 round trippers in 1932 fell two short of Babe Ruth's* then record 60. During that season (perhaps his best), he attained .364 batting and .749 slugging percentages, scored 151 runs, drove in 169 tallies, and slugged 100 extra-base hits. The financially strapped Mack traded the strongboy to the Boston Red Sox (AL) for cash and players in December, 1935. Taking advantage of Fenway Park's short left field wall, Foxx averaged 36 home runs per year from 1936 through 1941. In 1938 he hit 50 homers, scored 139 runs, and drove in 175 tallies.

By 1942 excess alcohol, too many late nights, and a sinus affliction caused his deterioration. In June he was waived to the Chicago Cubs (NL) and hit only .205 in 70 games. After doing war work in 1943, he returned to the Cubs the next season as a coach and fringe player and finished the season managing Portsmouth, VA (Pil). In 1945 he batted .268 in 89 games and pitched 9 contests for the Philadelphia Phillies (NL). Subsequently he managed St. Petersburg, FL (FIL), in 1947 and Bridgeport, CT (CtL), in 1949.

The easygoing Foxx then failed at several business ventures and could not hold jobs for sustained periods. A public admission of his destitute condition caused the Boston (AL) organization to enlist him as coach with the Minneapolis (AA) club during 1958. He continued drifting, holding intermittent jobs at different places. He suffered from heart disease, and choked to death at his brother Sam's house when a piece of meat lodged in his throat.

Nicknamed "Double X," he terrorized pitchers particularly left-handers and belted some of the longest, hardest hit homers ever seen in AL ballparks. Exceptionally strong, with broad shoulders, bulging biceps, moon face, square jaw, the well-liked, good-natured Foxx was affectionately called "The Beast" by his peers. The truly great slugger was elected to the National Baseball Hall of Fame in 1951. In twenty major league seasons, he batted .325, slugged .609, hit 458 doubles, 125 triples, and 534 homers, drove in 1,921 runs, walked 1,452 times, and struck out 1,311 times in 2,317 games. He won the AL Most Valuable Player Award in 1932, 1933, and 1938 and was selected as first baseman on *The Sporting News* Major League All-Star team five times. Foxx led the AL in strikeouts (seven times), slugging average (five times), home runs (four times), RBIs (three times), walks (twice), and batting average and runs (once) and batted .344 in three World Series.

Foxx, who married Helen Heite in 1928 and later divorced, wed Dorothy Anderson Yard in 1943. He had two children James Emory, Jr., and William Kenneth, by his first marriage, and two children, John and Nancy (Mrs. Canaday), by his second.

BIBLIOGRAPHY: Martin Appel and Burt Goldblatt, *Baseball's Best: The Hall of Fame Gallery* (New York, 1977); Bob Broeg, *Super Stars of Baseball* (St. Louis, 1971); Jimmy Burns, "Foxx Takes Post as Miller Coach; Many Offer Help," *TSN*, January 29, 1958; James E. Foxx file, National Baseball Hall of Fame Library, Cooperstown, NY, n.d.; Frederick G. Lieb, "Foxx, No. 3 on All-Time Homer List, Dead," *TSN*, August 5, 1967; Tom Meany, *Baseball's Greatest Hitters* (New York, 1950); *NYT*, July 22, 1967; Joseph L. Reichler, ed., *The Baseball Encyclopedia*, 6th ed. (New York, 1985), p. 924; *TSN*, February 4, June 10, 1943, February 7, 1951; Frank Yeutter, "Art of Home-Run Hitting Dying, Declares Foxx," *TSN*, February 14, 1951.

Frank V. Phelps

FREEDMAN, Andrew (b. 1 September 1860, New York, NY; d. 4 December 1915, New York, NY), executive, was the son of grocer Joseph and Elizabeth (Davies) Freedman, both German Jews. He attended public schools, graduated from City College of New York with a law degree, and entered the real estate business. He joined Tammany Hall at age 21 and became an intimate of future machine boss Richard Croker. Although never holding public office, he exercised enormous political influence through his association with Croker as a member of Tammany's Finance Committee and as national Democratic party treasurer in 1897. Freedman used his political ties to make many choice real estate and government bonding deals through the Maryland Fidelity and Guarantee Company, which he founded in 1898. His most important project comprised the bonding for the construction of the New York City subway.

Freedman first became involved in sports in the 1890s as the receiver of Manhattan Field, where the New York Giants (NL) played in 1889 and where Big Three college football teams subsequently performed. In January,

1895, Freedman purchased the controlling interest in the Giants for $48,000 from local Republican politicians. An extremely unpopular owner, he was criticized for operating his franchise like a Tammany fiefdom. The irascible, quick-tempered Freedman hired twelve managers in eight years and repeatedly fired pilots for no cause. He encouraged rowdyism on the field and fought with the anti-Semitic "Ducky" Holmes and other players. Freedman, a penurious owner, fined star hurler Amos Rusie* $200 in 1895 after the latter had won 24 games, causing him to sit out the next season. Journalists, who chastised the Giants owner, were barred from the ballpark, while Freedman used his political clout to bully fellow team owners. He sought to establish a national baseball trust to operate the sport on sound business pinciples, including exercising tight control over wages and shifting franchises to the most profitable sites. His scheme to pool profits ultimately was defeated in 1901.

Freedman's presence in New York proved a major stumbling block for the AL, which wanted to establish a franchise there. His political influence and his position in the real estate market enabled him to control most potential park sites. AL president Ban Johnson* also feared that Freedman could order streets built through any field the junior circuit might find.

In 1902 Freedman sold the Giants because the club did not make the anticipated profits and had caused him aggravation; he concentrated instead on the forthcoming subway construction. John T. Brush, who bought most of Freedman's stock for $200,000, just had sold his Cincinnati Reds (NL) to Freedman's friend, Mayor Julius Fleischmann, and other members of that city's Republican machine. Freedman assisted the new Giants owner by keeping Manhattan free of interlopers and using his influence as a director of the IRT to block the subway from subsidizing an AL team, scheduled to begin play in New York the following season. The AL was forced to find investors with personal political clout in Tammany Hall capable of overcoming Freedman's opposition and breaking into the potentially lucrative New York market.

Freedman, a lifelong bachelor who had accumulated an estimated $7 million fortune at his death, lived at Sherry's on Fifth Avenue and owned an estate at Red Bank, NJ. He belonged to fourteen clubs and admired fast horses and yachts. The bulk of his estate was used to construct a home for the aged in the Bronx.

BIBLIOGRAPHY: Pat Edith Aynes, *The Andrew Freedman Story* (New York, 1976); "Andrew Freedman," *DAB*, 7 (New York, 1931), p. 8; *NYT*, December 5, 1915; Steven A. Riess, *Touching Base: Professional Baseball and American Culture in the Progressive Era* (Westport, CT, 1980); Harold Seymour, *Baseball: The Early Years*, vol. 1. (New York, 1960).

Steven A. Riess

FRENCH, Lawrence Herbert "Larry" (b. 1 November 1907, Visalia, CA), player, married Thelma Grace Olmstead on June 2, 1928, and attended the University of California at Berkeley for one year. The 6 foot, 1 inch, 195 pound left-hander of English-Scotch descent entered professional baseball in 1926 with Portland, OR (PCL), and Ogden, UT (UIL), and spent the 1927 and 1928 seasons with Portland. French broke into the major leagues in 1929 with the Pittsburgh Pirates (NL). His 7–5 record that year was followed by a 17–18 mark, leading the NL in losses. During the early 1930s, however, French became the workhorse of the Pirates staff and twice won 18 games.

After the 1934 season, he was traded to the Chicago Cubs (NL). The trade gave Chicago a needed left-hander and paid immediate dividends with an NL pennant, as French contributed 17 wins and 2 saves. The amiable southpaw enjoyed some of his best years with the Cubs, hurling 20 shutouts (twice tying for the NL lead) and producing a 95–84 record in a little over six seasons. His 18–9 and 15–8 1936 and 1939 seasons were his finest campaigns there, while his 10–19 mark in 1938 proved his worst. In two World Series, he recorded a good 3.21 ERA. French compiled two losses and no wins in five appearances, as Chicago lost both World Series.

French fit in well with the strong Cubs teams of the 1930s. A "go-getter" with business acumen, he advised many of his teammates on business transactions and dabbled in real estate. After suffering an injured thumb and a miserable 5–14 start in 1941, French was sent to Brooklyn for the waiver price. He hurled one inning in the World Series for the Dodgers without any decision. In 1942 French rebounded brilliantly with his knuckleball to lead the NL in winning percentage (.789) with a 15–4 mark. He joined the U.S. Navy in World War II and became a career officer, retiring in 1969. Never a robust hitter, he enjoyed his finest season in 1942 with a .300 batting average. During his fourteen-year career, French won 197 games and lost 171, struck out 1,187 batters in 3,152 innings, hurled 40 shutouts, and compiled a 3.44 ERA.

BIBLIOGRAPHY: Warren Brown, *The Chicago Cubs* (New York, 1946); Larry French file, National Baseball Hall of Fame Library, Cooperstown, NY; Eddie Gold and Art Ahrens, *The Golden Era Cubs* (Chicago, 1985); Joseph L. Reichler, ed., *The Baseball Encyclopedia*, 6th ed. (New York, 1985), p. 1,729.

Duane A. Smith

FRICK, Ford Christopher (b. 19 December 1894, Wawaka, IN; d. 8 April 1978, Bronxville, NY), sportswriter and baseball executive, was the son of Jacob and Emma Frick and grew up in northern Indiana farming communities. After graduating from DePauw University in 1915, Frick spent six years as a teacher and journalist in Colorado. He married Eleanor Cowing in 1916 and had one son, Frederick. In Colorado, Frick taught high school and college, briefly played for an industrial league baseball team, wrote for a newspaper, and in 1918–1919 supervised rehabilitation for World War I veterans. His stories about a devastating flood for the Colorado Springs *Telegraph* after the war won national recognition.

Frick, who moved to New York City in 1922, became a sportswriter with the New York *Journal* and covered the New York Yankees (AL) from 1923 to 1934. His career blossomed when he agreed to ghostwrite newspaper articles for Babe Ruth* and subsequently wrote *Babe Ruth's Own Book of Baseball*. Between 1930 and 1934, Frick combined newspaper work with radio announcing and shared in the first radio broadcast of Brooklyn Dodgers (NL) games in 1931.

Frick left journalism in 1934 to become director of the NL Service Bureau, a publicity office, and began his climb to the top of baseball's hierarchy. Nine months later he was elected NL president to replace John A. Heydler,* who resigned after a dispute with a team owner but officially cited health reasons for his departure. Between 1934 and 1951, NL president Frick avoided conflict with club owners and concentrated on routine administrative matters. He stabilized NL affairs, found new capital for financially weak teams, and promoted the addition of a Hall of Fame to the baseball museum that opened at Cooperstown, NY, in 1939. Although apparently content with the major league's exclusion of black players, Frick accepted Jackie Robinson's* appearance for Brooklyn (NL) in 1947. Acting through the team owner, he warned St. Louis Cardinals players threatening not to play the Dodgers that they would be "barred from baseball even though it means the disruption of a club or a whole league."

Baseball Commissioner Albert B. Chandler,* who had upset team owners, resigned in 1951, opening the way for Frick's election as the game's third commissioner and first from within baseball's ranks. He served two seven-year terms, retiring in 1965, and was voted into the National Baseball Hall of Fame in 1970. Baseball faced serious challenges during his tenure as Commissioner: franchise shifts, major league expansion, player demands, congressional hearings into the business side of baseball, survival of the minor leagues, the impact of television, and competition from other professional sports. The Commissioner treated most challenges as "league matters" beyond his control. Frick deferred to the most powerful owners and, critics said, primarily to Walter O'Malley,* who moved his Dodgers from Brooklyn to Los Angeles in 1957. During Frick's administration, five teams relocated, the AL added teams in Los Angeles and Minnesota in 1961, and the NL established franchises in New York and Houston in 1962. In a controversial 1961 decision, Frick ruled that official records show that Yankee Roger Maris* surpassed Babe Ruth's* season mark of 60 home runs in 161 rather than 154 games.

In bland, sentimental memoirs, Frick praised baseball owners and defended his own record of executive restraint. An alternative view came from maverick owner Bill Veeck,* who complained that the succession of commissioners from Judge Kenesaw Mountain Landis* to Frick should appear as a perpendicular line on a chart. Instead, Frick may have embodied the dominance of club owners in the period and baseball's own smug certainty about the future.

BIBLIOGRAPHY: Lee Allen, *The National League Story* (New York, 1961); Ford C. Frick, *Games, Asterisks, and People: Memoirs of a Lucky Fan* (New York, 1973); Lee Lowenfish and Tony Lupien, *The Imperfect Diamond* (Briarcliff Manor, NY, 1980); Paul MacFarlane, ed., *Hall of Fame Fact Book* (St. Louis, 1982); *NYT*, April 9, 1978; Bill Veeck and Ed Linn, *Veeck—as in Wreck* (New York, 1972); David Quentin Voigt, *American Baseball*, vol. 3 (University Park, PA, 1983).

                                                                    Joseph E. King

FRISCH, Frank Francis, "Frankie," "The Fordham Flash" (b. 9 September 1898, New York, NY; d. 12 March 1973, Wilmington, DE), all-around athlete, baseball player, manager, and broadcaster, was the son of immigrant Franz Frisch, a wealthy lace linen manufacturer, and Katherine (Stahl) Frisch. He attended Fordham Prep School and graduated from Fordham University in 1919. Besides being a sprinter on the track team, he played catcher on the baseball squad. Frisch captained Fordham's baseball, basketball, and football squads and was named as halfback on Walter Camp's* (FB) mythical All-American football second team in 1918.

Frisch signed with the New York Giants (NL) baseball club in 1919 and never played in the minors. He married Ada E. Lucy in November 1922; they had no children. Although using an unorthodox cross-handed batting style in college, Frisch corrected his stance with the Giants to become one of baseball's finest switch-hitters. With the Giants, he played second and third base. From 1921 to 1924, Frisch's batting and fielding helped the Giants to four consecutive pennants and two world championships. Manager John McGraw* admired Frisch's ability and named him captain, but later clashed with him in 1926 when the Giants dropped into the second division. On December 20, 1926, Frisch and pitcher Jimmy Ring were traded to the St. Louis Cardinals (NL) for stellar player-manager Rogers Hornsby.* Although the Cardinals had just won the world championship, Hornsby had wrangled with owner Sam Breadon* over salary and other issues.

Frisch, who faced hostile St. Louis fans upset at losing the popular Hornsby, responded in 1927 with a brilliant season by fielding spectacularly, batting .337, and leading the league with 48 stolen bases. The second baseman led the NL in fielding and assists and set a major league record for total chances accepted. He struck out only 10 times in 153 games, setting a major league record for fewest strikeouts in a season by a switch-hitter. Frisch helped the Cardinals win NL pennants in 1928, 1930, and 1931, when he was selected as the NL's Most Valuable Player. He was named player-manager of the Cardinals on July 24, 1933, and led his team to another pennant in his first full season (1934) as pilot. In 1931 and 1934 the Cardinals won world championships. Frisch, who retired as a player in 1937, was released as Cardinals manager on September 10, 1938. Frisch piloted the Pittsburgh Pirates (NL) from 1940 through 1946 and the Chicago Cubs (NL) from June 10, 1949, through July 21, 1951. In sixteen major league seasons as manager, Frisch saw his clubs win 1,137 of 2,215 games for a .513 percentage. He announced over radio for the Boston Braves in 1939 and from 1947 through 1949 for the New York Giants.

As a player, Frisch appeared in 2,311 games, made 2,880 hits, slugged 466 doubles, knocked in 1,244 runs, stole 419 bases, and batted .316. Besides leading the NL in stolen bases in 1921(49), 1927(48), and 1931(28), Frisch set numerous fielding records for NL second basemen and various batting and fielding marks in his 50 World Series games. In 1947 he was elected to the National Baseball Hall of Fame.

BIBLIOGRAPHY: Bob Broeg, *Super Stars of Baseball* (St. Louis, 1971); Gene Karst and Martin J. Jones, Jr., *Who's Who in Professional Baseball* (New Rochelle, NY, 1973); *TSN*, March 24, 1973.

Gene Karst

G

GALBREATH, John Wilmer (b. 10 August 1897, Derby, OH), baseball executive, horse breeder, and sportsman, was the son of farmer Francis Hill and Belle (Mitchell) Galbreath. After graduating from Mt. Sterling High School, he worked his way through Ohio State University by washing dishes, waiting tables, and photographing fellow students. After his college graduation on 1920, he formed a real estate business. During the 1930s, he amassed a fortune by buying company-owned towns from U.S. Steel, Westinghouse, the Erie Mining Company, and other corporations. After renovating the houses, he sold them back to the workers. He made a second fortune by building, leasing, and managing skyscrapers. He married Helen Mauck on September 14, 1921, and had two children, Joan Hill and **Daniel Mauck Galbreath** (b. 15 June 1928, Columbus, OH). After Helen died in 1946, Galbreath married Dorothy Bryan Firestone on February 17, 1955.

Galbreath invested considerable money in two racing stables named Darby Dan Farms near Columbus, OH, and at Lexington, KY. In 1955 he paid a world record $2 million for 1955 Kentucky Derby winner Swaps* (OS). In 1959 he leased the undefeated Italian horse Ribot for five years at $1.35 million. When the animal's contrary disposition prevented its return to Italy, Galbreath leased the horse for life. Darby Dan Farms produced several notable horses, including Chateaugay (1963 Kentucky Derby and Belmont Stakes winner), Proud Clarion (1967 Kentucky Derby), Little Current (1974 Preakness and Belmont Stakes), and Graustark. When his horse Roberto (named for baseball player Roberto Clemente*) won the 1972 English Epsom Derby, Galbreath became the only person to win derbies on both sides of the Atlantic. Galbreath, among the most influential American horse racing figures, headed the committees building the Belmont and Aqueduct race tracks and modernizing the Saratoga racing plant in New York. He formed the group that bought up shares in the Kentucky Derby when a business conglomerate threatened to take it over.

In 1946 Galbreath joined a four-man syndicate, including singer-entertainer Bing Crosby, that purchased the Pittsburgh Pirates (NL). Four years later, he bought 70 percent of the club, named himself president, and hired Branch Rickey* as general manager to reverse the Pirates' dismal fortunes. During the next fifteen years, Galbreath lost an estimated $2 million. The 1952 Pirates, who lost 112 games and finished last in the NL by 54 1/2 games, rank among the worst baseball teams ever. Galbreath's patience, however, paid off. Led by outfielder Roberto Clemente and manager Danny Murtaugh, the Pirates upset the powerful New York Yankees four games to three in the 1960 World Series. As baseball owner, Galbreath helped to formulate the 1957 players' pension plan and to choose a successor to Commissioner Ford Frick.* By the late 1970s, Galbreath's honesty and even-handedness made him among America's most respected elder sportsmen.

His son, Daniel, executive, graduated from Amherst College in 1950 and earned a Master's degree in business administration from Ohio State University in 1952. He married Elizabeth Lind on July 17, 1954, and has three children, Laurie Lind, Lizanne, and John Wilmer II. Dan assumed many of his father's business interests in the 1950s and 1960s and was named president of the Pittsburgh Pirates in 1970. Under his leadership, the Pirates reached the NL Championship Series in 1970, 1971, 1974, 1975, and 1979. Pittsburgh captured the 1971 and 1979 World Series, defeating the Baltimore Orioles both times. Following the 1979 season, the club's fortunes and quality of play declined markedly. In 1985 the Galbreath family sold its majority interest in the Pirates to a unique public-private coalition consisting of the city of Pittsburgh and several local corporations and individuals.

BIBLIOGRAPHY: "Down the Mountain," *Time*, 76 (August 22, 1960), p. 56; Jack Mann, "Superfan and Super Achiever," *SI*, 24 (January 24, 1966), pp. 53–60; *WWA*, 3 (1982–83), p. 1,149.

John Hanners

GALVIN, James Francis "Pud," "Gentle Jeems," "The Little Steam Engine" (b. 25 December 1855, St. Louis, MO; d. 7 March 1902, Pittsburgh, PA), player and umpire, grew up in the Irish section of St. Louis known as Kerry Patch. He married Bridget Griffin on February 20, 1878 and had eleven children. Galvin began his professional pitching career in 1875 for St. Louis (NA). In 1876 he pitched for the St. Louis Red Stockings, an independent club, hurling no-hit, no-run games against Philadelphia on July 4 and the Cass Club of Detroit on August 17. The latter no-hitter probably was the first perfect game (no batters reaching base) ever by a pro pitcher. In 1877 Galvin pitched 4 shutouts in 19 games for Allegheny (IA), part of baseball's first minor league. For the 1878 pennant-winning Buffalo Bisons

(IA), Galvin pitched 106 of the team's 116 games, winning 72, losing 25, and tying 3. In addition, he recorded 17 shutouts, hurled 96 complete games, and won 10 of 15 games against NL clubs.

In 1879 Buffalo joined the NL. With Buffalo from 1879 to 1885, Galvin became one of the game's premier pitchers, winning 37, 20, 29, 28, 46, 46, and 13 games for a team never finishing above third place. Galvin pitched no-hit, no-run games against Worcester, MA, on August 20, 1880, and against Detroit on August 4, 1884. In 1884 Galvin shut out the Providence Grays, 2–0 to end their 20-game winning streak and stop Providence pitcher Hoss Radbourne,* who had won 18 consecutive contests. A workhorse of legendary reputation, Galvin pitched 593 innings in 1879, 656 innings in 1883, and 636 innings in 1884.

Early in the 1885 season, Buffalo sold Galvin to Allegheny (AA) for $2,500 and gave him $750 of the sale price. His $3,000 contract with the Allegheny club exceeded by $1,000 his salary at Buffalo. He hurled for Pittsburgh (NL) from 1887 to 1889 and in 1890 jumped to Pittsburgh (PL). When the PL folded after one season, Galvin returned to the Pittsburgh Nationals for the 1891 season and part of the 1892 season and completed his major league career with St. Louis (NL) in 1892. He failed in a comeback attempt with Buffalo (EL) in 1894 and umpired briefly in the NL. After his baseball career, Galvin resided in Pittsburgh, operated an unsuccessful saloon, and worked for a contractor and as a bartender. When he died in 1902, the impoverished Galvin left his wife and six surviving children.

He was nicknamed "Gentle Jeems" for his placid nature, "Pud" for making pudding out of opposing batters, and "The Little Steam Engine" for his vigorous pitching style. The 5 foot, 8 inch, 190 pound Galvin proved a superb fielder and strong hitter and often played in the outfield when not pitching. Besides using an intimidating fastball and a devastating change of pace, he developed a brilliant pickoff move. In an 1886 contest with Pittsburgh, he walked three men and then picked each one off first base. During his fourteen-year major league career, Galvin won 361 games; he is tied for sixth place among all pitchers. He ranks second only to Cy Young* in complete games (639), innings pitched (5,941 1/3), and games lost (310). He notched 1,799 strikeouts and recorded 57 shutouts. Despite these imposing credentials, he was not elected to the National Baseball Hall of Fame until 1965.

BIBLIOGRAPHY: James F. Galvin, correspondence with Buffalo Baseball Club, 1877, 1878, Joseph M. Overfield Collection, Tonawanda, NY; George Moreland, *Balldom* (New York, 1914); Joseph Overfield, "A Memorable Performer-Jim Galvin," *Baseball Research Journal*, 11 (1982), pp. 80–83; Joseph Overfield, "First Great Minor League Club," *Baseball Research Journal*, 6 (1977), pp. 1–6; Pittsburgh *Gazette*, March 8, 1902; Lowell Reidenbaugh, *Cooperstown: Where Baseball's Legends Live Forever* (St. Louis, 1983); *TSN*, February 13, 1965.

Joseph M. Overfield

GARDNER, William Lawrence "Larry" (b. 13 May 1886, Enosburg Falls, VT; d. 11 March 1976, St. George, VT), player, coach, and administrator, was signed from the University of Vermont campus by the Boston Red Sox (AL) in 1908. After being sent to Lynn, MA (NEL), for seasoning, he started from 1910 to 1917 as the Red Sox third baseman. The New Englander by birth and temperament felt more comfortable playing for Boston, especially after University of Vermont friend Ray Collins joined the Red Sox. Although few players from that era had attended college, the Boston Red Sox fielded more college players than any other major league team. Bill Carrigan, Duffy Lewis, Harry Hooper,* Chris Mahoney, and Marty McHale had attended college and welcomed Gardner.

In the dead ball era, he hit over .300 five times and retired with a .289 lifetime batting average. In 1,922 games, he made 1,931 hits, slammed 300 doubles, and knocked in 929 runs. Gardner, a good fastball hitter, always batted well against Walter Johnson.* Ty Cobb* alleged that he never beat out a bunt against Gardner. Years later Gardner told Cobb, "You clenched your jaw and clamped your lips together when you intended to bunt." Gardner shrewdly never told others how Cobb telegraphed the bunt, keeping the information secret. In 1914 Babe Ruth,* a raw, untutored youth, joined the Red Sox. Ruth's behavior shocked Gardner and the more cultivated team members, but his immense talent impressed them. Gardner starred on the AL championship teams of 1912, 1915, and 1916 and drove in the winning run in the final game of the 1912 World Series against the New York Giants. In the fourth game of the 1916 World Series against the Brooklyn Dodgers, his three-run homer off Rube Marquard* proved the deciding blow and the turning point of the Series.

In 1918 he was traded to the Philadelphia Athletics (AL), but manager Connie Mack* the next year gave his position to promising rookie Jimmy Dykes.* Gardner ended his career from 1919 to 1924 with the Cleveland Indians (AL). Although not excelling in the 1920 World Series, he was involved peripherally in its most celebrated play. A photo showed Gardner and a Brooklyn runner at third watching Bill Wambsganss making the final out of his unassisted triple play. Subsequently, Gardner coached baseball at the University of Vermont for twenty-five years and served as athletic director there for eight years. An articulate, well-read man who enjoyed campus life, he and Jack Coombs* were considered among the nation's finest collegiate coaches. Although respecting the players he coached, Gardner maintained that the players of his era were superior.

BIBLIOGRAPHY: Ty Cobb with Al Stump, *My Life in Baseball: The True Record* (New York, 1961); Lawrence Ritter, *The Glory of Their Times* (New York, 1966); *TSN*, March 27, 1978.

                                                                      Anthony J. Papalas

GARVEY, Steven Patrick "Steve" (b. 22 December 1948, Tampa, FL), player, is the only child of bus driver Joseph Patrick and Mildred (Winkler) Garvey. He graduated from Chamberlain High School in Tampa, where he starred in baseball and football. For the Michigan State University Spartans, he excelled as an All-American baseball player and starting defensive halfback in football. In 1971 he graduated from Michigan State with a Bachelor of Science degree in education. He married Cyndy Truhan (from whom he was since divorced) on October 29, 1971, and has two children.

Garvey was the first draft choice of the Los Angeles Dodgers (NL) in 1968 and assigned to Ogden, UT (PrL). After a three-game tryout the following year, he spent most of the season at Albuquerque (TL) and hit .373. In 1970 he rejoined the Los Angeles Dodgers. Originally a third baseman, he was switched to first base in 1973 and starred in the remarkable Dodgers infield with Davey Lopes, Bill Russell, and Ron Cey for a decade.

A steady, durable right-handed power hitter, Garvey through 1986 had 2,583 career hits, 438 doubles, 271 home runs, 1,299 RBIs, and a .295 batting average. Besides having six 200-hit seasons, he has accumulated five with over 100 RBIs and 20 home runs. His 33 round trippers in 1977 established a record for Dodgers first basemen. The same year he tied an NL mark with five extra-base hits (two homers and three doubles) in one game. In 1982 he batted a consistent .285 at home and .279 away, .280 on grass and .285 on artificial turf.

Garvey played the entire Dodgers schedule for seven seasons, breaking the NL consecutive game record. His streak ended in 1983 at 1,207 games, the fourth longest in major league history. An impeccable fielder with a .994 career average, Garvey has earned four Gold Gloves. In 1976 he set a league record for fewest errors (3) by a first baseman handling at least 1,500 chances. In the strike-shortened 1981 season, he missed a perfect 1.000 average by the margin of one error in 1,075 chances. Garvey did not make an error in 1,319 chances in 1984.

These performances have earned him eleven All-Star Game appearances, including eight in the starting lineup, and two awards as its Most Valuable Player. In 1977 he became the first National Leaguer to get over 4 million votes in the All-Star balloting. In 1974 he was chosen NL MVP. A reliable clutch hitter, Garvey has batted .393 in All-Star competition, .368 in one division series, .356 in five league Championship Series, and .319 in five World Series. After thirteen seasons with the Dodgers, he elected free agency in 1982 and negotiated a five-year, $6.6 million contract with the San Diego Padres (NL).

Garvey is a handsome, stalwart player considered to be as upright in character as in batting stance. In 1977 a junior high school in Lindsay, CA, was named after him. He serves as honorary chairman of the Multiple Sclerosis Foundation. An enterprising businessman, he is founder and chairman of Professional Athletes Career Enterprises, Inc. (PACE) of Barrington, IL. A national career counseling and placement service, PACE helps athletes adjust to the job market outside the world of sports.

BIBLIOGRAPHY: John Heins, "Stepping Into the Vacuum," *Forbes* 123 (April 30, 1984), p. 134; Gene Karst and Martin L. Jones, Jr., *Who's Who in Professional Baseball* (New Rochelle, NY, 1973); Los Angeles *Times*, September 11, 1977; Joseph L. Reichler, ed., *The Baseball Encyclopedia*, 6th ed. (New York, 1985), pp. 941–942; San Diego Padres *Media Guide, 1983*.

David L. Porter

GEHRIG, Henry Louis "Lou," "The Iron Horse," "Columbia Lou" (b. 19 June 1903, New York, NY; d. 2 June 1941, Riverdale, NY), player, was the son of skilled mechanic Heinrich and Christina (Flack) Gehrig, both German immigrants who settled in New York City. They had four children, but only Lou survived. Gehrig attended Public School No. 132 and New York's High School of Commerce, excelling in baseball, football, swimming, and other sports. Although entering Columbia University in 1921, Gehrig was barred from athletic competition for one year because he had played baseball briefly that summer for Hartford, CT (EL). The next year he participated in both football and baseball at Columbia, starring in the latter sport. In June, 1923, the New York Yankees (AL) signed him to a baseball contract. Gehrig played most of the 1923 and 1924 seasons at Hartford, where he won acclaim as a power-hitting first baseman. He did not become a regular player for the Yankees until June 1, 1925, when he began the 2,130 consecutive game streak which ran to the end of his career in 1939.

Gehrig experienced moderate success in 1925–1926, leading the AL with 20 triples the latter season. In 1927 he blossomed as a major slugging star and challenged teammate Babe Ruth* most of the season in home runs. Gehrig ended the season with 47 home runs, while Ruth slugged a then record 60 round trippers. He bested Ruth in most other departments, however, by batting .373, leading the AL with 52 doubles and 447 total bases, and setting a then major league record with 175 RBIs. Besides being voted the AL's Most Valuable Player, Gehrig helped the 1927 Yankees (whom most baseball authorities consider the greatest team of all time) sweep the World Series from the Pittsburgh Pirates in four games.

Gehrig continued playing exceptional ball, scoring and knocking in over 100 runs for thirteen consecutive seasons. In 1931 he slugged 46 home runs and became baseball's top run producer by scoring 163 and knocking in 184. He led the league in RBIs five times, runs scored and total bases four times, slugging percentage twice, and batting average once. Gehrig won the Triple crown (home runs, RBIs, and batting average) in 1934 and in 1927 and 1936 he won AL Most Valuable Player awards.

The left-handed slugger became the first AL player to hit four home runs in one game, connecting against the Philadelphia Athletics on June 3, 1932. Gehrig also compiled a career record of 23 grand slam homers. The powerfully built 6 foot, 210 pound slugger ran the bases well, stole home 15 times, and fielded adequately. Although quiet and modest off the field, Gehrig exhibited very competitive characteristics during game situations. His impressive career batting statistics included 535 doubles, 493 home runs, 1,188 runs scored, 1,990 RBIs, 1,508 walks, and a .340 batting average.

During spring training in 1939, Gehrig appeared to lack power and coordination. Shortly after the season started, on May 2, he removed himself from the lineup after playing in 2,130 consecutive games. A thorough examination at the Mayo Clinic in Rochester, MN, indicated that the 35-year-old star had contracted a rare muscle disease called amyothropic lateral sclerosis, and had a slim chance for survival. He continued as non-playing captain of the Yankees until the season's end. At Yankee Stadium on July 4, 1939, over 62,000 fans and a grateful nation honored the modest hero. In December, 1939, he was elected to the National Baseball Hall of Fame.

Mayor Fiorello LaGuardia named Gehrig New York City Parole Commissioner, a position he held until his health failed. Gehrig married Eleanor Twitchell of Chicago in September, 1933. They had no children. Lou Gehrig Plaza in the Bronx was named for him.

BIBLIOGRAPHY: Bob Broeg, *Superstars of Baseball* (St. Louis, 1971); *CB* (1940), pp. 330–332; *DAB*, Supp. 3 (1941–1945), pp. 294–295; Raymond J. Gonzalez, "The Gehrig Streak Reviewed," *Baseball Research Journal*, 4 (1975), pp. 34–37; Raymond Gonzalez, "Larrupin' Lou and 23 Skidoo," *Baseball Research Journal*, 12 (1983), pp. 22–26; Raymond Gonzalez, "Lou Who? Stole Home 15 Times," *Baseball Research Journal*, 7 (1978), pp. 109–111; Raymond Gonzalez, "Still the Greatest One-Two Punch," *Baseball Research Journal*, 6 (1977), pp. 98–101; Frank Graham, *Lou Gehrig, A Quiet Hero* (New York, 1942); *TSN Baseball Register, 1942* (St. Louis, 1942).

L. Robert Davids

GEHRINGER, Charles Leonard "Charlie," "The Mechanical Man" (b. 11 May 1903, Fowlerville, MI), baseball and football player, coach, and executive, grew up on a farm near Lansing, MI, and played baseball with his brother Al. Gehringer starred as a third baseman for his Fowlerville High School and town teams and played both baseball and football at the University of Michigan. After one year there, he entered professional baseball with the Detroit Tigers (AL) organization. Former Tigers outfielder Robert Veach* arranged Gehringer's tryout at Detroit's Navin Field. Gehringer impressed Tigers manager Ty Cobb,* who assigned him to London (MOL). At London, Gehringer was shifted to second base and batted .292 in 1924. After Gehringer hit .462 in five games with the Tigers at season's end, in 1925 he batted .325 with 25 home runs and 108 RBIs at Toronto and led

IL second basemen in fielding. He rejoined the Tigers for the final eight games of the season as a replacement for Frank O'Rourke.

The 5 foot, 11 1/2 inch, 185 pound Gehringer, who batted left-handed and threw right-handed, played his entire seventeen-year major league career (1926–1942) with Detroit and started at second base for sixteen seasons. An outstanding fielder, he possessed quick hands and proved graceful and virtually flawless with a glove. He paced AL second basemen in fielding percentage nine times, led or tied for the lead in assists seven times, and prevailed in putouts three years. Gehringer, a fine .320 lifetime batter, hit .277 his rookie year and batted at least .300 from 1927 to 1940 except for a .298 mark in 1932. His best marks included .356 in 1934, .354 in 1936, and .371 and an AL batting title in 1937. A consistent hitter, he possessed some power, with 1,427 career RBIs. He made over 200 hits in each of seven seasons, including five in succession from 1933 through 1937. In 2,323 career games, Gehringer stroked 2,839 career hits, including 574 doubles (10th), 146 triples, and 184 home runs. He scored 1,774 runs and recorded seven 100-plus RBI seasons.

With Gehringer at second base, Detroit often finished well and won AL flags in 1934, 1935, and 1940. He batted .379 in the 1934 World Series and .375 in the 1935 classic to help the Tigers win the world championship, but hit only .211 in the 1940 classic. Overall, Gehringer's .321 post-season batting average was one point above his career mark. Nicknamed "The Mechanical Man" because of his calm, consistent, superior play, Gehringer received many honors. He was named to *The Sporting News* Major League All-Star team in 1933, 1934, 1936, 1937, and 1938 and was selected AL Most Valuable Player in 1937. Gehringer played every inning of the first six All-Star games and hit .500, a record for players participating in at least five midseason classics. In 1949 he was named to the National Baseball Hall of Fame.

When his playing skills deteriorated in 1942, Gehringer became a Detroit Tigers coach. He then joined the U.S. Navy, serving in the Fitness Program for the duration of World War II. After the war, he became a manufacturer's agent until being named vice-president and general manager of the Detroit Tigers in 1951. He held both posts until the end of the 1953 season, when he hired Muddy Ruel as general manager. Gehringer, a bachelor, retired from the Detroit front office in 1959 and resides in Birmingham, MI.

BIBLIOGRAPHY: Lee Allen and Tom Meany, *Kings of the Diamond* (New York, 1965); Martin Appel and Burt Goldblatt, *Baseball's Best: The Hall of Fame Gallery* (New York, 1977); Paul MacFarlane, ed., *TSN Daguerreotypes of Great Stars of Baseball* (St. Louis, 1971); Joseph L. Reichler, ed., *The Baseball Encyclopedia*, 6th ed. (New York, 1985), p. 944. Ken Smith, *Baseball's Hall of Fame* (New York, 1978).

Douglas D. Martin

GIBSON, Joshua "Josh" (b. 21 December 1912, Buena Vista, GA; d. 20 January 1947, Pittsburgh, PA), player, was the son of sharecropper and millworker Mark and Nancy (Woodlock) Gibson. Josh had a brother, Jerry, who pitched for the Cincinnati Tigers, and a sister, Annie. Gibson attended public school through grade five in Buena Vista and studied at Allegheny Pre-Vocational School in Pittsburgh, where he began learning the electrician's trade. In 1930 he married Helen Mason, who later died giving birth to their twin children, Josh, Jr., and Helen.

In 1927 Gibson joined the semi-pro Pittsburgh Crawfords. Three years later, the powerfully built 6 foot, 1 inch, 215 pound Gibson joined the Homestead Grays (ANL) at midseason. His home runs at Yankee Stadium in New York and Forbes Field in Pittsburgh were the longest hit in each park. In 1931 the 19-year-old Gibson hit 75 home runs and quickly became a star of the first magnitude. From 1932 to 1936 he excelled for the Pittsburgh Crawfords (NNL) and caught for the legendary Satchel Paige.* In 1934 he slugged 69 home runs. From 1937 to 1940 he starred for the Grays and dominated the NNL in hitting. In 1940 he signed a contract for $6,000 (a $2,000 raise) with Vera Cruz (MEL). After returning to the Grays in 1942 he developed a brain tumor. Gibson refused to be operated on, and the brain tumor contributed to his early death.

From 1933 to 1945 Gibson played winter baseball in Puerto Rico, Cuba, Mexico, and Venezuela. In 1941 he compiled a remarkable .480 batting average and earned the Most Valuable Player Award in Puerto Rico. During the early 1940s, Gibson earned $6,000 in the NNL and $3,000 in Puerto Rico annually. Gibson's salary was surpassed only by that of Paige among black players. In contrast, Babe Ruth* earned a peak salary of $80,000 in the 1930–1931 era.

From 1937 to 1946, Gibson and Buck Leonard* were considered the NNL's Babe Ruth and Lou Gehrig* and helped the Grays win nine consecutive NNL titles. Gibson never played for a losing team. Due to poor record keeping, his home run hitting prowess cannot be fully documented. Estimates place his total homers around 960 and his lifetime batting average over .350 for his seventeen-year career. He hit four home runs in one game in 1938 in Washington's spacious Griffith Stadium and in 1943 hit eleven homers to left field there, a feat never duplicated by major leaguers.

Gibson batted .483 as a starting catcher in nine Negro East-West All-Star games played before large crowds at Comiskey Park in Chicago. Walter Johnson* rated Gibson superior to Bill Dickey,* while Roy Campanella* considered him an all-time great catcher. According to Johnson, Gibson combined superb defensive skills with impressive power hitting. In exhibition contests, he batted well against star major league pitchers Grover Cleveland Alexander,* Dizzy Dean,* and Bob Feller.* As a batter, he turned up his cap bill, rolled up his left sleeve, and hit from a flat-footed stance. Joe DiMaggio,* emulating Gibson's style, did not take a stride into the pitch.

In 1972 Gibson became the second player from the Negro leagues elected to the National Baseball Hall of Fame. Many baseball experts regard Gibson as the sport's greatest home run hitter in numerical and power terms.

BIBLIOGRAPHY: Martin Appel and Burt Goldblatt, *Baseball's Best: The Hall of Fame Gallery* (New York, 1977); William Brashler, *Josh Gibson* (New York, 1978); Robert W. Peterson, *Only the Ball Was White* (Englewood Cliffs, NJ, 1970); Pittsburgh *Courier*, January 25, 1947; Andrew S. Young, *Great Negro Baseball Stars* (New York, 1953); Andrew S. Young, *Negro Firsts in Sports* (Chicago, 1963).

Robert T. Bowen

GIBSON, Robert "Bob," "Hoot," "Gibby" (b. 9 November 1935, Omaha, NE), player and coach, is the seventh child of Pack Gibson, a millworker who died before Robert's birth, and Victoria Gibson. Despite suffering from rickets, asthma, pneumonia, hay fever, and a rheumatic heart as a child, Gibson starred in basketball and baseball at Omaha Technical High School from 1949 to 1953. After rejecting an offer from the Kansas City Monarchs (NAL), he accepted a basketball scholarship at Creighton University in Omaha in 1953 and broke numerous scoring records there. He married high school sweetheart Charline Johnson in April, 1957, and has two daughters, Renee and Annette.

In 1957 Gibson signed as a pitcher with the St. Louis Cardinals (NL) and was sent to Omaha (AA). In the autumn of 1957 he played basketball with the Harlem Globetrotters. Gibson displayed increased speed and better control at Rochester, NY (IL), and saw action with the Cardinals in 1959 and 1960, compiling 3–5 and 3–6 win-loss marks. After having respectable 13–12 and 15–13 seasons in 1961 and 1962, "Hoot" posted 18, 19, 20, and 21 victories with St. Louis from 1963 to 1966, respectively. Between 1962 and 1966, he averaged 230 strikeouts per year. Gibson's 9–2 mark the final six weeks of the 1964 season paced the Redbirds to their first NL pennant since 1946.

Although suffering a broken ankle in a July 15, 1967, contest, he returned in September to win three games, helping the Cardinals win another NL pennant. In 1968 the 6 foot, 1 inch, 193 pound right-hander enjoyed an extraordinary 22–9 season with 15 consecutive wins, 13 shutouts, 268 strikeouts, and a 92-inning stretch yielding only 2 runs. He compiled a 1.12 ERA, the lowest ever in the major leagues for at least 300 innings pitched. The season proved even more remarkable given the arthritis and chipped bone in Gibson's right elbow. Gibson set numerous World Series records in 1964, 1967, and 1968, including eight consecutive complete games pitched, seven consecutive victories, seventeen strikeouts in a game (1968), and three complete-game wins in a World Series (1967).

In 1969 and 1970 Gibson won 20 and 23 games, respectively, and averaged over 300 innings and 270 strikeouts per season. A torn thigh muscle slowed him to a 16–13 mark in 1971, but he hurled his fiftieth career shutout and on August 14 tossed an 11–0 no-hitter against the Pittsburgh Pirates. After rebounding to a 19–11 log in 1972, he missed two months of the 1973 campaign with a torn cartilage and finished at 12–10. Arthritis and knee injuries took a heavy toll, causing Gibson to finish his playing career with 11–13 and 3–10 marks. Gibson completed a seventeen-year Cardinals career with a 251–174 record, 56 shutouts, 3,117 strikeouts, and a 2.91 ERA. A good hitter, "Gibby" slugged 24 career home runs and batted .303 in 1970. His honors included two Cy Young* awards (1968, 1970), NL Most Valuable Player (1968), nine Gold Gloves, and overwhelming election to the National Baseball Hall of Fame in 1981. Gibson, pitching coach for the New York Mets (NL) in 1981 and for the Atlanta Braves (NL) from 1982 to 1984, is part-owner of a bank and a radio station in Omaha.

BIBLIOGRAPHY: Bob Broeg, "Fire-Breathing Gibby Was Cool," *TSN 1981 Baseball Yearbook* (1981), pp. 85–89; Bob Broeg, *Redbirds: A Century of Cardinals' Baseball* (St. Louis, 1981); *CB* (1968), pp. 145–148; John Devaney, *The Greatest Cardinals of Them All* (New York, 1968); Bob Gibson with Phil Pepe, *From Ghetto to Glory: The Story of Bob Gibson* (Englewood Cliffs, NJ, 1968); Jack Lang, "Gibby a Shoo-in with 84% of Vote," *TSN*, January 31, 1981, p. 43; David Lipman and Ed Wilks, *Bob Gibson: Pitching Ace* (New York, 1975).

                                                                Frank J. Olmsted

GILES, Warren Crandall (b. 28 May 1896, Tiskilwa, IL; d. 7 February 1979, Cincinnati, OH), executive, was the son of William F. and Isabelle S. Giles, who owned a contracting company. Giles graduated from high school in Moline, IL, and attended Staunton (VA) Military Academy (1914–1916) and Washington and Lee University for one semester before joining the U.S. Army in 1917. An infantry officer wounded in France, he returned to Moline to join his father's business. Giles' suggestions on how to improve the Moline (3IL) team earned him the club presidency in 1919 and started a fifty-year career in baseball administration.

Giles proved an able minor league executive. After winning the 1921 3IL pennant, he took a front office post with St. Joseph (WL), became part owner, and aided Branch Rickey* of the St. Louis Cardinals (NL) in searching for young players. When Rickey organized his farm system, Giles headed his top team at Syracuse (IL) in 1926–1927 and Rochester from 1928 to 1936. In nine years, Rochester won four pennants and two IL championships. Several Rochester managers, including Billy Southworth* and Bill Mc-Kechnie,* later piloted major league clubs. Giles' junior assistant, Gabe Paul,* became a major league executive. Giles married Mabel Skinner in October, 1932, and had one child, William, who became an executive with the Philadelphia Phillies (NL).

Challenged to save a debt-ridden team, Giles joined the Cincinnati Reds

(NL) as general manager from 1937 to 1947 and as president until 1952. Under the leadership of the stocky, convivial executive, the Reds regained financial strength and improved on the field with manager McKechnie and stars like Ernie Lombardi* and Bucky Walters.* Cincinnati won NL pennants in 1939 and 1940 and the 1940 World Series, but declined during World War II. Giles, who believed ballplayers should serve in the military even if it hurt the sport, resorted to playing 15-year-old pitcher Joe Nuxhall for one game in 1944.

In voting for a new baseball commissioner in 1951, owners stalemated between NL president Ford Frick* and Giles. After the seventeenth ballot, the Reds' president withdrew from contention. In 1952 Giles became the eleventh NL president and held that position until 1969. An active president, he thought that teams not well supported in one city could go elsewhere. Giles facilitated the move of the Braves from Boston to Milwaukee in 1953 and then to Atlanta in 1966, and the shift of the Brooklyn Dodgers and New York Giants to California in 1957. He added new franchises in New York, Houston, San Diego, and Montreal and favored the construction of new stadiums. In a strategy with long-range implications, Giles cooperated with efforts of NL teams to sign black and Latin American players, jumping ahead of the rival AL. During his eighteen-year presidency, the NL won ten world championships and fifteen All-Star games. A principal figure in shaping modern baseball administration, the affable, strong-willed Giles was inducted in 1979 to the National Baseball Hall of Fame.

BIBLIOGRAPHY: Lee Allen, *The National League Story* (New York, 1967); Warren Giles file, National Baseball Hall of Fame Library, Cooperstown, NY; Gene Karst and Martin J. Jones, Jr., *Who's Who in Professional Baseball* (New Rochelle, NY, 1973); Paul McFarlane, ed, *Hall of Fame Fact Book* (St. Louis, 1983); *NYT*, February 8, 1979.
                                                                                    Joseph E. King

GLASSCOCK, John Wesley "Jack," "Pebbly Jack" (b. 22 July 1857, 1859, or 1860, Wheeling, WV, then part of VA; d. 24 February 1947, Wheeling, WV), player and manager, was the son of carpenter Thomas Glasscock and Julia (Carrol?) Glasscock. He married Rhoda Rose Dubula (or Deubal), who died in 1925, and had four children. "Pebbly Jack," generally rated the best shortstop of the 1880s, possessed great range, sure hands, and a strong, accurate right arm and fielded barehanded until 1890. In seventeen major league seasons, the 5 foot, 8 inch, 160 pound right-handed Glasscock made 2,040 hits and batted .290, high for a shortstop. Glasscock's best performance (September 27, 1890) saw him hit six singles in six at bats. He led the NL in 1890 with a .336 hitting average and 172 hits, and in 1889 with 205 total base hits.

After playing sandlot baseball, he performed with the semi-pro Evening Standards of Wheeling in 1876, the Champion City Club of Springfield,

OH, in 1877, and Forest City of Cleveland in 1878 as a third baseman. When Cleveland joined the NL in 1879, Glasscock played second base and then switched to shortstop the next year. After jumping to Cincinnati (UA) in 1884, he played for St. Louis (NL) in 1885 and 1886. When the team moved to Indianapolis in 1887, he became field captain and then managed them to a 34–33 record in 1889. Allegedly he discovered pitcher Amos Rusie* at that time. When Indianapolis folded, Glasscock was sold to New York (NL) and played two seasons (1890–1891) for the Giants. He joined St. Louis (NL) in 1892 and was traded in June, 1893, to Pittsburgh (NL) for shortstop Frank Shugart. The Pirates released Glasscock, who had suffered arm and finger injuries, after the 1894 season. He played briefly with Louisville (NL) and Washington (NL) in 1895, and finished that season at first base for the Wheeling Stogies (ISL). Glasscock then performed at first base for St. Paul (WL) in 1896, 1897, and 1898, Fort Wayne, IN (ISL), in 1899 and early 1900, and Sioux City, IA (WL), in 1900, managing the last two clubs. Following his baseball career, he worked as a carpenter in Wheeling.

BIBLIOGRAPHY: Wheeling (WV) *Intelligencer*, February 24, 1947; John B. Glasscock file, National Baseball Hall of Fame Library, Cooperstown, NY; Harold W. Lanigan, "Jack Glasscock, 81, Recalls His Days of Fun and Fame as Barehanded Shortstop on Pebbly Diamonds," *TSN*, April 24, 1941; Paul MacFarlane, ed. *TSN Daguerreotypes of Great Stars of Baseball* (St. Louis, 1981), pp. 108–109; Joseph L. Reichler, ed., *The Baseball Encyclopedia*, 6th ed. (New York, 1985), pp. 90–191, 953, *TSN*, March 5, 1947; United States Census, 1860, 6th Ward, Wheeling, Ohio County, VA, 423, Microfilm M–653, Roll 368.

Frank V. Phelps

GOMEZ, Vernon Louis "Lefty," "Goofy," "The Gay Castillion," "El Gomez" (b. 26 November 1908 or 1909, Rodeo, CA), player and manager, is the son of Manuel and Mary Gomez, of Spanish and Irish ancestry, respectively, and owners of a cattle ranch. After completing grammar school in Rodeo, Gomez attended high school in nearby Richmond, CA. On February 26, 1933, Gomez married stage actress June O'Dea; he has four children. Gomez signed as a pitcher with San Francisco (PCL) in 1928 and was optioned to Salt Lake City (UIL) that year. Gomez pitched for San Francisco in 1929, when the New York Yankees (AL) purchased his contract. After spending part of the 1930 season at St. Paul (AA), Gomez played with New York through 1942 and pitched briefly in 1943 for the Boston Braves (NL) and Washington Senators (AL).

Gomez, one of the premier left-handed pitchers of the 1930s, pitched 2,503 innings, won 189 contests, and lost 102 games for a .649 percentage. During his career, he struck out 1,468 batters, compiled a 3.34 ERA, and registered 28 shutouts. In his best season (1934), Gomez recorded a 26–5 won-lost record, a 2.33 ERA, and 6 shutouts. Gomez played on seven pennant winners and won 6 World Series games without a loss. He led the AL in victories (1934, 1937), winning percentage (1934, 1941), and ERA (1934, 1937) twice, in shutouts (1934, 1937, 1938) and strikeouts (1933, 1934, 1937) three times, and in innings pitched (1934) and complete games (1934) once.

Eccentric, engaging, witty, friendly, voluble, and colorful, the 6 foot, 2 inch, 175 pound left-hander became a favorite of the press and was nicknamed "Lefty," "Goofy," and "El Gomez." Journalists frequently wrote vignettes featuring his offbeat humor. Sportswriters, for example, recounted the following story: "My first name was Quits. The day I was born my Dad came in and looked at me, and then said to my mother, " 'Let's call it Quits.' " Despite his self-deprecating badinage, the handsome, gray-eyed, brown-haired Gomez possessed shrewd intelligence.

From June, 1946, through the 1947 season, Gomez pitched four innings and managed the Binghamton Triplets (EL) to last place finishes. In 1948 he began a three-decade association as a spokesman with the Wilson Sporting Goods Company and resided in Fairfax, CA, during his later years.

Gomez's 1972 election to the National Baseball Hall of Fame attests to his ability and reflects the favorable circumstances under which he played. Players on New York or pennant-winning teams attract more publicity than those on less successful franchises in smaller localities. Moreover, the abundant anecdotes attributed to Gomez by the press demonstrate that baseball is both entertainment and sport.

BIBLIOGRAPHY: Martin Appel and Burt Goldblatt, *Baseball's Best: The Hall of Fame Gallery* (New York, 1977); Oscar Kahn, "Lefty Gomez—King of Diamond Comics," *TSN*, January 17, 1948, pp. 7–8; Howard Liss, *Baseball's Zaniest Stars* (New York, 1971); Tom Meany, *Baseball's Greatest Pitchers* (New York, 1951).

William M. Simons

GOSLIN, Leon Allen "Goose" (b. 16 October 1900, Salem, NJ; d. 15 May 1971, Bridgetown, NJ), player and manager, grew up on a New Jersey dairy farm and developed his strength and size through performing various farm chores. His father sold the farm in 1917 and moved to Salem, where "Goose" attended high school. In 1917 Goslin joined the semi-pro Salem All-Stars as a 16-year-old pitcher for $3 a game. The next year Goslin pitched for an industrial league team and impressed professional scouts with his baseball skills. The talented pitcher entered pro baseball with the Columbia, SC, club (SAL) in 1920. Goslin, who threw right and batted left-handed, often pinch-hit and played the outfield when not pitching. In 1921 he was switched permanently to the outfield and led the SAL in runs scored, hits, RBIs, and batting average (.390). At age 21, the 5 foot, 11 inch, 180 pound Goslin was purchased for $7,000 by the Washington Senators (AL). In 1922 he enjoyed a .324 batting average, his first of eleven seasons with at least a .300 mark.

Two years later, he batted .344 and led the AL with 129 RBIs. Eleven times Goslin knocked in at least 100 runs in a season. Goslin led the AL in triples in 1923 and 1925 and saw his batting average climb to .354 in 1926 and a .379 peak in 1928, stroking a single in his final at bat to edge Heinie Manush* by one point for the AL batting title. In 1928 he injured his arm in spring training by trying to throw a medicine ball like a baseball. The injury nagged him all season, causing him to experiment throwing left-handed and nearly ending his baseball career.

After being traded to the St. Louis Browns (AL) in 1930, Goslin returned to the Senators following the 1932 season. Goslin slugged three home runs in one game three times and led the Senators to three AL pennants (1924–1925, 1933) and a world championship (1924). He belted three home runs in both the 1924 and 1925 World Series and another in the 1933 classic. In 1924 he made four hits in game four and set a record for most consecutive hits in one series (six). Goslin was traded to Detroit (AL) in 1933 and helped lead the Tigers to two straight pennants (1934–1935). Goslin in 1935 drove home Mickey Cochrane* with a ninth-inning single in the sixth and decisive game to win the championship over the Chicago Cubs. In 32 World Series games, Goslin collected 37 hits and a .287 batting average. When Detroit released him in 1938, he signed with the Senators and played in only 38 games. Goslin served as player-manager (1939–1941) for Trenton, NJ (ISL), leading his teams to second, third, and fourth place finishes. Following his retirement from baseball, Goslin operated a boat and fishing tackle rental business in the Salem, NJ, area. Goslin, who married Marian Wallace in December, 1940, was elected to the National Baseball Hall of Fame in 1968.

An AL outfielder for eighteen seasons, Goslin ranks high on the all-time major league lists in several categories. He recorded 2,735 hits (34th), 4,325 total bases (28th), 1,609 RBIs (18th), 500 doubles (24th), and 173 triples (22nd), and in 1934 hit safely in 30 consecutive games. In 2,287 career games, he batted 8,655 times, scored 1,483 runs, slugged 248 home runs, and compiled a .316 lifetime batting and .500 slugging average. The free-spirited Goslin devised a striped bat in 1932 to confuse opposition pitchers and fielders, but the "zebra bat" caused such heated controversy that AL President Will Harridge* ruled it illegal.

BIBLIOGRAPHY: Gene Karst and Martin J. Jones, Jr., *Who's Who in Professional Baseball* (New Rochelle, NY, 1973); Paul MacFarlane, ed., *TSN Daguerreotypes of Great Stars of Baseball* (St. Louis, 1971); New York *World*, July 29, 1928; Joseph L. Reichler, ed., *The Baseball Encyclopedia*, 6th rev. ed. (New York, 1985), pp. 962–963; Lowell Reidenbaugh, *Cooperstown: Where Baseball's Legends Live Forever* (St. Louis, 1983); Lawrence S. Ritter, *The Glory of Their Times* (New York, 1966); Salem (NJ) *Sunbeam*, May 17, 1971; *TSN Official Baseball Record Book 1985* (St. Louis, 1985).

David S. Matz and John L. Evers

GOSSAGE, Richard Michael "Goose" (b. 5 July 1951, Colorado Springs, CO), player, is the son of landscaper Jack and Sue Gossage. At Wasson High School in Colorado Springs, Gossage starred in baseball and basketball. After his father died, Gossage signed as a pitcher with the Chicago White Sox (AL) in the 1970 free agent draft following graduation instead of accepting a college basketball scholarship. The 6 foot, 3 inch, 180 pound right-hander subsequently attended Southern Colorado State College and entered pro baseball with Sarasota, FL (GCL), in 1970. With Appleton, WI (ML), in 1971, Gossage compiled an 18–2 win-loss record and was named Player of the Year. In 1972 for the White Sox, he finished with a 7–1 record as a relief pitcher. After pitching with average success for Iowa (AA) and Chicago in 1973 and 1974 mostly in the minor leagues, Gossage was named Fireman of the Year in 1975 by earning 26 saves for the White Sox. He slumped to a 9–17 record as a starter in 1976 and was traded to the Pittsburgh Pirates (NL). He responded with 26 saves and established an NL record for most strikeouts by a relief pitcher in one season (151). Unable to agree on contract terms, Gossage signed with the New York Yankees (AL) as a free agent in 1977.

With the Yankees between 1978 and 1983, Gossage compiled a 41–28 record and saved 150 games. In 1978 and 1980 he led the AL in saves and was named 1978 Fireman of the Year. Gossage compiled a 1–0 record in six World Series appearances for the Yankees (1978, 1981) and did not allow a single run. A nine-time All Star (1975–1978, 1980–1982, 1984–1985), Gossage was the losing pitcher for the AL in 1978 and gained the save for the NL in 1984. Granted free agency in 1983, Gossage signed a multimillion dollar contract with San Diego (NL) in 1984. He led the Padres to the NL pennant with a 10–6 regular season record and 25 saves, but his team lost to the Detroit Tigers in the World Series. In 1985 he compiled a 5–3 mark, 1.82 ERA, and 26 saves in 50 appearances. The Padres suspended Gossage for a portion of the 1986 season, but he still recorded 21 saves. During his major league career through 1986, Gossage pitched 1,482 1/3 innings in 725 games, allowed 473 earned runs and 592 bases on balls, and struck out 1,275 batters. He has a 2.87 ERA, a 96–82 win-loss record, and 257 saves.

Gossage's greatest assets as a pitcher include fear and intimidation. He can throw a baseball upwards of 100 miles per hour and the batter knows it, making Gossage fully confident he can get the batter out. Although deadly serious and mean when pitching, he is mild, meek, and friendly around the clubhouse and at home with his wife Cornelia and sons Jeff and Keith.

BIBLIOGRAPHY: Tom Cushman, "Going with Goose," *TSN*, April 9, 1984, p. 3; Phil Pepe, "Golden Goose-Gossage Is Yanks' Bird of Paradise," *TSN*, August 22, 1981, pp. 2, 30; Phil Pepe, "The Goose Fires Golden Eggs for Yankees," *TSN*, September 30, 1978, p. 3; *TSN Official Baseball Register, 1985* (St. Louis, 1985).

John L. Evers

GRANT, Frank (b. 1867, Pittsfield, MA; d. 26 May 1937, New York, NY), player, was probably the best of the black players in organized baseball during the nineteenth century before the color line was drawn. Grant, primarily a second baseman, played all infield positions and the outfield during six years in the minor leagues. As a teenager, he pitched and caught for amateur clubs in Pittsfield, MA, and Plattsburg, NY. He began his professional career with Meriden, CT (EL), in 1866, but the club folded in midseason. Grant was then signed by Buffalo (IA) and led the Bisons with a .340 batting average. The following year, he again led Buffalo batters with a .366 mark. Despite his small stature, the 5 foot, 7 1/2 inch, 155 pounder led the IA in slugging with 27 doubles, 10 triples, and 11 home runs in 105 games.

In 1888 Grant topped the Bisons again by batting .326 in 95 games, mostly as an outfielder. The next year he could not reach contract terms with the Bisons and signed with the Cuban Giants, the preeminent nineteenth century black team. The Giants represented Trenton, NJ (MSL), that summer. Grant spent 1890 with Harrisburg, PA (EIL and AtA).

In his last year in white leagues (1891), he again played for the all-black Cuban Giants, who represented Ansonia, CT (CtSL). After the circuit dissolved in July, Grant and the Cuban Giants returned to barnstorming. Grant starred as a second baseman for the Giants for several years and spent his last year as a professional (1903) with the Lansing, MI, Colored Capital All-Americans.

Like the handful of other black players in white leagues during the nineteenth century, Grant suffered much discrimination on and off the field. Some white pitchers consistently threw at him, while base runners often tried to spike him at second base. Grant, whose Buffalo teammates refused to be photographed with him in 1888, sometimes was refused service at hotels and restaurants. Despite these handicaps, he earned the complimentary sobriquet "the black Dunlap." (Fred Dunlap of the St. Louis Browns was acknowledged as the best second baseman during the 1880s.)

BIBLIOGRAPHY: Jerry Malloy, "Out at Home," *The National Pastime* 2, (Fall, 1982), pp. 14–28; Robert W. Peterson, correspondence with Merl Kleinknecht, Raymond J. Nemec, Joseph M. Overfield, Robert W. Peterson Collection, Ramsey, NJ; Robert W. Peterson, *Only the Ball Was White* (Englewood Cliffs, NJ, 1970); Sol White, *History of Colored Base Ball* (Philadelphia, 1907).

Robert W. Peterson

GREENBERG, Henry Benjamin "Hank," "Hammerin' Hank" (b. 1 January 1911, New York, NY; d. 4 September 1986, Beverly Hills, CA), player and executive, was the son of Rumanian Jewish immigrants Sarah and David Greenberg. His father owned a cloth-shrinking business. After completing his public school education at New York City's James Monroe High School in 1929, he attended New York University for a semester. Greenberg married Carol Gimbel, the department store heiress, in February, 1946. The couple had three children before divorcing. He married Mary Jo Tarola in 1966.

Four varsity high school letters, an athletic scholarship from New York University, and overtures from professional baseball teams resulted less from natural grace than from size, strength, constant practice, and applied intelligence. Regarding Lou Gehrig* as a permanent fixture at first base, the 6 foot, 4 inch, 215 pound Greenberg rejected an offer from New York Yankees scout Paul Krichell and instead signed with the Detroit Tigers (AL) organization. Aside from two seasons in the outfield later in his career, Greenberg remained at first base throughout his playing days. He spent three years in the minor leagues (1930–1932), playing sequentially for Hartford (EL), Raleigh (Pil), Evansville (3IL), and Beaumont (TL). Greenberg appeared in a single game for Detroit at the end of the 1930 season, and, except for U.S. Army duty from 1941 to 1945, starred for the Tigers from 1933 to 1946. During World War II Greenberg served in the China-Burma-India theater with the first B–29 unit to go overseas. In 1947 he concluded his playing career with the Pittsburgh Pirates (NL).

Hired by Cleveland (AL) owner Bill Veeck* for the front office in 1948, he soon became the Indians' general manager. Leaders in the campaign to integrate baseball racially, the Indians won AL pennants in 1948 and 1954 and set attendance records. Following Veeck to Chicago (AL), Greenberg joined the White Sox in 1958 as part-owner and vice-president. In 1959 the White Sox won their first AL pennant in forty years. After severing his relationship with the White Sox in 1961, he became a successful investment banker in New York City and later moved to Beverly Hills, CA.

Due to four and one-half seasons lost to military service during World War II at the peak of his talents, Greenberg's career 331 home runs and 1,276 RBIs do not fully reflect his stature as a player. Despite the relative brevity of his career (the equivalent of ten full seasons), Greenberg became baseball's original "Hammerin' Hank" and ranks with the most powerful sluggers who ever played the game. After sharing the AL home run title with Jimmie Foxx* in 1935, he won the AL home run crown outright in 1938, 1940, and 1946. No right-handed batter has surpassed his 1938 total of 58 home runs. Greenberg drove in more runs than any other AL player four times (1935, 1937, 1940, and 1946). His 1937 183 RBIs came within one of the league record. In addition, he led the AL in doubles twice (1934, 1940) and runs scored once (1938). The generally steady but unspectacular fielder compensated for limited range through diligence and determination. Greenberg nevertheless paced first basemen in putouts twice, fielding average once, and assists twice. He also led the AL in errors twice, once each as a first baseman and an outfielder. In 1935 and 1940 he received the AL Most Valuable Player Award. Only four players have exceeded Greenberg's career slugging percentage of .605. Besides playing on four AL pennant-winning teams (1934–1935, 1940, 1945), he compiled a career .313 batting average. In 1,394 games, he made 1,628 hits and slammed 379 doubles.

Greenberg, elected to the National Baseball Hall of Fame in 1956, helped institutionalize the power hitting popularized by Babe Ruth* in the 1920s as a major element of strategy and promotion. He also served as an ethnic standard-bearer for co-religionists seeking assurance that Judaism and American secularism were compatible. Amid the rising anti-Semitism of the 1930s, Greenberg's baseball heroics took on symbolic meaning for many Jewish Americans.

BIBLIOGRAPHY: Bob Broeg, *Super Stars of Baseball* (St. Louis, 1971); Arthur Daley, *Kings of the Home Run* (New York, 1962); Jack Drees and James Miller, *Where Is He Now? (New York, 1973)*; Zander Hollander and Larry Fox, *The Home Run Story* (New York, 1966); William Simons, "The Athlete as Jewish Standard Bearer," *Jewish Social Studies* 44 (Spring, 1982), pp. 95–112.

William M. Simons

GREENLEE, William Augustus "Gus," "Big Red" (b. 1897, Marion, NC; d. July, 1952, Pittsburgh, PA), executive and boxing promoter, was known by nearly everyone in black Pittsburgh. Some patronized his nightclubs, others drank his bootleg liquor, while many more spent money on his numbers operations. Above all, they recognized Greenlee as black Pittsburgh's leading sportsman of the 1930s. They cheered his stable of boxers, especially John Henry Lewis* (IS), and witnessed numerous sporting events that he promoted at Greenlee Field. During the 1930s, black Pittsburgh knew Greenlee as owner of one of baseball's rarest teams, the Pittsburgh Crawfords (NNL). Although two of his brothers became doctors and a third practiced law, Gus left college after one year and became black Pittsburgh's "Mr. Big." With over 200 pounds padding his 6 foot, 3 inch frame, "Big Red" commanded attention both in the rackets and in local politics.

The son of a masonry contractor, Greenlee joined the migration north in 1916. Greenlee settled in Pittsburgh where he shined shoes, worked at a steel mill, and drove a taxi. After serving overseas during World War I, Greenlee bootlegged liquor and operated nightclubs. His best-known establishment, the world-renowned Crawford Grill, became a mecca for jazz afficionados and the hub of his numbers operation.

The Crawfords, one of the area's top sandlot teams, asked Greenlee in 1931 to become their owner. Before Greenlee arrived, the team relied mainly on local black youths. Greenlee built the club into one of the finest ever assembled; they became champions of the NNL by 1935. Between 1931 and 1938, Greenlee owned the Crawfords with future Hall of Famers Oscar Charleston,* Judy Johnson,* Cool Papa Bell,* Satchel Paige,* and Josh Gibson.* In 1932 Greenlee constructed one of the nation's finest black-controlled stadiums in the city's Hill District.

Greenlee not only promoted the Crawfords, but resurrected the NNL. The NNL broke ground for black professional sport in the 1930s, achieving financial stability and public presence unprecedented for a black sporting venture. Greenlee served as NNL architect and president during the league's first five seasons. His biggest contribution may have been the creation in 1933 of an annual all-star game, the East-West classic, in which black baseball's best players displayed their talents.

In 1937 Paige, Bell, and several other teammates decimated the Crawfords by jumping to the Dominican Republic to play for General Trujillo. Greenlee quit the NNL a season later, disbanded the Crawfords, and razed Greenlee Field, which never had become solvent. Greenlee, as promoter, sponsored Lewis, who became the first American black light-heavyweight champion by defeating Bob Olin in St. Louis on October 31, 1935.

Greenlee reentered black baseball in 1945 by forming the USL, a rival black circuit linked with Brooklyn Dodgers general manager Branch Rickey.* Considered by many a stalking horse for Rickey's plans to integrate baseball, the USL folded after two seasons. Greenlee then retreated to the Crawford Grill, which was destroyed by fire in 1951. White numbers men cut into his numbers operations, while the federal government pursued him over unpaid income taxes.

BIBLIOGRAPHY: Janet Bruce, *The Kansas City Monarchs: Champions of Black Baseball* (Lawrence, KS, 1985); Robert W. Peterson, *Only the Ball Was White* (Englewood Cliffs, NJ, 1970); Donn Rogosin, *Invisible Men: Life in Baseball's Negro Leagues* (New York, 1983); Robert L. Ruck, *Sandlot Seasons: Sport in Black Pittsburgh* (Champaign, IL, 1986).

Robert L. Ruck

GRIFFIN, Michael Joseph "Mike" (b. 20 March 1865, Utica, NY; d. 10 April 1908, Utica, NY), player and manager, generally was considered the best major league center fielder from 1887 to 1898. From an Irish-American family, Griffin attended the Maryst School, spent four years in the Advanced School, and married Margaret Esther Barney in 1890. According to his sons, Griffin began his professional baseball career in 1884 and helped Utica win an IL pennant in 1886. He played in three major leagues, with Baltimore (AA) from 1887 to 1889, Philadelphia (PL) in 1890, and Brooklyn (NL) from 1891 to 1898. Griffin led his position in fielding in 1892, 1894 and 1895 and in 1898 and combined outstanding defensive ability with speed and a potent bat. He led the AA in runs scored (152) in 1889, and the NL in doubles (36) in 1891. While captain for Brooklyn in 1898, he managed four games. He retired following the 1898 season, when Brooklyn sold him to St. Louis without his consent and under unacceptable conditions.

Griffin, who weighed 160 pounds, stood 5 feet, 7 inches tall, and batted and threw right-handed, hit a home run on April 16, 1887, in his first major league at bat and may have been the first player to accomplish that feat. After hitting the home run in the first inning, Griffin made two more extra-base hits. He hit at least .300 five seasons, including .301 (1887), .365 (1894), .335 (1895), .314 (1896), and .318 (1897). His lifetime statistics included a .299 batting average, 1,776 hits, 317 doubles, 110 triples, .410 slugging average, and 1,406 runs scored in 1,511 games. Despite these achievements, he never played on a major league championship team. An early players' rights advocate, Griffin in 1892 protested the terms of his contract. *Sporting Life* on February 27 reported, "Griffin has already received the ultimatum of the club [Brooklyn] and must take the Southern trip or look for center field honors elsewhere." After voluntarily retiring in his prime, he became a salesman in Utica, NY, and remained there until his death from pneumonia.

BIBLIOGRAPHY: Michael Griffin file, National Baseball Hall of Fame Library, Cooperstown, NY; Al Kermisch, "From a Researcher's Notebook," *Baseball Research Journal* 7 (1978), pp. 47–48; Paul MacFarlane, ed., *TSN Daguerreotypes of Great Stars of Baseball* (St. Louis, 1968), pp. 87–88; Joseph L. Reichler, ed., *The Baseball Encyclopedia*, 6th ed. (New York, 1985), p. 971; Alfred H. Spink, *The National Game* (St. Louis, 1911); *Sporting Life*, February 27, 1892, April 16, 1908; *TSN* undated supplement, 1899.

Mark D. Rucker

GRIFFITH, Calvin Robertson Griffith, Sr. See GRIFFITH, Clark Calvin.

GRIFFITH, Clark Calvin "The Old Fox" (b. 20 November 1869, Stringtown, MO; d. 27 October 1955, Washington, DC), player, manager, and owner, was the son of Sarah Wright and Isaiah Griffith, a commercial hunter and trapper. He married Addie Ann Robertson in December, 1900, and had no children. Upon the death of Mrs. Griffith's brother, she and Clark raised seven nieces and nephews in their home. They officially adopted several of the children, including baseball executive **Calvin Robertson Griffith, Sr.** (b. 11 December, 1911, Montreal, Canada). Calvin's sister Thelma married Joe Cronin,* while his brother Sherry Robertson played with the Washington Senators. His brothers William and James Robertson served as executives in the Senators' organization.

Griffith spent his youth near America's prairie country in a log cabin and became a professional trapper by age 10. He contracted malaria at age 13, precipitating a family move to more urban Bloomington, IL. By age 18, he pitched professionally in Illinois and signed his first professional contract in 1888. Griffith, his era's premier pitcher, spent three seasons with Milwaukee (WL) and jumped in 1891 to the newly formed AA with St. Louis and Boston. When the AA folded, he compiled a 13–7 record for Tacoma (PNL) in 1892 and a 30–18 mark for the Oakland Oaks (PCL) in 1893. He led a players' strike against Oaks' owners for back pay and joined other Oakland team members briefly as actors in San Francisco's Barbary Coast district. Griffith, nicknamed "The Old Fox," was signed by Adrian "Cap" Anson* for the Chicago Colts (NL) in 1893, remained there well into the 1900 season, and experienced many excellent years there. In 1900 he became a principal participant in the formation of the AL.

As vice-president of the Ball Players Protective Association (BPPA), Griffith in 1900 led the National Leaguers in a revolt. Players demanded raising the salary ceiling to $3,000 a year and uniforms paid for and supplied by team owners. Griffith obtained a strict pledge from all BPPA members not to sign contracts without the group's advice and consent, leading to the availability of high quality players for the AL. Griffith helped AL president Ban Johnson* secure thirty-nine major league stars and served as player-manager of the Chicago franchise in 1901 and 1902. Although an excellent pitcher who compiled the AL's best winning percentage in 1901, Griffith appeared mainly in relief roles thereafter. He started 30 of 35 games in 1901, but relieved in 18 of his 25 appearances by the 1905 season. His celebrated, revolutionary reliance on relief pitching, a new pitching/managing philosophy shared by Griffith's staunchest rival, John McGraw,* had begun. Griffith subsequently developed baseball's first great relievers, Allan Russell and Fred Marberry, with the Washington Senators (AL). During his twenty-year pitching career, he won 240 games, lost only 141 contests, and compiled a 3.31 ERA.

From 1903 to 1908, Griffith served as player-manager of the New York Highlanders (AL) and was mistreated by the owners, press, and fans. Griffith managed the Cincinnati Reds (NL) from 1909 through 1911, taking with him a lifelong animosity toward the Yankees. AL president Johnson coaxed him back to manage the Washington Senators, an ailing franchise in the standings and at the bank. Griffith mortgaged some property and used all his available cash to rescue the club. Besides receiving 10 percent of the team's stock, he was elected to its board of directors in 1912. After three consecutive losing seasons and resultant arguments with other stockholders, Griffith bought a controlling share of the stock in 1920, resigned as field manager, and became club president. Financial strife did not end for Griffith, although the Senators won the AL pennant in 1924 and 1925. He shrewdly maneuvered players via the trading block and guided the club to the 1933 pennant, but thereafter never fielded contenders. His clubs won 1,491 of 2,916 games, for a .522 winning percentage.

Griffith developed outstanding post–World War I baseball talent, including Walter Johnson,* Joe Cronin,* Fred Marberry, Bucky Harris,* and Leon "Goose" Goslin.* He welcomed any publicity and controversy, continually baiting umpires and utilizing a flamboyant, cunning "spitball" delivery. During his windup, he hid the ball with his body by bringing his leg up high and then cut the ball's hide on his spikes. Nevertheless, he led the movement in 1920 to enforce the ban of all forms of illegal pitches. Griffith's best pitch, the sinker, was learned from Charles "Old Hoss" Radbourne* before he signed his first contract. Griffith also helped invent the screwball with Christy Mathewson,* who called the pitch a "fadeaway." In 1894, as a publicity stunt, he became the first of many to "pitch" a baseball from the top of the Washington Monument. The first to use professional on-field entertainers, he hired former players Al Schact and Nick Altrock as baseball clowns. In 1934 he signed a pitcher from the House of David team so that he could claim the only bearded major league player. His administrative and scouting philosophies revolutionized baseball. He helped change the waiver rule governing the release and movement of players and establishing a single, base waiver claim fee. He signed the first modern-era player of Cuban descent (Armando Marsans) and imported several Latin Americans before and during World War II. He initiated use of a "speed gun" to time fastball pitcher Bob Feller* in a 1946 pre-game exhibition and frequently juggled Washington's pitching rotation to ensure weekend appearances for Walter Johnson,* his biggest gate attraction.

During both world wars, Griffith raised money to provide baseball equipment and related materials to American servicemen abroad, and converted the club's ballfield in Charlotte, NC, into a camp for soldiers on weekend leave from boot camp. He befriended government officials and became baseball's permanent liaison with President Franklin Roosevelt. In 1918 he appealed the drafting of his star catcher, Eddie Ainsmith, creating a flood of anti-Griffith sentiment. During World War II, he lunched weekly with the Selective Service head and received short-term deferments for many better players. His clubs played twenty-one night games yearly during the war, although other teams were restricted to fourteen because of blackout requirements. In 1945 he signed pitcher Bert Shepard, who had lost his leg during the war after a promising minor league career. Although Shepard pitched in only one game for the Senators, Griffith believed that he could be an inspiration to other disabled veterans.

Calvin, Griffith's nephew and adopted son, played baseball at Staunton Military Academy and George Washington University. As a youngster, he served as Senators mascot and batboy. After selling peanuts and running errands for the front office staff, he quickly learned the baseball business and was hired by Clark as team secretary of the Chattanooga Lookouts (SA) in 1935. In a surprise move, 25-year-old Calvin was named team president only two years later. During the early 1940s, he played semi-professional ball on a team organized by Joe Cambria, the Senators' chief Latin American scout. In 1942 he became head of the Senators' concessions. As his uncle grew older, Calvin assumed more responsibility for team operations. Upon Clark's death in 1955, Calvin became president of the Senators.

After several losing seasons and continued deficits inherited from his uncle, Calvin moved the AL team to Minnesota before the 1961 campaign. Under

Calvin, the Twins became a powerful club with hitters Harmon Killebrew* and Tony Oliva. The retirement of his better players, divisional reorganization, and the advent of free agency, however, renewed the club's money problems. Griffith continually sold his better players and prospects and ultimately fielded the youngest, least experienced team in either league. The last team organized by Griffith before he sold the franchise to Minneapolis banker Carl Polhad in 1984 managed an inspiring challenge for the divisional title before finishing second. Griffith remained with the franchise, coordinating and developing talent throughout the organization.

BIBLIOGRAPHY: Anthony J. Connor, *Baseball for the Love of It* (New York, 1982); Glenn Dickey, *The History of American League Baseball* (New York, 1980); Richard Goldstein, *Spartan Seasons* (New York, 1980); Gene Karst and Martin J. Jones, Jr., *Who's Who in Professional Baseball* (New Rochelle, NY, 1973); Paul MacFarlane, ed., *TSN Daguerreotypes of Great Stars of Baseball* (St. Louis, 1981); William B. Mead, *The Worst Ten Years of Baseball* (New York, 1978); *NYT*, December 29, 1943, October 23–26, 28–29, November 1, 1955; Shirley Povich, *The Washington Senators* (New York, 1954); Joseph Reichler, ed., *The Baseball Encyclopedia*, 6th ed. (New York, 1985), pp. 629, 1,754–1,755; Steven A. Reiss, *Touching Base* (Westport, CT, 1980); John Thorn, *The Relief Pitcher* (New York, 1979); *Time* 66 (November 7, 1955), p. 110; *TSN*, January 21, 1937.

                                                                                       Alan R. Asnen

GRIMES, Burleigh Arland "Ol' Stubblebeard" (b. 18 August 1893, Emerald, WI; d. 6 December 1985, Clear Lake, WI), player, manager, and scout, was the last legal major league spitball pitcher. After graduating from Clear Lake (WI) High School in 1911, he began his professional career with Eau Claire, WI (MWL), in 1912. Grimes also pitched at Ottumwa, IA (CA), in 1913, Chattanooga, TN (SA), in 1913–1914, Birmingham, AL (SA), from 1914–1916, and Richmond, VA (VL), in 1914. The Pittsburgh Pirates (NL) signed Grimes in 1916, but he lost 13 straight games for the last place club in 1917. With the Brooklyn Dodgers (NL) from 1918 to 1926, he enjoyed fine records of 23–11 (1920), 22–13 (1921), 21–18 (1923), and 22–13 (1924). Grimes pitched for the New York Giants (NL) in 1927 and the Pittsburgh Pirates in 1928 and 1929, compiling a 25–14 record in 1928. After joining the St. Louis Cardinals (NL) in 1930, he recorded 17 wins in 1931. He also hurled for the Chicago Cubs (NL) in 1932–1933, St. Louis (NL) in 1933–1934, and Pittsburgh (NL) in 1934.

His four World Series (1920, 1930–1932) resulted in a 3–4 overall record. Grimes defeated the Cleveland Indians in the second game of the 1920 Series and the Philadelphia Athletics twice in the 1931 classic despite a severely inflamed appendix. His major league record included 270 career wins against 212 losses, 35 shutouts, 495 games started, 314 games completed, and 1,512 strikeouts in 4,179 2/3 innings pitched and a 3.53 ERA. Grimes led the NL four times in complete games (1921, 1923–1924, 1928), three times in games started (1923–1924, 1928) and innings pitched (1923–1924, 1928), twice in wins (1921, 1928), appearances (1918, 1928), and hits surrendered (1923–1924), and once each in winning percentage (1920) and strikeouts (1921).

After ending his major league career in 1934 with the New York Yankees (AL), in 1935 he pitched and managed for Bloomington, IL (3IL). He then managed Louisville (AA) in 1936, the Brooklyn Dodgers (NL) to a 130–171 record in 1937–1938, Montreal (IL) in 1939, Grand Rapids (MISL) in 1940, Toronto (IL) in 1942–1944, 1947, and 1952–1953, and Rochester, NY (IL), in 1945–1946. Grimes also scouted for the AL New York Yankees (1947–1952), AL Kansas City Athletics (1956–1957), and AL Baltimore Orioles (1960–1971) and coached for Kansas City in 1955. Grimes, who married Inez Martin on May 15, 1940, served one year in the U.S. Navy (1918) and was elected to the National Baseball Hall of Fame in 1964.

BIBLIOGRAPHY: Burleigh Grimes file, National Baseball Hall of Fame Library, Cooperstown, NY; Gene Karst and Martin J. Jones, Jr., *Who's Who in Professional Baseball* (New Rochelle, NY, 1973); Joseph L. Reichler, ed., *The Baseball Encyclopedia*, 6th ed. (New York, 1985), pp. 629, 1,755–1,756.

Horace R. Givens

GRIMM, Charles John "Charlie," "Jolly Cholly" (b. 28 August 1898, St. Louis, MO; d. 15 November 1983, Scottsdale, AZ), player, manager, coach, broadcaster, and executive, played sandlot baseball and worked as a batboy in Sportsman's Park in St. Louis. He entered professional baseball with the Philadelphia Athletics (AL), batting .091 in twelve games as an outfielder and pinch hitter in 1916. After performing with Durham, NC (NCL), as an outfielder, pitcher, and first baseman in 1917, he played 50 games the next year with the St. Louis Cardinals (NL) before being sent to Little Rock, AR (SA), for seasoning at first base. In 1919 he hit .285 and led SA first basemen in putouts and fielding average. Near the end of the season, Grimm was sold to the Pittsburgh Pirates (NL) for $3,500 and hit .318 in 12 games. From 1920 through 1924, the left-handed, 5 foot, 11 1/2 inch, 173 pounder started at first base for Pittsburgh and continued excelling defensively. He led NL first basemen in fielding in 1920 and from 1922 through 1924 and eventually improved his hitting, batting a career-high .345 with 99 RBIs during the 1923 season.

In October, 1924, Grimm joined the Chicago Cubs (NL) in a six-player trade and spent the rest of his playing career (1925–1936) there. He led NL first basemen in fielding in 1928, 1929, 1930, 1931, and 1933, setting a major league record by leading nine seasons in fielding average. Although lacking power, he batted over .300 in four seasons for the Cubs (1925, 1927, 1931–1932) and hit .331 in 1931. Grimm played in two World Series with Chicago, hitting .389 and one home run in the 1929 loss to Philadelphia and .333 in the New York Yankees' sweep in 1932. Grimm's .290 career batting average included 2,299 hits, 394 doubles, 108 triples, 79 home runs, 908 runs scored, and 1,078 RBIs. His .993 fielding percentage proved even more impressive, as his 20,711 putouts and 22,087 chances accepted remain close to major league records.

Grimm enjoyed a long managerial career. He served as player-manager of the Chicago Cubs from 1932 through 1936 and continued as bench pilot until July, 1938. Chicago won NL pennants with 21 consecutive victories in 1932 and 100 triumphs in 1935. Grimm was replaced by Gabby Hartnett* as Cubs manager in July 1938 and spent the next two and one-half seasons in the broadcast booth. He returned to the Cubs as a coach briefly in 1941 and then managed Bill Veeck's* Milwaukee club (AA) through 1943, capturing a pennant and the Little World Series that year. He returned as Cubs manager from 1944 through 1949 and won another pennant in 1945, but lost the World Series to the Detroit Tigers. Grimm moved to the Chicago front office in 1949, but a dispute with the club business manager caused him to quit. After managing Dallas (TL) in 1950, he piloted Milwaukee again in 1951 and 1952 and won another AA pennant and Little World Series in 1951. In May, 1952, he became manager of the Boston Braves (NL) and kept the job when the Braves moved to Milwaukee in 1953. Grimm's Braves finished as contenders from 1953 through 1955, but did not win an NL pennant. In 1956 Grimm was fired and returned to the Chicago Cubs. He served as vice-president from 1957 through 1959, managed for 17 games in 1960, shifted to the broadcast booth, and coached on the field in 1961. He rejoined the front office, serving in various capacities until 1981. During retirement, he worked as a special consultant to General Manager Dallas Green. Grimm, one of baseball's most colorful and fun-loving figures and a highly competent player and manager (1,287 wins, 1,069 losses for a .546 winning percentage over nineteen years), died of cancer.

BIBLIOGRAPHY: Paul MacFarlane, ed., *TSN Daguerreotypes of Great Stars of Baseball* (St. Louis, 1971); *NYT*, November 17, 1983; Joseph L. Reichler, ed., *The Baseball Encyclopedia*, 6th ed. (New York, 1985), pp. 629, 973–974; *TSN*, November, 1983.
                                                                    Douglas D. Martin

GROH, Henry Knight "Heinie" (b. 18 September 1889, Rochester, NY; d. 22 August 1968, Cincinnati, OH), player, manager, and scout, attended local schools. From 1908 through 1910, Groh played shortstop with Oshkosh, WI (WSL). After subsequent minor league stops at Decatur, IL, (3IL) and Buffalo (EL), he in 1912 joined the New York Giants (NL). Although debuting in the major leagues at age 22, the 5 foot, 8 inch, 158 pound Groh looked so young that many spectators believed Manager John McGraw* had signed the team's batboy. Groh appeared in 27 games as a substitute infielder for the 1912 Giants. During early 1913, he was traded to the Cincinnati Reds (NL) with Red Ames, Josh Devore, and $20,000 for Art Fromme and Eddie

Grant and immediately became the Reds' regular second baseman. After being shifted to third base in 1915, he led the NL a record six times in double plays and fielding average and had a .967 lifetime fielding average. His .983 percentage in 1924 bettered the previous record by six points.

Groh, who starred for Cincinnati for nine years, managed the Reds the last ten games of 1918 and then returned to a playing role to help lead the 1919 squad to the world championship. In 1922 Giants manager McGraw shipped center fielder George J. Burns,* catcher Mike Gonzalez, and $100,000 to the Reds for the coveted Groh. With Groh at third base, the Giants won the NL pennant the next three years. Groh batted .474 in the 1922 World Series and later proudly displayed this figure on his auto license plate. Sidelined with a bad knee in late 1924, he lost his third base position to Fred Lindstrom.* After finishing his major league career with the NL pennant-winning Pittsburgh Pirates in 1927, Groh played for and managed minor league teams in Charlotte (Pil), Canton (CL), and Binghamton (EL). He later scouted for several major league teams, invested in bowling alleys, and worked as a cashier at River Downs Race Track in Cincinnati.

A dangerous right-handed hitter with his unique "bottle bat," Groh batted .292 lifetime. In 1,676 games, he made 1,774 hits, slugged 308 doubles, and knocked in 566 runs. He led the NL twice in doubles (1917–1918) and once each in runs (1918) and hits (1917). McGraw in 1912 suggested that Groh use a heavier bat to raise his batting average, but the latter could not find one he could grip comfortably. Finally he whittled down the handle of a Spalding bat to his satisfaction and used a similarly altered cudgel the rest of his career. Groh married Marguerite "Ruby" Bender in Cincinnati on February 24, 1915. The popular, highly newsworthy Groh had engaged in a whirlwind three-week courtship with Ruby that became the talk of the Queen City. Groh's brother Lew played briefly for the 1919 Philadelphia Athletics (AL).

BIBLIOGRAPHY: Joseph L. Reichler, ed., *The Baseball Encyclopedia*, 6th ed. (New York, 1985), p. 974. Lawrence S. Ritter, *The Glory of Their Times* (New York, 1966).

Dennis T. "Tom" Chase

GROVE, Robert Moses "Lefty," "Mose" (b. 6 March 1900, Lonaconing, MD; d. 22 May 1975, Norwalk, OH), player, was the son of coal miner John and homemaker Emma (Beeman) Grove. Grove, who left Lonaconing public school in eighth grade, married Ethel Gardner on January 30, 1921, and had two children, Robert G. and Doris. The shy, taciturn, gruff country lad distrusted and feared city strangers, but generously provided young area boys with baseball equipment. A dedicated, highly competitive pitcher, he occasionally displayed strong temper. On August 21, 1931, after 16 consecutive wins, he lost a 1–0 decision to the St. Louis Browns, denying him the AL consecutive win record. The infuriated Grove attributed his defeat to the authorized absence of batting star Al Simmons* from the team. Grove, a master psychologist, used his personal traits (6 foot, 3 inch frame, scowl, stare, speed, and wildness) to his pitching advantage. Teammates' occasional costly errors and failure to produce timely runs drew Grove's ire, as his second manager Joe Cronin* discovered.

The strong-armed Grove played first base in 1917 for a Midland, MD, team. In early 1920, he began his professional career pitching six games for Martinsburg, WV (BRL), at a monthly $125 rate. Jack Dunn, owner of the Baltimore Orioles (IL), bought his contract for $2,000. With the Orioles from 1920 to 1924, he compiled an outstanding 109–36 record and led the IL four times in strikeouts. By 1924 he earned a $7,500 annual salary. Philadelphia Athletics (AL) manager Connie Mack* persuaded Dunn to sell him for a record $100,000. He pitched for the Athletics from 1925 to 1933, when the Boston Red Sox (AL) bought him, Max Bishop, and Rube Walberg for two players and $125,000. After pitching for Boston from 1934 to 1941, Grove retired and operated a bowling alley in Lonaconing. Following his wife's death, he spent his remaining years in Norwalk, OH, at his daughter-in-law's home.

Grove holds the AL record for four consecutive seasons as ERA leader, shares the mark of 16 consecutive wins, and compiled the second highest AL career winning percentage (.680). With the Athletics, he topped the AL seven consecutive seasons in strikeouts, five times in ERA, and four times each in wins and winning percentage. At Boston, he led the AL four times in ERA and once in winning percentage. During nine years with the Athletics, he appeared in 402 games, pitched 2,401 innings, compiled a 195–79 record, a .711 won-lost percentage, and a 2.87 ERA, struck out 1,523 batters, and walked 740 hitters. With the Red Sox for eight seasons, he appeared in 214 games, pitched 1,539 innings, and compiled a 105–62 record, a .629 won-lost percentage, and a 3.34 ERA, struck out 743 batters, and walked 447 hitters.

During his seventeen-year career, he appeared in 616 games, pitched 3,940 2/3 innings, compiled a 300–141 record, a .680 won-lost percentage, and a 3.06 ERA, struck out 2,266 batters, and walked 1,187 hitters. On *The Sporting News* All-Star team from 1928 to 1932, he won the AL Most Valuable Player Award in 1931. He starred on the AL champion Athletics teams from 1929 to 1931 and hurled four World Series victories, helping his club win the 1929 and 1930 Series. Grove was elected to the National Baseball Hall of Fame in 1947 and was chosen by Boston fans in 1982 as the second left-hander on the Red Sox "dream team."

One of baseball's greatest left-handed pitchers, Grove was called "my best one" by manager Mack. According to manager Cronin, "He was all baseball. We all admired him and his dedication to the sport." Grove increased the popularity of baseball because of his skill and feisty character and drew large crowds whenever he pitched. An intelligent athlete constantly improving his effectiveness, he lengthened the time between pitches to improve his rhythm. His sore arm at Boston caused him to develop craftiness, a curve, a change-of-pace forkball, and better control, while his temper continually sparked teammates to play harder both in the field and at bat.

BIBLIOGRAPHY: Boston Red Sox, *Media Guide* (1984); Robert Broeg, "Grove's Badges: Hot Temper, Blazing Fast Ball," *TSN*, July 12, 1969, pp. 28–29; Ellery H. Clark, Jr., *Boston Red Sox: 75th Anniversary History* (Hicksville, NY, 1975); Ellery H. Clark, Jr., *Red Sox Fever* (Hicksville, NY, 1979); Ellery H. Clark, Jr., *Red Sox Forever* (Hicksville, NY, 1977); Ellery H. Clark, Jr., interviews with Lefty Grove, April, 1927, June, 1935, Cy Perkins, April, 1927, Howard Ehmke, December, 1944, Connie Mack, December, 1944, Max Bishop, January, 1950, Mrs. Robert Grove, May, 1983, Joe Cronin, July, 1983; Joseph L. Reichler, ed., *The Baseball Encyclopedia*, 6th ed. (New York, 1985), p. 1, 758.

Ellery H. Clark, Jr.

GUIDRY, Ronald Ames "Ron," "Louisiana Lightning," "Gator" (b. 28 August 1950, Lafayette, LA), player, is the son of railroad conductor Roland and Mary (Grace) Guidry. At Northside High School in Lafayette, Guidry starred in football, basketball, and track. He developed his pitching skills playing American Legion ball because his school did not field a team. The 5 foot, 11 inch, 160 pound Guidry in 1971 resigned his scholarship at the University of Southwest Louisiana to enter the professional baseball free agent draft and was signed by the New York Yankees (AL) as their third selection. The next few years in the Yankees farm system proved unspectacular. Guidry pitched with only moderate success with Johnson City (ApL) in 1971, Fort Lauderdale (FSL) in 1972, Kinston (CrL) in 1973, and West Haven, CT (EL) in 1974. In 1975 and 1976, Guidry divided time between the Yankees and their top Syracuse (IL) farm team.

With a sound arm and superior athletic ability, Guidry was destined to succeed. His incredible ability to throw hard (over 95 miles per hour) with sheer power defies his scant 160 pounds. In 1977 Guidry won 16 games and helped the Yankees win the AL pennant. He won one game in the World Series, as the Yankees defeated the Los Angeles Dodgers in six games. In 1978 the Cajun left-hander became the ace of the Yankees pitching staff. Guidry's 25–3 record ranked as the highest winning percentage (.893) in baseball history for pitchers winning at least 20 games. He compiled the lowest ERA for a left-hander in the AL since 1941 (1.74), most strikeouts by a Yankees pitcher (248), most strikeouts in one game by an AL left-hander (18), a major league high shutouts (9), and a Yankees record for victories at the start of the season (13). The Yankees again captured the AL pennant and World Series over the Dodgers in six games, with Guidry winning game three. For his efforts, Guidry was named *The Sporting News* Man of the Year, Major League Player of the Year, AL Pitcher of the Year, and AL Cy Young Award winner.

Still the mainstay of the pitching staff, Guidry made a 1–1 record in the 1981 World Series loss to the Dodgers. In 1985 Guidry compiled a 22–6 mark and 3.27 ERA, led the AL in victories, finished fourth in complete games (11), struck out 143 batters in 259 innings, and placed second in the Cy Young Award balloting. Through the 1986 season, Guidry has won 163 games and lost only 80 decisions for a .671 winning percentage and 3.24 ERA, and has struck out 1,650 batters in 2,219 1/3 innings. He was named to five All-Star teams (1978–1979, 1982–1983, 1985) and All-Star fielding team (1982–1986). Guidry married his hometown sweetheart, Bonnie Lynn Rutledge, in September, 1972, and has two children, Jamie Rachael and Brandon. After baseball, hunting dominates Guidry's life.

BIBLIOGRAPHY: Maury Allen, *Ron Guidry: Louisiana Lightning* (New York, 1979); *TSN Official Baseball Register, 1984* (St. Louis, 1984).

John L. Evers

H

HACK, Stanley Camfield "Stan," "Smiling Stan" (b. 6 December 1909, Sacramento, CA; d. 15 December 1979, Dixon, IL), player, manager, and coach, was a 6 foot, 175 pound third baseman who threw right-handed and batted left-handed. He played his entire major league baseball career with the Chicago Cubs (NL) from 1932 through 1947. Hack graduated from high school in Sacramento, where he participated in baseball. He worked as a bank clerk in Sacramento and played on a local city league team when the Sacramento Solons (PCL) offered him a tryout in 1931. Initially he was reluctant to surrender the security of his bank position for the uncertainty of a baseball career, but took a two-week vacation in March, 1931, to attend the tryout camp. The Solons were very impressed with Hack's performance and persuaded him to resign his bank post and sign a baseball contract. The 21-year-old Hack started for the PCL club and enjoyed a .352 batting average in 164 games. After being purchased by the Cubs (NL) for $40,000 in 1932, Hack opened the season as regular Cubs third baseman before being benched because of weak hitting. In 1933 he batted .299 in 137 games for Albany (IL) and hit .350 in 20 games for the Cubs later that season. Hack started at third base for the Cubs for the rest of his playing career and led Chicago to four World Series (1932, 1935, 1938, 1945), collecting 24 base hits in 18 games. Hack tied the fall classic record for most singles in four games (7) and most hits in one game (4) and compiled a .348 overall batting average. In game six of the 1945 Series, he doubled home the winning run in the bottom of the twelfth inning.

Selected the all-time Cubs third baseman, Hack recorded at least a .300 batting average during seven seasons, scored over 100 runs a season seven times, and paced the NL in hits (1940–1941) and stolen bases (1938–1939). Always among the defensive standouts, Hack topped NL third basemen in putouts five times (including 1937–1940), double plays three times, and twice each in assists and fielding average. He set a World Series record (since broken) by making twelve putouts in the 1945 fall classic. In four All-Star games (1938, 1939, 1941, 1943), Hack made six hits and a .400 batting average. During sixteen seasons with the Cubs, Hack played in 1,938 games, compiled 2,193 hits, 363 doubles, 81 triples, 57 home runs, 642 RBIs, and a .301 batting average. He also enjoyed a walk/strikeout ratio of better than two to one.

Hack in 1948 began managing in the Cubs' farm system with stops at Des Moines (WL), Springfield, MA (IL), and Los Angeles (PCL). Named manager of the Chicago Cubs (NL) in 1954, Hack experienced little success, finishing in seventh, sixth, and eighth place. After coaching for the St. Louis Cardinals (1957–1958), Hack piloted the NL club for the remainder of the 1958 season when manager Fred Hutchinson was fired. In four managerial seasons, Hack's clubs won 199 and lost 272 for a .423 mark. Hack also performed managerial stints at Denver (AA), Salt Lake City (PCL), and Dallas-Fort Worth (TL) before retiring from baseball in 1966. After divorcing his first wife, Dorothy Alice Weisel, Hack married Glennyce Mary Graf on November 30, 1957. He had one son and two daughters and owned and operated a restaurant in Grand Detour, IL.

BIBLIOGRAPHY: Stanley Hack file, National Baseball Hall of Fame Library, Cooperstown, NY; Jim Enright, *Chicago Cubs* (New York, 1975); Gene Karst and Martin J. Jones, Jr., *Who's Who in Professional Baseball* (New Rochelle, NY, 1973); Paul MacFarlane, ed., *TSN Daguerreotypes of Great Stars of Baseball* (St. Louis, 1971), Joseph L. Reichler, ed., *The Baseball Encyclopedia*, 6th ed. (New York, 1985), pp. 629, 980.

David S. Matz and John L. Evers

HAFEY, Charles James "Chick" (b. 12 February 1903, Berkeley, CA; d. 2 July 1973, Calistoga, CA), player, was one of five sons and three daughters of sewer contractor Charles and May Hafey. Hafey graduated from St. Mary's High School and at age 17 signed with the St. Louis Cardinals (NL). Hafey claimed to be age 18, thinking it would improve his chances. A right-handed pitcher, he excelled for the Shattuck Avenue Merchants team. In 1922 Hafey pitched batting practice for the St. Louis Cardinals. He married Bernice Stigliano on December 1, 1922, and had one son. In 1923 Cardinals manager Branch Rickey* switched the strong-armed, erratic pitcher to the outfield to utilize his powerful bat. Hafey already had demonstrated big league hitting potential by lashing line drives into the outfield. He batted .284 in 1923 for Fort Smith, AR (WA), .253 for St. Louis and .350 for Houston (TL) the next year. After appearing in 21 games for Syracuse (IL) in 1925, the Cardinals promoted him.

Hafey enjoyed a great career with the Cardinals, despite ill health, poor eyesight, and salary disputes. After Hafey was beaned several times in 1926, Dr. Robert Hyland told him to wear glasses. Hafey, one of the first outfielders to wear lenses, used three different pairs because his eyesight varied. A chronic sinus infection compounded his vision problems, requiring many operations the next few seasons. After hitting .336 in 1930, Hafey held out for $15,000. The Cardinals offered him only $12,000, causing him to report ten days late to spring training. Hafey eventually signed for $12,500, but Rickey fined him $2,100 for not being in playing condition. After winning the NL batting title in 1931 with a .349 mark, Hafey demanded a $17,000 salary, including a return of the $2,100 fine. Rickey traded Hafey to the Cincinnati Reds (NL) for $50,000 (a percentage of which he banked for himself), Bennie Frey, and Harvey Hendrick. From 1932 to 1935, Hafey saw limited service with the Reds. The quiet, soft-spoken Hafey became quite a practical joker, once tying the hands and feet of his roommate Ernie Lombardi* to the bedposts while he slept. A sinus condition forced him to retire after the 1935 season. He attempted a brief comeback with the Reds in 1937, but hit only .261.

Hafey batted with considerable power, slugging 82 homers and knocking in 343 runners from 1928 to 1930. During his career, he played in 1,283 games, batted 4,625 times, scored 777 runs, made 1,466 hits, slugged 164 homers, knocked in 833 runs, and compiled a .317 batting average. Although hitting only .205 in four World Series, he set a record for the most doubles (5) in a six-game set. Hafey, one of the game's best right-handed hitters, in 1929 made ten consecutive hits. In 1971 the Veterans Committee elected him to the National Baseball Hall of Fame. Hafey's older brother and three nephews also played professional baseball. Hafey raised sheep and cattle on his ranch, but suffered from emphysema and a disabling stroke.

BIBLIOGRAPHY: Bob Broeg, "Hafey's Dilemma," St. Louis *Post Dispatch*, July 8, 1973; Gene Karst and Martin J. Jones, Jr., *Who's Who in Professional Baseball* (New York, 1973); Frederick G. Lieb, *Comedians and Pranksters of Baseball* (St. Louis, 1958); Paul MacFarlane, ed., *TSN Daguerreotypes of Great Stars of Baseball* (St. Louis, 1981); Lawrence Ritter and Donald Honig, *The 100 Greatest Baseball Players of All Time* (New York, 1981); *TSN* (July 21, 1973).

William A. Borst

HAINES, Jesse Joseph "Pop" (b. 22 July 1893, Clayton, OH; d. 5 August 1978, Dayton, OH), player and coach, was the son of auctioneer Elias Haines. He married Carrie M. Weidner in 1915 and had one daughter. After attending public schools in Phillipsburg, OH, he pitched for Dayton, OH (CL), Saginaw, MI (SML), Fort Wayne, IN (CL),Springfield, OH (CL), Topeka-Hutchinson, KS (WL), Tulsa, OK (WL), and Kansas City, MO (AA) from 1914 through 1919 and had brief tryouts with the Detroit Tigers (AL) in 1915 and 1916 and the Cincinnati Reds (NL) in 1918. His record of 21 victories against only 5 defeats with Kansas City in 1919 induced St. Louis Cardinals (NL) manager Branch Rickey* to persuade several community stockholders to borrow $10,000 from a bank to buy Haines' contract. Haines represented a big gamble for the financially troubled club.

The 6 foot, 180 pound Haines excelled for the Cardinals. From 1920 through 1937, the right-hander won 210 games, lost only 158 (.571), and helped his club win the NL pennant in 1926, 1928, 1930, 1931, and 1934. Besides recording at least 20 victories three times (1923, 1927–1928), he pitched a no-hit, no-run game against the Boston Braves in 1924. In 1927 he led the NL in complete games (25) and shutouts (6). In six World Series games (1926, 1928, 1930, 1934), he won three of four decisions and compiled a low 1.67 ERA. His stellar .444 career World Series batting average included one home run. During his career, he pitched 3,208 2/3 innings, struck out 981 batters, and compiled a 3.64 ERA. Haines, who relied on a blazing fastball and knuckleball, coached in 1938 with the Brooklyn Dodgers (NL). After retirement from baseball, he served seven terms from 1938 through 1965 as auditor for Montgomery County, OH.

BIBLIOGRAPHY: Harold (Speed) Johnson, *Who's Who in Major League Baseball* (Chicago, 1933); Gene Karst and Martin J. Jones, Jr., *Who's Who in Professional Baseball* (New Rochelle, NY, 1973); *NYT*, July 26, 1978.

Gene Karst

HAMILTON, William Robert "Sliding Billy," "Good Eye Billy" (b. 16 February 1866, Newark, NJ; d. 15 December 1940, Worcester, MA), player, manager, scout, and executive, was the son of Samuel and Mary (McCutchin) Hamilton. Hamilton grew up in Clinton, MA, where he and his father worked in a cotton mill. Reputedly Hamilton signed with Waterbury, CT (EL), during 1886, but their box scores do not include his name. He batted .380 for Lawrence, MA (NEL), in 1886, and Salem, MA (NEL), in 1887, and .352 in 61 games for Worcester, MA (NEL), in 1888, before being sold in midseason to Kansas City, MO (AA). Hamilton's brilliant major league career saw him with Kansas City in 1888 and 1889, Philadelphia (NL) from 1890 through 1895, and Boston (NL) from 1896 through 1901. At Philadelphia, Hamilton, Ed Delahanty,* and Sam Thompson* formed one of baseball's all-time great outfields. The Phillies unwisely traded Hamilton to Boston for third baseman and field captain Billy Nash, who fizzled in Philadelphia. At Boston, he played with NL pennant winners in 1897 and 1898.

A left-handed batter and thrower, the stumpy, 5 foot, 6 1/2 inch, 165 pound Hamilton was selected for the National Baseball Hall of Fame in 1961. His outstanding fourteen-season major league statistics included 2,163 hits in 1,593 games, 1,692 runs (over one per game, an all-time record), 937 stolen bases (a record until recent years), 1,187 bases on balls, and a .344 batting average—despite shortened seasons in 1893 (typhoid fever), and 1898 and 1899 (knee injuries). He led his league twice in batting championships, four times in runs scored, five times in walks, and seven times in stolen bases. An ideal leadoff man, Hamilton hit many singles, batted for high average, and exercised sharp judgment and patience in waiting out pitchers for walks.

Hamilton seldom struck out, earning him a second nickname, "Good Eye Billy." His ability to get on base resulted in a .454 on-base average, second only to John McGraw* among nineteenth century regulars.

He proved the bane of infielders with his extreme speed and elusiveness on the basepaths and daringly hurtled himself at bases. Hamilton, who stole 117 bases in 1889, by 1896 had stolen over 100 two more times and over 90 three more times. Since these totals included extra bases taken by the base runner on batters' singles and doubles per scoring rules of that time, Hamilton's numbers are not comparable with those of Ty Cobb* and other notable twentieth century base stealers. Nevertheless, the popular "Sliding Billy" was the best base runner of his day. A superlative ball hawk, Hamilton became an ideal center fielder by combining extreme speed and sure-handedness with his uncanny crack-of-the-bat judgments of the direction and depth of batted balls and an acrobatic instinct for catching balls off-balance. Consequently, he ran down every possible catch and made spectacular grabs commonplace. His best single season came in 1894, when he batted .399 with 223 hits, led the NL in runs scored (an all-time season record, 196), bases on balls (126), on-base average (.523), and stolen bases (99), and sustained a 46 consecutive game hitting streak. His .344 lifetime batting average is eighth best in major league history.

After 1901 Hamilton played outfield and managed with Haverhill, MA (NEL), from 1902 through 1908, except 1905; Lynn, MA (NEL), 1909 and 1910; and Harrisburg, PA (outlaw TSL), in 1905 and 1906. He scouted for Boston (NL) during 1911 and 1912 and bench managed at Fall River (NEL) in 1913, Springfield (EL) in 1914, and Worcester (EL, as part-owner) in 1916. He married Rebecca Jane Carr in 1888 and had four daughters: Ethel (Mrs. Leroy E. Fields), Mildred (Mrs. Howard Prior), Ruth (Mrs. John C. Miller), and Dorothy (Mrs. H. P. Starr). Having invested earnings wisely and bought property, the Hamiltons lived comfortably in Clinton, MA, until his death.

BIBLIOGRAPHY: Martin Appel and Burt Goldblatt, *Baseball's Best: The Hall of Fame Gallery* (New York, 1977); William Hamilton file, National Baseball Hall of Fame Library, Cooperstown, NY; Paul MacFarlane, ed., *TSN Daguerreotypes of Great Stars of Baseball* (St. Louis, 1981); Joseph L. Reichler, ed., *The Baseball Encyclopedia*, 6th ed. (New York, 1985), p. 987; John Thorn and Pete Palmer, *The Hidden Game of Baseball* (New York, 1984); *TSN*, December 26, 1940, January 25, 1961; United States Census 1880, Massachusetts, Worcester County, T–9, Roll 565, 352; Worcester *Telegram*, December 16, 1940.

Frank V. Phelps

HANLON, Edward Hugh "Ned" (b. 27 August 1857, Montville, CT; d. 14 April 1937, Baltimore, MD), player, manager, and executive, was the son of a housebuilder and began his career as a pitcher for the Montville town team. After signing his first professional contract in 1876 with Providence, RI (NEL), he played for Fall River, MA, in 1877, Rochester, NY, in 1878, and Albany, NY, in 1879. His third base play for Albany earned a berth with the Cleveland Nationals (NL) for the 5 foot, 9 1/2 inch, 170 pounder. Hanlon played left field for Cleveland in 1880, leading the NL in errors and hitting .246. Cleveland sold Hanlon to Detroit (NL), where he was installed in center field. Hanlon quickly became a solid fielder, pacing NL outfielders in putouts in 1882 and 1884, total chances per game in 1882 and 1883, and double plays in 1883. He batted about .300 only in 1885, when he hit .302 and was named Detroit team captain. The Wolverines won the NL championship in 1887, but fell apart the next year and were sold.

In the 1888–1889 off-season, Hanlon joined an All-Star team that barnstormed against Adrian Anson's* Chicago White Stockings. The 32,000 mile tour included the United States, Hawaii, New Zealand, Australia, Ceylon, Arabia, Egypt, Europe, England, Scotland, and Ireland, bringing baseball to several countries for the first time. In 1889 Hanlon signed with Pittsburgh (NL) and assumed managerial responsibilities late in the season. In 1890 he joined the player revolt against the owners known as the Brotherhood War. Hanlon jumped to the Pittsburgh entry of the new PL as center fielder and manager and batted .278 for his sixth place team. When the NL owners crushed the upstart league, Hanlon in 1891 returned to Pittsburgh and batted .266 for his last place squad. He joined the Baltimore (NL) franchise the next year, but an injury ended his playing career after eleven games. The Hanlon-led Orioles finished last in 1892 and climbed to eighth in 1893. A .260 lifetime hitter, he proved a good, fast, strong-armed outfielder. In thirteen major league seasons, he made 1,317 hits, 159 doubles, and 79 triples, scored 930 runs, and stole 279 bases.

By trading shrewdly and often, Hanlon quickly built a championship team in Baltimore. He acquired John McGraw,* Joe Kelley,* and Wilbert Robinson* in 1893 and added Willie Keeler,* Hugh Jennings,* Dan Brouthers,* and others the next season to vault the Orioles into first place. Nine Orioles batted over .300, while eight drove in at least 92 runs. For three straight seasons (1894–1896), Baltimore won the NL championship. In 1897 and 1898, the Orioles finished second. The Orioles fielded one of the best teams in baseball history. Although the pitching staff lacked outstanding performers, the Orioles offense required only adequate hurlers. Triumphant Baltimore drove the opposition to distraction by executing "inside baseball" better than any team of that era. Scholars and contemporaries disagree as to who originated and refined the techniques, but Hanlon's Orioles implemented the strategy with relentless precision and verve. They hit and ran, used the squeeze play, and platooned right-handers versus left-handed pitchers and vice-versa. Hanlon also became the first Orioles manager to take his team south for spring training.

When the Baltimore franchise moved to Brooklyn (NL) in 1899 without McGraw and Robinson, Hanlon's team won pennants the next two years.

Of ten pennants contested from 1891 through 1900, Hanlon's clubs won five. The Brooklyn move made Hanlon baseball's highest paid manager. He retained that distinction upon joining Cincinnati in 1906, but met little success in two years there. Hanlon, who had lived in Baltimore since 1892, left Cincinnati in 1907 and became president of the Baltimore Orioles (EL). After selling the team to Jack Dunn, he tried unsuccessfully to buy the Boston Pilgrims in 1911 and invested much of his savings in the Baltimore franchise (FL) in 1914 and 1915. A civic leader, Hanlon served for twenty-one years as member of the City Park Board and from 1931 on as its president. He and Ellen Jane Kelly had five children, including three daughters and a son, Edward. Another son, Joseph, died in World War I. Hanlon's substantial contributions to baseball are not well recognized. His managerial contributions included five pennants in seven years, a 1,315–1,165 career record (.530), the building of one of baseball's legendary teams, and the use of innovative techniques. Several of Hanlon's players, including McGraw, Jennings, Kelley, Robinson, and Fielder Jones, enjoyed successful managerial careers.

BIBLIOGRAPHY: Lee Allen, *The National League Story* (New York, 1961); Baltimore *Sun*, April 15, 1937; James H. Bready, *The Home Team* (Baltimore, MD, 1979); Frank Graham, *McGraw of the Giants* (New York, 1944); *NYT*, April 15, 1937; Edwin Pope, *Baseball's Greatest Managers* (Garden City, NY, 1960); Joseph L. Reichler, ed., *The Baseball Encyclopedia*, 6th ed. (New York, 1985), pp. 630, 989–990; Robert Smith, *Baseball* (New York, 1947).

Douglas D. Martin

HARDER, Melvin Leroy "Mel," "Chief," "Wimpy" (b. 15 October 1909, Beemer, NE), player and coach, is the son of a Nebraska Power Company machinist. After his parents, Claus H. and Clara (Skala) Harder, moved to Omaha, Harder attended Druid Hill grade school and Omaha Technical High School (1924–1927). As a high school sophomore, he pitched his team to the city championship. During the spring of 1927, he signed with the Class A Omaha ballclub (WL) and was optioned to Dubuque, IA (MOVL). After Harder returned to Omaha, the Cleveland Indians (AL) purchased his contract.

Harder hurled for the Indians from 1928 to 1947, but the 18-year-old right-hander pitched only 49 innings his rookie season. At midseason the following year, the Indians briefly sent him to the New Orleans Pelicans (SA). Harder blossomed after developing a curveball to complement his fastball and adding weight to his 6 foot, 1 inch, 150 pound frame. From 1930 to 1933, he averaged 13 wins a season. On July 31, 1932, he pitched the inaugural game at Cleveland Municipal Stadium, losing 1–0 to Lefty Grove* of the Philadelphia Athletics. Harder married Hazel Claire Schmidt of Omaha in 1932 and has two daughters, Kathryn Gay and Penny Lyn.

Harder enjoyed his finest seasons in the mid-1930s, winning 20 games in 1934 and 22 games in 1935 against the likes of Lou Gehrig,* Charles Gehringer,* and Jimmie Foxx.* His 2.61 ERA in 1934 comprised the AL's second lowest. Nicknamed "Chief" and "Wimpy" by teammates, Harder earned national recognition by pitching five scoreless innings in the 1934 All-Star Game. He participated in the 1935, 1936, and 1937 All-Star games, hurling thirteen scoreless innings against National Leaguers.

After an impressive 12–3 start in 1936, Harder injured his arm and finished the season in pain with a disappointing 15–15 record. Harder won between 12 and 17 games annually for the next four years, but arm problems continued to plague him. Following a mediocre 5–4 season in 1941, he underwent surgery and hurled 13 victories in 1942. He pitched with Cleveland until retirement in 1947, amassing 223 career wins and 186 defeats and compiling more triumphs than any Indian except Bob Feller.* In 582 games, he pitched 3,426 1/3 innings, struck out 1,160 hitters, and posted a 3.80 ERA.

Harder returned to the Indians as a first base coach for the 1948 pennant-winning season and served as pitching coach there from 1949 through 1963. A mild-mannered, patient teacher, he contributed immensely to the pitching successes of Bob Lemon,* Early Wynn,* Mike Garcia, and Feller during the 1950s. The bespectacled Harder was said to possess a camera in his head, enabling him to spot a pitching flaw immediately. After wearing an Indians uniform longer than any other ballplayer (thirty-six years), Harder ended his coaching career with the New York Mets (1964), Chicago Cubs (1965–1966), and Cincinnati Reds (1967–1968), all of the NL, and the AL Kansas City Royals (1969).

BIBLIOGRAPHY: Cleveland *News*, September 10, December 6, 1941; Cleveland *Plain Dealer*, June 23, 1935, May 18, July 2, 1947, December 24, 1961, January 21, 23, October 24, 1962, June 26, 1963, February 17, 1974, March 26, 1976; James N. Giglio, correspondence with Mel Harder, February 4, 1984; Paul Green, "Mel Harder" (interview), *Sports Collectors Digest* 11 (June 22, 1984), pp. 64–78; Franklin Lewis, *The Cleveland Indians* (New York, 1949); David S. Neft et al., *The Sports Encyclopedia: Baseball*, 1st ed. (New York, 1974).

                                                                                James N. Giglio

HARRIDGE, William "Will" (b. 16 October 1883, Chicago, IL; d. 9 April 1971, Evanston, IL), executive, was born to poor English immigrant parents on Chicago's south side. He graduated from high school, attended night classes to learn stenography, and was employed by the Wabash Railroad in Chicago. Harridge's skill at scheduling transportation for AL teams and umpires impressed AL founder and president Ban Johnson.* Johnson made arrangements with the railroad in 1911 to hire the surprised railway clerk, who had never exhibited an interest in baseball, as his private secretary.

Harridge married Maude Hunter in June, 1911, and had one child, William, Jr.

The quiet, reliable Harridge served the occasionally tempestuous Johnson as personal secretary from 1911 to 1927. In 1927 Johnson's conflicts with team owners and Commissioner Kenesaw Mountain Landis* led to his ouster from the AL presidency and his replacement by Ernest S. Barnard* of the Cleveland Indians (AL). Club owners, perhaps recognizing that Harridge had handled many league matters during the difficult transition in AL presidents, appointed him AL secretary. When Barnard died in March 1931, Harridge was chosen interim president. With the strong support of owners Charles Comiskey* of the Chicago White Sox and Philip Ball of the St. Louis Browns, he was unanimously elected the third AL president two months later. Harridge was reelected president three times and remained the AL's chief executive for a record twenty-eight years. After resigning in 1958, he chaired the AL board until his death in 1971. A year later, Harridge was inducted into the National Baseball Hall of Fame.

Throughout his long tenure as AL head, Harridge concentrated on administrative matters and avoided publicity for himself and his office. When appearing before the public, Harridge spoke briefly, acted dignified and reserved, and represented the solemn, business orientation of the sport. His penchant for discreetly handling AL matters behind closed doors with little fanfare won him the respect and loyalty of team owners. In 1933 Harridge actively promoted AL participation in the first All-Star Game and championed the annual spectacle during his presidency. Besides firing and suspending players and managers for "baiting" umpires, he stopped Bill Veeck* from further using a midget pinch hitter for the 1951 St. Louis Browns (AL), and in 1948 dismissed umpire Ernest Stewart for trying to unionize AL umpires. Harridge also established new departments within his office to promote attendance at AL games. Harridge was inclined to let club owners rule the AL and proved a steady, cautious administrator, content with the daily routine of business at league headquarters in Chicago.

BIBLIOGRAPHY: Lee Allen, *The American League Story* (New York, 1965); William Harridge file, National Baseball Hall of Fame Library, Cooperstown, NY; Paul MacFarlane, ed., *TSN Hall of Fame Fact Book* (St. Louis, 1982); Eugene C. Murdock, *Ban Johnson: Czar of Baseball* (Westport, CT, 1981); *NYT*, April 10, 1971.

Joseph E. King

HARRIS, E. Victor "Vic" (b. 10 June 1905, Pensacola, FL; d. 23 February 1978, Mission Hills, CA), player, coach, and manager, was the son of William Harris and attended school in the South. After moving to Pittsburgh, PA, he attended McKelvy Grade School from 1914 to 1919 and Schenley High School from 1919 to 1922. Harris entered professional baseball in 1923 with the Cleveland Tate Stars and was signed the following year by Rube Foster* of the Chicago American Giants (NNL). He joined Cum Posey's* Homestead Grays (ANL) in 1925 and played there through 1948, except for spending 1934 with the Pittsburgh Crawfords (NNL) and working in 1943 and 1944 in a defense plant. He married Dorothy Smith on October 14, 1936, and had two children, Judith Victoria and Ronald Victor.

Although quiet and soft-spoken, Harris played with determination and aggressiveness. The left-handed batter and right-handed thrower became a fearsome base runner, formidable hitter, and a sure-handed outfielder. Available statistics indicate that Harris batted over .300 during his Negro league career. He participated in six East–West (Negro league) All-Star games, including the 1933, 1935, and 1939 classics, and played winter ball primarily in Puerto Rico and Cuba.

Harris, better remembered as a manager, was named Homestead field leader in 1935 and piloted the Grays to eight NNL pennants. From 1937 through 1945, Hall of Famers Josh Gibson* and Buck Leonard* paced the Grays to nine straight flags. The 1943 and 1944 titles came under James Taylor. Harris guided Homestead to NNL crowns from 1937 to 1942 and in 1945 and 1948, and managed the 1948 team to the Negro World Series championship. In 1949 he coached the Baltimore Elite Giants, winners of the NAL title. Harris finished his managerial career in 1950, directing the NAL Birmingham Black Barons to a 51–24 record. He also managed in the CUWL in 1938 and PRWL in 1936 and from 1947 to 1950.

During his era, Harris was considered the top Negro league manager. His teams posted a 382–238 mark in regular season play from available records and a 10–10 mark during post-season play. An excellent motivator, he was well liked and respected by his players.

BIBLIOGRAPHY: Baltimore *Afro-American*, September 20, 1947; William Brashler, *Josh Gibson* (New York, 1978); Vic Harris, with John Holway, "Vic Harris Managed Homestead Grays," *Dawn Magazine* (March 8, 1975); *Negro Player Reports* (Baseball Hall of Fame #1, courtesy of Cliff Kachline, January, 1972); Robert W. Peterson, *Only the Ball Was White* (Englewood Cliffs, NJ, 1970).

                                                                            Merl F. Kleinknecht

HARRIS, Stanley Raymond "Bucky" (b. 8 November 1896, Port Jarvis, NY; d. 8 November 1977, Bethesda, MD), player, manager, and scout, was of Swiss-Welsh descent and the son of a coal miner. Harris grew up in Pittstown, PA, and ended his formal education at age 13. The 5 foot, 9 1/2 inch, 156 pounder began his professional baseball career in Muskegon, MI (CL), in 1916 and played for Norfolk, VA (VL), the next season until the club disbanded. Harris, who batted and threw right-handed, completed 1917 with Reading, PA (NYSL), and spent the 1918 and 1919 seasons with Buffalo, NY (IL). In late 1919, the Washington Senators promoted Harris to their AL club.

During a twelve-year major league career, the slick-fielding second base-man compiled a .274 batting average, made 1,297 hits, knocked in 506 runs, and stole 166 bases. Besides setting a major league record in 1922 for most putouts (479) by a second baseman, he led his position in fielding (1927), putouts (1922–1923, 1926–1927), errors (1923), and double plays (1923, 1925). In 1924 Washington Senators owner Clark Griffith* named the youthful Harris player-manager. The 27-year-old "Boy Wonder" promptly led Wash-ington to its first AL pennant and World Series title. In the seven-game World Series against the New York Giants, Harris batted .333 with two home runs and handled 54 fielding chances. He established records for most putouts and assists by a second baseman in a series game (8 each) and for a seven-game series (26, 28). Harris the next year led Washington to the World Series and continued as Senators player-manager until 1928, when he was traded to the Detroit Tigers (AL) for infielder Jack Warner. Two years earlier Harris had married Elizabeth Sutherland, daughter of the U.S. Senator from West Virginia.

The perennial "available man," Harris managed in five different decades and piloted more major league games than anyone except Connie Mark* and John McGraw.* Harris, who ranks as the third winningest manager (2,159) and second in games lost (2,219), piloted the Tigers (1929–1933), AL Boston Red Sox (1934), AL Washington Senators (1935–1942), and NL Philadelphia Phillies (1943). After serving the 1944–1945 seasons as bench manager and front office executive with Buffalo (IL), Harris in 1947 joined the New York Yankees (AL) as manager. He led the Bronx Bombers to a 1947 World Series triumph over the Brooklyn Dodgers and was named Major League Manager of the Year by *The Sporting News*, but was replaced by Casey Stengel* after New York finished third in 1948. From 1950 to 1954 Harris managed the Washington Senators (AL) to five second division finishes and closed his managerial career on a winning note at Detroit (AL) in 1956. After being assistant to the general manager of the AL Boston Red Sox (1956–1960), he scouted for the AL Chicago White Sox (1962) and AL Washington Senators (1963–1971). In 1975 Harris was elected to the National Baseball Hall of Fame.

BIBLIOGRAPHY: Stanley Harris file, National Baseball Hall of Fame Library, Coo-perstown, NY; Paul MacFarlane, ed., *TSN Hall of Fame Fact Book* (St. Louis, 1983).
William Ivory

HARTNETT, Charles Leo "Gabby" (b. 20 December 1900, Woonsocket, RI; d. 20 December 1972, Park Ridge, IL), player, coach, and manager, was the eldest of fourteen children. He grew up in Millville, MA, where he finished elementary school and attended Dean Academy for two years. Hart-nett played baseball for Dean Academy and for a semi-pro team while work-ing in a local factory. After Hartnett began his professional career with

Worcester, MA (EL), in 1921, the Chicago Cubs (NL) purchased his contract for $2,500. During spring training of his rookie year (1922), he said nothing to reporters, who tagged him with the ironic nickname "Gabby." A right-handed catcher, the durable Hartnett played nineteen seasons for Chicago (1922–1940) and appeared in over 100 games twelve seasons. A solid hitter, he compiled a .297 lifetime batting average and achieved a career-high .354 mark in 1937. His most noteworthy hit, the "homer in the gloamin'," came in the bottom of the ninth inning on September 28, 1938, and enabled the Cubs to defeat the Pittsburgh Pirates and win the NL pennant. Hartnett once held the career home run mark for catchers with 236, made 1,912 hits and 396 doubles, and knocked in 1,179 runs.

An excellent defensive catcher and handler of pitchers, Hartnett helped lead the Chicago Cubs to NL pennants in 1929, 1932, 1935, and 1938. Hartnett paced NL catchers six times each in fielding percentage and assists and four times in putouts. He appeared in five All-Star games and was catcher for the NL when a line drive broke pitcher Dizzy Dean's* toe, effectively ending the latter's career. Dean had shaken off Hartnett's sign and thrown another pitch. During the 1938 season, Hartnett replaced Charlie Grimm* as Cubs manager. He directed the team to a 203–176 won-loss record through the 1940 season and spent 1941 as a player-coach with the New York Giants (NL). Minor league managing stints followed in Indianapolis (AA) in 1942, Jersey City (IL) in 1943, and Buffalo (IL) in 1946. After leaving baseball in 1947, he became successful in the insurance business and owned a bowling alley. Hartnett briefly returned to baseball as a coach in 1965 and as a scout in 1966 for the Kansas City Athletics (AL). On his seventy-second birthday, he died of cirrhosis of the liver. Described as a "beefy man with a tomato-red face who talked a lot," the 6 foot, 1 inch, 218 pound Hartnett spearheaded the successful Cubs teams of the 1930s. He was named Most Valuable Player by the Baseball Writers Association of America in 1935 and was elected to the National Baseball Hall of Fame in 1955.

BIBLIOGRAPHY: Bob Broeg, *Super Stars of Baseball* (St. Louis, 1971); Warren Brown, *The Chicago Cubs* (New York, 1946); Jim Enright, *Chicago Cubs* (New York, 1975); Charlie Grimm, *Jolly Cholly's Story* (Chicago, 1968); Gene Karst and Martin J. Jones, Jr., *Who's Who in Professional Baseball* (New Rochelle, NY, 1973); *Macmillan Baseball Encyclopedia* (New York, 1969); *NYT*, December 21, 1972; Lowell Reidenbaugh, *Cooperstown: Where Baseball's Legends Live Forever* (St. Louis, 1983).

John E. Findling

HEILMANN, Harry Edwin "Slug" (b. 3 August 1894, San Francisco, CA; d. 9 July 1951, Detroit, MI), player, coach, and announcer, attended St. Mary's High School in Oakland, CA, and Sacred Heart College. Portland, OR, signed him as an outfielder–first baseman out of college in 1913 for their NWL farm club. The Detroit Tigers (AL) drafted the 6 foot, 1 inch, 200 pound Heilmann in 1914, but he could not break into the stellar hitting outfield of Ty Cobb,* Sam Crawford,* and Bobby Veach.* He was sent in 1915 to San Francisco (PCL), where his hard hitting overcame weak fielding and lack of speed. From 1916 to 1929, he played for the Detroit Tigers. Since the Tigers had a plethora of slugging outfielders, Harry occasionally played first base. In 1919 and 1920 he led AL first basemen in errors. On October 5, 1920, he married Harriet Maynes.

Cobb, who became manager in 1921, permanently moved Heilmann to the outfield and markedly improved his batting average by changing his batting stance and grip. Nicknamed "Slug," Heilmann led the AL that year with 237 hits and a sparkling .394 batting average. In 1923, 1925, and 1927, he also won batting titles and attributed the strange sequence of dates to his two-year contracts. He particularly valued his 1921 title because he narrowly edged his close friend Cobb for that championship. Although not a home run hitter, Heilmann usually led his hard-hitting team in RBIs and eight times hit 40 or more doubles. After hitting .344 in 1929, Heilmann was sent to the Cincinnati Reds (NL). He batted .333 and hit 43 doubles in 142 games in 1930, but arthritis forced him to miss the next season. Heilmann retired in 1932 at age 37, finishing the year as club coach.

One of baseball's greatest hitters, with a lifetime .342 average, Heilmann batted and threw right-handed. In 2,146 games, Heilmann made 2,660 hits, 542 doubles, and 183 homers, and knocked in 1,551 runs. A fair fielder, he led the AL in outfield assists in 1924 with 31. Heilmann made three errors in one inning to tie a major league record for first basemen. His championship batting averages of .394, .403, .393, and .398 came within nine hits of giving him a nearly unprecedented .400 average for those four years. In 1925 he made six hits in nine at bats on the last day to surpass Tris Speaker* for the batting title. Two years later, he made seven for nine on the final day to narrowly edge Al Simmons.* Heilmann, who could have won either title by remaining on the bench, rarely beat out infield hits. His maximum home run production was 21 in 1922, while his best RBI mark was 139 in 1921. Despite Heilmann's hitting skills, the Tigers did not win an AL pennant. His career was interrupted by military service in 1918, a broken collarbone in 1922, sinus surgery in 1924, and arthritis in 1931, the latter ending his career. In 1952 he was elected to the National Baseball Hall of Fame.

Unlike many baseball players, Heilmann moved successfully into a second career. After an unsuccessful experience in the insurance business, he entered radio broadcasting and from 1933 until 1951 announced the Tigers' games. Although other announcers vied with one another in their shrillness, "Slug" told droll, low-key stories, demonstrated his superb knowledge of the game, and even took elocution lessons. Extremely popular with Michigan fans, he attracted a large following among younger listeners who had not known him as a player.

As player and announcer, he served the Detroit club for nearly thirty-four years. During spring training in 1951, Heilmann was found to have cancer; he was hospitalized in Florida and then in Detroit. He died the day before the annual All-Star Game, held in Detroit that year. Thousands of his fans crowded the Shrine of the Little Flower for the final services. He left his wife, Mae, and one son and one daughter.

BIBLIOGRAPHY: Lee Allen, *The American League Story* (New York, 1962); Martin Appel and Burt Goldblatt, *Baseball's Best: The Hall of Fame Gallery* (New York, 1977); Joe Falls, *The Detroit Tigers* (New York, 1975); David S. Neft, Richard M. Cohen, and Jordan A. Deutsch, *The Sports Encyclopedia: Baseball*, 5th ed. (New York, 1982); *NYT*, 1916–1951, June 12, 1924, July 10, 1951; Lowell Reidenbaugh, *Cooperstown: Where Baseball's Legends Live Forever* (St. Louis, 1983).

Thomas L. Karnes

HENDERSON, Rickey Henley (b. 25 December 1958, Chicago, IL), player, is the fourth of seven children of John Henderson and nurse Bobby Henderson. His father left when Rickey was two months old, after which his family moved to Arkansas and then settled in Oakland, CA. An All-American running back at Oakland Technical High School, Henderson was recruited by the University of Southern California, Arizona State University, and other football powers. Henderson, however, signed with the hometown A's (AL), who selected him in the fourth round of the 1976 draft.

With Modesto, CA (CaL), in 1977, he developed his batting stance and stole 95 bases. At Class AAA Ogden, UT (PCL), in 1979, he perfected his head-first slide. In his 89 games with the Oakland A's (AL) that year, he stole 33 bases. In his first full major league season (1980), the 5 foot, 10 inch, 180 pound speedster surpassed Ty Cobb's* 65-year-old AL stolen base record of 96 with 100 thefts. The strike in 1981 reduced his seasonal output to 56, but he stole 130 bases in 1982, 108 in 1983, 66 in 1984, 80 in 1985, and 87 in 1986. His 130 stolen bases in 1982 erased Lou Brock's* major league single season record of 118.

Henderson's base-stealing reputation overshadows his other accomplishments. According to *Baseball Abstracts* author Bill James, Henderson's .450-plus on-base percentage makes him this century's best leadoff hitter. Batting from a crouch to reduce his strike zone, he receives many walks. Henderson, whose 116 bases on balls in 1982 and 103 in 1983 led the AL, does not wait for walks. In 1981 Henderson, who throws left but bats right, paced the AL with 89 runs on 135 hits and batted a solid .319 average. Although usually batting for base hits, he demonstrates considerable power. In 1984 he slugged 27 doubles, 4 triples (down from 7 in 1983), and 16 homers. The next year, he led the AL in runs scored (146) and stolen bases (80) and finished fourth in batting average (.314) and on-base percentage (.419). Henderson also made 172 hits, 28 doubles, 24 home runs, and 72 RBIs, finishing third in the Most

Valuable Player balloting. In 1986 the lead-off batter paced the AL in runs scored (130) and stolen bases (87), and slugged a career-high 28 homers.

From 1979 to 1982, Henderson teamed with Dwayne Murphy and Tony Armas to form one of baseball's most effective outfields. Many rank Henderson the best left fielder in the majors. He consistently stands among the leaders in chances and putouts, leading the AL in the latter category with 327 and winning the Gold Glove award in 1981. After six seasons, the long-time Oakland resident and fan favorite was traded to the New York Yankees (AL) in 1984 for five players and signed for an estimated $8.65 million over five years. Through 1986, Henderson compiled a career .291 batting average with 862 runs on 1,182 hits, 188 doubles, 103 home runs, and 660 stolen bases. He still lives in Oakland, where his fiance, Pam Palmer is expecting their first child. In 1986 Henderson was named to the AL All-Star Team for the sixth time.

BIBLIOGRAPHY: Ron Fimrite, "He Finally Bagged It," *SI* 57 (September 6, 1982), pp. 14–19; Ron Fimrite, "A Well Matched Set," *SI* 56 (May 10, 1982), pp. 88–102; Peter Gammons, "Who's the Fastest Man in Baseball?" *Sport* 73 (May, 1982), pp. 44–48; Bill James, "So What's All the Fuss," *SI* 57 (September 6, 1982), pp. 30–34; Jim Kaplan, "No Slouch in the Crouch," *SI* 55 (September 14, 1981), pp. 52–54; Barry Siegel, ed., *TSN Official Baseball Register, 1984* (St. Louis, 1984); *TSN*, October 15, December 3, 17, 1984.

Gaymon L. Bennett

HERMAN, Floyd Caves "Babe" (b. 26 June 1903, Buffalo, NY), player, coach, and scout, is the son of Charles and Rose Etta (Caves) Herman and attended Glendale, CA, High School. Herman wanted to play football for the University of California, but signed as a first baseman and outfielder with the Brooklyn Dodgers (NL).

Nicknamed "Babe," the youthful Herman in 1921 hit .330 for Edmonton (WCaL). In 1922 he played for Reading, PA (IL) and Omaha (WL), where he hit .416. Herman hit .300 or better from 1923 to 1925 for other minor league teams, including Atlanta, Memphis, San Antonio, Little Rock, and Seattle. He married Anna Merriken on November 9, 1923, and has three sons and one daughter.

The very superstitious Herman played first base and later outfield for the famous NL "Daffy Dodgers" of Wilbert Robinson.* He laid his glove up in the field if facing a left-handed pitcher and face down if opposing a right-hander. He crowded the plate and could hit to all fields. A left-handed batter, the 6 foot, 4 inch, 190 pound Herman once doubled into a double play when three Dodgers runners wound up on third base in 1926. Herman was never hit on the head by a fly ball, but once was hit on the shoulder. He excelled at the plate, hitting .381 in 1929. Although batting .393 the following year, Herman lost the NL batting title to Bill Terry.* That same season, he hit

35 homers and knocked in 130 runs. Though Herman looked ungainly in the field, his lifetime .971 fielding average ranked almost ten percentage points higher than that of Ty Cobb.*

On March 14, 1932, the Dodgers traded Herman, Ernie Lombardi,* and Walt Gilbert to the Cincinnati Reds (NL) for Joe Stripp, Tony Cuccinello, and Clyde Sukeforth. Although he hit .326 and led the NL with 19 triples with Cincinnati, the Reds sent him to the Chicago Cubs (NL) in a multi-player deal in 1933. After Herman had two fair seasons, including a .304 batting mark in 1934, the Cubs traded him to the Pittsburgh Pirates (NL). With Herman struggling at .235 at mid-season the Pirates traded him back to the Reds. The Reds sent Herman to the Detroit Tigers (AL) after he posted a .279 average in 1936. The Tigers released him following seventeen games, after which he spent several seasons in the minor leagues with Toledo (AA), Jersey City (IL), and Hollywood (PCL). In 1945 the Dodgers recalled Herman, who hit .265 in 37 games.

During his major league career, Herman played in 1,552 games, compiled a .324 batting average, hit 399 doubles and 181 home runs, and knocked in 997 runs. In one 1933 game, he belted three homers against the Philadelphia Phillies. On July 10, 1935, with the Reds, Herman slugged the first home run hit during a night game against the Dodgers. Herman subsequently scouted for the NL Pittsburgh Pirates (1947–1950), AL New York Yankees (1953–1954, 1962–1963), NL Philadelphia Phillies (1955–1959), NL New York Mets (1961), and NL San Francisco Giants (1964) and coached for the Pirates (1951) and Seattle Reindeer (PCL) in 1952. The Glendale, CA, resident has raised turkeys, owned an orange grove, and grown prize-winning orchids.

BIBLIOGRAPHY: Maury Allen, *Baseball's 100* (New York, 1981); Harold H. Horowitz and Ralph Tolleris, *Big Time Baseball* (New York, 1950); Gene Karst and Martin J. Jones, Jr., *Who's Who in Professional Baseball* (New Rochelle, NY, 1973); John Lardner, "Unbelievable Babe Herman," *Sport Magazine's World of Sport* (New York, 1962); Ira Smith, *Baseball's Famous Outfielders* (New York, 1954); Red Smith, "Holy Name in Brooklyn," *NYT Biographical Service*, November, 1979.

William A. Borst

HERMAN, William Jennings "Billy," "Bryan" (b. 7 July 1909, New Albany, IN), player, coach, and manager, attended New Albany High School and pitched his church team to a league championship. As a minor leaguer, the 5 foot, 11 inch, 195 pound Herman played second base for Vicksburg, MS (CSL), and Louisville (AA) in 1928, Dayton (CL) in 1929, and Louisville (AA) from 1929 through 1931. After joining the NL, the right-handed batter and thrower performed as a second baseman for the Chicago Cubs (1931–1941), Brooklyn Dodgers (1941–1946), and Boston Braves (1946). In 1,922 games, he made 2,345 hits, slugged 486 doubles, scored 1,163 runs, and knocked in 839 runs. Herman, the second baseman on *The Sporting News* Major League All-Star team in 1943, compiled an impressive .304 lifetime batting average. Besides batting .433 in 10 All-Star games, he starred on four NL pennant-winning clubs (Chicago, 1932, 1935, 1938; Brooklyn, 1941). The stellar defensive second baseman holds NL records at his position for most years leading in putouts (7), most putouts in a doubleheader (16, June 28, 1933), and most seasons accepting at least 900 chances (1932–1933, 1935–1936, 1938).

Herman subsequently served as player-manager for the Pittsburgh Pirates (NL) in 1947 and Minneapolis (AA) in 1948 and played for Oakland (PCL) in 1950. He also managed Richmond (Pil) in 1951, the Boston Red Sox (AL) from 1964 to 1966, Bradenton, FL (GCRL), in 1968, and Tri-City (NWL) in 1969. Herman's major league clubs won 189 games and lost 274, perennially finishing in the second division. His major league coaching assignments included stints with the Brooklyn Dodgers (NL) from 1952 to 1957, Milwaukee Braves (NL) in 1958 and 1959, Boston Red Sox (AL) from 1960 to 1964, California Angels (AL) in 1967, and San Diego Padres (NL) in 1978 and 1979. The Oakland Athletics (AL) hired him as a scout from 1968 through 1974.

An expert at stealing opponents' signals, Herman was lauded by Casey Stengel* as "one of the . . . smartest players ever to come into the National League." Herman, who resides in Palm Beach Gardens, FL, married Hazel Jean Steproe on August 31, 1927, and later wed Frances Ann Antonucci on May 23, 1961. In 1975 he was elected to the National Baseball Hall of Fame.

BIBLIOGRAPHY: William J. Herman file, National Baseball Hall of Fame Library, Cooperstown, NY; Paul MacFarlane, ed., *TSN Hall of Fame Fact Book* (St. Louis, 1983).

Brian R. Kelleher

HERNANDEZ, Keith (b. 20 October 1953, San Francisco, CA), player, is the son of fireman John and Jacquelyn (Jordan) Hernandez. Hernandez's father, his number one fan and adviser, formerly played infield in the St. Louis Cardinals (NL) farm system. Hernandez, a 6 foot, 185 pound all-around athlete, quit the Capucino High School baseball team his senior year. Consequently, he was drafted only 42nd by the St. Louis Cardinals (NL) in 1971 and was the 783rd player selected. He attended the College of San Mateo and is an avid history buff.

Hernandez, who signed with the Cardinals for a $30,000 bonus despite his low selection, played first base for St. Petersburg (FSL) and Tulsa (AA) in 1972, and for Arkansas (TL) and Tulsa (AA) in 1973. He came up from Tulsa to St. Louis permanently at midseason in 1975 and led the Cardinals defensively with a .996 fielding average. From 1976 to 1983, Hernandez played first base for the Cardinals and paced the NL in many defensive categories. He consistently has ranked among the leaders in total chances and has led in assists in four seasons. His 146 assists in 1979 placed him fifth on the all-time single-season list. Besides topping the NL in putouts two times and double plays six times, he earned eight Gold Glove awards from 1978 through 1985.

Hernandez, a left-handed batter, also poses an offensive threat. The .302 lifetime hitter led the NL in intentional walks received in 1982 (19), consistently leads in on-base percentage, bats well with runners on base, and topped the NL with 21 game-winning RBIs in 1982. In 1979 he led the NL with 116 runs, 48 doubles, and a .344 batting average, being named NL Player of the Year by *The Sporting News* and NL co-Most Valuable Player. Three years later, Hernandez played in the league championship and World Series. Hernandez has made four All-Star teams, hitting .500 with a 1.000 fielding average.

On June 15, 1983, Hernandez was traded to the New York Mets. Although initially upset with the trade, he adjusted and led the Mets in 1984 to a second place finish in the NL East. In 1985 he led the NL in game-winning RBIs (23), placed sixth in hitting (.309), and tied for fifth in doubles (34). On July 4 he hit for the cycle in a 16–13 victory over the Atlanta Braves in 19 innings. In 1986 Hernandez was named to the NL All-Star Team for the fourth time. He finished fifth in the NL in batting (.310) and tied for first in on-base percentage (.413), helping the Mets to capture the NL pennant. In the NL Championship Series against the Houston Astros, Hernandez hit .269 and knocked in 3 runs. He batted .231 and knocked in 4 runs, as the Mets defeated the Boston Red Sox in the World Series. Through 1986, he has compiled 1,840 hits and a .302 batting average, scored 969 runs, slugged 372 doubles, and recorded 900 RBIs. He is tied for fifth place for lifetime fielding average (.994) with six other first basemen. Commissioner Peter Ueberroth* (OS) in February, 1986, suspended Hernandez for one year for his involvement with drugs. Hernandez avoided the suspension by donating 10 percent of his salary to a drug rehabilitation program, contributing one-hundred hours of community service, and agreeing to periodic testing. In 1986 Hernandez was named to the NL All Star Fielding Team for the ninth time. Hernandez, whose 1984 salary of $1.6 million ranked eighth highest in the majors, is separated from his wife Sue, has three daughters, Jessica, Melissa, and Mary, and lives in New York City.

BIBLIOGRAPHY: *Idaho Statesman*, December 15, 1984, p. 1B; Joe Jares, "KHrnnz Is Dng Jst Grt," *SI* 51 (September 17, 1979), pp. 50–51; Joseph L. Reichler ed., *The Baseball Encyclopedia*, 6th ed. (New York, 1985) p. 1,015; Barry Siegel, ed., *TSN Official Baseball Register*, 1984 (St. Louis, 1984); *TSN* July 24, 1984, p. 11; October 15, 1984, p. 35; December 3, 1984, p. 54; George Vecsey, "Keith Hernandez Historian at First Base," *NYT Biographical Service* (August, 1983), pp. 946–947; *WWA*, 42nd ed. (1982–1983), p. 1419.

Gaymon L. Bennett

HEYDLER, John Arnold (b. 10 July 1869, Lafargeville, NY; d. 18 April 1956, San Diego, CA), umpire, sportswriter, and executive, became a printer's apprentice at age 14 in Rochester, NY, and later worked for the Bureau of Printing and Engraving in Washington, DC. He reportedly recited "Casey at the Bat" to President Grover Cleveland, to whom he was presenting a draft of a printed document for approval. Heydler, an avid fan and amateur player, became involved in the sport as an occupation almost by accident when asked to umpire a game in 1895 because the regular official did not show up. He served as an assistant umpire in the NL from 1895 to 1898 and covered the game as a sportswriter from 1898 to 1903. His first important executive activity came in 1903, when he was named private secretary to NL president Harry Pulliam.* His principal responsibility comprised compiling statistics, thus preserving much of the game's early history.

After being selected NL secretary-treasurer in 1907, Heydler served as acting NL president in 1909 and as NL president in his own right in 1918. His tenure came after the sport had established itself as America's pastime and was experiencing its most difficult, disreputable period, culminating with the Chicago Black Sox scandal in 1919. As NL president, Heydler did not exhibit aggressive leadership or rigorously investigate suspected wrongdoing. Early in 1919 he exonerated Hal Chase,* who was later involved in the Black Sox scandal, from charges of betting on and throwing games in previous seasons. This action resulted in heavy criticism then and later. Nonetheless, Heydler became one of the last presidents to stand up to the owners. In 1920 he actively backed the selection of Judge Kenesaw Mountain Landis* as Commissioner of Baseball. Heydler clearly recognized the importance of creating a strong Commissioner's Office to tame the owners. His support of this move proved critical in changing the direction which baseball underwent thereafter.

The innovative Heydler, well regarded in the sport, helped establish the National Baseball Hall of Fame to honor the sports heroes and fix the sport of baseball in the national consciousness. He also proposed in 1929 that pitchers should not bat and suggested that a tenth man hit for them. He thus fathered the designated hitter system currently used in the AL. Upon retiring as president because of ill health in 1934, Heydler served as NL chairman of the board until his death. Heydler, a lifetime Lutheran, married Nancy Humphrey of Franklin, PA, on September 18, 1894, and apparently had no children.

BIBLIOGRAPHY: Gene Karst and Martin J. Jones, Jr., *Who's Who in Professional Baseball* (New Rochelle, NY, 1973); *NYT*, April 19, 1956; Marshall Smelser, *The Life That Ruth Built* (New York, 1975); *Time* 67 (April 30, 1956), p. 80; David Quentin Voigt, *American Baseball*, vol. 2 (Norman, OK, 1970).

Charles R. Middleton

HIGGINS, Michael Franklin, Jr. "Pinky" (b. 27 May 1909, Red Oak, TX; d. 21 March 1969, Dallas, TX), player, manager, scout, and executive, was the son of Dallas police officer Michael Higgins, Sr. The three Higgins sons, all talented high school athletes, played college sports. Clen played football at the University of Texas, while Jimmy performed for Southern Methodist University, and Mike played football and baseball at the University of Texas. After graduating from there in 1930, Higgins signed with Connie Mack's* Philadelphia Athletics (AL) and played in only 14 games, mainly at third base, on their world championship team. After spending 1931 with Dallas and San Antonio (TL) and 1932 with Portland, OR (PCL), he played third base for the Athletics from 1933 through 1936. He was then traded to the Boston Red Sox (AL), where he hit .302 and .303 his next two seasons and drove in 106 runs each season. From 1939 to 1944, the right-hander performed as the regular third baseman with the Detroit Tigers (AL). In 1935 he married Hazel French of Dallas; they had two daughters, Diane and Elizabeth. During World War II, he served in the U.S. Navy. He played in 18 games with Detroit in 1946 and was traded back to Boston (AL), where he finished his last season as a player. A clutch hitter and a solid fielder, the 6 foot, 1 inch, 185 pound Higgins compiled a .292 lifetime average with 1,941 hits, 374 doubles, 141 home runs, and 1,075 RBIs. In his first full season, Higgins batted .314, had eight hits in a June, 1933, doubleheader, and hit for the cycle in an August game. During the 1938 season with Philadelphia, he hit safely in 12 successive times at bat to break the AL record of 10 straight hits. In the 1940 World Series with Detroit, he batted .333, made 8 hits and 6 RBIs, recorded 30 composite putouts, and handled a record 10 chances in one game. In 64 games with Boston in 1946, Higgins helped the Red Sox win an AL pennant by batting .275 and delivering some clutch hits. After his playing career ended, he spent eight years managing in the Red Sox minor league system and developed a reputation as a winner and a patient, skillful handler of talent. After moving steadily up from Class B to AAA clubs, he became manager of the Red Sox in 1955. In his first year, he was named *The Sporting News* Manager of the Year and guided Boston to an 84–70 fourth place finish. Although not producing a pennant winner in eight seasons as Red Sox manager, he steered his teams to third place finishes in 1958 and 1959. As manager, Higgins gave players the benefit of the doubt when struggling with slumps or problems and earned their respect and loyalty with his easygoing, approachable manner. His last three years at Boston were spent as Red Sox executive vice-president and general manager. After being dismissed in 1965, he scouted for the Houston Astros (NL).

His car struck and killed a Louisiana state highway worker and injured three others in February, 1968. Pleading guilty to drunk driving, Higgins was sentenced to four years in prison. After serving less than two months of his sentence, he was paroled and died of a heart attack one day after his release.

BIBLIOGRAPHY: Gene Karst and Martin J. Jones, Jr., *Who's Who in Professional Baseball* (New Rochelle, NY, 1973); Howard Liss, *The Boston Red Sox* (New York, 1982); Tom Meany et al., *The Boston Red Sox* (New York, 1956); *NYT*, March 22, 1969, p. 33.

Douglas A. Noverr

HILL, J. Preston "Pete" (b. 1880, ?; d. 1951, Buffalo, NY), player and manager, ranked among the finest hitters in Negro baseball's early years. In 1904 the left-handed hitting Hill began his baseball career with the Philadelphia Giants. Hill, a line drive hitter with occasional home run power, teamed five years at Philadelphia with stars Rube Foster,* Grant "Home Run" Johnson,* Pete Booker, Charlie Grant, and Dan McClellan. The Philadelphia Giants played against all-white teams in the Philadelphia City League. The white teams fielded "Turkey Mike" Donlin,* Harry McCormick, Jake Stahl, "Topsey" Hartsel, and other major leaguers.

After jumping in 1909 to the Leland Giants of Chicago, he captained and was assistant manager of the incredible 123–6 1910 team. The Giants, managed by Rube Foster, included stars John Henry Lloyd,* Bruce Petway, and Frank Wickware. In the fall of 1910, he played a three-game series against his friend Frank Chance's* Chicago Cubs (NL). Hill, a part Indian who was known as Foster's "money hitter," played for the Chicago American Giants from 1911 to 1918. For six seasons he participated in winter baseball in Cuba and compiled a .307 composite batting average and a league-leading .365 mark in the 1910–1911 campaign. He batted four for four in 1909–1910 against 21-game winner Ed Willett of the Detroit Tigers (AL) and four for nine in 1910–1911 against Eddie Plank* and Chief Bender* of the Philadelphia Athletics (AL). In recorded games against white ballplayers, he batted an even .300.

From 1919 to 1921, he became player-manager of the Detroit Stars. The Stars entered the NNL in 1920. He played for and managed the Milwaukee Bears (NNL) in 1923 and returned to Detroit in 1924. After moving in midseason 1924 to the Baltimore Black Sox (ECL), he performed occasionally and served as club business manager through the 1925 season. Hill later formed the Buffalo Red Caps and worked at the Ford Motor Company in Detroit. His career spanned two distinct eras of black baseball. After participating on the great barnstorming teams of the century's first two decades, he starred in the early NNL years. Hill and the era's other great players gave relative stability to the Negro leagues.

BIBLIOGRAPHY: Terry A. Baxter, correspondence with Jorge Figueroda, 1984, Cuban League statistics, Terry A. Baxter Collection, Lee's Summit, MO; John Holway, "Pete Hill," John Holway Collection, Alexandria, VA; John Holway, *Rube Foster: The Father of Black Baseball* (Alexandria, VA, 1981); Joseph M. Overfield, correspondence with John Holway, December 26, 1983, John Holway Collection, Alexandria, VA; Robert W. Peterson, *Only the Ball Was White* (Englewood Cliffs, NJ, 1970);

James A. Riley, *The All-Time All-Stars of Black Baseball* (Cocoa, FL, 1983); *Sol White's Official Baseball Guide* (1907; reprint, Columbia, SC, 1984).

                                                             Terry A. Baxter

HINES, Paul A. (b. 1 March 1852, Washington, DC; d. 10 July 1935, Hyattsville, MD), player, starred as an outfielder in the NA, NL, and AA from 1872 to 1891. During his career he played with Washington (1872–1873, 1886–1887), Chicago (1874–1877), Providence (1878–1885), and Indianapolis (1888–1889). Although only 5 feet, 9 inches tall and 173 pounds, Hines possessed quickness afoot and remained a good base runner even in his late thirties. Hines played center field adequately throughout his career, effectively using his above average speed.

Hines' record as a right-handed batter made him a leading player of his generation. A consistently hard hitter, he compiled a lifetime .302 batting average in the NA and .301 marks in the NL and AA. Hines, who eleven times hit at least .300, only once batted below .270. His best performances came in his first two years (1878, 1879) with the powerful Providence team. In 1878 Hines became the first Triple Crown winner in major league history by leading the league with 4 home runs, 50 RBIs, and a .358 batting average. That feat was not duplicated until Hugh Duffy* performed it in 1894. In 1879 Hines finished second in batting (.357) and led the NL with 146 hits. In addition, he paced the NL in doubles in 1876, 1881, and 1884.

Hines starred on three championship teams: Chicago in 1876, and Providence in 1879 and 1884. As his skills deteriorated, Hines split the 1890 season with Pittsburgh and Boston (NL) and concluded his career as a substitute for Washington (AA) in 1891.

BIBLIOGRAPHY: Joseph L. Reichler, ed., *The Baseball Encyclopedia*, 6th ed. (New York, 1985), pp. 58, 1,022–1,023.

                                                             Gordon B. McKinney

HODGES, Gilbert Ray "Gil" (b. 4 April 1924, Princeton, IN; d. 2 April 1972, West Palm Beach, FL), player and manager, was the son of coal miner Charles and Irene (Horstmeyer) Hodges. He won varsity letters in four sports at Petersburg (IN) High School and played summer American Legion baseball. The Brooklyn Dodgers (NL) scouted and signed him in mid–1943, after Hodges spent three years at St. Joseph's College, Rensselaer, IN. Brooklyn used him as a third baseman in the season finale. Drafted into the U.S. Marine Corps, he served in the Pacific theater during World War II.

Discharged as a sergeant in February, 1946, he spent a season at Newport News, VA (Pil), learning to be a catcher. Hodges was recalled for 1947 and remained with the Dodgers in Brooklyn and Los Angeles through 1961. He became regular catcher in 1948 but was shifted to first base when Roy Campanella* was acquired. Hodges quickly mastered that position and subsequently won Gold Glove awards for defensive excellence there. Taken by the New York Mets (NL) in the 1961 expansion draft, he finished his playing days there in 1963. In early 1963, he was traded to Washington (AL) to be the Senators' manager. Hodges led the Senators from tenth place in 1963 to sixth in 1967 and then returned to the Mets as manager. New York finished ninth in 1968 but won the world championship in 1969 and came in third in 1970 and 1971. During the 1972 spring training season, Hodges suffered a fatal heart attack following a round of golf.

Despite some problems hitting the curveball and enduring prolonged slumps, the powerful 6 foot, 1 1/2 inch, 200 pound Hodges batted .273, slugged .487, hit 370 home runs, and drove in over 100 runs per season during seven consecutive years in his career. Hodges compiled 1,921 hits, 295 doubles, 1,105 runs, 1,274 RBIs, and 1,137 strikeouts in 2,071 games. On August 31, 1950, he knocked four homers into the left field stands at Ebbets Field to tie a major league record. As a manager, Hodges compiled a 660–754 record (.467). Frequently called the physically strongest baseball player, Hodges possessed unusually huge hands. Each hand measured almost twelve inches from thumb tip to little finger tip. The devout Catholic was an even-tempered, soft-spoken, gentle person, courageous in overcoming a fear of the tight pitch, and astute and meticulous in managerial operations. Hodges, who made Brooklyn his permanent home, married Joan Lombardi in 1948 and had four children, Irene, Barbara, Cindy, and Gilbert Ray II.

BIBLIOGRAPHY: Tom Fox, "Every Day Is Father's Day to Hodges," *TSN*, June 15, 1963, p. 3; Gil Hodges file, National Baseball Hall of Fame Library, Cooperstown, NY; Gil Hodges, player questionnaire, Washington Senators, 1964; Roger Kahn, *The Boys of Summer* (New York, 1972); Joe King, "Diamond Dossier . . . Gil Hodges," *TSN*, June 6, 1951, p. 13; Joe King, "Homer Festival Puts Hodges in Famed Society," *TSN*, September 13, 1950, p. 5; Roscoe McGowan, "Gil's Capable Hands Make Job Look Easy," *TSN*, March 13, 1957, p. 3; *NYT*, April 3, 1972, pp. 1, 52; Joseph L. Reichler, ed., *The Baseball Encyclopedia*, 6th ed. (New York, 1985), pp. 632, 1,025; Bill Roeder, "The Strong Man," in Tom Meany et al., *The Artful Dodgers* (New York, 1954), pp. 67–85; *TSN*, April 15, 1972, p. 5.

Frank V. Phelps

HOLMES, Thomas Francis "Tommy," "Kelly" (b. 29 March 1917, Brooklyn, NY), player, manager, scout, and executive, attended New York City public schools. On January 5, 1941, he married high school sweetheart Lillian Helen Petterson. They have a son and daughter and reside in Woodbury, NY. Following his high school career, he excelled as a strong-armed outfielder and left-handed hitter with the Brooklyn Bay semi-professional team. In 1937 the New York Yankees (AL) assigned outfielder Holmes to Norfolk, VA (Pil), where he batted .320 and did not miss a game. At Binghamton, NY, in 1938, he paced the EL with a .368 batting percentage, 200 hits, and 41 doubles. He played with Kansas City (AA) in 1939 and with Newark

(IL) from 1939 through 1941, hitting consistently above .300. In 1940 and 1941 he led the IL in hits with 211 and 190, respectively.

Since the Yankees possessed an all-star outfield of Joe DiMaggio,* Tommy Henrich, and Charlie Keller, manager Joe McCarthy* dealt Holmes to the Boston Braves (NL). From 1942 through 1950, he started as regular left fielder for the Braves. In 1951 the Braves assigned him as player-manager of their Hartford, CT (EL) team. At Boston, Holmes set a then NL record by hitting in 37 consecutive games from June 6 to July 11, 1945. Named the NL's Most Valuable Player in 1945, he had a sparkling .352 batting average and led the NL with 28 home runs, 47 doubles, and 224 hits. His consecutive game hits record was surpassed by Pete Rose* of Cincinnati with 44 in 1978. The Braves recalled Holmes in 1951 to succeed manager Billy Southworth.* As player-manager, he lifted the Braves to a fourth place finish and briefly served as pilot the following season. Holmes, however, preferred to manage in the minor leagues, helping to develop young players' batting techniques.

Holmes, who finished his eleven-year career with the Brooklyn Dodgers (NL) for the remainder of the 1952 season, compiled a .302 lifetime batting average, made 1,507 hits and 292 doubles, and knocked in 581 runs. In 1948 he batted .325 and excelled in left field to help the Braves win the NL pennant. The Cleveland Indians stilled Holmes' bat in baseball's only "Indian Summer" World Series, besting Boston in six games. In 1952 Holmes earned a second World Series ring with brief appearances against the New York Yankees. His subsequent minor league managerial assignments included Toledo (AA), 1953; Elmira (EL), 1954; Forth Worth (TL), 1955; Portland, OR (PCL), 1956; and Montreal (IL), 1957. After serving as a Los Angeles Dodgers (NL) scout in 1958, he returned to New York to be third director of the Greater New York Sandlot Baseball Foundation. Holmes became a sales executive at Hi-Temp Wires and Teflon Products and later manufacturer's representative for various metal products.

In 1973 the New York Mets (NL) designated Holmes as community relations director of the metropolitan area youth sandlot program. Sixty-five youngsters enrolled in the program have made the major leagues. With the Mets, he has established sandlot clinics, developed youth baseball programs, and has created a goodwill program between New York City and Tokyo. Holmes also serves as an executive of Kenko Sports, manufacturers of rubberized baseballs for young players. Holmes maintains a heavy speaking and public appearance schedule with the Mets and participates in many community endeavors on Long Island.

BIBLIOGRAPHY: *American League Red Book* (New York, 1941); Paul MacFarlane, ed., *TSN Daguerreotypes of Great Stars of Baseball* (St. Louis, 1981); *National League Green Book* (New York, 1942); *TSN World Series Record Book*, 1948, 1952 (St. Louis, 1948, 1952).

                                                                    Carl Lundquist

HOOPER, Harry Bartholomew (b. 24 August 1887, Elephant Head Homestead, CA; d. 18 December 1974, Santa Cruz, CA), player, manager, and coach, was the son of farmer Joseph and Kathleen (Keller) Hooper. He married Esther Henchy on November 26, 1912, and had three children, Harry Jr., Marie, and John. After graduating in 1907 with a civil engineering degree from St. Mary's College in Oakland, CA, he played outfield in 1907 and 1908 for Alameda and Sacramento (outlaw CaSL). Manager Charles Graham recommended him to Boston Red Sox (AL) owner John I. Taylor, who signed Hooper in 1909 for $2,850.

Hooper, one of the most intelligent, observant, dedicated, and innovative baseball players, performed for fun and placed winning far above money. Popular with players and fans alike, he became the only Red Sox player to participate on four world championship teams. Hooper played with Boston from 1909 to 1920 and for the Chicago White Sox (AL) from 1921 to 1925. In 1927 he served as player-manager for San Francisco (PCL). As baseball coach at Princeton University in 1931 and 1932, he compiled a mediocre 22–29–1 win-loss record. Subsequently he sold real estate in Santa Cruz, CA, and worked as a U.S. postmaster.

During seventeen major league seasons, he batted .281 in 2,308 games and hit 1,842 singles, 389 doubles, 160 triples, and 75 home runs. Hooper walked 1,136 times, reached base 3,602 times, stole 375 bases, knocked in 817 runs, and scored 1,429 times. From 1910 to 1915, he played alongside strong-armed outfielders Duffy Lewis and Tris Speaker.* The fast, aggressive Hooper still leads the Red Sox with 130 triples and 300 stolen bases.

Hooper relied on his own judgment and devised a signal system for teammate base runners. He credited Jesus Christ with answering his prayer in the deciding game of the 1912 World Series, when he made his famous barehanded catch of Larry Doyle's* drive to prevent the New York Giants from winning in regular innings. A member of the world champion Red Sox in 1912, 1915, 1916, and 1918, he starred in the fifth 1915 game by becoming the first player to hit two home runs in a single World Series contest. In 1971 he was elected to the National Baseball Hall of Fame.

Hooper, a remarkable leadoff batter for Boston, made 1,707 hits and walked 826 times for a .403 on-base percentage there. Defensively, he became the best outfielder to play the sunfield in Boston and made 344 assists, a record for right fielders. Hooper invented the "rump-slide," wherein he slid on one hip with feet forward and knees bent to catch many short fly balls. As Boston captain, he persuaded Red Sox manager Ed Barrow* to play Babe Ruth* in the outfield when he was not pitching. Hooper continually improved his batting, base-running, and outfield strategy and exemplified personal leadership in stressing combined individual effort to produce team successes. He greatly enhanced baseball's popularity by suggesting Ruth's timely move to the outfield.

BIBLIOGRAPHY: *Boston Red Sox Media Guide, 1984*; Ellery H. Clark Jr., *Boston Red Sox: 75th Anniversary History* (Hicksville, NY, 1975); Ellery H. Clark, Jr., correspondence with Harry Hooper, "Duffy" Lewis, Harry Hooper, Jr., John Hooper, Red Sox Analytical Letter Collection, Ellery H. Clark, Jr. Papers, Annapolis, MD; Ellery H. Clark, Jr., *Red Sox Fever* (Hicksville, NY, 1979); Ellery H. Clark, Jr., *Red Sox Forever* (Hicksville, NY, 1977); Joseph L. Reichler, ed., *The Baseball Encyclopedia*, 6th ed. (New York, 1985), pp. 1,031–1,032.

                                                                                    Ellery H. Clark, Jr.

HORNSBY, Rogers "Rajah" (b. 27 April 1896, Winters, TX; d. 5 January 1963, Chicago, IL), player, manager, coach, and scout, is ranked by many as the greatest right-handed hitter of all time. Hornsby, the son of cattle rancher and farmer Edward and Mary Dallas (Rogers) Hornsby, moved to a farm near Austin, TX, when his father died. The Hornsbys later moved to Fort Worth, where he attended school and excelled in baseball.

Hornsby began playing baseball professionally in 1914 at age 18 with Hugo, OK (TOL), and Denison, TX (WA). After being purchased by the St. Louis Cardinals (NL), he played in his first major league game on September 1, 1915. An aggressive, driving player with a fierce will to win, Hornsby played as a regular infielder (primarily a second baseman) for the Cardinals from 1916 through 1926 under managers Miller Huggins* and Branch Rickey.* From 1920 through 1925, Hornsby won six consecutive batting titles (an NL record). Batting above .400 three times, Hornsby holds the modern season record for highest average, hitting .424 in 1924. He led the NL in home runs (1922, 1925), RBIs (1920–1922, and 1925), base hits (1920, 1921, 1922, and 1924), and runs scored (1921–1922). One of the finest fielding infielders of his time, Hornsby led NL second basemen in 1922 with a .967 fielding average and completed his career with a .957 average.

In June, 1925, Hornsby succeeded Rickey as manager of the Cardinals. He led St. Louis to the 1926 pennant and world championship over the New York Yankees, the first club flag of the twentieth century. The NL's Most Valuable Player in 1925, the successful manager was idolized by St. Louis fans and demanded a three-year contract from Cardinals owners Sam Breadon* for $50,000 annually. When Breadon declined and an impasse followed, Hornsby on December 20, 1926, was traded to the New York Giants (NL) for Frankie Frisch* and Jimmy Ring. Protesting St. Louis fans, stunned at the trade of their hero, tried to get the trade cancelled. Many vowed to boycott the team, but the trade stood.

Controversy and adversity continually plagued Hornsby. Known for his unpredictable mood changes, the generally quiet Hornsby argued strenuously. His relations with team owners showed intolerance, suspicion, belligerence, and a lack of diplomacy. Hornsby's compulsive gambling on horse races caused him constant financial setbacks and home problems, with two of his three marriages ending in divorce. His first wife, Sarah, divorced him in 1923. Hornsby married Jeannette Pennington Hine in February, 1924, and they were later divorced. In January, 1957, he married Marjorie Bernice Frederick. He had two sons, Rogers, Jr., a U.S. Air Force pilot, and William, who played minor league baseball briefly.

The outspoken Hornsby lasted only one season with John McGraw's* Giants. Although he hit 26 homers, drove in 125 runs, and batted .361 in 1927, he was traded to the Boston Braves (NL). He became manager of the Braves in May, 1928, and led the NL in hitting with a .387 average, but was traded that November to the Chicago Cubs (NL) for five players and $200,000. Named the NL's MVP in 1929, Hornsby batted .380 and led the Cubs to the pennant. He managed the Cubs from September, 1930, until August, 1932, when unconditionally released because of problems with the front office. By this time, Hornsby was finished as a regular player and in considerable debt because of gambling losses.

In 1933 Hornsby returned to the Cardinals as a substitute infielder and signed that July as the manager of the St. Louis Browns (AL). He remained there until July, 1937, when fired because of his gambling activities. He managed the Browns again briefly in 1952 and the Cincinnati Reds (NL) later that same season and most of 1953. Between 1938 and 1943, Hornsby managed several minor league teams. These included Chattanooga (SA) in 1938, Baltimore (IL) in 1939, Oklahoma City (TL) in 1940 and 1941, and Fort Worth (TL) in 1942. In 1944 after taking over a last place team and leading them to 40 victories in 74 games, Hornsby was named Manager of the Year with Oklahoma City (TL). Between 1944 and 1949, Hornsby supervised a baseball school sponsored by the Chicago *Daily News*. He managed minor league teams in Beaumont, TX (TL), in 1950 and Seattle (PCL) in 1951, winning the league championship both seasons. In 1958 and 1959 he served as a coach with the Chicago Cubs (NL) and scouted and coached for the New York Mets (NL) in 1961 and 1962.

During Hornsby's major league career, he won seven batting titles and compiled a lifetime .358 batting average ranking second only to Ty Cobb's* .367. In 2,259 games, Hornsby made 2,930 hits (just 70 short of the coveted 3,000), 541 doubles, 169 triples, 301 home runs, and 1,584 RBIs, and scored 1,579 runs. His managerial record spanned thirteen seasons, producing 680 wins in 1,494 games, one pennant, and one world championship. In 1942 he was elected to the National Baseball Hall of Fame.

BIBLIOGRAPHY: Bob Broeg, *Super Stars of Baseball* (St. Louis, 1971); Gene Karst and Martin J. Jones, Jr., *Who's Who in Professional Baseball* (New Rochelle, NY, 1973); Tom Murray, *Sport Magazine's All-Time All Stars* (New York, 1977).

John L. Evers

HORTON, Willie Wattison (b. 18 October 1942, Arno, VA), player and coach, is the youngest of twenty-one children of James Thomas Clinton and Lillian (Wattison) Horton. He led Detroit Northwestern High School to a city championship in 1959 and signed with the Detroit Tigers (AL) in August, 1961, for a $50,000 bonus. On December 18 of that year, he married Patricia Strickland. After their divorce, he married Gloria Kendrick in 1981. These marriages produced three sons and four daughters.

Horton spent the 1962–1964 seasons in the minor leagues with Duluth-Superior (NoL) in 1962, Syracuse (IL) and Knoxville (SAL) in 1963, and Syracuse (IL) in 1964, briefly appearing with the Tigers in 1963 and 1964. In his first full major league season (1965), the 5 foot, 11 inch, 200 pound right-handed left fielder batted .273, belted 29 home runs, and knocked in 104 runs. These statistics resembled his standard performance the next decade, as Horton compiled a .273 lifetime batting average. Although a mediocre fielder, Horton exhibited physical strength widely respected around the league. In the Tigers' world championship 1968 season, Horton led the team in batting average (.285—fourth highest in the AL), slugging percentage (.543), and home runs (36). He batted .304 in the seven-game World Series against the St. Louis Cardinals.

When traded to the Texas Rangers (AL) in early 1977, Horton ranked among the top ten Tigers in home runs (262), total bases (2,549), and RBIs (886). Horton, who played in the 1965, 1968, 1970, and 1973 All-Star games, hit three homers in one game in 1970 and 1977. In 1977 and 1978, Horton played briefly for the Texas Rangers (AL), Cleveland Indians (AL), Oakland Athletics (AL), and Toronto Blue Jays (AL). As a designated hitter for the Seattle Mariners (AL) in 1979, he batted .279, slammed 29 home runs, made 106 RBIs, and was named Comeback Player of the Year. He finished his major league career with the Mariners in 1980, seven hits short of the 2,000 mark. In 2,028 career games, he slugged 284 doubles and 325 home runs and knocked in 1,163 runs. He played for the Portland, OR, Beavers (PCL) in 1981 and 1982 and in the MEL (1983), and served as a minor league batting instructor for the Oakland Athletics (1984) and Detroit Tigers (1985). In 1986 the Chicago White Sox (AL) named him as club batting coach.

BIBLIOGRAPHY: Joseph Reichler, ed., *The Baseball Encyclopedia*, 6th ed. (New York, 1985), p. 1,034; Fred Smith, *995 Tigers* (Detroit, 1981).

Sheldon L. Appleton

HOUK, Ralph George "Major" (b. 9 August 1919, Lawrence, KS), player, manager, coach, and executive, is the son of George Houk and the fourth of five children. Houk, who grew up on a farm near Lawrence, played baseball weekends as a youngster for the semi-professional Belvoirs, managed by his uncle, Charlie Houk. After performing in the outfield his first year with the Lawrence team, he switched to catching and played that position most of his career. "I liked catching," Houk recalled. "I had the whole game in front of me. I was in on every pitch. At fifteen I was as solid as a rock, 170 pounds of hard muscled flesh. I could block baserunners at home plate. In fact, blocking was easy for me."

Houk graduated from Lawrence High School, where he was selected All-State in football. New York Yankees (AL) scouts spotted Houk at a national tournament and signed him. Houk began his minor league career in 1939 as a $75-a-month rookie with the Neosho, MO, club (AML), where he hit .286. After moving up the minor league ranks, he hit .271 in 1941 with the Augusta, GA, club (SAL). His progress toward the major leagues was interrupted by army service in World War II, where he earned a Purple Heart and Silver and Bronze Stars and rose to the rank of major.

Upon returning to baseball in 1946, Houk played with Kansas City (AA) and Beaumont, TX (TL). In 1947 he was promoted to the New York Yankees as third-string catcher and played for Kansas City during the 1948 and 1949 seasons. Houk returned to the Yankees and completed his major league career as a reserve catcher there from 1950 through 1954. During his major league career, the right-handed Houk played in 91 games with a .272 batting average. He married Bette Porter on June 3, 1948, and has three children, Donna (Mrs. Walter Sloboden), Dick, and Robert.

The Yankees, impressed with Houk's leadership and baseball knowledge, appointed him manager of their Denver (AA) team in 1955. The Triple A club finished third that year and second in 1956, and won the Little World Series in 1957. This successful, short stint with Denver earned him a coaching position in 1958 with the New York Yankees, where he served until named New York club manager for the 1961 season. During his three years as coach, Houk refused several offers to manage other major league teams. He managed the Yankees to AL pennants and World Series titles in 1961 and 1962. Following his AL pennant-winning season in 1963, he was promoted to a front office position with the Yankees. He managed the Yankees again from 1966 through 1973, making a .539 winning percentage in eleven total seasons with New York. In 1974 he signed a contract to manage the Detroit Tigers (AL) and piloted them until retiring in 1978 with a composite five-season .450 winning percentage. From 1981 through 1984, Houk piloted the Boston Red Sox (AL) to a .542 winning percentage. In twenty managerial seasons, he guided major league clubs to 1,619 wins, 1,531 losses (.514), and three first place finishes. In November 1986 the Minnesota Twins (AL) named him a vice president.

BIBLIOGRAPHY: New York *Herald Tribune*, October 21, 1960, p. 24; *NYT*, October 21, 1960, p. 38; *NYT Magazine* (July 2, 1961); Joseph L. Reichler, ed., *The Baseball Encyclopedia*, 6th ed. (New York, 1985) pp. 632, 1,035; *Time* 78 (October 6, 1961), pp. 76–77.

                                                              Albert J. Figone

HOWARD, Frank Oliver "Hondo," "The Capital Punisher" (b. 8 August 1936, Columbus, OH), baseball and basketball player, manager, and coach, graduated in 1954 from South High School in Columbus, where he played baseball and basketball. At Ohio State University, the 6 foot, 7 inch, 255 pound Howard captained the basketball squad, was named to the All–Big Ten Conference basketball team, and starred in baseball. The Los Angeles Dodgers (NL) signed Howard for an $108,000 bonus baseball contract in 1958. After enjoying impressive minor league seasons as an outfielder with Green Bay (3IL) in 1958 and Victoria, TX (TL), and Spokane (PCL) in 1959 and 1960, he joined the Los Angeles Dodgers in 1960 and was named NL Rookie of the Year. His 23 home runs established a record for Dodgers rookies. Howard batted a career-high .296 in both 1961 and 1962 and hit .300 in the victorious 1963 World Series against the New York Yankees. Used primarily as an outfielder, he played with the Dodgers through 1964 before being traded to the Washington Senators (AL).

Howard enjoyed his greatest seasons with the Senators and set several records in 1968. He batted .274, drove in 106 runs, and led the AL with 44 home runs and a .552 slugging average in 1968. From May 3 through May 18, Howard belted an incredible 12 homers. This streak included setting major league records for most home runs in six consecutive games (10) and five straight games (8) and tying AL marks for most homers in four consecutive games (7) and most straight games with homers (6). Howard's career-high 48 home runs came in 1969, when he batted .296, recorded 111 RBIs, and compiled a .574 slugging percentage. Howard, who topped the AL in total bases with 330 in 1968 and 340 in 1969, won the AL home run title in 1970 with 44. He batted .283 with a .546 slugging average and led the junior circuit with a career-high 126 RBIs and 132 walks. In August, 1972, the Senators sold Howard to the Detroit Tigers (AL). During 1973, his final season as a player, he appeared mainly as a designated hitter.

The right-handed slugger belted 382 career home runs and batted .273 lifetime, with 1,774 hits and 1,119 RBIs. In 1,902 games, he hit 245 doubles, scored 864 runs, struck out 1,460 times, and had a .499 slugging percentage. Howard's tape-measure home runs led Ted Williams* to remark that the mammoth slugger hit balls farther and harder than anybody else he ever saw. After playing baseball in Japan in 1974, Howard embarked on a managerial and coaching career. He piloted Spokane (PCL) in 1976 and then coached with the Milwaukee Brewers (AL) from 1977 through 1980. The San Diego Padres (NL) named Howard manager for the 1981 season, during which he recorded a 41–69 mark. From 1982 through 1984, Howard served as a coach for the New York Mets (NL) and piloted them to a 52–64 slate on an interim basis for the last four months of the 1983 season. In October 1984, the Milwaukee Brewers hired Howard as a coach. As a manager, he garnered a 93–133 record (.412) and two sixth place finishes. Howard married Cecilia Ann Johanski on February 7, 1959, and has six children, Tim, Cathy, Dan, Mitchell, Mary, and Becky.

BIBLIOGRAPHY: Frank Howard file, National Baseball Hall of Fame Library, Cooperstown, NY; Paul MacFarlane, ed., *TSN Daguerreotypes of Great Stars of Baseball* (St. Louis, 1981); Joseph L. Reichler, ed., *The Baseball Encyclopedia*, 6th ed. (New York, 1985), pp. 632, 1,037; Ted Williams, *The Science of Hitting* (New York, 1971); *TSN Official Baseball Record Book, 1985* (St. Louis, 1985).

Robert J. Brown

HOY, William Ellsworth "Dummy" (b. 23 May 1862, Houcktown, OH; d. 15 December 1961, Cincinnati, OH), player, became a deaf mute because of a meningitis attack in infancy and could not attend local schools. In 1874 his parents sent him to Columbus, where he enrolled at the Ohio State School for the Deaf. He completed grade and high school in six years, graduating as valedictorian of his class. Hoy opened a small shoe shop in Houcktown and played for the town baseball team on weekends. In 1886 he joined Oshkosh, WI (NWL), where his speed and outfield defensive skills excited onlookers. After becoming a dependable hitter his second year with Oshkosh, he joined the major leagues.

The left-handed batting Hoy spent fourteen major league seasons with Washington (NL) in 1888–1889 and 1892–1893, Buffalo (PL) in 1890, St. Louis (AA) in 1891, Cincinnati (NL) 1894 through 1897, and 1902, Louisville (NL) in 1898–1899, and Chicago (AL) in 1901. A constant base-stealing threat, he led the NL with 82 thefts in 1888, his rookie season. His center field play helped the Chicago White Stockings win an AL championship in 1901. Hoy ended his professional career in 1903 with Los Angeles (PCL).

Although only 5 feet, 4 inches, and 150 pounds, Hoy demonstrated all-around offensive and defensive skills. Never a power hitter, he usually batted at or near the top of the lineup and reached base and scored frequently. In 1,798 major league games, he amassed 2,054 hits, scored 1,426 runs, stole 597 bases, and batted .288. A defensive standout, he is considered the first center fielder to play the position shallow. The speedy Hoy ran down balls hit behind him and possessed a powerful, accurate throwing arm. He threw out three runners at home plate on June 19, 1888, the first of only three players to accomplish this feat.

On October 26, 1898, Hoy married the deaf Anna Maria Lowery, who became a prominent teacher of the deaf in Ohio. After his playing career, Hoy purchased a farm in Mt. Healthy, OH. Born there were his son, Carson, later a distinguished Cincinnati jurist, and his daughter, Clover.

BIBLIOGRAPHY: Joseph M. Overfield, "William Ellsworth Hoy, 1862–1961," *The National Pastime* 2 (Fall, 1982), pp. 70–72; Joseph L. Reichler, ed., *The Baseball Encyclopedia*, 6th ed. (New York, 1985), p. 1,039.

Dennis T. "Tom" Chase

HOYT, Waite Charles "Schoolboy" (b. 9 September 1899, Brooklyn, NY; d. 25 August 1984, Cincinnati, OH), player and broadcaster, signed a major league contract at age 15 and became only the second player to have signed at such an early age. His father, Addison, worked as a businessman and sometime actor. Hoyt graduated from Erasmus High School in Brooklyn and chose to pursue a career in baseball rather than attend college. He pitched mostly for the New York Yankees (1921–1930) of the AL during his twenty-year major league career. Hoyt also hurled for the Boston Red Sox (1919–1920), Detroit Tigers (1930–1931), and Philadelphia Athletics (1931), all AL teams, and for the Brooklyn Dodgers (1932, 1937–1938), New York Giants (1918, 1932), and Pittsburgh Pirates (1933–1937), all of the NL. He compiled a lifetime record of 237 wins and 182 losses and a 3.59 ERA. In 1969 he was named to the National Baseball Hall of Fame and subsequently served for several years on its Veterans Committee. He married Ellen Burbank in May, 1933, and had one son.

Hoyt played in the minor leagues with Mt. Carmel (PSL) and Hartford-Lynn (EL) in 1916, Memphis (SA) and Montreal (IL) in 1917, and Nashville (SA) and Newark (IL) in 1918. Hoyt appeared in one game with the New York Giants in 1918 and was acquired in 1919 by the Boston Red Sox (AL). Following two mediocre seasons there, he was traded on December 15, 1920, to the New York Yankees (AL). Hoyt helped New York capture its first AL pennant in 1921 with a 19–13 mark and won 19 games again in 1922. In the 1921 World Series against the Giants, he pitched three complete games without allowing an earned run. The hard-throwing right-hander's best seasons came in 1927 and 1928, when he compiled 22–7 and 23–7 records, respectively. His .759 percentage and 2.63 ERA in 1927 led the AL. After being traded to Detroit (AL) in May, 1930, he was shuttled during the next two years to the Athletics, Dodgers, Giants, and Pirates, and remained in Pittsburgh until June, 1937. His last major league season came in 1938 with the Dodgers.

Following his retirement in 1938, Hoyt became a radio sportscaster in New York and from 1942 to 1965 broadcast games for the Cincinnati Reds. One of the first former ballplayers to become an announcer, he made notable "rain delay" narrations of interesting episodes in his baseball career. The handsome, popular Hoyt possessed a nimble wit and fine command of the English language. He made famous the phrase, "It's great to be young and a Yankee." Known as "the aristocrat of baseball," Hoyt proved a fiery, tough competitor with tremendous pride in the Yankee organization. He contended that the great New York teams of the 1920s developed a unique tradition, mystique, and winning style copied by later Yankees clubs.

BIBLIOGRAPHY: *Baseball Magazine* 38 (December, 1926), pp. 297–298, 328–330; "The Best of Waite Hoyt in the Rain," Personality Records (WHLP–537); *Liberty* (August 26, 1939), pp. 57–58; Paul MacFarlane, ed., *TSN Daguerreotypes of Great Stars of Baseball* (St. Louis, 1981); Eugene C. Murdock, interview with Waite Hoyt, March 12, 1976; *NYT*, June 4, 1967, February 7, 1969; *TSN*, February 10, 1938, December 4, 1941, April 2, 1942, October 15, 1952.

Eugene C. Murdock

HUBBARD, R. Cal. See *Biographical Dictionary of American Sports: Football.*

HUBBELL, Carl Owen "King Carl," "The Meal Ticket" (b. 22 June 1903, Carthage, MO), player, executive, and scout, grew up in Meeker, OK, where he picked cotton and pecans as a child. Hubbell married Lucille Harrington in January, 1930, and has two sons. Widowed in 1964, he wed Julia Stanfield. In 1947 he was elected to the National Baseball Hall of Fame. Nicknamed "King Carl" and "The Meal Ticket," the 6 foot, 175 pound left-hander utilized a slow, cartwheel-like delivery of the screwball to record five consecutive 20-win NL seasons (1933–1937). With sluggers Bill Terry* and Mel Ott* and pitcher Hal Schumacher, he helped the powerful New York Giants to the 1933, 1936, and 1937 World Series.

After beginning his career with Cushing, OK (OKSL), in 1923, he signed in 1924 with the Detroit Tigers (AL). He spent four mediocre seasons pitching in their minor league system and allegedly was instructed by Ty Cobb* to forsake the screwball. Hubbell was saved from obscurity by being traded to the New York Giants' organization and pitched in 1928 for Beaumont, TX (TL). Giants manager John McGraw* encouraged Hubbell to utilize his best pitch. Within several months, Hubbell in 1928 joined the Giants' (NL) roster. During his sixteen years (1928–1943) with the Giants, he won 253 games, lost 154 decisions, and posted only one losing record. Hubbell compiled a 2.97 ERA, struck out 1,678 batters, and led the NL in wins three times and in winning percentage twice.

Hubbell enjoyed his best seasons in 1933 and 1936, winning the NL Most Valuable Player award both years. A 1–0 victory over the St. Louis Cardinals on July 2, 1933, typified his 23-win performance that year. In 18 innings, he did not walk a batter and struck out 12 from the powerful Gas House Gang. In the 1933 World Series, he won two games, allowed no earned runs in 20 innings, and hurled 15 strikeouts. After receiving his MVP plaque, Hubbell made headlines at the 1934 All-Star Game. He struck out Hall of Famers Babe Ruth,* Lou Gehrig,* Jimmy Foxx,* Al Simmons,* and Joe Cronin* consecutively, starting this string with no outs and two men on base. On May 8, 1929, he tossed a no-run, no-hit victory over the Pittsburgh Pirates.

His most striking feats occurred in 1936. After compiling 10 victories and 6 defeats, Hubbell won 16 consecutive decisions from July 17 through the end of the season. He surrendered the winning home run to Lou Gehrig in game four of the 1936 World Series, but had defeated the Yankees in game one without allowing a single outfield chance. In the 1937 World Series, he secured the Giants' only victory over the Yankees. He finished with a 4–2 World Series career record and a strong 1.79 ERA in 50.1 innings pitched. From 1943 to 1978, he served as director of field operations for the Giants' minor league system. Since 1978 he has scouted for the Giants.

BIBLIOGRAPHY: Bob Broeg, *Super Stars of Baseball* (St. Louis, 1971); Anthony J. Connor, *Baseball for the Love of It* (New York, 1982); Glenn Dickey, *The History of National League Baseball* (New York, 1979); Paul MacFarlane, ed., *TSN Daguerreotypes of Great Stars of Baseball* (St. Louis, 1981); William B. Mead, *The Worst Ten Years of Baseball* (New York, 1978); NYT, July 11, 1934; Joseph L. Reichler, ed., *The Baseball Encyclopedia*, 6th ed. (New York, 1985), p. 1,800.

Alan R. Asnen

HUGGINS, Miller James "Hug," "The Mighty Mite" (b. 27 March 1879, or 1880 Cincinnati, OH; d. 25 September 1929, New York, NY), player and manager, was the third of four children born to grocer James Thomas and Sarah (Reid) Huggins. Miller, whose father had emigrated from England, attended public grammar and secondary schools in Cincinnati. An excellent student, he received a law degree from the University of Cincinnati and passed the Ohio bar exams in 1902.

He completed the law degree to please his father, but preferred to play baseball. His professional baseball career began in 1899 at Mansfield, OH (ISL), where he assumed the name Proctor because his father disapproved of Sunday baseball. From 1901 to 1903, the 5 foot, 6 1/2 inch, 140 pound Huggins batted .322, .328, and .308 at St. Paul MN (AA).

After being purchased by the Cincinnati Reds (NL), Huggins played second base there from 1904 to 1909. Although excellent defensively, he hit with little power. Huggins drew many bases on balls, showed good speed, and once batted .292 with the Reds. Traded to the St. Louis Cardinals (NL) following the 1909 season, "The Mighty Mite" twice drew over 100 walks and scored over 100 runs between 1910 and 1914 and hit a career-high .304 in 1912. He averaged around 30 stolen bases per season, but was caught 36 times in 68 attempts in 1914.

In 1913 Huggins became player-manager of a weak last place Cardinals team. From 1913 through 1917, St. Louis fielded only two winning teams under Huggins. He retired as a player in 1916, when Rogers Hornsby* replaced him at second base. After new Cardinals owners named Branch

Rickey* manager, Huggins piloted the New York Yankees (AL) to fourth and third place finishes in 1918 and 1919. The "Mite Manager" instructed the front office to acquire Boston Red Sox pitcher-outfielder Babe Ruth.* New York purchased Ruth for $125,000, changing baseball history forever. Ruth often criticized Huggins publicly and regularly broke club rules, but the slugger enabled Huggins to construct a dynasty that captured six AL pennants and three world championships from 1921 to 1928. Many authorities rank Huggins' 1927 Yankees as the greatest baseball team in history. With Ruth, Lou Gehrig,* Earle Combs,* Tony Lazzeri,* Herb Pennock,* Waite Hoyt,* and other stars, New York compiled a 110–44 record and four straight World Series wins over the Pittsburgh Pirates. In September 1929, Huggins began losing weight and energy and turned the team over to Art Fletcher with eleven games remaining. Huggins, a lifelong bachelor, lived with his sister, who cared for him in his final weeks. He suffered from neuritis and died from a blood infection caused by a cut beneath his eye.

In 1,585 games at second base, "Hug" made 1,474 hits, accumulated over 1,000 bases on balls, stole 324 bases, and batted .265. His 1,413 wins and 1,134 losses as a manager included a 1,067–719 slate as Yankees skipper. Huggins, acknowledged as one of the finest managers in baseball history, was elected to the National Baseball Hall of Fame in 1964.

BIBLIOGRAPHY: Martin Appel and Burt Goldblatt, *Baseball's Best: The Hall of Fame Gallery* (New York, 1977); Bob Broeg, *Redbirds: A Century of Cardinals' Baseball* (St. Louis, 1981); *DAB* 9 (1946), pp. 345–346; Edwin Pope, *Baseball's Greatest Managers* (New York, 1960); Lowell Reidenbaugh, *Cooperstown: Where Baseball's Legends Live Forever* (St. Louis, 1983).

Frank J. Olmsted

HUGHES, Samuel Thomas "Sammy" (b. 20 October 1910, Louisville, KY; d. 9 August 1981, Los Angeles, CA), player, ranked among the finest Negro League second basemen of the 1930s and 1940s. Hughes, the son of Henry and Susan (Cowherd) Hughes, attended school in Louisville through the eighth grade. The graceful 6 foot, 4 inch infielder began his professional career in 1929 with the Louisville White Sox. The Washington Pilots selected him in 1932 as a first baseman, where he joined stars Mule Suttles,* Chet Brewer, and Frank Warfield. When Warfield died of a hemorrhage, Hughes claimed the second base job. The Pilots' financial troubles caused Hughes to quit the team. He joined the Nashville Elite Giants (NNL) in 1933 and continued to play with the team when it transferred successively to Columbus, Washington, and Baltimore.

An excellent hitter and a smart base runner, Hughes unofficially hit .322 in his NNL career and batted .263 in five East-West All-Star games. In 1936 the Elite Giants won the Denver *Post* semi-pro tournament. The same year, Hughes played with Satchel Paige* and Josh Gibson* against Rogers Hornsby's* Major League All-Stars. Hughes posted a .353 batting average against major league players and batted .246 in Cuba in 1939–1940. He married Mildred Shannon in 1941 and had two children, Spencer and Barbara, before their divorce in the early 1950s. In 1956 he married Thelma Smith. Hughes jumped with Roy Campanella* to Mexico in 1941, but returned to the Baltimore Elite Giants (NNL) in 1942. A proposed tryout by the two ballplayers with the Washington Senators that year never materialized. Hughes entered the U.S. Army in 1943, participating in the New Guinea invasion with the 196th Support Battalion, and was discharged in 1946. Upon returning to the Baltimore Elite Giants in 1946, Hughes tutored future Brooklyn Dodgers infielder James "Junior" Gilliam. Hughes retired at the end of the season and worked for the Pillsbury Company and Hughes Aircraft Company in Los Angeles. Hughes helped bridge the gap between the Negro and major leagues. He and other Negro leaguers demonstrated the requisite skills to play in the major leagues.

BIBLIOGRAPHY: Terry A. Baxter, correspondence with Jorge Figueroda, 1984, Cuban League statistics, Terry A. Baxter Collection, Lee's Summit, MO; Terry A. Baxter, correspondence with Andrew Porter, 1984, Terry A. Baxter Collection, Lee's Summit, MO; Terry A. Baxter, correspondence with Donn Rogosin, 1984, Terry A. Baxter Collection, Lee's Summit, MO; Terry A. Baxter, telephone interview with Monford Irvin, 1984; Roy Campanella, *It's Good to Be Alive* (Boston, 1959); John B. Holway, monograph on Sammy T. Hughes, John Holway Collection, Alexandria, VA; John Holway, *Voices from the Great Black Baseball Leagues* (New York, 1975); Robert W. Peterson, *Only the Ball Was White* (Englewood Cliffs, NJ, 1970); James A. Riley, *The All-Time All-Stars of Black Baseball* (Cocoa, FL, 1983); Donn Rogosin, *Invisible Men: Life in Baseball's Negro Leagues* (New York, 1983).

Terry A. Baxter

HULBERT, William Ambrose "Bill" (b. 23 October 1832, Burlington Flats, NY; d. 10 April 1882, Chicago, IL), executive, moved to Chicago with his parents at age two. After attending Chicago public schools, he matriculated at Beloit College, entered the wholesale grocery business in Chicago, married Jennie Murray, and became a member of the Chicago Board of Trade. The big, energetic, robust Hulbert proved an optimistic civic booster and often said, "I would rather be a lamp post in Chicago than a millionaire in any other city."

In 1875 Hulbert entered baseball as president of the Chicago White Stockings (NA), hoping to build a winning team. He signed many premier players, starting with Albert G. Spalding* of the Boston Red Stockings. Spalding helped persuade Boston stars Cal McVey,* James "Deacon" White,* and Ross Barnes,* along with Philadelphia stars Adrian Anson* and Ezra Sutton, to sign secret contracts with Chicago. When the contracts, which violated the NA rule against signing players still under contract, became public knowledge, Hulbert and his signees faced possible expulsion from the NA.

Hulbert took the initiative in organizing a new league. Widespread support for a change already existed because the NA suffered from rumors of corruption, shifting membership, makeshift schedules, weak management, and competitive imbalance. In the fall of 1875, Hulbert and Spalding drafted a proposal for a new league. The St. Louis, Louisville, and Cincinnati clubs quickly accepted Hulbert's plan. He then arranged a meeting on February 2, 1876, in New York, where representatives from New York, Philadelphia, Boston, and Hartford joined the midwestern clubs in adopting Hulbert's proposal for a new league and named it the National League of Professional Base Ball Clubs.

Hulbert's NL constitution shifted control of the professional game from the players to the owners, attempted to assure respectability for the sport, and sought profits for the clubs. To these ends, he established a regular schedule of games, required clubs to maintain order at games, prohibited Sunday games, attempted to abolish gambling and the sale of alcohol in league parks, and restricted NL membership to one club per city. Morgan G. Bulkeley* of Hartford became the NL's first president in a drawing, but Hulbert assumed the helm after the first season.

Hulbert exercised strong leadership during the NL's first few years. He expelled clubs and players that he believed threatened the game's reputation. Besides being NL president, he continued to operate the Chicago club until his death of heart disease in 1882. In the overblown nineteenth century rhetoric, he was called the "saviour of the game" for organizing the NL, establishing club owners' control of the sport, and assuring the professional game's reputation for honesty.

BIBLIOGRAPHY: Arthur R. Ahrens, "The Chicago National League Champions of 1876," *Baseball Research Journal* 11 (1982), pp. 84–90; Lee Allen, *The National League Story* (New York, 1961); Glenn Dickey, *The History of National League Baseball since 1876* (New York, 1979); Peter Levine, *A. G. Spalding and the Rise of Baseball* (New York, 1985); Harold Seymour, *Baseball: The Early Years* (New York, 1960); Albert G. Spalding, *America's National Game* (New York, 1911).

William E. Akin

HUNTER, James Augustus "Catfish" (b. 18 April 1946, Hertford, NC), player, pitched for the Oakland Athletics (AL) and New York Yankees (AL). The fourth son of eight children born to Abbot and Millie Hunter, he was reared on a farm. Hunter frequently missed elementary school to hunt and fish. He loved sports and starred in football and baseball at Perguimans High School. Upon graduating from high school in 1964, Hunter signed with the Oakland Athletics (AL) for a $50,000 bonus. He spent the 1964 season pitching batting practice and serving in promotional stunts devised by Oakland owner Charles Finley.* In one of these stunts, Satchel Paige,* the colorful pitcher from the black baseball leagues, was pictured in a rocking chair with Hunter sitting on his lap. Finley nicknamed Hunter "Catfish."

On July 27, 1965, the 6 foot, 190 pound, right-handed Hunter pitched his first win in professional ball with the A's and finished his first full season with an 8–8 mark. He made the AL All-Star team in 1966 despite his 9–11 season record. In 1968 he pitched a perfect game against the Minnesota Twins. After enjoying his first winning season with an 18–14 record in 1970, he reached the 20-game victory plateau in 1971 with a 21–11 mark. In 1974 he was named the Cy Young Award winner and *The Sporting News* Pitcher of the Year with a 25–12 record. The same year, he sued Finley for breach of contract for not paying $50,000 of his $100,000 salary on a deferred basis. Hunter won his case and was declared a free agent, triggering a precedent-setting bidding war for his services. On January 1, 1975, he signed a five-year contract with the New York Yankees (AL) for an estimated $3.75 million.

Hunter pitched for the Yankees until retiring in 1979. His best year with them came in 1975, when he finished 23–14 for his fifth consecutive year with at least 20 victories. His career record with the Athletics and Yankees included 224 wins and 166 losses (.574) with 2,958 strikeouts in 3,448 1/3 innings pitched and a 3.26 ERA. Hunter compiled a 4–3 mark in six AL Championship Series and a 5–3 mark in six World Series (1972–1974, 1976–1978). He led the AL twice in victories (1974–1975), finished first in winning percentage twice (1972–1973), and led the AL once each in ERA (1974), games started (1970), complete games (1975), and innings pitched (1975).

Hunter's pitching style was controlled and intelligent, although not over-powering. That distinctiveness fostered his success but contributed to some of his pitching problems. His repetitive motion led to great control but caused him to surrender numerous home runs. Hunter was elected to the National Baseball Hall of Fame in January 1987. Married to his high school sweetheart, Helen, he has two children, Todd and Kimberly, and still lives on his North Carolina farm.

BIBLIOGRAPHY: Roy Blount, Jr., "Opening of the Catfish Season," *SI* 42 (March 17, 1975), p. 56; Peter Bonventre, "Pride of the Yankees," *Newsweek* 84 (March 24, 1975), p. 62; *CB* 36 (1975), pp. 196–199; Murray Chass, "Yankees Sign Up Catfish Hunter in Estimated $3.75 Million Deal," *NYT*, January 1, 1975, p. 1; Gerald Eskenazi, "Millionaire Pitcher James Augustus Hunter," *NYT* January 1, 1975, p. 12; Roy Fimrite, "A City on Pinstripes and Needles," *SI* 42 (April 2, 1975), pp. 24–27; J. Anthony Lukas, "The Catfish Enigma," *NYT Magazine* (September 7, 1975), pp. 19–40; Ted O'Leary, "Time for a Catfish Fry in KC," *SI* 38 (June 25, 1973), pp. 24–26.

Tony Ladd

I

IRVIN, Monford Merrill "Monte" (b. 25 February 1919, Columbia, AL),
player and executive, is the seventh of ten children born to farmer Cupid
and Mary Eliza (Henderson) Irvin. The Irvins moved in 1947 to Orange,
NJ, where Monte earned sixteen varsity letters and won All-State in four
sports for East Orange High School. He became perhaps the finest schoolboy
athlete in New Jersey history. Irvin declined a football scholarship to the
University of Michigan because his parents could not afford the train fare
to Ann Arbor and instead attended Lincoln University in Oxford, PA, for
two years, majoring in political science.

In 1937 the 6 foot, 1 inch, 195 pound Irvin joined the Newark Eagles
(NNL) under the assumed name of Jimmy Nelson. The Eagles, managed
by Willie Wells,* included several great baseball players. Irvin began as a
shortstop and was named in 1939 to the East All-Star team. Subsequently,
he played in four other Negro league All-Star games (1941, 1946–1948). Irvin
performed in both the infield and outfield for Newark and proved an excellent
fielder with a tremendous arm. He also displayed fine batting skills, hitting
.422 in 1940 and .396 in 1941. In 1942 Irvin hit .398 in Mexico. He spent
the next three years in the U.S. Army, partly preventing him from being
the first or among the first to break the major league color barrier. Irvin was
named Most Valuable Player of the 1946 PRWL and then returned to Newark, where he made NNL MVP by hitting .389 and scored the winning run
in the Negro World Series.

Since the breaking of the color barrier killed the Negro leagues, the Newark
Eagles disbanded in 1948. Irvin played winter baseball in Cuba before signing
with the New York Giants (NL) in 1949. The 30-year-old Irvin hit .373
with 9 home runs and 52 RBIs for Jersey City (IL) in 1949. After faring
poorly when called up by the Giants, he was among the first players cut in
the spring of 1950. At Jersey City, however, he hit 10 home runs, drove in
33 runs, and batted .510 in 18 games. In the second game after being recalled
by the Giants, he slugged a grand slam homer. By June, he started in left

field and then was moved to first base. For the 1950 season, he hit .299 with 15 home runs in 110 games. In 1951 Irvin returned to the outfield and befriended rookie Willie Mays.* Irvin batted over .400 the last six weeks of that season, as the Giants caught the Brooklyn Dodgers to set the stage for Bobby Thomson's playoff game home run. Although the New York Yankees won the World Series, Irvin hit .458 and stole home in game one. During 1951 Irvin batted .312 with 24 home runs, led the NL with 121 RBIs, and finished third in the MVP balloting.

In 1952 Irvin broke his ankle in spring training. He hit .310 after his return in August, but his speed had diminished. He hit .329 the next year, until reinjuring his ankle in August. Irvin delivered several key hits in the 1954 Giants pennant drive, but his batting average dropped to .262. Although the Giants swept Cleveland in the World Series, Irvin hit only .222. After batting .253 in 51 games in 1955, he was sent to Minneapolis (AA) and hit .352 in 75 games there. In 1956 Irvin joined the Chicago Cubs (NL), slugging 15 home runs and batting .271 in 111 games to finish his playing career. Negro league records suggest that Irvin ranked among the finest players of his era. With the Giants, he also displayed his superior talent at bat and in the field. In eight NL seasons, he batted .293, made 731 hits, 97 doubles, 31 triples, and 99 home runs, and knocked in 443 tallies. Irvin also batted a sparkling .394 in two World Series.

Although primarily a baseball player, Irvin displayed other interests. He owned a business and an apartment building and ran unsuccessfully for the New Jersey State Assembly in 1951. After retiring, he worked for a major brewery in Orange, NJ, and frequently spoke at banquets. Irvin scouted for the New York Mets (NL) in 1967 and 1968 and joined the Office of the Commissioner of Baseball in August, 1968, as a public relations represent-ative, a job he held for fifteen years. He also served on the committee to select deserving Negro league players to the National Baseball Hall of Fame and was chosen for baseball's highest honor in 1973. The Irvins live in retirement in Homosassa, FL.

BIBLIOGRAPHY: Martin Appel and Burt Goldblatt, *Baseball's Best: The Hall of Fame Gallery* (New York, 1977); Anthony J. Connor, *Voices from Cooperstown* (New York, 1982); John Holway, *Voices from the Great Black Baseball Leagues* (New York, 1975); Robert W. Peterson, *Only the Ball Was White* (Englewood Cliffs, NJ, 1970); Joseph L. Reichler, ed., *The Baseball Encyclopedia*, 6th ed. (New York, 1985), p. 1,046; Donn Rogosin, *Invisible Men: Life in Baseball's Negro Leagues* (New York, 1983); Ken Smith, *Baseball's Hall of Fame* (New York, 1979); Chris Stern, *Where Have They Gone? Baseball Stars* (New York, 1979).

                                                                                   Douglas D. Martin

J

JACKSON, Joseph Jefferson "Joe," "Shoeless Joe" (b. 16 July 1887 or 1888, Brandon Mills, SC; d. 5 December 1951, Greenville, SC), player, was the son of George and Martha Jackson. In the 1910–1920 era, Jackson joined Ty Cobb,* Tris Speaker,* and George Sisler* as the AL's outstanding hitters. He would have joined the others in the National Baseball Hall of Fame, but was one of the eight Chicago White Sox players who accepted money from gamblers to throw the 1919 World Series to the Cincinnati Reds.

Jackson's role in baseball's greatest scandal was partly related to his background and lack of sophistication. He came from a large, very poor southern white family, and his parents worked hard picking cotton and at a mill. Jackson, who received no formal education, began mill work at age 13 and soon excelled on the mill's baseball team. Manager Connie Mack* liked Jackson's great natural ability and induced the reluctant Southerner to play for his Philadelphia Athletics (AL) in 1908. Lacking Cobb's fierce competitiveness, Jackson experienced great difficulty adjusting to the urbanized North. From the outset, he reacted awkwardly and defensively because players and fans reminded him about his humble origins. Mack sought to provide him with a teacher to make him literate, but the self-conscious Jackson declined. He quit the team more than once, forcing Mack to release him after the 1909 season. The ever unsettled Jackson relied heavily on his wife, Katherine Wynn. They had no children.

Jackson, a rare natural athlete, resembled Babe Ruth* in classic batting stance, size, strength, and throwing arm. From 1910 to 1915, he compiled several fine batting averages ranging from .331 to :408 for the Cleveland Indians (AL). Financial exigencies forced his sale in 1915 to the Chicago White Sox (AL), owned by miserly Charles A. Comiskey.* At Chicago, Jackson never fully adjusted to his teammates or the owner. He led the AL thrice in triples (1912, 1916, 1920), and once each in doubles (1913), slugging percentage (1913), and total bases (1912). Although never winning a batting title, he finished several times among the first five. Despite Jackson's amazing

.408 batting average in 1911, Cobb won the AL batting title. Cobb allegedly shook Jackson's confidence to ensure the championship, but Jackson's biographer showed convincingly that the Detroit star consistently led Jackson in the latter part of the season. Jackson's career .356 batting average trails only those of the fabled Cobb and Rogers Hornsby.* In 1,330 games, Jackson made 1,774 hits, 307 doubles, and 168 triples, knocked in 785 runs, and stole 202 bases.

For his role in the 1919 World Series, Commissioner Kenesaw Mountain Landis* barred Jackson from organized baseball for life. Jackson tried unavailingly to be reinstated, winning considerable public sympathy by claiming that he performed at his best in the Series. He reluctantly accepted $5,000 of gamblers' money and had been promised $20,000. Jackson batted a resounding .375 but made a couple of questionable defensive gaffes. Since surroundings and companions easily influenced Jackson, he may have halfheartedly participated in the "fix." In admitting his involvement before a Chicago grand jury in 1920, he expressed both regret and relief.

When Jackson left the courtroom, a little boy supposedly told him, "Say it ain't so, Joe." Jackson always denied it. His involvement in the scandal resulted partly from his own passivity in bad company. Jackson also greatly resented Comiskey for paying him only $8,000 a year and for criticizing his shipyard job in World War I.

After his expulsion, Jackson lived in his native South Carolina and for several years played intermittent "outlaw" baseball. He invested his baseball earnings in moderately successful small businesses and received slight attention through occasional news items, old fans' sympathy, and rare visits from one-time fellow players. Numerous people regretted that Judge Landis found it necessary to terminate the career of such an outstanding performer.

BIBLIOGRAPHY: Eliot Asinof, *Eight Men Out* (New York, 1963); Donald Gropman, *Say It Ain't So, Joe!* (Boston, 1979); Frederick G. Lieb, *Baseball as I Have Known It* (New York, 1977); Victor Luhrs, *The Great Baseball Mystery* (New York, 1966); *NYT*, December 6, 10, 1959; Bill Veeck, *The Hustler's Handbook* (New York, 1965)
                                                                Lowell L. Blaisdell

JACKSON, Reginald Martinez "Reggie," "Mr. October" (b. 18 May 1946, Wyncote, PA), player, is the son of semi-pro baseball player and Philadelphia tailor Martinez Jackson and Clara Jackson. His grandmother on his father's side was of Spanish descent. Jackson grew up in suburban Philadelphia, graduating in 1964 from Cheltenham Township High School and playing four sports there. He received a football scholarship at Arizona State University, but quit after coach Frank Kush* (FB) switched him from offense to cornerback. Jackson turned to the university baseball team, which already included Sal Bando and Rick Monday. Jackson, an outfielder, became the first collegian to hit a home run out of Phoenix Stadium. In 1966 *The Sporting News* named him College Player of the Year.

In the first round of the 1966 amateur draft, the New York Mets bypassed him to pick a now-obscure catcher. Kansas City Athletics (AL) owner Charles O. Finley* selected Jackson in the second turn of that first round and signed him for a reported $90,000. A 6 foot, 206 pound left-hander, Jackson played with Lewiston, ID (NWL) and Modesto, CA (CaL), in 1966 and Birmingham (SL) in 1967 before joining Kansas City in 1967. He followed the franchise to Oakland, helping the A's win three consecutive World Series (1972–1974). In 1968 he married Hispanic college friend Jeannie Campos, but the marriage ended in divorce after five years. During early 1969, Jackson appeared likely to surpass the Babe Ruth*-Roger Maris* mark for most home runs in a season. Jackson, however, ended the season with 47 round trippers, but that still established an Oakland record. In the 1972 playoff against the Detroit Tigers, Jackson stole home. He was named 1973 AL Most Valuable Player, having made 32 home runs and 117 RBIs. Although Jackson tied for the AL home run lead with 36 in 1975, Finley became disenchanted with him and traded the outfielder to Baltimore (AL). Within a year of becoming a free agent, Jackson bided his time with the Orioles. The slugger was interested in playing in New York and previously had declared that the city would name a candy bar after him if he played there.

The New York Yankees (AL) selected Jackson in the first-ever free agent draft. He played five stormy years with New York, hitting 144 home runs and arguing publicly with Yankee owner George Steinbrenner and several managers. Yankees captain Thurman Munson was miffed that Jackson declared himself the team leader. The Reggie Bar also appeared. After a poor performance in strike-torn 1981, Jackson joined the California Angels (AL). Through the 1986 season, Jackson had compiled a .263 lifetime batting average with 2,510 hits in 2,705 games, hit 449 doubles and 548 home runs (6th best lifetime), and drove in 1,659 runs. On the other hand, he struck out over 2,500 times and was not considered a good fielder. Through 1984 he had slugged at a .498 clip and had about a .350 on-base percentage. Jackson appeared in 11 All-Star games and on 10 divisional winners. He led the AL five times in strikeouts, four times in homers, three times in slugging average, twice in runs scored, and once in RBIs.

In five World Series, Jackson became "Mr. October." His .755 slugging average in fall classics surpassed all players appearing in a significant number of games. Jackson belted 10 World Series home runs, placing fifth on the all-time list. In the deciding game of the 1977 Series, he hit three home runs on three consecutive pitches by Los Angeles Dodgers hurlers Burt Hooton, Elias Sosa, and Charlie Hough. Only Babe Ruth previously had hit three home runs in a World Series game. Jackson occasionally works as a sports caster. In July 1986, against the Boston Red Sox, Jackson hit his 537th career home run to surpass Mickey Mantle* for sixth place on the all-time list. The Angels released Jackson after the 1986 season.

BIBLIOGRAPHY: Maury Allen, *Mr. October* (New York, 1981); *CB* (1974), pp. 181–83; Dallas *Times-Herald*, August 27, 1978; Reggie Jackson, *Reggie*, 2nd ed. (New York, 1984); Robert Ward, "Reggie Jackson in No-Man's Land," *Sport* 64 (June, 1977), pp. 89–96.

John David Healy

JACKSON, Travis Calvin "Stonewall" (b. 2 November 1903, Waldo, AR), player, manager, and coach, attended public schools in the Waldo area and graduated from Ouachita Baptist College. Of Scotch-English descent, Jackson married Mary Blackman in January, 1928, and has one son and one daughter. Jackson began his professional baseball career with Little Rock (SA) in 1921 and the next season became the club's regular shortstop. Little Rock manager Norman "Kid" Elberfield arranged for New York Giants (NL) manager John McGraw* to see his talented player. McGraw met Jackson in April 1922 and purchased his contract after the Little Rock season ended. Jackson joined the Giants (NL) in September, 1922, going hitless in two plate appearances in his initial game. He became the Giants' regular shortstop in 1924 and played with no other major league team in a fifteen-year career, serving as the Giants' field captain the last five seasons. In 1,656 games, he batted .291 with 1,768 hits, 291 doubles, 135 home runs, and 929 RBIs.

The 5 foot, 10 inch, 160 pound Jackson excelled at shortstop, possessing among the most powerful arms and greatest ranges at the position. He led NL shortstops in assists four times, total chances three times, and fielding average and double plays twice. He suffered recurrent knee ailments, forcing him to shift to third base for the 1935 and 1936 seasons. Jackson, who made the 1934 NL All-Star squad, batted right-handed, proved a great bunter, and demonstrated surprising power.

Writer Arnold Hano captured the essence of the popular, workmanlike Jackson in the following description:

All through his career, one picture remains vivid, and that is the lean, dark-haired young man gliding to his right and rifling out runners at first. But he also ripped his share of base hits into the left-field corner, and he had another trait that nearly equaled his arm. On a team always known for its ability to bunt and squeeze out runs one at a time, Jackson was a master. He could sacrifice with deadly skill; better, he was one of the finest drag-bunters, for base hits, the game ever saw.

Jackson managed the Giants AAA farm team in Jersey City (IL), in 1937 and 1938 and coached for the Giants in 1938–1940 and 1947–1948. Before retiring in 1961, he managed eleven other minor league clubs, mostly in the Milwaukee Braves (NL) farm system. His managerial assignments included

Jackson, MS (SEL) in 1946, Tampa (FSL) in 1949, Owensboro, KY (KL) in 1950, Bluefield, WV (ApL) and Hartford, CT (EL) in 1951, Appleton, WI (WSL) in 1952 and 1953, Lawton, OK (SSL) from 1954 to 1957, Midland, TX (SpL) in 1958, Eau Claire, WI (NoL) in 1959, and Quad-City (ML) in 1960. In 1983 Jackson was elected to the National Baseball Hall of Fame.

BIBLIOGRAPHY: Frank Graham, *McGraw of the Giants* (New York, 1944); Arnold Hano, *Greatest Giants of Them All* (New York, 1967); Lowell Reidenbaugh, *Cooperstown: Where Baseball's Legends Live Forever* (St. Louis, 1983); Fred Stein, *Under Coogan's Bluff* (Glyddon, MD, 1979).

Fred Stein

JACOBSON, William Chester "Baby Doll" (b. 16 August 1890, Cable, IL; d. 16 January 1977, Orion, IL), player, was the son of an Illinois farm family. After attending Geneseo High School for three years, the 6 foot, 3 inch, 210 pounder began his professional baseball career as an outfielder with Rock Island (SML) in 1909. He played with Mobile and Chattanooga (SAL) from 1912 to 1914 and appeared in 71 games for the Detroit Tigers and St. Louis Browns (AL) in 1915. Female fans at Mobile nicknamed him "Baby Doll" because he was such a dream boat. After another stint at Little Rock (SA) in 1916, he rejoined the St. Louis Browns (AL) in 1917. After U.S. Army service in 1918, Jacobson stayed permanently in the major leagues. From 1919 to 1923, he combined with Ken Williams* and Johnny Tobin* of the Browns to form one of the most prolific outfields in baseball history. For those five years, each member of the outfield trio hit at least .300. The streak ended when Tobin slipped to .299 in 1924. In 1921 they averaged .350, as Williams and Jacobson each hit .352.

In 1922 the outfield propelled the Browns into an AL pennant fight and helped the club finish just one game behind the New York Yankees. Jacobson continued to surpass the .300 mark until being traded in 1926 to the Boston Red Sox (AL) as part of a three-cornered deal. He finished 1926 at .299 and saw service with the Cleveland Indians (AL) and Philadelphia Athletics (AL) the next season before being sent to Baltimore (IL) in 1928. From 1928 to 1930, "Baby Doll" still hit better than .300 in the minor leagues. He hit .304 with Quincy, IL (3IL), in 1930, before retiring to his Illinois farm.

His career statistics included 1,472 games, 1,714 hits, 787 runs scored, 328 doubles, 94 triples, 84 homers, 819 runs knocked in, and a .311 batting average. Jacobson, a superior center fielder, held thirteen fielding records at one time and made the most putouts and chances accepted in 1924. The right-handed Jacobson enjoyed his best year at the plate in 1920, when he hit .355 and knocked in 122 runs to place second behind Babe Ruth's* 137. In 1924 his 19 home runs put him third behind Ruth and Philadelphia's Joe Hauser. "Baby Doll," who married Vurl Cruse on March 6, 1919, and later Ida Rankin on April 5, 1948, had three sons and one daughter.

BIBLIOGRAPHY: Bill Borst, *Last in the American League* (St. Louis, 1976); Bob Broeg, St. Louis *Post Dispatch*, January 18, 1977; Gene Karst and Martin J. Jones, Jr., *Who's Who in Professional Baseball* (New Rochelle, NY, 1973).

William A. Borst

JAMIESON, Charles Devine "Charlie" (b. 7 February 1893, Paterson, NJ; d. 27 October 1969, Paterson, NJ), player, performed for eighteen major league seasons. Noted for his speed and spectacular fielding, the left-handed Jamieson on May 23 and June 9, 1928, became the only outfielder ever to initiate two triple-plays in one season. He married Edith Van Kirk in November, 1913, and had two daughters and one son. The 5 foot, 8 1/2 inch, 165 pound Jamieson played from 1912 to 1915 with Buffalo (IL), being used principally as a pitcher and part-time outfielder. The Washington Senators (AL) purchased him on August 15, 1915, for $3,000 and two players. After experiencing two mediocre seasons with the Senators as a pitcher-outfielder, he was waived in July 1917 to the Philadelphia Athletics (AL). He performed poorly with the Athletics in 1917 and 1918 and was dealt in March 1919 with Larry Gardner* and Elmer Myers to the Cleveland Indians (AL) for Bobby Roth.

At age 27, Jamieson blossomed into a star outfielder with the Indians. Although platooned in left field in 1920, he played a central role in helping Cleveland win its first AL pennant and world championship. The regular left fielder for the next ten years, he enjoyed his highest batting averages in 1922 (.323), 1923 (.345), and 1924 (.359). Jamieson led American Leaguers in hits in 1923 (222), averaged 206 hits for each of the three seasons, and compiled a lifetime .303 batting average. In 1,779 games, he made 1,990 hits and 322 doubles, scored 1,062 runs, and stole 132 bases. He also pitched in thirteen major league games, winning two of three decisions.

Jamieson's speed was reflected in his stolen base figures. Between 1922 and 1925, he stole 69 bases. His speed and hustle enabled him to lead the AL in singles several years. He often tricked opponents by bunting the ball rather solidly down the first base line and shielding it between his feet while dashing down the line. Jamieson, a superb, speedy outfielder, often made incredible diving catches, turned two or three somersaults, and landed on his feet prepared to throw. Blessed with a strong arm, he led all AL outfielders in 1928 with 22 assists. Veteran baseball writer Henry P. Edwards considered Jamieson the second best fielding left fielder behind Hugh Duffy* in the AL's first thirty years. After Cleveland released him in 1932, Jamieson spent his final season as a utility player with Jersey City (IL) in 1933.

BIBLIOGRAPHY: Cleveland *News*, 1931–1932; Cleveland *Plain Dealer*, January, 1931, March 16, 1932; S. Crosby, "Charles Jamieson of the World's Champions," *Baseball Magazine* 36 (May, 1926), pp. 549–550; Franklin Lewis, *The Cleveland Indians* (New York, 1949); Paul MacFarlane, ed., *TSN Daguerreotypes of Great Stars of Baseball* (St.

Louis, 1981); *TSN*, September 11, 1924, November 8, 1969; "Why It Pays to Hustle: Interview with Charles Jamieson," *Baseball Magazine* 36 (May, 1926), pp. 549–550.

Eugene C. Murdock

JENNINGS, Hugh Ambrose "Hughie," "Ee-Yah" (b. 2 April 1869, Pittston, PA; d. 1 February 1928, Scranton, PA), player, coach, and manager, grew up in the eastern Pennsylvania coal mining region, where his Irish immigrant father struggled in the mines to support his family. At about age 12, Jennings left school and worked in the mines as a breaker boy on the coal chutes for 90 cents a day, but soon made $5 a game playing semi-pro baseball on Sundays. In 1890 he entered professional baseball with Allentown (EIL). His hitting, base stealing, and deft infield play attracted the attention of a scout for the major league Louisville (AA) team. In 1891 Jennings joined Louisville for 90 games, hitting a promising .292 average. The next year he slumped to .222 against stronger pitching in the newly reorganized twelve-team NL and was sold to the Baltimore Orioles (NL).

Jennings excelled at Baltimore under manager and part-owner Ned Hanlon.* Featuring the talented, colorful third baseman John McGraw,* catcher Wilbert Robinson,* and outfielders Willie Keeler* and Joe Kelley,* the Orioles from 1894 to 1896 won three straight NL pennants. Jennings, captain and right-hand hitting shortstop, became one of that great team's mainstays, hitting .335, .386, and .398 in the three NL pennant-winning seasons and stealing an aggregate 160 bases. Although the Orioles finished second to Boston in 1897, Jennings hit an impressive .355 and stole 60 times. A typical Oriole, the 5 foot, 8 1/2 inch, 165 pound Jennings was hot-tempered and fiercely competitive. He crowded the plate and dared pitchers to throw at him, being hit 49 times in 1896. The next year he missed the last part of the season with a skull fracture from an errant pitch.

Following the 1898 season, Hanlon became manager and part-owner of the Brooklyn (NL) team and took Jennings, Keeler, and Kelley with him. Although he hurt his arm, Jennings still played regularly at first base on the club's 1899–1900 champions. After being sold to Philadelphia (NL) in 1901, Jennings became a part-time infielder-outfielder for the Phillies. He returned to Brooklyn (NL) briefly early in 1903 and then managed Baltimore (EL). During his major league career, Jennings compiled a .312 batting average with 1,531 hits, 235 doubles, and 359 stolen bases.* Jennings directed Baltimore (NL) to four successive first division finishes and played part-time in the infield. After the 1906 season, Detroit (AL) signed him as a player and manager.

From 1907 to 1920, Jennings ranked among baseball's most colorful managers. By stamping his feet, clawing handfuls of grass, and yelling his ear-splitting "Ee-yah" from the coaching box, he entertained AL fans. Sparked by the incomparable Ty Cobb, * sturdy Sam Crawford,* and strong pitching from the likes of Bill Donovan* and George Mullin,* Jennings' Tigers won three consecutive AL pennants and lost three World Series in his first three seasons (1907–1909). Otherwise his ballclubs finished second twice, third twice, fourth three times, sixth twice, and seventh twice. Jennings handled his players firmly except for the thin-skinned, volatile Cobb, whom he allowed considerable freedom. The often sarcastic and tempestuous Jennings became increasingly unpopular with Detroit's players. After a dreary seventh place finish in 1920, he yielded the managerial job to Cobb.

Jennings, who had earned a law degree from Cornell University more than a decade earlier, practiced law with his brother at Scranton, PA. In 1921 he joined the New York Giants (NL) as coach under his old Orioles teammate, the brilliantly successful John McGraw. From 1921 to 1924, Jennings picked up World Series shares with the Giants and managed the ballclub most of 1925, when McGraw was ill. After that grueling year, Jennings suffered both a nervous collapse and the onset of physical decline. At an Asheville, NC, sanitarium, physicians discovered that he had tuberculosis. He died at his Scranton home, leaving his wife, Nora O'Boyle Jennings, and one married daughter. In 1945 the Veterans Committee of the Baseball Writers Association of America selected the outstanding player-manager to the National Baseball Hall of Fame.

BIBLIOGRAPHY: Charles C. Alexander, *Ty Cobb* (New York, 1984); "Hugh Jennings: Why His Team Wins," *Outing* 54 (August, 1909), pp. 559–560; Frederick G. Lieb, *The Detroit Tigers* (New York, 1946); Paul MacFarlane, ed., *TSN Daguerreotypes of Great Stars of Baseball* (St. Louis, 1981); *TSN*, February 9, 1928.

Charles C. Alexander

JETHROE, Samuel "Sam," "Jet" (b. 20 January 1922, East St. Louis, IL), player, is the son of farmer Albert and domestic worker Janie Jethroe. After graduating from Lincoln High School, Jethroe played semi-pro ball with the East St. Louis Colts and St. Louis Giants. He joined the Cincinnati Buckeyes in 1942 as an outfielder and achieved immediate success by leading the NAL in batting average, runs scored, doubles, triples, stolen bases, and base hits. He married Elsie Allen on October 5, 1942, and has one daughter, Gloria. After moving with the Buckeyes to Cleveland in 1943, he led the NAL in hitting in 1944 (.353) and 1945 (.393) and paced the Buckeyes to a World Series sweep of the Homestead Grays in 1945. Jethroe tried out with the Boston Red Sox (AL) on April 16, 1945, but was not signed. He played winter ball in Cuba in 1947–1948 and 1948–1949, leading the CUWL in stolen bases both years.

The 6 foot, 1 inch, 178 pound Jethroe broke into organized baseball in midseason 1948, when the Buckeyes sold him to the Brooklyn Dodgers (NL). At Montreal (IL), the switch-hitting Jethroe batted .322 and stole 18 bases in 76 games. The next season he batted .326, slugged 17 homers, scored an

IL high 154 runs, and stole an IL record 89 bases. Reputedly among the fastest men ever to play organized baseball, Jethroe was sold to the Boston Braves (NL) for a reported $100,000 and became the team's first black player in 1950. He earned the Baseball Writers' Association Rookie of the Year honors by hitting .273, slugging 18 homers, and leading the NL in stolen bases with 35. Nicknamed "Jet," in 1951 he hit 18 home runs, batted .280, and again led the NL in stolen bases with 35. Poor eyesight contributed to his sub-par defensive skills and low .232 batting average in 1952, causing him to be relegated to the minor leagues. He appeared briefly with the Pittsburgh Pirates (NL) in 1954. During his major league career, Jethroe batted .261 with 460 hits, 49 home runs, 181 RBIs, and 98 stolen bases. He played with Toledo (AA) in 1953 and with Toronto (IL) from 1954 to his retirement in 1958. Jethroe, who performed in Cuba in 1954–1955, later participated in amateur ball and operated a bar and restaurant in Erie, PA.

Among the pioneers integrating major league baseball, Jethroe helped re-establish the stolen base as an offensive weapon. A double threat with his power and speed, he bridged the gap between the one-dimensional home run hitters of the 1930s and 1940s and today's complete players.

BIBLIOGRAPHY: Bob Ajemian, "$100,000 Jethroe May Be Flop in Outfield," *TSN*, March 29, 1950; Terry A. Baxter, correspondence with Jorge Figueroda, 1984, Cuban League statistics; Terry A. Baxter Collection, Lee's Summit, MO; Terry A. Baxter, correspondence with David Rutledge, 1984, Terry A. Baxter Collection, Lee's Summit, MO; Terry A. Baxter, telephone interview with Monte Irvin, 1984; Terry A. Baxter, telephone interview with Sam Jethroe, 1984; Cy Kritzer, "Bisons Walk Pitcher to Slow Up Royals' Base Rocket, Jethroe," *TSN*, July 27, 1949; Cy Kritzer and Lloyd McGowan, "Jethroe Ready for Jump to Stardom?" *TSN*, November 16, 1949; Lloyd McGowan, "Royals' Jet-Propelled Jethroe Sprints Toward New International League Theft Record," *TSN*, June 29, 1949; Gerry Moore, "Jethroe Recalls' 45 Tryout by Red Sox," *TSN*, November 23, 1949; Robert W. Peterson, *Only the Ball Was White* (Englewood Cliffs, NJ, 1970); Joseph L. Reichler, ed., *The Baseball Encyclopedia*, 6th ed. (New York, 1985), pp. 1,054–1,055; James A. Riley, *The All-Time All-Stars of Black Baseball* (Cocoa, FL, 1983); Donn Rogosin, *Invisible Men: Life in Baseball's Negro Leagues* (New York, 1983); *TSN Official Baseball Guide* 1949, 1950, 1954–1959, 1984 (St. Louis, 1949, 1950, 1954–1959, 1984); *TSN Baseball Questionnaire*, December 22, 1949; Jules Tygiel, *Baseball's Great Experiment: Jackie Robinson and His Legacy* (New York, 1983). Larry Whiteside, "The First to Play, Jethroe Came to Braves, But Sox Had First Crack," Boston *Sunday Globe*, July 22, 1979.

Terry A. Baxter

JOHN, Thomas Edward "Tommy" (b. 22 May 1943, Terre Haute, IN), player, is the son of utility employee Thomas and Ruth John. He played basketball and baseball at Terre Haute Gerstmeyer High School and was offered numerous college basketball scholarships. In 1961 the pitcher signed as a free agent with the Cleveland Indians (AL) for a reported $40,000 bonus.

After beginning his professional baseball career in 1961 at Dubuque, IA (ML), he pitched for Charleston, WV (EL), Jacksonville, FL (IL), and Portland, OR (PCL). After joining Cleveland in 1963, John in 1965 was traded to the Chicago White Sox (AL), won 82 games and lost 80 decisions there through the 1971 season and led the AL twice in shutouts. Between seasons, he attended Indiana State University. He married Sally Simmons in July, 1970, and has four children, Tommy, Travis, Tami, and Taylor.

On December 2, 1971, John was traded to the Los Angeles Dodgers (NL). The talented 6 foot, 3 inch, 190 pound southpaw enjoyed outstanding success there, winning 87 games and losing 42 contests through the 1978 season. He pitched in three World Series games in 1977–1978 for the Dodgers, winning one and losing one. Midway through the 1974 season, he suffered torn ligaments in his pitching arm and underwent the first ligament transplant surgery. Upon returning to the pitching mound in 1976, John won 10 of 20 decisions, received the Fred Hutchinson Award for his courageous effort, and was voted Comeback Player of the Year. After being granted free agency in 1978, he signed with the New York Yankees (AL). He won 62 games and lost 36 decisions through August, 1982, and was credited with one victory in the 1981 World Series. John was traded in August, 1982, to the California Angels (AL), winning 22 of 50 decisions through the 1985 season.

In twenty-three major league seasons through 1986, John pitched in 682 games, won 264 contests, lost 210 decisions, and hurled 45 shutouts. The three-time 20-game winner had a 3.23 ERA and recorded 2,083 strikeouts in 4,280 2/3 innings pitched. A member of the 1968 and 1978–1980 All-Star squads, he suffered the AL loss in 1980. In 1980 he led the AL in shutouts with six and was named the left-handed pitcher on *The Sporting News* AL All-Star team. John, a strong, fierce looking, confident, and self-assured competitor, has a strong desire to succeed and a determination to fight back when down. Off the field, he is a gentle, caring, thoughtful man and places his family first. He has strong religious convictions and a deep faith that nothing is impossible with God. He and his wife are co-authors of *The Sally and Tommy John Story*, describing their life and the tragic accident of their son Travis. At age 2, Travis had fallen from an upper-level window and was in a coma 15 days. The California Angels released John in June, 1985, after which he pitched briefly for Modesto, CA (CaL), and Madison, WI (ML), in the Oakland A's organization. The New York Yankees (AL) signed the sinkerball pitcher as a free agent in May 1986.

BIBLIOGRAPHY: Sally John and Tommy John, *The Sally and Tommy John Story* (New York, 1983); Gene Karst and Martin J. Jones, Jr., *Who's Who in Professional Baseball* (New Rochelle, NY, 1973); *TSN Official Baseball Register, 1984* (St. Louis, 1984).

John L. Evers

JOHNSON, Byron Bancroft "Ban" (b. 6 January 1863, Cincinnati, OH; d. 28 March 1931, St. Louis, MO), sportswriter and baseball executive, was founder and first president of the AL. His parents were Eunice Fox and Albert B. Johnson, a prominent school administrator in Cincinnati for almost fifty years. Johnson attended Marietta College for one year and the University of Cincinnati Law School for over a year before joining the staff of the Cincinnati *Commercial-Gazette*. From 1887 to 1894, he served as sporting editor of the *Commercial-Gazette*, met many baseball figures, and developed a deep knowledge of the game. He disliked rowdy behavior on the field and umpire abuse and sought to correct those two problems. In 1891 he married Sara Jane Laymon of Spencer, IN; they had no children.

His familiarity with baseball prompted owners of the revived WL to invite Johnson in November 1893 to lead their organization. Although intending to remain only one year, he continued as WL president through the 1899 season. During those six years, Johnson apprenticed in baseball administration and made the WL the most successful minor league. Johnson aspired to head a major league and in the winter of 1899–1900 saw his opportunity. The NL had dropped the bottom four teams from its twelve-club membership, which opened up important free territory. The WL agreement simultaneously expired and a major league players' group (Players' Protective Association) was formed. These developments inspired Johnson and his WL colleagues to move toward major league status. The WL became the AL before the 1900 season, but the circuit was bound by the National Agreement and remained a minor league.

In 1901, however, Johnson unsuccessfully pressed the NL to accept the AL as an equal. A two-year war broke out, during which time the NL hoped to crush the AL and the latter sought recognition as a second major league. During the "Great Baseball War," eighty-seven National Leaguers jumped to the AL and established the creditability of the new major loop. After the AL won the attendance battle in 1902, the NL sought peace. The "peace conference," held in Cincinnati in January, 1903, created the basic structure governing organized baseball over half a century.

Under the new National Agreement, a three-man ruling body, the National Commission, was established. Cincinnati owner Garry Herrmann chaired the commission, but Johnson proved its most influential figure. Although not having unlimited authority, he was called the "Czar of Baseball." During Johnson's era, from 1903 to 1920, baseball prospered as never before and became known as the national pastime. His creation of a second major league, along with his efforts to upgrade umpires, crack down on rowdy players and fans, and make baseball "respectable family entertainment," contributed largely to the game's success.

Between 1916 and 1919, Johnson became involved in four controversial player dispute decisions and antagonized a number of owners in both leagues. In the most critical case, he overruled the sale in July, 1919, of Carl Mays* by the Boston Red Sox to the New York Yankees. The New York State Supreme Court, however, later overruled Johnson, causing the latter's influence to decline. The National Commission also fell into disfavor because of Johnson's power over it and in 1920 was replaced by a single commissioner. With the election of Kenesaw Mountain Landis* to that post, Johnson's former influence vanished.

Thereafter AL president Johnson clashed frequently with Landis. The final dispute, precipitated when Landis published the correspondence in the Ty Cobb*-Tris Speaker* scandal in the winter of 1926–1927, led to Johnson's forced resignation as the junior circuit's chief executive in July, 1927. He refused to accept remuneration for the eight remaining years on his contract, a $320,000 sum. Johnson's already failing health worsened steadily after he left office. In 1937 he was elected to the National Baseball Hall of Fame.

BIBLIOGRAPHY: John B. Foster, "Ban Johnson's Twenty-five Years in the American League," Chicago *Daily News*, January 2, February 10, 1928; Ban Johnson, "Ban Johnson's Own Story," as told to John E. Wray and J. Roy Stockton, St. Louis *Post-Dispatch*, February 10, March 3, 1929; Ban Johnson, "My Thirty-four Years in Baseball," as told to Irving Vaughan, Chicago *Tribune*, February 24, March 3, 10, 1929; Eugene C. Murdock, *Ban Johnson: Czar of Baseball* (Westport, CT, 1982); Earl Obenshain, "Life of Ban Johnson," *Baseball World Inc. (December 3, 1928-February 3, 1929*; Branch Rickey (with Robert Riger), *The American Diamond* (New York, 1965).

Eugene C. Murdock

JOHNSON, Grant "Home Run" (b. 1874, Findlay, OH; d. ?), player and manager, attended Public School No. 9 in Findlay OH, and in 1894, at age 20, played shortstop for the strong semi-pro Findlay Sluggers. The following year he began his professional career and subsequently played with the era's greatest black teams. A star for the Page Fence Giants of Adrian, MI, the Columbus Giants of Chicago, and the Cuban X-Giants, Johnson was the most famous shortstop in black baseball before John Henry Lloyd.* During baseball's dead ball era, the right-handed slugger earned the lifetime sobriquet "Home Run." On Sol White's championship Philadelphia Giants of 1906, he teamed with greats Rube Foster,* J. Preston "Pete" Hill,* and Bill Monroe. When Foster assembled the Leland Giants team in Chicago, he recruited Johnson (as second baseman) and Hill. The trio joined Lloyd, Bruce Petway, Frank Wickware, and Pat Dougherty to form what was perhaps the greatest aggregation of talent in black baseball history. In 1910 the Giants compiled an incredible 123–6 record.

Johnson and Lloyd joined Louis Santop,* Joe Williams,* Dick Redding,* and Spot Poles* in 1911 on the great Lincoln Giants team. As at Chicago, Johnson played second base in deference to Lloyd's outstanding ability. After the team won the 1912 and 1913 championships and outclassed Foster's Chicago American Giants in the 1913 playoff, the Lincoln owner claimed that his club could defeat any major league team. Johnson subsequently excelled with the Lincoln Stars and Brooklyn Royal Giants, serving as player-manager with the latter team. In this same capacity, he guided the Lincoln Giants to a championship.

The star infielder also captained the Havana Reds to the CNL championship and became the first American to win a batting title there. The superior slugger hit .319 during five winters there and batted a sparkling .412 one season. After the 1910 season, the World Series champion Philadelphia Athletics (AL) played Johnson's Havana Reds in Cuba. Manager Connie Mack* pitched great moundsmen Eddie Plank,* Chief Bender,* and Jack Coombs,* but Havana captured the series. That same year, the line drive hitter batted .412 in exhibition games against the Detroit Tigers (AL) and outhit Hall of Fame outfielders Ty Cobb* and Sam Crawford.* In 19 exhibition games against major leaguers, Johnson batted .293.

During his latter years, he played with the Pittsburgh and Buffalo Colored Giants. The sturdy infielder kept in good physical condition and played thirty-eight years before retiring in 1932 at age 58. He continued to reside in Buffalo, where he worked with the New York Central Railroad Company.

BIBLIOGRAPHY: Robert W. Peterson, *Only the Ball Was White* (Englewood Cliffs, NJ, 1970); James A. Riley, *The All-Time All-Stars of Black Baseball* (Cocoa, FL, 1983); James A. Riley, interviews with former Negro league players, James A. Riley Collection, Cocoa, FL.

James A. Riley

JOHNSON, Robert Lee "Bob," "Indian Bob" (b. 26 November 1906, Pryor, OK; d. 6 July 1982, Tacoma, WA), player and manager, was the brother of outfielder Roy Johnson. He married Caroline Stout in December, 1924, and had two daughters. He later wed Elizabeth Pastore in September, 1950. Nicknamed "Indian Bob" because of his part-Cherokee Indian ancestry, Johnson became the mainstay of the Depression era Philadelphia Athletics (AL). From 1935 through 1941, he drove in at least 100 runs per season for Philadelphia manager Connie Mack.* In his first nine seasons, he never hit under 21 home runs. During his thirteen major league seasons, he slugged 288 homers and ranks among the top twenty career sluggers in average home runs per season. Johnson, who never batted under .265 and averaged over 150 hits per season, batted .296 lifetime, made 396 doubles, recorded 2,051 hits, and knocked in 1,283 career runs. In his second major league season (1934), he hit safely in 26 consecutive games and went six for six in an eleven-inning game on June 16. He set the AL record for the most RBIs in one inning (6) and in one game for a player driving in all of his team's runs (8). Johnson made seven All-Star teams, a feat bettered by only sixteen other AL players.

Johnson, who left school in the fifth grade when his family moved to

Washington, began his professional baseball career with Wichita-Pueblo (WL) in 1929 and played from 1929 through 1932 with Portland, OR (PCL). In 1933 he joined the Athletics and played there until traded in March, 1943, to the Washington Senators (AL). At Washington in 1943, Johnson experienced his worst season by batting .265 with only seven home runs. The 6 foot, 200 pound outfielder enjoyed fine seasons with the Boston Red Sox (AL) in 1944 and 1945, but then spent the remainder of his career in the minor leagues with Milwaukee (AA) in 1946, Seattle (PCL) in 1948, and Tacoma (WIL) in 1949. Johnson, who injured his knee in 1948, managed the Tacoma club in 1949 and attempted a comeback as a player with Tijuana, Mexico (IL) in 1951. He worked for a brewing company and as an engineer in the Glendale, CA, Fire Department before retiring to Tacoma, WA.

BIBLIOGRAPHY: Alan R. Asnen, interview with Jeff Kernan, August 21, 1984, National Baseball Hall of Fame Library, Cooperstown, NY; Gene Karst and Martin J. Jones, Jr., *Who's Who in Professional Baseball* (New Rochelle, NY, 1973); Paul MacFarlane, ed., *TSN Daguerreotypes of Great Stars of Baseball* (St. Louis, 1981); Joseph L. Reichler, ed., *The Baseball Encyclopedia*, 6th ed. (New York, 1985); *TSN Official Baseball Guide, 1983*, (St. Louis, 1983), p. 1,056.

Alan R. Asnen

JOHNSON, Walter Perry "The Big Train," "Barney" (b. 6 November 1887, Humboldt, KS; d. 10 December 1946, Washington, DC), player, manager, and announcer, was the son of farmer Frank Edwin and Minnie Johnson. In 1901 the Johnsons moved to Olinda, CA, where Walter attended Fullerton Union High School. In 1906 he turned professional and tried out with Tacoma (NWL). Since the NWL was too fast for the 16-year-old, he was sent to Weiser, ID (IdSL). Johnson pitched 75 scoreless innings there and averaged 15 strikeouts per game.

Johnson signed with the Washington Senators (AL) and lost his debut on August 2, 1907, against the Detroit Tigers 3–2. In his second start, Johnson beat Cleveland 7–2 to win the first of 416 decisions spanning twenty-one seasons (1907–1927) at Washington. He lost 279 games for a mostly second division club. Twelve times Johnson won at least 20 games during one season. He captured 32 victories in 1912 and a career-high 36 triumphs the following year. Besides pitching 110 career shutouts, he lost 65 games when the Senators were shut out. He fanned 3,508 batters, pitched in the most games in AL history (802), and hurled more complete games in modern times than any other major leaguer (531). Along with making 666 starts, he allowed only 1,902 runs in 5,923 2/3 innings and boasted a 2.17 career ERA. His lowest ERAs included 1.09 in 1913, 1.27 in 1918, and 1.49 in 1919. Twelve times Johnson led AL pitchers in strikeouts, with 313 in 1910 his one-season maximum. Johnson tied the AL mark for consecutive victories with 16 in 1912 and pitched three shutouts against the New York Yankees (then Highlanders) in four days in 1908. After striking out four Boston Red Sox hitters in one inning in 1911, he established an AL record by hurling 56 consecutive scoreless innings in 1913. Johnson, who pitched a no-hitter against Boston in 1920 and compiled numerous one-hitters, received the AL Most Valuable Player Award in 1913 and 1924.

Johnson pitched the opening game of the 1910 season with President William Howard Taft in attendance. This event marked the first of the "presidential openers" that became traditional in Washington. Johnson pitched 14 opening-day games, recording 7 shutouts. For the Senators, Johnson also pitched in the 1924 and 1925 World Series. Although losing his first two starts for the world champion Senators in 1924, he pitched four innings in the seventh and deciding game to earn the win. In 1925 he triumphed in his first two starts, but lost the crucial seventh game 9–7 to the Pittsburgh Pirates. In Washington, fans quickly accepted Johnson as everybody's country cousin. A big, modest hick with a behind-the-plow gait, he did not fit into city ways and was amazed that people thought he was so wonderful. The country bumpkin neither smoked nor drank and lived a social life of movie-going, hunting, and talking baseball with his longtime roommate Clyde Milan.* The backward, shy Johnson lived in constant fear of hitting an opposing batter with one of his fast pitches.

He married Hazel Lee Roberts, daughter of a Nevada Congressman, in 1914 and had three sons, Walter, Jr., Edwin, and Robert, and two daughters, Caroline and Barbara. In 1930 death came to his 36-year-old wife, a tragedy that there after left its mark on Johnson. Although a fabulous pitcher, he enjoyed somewhat less success as a manager. He piloted the Washington Senators (1929–1932) after managing Newark (IL) in 1928. His highest finish with Washington was second place in 1930. Johnson became manager of the Cleveland Indians (AL) in June, 1933, and guided the 1934 Indians to a third place finish, but was replaced as manager in August, 1935. His overall managerial record comprised 530 victories and 432 losses for a .551 percentage. After spending one season as a play-by-play radio announcer in Washington, he raised cattle on his farm and campaigned unsuccessfully for election to the U.S. Congress from Maryland. In 1936 Johnson, probably the fastest pitcher who ever lived, was elected one of the five charter members of the National Baseball Hall of Fame. He died of a brain tumor at age 59.

BIBLIOGRAPHY: Bob Broeg, *Super Stars of Baseball* (St. Louis, 1971); Gene Karst and Martin J. Jones, Jr., *Who's Who in Professional Baseball* (New Rochelle, NY, 1973); Tom Murray, *Sport Magazine All-Time All-Stars* (New York, 1948).

John L. Evers

JOHNSON, William Julius "Judy," "Jing" (b. 26 October 1899, Snow Hill, MD), player, scout, and coach, starred as a third baseman on the great Negro league Pittsburgh Crawfords teams of the 1930s. The son of William H. and Annie Johnson, he played childhood baseball in the Wilmington,

DE, area and attended Howard High School for one year. His father, a seaman, became athletic director of the Negro Settlement House in Wilmington. Johnson's first paid baseball job came with the semi-pro Chester Stars in Wilmington. In 1918 he worked on a loading dock in Deepwater Point, NJ, and then joined the Bacharach Giants, a fine eastern barnstorming team. After a tryout with the Darby, PA, Hilldale club, Johnson played with the Madison Stars. Hilldale purchased his contract in 1920 and made him regular third baseman the next year.

A superb defensive third baseman, Johnson played nine seasons with the Hilldales and starred on the pennant-winning ECL teams from 1923 through 1925 with batting marks of .280, .358, and .392. He married Anita T. Irons in 1923 and has one daughter, Loretta L., who married major league outfielder Bill Bruton. In 1924 the Hilldales met the NNL's Kansas City Monarchs in the first Negro World Series. Johnson batted .364 and made six doubles, a triple, and a homer in a losing cause. The Hilldales secured revenge in 1925. With Monarchs star pitcher Wilbur "Bullet" Rogan* injured, the Hilldales defeated the Monarchs four games to one. Johnson hit .300 and contributed solid defensive play. He remained with Hilldale until 1929, batting .302 in 1926, .243 in 1927, .231 in 1928, and .383 with 22 stolen bases in 1929. The Hilldales did not win any more ECL pennants during this period, but Johnson sharpened his skills in Cuban winter ball. In the 1926–1927, 1927–1928, and 1928–1929 winter league seasons, he hit .374, .331, and .341, respectively. His composite CUWL average over four years (including 1930–1931) was .334.

With the collapse of the ECL, Johnson in 1930 joined the independent Homestead Grays as player-manager. This team fielded Oscar Charleston,* "Smoky" Joe Williams,* and Josh Gibson,* whom Johnson lured from semipro ball. After a one year stint with the Darby, PA, Daisies, Johnson in 1932 returned to Homestead (EWL). In midseason, Johnson and most of the Grays jumped to Gus Greenlee's* Pittsburgh Crawfords (NNL). As field captain of the Crawfords, Johnson played with stars Walter "Buck" Leonard,* Gibson, Leroy "Satchel" Paige,* John Henry Lloyd,* and Charleston. That fall the Crawfords defeated Casey Stengel's* major league All Stars in five of seven games. Nicknamed "Jing" in Pittsburgh, Johnson batted .333 in 1934 and that fall helped the Crawfords defeat Dizzy Dean* in three games. An excellent shortstop and an outstanding fielding third baseman, Johnson batted .367 and helped the Crawfords win the 1935 NNL pennant and defeat the New York Cubans in the NNL playoffs. Johnson hit .282 in 1936, played against Rogers Hornsby* and Jimmie Foxx* that fall in Mexico, and then retired in 1937 with an unconfirmed .344 lifetime batting average. Johnson later worked as a supervisor for Continental Can Company in Wilmington and operated a general store with his brother in the 1940s.

Johnson, well respected for his intelligence and playing skills, later scouted and served as spring training instructor for the Philadelphia Athletics (AL),

Milwaukee Braves (NL), and Philadelphia Phillies (NL). The pinnacle of his baseball career came in 1975 with his induction into the National Baseball Hall of Fame. A gentleman in an era of rough ballplayers, Johnson excelled as a fine all-around player. As field captain of the Crawfords, he exerted a steadying influence on his teammates and helped them establish the excellence of Negro league play. As a scout, he participated in the early days of major league integration and coached young black players in organized baseball.

BIBLIOGRAPHY: Terry A. Baxter, correspondence with Jorge Figueroda, 1984, Cuban League statistics, Terry A. Baxter Collection, Lee's Summit, MO; Terry A. Baxter, correspondence with Judy Johnson, 1984, Terry A. Baxter Collection, Lee's Summit, MO; Terry A. Baxter, telephone interview with Judy Johnson, 1984; John Holway, "The Man Called Judy", John Holway Collection, Alexandria, VA; John Holway, *TSN*, July 5, 1982; Kevin Kerrane and Rod Beaton, "Judy Johnson, Reminiscences by the Great Baseball Player," *Delaware Today* (May 1977); Gordon 'Red' Marston, "A Mission Arranged by Judy Johnson," *TSN*, March 1954; Robert W. Peterson, *Only the Ball Was White* (Englewood Cliffs, NJ, 1970); Lowell Reidenbaugh, *Cooperstown: Where Baseball's Legends Live Forever* (St. Louis, 1983); James A. Riley, *The All-Time All-Stars of Black Baseball* (Cocoa, FL, 1983); Donn Rogosin, *Invisible Men: Life in Baseball's Negro Leagues* (New York, 1983); Jules Tygiel, *Baseball's Great Experiment: Jackie Robinson and His Legacy* (New York, 1983).

Terry A. Baxter

JONES, Samuel Pond "Sad Sam" (b. 26 July 1892, Woodsfield, OH; d. 6 July 1966, Barnesville, OH), player and coach, attended Woodsfield public schools. On his twenty-fourth birthday he married Edith Mae Kerr. A 6 foot, 170 pound right-handed pitcher, Jones began his professional baseball career in 1913. After playing for minor league teams in Zanesville, OH (TSL), Portsmouth, OH (OSL), and Cleveland (AA), in 1914 he relieved in one game for the Cleveland Indians (AL). Jones spent 1915 with the Indians, leading relievers in games and innings pitched. In early 1916, he was traded to the Boston Red Sox (AL) with infielder Fred Thomas and $50,000 for Tris Speaker.* Jones hurled sparingly the next two years for the pitching-rich Red Sox, but started regularly in 1918, winning 16 games and losing only 5 for an AL leading .762 winning percentage. In game five of the 1918 World Series, he lost 3–0 to Hippo Vaughn* of the Chicago Cubs.

Jones' 23 victories and AL-leading 5 shutouts in 1921 established him as one of baseball's top pitchers. The dynasty-building New York Yankees (AL) acquired Jones' contract and won three pennants during his five years with the club. Manager Miller Huggins* used him as both a starter and a reliever. In his best major league season (1923), Jones started 27 games, relieved in 12, and compiled a 21–8 won-lost record. On September 4 he pitched a no-hit game against Philadelphia, and on October 12 he started the first World Series game ever played at Yankee Stadium. He was defeated by the New York Giants' Art Nehf,* surrendering only Casey Stengel's* seventh inning home run. Three days later, he pitched two scoreless relief innings to save the deciding sixth game for the Yankees. Subsequently Jones pitched for the St. Louis Browns (1927), Washington Senators (1928–1931), and Chicago White Sox (1932–1935), all of the AL. His career totals included 229 wins, 217 losses, 36 shutouts, and a 3.84 ERA. In 1940 he served as a pitcher-coach for Toronto (IL).

Jones set an AL longevity record by pitching twenty-two consecutive seasons. He attributed his longevity to his disinclination to throw to first base to hold enemy base runners close, preferring to conserve his energy for the batter. Although nicknamed "Sad Sam," he did not possess a lugubrious personality. The sobriquet was bestowed by a rookie sportswriter who had never met Jones and was impressed by his serious demeanor on the field.

BIBLIOGRAPHY: Joseph L. Reichler, ed., *The Baseball Encyclopedia*, 6th ed. (New York, 1985), p. 1,820; Lawrence S. Ritter, *The Glory of Their Times* (New York, 1966).

Dennis T. "Tom" Chase

JOSS, Adrian "Addie" (b. 12 April 1880, Juneau, WI; d. 14 April 1911, Toledo, OH), player, was the son of farmers Jacob and Theresa (Stauden-meyer) Joss. After attending schools in Juneau and Portage, WI, he entered St. Mary's College and played on the baseball team there. He started his professional career with the Toledo Mudhens (ISL) in 1900. He married Lillian Shinivar on October 11, 1902, and had one son and one daughter.

Joss became a major league pitcher with Cleveland (AL) in 1902 and spent nine years with that team. He never experienced a losing season, winning 160 games while losing only 97. He pitched 234 complete games, hurled 46 shutouts, and compiled the second best lifetime ERA (1.88) in baseball history. In his major league debut on April 26, 1902, he pitched a one-hitter. He hurled six one-hitters in his major league career, but his greatest performance was the perfect game he pitched against the Chicago White Sox on October 2, 1908. Joss needed perfection to win 1–0 because his mound opponent, Ed Walsh,* struck out fifteen batters. He recorded a second no-hitter on April 20, 1910, also against Chicago. The 6 foot, 3 inch, 185 pound Joss possessed long arms and proved extremely graceful in fielding. AL president Ban Johnson* said of him, "He was one of the greatest pitchers the game has ever seen." In the off-season, Joss worked as a sportswriter for the Toledo *News Bee* and Cleveland *Press* and covered the 1907–1909 World Series for the *Press*.

Despite his stellar record, Joss experienced frequent illness. High fever cost him the last month of the 1903 season. He suffered a bout with malaria in April, 1904, and missed several starts in 1905 because of a bad back. On July 25, 1910, he left a game in the fifth inning because of a sore arm and never pitched again. He went to spring training in 1911, but became ill on April 3 and died of tubercular meningitis eleven days later at age 31. On

July 24, 1911, Cleveland played an All-Star team in a benefit game to raise over $13,000 toward defraying some debts that Joss had incurred from his illness. The Veterans Committee voted Joss into the National Baseball Hall of Fame in 1978.

BIBLIOGRAPHY: Martin Appel and Burt Goldblatt, *Baseball's Best: The Hall of Fame Gallery* (New York, 1977); Jordan Deutsch, Richard Cohen, Roland Johnson, and David Neft, *The Scrapbook History of Baseball* (New York, 1975); Paul MacFarlane, ed., *TSN Hall of Fame Fact Book* (St. Louis, 1983); *NYT Book of Baseball History* (New York, 1975).

Emil H. Rothe

JUDGE, Joseph Ignatius "Joe" (b. 25 May 1894, Brooklyn, NY; d. 11 March 1963, Washington, DC), player and coach, was the son of Joseph and Catherine Judge and attended New York City public schools. He married Alma Gauvreau in 1914 and had four children, Joseph, Jr., Catherine, Alma, and Dorothy. After playing minor league baseball in Lewiston, ME (NEL) in 1914 and Buffalo, NY (IL) in 1915 , he joined the Washington Senators (AL) in 1915. Judge, a left-handed hitting and fielding first baseman, played with Washington from 1915 to 1932, with the Brooklyn Dodgers (NL) in 1933, and with the Boston Red Sox (AL) in 1933 and 1934. Although a small first baseman, the 5 foot, 8 1/2 inch, 160 pounder sparkled at his position and was rivaled only by George Sisler.* Judge, chosen on Walter Johnson's * all-time Washington team, led AL first basemen in fielding six times. During his career, he made 19,277 putouts, 1,300 assists, and only 142 errors for a .993 fielding percentage. In 1920 he saved the only no-hitter Walter Johnson ever pitched by robbing the last Boston batter, Harry Hooper,* of a base hit.

Although not a great slugger and never leading the AL in any batting category, Judge hit very consistently and compiled a .298 lifetime batting average in 2,170 major league games. During his career, he reached the .300 mark eleven times. His 2,350 hits included 433 doubles, 159 triples, and 71 home runs. He scored 1,184 runs, drove in 1,037 runs, and pilfered 213 bases. In the 1924 and 1925 World Series, he batted .286 in 14 games with one home run. Judge, one of the most popular players ever to play in Washington, was honored in 1930 with $10,500 of the gate receipts and numerous other gifts. He managed Baltimore (IL) in 1934 and coached for the Washington Senators from 1945 to 1946. He also served as coach of the Georgetown College baseball team.

BIBLIOGRAPHY: Allison Danzig and Joseph L. Reichler, *The History of Baseball: Its Great Players, Teams, and Managers* (Englewood Cliffs, NJ, 1959); Ralph Hickok, *Who's Who in American Sport* (New York, 1971); "Joe Judge Dies, Former Nat's Star," Washington *Post*, March 11, 1963, pp. A23–24; Joseph L. Reichler, ed., *The Baseball*

Encyclopedia, 6th ed. (New York, 1985), p. 1,069; Washington *Post*, June 28, 1930, pp. 11–13; *Who's Who in American Sports* (Washington, DC, 1928).

James K. Skipper, Jr.

K

KAAT, James Lee "Jim" (b. 7 November 1938, Zeeland, MI), player, coach, and announcer, became one of few major leaguers appearing in four decades by pitching from 1959 through 1983. After attending Hope College in Holland, MI, he began his baseball career with Superior, NE (NeSL), in 1957. He pitched for Missoula, MT (PrL) in 1958 and led hurlers in games started (30) and shutouts (5). Kaat performed for Chattanooga (SA) in 1959 and Charleston, WV (AA), in 1960 and compiled a 1–7 record in brief appearances with the Washington Senators (AL) those seasons. The 6 foot, 5 inch, 195 pound left-hander played for the AL Minnesota Twins (1961–1973), AL Chicago White Sox (1973–1975), NL Philadelphia Phillies (1976–1979), AL New York Yankees (1979–1980), and NL St. Louis Cardinals (1980–1983). In July 1983 the Cardinals released Kaat.

In 898 regular season games, Kaat compiled a 283–237 won-lost record (237–191 in the AL; 46–43 in the NL), recorded a 3.45 ERA in 4,528 innings, and struck out 2,461 batters. The slick-fielding Kaat won sixteen consecutive Gold Glove awards from 1962 through 1977, made three AL All-Star teams (1962, 1966, 1975) and two of *The Sporting News* All-Star teams (1966, 1975), and was named AL Pitcher of the Year in 1966 by *The Sporting News*. His 16 career home runs paced active major league pitchers at the time of his retirement.

Kaat made major league history in the Cardinals' opening game on April 6, 1982, when he surpassed Early Wynn* to become the first pitcher to appear in twenty-four major league seasons. Besides establishing a major league record for most career sacrifice flies allowed (134), he set AL marks for most games lost by a left-handed pitcher (191) and most career sacrifice flies allowed (108). During his career, Kaat won at least 20 games three times (1966, 1974, 1975) and reached a career-high 25–13 mark with the 1966 Twins. He recorded at least ten victories for fifteen consecutive seasons (1962–1976) and participated on the 1965 AL champion Minnesota and 1982 world champion St. Louis teams. Kaat also helped Minnesota and Philadelphia win division titles in 1970 and 1976, respectively. A resident of Glen Mills, PA, the very durable Kaat married Julie Anne Moore in October 1959 and later wed Linda Jankowski. He has two children, Jim, Jr., and Jill. Kaat was the pitching coach for the Cincinnati Reds (NL) in 1984 and joined the New York Yankees (AL) as an announcer in 1986.

BIBLIOGRAPHY: St. Louis Cardinals *Media Guide* (1983); *TSN Official Baseball Register, 1984* (St. Louis, 1984).

Brian R. Kelleher

KALINE, Albert William "Al" (b. 19 December 1934, Baltimore, MD), player and announcer, is the youngest of the three children of broommaker Nicholas and housekeeper Naomi Kaline and has two older sisters, Margaret and Caroline. Nicholas, his two brothers, and his father played semi-profes-sional baseball on the Maryland Eastern Shore and encouraged Al to play sandlot ball in Baltimore. At age 8 Kaline suffered from osteomyelitis, a bone disease that forced surgeons to remove two inches of bone from his left foot. This condition caused Kaline problems throughout his career. As a high school star at Southern High School in Baltimore, he made the All-Maryland high school team four seasons and hit .488 his senior year. In 1953 the Detroit Tigers (AL) paid the 6 foot, 2 inch, 184 pound, right-handed Kaline a $30,000 bonus to sign. Kaline gave the money to his parents so that they could pay off their mortgage and finance an operation needed to save his mother's eyesight. Joining the Tigers after his graduation, Kaline hit only .250 in 30 games his initial season. In 1954 he raised his average to .276 and played a solid right field. Determined to become a consistent hitter, he improved his batting eye, swing, and arm and wrist strength. His remarkable 1955 season included leading both leagues with a .340 batting average (making him the youngest player ever to win a major league batting title), garnering 200 hits, driving in 102 runs, hitting 27 home runs, and producing 321 total bases. This phenomenal season at age 20 put tremendous pressure on Kaline, who was compared to Ty Cobb* and Joe DiMaggio.* Although never win-ning another batting championship or again reaching the 200-hit level, he proved a consistent hitter and a spectacular outfielder noted for his speed, rifle arm, and smart defensive play. His second best season came in 1959, when he hit .327 and led the AL with a .530 slugging average. In the 1968 World Series against the St. Louis Cardinals, he batted .379 with 11 hits and 8 RBIs. During his twenty-two years with the Tigers through 1974, Kaline hit over .300 nine times, amassed 3,007 hits, knocked in 1,583 runs, slugged 399 home runs, and compiled a .297 lifetime average. Like Mickey Mantle,* Kaline suffered numerous serious injuries and overcame them to return to the lineup with renewed dedication. The winner of eleven Gold Glove fielding awards, he became the first Tiger player to be paid over $100,000 a year. He married Louise Hamilton on October 16, 1954 and has two sons, Mark and Michael. The greatest Tigers player of the post–World War II era, Kaline was elected to the National Baseball Hall of Fame in 1980 in his first year of eligibility. Kaline's records speak for themselves, but his remarkable character, discipline, dedication, intensity of effort, and gentlemanly sportsmanship have enhanced his legend. Since retirement as an active player, he has served as an executive for a Detroit automotive engineering firm, a sportscaster of Tigers games with George Kell* for WDIV-TV, and a spring training coach for the Tigers. One of the most respected and honored players in Tigers baseball history, he was named by the fans in 1969 to the All-Time Tigers team.

BIBLIOGRAPHY: "Al Kaline: Better Than Most," *Inside Sports* 6 (October, 1984), pp. 54, 56, 58; Hal Butler, *Al Kaline and the Detroit Tigers* (Chicago, 1973); *CB* (1970), pp. 211–214; Joe Falls, *Detroit Tigers* (New York, 1975); Gene Karst and Martin J. Jones, Jr., *Who's Who in Professional Baseball* (New Rochelle, NY, 1973); Joe LaPointe, "Detroit's Real Home Tome," Detroit *Free Press Sunday Magazine* (September 23, 1984).

Douglas A. Noverr

KEEFE, Timothy John "Tim," "Sir Timothy" (b. 1 January 1857, Cambridge, MA; d. 23 April 1933, Cambridge, MA), player, umpire, and coach, was the son of Irish immigrants Patrick Keefe, a builder, and Mary (Leary) Keefe and grew up in Cambridge. A 5 foot, 10 1/2 inch, 185 pound, right-handed pitcher, Keefe began his baseball career with Utica, New Bedford, and Albany (NA) in 1879 and 1880. Upon moving to Troy, NY (NL), Keefe won 42 games and lost 59 over three seasons (1880–1882). With New York (AA) in 1883 and 1884, Keefe enjoyed his first big seasons. In 1883 he won 41 games for the Metropolitans and led the AA in innings pitched, strikeouts, and complete games. On July 4, 1883, Keefe allowed just one hit in the morning game against Columbus, returned that afternoon to hurl a two-hitter, and won both games. The following season, Keefe added 37 victories, pacing New York to the AA flag.

Keefe joined the New York Giants (NL) in 1885 and the next season posted an NL-tying 42 victories and topped the NL in strikeouts and complete games. He suffered a nervous breakdown in 1887 after one of his fastballs struck a batter in the temple. Keefe later teamed with Mickey Welch* to form one of the era's most potent mound duos. Over the next two seasons, Keefe won 63 games to lead the Giants to NL championships. Besides leading the NL in victories, strikeouts, and shutouts, Keefe established a major league record in 1888 by winning 19 consecutive games and won 4 games in a post-season series to help the Giants defeat the St. Louis Browns (AA). After his performance, Keefe demanded $4,500 and became the highest paid Giant.

Keefe in 1890 joined many other National Leaguers in deserting to the newly formed PL. After winning 17 games and losing 11 for the New York entry, Keefe returned to the Giants (NL) in 1891 and was traded to the Philadelphia Phillies (NL) in August of that year. Upon completing his playing career with the Phillies in 1893, Keefe became an NL umpire in 1894 and 1895. Keefe then returned to Cambridge to enter the real estate business and also coached baseball at Harvard, Tufts, and Princeton universities. Keefe, who married Clara A. Gibson on August 19, 1889, ranks high on the all-time major league lists for pitchers in numerous departments. During fourteen seasons, he compiled 344 victories (8th), 225 losses (16th), started 595 games, completed 558 games (63rd), and pitched 5,072 innings (8th). He allowed 4,552 hits and 2,468 runs (6th), struck out 2,533 batters (16th), and issued 1,231 bases on balls (33rd). Keefe posted at least 30 victories six times (2nd), 20 or more decisions seven times (5th), and 40 or more wins twice, and hurled 40 shutouts. In post-season play, he won 4 games and lost 3. The quiet, gentle Keefe avoided the spotlight and pioneered in the use of the change of pace to complement his fastball and curve. A master strategist, Keefe knew the weakness of every batter in the league. In 1964 he was elected to the National Baseball Hall of Fame.

BIBLIOGRAPHY: Gene Karst and Martin J. Jones, Jr., *Who's Who in Professional Baseball* (New Rochelle, NY, 1973); Paul MacFarlane, ed., *TSN Daguerreotypes of Great Stars of Baseball* (St. Louis, 1981); Lowell Reidenbaugh, *Cooperstown: Where Baseball's Legends Live Forever* (St. Louis, 1983).

John L. Evers

KEELER, William Henry "Willie," "Wee Willie" (b. 3 March 1872, Brooklyn, NY; d. 1 January 1923, Brooklyn, NY), player, was the son of a Brooklyn trolley car conductor and remained a bachelor throughout his life. From 1892 through 1910, he played with the Brooklyn Superbas, Baltimore Orioles, and New York Giants (NL), and the New York Highlanders (AL), and became one of few players to perform with all three traditional New York City teams. Although primarily a good defensive outfielder, the left-handed Keeler frequently played shortstop, second base, and third base. Contemporaries considered Keeler, whose slogan was "Keep your eye on the ball and hit 'em where they a'int," ranked among the best all-time bunters and place hitters. With the Orioles, he and John McGraw* perfected the hit-and-run play. Keeler originated the "Baltimore Chop," whereby he swung down, pounded the ball into the ground, and reached first base by the time the ball finally came down.

His 44-game hitting streak remains an NL record, although Pete Rose* tied it in 1978. Keeler's feat remained the major league record for forty-four years, until Joe DiMaggio* hit safely in 56 games in 1941. His .432 batting average in 1897 ranks as the third highest in major league history behind Hugh Duffy's* .438 mark in 1894 and Tip O'Neill's* .435 mark in 1887, while his lifetime .345 mark is the fifth highest in baseball history. If he had retired after ten major league seasons (which would still have made him eligible for the National Baseball Hall of Fame), Keeler would have batted a phenomenal .376 or nine points above Ty Cobb's* current all-time record career average. Keeler achieved the above averages despite being only 5 feet, 4 inches tall and weighing 140 pounds. He made 2,962 hits during his nineteen-year career and undoubtedly would have easily surpassed the 3,000-hit milestone had the media stressed its significance then. Far fewer than the traditional 154 games per season were scheduled during some of his earlier seasons.

From 1894 to 1900, he played on five NL pennant winners—the Baltimore Orioles (1894–1896) and the Brooklyn Superbas (1899–1900). Due to common forms of ownership and the then-legal interlocking directorates between Baltimore and Brooklyn, he moved from the Orioles to the Superbas with teammates Joe Kelley,* Hugh Jennings,* and manager Ned Hanlon.* Over a six-year period from 1894 to 1899, Keeler averaged 148 runs scored, 47 stolen bases, a .388 batting average, and 219 hits. He played briefly in the minor leagues at the beginning of his career with Binghamton (EL) in 1892 and 1893 and at the end with Toronto (IL) in 1911. After retiring, he lived in Brooklyn and prospered in real estate. His oft-quoted cliché, "Hit 'em where they a'int," was first credited to Keeler by Brooklyn *Eagle* sportswriter Abe Yager. Keeler choked up on the bat so much that Sam Crawford* once remarked that "it seemed like he used only half of it." Although serious on the field and an excellent rightfielder, he was a practical joker off the field. In 1939 Keeler was among the first two dozen figures elected to the National Baseball Hall of Fame.

BIBLIOGRAPHY: John Durant, *The Dodgers* (New York, 1947); Frank Graham, *The Brooklyn Dodgers* (New York, 1945); Tommy Holmes, *The Dodgers* (New York, 1972); Tot Holmes, *1979 Dodger Blue Book* (Gothenberg, NE, 1979); Donald Honig, *A Pictorial History of the Brooklyn Dodgers* (New York, 1982); Daniel Okrent and Harris Lewine, eds., *The Ultimate Baseball Book* (New York, 1981); David R. Phillips, ed., *That Old Ballgame* (New York, 1975); John Thorn, *A Century of Baseball Lore* (New York, 1974).

Ronald L. Gabriel

KELL, George Clyde (b. 23 August 1922, Swifton, AR), player, scout, and announcer, is the oldest of three sons of Melvin Clyde and Alma Kell. His father played semi-pro baseball, enabling George to grow up with the sport. After attending Arkansas State College at Jonesboro for one year, Kell played at Newport, AR (NEAL), in the 1940–1941 seasons and at Lancaster, PA (ISL), in the 1942–1943 seasons. In 1943 he led the ISL in batting (.396 average), hits, runs, triples, putouts, assists, and fielding as a third baseman.

After playing one game with the Philadelphia Athletics (AL) in 1943, Kell hit .268 as regular third baseman the following season. Manager Connie

Mack* guided Kell's development, continuing to play the youngster during batting slumps. Mack predicted that Kell would "never be a hitter." Accepting the challenge, Kell worked hard on his batting, changed his grip, used a lighter bat, and became a spray hitter. After hitting .272 in 1945, Kell was traded in 1946 to the Detroit Tigers (AL) for Barney McCosky. In 1946 he hit a sparkling .322 average, the first of nine seasons over .300.

In 1949 Kell dramatically captured the AL batting title. After trailing Ted Williams* by five percentage points, Kell surpassed the Boston star by two ten-thousandths of a point, .3429 to .3427. Although Kell could have won the title by not batting in the ninth inning in the season finale, he insisted on hitting since he did not want to be a "cheese champion." Kell, however, did not have to bat because his teammate hit into a double play to end the inning. In 1950 Kell batted .340, led the AL in hits (218) and doubles (56), and knocked in 101 runs. Billy Goodman of the Boston Red Sox won the batting title by hitting .354 with 217 fewer times at bat. Kell said philosophically, "I won a close one and lost a close one."

During the 1952 season, Kell was traded to the Boston Red Sox (AL). He played for the Chicago White Sox (AL) from 1954 through early 1956, was traded to the Baltimore Orioles (AL), and retired after the 1957 season. During fifteen major league seasons, Kell compiled a .306 lifetime batting average with 2,054 hits, 385 doubles, and 870 RBIs. A fine fielder, he led AL third basemen in double plays in 1945 and 1946, in fielding percentage in 1946–1947, 1950–1951, 1953, 1955 and 1956, in putouts in 1945 and 1946, and in assists in 1945–1947 and 1951.

Kell, "an undemonstrative, no flare type both in and out of uniform," relied on "sheer merit" rather than showmanship. He worked hard at all facets of the game, relying on constant practice rather than natural talent. His unflamboyant style may have caused the Baseball Writers Association to overlook him for the National Baseball Hall of Fame. In 1983 the eighteen-member Veterans Committee elected Kell to Hall of Fame membership. Brooks Robinson,* a player Kell had tutored at third base in 1957 at Baltimore, joined the Hall of Fame the same year. Kell scouted for the Detroit Tigers (AL) from 1971 through 1977 and teamed with former baseball standout Al Kaline* to telecast Detroit Tigers games.

BIBLIOGRAPHY: Detroit *Free Press*, March 11, 1983; Detroit *News*, March 11, 1983; "Detroit's Impossible Kell," *American Magazine*, 151 (March 1951), pp. 106–111; Joe Falls, *Detroit Tigers* (New York, 1975); Gene Karst and Martin J. Jones, Jr., *Who's Who in Professional Baseball* (New Rochelle, NY, 1973); Joseph L. Reichler, ed., *The Baseball Encyclopedia*, 6th ed. (New York, 1985), pp. 1,075–1,076.

Lawrence E. Ziewacz

KELLEY, Joseph James "Joe" (b. 9 December 1871, Cambridge, MA; d. 14 August 1943, Baltimore, MD), player, manager, scout, and coach, was 5 feet, 11 inches tall, weighed 190 pounds, and threw and batted right-handed. In 1891 he began his baseball career with Lowell, MA (NEL), and played twelve games with the Boston (NL) champions and two with Pittsburgh (NL). At Pittsburgh (NL) in 1892, he attracted the attention of Baltimore (NL) manager Ned Hanlon.* Hanlon traded George Van Haltren* to Pittsburgh for Kelley and $2,000. Kelley joined "Wee Willie" Keeler,* John McGraw,* and Hugh Jennings* as part of the Baltimore "Big Four." As Baltimore's center and left fielder from 1892 through 1898, Kelley ranked among NL leaders in slugging and stolen bases and placed second in the NL in stolen bases in 1896.

From 1899 through early 1902, Kelley played under Hanlon with the Brooklyn Superbas (NL). Baltimore, which had joined the new AL, raided Brooklyn to get Kelley back. New York Giants owner John T. Brush bought the Baltimore club in 1902, released its stars from their contracts, and urged those players to jump to the NL. Kelley left to manage Cincinnati (NL), taking "Cy" Seymour* and Mike Donlin* with him. As Cincinnati player-manager, Kelley released catcher Branch Rickey* in 1903 for refusing to play Sunday baseball. Kelley led the Reds to a third place finish in 1904, but was replaced by Hanlon after they dropped to fifth place in 1905. Kelley played for Cincinnati in 1906 and finished his major league career as player-manager for the 1908 Boston Braves (NL). Under Kelley's direction, his clubs won 337 games and lost 321.

During his seventeen-year major league career, Kelley batted .319 in 1,845 games, made 2,242 hits, including 356 doubles and 194 triples (9th best), stole 443 bases, scored 1,426 runs, knocked in 1,193 runs, and compiled a .453 slugging average. He played on championship teams at Boston (1891), Baltimore (1894–1896), and Brooklyn (1899–1900). In post-season play, he participated in four straight Temple Cups for Baltimore (1894–1897). He managed at Toronto (1907, 1909–1914), scouted for the AL New York Yankees (1915–1916), and coached for the NL Brooklyn Dodgers (1926). Kelley married Margaret Mahon, the daughter of prominent Maryland political figure John J. Mahon, and had two sons, Joseph J., Jr., and Ward. In 1971 the Veterans Committee elected him to the National Baseball Hall of Fame.

BIBLIOGRAPHY: Lee Allen, *The Cincinnati Reds* (New York, 1948); "Joe Kelley," *NYT*, August 15, 1943, p. 38; Paul MacFarlane et al., eds., *TSN Official Baseball Guide, 1971* (St. Louis, 1971); John J. McGraw, *My Thirty Years in Baseball* (repr. New York, 1974); Joseph L. Reichler, ed., *The Baseball Encyclopedia*, 6th ed. (New York, 1985), pp. 634, 1,077.

                                                                    Steven P. Savage

KELLY, George Lange "High Pockets" (b. 10 September 1895, San Francisco, CA; d. 13 October 1984, Burlingame, CA), player, coach, and scout, was the seventh of nine children of police captain James and Mary (Lange) Kelly and came from a baseball family. He was a nephew of Bill Lange,* a Chicago (NL) outfielder of the 1890s, and the elder brother of Reynolds "Ren" Kelly, who pitched seven innings for the Philadelphia Athletics (AL) in 1923. He married Helen O'Connor on November 3, 1927, and had three children. Kelly played sandlot baseball for an Owl Drug Company team while attending Polytechnic High School in San Francisco. He left during his senior year to begin his professional baseball career with Victoria (PNL) in 1914. Acquired by the New York Giants (NL) for $15,000 in 1915, the 6 foot, 4 inch, 195 pound Kelly became a regular in 1920. He spent sixteen years in the NL, mainly as first base anchor for great Giants infielders Frank Frisch,* Dave Bancroft,* and Heinie Groh.* Nicknamed "High Pockets," he missed the 1918 season serving in the U.S. Army Air Corps at Kelly Field, TX.

A long-ball hitter, Kelly led the NL in homers in 1921 with 23, twice hit three homers in one game (1923, 1924), and set an NL record in 1924 with seven home runs in six games. He twice led the NL in RBIs with 94 in 1920 and 136 in 1924, knocked in at least 100 runs in four consecutive seasons, and recorded 1,020 lifetime RBIs. By accounting for all the Giants' eight runs, the three-homer splurge in 1924 set an NL record. Kelly hit over .300 for six straight seasons, compiled a career .297 batting average, made 1,778 hits, and belted 337 doubles and 148 round trippers. During the Giants' four World Series appearances in the 1920s, he struck out 23 times and batted only .248. Over the years, manager John McGraw* said, Kelly made "more important hits for me than any player I ever had."

As a first baseman, Kelly is tied for third on the lifetime list for average per-game putouts (10.4) and chances (11.1). He has the second highest single-season mark for putouts (1,759) and the third highest for total chances (1,873), both set in 1920. In 1921 he made a brilliant throw to catch Yankee Aaron Ward sliding into third base and complete a game-ending, World Series winning double play. The right-handed Kelly, a placid, reserved, and adaptable performer, played 108 games at second base in 1925. McGraw wanted to keep his bat in the lineup after newcomer Bill Terry* took over at first base. Kelly even earned one pitching victory in five innings of relief against the Philadelphia Phillies and pitcher Joe Oeschger of longest game fame, in 1917.

Traded to the Cincinnati Reds (NL) in 1927 for Edd Roush,* Kelly moved to the Chicago Cubs (NL) in 1930 and ended his active career with the Brooklyn Dodgers (NL) in 1932. He coached for the NL Reds (1935–1937, 1947–1948) and the NL Boston Braves (1938–1943) and then returned to California as a scout and coach for Oakland (PCL). Off-season, he worked for many years as a machinist for a San Francisco engineering firm and as a ground transport dispatcher at San Francisco International Airport until retirement in 1960. Kelly helped incorporate Millbrae, CA, where he lived for fifty-four years, and served on its first city council in 1948. In 1973 he was named to the National Baseball Hall of Fame.

BIBLIOGRAPHY: Lee Allen, *The Cincinnati Reds* (New York, 1948); Joseph Durso, *The Days of Mr. McGraw* (Englewood Cliffs, NJ, 1969); W. B. Hanna, "Long George Kelly, a True Star of the Diamond," *Baseball Magazine* 37 (August, 1926), p. 411; Gene Karst and Martin J. Jones, Jr., *Who's Who in Professional Baseball* (New Rochelle, NY, 1973) David S. Neft, Richard M. Cohen, and Jordan A. Deutsch, *The Sports Encyclopedia: Baseball* 5th ed. (New York, 1981); Joseph L. Reichler, ed., *The Baseball Encyclopedia*, 6th ed. (New York, 1985), p. 1,078; Lowell Reidenbaugh, *100 Years of National League Baseball* (St. Louis, 1976); Harold Seymour, *Baseball: The Golden Age* (New York, 1971); A. D. Suehsdorf, telephone interviews with George Kelly, July 29, 1983, July 9, 1984.

A. D. Suehsdorf

KELLY, Michael Joseph "King" (b. 31 December 1857, Troy, NY; d. 8 November 1894, Boston, MA), player and manager, began his baseball career with the Troy Haymakers (1873–1875), Paterson, NJ, Olympics (1876), and Columbus, OH, Buckeyes (1877) and started his major league career with Cincinnati, OH (NL) in 1878 and 1879. A versatile athlete who performed at every position including pitcher, Kelly principally played outfield and catcher. He was considered his era's greatest player and number one idol, resulting in the title "King of Baseball."

After joining the Chicago White Stockings (NL) in 1880, Kelly sparked Cap Anson's* NL club to five championships (1880–1882, 1885–1886). Kelly, ranked among baseball's great hitters, also became one of the most daring base stealers of his time. He stole at least 50 bases over four successive years, including a season-high 84 in 1887. His sensational base running and sliding led fans to cheer him on and to yell, "Slide, Kelly, Slide!" Kelly led the NL in doubles (1881–1882) and runs scored (1884–1886), and with .354 and .388 batting averages (1884, 1886). After winning the batting crown, he was sold to Boston (NL) for a record $10,000 in one of the biggest deals of baseball's early history. Chicago fans were so upset that they boycotted their own team except when Boston played there. Besides having a .322 batting average in 1887, Kelly scored six runs in a game against the Pittsburgh Pirates on August 27.

Kelly in 1890 joined many other NL performers in deserting to the newly formed PL. Named player-manager of the Boston (PL) entry, Kelly stole six bases in one game and compiled a .326 batting average. His team captured the PL championship by posting a 81–48 record. In 1891 he was selected player-manager of Cincinnati (AA). After his team finished fifth in the AA, Kelly returned to play for Boston and helped them win two NL titles (1891–1892). Kelly played a few games for the New York Giants (NL) in 1893 at age 35 and then drifted to the minor leagues. In 1894 he managed Allentown, PA (PSL), and later Yonkers (EL).

Kelly performed on eight pennant winners in sixteen major league seasons and compiled a .307 batting average. He played in 1,463 games, batted 5,923 times, scored 1,363 runs, and collected 1,820 base hits, including 360 doubles, 102 triples, and 69 home runs. Kelly, who recorded a .300 or better batting average eight times, was elected to the National Baseball Hall of Fame in 1945. The imaginative, quick-thinking Kelly was credited by Anson with devising the hit-and-run play. He studied the rules, took every advantage, found ways to get around them, and caused the league to make changes. Colorful both on and off the field, Kelly acted with flair and was admired and adored by fans. He wore the finest tailored clothes and the most current styles. American billboards featured this handsome, happy-go-lucky Irishman as the nation's best dressed man. Kelly supplemented his income with off-season stage appearances and authored *Play Ball*. Following his retirement from baseball, he opened a saloon in New York. At age 36, he died of pneumonia en route to Boston to appear in the Palace Theater.

BIBLIOGRAPHY: Gene Karst and Martin J. Jones, Jr., *Who's Who in Professional Baseball* (New Rochelle, NY, 1973); *National Baseball Hall of Fame and Museum Brochure* (Cooperstown, NY, 1974); Lowell Reidenbaugh, *Cooperstown: Where Baseball's Legends Live Forever* (St. Louis, 1983).

John L. Evers

KILLEBREW, Harmon Clayton "Killer" (b. 29 June 1936, Payette, ID), player and announcer, is the youngest of four children of painter and sheriff H. C. Killebrew and Katherine Pearl (May) Killebrew. At Payette High School, he won letters in baseball, football, and basketball, and saw the school eventually retire his uniform number. He enrolled at the College of Idaho, declining an athletic scholarship from the University of Oregon. Senator Herman Welker of Idaho urged Clark Griffith,* owner of the Washington Senators (AL), to scout him. The 6 foot, 195 pound Killebrew was signed to a bonus contract on June 19, 1954, while hitting .847 in a semi-pro league. Under prevailing baseball rules, bonus players were kept on the major league roster for two seasons. This rule may have impeded young Killebrew's progress. In 1954–1955 he batted only 93 times, struck out 34 times, hit a combined .215 with 4 homers, and had defensive troubles.

After the bonus period expired, he was shuttled back and forth between Washington and the minor leagues until 1959. In 1959 Griffith decided that Killebrew was ready for the majors and traded third baseman Ed Yost. Killebrew attracted attention early in the 1959 season when he belted 8 home runs in twelve days. By midseason, he had slugged 28 homers and was chosen for the All-Star team. He finished with 42 home runs to tie for the AL title. Used at third base, the outfield, first base, and eventually as designated hitter, Killebrew played through the 1975 season. He moved in 1961 with Griffith's AL team to Minnesota, where he became the most famous and popular Twins player. He finished his career with the Kansas City Royals (AL) in 1975. Killebrew's home runs remain legendary, many being hit high and deep. He remains the leading right-handed home run hitter in AL history with 573, and ranks fifth on the all-time list. He led the AL in homers five times (tied for the lead twice) and RBIs three times and reached personal highs of 49 home runs and 140 RBIs in 1969, when he won the AL Most Valuable Player Award. Killebrew's home run total exceeded 40 in eight seasons, while his RBIs surpassed 100 nine times. He hit two round trippers in one game 46 times for eighth on the all-time list and connected for three in a game and four in one day in 1963. Eleven of his home runs came with the bases full. He homered every 14.22 at bats, third on the all-time list behind Babe Ruth* and Ralph Kiner.*

Killebrew was selected for thirteen All-Star games, hitting .308 and slugging home runs in the 1961, 1965, and 1971 games. He appeared in two league championship series with Minnesota (1969 and 1970), batting .211 with two homers. He played in the 1965 World Series for the Twins, hitting .286 with a home run against the Los Angeles Dodgers, after missing much of that season with an elbow injury. Although Killebrew's lifetime batting average is only .256, his enormous power made him one of the game's most feared hitters. In 2,435 games, he made 2,086 hits, 290 doubles, 1,283 runs scored, 1,584 RBIs, 1,559 walks (9th), 1,699 strikeouts (7th), and a .509 slugging average. In 8,147 career at bats, he was never asked to sacrifice bunt, a major league record. Killebrew, whose fielding improved after his first few seasons, once led AL first basemen in assists. Killebrew was inducted into the National Baseball Hall of Fame in 1984 and saw his uniform number (3) retired by the Minnesota Twins. The muscular, wide-shouldered Killebrew threw and batted right-handed. Although called "Killer," he is a modest, reserved, religious man. He married Elaine Roberts in October 1955 and has five children, Cameron, Kenneth, Sharon, Kathryn, and Erin. He has worked as a baseball announcer for the Twins, Oakland A's (AL), and California Angels (AL). He resides in Ontario, OR, enjoys hunting and fishing, and maintains an interest in a Boise, ID, insurance and securities firm.

BIBLIOGRAPHY: Wayne J. Anderson, *Harmon Killebrew, Baseball's Superstar* (Salt Lake City, 1965); *CB* (1966), pp. 218–220; *Minnesota Twins Media Guide, 1984*; *The Oregonian*, October 26, 1983, January 11, 12, 1984; Shirley Povich, "Strong Boy of the Twins," *SEP* 235 (September 15, 1962), pp. 54–55; *SI* (June 1, 1959), p. 18 (April 8, 1963), pp. 85ff.; *Time* 84 (August 14, 1964), p. 44.

Phillip P. Erwin

KINER, Ralph McPherran (b. 27 October 1922, Santa Rita, NM), player, executive, and announcer, is the son of baker Ralph Macklin and Beatrice (Grayson) Kiner. He graduated from Alhambra, CA, High School in 1940, and attended Pasadena Junior College from 1940 through 1942. Kiner married tennis star Nancy Chaffee in October 1951 and had three children, but their marriage ended in divorce in 1969. That same year he married Barbara Batchelder. After divorce terminated that union, Kiner married Di Ann Shugart in December, 1982.

Kiner spent the first two years of his professional baseball career (1941–1942) as an outfielder with Albany, NY (EL). He moved to Toronto (IL) in 1943, but was inducted into the U.S. Navy Air Corps after only 43 games and spent the balance of 1943 and all of 1944 and 1945 in military service. He was discharged in time to start the 1946 season with the Pittsburgh Pirates (NL). During that year, he started a home run record that neither Babe Ruth* nor any other slugger has ever equalled. For seven consecutive years, he led or shared the NL lead in home runs. In 1949 he also paced the NL in RBIs with 127. Kiner's most productive home run output came in 1947, when he slugged 51 round trippers and a major league record eight homers in four consecutive games. In two games that year, he made three consecutive home runs. Kiner, who belted 369 major league home runs, remains proudest of being the first National Leaguer to hit over 50 home runs in two seasons (51 in 1947 and 54 in 1949).

From 1946 through 1954, the durable Kiner appeared in 98 percent of his team's scheduled games and excelled as a "gamer." In the 1950 All-Star Game, his ninth inning homer tied the score and enabled his teammates to win the game eventually. At Chicago, a fever of 101° once prevented him from being in the lineup. Upon hearing that the Cubs had gone ahead 10–8 in the seventh inning, Kiner thought he might be needed to pinch-hit and reported to the dugout. He told Pirates manager Billy Meyer, "I have one good swing in me." Kiner's swing produced a game-winning grand slam homer.

Besides being selected four times by *The Sporting News* for its Major League All-Star team, Kiner in 1950 was named NL Player of the Year. During the 1953 season, Pittsburgh traded Kiner to the Chicago Cubs (NL) in a ten-player deal. He was traded to the Cleveland Indians (AL) in November, 1954, and finished his playing career with 113 games there in 1955. In ten seasons, Kiner batted .279 with 1,451 hits, 216 doubles, 971 runs scored, 1,015 RBIs, and 1,011 walks. From 1956 through 1960, he served as general manager of San Diego (PCL). He became a radio announcer for the Chicago White Sox (AL) in 1961 and has announced games over television for the New York Mets (NL) since 1962. In 1975 he was elected to the National Baseball Hall of Fame.

BIBLIOGRAPHY: Martin Appel and Burt Goldblatt, *Baseball's Best: The Hall of Fame Gallery* (New York, 1977); Richard Burtt, *The Pittsburgh Pirates* (Virginia Beach, VA, 1977); John F. Carmichael, *My Greatest Day in Baseball* (New York, 1963); Charles Einstein, *Fireside Book of Baseball* (New York, 1961); Joseph L. Reichler, ed., *The Baseball Encyclopedia*, 6th ed. (New York, 1985), p. 1,086.

Emil H. Rothe

KING, Charles Frederick "Silver" (b. Koenig, 11 January 1867 or 1868, St. Louis, MO; d. 19 May 1938, St. Louis, MO), player, was the third of seven children of bricklayer William and Dora Koenig. He married Stella (Adele, Della) Loring around 1900 and had four children. King turned professional as a pitcher in 1885 with a Jacksonville, IL, team and pitched the following year for pennant-winning St. Joseph (WL). A newspaperman there, struck by King's platinum-blond hair, nicknamed him "Silver." At season's end, he was given a trial by the Kansas City Cowboys (NL) and won one of four decisions. When that franchise folded in 1887, King joined his hometown St. Louis Browns (AA). This proved a difficult year for pitchers as strikes were increased to four while walks were reduced to five balls instead of seven and were scored as hits. The free base for hit batsmen was introduced. The Browns won the AA pennant, as King contributed 34 victories for the first of four consecutive over–30 seasons. In 44 starts, he recorded 43 complete games. In a post-season "Travelling World Series" around the two circuits, the Browns were walloped ten games to five by the NL's Detroit Wolverines. King took three losses and earned only one win.

While St. Louis captured its fourth consecutive pennant in 1888, King reached his zenith to lead the AA with 64 complete games in 65 starts, 45 wins, 21 losses, 585 2/3 innings pitched, 6 shutouts, and a 1.64 ERA. He faced 2,208 batters, allowing 437 hits, and posted a .208 batting average. The Browns again fared poorly against the NL, losing six of a ten-game series with the New York Giants. Exhibitions and post-season games saw King pitch 121 innings, giving him 707 for the season. King compiled a 33–17 record in 1889, hurling 47 complete games in 53 starts. He then jumped to the PL, winning 32 and losing 22 in 56 starts for a fourth place Chicago team and pacing the PL with his 2.69 ERA. He also pitched an unusual losing no-hitter against Brooklyn. Although Chicago was the home team, it elected to bat first. Since Brooklyn led 1–0 in the bottom of the ninth inning and did not bat, King was credited only with an eight-inning no-hitter.

After the Brotherhood collapsed, King returned to the NL in 1891 with Pittsburgh. He was paid the highest salary of his career ($5,000), but slumped to an NL-leading 29 losses against 14 wins for the last place Pirates. King pitched his final iron-man season for New York (NL) in 1892, winning 22 and losing 24 complete games in 47 starts spanning 419 1/3 innings. He split 1893 between New York and Cincinnati (NL), finishing with a meager 8–

10 record. The disgusted King sat out the next two seasons and worked instead at the bricklayer's trade. Washington (NL) coaxed him back, but his great skills had vanished. He won 10 and lost 7 in 1896 and finished with a 7–8 won-lost record in 1897.

His ten-year statistics included 206 victories, 152 defeats, and a 3.18 ERA. He pitched 329 complete games in 371 starts, ranking twenty-eighth on the all-time list. King, a well-built 6 foot, 170 pound right-hander with big hands, relied chiefly on his fastball. He threw the occasional curve, but never mastered the spitter, fadeaway, or other specialties of the next pitching generation. He continued in the contracting business until 1925 and built his own house. He lost all interest in baseball after his retirement and never saw another game.

BIBLIOGRAPHY: Al Kermisch, "From a Researcher's Notebook," *Baseball Research Journal* 9 (1980) p. 50; Paul MacFarlane, ed., *TSN Daguerreotypes of Great Stars of Baseball* (St. Louis, 1981), pp. 158–159; Charles King file, National Baseball Hall of Fame Library, Cooperstown, NY; *Reach's American Association Baseball Guide, 1888* (Philadelphia, PA, 1888); Joseph L. Reichler, ed., *The Baseball Encyclopedia*, 6th ed. (New York, 1985), pp. 1833–1834; Harold Seymour, *Baseball: The Early Years* (New York, 1960); *Spalding's Official Baseball Guide, 1888* (New York, 1888); St. Louis *Post-Dispatch*, June 20, 26, 1938; David Quentin Voigt, *American Baseball*, vol. 1 (University Park, PA, 1983).

A. D. Suehsdorf

KLEIN, Charles Herbert "Chuck" (b. 7 October 1904 or 1905, Indianapolis, IN; d. 28 March 1958, Indianapolis, IN), player and coach, became one of the greatest left-handed sluggers in NL history. After attending Southport (IN) High School, he worked on a construction road gang and hurled around 200 pound ingots in a steel mill. The sturdy 6 foot, 195 pound Klein signed a minor league baseball contract with Evansville (3IL) in 1927 and played less than one and a half seasons in the minors. The Philadelphia Phillies (NL) bought his contract for $5,000 from Fort Wayne (CL), outbidding the New York Yankees. After only 100 games in the minors, he joined the Phillies in July 1928, hit 14 doubles and 11 home runs, and batted .360.

Between 1929 and 1933, he assembled the five greatest years of any left-handed power hitter in NL history. During that stretch, he averaged 36 home runs, 139 RBIs, 131 runs scored, 229 hits, a .635 slugging average, and a .359 batting average. He also established several NL records for a left-handed hitter for one season (1930), including 445 total bases, and 158 runs scored. His 107 extra-base hits (1930) remain a single-season NL record. Klein also knocked in 170 runs that year. The superb defensive right fielder holds the one-season mark with 44 assists in 1930. With the Phillies, Klein won one batting title and Triple Crown, captured four home run championships, and twice was named *The Sporting News* NL Most Valuable Player. Klein's records were downplayed by some baseball authorities because the marks were made in Baker Bowl, with its short 280 foot right field fence. Although admitting that he benefited from the short dimensions, Klein remarked that he "also slammed a lot of drives off that tin that would have been home runs in bigger parks."

In November, 1933, the financially destitute Phils traded Klein to the Chicago Cubs (NL) for shortstop Mark Koenig, pitcher Ted Kleinhans, outfielder Harvey Hendrick, and $65,000. Klein's two and one-half seasons with the Cubs triggered his decline, although he hit .333 with one home run in the 1935 World Series. Upon returning to the Phillies in 1936, he enjoyed one more good season and drove in over 100 runs for the sixth time. He slugged four homers in a July, 1936, game against the Pittsburgh Pirates, the first National Leaguer to accomplish that feat in modern times.

He was sold to the Pirates (NL) in 1939, but returned to the Phillies the next year and completed his playing career as a part-time outfielder and pinch hitter. From 1942 to 1945, he also coached for the Phillies. Klein's career totals included 2,076 hits, 398 doubles, 300 home runs, 1,201 RBIs, and a .320 batting average. He still holds fourteen NL records, including most consecutive years with 200 or more hits (5; 1929–1933), most years with 400 or more total bases (3; 1929–1930, 1932) and most years with 150 or more runs in a season (2; 1930, 1932). After retiring as a player in 1944, he operated a bar until 1947 in the Kensington section of Philadelphia. Suffering from poor health due to heavy drinking, he moved back to Indianapolis in 1947 to live with his brother Edward and his wife. Klein, a semi-invalid the rest of his life, died of a cerebral hemorrhage brought on by heavy drinking. Married in May, 1936, to Mary Torpey, he was divorced twenty years later and had no children. In 1980 Klein was elected to the National Baseball Hall of Fame.

BIBLIOGRAPHY: Stan Baumgartner and Frederick G. Lieb, *The Philadelphia Phillies* (Philadelphia, 1953); Frank Bilovsky and Richard Wescott, *The Phillies Encyclopedia* (Philadelphia, 1984); Philadelphia *Evening Bulletin*, March 29, 1958; Philadelphia *Inquirer*, March 29, 1958.

John P. Rossi

KLEM, William Joseph "Bill," "The Old Arbitrator," "Catfish" (b. Klimm, 22 February 1874, Rochester, NY; d. 1 September 1951, Miami, FL), umpire, was nicknamed "The Old Arbitrator" and was of German descent. Before umpiring, he earned his living briefly as a baseball player, a bartender, and, with his brothers, a bridge-builder. Klem umpired in the CtSL (1902), NYSL (1903), and AA (1904). From 1905 to 1941, he umpired in the NL. He arbitrated in a record eighteen different World Series. Klem absorbed the physical and mental punishment that homeplate umpires underwent daily on a full-season schedule for sixteen consecutive years. From 1941 until his death, he served as the NL chief of umpires. He ranks as baseball's greatest umpire and was elected in 1953 to the National Baseball Hall of Fame, only one of five umpires so honored.

In his difficult and unpopular pursuit, Klem resisted the constant abuse and the lonely life of early day umpires. In his reminiscences, Klem graphically recalled how rowdiness and loneliness gradually affected old-time umpires. John Gaffney became an alcoholic and Hank O'Day a misanthrope, while Bob Emslie developed complete hirsutelessness. Klem repelled these dangers with his immense ego, which enabled him to reign supreme over any threatening players or fans. Klem assessed Judge Kenesaw Mountain Landis'* role in baseball as mere "window-dressing." He banished hotel room loneliness by having his childless wife, Marie Krans, whom he married in 1910, travel about with him during the regular season.

Klem's photos show him as average in size (5 feet, 7½ inches) and weight (157 pounds), smaller than most umpires. Facially slightly piscine, he was nicknamed "Catfish." In vision, voice resonance, accuracy, and knowledge of the rules, Klem ranked with numerous other first-class umpires. In several vital areas, however, Klem made distinctive contributions. He helped all later umpires by asserting control over a game and "drawing the line" against obnoxious, charging players. At Klem's initiative, the dignity of umpires was upgraded via increasing salaries, using multiple arbiters, providing adequate quarters, and compelling managers to bring their lineups to home plate before a game. Klem gave verbal and visual definition to many functions of an umpire, including audible strike calls, handwaving on foul-line calls, and the sweeping gesture of the thumb on the close "out." Enhancing the integrity of umpires, Klem always asserted, "I never missed one in my life!" During his long career, the NL office actually reversed him two or three times. At a ceremony honoring him at the Polo Grounds on September 2, 1949, "The Old Arbitrator" declared, "Baseball to me is not a game; it is a religion."

BIBLIOGRAPHY: Jocko Conlan and Robert Creamer, *Jocko* (Philadelphia, 1967); William J. Klem, "I Never Missed One in My Heart," *Collier's* 127, (March 31, 1951), pp. 30–31ff.; (April 7, 1951), pp. 30–31ff.; (April 14, 1951), pp. 30–31ff.; (April 21, 1951), pp. 30–31 ff.; *NYT*, September 17, 1951; *TSN*, October 12, 1983.

Lowell L. Blaisdell

KLING, John Gradwohl "Johnny," "Noisy" (b. 25 February 1875, Kansas City, MO; d. 31 January 1947, Kansas City, MO), player, manager, and executive, ranked among the great catchers of the early 1900s. The 5 foot, 9½ inch, 160 pound Kling, who threw and batted right-handed, began his career as a pitcher for the Kansas City Schmeltzers. Although only 18 years old, Kling served as team manager, pitcher, and first baseman. In 1895 he briefly joined the Rockford, IL (3IL), club, but then returned to the Schmeltzers. After a short trial with Houston (TL) he signed with St. Joseph, MO (WL) and was discovered there by the Chicago Cubs (NL). Kling remained with the Cubs from 1900 through part of 1911, except for holding out the entire 1909 season.

During this period, Kling performed most of the catching duties and helped lead Chicago to four NL flags (1906–1908, 1910) as a teammate of Joe Tinker,* Johnny Evers,* and Frank Chance.* The Cubs lost the 1906 World Series to the Chicago White Sox, but became world champions in 1907 and 1908. Chicago defeated Detroit both times, as the Tigers won only one game in the two series. The Cubs lost to the Philadelphia A's in the 1910 series, four games to one. Kling either holds or shares several World Series fielding records, including most chances accepted in a six-game Series (56), most double plays in a six-game Series (3), most players caught stealing in a five-game Series (6), most assists in a nine-inning game (4), most passed balls in a nine-inning game (2), and most passed balls in World Series play (5). A fine catcher with a great arm, Kling led NL catchers in fielding average four times (1902–1905) and in putouts six years (1902–1907). Only Roy Campanella* of the Brooklyn Dodgers and Gary Carter* of the New York Mets have equalled this mark. In 1,260 major league games, Kling compiled a .272 batting average and twice (1906, 1912) batted above .300.

During the 1911 season, Kling was traded to the Boston Braves (NL) and became player-manager in 1912. His club won 52 games, lost 101, and finished in eighth place. His final season in the major leagues came in 1913 with the Cincinnati Reds (NL). In thirteen seasons, Kling batted 4,241 times and collected 1,152 base hits, slugging 181 doubles, 61 triples, and 20 home runs, and compiled 513 RBIs. In four World Series, he played in 21 games and batted only .185. Kling became a successful businessman, operating a billiard hall and owning two Kansas City hotels and a dairy farm. He purchased Kansas City (AA) in 1934 and sold the club in 1937 to the New York Yankees.

BIBLIOGRAPHY: Richard M. Cohen, David S. Neft, and Roland T. Johnson, *The World Series* (New York, 1976); Gene Karst and Martin J. Jones, Jr., *Who's Who in Professional Baseball* (New Rochelle, NY, 1973); Joseph L. Reichler, ed., *The Baseball Encyclopedia*, 6th ed. (New York, 1985), pp. 635, 1,091.

John L. Evers

KLUSZEWSKI, Theodore Bernard "Ted," "Klu" (b. 10 September 1924, Argo, IL), baseball and football player and coach, is the son of John and Josephine (Guntarski) Kluszewski. He played football, basketball, baseball, and softball at Argo Community High School. After graduation in 1942, he worked for the Corn Products Refining Company in Argo, playing sandlot football on weekends. Offered a football scholarship by Indiana University, Kluszewski in 1945 won All–Big Ten Conference and honorable mention All-American citations at end. Besides catching game-winning passes against the universities of Michigan and Illinois, he threw a touchdown pass to Pete

Pihos* (FB) on an end-around play to defeat Northwestern University 6–0 and assure the Hoosiers an unbeaten season.

Kluszewski also played baseball at Indiana, where his hitting in the spring of 1945 impressed the Cincinnati Reds (NL), who were training at the Bloomington campus. Following the football season, he signed a professional baseball contract as a first baseman and celebrated by marrying Eleanor Rita Guckel on February 9, 1946. After winning batting titles for Columbia, SC (SAL), in 1946 and Memphis (SA) in 1947 with .352 and .377 marks, Kluszewski became Cincinnati's first baseman in 1948. Kluszewski averaged .294 at the plate and 15 home runs a season for his first five years with the Reds. To stress his intimidating 6 foot, 2 inch, 240 pound physique, he discarded the undershirt of his sleeveless uniform to reveal massive shoulders and biceps. Since Kluszewski's normal batting stroke was through the middle, hurlers pitched him inside in sheer self-defense. After Kluszewski taught himself to pull the ball in 1953, he became an awesome offensive force. From 1953 to 1955, he batted .319, slugged 40, 49, and 47 home runs, and led the NL in homers in 1954 to become one of the most popular Reds ever. An inept fielder initially, he improved vastly and set a major league record for consecutive years leading the league in fielding at first base (1951–1955). On May 1, 1955, his six double plays in an extra-inning game tied a major league record.

In 1957 physical problems began plaguing Kluszewski. Hampered by a slipped disc, he spent most of the 1957 season on the Reds' bench. He was traded to the Pittsburgh Pirates (NL) for Dee Fondy and played there a year and a half before the Chicago White Sox (AL) acquired him. A regular down the stretch, Kluszewski in 1959 helped the White Sox win their first AL pennant in forty years. He hit .391 and batted in a six-game record 10 runs in his only World Series opportunity. He finished his career with the expansion Los Angeles Angels (AL) in 1961. During his career, the left-handed Kluszewski slugged 290 doubles and 279 home runs, batted .298, made 1,766 hits, and knocked in 1,028 runs. He struck out only once every seventeen at bats, a remarkable ratio for a power hitter. Kluszewski, hired in 1970 as a coach by the Reds, became one of baseball's best teachers of hitting.

BIBLIOGRAPHY: Donald Honig, *The October Heroes* (New York, 1979); Earl Lawson, "The Redlegs' One Man Gang," *SEP* 227 (March 19, 1955), pp. 32–33.

Dennis T. "Tom" Chase

KONETCHY, Edward Joseph "Ed," "Big Ed" (b. 3 September 1885, La Crosse, WI; d. 27 May 1947, Fort Worth, TX), player and manager, was the son of Bohemian parents who settled in La Crosse. Konetchy was educated at La Crosse public schools and then worked dipping chocolates in a local candy factory. An outsanding sandlot baseball player, he began his professional career at age 20 with La Crosse (Class D WSL). For La Crosse, he batted .222 his rookie season and .277 his second year. Konetchy's .358 batting average at the start of the 1907 season landed him a contract with the St. Louis Cardinals (NL). The 6 foot, 2½ inch, 195 pound right-hander immediately became the starting Cardinals first baseman and stayed there through the 1913 season. He played with the Pittsburgh Pirates (NL) in 1914, Pittsburgh (FL) in 1915, Boston Braves (NL) from 1916 to 1918, and Brooklyn Robins (NL) in 1919, 1920, and 1921 and spent the last part of his final major league season with the Philadelphia Phillies (NL) in 1921.

An outstanding fielder with excellent range and a powerful throwing arm, he led NL first basemen in percentage seven times and in putouts and assists several times. Konetchy compiled a .281 lifetime batting average, hit over .300 four times, and possessed above average power. He paced the NL in doubles (38) in 1911 and made 10 consecutive hits (1919), an NL record he shares with nine other players. In 2,083 career games, he made 2,148 hits, 344 doubles, 181 triples, 74 home runs, 992 RBIs, and 255 stolen bases. Often cited in box scores as "Koney," he performed at first base the entire major league record 26-inning game for Brooklyn against Boston in 1920. Folowing his baseball career, he pursued business in Fort Worth, TX. He managed Fort Worth Cats (TL) from 1923 to 1939, playing with them from 1925 through 1927. He also piloted his old La Crosse (WSL) team from 1940 to 1942, but returned to Fort Worth as a foreman in the Convair plant during World War II.

BIBLIOGRAPHY: Gene Karst and Martin J. Jones, Jr., *Who's Who in Professional Baseball* (New Rochelle, NY, 1973); *NYT*, May 28, 1947; Joseph L. Reichler, ed., *The Baseball Encyclopedia*, 6th ed. (New York, 1985), p. 1,096.

Robert E. Jones

KOOSMAN, Jerome Martin "Jerry" (b. 23 December 1943, Appleton, MN), player, is the son of farmer Martin William and Lydia (Graese) Koosman. He attended the University of Minnesota, Morris, MN (1960–1961), and the State School of Science, Wahpeton, ND (1961–1962). From 1962 to 1964, Koosman served in the U.S. Army. He married La Vonne Kathleen Sorum in February, 1967, and has three children. The Chaska, MN, resident's prowess as a pitcher on the Fort Bliss Army baseball team impressed the New York Mets (NL), who signed him in 1964 to a professional contract and assigned him to Greenville, SC (WCL). The 6 foot, 2 inch, 225 pound left-hander compiled a mediocre 27–30 won-lost record for several minor league teams—Williamsport, PA (EL) in 1965, Auburn, NY (NYPL) in 1966, and Jacksonville, FL (IL) in 1967—and an unimpressive 0–2 mark for the Mets during his first three seasons (1965–1967). With the Mets in 1968, he won 19 games, posted a 2.08 ERA, captured *The Sporting News* NL Rookie of the Year Award, and tied an NL rookie record for most shutout games

won or tied (8). Beginning in 1967, Koosman and teammate Tom Seaver*
enjoyed several years as baseball's preeminent lefty-righty pitching duo.

In twelve seasons with the Mets (1967–1978), Koosman compiled a 3.09
ERA and a 140–137 record. Twenty-one of those victories came in 1976.
After the Mets traded him to the Minnesota Twins (AL), Koosman in 1979
won 20 games for a second time. He garnered a cumulative 62–53 mark and
3.95 ERA during five AL campaigns with the Twins and Chicago White
Sox (1979–1983). In 1984 he rejoined the NL with the Philadelphia Phillies
and compiled a 14–15 mark. In nineteen major league seasons, he won 222
games, lost 209, struck out 2,556 batters in 3,839 1/3 innings, hurled 33
shutouts, and compiled a 3.36 ERA.

Koosman's 3–0 World Series record includes the "Miracle Mets' " decisive
triumph over the Baltimore Orioles in 1969. Koosman has pitched in two
major league All-Star games (1968, 1969) and three Championship Series
games (1969, 1973, 1983). During the 1968 season, Koosman set a dubious
NL record for a pitcher by striking out 62 times. He led the NL in balks in
1970 and 1975 and surrendered Pete Rose's* 4,000th major league hit in
1984. In December 1985 the Phillies released Koosman.

BIBLIOGRAPHY: Richard M. Cohen, David S. Neft, and Jordan A. Deutsch, *The
World Series* (New York, 1979); Zander Hollander, *The Complete Handbook of Baseball
1979* (New York, 1979); Milwaukee *Journal*, April 14, 1984; Joseph L. Reichler, ed.,
The Baseball Encyclopedia, 6th ed., (New York, 1985), pp. 1,841–1,842; *TSN Official
Baseball Register* (St. Louis, 1984), pp. 252–253; WWA, 1984, 42nd ed. (1982–83), p.
1,859.

Thomas D. Jozwik

KOUFAX, Sanford "Sandy" (b. Sanford Braun, 30 December 1935, Brooklyn, NY), player, instructor, and sportscaster, is the son of Jack and Evelyn
Braun and was an overpowering lefthanded pitcher. After his parents divorced in 1938, his mother, an accountant, married attorney Irving Koufax.
The young Koufax developed into a muscular athlete by playing baseball
and basketball in the schoolyards and Jewish community clubs in Brooklyn
and starred on his high school basketball team there. In 1953 the University
of Cincinnati awarded him a basketball scholarship while he prepared for an
architecture career.

Koufax, however, impressed major league baseball scouts as a pitcher when
he struck out 51 batters in 32 innings for his college team. Despite his limited
baseball background, the Brooklyn Dodgers (NL) in 1954 signed Koufax to
a $20,000 contract containing a $14,000 bonus. Baseball's bonus rule required
that the 19-year-old immediately join the major league squad and remain
there two years. The Dodgers, contending for NL pennants in 1955 and
1956, assigned Koufax to the bench and gave him few opportunities to pitch;

Koufax appeared in 28 games, winning 4 and losing 6 in those seasons. Without minor league training, Koufax remained a raw talent. Although possessing blinding speed and a sharp curveball, he lacked control and pitching technique and finished 1957 with a mediocre 5–4 record in 104 1/3 innings.

Koufax began to pitch regularly for the Dodgers after the team moved to Los Angeles in 1958. Still plagued by control problems, he won 27 contests and lost 30 between 1958 and 1960, occasionally turning in brilliant performances. In 1959 Koufax struck out 18 Chicago Cubs hitters in nine innings and set a two-game major league strikeout record with 31. Pitching delivery changes resulted in an impressive 1961 season, including an 18–15 record, an NL-leading 269 strikeouts in 255 2/3 innings, and only 96 walks. For the next five seasons, Koufax proved a dominating pitcher. In tandem with strong right-hander Don Drysdale,* he led the Dodgers to NL pennants in 1963, 1965, and 1966 and world championships in 1963 and 1965.

Koufax claimed his place among the great baseball pitchers with several stellar accomplishments between 1962 and 1966. He won 111 games and lost 34 decisions, led the NL in ERA each season (averaging under two earned runs per game during this period), paced the NL in strikeouts (1963, 1965, and 1966) and shutouts (3 seasons), and pitched four no-hitters, including a perfect game in 1965. Although winning the Cy Young Award in 1963, 1965, and 1966 and Most Valuable Player Award in 1963, Koufax achieved these feats in pain. In 1963 a circulatory problem deadened the index finger on his pitching hand, causing wags to speak of the million-dollar arm with the ten-cent finger. Traumatic arthritis in his elbow the next year threatened permanent disability and hastened his retirement after the 1966 season. His twelve-year career produced 165 wins and 87 losses, a 2.76 ERA in 397 games, 2,396 strikeouts and 817 walks in 2,324 1/3 innings, 40 shutouts, and a lowly .097 batting average.

In an unprecedented maneuver in 1966, Koufax united with Drysdale in a joint holdout for higher salary and hired an agent to bargain with the Dodgers. The strategy secured Koufax a $130,000 contract and encouraged the use of player agents. Koufax' introspective, bookish manner earned him a reputation as an anti-athlete athlete and disinterested sports hero, views which he rejected in his 1966 autobiography.

After retiring from the game, Koufax worked as a sportscaster for NBC from 1967 to 1972, dealt in real estate, and served as pitching instructor for the Dodgers. He married Anne Widmark, the daughter of actor Richard Widmark, in 1969 and resides in California. In 1971, at age 36, Koufax became the youngest inductee to the National Baseball Hall of Fame.

BIBLIOGRAPHY: Bob Broeg, *Super Stars of Baseball* (St. Louis, 1971); Arnold Hano, *Sandy Koufax: Strikeout King* (New York, 1964); Sandy Koufax and Ed Linn, *Koufax* (New York, 1966); Bill Libby, "The Sophistication of Sandy Koufax," in Tom

Murray, ed., *Sport Magazine's All-Time All-Stars* (New York, 1977); *NYT*, 1963–1966; Mordecai Richler, "Koufax the Incomparable," *Commentary* 42 (November, 1966), pp. 87–89.

Joseph E. King

KUENN, Harvey Edward, Jr. (b. 4 December 1930, Milwaukee, WI), player and manager, is the son of shipping clerk Harvey, Sr., and Dorothy (Wrensch) Kuenn. He graduated from Milwaukee Lutheran High School and attended Luther College. Kuenn transferred to the University of Wisconsin, where he played baseball and basketball. His father, an amateur baseball player-manager, exposed him to the sport at an early age. Kuenn married Dixie Sarchet in October, 1955, and has two children, but that marriage ended in divorce. He married Audrey Cesar in 1974 and owns Cesar's Inn in West Milwaukee. Kuenn's son gave up a promising baseball career to manage the family business.

Kuenn started his professional baseball career as a shortstop with Davenport, IA (3IL), in 1952 and joined the Detroit Tigers (AL) for 19 games late that season. As Detroit's regular shortstop in 1953, he led the AL in hits (209), demonstrated excellent fielding, and earned Rookie of the Year recognition from the Baseball Writers Association and *The Sporting News*. After being shortstop his first three major league seasons, he played other infield positions and the outfield through 1966. In 1956 he was selected shortstop on *The Sporting News* Major League All-Star team. He led the AL in 1959 with a .353 batting average and maintained a .303 career average.

The day before the 1960 season opened, Kuenn was involved in a surprising trade. Detroit traded their 1959 batting champion to the Cleveland Indians (AL) for Rocky Colavito,* who won the 1959 home run crown. Kuenn was traded in early 1961 to the San Francisco Giants (NL) and in early 1965 to the Chicago Cubs (NL). The Cubs sold him in April, 1966, to the Philadelphia Phillies (NL), where he finished his active career that season. In 1,833 career games, he made 2,092 hits, slugged 356 doubles, scored 951 runs, and knocked in 671 runs. In 1967 and 1968 he announced sports for WVTV in Milwaukee. After selling printing supplies for the next two years, he coached for the Milwaukee Brewers (AL) from 1971 to 1982 and managed them from June 2, 1982, through 1983. Kuenn regards with pride winning the 1959 batting title, playing for San Francisco in the 1962 World Series, and managing his native Milwaukee to the AL championship in 1982. Kuenn, with Jim Smilgoff, authored *Big League Batting Secrets* (1958).

BIBLIOGRAPHY: Charles Einstein, ed., *The Third Fireside Book of Baseball* (New York, 1968); Paul MacFarlane, ed., *TSN Daguerreotypes of Great Stars of Baseball* (St. Louis, 1968), pp. 123–124; Joseph L. Reichler, ed., *The Baseball Encyclopedia*, 6th ed. (New York, 1985), pp. 635, 1,102.

Emil H. Rothe

KUHEL, Joseph Anthony "Joe" (b. 25 June 1906, Cleveland, OH; d. 26 February 1984, Kansas City, KS), player and manager, was the son of grocer Carl and Agnes Kuhel. Kuhel, a first baseman, began his professional baseball career at Flint, MI (MOL), in 1924 and starred with Kansas City (AA) from 1928 to 1930. He joined the Washington Senators (AL) at the end of the 1930 season. His unusual career was spent entirely with the Senators and Chicago White Sox (AL), between which he shifted on four occasions. The fast 6 foot, 180 pound Kuhel enjoyed his finest season in 1933, hitting .322 to help the Senators capture the AL pennant. On March 18, 1938, Kuhel was traded to the White Sox for Zeke Bonura, a first baseman who represented Kuhel's antithesis. The left-handed Kuhel fielded adeptly and hit mainly singles, while the right-handed Bonura fielded poorly and demonstrated considerable power. The transaction produced years of debate in both cities.

After hitting .300 in 1939, Kuhel exhibited declining hitting skills. He returned to Washington at the waiver price on November 23, 1943, and enjoyed two excellent seasons, hitting .285 for the second place Senators team in 1945. After batting only .150 in the first 14 games of the 1946 season, Kuhel requested his release and signed again with the White Sox. In early 1947, he became manager of the White Sox' farm club in Hot Springs, AR (CSL). Although mainly known for his fielding, Kuhel compiled impressive batting statistics. He made 2,212 hits in 2,105 games, batted .277, hit 412 doubles, 111 triples, and 131 home runs, knocked in 1,049 runs, and stole 178 bases. Kuhel managed the Senators in 1948 and 1949, when Washington finished last and lost 104 games with particularly weak personnel. Upon being dropped as manager, Kuhel observed, "You can't make chicken salad out of chicken feathers." He managed the Kansas City Blues (AA) in 1950 and thereafter engaged in sales work in the Kansas City area. He married Willette West on October 9, 1930, and had one child, Joseph, Jr.

BIBLIOGRAPHY: George W. Hilton, correspondence with Joseph A. Kuhel, Jr., George W. Hilton Collection, Los Angeles, CA; Joseph L. Reichler, ed., *The Baseball Encyclopedia*, 6th ed. (New York, 1985) pp. 635, 1,102; *TSN*, March 12, 1984; *Who's Who in Baseball, 1947* (New York, 1947).

George W. Hilton

KUHN, Bowie Kent (b. 28 October 1926, Takoma Park, MD), executive, is a descendant of frontiersman Jim Bowie and two Maryland governors. Kuhn, whose father worked in the retail oil business, grew up in Washington, DC, and attended Theodore Roosevelt High School. Besides being president of his senior class, Kuhn substituted on the basketball team and played on the golf team. The basketball squad was coached by later renowned Boston Celtics mentor Arnold "Red" Auerbach* (IS). During summer vacations,

Kuhn worked the scoreboard at Washington Senators' (AL) baseball games in old Griffith Stadium.

Kuhn studied at Franklin and Marshall College and Princeton University, where he received a Bachelor of Arts degree in 1947. He earned his law degree from the University of Virginia in 1950 and joined the law firm of Willkie, Farr, and Gallagher of New York City. Kuhn began to receive baseball assignments at the firm and from the late 1950s through the 1960s served as legal counsel to several baseball teams. In 1968 he represented the NL club owners in negotiations with the Major League Players' Association, which was threatening to strike.

On December 6, 1968, Commissioner of Baseball William D. Eckert* was forced to resign. Michael Burke and Charles Feeney* were the leading candidates to replace Eckert, but the owners selected Kuhn as a compromise. On February 4, 1969, the owners elected Kuhn to a one-year team as Commissioner pro tempore. Kuhn, who faced baseball problems courageously and effectively, coaxed the owners back to the bargaining table and forced a settlement to the pension dispute. Kuhn also commanded certain owners with interests in Las Vegas gambling to sell those interests. On August 13, 1969, the owners signed him to a seven-year contract.

Kuhn's strong and inventive administration fit baseball's needs. He fought to improve and protect the game's integrity. In a few years, however, the situation began to change. The striking down of the old reserve clause by the Players' Association, the shift of power from management to the players' union, and his battles with several owners turned the pendulum against Kuhn. Most observers considered Kuhn the best Commissioner possible under the restrictions imposed by the owners. The severest criticism leveled at Kuhn concerned his decision to keep Willie Mays* and Mickey Mantle* out of baseball after both took jobs with gambling casinos, his voiding in 1979 of Oakland executive Charlie Finley's* sale of three players for $3.5 million, and his failure to affect the 1981 player strike. Kuhn penalized several owners for violations, fining New York Yankees executive George Steinbrenner $250,000. Kuhn also clashed in court with Steinbrenner, Finley, and Atlanta Braves' owner Ted Turner* (OS). One-year suspensions of several players for drug involvement brought repercussions from the Major League Players' Association.

Kuhn survived a crisis the first time his contract came up for renewal in 1975 and received a second term. Although baseball enjoyed unparalleled attendance and lucrative TV contracts under Kuhn, the owners charged that he lacked the business expertise required to lead baseball and were opposed to his revenue-sharing plan. Kuhn's contract expired on August 12, 1983, but the owners could not find a replacement. He agreed to an interim appointment lasting until September 30, 1984. Peter Ueberroth* (OS) was elected Commissioner of Baseball on March 3, 1984, and took office on October 1, 1984.

After sixteen years as Commissioner, Kuhn returned to his New York City law firm. The 6 foot, 5 inch, 240 pound Kuhn, an impressive person and an articulate speaker, lives with his wife, Luisa Hegeler, and four children in Ridgewood, NJ. Kuhn's recreations include golf, gardening, chess, reading, watching Princeton football games, and attending baseball games.

BIBLIOGRAPHY: *CB* (1970), pp. 236–237; *TSN Official Baseball Guide, 1983* (St. Louis, 1983); *TSN Official Baseball Guide, 1984* (St. Louis, 1984); *TSN Official Baseball Guide, 1985* (St. Louis, 1985).

John L. Evers

L

LAJOIE, Napoleon "Nap," "Larry" (b. 5 September 1875, Woonsocket, RI; d. 7 February 1959, Daytona Beach, FL), player, manager, and executive, was the son of day laborer John and Celina (Guertin) Lajoie, both of French-Canadian descent. He married Myrtle Everturk in 1906 and in 1937 became the sixth player selected to the National Baseball Hall of Fame. The happy, laughing, confident, decisive Lajoie excelled as baseball's most graceful infielder and led AL second basemen in fielding six times. Best remembered for his hitting prowess, Lajoie enjoyed his most productive year in 1901 by pacing the infant AL in hits, doubles, home runs, runs scored, RBIs, and slugging percentage and established the AL record batting average of .422. During his major league career, he batted .339, made 3,251 hits (tenth all-time), slugged 648 doubles (sixth all-time), scored 1,504 runs, knocked in 1,599 runs, and won three major league batting titles. His last batting title came with the Toronto Maple Leafs (IL) in 1917, when he compiled a .380 mark in 151 games at age 42.

After leaving Globe Public School following the eighth grade, Lajoie worked in south-central New England mills, became a taxi driver, and played semi-pro baseball in Rhode Island as a catcher and first baseman. In 1896 he began his professional career with Fall River, MA (NEL). After Lajoie batted .429 the first three months, the Philadelphia Phillies (NL) acquired him as a "throw in" in another deal. Lajoie, nicknamed "Larry" by pitcher Bill Taylor, helped solidify the Phillies' infield for over four seasons. Despite his talent and considerable charm, the rather reserved Lajoie seldom received any notoriety there.

In early 1901, Connie Mack* and Clark Griffith* attempted to sign the NL's best players to AL contracts. After losing Lajoie and two teammates, the Phillies owners filed an injunction to prohibit them from playing in Philadelphia. Lajoie's claim that the Phillies violated his constitutional rights and could not prevent him from signing or playing with another team comprised the first official court challenge to major league baseball's reserve clause. The court initially ruled for Lajoie in May 1901, but the Phillies appealed and the State Supreme Court reversed that decision in April 1902. After one season with the fledgling Philadelphia Athletics (AL), Lajoie, Elmer Flick,* and Bill Bernhard were "transferred" by edict of AL president Byron Johnson* to the Cleveland Broncos. Within the first few months, that team was renamed the Naps in honor of Lajoie. Cleveland did not begin using the name Indians until 1915, when Lajoie was traded back to the Athletics.

The 6 foot, 1 inch, 195 pound, right-handed Lajoie often used a special bat with two handles, one higher up for a solid grip on bunts and short-stroked, slashing line drives. This uncommon device worked well against the St. Louis Browns on October 9, 1910, when Lajoie bunted for seven infield hits and swung for a triple in eight at bats. His batting average came within a few ten-thousandths of AL leader Ty Cobb* on that last day of the season. Byron Johnson* awarded the batting title to Cobb, but the official Chalmers Award, an automobile, was presented to both players. Johnson, however, banned Browns manager Jack O'Connor for life from the AL for allegedly ordering a loose defense on Lajoie. In 1981 *The Sporting News* discovered discrepancies in official records, indicating Lajoie as the true batting titlist. Commissioner Bowie Kuhn,* though, ruled that Johnson's decision should stand. Lajoie managed the Cleveland team to a 397–330 record (.546) from 1905 to 1909, but resigned to concentrate on playing. He later managed Toronto (IL) in 1917 and Indianapolis (AA) in 1918 and served briefly as commissioner of the OPL. After working as a tire salesman, he retired to Florida in 1922.

BIBLIOGRAPHY: Alan R. Asnen, interview with Jeff Kernan, August 21, 1984, National Baseball Hall of Fame Library, Cooperstown, NY; Bob Broeg, *Super Stars of Baseball* (St. Louis, 1971); Anthony J. Connor, *Baseball for the Love of It* (New York, 1982); Gene Karst and Martin J. Jones, Jr., *Who's Who in Professional Baseball* (New Rochelle, NY, 1973); Paul MacFarlane, ed., *TSN Daguerreotypes of Great Stars of Baseball* (St. Louis, 1981); Eugene C. Murdock, *Ban Johnson* (Westport, CT, 1982); *NYT*, February 8, 1959; Joseph L. Reichler, ed., *The Baseball Encyclopedia*, 6th ed. (New York, 1985), pp. 635, 1,106; Lawrence S. Ritter, *The Glory of Their Times* (New York, 1966); *TSN*, April 18, 1981; *TSN Baseball Record Book, 1982* (St. Louis, 1982).

Alan R. Asnen

LANDIS, Kenesaw Mountain (b. 20 November 1866, Millville, OH; d. 25 November 1944, Chicago, IL), executive, was the son of Army surgeon Abraham and Mary (Kumler) Landis, and was the first sole Commissioner of Baseball (1920–1944). Named Commissioner in 1920 amid the collapse of the old National Commission and the Chicago "Black Sox" scandal, he ruled baseball with an iron hand. Some argued that he restored the game to respectability. He was named for the June 1864 Civil War battle of Kennesaw Mountain , GA, where his father was wounded. Landis attended Logansport, IN, High School, but never graduated. After enrolling at the YMCA Law

School in Cincinnati, he received his law degree from the Union Law School of Chicago in 1891 and was admitted to the Illinois bar the same year. Landis practiced law in Chicago for the next fourteen years except for a stint from 1893 to 1895 in Washington as private secretary to Secretary of State Walter Q. Gresham. He married Winifred Reed in 1895 and had one son and one daughter.

In 1905 President Theodore Roosevelt named Landis federal judge in the Northern District of Illinois. He attracted national attention in 1907 by fining the Standard Oil Company $29,240,000 for illegal rebating practices, but a higher court overturned the ruling. His hatred for radicals, socialists, and World War I pacifists was reflected in numerous harsh jail sentences. Landis won the sympathy of the baseball establishment in 1915, when the FL antitrust suit against organized baseball was argued in his court. By refusing to render a decision until the FL war was over and the suit was dropped, he preserved organized baseball's unique monopoly status. When the National Commission collapsed in 1920, baseball leaders turned to Landis to restore integrity to the game. He accepted the post of Commissioner on November 12, 1920, but retained his seat on the federal bench until February, 1922. A move to impeach him for not immediately resigning his judgeship failed in the U.S. House of Representatives.

Upon assuming office, Landis demanded and received absolute power. No appeals of his rulings or public criticisms of his actions by owners were permitted. One writer commented, "No man in private life ever enjoyed such power as did Landis," while a federal judge called Landis "legally an absolute despot." Whenever owners challenged the judge's rule, he threatened to quit and the owners backed down. Although zealous in defense of players' rights, Landis in March 1921 barred Philadelphia Phillies pitcher Eugene Paulette for life for consorting with gamblers. In June 1921 he similarly blacklisted Cincinnati Reds pitcher Ray Fisher for negotiating with an "outlaw" team. He also disqualified New York Giants outfielder Benny Kauff, who had been indicted for and acquitted of auto theft. On August 3, 1921, the day after a jury acquitted the eight Chicago "Black Sox" of throwing the 1919 World Series, Landis banished the players permanently from organized baseball. In 1922 he blacklisted Giants pitcher "Shufflin' Phil" Douglas, who in a drunken state had hinted willingness to throw a game. In 1924 he permanently barred Jimmy O'Connell and "Cozy" Dolan for complicity in a bribe plot between the New York Giants and the Phillies. Phillies owner William D. Cox was expelled from the game in 1943 for betting on his own team.

In the last game of the 1934 World Series, Landis ordered from the field hard-hitting St. Louis leftfielder Joe Medwick,* who had been bombarded with fruit and garbage by Detroit fans. The Cardinals won the game and the Series, defusing the controversy over removal of the St. Louis star. Landis could not break up baseball's farm system, which he strongly opposed. He proclaimed as free agents close to 200 players whom he believed parent clubs were "covering up." He also waged unceasing war against baseball personnel with race track connections. Due to dissatisfaction with Landis' autocratic rule, club owners have never granted subsequent commissioners comparable power. Although tough, profane, and opinionated, Landis displayed a warm personal side off the bench. The judge made the dedicatory address officially opening the National Baseball Hall of Fame at Cooperstown, NY, on June 12, 1939, and was elected to the Hall of Fame within a month of his death.

BIBLIOGRAPHY: Gene Karst and Martin J. Jones, Jr., *Who's Who in Professional Baseball* (New Rochelle, NY, 1973); F. C. Lane, "Has Judge Landis Made Good?" *Baseball Magazine* 34 (February, 1925), pp. 393–395, 428–430; Eugene C. Murdock, *Ban Johnson: Czar of Baseball* (Westport, CT, 1982); Harold Seymour, *Baseball: The Golden Age* (New York, 1971); J. G. Taylor Spink, *Judge Landis and Twenty-five Years of Baseball* (New York, 1947); *TSN*, December 6, 1923, November 30, 1944, July 2, 1947.

Eugene C. Murdock

LANGE, William Alexander "Bill," "Little Eva" (b. 6 June 1871, San Francisco, CA; d. 23 July 1950, San Francisco, CA), player, coach, and scout, grew up in the Presidio section of San Francisco as the son of German-American parents. He quit the San Francisco public schools after the eighth grade and soon started his professional baseball career with Port Townsend, WA (1889–1890) and Seattle (1891–1892). Lange performed from 1893 to 1899 for Chicago (NL), where he played center field and served as team captain. After his rookie season, he batted over .300 for six consecutive season and compiled a .330 career average. His .389 average in 1895 remains the season's standard for the franchise. During his seven-year career, he made 1,055 hits, 133 doubles, 79 triples, and 40 home runs, scored 689 runs, and knocked in 578 runs. Although considered of gigantic size then, the 6 foot, 1 inch, 180 pound Lange possessed great speed and still holds the team records for season (84 in 1896) and career (399) stolen bases. His speed, strong arm, and almost reckless abandon made him one of the finest defensive outfielders before 1900.

Lange, with an ever present smile, ranked among the most colorful and popular players of the 1890s. When Lange retired, the Chicago *Tribune* described him as "the most popular man who ever wore a Chicago uniform." His reputation as one of Chicago's "Dawn Patrol Boys," who liked late hours, practical jokes, and women, delighted fans but frustrated the team's puritanical manager, Adrian Anson.* Lange's unusual nickname, "Little Eva," probably derived from his peculiar strut.

Lange quit baseball at the peak of his career. In 1899 the 28-year-old Lange left the game to marry Grace Geiselman of California, whose father forbade her to wed a pro baseball player. Despite numerous attractive offers, Lange refused to return as a player. He coached at Stanford University, scouted for the Cincinnati Reds (NL), and owned a real estate and insurance business in San Francisco until his death. After his first marriage ironically ended in divorce, he married Sarah Griffith in 1925 and had one son, William, Jr. Contemporary sportswriters rated him the equal of National Baseball Hall of Fame outfielders. A. H. Spink, founder and editor of *The Sporting News*, described Lange as "Ty Cobb* enlarged, fully as great in speed, batting skill and base running," while T. H. Murnane of the Boston *Globe* listed the game's best outfielders up to 1914 as Cobb, Joe Jackson,* and Lange.

BIBLIOGRAPHY: Arthur R. Ahrens, "Lange's Classic Catch Re-classified," *Baseball Research Journal* 9 (1980), pp. 87–90; Arthur R. Ahrens and Eddie Gold, *Day by Day in Chicago Cubs History* (West Point, NY, 1982); William E. Akin, "Bare Hands and Kid Gloves: The Best Fielders, 1880–1899," *Baseball Research Journal* 10 (1981), pp. 60–65; Adrian C. Anson, *A Ball Player's Career* (Chicago, 1900); Alfred H. Spink, *The National Game* (St. Louis, 1911).

William E. Akin

LAZZERI, Anthony Michael "Tony," "Poosh 'Em Up" (b. 6 December 1903, San Francisco, CA; d. 6 August 1946, Millbrae, CA), player and manager, was the son of boilermaker Augustin and Julia Lazzeri and grew up in San Francisco's Cow Hollow district. Upon leaving St. Theresa's Catholic School at age 15, the quiet youngster joined his father at the Maine Ironworks in San Francisco. He quickly developed into a lean, hard, 5 foot, 11 inch, 170 pounder and planned a career as a boxer. While playing semi-pro baseball, Lazzeri was signed as an infielder by Salt Lake City (PCL). He debuted professionally in 1922, batting an unimpressive .192 in 45 games. At Salt Lake City in 1925, however, he set PCL records with 60 home runs, 202 runs scored, and 222 RBIs, and compiled a .355 batting average. That winter, the New York Yankees (AL) purchased the powerful infielder for $75,000.

As the Yankees' regular second baseman from 1926 to 1937, the right-handed hitting Lazzeri helped the team capture six AL pennants and five world championships. He seven times drove in over 100 runs and five times surpassed the .300 mark. In 1929 he batted a career-high .354. Against the Chicago Cubs in the 1932 World Series, Lazzeri homered twice in one game. In the 1936 and 1937 World Series he hit a grand slam home run and batted .400 against the New York Giants. He is best remembered, however, for the 1926 World Series, when Grover Cleveland Alexander* struck him out with the bases loaded in the seventh game to help preserve the St. Louis Cardinals' victory. On May 24, 1936, Lazzeri set the AL single-game record with eleven RBIs by hitting a triple and three home runs. Two of those home runs came with the bases filled, a major league record since tied by six others. That same month, he set records for most home runs in three consecutive (6) and four consecutive games (7).

After the 1937 season, he moved to the NL and played for the Chicago
Cubs (1938), Brooklyn Dodgers, and New York Giants (1939). From mid–
1939 through 1943, he played and managed at Toronto (IL), San Francisco
(PCL), Portsmouth, VA (Pil), and Wilkes-Barre (EL). Lazzeri married Maye
Janes in April, 1923, and had one son. After leaving baseball, he operated
a tavern in San Francisco until his death. Lazzeri never led the AL in any
offensive category except strikeouts (96, in 1926), but was considered an
extremely valuable performer for his consistency, coolness under pressure,
and quiet leadership. For his major league career, he batted .292 with 1,840
hits, 334 doubles, 178 home runs, and 1,191 RBIs. He played on the first
AL All-Star team in 1933. Although an epileptic, he was never affected by
the disease on the playing field. The popular Lazzeri attracted thousands of
new fans to baseball from the nation's Italian-American population and became one of the most feared clutch hitters of his time.

BIBLIOGRAPHY: Frank Graham, *The New York Yankees: An Informal History* (New
York, 1943); Gene Karst and Martin J. Jones, Jr., *Who's Who in Professional Baseball*
(New Rochelle, NY, 1973); *NYT*, 1926–1939, August 9, 1946; *TSN*, December 11,
1930.

                                                                            Joseph Lawler

LEACH, Thomas William "Tommy," "the Wee" (b. 4 November 1877,
French Creek, NY; d. 29 September 1969, Haines City, FL), player, manager, and scout, was the third of five children of Nelson Leach, a farmer,
printer, and railroad worker, and Mary (Conway) Leach, both of English
and Irish descent. His family moved to Cleveland when he was age five. He
graduated from Immaculate Conception School and was apprenticed in bi-
cycle repair, painting, and printing. Leach signed with Hanover, PA (CbL),
in 1896 and then played third base with Petersburg, VA (VL). In 1897 he
contracted with Youngstown, OH (ISL), but was released upon being injured
and performed with Geneva, OH (independent). In 1898 he played with
Auburn, NY (NYSL), and was sold to the Louisville Colonels (NL). After
brief seasoning in Worcester, MA (NEL), he played third base at Louisville.
When the Louisville club disbanded in 1900, Leach joined the Pittsburgh
Pirates (NL). He played third base through 1908 and then moved to the
outfield in 1909 because of an injured hip. Leach was traded in 1912 to
Chicago (NL) and moved to Cincinnati (NL) after the 1914 season. He
managed Rochester, NY (IL), in 1916 and then played with Kansas City
(AA), in 1917 and Chattanooga (SA), in 1918. After rejoining Pittsburgh for
the second half of the 1918 season, he performed for Shreveport (TL) in
1919 and Tampa (FSL) from 1920 through 1922.

At 5 feet, 6 inches and 148 pounds, the speedy Leach numbered 274
doubles, 172 triples, and 62 home runs among his 2,144 lifetime hits. His
six home runs topped the NL in 1902, while his 1,355 runs included an NL-

leading 126 in 1909 and 99 in 1913. He batted .269 in 2,155 major league games, playing a prominent role on the 1901, 1902, 1903, and 1909 NL pennant-winning Pittsburgh clubs. In Pittsburgh's 1909 World Series victory over the Detroit Tigers (AL), he hit .320 and scored a Series-leading eight runs.

Leach retired to Haines City, FL, to manage his citrus properties. He helped form the FSL and managed Tampa from 1920 through 1923, Lakeland in 1924, and St. Petersburg for part of 1928. From 1935 to 1941, he scouted for the Boston Braves (NL). He married Augusta Papcke and had one son. After her death, he married Sara Merron Darling in 1910 and had one daughter. Named to at least one All-Decade All-Star team for 1900–1910, "Tommy the Wee" provided swift confirmation of the cliché about good things and small packages.

BIBLIOGRAPHY: Frederick G. Lieb, *The Pittsburgh Pirates* (New York, 1948); Lawrence S. Ritter, *The Glory of Their Times* (New York, 1966).

Luther W. Spoehr

LEEVER, Samuel "The Goshen Schoolmaster" (b. 23 December 1871, Goshen, OH; d. 19 May 1953, Goshen, OH), player and manager, was the fourth of eight children of farmer Edward C. and Ameridith Ardelia (Watson) Leever. After attending the district elementary school and Goshen High School, he taught for seven years before entering professional baseball. He married Margaret Molloy on February 27, 1904; they had no children. Leever signed as a pitcher with Richmond, VA (AtL), in 1897 at the advanced age of 25 and posted a 20–15 record, thus earning a tryout with the Pittsburgh Pirates (NL) the following spring. He reported with a sore arm and was returned to Richmond, where he contributed 14 triumphs to the club's pennant-winning season. Recalled by Pittsburgh in late 1898, he pitched one victory and began a thirteen-year career as a Pirates mainstay.

A sturdy 5 foot, 10½ inch, 175 pound right-hander with a quiet, somber temperament and excellent curve, Leever often was overshadowed by Pittsburgh stalwarts Deacon Phillippe* and Jesse Tannehill.* Nevertheless, he compiled an impressive record with 20 wins in 1899, 22 in 1906, and 25 in 1903. His other outstanding marks included appearing in an NL-leading 51 games in 1899, surrendering a mere two home runs in 232 2/3 innings of pitching in 1900, and recording the NL's best winning percentage of .781 in 1903. In 1902 Pittsburgh won the second of three straight NL pennants by the largest margin in major league history (27½ games), while the Pirates staff achieved 130 complete games in 141 starts. Leever completed 23 of 26 starts, winning 16 games and losing only 7.

Overall, 1903 comprised "The Schoolmaster's" greatest year. He led the NL in winning percentage, ERA (2.06), and shutouts, completed 30 of 34 starts, pitched one of his three career no-hitters, and won two of a remarkable string of six consecutive Pirates shutouts, still a major league record. Leever, however, injured his right shoulder in a trapshooting contest and developed a sore arm for the first World Series ever held, losing twice to the Boston Pilgrims.

Although enjoying respectable seasons through 1908, he managed only six wins against five losses in 1910, and retired that year. His 193 career victories and 101 defeats gave him a .656 winning percentage, third only to Christy Mathewson's* .665 among twentieth century NL pitchers and tenth on the all-time list. In 388 appearances, he completed 241 of 299 starts, struck out 847 batters, and compiled a 2.47 ERA. Leever pitched in 26 games for Minneapolis (AA) in 1911 and, two years later, briefly managed the Covington, KY–Kansas City, MO, franchise of the then independent, not yet outlaw FL. He retired to a seventy acre farm in Goshen, OH, acquired during his playing days and maintained his local reputation as an expert trapshooter.

BIBLIOGRAPHY: Clermont *Sun* (Batavia, OH), May 28, 1953; Richard M. Cohen, David S. Neft, and Jordan A. Deutsch, *The World Series* (New York, 1979); Hugh Fullerton, "Sam Leever's Sad Plight," *Liberty* (July 28, 1928), pp. 71–72; Raymond Gonzalez, "Pitchers Giving Up Home Runs," *Baseball Research Journal* 10 (1981), p. 26; Samuel Leever file, National Baseball Hall of Fame Library, Cooperstown, NY, biographical materials; Frederick G. Lieb, *The Pittsburgh Pirates* (New York, 1948); Paul MacFarlane, ed., *TSN Daguerreotypes of Great Stars of Baseball* (St. Louis, 1981), p. 166; Joseph L. Reichler, ed., *The Baseball Encyclopedia*, 6th ed. (New York, 1985), p. 1,859; Lowell Reidenbaugh, *100 Years of National League Baseball* (St. Louis, 1976); *Sporting Life*, December 1, 1906.

                                                                            A. D. Suehsdorf

LEMON, Robert Granville "Bob" (b. 22 September 1920, San Bernardino, CA), player, manager, scout, and coach, became possibly the most outstanding performer to shift from the infield or outfield to the mound. Lemon, the son of iceman Earl and Ruth Lemon, began playing baseball professionally as an outfielder and shortstop at Springfield, OH (MAL), in 1938, but minor league managers recognized his strong throwing arm and made him a third baseman. In 1941 and 1942, he played a single game at third base for the Cleveland Indians (AL), making one hit in nine times at bat. He played in 1942 at Baltimore (IL) and entered military service that year. On January 14, 1944, he married Jane H. McGee; they had three sons, Jeff, Jim, and Jerry.

Although he had pitched only two innings in the minor leagues, the 6 foot, 180 pound right-handed Lemon became a pitcher on his return to the Indians out of doubt that he had major league batting ability. In 1946 he played 12 games in the outfield and pitched in 32 contests, winning 4 and losing 5. In 1947 he spent only 2 games in the outfield and compiled an 11–5 record in 37 pitching appearances. Thereafter Lemon hurled full-time, rapidly establishing himself as one of the AL's premier right-handers. He won 20 or more games seven times, leading the AL in victories with 23 in 1950 and 1954 and with 18 in 1955. A strong, durable arm allowed him to pace the AL in innings pitched in 1948, 1950, 1952, and 1953, and in complete games in 1948, 1950, 1952, 1954, and 1956. Besides pitching a no-hit game against the Tigers in Detroit on June 30, 1948, Lemon the same year won two of the Indians' four World Series victories over the Boston Braves. In 1954 he lost two World Series games to the New York Giants. Leg and elbow injuries made Lemon ineffective after 1956 and caused him to retire in 1958. Over his career, Lemon compiled a 207–128 record in 460 games with 188 complete games in 350 starts—a remarkable performance given his late conversion to pitching. In 2,850 innings pitched, he struck out 1,277 batters and compiled a 3.23 ERA.

Lemon recorded a lifetime .232 batting average, made 31 pinch hits for a .291 pinch-hitting average, and slugged 37 home runs, one less than the major league record for a pitcher. In 1976 he was elected to the National Baseball Hall of Fame. Lemon managed the Kansas City Royals (AL) from 1970 to 1972 and the Chicago White Sox (AL) in 1977 and early 1978. He served as the New York Yankees (AL) manager twice, from July, 1978, through June, 1979, and from September, 1981, to April, 1982. Although winning AL pennants in 1978 and 1981, on both occasions he was replaced with his immediate predecessor, Billy Martin* and Gene Michael, respectively. In 1978 he became the first manager in AL history to win a pennant after shifting teams during the season. As a major league manager, he compiled 432 wins and 401 losses for a .519 mark. The aplomb with which he accepted discharge as part of managership was noted widely by journalists. Lemon also scouted for Cleveland (1959), Kansas City (1973), and New York Yankees (1982–); coached for Cleveland (1960), the NL Philadelphia Phillies (1961), and the AL California Angels (1967–1970); and AL New York Yankees (1976) and managed Honolulu (PCL) in 1964, Seattle (PCL) in 1965 and 1966, Sacramento (PCL) in 1974, and Richmond, VA (IL) in 1975.

BIBLIOGRAPHY: George W. Hilton, correspondence with Robert G. Lemon, 1984, George W. Hilton Collection, Los Angeles, CA; Joseph L. Reichler, ed., *The Baseball Encyclopedia*, 6th ed. (New York, 1985), pp. 636, 1,861; *TSN Official Baseball Guide, 1940–1983* (St. Louis, 1940–1983); *Who's Who in Baseball*, 53rd ed. (New York, 1958), p. 103.

George W. Hilton

LEONARD, Emil John "Dutch" (b. 25 March 1909, Auburn, IL; d. 17 April 1983, Springfield, IL), player and coach, grew up in central Illinois with parents of Belgian descent and graduated from Auburn High School. The 6 foot, 175 pound, Leonard married Rose Dolenc in May, 1934, and had two sons and one daughter. Leonard, a right-handed hurler, switched clubs frequently because of depressed minor league baseball conditions and the vagaries of his "out" pitch, the knuckleball. His minor league stops included Canton, OH (CL), and Mobile, AL (SA), 1930; St. Joseph, MO (WL), and Springfield-Quincy-Decatur, IL (3IL), 1931; Decatur (3IL), 1932; York, PA (NYPL), most of 1933; and Atlanta (SA), half of 1936 and 1937.

As a major league pitcher, Leonard frequently moved. The Brooklyn Dodgers (NL) employed him in 1934 and 1935 and for parts of 1933 and 1936. From 1938 to 1946, he pitched for the Washington Senators (AL). After the old knuckleballer hurled for the Philadelphia Phillies (NL) in 1947 and 1948, he spent his last years with the Chicago Cubs (NL) through 1953. Leonard pitched eighteen full and two partial major league seasons. He showed great knuckleball skill and outstanding control, proving equally adept in starting and relieving roles. Leonard spent his Dodgers and Cubs years mostly as a reliever and his campaigns with the Senators and Phillies as a starter. Once he led relievers in saves (1935) and won 20 games (1939). Although he pitched for losing teams all but three seasons, he compiled a 191–181 career won-lost record, struck out 1,170 batters, appeared in 640 games, and had a 3.25 ERA. His winning percentage exceeded that of the teams he served by a remarkable 61 points.

Leonard's most memorable victory occurred on October 1, 1944, when he defeated the Detroit Tigers 4–1 to enable the otherwise forlorn St. Louis Browns to win their only AL pennant. Before the game, he spurned a bribe to "throw" the game that far exceeded his annual $14,000 salary. The Illinois native served as a Cubs coach (1954–1956) and for many years conducted baseball clinics from his hometown, Auburn. Heart trouble caused his death.

BIBLIOGRAPHY: *NYT*, April 19, 1983; *TSN*, March 12, 1966, May 2, 1983.

Lowell L. Blaisdell

LEONARD, Walter Fenner "Buck" (b. 8 September 1907, Rocky Mount, NC), player, was a black baseball star never given the opportunity to play in the major leagues. He was elected to the National Baseball Hall of Fame in 1972. The son of a railroad fireman, he left public school at age 14 and worked the next twelve years as a shoeshine boy, mill hand, and for the Atlantic Coast Line Railroad. During this time, he also played semi-pro baseball around Rocky Mount with the Elks and the Black Swans. After losing his job with the railroad in 1933, he found his only job opportunity in professional baseball. This idea initially did not seem too firm. According to Leonard, "I had almost given up baseball. . . . I had just about decided I wouldn't play any more because twenty-five is a pretty good age around here in the semipro lots." Leonard, who still resides in Rocky Mount, eventually completed his high school education, graduating from the American School in Chicago on May 28, 1959, after taking a correspondence course. On

December 31, 1937, he married Sarah Wroten. They remained married until her death on February 22, 1966, and had no children.

In 1933 he signed a professional contract with the Baltimore Stars under manager–first baseman Ben Taylor,* whom Leonard credits with teaching him how to play first base. When the Stars went bankrupt later that year, Leonard joined the Brooklyn Giants. Smoky Joe Williams,* then tending bar in New York, persuaded him to sign with the Homestead Grays for 1934. Leonard remained with the Grays until 1950, when the NNL disbanded. There he teamed with Josh Gibson* to form a formidable offensive combination called the Babe Ruth* and Lou Gehrig* of black baseball. During these years, the Grays won NNL championships nine straight years (1937–1945) and again in 1948. Leonard was selected to play in the Negro league All-Star Game twelve times. In 1953, he batted .333 in 10 games for Portsmouth, VA (Pil).

Leonard played baseball year round, participating in winter league baseball in Puerto Rico, Cuba, and Venezuela between 1935 and 1955. At age 48, he played his last game in 1955. In 1962 he helped organize the Rocky Mount, NC (CrL) club and served as its vice-president. During the winter of 1943, he played on Satchel Paige's* All-Star team against a major league All-Star team in California and batted .500 in eight games. The teams played eight games before Commissioner Kenesaw Mountain Landis* ordered them halted. At least twice during their long careers with the Grays, Leonard and Gibson were approached by major league owners about the possibility of playing major league baseball. Since the Grays played their home games first in Pittsburgh and then in Washington, Pirates owner Bill Benswanger and Senators owner Clark Griffith* naturally approached them first. White owners feared introducing black players into the major leagues, while black management was apprehensive about what it would do to the black baseball leagues. Consequently, no offer was ever made to Leonard and Gibson.

Although statistics from the NNL are sparse, Leonard was clearly a superior hitter and fielder. Many experts contend that Leonard fielded like George Sisler* and Hal Chase* and hit for a high average and with power. John Holway asserts that "Leonard hit over .400 four times, and over .390 six times, the last in 1948 when he hit a league-leading .391 and tied Luke Easter for the league home run crown. His lifetime average was .355 against black big leaguers—and .382 against whites." Eddie Gottlieb* (IS) stated: "Buck Leonard was as smooth a first baseman as I ever saw. In those days, the first baseman on a team in the Negro League often played the clown. They had a funny way of catching the ball so the fans would laugh, but Leonard was strictly baseball: a great glove, a hell of a hitter, and drove in runs."

BIBLIOGRAPHY: Martin Appel and Burt Goldblatt, *Baseball's Best: The Hall of Fame Gallery* (New York, 1977); William Brashler, *Josh Gibson: A Life in the Negro Leagues* (New York, 1978); John Holway, *Voices from the Great Black Baseball Leagues* (New

York, 1975); Robert W. Peterson, *Only the Ball Was White* (Englewood Cliffs, NJ, 1970); Art Rust, Jr., *Get That Nigger off the Field!* (New York, 1976); Red Smith, "Fame on Sixty Cents a Day," *NYT, February 9, 1972*; Jules Tygiel, *Baseball's Great Experiment* (New York, 1983).

Leverett T. Smith, Jr.

LINDSTROM, Frederick Charles "Freddie," "The Boy Wonder," "Lindy" (b. Frederick Anthony Lindstrom, 21 November 1905, Chicago, IL; d. 4 October 1981, Chicago, IL), player, announcer, manager, and coach, was the youngest of five children of plumbing contractor Frederick Lindstrom, Sr., and Mary (Sweeney) Lindstrom. Lindstrom married Irene Kiedaisch, whom he had known since childhood, on February 14, 1928, and had three sons. Charles, the youngest son, caught one game for the Chicago White Sox (AL) in 1958. Fred pitched in the public parks and parochial schools of Chicago, but switched to the infield at Tilden High School there. He transferred to Loyola Academy, where he graduated in 1922 and where former major league pitcher Jake Weimer coached him. After Weimer recommended Lindstrom to New York manager John McGraw,* the Giants (NL) signed him.

Although only 16 years old, Lindstrom hit .304 in 18 games at Toledo (AA) in 1922. After playing for Toledo in 1923, he joined the Giants in 1924. He played very infrequently in 1924 until replacing regular third baseman Heinie Groh,* who injured his knee severely. Lindstrom hit .253 in 52 games, as the Giants won the NL pennant. At 18 years and 2 months of age, he became the youngest player to appear in a World Series game. Lindstrom batted .333 in the 1924 World Series against the Washington Senators, making ten hits altogether and four hits against Walter Johnson* in one game. A ground ball, however, bounced crazily over his head to bring in the Senators' World Series-winning run in the seventh and deciding game.

The 5 foot, 11 inch, 170 pound right-handed Lindstrom, one of his era's best fielding third basemen with a powerful arm and good range, excelled as an outfielder from 1931 through 1936. Hitting still remained his forte. Nicknamed "The Boy Wonder," he hit .358 in 1928 and .379 in 1930 and collected a remarkable 231 hits each season. Lindstrom compiled a .311 batting average, 1,747 hits, 301 doubles, 895 runs scored, and 779 RBIs over thirteen major league seasons. He exhibited sharp wit and spirited independence, and willingly spoke up to his bosses, including the fearsome McGraw. He suffered a major disappointment in June, 1932, when the Giants named Bill Terry* as McGraw's replacement. Lindstrom, who believed he had been promised the job, remained very bitter and was traded to the Pittsburgh Pirates (NL) after the 1932 season. He played with the Pirates (1933–1934), NL Chicago Cubs (1935), and NL Brooklyn Dodgers (1936) before retiring.

After conducting a radio sports program in Chicago in 1937–1938, he managed Knoxville (SA) in 1940–1941 and Fort Smith, AR (WA), in 1942. Lindstrom left organized baseball, but coached the sport at Northwestern University from 1951 to 1954. Subsequently he was named U.S. Postmaster in Evanston, IL, where he remained until his retirement in 1972. In 1976 Lindstrom was elected to the National Baseball Hall of Fame.

BIBLIOGRAPHY: Martin Appel and Burt Goldblatt, *Baseball's Best: The Hall of Fame Gallery* (New York, 1977); Frank Graham, *McGraw of the Giants* (New York, 1944); Fred Stein and Nick Peters, *Day by Day in Giants History* (New York, 1984).

Fred Stein

LLOYD, John Henry "Pop," "Cuchara" (b. 25 April 1884, Palatka, FL; d. 19 March 1965, Atlantic City, NJ), player and manager, was the son of Afro-American parents. Lloyd, whose father died when John was an infant, left grade school to work as a delivery boy. In 1905 Lloyd launched his professional baseball career as catcher for the Macon, GA, Acmes, a team that had no catcher's gear. After being hit by errant balls, he wore a wire basket over his face when catching. That winter Lloyd waited on tables and played baseball in Florida. In 1906 he played second base for the Cuban X-Giants, a Philadelphia black team. They lost to manager Connie Mack's* Philadelphia Athletics (AL) once, although Lloyd made four hits. He spent the next three seasons as shortstop with the Philadelphia Giants, managed by black baseball pioneer Sol White.

Lloyd frequently played in the strong CUWL, often competing with white major leaguers. The Cuban fans adored Lloyd and nicknamed him "Cuchara" (a scoop or shovel), perhaps because of his prominent chin or big hands. His finest performance perhaps came there in November, 1910, against Ty Cobb* of the Detroit Tigers. The Tigers sailed south for several games with the Havana Reds. Although Detroit won the series, Cobb did not steal a base in five games and was outhit by three Reds black stars. Lloyd batted .500 (11 for 22), while Grant Johnson* hit .412 and catcher Bruce Petway hit .388. Cobb finished as the fourth best hitter at .369 and vowed never to compete against blacks again. When the world champion Philadelphia Athletics came to Havana, Lloyd batted three for ten against Chief Bender* and Eddie Plank* and averaged a composite .438 versus top AL pitching. Available figures indicate that he posted a .305 career average off major league competition. In Cuba he enjoyed spectacular seasons with .388, .393, .367, .371 and .362 batting marks and won the 1916 batting crown with the .393 mark.

Lloyd first managed in 1911 and compiled his best record with the 1915 New York Lincoln Stars, who played the Chicago American Giants for the black championship. Each team won five times, as Lloyd paced hitters with a .390 batting average. In 1918 he worked at the U.S. Army Quartermaster Depot in Chicago. A left-handed batter, he played with several top black teams through 1932 and compiled a lifetime .365 to .370 Negro league batting average. His clubs included the Chicago Leland Giants, New York Lincoln Giants, Chicago American Giants (NNL), Brooklyn Royal Giants (ECL), Columbus Buckeyes, Atlantic City Bacharach Giants (ECL), Philadelphia Hilldale Club, and New York Black Yankees. Lloyd helped open Yankee Stadium to black clubs when his Lincoln Giants and the Baltimore Black Sox played the first game there on July 10, 1930.

Following his baseball career, he became a janitor in Atlantic City at the post office and in the school system. Lloyd and his wife Nan had no children, but he loved youngsters and served as the city Little League commissioner. In 1949 the $150,000 John Henry Lloyd Baseball Park was dedicated in Atlantic City. The clean-living, gregarious Lloyd always had kind words for those around him.

Honus Wagner* commented of Lloyd, "They called him the Black Wagner and I was anxious to see him play. . . . after I saw him I felt honored that they would name such a great player after me." Connie Mack stated, "You could put Wagner and Lloyd in a bag together, and whichever one you pulled out you couldn't go wrong." In 1977 Lloyd was elected to the National Baseball Hall of Fame.

BIBLIOGRAPHY: John Holway, "The Black Wagner: John Henry Lloyd," John Holway Collection, Alexandria, VA; Robert W. Peterson, *Only the Ball Was White* (Englewood Cliffs, NJ, 1970).

John Holway and Merl F. Kleinknecht

LOLICH, Michael Stephen "Mickey" (b. 12 September 1940, Portland, OR), player, began his association with organized baseball as the batboy for the Portland Beavers (PCL). His father, Steve, worked for the Portland Park Bureau, while his mother, Margaret, was a secretary for a lumber company. An only child, Lolich starred on his high school baseball team. The 6 foot, 1 inch, 170 pound Lolich, who attended Clark Junior College of Vancouver, WA, is the first cousin of former baseball players Ron and Frank Lolich. Bob Scheffing, then manager of a California minor league team, saw the left-handed Lolich pitch batting practice and recommended him to the Detroit Tigers (AL), who signed the 18-year-old pitcher in 1958 to a three-year contract and a $30,000 bonus.

After working in the minor leagues from 1959 to 1963, he was promoted to the Tigers from Syracuse (IL) in 1963 and compiled a 5–9 win-loss record in 33 appearances. Lolich quickly matured as a pitcher, winning 18 games and losing only 9 the next season and ranking among the best major league pitchers in ratio of strikeouts to bases on balls. From 1964 to 1974, Lolich won at least 14 games per season. He went from the losingest AL pitcher (19) in 1970 to its winningest hurler (25 wins) in 1971. His remarkable 1971 season included AL-leading figures in complete games (29), innings pitched

(376), and strikeouts (308). His 376 innings pitched comprised the highest since Grover Cleveland Alexander's* 388 innings hurled in 1917.

His greatest accomplishments included the 1968 World Series against the St. Louis Cardinals, with his three complete-game victories, a masterful five-hitter in the seventh game, and an overall 1.67 ERA for three games. When Lolich became a consistent, dependable pitcher, his salary rose over the $100,000 level. In 1972 he compiled a 22–14 record and a 2.50 ERA, the second lowest of his sixteen-year career. After two losing seasons with Detroit in 1974 and 1975, Lolich played with the New York Mets (NL) in 1976 and San Diego Padres (NL) in 1978 and 1979. In 1974 Lolich's fastball was clocked at 90.9 miles per hour. During his career, he averaged 7 strikeouts per nine-inning game, won 217 games, lost 191 contests, recorded 2,832 strikeouts, pitched 195 complete games, hurled 41 shutouts, and compiled a 3.44 ERA. Lolich entered private business and owns and operates a family doughnut shop in Lake Orion, MI. He married Joyce Fleenor in November 1964 and has three daughters, Kimberly, Stacy, and Jody Jo.

BIBLIOGRAPHY: Ross Drake, "For Six Boys of Summer Grown Older, the Game Has Ended, but There Is Life after Baseball," *People Weekly* 19 (April 11, 1983), pp. 78, 82; Joe Falls, *Detroit Tigers* (New York, 1975); Lloyd Graybar, "World Series Rarities—The Three-Game Winners," *Baseball Research Journal* 11 (1982), pp. 18–25; Gene Karst and Martin J. Jones, Jr., *Who's Who in Professional Baseball* (New Rochelle, NY, 1973); Edward Kiersh, *Where Have You Gone, Vince DiMaggio?* (New York, 1983); "Mickey Lolich: Just Working at a Job," *Inside Sports* 7 (October, 1984), pp. 58–61.

Douglas A. Noverr

LOMBARDI, Ernest Natali "Ernie," "Schnoz," "Bocci" (b. 6 April 1908, Oakland, CA; d. 26 September 1977, Santa Cruz, CA), player, was a powerful 6 foot, 3 inch, 230 pound right-handed batter who caught for seventeen years in the NL for the Brooklyn Dodgers (1931), Cincinnati Reds (1932–1941), Boston Braves (1942), and New York Giants (1943–1947). Lombardi received a trial with his hometown Oakland club (PCL) but was assigned to Ogden, UT (UIL), and batted .398 in 50 games in 1927. He pounded PCL pitching for .377, .366, and .370 batting averages for Oakland (1928–1930) before joining Brooklyn. The Dodgers, for whom Lombardi batted .297 in 1931, traded him to Cincinnati the following season. He achieved his highest batting average with .343 in 1935, hit .333 and .334 the next two seasons, and led the NL with a .342 mark in 1938. The NL Most Valuable Player that year, Lombardi became only the second catcher to win a batting title. Although his batting average dropped to .287 in 1939, Lombardi slugged 20 home runs and knocked in 85 runs to help lead the Reds to their first of two consecutive NL pennants. He batted .319 in 1940, when Cincinnati captured the world championship by defeating Detroit (AL) in seven games.

In 1942 Cincinnati sold Lombardi to Boston, where he won his second

NL batting crown with a .330 mark to become the only catcher to win two batting championships. After being traded to New York, he caught over 100 games (1943–1945) while batting over .300 twice. Following the 1947 season, the Giants released Lombardi, who closed out his active playing career with Sacramento (PCL) in 1948. Although grounding into the most double plays four different seasons, he compensated for his lack of speed with his power hitting. Lombardi batted over .300 ten times and compiled a .306 lifetime average. An excellent receiver, Lombardi caught over 100 games fourteen consecutive seasons and in five All-Star games. He caught pitching greats Eppa Rixey,* Paul Derringer,* Bucky Walters,* and Johnny Vander Meer, including the latter's consecutive no-hit pitching performances.

In 1,853 career major league games, Lombardi scored 601 runs, knocked in 990 runs, and collected 1,792 hits, 277 doubles, 27 triples, and 190 home runs. He caught 1,542 games and eleven times surpassed 100 hits in a season. Lombardi in 1935 equalled the major league record for most doubles in one game (4) and two years later tied an NL mark by making six hits in six consecutive times at bat. On five occasions, Lombardi made five or more hits in one game. Lombardi, who married Bernice Marie Ayres in June 1944, experienced difficulties after his baseball career. In 1953 he attempted suicide and later was employed by the New York Giants. Embittered over his failure to be elected to the National Baseball Hall of Fame, Lombardi worked as a gas station attendant prior to his death. In 1986 the Veterans Committee elected him to the National Baseball Hall of Fame.

BIBLIOGRAPHY: Paul MacFarlane, ed., *TSN Daguerreotypes of Great Stars of Baseball* (St. Louis, 1971); Frank Stevens, *Baseball's Forgotten Heroes* (Netcong, NJ, 1984); *TSN*, October 15, 1977, p. 51.

John L. Evers

LONG, Herman C. "Germany" (b. 13 April 1866, Chicago, IL; d. 17 September 1909, Denver, CO), player and manager, married Anna Hillock. A contemporary rated Long, a shortstop through most of his sixteen-year career, as "one of the most brilliant infielders the game ever produced." He entered professional baseball in 1887 with Arkansas City (KSL) and Emporia, KS (WL), and reached the majors two years later with Kansas City (AA). Boston (NL) purchased his contract in 1890 for $6,500. Long anchored its infield through the 1902 season, including the championship 1891–1893 and 1897–1898 campaigns. The 5 foot, 8½ inch, 160 pounder fielded brilliantly from the outset. In April, 1890, a reporter, who questioned whether his ability was overrated, confessed,"His brilliant stops would not make him the star player that he is were it not for the fact that he seems to be a remarkably quick man on his feet." A master at handling thrown balls and covering a "vast amount of territory," he was lauded as "the fastest and best playing shortstop in the National League."

Long's fame also came from his batting. This left-handed hitter, who threw right-handed, batted over .300 for four consecutive years (1894–1897) and compiled a career .279 batting average in 1,872 games. He showed both power and speed, slugging 92 career home runs and leading the NL with 12 homers in 1900. Long stole 534 career bases and scored 1,460 runs, topping the NL with 149 in 1893. Long moved to New York (AL) in 1903, but enjoyed little success there and was soon traded to Detroit (AL). After appearing in one game for Philadelphia (NL) the next year, he played for and managed Toledo (AA) in 1904, Des Moines (WL) in 1905, and Omaha (WL) in 1906. In 1905 he guided Des Moines to the WL championship. The intelligent, quick-witted Long ended his baseball career that season, allegedly because of his "love of drink and misdirected generosity." Since Long suffered from consumption, he traveled to Colorado in hopes that the clear, dry air would effect a cure. There he died, virtually penniless and friendless.

BIBLIOGRAPHY: Herman Long file, National Baseball Hall of Fame Library, Cooperstown, NY; Joseph L. Reichler, ed., *The Baseball Encyclopedia*, 6th ed. (New York, 1985), p. 1,133; *Spalding Base Ball Guide*, 1894–1898, 1900 (New York, 1894–1898, 1900).

Duane A. Smith

LOPEZ, Alfonso Ramon "Senor" (b. 20 August 1908, Tampa, FL), player and manager, is the son of Modesto and Faustina Lopez, who emigrated from Madrid to work in the cigar trade. Lopez attended high school in Tampa and at age 16 became a schoolboy celebrity by being selected to catch Walter Johnson* in an exhibition game. Lopez began his professional baseball career with Tampa (FSL) from 1925 to 1926, Jacksonville, FL (SEL), in 1927, and Macon, GA (SAL), in 1928. He joined the Brooklyn Dodgers (NL) for three games in 1928, but was sent to Atlanta (SA) in 1929. For the next six years, the 5 foot, 11½ inch, 165 pound, slightly built right-hander caught in at least 111 games for the Dodgers. Although not a power hitter, Lopez hit above .300 twice. He was traded to the Boston Braves (NL) in December 1935, Pittsburgh Pirates (NL) in June 1940, and Cleveland Indians (AL) in December 1946. In nineteen major league seasons, Lopez played in 1,950 games, batted 5,916 times, and collected 1,547 hits, including 206 doubles, 42 triples, and 52 home runs. He compiled a .261 lifetime batting average, with 613 runs scored and 652 RBIs. Lopez holds the major league record for most games caught during his career (1,918) and the NL record for most games caught (1,861). He tied the NL record for fewest passed balls in one season (none in 1941); shared the NL record of most years catching at least 100 games (12); and caught at least 100 games eight consecutive seasons.

Lopez began his managerial career with Indianapolis (AA) from 1948 to 1950, winning 278 of 460 games. Indianapolis fielded a pennant winner his first season and made two second place finishes. In 1951 Lopez moved to

Cleveland as manager and produced an AL champion three years later. The 1954 Indians compiled 111 victories (AL record) and were rated heavy favorites in the World Series, but lost to the New York Giants in four games. After moving to Chicago (AL) in 1957, Lopez two years later led the White Sox to their first AL title since 1919. Chicago, however, lost the World Series to the Los Angeles Dodgers in six games. Lopez exhibited skill in handling teams with limited talent, as his clubs consistently wielded the best AL pitching. In fifteen full seasons as manager, Lopez saw his team finish either first or second twelve times. Health problems forced Lopez to retire after the 1965 season, but he returned as White Sox manager for brief periods in 1968 and 1969. In seventeen seasons, his teams won 1,422 games and lost only 1,026 contests. Lopez married Evelyn Kearney on October 7, 1939, and had one son, Alfonso Ramon, Jr. In 1977 Lopez was elected to the National Baseball Hall of Fame.

BIBLIOGRAPHY: *CB* (1960), pp. 241–242; Gene Karst and Martin J. Jones, Jr., *Who's Who in Professional Baseball* (New Rochelle, NY, 1973); Lowell Reidenbaugh, *Cooperstown: Where Baseball's Legends Live Forever* (St. Louis, 1983).

John L. Evers

LUNDY, Richard "Dick," "King Richard" (b. 10 July 1898, Jacksonville, FL; d. 5 January 1962, Jacksonville, FL), player, coach, and manager, generally was acclaimed the outstanding Negro baseball league shortstop during the 1920s. His baseball career began with his hometown Jacksonville Duval Giants as a third baseman. He remained with them when they moved north to become the Atlantic City Bacharach Giants in 1916. Lundy then spent the following two seasons in Philadelphia with Ed Bolden's Hilldale club and split 1919 between Atlantic City and the Hilldales. This same year, the Bacharach Giants divided into two teams and based the second squad in New York City. In 1920 Lundy signed contracts with all three teams, but a Philadelphia court eventually awarded him to the New York Bacharachs.

In 1921 Lundy returned to Atlantic City (ECL) and remained there through 1928. He spent 1929 through 1932 with the Baltimore Black Sox (ANL), moved to the Philadelphia Stars (NNL) for 1933, and performed with the Newark Dodgers (NNL) in 1934 and New York Cubans (NNL) in 1935. He played in 1937 with the Newark Eagles (NNL) and then coached and managed them through 1948. The switch-hitting, 5 foot, 10 inch, 180 pound Lundy exhibited a smooth, graceful style of play that resulted in his sobriquet of "King Richard." Offensively, he proved an excellent hitter and base runner with good power. Defensively, he possessed sure hands, wide range, and a strong arm. Available statistics place his career batting average in the .330 range. He hit .289 in Black World Series competition (.325 in 1926 and .250 in 1927) and produced a .341 mark in eight CUWL seasons. Against white major league competition, he batted .344.

The soft-spoken Lundy, a natural leader, served as Atlantic City manager from 1925 through 1928. He led the Giants to ECL titles in 1926 and 1927, but lost both years to manager Dave Malarcher's Chicago American Giants in the Black World Series. Lundy also piloted the Stars, Dodgers, Eagles, and New York Black Yankees. As shortstop of the celebrated 1929 Baltimore infield featuring Jud Wilson* at first, manager Frank Warfield at second, and Oliver Marcelle* at third, he helped the Black Sox capture the ANL crown. In 1933 and 1934 Lundy was selected starting East shortstop for the first two East-West (Negro leagues) All-Star games played and went hitless in seven at bats.

Although only his father's surname is known, he was the son of Millie Ann (La Gere) Lundy. He died from a lingering illness and was survived by his wife, Elese, five daughters, Linda, Sandra, Millie, Barbara, and Elaine, and five sons, Richard Jr., Arnold, Ronald, Maurice, and Frank. He also spent several years as a Red Cap at the Jacksonville, FL, Terminal Station.

BIBLIOGRAPHY: Atlantic City *Press*, October 1–2, 5–7, 9, 11–12, 14–15, 1926; Baltimore *Sun*, August 28, 1977; Chicago *Defender*, October 9, 16, 23, 1926, October 8, 15, 22, 1927; Florida *Times Union*, January 7, 1962; John Holway, "Baltimore's Great Black Team," Baltimore *Sun*, 1977; Robert W. Peterson, *Only the Ball Was White* (Englewood Cliffs, NJ, 1970); Pittsburgh *Courier*, October 8, 15, 1927; James A. Riley, *The All-Time All-Stars of Black Baseball* (Cocoa, FL, 1983).

Merl F. Kleinknecht

LYLE, Albert Walker "Sparky" (b. 22 July 1944, DuBois, PA), player, ranked among modern baseball's premier relief pitchers and is the son of building contractor Albert and Margaret Lyle. Nicknamed "Sparky" by his father, Lyle grew up in Reynoldsville, PA, and played high school football and basketball there. Lyle played sandlot baseball, pitched for an American Legion team, and worked as a manual laborer after graduating from high school. The left-hander signed with the Baltimore Orioles (AL) in 1964 and pitched for Bluefield, WV (ApL), and Fox Cities, WI (ML), before the Boston Red Sox (AL) drafted him the next year. Lyle pitched for Red Sox farm clubs in Winston-Salem (CrL), Pittsfield, MA (EL), and Toronto (IL) until joining the parent club during the 1967 pennant drive. In his rookie season, he appeared in 27 games with a 2.28 ERA. An arm injury, however, kept him out of the 1967 World Series.

Lyle, famous for his slider and sense of humor, developed the former upon the advice of Ted Williams* and the latter at the expense of his teammates. The slider allowed Lyle to become an effective reliever without having an overpowering fastball. Although the 6 foot, 1 inch, 182 pound Lyle experienced modest success in his four and one-half seasons with the Red Sox, he enjoyed his best years following a trade to the New York Yankees (AL) in March 1972. During the 1972 season, he set an AL record with 35 saves and won the Fireman of the Year Award. He also exhibited a zest for club-house pranks. Lyle's best years came in 1974, 1976, and 1977. In 1974 he made 66 appearances, compiled a 9–3 mark, saved 15 games, and compiled a 1.66 ERA. Lyle slumped in 1975, but the following year led the AL with 23 saves. In 1977 he made 72 appearances, won 13 and lost 5, saved 26 games, and paced the AL with a 2.17 ERA in becoming the first AL relief pitcher to win a Cy Young Award. Lyle appeared in three AL Championship Series and three World Series with the Yankees (1976–1978).

Lyle played his last season with the Yankees in 1978. After a feud with owner George Steinbrenner over a lack of playing time, he was traded to the Texas Rangers (AL) in November 1978. Lyle pitched for the Rangers until September 1980, when he was acquired by the Philadelphia Phillies (NL). Lyle remained with Philadelphia until August 1982 and was sold to the Chicago White Sox (AL). The White Sox released him in October 1982. Lyle married Mary Massey in April 1977, and has three children, Dane (by an earlier marriage), Shane, and Scott. Lyle set records for the most innings pitched by a relief pitcher, lifetime (1,390 2/3), most consecutive relief appearances, lifetime (899), and most games by a relief pitcher without a start (899). He concluded his career with 99 wins, 76 losses, 238 saves, and a 2.88 ERA.

BIBLIOGRAPHY: *CB* (1978), pp. 261–263; Sparky Lyle and Peter Golenbock, *The Bronx Zoo* (New York, 1979); *Philadelphia Phillies Press Guide, 1982*; *TSN Baseball Register, 1983* (St. Louis, 1983).

Eric C. Schneider

LYNCH, Thomas J. "Tom," "King of the Umpires" (b. 1859, New Britain, CT; d. 27 February 1924, New Britain, CT), umpire and executive, was the son of Mr. and Mrs. Patrick Lynch, attended local schools, and starred as a catcher in local amateur leagues. He married Minnie Holmes in 1890 and had no children. Lynch umpired in the NL from 1888 to 1899 and officiated the first New York Giants game in 1897. Nicknamed "King of the Umpires" in the 1890s, he often left games when threatened by fans or players (a common occurrence in the game's early days) and did not appear when dissatisfied with the pay. In these and other ways, he contributed materially to the emergence of professionalism in the umpiring corps.

Lynch then managed the Lyceum Theatre, which he had helped found in New Britain in 1893. He became NL president as a compromise candidate in 1909, when the owners disagreed over John Heydler* as temporary president. A dapper man with bushy mustache, Lynch possessed a brusque manner and a strong personality and provided firm leadership at this critical juncture of NL history. His personal traits caused difficulties with the owners, especially when he backed umpires in disputes with managers and players. Owners, dissatisfied by four consecutive losses in the World Series by

NL teams, removed him in 1913. Lynch again managed the Lyceum Theatre and was a prominent leader in the New Britain arts community until his death.

BIBLIOGRAPHY: Gene Karst and Martin J. Jones, Jr., *Who's Who in Professional Baseball* (New Rochelle, NY, 1973); New Britain (CT) *Herald*, February 27, 1924; *NYT*, December 19, 1909, November 19, 20, 1913, February 28, 1924; Harold Seymour, *Baseball: The Early Years* (New York, 1960); Robert Smith, *Baseball* (New York, 1970); Hy Turkin and S. C. Thompson, *The Official Encyclopedia of Baseball*, 5th rev. ed. (New York, 1970).

Charles R. Middleton

LYNN, Fredric Michael "Fred" (b. 3 February 1952, Chicago, IL), player, is the only child of Fredric and Marie Lynn. He grew up in El Monte, CA, and starred in baseball, basketball, and football at El Monte High School. Drafted upon graduation by the New York Yankees (AL) in 1970, he chose instead an athletic scholarship (football initially, but switched to baseball) from the University of Southern California. A baseball All-American selection in 1972 and 1973, the outfielder helped USC to three consecutive College World Series titles and led the nation's collegians in home runs in 1972.

Lynn signed after his junior year with the Boston Red Sox (AL), who drafted him in the second round in 1973. He played at Bristol, CT (EL), in 1973 and Pawtucket, RI (IL), and for a few games at Boston in 1974. In 1975 Lynn enjoyed perhaps the most extraordinary rookie season in recent baseball history, becoming the only player to win both the AL Rookie of the Year and Most Valuable Player awards the same season. The center fielder in 1975 received many awards, including a Gold Glove, Associated Press and United Press International Athlete of the Year, and *The Sporting News* Player of the Year. Besides batting .331, Lynn led the AL in doubles (47, a record for rookies), slugging (.566, the only time a rookie has accomplished that feat), and runs (103), hit 21 home runs, and drove in 105 runs to help Boston capture the AL pennant.

The 6 foot, 1 inch, 185 pound left-hander continued with Boston through the 1980 season, enjoying probably his best all-around campaign in 1979. He won the AL batting title (.333), led the AL in slugging percentage (.637), and achieved personal highs in runs scored (116), hits (177), home runs (39), and RBIs (122). Lynn was traded to the California Angels (AL) in January 1981 and played there through 1984. Following the 1984 season, he entered the free agent draft and signed with the Baltimore Orioles (AL). Through the 1986 season, Lynn appeared in 1,537 games, made 1,632 hits, 336 doubles, and 241 home runs, scored 906 runs, knocked in 926 runs, and batted .292.

Lynn was selected for nine All-Star games from 1975 through 1983, batting .300 with four homers and ten RBIs. His grand slam home run in the 1983 game, the first ever in All-Star competition, earned him the game MVP Award. Lynn's four home runs rank him second to Stan Musial* and tie him with Ted Williams* in All-Star Game history. In 1975 post-season play with the Red Sox, Lynn hit .364 against Oakland in the AL Championship Series and batted .280 with a home run in the 1975 World Series against the Cincinnati Reds. His .611 slugging percentage for California against Milwaukee in the 1982 AL Championship Series stands as the AL playoff record and earned him MVP honors for that series. He has hit safely in all eight of his league Championship Series games.

One of the game's best outfielders, Lynn has won four Gold Glove awards and has succeeded in 76 percent of his basestealing attempts. His best hitting game of his career perhaps came on June 18, 1975, against Detroit, when he hit 3 homers, 1 triple, and 1 single for 16 total bases and 10 RBIs. Lynn married Diane May Minkle in 1974 and has one son, Jason, and one daughter, Jennifer. They reside in Anaheim, CA.

BIBLIOGRAPHY: *Baltimore Orioles Media Guide, 1985*; Peter Bonventre and Sylvester Monroe, "Classic Rookie," *Newsweek* (July 7, 1975), p. 63; *California Angels Media Guide, 1984*; Peter Gammons, "New Big Socker for the Sox," *SI* 50 (May 7, 1979), pp. 47–48; Vin Gilligan, "The Best Is Yet to Come," *Sport* 68 (November, 1979), pp. 91–93ff; Jim Kaplan, "Lynn Had a Grand Time," *SI* 59 (July 18, 1983), pp. 52, 54.

Phillip P. Erwin

LYONS, James "Jimmie," player and manager, exhibited incredible speed and proved an all-around baseball performer typifying Rube Foster's* style of play. A good hitter and an expert drag bunter, he utilized his speed at the plate, in the field, and on the bases. Lyons began his Negro league career in 1911 with the great Lincoln Giants, hitting .450 in limited action for manager John Henry Lloyd's* squad. With Spotswood Poles,* Lyons formed the fastest outfield duo in black baseball history. In an exhibition game against a white all-star team featuring Hall of Fame shortstop Honus Wagner,* the rookie leadoff batter collected two hits against Walter Johnson.* During the 1912 winter season in Cuba, Lyons hit .288. Four years later, he starred for Charles I. Taylor's* champion Indianapolis ABC's.

During World War I, he performed military duty in France with teammate Dave Malarcher and played baseball in the Allied Expeditionary Force league in LeMans, France. Ty Cobb's* brother, a teammate, claimed that Lyons played better than Ty. Returning stateside, Lyons was assigned by Foster to the Detroit Stars to provide better balance for the newly formed NNL. After a short stint, Lyons rejoined Malarcher on the Chicago American Giants (NNL) and helped make them the dominant black baseball team during the early 1920s. Lyons' all-around ability and .350 and .286 batting averages contributed heavily to successive Giants pennants in 1921 and 1922.

Lyons starred for several other teams, including the St. Louis Giants, Brooklyn Royal Giants (ECL), and Cleveland Browns. Lyons closed out his career in 1932 as manager of the Louisville Black Caps (NSL).

BIBLIOGRAPHY: Robert W. Peterson, *Only the Ball Was White* (Englewood Cliffs, NJ, 1970); James A. Riley, *The All-Time All-Stars of Black Baseball* (Cocoa, FL, 1983); James A. Riley, interviews with former Negro league players, James A. Riley Collection, Cocoa, FL.

James A. Riley

LYONS, Theodore Amar "Ted" (b. 28 December 1900, Lake Charles, LA; d. 25 July 1986, Sulphur, LA) player, manager, coach, and scout, was the son of rancher A. F. Lyons. He grew up in Vinton, LA, with two brothers and a sister and played infield for Vinton High School. With plans for law school, he attended Baylor University, made good grades, was elected president of his class, and played on the basketball team. After his baseball coach converted him to a pitcher, Lyons enjoyed exceptional success and abandoned his law plans. On his graduation in 1923, he declined an offer from the Philadelphia Athletics and signed with Charles Comiskey* (whose AL Chicago White Sox trained in Waco) for $300 a month and a $1,000 bonus. Lyons, who never pitched in the minors, joined the White Sox in St. Louis and relieved in the first major league game he ever saw. From 1924 through 1942, he started for the White Sox.

Lyons pitched well for the White Sox, who scarcely contended for the AL pennant and always finished at least eight games out of first place. In his second full year, 1925, he tied for the AL lead with 21 wins for a fifth place team and lost a no-hitter to the Washington Senators by yielding a ninth-inning, two-out single. In 1926 he accomplished a no-run, no-hit game against the Boston Red Sox. Lyons' greatest season perhaps came in 1927, when he compiled a 22–14 record, completed 30 of 34 starts, led the league in innings pitched (307 2/3), and tied for first in wins, for a fifth place club. His career record included 260 wins, 230 losses, and a 3.67 ERA. Although not famed for strikeouts, he walked only 1,121 men in 4,161 innings. Consequently, he pitched very fast games, one taking only an hour and eighteen minutes.

After injuring his arm during spring training in 1931, Lyons lost his fastball and fashioned a second career by perfecting the knuckleball. In 1939 Lyons became a Sunday pitcher for manager Jimmy Dykes* to save his arm and draw crowds. Lyons followed this pattern each year through the 1942 season, and curiously compiled his best marks. During his last four full years, Lyons won 52 and lost 30 for a .634 percentage and completed 72 games out of 85 starts. In his last year (1942) at age 41, the right-hander completed every game started (20), won 14, maintained an AL-leading 2.10 ERA and walked only 26 men in 180 1/3 innings for the sixth place White Sox. After defeating the Cubs in the City Series, he enlisted in the U.S. Marines and served part of his three years in combat duty in the South Pacific. The 5 foot, 11 inch, 200 pound, switch-hitting Lyons often pinch-hit and ranked among the best fielding pitchers of his era. He made the AL All-Star team in 1939 and was elected to the National Baseball Hall of Fame in 1955. In 1940 Chicago honored him with thousands of dollars in gifts, although the White Sox asked people to give only dimes because of Lyons' popularity with children. Lyons, who never married, managed the White Sox to a 185–245 mark for three years (1946–1948), coached for the AL Detroit Tigers (1949–1953) and NL Brooklyn Dodgers (1954), and scouted for the White Sox (1955–1966) before retiring to manage a Louisiana rice plantation with his sister.

BIBLIOGRAPHY: Lee Allen, *The American League Story* (New York, 1952); Martin Appel and Burt Goldblatt, *Baseball's Best: The Hall of Fame Gallery* (New York, 1977); Warren Brown, *The Chicago White Sox* (New York, 1952); Thomas L. Karnes, Interviews and correspondence with Dr. Edward Compere, John B. Conlan, Lew Fonseca, Charles J. Grimm, Yosh Kawana, Robert Kennedy, Thornton Lee, and Edward Prell, 1983–1984, Thomas L. Karnes Collection, Tempe, AZ; Richard Lindberg, *Who's On Third?* (South Bend, IN, 1983); David S. Neft, Richard M. Cohen, and Jordan A. Deutsch, *The Sports Encyclopedia: Baseball*, 5th ed. (New York, 1982); Lowell Reidenbaugh, *Cooperstown: Where Baseball's Legends Live Forever* (St. Louis, 1983).

Thomas L. Karnes

M

McCARTHY, Joseph Vincent "Joe," "Marse Joe" (b. 21 April 1887, Philadelphia, PA; d. 13 January 1978, Buffalo, NY), player and manager, grew up in the Germantown section of Philadelphia and of Irish descent. McCarthy, his era's most successful baseball manager, suffered a broken kneecap as a boy, thwarting a possible major league career. After attending Niagara University, he joined Wilmington, DE (TSL), in 1907 as a shortstop and third baseman. He played with numerous minor league teams through 1921.

After finishing the 1907 season at Franklin, PA (TSL), he performed with the Toledo Mud Hens (AA) from 1908 to 1911 and briefly in 1911 with Indianapolis (AA). In 1912 he was sold to Wilkes-Barre (NYSL) and the next year was appointed manager and achieved a career-high .325 batting average. From 1914 through 1915, he participated with Buffalo (IL). In 1916 he signed with the FL, which collapsed before the season opened. McCarthy instead joined the Louisville Colonels (AA) and in July 1919 became manager there. He closed his playing career in 1921 and managed the Colonels to their first AA pennant. McCarthy, who became known nationally as perhaps the best minor league manager, piloted Louisville in 1925 to another AA pennant.

In 1926 William Wrigley, Jr., chewing-gum millionaire and Chicago Cubs owner, hired McCarthy as manager of his last place NL club. McCarthy sold Grover Cleveland Alexander,* whom he considered uncooperative. Under McCarthy's firm leadership, the Cubs finished fourth in 1926 and 1927, and third in 1928. In 1929 Chicago won the NL pennant and lost the World Series to Connie Mack's* Philadelphia Athletics. Bitter fan disappointment over that World Series loss caused McCarthy to resign in September, 1930. Rogers Hornsby,* whom McCarthy had purchased for the Cubs in 1928, became manager.

McCarthy replaced Bob Shawkey as New York Yankees (AL) manager in 1931. After finishing second in the AL in McCarthy's initial season, the Yankees in 1932 won the AL pennant and defeated the Chicago Cubs in the

World Series. From 1933 through 1935, the Yankees remained in second place. In 1935 Babe Ruth* left the Yankees to join the Boston Braves, giving McCarthy complete control of the club. From 1936 through 1945, McCarthy enjoyed one of the greatest managerial tenures in major league history. Joe DiMaggio* joined the Yankees in 1936 and helped the club clinch the AL pennant on September 9, 1936, the earliest in the league's history to that time. The Yankees overpowered rivals for four AL pennants and World Series titles, drawing heavily upon farm club talent from the Newark Bears (IL) and the Kansas City Blues (AA). The new talent included Phil Rizzuto,* Red Rolfe, and Joe Gordon. The Yankees won 102 games in both 1936 and 1937, 99 games in 1938, and 106 games in 1939. After losing the 1940 pennant, the Yankees captured the 1941 through 1943 pennants, and clinched the 1941 AL pennant on September 4. In the 1943 World Series, the Yankees beat the St. Louis Cardinals in five games and provided McCarthy with his seventh world title in eight seasons. World War II, however, depleted McCarthy's talent following the 1943 season.

McCarthy, beset by a stomach ailment and a personality clash with new Yankees president Larry MacPhail, Sr.,* resigned in 1946. He did not manage in 1947, but the next two seasons piloted the Boston Red Sox (AL). After the Red Sox lost photo-finish pennants to the Cleveland Indians in 1948 and the Yankees in 1949, McCarthy permanently retired in June, 1950.

McCarthy's Yankees teams demonstrated impressive teamwork. Although the team comprised great stars, McCarthy instilled cooperation masterfully in his players. McCarthy, a strict disciplinarian, always reprimanded his players in private and thus earned the utmost respect in return. He remained very close to his players and was disliked by only a few. His .627 winning percentage as a Yankees manager ranked as the best in history. In his twenty-four-year major league managerial career, his clubs won 2,126 games and lost 1,335 (.614), the highest percentage in major league history.

Nicknamed "Marse Joe" by Harry Neily of the Chicago *Evening American*, the 5 foot, 8 inch, 190 pound McCarthy was married in February, 1921, to Elizabeth "Babe" McCave and lived for many years on a sixty-one-acre farm near Buffalo, NY. McCarthy, whose wife died on October 18, 1971, managed seven AL All-Star teams and was elected in 1957 to the National Baseball Hall of Fame. He spent his retirement quietly in his colonial house far from the tumultuous scenes of his Yankees heyday and died from pneumonia.

BIBLIOGRAPHY: Gene Karst and Martin J. Jones, Jr., *Who's Who in Professional Baseball* (New Rochelle, NY, 1973); *NYT*, January 15, 1978; Joe McCarthy, "An Old Yankee Manager Recalls the Joy of His Job," *NYT*, September 25, 1977; Red Smith, "Joe McCarthy," *NYT*, January 22, 1978.

                                                                Arthur F. McClure

**McCARTHY, Thomas Francis Michael "Tommy," "Pudge," "The Kid,"
"Little Mac"** (b. 24 July 1864, South Boston, MA; d. 5 August 1922, Boston,
MA), player, manager, scout, and coach, was the son of liquor dealer Daniel
and Sarah (Healy) McCarthy. Of Irish descent, he graduated from Andrew
Grammar School in 1877 and then worked in the clothing business. On the
Boston sandlots, he starred with the bundle boys, the Actives and Chickering
Piano. In 1884 manager Tim Murnane of Boston in the ill-fated UA discov-
ered the speedy outfielder playing for Emerson Piano (CmA). Not yet age
21, McCarthy was held hitless in his July 10 major league debut by Chicago's
Hugh "One Arm" Daily. For the 1884 season, McCarthy lost all seven
decisions as a pitcher and batted .215 in 53 games.

In the NL with Boston (1885) and Philadelphia (1886–1887), he batted
.184 in 66 contests. McCarthy finished the 1885 season in Haverhill, MA
(NEL), and spent most of 1886 at Providence (EL) and Brockton, MA (NEL),
where he batted an improved .327 in 76 games. After starring on a pennant-
winning Oshkosh (NWL) team in 1887, McCarthy enjoyed a superb spring
series with the St. Louis Whites in 1888. Charles Comiskey* promoted him
to the St. Louis Browns of the major league AA. McCarthy helped the
Browns to their fourth straight AA pennant by batting .274, stealing 93
bases, scoring 107 runs, and leading outfielders with 44 assists and 12 double
plays. On July 17, he batted five for five, stole six bases, and scored three
runs.

During four seasons with the Browns (1888–1891), McCarthy batted .307
and averaged 127 runs scored, 68 stolen bases, and 31 outfield assists. In
1890 he batted .350. A widely respected, "smart" ballplayer, he perfected
the outfield trap play by juggling fly balls to catch base runners. McCarthy's
tactics inspired the "infield fly" and "tag up" rules. He also popularized the
fake bunt, the hit-and-run play, and sign stealing. At 5 feet, 7 inches and
ranging from 145 to 200 pounds, he was nicknamed "Pudge," "The Kid,"
and "Little Mac."

McCarthy enjoyed his greatest fame with the hometown Boston Bean-
eaters, whom he helped win NL championships in 1892 and 1893. Joining
Hugh Duffy* in the "Heavenly Twins" outfield, McCarthy from 1892
through 1895 averaged .304, 109 runs scored, and 40 stolen bases for Boston.
After being sold to Brooklyn (NL), he retired following the 1896 campaign.
The right-handed batting and throwing McCarthy compiled a .292 lifetime
batting average and was elected in 1946 to the National Baseball Hall of
Fame. In 1,275 games, he made 1,496 hits and 192 doubles, scored 1,069
runs, knocked in 665 runs, walked 537 times, and stole 467 bases.

Subsequently he operated a Boston bowling alley and saloon, "Duffy and
McCarthy." Later, he scouted for the NL Cincinnati Reds (1909–1912), NL
Boston Braves (1914, 1917), and AL Boston Red Sox (1920). After managing
the St. Louis Browns briefly in 1890 to 13 wins and 13 losses, he piloted

Newark (IL) in 1918 and coached baseball at Dartmouth, Holy Cross, and Boston colleges. McCarthy was married to Margaret McCluskey, who died in 1897. They had three daughters, Sadie, Edith, and Margaret ("Reta").

BIBLIOGRAPHY: Martin Appel and Burt Goldblatt, *Baseball's Best: The Hall of Fame Gallery* (New York, 1977); John Gruber, "Tom McCarthy," *TSN*, February 12, 1914, p. 8; "Hundreds Mourn for Tom McCarthy, One of Greatest Outfielders of All Time," Boston *Herald*, August 6, 1922, p. B–2; Ken Smith, *Baseball's Hall of Fame* (New York, 1947); "Tom McCarthy, Noted Old Ball Player, Dead," Boston *Evening Globe*, August 5, 1922, p. 8.

James D. Smith III

McCORMICK, Frank Andrew "Buck" (b. 9 June 1911, New York, NY; d. 21 November 1982, Manhasset, NY), player, manager, coach, and scout, was the son of railroad worker Andrew and Ann McCormick. The 6 foot, 4 inch, 210 pound McCormick's physique was well suited for first base, the position he played in the major leagues except for very brief appearances in 1937 at second base and in the outfield. McCormick also excelled at high school and church league basketball in New York City. After attending high school in the Yorkville section of New York, he was invited to major league tryouts with the Philadelphia Athletics, Washington Senators, and New York Giants. McCormick, however, failed to impress scouts enough to sign him to a professional contract. The determined McCormick borrowed $50 from his uncle and took a bus to the Cincinnati Reds' (NL) tryout camp in Beckley, WV. Roderick Wallace,* former major league shortstop and scout, recommended that the Reds sign him. He played first base for Beckley (MAL) in 1934 in his initial pro baseball season. McCormick batted .347 in 120 games and then joined Cincinnati at the end of the campaign. After playing in the minors in 1935, 1936, and part of the 1937 season, he started with Cincinnati from 1938 through 1945. On October 8, 1938, he married Vera Preedy in Hamilton, OH. They had two daughters, Judith and Nancy.

McCormick hit above .300 in five of his eight full seasons with Cincinnati and led NL batters in hits in 1938, 1939, and (tied) 1940, RBIs in 1939, doubles in 1940, and fewest strikeouts (150 games or more) in 1938, 1939, and 1941. He played major roles in Cincinnati's 1939 and 1940 NL pennants and 1940 World Series title over the Detroit Tigers, earning the NL's Most Valuable Player Award in 1940. He was sold to the Philadelphia Phillies (NL) in December, 1945, and played the 1946 season and part of the 1947 season there before being released. He quickly joined the Boston Braves (NL) and batted .354 for the remainder of the 1947 campaign. The following year, he played part-time and assisted the Braves in their NL pennant triumph. From September 26, 1945, through September 23, 1946, he played 138 consecutive games at first base without committing an error. In thirteen major league campaigns, McCormick batted .299, made 1,711 hits, 334 doubles, and 128 home runs, knocked in 954 runs, and struck out only 189 times.

Following the 1948 season, McCormick retired as a player and remained in baseball in other capacities. Besides managing in the minor leagues, he coached, scouted, and conducted tryout camps for Cincinnati and handled television broadcasts of Reds games. Prior to his death, he served as director of group and season ticket sales for the New York Yankees (AL).

BIBLIOGRAPHY: Richard Goldstein, *Spartan Seasons: How Baseball Survived the Second World War* (New York, 1980); Donald Honig, *Baseball When the Grass Was Real* (New York, 1975); Joseph L. Reichler, ed., *The Baseball Encyclopedia*, 6th ed. (New York, 1985), p. 1,177; Ira L. Smith, *Baseball's Famous First Basemen* (New York, 1956).

Albert J. Figone

McCORMICK, James "Jim" (b. 1856, Glasgow, Scotland; d. 10 March 1918, Paterson, NJ), player and manager, became one of baseball's most durable pitchers and ranks tenth in major league complete games with 466. McCormick, the son of James and Rose (Lowrey) McCormick, came to the United States at an early age and grew up in Paterson. In 1873 he and boyhood friend Mike Kelly* helped form a baseball club there. McCormick became the club's pitcher in 1876, and the next year pitched for the Buckeye Club of Columbus. He entered the NL in 1878, pitching 14 games for Indianapolis. The following year, he joined Cleveland (NL) as pitcher and manager.

In his two years as manager, McCormick pitched in over 81 percent of Cleveland's games. In 1879 he won 20 games and lost 40 for his 27–55 sixth place club. The next year, McCormick lowered his ERA .57 points to 1.85. Cleveland raised its batting and fielding averages 9 and 21 points over the previous season and rose to third place with a 47–37 won-lost record. McCormick led NL pitchers with 72 complete games and 45 wins (against 28 losses) and finished second in strikeouts and shutouts.

Although replaced as manager after 1880, McCormick remained Cleveland's leading pitcher until mid-1884. In 1881 and 1882, he again paced the NL in complete games with 57 and 65. His won-lost record slipped to 26–30 in 1881, but he rebounded in 1882 to lead the NL a second time in wins with his 36–29 record. In 1883 McCormick and Cleveland appeared headed for their finest season. McCormick already had won 27 games (losing only 13) when an injured arm sidelined him for the rest of the season. His estimated 1.84 ERA and .675 winning percentage led the NL, but Cleveland slipped from first place to fourth after his injury.

In the midst of a disappointing 19–22 season in 1884, McCormick and two teammates deserted Cleveland for Cincinnati in the outlaw UA. At Cincinnati his fortunes improved, as he led the UA in ERA (estimated 1.54) and shutouts (7), and won 21 of 24 decisions. McCormick returned to the NL with Providence in 1885, but saw little action (1 win, 3 losses) before joining Chicago (NL) in midseason. He helped Chicago win NL pennants that year (20 wins, 4 losses) and the next (31–11), but broke club regulations against drinking and was sold to Pittsburgh. In 494 career games, he compiled a 264–214 record (.552), struck out 1,704 batters in 4,275.2 innings, hurled 33 shutouts, and made a 2.43 ERA.

Following an ineffective season (13 wins, 23 losses) at Pittsburgh (NL) in 1887, McCormick left baseball because he could not gain his release from the club. He operated a cafe for many years in Paterson, retiring a few years before his death from cirrhosis of the liver. McCormick married about 1883 and was survived by a son, James, and a daughter, Mrs. Francis Dunkerly.

BIBLIOGRAPHY: Henry Chadwick Scrapbooks, Albert Spalding Collection, New York Public Library; Mike Kelly, *Play Ball* (Boston, 1888); Paul MacFarlane, ed., *TSN Daguerreotypes of Great Stars of Baseball* (St. Louis, 1981); James McCormick file, National Baseball Hall of Fame Library, Cooperstown, NY; Paterson (NJ) *Evening News*, March 11, 1918; Joseph L. Reichler, ed., *The Baseball Encyclopedia*, 6th ed. (New York, 1985), pp. 1,177–1,178, 1,895–1,896; John C. Tattersall Scrapbooks, National Baseball Hall of Fame Library, Cooperstown, NY.

Frederick Ivor-Campbell

McCOVEY, Willie Lee "Stretch," "Big Mac" (b. 10 January 1938, Mobile, AL), player and executive, was nicknamed "Stretch" and later "Big Mac," and quietly shared the limelight alongside Willie Mays* as the best power hitters in San Francisco Giants (NL) history. The shy first baseman exhibited considerable power during a twenty-two-year NL career spanning three decades from 1959 to 1980. He is tied with Ted Williams* in ninth place on the all-time home run list and led all NL left-handed batters with 521 round trippers. He ranked tenth all-time in home run percentage (6.4) and struck out (1,550) times. In 2,588 career games, he compiled 2,211 hits, 353 doubles, 1,229 runs, 1,555 RBIs, a .270 batting average, and a .515 slugging percentage. Additionally, he holds the NL records for home runs by a first baseman (439), grand slam home runs (18), pinch hit grand slams (3, tied for the major league record), and intentional walks in a single season (45 in 1969). McCovey led the NL in home runs and slugging percentage three times, RBIs twice, and walks once (137 in 1970). He paced the NL in home run percentage five times, including an incredible four consecutive seasons from 1967 to 1970. In 1969 he earned NL Most Valuable Player honors with 45 home runs (9.2 percent of his at bats for the highest major league percentage that season), 126 RBIs, and a remarkable .656 slugging percentage. In his third of six All-Star games, he led the NL in 1969 to a 9–3 victory with two home runs and three RBIs.

A dead pull hitter, McCovey consistently slashed line drives to right field, proved a constant threat to reach the fence, and made numerous marks with his long balls. In 1970 the 6 foot, 4 inch, 198 pound left-hander homered in all twelve NL parks. He slugged three consecutive home runs twice in his career and belted two home runs in the same inning twice. In June, 1977, he hit grand slam and solo homers in the same inning against the defending NL champion Cincinnati Reds. McCovey debuted in the major leagues with four hits in four at bats, including two triples, against Robin Roberts* and earned NL Rookie of the Year honors.

McCovey's path to the major leagues included stops at Sandersville, GA (GSL), in 1955, Danville, VA (CrL), in 1956, Dallas (TL) in 1957, and Phoenix (PCL) in 1958. After beginning the 1959 season at Phoenix, he was called up to the parent Giants' club. Except for briefly returning to the minors with Tacoma (PCL) in 1960, McCovey remained with the Giants through 1973. The San Francisco management rankled fans, however, by trading Mays to the New York Mets (NL) in 1972 and McCovey to the fledgling San Diego Padres (NL) before the 1974 season. Attendance at Candlestick Park in San Francisco declined dramatically following McCovey's departure. McCovey had mediocre performances with the Padres for three seasons before being traded in August 1976 to the Oakland Athletics (AL), for whom he never played. After being invited to spring training by new management, McCovey made the San Francisco Giants roster in 1977, brought back the fans, and helped lead the club back into contention. He retired midway through the 1980 season, joining the Giants' public and community relations staff.

McCovey appeared in only one Championship Series, batting .429 with two home runs and six RBIs against the Pittsburgh Pirates in 1971. In the 1962 World Series, he played a key role against the New York Yankees. Facing Ralph Terry in the second game, he belted a two-run homer to give the Giants a 2–0 victory. McCovey confronted Terry again in the seventh game with two men out, a runner in scoring position, and the club one run behind in the ninth inning. McCovey lined a drive toward right field, but Yankees second baseman Bobby Richardson timed a perfect leap and dramatically ended the Series. McCovey's at bat was discussed repeatedly and even became the subject of a series of "Peanuts" cartoon strips. In 1986 he was elected to the National Baseball Hall of Fame.

BIBLIOGRAPHY: Charles Einstein, *Willie Mays* (New York, 1963); Charles Einstein, *Willie's Time* (New York, 1979); Paul MacFarlane, ed., *TSN Daguerreotypes of Great Stars of Baseball* (St. Louis, 1981); *NYT*, November 21, 1969; Joseph L. Reichler, ed., *The Baseball Encyclopedia*, 6th ed. (New York, 1985), pp. 1,178–1,179.

Alan R. Asnen

McDANIEL, Lyndall Dale "Lindy" (b. 13 December 1935, Hollis, OK), player, is the son of farmer Newell McDaniel and was salutatorian of his senior class at Arnett High School. After attending Oklahoma University and Abilene Christian College for two years, McDaniel signed as a pitcher with the St. Louis Cardinals (NL) for a $50,000 bonus in 1955. Brothers Kerry and Von also signed with St. Louis. Named after aviator Charles Lindbergh, McDaniel pitched in four games for the Cardinals in 1955 without any minor league experience. He hurled an impressive 15–9 season in 1957, but slumped badly the next year and was sent to Omaha (AA). McDaniel switched to the bullpen after having started his first four seasons and rebounded to become one of the best relief pitchers in baseball history. A sidearm pitcher, he also changed his motion to three-quarters.

The Cardinals traded him to the Chicago Cubs (NL) in a multiplayer deal in October 1962. McDaniel pitched with the San Francisco Giants (1966–1968) and found a successful niche with the New York Yankees (AL) in July 1968. He had developed a highly effective forkball by this time and enjoyed some of his most successful years as a Yankee. That year he retired 32 consecutive batters in one period. In 1970 he recorded a career-high 29 saves, but did not lead the AL. In 1973 he hurled a complete game in his first start since 1960. McDaniel finished his twenty-one-year career with the Kansas City Royals (AL) in 1974 and 1975.

In 987 career games, he compiled a 141–119 record, a 3.45 ERA, and 119 relief wins, second behind Hoyt Wilhelm.* He played in 225 NL games without committing an error, an NL record. He was voted the Fireman of the Year by *The Sporting News* in 1960 and 1963, when he led the NL in saves with 26 and 22, respectively. McDaniel led the NL in wins with 15 in 1959 and tied an NL mark by allowing three grand slams in 1963. The father of two boys and a girl, McDaniel married Audrey Kahn on January 24, 1957. A devout Christian, McDaniel manages a Bible Book Store in Kansas City and lectures and publishes on the values of religion, family, and the Bible.

BIBLIOGRAPHY: Bob Broeg, *Redbirds: A Century of Cardinal Baseball* (St. Louis, 1981); Gene Karst and Martin J. Jones, Jr., *Who's Who in Professional Baseball* (New Rochelle, NY, 1973); Richard Marazzi and Len Fiorito, *Aaron to Zuverink* (New York, 1982).

William A. Borst

McGILLICUDDY, Cornelius. See MACK, Connie

McGINNITY, Joseph Jerome "Joe," "Iron Man," "The Blond Giant" (b. 19 March 1871, Rock Island, IL; d. 14 November 1929, Brooklyn, NY), player, coach, manager, and scout, was selected in 1946 to the National Baseball Hall of Fame. The 5 foot, 11 inch, 206 pound right-handed pitcher, who never experienced a losing major league season, was nicknamed "Iron Man" for his staying power and for his off-season work in an iron foundry. Known as the "Blacksmith from Indian Territory" and the "Blond Giant," McGinnity joined Christy Mathewson* and Jack Chesbro* among the era's highest paid players and earned over $5,000 in 1904 at the height of his career. He led the NL in wins five times between 1899 and 1906. In 1904 he recorded a career-high 35 victories and paced the NL with an .814 winning percentage, a 1.61 ERA, 9 shutouts, and 5 saves. The previous season, he had established a major league record by pitching both games on the same day five times and an NL record for pitching most innings in one season (434). He led the NL in appearances seven times between 1900 and 1907, including 55 games in 1903, and in innings pitched five times between 1899 and 1904. In his only World Series performance, McGinnity allowed no earned runs in seventeen innings, but was the victim of poor fielding and emerged with a 1–1 record in the famous "Pitchers' Series" of 1905 against the Philadelphia Athletics.

McGinnity's thirty-six-year professional career began with Montgomery (SA) in 1893 and continued at Kansas City (WL) the next year. After marrying in the midst of a nationwide financial depression, he left pro baseball for three years. McGinnity pitched in a semi-pro league in Decatur, IL, and worked at his father-in-law's iron foundry. A solid 10–3 season at Peoria (WL) in 1898 led the NL's Baltimore Orioles to sign him in 1899. In several financial maneuvers engineered by co-player John McGraw,* McGinnity and fifteen other Orioles were released. Several players, including McGinnity and McGraw, ended up with former Baltimore manager Wilbert Robinson,* pilot of the Brooklyn Superbas (NL). These actions quickly brought the demise of the Baltimore franchise, rumored to be part of a plan by McGraw, Ban Johnson* (then trying to form the AL), and others. McGinnity and McGraw enjoyed a successful season in Brooklyn and played for Baltimore's newly formed AL franchise in 1901. McGinnity, who became involved in the developing feud between McGraw and Johnson, experienced mediocre seasons in 1901 and 1902. In July 1902, he joined McGraw and others in jumping to the New York Giants (NL). McGinnity began a string of six remarkable seasons (1903–1908), rarely equalled in overall domination of the competition. His ten-year major league career ended in 1908 with 247 wins, 144 losses, and a sterling 2.64 ERA. McGinnity completed 314 of 381 starts, struck out 1,068 batters in 3,458.2 innings pitched, and hurled 32 shutouts.

McGinnity joined Newark (EL), as the team owner and manager in 1909, and led the league in games (55), innings pitched (422), and wins (29). He journeyed through the minor leagues as a player-manager for sixteen years with Tacoma, WA (NWL), Venice, CA (PCL), Butte (NWL), Vancouver (PCL), and Danville/Dubuque (MVL), amassing over 200 additional wins. In 1923 he incredibly garnered 15 victories as pitcher/manager at Dubuque at age 52. In 1926 manager Wilbert Robinson hired McGinnity as a pitching instructor and first base coach for the Brooklyn Dodgers (NL). Robinson, who later regretted his choice, remarked, "Every time I give Joe a sign, it's like ringing a fire alarm. I don't know if the players are gettin' the sign, but I know everybody in the park is, including the peanut vendor." After conducting laboratory work for several Brooklyn physicians in 1927, McGinnity scouted for the Dodgers from 1928 until succumbing from cancer the next year. He also coached baseball at Williams College.

McGinnity utilized a sidearm (nearly underhanded) delivery of a most effective rising curveball he nicknamed "Old Sal." In 1908 he was involved in the famous Merkle play that ultimately caused the Giants to lose the NL championship. After Giant Fred Merkle failed to touch second base on what appeared to be the game-winning hit, the Chicago Cubs appealed the play and the game officially was declared a tie. McGinnity claimed to have thrown the actual game ball into the stands. Some observers contended that Mc-Ginnity acted too exuberantly, while others commented that McGinnity shrewdly noticed his teammate's error and that the Cubs had used a spare ball supplied from their dugout. This contest became one of the most controversial baseball games ever played.

BIBLIOGRAPHY: Gordon H. Fleming, *The Unforgettable Season* (New York, 1981); Paul MacFarlane, ed., *TSN Daguerreotypes of Great Stars of Baseball* (St. Louis, 1981); Eugene C. Murdock, *Ban Johnson* (Westport, CT, 1982); *NYT*, October 22, November 15–19, 1929; Joseph L. Reichler, ed., *The Baseball Encyclopedia*, 6th ed. (New York, 1985), p. 1,900; Lowell Reidenbaugh, *Cooperstown: Where Baseball's Legends Live Forever* (St. Louis, 1983); Steven A. Reiss, *Touching Base* (Westport, CT, 1980); Lawrence S. Ritter, *The Glory of Their Times* (New York, 1966); John Thorn, *The Relief Pitcher* (New York, 1979).

Alan R. Asnen

McGRAW, John Joseph "Little Napoleon" (b. 7 April 1873, Truxton, NY; d. 25 February 1934, New Rochelle, NY), player and manager, was the son of Irish-born Civil War veteran John McGraw, who settled in Truxton in 1871. The elder McGraw married Ellen Comerfort and had eight children, four of whom died in infancy. Young John attended a local grade school and worked as a farmhand and candy butcher on the Elmira, Cortland, and Northern Railroad. He married Blanche Sindall in January, 1902, and had no children.

McGraw pitched for the Truxton town team and began his professional baseball career with Olean, NY (NYPL), in 1890. Although an unsuccessful pitcher with Olean, McGraw played well at shortstop and joined Cedar Rapids (3IL) in 1891. In August, 1891, he signed with the Baltimore Orioles (AA) and hit .270 in 33 games. In 1892 the Baltimore club merged into an expanded twelve-team NL. McGraw performed brilliantly for the famous rough-and-ready Orioles through the 1899 season. The scrappy 5 foot, 7 inch, 155 pound McGraw played third base for the Orioles and hit over .320 seven straight seasons, leading the NL twice in both runs and walks. McGraw and teammate "Wee Willie" Keeler* developed the hit-and-run play, one of the Orioles' major innovations. McGraw, who hit .334 in his sixteen-year major league career, managed Baltimore in 1899. After moving to St. Louis

(NL) as a player in 1900, he jumped to the new AL and accepted Ban Johnson's* offer to manage the Baltimore club in 1901. In 1,099 games, he made 1,308 hits, scored 1,026 runs, walked 836 times, stole 436 bases, and knocked in 462 runs.

McGraw feuded with AL founder and president Johnson when the latter consistently backed his umpires in battles with the fiery McGraw. McGraw consequently accepted the offer of owner Andrew Freedman* to manage the New York Giants (NL) in July, 1902. Nicknamed "Little Napoleon," McGraw guided the ineffectual Giants to second place in 1903 and an NL pennant in 1904. The Giants became the most successful NL team for the next thirty years under McGraw's leadership. McGraw engendered high excitement and emotions as manager. Famed sportswriter Grantland Rice* (OS) wrote of McGraw: "His very walk across the field in a hostile town is a challenge to the multitude." Most fans either loved or disliked him intensely, but he helped bolster attendance at baseball games. McGraw stimulated the growth of baseball from the early 1900s until the 1920s, when the lively ball era further elevated the sport's popularity and commercial importance.

Most experts consider McGraw the greatest manager ever. He ranks second only to Connie Mack* in major league games managed (4,879) and in games won (2,840). He captured ten NL pennants and three world championships over thirty seasons with the Giants and guided New York to only two second division finishes. McGraw's managerial genius produced strategic and tactical innovations and attracted and developed superb players. He had continuing impact on the game through the leadership exerted by his players. McGraw's career evoked continuous arguments, fistfights, and controversies with NL presidents, owners, umpires, opposing managers and players, and off-the-field acquaintances. The bon vivant, raconteur, and man of varied non-baseball interests helped downtrodden players.

McGraw demanded unquestioning obedience from his players and strict compliance with curfew rules. His iron-fisted approach succeeded admirably until the mid–1920s, when several players rebelled openly against his long clubhouse diatribes, vicious tongue-lashings, and fines. Not surprisingly, McGraw failed to win another NL pennant from 1925 through June 3, 1932, when he relinquished managerial duties to first baseman Bill Terry.* In 1937 McGraw was elected to the National Baseball Hall of Fame.

BIBLIOGRAPHY: Martin Appel and Burt Goldblatt, *Baseball's Best: The Hall of Fame Gallery* (New York, 1977); Frank Graham, *McGraw of the Giants* (New York, 1944); Joe King, *The San Francisco Giants* (Englewood Cliffs, NJ, 1958); Daniel Okrent and Harris Lewine, eds., *The Ultimate Baseball Book* (Boston, 1979); Lawrence Ritter, *The Glory of Their Times* (New York, 1966); Fred Stein and Nick Peters, *Day by Day in Giants History* (New York, 1984).

Fred Stein

McHALE, John Joseph (b. 21 September 1921, Detroit, MI), player and executive, is the son of John and Catherine (Kelly) McHale and graduated in 1947 from the University of Notre Dame, where he played football two years. The 6 foot, 200 pound McHale joined the Detroit Tigers (AL) organization as a first baseman. Between 1943 and 1948, he performed at first base for Muskegon, MI (MISL), Beaumont, TX (TL), Winston-Salem (CrL), and Buffalo (IL). He played several games with the Detroit Tigers in 1945 and 1947 and made brief appearances in 1943, 1944, and 1948. McHale, who served in the U.S. Navy from 1943 to 1944, threw right-handed and batted left-handed. In 64 major league games, he collected 22 hits, 1 double, 3 home runs, and 12 RBIs, and compiled a .193 batting average. McHale made three pinch-hitting appearances for Detroit against the Chicago Cubs in the 1945 World Series.

After failing to win the regular first base position, McHale moved to the Tigers' front office. Under general managers "Red" Rolfe, Charles Gehringer,* Muddy Ruel, and Spike Briggs, McHale served as assistant director of minor league clubs (1948), assistant farm director (1948–1953), director of minor league clubs (1954–1955), and director of player personnel (1956–1957) before becoming general manager on April 30, 1957. The Milwaukee Braves (NL) made him their vice-president and general manager in early 1959 and named him club president two years later. McHale remained in that position until becoming administrative assistant to the Commissioner of Baseball for the 1967 and 1968 seasons.

In 1968 McHale was appointed president and chief executive officer of the Montreal Expos when the Canadian team entered the NL. Besides serving on the board of directors and continuing as president with the Expos, he has been NL vice-president since 1970. Several months after accepting the Montreal job, McHale was seriously considered for the Commissioner of Baseball position when General William Eckert* was dismissed. McHale, however, later withdrew his application to remain with the Expos. He chairs the Major League Baseball Promotion Corporation and belongs to both baseball's executive council and the board of directors of the Perini Corporation, which formerly owned the Boston and Milwaukee Braves. McHale married Patricia Ann Cameron on February 15, 1947, and has six children, Patricia, John, Kevin, Anne, Brian, and Mary.

BIBLIOGRAPHY: Gene Karst and Martin J. Jones, Jr., *Who's Who in Professional Baseball* (New Rochelle, NY, 1973); Joseph L. Reichler, ed., *The Baseball Encyclopedia*, 6th ed. (New York, 1985), p. 1,185; *WWA*, 39th ed. (1976–1977) p. 2,112.

                                                                                    John L. Evers

McINNIS, John Phalen "Stuffy" (b. 19 September 1890, Gloucester, MA; d. 16 February 1960, Ipswich, MA), player, manager, and coach, batted .308 lifetime and set numerous fielding records for first basemen during a nineteen-year major league career. McInnis was the son of Stephen and Udavilla (Grady) McInnis of Gloucester. His father worked as a caretaker, chauffeur, and assistant chief of the town's fire department. After attending Babson Elementary School, McInnis graduated from Gloucester High, where he played on the baseball team. In 1908 the teenager McInnis jumped from semi-pro baseball to the minors with Haverhill, MA (NEL). The next year, he joined the Philadelphia Athletics (AL) and stayed there through 1917.

After two seasons as a substitute shortstop, he became the regular Philadelphia first baseman in 1911 and joined Eddie Collins*, Jack Barry, and "Home Run" Baker* to form the famed "$100,000 Infield," still considered among the best of all time. During his nine years with the Athletics, McInnis batted below .300 as a regular only one season (.295 in 1916). The Athletics won four AL pennants and captured three world championships by defeating the Chicago Cubs in 1910 and the New York Giants in 1911 and 1913. In the 1914 World Series McInnis and his teammates were swept in four games by the underdog Boston Braves.

McInnis was traded to the Boston Red Sox (AL) in January 1918 and helped them capture the pennant and world championship that year. Another trade sent McInnis to the Cleveland Indians (AL) in December 1921. The 1923 season found him back in Boston, where the Braves (NL) had claimed him on waivers. After being released by the Braves in April, 1925, he signed with the Pittsburgh Pirates (NL) and sparked them to a pennant and World Series victory by batting .368 in 59 games.

As manager of the 1927 Philadelphia Phillies (NL), McInnis completed his major league playing career by appearing in one game and led the team to a last place finish with a 51–103 record. He returned to the NEL in 1928, closing out his player-manager days with the Salem club. From 1929 through 1954, McInnis coached baseball at Norwich University, The Brooks School, and Harvard University. McInnis married Elsie Sherman Dow in 1918 and had one daughter.

Although just 5 feet, 9½ inches tall and 162 pounds, the right-hander became a superb first baseman. A league leader in fielding average five times, putouts three times, and assists twice, he compiled a .991 career average. His records included the major league season marks for highest average (.999), fewest errors (1), and most chances accepted without error (1,300), all in 1921. That same season he played 119 consecutive errorless games, an AL record. Over a two-year span (1921–1922), he played 163 straight games without an error, another major league record. In 20 World Series games, he committed just one error in over 200 chances.

McInnis, although renowned for his glovework, proved a dangerous contact hitter, seldom struck out, and consistently batted at or near the .300 mark throughout his long career. In 2,128 games, he made 2,406 hits, drove in 1,060 runs, and compiled 312 doubles, 101 triples, 20 home runs, 872 runs scored, and 172 stolen bases. His best year came in 1912, when he batted .327, drove in 101 runs, and led the AL in putouts, assists, and double plays.

BIBLIOGRAPHY: Gloucester *Daily Times*, March 4, 1972; Gene Karst and Martin J. Jones, Jr., *Who's Who in Professional Baseball* (New Rochelle, NY, 1973); John McInnis file, National Baseball Hall of Fame Library, Cooperstown, NY; *NYT*, February 17, 1960; Providence *Journal*, February 17, 1960.

Joseph Lawler

MACK, Connie "The Tall Tactician" (b. Cornelius Alexander Mc-Gillicuddy, 22 December 1862, East Brookfield, MA; d. 8 February 1956, Germantown, PA), player, manager, and executive, was the son of Irish immigrants Michael and Mary McGillicuddy. His father fought in the Civil War and worked in the cotton mills and shoe factories around Brookfield. Mack left school as a teenager for a job in the shoe factory to help support his family after his father's death. The tall, lanky 6 foot, 1 inch, 150 pound Mack began an undistinguished baseball playing career in 1884 by catching for Meriden, CT (CtL) and caught for Hartford, CT (NECSL) in 1885 and (EL) in 1886. Between 1886 and 1889, he played for Washington (NL). Although known more for his defensive than hitting skills, he jumped to Buffalo (PL) in 1890 and enjoyed his most active year as a player (123 games) there. Mack performed with Pittsburgh (NL) from 1891 to 1896 and became playing manager in 1894 partly because of his reputation as a tricky catcher who distracted hitters by talking and tipping their bats. From 1894 to 1896, Mack managed Pittsburgh to a 149–134 won-loss record. He compiled a lifetime .245 batting average with 659 hits, 391 runs, and 265 RBIs. Mack was married twice: in 1887 to Margaret Hogan, who died in 1892 and had children Roy, Earle, and Margaret; and in 1910 to Katherine A. Hallahan, who had Mary, Connie, Jr., Ruth, Rita, and Elizabeth.

A friendship with Byron Johnson* won Mack the managing job at Milwaukee (WL) from 1897 to 1900, when the former granted Ben Shibe* and Mack the Philadelphia franchise in the new AL. The part-owner of the Athletics and manager for a record fifty years, Mack symbolized the game's striving for respectability and a public image of gentlemanly conduct on and off the field. He provided that model through his abstemious habits, mild manners, devotion to family, and conservative managing style. Mack always remained a shrewd businessman, who enticed members from the crosstown Phillies to build his team and kept a tight rein on player salaries. Mack played collegian Eddie Collins* in the majors under a false name, costing the latter his amateur standing at Columbia University.

Known as "The Tall Tactician," he built and dismantled great A's teams. Mack's clubs won four AL pennants and three World Series between 1910 and 1914 by combining good pitching and the "$100,000 infield," led by Collins and "Home Run" Baker.* Refusing to meet higher salaries offered to team members by the upstart FL, Mack sold his stars in 1915. The A's consequently dropped into last place from 1915 through 1921. The AL pennant returned to Philadelphia between 1929 and 1931 and world championships came in 1929 and 1930, due to Mack's impressive blend of power pitcher Lefty Grove* and sluggers Al Simmons,* Jimmie Foxx,* and Mickey Cochrane.* Once again, however, he broke up a winning combination, claiming operating losses from the Great Depression. Mack reportedly commented that good teams, with high-paid stars, proved less profitable than his poor ones. He retired from managing after the 1950 season, leaving a record of nine AL pennants, five World Series championships, seventeen cellar finishes, and first place among managers in total games (7,878), wins (3,776), and losses (4,025) for a .484 mark.

Remembered for wearing street clothes on the bench and waving his scorecard to give directions, Mack appeared aloof and taciturn. He earned the respect of players with his gentle and patient manner, a style often contrasted earlier with the pugnacious ways of New York Giants manager John J. McGraw.* He proved a keen judge of playing talent and a skillful handler of diverse personalities, ranging from college stars Collins, Eddie Plank,* and Chief Bender,* to the man-child Rube Waddell,* who won 130 games for the A's between 1902 and 1907. Mack adjusted to the changing style of the game, building great teams in both the dead and live ball eras. Philadelphia honored Mack for his service to the city with the prestigious Bok Award in 1930. In 1937 Mack was named to the National Baseball Hall of Fame.

BIBLIOGRAPHY: Bob Considine, "Mister Mack," *Life* 25 (August 9, 1948), pp. 92–98; Frederick G. Lieb, *Connie Mack* (New York, 1945); Connie Mack, *My Sixty-six Years in the Big Leagues* (Philadelphia, 1950); Jerome C. Romanowski, *The Mackmen* (Upper Darby, PA, 1979); Wilfrid Sheed, "Mr. Mack and the Main Chance," in Daniel Okrent and Harris Lewine, eds., *The Ultimate Baseball Book* (Boston, 1979); John R. Tunis, "Connie Mack: First Citizen of Philadelphia," *Atlantic Monthly* 166 (August, 1940), pp. 212–216.

Joseph E. King

McKEAN, Edward John "Ed," "Mack" (b. 6 June 1864, Grafton, OH; d. 16 August 1919, Cleveland, OH), player and manager, captained and played shortstop for the Cleveland Spiders (NL) in the 1890s. He grew up in Cleveland, where he and his wife Belle had three sons and one daughter. He started his professional baseball career with Youngstown (IOL) in 1884 and played for Providence (EL) and Rochester, NY (IL), in 1886 before making the major leagues.

In 1887 he joined his hometown Cleveland club, an AA team until shifting to the NL two years later. The 5 foot, 9 inch, 160 pound right-handed McKean was known for hustle, aggressive play, and umpire baiting, leading him to be named team captain in 1891. The following year, Cleveland joined Boston and Baltimore as the dominant teams when Denton "Cy" Young* and Jesse Burkett* came to the Spiders. In 1892 Cleveland captured the second half championship of the NL's only scheduled split season after Boston had easily won the first half. When Boston swept the Spiders in the post-season playoffs, the NL abolished the split season format and instituted the Temple Cup series between first and second place finishers. In the 1895 series, second place Cleveland upset the Baltimore Orioles four games to one. Burkett and McKean, who hit .300, gave Cleveland a strong one-two combination to back Young's three pitching victories. The two clubs again played for the cup in 1896, but the Orioles swept the series.

McKean enjoyed his best seasons between 1893 and 1896, batting over .300 (.357 in 1894, .342 in 1895, and .338 in 1896), scoring over 100 runs, driving in at least 100 runs for four straight seasons, and fielding well. The performance of McKean and Cleveland declined after 1896. McKean finished his thirteen-year major league career with St. Louis (NL) in 1899 and compiled a .302 lifetime batting average. In 1,654 games, he made 2,083 hits, 272 doubles, 158 triples, 635 walks, and 323 stolen bases, scored 1,227 runs, and knocked in 1,069 runs. Following his major league career, McKean managed minor league teams at Rochester, NY, Springfield, and Dayton.

BIBLIOGRAPHY: Lee Allen, *The National League Story* (New York, 1961); Joseph Durso, *The Days of Mr. McGraw* (Englewood Cliffs, NJ, 1969); Franklin Lewis, *The Cleveland Indians* (New York, 1949).

William E. Akin

McKECHNIE, William Boyd "Bill," "Deacon" (b. 7 August 1886 or 1887, Wilkinsburg, PA; d. 29 October 1965, Bradenton, FL), player, manager, and coach, was the son of Scottish immigrants and grew up in a devout Methodist-Episcopal home. After attending high school in Wilkinsburg, McKechnie signed professionally with Washington, PA, and from 1906 to 1909 played third base for Washington, PA (POML), Canton, OH (OPL), and Wheeling, WV (CL). He received a brief trial with the Pittsburgh Pirates (NL) in 1907. After marrying Beryl Bien on June 15, 1911, he had four children, William, Jr., president of the PCL from 1968 to 1973, Beatrice, James, and Carol.

McKechnie spent from 1910 to 1912 as a utility infielder with the Pirates. After starting the 1913 season with St. Paul (AA), he played briefly for the Boston Braves (NL) and New York Yankees (AL). In 1914 he jumped to the

FL and hit .304 with Indianapolis. After the franchise shifted to Newark, the 27-year-old third baseman was named player-manager in June, 1915, and led the club to a 54–45 record. The New York Giants (NL) signed the 5 foot, 10 inch, 180 pound switch-hitter in 1916, but traded him in July to the Cincinnati Reds (NL). In 1918 Cincinnati sold McKechnie to Pittsburgh (NL), where he hit .255. Although temporarily retiring in 1919, he returned as a utility infielder with the Pirates in 1920 and played for Minneapolis (AA) in 1921. His major league statistics included 713 hits, 319 runs scored, 240 RBIs, 127 stolen bases, and a .251 batting average in 845 games.

McKechnie, named manager of the Pirates in July, 1922, led Pittsburgh to a 47–26 second half. After making strong third place finishes in 1923 and 1924, he led the 1925 Pirates, which had few stars, to a world championship over the Washington Senators and Walter Johnson.* He finished third in 1926 and joined the St. Louis Cardinals (NL) coaching staff the next year. McKechnie was appointed Redbird pilot in 1928 and led St. Louis an NL pennant by two games over John McGraw's* Giants. After dropping four straight contests to the New York Yankees in the World Series, he was demoted to manage the Rochester, NY, farm club (IL). When St. Louis faltered in 1929, however, McKechnie returned to manage the Cardinals.

McKechnie became manager of the cellar-dwelling Boston Braves (NL) in 1930 and guided them eight seasons. In 1937 he was named Manager of the Year for leading the hapless Braves to a 78–73 finish. In 1938 McKechnie was hired to manage the Cincinnati Reds (NL) for $25,000. From 1938 through 1946, he led the Reds to two NL pennants (1939, 1940), a world championship (1940), and seven upper division finishes. McKechnie's twenty-five-year managerial career record of 1,898 wins and 1,724 losses places him in the top ten for total games, wins, and losses as a pilot. He coached with the AL Cleveland Indians (1947–1949) and Boston Red Sox before retiring to Bradenton, FL, in 1953.

McKechnie sang in a Methodist church choir for twenty-five years and impressed others as generous, honest, and pleasant. He owned several oil wells and considerable real estate in Pittsburgh and Florida. McKechnie, recognized as one of the finest managers in baseball history for his expertise on pitching and defense, was elected to the National Baseball Hall of Fame in 1962.

BIBLIOGRAPHY: Martin Appel and Burt Goldblatt, *Baseball's Best: The Hall of Fame Gallery* (New York, 1977); Bill Borst, *The Pride of St. Louis: A Cooperstown Gallery* (St. Louis, 1984); Bob Broeg, *Redbirds: A Century of Cardinal Baseball* (St. Louis, 1981); *DAB*, Supp. 7, (1961–1965), pp. 501–502; *NYT*, October 30, 1965; Lowell Reidenbaugh, *Cooperstown: Where Baseball's Legends Live Forever* (St. Louis, 1983); Ken Smith, *Baseball's Hall of Fame*, rev. ed. (New York, 1970).

Frank J. Olmsted

MACKEY, Raleigh "Biz" (b. 27 July 1897, Eagle Pass, TX; d. ?, Los Angeles, CA), player and manager, excelled in the Negro leagues. After moving to Luling, TX, as an infant, he grew up and learned to play baseball there. At age 18 he joined the good local Prairie League baseball team, which also included his brothers Ray and Ernest. Mackey, who threw right-handed and learned to be a switch-hitter, played two years for the Luling Oilers and then began his professional career in 1918 as a catcher with the San Antonio Black Aces. Mackey played with San Antonio until being sold with several other players to the Indianapolis ABCs in 1920. Indianapolis, under manager C. I. Taylor,* fielded one of the era's strongest clubs and featured Oscar Charleston* in the outfield and Ben Taylor* at first base. After the 1922 season, Mackey jumped to the Philadelphia Hilldale team. The versatile Mackey remained with Hilldale for six years and supposedly played every position. In 1923 Hilldale won the first ECL pennant, as Mackey led the league with a .440 batting average. Hilldale repeated as ECL champions in 1924, but lost the Negro World Series to the Kansas City Monarchs five games to four. In 1925 Hilldale again won the ECL pennant and defeated Kansas City five games to one in the Negro World Series, as Mackey batted .375.

In 1929 Mackey joined the Baltimore Black Sox (ANL). The Black Sox won the ANL pennant and fielded one of the strongest teams until the Depression caused the league to fold. In 1934 Mackey joined the Philadelphia Stars, an NNL club based on the Hilldale team. After playing with the short-lived Washington Elite Giants (NNL) in 1936, he became player-manager of the Baltimore Elite Giants (NNL) the following year and signed catcher Roy Campanella.* In 1939 Baltimore owner Tom Wilson, confident that the Mackey-trained Campanella could handle the catching responsibilities, traded Mackey to the Newark Eagles (NNL). Mackey remained with Newark from 1939 through 1948. He initially was used as a catcher and began managing the club in 1946. Mackey's Eagles won both halves of the NNL season and then defeated the Kansas City Monarchs in the Negro World Series. The next year, Newark won the first half of the season and finished second overall. As Eagles manager, Mackey handled interference by owner Effa Manley in team operations fairly well. Mackey's players at Newark included future major leaguers Larry Doby,* Monte Irvin,* and Don Newcombe.* After the major league color barrier was broken, the Negro leagues experienced hard times. The Eagles disbanded following the 1948 season, ending Mackey's managerial career.

Mackey, one of his era's great players, still caught regularly and batted .307 in 1945 at age 48. The fiercely competitive Mackey handled pitchers very well and may have been the best all-around catcher produced by the Negro leagues. Josh Gibson* possessed better offensive skills and a stronger arm, but Mackey had few peers as a defensive catcher. He played in five

East–West All-Star games (1933, 1935–1936, 1938, and 1947), the last at age 50. In a 1954 Pittsburgh *Courier* poll, Mackey edged Gibson as the greatest Negro league catcher. As a manager, Mackey also enjoyed success with the Baltimore Elite Giants and Newark Eagles and helped develop several future major league players.

BIBLIOGRAPHY: William Brashler, *Josh Gibson* (New York, 1978); Roy Campanella, *It's Good to Be Alive* (New York, 1959); Anthony J. Connor, *Voices from Cooperstown* (New York, 1982); John Holway, *Voices from the Great Black Baseball Leagues* (New York, 1975); Raleigh Mackey file, National Baseball Hall of Fame Library, Cooperstown, NY; Robert W. Peterson, *Only the Ball Was White* (Englewood Cliffs, NJ, 1970); Donn Rogosin, *Invisible Men: Life in Baseball's Negro Leagues* (New York, 1983).

Douglas D. Martin

McMAHON, John Joseph "Sadie" (b. 19 September 1867, Rising Sun, DE; d. 20 February 1954, Delaware City, DE), player, grew up in the Wilmington, DE, area and finished high school at age 17. The 5 foot, 9 inch, 185 pound McMahon worked as a carpenter for a few years and played amateur baseball in Wilmington with the Blue Rose Club in 1886 and later with the Americas Club. After signing professionally with Norristown, PA, in 1889, he joined the Philadelphia Athletics (AA) later that year and won 16 of 28 decisions. In late 1890, manager Bill Barnie convinced right-handed McMahon and battery mate Wilbert Robinson* to move to his Baltimore team (AA). He pitched seven seasons for Baltimore, two in the AA (1890–1891), and five in the NL (1892–1896). McMahon helped the fabulous Orioles to NL pennants in 1894, 1895, and 1896, playing with Robinson, "Wee Willie" Keeler,* Hughie Jennings,* and John McGraw.* His heroic work in the stretch drive of 1895 proved crucial. After returning from a pulled shoulder tendon, McMahon pitched 18 games in the season's last six weeks, won 10 and lost 3, and hurled 3 late victories over Cleveland to wrest the NL championship from them. He also pitched several wins in the Temple Cup competition.

In 1890 he led the AA in games appeared in (60), games started (57), complete games (55), innings pitched (509), strikeouts (291), and wins (36). The following year, he paced again in games started (58), complete games (53), innings pitched (503), and wins (34). He hurled the most shutouts in 1891 (5) and 1895 (4). In compiling a 177–125 lifetime record and 3.49 ERA, he won 36 games in 1890, 34 in 1891, 20 in 1892, 24 in 1893, and 25 in 1894. When the Brooklyn Dodgers (NL) hired Baltimore manager Ned Hanlon* in 1897, McMahon joined him and played his last major league season there. He played sporadically around Wilmington for a few years and in 1903 was coaxed out of retirement by manager Jennings of the EL's Baltimore Orioles. He won the second game of a doubleheader with Newark on August 15, driving in the winning run. McMahon scouted for the New York Giants (NL) from 1911 to 1925, but claimed that the game took too much out of him.

BIBLIOGRAPHY: Al Kermisch, "From a Researcher's Notebook," *Baseball Research Journal* 10 (1981), pp. 69–70; John McMahon file, National Baseball Hall of Fame Library, Cooperstown, NY; Joseph L. Reichler, ed., *The Baseball Encyclopedia*, 6th ed. (New York, 1985), pp. 1,905–1,906; Wilmington (DE) *Star*, December 23, 1951, February 21, 1954.

Mark D. Rucker

McNALLY, David Arthur "Dave" (b. 31 October 1942, Billings MT), player, is the son of oil salesman James and social case worker Beth McNally. His father served in World War II and was killed in action in Okinawa in July 1945. McNally attended Billings Central Catholic High School, which fielded no baseball team. In 1960 he led Post No. 4 to the American Legion World Series with an 18–1 pitching mark and five no-hitters. Later that year, the Baltimore Orioles (AL) signed him for a reported $80,000. McNally married Jean Marie Hoefer in 1961 and has five children, Jeff, Pamela, Susan, Annie, and Michael. After minor league seasons with Victoria, TX (TL) and Fox Cities, WI (3IL) in 1961 and Elmira, NY (EL) in 1962, McNally joined the Baltimore Orioles in late 1962. In his major league debut at age 19, he hurled a two-hit shutout over Kansas City in 1962. Following two uneventful years, he pitched well in 1965 and 1966 and shut out the Los Angeles Dodgers in the 1966 World Series. An arm ailment lessened his effectiveness in 1967.

From 1968 through 1971, the 5 foot, 11 inch, 190 pound left-hander became the most successful hurler in baseball by winning 87 of 118 decisions (plus 6 in post-season play). Only one other hurler, Ferguson Jenkins, won as many contests, while McNally's .737 winning percentage was .078 above that of his nearest competitor. In 1968 McNally finished 22–10 with a 1.95 ERA and 202 strikeouts and allowed only 5.8 hits per nine innings. His 24 victories led the AL in 1970. In 1971 he compiled a 21–5 mark despite missing five weeks with an elbow injury. From September 22, 1968, through July 30, 1969, McNally won 17 straight decisions to tie AL records for consecutive victories and wins at the beginning of a season (15). He was named to All-Star teams in 1969, 1970, and 1972, appearing in two, and made *The Sporting News* All-Star team in 1968. In post-season play, he pitched for the Orioles in the 1969, 1970, 1971, 1973, and 1974 Championship Series, and in the 1966, 1969, 1970, and 1971 World Series. McNally compiled a 3–2 mark and 2.68 ERA in playoffs and a 4–2 slate with a 2.34 ERA in World Series.

A right-handed batter, he slugged nine regular season home runs, remains the only pitcher to belt a grand slam home run in the World Series, and is one of the only two pitchers to hit two World Series homers. The good fielding southpaw made only one error in each of the seasons from 1967 through 1971.

In December 1974 McNally was traded to the Montreal Expos (NL). He then held lifetime Orioles records for games pitched, innings, wins, complete games, shutouts, strikeouts, and walks, plus several single-season records. He retired at age 32 after pitching 12 games for the Expos. In fourteen seasons, he compiled a 184–119 (.607) mark, 3.24 ERA, struck out 1,512 batters in 2,729 1/3 innings, and hurled 33 shutouts. In 1975 McNally and Andy Messersmith challenged the reserve clause, which had bound players to their teams for as long as the team wished. An arbitrator ruled that, by playing for a year without contracts, the players had fulfilled their legal obligations and were free agents. This decision led to other cases, permanently altering labor relations in baseball.

BIBLIOGRAPHY: *Baltimore Orioles Press Guide, 1974*, pp. 74–75; Billings (MT) *Gazette*, July 28, 1945; Roy Blount, Jr., "Three Birds Who Mainly Stay," *SI* 33 (October 12, 1970), pp. 30–32; Peter Bonventre, "Off the Reservation," *Newsweek* 87 (January 5, 1976), p. 51; "Flying High," *Time* 94 (July 11, 1969), pp. 45–46; "Highlight," *SI* 30 (June 16, 1969), p. 80; Gene Karst, and Martin J. Jones, Jr., *Who's Who in Professional Baseball* (New Rochelle, NY, 1973); *Montreal Expos Press Guide, 1975*, p. 66; *NYT*, June 10, 1975, p. 50; Joseph L. Reichler, ed., *The Baseball Encyclopedia*, 6th ed., (New York, 1985), p. 1,906; *TSN Official Baseball Guide, 1968–1975* (St. Louis, 1968–1975); *TSN Official Baseball Register, 1962–1976* (St. Louis, 1962–1976).

Bruce Erricson

MacPHAIL, Leland Stanford, Sr. "Larry" (b. 3 February 1890, Cass City, MI; d. 1 October 1975, Miami, FL), executive, was the son of William Curtis MacPhail, a Scottish immigrant storekeeper and banker. MacPhail attended various Michigan schools and Staunton Military Academy in Virginia. At age 16 he passed the entrance exam for the U.S. Naval Academy at Annapolis, but instead enrolled at Beloit College. MacPhail subsequently attended the University of Michigan Law School and George Washington University and passed the bar exams of Michigan, Illinois, and Washington, DC. After practicing law in Chicago, he became chief of a Nashville, TN, department store. During World War I, MacPhail enlisted in the U.S. Army as a private, rose to captain, served in France, and was wounded. After the armistice, he and others tried unsuccessfully to capture Kaiser Wilhelm, who was in exile in Holland. MacPhail, though, claimed that he took the Kaiser's ashtray as a souvenir.

MacPhail tried several unsuccessful business ventures in Ohio and refereed Big Ten Conference football games on weekends. He obtained an option on the impoverished Columbus baseball club (AA) and sold it to the St. Louis Cardinals (NL) to become a farm club. St. Louis made MacPhail president of the Columbus team, although he had no previous experience administering a baseball club. The Cardinals built a new ballpark and installed lights at Columbus. MacPhail implemented innovative, successful promotions, but was fired by the Cardinals in June 1933 for his personal actions in and out of baseball.

A bank that had reluctantly taken over the financially struggling Cincinnati

Reds (NL) hired MacPhail before the 1934 season. He contacted Powel Crosley, Jr.,* owner of radio stations and factories that produced electrical appliances and radio receivers. Crosley knew nothing about baseball, but was persuaded to take an option on the baseball club partly as a civic duty. With Crosley's financial backing, MacPhail immediately instituted several changes in the stadium, obtained new players, and persuaded club owners to permit night baseball for the first time in major league history. MacPhail persuaded President Franklin D. Roosevelt in May, 1935, to touch the signal in the White House turning on the lights for the historic first night game. Night baseball, along with MacPhail's mammoth fireworks displays, attracted almost capacity crowds. In June 1936 Crosley exercised his option to buy the ball club from the bank.

Although attendance improved greatly at Cincinnati ball games, MacPhail and Crosley parted at the end of the 1936 season. MacPhail spent 1937 in Michigan in the banking business. In 1938 a bank called on MacPhail to rescue the Brooklyn Dodgers (NL) from severe financial problems. Breaking with tradition again, MacPhail persuaded the bank to put up the cash to install lights in Ebbets Field. He also ended the agreement with the New York Yankees and New York Giants barring play-by-play broadcasts of baseball games in the New York area, and brought Red Barber* (OS) from Cincinnati to announce the Dodgers games. MacPhail talked the bank into advancing cash to buy prominent players Dolf Camilli, Mickey Owen, Pee Wee Reese,* Whitlow Wyatt, Fred "Dixie" Walker,* Billy Herman,* Joe Medwick,* and Kirby Higbe. He hired Leo Durocher* as manager and made the Dodgers into a contender for the top NL spot. During the MacPhail regime, Brooklyn finished seventh, third, and second and placed first in the NL in 1941. The Dodgers finished second in 1942, when the United States again was at war. MacPhail returned to the army as a colonel, serving as a special assistant to the Secretary of War.

After VJ Day, MacPhail promoted a partnership backed by Dan Topping* and Del Webb to buy the New York Yankees (AL) from the heirs of the late Colonel Jacob Ruppert* for $2.8 million. The bargain deal included Yankee Stadium, the team's minor league farm system, and considerable real estate. MacPhail received one-third interest in the partnership and a ten-year contract to administer the ball club. Once more MacPhail instituted many innovations, including installing lights in Yankee Stadium for the first time in history. The Yankees finished in third place in 1946 and captured the 1947 AL pennant and World Series. During a victory celebration on the day the Yankees won the world championship, MacPhail engaged in a loud public brawl. The next day, Topping and Webb terminated MacPhail's contract for a $1.5 million payoff.

MacPhail retired to a Maryland farm, where he raised Black Angus cattle, and briefly became president of Bowie Race Track. In 1978 he was elected to the National Baseball Hall of Fame. MacPhail married Inez Thompson

of Oak Park, IL, and had three children, Leland S. Jr. (Lee),* William, and
Marian McDermott. Lee became AL president, while William served as a
television executive and Marian headed research at *Time* magazine. After
being divorced, MacPhail married Jean Bennett Wanamaker in 1945 and had
one daughter, Jennie.

BIBLIOGRAPHY: Gene Karst and Martin J. Jones, Jr., *Who's Who in Professional Baseball*
(New Rochelle, NY, 1973); *NYT*, October 2, 1975.

Gene Karst

MacPHAIL, Leland Stanford, Jr., "Lee" (b. 25 October 1917, Nashville,
TN), executive, is the son of Leland Stanford MacPhail, Sr.,* and Inez
(Thompson) MacPhail. In 1939 he received the Bachelor of Arts degree from
Swarthmore College and married Jane M. Hamilton. They have four chil-
dren, Leland Stanford III, Allen, Bruce, and Andrew. After a year in cor-
porate management, MacPhail launched a career in baseball administration.
Assistance and encouragement came from his father, a prominent major
league executive.

MacPhail's initial assignments included being business manager of Reading, PA (ISL), in 1941, and general manager of Toronto (IL) in 1942–1943.
Following a tour of duty as a U.S. Navy lieutenant (j.g.) during World War
II (1944–1945), he served as general manager of the New York Yankees farm
team at Kansas City (AA) from 1946 to 1948. (His father was co-owner and
executive vice-president–general manager of the Yankees from 1945 to 1947.)

As director of player personnel for the Yankees from 1948 to 1958,
MacPhail helped to assemble the talent that produced nine AL pennants and
seven World Series championships in ten years. He then joined the lowly
Baltimore Orioles (AL) as president and general manager (1958–1965), and
supervised the building of a team that won the 1966 World Series. When
William D. Eckert* was named Commissioner of Baseball in November,
1965, MacPhail became his chief administrative assistant and the real baseball
authority in the office. For his achievements, *The Sporting News* named him
Major League Executive of the Year for 1966. MacPhail returned to the
Yankees in October 1966 as executive vice-president and general manager.
In October 1973 he was chosen AL president and took office on January 1,
1974. He resigned that office at the end of 1983. Since January 1, 1984, he
has served as president of the Major League Player Relations Committee,
the agency representing the owners in negotiations with the Major League
Baseball Players Association.

As a baseball executive, MacPhail's quiet, soft-spoken, introverted personality sharply contrasted with that of his explosive, outspoken, extroverted
father. But like Larry, Lee emphasized the farm system as the best way to
build strong teams. When AL president, he preserved the controversial designated hitter rule. As AL president and head of the Major League Player

Relations Committee, he defended the financial interests of club owners in an era of arbitration, free agency, and collective bargaining by the Players Association.

BIBLIOGRAPHY: Gene Karst and Martin J. Jones, Jr., *Who's Who in Professional Baseball* (New Rochelle, NY, 1973); *NYT*, November 6, 1958, December 12, 1959, November 18, 1965, October 14, 1966, October 24, 1973, December 5, 1983; *TSN*, December 3, 1966, September 12, 1981, June 27, 1983; *WWA*, 42nd ed. (1982–1983), p. 2,101.

Larry R. Gerlach

McPHEE, John Alexander "Biddy," "Bid" (b. 1 November 1859, Massena, NY; d. 3 January 1943, San Diego, CA), player, manager, and scout, was the fourth of five children of saddler John and Maria (Button) McPhee. In 1866 the McPhees moved to Keithsburg, IL, where young John learned to play baseball. He entered professional baseball with Davenport, IA (NWL), in 1877, first as a catcher and then as a second baseman and outfielder. In 1879 he worked as a clerk at a Davenport commission house. After returning to baseball a year later as a second baseman with a semi-pro team in Akron, he signed in 1882 with the Cincinnati entry in the newly formed AA. Thereafter, he owned second base in Cincinnati, playing eight fine seasons with the Red Stockings (AA) and ten with the Reds (NL).

A capable leadoff hitter, McPhee compiled a .275 career batting average with 2,291 hits in 2,138 games. His specialty was hitting triples, ranking eleventh on the all-time list (189). A right-handed batter, he led the AA with 19 triples in 1887, hit 22 for the Reds in 1890, and made 3 in one game against the New York Giants in 1890. He also tallied over 100 runs in ten different seasons, placing twenty-first lifetime. He stole 528 bases, mostly between 1887 and 1897, when bases advanced on a teammate's hit or out were scored as thefts. McPhee also made 307 doubles, scored 1,684 runs, knocked in 726 runs, and walked 981 times.

Although his career .945 fielding average frequently has been exceeded in the modern era, he ranked among the premier nineteenth century second basemen. He led his league in fielding average ten seasons, finished second four times, and never placed below fourth. McPhee also paced his league for eleven years in double plays, eight in putouts, and six in assists. For second basemen, McPhee's .978 fielding average in 1896 comprised the best in the major leagues during his eighteen-year career, and his 529 putouts in 1886 remain a single-season record. Overall, McPhee ranks second for putouts (6,300), total chances (13,658), and total chances in one season (1,058), third in average putouts per game (3), fifth in assists (6,593), fourth in average chances per game (6.4), and eleventh in total double plays (1,145). McPhee's records are the more remarkable because he was one of the last barehanded players. Although gloves were in general use by 1886, he disdained them until 1897, when his career was nearly ended.

During McPhee's first season, the AA used color-coded uniforms to familiarize new fans with each player's position. As a second baseman, he wore orange and black. The same year he participated in the first post-season Championship Series against the Chicago White Stockings (NL). The teams split two games before an interleague dispute ended the competition. McPhee also adjusted to fundamental changes in how baseball was played. Pitchers threw underhand from 45 feet his first two seasons, overhand from 50 feet for the next nine, and from the modern distance of 60½ feet for his last seven campaigns.

In 1899 he played in 111 games, batted .279, and led the NL for the fourth time in fielding average with .958. To the city's dismay, McPhee, nearly 40 years old, retired before the 1900 season, proud of never having been fined or ejected from a game. Although exciting to watch in an era that appreciated fine fielding, McPhee personally lacked color. The trim 5 foot, 8 inch, 152 pounder wore the typical center part and curly mustache of his time, conducted himself soberly, and always remained in shape. He managed the Reds to an eighth place finish in 1901 and to seventh in 1902, resigning part way through the season. On August 7, 1902, he married Julia Caroline Broerman; they had no children. From 1903 through 1909, McPhee served as a Reds scout. He retired to Southern California in 1917.

BIBLIOGRAPHY: William E. Akin, "The Great Fielders of 1880–1899," *Baseball Research Journal* 10 (1981), pp. 62–65; Lee Allen, *The Cincinnati Reds* (New York, 1948); *Lee Allen, "The Cincinnati Reds: The Oldest Club in Baseball," Sport* 11 (May, 1951), p. 52: Cincinnati *Enquirer*, April 12, 1890; Cincinnati *Times-Star*, January 4, 1943; John Alexander McPhee file, National Baseball Hall of Fame Library, Cooperstown, NY; Joseph L. Reichler, ed., *The Baseball Encyclopedia*, 6th ed. (New York, 1985), p. 1,192; Harold Seymour, *Baseball: The Early Years* (New York, 1960); *Sporting Life*, April 7, 1900, p. 3; *TSN*, June 5, 1897; David Quentin Voigt, *American Baseball*, vol. 1 (University Park, PA, 1983).

A. D. Suehsdorf

McRAE, Harold Abraham "Hal," "Mr. Ribbie" (b. 10 July 1946, Avon Park, FL), player, is one of ten children of custodian-gardener-citrus worker Willie and Virginia (Foster) McRae. McRae graduated from Douglas High School in Sebring, FL, where he lettered in baseball, basketball, and football. McRae, who played baseball at Florida A&M University, married Johncyna Williams on April 21, 1966, and has three children. He entered professional baseball with Tampa (FSL) in 1965 and played second base with Peninsula, VA (CrL), in 1966 and Knoxville (SA) and Buffalo (IL) in 1967. McRae switched to the outfield with Indianapolis (AA) in 1968 and 1969. A part-time player with the Cincinnati Reds (NL) for four years, McRae excelled in the 1972 World Series by batting four for nine against the winning Oakland A's. As a National Leaguer, he compiled a .257 batting average.

His stardom, however, was achieved in the AL after being traded before the 1973 season to the Kansas City Royals. With the Royals chiefly as a designated hitter, McRae hit the ball to all fields and enjoyed six seasons of hitting at least .303. He averaged .293 for the Royals through 1986 and was named the AL's top designated hitter five times. A student of the renowned Charlie Lau and Rocky Colavito,* McRae kept his strikeouts to a minimum and still hit with power. In 1976 teammate George Brett* hit an inside-the-park homer on what appeared to be a catchable fly ball to win a controversial batting crown over McRae. McRae won only two hitting categories in his career, leading the AL in doubles with a club record 54 in 1977 and tying for the lead in doubles with 46 in 1982. In 1982 he won the RBI title with 133, a Royals record and highest ever for an AL designated hitter. Nicknamed "Mr. Ribbie" by teammates for his clutch hitting, he set Royals records for total bases (330) and extra-base hits (86) in 1977.

Besides his hitting, McRae exhibited a hard-sliding, aggressive, running style of play and consequently suffered several injuries. He missed an entire season (1969) on the disabled list, breaking a leg in four places by sliding into home plate during a Puerto Rican game in winter ball. The fiery, out-spoken leader played brilliantly in three World Series, hitting 18 for 44, batting .409, and slugging 6 doubles and 6 RBIs. McRae batted consistently, very rarely played two or three straight games without a hit, and generally made hits in three of every four games. When the Royals captured the Western Division title in 1985, McRae knocked in 70 runs in 320 at bats and made 9 game-winning hits as a designated hitter. He batted .261 and knocked in three runs in the Royals' successful AL Championship Series against the Toronto Blue Jays. Since the DH was not used in the 1985 World Series triumph over St. Louis, McRae made only one official at bat. At the close of the 1986 season, McRae's lifetime statistics included 2,081 hits, 481 doubles, 66 triples, 190 home runs, 1,088 RBIs, and a .290 batting average. McRae, twice named Kansas City Player of the Year (1974, 1982), participated in two All-Star games (1975, 1982) and was named to *The Sporting News* All-League team four times (1976, 1977, 1982, 1983).

BIBLIOGRAPHY: John E. DiMeglio, correspondence with Johncyna McRae, John E. DiMeglio Collection, Mankato, MN; Ron Fimrite, "The Dean of the DHs," *SI* 57 (July 19, 1982), pp. 26–27ff.; Jim Selman, "Hal McRae; A Premier DH in Twilight of His Career," *Baseball Digest* 43 (August, 1984), pp. 69–70.

John E. DiMeglio

McVEY, Calvin Alexander "Cal" (b. 30 August 1850, Montrose, IA; d. 20 August 1926, San Francisco, CA), player and manager, excelled as a hitter in the early years of professional baseball. He played every position, including pitcher, during his career, and starred as a catcher and right fielder. After moving with his family at age 11 to Indianapolis, McVey in his mid-teens played amateur ball for several Indianapolis clubs. In 1869 manager Harry

Wright* hired him to play for the Cincinnati Red Stockings, baseball's first openly professional club. In 1871 McVey accompanied Wright to the Boston Red Stockings of the newly formed NA, baseball's first professional league. Following two years as Boston's catcher, McVey played in 1873 for Baltimore (also managing the club part of the season to a 23–14 won-lost record) and returned to Boston for two more years. McVey led the NA once in hits (1874) and once in runs scored (1874). His five-year .362 batting average ranked second in the NA to Ross Barnes'* .379. In three of his four years with Boston, he helped the club win the NA championship.

When the NA gave way to the NL, McVey became one of the notorious "big four" (which included Barnes, Al Spalding,* and Deacon White*) who deserted Boston for the Chicago White Stockings and led them to the NL's first championship in 1876. McVey batted .347 in 1876, fifth highest in the NL. In 1877 he raised his batting average to .368, third best in the NL, and ranked second in hits, runs, and total bases. Chicago, however, fell to fifth place in the six-club league. McVey concluded his NL career as infielder and manager at Cincinnati. In 1878 he managed the club to second place with a 37–23 won-lost record, but his 35–29 1879 record in a partial season as manager produced only a fifth place finish. During his four NL seasons, McVey batted .328 to give him a nine-year .346 major league batting average.

McVey remained active in baseball for another decade in California. He organized and managed clubs in Oakland, Hanford, and San Diego, working as an irrigation company superintendent and owner of a stock farm. In 1906 he lost his home and possessions in the San Francisco earthquake and—with his aged father William and his invalid wife—was reduced to living in a shack. In 1913 he was injured severely in a thirty-foot fall in a Nevada mine. With encouragement and financial assistance from baseball friends, McVey recovered from each adversity. One former teammate found him at age 73 in good health and employed as night watchman for a lumber company. In 1968 McVey was elected to the Iowa Sports Hall of Fame.

BIBLIOGRAPHY: Bill Bryson, "Cal McVey Joins 'Hall,' " Des Moines *Sunday Register*, April 14, 1968; Seymour R. Church, *Base Ball* (San Francisco, 1902; repr. Princeton, NJ, 1974); Cal McVey file, National Baseball Hall of Fame Library, Cooperstown, NY; Joseph L. Reichler, ed., *The Baseball Encyclopedia*, 6th ed. (New York, 1985), pp. 62, 641, 1,194.

Frederick Ivor-Campbell

MADLOCK, Bill, Jr., "Mad Dog" (b. 12 January 1951, Memphis, TN), player, grew up in difficult family circumstances without his father, Bill, Sr. Before he was one month old, he was sent to live with his grandmother, Annie Polk. At age 2, Madlock moved with his grandmother to Decatur, IL. His aunt and uncle, Sarah and Wardie Sain, assisted in his upbringing there. Madlock attended Dwight D. Eisenhower High School in Decatur, where he earned nine letters in various sports and made All-State halfback in football. He married Cynthia Johnson in 1969 and has four children, Sarah, Stephen, William, and Jeremy. In 1969 Madlock rejected over 100 football scholarships to play baseball for Southeastern Community College in Keokuk, IA.

In January 1970 Madlock signed a professional baseball contract with the Washington Senators (AL), who had selected him in the secondary phase of the draft. His first season (1970) saw him play for Geneva, NY (NYPL) where he toiled at shortstop, batted .269, and slugged 6 home runs. During the next two years, he played for Pittsfield, MA (EL), under manager Joe Klein. Klein helped Madlock develop a more disciplined swing which contributed to a .328 batting average in 1972. During a banner 1973 season with the Spokane Indians (PCL), Madlock batted .338, belted 22 home runs, contributed 90 RBIs, and led the league in runs scored with 119. In late 1973 Madlock was promoted to the Texas Rangers (AL) and batted .351 in their final 21 games.

From 1974 to 1976, the right-handed Madlock played second base for the Chicago Cubs and twice led the NL in batting average, with .354 (1975) and .339 (1976) percentages. In 1977 Madlock was dealt to the San Francisco Giants (NL), where he continued his .300-plus hitting. Madlock remained with the Giants until traded on June 28, 1979, to the Pittsburgh Pirates (NL). In the 85 remaining games, Madlock batted .328 and played outstanding third base to help the Pirates win the Eastern Division and NL pennant. Furthermore, Madlock provided instrumental help in the Pirates' World Series victory over the Baltimore Orioles by batting .375 in the championship games.

In the strike-shortened 1981 season, Madlock won his third batting title with a healthy .341 mark to become only the sixth major league player to win batting titles with two different clubs. Madlock won his fourth batting title with a .323 average in 1983, becoming one of only eleven major league players to have captured that many batting titles. In August 1985 he was traded to the Los Angeles Dodgers (NL) for three players and helped them capture the 1985 Western Division title. Madlock batted .333 in the NL playoffs against St. Louis with 3 homers, 1 double, and 7 RBIs. Through the 1986 season, he batted .307 with 1,906 hits, 330 doubles, 146 home runs, 803 RBIs, and 170 stolen bases.

Although not known for his power, the 5 foot, 11 inch, 190 pound Madlock in 1982 belted 19 home runs and drove in 95 runs. His career was somewhat tarnished in 1980 when he hit umpire Jerry Crawford in the face with a glove during an argument. Madlock, nicknamed "Mad Dog" because of the incident, was assessed the largest fine ever levied for an on-the-field incident ($5,000) and the second longest suspension in major league history (15 days).

Following the incident, Madlock's temperament rebounded admirably, and his leadership qualities blossomed. In September 1982 he was named captain of the Pirates. Off the field, Madlock collects clocks, is a partner in the restaurant business, and advises the President's Council on Physical Fitness and Sports.

BIBLIOGRAPHY: Zander Hollander, ed., *The Complete Handbook of Baseball, 1983* (New York, 1983); Harris Lewine and Daniel Okrent, eds., *The Ultimate Baseball Book* (New York, 1983); William C. Matney, ed., *Who's Who Among Black Americans* (Northbrook, IL, 1977); Robert Obojski, *Bush League: A History of Minor League Baseball* (New York, 1975); Steve Wulf, "Glad Times for Mad Dog," *SI* 58 (May 9, 1983), pp. 48–57.

Samuel John Regalado

MAGEE, Sherwood Robert "Sherry" (b. 6 August 1884, Clarendon, PA; d. 13 March 1929, Philadelphia, PA), player and umpire, was a son of oilfield worker James S. and Drusilla (Hall) Magee. He entered professional baseball in 1903 at Allentown, PA, and began the 1904 season at Carlisle, PA, where Philadelphia (NL) scout Jim Randall signed him. The burly 5 foot, 11 inch, 179 pound right-hander reported to Philadelphia in June, 1904, and played left field for the Phillies through 1914, serving as field captain in 1914. After disappointment at not being named manager, he was traded at his own request to Boston (NL) in 1915. Magee was waived to Cincinnati (NL) in August 1917 and finished his NL career there in 1919. Subsequently he played for Columbus (AA) in 1920, Minneapolis (AA) in 1921 and 1922, St. Joseph (WL) in 1923, Milwaukee (AA) in 1923, 1924, and 1925, and Baltimore (IL) in 1925 and 1926.

Although playing during the dead ball era, Magee batted .291 in 2,085 NL games, with 2,169 hits, 1,112 runs, 1,182 RBIs, 441 stolen bases, and a .427 slugging percentage. During his eleven seasons with Philadelphia, he hit .299, usually as the fourth batter in the lineup, and slugged .447 (35 percent above the NL average). In 1910 he hit .331 to win the NL batting championship and led the NL in runs scored (110), RBIs (123), and slugging average (.507). In 1914 he paced the NL in hits (171), doubles (39), RBIs (103), and slugging average (.509). He also topped the NL in RBIs in 1907 (85) and 1918 (76).

The smart, aggressive Magee, a fast, excellent fielder with a strong, accurate throwing arm, proved a superior base runner and hit sharp line drives to all fields. He always played hard to win, constantly scolded teammates and himself for mistakes and lapses, and experienced difficulties because of his hot temper. On July 10, 1911, he knocked out umpire Bill Finneran with one punch after the latter ejected him for exhibiting displeasure over a called third strike. Although originally suspended for the season, he subsequently was reinstated on August 16. Off the field, however, "Sherry" was a gentle, warm person, exhibited much wit and humor, abstained from hard liquor, and remained extremely popular.

Magee began umpiring in 1927 in the NYPL and received such favorable notice that NL president John Heydler* appointed him to the NL staff. Contrary to some expectations, Magee worked efficiently and got along well with players during his rookie 1928 season. Before the next season, however, he contracted pneumonia and died. Magee was survived by his widow, Edna May (Cary) Magee, whom he married in 1905, and three children, Erwin, Robert, and Charlotte.

BIBLIOGRAPHY: *The Evening Bulletin* (Philadelphia), March 14, 1929; Paul Mac-Farlane, ed., *TSN Daguerreotypes of Great Stars of Baseball* (St. Louis, 1981), pp. 177–178; Sherwood Magee file, National Baseball Hall of Fame Library, Cooperstown, NY; *The North American* (Philadelphia), July 11, 16, 1911; Frank V. Phelps, correspondence with Derek B. McKown, Curator, Warren County (PA) Historical Society, October 23, 1985, Frank V. Phelps Collection, King of Prussia, PA; The Philadelphia *Inquirer*, March 14, 17, 1929; *Public Ledger-Philadelphia*, March 14, 15, 1929; Joseph L. Reichler, ed., *The Baseball Encyclopedia*, 6th ed. (New York, 1985), p. 1147.

Frank V. Phelps

MANTLE, Mickey Charles "The Commerce Comet" (b. 20 October 1931, Spavinaw, OK), player and coach, is the oldest of five children of Elvin "Mutt" and Lovell (Richardson) Mantle. The elder Mantle, a former semi-pro player and zinc miner, vowed that his son would never have to be a miner and taught Mickey, named after Detroit Tiger catcher Mickey Cochrane,* baseball's fine points. With Mickey's grandfather, "Mutt" made Mantle into a switch-hitter by age 7. Mantle, a star football player for Commerce (OK) High School, was kicked in the shins in a freak accident in 1946 and developed a chronic bone infection that plagued him throughout his career.

Mantle played baseball for a local team called the Whiz Kids and impressed a scout for the New York Yankees (AL). Three weeks after his high school graduation, Mantle signed a contract for a $1,000 bonus with Tom Greenwade of the Yankees. He joined Independence, MO (KOML), as a shortstop in Class D at $140 a month. In 1950 Mantle hit .383, made 199 hits, and slugged 26 home runs for Joplin, MO (WA). Mantle led the WA in hitting, but made 55 errors at shortstop. He joked later that he played 1,000 percent, hitting .250 and fielding .750.

In 1951 the Yankees signed him to the parent club for $5,400. Playing alongside Joe DiMaggio* in right field, Mantle experienced some difficulty adjusting to the major leagues. His first home run, a gargantuan shot, went over 450 feet to the deepest part of Chicago's Comiskey Park. On July 15, the Yankees optioned him to Kansas City (AA) to regain his confidence. Mantle, however, suffered a batting slump and considered quitting baseball. Mantle's father, terminally ill with Hodgkins disease, visited Kansas City and talked him out of it. Mantle returned to Yankee Stadium and appeared in the World Series against the "Miracle" New York Giants. In the second game, Willie Mays* hit a fly to right center that DiMaggio caught. Mantle tripped over an uncapped drain, severely spraining his knee. The muscular 5 foot, 11½ inches, 195 pound Mantle suffered several serious injuries in his eighteen-year career. He did not follow a strict exercise regimen and preferred instead to have fun because no male in the Mantle family had lived to age 40. Carousing with drinking buddies Whitey Ford* and Billy Martin* attracted him more than staying in perfect shape, probably shortening his career by at least three years.

Despite his physical ailments, Mantle achieved incredible diamond accomplishments. Mantle, who hit home runs from both sides of the plate in the same game ten times, scored 1,677 runs and made 2,415 hits in only 2,401 games. He knocked in 1,509 runs, slugged 344 doubles and 536 homers, and compiled a .298 career batting average. Three times (1956, 1957, 1962) he won the AL's Most Valuable Player Award. In 1956 he won the coveted Triple Crown with a .353 batting average, 52 homers, and 130 RBIs.

Mantle compiled outstanding World Series statistics, setting major league marks with 18 home runs, 42 runs scored, 40 RBIs, 123 total bases, 26 extra-base hits, 43 walks, and 54 strikeouts. Only his .257 World Series average seemed ordinary. In game five of the 1953 World Series, Mantle hit a grand slam home run off Brooklyn Dodger pitcher Russ Meyer. In 1974 Mantle was elected to the National Baseball Hall of Fame.

After his retirement in 1968, Mantle served as a batting instructor with the Yankees (1970) and did promotional work for gambling casinos in Atlantic City and for other corporations. Mantle's casino connections caused Commissioner Bowie Kuhn* to exclude him from active involvement with baseball. In 1985 Commissioner Peter Ueberroth* (OS) lifted the ban. Mantle pursues his business interests with the Robert J. True firm in Dallas, and plays golf on two very sore knees. In 1983 he signed a book contract for his life story with a $150,000 advance, the highest ever paid for a ballplayer's life. Mantle married Merlyn Johnson on December 23, 1951, and has four sons.

BIBLIOGRAPHY: Jim Bouton, *Ball Four* (New York, 1970); *Colliers* 127 (June 2, 1951), p. 24; *CB* (1953), pp. 411–413; Whitey Ford, Mickey Mantle, and Joseph Durso, *Whitey and Mickey* (New York, 1977); Gene Karst and Martin J. Jones, Jr., *Who's Who in Professional Baseball* (New Rochelle, NY, 1973); *Life* 33 (April 30, 1951), p. 71; *Look* 16 (August 12, 1952), p. 61; Mickey Mantle, *The Education of a Baseball Player* (New York, 1967); Mickey Mantle and Herb Gluck, *Mick* (New York, 1985); *NYT*, April 8, 1951; *NYT Magazine*, June 3, 1951, p. 23; *SEP* 225 (April 18, 1953), p. 31; *Time* 61 (June 15, 1953), p. 64; *WWA*, 41st ed. (1980–1981), p. 2,140.

William A. Borst

MANUSH, Henry Emmett "Heinie" (b. 20 July 1901, Tuscumbia, AL; d. 12 May 1971, Sarasota, FL), player, manager, scout, and coach, was one of seven sons, six of whom played professional baseball. As a 17-year-old student at Massey Military Academy in Pulaski, TN, Manush struck out on his own. He worked in his brother's plumbing business in Burlington, IA, and then drifted westward. Manush made his baseball debut in 1921 with the Edmonton (WCaL) club. After playing at Omaha (WL) in 1922, 21-year-old Manush joined the Detroit Tigers (AL) in 1923 to begin a seventeen-year major league career.

The 6 foot, 1 inch, 200 pound, left-handed Manush played outfield for the Tigers from 1923 to 1927. Manush won the AL batting title with a .378 average in 1926, edging Babe Ruth* with six hits in nine at bats in the closing day's doubleheader. After slumping to a .298 mark in 1927, Manush was traded to the St. Louis Browns (AL) and hit .378 again in 1928. Manush lost the crown by one point to Goose Goslin,* for whom he was exchanged two years later. In 1928 he paced the AL in base hits (241) and tied for the lead in doubles (47). The Browns traded Manush on June 30, 1930, to Washington (AL), where he performed for the Senators through 1935. Besides finishing runner-up to Jimmie Foxx* with a .336 batting average, Manush in 1933 led the AL with 221 hits and 17 triples and helped the Senators win the AL pennant. Washington lost the World Series in five games to New York (NL), as Manush became the first player in the history of the classic to be ejected from a game. In an argument with umpire Charley Moran* (FB), Manush was banished from the game. Commissioner Kenesaw Mountain Landis* backed Moran's action, but ruled that henceforth only the commissioner could eject a player in a World Series. A .349 batting mark in 1934 earned Manush his only All-Star game selection. After being traded to Boston (AL) in December, 1935, Manush closed out his major league career with the Brooklyn Dodgers (NL) in 1937 and 1938 and Pittsburgh Pirates (NL) in 1938 and through 1939.

In 2,009 major league games, Manush scored 1,287 runs, collected 2,524 hits, 491 doubles (29th on the all-time list), 160 triples (39th), 110 home runs, 1,173 RBIs, and compiled a .330 batting average (25th). He batted over .300 eleven seasons, including seven consecutive campaigns, and made over 200 hits four seasons. Only ten players have topped his .334 batting average as a rookie. Manush made at least five hits on seven different occasions and batted safely in 33 consecutive games in 1933. His 241 base hits in the 1928 season placed him tenth on the all-time list.

Manush played for Toronto (IL) in 1938 and 1939 and served as player-manager for Rocky Mount, NC (Pil), Greensboro, NC (Pil), and Roanoke, VA (Pil), from 1940 to 1943. He piloted Scranton (EL) in 1944 and Martinsville, VA (CrL), in 1945 and scouted for Boston and Pittsburgh (NL) from 1946 to 1948. Manush coached (1953–1954) and scouted (1961–1962) for the Washington Senators before leaving baseball. Married to Betty Lloyd in 1928, Manush was enshrined in the National Baseball Hall of Fame in 1964.

BIBLIOGRAPHY: Paul MacFarlane, ed., *TSN Daguerreotypes of Great Stars of Baseball* (St. Louis, 1971); *National Baseball Hall of Fame and Museum Brochure* (Cooperstown, NY, 1974); Lowell Reidenbaugh, *Cooperstown: Where Baseball's Legends Live Forever* (St. Louis, 1983).

John L. Evers

MARANVILLE, Walter James Vincent "Rabbit" (b. 11 November 1891, Springfield, MA; d. 5 January 1954, New York, NY), player and manager, attended Springfield High School for one year and played semi-pro baseball several years. Maranville, who began his career in 1911 with New Bedford, MA (NEL), for $125 per month, joined the Boston Braves (NL) at the end of the 1912 season for $3,000 and became regular shortstop next year. After helping the 1914 "Miracle Braves" win the NL pennant, he batted .308 in the World Series sweep of the Philadelphia Athletics. During his twenty-three-year major league career, he played with the Braves (1912–1920, 1929–1935), Pittsburgh Pirates (1921–1924), Chicago Cubs (1925), Brooklyn Dodgers (1926), and St. Louis Cardinals (1927–1928), all of the NL. In 10,078 career at bats, he made 2,605 hits, 380 doubles, 177 triples, 884 RBIs, 1,255 runs scored, and 291 stolen bases. His .258 lifetime batting average included a single-season high of .295 in 1922. Noted for his fielding, Maranville led the NL in putouts, assists, and fielding percentage several times, at both shortstop and second base.

Known for his off- and on-field escapades, he once swam the Charles River in Boston rather than walk to a bridge, crawled between the legs of umpire Hank O'Day, and often sat on opposing players after tagging them out at second base. After being demoted to Rochester, NY (IL), by Brooklyn in 1927, Maranville stopped drinking and launched a comeback at age 35. He became regular shortstop for the St. Louis Cardinals in 1928 and batted .308 in the World Series loss to the New York Yankees. Maranville, who served in the U.S. Navy in 1918, married Elizabeth Shea on November 11, 1914. He later wed Helene Bertrand on February 20, 1921. As manager of the Chicago Cubs (NL) in 1925, he piloted the club to a 23–30 record. Maranville also managed Elmira, NY (NYPL), in 1936, Montreal (IL) in 1937–1938, Albany (EL) in 1939, and Springfield, MA (EL), in 1941. He set the NL record (since broken) for years as a player with twenty-three and was enshrined by the National Baseball Hall of Fame in 1954.

BIBLIOGRAPHY: Gene Karst and Martin J. Jones, Jr., *Who's Who in Professional Baseball* (New Rochelle, NY, 1973); Walter Maranville file, National Baseball Hall of Fame Library, Cooperstown, NY; Joseph L. Reichler, ed., *The Baseball Encyclopedia*, 6th ed. (New York, 1985), pp. 638, 1,155–1,156.

Horace R. Givens

MARCELLE (also spelled MARCELL and MARCEL), Oliver H. "Ghost"
(b. 24 June 1897, Thibodaux, LA; d. 12 June 1949, Denver, CO), player,
completed eighth grade at Tomey Lafon Elementary School and attended
high school at New Orleans University. The 5 foot, 9 inch, 160 pound
infielder began his Negro league baseball career in 1914 and four years later
joined the Brooklyn Royal Giants (ECL). A superior defensive third baseman,
he outperformed all other black players at his position in the 1920s. Whether
making spectacular plays to his left or right or fielding bunts like a master,
he delighted the fans who idolized him. After joining the Atlantic City
Bacharach Giants (ECL), he teamed with Dick Lundy* to form an almost
impregnable left side of the infield and helped his club win the 1926–1927
ECL pennants. In the 1926 Negro World Series against the Chicago American Giants, he hit a solid .293 in a losing effort.

After the ECL dissolved, Marcelle moved with Lundy to the Baltimore
Black Sox (ANL) and batted a respectable .288 in 1929. A good hitter and
a dangerous clutch performer, he batted .335 lifetime in Negro league competition. During eight winter seasons in Cuba, "Ghost" compiled a .305
average and led the league with .371 in 1923–1924 and hit .333 in exhibitions
against major leaguers. The competitive Creole also played for the Lincoln
Giants (ANL) and Detroit Stars (NNL). Marcelle's quick and fiery temper
frequently antagonized umpires, opponents, and teammates and indirectly
led to his withdrawal from league play.

Married to Hazel Taylor, he had two sons, Oliver, Jr., and Everett "Ziggy"
Marcelle. Ziggy played baseball for ten years in the NNL and for two years
in organized baseball at Quebec and also played professional basketball for
the Harlem Globetrotters. After retiring from baseball in 1934, Marcelle
worked as a painter in Denver, and died there of arteriosclerosis. Marcelle
was selected as the greatest third baseman in black baseball history in a 1952
Pittsburgh *Courier* poll.

BIBLIOGRAPHY: Oliver Marcelle file, National Baseball Hall of Fame Library, Cooperstown, NY; Robert W. Peterson, *Only the Ball Was White* (Englewood Cliffs, NJ,
1970); James A. Riley, *The All-Time All-Stars of Black Baseball* (Cocoa, FL, 1983);
James A. Riley, interviews with former Negro league players, James A. Riley Collection, Cocoa, FL.

James A. Riley

**MARICHAL, Juan Antonio Sanchez "Manito," "The Dominican
Dandy," "Laughing Boy"** (b. 20 October 1938, Laguna Verde, Dominican
Republic), player, grew up in a palm bark shack. His father, an impoverished
farmer, died when Juan was only 3 years old, after which his mother and
older brother Gonzalo brought him up. Gonzalo and Prospero Villona, Juan's
brother-in-law, stimulated his interest in baseball. Juan quit high school after
the eleventh grade and played amateur baseball as a shortstop and pitcher

for Monte Cristi, the United Fruit Company, and the Dominican Air Force and professionally with the Escogido Leones. He married 16-year-old Alma Rosa Carrajal on March 28, 1962, and has three children.

In 1958 San Francisco Giants (NL) scouts Horacio Martinez and Alex Pompez signed Marichal for a $500 bonus. Marichal pitched for Michigan City, IN (ML) in 1958, Springfield, MA (EL), in 1959, and Tacoma (PCL) in 1960 until joining the San Francisco Giants (NL) at midseason. The ML and EL leader in several pitching categories, the 6 foot, 185 pound, high-kicking right-hander varied his deliveries of the fastball, curve, and slider. His incredible control led to 575 strikeouts and only 131 walks in 655 minor league innings pitched. Marichal's chubby face, impish grin, agility, and grace masked his fierce determination. In his major league debut on July 19, 1960, he shut out the Philadelphia Phillies 2–0 and surrendered only an eighth-inning single by Clay Dalrymple. A 6–2 mark and 2.66 ERA highlighted his rookie season. In 1962 he compiled an 18–11 slate to help the Giants capture the NL pennant, but pitched only four innings in the World Series loss to the New York Yankees because of an injured finger.

From 1963 to 1969, Marichal compiled six 20-game victory seasons as the period's winningest hurler. During that span, Marichal enjoyed four consecutive 20-game victory seasons (1963–1966) and led the NL twice in victories (1963, 1968), complete games (1964, 1968), innings pitched (1963, 1968), and shutouts (1965, 1969) and once in best pitching percentage (1966) and ERA (1969). His 20-game victory seasons included 25–8 in 1963, 21–8 in 1964, 22–13 in 1965, 25–6 in 1966, 26–9 in 1968, and 21–11 in 1969. He compiled ERAs below 3.00 nine times, struck out over 200 batters six seasons, pitched over 300 innings four times, won at least 25 games three times, and walked at least 60 batters only twice. In 1971 he recorded an 18–11 slate to help the Giants win the Western Division title. The Giants lost the Championship Series to the Pittsburgh Pirates, as Marichal dropped his only decision. Marichal, who did not experience a losing season until 1972, was sold by the Giants following the 1973 campaign. He posted a 5–1 mark with the Boston Red Sox (AL) in 1974 and pitched briefly for the Los Angeles Dodgers (NL) in 1975 before retiring to his 1,000 acre mechanized farm in Santo Domingo.

During his sixteen-year major league career, the injury-prone Marichal won 243 games, lost 142 decisions, and recorded a 2.89 ERA in 471 contests. He completed 244 of 457 starts, struck out 2,303 batters and walked only 709 in 3,509.1 innings, and hurled 52 shutouts. San Francisco manager Alvin Dark* once commented, "Put your club a run ahead in the later innings, and Marichal is the greatest pitcher I ever saw." An eight-time NL All Star, Marichal surrendered only two runs in eighteen innings. He won the first 1962 All-Star Game and the 1964 All-Star Game and was named the Most Valuable Player of the 1965 contest. *The Sporting News* named Marichal to its NL All-Star team in 1963, 1965–1966, and 1968. He hurled a no-hit game on June 15, 1963, against the Houston Colt 45s and a one-hit shutout on August 2, 1966, against the Dodgers. In June 1963 he outdueled Warren Spahn* of the Milwaukee Braves 1–0 in 16 innings. Marichal's six opening season games (1962, 1964, 1966, 1971–1973) set another NL record.

At Candlestick Park on August 22, 1965, the normally easygoing, good-natured Marichal struck Los Angeles catcher John Roseboro on the head with his bat in the third inning. Dodgers pitcher Sandy Koufax* had just pitched inside, and Roseboro had fired the ball hard back to the pitcher just past Marichal's ear. Marichal was ejected from the game, suspended for nine days, and fined $1,750, then the stiffest penalty in NL history. In 1983 he became the first Latin American player chosen to the National Baseball Hall of Fame through the regular selection process.

BIBLIOGRAPHY: "The Dandy Dominican," *Time* 87 (June 10, 1966), pp. 88–92; Charles Einstein, "Juan Marichal at the Crossroads," *Sport* 45 (April, 1968), pp. 58–60, 88; Charles Einstein, "The Juan Marichal Mystery," *Sport* 35 (June, 1963), pp. 49–51, 72; "Juan Marichal," in *The Lincoln Library of Sports Champions*, vol. 8 (Columbus, 1974); Joseph L. Reichler, ed., *The Baseball Encyclopedia*, 6th ed. (New York, 1985), p. 1,883; Lowell Reidenbaugh, *Cooperstown: Where Baseball's Legends Live Forever* (St. Louis, 1983); Al Stump, "Always They Want More, More, More," *SEP* 240 (July 29, 1967), pp. 68–71; *TSN Baseball Register, 1967, 1975* (St. Louis, 1967, 1975).

David L. Porter

MARION, Martin Whitford "Marty," "Slats," "The Octopus" (b. 1 December 1917, Richburg, SC), player, manager, and executive, was the mainstay of the St. Louis Cardinals (NL) infield from 1940 to 1950 and one of the greatest fielding shortstops in baseball history. A descendant of Francis Marion ("The Swamp Fox" of Revolutionary War fame), he was one of the four sons of John and Virginia Marion and younger brother of Washington Senators outfielder John Marion. The 6 foot, 2 inch, 170 pound Marion grew up in the Atlanta, GA, area and attended Georgia Institute of Technology for one year. After the Cardinals signed him in 1936 to a four-year contract averaging about $3,000 annually, he played with Huntington, WV (MAL), in 1936 and Rochester, NY (IL), from 1937 through 1939. Joining the parent Cardinals in 1940, he batted .278 in 125 games and rapidly became one of the decade's dominant infielders. Never a high average or power hitter, he batted .263 and belted 36 home runs in a thirteen-year career. In 1,572 games, he made 1,448 hits and 272 doubles, and knocked in 624 runs. Marion developed into a clutch hitter, leading the NL in doubles (38) in 1942 and adeptly hitting to the opposite field.

Marion is best remembered as a fielder. Nicknamed "The Octopus," the tall, lanky Marion possessed sure hands, vast range, and a strong, accurate arm. Equally adept at charging balls and going behind second base, he made easy, precise throws. In the last (fifth) game of the 1942 World Series, Marion and catcher Walker Cooper collaborated on a dramatic pickoff play of Joe Gordon to climax the Cardinals' rout of the New York Yankees. In 1944 Marion batted .267 and was voted both the NL's Most Valuable Player and baseball's Player of the Year. A member of four NL pennant winners (1942–1944, 1946), he helped the Cardinals capture three World Series championships.

A childhood leg injury kept Marion from World War II military service and combined with recurrent back trouble to shorten his career. After the Cardinals' first second division finish in over a decade, he replaced Eddie Dyer in 1951 as manager and guided St. Louis to a respectable 81–73 mark and a third place finish. In 1952 he joined the crosstown AL Browns and piloted them to two losing seasons. He managed the Chicago White Sox (AL) in 1955 (91–63) and 1956 (85–69) to third place finishes. In six years as manager, Marion compiled 356 wins, 371 losses, and a .490 percentage.

After retiring from playing and managing, Marion owned the Houston (TL) franchise in 1960 and managed the St. Louis Stadium Club (a center for area sportsdom) for eighteen years. The suburban St. Louis resident married Mary Dallas in December 1937, has four daughters, farms near St. Louis, and duck hunts. His biggest baseball thrill came in 1942, when the Cardinals upset the Yankees. Marion played a considerable role in bringing the Cardinals from nine and one-half games behind the Brooklyn Dodgers in mid-August to capture the pennant. Like many right-handed batters of his era, he considered Ewell Blackwell of the Cincinnati Reds as the toughest pitcher. Marion regarded Frank Crespi, maimed in World War II, as the greatest single-season (1941) second baseman he teamed with.

BIBLIOGRAPHY: Bob Broeg, *Redbirds: A Century of Cardinals' Baseball* (St. Louis, 1981); William B. Mead and Harold Rosenthal, *The Ten Worst Years of Baseball* (New York, 1978); Stan Musial, *Stan Musial: The Man's Own Story*, as told to Bob Broeg (New York, 1964); Joseph L. Reichler, ed., *The Baseball Encyclopedia*, 6th ed. (New York 1985); Lawrence Ritter and Donald Honig, *The Image of Their Greatness* (New York, 1979).

Leonard Frey

MARIS, Roger Eugene (b. Maras, 10 September 1934, Hibbing, MN; d. 14 December 1985, Houston, TX), player, was the son of Rudolph and Connie Maras, whose family name was legally changed to Maris. His father worked as a railroad supervisor and played town and semi-pro baseball. Maris moved at age 12 with his parents to Fargo, ND, and completed his education at Shanley High School, where he excelled in football, basketball, and track and field. He played Little League baseball, but his high school had no organized team. Maris instead performed for the Fargo American Legion baseball team and was named its Most Valuable Player in 1950. The Cleveland Indians (AL) signed Maris for $15,000 in 1953 and assigned the outfielder to his hometown Fargo-Moorehead, MN (NoL), team, where he hit .325 and belted 9 home runs. At Keokuk, IA (3IL) the following year, he blossomed into a long-ball hitter with 32 home runs, 111 RBIs, a .315 batting average, and 25 stolen bases. Brief stints followed at Tulsa (TL), Reading, PA (EL), and Indianapolis (AA) before Maris joined the Cleveland Indians in 1957.

Maris batted .235 his rookie year with 14 homers and 51 RBIs for Cleveland. In June, 1958, he was traded in a multi-player deal to the Kansas City Athletics (AL), where he batted .240, slugged 28 home runs, and drove in 80 runs. Although stricken with appendicitis the following year, he still compiled a .273 batting average and 16 home runs. On December 11, 1959, the New York Yankees (AL) traded established players Hank Bauer, Norm Siebern, Marv Throneberry, and Don Larsen to Kansas City for the hard-hitting, solid-fielding Maris and infielders Joe DeMaestri and Kent Hadley. With the Yankees, the 6 foot, 200 pound, pull-hitting right fielder reached his potential as a player and left an indelible mark on baseball history. In 1960 Maris helped the Yankees win the AL pennant by batting .283 with 39 homers and 112 RBIs. His RBI figure and .581 slugging percentage paced the AL. This outstanding effort earned Maris both the AL MVP and Gold Glove (.985 fielding average) awards and an AL All-Star team selection.

Maris made 1961 an exciting, memorable baseball year by dueling teammate Mickey Mantle* for the home run title. After hitting only 1 homer in April, he belted 11 in May, 15 in June, 13 in July, 11 in August, and 9 in September. His record-setting 61st round tripper came on October 1 against Boston Red Sox right-hander Tracy Stallard. This home run, hit on the last day of the regular season, enabled the mentally and physically exhausted Maris to surpass the legendary Babe Ruth* as the major league player with the most homers in a single season. He also won the RBI (142) and runs scored (132) titles, led the AL in total bases (366), tied Lou Gehrig's* record for most home runs (30 in a single season at Yankee Stadium), belted seven homers in six consecutive games (August 11–16), and tied an AL standard for most homers in a doubleheader (4) on July 25, hitting two in each game. Maris also had to endure the intense media and psychological pressure associated with his feat. Baseball Commissioner Ford Frick* ruled that the new home run record would have an asterisk attached because it was accomplished in 162 games rather than within the 154 game schedule of the Ruth era. The many accolades and awards for that exceptional season included Maris being named AL MVP again and recipient of the Hickok Belt as the world's top pro athlete.

In 1962 Maris hit 33 homers, drove in 100 runs, and batted .256, but his home run and RBI productions thereafter gradually declined due to several nagging injuries. He was traded to St. Louis (NL) in December, 1966, and helped the Cardinals win pennants in 1967 and 1968. After retiring from baseball following the 1968 campaign, the Gainesville, FL, resident operated an Anheuser-Busch distributorship (Maris Distributing Company). In twelve major league seasons, Maris batted .260 with 1,325 hits, 195 doubles, 275 home runs, 851 RBIs, and a .476 slugging average. The outstanding right fielder compiled a .982 lifetime fielding average. He played in five World Series with the Yankees (1960–1964) and two with the Cardinals (1967–1968), making 33 hits, 6 home runs, 18 RBIs, and a .217 batting average. From 1959 through 1962, he made the AL All-Star team. Maris, who died of cancer, married Patricia Ann Carvell on October 13, 1956, and had six children, Susan, Roger, Jr., Kevin, Richard, Sandra, and Randy.

BIBLIOGRAPHY: Maury Allen, *The Record Breakers* (Englewood Cliffs, NJ, 1968); Arthur Daley, *Kings of the Home Run* (New York, 1962); Mark Gallagher, *Fifty Years of Yankee All Stars* (New York, 1984); Zander Hollander and Larry Fox, *The Home Run Story* (New York, 1966); Paul MacFarlane, ed., *TSN Daguerreotypes of Great Stars of Baseball* (St. Louis, 1981); Roger Maris file, National Baseball Hall of Fame Library, Cooperstown, NY; Roger Maris and Jim Ogle, *Roger Maris at Bat* (New York, 1962); Richard Rainbolt, *Baseball's Home Run Hitters* (Minneapolis, 1975); Joseph L. Reichler, ed., *The Baseball Encyclopedia*, 6th ed. (New York, 1985), p. 1,156; Ray Robinson, *The Greatest Yankees of Them All* (New York, 1969); Milton J. Shapiro, *Champions of the Bat: Baseball's Greatest Sluggers* (New York, 1970); Milton J. Shapiro, *The Day They Made the Record Book* (New York, 1968); Leonard Shecter, *Roger Maris: Home Run Hero* (New York, 1961).

Louis J. Andolino

MARQUARD, Richard William "Rube" (b. 9 October 1889, Cleveland, OH; d. 1 June 1980, Pikesville, MD), player, manager, scout, and coach, was the son of Cleveland's chief engineer. He married three times and did not have any children. In 1913 he wed actress Blossom Seeley and appeared with her in a vaudeville dance routine during the off-season. After the couple divorced in 1920, Marquard in 1921 married Naomi Wrigley of Baltimore. Following her death in 1954, he wed Jane Ottenheimer of Baltimore. Although nicknamed "Rube" because of his resemblance to Philadelphia Athletics left-hander Rube Waddell,* the far more sophisticated Marquard never smoked, drank, or missed curfew.

Marquard at age 15 pitched (and won) one game for Waterloo, IA (IoSL) but quit the club when not offered a contract. When the 1907 baseball season opened, Marquard worked for a Cleveland ice cream plant and pitched for the company baseball team. Later that season, he signed with Indianapolis (AA) and was optioned to Canton, OH, where he led the CL in victories with a 23–13 record. In 1908 he pitched superbly for Indianapolis, pacing the AA with 28 wins. The New York Giants (NL) outbid several other major league clubs and purchased Marquard's contract for $11,000, then a record price for a minor league player. The 6 foot 3 inch, 180 pound, 18-year-old left-hander was initially labeled "the $11,000 beauty," but was called the "$11,000 lemon" after losing 13 of 18 decisions. Following another mediocre season in 1910, Marquard in 1911 mastered control of his curveball and blossomed into a 24–7 pitcher. That year he and his roommate Christy Mathewson* led the Giants to the first of three consecutive pennants.

Marquard enjoyed his most notable season in 1912, compiling a 26–11 record. He won his first 19 decisions, a major league one-season consecutive game-winning record shared with old-time Giants right-hander Timothy Keefe.* Due to then-existing rules, Marquard was denied one win he would have been awarded now. In 1913 he won 23 games and lost only 10. Marquard's fortunes reversed in 1914, when he lost 12 straight games and dropped to a 12–22 record. Although winning a remarkable 21-inning triumph over the Pittsburgh Pirates, Marquard helped cause the Giants to drop to second place. The Boston Braves moved from last place on July 4 to a "miracle" NL pennant win. In 1915 Marquard pitched a no-hitter against Brooklyn on April 15, but pitched inconsistently thereafter. When permitted by disenchanted manager John McGraw* to arrange a deal, Marquard was sold to the Brooklyn Dodgers (NL) for $7,500 later that season. He remained with Brooklyn through its NL pennant-winning season in 1920 and played the 1921 season for the Cincinnati Reds (NL). The Reds traded Marquard to the Boston Braves (NL), for whom he pitched the last four years of his major league career. Marquard compiled a 204–179 record over eighteen major league seasons, winning over 20 games three seasons. He appeared in 536 games, struck out 1,593 batters, and compiled a 3.08 ERA.

Subsequently Marquard managed and pitched part-time for Providence (EL) in 1926, Baltimore (IL) and Birmingham, AL (SA), in 1927, and for Jacksonville, FL (SEL), in 1929–1930. After umpiring in the EL and being assistant coach at Assumption College, he coached and scouted for Atlanta (SA) in 1932 and completed his baseball career at age 43 by managing Wichita in 1933. Marquard settled in Baltimore in 1930 and remained there, working in mutuel windows at various race tracks for many years. In 1971 he was elected to the National Baseball Hall of Fame.

BIBLIOGRAPHY: Martin Appel and Burt Goldblatt, *Baseball's Best: The Hall of Fame Gallery* (New York, 1977); Frank Graham, *McGraw of the Giants* (New York, 1944); Gene Karst and Martin J. Jones, Jr., *Who's Who in Professional Baseball* (New Rochelle, NY, 1973).

Fred Stein

MARTIN, Alfred Manuel "Billy" (b. 16 May 1928, Berkeley, CA), player, scout, coach, manager, and announcer, is the son of itinerant Portuguese musician Alfred Manuel Martin, who deserted his mother, Joan (Salvini) Downey. Billy's feisty, outspoken mother became the major influence on her son. Martin grew up in the tough region of West Berkeley, where, as he remembered, "From the time I was twelve years old until I was maybe fifteen, I awoke every morning knowing that there was a good chance I was going to have to get in a fight with somebody." He attended public schools but showed classroom ability only in history and other subjects that he liked. Sports, especially baseball, kept him out of serious conflicts with the law. As a high school ballplayer, he impressed Casey Stengel,* the Oakland Oaks' (PCL) manager. Martin's professional baseball career started as a second and third baseman on Oakland's Idaho Falls (PrL) team in 1946 and at Phoenix (ArTL) in 1947. In 1948 he played under Stengel at Oakland. Stengel, who became the New York Yankees' (AL) manager in 1949, remembered his brash pupil. In 1950 Martin joined the Bronx Bombers after spending the first 29 games with in the Yankees farm club at Kansas City (AA).

As a major leaguer, the 5 foot, 11 inch, 170 pound Martin compensated for a lack of size and skills with intelligence and drive. Martin's mediocre .257 career batting average belied his skills in the clutch. After saving the 1952 World Series with a desperation catch, he won the 1953 classic Most Valuable Player Award by hitting .500 with a record 12 hits in a six-game series. As a New York Yankee from 1950 to 1957, he became Stengel's favorite and absorbed many of the "Old Professor's" insights into managing. Martin's off-the-field conduct, however, displeased the team ownership, which viewed him as a harmful influence on his drinking buddy, team star Mickey Mantle.* After a brawl at the Copacabana night club, Martin was traded to the Kansas City Athletics (AL). His nondescript post-Yankees career saw him play with Kansas City in late 1957, the Detroit Tigers (AL) in 1958, Cleveland Indians (AL) in 1959, Cincinnati Reds (NL) in 1960, and Milwaukee Braves (NL) and Minnesota Twins (AL) in 1961. In 1,021 games, he amassed 877 hits, 137 doubles, 28 triples, and 64 home runs, scored 425 runs, and knocked in 333 runs.

Martin's off-the-field life was troubled. His first marriage to Lois E. Berndt on August 4, 1950, produced a daughter, Kelly Ann, but ended in divorce in 1953. Martin married Gretchen Winkler in October 1959 and has a son, Billy Joe. Martin's reputation for fighting and drink led to several incidents that overshadowed a generosity and attachment to friends that seldom received publicity.

After serving as a scout and coach with Minnesota from 1962 through 1967, Martin began managing with the Denver Bears (AA) in 1968. He began major league managing the next year by leading the Twins to the division championship. Thereafter his managerial career fell into a predictable if exciting pattern. He produced winners on the field, but off-the-field troubles with owners and incidents resulted in his being fired or resigning. He managed Minnesota in 1969, Detroit from 1971 to September 1, 1973, the Texas Rangers (AL) from September 8, 1973 to July 1975, the Oakland A's (AL) from 1980 to 1982, and the New York Yankees on four different occasions from 1975 to 1985. In each place except Texas, he produced at least one division winner. With the lowly Rangers, he secured the highest finish in the history of the franchise. Martin's success resulted from his intense study of the game and ability to motivate players. An active manager, Martin sought to control most aspects of play, from calling pitches to approving attempted steals. He seemed best at propelling average players to good performances, but sometimes encountered difficulties with superstars and young players.

The most publicized and longest running of Martin's managerial efforts involved the New York Yankees. Hired by owner George Steinbrenner to rekindle Yankees greatness in late 1975, Martin delivered the first Yankees AL pennant in eleven years in 1976. The Cincinnati Reds, however, defeated the Yankees in four straight games in the World Series. In 1977 Steinbrenner added slugger Reggie Jackson,* initiating several highly publicized feuds between manager and superstar. Highlights included a near fight in a nationally televised game, the benching of Jackson in the AL Championship Series, and the star's record-shattering performance leading the Yankees to victory in the 1977 World Series. The next year Steinbrenner first fired Martin in midseason and then promised to rehire him. Martin returned as manager in 1979, only to be dismissed after an off-the-field incident. Between Yankees firings, Martin managed Oakland and won a divisional flag there in 1981 before being relieved in 1982. He again managed the Yankees in 1983, was relieved, and returned as the club's manager in 1985. Martin piloted the Yankees to a 91–54 mark for the remainder of 1985, but then was replaced by Lou Piniella. He ended his 1985 assignment with a career managerial record of 1,218 wins and 990 losses, a .552 winning percentage, five divisional championships, two AL titles, and one World Series championship. In 1986 he joined the New York Yankees' announcing team.

BIBLIOGRAPHY: Robert W. Creamer, *Stengel* (New York, 1984); Frank Deford, "Love, Hate and Billy Martin," *SI* 42 (June 2, 1975), p. 70; Peter Golenbock, *Dynasty: The New York Yankees, 1949–1964* (New York, 1975); Reggie Jackson with Mike Lupica, *Reggie* (New York, 1984); Larry Keith, "Billy Boy Is Back," *SI* 51 (July 2, 1979), pp. 14–18; Ed Linn, *Steinbrenner's Yankees* (New York, 1982); Sparky Lyle and Peter Golenbock, *The Bronx Zoo* (New York, 1979); Billy Martin and Peter Golenbock, *Number 1* (New York, 1980); Craig Nettles, *Balls* (New York, 1984); B. J. Phillip and P. A. Witteman, "Happy Playing Billy Ball," *Time* 117 (June 4, 1981), p. 88; *TSN Baseball Register—1978*, (St. Louis, 1978), pp. 449–450; *WWA*, 43rd ed. (1984–1985), p. 2,116.

James W. Harper

MARTIN, Johnny Leonard Roosevelt "Pepper," "The Wild Hoss of the Osage" (b. 29 February 1904, Temple, OK; d. 5 March 1965, McAlester, OK), player, coach, and manager, was the son of Oklahoma prairie farmer George Washington and Celia Martin. Nicknamed "Pepper," Martin attended high school for two years at Classen, OK, and served in the Reserve Officer Training Corps. Friends called Martin "Johnny" because he disliked the nickname "Pepper." A Rochester, NY, reporter later called him "The Wild Hoss of the Osage" because of his gridiron exploits at age 19 for Guthrie in Osage County, OK. Martin began his professional baseball career with Greenville, TX (ETL) in the St. Louis Cardinals farm system in 1924 and played at Fort Smith, AR (WA) in 1925, Syracuse, NY, and Rochester, NY (IL), in 1926 and 1930, and Houston (TL) in 1927. Although a pinch runner with the Cardinals (NL) in 1928, he did not win a permanent place on the roster as an outfielder until 1931.

Martin's aggressive spirit and desire to play the game abounded in the 1931 World Series, in which he virtually defeated the Philadelphia Athletics single-handedly by making a record of 12 hits, batting .500, and stealing 5 bases. In 1932 the 5 foot, 8 inch, 170 pound Martin slumped to a .238 average. He had spent a night sleeping in tall, wet grass on a hunting trip, causing a persistent skin infection that severely hampered his play. He also suffered a broken hand, compounding his misfortunes. In 1933 he switched to third base and raised his batting average to .316. Although a steady outfielder, Martin played the infield adventurously. He discouraged bunting by aiming throws at the runner going down the line.

Martin learned his head-first sliding style, characteristic of the "Gas House Gang," from manager Frankie Frisch.* The fiery Martin, who never wore sanitary hose or underwear, led the NL in runs scored (122) and stolen bases (26) in 1933. Twice more (1934, 1936) he led the NL in stolen bases with 23. Martin also organized a highly publicized band, The Mudcats. He returned to the minors after the 1940 season, although he had hit .316 that year. An itinerant minor league manager, he made stops at Sacramento (PCL) and Miami and Fort Lauderdale (FIL). During 1944 he returned briefly to the Cardinals and hit .279. In 1,189 career games, he made 1,227 hits and 270 doubles, scored 756 runs, knocked in 501 runs, and batted .298. In three World Series, he hit a superlative .418. Martin was planning to coach for the Tulsa Oilers (TL) when he was stricken with a fatal heart attack. His last major league appearance came as a Chicago Cubs' (NL) coach in 1965. He left his widow, Ruby, whom he had married on November 9, 1927, and three married daughters.

BIBLIOGRAPHY: Bill Borst, *Baseball Through a Knothole* (St. Louis, 1978); Bob Broeg, *Redbirds* (St. Louis, 1981); Robert Hood, *The Gas House Gang* (New York, 1976); Gene Karst and Martin J. Jones, Jr., *Who's Who in Professional Baseball* (New Rochelle, NY, 1973); Frederick G. Lieb, *The St. Louis Cardinals* (New York, 1945); Frederick G. Lieb, *The Story of the World Series* (New York, 1965); Paul MacFarlane, ed., *TSN Daguerreotypes of Great Stars of Baseball* (St. Louis, 1981); *NYT*, March 6, 1965.

William A. Borst

MATHEWS, Edwin Lee, Jr., "Eddie" (b. 13 October 1931, Texarkana, TX), player, coach, and manager, is the son of Western Union telegraph operator Edwin L. Mathews, Sr. and spent fifteen of seventeen major league seasons with the Braves (NL). He signed with the Boston Braves for a $6,000 bonus on graduation from Santa Barbara High School. Mathews played third base with High Point-Thomasville (NCSL) in 1949, Atlanta (SA) in 1950 and 1951, and Milwaukee (AA) in 1951. After joining the Boston club in 1952, he played with the Braves in Milwaukee (1953–1965) and Atlanta (1966). His final two seasons were spent with the Houston Astros (NL) and the Detroit Tigers (AL). The 6 foot, 1 inch, 190 pound Mathews performed primarily as a third baseman, but played first base his final two seasons. Mathews, an above average third baseman, exhibited hitting prowess that attracted widespread attention. In his first season, he broke Ralph Kiner's* record for home runs by a rookie by slugging 25. That season he hit a rookie record three home runs in one game. He learned quickly in the batter's box, leading the NL with 115 strikeouts and drawing only 59 walks his rookie season. Two years later, he struck out only 61 times and walked on 113 occasions. He never again led the NL in strikeouts, but paced in walks four times.

A left-handed batter who threw right-handed, Mathews led the major leagues in homers in 1953 and 1959 by hitting 47 and 46, respectively. He slugged 512 home runs in his major league career, averaging over 30 per season. Contemporary sluggers Mickey Mantle* and Willie Mays* averaged fewer home runs per season. Blessed with good health and good luck, Mathews played in 134 or more games in each of his first sixteen seasons and batted at least 436 times per season over that span. Since Hank Aaron* played on the Braves, opposing catchers could not pitch around Mathews. Mathews and Aaron combined for 1,267 home runs, exceeding Babe Ruth* and Lou Gehrig* by 60 career round trippers. In 2,388 games, he made 2,315 hits, slammed 354 doubles, knocked in 1,453 runs, walked 1,444 times, struck out 1,487 times, and batted .271. Mathews participated in the 1957 and 1958 World Series with Milwaukee and in the 1968 fall classic with Detroit. His 1957 and 1968 teams won World Series championships. Mathews later coached and managed the Atlanta Braves from 1972 through 1974 and served as a minor league instructor-scout for the Milwaukee Brewers (AL) from 1975 through 1978. His squads compiled losing records (149–161), with his best team finish being fourth place. In 1978 he was elected to the National Baseball Hall of Fame in his first year of eligibility.

BIBLIOGRAPHY: Joseph L. Reichler, ed., *The Baseball Encyclopedia*, 6th ed. (New York, 1985), p. 1,164; Lowell Reidenbaugh, *Cooperstown: Where Baseball's Legends Live Forever* (St. Louis, 1983).

Stephen D. Bodayla

MATHEWS, Robert T. "Bobby," "Little Bobby" (b. 21 November 1851, Baltimore, MD; d. 17 April 1898, Baltimore, MD), player, performed for ten baseball teams from 1868 through 1887. His clubs included the Fort Wayne Kekiongas (1871), Lord Baltimores (1872), and New York Mutuals

(1873–1875) of the NA, the Mutuals of New York (1876), Cincinnati (1877), Providence (1879–1881), and Boston (1881–1882) of the NL, and Philadelphia (1883–1887) of the AA. From 1871 through 1887, the masterly 5 foot, 5½ inch, 145 pound right-hander compiled a 298–249 win-loss record. After winning 132 and losing 111 decisions in the NA from 1871 to 1875, he won 166 and lost 138, struck out 1,199 batters, and compiled a 3.00 ERA in the NL from 1876 to 1887. A star pitcher for the famed New York Mutuals, he reached a career high 42 wins and 23 losses in 1874. A *New York Times* sportswriter lauded his 2–0, three-hit victory on May 30, "undoubtedly the best ever played in this vicinity and with one exception—Kekionga and Forest City, the best ever played in the United States." Coincidentally, Mathews also hurled that earlier game, helping Fort Wayne defeat Cleveland's Forest City on May 4, 1871. In a day characterized by much higher scores, Mathews' five-hit shutout was considered a remarkable feat and comprised the "smallest score made in a regular match during the season." During 1875 and 1876, he won 29 and 21 victories, respectively, and yet experienced losing seasons because his teams sagged. In 1875 he led the NA with 38 losses.

In 1877 he encountered his worst season by winning only 3 of 15 decisions. Surviving changing pitching rules and techniques, "Little Bobby" quickly regained his pitching ability. From 1883 to 1885, he compiled three superb 30-game victory seasons for Philadelphia (AA) and in 1883 led them to the championship. Mathews, a control expert, threw within a hair's breadth of a mark. Relying on mastery of pitches rather than overpowering speed, he "generally outguessed the batter." He struck out sixteen batters in one game in 1884 and averaged over six strikeouts per game the next year. During his three 30-game seasons, Mathews walked only 137 batters and struck out 775. Several contemporary reporters credited him with developing the curveball, but this claim has since been challenged. To keep hitters off balance, he threw a variety of pitches ("hardly ever using the same delivery twice"). He was hailed as "without doubt the most versatile boxman of his day." Hank O'Day, later manager of the Chicago Cubs, claimed that Mathews threw an early-day spitball and controlled the pitch with remarkable skill.

Mathews' inept hitting, however, pleased opposing teams. From 1871 through 1875, he batted .212. He averaged only .192 from 1876 to 1887 and occasionally played the outfield and infield. The slightly built Mathews did not need to rely on his hitting because he was a scientific pitcher who "occupied the spotlight of the baseball stage for fourteen years." Physical ailments limited him to seven games in 1887 and forced Mathews to retire from baseball. The Baltimore *Sun* on April 18, 1898, recounted his sad post-baseball career: "From that time until his mind failed he tried a number of occupations, and was in rather straitened circumstances, having saved little in his prosperous days."

BIBLIOGRAPHY: *Base Ball Player*, 1872–1876; *De Witt's Base Ball Guide*, 1876–1881; Robert Mathews file, National Baseball Hall of Fame Library, Cooperstown, NY;

NYT, 1873–1874; Joseph L. Reichler ed., *The Baseball Encyclopedia*, 6th ed. (New York, 1985), pp. 61, 1, 164, 1, 888; *Spalding's Base Ball Guide, 1880–1888* (New York, 1880–1888); *The* (Baltimore) *Sun*, April 18, 1898.

                                                                            Duane A. Smith

MATHEWSON, Christopher "Christy," "Big Six" (b. 12 August 1880, Factoryville, PA; d. 7 October 1925, Saranac Lake, NY), player, coach, manager, and executive, was the son of gentleman farmer Gilbert B. and Minerva J. (Capwell) Mathewson. After prepping at Keystone Academy in Factoryville, he entered Bucknell College in 1898 on a scholarship. He played football, basketball, and baseball there, but did not graduate. He married Jan Stoughton and had one child, Christopher, Jr. His brother Henry briefly pitched with the New York Giants. An outstanding college pitcher, Mathewson began his professional baseball career in 1899 with Taunton, MA (NEL), and started the 1900 season with Norfolk, VA (VL). Norfolk sold the 20-2 Mathewson in midsummer to the New York Giants (NL), where he pitched for seventeen years and became one of the NL's greatest pitchers.

The 6 foot, 1½ inch, 195 pound right-handed "Matty" specialized in his "fadeaway," described by journalist John Kieran* (OS) as "a ball that dropped deceptively and on the 'inside' for a right-handed batter." "Big Six" won 373 games, third highest in major league history, and compiled a .665 winning percentage, the seventh best all-time mark. Mathewson lost only 188 games, completed 435 of 552 starts, pitched 4,782 innings, struck out 2,502 batters, and walked only 846. A 37-game winner in 1908, the consistent Mathewson triumphed in at least 22 games per season from 1903 through 1914. Five times he led the NL in ERA, including a sparkling 1.14 in 1909. His 2.13 career ERA stands as baseball's fifth best. Seldom pitching under 300 innings, he hurled 390.2 innings to lead the NL in 1908 and completed 34 games. An overpowering pitcher, he five times led the NL in strikeouts and exhibited great control. Only two pitchers have surpassed his 80 career shutouts. Mathewson's World Series record augmented his fame. Although winning only five of ten decisions in four World Series, in 1905 he incredibly hurled three shutouts against the Philadelphia Athletics. Besides holding the record for most World Series shutouts (4) and complete games (10), he failed to complete only one World Series game that he started and compiled a composite 1.15 ERA.

In early 1916, Mathewson became manager of the Cincinnati Reds (NL) and won in his only mound appearance there. From 1916 to 1918 he piloted the Reds to 164 wins, 176 losses, and two fourth place finishes. On August 20, 1917, he and Giants manager John McGraw* were arrested because their teams had violated a New York law prohibiting games on Sunday. The episode publicized the movement to secure Sunday baseball in New York, particularly because Mathewson had promised his mother never to play on the Sabbath. In 1918 Mathewson enlisted in the U.S. Army as a captain and served overseas in the Gas and Flame Division of the American Expeditionary Force in France. A poisonous gas victim, he suffered pulmonary tuberculosis thereafter. Mathewson rejoined the Giants as a coach after World War I and remained with the club until 1920. During that span, Mathewson spent much time at Saranac Lake, NY, recuperating from tuberculosis. In 1923 the lowly Boston Braves (NL) made him president as a public relations ploy because Mathewson could work only part-time.

Mathewson, a public hero, substantially elevated the professional baseball player's image. The college man epitomized the Christian athlete, did not smoke or drink, and acted as a gentleman and scholar. Lester Chadwick's "Baseball Joe," a series of juvenile sports books, used Mathewson as a model. John Wheeler ghostwrote juvenile books under Mathewson's name, among them *Pitching in a Pinch* and *Pitcher Pollock*. After Mathewson's death, newspapers and periodicals throughout the United States eulogized him. *Commonweal* wrote,

No other pitcher ever loomed so majestically in young minds, quite overshadowing George Washington and his cherry tree or even that transcendant model of boyhood, Frank Merriwell. Such men have a very real value above and beyond the achievements of brawn and sporting skill. They realize and typify in a fashion the ideal of sport—clean power in the hands of a clean and vigorous personality.

In 1936 Mathewson was elected to the National Baseball Hall of Fame in the very first year of balloting.

BIBLIOGRAPHY: Chicago *Daily News*, July 5, 7, 1913; *Commonweal* 2 (October 21, 1925), p. 579; *DAB* 12 (1933), pp. 407–408; John McGraw, *My Thirty Years in Baseball* (New York, 1923); *NYT*, 1900–1916, August 21, 22, 1917, October 8, 1925; Joseph L. Reichler, ed., *The Baseball Encyclopedia*, 6th ed. (New York, 1985), pp. 639, 1,888–1,889; Steven A. Riess, *Touching Base: Professional Baseball and American Culture in the Progressive Era* (Westport, CT, 1980); Lawrence S. Ritter, *The Glory of Their Times* (New York, 1966); Harold Seymour, *Baseball*, vol. 2, *The Golden Age* (New York, 1971); Christopher Mathewson file, National Baseball Hall of Fame Library, Cooperstown, NY; David Quentin Voigt, *American Baseball, From the Commissioners to Continental Expansion*, vol. 2, (Norman, OK, 1970); Douglas Wallop, *Baseball: An Informal History* (New York, 1969).

Steven A. Riess

MAY, Lee Andrew (b. 23 March 1943, Birmingham, AL), player and coach, is the brother of outfielder–first baseman Carlos May and starred for the Cincinnati Reds (NL), Houston Astros (NL), and Baltimore Orioles (AL). May's father strung together mattresses, while his mother plucked chickens. After his parents divorced, he lived with his grandmother. He married childhood sweetheart Terrye Perdue in January, 1962, and has three children. Upon graduating from high school, May attended Miles College in Birmingham and then signed with the Cincinnati Reds (NL) for $12,000. He played with Tampa (FSL) in 1961 and 1962, Rocky Mount, NC (CrL) in 1963, Macon (SL) in 1964, San Diego (PCL) in 1965, Buffalo (IL) in 1966, and the Reds from 1965 through 1971. In a July 15, 1969, doubleheader, May slugged four home runs and knocked in ten runs. In 1970 May set a club record by hitting three grand slam homers and striking out 142 times. A star of the 1970 NL championship team, he hit .389 in the World Series against the Baltimore Orioles. After the next season, however, May was sent to the Houston Astros (NL) in an eight-player trade. In the sixth inning of an April 29, 1974, game against the San Diego Padres, May became the twentieth major leaguer to belt two home runs in one inning. He was traded to the Baltimore Orioles (AL) after the 1974 season and led the AL in 1976 in RBIs (109). In 1981 and 1982, he played with the Kansas City Royals (AL). He retired in 1983, but the Royals hired him as a batting instructor in 1984. During his career, May appeared in 2,071 games, made 2,031 hits, slugged 340 doubles and 354 home runs, batted .267 lifetime, knocked in 1,244 runs, and compiled a .459 slugging average. His 1,570 strikeouts ranked him among the ten highest on the all-time list. A 6 foot, 3 inch, 200 pound right-hander, May hit with power to all fields by "going with the pitch." Critics noted that the slow May stole only 39 career bases and played only adequately on defense.

BIBLIOGRAPHY: Cincinnati *Enquirer*, July 16, 1969; Houston *Post*, April 30, 1974; Mark Ribowsky, "May Gives Orioles Edge in AL East," *Black Sports* (August, 1975), pp. 48–51; *TSN*, February 20, 1984.

John David Healy

MAYS, Carl William "Sub" (b. 12 November 1893, Liberty, KY; d. 4 April 1971, El Cajon, CA), player and scout, excelled as a right-handed "submarine pitcher" in both the AL and NL (1915–1929). Mays, one of eight children born to William Henry Mays, a Methodist minister and farmer, and Louisa (Callie) Mays, was forced to leave school when his father died in 1904. The 5 foot, 11½ inch, 195 pound Mays began his professional baseball career with Boise (WTL) in 1912. He pitched with Portland, OR (NWL), in 1913 and compiled a 24–8 mark with Providence (IL) in 1914. He joined the Boston Red Sox (AL) and became one of their mound mainstays from 1915 to July, 1919.

On July 13, 1919, Mays quit the Red Sox in the middle of a game, claiming that he "could not win" for the team. Two weeks later, he was traded to the New York Yankees (AL). Ban Johnson,* AL president, tried to block the deal, but the New York State Supreme Court overruled him. Mays enjoyed very good seasons with the club in 1920 and 1921, but feuded with Yankees manager Miller Huggins* and was waived to the NL after the 1923 season. He appeared in the 1916 and 1918 World Series with Boston and in the 1921 and 1922 fall classics with New York, winning three of seven decisions with a 2.20 ERA. On August 16, 1920, Mays struck Cleveland shortstop Ray Chapman on the left temple with a pitch in the strike zone. Chapman died that night, the only major league fatality in history. Mays was absolved of all blame in the tragedy when a move to bar him from the game failed.

Mays spent five years with the Cincinnati Reds (NL) from 1924 to 1929, experiencing two good seasons there, and finished his major league career with the New York Giants (NL) in 1929. He hurled for Portland, OR (PCL), in 1930 and for Toledo-Louisville (AA) in 1930–1931, retiring following the latter season. Mays won at least 20 games five times in the major leagues, compiled a lifetime record of 208 wins and 126 losses (.623), completed 231 of 325 starts, struck out 862 batters, hurled 29 shutouts, and compiled a 2.92 ERA. In his best year (1921), Mays finished 27–9 and led the AL in games won, best percentage (.750), games (49), and innings pitched (336.1). In retirement Mays scouted for the AL Cleveland Indians (1958–1961), Kansas City Athletics (1962), and NL Milwaukee Braves (1963), in the northwest and operated a boys' baseball school.

BIBLIOGRAPHY: Gene Karst and Martin J. Jones, Jr., *Who's Who in Professional Baseball* (New Rochelle, NY, 1973); F. C. Lane, "Carl Mays' Cynical Definition of Pitching Efficiency," *Baseball Magazine* 37 (August, 1928), pp. 391–392; Paul MacFarlane, ed., *TSN Daguerreotypes of Great Stars of Baseball* (St. Louis, 1981); Bob McGarigle, *Baseball's Greatest Tragedy: The Story of Carl Mays—Submarine Pitcher* (Hicksville, NY, 1972); Carl Mays, "Is Hornsby Baseball's Greatest Hitter?" *Baseball Magazine* 34 (February, 1925), pp. 391–392; Carl Mays, "My Attitude Towards the Unfortunate Chapman," *Baseball Magazine* 25 (November, 1920), pp. 575–577, 607; Eugene C. Murdock, *Ban Johnson: Czar of Baseball* (Westport, CT, 1982); Eugene C. Murdock, taped interview with Waite Hoyt, March 12, 1976; *TSN*, February 14, 1944, August 10, 1963, April 17, 1971.

Eugene C. Murdock

MAYS, Willie Howard "Say Hey" (b. 6 May 1931, Westfield, AL), player and coach, is the son of steel mill worker William and Ann Mays, both excellent athletes. Since Mays' parents were divorced soon after his birth, he grew up with his Aunt Sarah in Fairfield, AL. Mays attended Fairfield Industrial High School, where he starred in basketball, football, and especially baseball. A semi-pro baseball player early, Mays joined the Birmingham, AL, Barons (NNL) at age 17. In 1950 the New York Giants (NL) purchased the 5 foot, 10½ inch, 170 pound right-handed outfielder and assigned him to Trenton (ISL). After 35 games with Minneapolis in 1951, Mays joined the Giants. Under manager Leo Durocher,* Mays became the regular center fielder and helped the Giants win the NL pennant after being 13½ games behind the Brooklyn Dodgers. He was named NL Rookie of the Year.

After serving in 1952 and 1953 in the U.S. Army, Mays in 1954 returned to the Giants and captured the NL batting title with a .345 average. He led the Giants to the NL pennant and world championship in four games over the Cleveland Indians and made an unbelievable catch of a towering drive by the Indians' Vic Wertz. No player ever made a more publicized catch, which many considered to be the greatest ever made on any baseball diamond. This feat epitomized Mays' career. His defensive play, ranging from his famous basket-catch to nailing a runner at home plate with a perfect throw, was accomplished with a unique flair.

With the Giants in New York (1951, 1954–1957) and San Francisco (1958–1971), Mays continually amazed baseball crowds and batted above .300 ten times. He led the NL in home runs four times, slugging 51 in 1955 and 52 ten years later, hit at least 30 home runs eleven different seasons, and scored over 100 runs twelve consecutive seasons. Besides winning the NL's Most Valuable Player Award (1954, 1965), he was named *The Sporting News* Outstanding NL Player (1954, 1965), outfielder on All-Star major league teams (1954, 1957–1960) and on NL All-Star fielding teams (1958–1968), and baseball's Player of the Decade (1960–1969). Mays slugged four home runs in one game once and three in one game twice and set the NL record by hitting two or more round trippers in one game 63 times. The first major league player to hit at least 50 homers and steal at least 20 bases in a season (1955), he remains one of five players in major league history to slug 30 home runs and steal 30 bases in the same season (1956–1957).

Between 1954 and 1973, Mays played in every All-Star game with a composite .315 batting average. He participated in 20 World Series games (1951, 1954, 1962, and 1973) and batted .239. An excellent base runner, Mays stole 40 bases in 1957 and 338 career bases. He also set NL standards for most putouts (7,095) and chances (7,431) accepted by an outfielder. In May 1972 Mays was traded to the New York Mets (NL). The Mets ownership assumed his playing contract and signed him to a ten-year pact (as a goodwill ambassador and part-time coach), taking effect after his retirement. Mays helped the Mets win the NL flag in 1973, but New York lost the World Series to the Oakland A's.

Mays retired at the end of the 1973 season. In his twenty-two-year career, he played in 2,992 games, with 10,881 at bats, 2,062 runs scored, 3,283 hits, 523 doubles, 140 triples, 660 home runs, 1,903 RBIs, a .981 fielding average, and a .302 batting average. His 660 home runs rank third on the all-time list behind Henry Aaron* and Babe Ruth.* Within three months after his induction into the National Baseball Hall of Fame (1979), Mays was ordered by Commissioner Bowie Kuhn* to choose between employment by the Mets and a company owning a hotel gambling casino. On October 29, 1979, Mays signed a ten-year contract with the Bally Manufacturing Corporation and ended his participation in baseball. In 1985 Commissioner Peter Ueberroth* (OS) lifted the ban on Mays' involvement in baseball. Mays married Marghuerite Wendell Kennedy Chapman in February 1956 and adopted a son, Michael. After the marriage ended in divorce in 1961, Mays wed social worker Mae Allen in 1971.

BIBLIOGRAPHY: Charles Einstein, *Willie Mays: My Life In and Out of Baseball* (Greenwich, CT, 1972); Tom Murray, *Sport Magazine's All-Time All Stars* (New York, 1977); *TSN Official Baseball Register, 1974* (St. Louis, 1974).

John L. Evers

MAZEROSKI, William Stanley "Bill," "Maz" (b. 5 September 1936, Wheeling WV), player and coach, set several major league fielding records as Pittsburgh Pirates (NL) second baseman from mid–1956 through 1972. A graduate of Warren Consolidated High of Tiltonsville, OH, he played basketball and pitched baseball there. He began his professional baseball career as a 17-year-old shortstop with Williamsport, PA (EL), in 1954. Midway through the following season, he joined the Hollywood Stars (PCL) as a second baseman. After 80 games there in 1956, he came to Pittsburgh as the NL team's second baseman. Although chosen for the first of seven years of All-Star appearances in 1958, Mazeroski did not attract national fame until he hit a home run in the 1960 World Series. In the deciding seventh game on October 13, Mazeroski slugged a dramatic homer in the last half of the ninth inning in a tie game to give the Pirates the championship over the New York Yankees.

During his career with Pittsburgh, he played 2,163 games, made 2,016 hits, including 294 doubles, 62 triples, and 138 home runs, drove in 853 runs, and compiled a .260 batting average. A superior fielder, he led the NL's second basemen five years in putouts, nine years in assists, and three years in fielding percentage. He also played in three league Championship Series and in two World Series, hitting .308. Mazeroski established major league records among second basemen for most double plays and games played in a season, most years leading the league in assists and double plays, most consecutive years pacing in double plays, and most lifetime double plays. His NL records for second basemen included most years leading the league in chances accepted, most career games, chances accepted, putouts, and assists.

Mazeroski, named Major League Player of the Year by *The Sporting News* in 1960, was selected as second baseman on NL All-Star fielding teams seven years and on several all-league and all-majors teams by other publications and news services. Mazeroski served as a coach for the Pittsburgh Pirates in 1973 and Seattle Mariners (AL) in 1979–1980 and as a minor league batting instructor. A right-handed batter and thrower, he stood 5 feet, 11 inches and weighed from 180 to 195 pounds during his playing career. Mazeroski married Milene Ruth Nicholson on October 11, 1958, has two sons, Darren and Daun, and lives near Greensburg, PA. A hunting and fishing enthusiast, he owns and operates a golf course at Rayland, OH, and a nearby restaurant and bar at Yorkville, OH. As a major league player-participant, Mazeroski won several Astrojet golf tournaments conducted for professional athletes by an airline. Besides being inducted into several local sports halls of fame, he was named to the Pennsylvania Sports Hall of Fame in 1985.

BIBLIOGRAPHY: Greensburg (PA) *Tribune-Review*, 1956–1972; *Pittsburgh Pirates News Media Guides*, 1956–1972; Pittsburgh *Post-Gazette*, 1956–1972; Pittsburgh *Press*, 1956–1972; Chet Smith and Marty Wolfson, *Greater Pittsburgh Illustrated History of Sports* (Pittsburgh, 1969); Robert B. Van Atta, interview with Bill Mazeroski, n. d.

                                                                                              Robert B. Van Atta

MEDWICK, Joseph Michael "Joe," "Ducky," "Muscles" (b. 4 or 24 November 1911, Carteret, NJ; d. 21 March 1975, St. Petersburg, FL), player, manager, and coach, was the son of factory worker John and Elizabeth Medwick. A star athlete at Carteret High School, Medwick rejected an offer to play football at Notre Dame University to sign as an outfielder in 1929 with the St. Louis Cardinals (NL). In 1930 he hit .419 his first season at Scottdale, PA, to lead the MAL. After batting .354 at Houston (TL) in 1932, he joined the Cardinals and hit .349 that same season. During the next ten seasons, Medwick hit at least .300 in the major leagues. In 1937 he won the coveted Triple Crown with a .374 batting mark, 31 homers, and 154 RBIs.

In June 1940 the Cardinals traded Medwick to the Brooklyn Dodgers (NL) with pitcher Curt Davis for four players and $125,000. In one of his first appearances against his old teammates, Cardinals pitcher Bob Bowman beaned the 5 foot, 10 inch, 187 pound, right-handed hitting slugger, putting him in the hospital with a severe concussion. Medwick survived the incident, which was investigated by Commissioner Kenesaw Mountain Landis* and a New York district attorney, but thereafter lacked his fierce edge at the plate. Although retaining his philosophy of "basehits and bucks," he lost his competitive determination. Medwick hit .337 for the New York Giants (NL) in 1944 but was traded to the Boston Braves (NL) in June of the next season. He returned to Brooklyn (NL) in 1946 and spent 1947 and part of 1948 with the Cardinals (NL). Subsequently, he served as minor league player-manager at Houston (TL) in 1948, Miami Beach (FSL) in 1949, Raleigh (CrL) in 1951 and Tampa (FIL) in 1952. Medwick also was assistant baseball coach at St. Louis University from 1961 to 1965 and farm system hitting instructor for the St. Louis Cardinals (NL) from 1966 to 1975.

Medwick's National Baseball Hall of Fame (1968) career produced 2,471 hits in 1,984 games, 540 doubles, 113 triples, 205 home runs, 1,383 RBIs, a .324 batting average, and .505 slugging average. Medwick hit .326 in two World Series, but became the only player ever removed from a game for safety reasons. Angry Detroit Tigers fans bombarded him with fruit and garbage following his scuffle with Tigers third baseman Marv Owen in the final 1934 Series game. In July 1936 Medwick equalled the NL mark by making ten consecutive hits. Besides setting the NL mark with 64 doubles the same season, he tied the major league mark by leading the NL in RBIs from 1936 through 1938. On June 29, 1935, Medwick made a single, double, triple, and home run. He hit 40 or more doubles seven consecutive years from 1933 through 1939, made *The Sporting News* All-Star team from 1935 through 1939, and won the NL's Most Valuable Player Award in 1937.

Known as "Muscles" to his friends, Medwick received the nickname "Ducky" from a woman fan in Houston during the 1931 season. A manufacturer named a candy bar "The Ducky-Wucky," a name he truly despised. He married Isabelle Heutel of St. Louis on August 24, 1936, and had one son and one daughter.

BIBLIOGRAPHY: Bill Borst, *Baseball Through a Knothole* (St. Louis, 1977); Bob Broeg, *The Redbirds* (St. Louis, 1981); Robert Hood, *The Gashouse Gang* (New York, 1976); Gene Karst and Martin J. Jones, Jr., *Who's Who in Professional Baseball* (New Rochelle, NY, 1973); Frederick G. Lieb, *The St. Louis Cardinals* (New York, 1945); *Newsweek* 85 (March 31, 1975), p. 53; *NYT*, March 24, 1975, p. 34; *Time* 105 (March 31, 1975), p. 83.

William A. Borst

MEUSEL, Emil Frederick "Irish" (b. 9 June 1893, Oakland, CA; d. 1 March 1963, Long Beach, CA), and **Robert William "Long Bob" MEUSEL** (b. 19 July 1896, San Jose, CA; d. 28 November 1977, Downey, CA), players, were the last of six children of teamster Charles F. and Mary (Smith) Meusel. They were educated in Los Angeles schools, with Emil completing three years at Manual Arts High School and Robert graduating from Los Angeles High School. Emil married Evangeline R. Proctor on May 17, 1917, and Estella R. Dansereau on October 1, 1945, having an adopted son in the first marriage. Robert wed Edith Cowan on December 14, 1921, and had one daughter.

For six years, the brothers were outfield rivals on the two New York teams. Emil played for the Giants (NL) and Robert for the Yankees (AL). From 1921 to 1923, they opposed each other in the World Series. The Meusels reached the major leagues rather late. Emil, nicknamed "Irish" because of a ruddy complexion and presumably Irish appearance, spent five seasons in the minors before being drafted by the Philadelphia Phillies (NL) in 1918 at age 25. Robert joined the Yankees in 1920 at age 24, after three seasons with Vernon, CA (PCL), and a U.S. Navy hitch.

The 5 foot, 11 1/2 inch, 178 pound Irish was traded to the Giants (NL) in 1921, when he achieved a career-high .343 batting average. Released after the 1926 season, he played briefly for Brooklyn (NL) and Toledo (AA) in 1927, returned to the PCL with Oakland in 1928 and Sacramento in 1929, and in 1930 rejoined the Giants (NL) as coach. After a few games with Omaha (WL) in 1931, he retired from baseball. For fifteen years until his death, he served as a gate guard at the Santa Anita and Hollywood Park race tracks in California. A solid, non-spectacular left fielder, the right-handed Irish compiled a .310 career average over eleven seasons (he had a one-game tryout with Washington [AL] in 1914), but was hampered by a weak throwing arm. He made 1,521 hits, 250 doubles, and 106 home runs, scored 701 runs, and knocked in 819 runs. In 1923 he led the NL with 125 RBIs. He averaged .276 in four World Series, outhit Robert in the 1921–1923 contests, and was regarded as a hard out with men on base.

Robert batted one point less than his brother (.309) in eleven years with the AL Yankees (1920–1929) and NL Cincinnati Reds (1930). His batting average in six World Series was only .225 and included 24 strikeouts, ranking eighth on the all-time list. In 1,407 games, he made 1,693 hits, 368 doubles, and 156 home runs and struck out 619 times. Nevertheless, Robert proved the superior player. Batting right-handed, the 6 foot, 3 inch, 190 pounder exceeded .300 in seven of his first eight seasons in New York. In 1925, his one off-year for average (.290), he led the AL in home runs (33) and RBIs (138). Only two other players have equalled his mark of hitting for the cycle (single, double, triple, and home run in one game) three times. Although many have exceeded his career 1,067 RBIs, he ranks eleventh all-time for productivity with a remarkable .76 runs driven in per game. He became a legitimate member of the Yankees' famed "Murderers' Row."

Meusel patrolled left field (the Yankee sun field) and compensated for his sometimes casual pursuit of fly balls with one of baseball's strongest, most accurate throwing arms. Since his throwing motion imparted a spin to the ball that made it bounce eccentrically, he threw on the fly like an infielder. Even Ty Cobb* held third base on sacrifice flies to Meusel. "Bob" tied for the AL lead in outfield assists in 1921 with 28 and led the following year with 24. After being released by Cincinnati in 1930, he played two years in the minors. In his last fifteen years, he served as a security guard at a U.S. Navy installation. In contrast to the ebullient Irish, handsome Bob was taciturn and self-contained. Reputedly, he said "Hello" to his teammates at the beginning of the season, "Good-bye" at the end, and little else in between.

BIBLIOGRAPHY: Joseph G. Donnor, "Hitting for the Cycle," *Baseball Research Journal* 10 (1981), pp. 75–81; Joseph Durso, *Casey* (Englewood Cliffs, NJ, 1967); Donald Honig, *Baseball When the Grass Was Real* (New York, 1977); Donald Honig, *October Heroes* (New York, 1979); Los Angeles *Times*, March 16, 1963; Emil Meusel and Robert Meusel files, National Baseball Hall of Fame Library, Cooperstown, NY; John Mosedale, *The Greatest of All* (New York, 1975); *NYT*, November 30, 1977; Lawrence S. Ritter, *The Glory of Their Times* (New York, 1966); George Herman Ruth, *Babe Ruth's Own Book of Baseball* (New York, 1928); A. D. Suehsdorf, interviews with Mark Koenig, July 12, 22, 1983.

A. D. Suehsdorf

MEUSEL, Robert William "Long Bob." See under MEUSEL, Emil Frederick "Irish".

MEYERLE, Levi Samuel "Long Levi" (b. July 1845, Philadelphia, PA; d. 4 November 1921, Philadelphia, PA), player, was the son of laborer-shoecutter Jacob and Margaret Meyerle, of German descent. Meyerle was educated in the Philadelphia schools and learned the building trades, but preferred sharpening his athletic skills on the city's fields during the post-Civil War baseball boom. As a pitcher, he played for the Geary Base Ball Club of Philadelphia in 1867. By 1869 he became "first substitute" for the Philadelphia Athletics, appearing as catcher, pitcher, third baseman, and right fielder in 34 of the team's 49 games. Teamed with Alfred Reach* and other notables, he developed into an excellent batter. The following season, Meyerle joined the original professional Chicago White Stockings for $1,500 annually. Meyerle concentrated on third base, the position he played most frequently through 1884.

In 1871 Meyerle returned to the Athletics of the newly formed NA and led them to the championship with a superlative .492 batting average. By a decisive margin he won pro baseball's first batting crown. Meyerle remained with the A's in 1872 but performed for the rival Philadelphias (NA) in 1873 and 1875. In 1874 he starred for the Chicago White Stockings (NA). During these five NA seasons, the right-handed batting and throwing Meyerle compiled a .353 batting average, made 386 hits, and scored 245 runs in 221 games. The 6 foot, 1 inch, 177 pound Meyerle earned the nickname "Long Levi" in an era of much smaller players. Defensively, he lacked quickness and agility and was described by the press as "good hit, no field." Alfred H. Spink stated, "Meyerle was a very fair fielder, but his best asset was his ability to hit the ball hard."

On April 21, 1876, Meyerle played for the Philadelphia Athletics in the first NL game. For a weak team, he batted .340 and fielded only .791. In December the NL expelled the Athletics and New York Mutuals for failing to play out the schedule. This move virtually ended the major league career of Meyerle, a Philadelphia favorite. He batted .327 in 27 games for the woeful Cincinnati (NL) club of 1877 and briefly returned to the majors in 1884 for three UA games with the Philadelphia Keystones. From 1877 to 1883, Meyerle made minor league stops in Philadelphia, Springfield, MA, Washington, DC, and Rochester, NY. In 85 NL games, he batted .329 with 123 hits, 57 runs scored, and 49 RBIs. "Long Levi" and his Irish bride, Anna, had no children. After 1884 they remained in Philadelphia, where he worked as a lather, plasterer, painter, and carpenter.

BIBLIOGRAPHY: Lee Allen, "Cooperstown Corner: Pro Ball's First Batting Champ," *TSN*, (August 31, 1968), p. 6; Weston Fisler, notebook, National Baseball Hall of

Fame Library, Cooperstown, NY; "Levi Meyerle," New York *Clipper* 27 (June 21, 1879), p. 101; Alfred E. Spink, *The National Game* (St. Louis, 1911).

James D. Smith III

MILAN, Jesse Clyde "Deerfoot" (b. 25 March 1887, Linden, TN; d. 3 March 1953, Orlando FL), player, manager, coach, and scout, began his professional baseball career in 1906 with Wichita (WA) and joined the Washington Senators (AL) in 1907. Cliff Blankenship, a convalescent catcher, was sent to Wichita to sign Milan. Before returning to Washington, Blankenship scouted and signed Walter Johnson* in Weiser, ID. Milan and Johnson both came from rural areas and became roommates and inseparable friends. The more competitive 5 foot, 9 inch, 185 pound Milan, who batted left and threw right-handed, often drove Johnson when he became lackadaisical. During the winter months, they invariably hunted together in either Texas or Tennessee. Considered faster than Ty Cobb,* Milan made an excellent center-fielder with Washington and played shallow like Tris Speaker.* Although an average player for manager Joe Cantillon (1907–1909), he starred under Jimmy McAleer (1910–1911). After a lengthy hold-out with Johnson in 1911, he hit .315. Besides achieving a lifetime .285 batting average, he made 2,100 hits, 242 doubles, and 104 triples, scored 1,004 runs, stole 495 bases, and knocked in 617 runs.

During Milan's first four years, the Senators finished last three times and seventh once. Clark Griffith,* who became manager in 1912, improved the team partially by fully utilizing Milan's speed. Milan dethroned Cobb as base-stealing champion by pilfering 88 bases in 1912 and retained the title the following year with 75 thefts. The Senators reached second place those years, but Milan never played in a World Series. In 1922 he managed the Senators and led a relatively talented team to a sixth place finish. Griffith fired Milan, who was bothered by ulcers, at the end of the season, but kept him in the Washington organization. Milan managed Minneapolis (AA) in 1923, New Haven (EL) in 1924, Memphis (SA) in 1925–1926, Birmingham, AL (SA), from 1930 to June 1935, and Chattanooga (SA) from June 1935 to 1937. He also coached for the Senators in 1928 and 1929 and from 1938 through 1952, and scouted for them in 1937. In 1953 coach Milan died at spring training while hitting fungoes. Milan married Margaret Bowers in November, 1913, and had two daughters.

BIBLIOGRAPHY: Shirley Povich, "Necrology," *TSN*, March 11, 1953; Shirley Povich, *The Washington Senators* (New York, 1954); Lawrence S. Ritter, *The Glory of Their Times* (New York, 1966); Roger Treat, *Walter Johnson—King of Pitchers* (New York, 1948).

Anthony J. Papalas

MILLER, Edmund John "Bing" (b. 30 August, 1894, Cheney, IA; d. 7 May 1966, Philadelphia, PA), player and coach, was the son of farmer Norman Eugene and Philomena Miller. His father, along with two brothers, played organized baseball. Nicknamed after the comic strip character George Washington Bings, he attended Polk No. 7 rural grammar school in Benton County, IA. Miller starred as a 16-year-old pitcher for the Vinton, IA, Cinders and signed in 1914 as a pitcher-outfielder for $80 a month with Clinton, IA (CA). As a minor leaguer, he played outfield with Clinton from 1914 to 1917, with Peoria (CA) in 1917, and with Atlanta (SA) in 1919. After Miller hit .322 with Little Rock (SA) in 1920, the Washington Senators (AL) and Pittsburgh Pirates (NL) both claimed him. Commissioner Kenesaw Mountain Landis,* in his first major decision, ruled that Washington owned Miller's contract. Miller married Helen Fetrow of Philadelphia in March, 1930, and had no children.

Miller played outfield sixteen AL seasons with Washington (1921), the Philadephia Athletics (1922–1926, 1928–1934), St. Louis Browns (1926–1927), and Boston Red Sox (1935–1936). In 1,821 games, the 6 foot, 185 pound Miller made 1,937 hits and compiled a .312 career batting average. Miller, who played with Hall of Famers Jimmie Foxx,* Al Simmons,* Mickey Cochrane,* and Lefty Grove,* batted over .300 nine times. A powerful hitter, he slugged 117 home runs, 95 triples, and 389 doubles, scored 947 runs, and knocked in 990 runs. Defensively, he handled right field with finesse and compiled a lifetime .971 fielding percentage. In a 1930 World Series contest against the St. Louis Cardinals, he made a record seven putouts.

The humorous, flamboyant Miller reached peak performance with Connie Mack's* Athletics. A line drive hitter, he batted .336 in 1922 and a career pinnacle .342 in 1924. Miller helped the Athletics capture AL pennants from 1929 through 1931 as well as the 1929 World Series championship. In 1929 he batted .335 during the regular season and .368 in the World Series against the Chicago Cubs. Miller participated in Philadelphia's dramatic, come from behind ten-run seventh inning to erase a 7–0 Chicago lead in game four. In the ninth inning of the final game, Miller drove in the winning run with a towering double. He led the AL in pinch hits in 1934 and 1935. After retiring as an active player in 1936, he coached in the AL for the Boston Red Sox (1937–1938), Detroit Tigers (1939–1941), Chicago White Sox (1942–1949), and Philadelphia Athletics (1950–1953), the latter two stints at the request of his very close friend Jimmy Dykes.* In May, 1966, he died of a heart attack following an automobile accident.

BIBLIOGRAPHY: Des Moines *Register*, March 26, 1961, May 8, 1966; Ed Fitzgerald, ed., *The American League* (New York, 1963); Frederick G. Lieb, *Connie Mack: Grand Old Man of Baseball* (New York, 1945); George S. May, "Major League Baseball Players from Iowa," *The Palimpsest* 36 (April, 1955), pp. 133–165; Tom Meany, *Baseball's Greatest Teams* (New York, 1949); *NYT*, May 8, 1966; David L. Porter, correspondence with Mrs. Eddie Dyson, April 27, 1984, David L. Porter Collection, Oskaloosa, IA; David L. Porter, correspondence with Mrs. Ida Grubbs, May 6, 1984, David L. Porter Collection, Oskaloosa, IA; Joseph L. Reichler, ed., *The Baseball Encyclopedia*, 6th ed. (New York, 1985), p. 1,206.

David L. Porter

MILLER, Marvin Julian (b. 14 April 1917, New York, NY), executive, served as executive director of the Major League Players Association (MLPA) from 1966 to 1983 and is the son of clothing salesman Alexander and Gertrude (Wald) Miller. A gifted student, Miller graduated from high school at age 15, worked his way through New York University, and graduated from there with a degree in economics in 1938. In 1939 he married psychology professor Theresa Morgenstern; they have two children. As an economist for the U.S. government, Miller trained labor mediators during World War II. In 1950 he became research director of the United Steel Workers of America. The frequently promoted Miller served as assistant to USW presidents David McDonald and I. W. Abel.

At the suggestion of Wharton School professor George Taylor, a search committee of the Major League Players Association asked Miller in 1966 to become their paid executive director because the foundering organization needed strong leadership. Founded in 1953, the MLPA comprised the fifth attempt by major league players to organize in quest of bargaining rights with club owners. The four previous efforts had failed. Miller's appointment was approved 489–136 by the major league players but was opposed by club owners and league officials.

Opponents' fears of Miller were not misplaced. He transformed the MLPA into a strong bargaining agency within two years and became one of the most powerful figures in major league baseball by the end of his tenure. By rallying players behind his goals and methods, Miller helped MLPA membership swell to 600 by 1968. Using National Labor Relations Board procedures, Miller forced owners to bargain collectively with the MLPA and promulgate formal contracts.

During Miller's tenure, five labor contracts (Basic Agreements) were concluded. The first increased owner contributions to the pension fund, raised the minimum salary of players, and exacted a promise from owners to review the reserve clause. Ratified in 1970, the second agreement recognized the MLPA as the players' official bargaining agency in all matters except salary disputes, allowed players to be represented by agents in salary negotiations, and permitted arbitration of disputes between players and owners. This pact expired in 1971 without any successor, and in 1972 Miller led the players in a brief strike yielding a new contract. This third agreement extended the arbitration principle to salary disputes, a concession sending salary levels sharply upward.

In 1975 an arbitration panel headed by Peter Seitz circumvented the reserve clause by ruling that players Andy Messersmith and Dave McNally* had played out the option year of their contracts and could negotiate contracts with other clubs. When sustained by a federal court, this judgment precipitated a lockout by angry owners in 1976. A fourth agreement compromised on this issue by limiting free agency to six-year veterans, who could participate in newly established re-entry drafts.

Such drafts augmented soaring salaries and prompted angry owners to demand as compensation established major league players for any players lost to re-entry drafts. This impasse precipitated the 1981 player strike, which lasted fifty days and ended in a compromise. The fifth agreement compensated owners losing players in re-entry drafts by allowing them to pick established players from a general pool, but the MLPA emerged from the strike stronger than ever.

Miller was the catalyst that forged the MLPA into a powerful force. By masterly use of labor laws and charismatic leadership, Miller scored successes at bargaining tables empowering players, improving working conditions, and raising salaries and pension rights to the highest level in pro sports. At his retirement in 1984, MLPA members hailed Miller as "the players' Commissioner."

BIBLIOGRAPHY: "Baseball's Misbegotten Season," *Time* 118 (October 19, 1981), pp. 83, 86; R. H. Boyle, "This Miller Admits He's a Grind," *SI* 40 (March 11, 1974), pp. 22–23, 25–26; Curt Flood and Richard Carter, *The Way It Is* (New York, 1971); Lee Lowenfish and Tony Lupien, *The Imperfect Diamond* (New York, 1980); Lance Morrow, "Summer of Our Discontent," *Time* 117 (June 29, 1981), pp. 12–13; Harold Parrott, *The Lords of Baseball* (New York, 1975); B. J. Phillips, "Baseball Heads for the Showers," *Time* 117 (June 22, 1981), p. 55; David Quentin Voigt, *American Baseball*, vol. 3 (University Park, PA, 1983).

David Quentin Voigt

MIZE, John Robert "Johnny," "Big Cat" (b. 7 January 1913, Demorest, GA), player, scout, and coach, excelled in baseball and tennis at Tipton (GA) High School and attended Piedmont College for two years. Mize became one of the foremost baseball performers in the history of the St. Louis Cardinals (NL), New York Giants (NL), and New York Yankees (AL). After playing for Greensboro, NC (Pil), Elmira, NY (NYPL), and Rochester, NY (IL), between 1930 and 1935, Mize debuted with St. Louis in 1936, and was named NL Rookie of the Year. The 6 foot, 2 inch, 215 pound left-handed first baseman followed right-handed slugger Joe Medwick* in the lineup to make one of baseball's finest one-two combinations. Mize, who batted .329, .364, and .337 from 1936 through 1938 as Medwick's counterpart, led the NL in 1939 with a .349 mark. Besides his outstanding hitting achievements, Mize proved an excellent fielder.

After the 1941 season, the Cardinals traded Mize to the New York Giants

(NL). Mize spent three years in the U.S. Navy and in 1947 became the only NL left-handed batter to hit 50 or more home runs in one season, tying Ralph Kiner* for the NL lead with 51. New York made plans for a running team and consequently sold Mize in August 1949 to the New York Yankees (AL). Under manager Casey Stengel,* the Yankees drove to their first of five consecutive world championships and used Mize as an excellent part-time player in pinch-hitting and reserve situations. Mize played on five world championship teams (1949–1953), slugging three home runs and batting .400 to lead the Yankees past Brooklyn (NL) in seven games in 1952. He became only the second player in World Series history to make a pinch hit home run. In 1953 he established an AL record by getting five consecutive pinch hits and finished the season with 19 pinch hits, just one short of the league record. Mize's 53 career pinch hits included eight home runs.

In his major league career, Mize paced the NL or tied for the lead in home runs four times and won four slugging titles, three RBI crowns, and one batting championship. Mize shared the NL lead in doubles in 1941 and in 1938 paced the circuit with 16 triples. He slugged three homers in one game six times (a record unequalled) and two home runs in one game 30 times, collected over 100 RBIs eight times, made over 100 hits eleven times, and batted over .300 nine consecutive times. Mize hit for the cycle in a 1940 contest, holds the St. Louis club record for most home runs in a season (43), and belted homers in all fifteen ballparks in use during his career.

In 1,884 games, Mize scored 1,118 runs, collected 2,011 hits, 367 doubles, 83 triples, 359 home runs (33rd on the all-time list), and 1,337 RBIs, and compiled a .312 lifetime batting average. His .577 NL slugging average ranks second only to Rogers Hornsby's* .578 mark. After retiring as an active player following the 1953 season, Mize scouted for the Giants (1955) and served as a coach in 1961 for the Kansas City A's (AL). He married Jane Adams in August, 1937. Mize and his present wife, Marjorie, owned and operated orange groves in Florida for several years. In 1981 Mize was en-shrined in the National Baseball Hall of Fame.

BIBLIOGRAPHY: Paul MacFarlane, ed., *TSN Daguerreotypes of Great Stars of Baseball* (St. Louis, 1971); Joseph L. Reichler, *The Great All-Time Baseball Record Book* (New York, 1981); Lowell Reidenbaugh, *Cooperstown: Where Baseball's Legends Live Forever* (St. Louis, 1983).

John L. Evers

MORGAN, Joe Leonard (b. 19 September 1943, Bonham, TX), player and announcer, grew up in Oakland, and developed as an athlete there. Morgan attended Castlemount High School, where he excelled in baseball as a second baseman. After graduation, he in April, 1967, married high school sweetheart Gloria Stewart with whom he has two daughters, Lisa and Angela. After attending Merritt Junior College and earning all-conference honors on the baseball team there, he enrolled at California State University at Hayward. In 1963 he began his professional baseball career with the Houston Colt 45s (NL) organization at Modesto, CA (CaL), and spent two years in the minor leagues. After batting .332 at Durham, NC (CrL), in 1963, he batted .323 the following year, collected 160 hits, and belted 12 home runs for San Antonio (TL) and won the TL Most Valuable Player Award.

As a rookie with the Houston (NL) club in 1965, the left-handed batting Morgan collected 163 hits, contributed 14 home runs, and led the NL with 97 bases on balls. Those achievements earned him *The Sporting News* NL Rookie of the Year Award. Morgan continued performing for Houston until 1972, when he was traded to the Cincinnati Reds (NL). The 5 foot, 7 inch, 164 pound second baseman enjoyed his finest years with the Reds and had banner seasons in 1975 and 1976. In 1975 he batted .327, made 163 hits and 17 homers and knocked in 94 runs. In addition, he stole 67 bases and led the NL with 132 walks. In 1976 the talented Morgan hit .320, belted 27 home runs, drove in 111 runs, and stole 60 bases. Both years he served as the chief catalyst in the Reds' championship drives and earned two consecutive NL MVP awards. Morgan's fielding proved equally impressive during his stay at Cincinnati, as the right-handed second baseman set a major league record with 91 straight errorless games in 1977–1978.

Before the 1980 season, Cincinnati returned Morgan to the Houston Astros (NL). After one season there, he was traded to the San Francisco Giants (NL) and spent the 1981 and 1982 seasons with them. Morgan's second season with the Giants saw him belt 14 home runs, drive in 61 runs, and contribute a .289 batting average. His achievements that year earned him the NL Comeback Player of the Year Award. After that season, Morgan was dealt to Philadelphia (NL) and helped lead the Phillies to the 1983 NL crown. Morgan's last year in the major leagues was spent with the Oakland Athletics (AL) in 1984. Shortly after that season, he retired and became an announcer for the Cincinnati Reds. In 1986 he joined the San Francisco Giants (NL) and the NBC Game of the Week as an announcer. Morgan finished his career with a .271 batting average, 2,518 hits, 449 doubles, 96 triples, 268 homers, 689 stolen bases, 1,134 RBIs, and 1,865 walks—the latter being an NL record. Besides these accomplishments, Morgan made the NL All-Star team nine times and won five Gold Glove awards.

Off the field, Morgan enjoys playing golf, tennis, billiards, and dominos. Although using his activities for exercise, Morgan claims that they also strengthen his concentration and coordination.

BIBLIOGRAPHY: Nathan Aaseng, *Little Giants of Pro Sports* (New York, 1980); Mark Mulvoy, "The Little Big Man," *SI* 44 (April 12, 1976), pp. 52–60; Robert Obojski, *Bush League: A History of Minor League Baseball* (New York, 1975); Tom Seaver, *Tom Seaver's All-Time Baseball Greats* (New York, 1984); *Time* 109 (June 13, 1977), p. 76; *WWA*, 41st ed. (1980–1981), p. 2,366.

                                                          Samuel John Regalado

MOSES, Wallace, Jr. "Wally," "Peep Sight" (b. 8 October 1910, Uvalda, GA), player, coach, and scout, was the archetype of the small, speedy, hustling outfielder. A non–power hitter, he made 2,138 hits, batted .291, and hit 89 home runs in seventeen AL seasons with the Philadelphia Athletics (1935–1941, 1949–1951), Chicago White Sox (1942–1946), and Boston Red Sox (1946–1948). Moses came to the AL at age 25 after playing outfield with Augusta and Elmira, NY (Pol), in 1931, Monroe, LA (CSL), and Tyler, TX (TL), in 1932, and Galveston (TL) in 1933 and 1934. Moses hit over .300 for the Philadelphia A's each year from 1935 to 1941. His best year on the basepaths came with the White Sox in 1943, when he pilfered 56 bases. He led the AL with 12 triples in 1943 and 35 doubles in 1945.

A career marked by holdouts and toiling for second division clubs culminated in 1946, when the Boston Red Sox (AL) purchased the veteran as pennant insurance. The left-handed, 5 foot, 10 inch, 160 pound Moses hit .239 during the season and batted 5 for 12 in his only World Series for a .417 mark against the St. Louis Cardinals. In 2,012 career games, he made 435 doubles, 110 triples, 821 walks, and 174 stolen bases, scored 1,114 runs, and knocked in 679 runs. Moses retired as a player in 1951 and enjoyed a distinguished career as one of the game's best batting coaches for the Philadelphia Athletics (1952–1954), NL Philadelphia Phillies (1955–1958), NL Cincinnati Reds (1959–1960), AL New York Yankees (1961–1963, 1966), and AL Detroit Tigers (1967–1970). From 1964 through 1966, he scouted for the New York Yankees. Nicknamed "Peep Sight" with the White Sox for his fine batting eye, he taught his skills of placing the ball, running down the first base line fast, and catching flaws in a batting stroke. He tutored batting champions Ferris Fain and Richie Ashburn,* both of whom hit in Moses' basic style. December 2, 1936, Moses married Billie Mae Haines.

BIBLIOGRAPHY: Warren Brown, *The Chicago White Sox* (New York, 1952); Frederick G. Lieb, *Connie Mack: Grand Old Man of Baseball* (New York, 1945); Wally Moses file, National Baseball Hall of Fame Library, Cooperstown, NY.

Eric Solomon

MULLANE, Anthony John "Tony," "Count," "The Apollo of the Box" (b. 20 February 1859, Cork, Ireland; d. 25 or 26 April 1944, Chicago, IL), player, emigrated from Ireland with his parents as a child. The gifted athlete proved a fine skater and boxer and pursued baseball when the sport was becoming the "national pastime" of post–Civil War America. Mullane began his professional baseball career in 1880 as a right-handed pitcher with an independent team in Akron. During the 1881 season, he joined the Detroit Wolverines (NL) and began pitching with his left arm following an injury to his right arm. The recovery of Mullane's right arm enabled him to pitch with either arm, but he rarely hurled left-handed. His ambidexterity allowed the barehanded pitcher to field and throw with either hand and gave him a devastating pickoff move.

In 1882 Mullane joined Louisville in the new AA and won 30 of 54 decisions for the first of five consecutive 30-victory seasons. He moved in 1883 to the St. Louis Browns (AA), where he enjoyed another fine season with a career high 35 wins. Before the 1884 season, Mullane jumped his contract with the Browns and temporarily signed with the St. Louis franchise of the upstart UA. Before joining the UA, however, he switched to Toledo (AA) when that franchise agreed to meet his salary request for 1884. At Toledo he formed a popular battery with Moses Fleetwood Walker,* the first black major league baseball player. Since the Toledo franchise collapsed after the 1884 season, Mullane was sold back to the Browns (AA). Refusing to report to the Browns, he instead signed with Cincinnati (AA) for 1885. Protests from Browns owner Chris Von der Ahe* culminated in Mullane's suspension for the entire 1885 season. He nevertheless remained with Cincinnati from 1886 to June 1893 (in 1890 the franchise shifted to the NL), except for a brief stint with Butte (MtL) because of an 1892 salary dispute. He was traded to the Baltimore Orioles (NL) in 1893 and split his last major campaign (1894) between the Orioles and the Cleveland Spiders (NL). After pitching for St. Paul (WL) from 1895 to 1897, he ended his playing career with Toronto (EL) in 1899.

Mullane's major pitching career included 556 games, 4,540 1/3 innings pitched, 1,812 strikeouts, 285 wins, 215 losses, and a 3.05 ERA. His 31 career shutouts included a no-hit victory against Cincinnati on September 11, 1882, the first AA no-hitter. Mullane led the AA twice in shutouts (1884, 1887) and once each in pitching percentage (1883), games started (1882), walks, and strikeouts (1882). Besides pitching, he played all positions except catcher. The hard-hitting Mullane compiled a .243 lifetime batting average and swung mostly right-handed. The 5 foot, 10 1/2 inch, 165 pound Mullane ranked among the era's most colorful, popular players. Sporting a handlebar mustache, he was nicknamed "Count" for his elegant attire. After his baseball career, he became a police officer in Chicago and worked as a detective from 1904 until his retirement in 1924. He spent his retirement years in a predominantly Irish neighborhood on the south side of Chicago, married several times, and was survived by one daughter.

Although one of the leading players of the 1880s, Mullane remains largely forgotten today because he never played on a championship team, enjoyed his great years in the neglected AA, and (though exonerated) was once charged with throwing games. Mullane's showmanship, independence, and all-around athletic ability made him the embodiment of the nineteenth century baseball hero.

BIBLIOGRAPHY: Chicago Daily Tribune, April 27, 1944; Paul MacFarlane, ed., TSN Daguerreotypes of Great Stars of Baseball (St. Louis, 1981); Harold Seymour, Baseball: The Early Years (New York, 1960).

                                                        Clark Nardinelli

MULLIN, George Joseph "Wabash George" (b. 4 July 1880, Toledo, OH; d. 7 January 1944, Wabash, IN), player, began his baseball career in 1898 with a semi-pro team in Fort Wayne, IN. He shared pitching duties with rookie Addie Joss,* who later starred with the Cleveland Indians. In 1901 Mullin began his professional career with Ft. Wayne (WA) and then broke a contract with the Brooklyn Dodgers (NL) to accept a more lucrative offer from the Detroit Tigers (AL). Although his 1902 rookie record of 13 wins, 16 losses, and 3.67 ERA proved unimpressive, he debuted with three doubles. Mullin, an excellent hitter with a .263 lifetime batting average, became one of only three pinch hitters for Ty Cobb.* In 1911 Cleveland left-hander Eugene Krapp entered the ninth inning with a big lead. Mullin batted for Cobb, who had taken an early shower, not expecting to bat again.

In 1903 the right-hander became a star by winning 19 games, losing 15, and lowering his ERA to 2.25 for a fifth place club. Mullin won the respect of New York manager Clark Griffith,* who considered him one of baseball's premier pitchers. Mullin's duels with New York ace Jack Chesbro* became classics, appreciated by fans of the fledgling AL. Griffith arranged with Detroit general manager Ed Barrow* to add Mullin to his New York High-landers staff, but Detroit's new owner, William Yawkey, cancelled the deal.

Mullin led the Detroit pitching staff with 66 wins during the AL pennant seasons of 1907–1909. In 1909 he paced major league pitchers by winning 29 out of 37 decisions and posted a 2.22 ERA and two World Series victories against the Pittsburgh Pirates. Mullin, who relied on an excellent fastball, a good curve, and exceptional control, used psychological ploys such as talking to batters and stalling at critical times to counter incipient rallies. On several occasions he intentionally threw the ball over the catcher's head and off the wooden grandstands at Bennett Park. The ball bounced back to the catcher, who tagged out runners trying to score from third base. Despite his skill and cunning, Mullin believed that his success largely came from luck. During the 1908 and 1909 seasons, he attributed his victories partly to a black orphan and Detroit mascot, Lil Rastus.

Mullin, among the most sociable Detroit players, maintained close relations with Ty Cobb* and often visited him at his Augusta, GA, home. For a time, his best friend was Christy Mathewson.* In 1911 he won a friendly wager with Mathewson by backing the Philadelphia Athletics against the New York Giants in the World Series. Mullin won 21 and lost 12 in 1910 and posted an 18–10 record the following year. He began the 1912 season well and peaked with a July 4 no-run, no-hit game against the St. Louis Browns. Slumping the rest of the season, he finished with 12 victories against 17 defeats. After 1 win and 6 losses in 1913, he was sold to the Washington Senators (AL). Manager Clark Griffith,* however, failed to restore Mullin to his former greatness. The 5 foot, 11 inch, 188 pound Mullin, over-weight for most of his career, liked the bright lights and fast life and did not keep in good condition.

After completing the 1913 season with Washington, he jumped to Indianapolis (FL) in 1914 and ended his major league career with Newark (FL) in 1915. He won 16 and lost 12 in his two-year FL stint. After playing semi-pro ball the next five years in Indiana and Ohio, he settled with his wife, Grace, and daughter in Toledo in 1920 and became a police officer. Mullin won 228 games and lost 196 (.538) in a fourteen-year major league career. He compiled a 2.82 ERA in 488 games, completed 353 of 428 starts, hurled 35 shutouts, and struck out 1,482 batters in 3,686 2/3 innings pitched. Besides being a clutch pitcher, he was considered nearly unbeatable in big games in his peak years. Mullin achieved near National Baseball Hall of Fame statistics and probably fell only one good season short of being elected to that august institution.

BIBLIOGRAPHY: Detroit Baseball Club Letterbooks, 12 vols. (1900–1912), Ernie Harwell Collection, Detroit Public Library; Detroit *News*, 1905–1912, January 8, 1944; Frederick G. Lieb, *The Detroit Tigers* (New York, 1946).

Anthony J. Papalas

MURPHY, Dale Bryan (b. 12 March 1956, Portland, OR), player, is the son of Charles and Betty M. Murphy. He planned to attend Arizona State University on a baseball scholarship after graduation from Woodrow Wilson High School in Portland, but instead signed with the Atlanta Braves (NL) after being selected in the first round of the 1974 free agent draft. Murphy, who attended Portland Community College and Brigham Young University, married Nancy Thomas in 1979 and has three children, Chad, Travis, and Shawn.

Touted as "the next Johnny Bench*," Murphy began his career as a catcher with Kingsport, TN (ApL), and moved quickly through Greenwood, SC (WCL), Savannah (SL), and Richmond, VA (IL), to the majors in 1976. A mental block that produced erratic throws to second base led to experiments with him playing first base and the outfield. The Braves moved the 6 foot, 4 inch, 220 pound Murphy to the outfield permanently in 1982 to utilize his strong throwing arm and excellent speed.

Since moving to center field, the right-handed Murphy has emerged as a superstar with unusually consistent performances. From 1982 through 1984, he played in all 162 games each season, hit 36 home runs each year, and averaged 174 hits, 110 RBIs, 24 stolen bases, and a .290 batting average. For each of those three years, *The Sporting News* named him to the NL All-Star Fielding (Gold Glove) and Silver Slugger teams. The six-time All-Star team selection (1980, 1982–1986) was named in 1982 and 1983 the NL Most Valuable Player by the Baseball Writers Association and Player of the Year by *The Sporting News*, making Murphy the youngest player ever to win those honors in consecutive years. In 1985 he again played in 162 games, led the NL in home runs (37) and runs scored (118), and finished second in RBIs

(111), third in slugging percentage (.539), and fifth in hits (185) and on-base percentage (.388). Murphy, whose consecutive game streak ended at 740 in July, 1986, became the eighty-fifth major league player to hit 250 career home runs in a June 30, 1986, game against the San Francisco Giants. In nine full major league seasons, he has led or tied in games played (1982–1985), RBIs (1982–1983), slugging average (1983–1984), and total bases (1984). His career totals through 1986 include 1,360 games, 1,388 hits, 214 doubles, 266 home runs, 813 runs scored, 822 RBIs, 129 stolen bases, around .490 slugging average, and .277 batting average. Murphy won Gold Glove awards in 1985 and 1986.

Excelling in every phase of the game on the field, Murphy off the field is a model of decorum, a soft-spoken, unassuming athlete who does not use alcohol, tobacco, or profanity and objects strenuously to the presence of female sportswriters in the locker area after games. According to former manager Joe Torre*: "Murphy is the closest thing there is to the all-American boy. He's a complete ballplayer. All he does is play baseball better than anyone else."

BIBLIOGRAPHY: Michele Bartmess, "Dale Murphy: Nice Guys Don't Always Finish Last," *This People* 4 (April/May, 1983), pp. 42–46; Joseph Dalton, "Too Good for His Own Good," *Sport* 75 (June, 1984), pp. 24–30; Val Hale, "Dale Murphy," *This People* 5 (February, 1984), pp. 60–61; Joseph L. Reichler, ed., *The Baseball Encyclopedia*, 6th ed. (New York, 1985), p. 1,235; Rick Reilly, "So Good, He's Scary," *SI* 62 (June 3, 1985), pp. 74–88; Barry Siegel, ed., *TSN Official Baseball Register 1985* (St. Louis, 1985); Wayne Stewart, "Dale Murphy: Will He Win a Third Straight MVP Award?" *Baseball Digest* 43 (March, 1984), pp. 18–22; *TSN*, September 20, 1982, November 21, 28, 1983; Tim Tucker, "Is Dale Murphy for Real?" *Inside Sports* 5 (November, 1983), pp. 36–40; *WWA*, 43rd ed. (1984–1985), p. 2361; Steve Wulf, "Murphy's Law Is Nice Guys Finish First," *SI* 59 (July 4, 1983), pp. 24–31.

Larry R. Gerlach

MURRAY, Eddie Clarence (b. 24 February 1956, Los Angeles, CA), player, is the eighth of twelve children born to hourly worker Charles and Carrie Murray. All five Murray boys have played professional baseball, Richard having performed with the San Francisco Giants (NL) and in the Cleveland Indians (AL) farm system. Murray learned to bat by hitting tennis balls with a stick and played Little League, Babe Ruth, and Connie Mack League baseball. He also participated in baseball at Locke High School with future major leaguers Ozzie Smith and Darrell Jackson. The Baltimore Orioles (AL) selected Murray in the third round of the June, 1973, amateur draft and signed him for a $25,000 bonus. Murray spent four seasons in the minor leagues. At Bluefield, WV (ApL), in 1973, he hit .287 with 11 home runs. In 1974 he belted 12 homers and batted .289 for Miami (FSL) and played two games for Asheville, NC (SL). For Asheville in 1975, Murray played both first base and third base, hit .264, and slugged 17 home runs. Murray hit .298 and made 12 homers in 88 games at Charlotte, NC (SL), in 1976 before joining Rochester, NY (IL). At Rochester, he played first base, third base, and outfield and batted .274 with 11 home runs and 40 RBIs in 54 games. In each minor league season, Murray contended for the league lead in home runs and made the league All-Star team. With Asheville, the 6 foot, 2 inch, 190 pound right-hander began switch-hitting.

Murray has played ten seasons with the Baltimore Orioles through 1986. In 1977 he performed at first base and in the outfield but was used mostly as a designated hitter. He batted .283 with 27 round trippers and 88 RBIs to win AL Rookie of the Year honors. He became the regular first baseman in 1978 and steadily improved his fielding, earning three consecutive Gold Gloves from 1982 through 1984. Despite his excellent fielding, however, Murray has made the most impact with his bat, ranking consistently among AL leaders in home runs, RBIs, walks, slugging percentage, and on-base average. Through 1986 he hit 275 home runs, with his next to lowest portion of 22 leading the AL in the strike-shortened 1981 campaign. He has averaged over 101 RBIs per season, including an AL-leading 78 in 1981. Murray stands third on the all-time list of home run production by switch-hitters behind Mickey Mantle* and Reggie Smith,* with the trio being the only switch-hitters to have multiple 30-homer seasons. After leading the AL in walks (107) in 1984, he finished second in RBIs, third in runs scored, fourth in slugging percentage and game-winning hits, and fifth in on-base percentage in 1985. Murray improved steadily at the plate, hitting a career-high .316 in 1982 and enjoying a .299 career batting average. Through the 1986 season, he compiled 1,679 hits, 296 doubles, 884 runs scored, and 1,015 RBIs. The premier offensive player has been named to seven All-Star teams (1978, 1981–1986) and appeared in two World Series (1979, 1983). The AL Player of the Month several times, he was mentioned in the Most Valuable Player balloting eight seasons and finished second to Robin Yount* in 1982 and teammate Cal Ripken in 1983. Murray has been chosen Most Valuable Oriole four times (1978, 1981–1982, 1984), and ranks among the highest-paid major league players. Active in charity and community work, he resides in Phoenix, MD, and Los Angeles, CA.

BIBLIOGRAPHY: *American League Red Book, 1977–1985* (New York, 1977–1985); *Baltimore Orioles Media Guide, 1977–1985*; James H. Bready, *The Home Team* (Baltimore, 1979); Skip Dorer and Wayne Kaiser, *In the O-Zone* (Cherry Hill, NJ, 1980); Dan Schlossberg, *Baseball Stars 1985* (New York, 1985).

                                                                Douglas D. Martin

MUSIAL, Stanley Frank "Stan," "Stan the Man," "The Donora Greyhound" (b. 21 November 1920, Donora, PA), player and executive, is the son of mill worker Lukasz and Mary (Lancos) Musial. After graduating from Donora High School in 1938, he rejected a University of Pittsburgh basketball scholarship to sign a professional baseball contract as a pitcher with the St. Louis Cardinals (NL). In November, 1939, on his nineteenth birthday, he married Lillian Labash of Donora and has four children. Musial began his professional career in 1938 with Williamson, WV (MtnSL). During his third minor league season (1940), the left-handed Musial compiled an impressive 18–5 record with Daytona Beach (FSL). The hard-throwing 6 foot, 175 pound Musial, however, damaged his shoulder trying to make a tumbling catch in the outfield. Musial, an accomplished gymnast, had made many outstanding tumbling catches, but the ironic injury permanently weakened his throwing arm. Dickie Kerr, his manager of 1919 World Series fame, converted Musial to a full-time outfielder and refused to change his unique peek-a-boo batting stance.

In 1941 the left-handed batting Musial enjoyed a meteoric rise from Class C Springfield, MO (WA), where he hit .379 and compiled a .738 slugging average, to Class AA Rochester, NY (IL), where he batted .326. At the end of the 1941 season, he played 12 games with the parent St. Louis (NL) club and hit a phenomenal .426. From 1941 through 1963, Musial performed at all three outfield positions and first base for the Cardinals. During 1945 he served in the U.S. Navy. Musial, dubbed "The Man" by Brooklyn fans for his devastating hitting in Ebbets Field, hustled constantly and played all out. Nicknamed "The Donora Greyhound," he displayed considerable speed. During Musial's first four full major league seasons, the Cardinals captured four NL pennants and three world championships. Although the Cardinals won no other NL titles during his career, Musial won seven batting championships (1943, 1946, 1948, 1950–1952, 1957) and in 1948 hit a career-high .376 mark.

Musial led the NL in doubles eight times, in base hits, total bases, and slugging average six times, in triples and runs scored five times, and in RBIs twice. Until Henry Aaron* broke them, Musial held NL career records for games played (3,026), at bats (10,972), runs scored (1,949), and RBIs (1,951). Although Musial still holds the NL record for doubles with 725, Pete Rose* passed his NL mark for hits (3,630). Aaron also broke Musial's major league career records for most total bases (6,134) and extra-base hits (1,377). Musial batted .340 through the 1958 season, but his lifetime average subsequently dropped to .331. The aging, injury-plagued Musial averaged only .283 over his final five seasons. Although his 3,630 hits were equally divided home and away, Musial compiled a .336 batting average in home games and .326 in road contests. He hit an impressive .340 in daylight, much higher than his .320 in night games. In 24 All-Star game appearances, he averaged .317, made 20 hits, and slugged 6 home runs.

In 1969, his first year of eligibility, Musial was named to the National Baseball Hall of Fame. Besides being named the NL's Most Valuable Player three times (1943, 1946, and 1948), he was selected as *The Sporting News* National League Player of the Year in 1943, 1948, 1951, and 1957, *The Sporting News* Major League Player of the Year in 1946 and 1951, and its first Player of the Decade in 1956. Twelve times Musial made *The Sporting News* All-Star Major League team. Alongside his records, Musial exhibited gentlemanly behavior, friendliness, openness, and cheerfulness.

In active retirement, Musial continued as a popular restauranteur, served in the Cardinals front office, owned hotels and other real estate, and participated in numerous civic and charity affairs. Musial's extensive travels included an audience with the Pope, visits to Poland, and big game hunting in Kenya and Tanzania. In 1964 President Lyndon Johnson named him head of the national physical fitness program.

BIBLIOGRAPHY: Furman Bisher, "Get Any Hits, Stan?" *SEP* 236 (May 25, 1963), pp. 30ff.; Bob Broeg, *The Man Stan: Musial, Then and Now* (St. Louis, 1977); Roger Kahn, *A Season in the Sun* (New York, 1978); Theodore M. O'Leary, "Last Time Around with Stan," *SI* 19 (October 7, 1963), pp. 20–25; Harry T. Paxton, "A Visit with Stan Musial," *SEP* 230 (April 19, 1958), pp. 32–33ff.; John Reddy, "Stan, the Incredibly Durable Man," *Reader's Digest* 82 (April, 1963), pp. 175–180.

John E. DiMeglio

MYER, Charles Solomon "Buddy" (b. 16 March 1904, Ellisville, MI; d. 31 October 1974, Baton Rouge, LA), player, was the son of Charles and Maud Myer. His father, a merchant and cotton buyer, had German Jewish antecedents, while his mother noted an English lineage. After attending public schools in the Ellisville area, Myer matriculated in 1921 at Mississippi Agricultural and Mechanical College and excelled at college basketball and baseball. On February 10, 1927, he married Minnie Lee Williams; they had two sons. In 1925 Myer left Mississippi A & M before graduation to join the spring training camp of the Cleveland Indians (AL). After the Indians failed to retain him, Myer joined New Orleans (SA) and hit .336. Late in the the 1925 season, the Washington Nationals (AL) purchased Myer's contract. Washington traded shortstop Myer to the Boston Red Sox (AL) in May 1927 but reacquired him after the 1928 season. From 1929 until his 1941 release, Myer remained with Washington, mainly at second base, and captained the team for several years.

Although not a superstar, Myer played seventeen years in the major leagues as one of the era's better infielders defensively and offensively. Primarily a second baseman, the 5 foot, 10 1/2 inch, 163 pound Myer also played shortstop, third base, and the outfield. With a lifetime .968 fielding average, he led AL second basemen in fielding once (1938) and tied for the AL leadership on another occasion (1931). Myer exceeded the .300 mark nine times and compiled a .303 lifetime batting average. During his career he made 2,131 hits, drove in 850 runs, scored 1,174 runs, stole 156 bases, accumulated 130 triples, and registered 353 doubles. Myer won the 1935 AL batting title with a .349 average and led the AL with 30 stolen bases in 1928.

The underrated player lacked recognition because post–1920 baseball tended to overvalue home run hitters. The left-handed hitting, right-handed throwing Myer slugged just 38 home runs during his career. He played for only two AL pennant winners (1925, 1933) and frequently labored on second division teams. Since Babe Ruth's* power hitting revolutionized baseball, batters having a high batting average and few home runs rarely receive significant media attention unless they perform for successful teams. Myer's reserve was leavened by pride and determination. Several times he fought anti-Semitic opponents. Despite offers to manage, Myer retired from baseball after his playing days to Baton Rouge and became a successful mortgage banker.

BIBLIOGRAPHY: Morris Bealle, *The Washington Senators: An 87-Year History* (Washington, DC, 1947); Bob Broeg, "Myer Uncrowned Super Star," *TSN*, November 16, 1974, p. 52; "Charles Solomon (Buddy) Myer," *TSN*, November 16, 1974, p. 74; Shirley Povich, *The Washington Senators: An Informal History* (New York, 1954); Harold Ribalow, *The Jews in American Sports*, rev. ed. (New York, 1954).

                                                                      William M. Simons

N

NAVIN, Frank "Lucky Frank," "The Jap" (b. 7 March 1871, Adrian MI; d. 13 November 1935, Detroit, MI), executive, was the son of Irish-born parents. His father, a railroad worker, sent Navin to study business and law at the Detroit College of Law. Navin's brother Tom, a prominent Republican politician in Michigan, influenced him to seek the office of justice of the peace. Navin's subsequent defeat and his brother's imprisonment for embezzling a large sum of money convinced Navin to quit politics. Although a good student of jurisprudence, he never practiced law. Navin instead worked as an accountant for Sam Angus, insurance company owner and chief Detroit Baseball Club (AL) stockholder. Navin kept accounts for the ballclub and toiled in a gambling establishment, acquiring a shady reputation. He avoided payment of a gambling debt to Frank Croul, later police commissioner. A vindictive Croul made it difficult for Navin to have Sunday baseball in Detroit.

With Angus' finances in disarray, Navin persuaded William Yawkey, the scion of a wealthy Michigan family, to purchase the Tigers. Navin bought a small share of the Detroit club with a packet won in a card game. Navin, who believed that receipts should balance with expenditures, clashed with the club's general manager Ed Barrow.* Barrow wished to make liberal use of Yawkey's money to build a winning team. Navin, however, gained Yawkey's confidence and forced Barrow to resign. Although not having a professional grasp of baseball, he became Tigers general manager and learned much from manager William Armour. Armour persuaded Navin to purchase a pugnacious teenager, Ty Cobb.* Navin resisted pressure to trade the Georgia troublemaker and made several other astute acquisitions to build the 1907–1909 AL championships teams. In gratitude, Yawkey gave Navin half ownership of the club. Nicknamed "Lucky Frank," he became a solid Detroit citizen and contributed to many charities. He managed to have the ballpark named in his honor and conducted widely publicized annual contract negotiations with Cobb.

Walter Briggs* purchased a substantial share of the Tigers when Yawkey died in 1920. Although attendance skyrocketed and Navin became wealthy, Detroit did not win an AL championship that decade. Critics blamed Navin's parsimonious policies and Cobb's inept managing. In 1931 Navin was nearly ruined by the Depression and horse racing gambling losses and did not have enough money to take the Tigers to spring training. Briggs bought most of the club stock and pumped funds into the operation, building the 1934 and 1935 AL championship teams. Nicknamed "The Jap" because of his inscrutable features, Navin was an emotional man who often used pithy, colloquial language in intimate and business letters. Navin's intimates appreciated his fine sense of humor and generosity, particularly to old ball players. When Navin died, the city of Detroit mourned "Mr. Baseball."

BIBLIOGRAPHY: W. Malcolm Bingay, *Detroit Is My Home Town* (New York, 1951); W. Malcolm Bingay, *Of Me I Sing* (New York, 1949); Detroit Baseball Club Letterbooks, vols. 1–12, Ernie Harwell Collection, Detroit Public Library; Detroit *News*, November 13, 1935; Frederick G. Lieb, *The Detroit Tigers* (New York, 1946); John L. Lodge, *I Remember Detroit* (Detroit, 1949).

Anthony J. Papalas

NEHF, Arthur Neukom "Art," "The Terre Haute Terror" (b. 31 July 1892, Terre Haute, IN; d. 18 December 1960, Phoenix AZ), player, was a slightly built 5 foot, 9 inch, 170 pound southpaw pitcher. After attending a Terre Haute high school, he played baseball at Rose Polytechnic Institute (IN) and earned a Bachelor of Science degree there in 1913. Since engineers received low salaries in that era, Nehf pursued a professional baseball career. Chicago Cubs (NL) president Charles Webb Murphy offered Nehf a tryout, but field manager John Evers* considered him too small. Nehf pitched for Kansas City (AA) and Sioux City (WL) in 1913 and won 30 games and lost only 17 for Terre Haute (CL) the next two seasons. In 1915 he led the CL with 218 strikeouts and a sparkling 1.38 ERA.

After joining the Boston Braves (NL) for a reported $3,500 in 1915, Nehf compiled a 52–41 record there until traded on August 17, 1919, to John McGraw's* New York Giants (NL) for four players and $40,000. Nehf hurled for the Giants until developing arm problems and was sold in May, 1926, to the Cincinnati Reds (NL). Nicknamed "The Terre Haute Terror," Nehf won 87 games between 1920 and 1924, compiled a 107–60 overall win-loss mark with the Giants, and led them to four consecutive NL pennants (1921–1924). From 1921 to 1924, he finished with 20–10, 19–13, 13–10, and 14–4 marks. Nehf lost his first two World Series starts against the New York Yankees in 1921, but shut them out on four hits in the seventh and deciding game to win the world championship for the Giants. He pitched three complete games, allowing a record low 13 base hits. In the 1922 World Series, Nehf defeated the Yankees 5–3 in the fifth game to wrap up another world championship. He pitched a shutout victory over New York in the third game of the 1923 World Series, but the Yankees won their first title four games to two. Nehf bested Walter Johnson* in the first game of the 1924 World Series in Washington, DC, but lost the sixth game as the Senators won the title in seven games. In twelve World Series games, he pitched 79 innings, won four, lost four, and had a 2.16 ERA. After pitching for the Reds (1926–1927), Nehf signed with the Chicago Cubs (NL) in August, 1927. He won eight games in his final major league season (1929) and appeared in one more World Series, but did not figure in any decisions.

During his fifteen major league seasons, Nehf pitched in 451 games, recorded 184 victories and 120 losses, and compiled a 3.20 ERA. He hurled 2,707 2/3 innings and completed 182 games, including 30 shutouts. On August 1, 1918, Nehf pitched a 21-inning 2–0 loss against the Pittsburgh Pirates. He participated in 12 double plays in 1920, equalling the NL record for a pitcher. In 1918 he completed 28 games and surrendered 274 base hits and 107 runs, leading the NL in each category. After retiring from baseball, the arthritic Nehf was employed by Cubs owner William Wrigley in hotel management and later entered the real estate business in Arizona. Nehf married Elizabeth Bird May on November 1, 1916, and was honored when Rose Polytechnic Institute named its baseball field after him.

BIBLIOGRAPHY: Arthur Nehf file, National Baseball Hall of Fame Library, Cooperstown, NY; Gene Karst and Martin J. Jones, Jr., *Who's Who in Professional Baseball* (New Rochelle, NY, 1973); Paul MacFarlane, ed., *TSN Daguerreotypes of Great Stars of Baseball* (St. Louis, 1971); Joseph L. Reichler, ed., *The Baseball Encyclopedia*, 6th ed. (New York, 1985), p. 1,937; *TSN*, October 10, 1915, December 4, 1965.

David S. Matz and John L. Evers

NEWCOMBE, Donald "Don," "Newk" (b. 14 June 1926, Madison, NJ), player, became one of the first successful black pitchers in modern major league baseball. The 6 foot, 4 inch, 230 pound Newcombe pitched for the Brooklyn Dodgers (NL) from 1949 to 1957 and moved with the club to Los Angeles at the start of the 1958 season. After only 11 games on the West Coast, Newcombe was traded to the Cincinnati Reds (NL) and pitched there until midway through the 1960 season. He completed his major league career that season with the Cleveland Indians (AL). Prior to entering the major leagues, Newcombe pitched for the Negro Newark Eagles (NNL), and the Nashua Dodgers, (NEL), in 1946 and 1947 and Montreal Royals (IL) in 1948 and 1949.

Newcombe's ten major league baseball seasons included 344 appearances and 294 starts. Newcombe struck out 1,129 batters and walked only 490 in 2,154 2/3 innings pitched and compiled a 3.56 ERA. His career .623 winning percentage (149 wins, 90 losses) ranks him thirty-second among all major league pitchers with at least 100 career victories. Newcombe won 20 games in 1951 and 1955, and led the NL in 1956 with 27 victories and a .794 winning percentage. His other NL leading performances included winning percentage (.800, 20–5) in 1955, strikeouts (164) in 1951, and shutouts (5, tied with three others) in 1949. Newcombe was selected NL Rookie of the Year in 1949, NL Most Valuable Player in 1956, and initial recipient of the Cy Young* Award in 1956. He pitched for the Dodgers in the 1949, 1955, and 1956 World Series, compiling a 0–4 record. An NL All-Star performer in 1949 and 1951, he was the losing pitcher in the former contest.

Newcombe, an exceptionally able batter, often pinch-hit for the Dodgers. He posted a .271 career batting average (seventh among pitchers with at least 500 at bats), .367 slugging average (twelfth on the career list), 15 lifetime home runs, and 108 RBIs. In 1955 he batted .359 with a .632 slugging percentage in 117 at bats, the latter still a modern major league record for pitchers. Newcombe, who married Freddie Cross, has two children, engages in business, and lives in Los Angeles.

BIBLIOGRAPHY: *CB* (1957), pp. 399–401; Edwin B. Henderson and the Editors of *Sport* Magazine, *The Black Athlete: Emergence and Arrival* (Cornwall Heights, NJ, 1979); Gene Karst and Martin J. Jones, Jr., *Who's Who in Professional Baseball* (New Rochelle, NY, 1973).

William J. Serow

NEWHOUSER, Harold "Hal," Prince Hal" (b. 20 May 1921, Detroit MI), player and scout, is the son of patternmaker Theodore and homemaker Emilie Newhouser. He grew up in Detroit, where he became an outstanding Sandlot Class E Pitcher and starred for the American Legion Post 286 team. Detroit Tigers (AL) scout Wish Egan encouraged the high school youth to practice pitching at Briggs Stadium outside the foul lines. After graduation from Wilbur Wright High School, 17-year-old Newhouser accepted a $400 bonus and $150 a month salary to sign with the Tigers.

After spending 1939 with Alexandria, LA (EvL), and Beaumont, TX (TL), the 6 foot, 2 inch, 180 pound left-hander pitched from late 1939 to 1953 with the Tigers and finished his career in 1954 with the Cleveland Indians (AL). During 1944, 1945, and 1946, he stood at the forefront of major league pitchers. In 1945 he led the AL in eight categories, compiling a 25–9 record and 1.81 ERA. He holds the Tigers record for the lowest single-season ERA (1945) and most season victories by a left-hander (29 wins in 1944). *Baseball Digest* ranked his 1944 win-loss record the best achievement by an AL pitcher in the 1940s.

Although prone to surrendering walks and hits, Newhouser frequently pitched out of difficult situations and usually made timely outs. From 1944 to 1950, he averaged over 21 victories in a season and made the AL All-Star team six times. After hurting his arm in the 1948 finale, Newhouser experienced declining effectiveness. A loyal hometown boy, Newhouser could have jumped his bonus contract with the Tigers and signed with Cleveland for $15,000 and a new car. Newhouser wanted to serve in the U.S. Army during World War II but was rejected because of a heart problem. He married Beryl Margaret Steele on December 20, 1941, and has two daughters.

Newhouser, who compiled 207 career wins and 150 losses (.580 winning percentage), also hurled over 20 victories in 1946 and 1948. In 1945 he pitched the AL pennant-clinching win and two key victories in the World Series against the Chicago Cubs. In 1944 and 1945 he became the first of few players to win consecutive AL Most Valuable Player awards. In 488 appearances, he completed 212 of 374 starts, pitched 2,992 2/3 innings, struck out 1,796 batters, and hurled 33 shutouts. After retirement in 1955, Newhouser scouted for the AL Baltimore Orioles (1956–1961), Cleveland Indians (1961–1964), and NL Houston Astros (current) and became a bank executive in Pontiac, MI. He is active in community affairs, including the YWCA, Boy Scouts, and fund-raising efforts.

BIBLIOGRAPHY: Glenn Dickey, *The History of the American League Since 1901* (New York, 1980); Joe Falls, *Detroit Tigers* (New York, 1975); Richard Goldstein, *Spartan Seasons: How Baseball Survived the Second World War* (New York, 1980); Gene Karst and Martin J. Jones, Jr., *Who's Who in Professional Baseball* (New Rochelle, NY, 1973); George Voss, "Top Player Achievements of the Last Four Decades!" *Baseball Digest* 41 (August, 1982), p. 61.

Douglas A. Noverr

NICHOLS, Charles Augustus "Kid" (b. 14 September 1869, Madison, WI; d. 11 April 1953, Kansas City, MO), player, manager, and coach, starred as a pitcher between 1890 and 1905 and ranked among the steadiest all-time winners. The 5 foot, 10 1/2 inch, 175 pound right-hander hurled for Kansas City (WA), Omaha (WA), and for Memphis (SL) between 1887 and 1889. After joining Boston's NL team in 1890, Nichols topped the 25-victory mark nine consecutive seasons. An overhand pitcher with a smooth delivery, Nichols depended on speed and good control and possessed a durable arm. In his first five major league seasons, he compiled impressive innings-pitched totals of 427, 425, 454, 425, and 407. He toiled over 300 innings in seven of the next eight years. As a 20-year-old rookie, Nichols led Boston pitchers with 27 victories (including 7 shutouts) and then achieved seven consecutive seasons with 30 or more triumphs. In his first nine seasons, Nichols sparked Boston to five championships and led his team in victories. He recorded his most victories (35) in 1892 and paced the NL in wins three years in succession (1896–1898).

Following the 1901 season, Nichols bought a part-interest in the Kansas City (WA) club and pitched 48 victories (1902–1903) as their player-manager. As pitcher-manager for St. Louis (NL) in 1904 and part of 1905, Nichols guided the Cardinals to 94 wins in 202 games. In 1904, he won 21 games for the Cardinals and on August 11 struck out 15 Brooklyn batters in a 17-inning game. After being released as Cardinals manager in mid-June, Nichols joined Philadelphia (NL) and completed the season with an 11–11 record. Early in 1906 he retired from baseball at age 36.

Nichols won 360 games in his major league career and, at nine months and twenty-three days past his thirtieth birthday, became the youngest pitcher ever to win 300 games. Only five moundsmen, Cy Young,* Walter Johnson,* Christy Mathewson,* Grover Alexander,* and Warren Spahn,* have registered more victories, while only three pitchers have hurled more complete games. No other pitcher has ever won 30 games in seven consecutive seasons. Although Nichols did not attain the win standards achieved by Young and Johnson, he nevertheless remains one of the five premier nineteenth century baseball pitchers with Tim Keefe,* John Clarkson,* Charles Radbourne,* and Young.

Nichols, who ranks high on the all-time major league lists for pitchers in numerous statistical categories, participated in 621 contests, started 562 games (17th), completed 533 games (4th), pitched 5,084 innings (7th), struck out 1,885 batters, walked 1,282 batters, and hurled 48 shutouts (25th). In fifteen seasons, Nichols compiled 202 losses (35th) and won 20 or more contests eleven years (5th) and at least 30 games seven years (1st).

Subsequently, Nichols entered the motion picture business and real estate and also managed one of the largest bowling alleys in Missouri, gaining recognition as one of the finest bowlers in Kansas City. At age 64, Nichols won the Class A Championship. Nichols also coached the Missouri Valley College baseball team in Marshall, MO, and in 1949 was enshrined in the National Baseball Hall of Fame.

BIBLIOGRAPHY: Paul MacFarlane, ed., *TSN Daguerreotypes of Great Stars of Baseball* (St. Louis, 1971); *National Baseball Hall of Fame and Museum Brochure* (Cooperstown, NY, 1974); Lowell Reidenbaugh, *Cooperstown: Where Baseball's Legends Live Forever* (St. Louis, 1983).

John L. Evers

NIEKRO, Joseph Franklin "Joe" (b. 7 November 1944, Martins Ferry, OH), player, is the son of coal miner Philip and Henrietta (Klinkoski) Niekro. The younger brother of major league pitcher Phil Niekro,* he followed his footsteps by excelling in baseball and basketball at Bridgeport (OH) High School. After attending West Liberty State College in West Virginia, the 6 foot, 1 inch, 190 pound right-hander pitcher signed in 1966 with the Chicago Cubs (NL).

Niekro pitched with Treasure Valley, ID (PrL), Quincy, IL (ML), and Dallas-Fort Worth (TL) before making the Cubs roster in 1967. He recorded 24 victories with Chicago until traded to the San Diego Padres (NL) in April, 1969. Niekro hurled against brother Phil of the Atlanta Braves on July 4,

1967, and lost 8–3, marking the first time that brothers opposed each other on the mound in the NL. They met again in eight other encounters, with Joe winning five and Phil three. Joe's only major league home run came off Phil in May, 1976. After being traded to the Detroit Tigers (AL) following the 1969 season, Niekro hurled for the Tigers and Toledo (IL) until sold on waivers to the Atlanta Braves (NL) in August, 1973. Niekro captured 21 composite decisions for the Tigers and pitched a seven-inning, 2–0 perfect game for Toledo against Tidewater, VA (IL), on July 16, 1972. At Atlanta and Richmond (IL) Niekro collected 13 victories in 1973 and 1974 before being sold to the Houston Astros (NL) in April, 1975.

Following seven appearances for Iowa (AA) in 1975, Niekro became one of the leading Astros pitchers. On July 2, 1985, Niekro collected his 200th career major league victory with a 3–2 win over San Diego. Niekro, a knuckleball artist, recorded 144 victories with Houston from 1975 to 1985 and boasted 21 wins in 1979, both club records. Besides topping the NL in wins and tying for the lead in shutouts (1979), Niekro paced the NL in games started with 38 (1983–1984).

Named *The Sporting News* NL Pitcher of the Year and to the All-Star team (1979), Niekro pitched in two post-season playoff games (1980–1981). Although failing to gain a decision, Niekro did not allow a single run in 18 innings. Niekro remains one of only sixty-eight major league pitchers to start 400 or more games and one of only eighty-three hurlers to have 200 victories. In September, 1985, he was sent to the New York Yankees (AL) and joined his brother Phil there. Through 1986 Niekro had pitched in 670 games and 3,426 innings with 213 wins, 190 losses, 1,656 strikeouts, 29 shutouts, and a 3.50 ERA.

BIBLIOGRAPHY: Gene Karst and Martin J. Jones, Jr., *Who's Who in Professional Baseball* (New Rochelle, NY, 1973); *TSN Baseball Register, 1985*; (St. Louis, 1985); Steve Wulf, "Knucksie Hasn't Lost His Grip," *SI* 60 (June 4, 1984), pp. 91–94ff.

John L. Evers

NIEKRO, Philip Henry "Phil" (b. 1 April 1939, Blaine, OH), player, is the son of Philip and Henrietta (Klinkoski) Niekro, and brother of major league pitcher Joe Niekro.* His parents, both native Americans of Polish extraction, settled in eastern Ohio, near Wheeling, WV. His father, a coal miner and sandlot baseball player, taught the sport to Phil and Joe. Phil attended grade school in Lansing and high school in Bridgeport, OH, where he excelled in athletics. Although offered a college baseball scholarship, he instead signed a professional baseball contract with the Milwaukee Braves (NL). From 1959 to 1966 (except for military service in 1963), Niekro pitched for minor league clubs in Wellsville, NY (NYPL), McCook, NE (NeSL), Jacksonville, FL (SAL), Louisville (AA), Austin, (TL), Denver (AA), and Richmond (IL). He utilized the knuckleball, taught to him by his father.

Niekro's minor league progress proved slow, primarily because catchers encountered difficulty catching his knuckleball.

The 6 foot, 1 inch, 180 pound right-hander pitched his first major league game for Milwaukee (NL) in 1964 and was farmed out each season until 1967, by which time the franchise had been shifted to Atlanta. In his first full season, 1967, he led the NL with a 1.87 ERA. In 1969 he won 23 games and led the Braves to the Western Division title, the first year that the expansion system was used. Although pitching good ball, including a no-hit game over San Diego in 1973, Niekro did not win many more games than he lost because Atlanta fielded average teams.

In 1974 he led the NL in innings pitched and again won 20 games. Despite advancing years, Niekro became the NL workhorse. From 1977 through 1979, he led the NL in games started, games completed, and innings pitched. He also paced the NL with 262 strikeouts in 1977 and, at age 40 in 1979, tied his brother Joe of the Houston Astros for the NL lead in games won with 21. During their long major league careers, the Niekro brothers faced each other nine times. Joe won five of these games, including a 1–0 thriller on July 13, 1969, while Phil took four. On May 29, 1976, Joe hit his only major league home run off his brother Phil in a 4–3 victory. These fraternal confrontations posed a dilemma for their parents in this close-knit family.

Niekro ended his long association with the Braves after winning 11 of 21 decisions in 1983. Before the 1984 season, the New York Yankees (AL) signed him to a two-year contract. Niekro compiled an impressive 16–8 mark and 3.09 ERA in 1984 and a 16–12 record and 4.09 ERA in 1985. On October 8, 1985, Niekro recorded his 300th victory in an 8–0 four-hitter over Toronto and became the oldest major league pitcher ever to hurl a shutout. Niekro signed with the Cleveland Indians (AL) after being released by the Yankees in March 1986. His career record through 1986 included 838 games pitched, 311 wins, 261 losses, 45 shutouts, 3,278 strikeouts in 5,265 innings pitched, and a 3.27 ERA. The knuckleball, although slowing his progress to the majors in the 1960s, prolonged his career beyond age 40. An excellent fielding pitcher, he won Gold Gloves at that position four years.

The fierce, competitive Niekro is loquacious, friendly, and trusting off the field. During the off-season, he participates extensively in community service activities. This volunteer work has brought him humanitarian and service awards named for the late Lou Gehrig,* Roberto Clemente,* and Brian Piccolo. Niekro married Nancy Ferrand, a former airline stewardess, in Richmond, VA, in August, 1966, and has three sons, Michael, John, and Philip.

BIBLIOGRAPHY: Larry Amman, "Baseball Brothers," in L. Robert Davids, ed., *Insider's Baseball* (New York, 1983), pp. 111–120; Furman Bisher, "Niekro, a Real Phil for the Game," *Atlanta Braves Yearbook, 1979*; Jim Bouton, "Baseball's Working Class Hero," *Inside Sports* 4 (May, 1982); Gene Karst and Martin J. Jones, Jr., *Who's Who in Professional Baseball* (New Rochelle, NY, 1973); Phil Niekro file, National Baseball Hall of Fame Library, Cooperstown, NY.

L. Robert Davids

O

OLIVER, Albert, Jr. "Al," "Mr. Scoop" (b. 14 October 1946, Portsmouth, OH), player, is the son of bricklayer Albert Oliver, Sr., and attended Kent State University. His mother died when he was age 11, while his father died the day he was called up to the major leagues. A left-handed baseball catcher in high school, he rejected a basketball scholarship at Kent State to sign with the Pittsburgh Pirates (NL) in 1964 for $5,000. Oliver began his professional baseball career with Salem, VA (ApL), but did not play. As a left-handed hitting first baseman with Gastonia, NC, in 1965, he led the WCL with 159 hits. He performed with Raleigh (CrL) in 1966, Macon (SL) and Raleigh (CrL) in 1967, and Columbus (IL) in 1968.

The 6 foot, 1 inch, 200 pound Oliver joined the Pittsburgh Pirates as a part-time first baseman in 1969 and spent nine seasons there in the outfield and at first base, batting above .300 four times and usually finishing among NL leaders in batting average, total bases, and doubles. He played in five NL Championship Series between 1970 and 1975 and batted .211 in the Pirates' 1971 World Series triumph over the Baltimore Orioles. After the 1977 season, Oliver was traded to the Texas Rangers (AL). He hit well above .300 each season there and seldom struck out. In March 1982 Oliver was traded to the Montreal Expos (NL), where he enjoyed the finest season of his career. Besides hitting at a .331 NL-leading clip, he paced the NL with 204 hits and 43 doubles for 317 total bases and tied for the NL lead with 109 RBIs. An average defensive player, he led NL first basemen with 19 errors in 1982. Montreal traded Oliver in February 1984 to the San Francisco Giants (NL), where he played half a season before being sent in August to the Philadelphia Phillies (NL). He spent 1985 with the Los Angeles Dodgers (NL) and Toronto Blue Jays (AL). In the 1985 AL Championship Series against Kansas City, Oliver batted .375, knocked in three runs, doubled once, and delivered two game-winning hits.

Oliver appeared in seven All-Star games between 1972 and 1983, but started only in the last contest. If not underrated, he remained under-recognized. In contrast with well-known Reggie Jackson,* Oliver in two less major league seasons produced 233 more hits and a .303 batting average, 40 points higher than Jackson's. Oliver's 2,743 hits ranked him thirty-fourth on the all-time list. His 529 doubles placed him seventeenth on the lifetime list. Oliver's .303 batting average, 1,189 runs scored, and 1,326 RBIs also ranked high among active players at his retirement. The Burlington, TX, resident hit 77 triples and 219 home runs, and stole 84 bases. Oliver retired from pro baseball after being released by the Blue Jays in November 1985.

BIBLIOGRAPHY: Jim Laise, "Al Oliver: The Solution or Part of the Problem?" *Sport* 73 (October, 1982), p. 44; Joseph L. Reichler, ed. *The Baseball Encyclopedia*, 6th ed. (New York, 1985); p. 1,263; W. C. Rhoden, "Oliver: Quiet Brilliance," *NYT Biographical Service* (August, 1983), pp. 977–978; *TSN Official Baseball Register, 1985*, (St. Louis, 1985); Steve Wulf, "You Don't Know Me, Says Al," *SI* 52 (April 21, 1980), pp. 58–63; *WWA*, 43rd ed. (1984–1985), p. 2,519.

Gaymon L. Bennett

O'MALLEY, Walter Francis (b. 9 October 1903, New York, NY; d. 9 August, 1979, Rochester, MN), executive, was the most influential club owner of baseball's early expansion era. The son of wealthy New York City Commissioner of Public Markets Edwin J. and Alma (Feltner) O'Malley, he attended Jamaica High School in Queens and Culver Military Academy in Indiana. He graduated from the University of Pennsylvania in 1926 and earned a law degree from Fordham Law School. O'Malley practiced law for twenty years before concentrating on operating the Brooklyn Dodgers (NL) baseball team. He married Kay Hanson in 1931 and had two children, including eventual club president Peter.

In 1941 O'Malley became the Dodgers' attorney and began investing in the team. He gained control in 1950 by driving his rival, Branch Rickey,* whose flamboyant leadership O'Malley resented, from the presidency and forcing him to sell his quarter interest for $1.05 million. O'Malley then purchased the remaining 50 percent of the stock from the Ebbets estate for $1 million, cheaply acquiring the NL's most prominent franchise. From 1950 through 1956, the Dodgers won four NL pennants and a world championship and led the NL in attendance. Although Rickey built the farm system and signed star black players, O'Malley saw that the team maintained its formidable player development program.

Dodgers owner O'Malley concentrated on baseball interests and soon became a power in the baseball establishment. Although keeping a low profile, he served on key committees and became the most powerful voice in league councils. In 1950 he led a successful movement to oust assertive Commissioner Albert B. "Happy" Chandler* and proved instrumental in choosing more compliant successor Commissioners Ford Frick,* William Eckert,* and Bowie Kuhn.*

Despite the strength and profitability of his Brooklyn Dodgers, O'Malley fretted over the inadequacy of Ebbets Field. Determined to expand his profit base, he pressured New York State politicians for land for a new park. When disputes over location and cost reached an impasse, O'Malley moved his team west to lucrative Los Angeles. O'Malley persuaded New York Giants owner Horace Stoneham* to join him in 1959 in the westward move, ushering in major league baseball's expansion era.

The move triggered a storm of protest and made O'Malley's name anathema to New Yorkers. O'Malley testified before Congressional investigators that he had permission from his colleagues and had acquired the territorial rights to the Los Angeles area. Los Angeles politicians allowed him to purchase cheaply 300 acres of public land and also financed access roads for the new stadium, which O'Malley agreed to pay for. As his team played four seasons in the Los Angeles Coliseum, O'Malley supervised construction of $16 million Dodger Stadium. The Dodgers occupied the new facility in 1962. With its 56,000 seating capacity, the stadium annually attracted 2 million paid fans and in 1979 set a major league record by passing the 3 million paid mark. A promotional genius, O'Malley kept ticket prices low and profited from concession sales and a shrewd local television policy. In 1977 O'Malley's Dodgers enterprise was worth an estimated $50 million, twice the value of the average major league franchise.

In 1970 O'Malley turned the presidency over to his son Peter, but remained chairman of the board until his death. As unofficial adviser to commissioners, O'Malley continued to be a formidable power. Above all, he was the catalyst to the game's continental expansion. His westward move triggered the rival CntL movement of 1959. O'Malley helped defuse this movement by persuading major league owners to add two teams to each existing major league in 1961–1962, preempting key cities eyed by CntL promoters. In 1969 a second round of expansion swelled major league membership to twenty-four teams. Eight years later, the AL's unilateral expansion raised membership to twenty six. Such dynamic growth was credited to O'Malley's initial decision to move westward.

BIBLIOGRAPHY: Cary S. Henderson, "Los Angeles and the Dodger War, 1957–1962," *Southern California Quarterly* 62 (Fall, 1980); Roger Kahn, *The Boys of Summer* (New York, 1973); Richard Kowet, *The Rich Who Own Sports* (New York, 1977); Lee Lowenfish, "A Tale of Many Cities: The Westward Expansion of National Baseball in the 1950s," *Journal of the West* 17 (July, 1978); Harold Parrott, *The Lords of Baseball* (New York, 1975); Al Stump, "On Deck for the Dodgers—O'Malley the Younger," *Signature* (August, 1971); Bill Veeck, "The Baseball Establishment," *Esquire* 62 (August, 1964), pp. 45–47ff.

David Quentin Voigt

O'ROURKE, James Henry "Jim," "Orator Jim" (b. 24 August 1852, Bridgeport, CT; d. 8 January 1919, Bridgeport, CT), player, manager, umpire, and executive, ranks as perhaps the most versatile performer in major league history. The only player to perform in at least 100 games at six fielding positions, he covered all three outfield spots, catcher, first base, and third base. O'Rourke fielded adequately, lacked a strong arm, and possessed about average speed. The muscular 5 foot, 8 inch, 185 pounder remained a powerful right-handed hitter throughout his career. Born into an Irish family and the brother of major leaguer John O'Rourke, he began his career with the Osceola Club of Bridgeport in 1871. The next year he entered professional baseball with the Middletown Mansfields (NA).

From 1873 to 1880, he played with the powerful Boston Red Stockings (NA through 1875, NL thereafter) except for spending the 1879 season with Providence (NL). Starting in 1881, he played four seasons with Buffalo (NL). From 1885 to 1892, he starred for New York (NL) except for one season (1890) with New York (PL). He concluded his career with Washington (NL) in 1893, but returned for a single game with the New York Giants (NL) in 1904 at age 52. A consistent hitter, O'Rourke batted at least .300 thirteen times in his twenty-three-year career. He compiled a four-year .317 average in the NA and a .310 mark in the NL and PL. One of the era's power hitters, he produced 414 doubles, 132 triples, and 51 home runs in the NL and PL. O'Rourke also made 2,304 hits, scored 1,446 runs, knocked in 830 runs, and stole 177 bases.

O'Rourke, unlike most ball players, successfully shifted from the playing field to the front office. As player-manager in Buffalo from 1881 to 1884, O'Rourke piloted four teams to a composite 206–169 winning record. He served as player-manager of the 1893 Washington (NL) team and as a major league umpire the next year. His managerial record in the major leagues comprised 246 wins and 258 losses (.488). After spending two years (1895–1896) as manager of the independent Victors of Bridgeport, he returned to professional baseball as pilot of Bridgeport (CtL) from 1897 to 1908 and played there from 1904 to 1907. From 1907 through 1913, he served as CtL President. O'Rourke, EL president in 1914, was elected to the National Baseball Hall of Fame in 1945.

BIBLIOGRAPHY: Paul MacFarlane, ed., *Hall of Fame Fact Book* (St. Louis, 1982); Joseph L. Reichler, ed., *The Baseball Encyclopedia*, 6th ed. (New York, 1985), pp. 64, 1,267–1,268; *Spalding's Official Base Ball Guide 1887* (New York, 1887).

                                                                    Gordon B. McKinney

ORR, David L. "Dave," "Big Dave" (b. 29 September 1859, New York, NY; d. 3 June 1915, Brooklyn, NY), player and manager, was the son of laborer James and Rachel Orr, of Scotch-Irish descent. Orr attended New York elementary school, but did not excel. He worked odd jobs and began his baseball career on the city's independent teams, including the Alaskas of Brooklyn. A right-handed batter and thrower, Orr in 1883 played for the Metropolitan Reserves of Newark (later Hartford, CT). In 1883 colorful manager Jim Mutrie recruited Orr to play 13 games for the original New York Metropolitans (AA). Orr also replaced Roger Connor* for a single game with the New York Giants (NL). During an eight-season major league career ended prematurely by a crippling disability in 1890, "Big Dave" hit .342 lifetime and never batted below .300. Besides playing with New York (AA) from 1884 to 1887, he performed for Brooklyn (AA) in 1888, Columbus (AA) in 1889, and Brooklyn (PL) in 1890.

Teamed with Timothy Keefe,* Orr in 1884 placed second in the AA in batting (.354) and hits (162). He powered the Mets to a championship and the first "World Series" title. In December he heroically saved a child's life in a railroad accident. During the following two seasons, his slugging fame blossomed. Orr led the AA in triples each season, with his 31 in 1886 the second highest mark ever. He also paced the AA with seven home runs and became the first player to surpass 300 total bases in a single season. The immensely strong Orr stood just under 6 feet and eventually weighed nearly 250 pounds. His size regularly cost him extra bases and often aggravated injuries. Although plagued by leg problems, Orr in 1887 batted .368 and stole 17 bases. He also served as interim manager (28 wins, 36 losses) of the now-decimated Mets in their second year as "Indians" on Staten Island. At season's end, Charles Byrne and Charles Ebbets* of Brooklyn (AA) purchased the team. After a single season with the Bridegrooms, Orr was sold to the new Columbus (AA) team. In 1889 he led AA first basemen in assists, one of several times he led in fielding categories.

With John M. Ward's* Brooklyn team (PL), Orr in 1890 batted .373 and knocked in 124 runs. After sustaining two broken ribs from being hit by a pitch in July, he suffered a stroke at season's end that paralyzed his left side and terminated his career. A powerful home run hitter (37 lifetime), Orr was one of only four nineteenth century players to compile a lifetime .500 slugging mark. In 791 games, he made 1,126 hits, 198 doubles, 108 triples, and 536 runs scored, and batted .342. Subsequently, he resided in Brooklyn and Manhattan and worked as a stonecutter and stagehand. When Ebbets Field was built, he was named caretaker. When the Brooklyn Feds opened at Washington Park in 1914, Ward made Orr responsible for the press box. Orr, whose wife, Emily Ann, died in 1906, had no children.

BIBLIOGRAPHY: " 'Dave' Orr, Famous Ball Player, Dies," Brooklyn *Daily Eagle*, June 3, 1915, p. 20; Preston Orem, *Baseball 1845–1881* (Altadena, CA, 1961); "Orr, Mighty Hitter of the Eighties, Dead," *TSN*, June 10, 1915, p. 3.

James D. Smith III

ORTH, Albert Lewis "Al," "Smiling Al," "The Curveless Wonder" (b. 5 September 1872, Sedalia, MO; d. 8 October 1948, Lynchburg, VA), player, coach, and umpire, was the son of the Lewis Orth. After being educated in the Danville, IN, public schools and at DePauw University, he married Jimmie Allen and had two sons. "Smiling Al" Orth, a pitcher nick-named "The Curveless Wonder," broke into the major leagues in 1895 after an outstanding season at Lynchburg, VA (VL), where he won 28 games by August 8. This feat impressed Philadelphia (NL), which purchased his con-tract for $1,000. Orth continued his winning ways there with a 9–1 record. In 1899 he compiled a 13–3 mark and led the NL with a 2.49 ERA. *Spalding's Base Ball Guide* praised him for "being especially effective against the five first division clubs." The right-handed Orth jumped to Washington (AL) in 1902 and finished his career with New York (AL). In fifteen seasons, the 6 foot, 200 pounder won 202 games, lost 184, and triumphed in at least 20 games twice. Besides completing 324 of 394 starts, he struck out 948 batters in 3,354 2/3 innings and recorded a 3.37 ERA.

A "wily boxman" who knew the batters well, Orth became famous for his spitball. According to Manager Clark Griffith,* "He mastered his delivery, which was rapidly falling into disuse, more completely than any other pitcher in the American League. He pitches easily, but he has excellent control of the wet ball." The skillful Orth still ranks among major league leaders in fewest walks per game (1.77) during his career. During his banner 27–17 1906 season, he walked only 66 batters in 338 2/3 innings and completed 36 of 39 games started. Orth's .273 career batting average, including 12 home runs, ranks him as the sixth best hitting pitcher in major league history. The left-handed hitting Orth batted over .300 five seasons and also played in the outfield and infield occasionally. Following his retirement, he briefly managed the Lynchburg (VL) squad in 1909 and umpired in the NL (1913–1916) and VL (1912, 1920–1923) until a knee injury ended his career. Orth later coached baseball at Washington and Lee University and Virginia Military Institute. The Lynchburg *News* (October 9, 1948) eulogized him: "Baseball today could use a young Al Orth who could win games on either side of the plate. That was Al Orth's almost unique versatility."

BIBLIOGRAPHY: Lynchburg *News*, October 9, 1948; Albert L. Orth file, National Baseball Hall of Fame Library, Cooperstown, NY; Joseph L. Reichler, ed., *The Baseball Encyclopedia*, 6th ed., (New York, 1985), pp. 1,269, 1,951–1,952; *Spalding's Base Ball Guide, 1895–1900* (New York, 1895–1900).

Duane A. Smith

OTIS, Amos Joseph (b. 26 April 1947, Mobile, AL), player, attended St. Peter Claver grade school and graduated in 1965 from Williamson High School, Mobile, AL, where he starred in football and played basketball and baseball. Otis, who played Little League baseball in Mobile, married Alice

Bowick on October 10, 1964, and has three children. The 5 foot, 11 1/2 inch, 165 pound, right-handed Otis was signed out of high school by the Boston Red Sox (AL) and assigned to Harlan, KY (ApL), where he played third base and batted .329. After a modest season at Oneonta, NY (NYPL), he was drafted by the New York Mets (NL) in November, 1966. He played the 1967 season with Jacksonville, FL (IL), and appeared in 19 games with the Mets in September. Although connecting for a .327 batting average for Tidewater, VA (IL), in 1969, Otis batted only .151 in 48 games for the Mets and was traded with pitcher Bob Johnson over the winter to the Kansas City Royals (AL) for third baseman Joe Foy.

For fourteen seasons, Otis played regular center fielder for the Royals. Besides hitting .301 in 1971 and .300 in 1973, he led the AL in stolen bases with 52 in 1971 and slugged a career-high 26 home runs in 1973. In 1970 and 1971 Otis led AL outfielders in total chances and putouts. Otis won Gold Glove awards for his fielding excellence in 1971, 1973, and 1974, and was voted Kansas City Royals Player of the Year in 1971, 1973, and 1978 by the local chapter, Baseball Writers' Association. After the 1976 season, Otis was traded to the Pittsburgh Pirates (NL) with Cookie Rojas. Rojas, however, voided the deal. Otis starred for the Royals in 1978 and 1979 by hitting .298 and .295 and leading AL outfielders in fielding average.

In his only World Series, Otis belted three home runs and batted .478 in 1980 against the Philadelphia Phillies. Otis signed a $1.27 million contract with the Royals for 1982–1983, but Kansas City did not take a third-year option on his contract. He joined the Pittsburgh Pirates (NL) on December 19, 1983, but injuries and a .165 average led to his release on August 5, 1984. Although a slick fielder, he often was criticized for his easy style and one-handed catches. Otis, who smoked four packs of cigarettes a day until 1976, was selected to the AL All-Star team five times. He finished his major league career with 2,020 hits, 374 doubles, 193 home runs, 341 stolen bases, 1,092 runs scored, 1,007 RBIs, and a .277 batting average.

BIBLIOGRAPHY: Del Black, " 'I'm Your Centerfielder," Otis Tells Royals," *TSN*, March 24, 1979; Charley Feeney, "Otis Becomes a Tanner Fan," *TSN*, April 16, 1984; Zander Hollander, *The Complete Handbook of Baseball, 1977* (New York, 1977); Zander Hollander, *The Complete Handbook of Baseball, 1982* (New York, 1982); Joe McGuff, "One-Handed Grabs Are Trademark of Royals' Otis," *TSN*, July 10, 1971, p. 9; Amos Otis file, National Baseball Hall of Fame Library, Cooperstown, NY.

Frank J. Olmsted

OTT, Melvin Thomas "Mel," "Master Melvin" (b. 2 March 1909, Gretna, LA; d. 21 November 1958, New Orleans, LA), player, manager, and broadcaster, was the son of oil refinery worker Charles Ott and played baseball, football, and basketball at Gretna High School. Ott, who married Mildred Mattigny in October, 1930, and had two daughters, was elected to the National Baseball Hall of Fame in 1951. One of few major league players to spend his entire career with one franchise, he starred with the New York Giants (NL) from 1926 to 1947. Ott became the first National Leaguer to slug over 500 home runs and ranked third in lifetime home runs (511) behind Babe Ruth* and Jimmie Foxx* when he retired. He led the NL in home runs six times, slugging a career high 38 in 1932. Ott, nicknamed "Master Melvin," proved a consistent performer whose steady production paced a powerful lineup and helped the Giants capture three NL championships in the 1930s. Defensively, he led NL outfielders in double play assists twice and played third base when needed in the late 1930s. Twice Ott scored six runs in one game. Ott's patience at the plate netted him the NL record for most walks (1,708), a mark Joe Morgan* surpassed in 1982. Ott also holds the NL mark for the most seasons with over 100 bases on balls (10).

Ott, perhaps best remembered for his personality and unique batting stance, played semi-pro ball in 1926 for the Paterson, NJ, Grays, whose owner Harry Williams knew Giants manager John McGraw* very well. At age 16, Ott received a penny postcard from the Giants' front office, stating, "Report to McGraw, Polo Grounds," and immediately dismissed the message as a prank by one of his teammates. Williams physically put Ott on a train to New York, where he quickly became McGraw's personal development project. McGraw decided that Ott lacked major league catching skills, being too small (5 feet, 9 inches and 170 pounds), too quiet, and too much of a "southern gentleman." After witnessing Ott's classic "foot in the bucket" batting style, McGraw kept the teenager at his side on the Giants bench rather than entrust him to any minor league manager. Casey Stengel* offered to assist young Ott at Toledo (AA), but McGraw insisted, "Ott stays with me!" Nurturing the soft-spoken Louisiana native slowly, McGraw did not use Ott regularly until three seasons later.

Ott's unusual natural swing would have been altered by any minor league manager or coach. By stepping high and into each pitch with his bat slung low and nearly parallel to his upper arm, Ott produced a smooth, rhythmic swing resulting in a .304 lifetime batting average and 2,876 base hits. In 2,732 games, he made 488 doubles, 1,859 runs (9th best), 1,860 RBIs (8th best), 1,708 walks (6th best), and a .533 slugging percentage. No other player duplicated Ott's motion with any great success, however, and Ott never tried to teach anyone his swing. Ott proved too easygoing to insist on anyone doing anything in particular and compiled a 464–530 (.467) record as Giants manager from 1942 to 1948. In 1947 Ott's soft-spoken managerial style prompted Leo Durocher* to comment, "Nice guys finish last." The next season, Ott was fired by owner Charles Stoneham* and replaced by Durocher. The trials of major league managing may have caused Ott to lose much of his famed good humor. Nevertheless, he was one of only five baseball personalities selected to tour European battlefields with the USO during 1944–1945.

After three seasons with the Giants' farm system, Ott piloted the Oakland Oaks (PCL) in 1951 and 1952. He retired in 1953 and moved into the front office of a local Louisiana construction firm. During the late 1950s, he broadcast Detroit Tigers (AL) games. On November 14, 1958, he and his wife were seriously injured in a head-on automobile collision. Ott died from complications due to the accident at a New Orleans hospital.

BIBLIOGRAPHY: Bob Broeg, *Super Stars of Baseball* (St. Louis, 1971); Richard Goldstein, *Spartan Seasons* (New York, 1980); Paul MacFarlane, ed., *TSN Daguerreotypes of Great Stars of Baseball* (St. Louis, 1981); William B. Mead, *The Worst Ten Years of Baseball* (New York, 1978); *NYT*, November 22, 1950; Joseph L. Reichler, ed., *The Baseball Encyclopedia*, 6th ed. (New York, 1985), pp. 644, 1,271–1,272; Lowell Reidenbaugh, *Cooperstown: Where Baseball's Legends Live Forever* (St. Louis, 1983).

Alan R. Asnen

P

PAIGE, Leroy Robert "Satchel" (b. 7 July 1906, Mobile, AL; d. 8 June 1982, Kansas City, MO), player and coach, excelled as the Negro leagues' main star attraction. His athletic prowess, phenomenal durability, and incredible showmanship guaranteed large crowds wherever he pitched for over three decades. From his birth in a shotgun house in black Mobile, AL, to gardener John and washerwoman Lula Paige until his belated selection to the National Baseball Hall of Fame in 1971, Paige embodied Negro league life.

Although probably making more money than any other Negro leaguer, Paige was banned from the white major leagues until the color barrier ended in 1947. The following year, 42-year-old Paige became the oldest rookie in major league history and the first black pitcher in the AL. Bill Veeck* of the Cleveland Indians signed him for the 1948 AL pennant drive. His major league statistics, including 28 wins and 31 losses, 476 innings pitched, and a 3.29 ERA, represent the tip of an iceberg hidden beneath the nation's racial blindness.

In 1961 Paige concluded that he had pitched in about 2,500 games and won over 2,000 contests. His varied opponents included sandlot, semi-pro, Negro league, Caribbean, and barnstorming white major league teams. Opponents almost unanimously judged Paige about the best pitcher they had ever faced. On at least 55 occasions, he blanked the opposition without a hit or run. In other instances, he called his outfielders in and struck out the side. As teammate Jimmie Crutchfield* noted, "When Satchel got to that ball park it was like the sun just came out."

From his first season with the black semi-pro Mobile Tigers in 1924 until his last summer riding the bus with the Indianapolis Clowns in 1967, Paige pitched before an estimated 10 million fans. Between 1929 and 1958, he annually played both summer and winter ball and may have been the most widely seen player ever. His "have arm—will pitch" style carried him through Canada, the United States, the Dominican Republic, Cuba, and Mexico.

Baseball aficionados throughout the Western Hemisphere carry vivid memories of the gangly 6 foot, 3 inch, 180 pound Paige with his "bee ball," hesitation pitch, and pinpoint control.

Paige acquired his nickname as a 7-year-old by carrying satchels from the Mobile train station. At age 12, he was sent to the Mt. Meigs, AL, reform school for black youths after stealing several toy rings from a store. Although he had played for his W. C. Council school team, Paige blossomed as a pitcher during his five years at reform school. After reform school, Paige pitched for the Mobile Tigers in 1924 and 1925 and joined the Chattanooga Black Lookouts (NSL) in 1926. Two years later, he was sold to the Birmingham Black Barons (NNL). In 1931 the Nashville Elite Giants (NSL) bought the hard-throwing right-hander. The franchise moved to Cleveland during the season, but faced fiscal problems and disbanded.

Gus Greenlee,* the Pittsburgh numbers mogul who had recently assumed control of the Crawfords (NNL), quickly persuaded Paige to join his team. Through the 1933 season, Paige pitched for the barnstorming Crawfords and several semi-pro clubs that hired him on a per game basis. He jumped in 1934 to a white semi-pro club in Bismarck, ND, but returned to Pittsburgh (NNL) for the 1936 season. During spring training in 1937, Paige traveled to the Dominican Republic to pitch for dictator Rafael Trujillo's team, and resumed barnstorming for the Trujillo All-Stars upon returning to the United States. When Greenlee sold him to the Newark Eagles (NNL), Paige headed to Mexico. He developed arm trouble during the summer of 1938 and, with his future in doubt, returned to the United States.

After most Negro league clubs bypassed him, Paige signed with the Kansas City Monarchs' (NAL) second team, which toured the Northwest and Canada. Appearing a few innings each day, the once formidable athlete seemed finished. When his arm revived that summer, however, Paige never looked back again. Between 1939 and 1947, Paige anchored the Monarchs' pitching staff. In the 1942 Negro League World Series (the first played since 1927), Paige won three of his team's four victories over the Homestead Grays.

In 1948 Paige joined the white major leagues and helped the Cleveland Indians win the AL pennant with his 6–1 record. His first three starts drew over 200,000 fans and helped set night game attendance records in Cleveland and Chicago. Paige was released after the 1949 season and barnstormed until 1951, when Veeck, now owner of the St. Louis Browns (AL), signed him. In 1952 Paige won 12 games and was selected to the AL All-Star team. He remained with the Browns until 1953 and then barnstormed except for stints with Miami (IL) from 1956 to 1958 and Portland, OR (PCL), in 1961. In 1965 Paige made his last major league appearance in a three-inning outing with the Kansas City Athletics (AL). Paige played with the barnstorming Indianapolis Clowns in 1967 and coached for the Atlanta Braves (NL) in 1968. In his autobiography, *Maybe I'll Pitch Forever* (1964), Paige advised his readers to "keep the juices flowing by jangling around gently as you move." He succumbed in June, 1982, after a long siege of heart trouble and emphysema.

BIBLIOGRAPHY: Janet Bruce, *The Kansas City Monarchs: Champions of Black Baseball* (Lawrence, KS, 1985); Leroy Satchel Paige, as told to David Lipman, *Maybe I'll Pitch Forever* (Garden City, NY, 1962); Robert W. Peterson, *Only the Ball Was White* (Englewood Cliffs, NJ, 1970); Donn Rogosin, *Invisible Men: Life in Baseball's Negro Leagues*, (New York 1983).

Robert L. Ruck

PALMER, James Alvin "Jim" (b. 15 October 1945, New York, NY), player and announcer, was adopted two days after birth by Moe Wiesen, a Jewish dress manufacturer, and Polly Kiger Wiesen, a Catholic boutique owner. His early years were spent in the luxury of a Park Avenue apartment and Westchester County estates. When his father died in 1954, the family moved to California. His mother married Max Palmer, a television character actor. The family lived briefly in Beverly Hills before her arthritis prompted a move to Scottsdale, AZ. At Scottsdale High School, Palmer made All-State in football, basketball, and baseball. After graduating from high school, he signed a baseball contract with the Baltimore Orioles (AL) for a $60,000 bonus in August, 1963. Six months later he married his high school sweetheart, Susan Ryan. Palmer, who has two daughters, Jamie and Kelly, briefly attended Arizona State University and Towson (MD) State College.

After a brilliant rookie year in the minors in 1964, when he compiled an 11–3 record and a no-hitter for Aberdeen, SD (NoL). Palmer was promoted to the majors in 1965. He became a starting pitcher in 1966, and in the World Series that year threw a shutout against the Los Angeles Dodgers, at age 20 the youngest hurler ever to pitch a shutout in a World Series and the youngest in a half-century to pitch a complete World Series game. Arm and back problems forced his return to the minor leagues in 1967–1968, but he made a brilliant comeback in 1969 and pitched a no-hitter against Oakland on August 13. Except for 1974, which he spent on the disabled list, Palmer won at least 20 games eight of the next nine years (1970–1978) to become the first AL pitcher to record eight 20-game seasons since Lefty Grove* in 1935. The only AL pitcher to win the Cy Young Award three times (1973, 1975–1976), Palmer was named to the All-Star team six times (1970–1972, 1975, 1977–1978) and received four Gold Gloves for fielding excellence (1976–1979).

Despite recurring physical ailments, the 6 foot, 3 inch, 190 pound right-handed fastballer ranked among the most consistent pitchers in major league history. In nineteen years with Baltimore, he compiled 268 wins and 152 losses for a .638 winning percentage. Appearing in 558 games, 521 as a starter, he pitched 3,948 innings, struck out 2,212 batters, and posted a 2.86

ERA. He led the AL four times in innings pitched (1970, 1976–1978), three times in wins (1975–1977), and twice in ERA (1973, 1975) and winning percentage (1969, 1982). At his best in important games, Palmer enjoyed a 4–1 record in six Championship Series and a 4–2 record in six World Series.

The intelligent, articulate, and opinionated Palmer engaged in legendary feuds with manager Earl Weaver.* Teammates jokingly called him "Reginald" because of his wealthy background and "Cakes" because of his Jockey underwear commercials. After his retirement from baseball in May, 1984, Palmer began a career in broadcasting as a sports commentator for ABC television and an analyst for local Baltimore baseball telecasts.

BIBLIOGRAPHY: *CB* (1980), pp. 301–303; Joel H. Cohen, *Jim Palmer: Great Comeback Competitor* (New York, 1978); Frank Deford, "In a Strike Zone of His Own," *SI* 45 (July 26, 1976), pp. 28–34; Ron Fimrite, "Kings of the Hill Again," *SI* 43 (July 21, 1975), pp. 14–17; Jackie Lapin, "Jim Palmer of the Orioles," *Sport* 60 (March, 1975), pp. 66, 71–77; Jim Palmer with Joel H. Cohen, *Pitching* (New York, 1975); Joseph L. Reichler, ed. *The Baseball Encyclopedia*, 6th ed., (New York, 1985), p. 1,957; Mark Ribowsky, "Jim Palmer," *Sport* 68 (May, 1979), pp. 69–75; Barry Siegel, ed., *TSN Official Baseball Register, 1985* (St. Louis, 1985); Robert Ward, "Jim Palmer," *Sport* 74 (April, 1983), pp. 21–26; Steve Wulf, "The Biggest Bird in the Bushes," *SI* 59 (August 15, 1983), pp. 44–45.

Larry R. Gerlach

PAPPAS, Milton Steven "Milt," "Gimpy" (b. 11 May 1939, Detroit, MI), player, pitched for Cooley High School in Detroit and starred in Junior Legion ball. In 1957 former pitcher Hal Newhouser* scouted Pappas and signed him with the Baltimore Orioles (AL) for $4,000. The same year, Pappas pitched three games for Knoxville (SAL), made his major league debut with Baltimore on August 10 in relief against the New York Yankees, and performed four other relief stints. In 1958 Pappas started 21 games and garnered a 10–10 record for the sixth place Orioles. Since Pappas was the youngest AL starter, manager Paul Richards invariably pulled him after 70 pitches to protect his arm. Pappas continued to hurl for Baltimore through 1965 and won 16 games in 1963 and 1964. For Baltimore, he never experienced a losing season and amassed 110 wins despite injuries. Pappas, who married Carole Tragge in February, 1960, and had two children, pitched in three All-Star games (in both 1962 games and in 1965). In December 1965 the Orioles traded Pappas and two other players to Cincinnati (NL) for Frank Robinson.*

Pappas spent the rest of his career in the NL, finishing at 12–11 in 1966 and 16–13 in 1967 with Cincinnati. He compiled a 2–5 slate in 1968 until traded in June to the Atlanta Braves. After recording a 10–8 mark for the remainder of the 1968 season, he fell to a 6–10 record the following year. He relieved in game two of the 1969 NL Championship Series against the New York Mets. In 1970 he compiled a 2–2 slate until being sold to the

Chicago Cubs in June. At Chicago he finished with a 10–8 standard and 3.34 ERA. Pappas enjoyed 17–14 and 17–7 records in 1971 and 1972 and the latter year made his best ERA (2.77) since 1965. In 1972 Pappas hurled for a fifth place team in the NL East and recorded an 8–0 no-hitter against the San Diego Padres on September 2. The Cubs dropped to last place in the NL East in 1973, as Pappas won only 7 of 19 decisions. Overall, Pappas recorded 99 victories for three NL teams.

During his seventeen-year career, Pappas compiled a 209–164 record and 3.40 ERA, pitched 43 shutouts, struck out 1,728 batters and walked only 858 in 3,185 2/3 innings. Pappas remains one of only two major league pitchers having at least 200 wins without a 20-victory season. His 99 NL victories left him only one triumph short of joining Cy Young* and Jim Bunning* as the only hurlers to have gained 100 wins in each major league. In 1985 Pappas was selected as the twelfth member of the Baltimore Orioles Hall of Fame. His wife disappeared in September 1982 and neither she nor her car has ever been found. Pappas remarried in 1984, has one new daughter, lives in Wheaton, IL, and works for Metropolitan Supply Company. His son is a computer programmer, while his older daughter attends college.

BIBLIOGRAPHY: *Baltimore Orioles Official Yearbook, 1958–1965*; *Baltimore Orioles Scorebook 1985*; *Baltimore Sun*, September 17, 1982, June 2, 1985; James H. Bready, *The Home Team* (Baltimore, MD, 1979); *NYT*, September 17, 1982; Joseph L. Reichler, ed., *The Baseball Encyclopedia*, 6th ed. (New York, 1985), p. 1,958.

Douglas D. Martin

PARKER, David Gene "Dave," "The Cobra" (b. 9 June 1951, Jackson, MS), player, is the son of foundry worker Richard and Dannie (Fox) Parker. His father moved the family of six children to Cincinnati when Dave was three years old. A knee injury Parker's senior year at Cincinnati Courter Tech High School kept him out of football, limited his baseball activity, and caused the strong prospect to be drafted late. After being selected in 1970 by the Pittsburgh Pirates (NL) in the fourteenth round of the free agent draft, the 6 foot, 5 inch, 230 pound outfielder played for Bradenton, FL (GCL), in 1970, Waterbury, CT (EL), and Monroe, NC (WCL), in 1971, and climaxed his minor league career in 1972 at Salem, VA, by winning the CrL Most Valuable Player Award. He joined the Pittsburgh Pirates from Charleston, WV (IL), the next year and became a regular in 1975.

Parker, who throws right-handed and bats left-handed, played eleven seasons for Pittsburgh, primarily in right field, and helped lead the Pirates to NL pennants in 1974, 1975, and 1979. During the late 1970s, Parker became the team's "franchise player" and constantly hit above .300 from 1975 to 1979. In 1977 he topped the NL in hits (215), doubles (44), and batting average (.338). Supporting his claim as "the complete player," Parker also led the NL in putouts (389) and assists (26). Many of Parker's 15 errors that season came from his all-out play. He led NL outfielders in chances accepted (430) and double plays (9) and received the first of his three Gold Glove awards.

In 1978 Parker, nicknamed "The Cobra" for his quick-striking swing, again won the NL batting championship with a .334 average. He paced the NL with 340 total bases for a .585 slugging percentage and won the NL MVP Award. The next year, he batted .345 and made 10 hits to lead the Pirates to the World Series championship over the Baltimore Orioles. Although popular with his teammates for giving 100 percent and often playing with injuries, he became unpopular with some Pittsburgh journalists and fans. After his five-year $5 million contract in 1979 made him the highest paid player in baseball, Parker began to receive negative press coverage and fan abuse. The criticism worsened in 1981 and 1982, when injuries lowered his batting average to .258 and .270.

Granted free agency after an improved 1983 season, Parker signed with the Cincinnati Reds (NL) in his hometown. In 1984 he batted .285, made 173 hits (44 for extra bases), scored 73 runs, and produced 94 RBIs for a fifth place team. Inspired by the return of Pete Rose* as player-manager, Parker regained his 1970s form in 1985. Parker's 1985 season included a .312 batting average, 198 hits, 42 doubles, a .551 slugging percentage, and a career-high 34 home runs and 125 RBIs. Besides finishing second in the NL MVP balloting, he led the NL in doubles and RBIs, placed second in hits, home runs, and slugging percentage, and tied for second in game-winning hits (18). In 1986 Parker finished second in the NL in RBIs (116) and tied for second in home runs (31).

Through 1986, Parker had scored 978 runs on 2,024 hits with 1,093 RBIs. Combining power and average, he has hit 397 doubles and 247 home runs and batted .301. A participant in six All-Star games (four as a Pirate), he established the record for most assists in a game by an outfielder with two. Parker and his wife Kellye have two children and live in Cincinnati, where Parker is involved in commercial real estate. His hobbies include archery, photography, fishing, and bicycling. Commissioner Peter Ueberroth* (OS) in February, 1986, suspended Parker for one year for his involvement in drugs. Parker avoided the suspension by donating 10 percent of his salary to a drug rehabilitation program, contributing 100 hours of community service, and agreeing to periodic testing.

BIBLIOGRAPHY: Joseph Dalton, "For Sale: Dave Parker," *Sport* 74 (October, 1983), pp. 41–48; Jim O'Brien, "The Cobra Strikes Back," *Sport* 72 (June, 1981), pp. 13–18; "Plutocrat from Pittsburgh," *Time* 113 (April 16, 1979), p. 88; Joseph L. Reichler, ed., *The Baseball Encyclopedia*, 6th ed. (New York, 1985); p. 1,277; Derek A. Reveron, "Dave Parker: Big Man, Big Bat, and Baseball's Biggest Salary," *Ebony* 34 (October, 1979), pp. 84–921; *TSN Official Baseball Register, 1985* (St. Louis, 1985); *WWA*, 43rd ed., (1984–1985), p. 2,465.

Gaymon L. Bennett

PAUL, Gabriel Howard, Sr. "Gabe" (b. 4 January 1910, Rochester, NY), baseball executive and sportswriter, is one of ten children born to tailor Morris and Cecelia (Snyder) Paul and played sandlot baseball. In 1924 he became batboy for the Rochester Red Wings (IL) St. Louis Cardinals farm club. Two years later, Paul began reporting local sports for the Rochester *Democrat & Chronicle*. Warren Giles* hired Paul as Red Wings publicity director in 1928 and promoted him to road secretary in 1934. Paul married Mary Frances Copps on April 17, 1935, and has four sons and one daughter. His eldest son, Gabe, Jr., serves as director of stadium operations for the Milwaukee Brewers (AL).

In 1937 Giles joined the Cincinnati Reds (NL) and designated Paul publicity director. Paul then served as traveling secretary (1938–1948) except for a stint in the U.S. Army in World War II, assistant to the president (1948–1949) and vice-president (1949). When Giles became NL president in 1950, Paul was named Cincinnati club president. Paul presided over the Cincinnati organization for a decade, making eighty-six separate trades in a continuing effort to improve a mediocre team. Cincinnati's best year came in 1956 with a third place finish, when Paul was selected Major League Executive of the Year, Birdie Tebbetts was named Manager of the Year, and Frank Robinson* became Rookie of the Year. After 1956, however, Cincinnati slipped back into the second division. Paul opposed an attempt by owner Powel Crosley, Jr.,* to move the club and resigned in October, 1960. He became the first general manager of the Houston (NL) franchise, but was replaced by Paul Richards in April, 1961.

Paul joined the Cleveland Indians (AL) as general manager (1961–1963) and then served as president (1963–1972). Despite making 110 trades, however, the Indians remained mired in the second division. At Cleveland, Paul met local businessman George Steinbrenner. After Cleveland owner Vernon Stouffer sold the team in 1972, Paul helped forge the group that bought the New York Yankees (AL) from CBS in 1973. After the ouster of a major partner in the new Yankee ownership, Paul became New York club president. Paul's years with the Yankees proved both turbulent and fruitful. The turbulence stemmed from primary owner George Steinbrenner's personal involvement in the daily operation of the organization even though he knew little about baseball and his desire to improve the team by seeking high-priced talent to remain competitive with the New York Mets for both media attention and the fans' dollars.

During these fruitful years, New York bought top quality players. Paul, however, could not make any deal without Steinbrenner's approval, which he did not always receive. Nevertheless, Paul acquired several excellent players, including Chris Chambliss, Willie Randolph, Oscar Gamble, Bucky Dent, and Mickey Rivers through trades and also signed Reggie Jackson,* Jim Hunter,* and others through free agency. Paul was named Major League Executive of the Year in 1974 and received other honors in 1975 and 1976.

Paul's reconstructed team won AL pennants from 1976 through 1978 and the World Series the latter two years. By December, 1977, however, Paul resigned in a dispute over Steinbrenner's handling of volatile Billy Martin.*

Paul immediately was hired as president of the Cleveland Indians (AL), where he completed his major league career. Again he turned to trades to construct a contender, but was hampered by the organization's relative poverty. Paul made sixty-eight trades between 1978 and 1984, with twenty-one of the club's forty-man 1982 roster being through trade or acquistion. Only two players in Cleveland's 1984 opening day lineup had belonged to the 1982 squad. By Paul's retirement in 1984, the Indians had acquired a core of good, young players and provided a base upon which others would build. Paul, the traditional baseball executive, spent his adult career with four major league franchises. He made over 500 trades and also changed with the times. He showed at New York and Cleveland that he would seek talent through free agency, but undoubtedly preferred the wheeling and dealing of the pre–free agency era. Still on the Cleveland Indians Board of Directors, Paul lives with his wife in Tampa, FL.

BIBLIOGRAPHY: *Cleveland Indians Press-Radio TV Guide*, 1978–1984; *Cleveland Indians Yearbook*, 1979; Alvin Dark and John Underwood, *When in Doubt, Fire the Manager* (New York, 1980); Sparky Lyle and Peter Golenbock, *The Bronx Zoo* (New York, 1979); Billy Martin and Peter Golenbock, *Number One* (New York, 1980); Douglas D. Martin, telephone interview with Gabriel Paul, Jr., June, 1985; Graig Nettles and Peter Golenbock, *Balls* (New York, 1984); Joseph L. Reichler, ed., *The Baseball Trade Register* (New York, 1984); Dick Schaap, *Steinbrenner!* (New York, 1982).

Douglas D. Martin

PEARCE, Richard J. "Dickey" (b. 2 January 1836, Brooklyn, NY; d. 18 September 1908, Onset, MA), player, manager, and umpire, was the son of William and Louisa Pearce and began playing in Brooklyn. Although only 5 feet, 3 1/2 inches and 161 pounds, Pearce ranked among his era's greatest professional baseball players. From the 1850s through the mid–1870s, Pearce played shortstop primarily for the Brooklyn Atlantics (1856–1870, 1873–1874), New York Mutuals (1871–1872), and St. Louis (1875–1877). Pearce averaged .254 and made 306 hits in 257 games for the 1871–1875 NA seasons. In the NA, he managed New York to a 34–20 record in 1872 and St. Louis to a 39–29 mark in 1875. Although playing as early as 1856 for the Brooklyn Atlantics, he first gained attention in the 1858 series between the Brooklyn and New York "match" nines. A participant in two of the three games at shortstop, he scored seven runs for Brooklyn and was credited with playing "remarkably well." Throughout the next decade, he generally batted first and played various positions. Pearce caught, played shortstop and right field, and even pitched occasionally for the powerhouse Brooklyn team. A reporter noted that he showed "pluck in facing hot balls." The veteran had appeared in over 200 games by 1870 and scored 907 runs for the Atlantics.

Even in losing efforts, Pearce was recognized for his distinguished play. The *New York Times* (July 20, 1860) credited him "for some good play as catcher and at short," although his team lost 23–4. A decade later, he played an instrumental part in ending the long two-season 78-game winning streak of the Cincinnati Red Stockings. When the Atlantics beat the Red Stockings 8–7 in eleven innings, Pearce earned praise for his "work" and his adept base running in scoring the tying run. Pearce, who married, ended his long playing career with St. Louis (NL) in 1876 and 1877, hitting only .198 for 33 games. Pearce invented the "fair-foul" hit by artfully striking the ball down, "blocking it in front of the home base, from which point it bounded off into foul ground." This type of hit was abolished in 1876, probably helping to end his career. Following his retirement, Pearce umpired until at least the late 1880s.

BIBLIOGRAPHY: Henry Chadwick Scrapbooks, Albert Spalding Collection, New York Public Library; *Base Ball Player*, 1861–1877; *NYT*, 1858–1877; Preston Orem, *Baseball, 1845–1881* (Altadena, CA, 1961); Harry C. Palmer et al., *Athletic Sports in America, England and Australia* (Philadelphia, 1889); David Quentin Voigt, *American Baseball*, vol. 1 (Norman, OK, 1966).

Duane A. Smith

PENNOCK, Herbert Jeffries "Herb," "The Knight of Kennett Square" (b. 10 February 1894, Kennett Square, PA; d. 30 January 1948, New York, NY), player, coach, and executive, attended a Friends' School in West Town, PA, Cedar Croft School, and Wenonah Military Academy. Pennock, who married Esther Freck of Kennett Square on October 28, 1915, and had two children, was an avid fox hunter and raised silver foxes on his farm. After Pennock pitched a no-hitter in 1911 with the Atlantic City Collegians, catcher Earle Mack persuaded his father, Philadelphia's Athle76s manager Connie Mack,* to sign him. In 1912 the tall, slender 6 foot, 165 pound southpaw joined the Athletics (AL). Pennock was claimed on waivers by the Boston Red Sox (AL) in June, 1915, and was traded to the New York Yankees (AL) in January, 1923. He pitched with the Yankees through the 1933 season and spent his final campaign in 1934 with the Red Sox (AL). Nicknamed the "Knight of Kennett Square," Pennock exhibited a stylish, smooth, effortless delivery during his twenty-two year major league career. Besides his excellent curveball, he possessed masterful control and a baffling change of pace. In many games, he did not throw over one dozen fastballs.

Pennock compiled a 240–162 lifetime win-loss record in 617 games and toiled 3,558 1/3 innings. Elected to the National Baseball Hall of Fame in 1948, Pennock also recorded 35 shutouts, walked only 916 batters, and had a 3.61 ERA. From 1919 to 1923, the workhorse hurler appeared in over 30 games

per season with the Red Sox. Although New York manager Miller Huggins*
thought Pennock's best years were behind him, the Yankees acquired him in
1923 as a stopgap measure. The veteran southpaw became the ace of the Yankees staff, winning 115 games the next six seasons. Pennock compiled a 19–6
record for the best AL winning percentage (.760) in 1923 and made *The Sporting News* Major League All-Star team in 1926. Manager Huggins called Pennock the greatest left-handed pitcher of all time. On July 5, 1925, he bested
Lefty Grove* of the Athletics 1–0 in fifteen innings. Pennock faced the minimum eighteen batters the first six innings and only twenty-one batters in the
final seven frames.

Unbeatable in World Series competition, he won two games each in the
1923 and 1926 fall classics and one contest in 1927 and posted an impressive
1.95 ERA in 10 games. In the 1927 World Series, Pennock no-hit the Pittsburgh Pirates for 7 1/3 innings and eventually beat the club, noted for hitting
southpaws, by an 8–1 margin. Pennock later served as coach (1936–1940) and
farm system supervisor (1941–1943) for the Boston Red Sox (AL) and as general manager of the Philadelphia Phillies (NL) from 1944 until his death.

BIBLIOGRAPHY: Frank Graham, *The New York Yankees* (New York, 1943); Harold
(Speed) Johnson, *Who's Who in Major League Baseball* (Chicago, 1933); Paul MacFarlane,
ed., *TSN Daguerreotypes of Great Stars of Baseball* (St. Louis, 1968), p. 165; John Mosedale, *The Greatest of All: The 1927 New York Yankees* (New York, 1974); Nathan
Salant, *This Date in New York Yankee History* (New York, 1979).

B. Randolph Linthurst

PERRY, Gaylord Jackson. See PERRY, James Evan "Jim"

PERRY, James Evan "Jim" (b. 3 October 1936, Williamston, NC) and
PERRY, Gaylord Jackson (b. 15 September 1938, Williamston, NC), players, grew up in Farm Life, ten miles from Williamston. The children of
tenant farmers Evan and Ruby Perry, the right-handers won 529 games and
lost 439 decisions between them in the major leagues and compiled more
victories than any other brother combination. Both brothers attended Williamston High School in the 1950s. Jim headed the pitching staff as Williamston won the 1955 state tournament, while Gaylord played third base
and also pitched. In *Me and the Spitter: An Autobiographical Confession*, Gaylord
commented that "baseball was everything when Jim and I were growing up.
It was work the fields, go to worship on Sunday and play ball."

Six foot, 4 inch, 190 pound Jim graduated from Campbell Junior College
(now Campbell University) in Buies Creek, NC, and received a $4,000 bonus
for signing a professional contract with the Cleveland Indians (AL) in 1956.
He began his career that same year with North Platte, NE (NeSL) and joined
the Cleveland Indians (AL) in 1959. Six foot, 4 inch, 205 pound Gaylord
finished his senior year at Williamston High School and then attended Camp-

bell Junior College. He signed his first professional contract with the San Francisco Giants (NL) in 1958 and received a $60,000 bonus. He pitched with St. Cloud, MN (NoL), that year and first joined the Giants in 1962. Both Perrys are characterized as strong family men. Jim married Daphne Kay Snell in December, 1960, and has three children, Chris, Pam, and Michelle. Gaylord wed Blanche Hodges Manning in December, 1959, and has four children, Amy, Beth, Allison, and Jack.

Jim spent his entire seventeen-year career (1959–1975) in the AL, winning 215 games and losing 174 (.553) for the Cleveland Indians (1959–1963, 1974–1975), Minnesota Twins (1963–1972), Detroit Tigers (1973), and Oakland Athletics (1975). In 630 games, he struck out 1,576 batters in 3,286.1 innings, hurled 32 shutouts, and compiled a 3.45 ERA. With Cleveland in 1960, he led the AL in games won (18). He repeated in 1970 with Minnesota (24), winning the Cy Young Award as the AL's best pitcher. Both Perrys played together the 1974 season, combining for 38 wins, and for part of the 1975 season at Cleveland. They pitched against each other just twice, once in a regular season game and once at the 1970 All-Star Game. No brothers previously had pitched against one another at an All-Star game.

Gaylord pitched in both major leagues for twenty-two years, winning the Cy Young Award in the AL in 1972 with Cleveland and in the NL in 1978 with the San Diego Padres. No other pitcher has won the award in both leagues. During his career, he won 314 games and lost 265. In 777 games, he struck out 3,534 batters in 5,351 innings and compiled a 3.10 ERA. The majority of the victories came in the NL, where he finished 175–135 for San Francisco (1962–1971), San Diego (1978–1979), and the Atlanta Braves (1981). He compiled a 139–130 mark for five AL clubs: the Cleveland Indians (1972–1975), New York Yankees (1980), Texas Rangers (1980), Seattle Mariners (1982–1983), and Kansas City Royals (1983). Gaylord led the NL in victories (23) in 1970 with San Francisco and in 1978 (21) with San Diego. His 24 victories for Cleveland paced the AL in 1972. He also topped the NL in innings pitched in 1969 (325) and 1970 (329). On September 17, 1968, he pitched a no-hit, no-run game against the St. Louis Cardinals and bested Bob Gibson* 1–0 on a first-inning home run by Ron Hunt.

The extraordinary tenacity of the Perry brothers may be attributed to their rural upbringing: "work that instills great doggedness and tensile strength, if not 100% fluidity; a desire for some sociable and celebrated outlet for persistence than just hard work; an attunement to long, hot, ordered periods of time, compared to which six-run innings are brisk; and an urge to get away to the city." Of the two brothers, Gaylord earned more notoriety. Called "the most infamous spitball pitcher of modern times," he mastered and used variants of the spitball between 1966 and 1973. Perry's notoriety led to considerable rule changes regarding the spitball after the 1973 season. Although Gaylord claimed that he developed a new pitch in 1973 to substitute for the spitter, many opposing managers and players disagreed. Perry consequently achieved the status of a trickster hero, one who dominates through craft and intensity.

BIBLIOGRAPHY: Pete Axthelm, "The Conquering Con Man," *Newsweek* 99 (May 17, 1982), pp. 89–90; Ray Blount, Jr., "Return of the Natives," *SI* 34 (March 29, 1971), pp. 58–75; A. J. Carr, "Pitching Perry's Share Family Fame," Raleigh *News & Observer*, April 29, 1984, p. 28; *CB*, (1982), pp. 315–318; Glenn Dickey, *The Great No-Hitters* (Radnor, PA, 1976); Ron Fimrite, "Bound for Glory," *SI* 55 (August 24, 1981), pp. 92–106; Gaylord Perry with Bob Sudyk, *Me and the Spitter: An Autobiographical Confession* (New York, 1974).

Leverett T. Smith, Jr.

PESKY, John Michael "Johnny" (b. John Michael Paveskovich, 27 September 1919, Portland, OR), player, manager, coach, and broadcaster, is the son of mill worker Jacob and Maria (Bejama) Paveskovich; he had his name legally changed to Pesky in 1947. He married Ruth Hickey on January 10, 1945, and has one son. Pesky entered professional baseball as a shortstop with Rocky Mount, NC (Pil), in 1940 and played with Louisville (AA) in 1941. The 5 foot, 9 inch, 168 pound Pesky debuted with the Boston Red Sox (AL) in 1942 and replaced longstanding All-Star shortstop and manager Joe Cronin.* Pesky, who batted left and threw right-handed, led the major leagues in hits (205), batted .331, scored 105 runs, and was named AL Rookie of the Year in 1942.

After spending the next three years in the military, Pesky in 1946 led the AL in hits (208), batted .335, pounded 43 doubles, scored 115 runs, and helped the Red Sox win their first pennant since 1918. Pesky again led the AL in hits (207) in 1947, tying the major league record for consecutive years leading a league in hits. He batted .324 and struck out only 22 times in 638 at bats. In 1948 new Red Sox manager Joe McCarthy* moved Pesky to third base, where the latter led both leagues in double plays by a third baseman (48). His batting average, however, dropped to .281. Pesky rebounded by batting .306, .312, and .313 the next three seasons, but then injuries removed him from regular starting status. After being traded to the Detroit Tigers (AL) during the 1952 season in an eight-player deal, he ended his playing career with the Washington Senators (AL) in 1954. Pesky compiled 1,455 hits and struck out only 218 times in 4,745 at bats, hitting .307 in his ten-year career. Pesky made 226 doubles, 50 triples, 867 runs scored, 663 walks, and 404 RBIs.

After batting .343 as a player-coach at Denver (AA) in 1955, Pesky managed at Durham, NC (CrL); Birmingham, AL (SA); Lancaster, PA (EL); Knoxville (SAL) and Victoria, TX (TL) in the Detroit organization from 1956 through 1960. After managing the Red Sox' Seattle (PCL) farm team in 1961 and 1962, he piloted the Boston Red Sox (AL) in 1963 and 1964 to a 146–175 record before being fired. Pesky coached at Pittsburgh (NL) from 1965 to 1967, managed Columbus (IL) in 1968, and served as Red Sox broadcaster (1969–1974). From 1975 to 1984 Pesky coached for the Red Sox. In 1980 he compiled a 1–3 record as an interim manager with Boston.

BIBLIOGRAPHY: Ellery H. Clark, Jr., *Boston Red Sox: 75th Anniversary History* (Hicksville, NY, 1975); John E. DiMeglio, correspondence with Johnny Pesky, 1984, John E. DiMeglio Collection, Mankato, MN; John E. DiMeglio interview, Johnny Pesky, 1984; Frederick G. Lieb, *The Boston Red Sox* (New York, 1947).

John E. DiMeglio

PHILLIPPE, Charles Louis "Deacon" (b. 23 May 1872, Rural Retreat, VA; d. 30 March 1952, Avalon, PA), player, married Belle M. Phillippe and had one daughter. The 6 foot, 180 pound right-hander ranked among the best pitchers at the turn of the century. He first played baseball on the South Dakota prairies until the Minneapolis club (WL) signed him in 1897. Louisville (NL) drafted Phillippe in 1898. The next year, he finished with a 20–17 mark for Louisville and hurled a no-hitter against New York.

After joining Pittsburgh (NL) in 1900, Phillippe became a Pirates mound mainstay for the next eleven years and helped them capture pennants in the 1901–1903 and 1909 seasons. His most outstanding campaigns came in the first three pennant-winning seasons, when he compiled 22–12, 20–9, and 24–7 marks. Thereafter he enjoyed only one more 20-victory season (1905). In his last successful year (1910), he finished with a 14–2 mark and boasted a 7–1 record as a relief pitcher. Although appearing in relief as early as 1899, he never repeated his 1910 performance. Phillippe was never considered an overpowering pitcher, but he exhibited outstanding control. He walked only 363 batters while striking out 929 during his career.

Perhaps his finest moment in baseball came in the first World Series in 1903. Although Pittsburgh lost the Series to Boston, Phillippe paced the Pirates' injured and decimated pitching staff. A local paper crowed, "Deacon Phillippe has the American League Champions at his mercy." Since Phillippe completed five games and won three, appreciative fans presented him with a diamond stickpin. Having no other choice, manager Fred Clarke* asked him to pitch the last two games. As the paper said, the worn out Phillippe "went to the rubber too often." He lost both games, the last one 3–0. Weak team hitting crippled Pittsburgh's chances more than their pitching.

The quiet pitcher avoided the limelight throughout his career. His 186–108 career record (.633) included a 2.59 ERA over 372 games and 2,607 innings. Phillippe completed 242 of his 288 starts and pitched 27 shutouts during his thirteen major league years. Phillippe batted only .189, with a personal high of .244 in 1906. Following his retirement from baseball, he worked in a Pittsburgh steel mill and then as a bailiff in a local court. In 1969 Pittsburgh fans voted him Pittsburgh's all-time right-hander.

BIBLIOGRAPHY: Charles Phillippe file, National Baseball Hall of Fame Library, Cooperstown, NY; Joseph L. Reichler, ed., *The Baseball Encyclopedia*, 6th ed. (New York, 1985) p. 1,971; *Spalding Base Ball Guide, 1900* (New York, 1900).

Duane A. Smith

PIERCE, Walter William "Billy" (b. 2 April 1927, Detroit, MI), player and scout, ranked among baseball's leading left-handed pitchers and is the son of pharmacist Walter and Julia Pierce. An outstanding high school pitcher in Detroit, Pierce signed with the Detroit Tigers (AL) and spent the 1945–1947 seasons with the Buffalo (IL) farm club. Pierce pitched briefly with the Tigers at the end of 1945 and compiled a 3–0 record there in 1948, but the management questioned his control and, in November 1948, traded him to the Chicago White Sox (AL) for catcher Aaron Robinson. The transaction proved one of the most favorable in White Sox history because the 5 foot, 10 inch, 160 pound Pierce helped make Chicago a contender in the 1950s beginning in 1951 and the 1959 AL pennant winner.

After two losing seasons, Pierce in 1951 compiled a 15–14 record. He quickly became one of baseball's best left-handers, peaking in 1956 and 1957 with 20–9 and 20–12 records. He led the AL in every positive category: victories in 1957, ERA (1.97) in 1955, strikeouts (186) in 1953, and complete games (21, 16, and 19) from 1956 through 1958. He started the All-Star games of 1953, 1955, and 1956, losing the 1956 game. An excellent base runner, Pierce was used frequently as a pinchrunner. He never pitched a no-hit game, but came within a single out of a perfect game on June 27, 1958, when Ed FitzGerald batted for the Washington Senators' pitcher and doubled with two out in the ninth inning. In 1959 he won 14 games and made 3 relief appearances in the World Series against the Los Angeles Dodgers.

After the 1961 season, Pierce was traded to the San Francisco Giants (NL). Pierce enjoyed one of his finest seasons (16–6), never lost at home, and retired the Los Angeles Dodgers in the ninth inning of a playoff to clinch the 1962 NL pennant. He started two games in the World Series, winning one and losing one. Pierce retired at the end of the 1964 season, during which his 3–0 record ironically matched his first record in Detroit. In 585 games, Pierce won 211 and lost 169, pitched 38 shutouts, struck out 1,999 batters, and compiled a 3.27 ERA. His 186 victories for the White Sox established the club record for left-handed pitchers. Pierce married Gloria McCreadie on October 22, 1949, and has three children, William, Patti, and Robert. Following his baseball career, he engaged in sales work and developed an excellent reputation as a White Sox scout.

BIBLIOGRAPHY: George W. Hilton, correspondence with W. William Pierce, George W. Hilton Collection, Los Angeles, CA; Paul MacFarlane, ed., *TSN Daguerreotypes of Great Stars of Baseball* (St. Louis, 1981); *TSN Baseball Register, 1950–1964* (St. Louis,

1950–1964; *TSN Official Baseball Guide, 1946–1965* (St. Louis, 1946–1965); *Who's Who in Baseball, 1949–1964* (New York, 1949–1964).

George W. Hilton

PINSON, Vada Edward, Jr. (b. 8 or 11 August 1938, Memphis, TN), player and coach, moved at age 6 to Oakland, CA, where his father, Vada, Sr., worked as a longshoreman. Until age 15, Pinson was influenced by his natural grandmother, Lily Perkins, to practice the trumpet as much as baseball. He attended McClymonds High School, noted for Curt Flood,* Frank Robinson,* and other professional athletes. Robinson, a senior, played on the same baseball team with Pinson. Under the tutelage of high school coach George Powles, the left-handed hitting and fielding Pinson developed baseball skills to complement his natural speed. Pinson, who married Jacqueline Garibaldi in February 1960, was timed running to first base in 3.3 seconds.

After being signed by the Cincinnati Reds (NL), he hit .278 in 1956 as a first baseman for Wausau, WI (NoL). The following year at Visalla, CA (CaL), he batted .361 with 20 home runs and 53 stolen bases. After batting .343 for Seattle (PCL) in 1958, he finished the season as an outfielder with Cincinnati (NL) and remained there through the 1968 campaign. Pinson enjoyed his best years with the Reds, where he batted a career-high .343 in 1961. He led the NL in at bats twice (648 in 1959, 652 in 1960), runs scored once (131 in 1959), hits twice (208 in 1961, 204 in 1963), doubles twice (47 in 1959, 37 in 1960), and triples twice (14 in 1963, 13 in 1967). At one stretch, the 5 foot, 11 inch, 180 pounder played in 505 consecutive games for Cincinnati. In his one World Series, Pinson hit only .091 in 5 games in 1961 against the New York Yankees.

Pinson was traded in 1969 to the St. Louis Cardinals (NL), where he combined with Flood and Lou Brock* to make one of baseball's fastest modern outfields. The next two years, he played with the Cleveland Indians (AL) and slugged a career-high 24 home runs in 1970. He played for the California Angels (AL) in 1972 and 1973 and finished his career with the Kansas City Royals (AL) in 1974 and 1975. Pinson never achieved the superstar status of his high school classmate Robinson, nor did he take full advantage of his blinding speed in stealing bases. His lifetime statistics nevertheless included a .286 batting average, 1,366 runs scored, 1,170 RBIs, 2,757 hits, 485 doubles, 127 triples, 256 home runs, and 305 stolen bases. Pinson served as a minor league hitting instructor for the Seattle Mariners (AL) and in 1985 became hitting coach for the Detroit Tigers (AL).

BIBLIOGRAPHY: Furman Bisher, "Is He the Nearest-Perfect Player?" *SEP* 233 (July 16, 1960), pp. 72–78; "Cincinnati's Vada Pinson," *Look* 25 (August 25, 1961), pp. 84–86; Gene Karst and Martin J. Jones, Jr., *Who's Who in Professional Baseball* (New Rochelle, NY, 1973); Joseph L. Reichler, ed., *The Baseball Encyclopedia*, 6th ed. (New

York, 1985), p. 1,296; "Rookie with a Wallop," *Newsweek* 53 (April 27, 1959), p. 100; *Who's Who Among Black Americans* (Northbrook, IL, 1976).

James K. Skipper, Jr.

PLANK, Edward Stewart "Eddie," "Gettysburg Eddie" (b. 31 August 1875, Gettysburg, PA; d. 24 February 1926, Gettysburg, PA), player, won more games than any left-handed pitcher in AL history during a seventeen-year major league career. The son of the David Planks, he grew up on his father's farm and attended Gettysburg Academy. At age 21 he entered Gettysburg College, where he played organized baseball for the first time. Plank was persuaded to try out for the team by coach Frank Foreman, a former major league pitcher, and became one of the top collegiate players in Pennsylvania.

Upon graduation from Gettysburg College in 1901, Plank signed with the Philadelphia Athletics of the AL, then in its first year as a major circuit. With no minor league experience, the 25-year-old rookie won 17 and lost 13 his initial season. He remained in the major leagues until his retirement in 1918. Plank, who recorded four consecutive 20-win seasons (1902–1905), joined teammates Rube Waddell,* Chief Bender,* Jack Coombs,* and Andy Coakley to form one of the finest pitching staffs of all time. Under manager Connie Mack,* the Athletics won AL pennants in 1902, 1905, 1910–1911, 1913, and 1914 and world championships in 1910, 1911, and 1913.

Throughout his career, Plank exhibited excellent control, hurled numerous complete games and shutouts, and compiled consistently low ERAs. The 5 foot, 11 1/2 inch, 175 pounder used a fastball and curve from a sidearm delivery to baffle opposing batters. An extremely slow worker, he infuriated the opposition, umpires, and spectators with long delays between pitches. Plank pitched for the Athletics from 1901 through 1914 and won at least 20 games seven times. His season high for wins (26) came in both 1904 and 1912. He led the AL twice in shutouts (1907, 1911), and recorded the most complete games once (1905).

Plank suffered hard luck in World Series competition. He played in the 1905, 1911, 1913, and 1914 Series and appeared in seven games, winning two, losing five, and posting a 1.32 ERA. Four of his five defeats were by shutouts, while his teammates scored a total of only eight runs in the games. His greatest World Series performance came against the New York Giants in 1913, when he bested Christy Mathewson* 3–1 in the fifth game to clinch the championship for Philadelphia. Plank, who had lost in the tenth inning after pitching nine scoreless frames in game two, allowed just two hits in this deciding contest. In two previous Series matchups, Mathewson had beaten Plank by identical 3–0 scores.

Plank was released after the 1914 season and signed with the St. Louis Terriers (FL). The veteran hurler won 21 games and finished second in ERA with a 2.08 mark. When the FL folded in 1916, Plank was awarded to the AL St. Louis Browns. Although past age 40, the still effective Plank compiled 16–15 and 5–6 records in his two seasons with the Browns. In 1917 he produced a 1.79 ERA, the second best of his career. Plank was traded to the New York Yankees (AL) in January, 1918, but retired and returned to his home in Gettysburg. During off-seasons, Plank worked as a tour guide at the Gettysburg battlefield. After retiring from baseball, he farmed and also operated an automobile business until a few years before his death. For a few years, he pitched in the semi-professional BeL. Married to Anna Myers in 1915, Plank had one son.

Plank pitched in 622 games, won 327, lost 193 (.629), issued 1,072 bases on balls, and struck out 2,246 batters. He ranks fifth on the all-time list of shutout leaders (69) and compiled a 2.34 ERA. Plank holds the major league record for most complete games by a left-hander (412) and AL records for most shutouts (63) and most games won by a left-hander (306). He shares the AL record for most consecutive years of 100 or more strikeouts (13, from 1902 to 1914). In 1–0 games, Plank won 15 and lost 11 and ranks near the top in these categories. The quiet, serious Plank lacked the color of many of his contemporaries and never was a great favorite of the sportswriters. During the first two decades of this century, however, he became major league baseball's most successful left-handed pitcher. His victory total stood until 1961, when Warren Spahn* became the game's winningest left-hander. In 1946 Plank was elected to the National Baseball Hall of Fame.

BIBLIOGRAPHY: Lee Allen and Tom Meany, *Kings of the Diamond* (New York, 1965); Martin Appel and Burt Goldblatt, *Baseball's Best: The Hall of Fame Gallery* (New York, 1977); Gene Karst and Martin J. Jones, Jr., *Who's Who in Professional Baseball* (New Rochelle, NY, 1973); Tom Meany, *Baseball's Greatest Pitchers* (New York, 1951); *NYT*, February 25, 26, 27, 28, 1926; Edward Plank File, National Baseball Hall of Fame Library, Cooperstown, NY.

Joseph Lawler

POLES, Spottswood "Spot" (b. 1887, Winchester, VA; d. 1962, Harrisburg, PA), player, was a fleet-footed, sharp-hitting center fielder in the early twentieth century Negro leagues. Poles usually batted in the leadoff position to utilize his incredible speed, rivaling that of James "Cool Papa" Bell.* Poles began his professional baseball career with the Harrisburg Colored Giants in 1906 at age 19 and three years later joined Sol White's Philadelphia Giants. In 1911 he moved with White to the New York Lincoln Giants. Known as the black Ty Cobb,* the left-handed Poles batted .440 and .398 in 1911 and 1912, respectively, and stole 41 bases in only 60 games the former year. Superstar teammates with the Lincolns included John Henry Lloyd,* Smoky Joe Williams,* Dick Redding,* Louis Santop,* and Grant "Home Run" Johnson.* John McGraw* listed Poles, Lloyd, Williams, and Redding as the players that he would have selected for the New York Giants if the major leagues had integrated then.

After the Lincolns soundly defeated Rube Foster's* Chicago American Giants in the 1913 playoff for their second consecutive championship, the club owner boasted that his team could beat any team including major league squads. The following year (1914), Poles compiled an even more impressive .487 batting average. The speedster averaged .319 at bat for four winters spent in Cuba and batted .594 in frequent exhibitions there against the Philadelphia Phillies, Philadelphia Athletics and other major league teams. In 1917, at age 30, Poles began his World War I military service as a member of the 369th infantry and was decorated for his combat experience in France. He played with the Lincolns and Brooklyn Royal Giants (ECL) until 1923, retiring after fifteen seasons of top-level competition in black baseball. After ending his baseball career, Poles owned a small fleet of taxicabs and retired in Harrisburg, PA.

BIBLIOGRAPHY: John Holway, "Spottswood Poles," *Baseball Research Journal* 4 (1975); Robert W. Peterson, *Only the Ball Was White* (Englewood Cliffs, NJ, 1970); James A. Riley, *The All-Time All-Stars of Black Baseball* (Cocoa, FL, 1983); James A. Riley, interviews with former Negro league players, James A. Riley Collection, Cocoa, FL.

James A. Riley

POSEY, Cumberland Willis, Jr., "Cum" (b. 20 June 1890, Homestead, PA; d. 28 March 1946, Pittsburgh, PA), baseball player, manager, and executive, and basketball player, owned the powerful Homestead Grays (NNL) team. Posey also participated in professional basketball as an organizer and player. Posey's father, Cumberland W. Posey, Sr., worked as a riverboat engineer on the Ohio River and reputedly was the first so licensed. He later became general manager of Delta Coal Company and pursued banking and real estate interests. Posey's mother became the first black to graduate from and teach at Ohio State University.

After growing up in Homestead, Posey attended Pennsylvania State College in 1909 and 1910 and played basketball there both years. He also joined the then semi-pro Homestead Grays in 1910 as an outfielder and began a lifetime association there. In 1910 he organized a semi-pro basketball team and ranked among the nation's greatest basketball players. Besides working as a mail clerk in Pittsburgh, Posey in 1912 became the booking agent for the Grays and put the team on a full-time schedule. Posey, who married Ethel Truman in 1913 and had five daughters, attended the University of Pittsburgh in 1913. He formed and played through 1925 for the Loendi Big Five basketball team, the nation's first great black team. Loendi played several games against the New York Celtics and, by 1919, claimed the national championship. The slightly built 5 foot, 9 inch, 145 pound Posey enrolled at Holy Ghost College (later Duquesne University) in 1915 as Charles W.

Cumbert. He led the basketball team in scoring and captained the golf team. That year he became field captain of the Grays and held that post until his retirement as a player in 1928.

From 1919 to 1935, Posey managed the Grays. The Grays dominated Pennsylvania, Virginia, and Ohio until 1922, when the Pittsburgh Keystones attempted to raid them. Posey gained control of the team by attaining financing from Charles Walker, placed all his players on a salary basis, and made a deal for the Grays to use Forbes Field when the Pittsburgh Pirates were on the road. The Keystones eventually left town. Posey's Grays refused to join the EL in 1923 and raided many teams of their stars, including Sam Streeter, George Scales, "Smoky Joe" Williams,* Martin Dihigo,* and Vic Harris.* These players helped the Grays compile a 140–13 record in 1926 and win 43 straight games. That fall they defeated a big league team with stars Lefty Grove* and Goose Goslin* in three out of four games.

Nicknamed "Cum" by friends, Posey in 1927 formed the Grays basketball team and beat the great New York Celtics in three of five games. An excellent booking agent, Posey made more money than the Negro league teams and enlisted Oscar Charleston,* Judy Johnson,* and Josh Gibson* for his baseball squad by 1930. That year the Grays defeated the Lincoln Giants to claim the Negro Championship. In 1931 the Grays won 136 games and beat Connie Mack's* All Stars twice. Gus Greenlee* formed the Pittsburgh Crawfords in 1932 and snatched Johnson, Charleston, Gibson, and others from the Grays. Posey also formed the short-lived Detroit Wolves that year.

Financial troubles plagued Posey's Grays through the early and middle 1930s. After the Grays joined the NNL in 1935, Posey lured stars Buck Leonard,* Satchel Paige,* and even Gibson back to the Grays when the Crawfords collapsed in 1937. Posey built a powerhouse club, winning nine straight NNL pennants as well as Negro World Series titles in 1943 and 1944. The 1937 team won 152 games and lost only 24. In 1940 the Grays began playing many games in Washington, DC's Griffith Stadium. By 1942 they drew 102,000 fans in ten games, providing a financial boon to the Grays.

Posey continued securing the best talent in Negro baseball, signing Roy Partlow, Johnny Wright, Jud Fields, and James "Cool Papa" Bell.* Posey also served on the Homestead school board, worked as the NNL secretary, and wrote occasionally for the Pittsburgh *Courier*. The integration of baseball in 1945 ended the great Washington-Homestead Grays teams. After losing players Luke Easter, Wright, Partlow, Bob Thurman, and Luis Marquez, Posey protested that the major leagues did not pay for his stars. In 1946 Posey died of lung cancer.

Besides organizing both baseball and basketball teams, Posey served as a baseball player, manager, owner, talent scout, and league official, created among the finest baseball teams in history, and became one of the first black executives to pay salaries and ensure adequate meals and lodging. His move to Griffith Stadium in Washington and its consequent financial rewards demonstrated conclusively that people would pay to see black stars and provided a large boost to the integration of baseball.

BIBLIOGRAPHY: Edward Bolden, Amsterdam *News*, September 16, 1944; John Holway, "The Long Gray Line, Cum Posey" (Alexandria, VA), n.d.; John Holway Collection; Robert W. Peterson, *Only the Ball Was White* (Englewood Cliffs, NJ, 1970); Jules Tygiel, *Baseball's Great Experiment: Jackie Robinson and His Legacy* (New York, 1983).

Terry A. Baxter

POWELL, John Joseph "Jack" (b. 9 July 1874, Bloomington, IL; d. 17 October 1944, Chicago, IL), player and umpire, was the son of boilermaker John W. and Mary A. Powell. He spent most of his adult life in St. Louis, where he pitched for both of its major league teams and operated a saloon with his former battery mate and brother-in-law, Jack O'Connor. Powell married O'Connor's sister Nora, but the marriage ended in divorce in 1907. The Powells had one son, Jim, who played and managed in the minor leagues.

After pitching one year of minor league ball with Fort Wayne, IN (WA), in 1895, the 5 foot, 11 inch, 195 pound, right-handed Powell hurled for the Cleveland Spiders (NL) in 1897 and 1898. In 1899 the franchise was moved to St. Louis as the Cardinals. Powell became one of the Cardinals pitching aces until joining the St. Louis Browns (AL) in 1902. Powell was traded to the New York Highlanders (AL) in 1904 and won 23 games that season. He combined with Jack Chesbro* to hurl 64 victories, the all-time AL high. Powell returned to St. Louis (AL) in September, 1905, and pitched for the Browns through the 1912 season. He pitched for the Louisville Colonels (AA) and Venice, CA (PCL), in 1913 and 1914. He played semi-pro baseball (1916–1917), tried an unsuccessful comeback at age 44 with the Browns in 1918, and became an umpire for several years.

Powell, who pitched nine seasons for the Browns, placed at or near the top in several club statistical categories. He ranks first in games started (265), compelete games (215), innings pitched (2,160), strikeouts (884), shutouts (27), and games lost (142); second in games pitched (294) and games won (118), and fifth in ERA (2.71). In sixteeen major league seasons, Powell pitched in 577 games, struck out 1,621 batters, walked 1,021 hitters, and compiled a 2.97 ERA. He ranks high on the all-time major league lists for pitchers in several departments. Powell recorded 246 victories (40th), 255 losses (6th), started 517 games (25th), completed 422 games (14th), pitched 4,388 innings (24th), hurled 47 shutouts (26th), surrendered 4,319 hits (19th), and allowed 1,976 runs (21st). His most productive season came with Cleveland in 1898, when he recorded 24 victories and an NL-leading 6 shutouts. Powell paced the NL in games started (43) and complete games (40) in 1899 and in games pitched (45) in 1901.

BIBLIOGRAPHY: Paul MacFarlane, ed., *Daguerreotypes of Great Stars of Baseball* (St. Louis, 1971); *TSN* October 26, 1944; *TSN Official Baseball Record Book, 1985* (St. Louis, 1985).

                                                                John L. Evers

POWELL, John Wesley "Boog" (b. 17 August 1941, Lakeland, FL), player, ranked among his era's most feared hitters and proved a fine defensive first baseman. His father, a car salesman, nicknamed him "Boog" or "Booger" because of his mischievous childhood pranks. The Powells moved in 1957 to Key West, where Boog starred in three sports at Key West High School. Spurning several college football scholarship offers, he signed in 1958 with the Baltimore Orioles (AL) baseball club for a reported $35,000. In 1959 he began his professional career with Bluefield, WV (ApL). After playing at Fox Cities, WI (3IL), in 1960, Powell slugged 32 home runs and batted .321 for Rochester, NY (IL), in 1961. He joined the Baltimore club in 1962 and married Janet Swinton, a Kent State University student, on July 9 of that year.

From 1962 until 1974, Powell starred for Baltimore. An outfielder and later an All-Star first baseman, he belted 39 home runs and made a league-leading .606 slugging average in 1964. In 1970 he was voted AL Most Valuable Player. During his seventeen-year major league career, Powell made 1,776 hits, slugged 270 doubles, knocked in 1,187 runs, and hit .266. His 339 career home runs ranked fortieth as of 1986 among lifetime batting leaders. He appeared in five Championship Series and the 1966, 1969, 1970, and 1971 World Series. In the 1966 World Series, Powell batted .357 to lead his team to a four-game sweep over the Los Angeles Dodgers.

The 6 foot, 4 1/2 inch, 230 to 290 pound Powell enjoyed widespread popularity among fans and fellow players and was among the biggest men ever to play major league baseball. In the mid–1960s, the Baltimore team physician, an endocrinologist, and a psychologist sought unsuccessfully to curb his eating habits. In his MVP year (1970), Powell reportedly weighed 280 pounds. He was traded to the Cleveland Indians (AL) in February, 1975, where he batted .297 in 134 games. After several minor injuries, he ended his career in 1977 with the Los Angeles Dodgers (NL).

BIBLIOGRAPHY: Phil Jackman, "The Ball's Going Pffft," *SI* 40 (May 13, 1974), p. 70; "People on the Way Up," *SEP* 23 (May 5, 1962), p. 28; J. D. Reed, "Always Ready to Chew the Fat," *SI* 39 (July 16, 1973), pp. 65–72, 74.

                                                                John Hanners

PRATT, Derrill Burnham "Del" (b. 10 January 1888, Wallhalla, SC; d. 30 September 1977, Texas City, TX), player and manager, performed for the University of Alabama from 1907 through 1909. In 1910 he debuted professionally with Montgomery (SA) and batted a disappointing .232 mark in 51 games. Pratt was demoted to Hattiesburg, MS (CSL), where his .367 average earned him a ticket back to Montgomery the next season. After batting .310 there, he was sold to the St. Louis Browns (AL) for players and cash. With St. Louis (1912–1917) Pratt became a steady performer, usually batted well, and played second base in virtually all the team's games. His best season with St. Louis came in 1912, when he hit .302. Pratt stole 37 bases in both 1913 and 1914 and pilfered 174 altogether for the Browns to rank third on their all-time list just behind George Sisler* and Burt Shotton. He also ranked high on their all-time list of doubles and triples leaders. In 1915, the 5 foot, 11 inch, 175 pound right-hander, appeared in 159 games, a league record until the schedule was expanded in 1961.

In 1918 Pratt and teammate Doc Lavan sued Browns owner Phil Ball for $50,000 for saying they were "lazy" and implying that they had accepted money to throw baseball games. When Ball refused to retract the statement, AL president Byron Johnson* persuaded the players to settle out of court. Lavan was traded to the Washington Senators (AL), while Pratt and pitcher Eddie Plank* were shipped to the New York Yankees (AL) in January 1918 for pitchers Urban Shocker and Nick Cullop, catcher Les Nunamaker, infielders Joe Gedeon and Fritz Maisel, and $15,000. After a clubhouse hassle involving the disposition of the 1920 World Series shares, Pratt was traded with Muddy Ruel to the Boston Red Sox (AL) in December for Wally Schang and Waite Hoyt.* After the 1922 season, the Red Sox sold Pratt and Warren Collins to the Detroit Tigers (AL) for three players and cash.

Pratt ended his thirteen-year career in a Detroit Tigers uniform following the 1924 season. He became player-manager of the Waco, TX, Navigators (TL) in 1925 and stayed there through the 1930 season. He managed Galveston (TL) for two seasons and Fort Worth (TL) until his retirement after the 1934 season. Pratt remained in Texas thereafter. He enjoyed his best batting average in 1921 by hitting .324 in 135 games and led the AL in RBIs (1916) with 103. During thirteen major league seasons, he played in 1,835 games and compiled 1,996 hits, 392 doubles, 117 triples, 43 homers, 856 runs scored, 966 RBIs, 246 stolen bases, and a lifetime .292 batting average. On September 1, 1914, he married Leotine Mindora Ramsauer.

BIBLIOGRAPHY: Bill Borst, *Last in the American League* (St. Louis, 1976); Harold Seymour, *Baseball: The Golden Age* (New York, 1971); *Who's Who in Baseball, 1924*, 9th ed. (New York, 1924).

William A. Borst

PULLIAM, Harry Clay (b. 8 February 1869, Scottsville, KY; d. 29 July 1909, New York, NY), executive, was named for his tobacco farmer father, who had three sons and two daughters. After graduating from Louisville High School, he attended law school at the University of Virginia and became a reporter and city editor for the Louisville *Commercial*. A bachelor, he was elected in 1897 to the Kentucky Assembly, wore gala colored waistcoats, and often quoted Shakespeare. *Sporting Life* described him as "an idealist, a dreamer, a lover of solitude and nature." When Barney Dreyfuss* purchased the NL franchise in Louisville, he persuaded Pulliam to become the club's secretary. In 1900 Pulliam moved with Dreyfuss to Pittsburgh as the Pirates' secretary-treasurer. Pulliam's reputation for honesty, his businesslike approach to baseball, and his support of Dreyfuss led NL owners to elect him league president in 1902.

Pulliam quickly moved to smooth relationships between the NL and the rival AL and minor leagues. In January, 1903, Pulliam, AL president Ban Johnson,* and a committee of owners reached the National Agreement, which established the governance of organized baseball for two decades. Pulliam quickly became frustrated with his limited authority and constant conflicts with club owners and managers, especially New York's president John T. Brush and manager John McGraw.* Pulliam, however, exercised stronger leadership than his predecessor, Nicholas Young,* giving firm control of the game on the field to the umpires. He also helped sportswriters organize the Baseball Writers Association in 1908.

Bitter conflicts with the New York club and press culminated in the famous Fred Merkle decision of 1908. Pulliam followed his established pattern of supporting the umpires and received unmerciful criticism from McGraw and the press when his decision contributed to the Giants' losing the pennant to Chicago. A ticket scalping controversy at the 1908 World Series created a rift between Pulliam and Chicago owner Charles W. Murphy. These controversies undid Pulliam, who became paranoid, moody, and uncommunicative. He committed suicide in his New York Athletic Club apartment. Although temperamentally unsuited to be NL president, he nonetheless brought some order and respectability to the game after the turbulent 1890s.

BIBLIOGRAPHY: Lee Allen, *The National League Story* (New York, 1961); Joseph Durso, *The Days of Mr. McGraw* (New York, 1969); Francis C. Richter, "Passing of Pulliam," *Sporting Life* (August 7, 1909); Harold Seymour, *Baseball: The Golden Age* (New York, 1971); David Quentin Voigt, *American Baseball: From Gentleman's Sport to the Commissioner System* (Norman, OK, 1966).

William E. Akin

Q

QUINN, John Picus "Jack" (b. John Quinn Paykos, 5 July 1884, Jeanesville, PA; d. 17 April 1946, Pottsville, PA), player, grew up in eastern Pennsylvania. Very little is known of his early life. Although his family name was Paykos (modified to Picus), he played baseball as Jack Quinn. He first pitched for semi-pro coal-mining teams and in 1907 entered organized baseball with Macon (SAL). After his spectacular 14–0 season with Richmond, VA (VL), in 1908, he was drafted by the New York Yankees (AL). He spent four seasons with the Yankees, winning 18 games in 1910. After parts of two seasons with Rochester, NY (IL), he was purchased by the Boston Braves (NL) in August, 1913. Quinn soon jumped to Baltimore in the newly up-graded FL for the 1914–1915 seasons. He won 26 games the first season but lost 22 decisions in 1915. His performance for Vernon, CA (PCL), resulted in his purchase by the Chicago White Sox (AL) in 1918. He won five of six games, causing the Yankees to reclaim him. After lengthy deliberation, the National Commission awarded him to New York, with whom he spent three more seasons. He pitched in the 1921 World Series but then was traded to the Boston Red Sox (AL) that December.

Quinn, a steady but not spectacular hurler, possessed good control of his low-breaking spitball and did not allow many home runs. His fame grew primarily from his remarkable longevity, although there was uncertainty about his exact age then. After Connie Mack* purchased him for the Philadelphia Athletics (AL) in 1925, the 41-year-old 6 foot, 196 pound right-hander responded with several good seasons. He pitched on the AL pennant-winning 1929 and 1930 Athletics teams and on October 4, 1930, became the oldest player (age 46) to participate in a World Series game. With the Brooklyn Dodgers in 1931–1932, he ranked among the leading NL relief hurlers. He hurled briefly with the Cincinnati Reds (NL) in 1933, but was released shortly after his forty-ninth birthday on July 5. Although several players have made token appearances after age 50, Quinn was the oldest regular roster player in major league history and the oldest player to hit a home run

(June 27, 1930) and win a game (August 14, 1932). In twenty-three seasons, he won 247 games, lost 217 decisions, and compiled a 3.27 ERA. In 755 games, he pitched 3,934 2/3 innings, struck out 1,329 batters, and hurled 28 shutouts.

Quinn pitched a few games for Hollywood (PCL) in 1934 and the next year returned to Pennsylvania, where he managed Johnstown (MAL) in 1935. He lived the rest of his life in or near Pottsville, PA. His wife, the former Jean Lambert, whom he married in November 1910, died in 1940.

BIBLIOGRAPHY: Lee Allen, "Jack Quinn Big Leaguer at 49," *TSN* (September 9, 1967); Tom Hufford, "Minoso One of the Oldest," *Baseball Research Journal* 6 (1977), pp. 30–36; Gene Karst and Martin J. Jones, Jr., *Who's Who in Professional Baseball* (New Rochelle, NY, 1973); Paul MacFarlane, ed., *TSN Daguerreotypes of Great Stars of Baseball* (St. Louis, 1981); John Quinn file, National Baseball Hall of Fame Library, Cooperstown, NY.

L. Robert Davids

QUISENBERRY, Daniel Raymond "Dan" (b. 7 February 1953, Santa Monica, CA), is the son of John Quisenberry, an automobile salesman and horse breeder, and Reberta (Meola) Quisenberry. After graduating from Costa Mesa (CA) High School in 1971, he attended Orange Coast College (1971–1973), La Verne College (1973–1975), and Fresno Pacific College (off-season, 1978–1979). At La Verne, he made the National Association of Intercollegiate Athletics All-American team as a pitcher and set school records for most wins, innings pitched, and games pitched in one season. In 1984 he was named to the NAIA Hall of Fame. At college in 1975, Quisenberry became a sidearm hurler because the fatigue caused by his record 194 innings pitched led him to alter his pitching motion. Quisenberry's unique delivery dropped into the "submarine" position after he worked with Pittsburgh (now Philadelphia) star relief pitcher Kent Tekulve in spring training of 1980. Since 1980 he has become one of the finest relief pitchers in baseball.

Despite his outstanding amateur career, Quisenberry was not drafted by a professional team. The Kansas City Royals (AL) signed him as a free agent in 1975. After starting his first professional game, Quisenberry was moved to the bullpen because his Waterloo, IA (ML), team lacked a reliever with good control. His extraordinary control marked a four-year rise through the minor leagues at Jacksonville, FL (SL), and Omaha (AA) and created much of his great success in Kansas City. Since 1980 Quisenberry has led major league relief pitchers in saves (229), innings pitched (845 1/3), fewest walks per inning, and percentage of games finished. He has paced the AL in saves five times, in 1983 setting a major league record of 45, broken by New York (AL) reliever Dave Righetti in 1986. In 1980 and 1982–1985, he was named AL Fireman of the Year. Due to Quisenberry's effectiveness, he rarely needs to be relieved. In 1980, 1982, 1983, and 1985, he led the AL in games finished in relief. Quisenberry was selected to the AL All-Star team from 1982 through 1984. In 1980 his heroics extended to the World Series. Quisenberry set records by appearing in and completing all six games of the Royals' losing effort against the Philadelphia Phillies. In 1985 he helped the Royals win the Western Division title by winning 8 games and saving 37 others. Quisenberry lost game two of the AL playoffs against Toronto, but picked up a save in game six. He made four appearances in the Royals' World Series winning effort against the St. Louis Cardinals and won game six. Through 1986, he has appeared in 506 games, won 47, lost 42, and compiled a 2.51 ERA.

Quisenberry married Janie Ann Howard on September 11, 1976, has two children, and now resides in Kansas City, MO. A devoted family man and committed Christian, Quisenberry spends much of the off-season in religious work. He is also a popular public speaker, renowned for a delightful sense of humor.

BIBLIOGRAPHY: Sid Bordman, "Royals: Quisenberry Is Tekulve Disciple," *TSN*, June 28, 1980; Pat Jordan, "Oh What a Relief He Is," *Sport* 71 (November, 1980), pp. 68–71; Jonathan Rand, "Dan Quisenberry: Baseball's Best Reliever Is an Underhanded Guy," *TSN* August 22, 1983, p. 2; Steve Wulf, "Special Delivery from Down Under," *SI* 59 (July 11, 1983), pp. 74–78ff.

Allen E. Hye

R

RADBOURNE, Charles Gardner "Old Hoss" (b. 11 December 1854, Rochester, NY; d. 5 February 1897, Bloomington, IL), player, was nick-named "Old Hoss" and ranked for six years (1882–1887) among the top four National Leaguers in complete games and innings pitched. The right-hander's 489 major league complete games rank seventh all-time, and his 59 complete-game victories in 1884 established a major league record not likely to be surpassed. Radbourne received a grammar school education in Bloomington, IL, where he had moved as an infant from Rochester, NY, with his parents—English immigrants Charles, a butcher, and Caroline (Gardner) Radbourne. Through professional baseball, Radbourne found escape from employment as a slaughterhouse butcher and railroad brakeman. In 1878 he barnstormed as pitcher and right fielder for the Peoria, IL, Reds. The next year he joined Dubuque in the newly formed NWL.

Although signed to pitch for Buffalo (NL) in 1880, Radbourne injured his arm and played only six games, as outfielder and second baseman. He fared better the next year with the Providence Grays (NL), sharing pitching duties with Monte Ward* and winning 25 games. Replacing Ward as the Grays' workhorse, Radbourne from 1882 to 1884 pitched in over two-thirds of the team's championship games. His 140 wins accounted for 72 percent of the Grays' victories. In each of these years, he ranked either first or second in the NL in innings pitched, complete games, ERA, wins, and strikeouts. His 49 victories in 1883 set an NL record, which he shattered the next year.

Radbourne reached his peak in 1884. For the first half of the season, he shared the Grays' pitching with young Charlie Sweeney. Sweeney, however, was expelled from the NL for deserting the club in the middle of a game, and Radbourne offered to take up the slack. During one stretch, he pitched 30 of 32 games (including 22 consecutive ones). He won 26 games, among them a then record 18 in succession. His 73 complete games and 678 2/3 innings pitched rank second in major league history to Will White's* 75 complete games and 680 innings pitched in 1879. Radbourne led the NL with a 1.38 ERA, a personal best, and 441 strikeouts, the fourth highest major league season total ever. His 59 pitching wins (or 60, if one counts a win he is often credited with in one of his two relief appearances) form one of baseball's most enduring records. Radbourne's pitching in 1884 brought Providence the NL championship. In baseball's first "world series" that October, he pitched and won all three games over the AA champion New York Metropolitans.

Changes in the pitching rules (Radbourne's famous leaping delivery was outlawed in 1885) and the wear and tear on his arm diminished Radbourne's effectiveness after 1884. Although winning at least 20 games five of the next seven seasons, he pitched less often and saw his ERA rise and his winning percentage decline.

After Providence folded following the 1885 season, Radbourne pitched four years for the Boston Red Stockings (NL), winning 78 and losing 80. Jumping in 1890 to the Boston club in the outlaw PL, he enjoyed his finest season since 1884, with 27 victories, and helped Boston win the PL pennant. After pitching for Cincinnati (NL) in 1891, Radbourne retired from baseball with 308 major league wins and 191 losses.

Back home in Bloomington, Radbourne operated a pool hall/saloon purchased in 1887. He lost his sight in one eye in a hunting accident in 1894 and died less than three years later of paresis. He was survived by both parents, three brothers, and four sisters, his wife Carrie, and his stepson, Charles Stanhope. In 1939 he was elected to the National Baseball Hall of Fame.

BIBLIOGRAPHY: Frank C. Bancroft, " 'Old Hoss' Radbourne," *Baseball Magazine* 1 (July, 1908), pp. 12–14; Bloomington (IL) *Daily Pantagraph*, February 6, 1897; Sam Crane, "Charles Radbourne," New York *Journal*, January 12, 1912; Paul MacFarlane, ed. *TSN Daguerreotypes of Great Stars of Baseball* (St. Louis, 1981); Charles Radbourne file, National Baseball Hall of Fame Library, Cooperstown, NY; Joseph L. Reichler, ed., *The Baseball Encyclopedia*, 6th ed. (New York, 1985), pp. 1,309, 1,986; *Sporting Life*, 1884, February 13, 1897; Ted Sullivan, "Without an Equal," *TSN*, February 4, 1905.

                                                                Frederick Ivor-Campbell

REACH, Alfred James "Al" (b. 25 May 1840, London, England; d. 14 January 1928, Atlantic City, NJ), player, manager and manufacturer, was the son of Benjamin and Elizabeth (Dyball) Reach and entered baseball in 1855 with the newly formed Eckford team. Reach joined the Philadelphia Athletics in 1865 at a $25 a week salary "for expenses," a guise to maintain the sport's amateur status; he thus became the first paid player in the game's history. He married Louise Betts on December 25, 1866, and had four children. The 5 foot, 6 inch, 155 pound Reach played second base and outfield, was "clever" on the bases, and proved a remarkably hard-hitting left-handed batter. He played with the Athletics from 1865 through 1875 and managed Philadelphia the last two seasons. In the NA from 1871 to 1875 Reach compiled a .252 lifetime batting average, a real accomplishment in the dead ball era, and was selected for the first All-American team chosen in 1876. In 81 games from 1871 to 1875, he scored 89 runs and made 98 hits. As a manager, he guided the Athletics to 33–23 and 53–20 marks in 1874 and 1875, respectively.

Reach continued to have an active interest in baseball. In 1876 he named and backed the new Philadelphia Phillies (NL) and did not sell his interest until 1903. During those decades, A. J. Reach & Company made him a millionaire. This venture began as a cigar store and gathering place for sportsmen, but was transformed into a sporting goods store and became one of the largest companies of its type. Reach's company specialized in manufacturing baseballs by using a machine he allegedly developed personally to wind them more tightly. It also became one of the first mail-order houses and regularly sent out catalogues in the 1880s. These successful ventures enabled him to pursue his baseball interests. In 1883 he began publishing the avidly read *Reach's Official Base Ball Guide*, which probably contributed to the early development of baseball's mania for records and statistics. His successful company came under the watchful gaze of the emerging sporting goods giant Spalding & Company. He was given $100,000 and an executive position in 1889, when his own company became a division of the Spalding business. Reach, who sold out in 1892, spent his later years helping to popularize baseball. He served in 1907–1908 on the National Commission, which established the definitive American roots of the game and enabled it to become the national pastime.

BIBLIOGRAPHY: Gene Karst and Martin J. Jones, Jr., *Who's Who in Professional Baseball* (New York, 1973); *DAB*, 15 (1935), pp. 418–419; Joseph L. Reichler, ed., *The Baseball Encyclopedia*, 6th ed. (New York, 1985), pp. 65; Harold Seymour, *Baseball: The Early Years* (New York, 1960); David Quentin Voigt, *American Baseball*, vol. 1 (Norman, OK, 1966); Douglass Wallop, *Baseball: An Informal History* (New York, 1969).

Charles R. Middleton

REDDING, Richard "Dick," "Cannonball Dick" (b. 1891, Atlanta, GA; d. ?, Long Island, NY), player and manager, excelled as a pitcher in the early black baseball leagues and was nicknamed "Cannonball Dick" because of his overpowering fastball. A superb pitcher who was compared to Walter Johnson,* the 6 foot, 4 inch, right-handed Redding hurled his peak seasons with the New York Lincoln Giants between 1911 and 1915. He began pitching with small clubs in Atlanta as a youth. In 1911 the Philadelphia Giants recognized his ability and took him with them on tour. Later that season, Redding joined the Lincoln Giants and won 17 consecutive games for that outstanding team as a rookie. In 1912 he performed at his peak as a fast-throwing pitcher, winning 43 games and losing 12 and pitching several no-hitters. Against the Jersey City Skeeters (EL), Redding hurled a perfect game with 17 strikeouts. Redding pitched against a team comprised of minor league players that same season and tossed a three-hitter with 24 strikeouts, a semi-pro baseball record. The Lincoln Giants were among the great teams in black history with John Henry Lloyd,* Spottswood Poles,* Louis Santop,* and the fine pitching duo of Smoky Joe Williams* and Redding. In 1915 Redding won 20 consecutive games for the Lincoln Stars and defeated several teams made up of major league players. After playing with the Brooklyn Giants in 1916, Redding in 1917 pitched the Indianapolis ABC's to a championship.

After U.S. Army combat service in France during World War I, Redding performed with the Chicago American Giants and the Brooklyn Royal Giants for the 1919 season and did not regain his early greatness. The following season Redding joined the Atlantic City Bacharach Giants, where he pitched and managed through 1922. That winter Redding journeyed to Cuba for his fifth season, but enjoyed only average success there with an 18–23 overall record. Redding returned to the Brooklyn Royal Giants (ECL and later ANL) in 1923 and pitched and managed there until 1938. The Royal Giants lacked the talent of the other league clubs and usually finished in last place. Redding was not considered a great manager, but players liked him and performed hard for him. The clean-cut, clean-living Redding proved easygoing and good natured and enjoyed life.

Credited with 30 career no-hitters, Redding pioneered the no-windup delivery and developed a very effective, crowd pleasing hesitation pitch long before it was popularized by Satchel Paige.* Redding showed the batter his back for a few seconds, balanced on his right foot, and then turned and fired his fastball toward the plate. He died shortly after his retirement.

BIBLIOGRAPHY: John Holway, *Smokey Joe and the Cannonball* (Alexandria, VA, 1983); Robert W. Peterson, *Only the Ball Was White* (Englewood Cliffs, NJ, 1970); James A. Riley, *The All-Time All-Stars of Black Baseball* (Cocoa, FL, 1983).

                                                                                                    John L. Evers

REESE, Harold Henry "Pee Wee," "The Little Colonel" (b. 23 July 1918, Ekron, KY), player, coach, and announcer, is the son of railroad detective Carl Reese. He grew up in Louisville, KY, attended Louisville public schools, and graduated from DuPont Manual High School. Reese, whose nickname bears no reference to his 5 foot, 10 inch height and 160 pound weight, (he was nicknamed "Pee Wee" because he was a marble-shooting champion during his adolescent years), married Dorothy Walton on March 29, 1942, and has one daughter, Barbara, and one son, Mark. A .269 lifetime right-handed batter, Reese played shortstop for the Brooklyn Dodgers from 1940 to 1957 (with time out from 1943 to 1945 for military service) and Los Angeles Dodgers (1958) of the NL. The captain of the famed

"Boys of Summer," Reese held that star-filled team together. His National Baseball Hall of Fame plaque cites his "subtle leadership," "professional pride," and "easing acceptance of Jackie Robinson."*

Reese excelled with Brooklyn in many batting categories. He led all Dodgers in career stolen bases (231) and runs scored (1,317); ranked second in games played (2,107), hits (2,137), doubles (323), singles (1,612), and at bats (7,911); placed fifth in triples (78) and RBIs (868) and stood eighth in home runs (122). With Los Angeles in 1958, he added 33 hits, 7 doubles, 2 triples, 4 home runs, 21 runs scored, 17 RBIs, and 1 stolen base. Reese became the focal point of a ceremony unique in baseball history. The Dodgers celebrated his birthday in 1955 with Pee Wee Reese Night. Before the game at Ebbets Field, the lights were turned out and over 33,000 fans lit candles and sang "Happy Birthday" to him.

He began his professional baseball career in 1938 and 1939 with the Louisville Colonels (AA). In 1940 Brooklyn purchased the entire Louisville team just to secure Reese's services. The shortstop spanned two generations of Dodgers players, with his early teammates including Pete Reiser, Fred "Dixie" Walker,* Fred Fitzsimmons,* player-manager Leo Durocher,* Hugh Casey, Billy Herman,* Dolf Camilli, and Cookie Lavagetto. His later teammates, subsequently nicknamed "The Boys of Summer," included Jackie Robinson, Gil Hodges,* Roy Campanella,* Preacher Roe, Carl Furillo, Carl Erskine, Don Newcombe,* and Billy Cox. After ending his playing career with Los Angeles in 1958, Reese served as a coach there in 1959. Although Brooklyn allegedly had offered him the managerial post twice, he preferred to continue solely as their shortstop and captain. Subsequently, Reese worked as an announcer and banker and owned a storm window business and bowling alley in Louisville. He was an executive with the Hillerich and Bradsby Corporation, maker of Louisville Slugger baseball bats. Besides being elected to the National Baseball Hall of Fame in 1984, he also was inducted into the Brooklyn Dodgers Baseball Hall of Fame as a charter member on June 7, 1984.

BIBLIOGRAPHY: Red Barber and Barney Stein, *The Rhubarb Patch* (New York, 1954); *Brooklyn Dodgers Yearbooks, 1947, 1949–1957*; Leo Durocher, *The Dodgers and Me* (New York, 1946); Ed Fitzgerald, ed., *The Story of the Brooklyn Dodgers* (New York, 1949); Harvey Frommer, *New York City Baseball: The Last Golden Years* (New York, 1980); Peter Golenbock, *Bums: An Oral History of the Brooklyn Dodgers* (New York, 1984); Roger Kahn, *The Boys of Summer* (New York, 1972).

                                                              Ronald L. Gabriel

REULBACH, Edward Marvin "Ed," "Big Ed" (b. 1 December 1882, Detroit, MI; d. 17 July 1961, Glens Falls, NY), player, was the son of bookkeeper Edward J. and Catherine M. (Paulus) Reulbach. He attended elementary school in Detroit and Manual Training High School in St. Louis.

He studied electrical engineering at the University of Notre Dame and pre-medicine at the University of Vermont without graduating from either institution. While starring on the mound for Notre Dame, Reulbach played minor league ball under assumed names. As "Lawson," he pitched three summers (1901–1903) for Sedalia, KS (MVL). As "Sheldon," he pitched for Montpelier, VT (GML), in 1904. Confused scouts thought that they were tracking three different pitchers. He was signed as Reulbach for the Chicago Cubs (NL) in May, 1905 by George Huff, Illinois athletic director and former Dartmouth catcher and football star.

The big 6 foot, 1 inch, 190 pound right-hander pitched impressively from the outset. In 1905 he won 18 games, 9 consecutively, and scored a 20-inning 2–1 victory over Philadelphia. In 29 starts, he achieved 28 complete games, 292 innings pitched, and a 1.42 ERA. On August 13, 1906, he married Mary Ellen "Nellie" Whelan, with whom he had one son. He won 19 of 23 decisions and finished the season with a 12-game winning streak and a 1.65 ERA. For the first of three straight years, he compiled the NL top winning percentage (.826). Only Lefty Grove* has equalled this record. Reulbach enjoyed his finest year in 1908, winning 24 games, pitching 297.2 innings, and recording a 2.03 ERA. Nine wins came against Brooklyn, two of them in a unique shutout doubleheader to tie an NL mark. At season's end, he pitched 44 consecutive shutout innings to help the Cubs edge past the New York Giants by a game to win the NL pennant.

In 1909 Reulbach recorded a 14-game winning streak on the way to 19 victories and a 1.78 ERA. He continued through 1912 with winning percentages above .600, but his ballooning ERA's indicated that his great years were past. Traded to Brooklyn (NL) in mid–1913, he compiled an 11–18 record the next season in 256 innings of pitching. He jumped to the FL in 1915, becoming the ace of the Newark Peps' staff. His 20 victories, however, reflected the FL's weakness rather than his arm's rejuvenation. He won 7 of 13 decisions for the Boston Braves (NL) in 1916 and had one loss in 1917, when released to Providence (IL).

Reulbach's career statistics confirm his pitching renown. His .633 winning percentage (181 victories against 105 defeats) place him twentieth on the all-time list, his 2.28 ERA eleventh. He completed 200 of 299 starts, hurled 40 shutouts, and struck out 1,137 batters. For thirteen seasons, Reulbach's innings pitched exceeded his hits allowed. This superlative pitcher achieved modest World Series success and won two World Series decisions, including a scintillating one-hitter against the Chicago White Sox in 1906. In three other games, he was hit hard and removed.

A brainy pitcher, he threw perhaps the best curve in either league. Great contemporaries, including Mordecai "Three Finger" Brown* and Ed Walsh,* overshadowed him. For many, he became "the third best pitcher in Chicago" and its second "Big Ed." Reulbach served as founding director and secretary (1914–1915) of the short-lived Base Ball Players' Fraternity, organized to better working conditions, oppose contract abuses, and advise players with grievances. After leaving baseball, he worked for a piano manufacturer and operated a tire business which was bankrupted by the expenses of his son's long illness and eventual death. For twenty years thereafter, he was associated with a construction company.

BIBLIOGRAPHY: "Daguerreotypes," *TSN*, October 12, 1939; John J. Evers, with Hugh S. Fullerton, *Touching Second* (Chicago, 1910); Cappy Gagnon, "Ed Reulbach Remembered," *Baseball Research Journal* 11 (1982), pp. 77–79; J. Warren McEligot, "Ed Reulbach—A Sad, Quiet Man of 50," Chicago *Tribune*, December 29, 1932; Joseph L. Reichler, ed., *The Baseball Encyclopedia*, 6th ed. (New York, 1985), p. 1,994; Edward Reulbach file, National Baseball Hall of Fame Library, Cooperstown, NY; Harold Seymour, *Baseball: The Golden Age* (New York, 1971); David Quentin Voigt, *American Baseball*, vol. 2 (University Park, PA, 1983).

A. D. Suehsdorf

REYNOLDS, Allie Pierce "Superchief" (b. 10 February 1915, Bethany, OK), player, ranked among the leading right-handed pitchers of the 1940s and early 1950s. The son of fundamentalist minister D. L. Reynolds, he was one-quarter Creek Indian and starred in track and football at Capitol High School in Oklahoma City. Although entering Oklahoma A & M University on a track scholarship, he impressed coach Hank Iba* (IS) while pitching batting practice and launched his baseball career in 1937. He also starred as one of the best football running backs in the Missouri Valley Conference. Reynolds graduated in 1939 with a Bachelor of Science degree and was drafted by both the New York Giants (National Football League) and Cleveland Indians (AL). In the Indians' minor league system at Springfield, OH (MAL), Cedar Rapids, IA (3IL), and Wilkes-Barre, PA (EL), he caught, played the outfield, and pitched.

After joining the Indians (AL) in 1942, he won 51 games over the next four years and hurled 18 victories in 1945. Traded after the 1946 season to the New York Yankees (AL) for popular second baseman Joe Gordon, Reynolds became perhaps the mainstay of the Yankees pitching staffs of manager Bucky Harris* and Casey Stengel* in the world championship seasons of 1947, 1949, 1950, 1951, 1952, and 1953. From 1947 to 1954, he won 131 and lost only 60 and compiled 19 victories in 1947 and 20 triumphs in 1952. The fastball pitcher overcame wildness to post an impressive 1,423 strikeouts in a thirteen-year career.

Reynolds did not reach the majors until age 27 and had to overcome several physical and psychological obstacles. Often bothered by bone chips in his pitching elbow, he suffered through a successful 17–6 season in 1949. The fans and press derided his inability to finish games that year and named the Yankees' best pitcher "Reynolds-Page." In the 1949 World Series opener against the Brooklyn Dodgers' formidable Don Newcombe,* he pitched a masterful 1–0 victory decided by a ninth-inning Tommy Henrich home run. His World Series career proved outstanding, as his seven wins placed him with Red Ruffing* and Whitey Ford* among the most successful clutch pitchers in the history of post-season play. In 1951 he led the AL in shutouts (7) and joined Johnny VanderMeer as one of only two pitchers at that time with two no-hitters in the same season (against Cleveland in July and Boston in September, the latter game clinching the AL pennant).

Reynolds, a devout Methodist, retired after the 1954 season and now serves as chairman of the board of New Park Mid-Continental Drilling Company in Oklahoma City. He married Dale Jones in 1935 and has two sons and one daughter. During his career, he won 182 games, lost 107 contests, hurled 36 shutouts, and compiled a 3.30 ERA.

BIBLIOGRAPHY: Harry Molter, *Famous American Athletes of Today*, 13th series (Boston, 1953); Joseph L. Reichler, ed., *The Baseball Encyclopedia*, 6th ed. (New York, 1985), p. 1,995.

Leonard Frey

RICE, Edgar Charles "Sam" (b. 20 February 1890, Morocco, IN; d. 13 October 1974, Rossmor, MD), player, was the son of farmers Charles and Louise Christine (Newmyre) Rice. He attended Rhode Island Country School in Iroquois County, IL, where classmates remembered him as a good athlete with exceptional speed. Rice married Beulah Stam on September 17, 1908, moved to Watseka, IL, and had two children. He played pick-up and town team baseball but sought unsuccessfully four years to become a pitcher with a CA team. In April 1912 Rice's entire family (parents, siblings, wife, and children) was killed in a tornado. Following this tragedy, he made some last attempts at local baseball, wandered the nation working odd jobs, and joined the U.S. Navy in 1913.

After playing baseball in the Navy during tours of Mexico and Cuba, he pitched for Petersburg, VA (VL), in 1914 and posted a 9–2 record. In 29 appearances in 1915, Rice compiled an 11–12 mark. The Washington Senators (AL) secured him as payment for a Petersburg debt to owner Clark Griffith.* The 5 foot, 9 inch, 150 pound Rice saw limited action as a right-handed Washington pitcher, but enjoyed success as a pinch hitter and moved to right field. In 1917 the 27-year-old "rookie" batted .302 and stole 35 bases. Rice served in the U.S. Army in 1918 and then started as the Senators' right fielder from 1919 through 1931. He saw only limited action the following three seasons and finished his career with the Cleveland Indians (AL) in 1934. He married his second wife, Mary Kendal, on July 4, 1929, and retired with their daughter to his Maryland farm.

During his twenty-year major league career, Rice posted a .322 batting average and retired only thirteen hits short of the magic 3,000 mark. In 2,404 games, the left-handed Rice slugged 497 doubles and 184 triples, scored

1,515 runs, knocked in 1,079 runs, walked 709 times, and stole 351 bases. He batted .302 in three World Series (1924, 1925, and 1933) and achieved immortality in the 1925 Series, when he tumbled over a right field barrier and emerged with the ball in his glove. Although the umpire ruled the batter out, controversy raged for years. Rice was overshadowed by contemporaries Babe Ruth,* Ty Cobb,* and Lou Gehrig,* and he never earned over $18,000 a season. His achievements included having 200 or more hits in six different seasons, leading the AL in hits in 1924 and 1926 (216), and setting an AL record with 182 singles in 1925. Besides leading AL outfielders in putouts with 454 in 1920 and 385 in 1922, he paced the AL in stolen bases with 63 in 1920. Rice batted more than 600 times during eight seasons and struck out only 275 times during 9,269 career at bats.

The durable, consistent Rice belatedly was elected to the National Baseball Hall of Fame by unanimous vote of the Veterans Committee in 1963. He remained active in baseball, making his last appearance at the Hall only months before his death. Rice, a gifted athlete, overcame tremendous odds of age, inexperience, and great personal tragedy to achieve success in professional baseball.

BIBLIOGRAPHY: Martin Appel and Burt Goldblatt, *Baseball's Best: The Hall of Fame Gallery* (New York, 1977); Mary Lou Le Compte, correspondence with Thomas R. Heitz, Mary Lou Le Compte Collection, Austin, TX; Joseph L. Reichler, ed., *The Baseball Encyclopedia*, 6th ed. (New York, 1985), p. 1,325; "Sam Rice, Hall of Fame Outfielder, Dies," *NYT*, October 15, 1974; John Yost, "Edgar Charles 'Sam' Rice, Enterprise Profile," Newton County (IN) *Enterprise*, June 7, 1984, p. 9.

Mary Lou LeCompte

RICE, James Edward "Jim," "Ed" (b. 8 March 1953, Anderson, SC), player, is the best right-handed slugger for the Boston Red Sox (AL) since Jimmie Foxx* and is the fourth of nine children of True Temper Company supervisor Roger Rice and Julia Mae Rice. Nicknamed "Ed," Rice excelled as an all-around athlete at Westside and Hanna high schools in Anderson, SC. An All-State football player, he also attracted numerous major league baseball scouts. Shortly after Rice graduated, the Red Sox selected him in the first round of the June, 1971, amateur draft. Rice signed with Boston shortly thereafter for a reported $45,000 bonus and began his professional career as an outfielder in 1971 at Williamsport, PA (NYPL). Rice played at Winter Haven, FL (FSL), in 1972 and Bristol, CT (EL), in 1973, batting .317 to lead the EL. He moved up to Pawtucket, RI (IL), late in 1973 and enjoyed a superb season there in 1974. After winning the Triple Crown (25 home runs, 93 RBIs, .337 batting average), he was named Minor League Player of the Year by *The Sporting News* and IL Most Valuable Player. In September, 1974, Rice joined the Red Sox (AL).

In 1975 Rice and fellow rookie Fred Lynn* led the Red Sox to the AL pennant. Since 1975 Rice has led the AL three times in home runs (1977–1978, 1983), twice in RBIs (1978, 1983), twice in slugging percentage, and once each in triples (1978) and hits (1978), and made the AL All-Star team eight times (1977–1980, 1983–1986). In his finest season, 1978, he batted .315 and led the AL in games (163), at bats (677), hits (213), triples (15), home runs (46) RBIs (139), total bases (406), and slugging percentage (.600). The same year, he was voted AL MVP. In 1986 Rice ranked 5th in the AL in batting (.324), 4th in RBIs (110), tied for 3rd in doubles (39), and tied for 5th in hits (200), helping the Red Sox capture the AL pennant and finishing third in the AL MVP balloting. Although he batted only .161 in the AL Championship Series against the California Angels, he slugged 2 home runs and one double and knocked in 6 runs. Rice batted .333 and made one double and one triple in the World Series, which was won by the New York Mets. Through 1986, Rice's career totals included 2,163 hits, 1,104 runs scored, 331 doubles, 351 home runs, 1,289 RBIs, a .303 batting average, and a slugging average of over .500. At Fenway Park through 1983, his effective totals included 153 homers, 535 RBIs, .327 batting average, and .577 slugging percentage. Since Rice already ranks among the era's best players, his performance in the next few years will determine his position among baseball's all-time greats. Rice married Corine Gilliard in 1972 and has one child, Chauncy.

BIBLIOGRAPHY: Anderson (SC) *Independent*, 1971–1983; *SI* 50 (April 9, 1979), pp. 53–61; *TSN Baseball Register, 1983* (St. Louis, 1983).

Clark Nardinelli

RICKEY, Wesley Branch "The Mahatma" (b. 20 December 1881, Lucasville or Stockdale, OH; d. 9 December 1965, Columbia, MO), player, manager, and executive, was the son of farmer Franklin and Emily (Braum) Rickey. A gifted student, Rickey worked his way through Ohio Wesleyan College and the University of Michigan Law School by teaching and coaching sports. He married Jane Moulton of Lucasville, OH, in 1906 and had six children. As a mediocre catcher, Rickey played three seasons of minor league baseball at Terre Haute, IN (3IL) and Le Mars, IA (ISDL) in 1903 and Dallas (TL) in 1904 and 1905 and three years with the St. Louis Browns (1905–1906) and New York Highlanders (1907) of the AL. Injuries and tuberculosis ended his brief professional career in 1907. In 119 games, he batted .239 and knocked in 39 runs. His brilliant reputation as a coach returned the bespectacled, scholarly Rickey to the major leagues, where he became this century's most brilliant, innovative baseball executive. After joining the St. Louis Browns (AL) in 1913 as field manager and executive director, he acquired young players cheaply by negotiating working agreements with minor league teams. Under Rickey, the Browns finished with 139 wins and 179 losses from 1913 through 1915 and in the second division.

In 1916 Rickey joined the St. Louis Cardinals (NL) in the same dual capacity. Following World War I service as a major in the chemical warfare branch, Rickey returned in 1919 and shaped the lackluster Cardinals into a perennial contender. Rickey served as Cardinals manager through early 1925 and guided the club to two third place finishes. During his ten-year managerial career, he posted 597 wins and 664 losses (.473). By building a network of minor league farm clubs, Rickey acquired and developed a steady flow of young talent. No major league rival matched the efficiency of the Cardinals farm system, which included thirty-three teams by 1940. The system's productivity stemmed from tryout camps, brilliant teaching and evaluative techniques, and other Rickey innovations. During Rickey's tenure through 1942, the Cardinals won six NL pennants (1926, 1928, 1930–1931, 1934, 1942) and four world championships. Rickey profited from his percentage on the sale of surplus players, which aroused the enmity of owner Sam Breadon.*

Fired by Breadon in 1942, Rickey became president and general manager of the Brooklyn Dodgers (NL) and built their superb farm system. By his bold, successful experiment of selecting Jackie Robinson* as the first black player to play in the majors in this century, he cornered the market on black and Hispanic players. Rickey's efforts made the Dodgers a perennial NL power and 1947 and 1949 NL champions. Rickey was forced out of his Dodgers post in 1950 by Walter O'Malley,* who sought full ownership of the club and resented Rickey's flamboyant leadership. Rickey signed a five-year contract as executive vice-president of the Pittsburgh Pirates (NL) and laid the groundwork for their 1960 world championship.

In 1959 the 77-year-old Rickey surfaced as president of the CntL. Although it did not become a major league, the CntL forced the established majors to expand and brought major league baseball to hitherto excluded urban centers. The author of *The American Diamond* (1965), Rickey was elected to the National Baseball Hall of Fame in 1967. Rickey's innovations as baseball executive, dominant role in the racial integration of organized baseball, and stimulus to the game's expansion place him among this century's most influential baseball leaders.

BIBLIOGRAPHY: David Lipman, *Mr. Baseball: The Story of Branch Rickey* (New York, 1966); Arthur Mann, *Branch Rickey: American in Action* (Boston, 1957); Robert Obojski, *Bush League: A History of Minor League Baseball* (New York, 1975); Branch Rickey and Robert Rieger, *The American Diamond: A Documentary of the Game of Baseball* (New York, 1965); Jackie Robinson (with Alfred Duckett), *I Never Had It Made* (New York, 1972); Jules Tygiel, *Baseball's Great Experiment: Jackie Robinson and His Legacy* (New York, 1983); David Quentin Voigt, *American Baseball*, vols. 2, 3 (University Park, PA, 1983).

David Quentin Voigt

RIXEY, Eppa, Jr., "Eppa Jephtha" (b. 3 May 1891, Culpeper, VA; d. 28 February 1963, Cincinnati, OH), player, was the son of banker Eppa Rixey, Sr., and Willie Alice (Walton) Rixey. He attended grade school in Culpeper and moved with his family at age 11 to Charlottesville, VA. He attended high school in Charlottesville and enrolled at the University of Virginia, where he played baseball. In 1912, the left-handed Rixey moved directly from college to the Philadelphia Phillies (NL) without playing in the minor leagues. From 1912 to 1920, he won 87 games and lost 103 for the Phillies. In 1921 he joined the Cincinnati Reds (NL) and won 179 and lost 148 over the next thirteen seasons. During his twenty-one year career, he compiled 266 wins and 251 losses for a 3.15 ERA. In the 1915 World Series he lost his only decision to the Boston Red Sox.

Rixey appeared in 692 games, starting 552 and completing 290. He pitched 4,494.2 innings, gave up 4,633 hits, walked 1,082, and struck out 1,350, and threw 39 shutouts. In relief appearances, he won 20, lost 17, and saved 14. These accomplishments place him among the most successful pitchers in baseball history. Rixey's 6 foot, 5 inch, 210 pound frame, reliable pitching strength, and strange name made him a fan favorite. Although many references cite his full name as Eppa Jephtha (or Jeptha) Rixey, Jr., "Jephtha" was probably invented by a Cincinnati sportswriter. Rixey's twenty-one seasons set a longevity record among NL left-handers until Steve Carlton* broke it in 1986. In 1969 Cincinnati fans named Rixey the Reds' most outstanding left-hander. On October 29, 1924, he married Dorothy Meyers; they had two children. From his retirement until his death, Rixey managed a successful insurance business in Cincinnati. He was elected to the National Baseball Hall of Fame in 1963, one month before his death.

BIBLIOGRAPHY: Martin Appel, and Burt Goldblatt, *Baseball's Best: The Hall of Fame Gallery* (New York, 1977); Danny Diehl, "Eppa Rixey—Culpeper Baseball Hall of Fame," Culpeper (VA) *News*, July 21, 1983; Randy Hask and Linda Queen, "Eppa Jeptha Rixey" (photocopied), Culpeper High School, Culpeper, VA, n.d.; Gene Karst and Martin J. Jones, Jr., *Who's Who in Professional Baseball* (New Rochelle, NY, 1973); Joseph L. Reichler, ed., *The Baseball Encyclopedia*, 6th ed. (New York, 1985), p. 2,001; Robert Weaver, correspondence with Guinn, August 26, 1983, Robert G. Weaver Collection, Petersburg, PA.

                                                                                    Robert G. Weaver

RIZZUTO, Philip Francis "Phil," "Scooter" (b. 25 September 1918, New York, NY), player and announcer, is the son of Rose (Angotti) and trolley car conductor Philip Rizzuto. He attended Richmond Hill (NY) High School, where he starred as a third baseman and football quarterback, but Rizzuto dropped out of school at age 16 to play baseball and received his diploma in 1948 as special recognition of his diamond success. Paul Krichell, Rizzuto's high school baseball coach, arranged several tryouts for him. Brooklyn Dodgers manager Casey Stengel* rejected the short 5 foot, 6 inch, 150 pound Rizzuto and told him, "Go get a shoebox!" The New York Yankees (AL) signed him and assigned him to Bassett, VA (BSL), in 1937. With Kansas City (AA) in 1939, the right-handed Rizzuto teamed with second baseman Jerry Priddy to form "the Heavenly Twins." Teammate Billy Hitchcock nicknamed him "Scooter" for his swift motion from shortstop to second base. Rizzuto led the AA with 35 stolen bases and was named Minor League Player of the Year in 1940.

Rizzuto, who joined New York Yankees (AL) in 1941, married Cora Esselborn on June 24, 1943, and has three daughters. The deeply religious Rizzuto was plagued with sickness and injuries most of his career. He suffered many head injuries, the most serious being a 1946 beaning by Nelson Potter of the St. Louis Browns. Dizzy spells, ulcers, and malaria later developed from his U.S. Navy stint during World War II. In 1950 he hit .324 and was named the AL's Most Valuable Player. He played in five All-Star games (1942, 1950–1953) and led AL shortstops in putouts (1942, 1950), assists (1952), fielding average (1949–1950), and double plays (1941–1942, 1952). An outstanding bunter, he paced the AL from 1949 to 1953 in sacrifice bunts.

With the Yankees through 1956, he hit .273 in 1,661 games, made 1,588 hits, slugged 239 doubles, 62 triples, and 38 homers, scored 877 runs, knocked in 562 runs, and stole 149 bases. In nine World Series, he hit .246 in 52 games, made two homers, knocked in 8 runs, and walked 30 times. Rizzuto, who lives in Hillside, NJ, has broadcast for the New York Yankees since his release in 1956. His infectious enthusiasm is evident in his characteristic expression, "Holy Cow."

BIBLIOGRAPHY: Maury Allen, *Baseball's 100* (New York, 1981; *CB* (July, 1950), pp. 494–496; Gene Karst and Martin J. Jones, Jr., *Who's Who in Professional Baseball* (New York, 1973); *Look* 14 (May 9, 1950), p. 80; *Look* 22 (August 5, 1958), pp. 31–32; Richard Marazzi and Len Fiorito, *Aaron to Zuverink* (New York, 1982); "Professor Rizzuto's Baseball Academy," *Reader's Digest* (March, 1953), pp. 26–28; Joe Reichler, *Inside the Majors* (New York, 1952); Harold Rosenthal, *Lucky He's Still a Yankee* (New York, 1953); "Scooter Spared," *Time*, (April 14, 1941), p. 14; Gene Shoor, *The Scooter* (New York, 1982); Joe Trimble, *Phil Rizzuto* (New York, 1951); *WWA*, 41st ed. (1980–1981), p. 2,785.

William A. Borst

ROBERTS, Robin Evan (b. 30 September 1926, Springfield, IL), player and coach, was a sturdy right-handed pitching star for nineteen major league seasons. Roberts played with the Philadelphia Phillies (1948–1961) of the NL, Baltimore Orioles (1962–1965) of the AL, and Houston Astros (1965–1966) and Chicago Cubs (1966–1967) of the NL. His father, Tom, a Welsh coal miner, and his mother, Sarah, came to the United States from England in 1921. One of five children, Robin grew up in the Springfield, IL, area and became interested in sports. An accomplished high school basketball player, he was offered a scholarship at Michigan State University. When World War II intervened, he served as a U.S. Army Air Force flying cadet (1944–1945).

After his discharge in 1945, he enrolled at Michigan State and earned a Bachelor of Science degree in physical education there. At Michigan State, his interest and talent in baseball began blossoming. He pitched two no-hitters, including one against Michigan, then coached by former big league pitcher Ray Fisher. Fisher spent his summers managing the Montpelier, VT team in a semi-pro league that used college players who desired to have professional status. In 1946 Roberts began spending his summers with Fisher and within two years attracted the attention of major league scouts. Five clubs—the Boston Braves, Philadelphia Phillies, Boston Red Sox, Detroit Tigers, and New York Yankees—offered him contracts. The $25,000 bonus given by the Phillies (NL) proved the persuading factor. He was sent to Wilmington, DE, the Phillies' farm team in the ISL.

Roberts soon demonstrated that he pitched too well for the ISL. By the middle of June, he had started 11 games and compiled a 9–1 record. On June 17, 1948, he joined Philadelphia (NL). The next day, Roberts lost his first major league game 2–0 to Pittsburgh, but pitched well and allowed only five hits. In his next appearance, he defeated Cincinnati for his first major league victory. After a 7–9 record his first year, he finished 15–15 in 1949. In 1950 he achieved the first of six consecutive 20-win seasons, and narrowly missed a seventh (19) in 1956. Roberts led the NL in games started six times, complete games, innings pitched and hits surrendered five times, wins four times, and strikeouts and shutouts twice. Over the ensuing years, he amassed 286 career wins, 245 losses, and a 3.41 ERA.

He starred as a pitcher on the 1950 NL pennant-winning Phillies "Whiz Kids." He earned the NL pennant-clinching win with his twentieth win of the year in the final game against Brooklyn. In the World Series against the Yankees, he lost his only start by 2–1 in ten innings. Over the years, Roberts became a control pitcher, walking only 902 batters in 4,688 2/3 innings or an average of one every five to six innings. Since good control reduces the anxiety index, batters tagged him 502 times for home runs, a major league record.

The years 1959–1960 saw a decline in his pitching effectiveness. His dismal 1–10 record in 1961 ended his usefulness to the Phillies. He was sold to the New York Yankees (AL) and trained with them in 1962, but appeared in no games for them. On May 21 the Baltimore Orioles (AL) picked him up. Roberts enjoyed three good seasons with Baltimore, winning 42 and losing 36. When the Orioles released him in July, 1965, he signed with Houston (NL) and logged a 5–2 record. A year later, he captured three of eight decisions for the Astros before being released. Roberts completed his major league career with the Chicago Cubs (NL) in 1966 by posting a 2–3 mark in 11 games. The following year (1967) was supposed to be a rehabilitation one with Reading, PA (EL), but persistent arm trouble ended his hopes of returning to the major leagues.

Roberts married Mary Ann Kaines in 1949 and has four sons. He participated in the Players Association and made significant contributions to the welfare of players. Roberts won *The Sporting News* Pitcher of the Year Award in 1952 and 1955. In thirteen of his nineteen years, he was elected as opening game pitcher. Roberts appeared in five All-Star games and was elected to the National Baseball Hall of Fame in 1976. He coached baseball at the University of South Florida and in November, 1985, was named coordinator of minor league instruction for the Philadelphia Phillies.

BIBLIOGRAPHY: Martin Appel and Burt Goldblatt, *Baseball's Best: The Hall of Fame Gallery* (New York, 1977); Joseph L. Reichler, ed., *The Baseball Encyclopedia*, 6th ed. (New York, 1985), p. 2,002.

Robert G. Weaver

ROBINSON, Brooks Calbert, Jr. (b. 18 May 1937, Little Rock, AR), player, is the son of fireman Brooks Calbert and Ethel Mae (Denker) Robinson. In 1955 he signed for a $4,000 bonus with the Baltimore Orioles (AL) immediately upon graduation from Little Rock Central High School. Although primarily a third baseman, Robinson also played second base and shortstop early in his career. He played a portion of four of his first five seasons (1955–1959) with minor league clubs in York, PA (Pil), San Antonio (TL), and Vancouver (PCL). The balance of each season he played with the AL Orioles. At 180 pounds, the 6 foot, 1 inch Robinson slugged at least 20 home runs on six occasions and 268 career homers. He batted over .300 and knocked in over 100 runs twice each. He won the AL's Most Valuable Player Award in 1964, when he slugged 28 home runs, led the AL with 118 RBIs, and batted .317. In 2,896 games, he batted 10,654 times, made 2,848 hits, 482 doubles, and 68 triples, scored 1,232 runs, knocked in 1,357 runs, and batted .267.

The right-handed Robinson became the premier AL third baseman for most of his career. He topped the AL's third basemen in fielding average from 1960 through 1964, 1966 through 1969, and in 1972 and 1975. Frequently, he also paced his position in assists and double plays. He ranks as the major league career leader at his position in total chances (9,165), double plays (618), assists (6,205), putouts (2,697),and fielding average (.971), and won twelve Gold Glove awards. Robinson participated in four World Series with the Orioles, helping them win world championships in 1966 over the Los Angeles Dodgers and in 1970 over the Cincinnati Reds. He starred in the 1966 and 1967 All-Star games, making three hits in the former and homering for the only AL run in the latter. Perennially Robinson made third base on the AL All-Star teams. In 1970 he was selected as Hickok Professional Athlete of the Year.

Robinson, who retired in 1977 after twenty-three major league seasons, ranks among the best third basemen in baseball history. In 1983 he was elected to the National Baseball Hall of Fame in his first year of eligibility. Robinson married Constance Louise Butcher in October 1960 and has three sons and one daughter.

BIBLIOGRAPHY: *CB* (1973), pp. 361–363; Joseph L.Reichler, ed., *The Baseball Encyclopedia*, 6th ed. (New York, 1985), p. 1,336; Lowell Reidenbaugh, *Cooperstown: Where Baseball's Legends Live Forever* (St. Louis, 1983); Jack Zanger, *The Brooks Robinson Story* (New York, 1967).

Stephen D. Bodayla

ROBINSON, Frank (b. 31 August 1935, Beaumont, TX), player, coach, and manager, is the son of Frank and Ruth (Shaw) Robinson. One of ten children, Robinson attended school in Oakland, CA, and excelled in baseball there. He played on the Oakland American Legion team, winners of two consecutive national titles (1949–1950). Following high school graduation in 1953, the right-handed Robinson signed with the Cincinnati Reds (NL) and played for Ogden, UT (PrL), Tulsa (TL), and Columbia, SC (SAL), between 1953 and 1955. After joining the Reds in 1956, Robinson led the NL in runs scored and tied a major league record by hitting 38 home runs as a rookie. In 1959 he batted for the cycle and belted three home runs in one game. The 6 foot, 1 inch, 194 pound Robinson, who was an outfielder–first baseman for Cincinnati (1956–1965), won NL Rookie of the Year honors in 1956 and the Most Valuable Player Award in 1961. Besides helping the Reds win the NL pennant in 1961, Robinson led the NL in slugging percentage (1960–1962) and runs scored and doubles (1962).

Robinson was traded to the Baltimore Orioles (AL) following the 1965 season and the next year became one of just eleven players to win baseball's Triple Crown. He paced the AL in home runs (49), RBIs (122), and runs scored (122), and compiled a .316 batting average. Selected as the AL's MVP, he became the only player to achieve this feat in both leagues. In 1970 Robinson tied a major league record by slugging grand slam home runs in two successive times at bat. Robinson helped the Orioles win four AL pennants (1966, 1969–1971) and two world championships (1966, 1970) and was selected as the MVP in the 1966 World Series. In 26 World Series games, Robinson batted 92 times, collecting 23 hits, 8 homers, 14 RBIs, and a .250 batting average. Robinson performed in eleven All-Star games and was named the MVP in the 1971 classic. He belted a two-run home run for the AL, making him the only player in All-Star competition to hit a home run for each league. After playing with to the Los Angeles Dodgers (NL) in 1972, California Angels (AL) in 1973, and Cleveland Indians (AL) in 1974, Robinson in 1975 was chosen Indians player-manager and became the first black major league manager. Replaced in 1977, he then piloted Rochester,

NY (IL), in 1978, and coached for the Orioles (1979–1980). Named manager of the San Francisco Giants (NL) in 1981, Robinson remained there until dismissed during the 1984 season. As a major league manager, Robinson piloted his teams to 450 wins and 466 losses. His highest finish (third place) came in 1982, when he was named NL Manager of the Year.

In his twenty-one-year major league playing career, Robinson batted at least .300 nine times, knocked in 100 or more runs six times, slugged 30 or more home runs eleven times, belted 2 or more home runs in one game 54 times, and scored at least 100 runs eight times. On the all-time major league lists, Robinson ranks high in nearly all statistical categories. He played in 2,808 games (11th), batted 10,006 times (14th), scored 1,829 runs (9th), and collected 2,943 hits (20th), 528 doubles (18th), 72 triples, 586 home runs (4th), 1,812 RBIs (12th), and 5,373 total bases (8th). Robinson received 1,420 bases on balls (15th), struck out 1,532 times (13th), compiled a .537 slugging average (17th), and batted .294 lifetime. Robinson married Barbara Ann Cole in 1961 and has one son, Frank Kevin, and one daughter, Michelle. The co-author of *My Life in Baseball*, Robinson in 1982 was elected to the National Baseball Hall of Fame and became only the thirteenth player to achieve this honor in the first year of eligibility. Still active in baseball, Robinson coaches for the Baltimore Orioles.

BIBLIOGRAPHY: Phil Jackman, "Orioles' Rivals Celebrating the Departure of F. Robby," *TSN*, December 18, 1971, p. 50; Lowell Reidenbaugh, *Cooperstown: Where Baseball's Legends Live Forever* (St. Louis, 1983); *TSN Official Baseball Record Book 1985* (St. Louis, 1985); *TSN Official Baseball Register 1984* (St. Louis, 1984).

John L. Evers

ROBINSON, Jack Roosevelt "Jackie" (b. 31 January 1919, Cairo, GA; d. 24 October 1972, Stamford, CT), player and all-around athlete, was the first black to play baseball in the modern major leagues and the youngest child of sharecropper Jerry and Mallie (McGriff) Robinson. After his father deserted the family in 1920, his mother moved her five children to Pasadena, CA. Robinson's athletic versatility allowed him to escape an impoverished life. After excelling at track, baseball, football, basketball, and tennis at Muir Technical High School, 5 foot, 11 1/2 inch, 195 pound right-hander starred in baseball at Pasadena Junior College and in baseball, basketball, and football at UCLA. In 1941 financial pressures forced Robinson to leave UCLA without earning a degree. After playing professional football briefly, he enlisted in the U.S. Army in 1942 and the next year was commissioned a second lieutenant. Robinson's opposition to racial discrimination led to a court martial for insubordination and subsequent acquittal. In November, 1944, he was honorably discharged.

Robinson's stellar play as a $400 a month second baseman with the 1945 Kansas City Monarchs of the segregated NAL excited the interest of Clyde

Sukeforth, who scouted the black majors for Brooklyn Dodgers (NL) president Branch Rickey.* A brilliant baseball innovator, Rickey knew that the changing social climate must soon end major league baseball's segregation policy. Despite hostile colleagues, Rickey signed Robinson to a Dodgers contract and made him a *cause célèbre* in integrating major league baseball. In 1946 Robinson paced the IL in batting and led the Montreal Royals to the Little World Series championship. After promotion to the NL Dodgers in 1947, Robinson played first base and maintained a docile posture amidst controversy surrounding his presence. By batting .297 and leading the NL in stolen bases (29), Robinson won Rookie of the Year honors and helped the Dodgers to the NL pennant. In 1949 he captured the NL batting championship (.342) and the NL's Most Valuable Player Award as a second baseman. The admission of other black players enabled pathfinder Robinson to change his docile posture. An aggressive team leader and perennial All Star, he outspokenly advocated integrated baseball. His sallies against continuing discrimination caused some to label him a troublemaker.

From 1947 to 1956 with the Dodgers, he compiled a .311 batting average and helped his club win six NL pennants (1947, 1949, 1952–1953, 1955–1956) and a world title (1955). In 1962 sportswriters voted him into the National Baseball Hall of Fame. In 1,382 games, he made 1,518 hits, slugged 273 doubles, 54 triples, and 137 home runs, scored 947 runs, knocked in 734 runs, and stole 197 bases. From 1956 to 1972, Robinson pursued business interests and fought for broader participation and civil rights for black Americans. As a vice-president of Chock Full o' Nuts Company, he hired many blacks. Four semi-autobiographical books appeared disclosing Robinson's changing views of his quest to integrate baseball. Robinson concluded that he had done little for himself and his people as a black man "who never had it made" in a white world. When Robinson died of heart disease in 1972, he was afforded a hero's funeral. Robinson was extolled as an authentic All-American "who made a memorable impact for good in his country and his time." The nationally acclaimed pathfinder paved the way for black American and dusky Hispanic players, whose batting feats dominated baseball's early expansion era. In 1945 he married Rachel Isum of Los Angeles; they had three children, two of whom survived him.

BIBLIOGRAPHY: Roger Kahn, *The Boys of Summer* (New York, 1972); Jack Robinson and Alfred Duckett, *Breakthrough to the Big Leagues: The Story of Jackie Robinson* (New York, 1965); Jack Robinson with Alfred Duckett, *I Never Had It Made: An Autobiography* (New York, 1972); Jack Robinson with Bill Roeder, *Jackie Robinson* (New York, 1950); Jack Robinson and Carl T. Rowan, *Wait Till Next Year: The Story of Jackie Robinson* (New York, 1960); Jack Robinson and Wendell Smith, *Jackie Robinson: My Own Story* (New York, 1948); Jackie Robinson with Charles Dexter, *Baseball Has Done It* (Philadelphia, 1964); Jules Tygiel, *Baseball's Great Experiment: Jack Robinson and His*

Legacy (New York, 1983); David Quentin Voigt, *American Baseball: From Postwar Recovery to the Electronic Age*, vol. 3 (University Park, PA, 1983).

David Quentin Voigt

ROBINSON, Wilbert "Uncle Robbie" (b. 2 June 1863 or 1864, Hudson, MA; d. 8 August 1934, Atlanta, GA), player, manager, and executive, was the son of butcher Henry and Lucy Robinson and the younger brother of Fred Robinson, who played with Cincinnati (UA) in 1884. "Uncle Robbie," a Falstaffian figure with sound baseball knowledge, attended only the first few grades of the Hudson public school. Robinson's limited education hampered him as a baseball manager. As pilot of the Brooklyn Dodgers (NL) in the 1920s, Robinson removed Oscar Roettger from his lineup because he could not spell his name.

The 5 foot, 8 1/2 inch, 215 pound right-hander began his professional baseball career with Philadelphia (AA) in 1886 and caught with the Athletics until 1890, when he joined the Baltimore Orioles (AA). He stayed with the Orioles when the team moved to the NL the following season. With manager Ned Hanlon's* team, Robinson befriended John McGraw.* In February 1900 the Orioles traded both men to the St. Louis Cardinals (NL). The next year Robinson returned to Baltimore, now in the AL under player-manager McGraw, and played there through the 1902 season. In 1902 he managed Baltimore to a 22–54 record. During the 1903 and 1904 seasons, Robinson caught for Baltimore (EL). A broken hand forced him to retire at age 40.

His impressive National Baseball Hall of Fame (1945) statistics include his batting .273 in 1,374 games, making 1,388 hits, slugging 212 doubles, 51 triples, and 18 home runs, scoring 640 runs, knocking in 621 runs, and stealing 163 bases. He hit at least .300 four times, peaking with .353 in 109 games in 1894. On June 19, 1892, Robinson set a major league record (since tied by Pittsburgh's Rennie Stennett) by making seven hits in seven at bats in a nine-inning game. After working seven years in his father's butcher shop, Robinson joined the New York Giants (NL) as a coach under McGraw. Robinson coached them from 1911 to 1913, but a bitter argument with manager McGraw over a missed sign caused him to join the Brooklyn Dodgers (NL) as manager in 1914.

Robinson managed the Dodgers eighteen seasons, guiding his players to NL pennants in 1916 and 1920 and to a 1,397–1,395 (.500) career mark. Since Robinson was one of the most popular Brooklyn figures ever, the team was renamed the Robins in 1920. Robinson excelled at developing pitching talent but proved a very lax disciplinarian. His players played cards or caroused all night and openly read newspapers on the bench. Robinson hoped to eliminate stupid plays by instituting the "Bonehead Club," but became its first and last member when he posted the wrong lineup card. In 1915 Robinson set the tone for the "Daffy Dodgers" by boasting that he could catch a baseball thrown from a plane. Madcap Casey Stengel* substituted a grapefruit that exploded on impact, causing Robinson to think momentarily that he had been killed.

Robinson served as the president of the Dodgers from 1926 to 1929 and held a similar post with the Atlanta Crackers (SA) from 1933 until his death from a stroke in 1934. He married Mary O'Rourke around 1890 and had four children.

BIBLIOGRAPHY: Gene Karst and Martin J. Jones, Jr., *Who's Who in Professional Baseball* (New York, 1973); Paul MacFarlane, ed., *TSN Daguerreotypes of Great Stars of Baseball* (St. Louis, 1981); *NYT*, August 9, 1934, p. 17; August 10, 1934, p. 22; August 12, 1934, p. 22.

William A. Borst

ROGAN, Wilbur "Bullet Joe" (b. 28 July 1889, Oklahoma City, OK; d. 4 March 1964, Kansas City, MO), player, manager, and umpire, was of Afro-American descent. The 5 foot, 5 inch, 155 pound right-hander became a versatile performer, starring as a hitter and pitcher as did Hall of Famers Martin Dihigo* and Babe Ruth.* Rogan grew up in Kansas City, KS, and began his career there as a catcher for Fred Palace's Colts in 1908. He also performed for the black Kansas City Giants before joining the U.S. Army in the autumn of 1911. Rogan remained in the service through 1919 primarily with units in the Philippines, Honolulu, and the American Southwest, but pitched briefly for the Los Angeles White Sox (CWL) in 1917.

Rogan honed and exhibited his baseball skills in the Army and was recommended to J. L. Wilkinson,* white owner of the Kansas City Monarchs (NNL) by Pittsburgh Pirates outfielder Casey Stengel.* He joined Kansas City in 1920 and remained there through 1938. Long before Don Larsen, Rogan employed a quick no-wind up delivery, his nearly sidearm motion propelling him to the pinnacle then attainable for a black baseball player. Rogan's pitches included a blazing fastball, resulting in his nickname, "Bullet Joe." Available statistics indicate that Rogan compiled 106 regular season wins and 44 losses against top black competition and an 8–3 post-season mark from 1920 through 1930.

Rogan, an excellent hitter, often batted cleanup for powerful Monarchs teams and posted a regular season .340 batting average in the 1920s. His .325 batting mark in the 1924 Negro World Series and .500 and .583 averages in the 1925 and 1926 NNL Championship Series gave him an incredible .410 standard in post-season competition. In 25 games against white major leaguers, Rogan hit .329. During Rogan's tenure, Kansas City claimed NNL titles in 1923, 1924, 1925, and 1929. The Monarchs added the NAL crown in 1937 and split a pair of black World Series with the Philadelphia Hilldale Club in 1924 (won) and 1925 (lost). The 1926 unit, managed by Rogan, captured the NNL first half, but lost the Championship Series to the second half winner and eventual black world champion Chicago American Giants.

Rogan exhibited knowledgeable, capable leadership while captaining Army teams, managed with a military-like manner, and piloted the 1929 champions. He participated in the 1936 East-West (Negro) All-Star Game. Rogan's personal qualities ranged from being easygoing, jolly, quiet, gentlemanly, and free with advice to being arrogant, uncooperative, and demanding of his players. The trim, square-shouldered Rogan possessed slim legs and hips and a soldierly bearing. After retirement from the Monarchs, he umpired NAL games through 1946, worked in the post office, and lived quietly with his wife on their farm by a lake until his death.

BIBLIOGRAPHY: Janet Bruce, *The Kansas City Monarchs: Champions of Black Baseball* (Lawrence, KS, 1985); John Holway, *Bullet Joe and the Monarchs* (Alexandria, VA, 1984).

Merl F. Kleinknecht and John Holway

ROMMEL, Edwin Aloysious "Eddie" (b. 13 September 1897, Baltimore, MD; d. 26 August 1970, Baltimore, MD), player, coach, manager, and umpire, was a son of merchant Frederick Rommel and German-born Louisa Rommel. (Most baseball record books state his middle name as "Americus," but Rommel wrote it as "Aloysious" when completing a questionnaire.) After attending Baltimore Public School No. 94 and playing sandlot baseball, he began professionally in 1916 with a Seaford, DE, independent team. The pitcher entered organized baseball with a 12–15 win-loss record for Newark (IL) in 1918. He participated in spring training in 1919 with the New York Giants (NL) but was returned to Newark, where he compiled an impressive 22–15 mark and pitched a no-hit game. Manager Connie Mack* saw him hurl and bought him for Philadelphia (AL). He pitched for the Athletics from 1920 through 1932, winning 171 games, losing 119 contests, allowing 3.54 earned runs in 2,556 1/3 innings, and playing in two World Series. His best seasons came in 1922 and 1925 with 27–13 ad 21–10 marks, respectively. Rommel led the AL three times in relief victories and twice in games won, games lost, and appearances. He coached for the Athletics in 1933 and 1934 and managed Richmond, VA (Pil) briefly in 1935 before a salary dispute prompted his resignation.

At Newark, Rommel initially specialized with the spitball. When the talkative, 6 foot, 2 inch, 197 pound right-hander realized that the spitter would be banned shortly, he developed a new mainstay. A Baltimore friend showed him how to throw the knuckler. Rommel perfected his delivery of it so well that he is regarded as the first of the great knuckleball pitchers. A better than average hitting pitcher, he batted .199 during his career and became an excellent bunter. Subsequently he umpired in the NYPL in 1936 and the IL in 1937 before the AL purchased his contract. He umpired in the AL for twenty-two years, from 1938 through 1959, during which time he participated in two World Series and six All-Star games and demonstrated fairness and an ability to get along with the players.

The lifetime Baltimore resident married Emma Elizabeth Fahey in September, 1922, and had one son, Edwin A. Jr., and one daughter, Patricia Ruth. Rommel, whose hobbies included golf and bowling, became an outstanding duck pin bowler. After leaving baseball, Rommel in 1959 became an aide to Maryland's Governor Millard Tawes.

BIBLIOGRAPHY: Dan Daniel, "Batters Going Batty from Butterflies," *TSN*, June 12, 1936; *NYT*, August 28, 1970; Joseph L. Reichler, ed., *The Baseball Encyclopedia*, 6th ed. (New York, 1985), p. 2,006; Eddie Rommel file, National Baseball Hall of Fame Library, Cooperstown, NY; *TSN Baseball Register, 1958* (St. Louis, 1958), pp. 308–309; *TSN*, April 25, 1940, February 29, 1956, September 12, 1970, May 22, 1971; United States Census, 1900, Maryland, Baltimore City, Enumeration District 37, Sheet 2.

Frank V. Phelps

ROOT, Charles Henry "Charlie," "Chinski" (b. 17 March 1899, Middletown, OH; d. 5 November 1970, Hollister, CA), player, manager, and coach, was of German descent, grew up in southwestern Ohio and attended grammar school. At age 22, he became a professional baseball player. The 5 foot, 10 1/2 inch, 190 pound right-hander married Dorothy Hartman in May, 1918, and had two children. After pitching for Terre Haute (3IL) in 1922–1923, he compiled an 0–4 record for the St. Louis Browns (AL) in 1923. At Los Angeles (PCL), he enjoyed 20-plus victory seasons in 1924 and 1925 and returned to the major leagues.

From 1926 through 1941, Root pitched for the Chicago Cubs and led the NL once each in total wins (26) in 1927, most games pitched (48) in 1927, winning percentage (.760) in 1929, shutouts (4) in 1930, and relief wins (4) in 1931. In his outstanding single-game achievement, he pitched the NL pennant clincher in 1938 to help the Cubs edge the Pittsburgh Pirates. He ended his career with 201 triumphs, 160 losses, and a .557 percentage and became the only pitcher to win over 200 games as a Cub. In 632 games, he pitched 3,198 1/3 innings, struck out 1,459 batters, hurled 21 shutouts, and compiled a 3.58 ERA.

Unfortunately, Root is chiefly remembered for his World Series catastrophes. In four starts, he lost three times and surrendered seven home runs—all to National Baseball Hall of Fame sluggers. In the 1929 Series, he started the famous fourth game that saw the Philadelphia Athletics rally for a ten-run inning to defeat the Cubs. Moreover, he surrendered Babe Ruth's* fabled "Called Shot" home run on October 1, 1932. Ruth always claimed forecasting the homer, but Root vehemently denied it.

During World War II, Root pitched in the minor leagues at Hollywood

(PCL) from 1942 to 1944 and at Columbus (AA) in 1945. He pitched a few more games at Columbus in 1946 and at Billings, MT (PrL), in 1948. Root managed in the minor leagues at Hollywood (PCL) in 1943 and 1944; Columbus (AA) in 1945 and 1946; Billings (PrL) in 1948; Des Moines (WL) in 1950; and Eau Claire, WI (NoL), in 1954. He coached with Hollywood (PCL, 1949), the Chicago Cubs (1951–1953), and the NL Milwaukee Braves (1956–1957). He died on his ranch near Hollister, CA.

BIBLIOGRAPHY: *NYT*, November 6, 1970; *TSN*, November 21, 1970; October 18, 1982.

Lowell L. Blaisdell

ROSE, Peter Edward "Charlie Hustle" (b. 14 April 1941, Cincinnati, OH), player and manager, is one of four children of bank cashier Harry "Pete" and La Verne (Bloebaum) Rose. His father, an outstanding semi-pro athlete in the Cincinnati area, began encouraging his son at age 3 to participate in sports. Rose became so absorbed in sports that he required an extra year to finish at Western Hills High School. Although he weighed under 150 pounds by graduation in 1960, Rose was offered a football scholarship from Ohio's Miami University. He declined, hoping to play professional baseball, but only the Baltimore Orioles and his hometown Cincinnati Reds (NL) expressed interest in him. Buddy Bloebaum, Rose's uncle and a Reds scout, persuaded the Reds to offer Rose a modest bonus, arguing that men in their family matured late. Phil Seghi, the Reds official who signed him, recalled that Rose demonstrated "purpose and desire and dedication and ambition. . . . He wanted to make it and he made it, but it wasn't easy."

Assigned to Geneva, NY (NYPL), the switch-hitting Rose struggled his first year in organized baseball. Despite batting only .277 and failing to sparkle at second base, he still moved up two notches in the Reds' minor league system. Off-season work lifting crates for the Railway Express Agency in Cincinnati helped Rose mature physically. During his next two minor league seasons, the 5 foot, 11 inch, 190 pound Rose averaged well over .300. In 1963 Rose became the Reds' second sacker. Whitey Ford* nicknamed him "Charley Hustle" upon seeing him run to first base in a spring training camp after drawing a base on balls (a habit Rose had acquired from hearing his father praise the aggressive play of Enos Slaughter*). Rose married Karolyn Ann Englehardt in January 1964 and they had two children, but were divorced in 1980. In April, 1984, he wed Carol Woliung; they have one child.

Although his .273 average earned him NL Rookie of the Year honors in 1963, he still exhibited fielding deficiencies going to his right and making the double play pivot. Rose slumped badly at the plate the first half of the following season and was benched in August. After returning to the starting lineup, he hit well and raised his season's average to .269. Off-season drills and playing Venezuelan winter ball developed Rose into a star. In 1965 he hit over .300 for the first of fifteen seasons. Besides leading the NL with 209 hits, he exhibited good power for a leadoff man with 35 doubles, 11 triples, and 11 home runs. Never more than adequate at second base, Rose in 1967 demonstrated his versatility and team spirit by shifting to the outfield. "If I can make the All Star team as an infielder, I can make it as an outfielder," he correctly declared. As an outfielder in 1968 and 1969, he won consecutive NL batting titles with .335 and .348 averages. His third batting title came in 1973, when he hit .338 and was named the NL's Most Valuable Player.

Although the Reds rarely contended during Rose's first six seasons, stars Tony Perez, Johnny Bench,* and Joe Morgan* joined Rose on a hard-hitting team he dubbed "The Big Red Machine." Rose started for the Reds in the 1970, 1972, 1975, and 1976 World Series at right field, left field, and third base and was selected 1975 World Series MVP. He played first base for the Philadelphia Phillies (NL) in the 1980 and 1983 World Series. *The Sporting News* named him its Player of the Decade for the 1970s.

Rose remains the only player to appear in over 500 games at five different positions (second base, left field, right field, third base, and first base) and made NL All Star at each. Rose, remembered chiefly for his hustle, thrilling head-first slides, and numerous batting records in twenty-four seasons through 1986, played with the Cincinnati Reds (1963–1978, 1984–1986), Philadelphia Phillies (1979–1983), and Montreal Expos (1984) of the NL. He had joined the Phillies as a free agent after the 1978 campaign. He passed the 1,000 hit mark in 1968 and reached 2,000 hits on June 19, 1973, having become the Reds' all-time base hit leader the previous year. On May 5, 1978, he became the thirteenth and youngest player to achieve 3,000 hits. On August 10, 1981, Rose broke Stan Musial's* NL record of 3,630 hits, and in 1982 he climbed past Hank Aaron* into second place behind Ty Cobb.*

Rose's batting average declined from .325 in the strike-shortened 1981 season to .271 in 1982, to a punchless .245 in 1983. He was benched for the first time since his sophomore campaign, leaving doubts about his ability to play regularly for the two or more seasons he needed to pass Cobb. Rose, however, kept in good shape, never smoked, drank only occasionally, and kept his weight at or below 200 pounds. After joining the Montreal Expos as a free agent on January 20, 1984, Rose opened the season in left field, hit well, and made his 4,000th hit against the Phillies on April 13. An injury caused him to sit out several games, after which he returned to the lineup at first base and slumped with his team. Desperate for power, the Expos benched Rose in late July.

Rose took his latest setback with dignity, but barely two weeks later was traded to the Reds to become player-manager of this struggling team. Although the front office emphasized that he would be a manager first and player second, Rose's homecoming electrified the Cincinnati team and city. He played first base in his first three games as manager, pounding out eight hits and leading the team to victory in his debut. The crowds cheered his every move and gave him numerous standing ovations. Thereafter, he played occasionally and concentrated on managing, but still raised his average to .286 by season's end. On September 11, 1985, Rose singled in the first inning off of Eric Show of the San Diego Padres for his 4,192nd hit to break Cobb's longstanding major league mark. In 119 games, Rose batted .264, made 107 hits, and supplied 6 game-winning hits in 1985. Rose's qualities of leadership also made him a successful manager. After piloting the Reds to a 19–22 mark for the remainder of 1984, he guided Cincinnati to an 89–72 record and a surprising second place finish in the Western Division in 1985. *The Sporting News* named Rose Man of the Year for his 1985 achievements. Rose guided the Reds to an 86–76 record and another second place Western Division finish in 1986, but slumped to a career-low .219 batting average and removed his name from the team's 40 man winter roster.

His playing career has been a remarkable one. After the 1986 season, Rose ranked first in major league career totals in games played (3,562), times at bat (14,053), singles (3,217), and hits (4,256), second in doubles (746), fourth in runs scored (2,165), and sixth in total bases (5,754). Ten times (the most recent being 1979), he made over 200 hits in a season, a major league record. In each of his first twenty-three seasons, he made a major league record of at least 100 hits. Rose incredibly made over 1,000 hits after reaching age 38. A lifetime .303 batter, he and Ty Cobb remain the only players to have amassed 4,000 hits. Rose was selected 17 times to the NL All-Star Squad (1965, 1967–1971, 1973–1982, 1985). His own words best summarize his career: "I've been the most consistent player of my generation. There are a lot of players better than me, but I do the same thing day in and day out, year in and year out."

BIBLIOGRAPHY: Si Burick, "200 Grounders a Day!" *Baseball Digest* 24 (July, 1965), pp. 79–80; *CB* (1975), pp. 361–363; Dwight Chapin, "Pete Rose Alias—Charlie Hustle," *Baseball Digest* 28 (May, 1969), pp. 51–52; Cincinnati *Enquirer*, August 18–19, 1984; Cincinnati *Post*, August 17, 1984; Ron Fimrite, "Pete's Out to Prove He Can Pull His Weight," *SI* 60 (February 13, 1984), pp. 42–47; Pete Harmon to author, August 25, 1983, February 22, 1984; Reuben Katz to author, January 14, February 10, 1984; Lexington *Herald*, October 20, 1983, January 20, March 21, April 12, 14, October 1, 6, 1984; Bill Libby, *Pete Rose: They Call Him Charlie Hustle* (New York, 1972); Jack Mann, "Joe Hustle May Bring Flag to the Reds," *SI*, 23 (September 20, 1965), pp. 114–115; *NYT*, June 20, 1973, May 6, 1978, August 11, 1981, June 23, 1982; Pete Rose as told to Dick Kaplan, "Memories of My Dad," *Sport* 51 (April, 1971), pp. 16, 18, 52–53; Pete Rose with Bob Hertzel, *Charlie Hustle* (Englewood Cliffs, NJ, 1975); Jayson Stark, "Pete Rose Is Climbing High on Baseball's Hit List," *Street and Smith's Official Baseball Yearbook* (New York, 1982), pp. 6–10; *TSN*, January 30, 1984, p. 38; *World Series Program* (October 20, 1972), p. 19; Steve Wulf, "For Pete's Sake, Look Who's Back," *SI* 61 (August 27, 1984), pp. 16–22.

Lloyd J. Graybar

ROUSH, Edd J. "Eddie" (b. 8 May 1893, Oakland City, IN), player and coach, is one of twin sons of farmer William C. and Laura (Herrington) Roush and began his baseball career in 1909 as a high school student with the hometown semi-pro Walk-Overs. After two years at Oakland City Baptist College, he turned professional in 1912 with Evansville, IN (KL). He earned a nine-game tryout with the Chicago White Sox (AL) in 1913 and the following year joined Indianapolis of the new FL. With a $225 monthly salary, he considered himself wealthy enough to marry his Oakland City sweetheart, Essie Mae Swallow, on April 27, 1914; he has one child. After the FL collapsed, Roush and leading hitter Benny Kauff were acquired by the New York Giants (NL). John McGraw* mistakenly kept Kauff and included Roush in the July 1916 deal that sent Christy Mathewson* to Cincinnati (NL).

The 5 foot, 11 inch, 190 pound Roush, a remarkably consistent hitter and a nonpareil in center field, soon became Cincinnati's most popular player. The left-handed wrist hitter shifted his stance with the pitch, rarely struck out (once every 33 at bats), and sprayed line drives to all fields. Of these, 29 were inside-the-park home runs. Swinging the NL's heaviest bat (48 ounces), he won the NL batting championship in 1917 (.341) and 1919 (.321), and lost out in 1918 to Zack Wheat* by .002 points (.335 to .333). From 1921 through 1923, his averages varied only a single point: .352, .352, and .351. Twice he led the NL with 27-game hitting streaks. In a June, 1927, doubleheader, he made five singles, one double, and two home runs in 12 at bats. Afield, the left-hander made notable long sprints and circus catches of seemingly sure extra-base hits. "Oh, what a beautiful and graceful outfielder that man was," teammate Rube Bressler reminisced. Many experts considered Roush the equal of Tris Speaker,* although the "Gray Eagle" possessed a better arm.

Roush was traded back to the Giants (NL) in February 1927 for George Kelly* and returned to the Reds (NL) for his final year in 1931. In thirteen of his eighteen seasons, he hit over .300. Roush batted .323 lifetime and hit 182 triples to place seventeenth on the all-time list. Eleven times he hit 10 or more triples and in 1924 led the NL with 21. He also enjoyed eleven seasons with 20 or more doubles, including an NL-leading 41 in 1923. In 1,967 games, he made 2,376 hits, 339 doubles, 182 triples, and 68 home runs, scored 1,099 runs, knocked in 981 runs, and stole 268 bases.

Above all, Roush possessed a strong mind and a keen sense of his own value. He held out frequently for a better contract and to avoid spring training. He considered it foolish to risk injury (or the charley horse, to which he was prone) in meaningless games and always kept in condition. "All that fella has to do," Manager Pat Moran once said, "is wash his hands, adjust his cap, and he's in shape to hit." When his salary terms were not met, however, he stubbornly sat out most of the 1922 season at Cincinnati and all of the 1930 season at New York. After one year (1938) as a Cincinnati coach, he retired to Oakland City, independently wealthy from shrewd investments in blue-chip stocks. In 1962 he was voted into the National Baseball Hall of Fame.

BIBLIOGRAPHY: Lee Allen, *The Cincinnati Reds* (New York, 1948); Lee Allen and Tom Meany, *Kings of the Diamond* (New York, 1965).

David L. Porter

RUFFING, Charles Herbert "Red" (b. 3 May 1905, Granville, IL, d; 17 February 1986, Mayfield, OH), player, manager, coach, and scout, grew up in the coal-mining area of north-central Illinois and was the son of the German-born John and Frances Ruffing. The burly redhead played first base for his father's Nakomis mine team at age 15, when he lost three toes because a mining car ran over his left foot. Unable to run well thereafter, he switched to the mound and became a premier pitcher. He married Pauline Mulholland on October 6, 1934. After starring on local teams, he signed a professional contract in 1923 with Danville, IL (3IL). He won 12 games and lost 16 at Danville and posted a 4–7 record for Dover, DE (ESL), in 1924 before being purchased by the Boston Red Sox (AL). Ruffing appeared in eight games without decision to launch his seventeen-year major league career. The hard-throwing right-hander won 273 games and lost 225 for the Red Sox (1924–1930), AL New York Yankees (1930–1942, 1945–1946), and AL Chicago White Sox (1947). He lost the entire 1943 and 1944 seasons to military service and was released by Chicago on July 16, 1947.

The 6 foot, 2 inch, 210 pound Ruffing hardly seemed destined for the National Baseball Hall of Fame after his six years with Boston. By the 1930 season, he had won just 36 games against 96 losses for a .289 percentage, and had twice lost over 20 games. On May 6, 1930, he was traded to the Yankees (AL) for outfielder Cedric Durst and $50,000. "I was so tickled to death I couldn't wait 'till I got there," Ruffing recalls. Boston had finished last in the AL five consecutive years. In 1930 Ruffing finished with a 15–8 mark. After going 18–7 and leading the AL in strikeouts with 190 in 1932, the fastballer competed in his first World Series. Against the Chicago Cubs, he notched the first of his seven World Series wins and struck out ten batters. From 1936 through 1939, he relied on his fastball and pinpoint control. "Red" won 20, 20, 21, and 21 games these seasons and led the AL with a 21–7 mark and .750 percentage in 1938. From 1937 through 1939, he compiled a 4–0 mark in World Series games.

After winning 14 of 21 games in 1942, the redhead was drafted into the U.S. Army. Upon his return in 1945, he won 7 of 10 decisions. Sparingly used in 1946 because of a broken kneecap, he finished 5–1 before the Yankees released him on September 20. Ruffing signed with the White Sox (AL) primarily as a pinch hitter and completed his career in 1947 with 3 wins and 5 losses. By age 37, Ruffing had earned 258 career wins and had a postwar

15–9 mark. Most experts, along with Ruffing, believe that his military stint cost him a 300-win career. For his career, Ruffing appeared in 624 games, pitched 4,344 innings (over 200 for thirteen consecutive seasons), compiled a 273–225 record (.548), and recorded a 3.80 ERA. He finished with 48 shutouts, twice leading the AL. From 1930 to 1942, he and Lefty Gomez* won 408 games to make the third best righty-lefty duo in history. In ten World Series games, he finished 7–2 (.778) with a 2.63 ERA in 85 2/3 innings.

The competitive Ruffing ranked among the outstanding batters for pitchers, with a lifetime .269 average, 521 hits (third among pitchers), and a season high of .364 in 1930. His 36 lifetime home runs ranked third behind Wes Ferrell* (38) and Bob Lemon* (37). He slugged five homers in 1936, including two on June 7. In 1939 he supplemented his 21 wins with a .307 average. His 58 pinch hits rank second among pitchers, while his 273 RBIs remain unsurpassed.

After his retirement, Ruffing managed in the minor leagues and scouted and coached for the White Sox, Cleveland Indians (AL), and New York Mets (NL). (He served as Casey Stengel's* first pitching coach.) He suffered a stroke in 1973 and was confined to a wheelchair in his Cleveland home thereafter. Bill Dickey,* the Yankees' great catcher, called Ruffing the best pitcher he ever caught. Yankees manager Joe McCarthy* named Ruffing, Gomez, and Spud Chandler* as his best pitchers ever. Ruffing, who made *The Sporting News* Major League All Star teams in 1937, 1938, and 1939, was selected for the National Baseball Hall of Fame in 1967.

BIBLIOGRAPHY: Maury Allen, *Baseball's 100* (New York, 1981); Dave Anderson and Robert Creamer, *The Yankees* (New York, 1979); Daniel Okrent and Harris Lewine, eds., *The Ultimate Baseball Book* (Boston, 1981); Paul Green, "Red Ruffing," *Sports Collectors Digest* 11 (September 28, 1984), pp. 114–126; Lowell Reidenbaugh, *Cooperstown: Where Baseball's Legends Live Forever* (St. Louis, 1983).

Douglas G. Simpson

RUNNELS, James Edward "Pete" (b. 28 January 1928, Lufkin, TX), player and manager, is the son of Pete Runnels and played semi-professional baseball before graduating from high school. After enlisting in the U.S. Marine Corps, the 6 foot, 170 pound Runnels played third base for the San Diego Naval Air Station until discharged in 1948. Runnels, who married Betty Ruth Hinton on October 29, 1949, entered Rice Institute in 1948, but joined the St. Louis Cardinals (NL) for their 1949 spring training camp. The Cardinals assigned him to Albany, GA (GFL), and Winston-Salem (CrL). Runnels, who threw right-handed and batted left-handed, left the Cardinals organization and signed with Chickasha, OK (SSL), in 1949, leading the circuit with a .372 batting average. The following year, he batted .330 with Texarkana (BStL). The Washington Senators (AL) purchased Runnels and sent him to Chattanooga (SA), where he batted .356 in 1951.

A line drive hitter, Runnels played with the Washington Senators from midseason of 1951 through 1957, Boston Red Sox (AL) between 1958 and 1962, and Houston Astros (NL) in 1963 and 1964. He performed at virtually every infield position, playing over 600 games at both first base and second base and over 400 contests at shortstop. In 1958 he batted .322 with 183 hits and finished runner-up in the batting race to teammate Ted Williams,* whom Runnels credited for making him a consistent .300 hitter. After batting .314 in 1959, he topped the AL the next year with a .320 mark and hit .317 in 1961. His best season came in 1962, when he regained the batting crown with a .326 average and made 183 hits. An outstanding defensive infielder, Runnels paced all AL second baseman in fielding in 1960 and performed the same feat at first base the next year. On June 23, 1957, he tied an AL record by starting three double plays in a game at third base.

In fourteen major league seasons, Runnels hit .291 in 1,799 games with 1,854 hits, 876 runs scored, 283 doubles, 64 triples, 49 home runs, 630 RBIs, and 37 stolen bases. Besides batting above .300 and hitting at least 20 doubles six times, he tied a major league mark with nine hits in a doubleheader on August 30, 1960. Runnels played in the 1959, 1960, and 1962 All-Star games for the AL squad, becoming the first player to execute an unassisted double play in the summer classic and slugging a pinch hit home run in the 1962 contest. In 1966 he guided the Boston Red Sox to an 8–8 mark as interim manager. Following his retirement from baseball, Runnels returned with his wife and children to Texas and became co-director of a children's camp and co-owner of a sporting goods store in Pasadena. Runnels was elected in 1982 to the Texas Sports Hall of Fame and three years later to the Texas Baseball Hall of Fame.

BIBLIOGRAPHY: Paul Green, "SCD Interviews Pete Runnels," *Sports Collectors Digest* 12 (August 16, 1985), pp. 112–113, 117, 120–134; Al Hirshberg, "Secrets of a Batting Champion," *SEP* 234 (April 22, 1961), pp. 30, 113–114; Gene Karst and Martin J. Jones, Jr., *Who's Who in Professional Baseball* (New Rochelle, NY, 1973); Joseph L. Reichler, ed., *The Baseball Encyclopedia*, 6th ed. (New York, 1985), p. 1,353.

John L. Evers

RUPPERT, Jacob, Jr., "Colonel" (b. 5 August 1867, New York, NY; d. 13 January 1939, New York, NY), executive, was the son of brewery owner Jacob and Anna (Gillig) Ruppert. His father founded the Ruppert Brewery in 1867 and built it into a successful enterprise. The younger Ruppert graduated from Columbia Grammar School and was accepted at the Columbia School of Mines, but never attended there. After entering the family business at age 19, Ruppert became general superintendent four years later. He assumed the brewery presidency upon his father's death in 1915 and invested heavily and successfully in real estate. Ruppert's wealth placed him in the highest New York City social circles, in which he moved with ease. Although he never married, the outgoing Ruppert entertained often and continually was seen in the company of women. Ruppert also pursued politics. A colonel with the Seventh Regiment of the New York National Guard, he served as an aide-de-camp on the staff of New York Governor David B. Hill. Ruppert carried the designation "Colonel" as his preferred title to his death. After leaving the governor's staff, the Democrat represented New York City's fifteenth district in the U.S. Congress for four terms from 1899 to 1907.

Ruppert followed baseball closely since boyhood. Upon the advice of John McGraw,* he and Tillinghast Huston purchased the New York Americans (AL) in 1914 for $450,000. In 1918 Ruppert lured Miller Huggins* from the St. Louis Cardinals (NL) to manage the newly named Yankees. The following year, Ruppert and Huston bought Babe Ruth* from the Boston Red Sox (AL) for $100,000 and a $350,000 loan secured by the mortgage on Fenway Park. Ed Barrow,* who was hired as general manager in 1920, assembled the Yankees dynasties of the next two decades. Ruppert operated the Yankees from a distance, letting Huggins and Barrow conduct daily operations. The famous Yankee pinstripes were designed by Ruppert, who thought they made the bulky Ruth look slimmer. During Ruppert's reign, the Yankees introduced uniform numbers corresponding to the player's slot in the batting order. In 1919 Red Sox pitcher Carl Mays* jumped to his club. After Red Sox owner Harry Frazee sold Mays' contract to the Yankees, AL president Ban Johnson* voided the sale and suspended Mays. Ruppert secured a court injunction against Johnson's action and was joined by other rebellious AL owners. One year later, new baseball commissioner Judge Kenesaw Mountain Landis* assumed Johnson's power.

In 1919 Ruppert bought a plot of land directly across the Harlem River from the Polo Grounds for $600,000. Yankee Stadium was built there in 1922 and opened for play the next year. Yankee Stadium, which became "The House that Ruth Filled," was built by Ruppert and Huston for $2,500,000 and held 62,000 spectators. Ruppert contracted phlebitis in April, 1938, and died nine months later in his New York City apartment. One of his last visitors was Babe Ruth.

BIBLIOGRAPHY: *Biographical Dictionary of the American Congress* (Washington, DC, 1961), p. 1,549; Robert Creamer, *Babe* (New York, 1974); *DAB*, Suppl. 2, p. 589–590; *National Cyclopedia of American Biography*, vol. 29 (New York, 1941), p. 489.

                                                                      Robert E. Jones

RUSIE, Amos Wilson "The Hoosier Thunderbolt" (b. 30 or 31 May 1871, Mooresville [Moores Hill], IN; d. 6 December 1942, Seattle, WA), player, excelled as a right-handed pitcher and married May Smith in 1890. His wife predeceased by two months, leaving one daughter, Mrs. C. E. Spalding. Rusie generally was considered the best NL pitcher from 1891 through 1899, being ranked even better than Cy Young.* Nicknamed "The

Hoosier Thunderbolt," he resembled Walter Johnson* by throwing a blinding fastball. Manager Connie Mack,* who saw the major fastball hurlers through Bob Feller,* and John McGraw* both labeled Rusie the fastest moundsman ever. New York catcher Richard Buckley admitted adding lead wrapped in a handkerchief and a sponge when handling Rusie's pitches. The 6 foot, 1 inch, 210 pounder, however, considered the outdrop his favorite pitch. Elected to the National Baseball Hall of Fame in 1977, he remarkably finished all but 35 of his 427 starts.

Rusie quit Indianapolis public schools early to work in a factory and played outfield for an Indianapolis city league team. Rusie joined his hometown Indianapolis (NL) team in 1889 and accompanied the club when the franchise shifted the next season to New York. He became the ace of the New York (NL) staff with 94 wins over the next three years. His walks (289, 262, and 267) and strikeouts (345, 337, and 303) usually paced the NL from 1890 through 1892. He pitched New York's first no-hitter on July 31, 1891, against Brooklyn and led the NL in shutouts (6) that year. The pitching mound was moved from 50 feet to 60 feet, 6 inches from home plate partly because of Rusie. He set several single-season marks in 1893 by starting 52 games, completing 50 contests, pitching 482 innings, and walking 218 batters. Rusie also led the NL in hits surrendered (451), strikeouts (208), and shutouts (4). He beaned Hughie Jennings,* who was feared dead, and was hit by a line drive leaving him partially deaf.

In 1894 he led New York to the NL championship by winning 36 contests, including 26 of his last 30 decisions, and two Temple Cup games. Rusie paced the NL in victories, ERA (2.78), games started (50), walks (200), strikeouts (195), and shutouts (3). Rusie's win total dropped to 22 in 1895, but he still topped the NL in strikeouts (201) and shutouts (4). New York fined Rusie $200 for breaking training rules, a claim the latter vigorously denied. When New York asked Rusie to accept a $600 pay cut, the hurler sat out the 1896 season and then sued the Giants for $5,000 in damages and his release. The other owners raised the $5,000 to settle out of court, keeping the reserve clause intact.

In 1897 Rusie won 29 games for New York and led the NL with a 2.54 ERA. During a creditable 20-victory 1898 season, he hurt his arm picking Chicago's William Lange* off first base. Rusie remained out of baseball two years, during which time he drank heavily. Before the 1901 season, the Giants traded Rusie to Cincinnati (NL) for rights to Christy Mathewson.* Rusie's arm injury and heavy drinking aborted his attempted comeback with Cincinnati in 1901. He then retired, having won at least 20 games each of his eight seasons with the Giants and setting the record for most walks allowed (1,716). The latter record stood until after World War II. Overall, Rusie won 243, lost 160, completed 392 of 427 starts, struck out 1,957 batters in 3,769.2 innings, hurled 30 shutouts, and compiled a 3.07 ERA.

Rusie worked in a Muncie, IN, paper and pulp mill for three years, engaged in fresh water pearling in Vincennes, IN, and held a steamfitting job in Seattle from 1911 to 1921. John McGraw hired him as superintendent of the Polo Grounds in New York in 1921 and kept him there through the 1928 season. In 1929 Rusie moved to Seattle for health reasons and opened a small chicken ranch in Auburn. He lived in Seattle until his death.

BIBLIOGRAPHY: Paul McFarlane, ed., *TSN Daguerreotypes of Great Stars of Baseball* (St. Louis, 1981); New York *Herald Tribune*, December 8, 1942; Joseph L. Reichler, ed., *The Baseball Encyclopedia*, 6th ed. (New York, 1985), pp. 1,353, 2,012; Lowell Reidenbaugh, *Cooperstown: Where Baseball's Legends Live Forever* (St. Louis, 1983); Seattle *Sunday Times*, June 9, 1929, p. 5; *TSN*, December 28, 1939.

David B. Merrell

RUTH, George Herman, Jr., "Babe," "The Sultan of Swat," "The Bambino") (b. 6 February 1895, Baltimore, MD; d. 16 August 1948, New York, NY), player and coach, became the most celebrated baseball player and perhaps America's leading all-time sports hero. Ruth was the son of saloonkeeper George Herman and Katherine (Shamborg) Ruth. Frustrated by young George's incorrigible behavior, his parents committed him at age 7 to St. Mary's Industrial School for Boys. Ruth learned sports and a trade there. By 1914 Ruth's remarkable prowess as a left-handed pitcher prompted Jack Dunn, owner of the Baltimore Orioles (IL), to adopt and sign him. With the Orioles, he received the nickname "Babe." After being sold in 1914 to Boston (AL), he helped the Red Sox win the 1915 and 1916 world championships. During six seasons with the Red Sox, Ruth compiled a brilliant 89–46 won-lost pitching record and set a record for scoreless innings pitched in World Series play. In 163 games, he completed 107 of 148 starts, struck out 488 batters, pitched 17 shutouts, and compiled a 2.28 ERA. Ruth's slugging prowess, however, persuaded manager Ed Barrow* to assign him to outfield duty. In 1919 the 6 foot, 2 inch, 215 pound left-hander set a major league record with 29 home runs, ushering in a long-distance hitting style still prevalent in major league offenses.

Baseball fans were electrified in 1920 when the Red Sox sold Ruth to the New York Yankees (AL) for $125,000 and a $300,000 loan. Since the amount set a record, the sale enhanced the fame of both Ruth and the Yankees. From 1920 until his release in 1934, the New York media treated Ruth as a national celebrity. The Yankees superstar led the Yankees to seven AL pennants (1921–1923, 1926–1928, 1932) and four World Series titles. The AL's home run king twelve times, Ruth belted 60 homers in 1927 to set an all-time record for a 154-game season. His 714 career round trippers were unsurpassed until 1974. Since Ruth also compiled a lifetime .342 batting average, many experts rated him the sport's best offensive player. In 2,503 games, he made 2,873 hits, 506 doubles, and 136 triples, scored 2,174 runs, knocked in 2,211 runs, walked 2,056 times, and compiled a .690 slugging average. His fielding and earlier pitching success made him perhaps the sport's most versatile player.

Ruth became the most highly touted player ever. Besides having vast popularity, he earned enormous annual salaries and large endorsement incomes. Ruth was paid $80,000 for the 1930 season and reportedly received $2 million during his twenty-two-year major league career. Although he spent much in high living, prudent advice from investment counsellors enabled him to live comfortably in retirement. Ruth's lofty salaries helped raise earnings of other stars. As baseball's leading celebrity, Ruth christened newly built Yankee Stadium in April 1923, by blasting a homer on the day it opened. The structure was soon dubbed "the house that Ruth built." As "the Babe," "the Sultan of Swat," and "the Bambino," he became the most photographed and heralded hero of his day. Like his homeric feats, his misdeeds and off-the-field promotions and excesses only enhanced his image.

When Ruth retired in 1935, his undisciplined reputation kept him from being selected a manager. After leaving the Yankees, he played briefly in 1935 for the Boston Braves (NL) and also coached for the Brooklyn Dodgers (NL) in 1938. For the remainder of his life he remained popular with baseball fans. In 1936 he was voted a charter member of the newly established National Baseball Hall of Fame. His popular mystique made him the stuff of enduring legends. In 1946 Ruth headed the Ford Motor Company's junior baseball program. In 1969 a panel of sportswriters named him the most famous figure in American sports history. He also was named the greatest baseball figure of the first half of the twentieth century. Ruth died of cancer in 1948 in New York City. The nation mourned his passing, as 100,000 people viewed his bier as it rested in the rotunda of Yankee Stadium. Twice married (to waitress Helen Woodford, who died in 1929, and then to actress-model Claire Merritt Hodgson in 1929), Ruth raised two adopted daughters.

BIBLIOGRAPHY: Bob Considine, *The Babe Ruth Story* (New York, 1948); Robert W. Creamer, *Babe: The Legend Comes to Life* (New York, 1974); Frank Graham, *The New York Yankees* (New York, 1943); Waite Hoyt, *Babe Ruth as I Knew Him* (New York, 1948); Louis J. Leisman, *I Was with Babe Ruth at St. Mary's* (Baltimore, 1956); Tom Meany, *Babe Ruth: Big Moments of the Big Fella* (New York, 1947); Claire M. Ruth with Bill Slocum, *The Babe and I* (New York, 1959); Marshall Smelser, *The Life that Ruth Built* (New York, 1975); Ken Sobol, *Babe Ruth and the American Dream* (New York, 1974); David Quentin Voigt, *American Baseball: From the Commissioners to Continental Expansion*, vol. 2 (University Park, PA, 1983); Christy Walsh, *Adios to Ghosts* (New York, 1937); Martin Weldon, *Babe Ruth* (New York, 1948).

David Quentin Voigt

RYAN, James E. "Jimmy" (b. 11 February 1863, Clinton, MA; d. 26 October 1923, Chicago, IL), player and manager, attended Holy Cross College and joined Bridgeport, CT (EL), in 1885 as a left-handed throwing baseball shortstop and outfielder. Ryan, who batted right-handed, joined the

Chicago White Stockings (NL) late that season. He became manager Cap Anson's* regular right fielder in 1886, hitting .306 in 84 games and helping Chicago win its second straight NL pennant. When Chicago lost a post-season "World Series" to the St. Louis Browns (AA), disappointed owner Albert G. Spalding* sold several front-line players, including Michael "King" Kelly,* pitcher Jim McCormick,* and outfielders Abner Dalrymple and George Gore.

The fleet-footed, 5 foot, 9 inch, 162 pound Ryan was moved to center field, where he starred for the next three seasons (1887–1889) by averaging 189 hits, 124 runs, and over 50 stolen bases per season. In 1888 he led the NL in hits (182), doubles (33), homers (16), and total bases (283) and finished second to Anson in batting (.332). Ryan jumped to Charles Comiskey's* Chicago entry in the short-lived PL in 1890, but returned as the White Stockings' center fielder in 1891. He remained in the Chicago outfield for the next decade, switching from center field to the right field to make room for promising newcomer Bill Lange* in 1894 and then moving to left field in 1898. Ryan hit over .300 in six consecutive seasons (1894–1899), including a career-high .360 in 1894.

When Ryan slumped to a .277 batting average in 1900, Chicago released him. The following season he signed with St. Paul (WL), where he hit .323 in 108 games as a player-manager. He returned to the majors for the 1902–1903 seasons as an outfielder for Washington (AL) and finished his pro base-ball career managing Chicago Springs (WL) in 1904. Ryan stayed in Chicago, where he worked many years in the assessor's office and later as a deputy in the sheriff's office. He also managed the Rogers Parks, an amateur baseball club on Chicago's near north side, and played on the team until he was 51 years old. Ryan died suddenly of heart failure at his Chicago home in 1923.

In eighteen seasons, Ryan appeared in 2,012 major league games, collected 2,529 hits, made 451 doubles, 157 triples, and 118 home runs, scored 1,643 runs, knocked in 1,093 runs, and compiled a .309 batting average. Although best known for his outfield play, he occasionally played the infield and compiled a lifetime 6–1 mark as a pitcher in 24 games. Ryan made five hits in one game on five separate occasions and four extra-base hits in a game twice. He batted for the cycle two times (in 1888 and 1891) and scored six runs in a July 1894 game. He batted first throughout most of his career and led off 22 games with home runs, third best on the all-time list.

BIBLIOGRAPHY: Warren Brown, *The Chicago Cubs* (New York, 1946); Chicago *Daily Tribune*, October 30, 1923; Paul MacFarlane, ed., *TSN Daguerreotypes of Great Stars of Baseball* (St. Louis, 1981); Joseph L. Reichler, *The Great All-Time Baseball Record Book* (New York, 1981); Joseph L. Reichler, ed., *The Baseball Encyclopedia*, 6th ed. (New York, 1985), p. 1,356; David Quentin Voigt, *American Baseball*, vol. 1 (Norman, OK, 1966).

Raymond D. Kush

RYAN, Lynn Nolan (b. 31 January 1947, Refugio, TX), player, is the son of oil field supervisor Lynn Nolan and Mary (Haneal) Ryan. Ryan grew up in the small town of Alvin, TX, where he idolized Sandy Koufax.* A star right-handed pitcher at Alvin High School, he appeared in 24 of the team's 36 games during his senior year. He attended Alvin Junior College (1966–1969), married childhood sweetheart Ruth Elise Holdruff on June 26, 1967, and has one son, Reid.

An eighth round selection by the New York Mets (NL) in 1965, Ryan pitched in the minors for Marion, SC (ApL), in 1965; Greenville, NC (WCL) and Williamsport, PA (EL), in 1966; and Winter Haven, FL (FSL), and Jacksonville, FL (IL), in 1967. He reached the major leagues to stay in 1968 with a record-setting fastball, a devastating curve, and, in his own words, without "the slightest idea where the ball was going." Ryan's wildness led the Mets to trade him to the California Angels (AL) for infielder Jim Fregosi after the 1971 season. With the Angels from 1972 to 1979 and Houston Astros (NL) after becoming a free agent in 1980, the handsome 6 foot, 2 inch, 190 pound Ryan emerged as the premier power pitcher in a period boasting eight of baseball's ten all-time leading strikeout pitchers. Ryan reached a new plateau against the New York Mets on July 11, 1985, when he became the first pitcher ever to record 4,000 lifetime strikeouts. He struck out Danny Heep of New York on three pitches at the start of the sixth inning to break the 4,000 barrier.

Ryan, the only pitcher to have three straight seasons with at least 300 or more strikeouts (1972–1974), remains the only hurler to have pitched five no-hit games (against the Kansas City Royals [AL] and Detroit Tigers [AL] in 1973, Minnesota Twins [AL] in 1974, Baltimore Orioles [AL] in 1975, and Los Angeles Dodgers [NL] in 1981). Through 1986 he also had established major league marks for the most games with 15 or more strikeouts (19) and 10 or more strikeouts (162), and most seasons with 300 or more strikeouts (5). He holds the AL record for the most seasons with 200 or more strikeouts (7). On the negative side, he set the major league record for the most walks (2,268 through 1986) and prompted observers to suggest that he probably had thrown more pitches than any hurler in the game's long history. Ryan led the AL in strikeouts seven times (1972–1974 and 1976–1979) and in walks six times (1972–1974 and 1976–1978). He topped the NL in ERA in 1981 and in walks twice (1980 and 1982). The fascination with Ryan's numbers was perhaps underscored best by the numerous attempts to clock the speed of his fastball (at least 100.9 miles per hour), despite considerable evidence that his sharp-breaking curveball produced many of his strikeouts. Ryan was selected for the AL All-Star team in 1972, 1973, 1975, and 1979, and for the NL All-Star team in 1981 and 1985.

Ryan's records failed to evoke universal praise because critics stressed his .528 won-lost percentage and paucity of 20-victory seasons (1973 and 1974) and questioned whether he was more show than substance. Ryan expressed his own disappointment that, despite being a key figure in three division championships (California, 1979, and Houston, 1980, 1986), his only World Series experience had come early in his career with New York in 1969. Through 1986, Ryan had won 253, lost 226, struck out 4,277 and walked 2,268 batters in 4,115 1/3 innings, and compiled a 3.15 ERA.

BIBLIOGRAPHY: Ron Fimrite, "Bringer of the Big Heat," *SI* 42 (June 16, 1975), pp. 32–33; Ron Fimrite, "Speed Trap for an Angel," *SI* 41 (September 16, 1974), pp. 98ff; William Leggett, "Angel Who Makes the Turnstiles Sing," *SI* 38 (May 14, 1973), pp. 26–27; 32–33; Nolan Ryan with Steve Jacobsen, *Nolan Ryan Strikeout King* (New York, 1975); Nolan Ryan with Bill Libby, *Nolan Ryan: The Other Game* (New York, 1977); Nolan Ryan with Joe Torre, *Pitching and Hitting* (New York, 1977); "Ryan Records Special K," *TSN*, July 22, 1985, p. 6; *TSN Baseball Register 1985*, (St. Louis, 1985), pp. 428–429; "Throwing Smoke," *Time* 105 (June 2, 1975), pp. 37–38.

James W. Harper

S

SANTO, Ronald Edward "Ron" (b. 25 February 1940, Seattle, WA), player, is of Italian-Swedish descent, graduated from high school in Seattle, and starred in baseball in secondary school. He married Judy Lynn Scott in January, 1960, and has two sons. The 6 foot, 190 pound right-hander possessed an excellent build for a third baseman. After entering professional baseball at age 19, Santo spent the 1959 season at San Antonio (TL). Santo began 1960 at Houson (AA), but joined the Chicago Cubs (NL) in late June. He spent fourteen seasons with the Cubs and played more games at third base than any other Bruin. By a wide margin, he became the team's hardest-hitting third baseman.

During his career, Santo tied for the NL lead in triples once (13 in 1964) and led in bases on balls four times (1964, 1966–1968). Repeatedly he ranked among the first five in RBIs, home runs, total bases, and slugging average. Defensively, he led NL third basemen seven consecutive seasons in assists, eight times in total chances, six times in double plays, twice in games played, and once in fielding percentage. Santo ranks ninth lifetime in assists and tenth in single-season assists. Besides standing third in career games (2,130) and assists (4,581) at the hot corner, he ranks second in lifetime total chances (6,853), and fourth in double plays (395). Santo batted .285 in seven All-Star games and compiled a .277 lifetime batting average. In 2,243 games, he made 2,254 hits, 365 doubles, 67 triples, and 342 home runs, scored 1,138 runs, knocked in 1,331 runs, walked 1,108 times, and stole 35 bases. During Santo's career, the Cubs came close to winning the championship only in 1969 and 1970 and never played in a World Series. In 1974 Santo moved crosstown to the Chicago White Sox (AL) and played one season there. In retirement, he has prospered as an executive in the oil business.

BIBLIOGRAPHY: Leo Durocher, *Nice Guys Finish Last* (New York, 1975); Jim Langford, *The Game Is Never Over* (South Bend, IN, 1980); *TSN*, November 8, 1961, January 16, 1965, December 13, 1974.

Lowell L. Blaisdell

SANTOP, Louis Loftin "Top," "Big Bertha" (b. Louis Loftin, 17 January 1890, Tyler, TX; d. 6 January 1942, Philadelphia, PA), player, batted left-handed and became the first of the great Negro league sluggers. Nicknamed "Big Bertha" after the monstrous German siege gun of World War I, the gigantic 6 foot, 5 inch catcher, who weighed 245 pounds, switched his last name to Santop for baseball games. After beginning professionally in 1909 with the Fort Worth Wonders, he played the following year with Sol White's Philadelphia Giants and teamed with husky rookie "Cannonball Dick" Redding* to form the famous kid battery. From 1911 through 1914, Santop caught for the powerful New York Lincoln Giants and combined with "Smoky Joe" Williams* to form one of the all-time greatest batteries. Redding later joined the Lincolns, giving Santop two premier fastball pitchers to handle.

He performed through 1926 for several teams, including the Brooklyn Royal Giants, Chicago American Giants, New York Lincoln Stars, and Philadelphia Hilldale Club, and served in the U.S. Navy in 1918 and 1919. From 1922 to 1926, he played exclusively for Ed Bolden's Hilldale Club (ECL) and then left black baseball. During his career, he caught in black World Series in 1915 for the New York Lincoln Stars and in 1921, 1924, and 1925 for the Hilldales. Philadelphia defeated the Chicago American Giants for the 1921 title and the Kansas City Monarchs in the 1925 classic, while the 1915 set ended in a draw between the Stars and American Giants. Santop's best series came in a losing effort in 1924, when he batted .333 in nine games versus the Monarchs.

The gruff-voiced Santop often boasted to opposing pitchers about how far he would belt their deliveries and occasionally predicted his home runs. In 1912 he hit one ball over a 485 foot fence in Elizabeth, NJ, in the dead ball era. At Philadelphia's Shibe Park on October 12, 1920, Babe Ruth* led a semi-pro team against the Hilldales. Santop outperformed Ruth with a double and two singles in four at bats against Carl Mays* of the New York Yankees and Slim Harriss of the Philadelphia A's. Ruth made no hits in three official at bats and walked once, as the Hilldales won 5–0.

Although best remembered for his power, Santop consistently batted for high averages. He proved a durable, strong-armed catcher, occasionally played the outfield, and once caught a doubleheader with a broken thumb. His widow, Mrs. Eunice Taylor, described Santop as fiery and added, "But if you didn't rub his fur the wrong way, he was a lovely person." Santop's fine talent and showboat tendencies made him a top crowd drawer and earned him a salary of around $450–$500 a month in his prime.

BIBLIOGRAPHY: John B. Holway, "The Big Bertha: Louis Santop," John Holway Collection, Alexandria, VA; Robert W. Peterson, *Only the Ball Was White* (Englewood Cliffs, NJ, 1970).

John B. Holway and Merl F. Kleinknecht

SCHALK, Raymond William "Ray," "Cracker" (b. 12 August 1892, Harvel, IL; d. 19 May 1970, Chicago, IL), player, manager, and scout, was a durable catcher with the Chicago White Sox (AL) for seventeen years. Despite his slender 5 foot, 9 inch, 155 pound frame, Schalk caught at least 100 games for twelve seasons, including eleven in succession. Schalk started playing baseball when invited to catch for his Litchfield, IL, town team. Before joining the White Sox in 1912 he played professionally at Taylorville, IL (IML), in 1911 and Milwaukee (AA) in 1911 and 1912. He never attained a .300 season and hit only 12 home runs before ending his eighteen-year major league career in 1929 with the New York Giants (NL). Exceptional defensively, Schalk became one of the game's all-time best catchers and compiled numerous records. He holds major league catching standards for most years leading in fielding (8) and putouts (9), most double plays (221), and most assists in one league (1,811). Schalk tied major league marks by making three assists in one inning and leading in chances accepted the most years (8). His records included being the only catcher to handle four no-hit games: those by Jim Scott and Joe Benz in 1914, Ed Cicotte* in 1917, and Charley Robertson (perfect game) in 1922.

Besides being credited as the first receiver to back up plays at first and third base, Schalk even made putouts at second base. He played on Chicago's 1917 world championship team and on the 1919 squad in the "Black Sox Series," but was not involved in the scandal. Schalk batted .286 in 14 World Series games. Behind the plate in 1,726 games (5th on the all-time list), Schalk played in 1,760 games, collected 1,345 hits, scored 579 runs, drove in 594 runs, and compiled a .253 batting average.

Schalk managed the White Sox to fifth place in 1927 but was fired when Chicago faltered the next year. As a major league mentor, he compiled a 102–125 mark. He managed minor league teams in Buffalo (IL) from 1932 to 1937 and in 1950, Indianapolis (AA) from 1938 to 1939, and Milwaukee (AA) in 1940. His Buffalo teams won the IL playoffs in 1933 and 1936. Schalk, who later scouted for the Chicago Cubs (NL), operated a bowling establishment in Chicago, served as an assistant baseball coach for eighteen years at Purdue University, and directed the baseball program for Mayor Richard Daley's Chicago Youth Foundation. He married Lavina Graham on October 25, 1916, had at least one daughter, Mrs. Pauline Brinxon, and in 1955 was elected to the National Baseball Hall of Fame.

BIBLIOGRAPHY: Lowell Reidenbaugh, *Cooperstown: Where Baseball's Legends Live Forever* (St. Louis, 1983); *TSN*, June 6, 1970, p. 44; Paul MacFarlane, ed., *TSN Daguerreotypes of Great Stars of Baseball* (St. Louis, 1971).

John L. Evers

SCHMIDT, Michael Jack "Mike" (b. 27 September 1949, Dayton, OH), player, became the greatest power hitter in Philadelphia Phillies (NL) history. The only son of Jack and Lois Schmidt, managers of a restaurant at a popular Dayton swim club, he has one sister, Sally. After graduating from Fairview High School in Dayton in 1967, Schmidt won a baseball scholarship to Ohio University. After a sluggish start, Schmidt eventually established Ohio University single-season hitting records for runs scored (45), home runs (10), and walks (38) and was named College All-American his senior year. After graduating in 1971 with a Bachelor of Arts degree in business administration, he was selected in the second round of the free agent draft by Phillies scout Tony Lucadello. At Reading, PA (EL), he batted only .211 with 8 home runs and 31 RBIs in 1971. An excellent 1972 season followed with Eugene, OR (PCL), where Schmidt hit .291 with 26 home runs and 91 RBIs. Following promotion to the Phillies (NL) in September, 1972, he shared third base with Cesar Tovar in 1973 and experienced a frustrating year. He showed signs of defensive brilliance and power (18 home runs), but struck out 136 times and hit only .196.

The 6 foot, 2 inch, 200 pound right-hander blossomed in 1974 and won three consecutive home run titles (36, 38, 38). Altogether, he led the NL in homers for eight seasons (1974–1976, 1980–1981, 1983–1984, 1986), breaking Ralph Kiner's* record. Schmidt also paced the NL five times in slugging average, four times in RBIs, walks, and strikeouts, and once in runs scored. Schmidt's 495 career home runs through 1985 rank him second among active players behind Reggie Jackson* and first among National Leaguers. He surpassed Eddie Mathews* (481) for most career home runs by a third baseman. Schmidt hit 48 HRs in 1980, the most in major league history by a third baseman. Schmidt's defensive brilliance earned him ten Gold Gloves, second among third basemen to Brooks Robinson.* Through 1986, he had made 2,257 putouts, 4,342 assists, and 280 errors for .959 percentage. Schmidt slugged four home runs in a game against the Chicago Cubs in April 1976, the first in the NL to accomplish that dramatic feat since Willie Mays* in 1965.

Schmidt, the NL Most Valuable Player Award winner in 1980, 1981, and 1986, led the Phillies to the 1980 World Series title over the Kansas City Royals and captured the World Series MVP Award. In 1983 he helped lead Philadelphia to the World Series, but managed only one hit as the Baltimore Orioles won the title. Along with 495 home runs, Schmidt has 1,392 RBIs and a .268 lifetime batting mark. He has hit a homer an average of nearly 7 percent of his times at bat to stand fifth on the all-time list and ranks fourteenth on the all-time home run list. Schmidt made the NL All-Star team in 1974, 1976–1977, 1979–1984, and 1986 and holds most Phillies slugging records, including being first in round trippers, walks, extra-base hits, total bases, and strikeouts, and second in RBIs. Schmidt lives in suburban Philadelphia with his wife, Donna, and two children, Jessica and Jonathan. During the off-season, he participates in the Philadelphia Child Guidance Clinic and various other charitable enterprises. His hobbies include collecting toy trains and golf. During the 1986 season, Schmidt surpassed Stan Musial,* Willie Stargell* and Lou Gehrig* on the all-time home run list.

BIBLIOGRAPHY: Stan Baumgartner and Frederick G. Lieb, *The Philadelphia Phillies* (Philadelphia, 1953); Jim Wright, *Mike Schmidt* (New York, 1979).

John P. Rossi

SCHOENDIENST, Albert Fred "Red" (b. 2 February 1923, Germantown, IL), player, coach, and manager, is one of seven children of Joseph and Mary Schoendienst. His father, a coal miner and farmer, played semi-pro baseball. Nicknamed "Red" because of his freckles and fiery hair, Schoedienst left New Baden School at age 14, worked at odd jobs, and in 1939 joined the Civilian Conservation Corps. After a staple became embedded in his left eye, he started switch-hitting to favor his bad eye. He was employed as a civilian clerk at Scott Air Force Base when St. Louis Cardinals (NL) scout Joe Mathes signed him. After playing for Union City, TN (KL), and Albany, GA (GFL), in 1942, he hit .337 for Rochester, NY, in 1943 and was named the IL's Most Valuable Player.

The 6 foot, 170 pound Schoendienst played the outfield for the St. Louis Cardinals (NL) in 1945 but switched to second base the next season. For many years, he formed a great hitting tandem with roommate and close friend Stan Musial.* In the 1950 All-Star Game, he slugged the game-winning home run off Ted Gray of the Detroit Tigers in the fourteenth inning. Schoendienst was elected to ten All-Star teams and five of *The Sporting News* starting teams. He was traded to the New York Giants (NL) in a multi-player deal in June 1956 and the next year to the Milwaukee Braves (NL) for Ray Crone, Bobby Thomson, and Danny O'Connell. He spent the 1959 season mostly on the disabled list, as his right lung was removed. After the Braves released him in 1960, he spent the next three seasons with the St. Louis Cardinals as a player-coach and made 22 pinch hits in 1963. His career record included a .289 batting average in 2,216 games, 2,449 hits, 427 doubles, 78 triples, 84 home runs, 1,223 runs scored, 89 stolen bases, and 773 RBIs. In 1945 he led the NL in stolen bases with 26. His fielding records included the most years at second base (17) and the season's leading second basemen in fielding average (7). In 1948 the right-handed fielder tied a record with six doubles in a double header.

From 1964 to 1976, he managed the St. Louis Cardinals, piloting the club longer than anyone else. His teams won 1,010 games and lost 925 for a .522 winning percentage. In his two World Series as manager, St. Louis defeated the Boston Red Sox in 1967 and lost to the Detroit Tigers in 1968. After coaching with the Oakland Athletics (AL) in 1977 and 1978, he returned to the St. Louis Cardinals as coach. He married Mary Eileen O'Reilly on September 20, 1947, and has four children. His one son, Kevin, plays in the Chicago Cubs organization.

BIBLIOGRAPHY: Bob Broeg, "Red Loves to Take Charge," *SEP* 223 (July 22, 1950), p. 223–228; Hal Butler, *Sports Heroes Who Wouldn't Quit* (New York, 1973); *CB* 25 (1964), pp. 22–23; Tim Cohane, "Glue That Made Milwaukee Famous," *Look* 22 (May 2, 1958), pp. 74–76; Gene Karst and Martin J. Jones, Jr., *Who's Who in Professional Baseball* (New Rochelle, NY, 1973); Harry Molter, *Famous American Athletes* (New York, 1982); *NYT*, November 18, 1957.

William A. Borst and Frank J. Olmsted

SEAVER, George Thomas "Tom," "Tom Terrific" (b. 17 November 1944, Fresno, CA), player, is the son of Charles Seaver, a 1932 Walker Cup golfer, and Betty (Cline) Seaver. In 1962 the 5 foot, 9 inch, 160 pound senior compiled a 6–5 record for Fresno High School and received no baseball offers. After a stint in the U.S. Marine Corps and experience with the semi-pro Alaska Goldpanners, he had gained 3 inches and 30 pounds by 1965 and starred for the University of Southern California. He eventually earned a Bachelor's degree in public relations there in 1974.

The Los Angeles Dodgers (NL) drafted Seaver in 1965 but did not offer him a contract. When the Atlanta Braves (NL) made him an offer with a reported $40,000 bonus in February, 1966, Commissioner William Eckert* nullified the contract by claiming that it violated the "college rule." Ironically, at the same time, the National Collegiate Athletic Association declared him ineligible. Eckert then made him available to any team willing to match the Braves' offer. When three teams indicated their interest, the New York Mets (NL) won the right to sign him in a drawing. He signed for a $50,000 bonus and pitched for Jacksonville, FL (IL).

After an impressive spring in 1967, the Mets brought the 6 foot 1 inch, 210 pound right-hander up to New York. Seaver enjoyed a winning season on a losing ballclub. Two years later, "Tom Terrific" led the "Amazin' Mets" to the World Series with a major league leading 25–7 record. He was rewarded with a record $100,000-plus annual salary after only five seasons. Seaver proved the mainstay on the Mets pitching staff from 1967 to 1977, providing almost one-quarter of the team's victories. He led the NL in wins twice, with 25 in 1969 and 22 in 1975, and in strikeouts five times, establishing major league records for most seasons (10) registering 200 or more strikeouts (including a record nine in a row from 1968 to 1976). In 1970 he tied the then major league record of 19 strikeouts in one game and established the mark for most consecutive strikeouts (10). Three times he paced the NL in ERA, with his 1.76 in 1971 and 2.08 in 1973 being major league bests. In his first eleven seasons, he hurled 46 shutouts, topping the NL with 7 in 1977.

In 1967 Seaver was honored as NL Rookie of the Year. He was named NL Pitcher of the Year in 1969 and 1975 by *The Sporting News* and three times—in 1969, 1973, and 1975—won the Cy Young Award. He was named to the NL All-Star team twelve times—nine as a Met—and pitched the Mets to NL titles in 1969 and 1973 and a World Series championships in 1969. After a dispute with the Mets ownership in 1977, Seaver was traded to the Cincinnati Reds (NL). He spent six seasons in Cincinnati, where his five shutouts and .727 winning percentage in 1979 topped the NL, and his .875 win-loss percentage in 1981 led the majors. On June 10, 1978, he pitched a 4–0 no hitter against the St. Louis Cardinals. After the 1982 season, Seaver was traded back to the Mets, ostensibly to play out his career in Shea Stadium. When the team left Seaver unprotected during the 1984 free agent compensation draft, however, the Chicago White Sox (AL) selected him. In his first season with the White Sox, he led all Chicago starters with 15 wins and posted a 3.95 ERA.

Through the 1986 season, Seaver had compiled a 311–205 mark for a .603 winning percentage and 2.86 ERA. In 1985 he again paced the White Sox staff with a 16–11 mark and a 3.17 ERA. On August 4, 1985, he became the seventeenth major league pitcher to win 300 games by defeating the New York Yankees 4–1. On October 4, 1985, he struck out seven Seattle Mariners to pass Gaylord Perry* for third place in all-time strikeouts. He ranked first among active pitchers in shutouts (61), second in total victories (311), and third in strikeouts (3,640). In 4,782 2/3 innings, he has surrendered only 1,390 walks. Seaver threw a 98 mile-an-hour fastball as a rookie, although never labeled a fireballer. He has succeeded with superb pitch selection and placement, claiming that on a good day all but five pitches in a game will be on target. Seaver, who can still throw the fastball 93 miles an hour, pioneered training with weights for arm strength and pitching speed and developed a mechanically perfect delivery by eliminating unnecessary motion and using his entire body.

Although the picture of concentration on the mound and refined in public, Seaver is fun-loving and prankish in the clubhouse. He is a family man who enjoys reading, hunting, fishing, golfing, traveling, and playing bridge. The co-author of two baseball books, he has succeeded in many business and broadcasting ventures. He and his wife Nancy have two daughters and live in Greenwich, CT. Chicago traded Seaver on June 28, 1986 to the Boston Red Sox (AL) for centerfielder-third baseman Steve Lyons, enabling the veteran pitcher to be closer to home. Seaver started several games for the AL pennant winning Red Sox, but a knee injury prevented him from participating in either the Championship Series or World Series.

BIBLIOGRAPHY: *CB* (1970), pp. 384–386; Murray Chass, "Compensation System Showing Flaws," *TSN*, February 6, 1984, p. 40; Frank Deford, "Behind the Fence," *SI* 55 (July 27, 1981), pp. 50–64; Joseph Durso, "The Ordeal of George Thomas

Seaver," *Saturday Review* 2 (April 19, 1975), pp. 12–13; "How the Franchise Went West," *Time* 109 (June 27, 1977), p. 49; Joe Jares, "The Mets Find a Young Phenom," *SI* 26 (June 26, 1967), pp. 64–66; Pat Jordan, "Tom Terrific and His Mystic Talent," *SI* 37 (July 24, 1972), pp. 22–31; William Leggett, "Sportsman of the Year," *SI* 31 (December 22, 1969), pp. 32–37; Melissa Ludtke Lincoln, "TV Radio Making Another Kind of Pitch," *SI* 49 (September 18, 1978), p. 50; Joseph L. Reichler, ed., *The Baseball Encyclopedia*, 6th ed. (New York, 1985), p. 2,029; Barry Siegel, ed., *TSN Official Baseball Register, 1984* (St. Louis, 1984); *Washington Post*, April 19, 1985, p. E7.

Gaymon L. Bennett

SELEE, Frank Gibson (b. 26 October 1859, Amherst, NH; d. 5 July 1909, Denver, CO), player, manager, and executive, was the second of three children of Methodist-Episcopal clergyman Nathan P. and Annie Marie (Cass) Selee. The Selees moved to Melrose, MA, when Frank was still an infant. He attended local public schools and belonged to the town's Alpha baseball club. His professional baseball career began in 1884, when he left a job with the Waltham Watch Company to organize a town entry in the MasL. Although "without any practical experience as a manager or player," Selee wrote that he raised a capital fund of $1,000, played some outfield, and quickly found his métier as manager. In 1885–1886 he managed Haverhill, MA (NEL), and made his "real start in baseball" in 1887 with Oshkosh, WI (NWL), where he won his first pennant. The following year, the league became the WA. Selee shifted to Omaha and in 1889 won another pennant.

In 1890 the Boston Beaneaters (NL) signed Omaha's ace right-hander Kid Nichols* and hired Selee as manager. Undaunted by the loss of ten Beaneaters to the Boston franchise of the PL, Selee combined the remaining loyalists with shrewd acquisitions from other leagues to finish first. Over the next nine years, he managed Boston to five NL pennants (1891–1893, 1897–1898), won 849 games, and lost only 508 contests for a .626 percentage. His 1892 and 1898 teams became the first clubs to win over 100 games in one NL season. The 1894 powerhouse finished third, but set the major league single-season record of 1,222 runs scored. Seven regulars tallied over 100 runs each for a team that was never shut out in 132 games. No other major league club between 1884 and 1920 hit over 100 home runs (103) in a season.

It was as a master of inside baseball that Selee made his reputation. He favored the hit-and-run, the strategically stolen base, and signals to deploy his team defensively. In a rowdy era, he proved "modest and retiring," "courteous and mild-mannered." He represented an emerging breed of manager who directed his team from the bench and knew baseball without having been a star player. His eye for talent was so keen that he supposedly could "tell a ball player in his street clothes." The Boston years demonstrated his skill in player selection and development. Fred Tenney,* a left-handed college-educated catcher, was switched to first base and taught to execute the game's first 3–6–3 double plays. Jimmy Collins,* a minor league outfielder, became a National Baseball Hall of Fame third baseman. Six other Hall of Famers played for Selee in Boston, while four others did in Chicago. Two potential stars he supposedly rejected, however, were Honus Wagner* and Napoleon Lajoie.*

After a fifth place finish in 1901 and three years without a pennant, Boston released Selee. The sixth place Chicago Cubs (NL) promptly signed him. Undertaking again to create a new team, Selee raised the Cubs a notch in 1902. Frank Chance,* a catcher and part-time outfielder, was shifted to first base, while third baseman Joe Tinker,* acquired from Portland, OR (PNL), moved to shortstop. Johnny Evers,* an infielder from Troy (NYSL), joined the team on Labor Day and became the second baseman. On September 15 the Tinker-Evers-Chance combination made its first double play.

The Cubs advanced to third place in 1903 and to second in 1904. Selee added "Wildfire" Schulte and persuaded St. Louis (NL) to accept an aging pitcher and second-string catcher for Mordecai "Three Finger" Brown.* In May 1905 Ed Reulbach* was signed. After 90 games that season, the Cubs' management shifted to "Husk" Chance. The never robust Selee was gravely ill with tuberculosis and was given an indefinite leave of absence to regain his health. He moved to Denver, bought an interest in the Pueblo Indians (WL), and served as club president from mid–1906 to June 1907. He also became a partner in a Denver hotel.

He was buried in Melrose, MA, where he had operated a clothing store with Sidney Farrar, one-time first baseman for Philadelphia in the NL and PL and father of the great operatic soprano, Geraldine Farrar. In sixteen years as major league manager, Selee won 1,299 games and lost 872 for a .598 percentage, the fourth highest in baseball history. None of his teams ever finished lower than fifth. With the Cubs he developed winning pennants from 1906 to 1908 and in 1910 for Chance. Survived by his wife May, he had no children.

BIBLIOGRAPHY: Lee Allen, *The National League Story* (New York, 1961); Chicago *Tribune*, July 29, 1905; July 6, 1909; Cincinnati *Enquirer*, July 7–8, 12, 1909; Allison Danzig and Joe Reichler, *The History of Baseball* (Englewood Cliffs, NJ, 1959); Denver *Republican*, July 9, 1909, p. 9; Denver *Times*, July 9, 1909, p. 8; John L. Evers, with Hugh S. Fullerton, *Touching Second* (Chicago, 1910); Ralph Hickok, *Who Was Who in American Sports* (New York, 1971); Harold Kaese, *The Boston Braves* (New York, 1948); Frederick G. Lieb, *The Baseball Story* (New York, 1950); Melrose (MA) *Free Press*, July 9, 16, 1909; February 9, 1912; Pueblo (CO) *Chieftain*, March 26, May 25, July 6, 1909; Joseph L. Reichler, ed., *The Baseball Encyclopedia*, 6th ed. (New York, 1985), p. 647; Joseph L. Reichler, ed., *The Baseball Trade Register* (New York, 1984); Frank G. Selee, "Twenty-one Years in Baseball," *Baseball Magazine* 8 (December, 1911), pp. 53–56; Harold Seymour, *Baseball: The Early Years* (New York, 1960); Harold Seymour, *Baseball: The Golden Age* (New York, 1971); *Spalding's Official Base Ball Guide, 1906* (New York, 1906); *Sporting Life*, August 5, 12, 19, 26, 1905, June 8, 1907, July 24, 1909; David Quentin Voigt, *American Baseball*, vol. 1 (University Park, PA, 1983).

A. D. Suehsdorf

SEWELL, Joseph Wheeler "Joe" (b. 9 October 1898, Titus, AL), baseball and football player, coach, and scout, is the son of Jabez Wesley and Susan (Hannon) Sewell and one of three brothers to play professional baseball. James Luther "Luke" Sewell caught for several major league teams and managed the St. Louis Browns to the AL pennant in 1944, while Thomas played briefly for the Chicago Cubs (NL) in 1927. Sewell attended the Wetumpka, AL, public schools and enrolled at the University of Alabama in 1916 to study medicine. At Alabama, Sewell played college football and baseball with his brother Luke and Riggs Stephenson.* During this period, Alabama won four Southern Intercollegiate Athletic Association baseball championships and compiled a 58–17 overall record.

With one year (1918) out for military service, Sewell graduated from Alabama in 1920 and began his professional baseball career with New Orleans (SA). His contract was purchased later that year by the Cleveland Indians (AL) because their shortstop, Ray Chapman, had died from being beaned by New York Yankees pitcher Carl Mays.* The 5 foot, 9 inch, 155 pound shortstop and later third baseman played for Cleveland through 1930 and then joined the New York Yankees (AL) for the 1931–1933 seasons. Besides playing in 1,103 consecutive games, he compiled a .312 batting average. Famous for his bat control, the left-handed swinging and right-handed throwing Sewell proved the hardest hitter in baseball history to strike out. In 1925, 1929, and 1933, he batted over 500 times each season and struck out only four times. In 7,132 career at bats, Sewell struck out only 114 times, made 2,226 hits, scored 1,141 runs, and knocked in 1,051 runs. In 1924 he led the AL in doubles with 45.

Sewell married Willie Veal on December 31, 1921, and has three children, Joseph, Jr., James, and Mary Sue. Following his playing days, Sewell coached for the Yankees (1934–1935) and scouted for both the Indians (1952–1962) and the New York Mets (1963). He operated a hardware store in Tuscaloosa, AL, for several years and worked in public relations with a local dairy. At the behest of Alabama football coach Paul "Bear" Bryant* (FB), Sewell in 1964 became head Crimson Tide baseball coach. Alabama won the 1968 Southeastern Conference championship, earning him Southeastern Conference Coach of the Year honors. He was elected to the Alabama Sports Hall of Fame in 1970 and the National Baseball Hall of Fame in 1977.

BIBLIOGRAPHY: *CB* (1944), pp. 606–609; Cecil Hurt, "Hall of Famer Joe Sewell," *Bama* (April, 1981), pp. 24–25; Gene Karst and Martin J. Jones, Jr., *Who's Who in Professional Baseball* (New Rochelle, NY, 1973); Joseph L. Reichler, *The Great All-Time Baseball Record Book* (New York, 1981); Joseph L. Reichler, ed., *The Baseball Encyclopedia*, 6th ed. (New York, 1985), pp. 1,380–1,381; Joseph Sewell file, National Baseball Hall of Fame Library, Cooperstown, NY.

Horace R. Givens

SEYMOUR, James Bentley "Cy" (b. 9 December 1872, Albany, NY; d. 20 September 1919, New York, NY), player, was the son of a carpenter and first gained notice in baseball with the Ridgefield Athletic Club of Albany, NY. He pitched for Plattsburg, NY, in 1895 and Springfield, MA (EL), in 1896 before joining the New York Giants (NL) late in 1896. Seymour's pitching wildness and strong hitting caused him to switch to the outfield. After jumping to the Chicago Americans (AL) in late 1900, Seymour joined Baltimore (AL) in 1901. He moved during July 1902 to Cincinnati (NL), where he hit over .300 every year through 1905. During the 1906 season, New York (NL) purchased his contract for $10,000. Although a solid performer the next four years, he did not achieve the level he had established at Cincinnati. In 1908 he misplayed into a triple a long fly ball hit by Chicago's Joe Tinker* in the playoff game for the NL pennant, resulting in three runs scored. He played for Baltimore (EL) in 1910–1911, Newark (IL) in 1912, and Boston (NL), Buffalo (IL), and Newark (IL) in 1913.

A left-handed pitcher, the 6 foot, 200 pound Seymour compiled 63 wins and 54 losses in 140 appearances. He led the NL in strikeouts in 1897 and 1898, but also paced the NL in walks in 1897, 1898, and 1899. Seymour appeared in 1,333 major league games as an outfielder. A left-handed batter, he hit .303 in sixteen major league seasons, with 1,723 hits, 229 doubles, 96 triples, 52 home runs, 799 RBIs, and 222 stolen bases. In 1905 he hit .377 to defeat Honus Wagner* for the NL batting championship. Seymour's 219 hits, 40 doubles, 21 triples, 121 RBIs, and .559 slugging percentage also led the NL. Seymour, who married, became one of the few major leaguers to convert successfully from pitcher to everyday player. He proved a notable member of baseball's supporting cast at the turn of the twentieth century.

BIBLIOGRAPHY: Lee Allen, *The Cincinnati Reds* (New York, 1948); Frank Graham, *The New York Giants* (New York, 1952); Joseph L. Reichler, ed., *The Baseball Encyclopedia*, 6th ed., (New York, 1985), pp. 1,381–1,382, 2,032.

Luther W. Spoehr

SHAWKEY, James Robert "Sailor Bob," "Bob the Gob" (b. 4 December 1890, Sigel, PA; d. 31 December 1980, Syracuse, NY), player, coach, and manager, was the second of four children of farmer John W. and Sarah C. Shawkey, attended a country schoolhouse and spent one year at Slippery Rock Teachers College. He married Anna Blauser around 1910, had one daughter, and later wed Gertrude Weiler Killian on December 12, 1943. Shawkey's nautical nicknames derived from his year of service in the U.S. Navy aboard the battleship *Arkansas* during World War I. He pitched for Bloomsburg, PA (MtnL) in 1910 and worked as a tool dresser in the Pennsylvania oil fields. The following year, he left a job as fireman for the Pennsylvania Railroad and turned professional with Harrisburg, PA (TSL).

After signing with the Philadelphia Athletics (AL) in 1913, he won 16 games in 1914 and lost the fourth game of the World Series sweep by Boston's "Miracle Braves." When Connie Mack* began breaking up his team, Shawkey was dealt to the New York Yankees (AL) in July 1915 and promptly became their pitching ace. He won 168 of his 196 major league victories for the Yankees, including 24 in 1916 and 20 each in 1919, 1920, and 1922. During fifteen seasons, he lost 150 games, completed 194 of 333 starts, struck out 1,360 batters in 2,937 innings, hurled 33 shutouts, and compiled a 3.09 ERA. He led the AL with 10- and 11-game winning streaks in 1919 and 1920 and a 2.45 ERA in 1920. During his career, he pitched a Yankees record seven 1–0 victories. He also achieved 15 strikeouts against the Athletics in 1919 and won one of four decisions in five World Series. In 1923 he pitched and won the first game played at Yankee Stadium, hitting the park's second home run. (Babe Ruth* blasted the first.) He surrendered an AL-leading 17 home runs during that season.

A strong, confident, 5 foot, 11 inch, 168 pound right-hander, Shawkey exhibited an unassuming manner and a mild temperament and wore a distinctive red-sleeved sweatshirt under his uniform. After his playing career ended in 1927 with Montreal (IL), he returned to the Yankees as coach in 1929 and manager in 1930. Dismissed after a third place finish, he managed Jersey City (IL) in 1931, Scranton (NYPL) in 1932–1933, Newark (IL) in 1934–1935, Watertown, NY (BL) in 1947, and Tallahassee (GFL) in 1949. He served as a pitching coach in the Pittsburgh Pirates and Detroit Tigers farm systems and baseball coach at Dartmouth College between 1952 and 1956.

BIBLIOGRAPHY: Robert W. Creamer, *Babe: The Legend Comes to Life* (New York, 1976); Dan Daniel, New York *Telegram*, October 13, 1929; Dartmouth College Sports Information Department, Hanover, NH; Mark Gallagher, *The Yankee Encyclopedia* (New York, 1982); Donald Honig, *The Man in the Dugout* (Chicago, 1977); Gene Karst and Martin J. Jones, Jr., *Who's Who in Professional Baseball* (New Rochelle, NY, 1973); Ronald G. Liebman, "Winning Streaks by Pitchers," *Baseball Research Journal* 7 (1978), pp. 35–42; Paul MacFarlane, ed., *TSN Daguerreotypes of Great Stars of Baseball* (St. Louis, 1981); John Mosedale, *The Greatest of All: The 1927 New York Yankees* (New York, 1975); *NYT*, January 4, 1981, p. 26; Joseph L. Reichler, ed., *The Baseball Encyclopedia*, 6th ed. (New York, 1985), pp. 2,033–2,034; Lawrence S. Ritter, *The Glory of Their Times* (New York, 1966); Bob Shawkey, "The Veteran of the Yankee Hurling Staff" (interview) *Baseball Magazine* 37 (July, 1926), p. 349; A. D. Suehsdorf, telephone interview with Mrs. Dorothy Shawkey Hitchcock, December 20, 1983.

A. D. Suehsdorf

SHECKARD, Samuel James Tilden "Jimmy" (b. 23 November 1878, Upper Chanceford, PA; d. 15 January 1947, Lancaster, PA), player, coach, and manager, was of German descent and was born on a farm in York County near Columbia in southeastern Pennsylvania. Sheckard only attended grammar school and wed Cora Seicrest. Later, in May 1922, he married Frances

Ewes. The 5 foot, 9 inch, 175 pound Sheckard entered professional baseball in 1896 at age 17 with Portsmouth, VA (VL). After spending the next season at Brockton, MA (NEL), he joined the Brooklyn Dodgers (NL) in late 1897. He played outfield with Brooklyn through 1905, except for a one-year stint with Baltimore (NL) in 1899 and a brief time in 1902 when the latter city was in the AL. He performed from 1906 to 1912 with the Chicago Cubs (NL), split the 1913 campaign between the St. Louis Cardinals and Cincinnati Reds, and finished his career in 1914 as player-manager for Cleveland (AA). In 1917 he served as coach for the Chicago Cubs.

The left-handed batting and right-handed throwing Sheckard, a fine base runner, clever, coaxing batter, and skillful outfielder and thrower, led the NL in stolen bases with 77 in 1899 and 67 in 1903. He paced the NL in triples (19) and total bases (299) in 1901, runs scored (121) and bases on balls (147) in 1911, and walks (122) in 1912. His 147 walks in 1911 remained the NL record until 1945. In 1903 he led the NL in home runs (9). For his career, Sheckard batted .275, with 2,095 hits, 356 doubles, 136 triples, 56 home runs, 1,296 runs scored, 813 RBIs, 1,135 walks, and 465 stolen bases. A fine fielder, he participated in 14 double plays in 1899, made 36 assists in 1903, and led outfielders in putouts in 1902.

Sheckard played for the great 1906–1910 Chicago Cubs squads. The superlative 1906 team lost the World Series in six games to the Chicago White Sox partly because Sheckard made no hits in 21 at bats and hit only one ball out of the infield. Sheckard, however, performed better in the Cubs' 1907 and 1908 World Series triumphs and drove in the winning run in the lone 1910 Cubs victory against the Philadelphia Athletics. Ill luck subsequently dogged Sheckard, who lost his modest savings in the stock market crash. He later worked as a physical laborer, delivered milk, and held a filling station job. His death came from being struck by a car.

BIBLIOGRAPHY: Gregg Dubbs, "Jim Sheckard in the Dead-Ball Era," *Baseball Research Journal* 9 (1980), p. 134–139; *NYT*, January 16, 1947; Philadelphia *Bulletin*, January 15, 1947; Philadelphia *Inquirer*, January 16, 1947.

Lowell L. Blaisdell

SHIBE, Benjamin Franklin "Ben" (b. 1838, Philadelphia, PA; d. 14 January 1922, Philadelphia, PA), executive, joined Connie Mack* in helping establish the AL franchise in Philadelphia in 1901. Shibe, a horse car driver in Philadelphia, became an enthusiastic baseball fan in the late 1800s. Although unable to play because of a leg injury that required him to wear a steel brace, he helped develop baseball equipment. A flair for making baseballs led him in 1882 to join the sporting goods firm of Alfred J. Reach.* Shibe later developed the two-piece baseball cover and invented the cork center baseball. Shibe's partnership with Reach established his fortune, estimated at over $1 million by his death.

When Ban Johnson* formed the AL in 1901, he approached Shibe about establishing a team in Philadelphia. In partnership with field manager Mack, Shibe effectively directed business operations for the new team and saw the Athletics dominate the first decade of the AL. From 1901 to 1914, the Athletics won 6 AL pennants, 3 World Series titles, and finished in second place twice. In 1909 he played an instrumental role in moving the Athletics to the modern Shibe Park. He also became one of the first baseball executives to adopt the scoreboard, enabling fans in all parts of the stadium to follow the game. Shibe served as president of the Athletics until his death, two years after involvement in a serious automobile accident. Shibe, whose wife predeceased him, left four children, Thomas, John, Mrs. Frank MacFarlane, and Mrs. George Reach. His son Thomas (1866–1936), who had served as vice-president of the Athletics and chief officer of the Reach Company, became club president.

BIBLIOGRAPHY: Connie Mack, *My Life in Baseball* (Philadelphia, 1953); Philadelphia *Bulletin*, January 15, 1922, February 17, 1936; Philadelphia *Inquirer*, January 14, 1922; Philadelphia *Public Ledger*, January 15, 1922, February 17, 1936; Philadelphia *Record*, February 17, 1936.

John P. Rossi

SIMMONS, Aloysius Harry "Al," "Bucketfoot Al" (b. Syzmanski, 22 May 1902, Milwaukee, WI; d. 26 May 1956, Milwaukee, WI), player, was the son of Polish immigrants and was nicknamed "Old Bucketfoot." He grew up in Milwaukee, briefly attended Stevens Point Teachers College, and played semi-pro baseball for a Juneau, WI team. The Milwaukee Brewers (AL) signed him in 1922 and farmed him to Aberdeen, SD (DL), where he hit .365 in 99 games. After Simmons batted .360 in 1923 for Shreveport (TL), the Brewers recalled him for the team's final 24 games. His .398 average impressed manager Connie Mack,* who bought him for the Philadelphia Athletics (AL). Simmons played every game in 1924 for Philadelphia and received much derision for his strange batting stance. A right-handed hitter and thrower, he pointed his left foot almost straight down the third base line. But Mack refused to alter the stance, as the rookie hit .308 and batted in 102 runs. Simmons hit over .300 in fourteen seasons, including eleven consecutive ones.

Simmons, who stood 6 feet tall and weighed about 200 pounds, possessed a very strong throwing arm and thrice led the AL outfielders in fielding average. But he was best known for his heavy hitting and high average. In 2,215 games, he made 2,927 hits and slugged 539 doubles, 149 triples, and 307 home runs. Besides knocking in 1,827 runs, he compiled a career .334 batting average and .535 slugging percentage. He led the AL in hitting twice (.381 in 1930, .390 in 1931) and finished second two times. His career peak .392 batting average in 1927 ranked second behind Harry Heilmann's* .398.

He led the AL in total hits twice (253 in 1925 and 216 in 1932) and in RBIs (157) in 1929. Although never leading in home runs, in 1930 he slugged 36 homers and 41 doubles among his 211 total hits. In 1929 he was chosen the AL's Most Valuable Player.

During Simmons' nine seasons with Philadelphia, the Athletics always contended and won three consecutive AL pennants (1929–1931). In those three World Series, he hit .333 in 18 games and batted in 17 runs. His .364 average in 1930 paced both teams, while his homer and single in the seventh inning of the dramatic fourth game of the 1929 World Series helped the Athletics overcome an 8–0 Cubs lead. The Athletics won that Series 4 games to 1, beat the St. Louis Cardinals 4–2 in 1930, and lost to the Cardinals 4–3 in 1931. Simmons also played one game in the 1939 World Series for the Cincinnati Reds (NL). His 253 hits in 1925 perhaps represented his greatest baseball achievement.

After the 1932 season, manager Mack began reducing his expenses by selling his stars. Simmons moved to the Chicago White Sox (AL) and batted .331 and .344 in 1933 and 1934. After his average declined to .267 in 1935, he was traded to the Detroit Tigers (AL) and enjoyed a fine year there. Nearing the end of his career, he was traded to Washington (AL) in 1937, Boston (NL) in 1939, Cincinnati (NL) in 1939, Philadelphia (AL) in 1940, and Boston (AL) in 1943. Simmons, who ended his playing career with Philadelphia (AL) in 1944, was elected to the National Baseball Hall of Fame in 1953. Simmons coached for the Philadelphia Athletics (AL) from 1940 to 1942 and 1944 to 1948 and Cleveland Indians (AL) in 1950. He married Doris Lynn Reader of Chicago in August, 1934, and had one son, John, before their subsequent divorce. Simmons died of a heart attack.

BIBLIOGRAPHY: Lee Allen, *The American League Story* (New York, 1962); Martin Appel and Burt Goldblatt, *Baseball's Best: The Hall of Fame Gallery* (New York, 1980); Warren Brown, *The Chicago White Sox* (New York, 1952); Donald Honig, *Baseball's Ten Greatest Teams* (New York, 1982); Richard Lindberg, *Who's on Third?* (South Bend, IN, 1983); *Literary Digest* 116 (December 23, 1933), p. 26; David Neft, Richard Cohen, and Jordan Deutsch, *The Sports Encyclopedia: Baseball*, 6th ed. (New York, 1985), p. 1,393; *NYT*, 1923–1956, September 22, 1927, June 3, 1930, August 11, 1934, May 27–28, 1956; Lowell Reidenbaugh, *Cooperstown: Where Baseball's Legends Live Forever* (St. Louis, 1983).

Thomas L. Karnes

SIMMONS, Ted Lyle "Simba" (b. 9 August 1949, Highland Park, MI), player, is the son of Finis Simmons, owner, trainer, and occasional driver of harness horses. After graduating from Southfield (MI) High School, Simmons attended the University of Michigan and Wayne State University. In 1970 Simmons married Maryane Ellison, the daughter of his Little League baseball coach. They have two sons, John and Mathew, and reside in St. Louis, where Simmons has worked in the banking industry during off-seasons. Simmons idolized Al Kaline,* the Detroit Tigers' outstanding outfielder, and became a switch-hitter at age 13. At Southfield High School, he was named Most Valuable Player in baseball, all-league in basketball, and All-State in football. Despite football scholarship offers from several universities, the 6 foot, 200 pound Simmons instead signed a $50,000 baseball contract as a free agent with the St. Louis Cardinals (NL) in June, 1967.

Simmons divided his first professional baseball season in 1967 between Sarasota (GCL) and Cedar Rapids (ML). He won both Rookie of the Year and Most Valuable Player honors with Modesto, CA (CaL), in 1968. The following year, he advanced to Tulsa (AA) and won another MVP Award. In his first full major league season, Simmons batted .304 in 1971 for the Cardinals. He has hit above .300 seven times since then and attained a personal high .332 mark in 1975, finishing second in the NL. Besides hitting 20 or more home runs at least six seasons, "Simba" has driven in at least 100 runs three times.

During ten years as a regular with Cardinals (1971–1980), Simmons was primarily a catcher but occasionally played first base, third base, and the outfield. A line drive hitter who seldom strikes out, he set NL records for most hits by a catcher in a season (188 in 1975) and most career home runs by a switch-hitter (172). He was named to six midseason All-Star teams and three post-season *The Sporting News* All-Star teams as a National Leaguer. The right-handed throwing Simmons led the NL three times in total chances and twice each in intentional walks, assists, and putouts. Conversely, he paced the NL three times in passed balls and once in grounding into double plays.

In December 1980 Simmons was traded to the Milwaukee Brewers (AL). Simmons played in one World Series (1982) with Milwaukee, hitting two homers, and in two All-Star games (1981 and 1983). With the Brewers, he was a designated hitter, catcher, first baseman, and third baseman. Through 1986, he has appeared in 2,305 games, scored 1,048 runs, made 2,402 hits, slugged 469 doubles, 47 triples, and 242 home runs, knocked in 1,348 runs, and batted .286. In March 1986 he was traded to the Atlanta Braves (NL).

BIBLIOGRAPHY: Bob Broeg, "A Batting Title in Store for Ted Simmons?" *Baseball Digest* 37 (May, 1978), pp. 38–40; Jim Brosnan, *The Ted Simmons Story* (New York, 1977); Mac Hoffman, "Ted Simmons—Finally out of the Shadows," *Sport World* 18 (August, 1979), pp. 16, 80; Zander Hollander, ed., *The Complete Handbook of Baseball, 1979, 1984* (New York, 1979, 1984); *1983 Milwaukee Brewers Media Guide 1983*; *TSN Official Baseball Register, 1984* (St. Louis, 1984); *WWA*, 42nd ed. (1982–1983), p. 3,081.

Thomas D. Jozwik

SINGLETON, Kenneth Wayne "Ken" (b. 10 June 1947, New York, NY), player, grew up in Mount Vernon, NY, and became a New York Giants (NL) fan. An admirer of Willie Mays* and Willie McCovey,* he learned to be a switch-hitter to imitate them in sandlot games. After entering Hofstra

University in 1966, he was drafted by the New York Mets (NL) in 1967 as their first choice and given a $10,000 bonus. Singleton, who threw right-handed, played outfield and first base in the minor leagues at Winter Haven FL (FSL), Raleigh-Durham (CrL), Visalia, CA (CaL), Jacksonville, FL (IL), and Memphis (TL) from 1967 through 1970, ending that portion of his career at Tidewater, VA (IL).

He was called up to the New York Mets in 1970 and traded in April, 1972 to the Montreal Expos (NL). Singleton played outfield for Montreal from 1972 through 1974 and led the club in runs, hits, and doubles in 1972. From 1975 to 1984, he performed in the outfield and as designated hitter with the Baltimore Orioles (AL). After leading the team in hitting in 1975 and 1976, he earned a five-year contract, at that time the longest ever given to an Oriole. He won Baltimore's Most Valuable Player Award in 1975. In 1977 he hit .328 to break the modern Orioles single-season batting average record. The 6 foot, 4 inch, 210 pound Singleton always hit with considerable power. Upon entering the NL, he was thought to have the potential to become the strongest home run hitter since Mickey Mantle.* An intelligent hitter with a sharp eye, he consistently compiled one of the highest on-base percentages in the majors. Like most power hitters, however, he struck out frequently.

His career never prospered to full expectations. He played with noncontending teams in the early 1970s and consequently remained relatively unknown. By the late 1970s, his fielding career declined, partly due to arm trouble. Surgical removal of a bone chip in December, 1977, helped Singleton, but his speed slowed further. His designated hitter role prolonged his career, making him a valued team member. During fourteen major league seasons, he compiled a .282 batting average with 985 runs, 2,029 hits, 317 doubles, 25 triples, 246 home runs, and 1,065 RBIs. Singleton appeared in the 1979 and 1983 World Series, batting .357 and making 10 hits against the Pittsburgh Pirates in 1979. Singleton and his wife Colette have one son, Matthew.

BIBLIOGRAPHY: Ron Fimrite, "Looking for an Argument? Then Name Your MVP," *SI* 51 (September 24, 1979), pp. 20–22ff; Larry Keith, "Beat Feet but Eyes Right," *SI* 47 (July 25, 1977), pp. 38ff; *NYT*, July 25, 1970, March 23, 1971; *Who's Who Among Black Americans* (Northbrook, IL, 1978).

Charles R. Middleton

SISLER, George Harold "Gorgeous George" (b. 24 March 1893, Manchester, OH; d. 26 March 1973, St. Louis, MO), player, manager, coach, and scout, came from a prominent Ohio family. His parents graduated from Hiram College, while an uncle served as mayor of Akron. Sisler graduated from the University of Michigan in 1915 with a mechanical engineering degree. When Branch Rickey* served as the Michigan baseball coach, Sisler became his first outstanding find. As a star pitcher, Sisler reputedly compiled an incredible 50–0 mark for the Wolverines. The 5 foot 10 1/2 inch, 170 pound Sisler possessed excellent coordination and speed and proved a superb athlete. Upon his graduation, several major league clubs wanted him for their parent rosters.

Although sought by the Pittsburgh Pirates (NL), he signed with the St. Louis Browns (AL) and played under manager Rickey. Like Babe Ruth,* he began as a left-handed pitcher and compiled a 5–6 lifetime record. His decisions included 2–1 and 1–0 wins over Washington standout Walter Johnson* and one loss to the fellow National Baseball Hall of Famer. Sisler, a great left-handed batter, soon was converted to a first baseman. He hit .407 in 1920 and .420 in 1922, the latter equaling Ty Cobb's* highest AL batting percentage. Besides holding the major league record for single-season hits (257 in 1920), he won the AL batting championship in his two .400-plus years. He led the AL in total bases in 1920, triples (18) in 1922, and stolen bases in 1918 (45), 1921 (35), 1922 (51), and 1927 (27). In 1922 he compiled a 41-game hitting streak, exceeded only by Joe DiMaggio* and Pete Rose* in this century. The same year he won the AL Most Valuable Player Award. Sisler's lifetime .340 batting average over fifteen seasons ranks him fifteenth among all hitters. In 2,055 games, he made 2,812 hits, 425 doubles, 165 triples, 100 home runs, 1,284 runs scored, 1,175 RBIs, and 375 stolen bases. In 1939 he was named to the National Baseball Hall of Fame.

The agile, hard-throwing Sisler made a fine first baseman. He led AL first sackers in assists six times, including a one-season record in 1920 (140), and paced the NL once. Sisler ranks first in lifetime total assists at his position (1,528). Unfortunately, Sisler missed the entire 1923 season due to a severe sinus infection. Although he hit well thereafter, eye trouble prevented him from achieving his previous greatness. From 1924 through 1927, "Gorgeous George" served reluctantly as the Browns player-manager and compiled a 218–241 (.475) mark. After very brief service with the Washington Senators (AL) in 1928, Sisler played from May 1928 through 1930 for the Boston Braves (NL) and ended his major league career there. He played one season each in the minors with Rochester, NY (IL), and Shreveport, LA–Tyler, TX (TL), managing briefly in the latter location.

Sisler led an exemplary life, neither drinking nor smoking. Comedian W. C. Fields, a baseball fan, admired Sisler's play. When Sisler refused a drink poured by Fields, the comedian responded, "Even the perfect ball player isn't perfect in everything." Sisler married Kathleen Holznagle in 1916 and had three sons and one daughter. Sons Dick and Dave achieved prominence as major league players, while George, Jr. served as IL president. George, Sr. later served under old mentor Rickey as scout and batting instructor for the NL Brooklyn Dodgers (1943, 1946–1950) and NL Pittsburgh Pirates (1951–1966), engaged in printing and sporting goods enterprises, and supervised the National Semi-Professional Baseball Tournament.

BIBLIOGRAPHY: Paul Greenwell, "The 1922 Browns-Yankees Pennant Race," *Baseball Research Journal* 6 (1977), pp. 68–73; Ronald G. Liebman, "George Sisler the Pitcher," *Baseball Research Journal* 8 (1979), pp. 94–98; *NYT*, March 27, 1973; Lowell Reidenbaugh, *Cooperstown: Where Baseball's Legends Live Forever* (St. Louis, 1983); *TSN*, April 14, 1973.

Lowell L. Blaisdell

SLAUGHTER, Enos Bradsher "Country" (b. 27 April 1916, Roxboro, NC), player, manager, and coach, is the son of farmer Zadok and Lonnie (Gentry) Slaughter. He graduated from Bethel Hill High School (NC) in 1934, married five times, and had five daughters. After signing with the St. Louis Cardinals (NL) in 1934, he played outfield the next year with Martinsville, VA (BSL). At Columbus, GA, in 1936, he hit .325 and led the SAL in triples. In 1937 with Columbus, OH, he paced the AA with 245 hits, 147 runs scored, and a .382 batting average.

From 1938 through 1953 (except for 1943–1945, spent in military service), Slaughter played with the St. Louis Cardinals. Besides having an accurate rifle arm from right field, the right-handed throwing Slaughter made many thrilling catches. With the Cardinals, Slaughter, a left-handed hitter, made 2,064 hits and compiled a .305 composite batting average. Slaughter twice led the NL in triples (17 in 1942, 13 in 1949), double plays by an outfielder (1939 and 1940), and assists (18 in 1939, 23 in 1946). He paced the NL once each in fielding percentage (.996 in 1953) and RBIs (130 in 1946). After being traded to the New York Yankees (AL) in 1954, Slaughter batted only .248. He split the 1955 season between the Yankees and the Kansas City Athletics (AL), hitting .315. In August, 1956, he returned to the Yankees and helped New York win the AL pennant and the World Series. Against the Brooklyn Dodgers, he made seven hits in twenty tries, scored six runs, and belted a game-winning three-run homer. He split the 1959 season with New York (AL) and Milwaukee (NL) before leaving the major leagues.

During his nineteen-year major league career, Slaughter made 2,383 hits, including 413 doubles, 148 triples, and 169 home runs, and compiled a .453 slugging and .300 batting average. In 2,380 games, he scored 1,247 runs, knocked in 1,304 runs, and walked 1,019 times. Over five World Series, he hit .291. The ten-time All-Star made two hits, scored two runs, batted in one tally, and made a diving catch in the NL's 5–1 victory in 1953. *The Sporting News* named Slaughter to their 1942 and 1946 Major League All-Star teams. His career highlight came in game seven of the 1946 World Series, when he scored the winning run from first base on a double to left center field against the Boston Red Sox. Nicknamed "Country," Slaughter hustled constantly and played back-alley baseball. Manager Eddie Dyer called Slaughter "a professional who plays like one of those starry-eyed amateurs." In 1985 Slaughter belatedly was selected for the National Baseball Hall of Fame. He served as player-manager in 1960 with Houston (AA) and in 1961 with Raleigh (CrL). From 1971 to 1977, he coached baseball at Duke University. Slaughter raises tobacco on a Roxboro, NC, farm and lives in his self-built home.

BIBLIOGRAPHY: Jack Drees, *Where Is He Now?* (Middle Village, NY, 1973); Ralph Knight and Bob Broeg, "Country Keynotes the Cards," *SEP* 219 (May 17, 1947), pp. 23ff.; Tom Wicker, "Player: Enos Slaughter, on His Toes," in Daniel Okrent and Harris Lewine, eds., *The Ultimate Baseball Book* (Boston, 1979), pp. 230–246.

John E. DiMeglio

SMITH, Carl Reginald "Reggie" (b. 2 April 1945, Shreveport, LA), player, grew up in southern California and graduated from Centennial High School, where he starred in baseball and football. A natural right-handed hitter, Smith was converted to switch-hitting by his high school coach. The young shortstop, sought by several major league teams, signed with the Minnesota Twins (AL) in 1963. At Wytheville, VA (ApL), in 1963, he displayed a strong, inaccurate arm at shortstop. Following the 1963 season, he was drafted by the Boston Red Sox (AL) and played third base in 1964 at Reading, PA (EL), and Waterloo, IA (ML). In 1965 Smith became the regular center fielder for the Pittsfield, MA (EL), club. At Toronto in 1966, he won the IL batting championship with a .320 average.

Smith joined the AL pennant-winning Boston Red Sox in 1967 and hit .250 in the World Series against the St. Louis Cardinals. He batted over .300 for the Red Sox in 1969, 1970, and 1973 before being traded in October, 1973, to the St. Louis Cardinals (NL). After hitting over .300 the next two seasons with St. Louis, he was sent to the Los Angeles Dodgers (NL) on June 15, 1976. In 1977 and 1978, Smith set an NL record for homers (61) by a switch-hitter over two consecutive seasons. His 17 home runs on the road in 1977 established an NL mark for a switch-hitter. Smith belted a career-high 32 homers in 1977 and joined Steve Garvey,* Dusty Baker, and Ron Cey in making the Dodgers the first major league club in history to have at least four players hitting 30 or more home runs. During the 1980 season, Smith batted a career-high .322 for Los Angeles. A severe shoulder injury diminished his playing time to only 68 games in 1979, 92 contests in 1980, and 41 games in 1981 and limited him to playing first base and pinch-hitting. After hitting only .200 in 1981, Smith was released by the Dodgers. He batted .284 in 106 games with the San Francisco Giants in 1982. On December 10, 1982, Smith signed with the Tokyo Giants.

In seventeen major league seasons, Smith batted over .300 seven times, led the AL in doubles twice (1968, 1971), and hit .247 in four World Series. His final three World Series came in 1977, 1978, and 1981 against the New York Yankees. The 6 foot, 185 pound outfielder compiled a lifetime .287 batting average, 2,020 hits, and 1,092 RBIs. Smith's 314 career home runs rank second only to Mickey Mantle* among switch-hitters. In 1,987 games, he scored 1,123 runs, hit 363 doubles, and stole 137 bases. A fine defensive outfielder, he possessed one of the best throwing arms in baseball. Smith married Ernestine Mary Alexander on September 6, 1964, and has two children, Carl Reginald, Jr., and Nicole La Shann.

BIBLIOGRAPHY: *Los Angeles Dodgers 1981 Media Guide*; David S. Neft and Richard M. Cohen, *The Sports Encyclopedia: Baseball*, 6th ed., (New York, 1985); Joseph L. Reichler, ed., *The Baseball Encyclopedia*, 6th ed. (New York, 1985), p. 1,408; Reggie Smith file, National Baseball Hall of Fame Library, Cooperstown, NY; *TSN Official Baseball Record Book*, 1985 (St. Louis, 1985); Harry Xanthakos, "Smith's Bat Keeps Cards in Contention," *Black Sports* (September, 1974), pp. 26, 28, 38.

Robert J. Brown

SMITH, Charles "Chino" (b. 1903, Greenwood, SC; d. 1930 ?), player, was ranked by pitcher Satchel Paige* as one of the two greatest Negro league hitters. The compact, scrappy 5 foot, 6 inch Smith excited fans and intimidated pitchers. Nicknamed "Chino" because of a slant across his eyes, he rocketed through the black baseball world like a meteor in his brief, bright career. The left-handed batter and fielder excelled as a defensive outfielder and gained most notoriety as a hitter. A line drive spray hitter, the keen-eyed Smith rarely struck out. The supremely confident slugger hit virtually all pitches and displayed no major batting weaknesses.

As a young adult, he worked summers as a redcap in New York's Pennsylvania Station and played second base on their baseball team. He performed in 1924 with the Philadelphia Giants and the next four seasons with the Brooklyn Royal Giants (ECL), recording .341, .326, and .439 batting averages the first three seasons. After joining the Lincoln Giants (ANL) in 1929, Smith the next year hit two home runs and one triple in the first game played by Negroes in Yankee Stadium. He teamed with John Beckwith,* John Henry Lloyd,* Norman "Turkey" Stearns*, Clint Thomas,* and Clarence "Fats" Jenkins* (IS) on the powerful Lincoln Giants and compiled superior marks batting third in the lineup. In an abbreviated career from 1924 to 1930, Smith batted .446 lifetime in regular season play, .423 in exhibitions against major leaguers, and .335 in the Cuban winter leagues. In 1929 he also belted 23 home runs and led the ANL in hitting and homers. Smith enjoyed his best season in 1930 and then died, possibly from yellow fever. Baseball historians wonder what Smith would have accomplished if he had enjoyed a long career.

BIBLIOGRAPHY: John Holway, "Charlie 'Chino' Smith," *Baseball Research Journal* 7 (1978), pp. 63–67; Robert W. Peterson, *Only the Ball Was White* (Englewood Cliffs, NJ, 1970); James A. Riley, *The All-Time All-Stars of Black Baseball* (Cocoa, FL, 1983); James A. Riley, interviews with former Negro leagues players, (collection). Riley, Cocoa, FL.

James A. Riley

SMITH, Hilton Lee (b. 27 February 1912, Giddings, TX; d. 18 November 1983, Kansas City, MO), player and scout, was the son of school teacher John and Mattie Smith. Smith's amateur career began in 1927, when he played town ball with his father. He attended Prairie View A&M (TX) College for two years and pitched there his final year. After pitching for the semi-pro Austin Senators in 1931, the right-hander hurled for the Monroe, LA, Monarchs in the Negro Southern Conference from 1932 to 1935. He married Louise Humphrey in 1934 and had two children, Hilton and DeMorris. In 1935 and 1936, Smith compiled a 5–0 record on semi-pro teams in the National Baseball Congress tournament in Wichita, KS. During the fall of 1936, he barnstormed with the Kansas City Monarchs (NAL).

Smith, who threw one of the best curveballs in Negro baseball, joined the Kansas City Monarchs full time in 1937 and pitched a perfect game in his NAL debut against the Chicago American Giants. Reputedly the equal of Satchel Paige,* Smith compiled an unofficial 161–22 record for the Monarchs in NAL play from 1937 to 1948. A sore arm limited his effectiveness in 1943 and 1944. Counting non-league games, he won at least 20 games every season from 1937 to 1948. An excellent hitter, he played many games in the outfield and occasionally batted fourth. Smith, an intelligent pitcher, enjoyed great success against major league players. He shut out an All-Star team with Bob Feller* and Johnny Mize* in 1937, and in 1946 beat Feller's All-Star team 3–2. The next spring in Caracas, Venezuela, he pitched five scoreless innings against the New York Yankees, missing only Joe DiMaggio.*

In two CUWL seasons (1937–1938 and 1939–1940), Smith won 10 games and lost 5. He pitched six consecutive East-West All-Star games from 1937 to 1942 and triumphed in the 1938 game, striking out 13 batters to tie Satchel Paige for second place on the All-Star list. He won one game in both the 1942 and 1946 Negro World Series. Smith in 1945 recommended Jackie Robinson* to the Monarchs after having played with him in the CUWL. He declined an offer to play in the Brooklyn Dodgers (NL) organization in 1946 and finished his pro career in 1948 with Kansas City. After two semi-pro seasons in Fulda, MN, he worked for Armco Steel in Kansas City and became a foreman there until 1978. He served as an associate scout for the Chicago Cubs (NL) at the time of his death. Smith, a superlative Negro league pitcher, played in the generation immediately preceding the entrance of blacks into organized baseball. He joined others establishing the excellence of Negro league baseball and paving the way for integration of the major leagues.

BIBLIOGRAPHY: Terry A. Baxter, correspondence with Jose Figueroda, 1984, Cuban League statistics, Terry A. Baxter Collection, Lee's Summit, MO; Terry A. Baxter, telephone interview with Monte Irvin, 1984; Terry A. Baxter, telephone interview with John "Buck" O'Neill, 1984; Terry A. Baxter, telephone interview with Mrs. Hilton Smith, 1984; Terry A. Baxter, telephone interview with Quincy Troupe, 1984; Janet Bruce, *The Kansas City Monarchs: Champions of Black Baseball* (Lawrence,

KS, 1985); John Holway, "They Made Me Survive," *TSN* (July 18, 1981); John Holway, *Voices from the Great Black Baseball Leagues* (New York, 1975); "Monarchs' Hilton Smith Dies at 71," Kansas City *Star*, November 20, 1983; National Baseball Congress, *Official Baseball Annual* (Wichita, KS, 1957); James A. Riley, *The All-Time Stars of Black Baseball* (Cocoa, FL, 1983); Donn Rogosin, *Invisible Men: Life in Baseball's Negro Leagues* (New York, 1983); Quincy Troupe, *Twenty Years Too Soon* (Los Angeles, 1977).

Terry A. Baxter

SNIDER, Edwin Donald "Duke," "Silver Fox" (b. 19 September 1926, Los Angeles, CA), player, scout, manager, and announcer, is the son of naval shipyard worker Ward and Florence (Johnson) Snider. The elder Snider, a former semi-pro player, nicknamed his 6-year-old son "Duke" because he acted like royalty. He also taught his right-handed child to bat left-handed because most baseball parks favored southpaws. Snider starred at Compton High School in football and baseball and signed with the Brooklyn Dodgers (NL) in 1944 for $750. At Newport News, Snider in 1944 led the Pil in doubles and homers and began a lifetime problem hitting southpaw curveball pitchers.

The petulant 6 foot, 179 pound Snider joined the Brooklyn Dodgers in 1947, following two years in the U.S. Navy, including eleven months on a submarine in the Pacific. After hitting only .241, Snider was farmed out to St. Paul (AA) and hit .316 there. He was recalled by the Dodgers to help in their NL pennant fight. Although ineligible to play against the New York Yankees, he received a $1,000 World Series share. Snider split the 1948 season between the Dodgers and the Montreal Royals (IL), often swinging at balls out of the strike zone and having problems with left-handed curveball pitchers. With Brooklyn in 1949, he led the NL in strikeouts with 91.

During the 1952 World Series, he made ten hits against the New York Yankees and tied the existing record by slugging four home runs. He duplicated this feat in 1955, leading Brooklyn to its only World Series championship. In 1955 he led the NL for the third consecutive year in runs scored (126) and paced both leagues with 136 RBIs. Nicknamed the "Silver Fox" because his hair had turned prematurely gray, he hit at least 40 home runs each season from 1953 through 1957. He slugged three homers in single games on May 30, 1950, and June 1, 1955, and set an NL mark (since broken) of eleven World Series home runs. *The Sporting News* named Snider the Major League Player of the Year in 1955 and selected him for its All-Star team in 1950 and 1952–1955. Snider played on the NL All-Star team in 1950, 1952–1956, and 1963, batting .273 composite. In 2,143 career games, Snider made 2,116 hits, scored 1,259 runs, slugged 358 doubles, 85 triples, and 407 home runs, knocked in 1,333 runs, struck out 1,237 times, and batted .295. He was elected to the National Baseball Hall of Fame in 1980.

After ending his active career with the New York Mets (NL) in 1963 and San Francisco Giants (NL) in 1964, he scouted for the Los Angeles Dodgers

(1965), managed Spokane (PCL) in 1965, and piloted Kennewick, WA (NWL), in 1966. After scouting for the Dodgers in 1967 and 1968, and for the San Diego Padres (NL) in 1969, he managed Alexandria, LA (TL), in 1972. He served as a batting instructor with the Montreal Expos (NL) in 1974–1975 and became one of their regular announcers. He married Beverly Null on October 25, 1947, and has one son and one daughter.

BIBLIOGRAPHY: Bill Borst, *The Brooklyn Dodgers: A Fan's Memoir, 1953–57* (St. Louis, 1982); *CB (1956), pp. 590–591;* Roger Kahn, *The Boys of Summer* (New York, 1972); Roger Kahn, "I Play Baseball For Money, Not Fun," *Collier's* 137 (May 25, 1956), p. 42; Gene Karst and Martin J. Jones, Jr., *Who's Who in Professional Baseball* (New Rochelle, NY, 1973); Tim Cohane, "He Reaches for Greatness," *Look* 19 (June 28, 1955), p. 107, 590–591; Paul MacFarlane, ed., *TSN Daguerreotypes of Great Stars of Baseball* (St. Louis, 1981); *NYT*, March 27, 1953, June 7, 1955; *SI* 2 (June 27, 1955), p. 17.

William A. Borst

SOCKALEXIS, Lewis M. "Chief" (b. 24 October 1871, Old Town, ME; d. 24 December, 1913, Burlington, ME), player and manager, was the son of American Indians Francis P. and Frances (Sockabeson) Sockalexis and grew up at Indian Island, Old Town, the Penobscot tribe reservation. Sockalexis, whose father worked as a guide, excelled in all sports. After playing semi-pro baseball in Maine and upstate New York, he enrolled at Holy Cross College in Worcester, MA. Michael "Doc" Powers, who had played summer baseball with Sockalexis, knew that the stocky Indian could strengthen the Holy Cross baseball program. Sockalexis, who batted left-handed and threw right-handed, helped the Crusaders become among the best baseball teams in the eastern United States. In February, 1897, Sockalexis joined Powers in moving to the University of Notre Dame and quickly became the team's best athlete.

After approximately one month at South Bend, Sockalexis borrowed money from Notre Dame to travel by train to Cleveland, and signed professionally with the Cleveland Spiders (NL) baseball team. Sockalexis, the first native American professional athlete, quickly proved an outstanding hitter and a marvelous fielder with a strong, accurate throwing arm and tremendous crowd appeal. At each city the Spiders played, he was greeted with derisive "war whoops" that turned to cheers because of his adept field play. In 1897 right fielder Sockalexis batted third in the lineup and only twice went without a hit in two consecutive games. His batting average never dropped below .300 after the seventh game of the season and rose to .386 on May 17.

In four consecutive games before July 4, he compiled 11 hits in 21 at bats. On July 4, however, Sockalexis engaged in a night of protracted drinking and could not play for two days. Upon returning to the lineup, he made two hits in each of his next three games. Sockalexis, however, began to stumble in the outfield and made errors attributed to his being intoxicated. In mid-July, Cleveland manager Patsy Tebeau began assigning players to check on Sockalexis so that he would not get drunk. Sockalexis sneaked out of his second floor hotel room one night and jumped or fell to the ground, severely injuring his ankle. He played one game a few weeks later, was benched for another month, and made two more outfield errors in his final game. During 1897 he batted .338, made 94 hits, and knocked in 42 runs in 66 games. *Sporting Life* observed: "Much of the stuff written about his dalliance with grape juice and his trysts with palefaced maidens is purely speculation. . . . Too much popularity has ruined Sockalexis by all accounts. It is no longer a secret that the Cleveland management can no longer control Sockalexis."

The Cleveland club still held out hope for Sockalexis for the 1898 season. Unfortunately, he returned to his old ways and batted only .224 in 21 games. Seven similar games in 1899 finished his major league baseball career. In 94 career games, he batted .313 with 115 hits and 55 RBIs. The single Sockalexis drifted to minor league teams in New England, occasionally umpired, and worked as a woodsman near the reservation until dying in 1913 of chronic alcoholism. Two years later, a contest was held to rename the Cleveland baseball team. The Indians, a team nickname when Sockalexis was playing, was selected. His exploits during a short stay with Cleveland still inspired Indians two decades later. More than seventy years later, the team nickname remains.

BIBLIOGRAPHY: Harry Grayson, *They Played the Game* (New York, 1945); Franklin Lewis, *The Cleveland Indians* (New York, 1949); Joseph L. Reichler, ed., *The Baseball Encyclopedia*, 6th ed. (New York, 1985), p. 1,412; *Sporting Life* (April, August, September, 1897).

Cappy Gagnon

SOMERS, Charles W. (b. 13 October 1868, Newark, OH; d. 29 June 1934, Put-In-Bay, OH), executive, was one of the AL's founding fathers and the son of businessman Joseph Hook and Philenia M. Somers. He married Mae (Gilbert) Somers and had one daughter, Dorothy (Somers) Clarke. In 1900, at age 31, he and John F. Kilfoyle organized and financed the Cleveland club in Ban Johnson's* new AL. Somers' father disapproved of his son's involvement with "such a foolish and unprofitable thing as baseball" and suggested that it would be more worthwhile if Charles devoted his energies to the J. H. Somers Coal Company. Despite his father's protests, young Somers continued his involvement in the fledgling AL by bankrolling the Cleveland franchise and holding financial interests in the Philadelphia, Boston (president, 1901–1904), and Chicago clubs. The shy Somers, who served as AL vice-president from 1901 through 1916, avoided the glare of publicity.

Somers proved instrumental in signing several established NL stars, including Nap Lajoie,* Bill Bernhard, and Elmer Flick,* for his Cleveland team. He also helped bring into organized baseball Ernest S. Barnard,* who succeeded Johnson as AL president. In 1913 Somers purchased the New Orleans Pelicans (SA) and again remained in the background. He selected A. J. Heinemann, who had been merely an office clerk, as club president. But Somers possessed a gift for recognizing and developing administrative talent, as Heinemann became an excellent president. Three years later, Somers' fortunes declined. Since his Cleveland club struggled on the field and at the gate, he sold the team in 1916 to James Dunn. Contemporary reports indicate that Somers lost much money in the last few years that he owned the franchise.

Somers still maintained control over the New Orleans Pelicans, although few people knew it, and allowed Heinemann free rein to run the club. When Heinemann died suddenly, Somers assumed a more active role in June, 1930. Once again, he delegated much authority and responsibility to new president Larry Gilbert. Somers received less publicity and acclaim than magnates Johnson, Charles Comiskey,* and Clark Griffith,* but his influence, wealth, and business acumen played an equally important part in the development of baseball in the early twentieth century.

BIBLIOGRAPHY: Cleveland *Plain Dealer*, June 29, 1934; Charles Somers file, National Baseball Hall of Fame Library, Cooperstown, NY; *NYT*, June 30, 1934.

                                                                David S. Matz

SOUTHWORTH, William Harrison "Billy" (b. 9 March 1893, Harvard, NE; d. 15 November 1969, Columbus, OH), player and manager, began his professional baseball career with Portsmouth, OH (OSL) in 1912 for $5 a day. The 5 foot, 9 inch, 170 pound Southworth, who batted left-handed and threw right-handed, played outfield with Portsmouth into 1913, Toledo (AA) in 1913, Cleveland (AA) in 1914–1915, Portland, OR (PCL) in 1915–1916, and Birmingham (SA) in 1917–1918. After brief trials with the Cleveland Indians (AL) in 1913 and 1915, Southworth performed in the major leagues as an NL outfielder with the Pittsburgh Pirates (1918–1920), Boston Braves (1921–1923), New York Giants (1924–June 1926), and St. Louis Cardinals (June 1926–1929). Southworth hit .300 or better six times and tied for the NL lead in triples with 14 in 1919. He enjoyed his greatest playing day on September 24, 1926, when he hit a two-run home run against his former manager, John McGraw,* and the New York Giants to put the Cardinals into first place. The Cardinals won the NL pennant and defeated the awesome New York Yankees in a seven-game World Series. In thirteen major league seasons, Southworth compiled a lifetime .297 batting average with 1,296 hits, 173 doubles, 91 triples, 52 home runs, 661 runs scored, 561 RBIs, and 138 stolen bases in 1,192 games.

After piloting successfully at Rochester, NY (IL), in 1928, Southworth the next year was named Cardinal manager. Since the Cardinals faltered, however, Southworth returned as Rochester pilot in July, 1929, and managed there through the 1932 season. After serving as a coach with the New York Giants (NL) in 1933, he managed at Asheville, NC (Pil), in 1935–1936, Memphis (SA) from July, 1936, through 1938, and Rochester, NY (IL), in 1939–1940. Southworth, who married Mabel Stemen on January 7, 1934, replaced Ray Blades as Cardinal manager in June, 1940. He piloted the Cardinals six seasons, winning three consecutive NL pennants (1942–1944) as well as World Series titles over the 1942 New York Yankees and 1944 St. Louis Browns. In 1943 the Cardinals lost the World Series to the Yankees. Southworth, named *The Sporting News* Manager of the Year in 1941 and 1942, signed with the Boston Braves (NL) as manager in 1945 while still under contract to the Cardinals. Cardinals owner Sam Breadon* permitted Southworth to join the Braves only after Eddie Dyer agreed to manage St. Louis. In 1948 Southworth piloted the Braves to their first NL pennant in thirty-four years, but his club lost the World Series to the Cleveland Indians in six games. Southworth, who managed Boston until removed during the 1951 season, compiled 1,064 wins and only 729 losses for a .593 mark (6th) in thirteen major league seasons as manager.

BIBLIOGRAPHY: John P. Carmichael, *My Greatest Day in Baseball* (New York, 1946); Ed Fitzgerald, *The National League* (New York, 1952); David S. Neft et al., *The Sports Encyclopedia: Baseball* (New York, 1976); *NYT*, November 16, 1969.

Edward J. Walsh

SPAHN, Warren Edward (b. 23 April 1921, Buffalo, NY), player, coach, and manager, attended Park High School in Buffalo and by age 15 played for three teams six days a week. Spahn's life was greatly influenced by his father Edward, a wallpaper salesman who taught him the fundamentals of pitching. After signing with the Boston Braves (NL) in 1940, the 6 foot, 183 pound Spahn began his professional career as a left-handed pitcher for Bradford, PA (Pol). The next season, Spahn hurled for Evansville, IN, and led the 3IL in victories. After a short stay with Boston, Spahn was sent to Hartford, CT (EL), to complete the 1942 season. He served in the U.S. Army (1943–1946) and was cited for bravery with the engineers in Germany. Following his discharge, Spahn excelled in his first full major league season (1947) by winning 21 games, losing 10, and pacing NL pitchers in ERA (2.33).

Spahn pitched for the Boston Braves (1942, 1946–1952) and Milwaukee Braves after the franchise was switched (1953–1964). In 1965 he finished his major league career with the New York Mets (NL) and San Francisco Giants (NL). During his twenty-one-year pitching tenure, Spahn established major league records for most seasons winning 20 or more games by a left-handed pitcher (13), most years leading in games won (8), most consecutive years pacing the NL in complete games (7), most career games won by a left-handed pitcher (363), most career strikeouts by a left-handed pitcher (2,583, since broken), and most consecutive years with at least 100 strikeouts (17). He established NL records, some since broken, for most career shutouts by a left-handed pitcher (63), most career games started (665), most seasons with at least 100 strikeouts (17), most seasons pitching for one team (20), and most career games pitched (750). Spahn also paced NL pitchers in strikeouts (1949–1952), innings pitched (1947, 1949, 1958–1959), ERA (1947, 1953, 1961), and complete games (1949, 1951, 1957–1963), and led or tied for the league lead in shutouts (1947, 1959, 1961).

Spahn pitched no-hit victories against the Philadelphia Phillies in 1960 and San Francisco Giants in 1961. At age 42, he posted a 23–7 record for his final big season. The good-hitting Spahn cracked 35 lifetime home runs, an NL record for pitchers. Named by *The Sporting News* as outstanding NL pitcher (1953, 1957–1958, 1961) and Major League Pitcher of the Year (1961), Spahn won the Cy Young Award as the best major league pitcher (1957). Combining with Johnny Sain and later Lew Burdette,* Spahn helped lead the Braves to three NL pennants (1948, 1957–1958) and one world championship (1957). In eight World Series games, Spahn won four and lost three. He pitched in seven All-Star games and was the NL's winning pitcher in the 1953 classic.

Elected to the National Baseball Hall of Fame in 1973, Spahn ranks near the top of the all-time major league lists for pitchers in nearly every category. Spahn compiled 363 victories (5th) and 245 losses (8th), started 665 games (6th), pitched in 750 games (17th), and completed 382 games (19th). He pitched 5,244 innings (6th), allowed 4,830 hits (7th), and 2,016 runs (16th), issued 1,434 bases on balls (11th), struck out 2,583 batters (14th), recorded 20 or more victories thirteen times (3rd), and compiled a career 3.09 ERA.

After hurling a few games in Mexico City, Spahn managed at Tulsa from 1967 to 1970. His Oilers captured a PCL championship (1968) and finished second (1969–1970) when the franchise was switched to the AA. In 1971 he was a scout and minor league pitching instructor for the St. Louis Cardinals (NL). He was pitching coach for the Cleveland Indians (AL) in 1972 and 1973, and a minor league pitching instructor for the California Angels (AL) since 1978. Spahn operates a 2,800 acre cattle ranch in Hartshorne, OK. He married Lorene Southard in August, 1946, and has one son, Gregory. The craftiest pitcher of his day, Spahn overcame knee surgery three times to return to the mound. A master of control, he consistently placed pitches and continually kept batters off stride. Besides having an excellent fastball, curve, and change of pace, Spahn developed the screwball and slider.

BIBLIOGRAPHY: Bob Broeg, *Super Stars of Baseball* (St. Louis, 1971); *TSN Official Baseball Record Book, 1985* (St. Louis, 1985); *TSN Official Baseball Register, 1973* (St. Louis, 1973).

John L. Evers

SPALDING, Albert Goodwill "Al" (b. 2 September 1850, Byron, IL; d. 9 September 1915, Point Loma, CA), player, manager, owner, and manufacturer, was the son of Harriet and James Spalding, attended Byron and Rockford public schools, and completed his formal education at the Rockford Commercial College. He married Sarah Keith and had one son. After her death in 1899, he married Mrs. Elizabeth Mayer the next year. During baseball's first half century, no other individual so dominated the sport as player, owner, and business entrepreneur. A product of the Illinois prairies, Spalding pitched well for the Forest City Club of Rockford in the 1860s and then joined Boston (NA) in 1871, leading them to four consecutive NA championships (1872–1875). From 1871 to 1875, he compiled an amazing 207–56 won-lost record (.787) and became baseball's first 200-game winner. Spalding twice won over 50 decisions in a season, with 52–18 and 57–5 marks in 1874 and 1875, respectively. Spalding also compiled 37–8 and 41–15 won-lost records in 1872 and 1873. An excellent batter, he made 462 hits in 284 games and hit .320 from 1871 to 1875.

"The champion pitcher of the world" surprised the baseball community by jumping in 1876 to the Chicago White Stockings of the NL. During that season, the right-hander won 47 of 60 decisions for a 1.75 ERA, batted .312, and managed his club to the championship. He hurled shutouts in his first two appearances and threw eight for the season. This represented the last hurrah for the crafty 6 foot, 1 inch, 170 pound "gentlemanly and effective pitcher," who played rarely thereafter and retired following the 1878 season. In the NL, he won 48, lost 13 (.787), boasted a 1.78 ERA, and completed 53 of 61 starts. He played mainly first base and some second base in 1877 and batted .256. From 1876 to 1878, he appeared in 127 games, made 158 hits, 21 doubles, and 8 triples, scored 83 runs, and knocked in 79 runs.

Spalding already had charted another career. The Chicago *Tribune* announced his opening in February, 1876, of a "large emporium in Chicago, where he will sell all kinds of baseball goods and turn his place into the headquarters for the Western Ball Clubs." His company, eventually named A. G. Spalding & Brothers, emerged as the generation's dominant sporting goods firm. The NL gave Spalding exclusive authority to supply its official baseballs and to publish *Spalding's Official Base Ball Guide*. Spalding proved a skilled businessman, capitalizing on his fame as a ballplayer to promote his company. His favorite motto, "Everything is possible to him who dares," guided his company's growth. With a fierce drive to succeed, Spalding became a captain of industry and developed as tight a monopoly as Andrew Carnegie and other business leaders. With superior organization, imagination, and ruthlessness, he virtually eliminated competition.

While developing and expanding his business, he served from 1882 to 1891 as president of the Chicago (NL) team (eventually renamed the Cubs). A hard worker, he sought to improve baseball's image around ballparks by reducing rowdiness and eliminating gamblers' influence; he even hired detectives to check up on his players, creating a Chicago press and public upheaval in the 1880s. When the PL was formed in 1890, Spalding led the fight against it and probably saved the NL from extinction by helping crush the rival league. A skillful diplomat and first-rate organizer, Spalding promoted baseball's interests nationally and internationally and simultaneously furthered his own sporting goods enterprises. In 1874 he arranged a tour of England and Ireland for two baseball teams and in 1888–1889 led the first world baseball tour. His Chicago team and a squad of "All Star" players performed at such widely separated stops as Australia, Egypt, Italy, and England. Although it did not succeed financially, the latter tour publicized baseball and Spalding's company abroad.

By 1900 Spalding was acknowledged as the "Father of Baseball" and of the NL. Spalding's classic baseball history, *America's National Game* (1911) further enhanced his reputation and provided the best comprehensive early examination of the sport. His compulsion to prove that baseball's origins were American led him to advance the myth that Abner Doubleday founded the sport at Cooperstown, NY, in 1839. Since Spalding recorded games played before 1839 in his book, he personally may not have believed the myth.

An all-around sportsman, Spalding was selected American commissioner for the 1900 Olympic games in Paris and later received the rosette of the Legion of Honor from France for his work. Upon his death, the *New York Times* praised his versatile ability as a player, positive genius as a manager, exceptional executive ability, and personal magnetism. These qualities held organized baseball together throughout its "earlier tribulations." In 1939 he was elected to the National Baseball Hall of Fame. Spalding's plaque in the Baseball Hall of Fame acclaimed him as the "organizational genius of baseball's pioneer days" and a star pitcher.

BIBLIOGRAPHY: Arthur Bartlett, *Baseball and Mr. Spalding* (New York, 1951); *Base-Ball Player*, 1869–1877; Peter Levine, *A. G. Spalding and the Rise of Baseball* (New York, 1985); Harold Seymour, *Baseball: The Early Years* (New York, 1960); Robert Smith, *Pioneers of Baseball* (Boston, 1978); Albert G. Spalding, *America's National Game* (New York, 1911); Albert G. Spalding Collection, New York Public Library; Albert Spalding file, National Baseball Hall of Fame Library, Cooperstown, NY; David Quentin Voigt, *American Baseball*, vol. 1 (Norman, OK, 1966).

Duane A. Smith

SPEAKER, Tristram E. "Tris," "The Gray Eagle," "Spoke" (b. 4 April 1888, Hubbard City, TX; d. 8 December 1958, Lake Whitney, TX), player, manager, executive, and sportscaster, was the son of merchant Archie and homemaker Nancy Jane (Peer) Speaker and married Mary Frances Cudahy on January 15, 1925. Speaker, who exhibited dedication, desire for athletic perfection, and self-confidence, steadfastly recognized his potential before others became believers and was outspoken when exposed to criticism. Nicknamed "The Gray Eagle," he worked as a telegraph linesman and cow puncher as a youth and excelled as an all-around athlete in high school. In 1906 18-year-old Speaker began his professional baseball career as a pitcher–right fielder for Cleburne, TX (NTL), and batted .268. In 1907 this franchise was transferred to Houston (TL), where he raised his average to .314. After the Boston Red Sox (AL) bought his contract in August, 1907, for $750, Speaker hit .158 in seven games. Boston did not send Speaker a 1908 contract, but he paid his own expenses to their Little Rock training camp. Boston left him with the Little Rock club in lieu of ground rent payment with $500 purchase rights to him. After leading the SA in batting that year with .350, Speaker rejoined Boston (AL) and hit .220 in 31 games.

With the Red Sox from 1909 to 1915, Speaker became an AL star. The winner of the Chalmers Award in 1912, he helped the Red Sox capture world championships in 1912 and 1915 and made 161 assists from 1910 to 1915 as center fielder in the superb "Duffy" Lewis–Speaker–Harry Hooper* trio. During the winter of 1915–1916, Boston owner Joe Lannin proposed cutting Speaker's salary from $11,000 to $9,000. The furious Speaker held out and was traded on April 12, 1916, to the Cleveland Indians (AL) for two players and $50,000. With Cleveland for eleven seasons, he batted .354, frequently led the Indians in offensive categories, and paced the AL four consecutive years in doubles. As Cleveland manager, he compiled a 616–520 won-lost mark (.542) from 1919 through 1926. In 1920 he led Cleveland to its first AL pennant and world championship, beating the Brooklyn Dodgers (NL) five games to two. Following a delayed scandal over a questionable 1919 AL game, league president Ban Johnson* in late 1926 persuaded managers Speaker and Ty Cobb* of the Detroit Tigers to resign. Speaker ended his major league career with one season each for the Washington Senators (AL) and Philadelphia Athletics (AL). After spending 1929 and early 1930 as manager-player of Newark (IL), he later served as a broadcaster and briefly as part-owner and manager of Kansas City (AA).

A major leaguer for twenty-two years, Speaker still leads the majors in career doubles (793), outfield assists (448), and double plays (139), and paces the AL in outfield putouts (6,791). The eight-time AL leader in doubles ranks fifth in major league hits, sixth in batting average (.344) and triples (223), eighth in runs scored (1,881), and ninth in both total bases and extra-base hits (1,133). Of his 3,515 career hits, 68 percent were singles, 23 percent doubles, 6 percent triples, and 3 percent (117) home runs. Speaker knocked in 1,559 runs, walked 1,381 times, struck out only 220 times, and stole 433 bases. In 1937 he was elected to the National Baseball Hall of Fame. Speaker, whose Hall of Fame plaque correctly cites him as "the greatest centerfielder of his day," made an outstanding impact on the development of his position, batting, and base running skills. Defensively, he quickly determined the eventual direction and distance of fly balls when a hitter's bat made contact

with the ball. His great speed and accurate estimates frequently enabled him
to get a jump on the ball. He deliberately played shallow, helping him set
a major league outfield record for double plays. An extremely versatile batter,
he used aggressiveness, speed, and deception on the base paths.

BIBLIOGRAPHY: *Boston Red Sox Media Guide, 1984*; Ellery H. Clark, Jr., *Boston Red
Sox: 75th Anniversary History* (Hicksville, NY, 1975); Ellery H. Clark, Jr., [Red Sox
Analytical Letter Collection], correspondence with Harry Hooper, "Duffy" Lewis,
Ellery H. Clark, Jr. papers, Annapolis, MD; Ellery H. Clark, Jr., *Red Sox Fever*
(Hicksville, NY, 1979); Ellery H. Clark, Jr., *Red Sox Forever* (Hicksville, NY, 1977);
Ellery H. Clark, Jr., Interviews, Everett Scott, September, 1924; Tris Speaker, June,
1926, June 1927; Bill Carrigan, May, 1928; Marty McHale, May, 1950; Ray Collins,
July, 1950; "Duffy" Lewis, June, 1973, August, 1974; Marty McHale, "A Closeup
of Tris Speaker," Ellery Clark collection, Annapolis, MD; Joseph L. Reichler, ed.,
The Baseball Encyclopedia, 6th ed. (New York, 1985), pp. 1,414–1,415.

Ellery H. Clark, Jr.

STARGELL, Wilver Dornel "Willie," "Pops" (b. 6 March 1941, Earlsboro,
OK), player and coach, is the son of William and Verlene Stargell and moved
as a small boy with his family to Oakland, CA, where he starred in baseball,
basketball, and track at Encinal High School. He played baseball briefly at
Santa Rosa Junior College before the Pittsburgh Pirates (NL) signed him for
a $1,200 bonus in 1958. After four minor league seasons with Roswell, NM
(SpL), in 1959, Grand Forks, ND (NoL), in 1960, Asheville, NC (SAL), in
1961, and Columbus (IL) in 1962, Stargell joined the Pirates in 1962 and
remained with Pittsburgh for twenty-one seasons, retiring after the 1982
season.

Stargell played the outfield in his early years, but shifted permanently to
first base in the 1970s. A feared slugger, Stargell hit 475 home runs to tie
for sixteenth place on the all-time list with Stan Musial.* He compiled a
.282 lifetime batting average and drove in 1,540 runs to place twenty-seventh
on the all-time list. In 2,360 games, he made 2,232 hits, 423 doubles, 1,195
runs scored, and 1,936 strikeouts, second on the all-time list. Stargell's home
run output might have been considerably higher had he not played much of
his career in spacious Forbes Field. During sixty-two seasons of major league
play at Forbes Field, only 18 homers were hit completely out of the stadium;
Stargell slugged 7 of those. After the Pirates moved to Three Rivers Stadium,
Stargell led the NL with 48 home runs in 1971 and 44 home runs in 1973.

Stargell helped the Pirates win six NL Eastern Division championships
in the 1970s and NL pennants and World Series titles in 1971 and 1979. In
1979 the 38-year-old Stargell provided on- and off-field leadership that enabled the underdog Pirates to win the World Series. As "Pops" of the Pirate
"Family," Stargell hit .281 with 32 home runs in 1979 and shared the NL's
Most Valuable Player Award with Keith Hernandez* of St. Louis. He batted
.455 and hit two homers in the Pirates' sweep of the Cincinnati Reds in the

NL Championship Series. In the World Series against the Baltimore Orioles, Stargell hit .400 and slugged three home runs, including a decisive two-run homer in the seventh game.

Used primarily as a pinch hitter his last two campaigns, Stargell retired as an active player following the 1982 season and rejoined the Pirates as a coach in 1985. Before the 1986 season, Stargell joined the Atlanta Braves (NL) as a coach. He participated in various civic and charitable activities, serving as chair of an organization of athletes raising money for research on sickle-cell anemia. Stargell and his wife, Dolores, have three children. A dangerous power hitter, fierce competitor, and clubhouse leader, Stargell excelled as one of baseball's greatest left-handed sluggers.

BIBLIOGRAPHY: Roy Fimrite, "Two Champs from the City of Champions," *SI* 51 (December 14, 1979), pp. 36–42; Arnold Hano, "Willie Stargell and the Beautiful Challenge," *Sport* 15 (August, 1971), pp. 61–70; Hank Nauer, "Willie Stargell: The Pride of Pittsburgh," *SEP* 7 (May/June, 1980), pp. 29–38.

Fred M. Shelley

START, Joseph "Joe," "Old Reliable" (b. 14 October 1842, New York, NY; d. 27 March 1927, Providence, RI), player, enjoyed a three-decade baseball career and became a national hero in the 1860s as a power hitter. Of Dutch-American parents, Start attended the Bedford Avenue and Monroe Street Elementary School. A first baseman practically his entire career, the 5 foot, 9 inch, 165 pound left-hander joined the Enterprise Club of Brooklyn in 1860 at age 17. He played there with John Chapman for two seasons until both moved to the mighty Brooklyn Atlantics in 1862. For Brooklyn from 1862 to 1870, Start enjoyed his strongest seasons, batting third, fourth, and fifth, and helping the Atlantics win championships from 1865 through 1866. In 1869 the Atlantics defeated the legendary Cincinnati Red Stockings in two out of three games, the only club to do so. Start jumped to the Mutual team of New York in 1871, a charter member of the new NA, baseball's first professional league. The same year, he married Angeline Creed.

The first available statistical records of Start's accomplishments appeared in the NA. During five full seasons, he compiled a .282 batting average, scored 266 runs, and made 382 hits in 273 games, and peaked in 1871 with a .339 percentage. He remained with New York when the NL was formed in 1876. Start batted .332 with Hartford (1877) and .351 at Chicago (1878), leading the NL in at bats (285) and hits (100). In 1879 he joined Providence and helped them to the NL championship that year and in 1884. He remained with Providence through 1885, hitting .319 in 1879, .328 in 1881, and .329 in 1882, and finished his playing career at Washington (NL) in 1886. During eleven NL seasons, Start hit .300 in 798 games. Before retiring at age 44, he collected 1,031 hits, scored 590 runs, and knocked in at least 220 runs, switching from a power to a percentage hitter. He belted 107 doubles, 55 triples, and 7 home runs and walked 150 times. Start, who later became an innkeeper in Providence, was one of the few early stars to participate in the pre-professional, NA, and young NL eras.

BIBLIOGRAPHY: Preston D. Orem, *Baseball, 1845–1881* (Altadena, CA, 1961); Joseph L. Reichler, ed., *The Baseball Encyclopedia*, 6th ed. (New York, 1985), pp. 68, 1,423; Joe Start file, National Baseball Hall of Fame Library, Cooperstown, NY.

Mark D. Rucker

STAUB, Daniel Joseph "Rusty" (b. 1 April 1944, New Orleans, LA), player, coach, scout, and announcer, resides in Houston and owns Rusty's Restaurant in New York City. Staub, a bachelor who bats left and throws right, is 6 feet, 2 inches tall and weighs 190 pounds. In 1961 Staub was named Louisiana Scholastic Athlete of the Year and an All-State selection in basketball and baseball at Jesuit High School in New Orleans. The same year, at age 17, Staub signed his first professional contract with the Houston Colt .45's (NL) organization. He started in 1963 at outfield for the Houston Astros. In January 1969 the red-orange haired Staub was traded to the Montreal Expos (NL), where he became the first baseball hero in the expansion team city and was dubbed "Le Grand Orange" by the fans.

After joining the New York Mets (NL) in 1972, Staub established several records. In the 1973 Championship Series, he set records for most home runs in a series (3) and most homers in two consecutive innings (2). During the 1973 World Series against the Oakland A's, Staub tied a record by reaching base safely five times in one game, batted .423, drove in six runs, and became one of forty-two players to get four hits in one game. Two years later, Staub became the first Met to drive in over 100 runs in a season and then was traded to the Detroit Tigers (AL). As a Tiger, Staub in 1978 was voted the AL's Outstanding Designated Hitter by batting .273 and knocking in 121 runs in 162 games. After brief stints with Montreal (NL) in 1979 and the Texas Rangers (AL) in 1980, Staub twice became a free agent and was re-signed both times by the NL New York Mets (1980, 1985).

In 1983 he pinch-hit in 104 games, made 24 pinch hits, compiled a .296 batting average, and tied major league records with 8 consecutive pinch hits and 25 RBIs as a pinch hitter. In 1984, at age 40, Staub again led the NL in pinch hits and RBIs as a pinch hitter. He became only the second player in baseball history to hit major league home runs as a teenager and 40-year-old.

Staub, one of forty-one players in major league history to amass over 4,000 total career bases, played in five straight All-Star games with the NL (1967–1971) and was voted an AL starter in 1976. Staub, who retired following the 1985 season, scored 1,189 runs, made 2,716 hits, slugged 499 doubles, 47 triples, and 292 homers, knocked in 1,466 runs, and batted .279. In 1986 the New York Mets (NL) named him a spring training instructor, special scout, talent evaluator, and announcer.

BIBLIOGRAPHY: Roger Angell, "My Summer Vacation," *New Yorker 60 (May 7, 1984), pp. 74–120; Larry Keith, "He's Still Le Grand Orange," SI* 49 (August 21, 1978), pp. 58–59; Mark Mulvoy, "In Montreal They Love Grand Orange," *SI* 33 (July 6, 1970), pp. 38–39; *New York Mets 1984 Information Guide* (New York, 1984); *NYT*, February 13, 1982; Joseph L. Reichler, ed., *The Baseball Encyclopedia*, 6th ed. (New York, 1985) pp. 1,423–1,424; Gary Ronberg, "Houston's Boy Is Now a Man," *SI* 27 (August 14, 1967), pp. 54–56; *TSN Official Baseball Register, 1985* (St. Louis, 1985).

Leslie Eldridge

STEARNS, Norman "Turkey" (b. 8 May 1901, Nashville, TN; d. 4 September 1979, Detroit, MI), player, was the son of Will and Mary (Everett) Stearns and pitched for the Pearl High School baseball team. Following his father's death, Stearns left school to work at age 15 and played baseball in his spare time. Stearns performed with the Montgomery Grey Sox in 1921 and with a Memphis team the following year, when Bruce Petway of the Detroit Stars recruited him. Since Stearns desired to finish school and needed full-time employment, he accepted the Detroit offer. In 1923 the 6 foot, 1 inch, 170 pound switch-hitting outfielder began working for the Briggs Manufacturing Company and playing for the Detroit Stars (NNL). He quickly was recognized as an outstanding outfielder by slugging 50 home runs in 1924, and remained with Detroit through the 1931 season. Although they usually contended during those years, the Detroit Stars finished at the top only in the first half of the 1930 season and were defeated that year by the St. Louis Stars for the NNL pennant.

After the Depression terminated the NNL, Stearns performed for several other clubs over the next decade. He played briefly for the Philadelphia Stars and Lincoln Giants and then patrolled the outfield for Cole's American Giants and the Chicago American Giants under manager Dave Malarcher. Stearns learned there to bunt, something the free-swinging power hitter hitherto had not done very often. At Chicago, Stearns teamed with "Steel Arm" Davis and Nat Rogers to form one of the better outfields in black baseball. During the late 1930s, he returned to the Detroit Stars (NAL) and Black Sox. He slugged 35 home runs in 1937 and performed with "Cool Papa" Bell* and Davis in the outfield. Stearns, who finished his playing career with the Kansas City Monarchs (NAL) in 1940 and 1941, played winter ball in California and Cuba. Despite the paucity of actual box scores and other statistical records, Stearns clearly ranked among the best outfielders of his time. He performed well enough during the 1930s to play center field in four of the first five East-West Negro All-Star games (1933–1935, 1937). After quitting baseball, Stearns worked until 1964 in the rolling mills of Detroit, married Nettie MacArthur on May 8, 1946, and had two children.

BIBLIOGRAPHY: William Brashler, *Josh Gibson* (New York, 1978); John Holway, *Voices from Great Black Baseball Leagues* (New York, 1975); Robert W. Peterson, *Only the Ball Was White* (Englewood Cliffs, NJ, 1970); Donn Rogosin, *Invisible Men: Life in Baseball's*

Negro Leagues (New York, 1983); Norman "Turkey" Stearns file, National Baseball Hall of Fame Library, Cooperstown, NY.

                                                                                       Douglas D. Martin

STENGEL, Charles Dillon "Casey," "Dutch," "The Old Professor" (b. 30 July 1890, Kansas City, MO; d. 29 September 1975, Glendale, CA), player and manager, was the son of the Irish-German Louis Stengels of Kansas City. Nicknamed "Dutch" and later "Casey," he attended Woodland Grade School, starred in baseball, football, and basketball at Central High School, and spent three years studying dentistry at Western Dental College. In 1910 he quit his studies and signed for $75 a month as an outfielder for Kankakee, IL (NoA). When the NoA disbanded that July, he played with Shelbyville–Maysville, KY (BGL), batting .223 and fielding .987. For Aurora, IL (WIL), in nearly 1911, he nearly won the batting title with a .352 average and led the WIL in stolen bases. The left-handed Stengel in 1912 performed with Montgomery, AL (SL), and was purchased by the Brooklyn Dodgers (NL) for $300.

Stengel played 17 games with Brooklyn in 1912, debuting with four hits in four at bats. He batted .316 during that short season and compiled a .284 mark over fourteen NL seasons as an outfielder with the Dodgers (1912–1917), Pittsburgh Pirates (1918–1919), Philadelphia Phillies (1920–July 1921), New York Giants (July 1921–1923), and Boston Braves (1924–1925). He hit .316 in 126 games in 1914, achieved career highs of 141 hits, 73 RBIs, and 69 runs scored with the Dodgers in 1917, and hit .364 in his first World Series in 1916. After being traded in January 1918 to Pittsburgh (NL), he hit .246 and fielded .957. He was dealt in September, 1919, to Philadelphia (NL) and in July 1921 to John McGraw's* New York Giants. His 1922 batting average reached a career-high .368 mark. He batted .339 in 1923 for the Giants and starred in the 1922 and 1923 World Series. He hit .400 in the 1922 classic and .417 in the 1923 Series against the New York Yankees, winning two 1923 games with crucial home runs. Stengel was traded to Boston in November 1923 and played his last two major league seasons there. In 1,277 games, he compiled 1,219 hits, 182 doubles, 89 triples, 60 homers, 575 runs scored, 535 RBIs, and 131 stolen bases.

Stengel managed Worcester (EL) in 1925 and the Toledo Mudhens (AA) from 1926 to 1931 and coached at Brooklyn (NL) in 1932 and 1933. When the Dodgers fired pilot Max Carey* in 1934, Stengel began his major league managerial career. He endured nine barren years with Brooklyn and the Boston Braves (NL). After 1936, the Dodgers paid him to sit out the fourth year of his contract. Hired by the Braves in 1938, he experienced six struggling years. The Braves finished fifth in 1938, seventh the next three seasons, and sixth in 1942. Stengel, who resigned in 1943, was hired the next year by Bill Veeck* as manager of the Milwaukee Brewers (AA). After finishing first there, he managed his hometown Kansas City Blues (AA) in 1945 and Oakland (PCL) from 1946 to 1948. On October 13, 1948, he signed to manage the New York Yankees (AL) for $25,000, succeeding Bucky Harris.* General manager George Weiss* had tried for years to bring Stengel to the Yankees. There Stengel recorded an unprecedented ten AL pennants and seven World Series titles in twelve years. From 1949 to 1953, the Yankees won five straight AL pennants in Stengel's first five years. His 1954 Yankees won 103 games but finished eight games behind the Cleveland Indians.

Stengel rewrote managing rules. When the Yankees suffered eleven injuries in 1949, he skillfully platooned his players, followed intuition, gambled on percentages, and abruptly became "The Old Professor." After being released in 1960 by the Yankees, he returned to Oakland as a millionaire and served as a bank director. From 1962 to 1965, Stengel managed the New York Mets (NL) to four tenth place finishes. In twenty-five years as a major league manager, Stengel compiled 1,926 wins and 1,867 losses (.508). He was elected to the National Baseball Hall of Fame in 1966 and saw his uniform number, 37, retired by the Yankees. He married Edna Lawson on August 16, 1924, and had no children. Stengel, who died of cancer, may have held more public affection than any other baseball figure since Babe Ruth.*

BIBLIOGRAPHY: Robert W. Creamer, "Casey Stengel—An Appreciation," *SI* 43 (October 13, 1975), p. 41; Robert W. Creamer, *Stengel* (New York, 1984); Mark Gallagher, *The Yankee Encyclopedia* (New York, 1982); Red Smith, "Leave Him to the Angels," *NYT*, January 18, 1981.

Arthur F. McClure

STEPHENS, Vernon Decatur "Junior," "Buster" (b. 23 October 1920, McAlister, NM; d. 3 November 1968, Long Beach, CA), player, ranked among the leading power hitters and shortstops of the 1940s and early 1950s. His father, a farmer and WL umpire, moved the family to Long Beach in the early 1920s. Stephens grew up in an athletic environment with baseball and basketball, but weighed under 100 pounds and was too small for high school competition. After a regimen of body building and swimming, he developed rapidly as a star baseball shortstop in American Legion play. In 1936 he tentatively was signed by the St. Louis Browns (AL) organization while studying journalism at Long Beach Junior College. He reported to the Browns' Springfield, IL (3IL), farm and spent four seasons in the minors. As a minor leaguer, he batted .290 and fielded brilliantly but erratically.

Stephens joined the St. Louis Browns (AL) in 1942 and starred immediately with a .294 batting mark and 92 RBIs. Browns manager Luke Sewell claimed that he never saw a player develop as rapidly as Stephens. During the next five years with St. Louis, Stephens batted around .290 with impressive RBI statistics, showed a formidable throwing arm, and was named to the AL All-Star teams in 1943–1944, 1946, and 1948. An early knee injury exempted him from military service. In 1944 he helped the Browns capture their first AL pennant by leading the AL with 109 RBIs. Traded in November 1947 with Jack Kramer to the Boston Red Sox (AL), Stephens starred in a potent lineup that included Ted Williams,* Bobby Doerr,* Johnny Pesky* and Dom DiMaggio. Batting behind Williams, he averaged 35 homers and 145 RBIs the next three years and tied for the AL lead in RBIs with 159 in 1949 and 144 in 1950. After an injury-shortened 1952 season, he divided 1953 between the Chicago White Sox (AL) and the Browns (AL) and 1954 and 1955 (his last major league season) between the Baltimore Orioles (AL) and the White Sox.

The 5 foot, 10 inch, 180 pound Stephens was renowned for his clutch hitting and frequent brilliance afield. At Boston, his hitting ranked second to Williams in one of the most lethal batting orders in major league history. In 1,720 major league games, he made 1,859 hits, 307 doubles, 247 home runs, and 1,174 RBIs, and batted .286. He married Bernice Hood in 1940 and was survived by his wife and two sons.

BIBLIOGRAPHY: Joseph L. Reichler, ed., *The Baseball Encyclopedia*, 6th ed. (New York, 1985), p. 1,427; Frank Waldman, *Famous American Athletes of Today*, 11th series (Boston, 1949).

                                                                                    Leonard Frey

STEPHENSON, Jackson Riggs "Old Hoss" (b. 5 January 1898, Akron, AL; d. 15 November 1985, Tuscaloosa, AL), baseball and football player and manager, attended high school in Guntersville, AL, graduated from the University of Alabama with a Bachelor of Science degree in 1921, and served one year (1918) in the U.S. Army. At Alabama, Stephenson made All–Southern Conference football squads his junior and senior years, and in 1920 was named All–Southern Conference fullback. Baseball became Stephenson's primary sport at Alabama, where he played shortstop from 1918 to 1920, joining lifelong friend Joe Sewell.* In 1921 the 5 foot, 10 inch, 185 pound Stephenson signed a contract for $300 a month with Cleveland (AL) and expected to join the Indians after the college season. Stephenson, however, was called up by Cleveland before opening day to replace the injured Bill Wambsganss at second base.

Although a great hitter, the right-handed Stephenson proved only a mediocre infielder and possessed a weak arm due to a boyhood accident. Cleveland manager Tris Speaker* in 1925 optioned Stephenson to Kansas City (AA) to become an outfielder, but Kansas City traded him the same year to Indianapolis (AA) for Johnny Hodapp. When Louisville manager Joe McCarthy* became the Chicago Cubs pilot the next year, he quickly obtained Stephenson. With Stephenson in left, Lewis "Hack" Wilson* in center, and Kiki Cuyler* in right, the Cubs (NL) wielded one of the hardest hitting outfields of all time. Stephenson played outfield nine years for Chicago and helped the Cubs win NL pennants in 1929 and 1932, but his club lost the World Series in 1929 to the Philadelphia Athletics and in 1932 to the New York Yankees. Stephenson led Cubs batters in the 1932 World Series with a .444 average and hit .316 in 1929 against the A's.

During the regular season, Stephenson compiled batting averages of .362 in 1929 and .367 in 1930 for Chicago. Although not considered a long-ball hitter, he led the NL in doubles in 1927 (46). Stephenson had a .336 career batting average as well as 773 RBIs, 714 runs scored, 1,515 hits, 321 doubles, and only 247 strikeouts in 4,508 at bats in fourteen seasons. After being released by the Cubs, Stephenson joined Indianapolis (AA) in 1935 and Birmingham, AL (SA), as player-manager in 1936 and 1937. His Birmingham team finished third in 1936 and won the SA playoffs defeating Nashville and New Orleans. He managed Helena, AL (CSL), in 1938 and Montgomery, AL (SEL) in 1939 before retiring from baseball. Stephenson married Norma Chadwick on January 10, 1934 and had one daughter.

BIBLIOGRAPHY: Gene Karst and Martin J. Jones, Jr., *Who's Who in Professional Baseball* (New Rochelle, NY, 1973); Laurie Kiely, "A Football Star Turned Baseball Pro," *Bama* (March, 1983), pp. 23–25; Joseph L. Reichler, *The Great All-Time Baseball Record Book* (New York, 1981); Joseph L. Reichler, ed., *The Baseball Encyclopedia*, 6th ed. (New York, 1985), p. 1,428; Riggs Stephenson file, National Baseball Hall of Fame Library, Cooperstown, NY.

Horace R. Givens

STIVETTS, John Elmer "Jack," "Happy Jack" (b. 31 March 1868, Ashland, PA; d. 18 April 1930, Ashland, PA), player, won over 200 games as a pitcher and batted near .300 during an eleven-year major league career. Stivetts, the son of coal miner Adam and Ameila (Cooper) Stivetts, attended the Ashland public school for eight years, worked around the anthracite mines, and pitched for the town baseball team. He first played professionally for York, PA, and Allentown, PA (CL), and in 1889 signed with the major league St. Louis Browns (AA). The 6 foot, 2 inch, 185 pound right-hander displayed exceptional skill at the plate and on the mound and often was used at other positions to take advantage of his powerful hitting. As a rookie in 1889, Stivetts appeared in 26 games, won 13, lost 7, and struck out 143 batters. The following year, he finished among the AA's top five pitching and batting leaders. His 29 victories and 289 strikeouts placed him fourth and second, respectively, in those categories. He hit 7 home runs to tie for third place in the final standings. Besides improving to 33 wins and an AA-leading 259 strikeouts in 1891, Stivetts also hit .305, drove in 54 runs, and again slugged 7 home runs.

With the demise of the AA, Stivetts in 1892 signed with Boston, the defending NL champions and one of the decade's dominant teams. Stivetts strengthened an already formidable pitching staff led by Charles "Kid" Nichols,* a perennial 30-game winner. In his first NL season, Stivetts recorded 35 victories and batted .296. On August 6, 1892, he became the first Boston pitcher to hurl a no-hit, no-run game when he blanked Brooklyn 11–0. He also hurled a five-inning no-hitter against Washington on October 15 in a game shortened to allow the Boston team to catch a train.

Behind the pitching of Stivetts and 35-game winner Nichols, Boston clinched the second half pennant in the NL experimental split season schedule. A post-season playoff between Boston and first half leader Cleveland decided the overall championship. In the opening game, Stivetts dueled Cy Young* through eleven scoreless innings before darkness ended the contest. The two faced each other again in game three, with Stivetts emerging the winner. He triumphed again in the fifth game, as Boston swept to the championship without defeat. Injuries, along with difficulties adjusting to the new pitching distance of 60 feet, 6 inches, hampered Stivetts in 1893. Although dropping to 19 victories, he batted .297 to help Boston capture its third consecutive NL pennant. Stivetts came back in 1894 to win 28 games and bat .328, with career highs in home runs (8) and RBIs (64). He recorded 17 and 21 wins and .190 and .344 batting averages, respectively, the next two seasons. After 1896 Stivetts pitched less and played most often in the outfield. He batted a career-high .367 in 1897 and .252 the following season, as Boston won two more NL pennants.

Stivetts was sold to Cleveland (NL) in 1899 and ended his major league career with a 0–4 pitching mark. Cleveland compiled the worst record (20–134) in major league history that season. After retiring from baseball, Stivetts returned to Ashland, PA, where he worked as a carpenter and umpired local baseball games. Stivetts married Margaret Ann Thomas in June, 1886, and had five daughters and one son.

As a pitcher, Stivetts compiled a 207–131 lifetime record and one of the best win-loss percentages (.612) of the pre–1900 era. He registered 1,223 strikeouts, completed 278 of his 332 starts, and had a 3.74 ERA. For three consecutive years (1890–1892), he pitched over 400 innings and completed over 40 starts. Stivetts batted .297 lifetime with 35 home runs, including 20 as a pitcher. He made 592 hits, including 84 doubles and 46 triples, and knocked in 314 runs. On three occasions, he slugged two home runs in a single game. He belted three homers as a pinch hitter, becoming the first pitcher to accomplish this feat. Considered among the fastest throwers of his time, Stivetts also ranks among the greatest hitting pitchers in major league history and showed extraordinary versatility by playing every position except catcher. The friendly, good-natured Stivetts won the admiration of teammates and fans through his dedication, selflessness, and hard work on the field.

BIBLIOGRAPHY: Harold Kaese, *The Boston Braves* (New York, 1948); Gene Karst and Martin J. Jones, Jr., *Who's Who in Professional Baseball* (New Rochelle, NY, 1973); Providence *Journal*, April 20, 1930; John Stivetts file, National Baseball Hall of Fame

Library, Cooperstown, NY; George V. Tuohey, comp., *A History of the Boston Base Ball Club* (Boston, 1897).

Joseph Lawler

STONEHAM, Charles (b. 5 July 1876, Jersey City, NJ; d. 6 January 1936, Hot Springs, AR), owner and executive, played a major role administering the New York Giants (NL) Baseball Club. Stoneham married Margaret Leonard and had four children, Horace, Mary, Jane, and Russell. An altar boy as a youth, Stoneham became a runner for a major stockbroker and then a stock salesman. New York Curb Exchange activity represented a far cry from his church duties, but could mean millions in earnings for an industrious person. In 1913 he established Charles A. Stoneham and Company with a sizeable portion of his earnings. The balance, including some accumulated earnings, was spent in 1919 when he, John McGraw,* and New York City magistrate Francis McQuade formed a syndicate to purchase the New York Giants from the estate of John T. Brush. The three simultaneously purchased numerous Cuban properties, including a racetrack, casino, and newspaper in Havana. After the company disbanded in 1921, the syndicate encountered legal difficulties. In 1923 Stoneham was indicted on charges of perjury and mail fraud because of activities involving his Cuban holdings and stock transfers for company customers. He was cleared of the mail fraud charges, but found guilty of perjury in 1925 and fined heavily. During the nearly three-year ordeal, Stoneham was pressured constantly to leave the baseball arena by both newspapermen and other owners. Stoneham, who had paid $1 million for his 1,300 shares, intended to keep them and pass them on to his son.

Horace Stoneham (27 April 1903, Newark, NJ), owner and executive, also figured prominently in administering the New York Giants Baseball Club. He attended prep school at Loyola, Hunter, and Pawling and graduated from Fordham University, where he played both baseball and hockey. Stoneham worked at a California copper mine and married Valleda Pyke in April 1924. Stoneham, who had three children, Mary, Horace, Jr., and Peter, became involved in the Giants' administrative organization in 1929. When his father contracted Brights disease, Horace assumed more daily operational responsibility in the front office. By the time Charles died in 1936, Horace had already performed his father's duties for nearly a year. On January 16, 1936, Horace was voted president and part-owner of the Giants and became the youngest owner in baseball history. Charles was considered a sharp-witted, often ruthless businessman, who frequented after-hours gambling clubs on nightly free-spending binges. By contrast, Horace seemed overly sentimental, too close to the game, and too business-minded, and limited his gambling to very risky, often criticized trades.

Horace, one of the few owners in history to concentrate on baseball as an interest and business, joined Bill Terry* in building the Giants minor league system and held the same commitment to his farm club and Polo Grounds customers. When Willie Mays* was advanced to the major leagues in 1951, Stoneham used a full page in the Minneapolis papers to apologize to the Millers fans for his action. Earlier Stoneham had promised that Mays would stay at the Triple A level AA club for another year. During the late 1940s and early 1950s, Stoneham proved instrumental among the owners in bringing black and Latin American talent into organized baseball. After his NL team swept the Cleveland Indians in the 1954 World Series, Stoneham was named *The Sporting News* Executive of the Year. Despite this success on the field, Stoneham lost money at the gate. Nevertheless, he rejected a $1 million offer by August Busch* of the St. Louis Cardinals for Mays in 1956. Financial insecurity, the changing baseball market in New York, and numerous other factors convinced Stoneham to move his team initially to Minneapolis, where he had a ready-made, baseball-hungry audience. He was talked out of this location by Dodgers executive Walter O'Malley,* who desperately needed a California rival to accompany his own team's move to Los Angeles. Business and baseball did not treat Stoneham very well after his move to San Francisco. Despite further expansion on the West Coast, a new stadium, and some truly awesome baseball talent, he regularly lost large sums of money on the franchise. Stoneham, who refused to sell the team to Labatts Brewery of Toronto, sold the club in 1976 to local real estate magnate Robert Lurie. Both Charles and Horace were seldom seen or heard except during spring training, watching all the games from their offices rather than from the field. After selling the Giants, Stoneham retired from public life.

BIBLIOGRAPHY: Alvin Dark and John Underwood, *When in Doubt, Fire the Manager* (New York, 1980); Charles Einstein, *Willie Mays* (New York, 1979); Frank Graham, *The New York Giants* (New York, 1952); Russ Hodges, *My Giants* (Garden City, NY, 1963); *NYT*, January 7, 9–11, 16; April 2, 16, 1936.

                                                                Alan R. Asnen

STONEHAM, Horace. See under STONEHAM, Charles

STOVEY, Harry Duffield (b. Harry Duffield Stow, 20, 26, or 28 December 1856, Philadelphia, PA; d. 20 September 1937, New Bedford, MA), player, was the son of watchman John and Lizzie Stow. His father was descended from bellmaker and foundry owner Charles Stow, who recast the Liberty Bell after it had been cracked. When Stow began playing professional baseball, he changed his name to Stovey so that his mother, who forbade him to play, would not see his name in the newspapers. Although he had little formal education, Stovey became one of his era's most articulate, knowledgeable players. In 1876 the right-handed, 5 foot, 11 1/2 inch, 180 pound

Stovey began his pro baseball career as a pitcher for the old Defiance Club of Philadelphia. Two years later, he played first base for Frank Bancroft's New Bedford, MA, Clam-Eaters. He married Mary L. Walker in 1879 and had three children.

Noted for his gentlemanly behavior, Stovey in 1880 started his major league career as an outfielder–first baseman for Worcester, MA (NL). After Worcester disbanded in 1882, Stovey played from 1883 to 1889 for the Philadelphia Athletics (AA) and joined Boston of the short-lived PL in 1890. The NL and AA quarreled over the ownership of Stovey and Louis Bierbauer, resulting in a twelve-club NL. When the Board of Control ruled that the Boston (NL) club owned the rights to Stovey, he signed in 1891 with the Nationals. The Boston team experienced financial problems, and Stovey's skills faded, causing his release in June 1892. Stovey played with Baltimore (NL) until August 1893 when Brooklyn (NL) signed him. After playing briefly for Michael "King" Kelly's* Allentown, PA (PSL), club in 1894, he finished his playing career that same year as captain of New Bedford (NEL). In 1895 Stovey joined the New Bedford police force and served as captain from 1915 until his retirement in 1923.

A swift base runner and power hitter in the dead ball era, Stovey also exhibited a strong arm. Stovey led the AA in batting (.404) in 1884, in doubles (32) in 1883, in runs scored four times (1883–1885, 1889), and in RBIs (119) in 1889. The first player to wear sliding pads, he led base stealers of his era and reached a career high 97 in 1890 for Boston. Besides allegedly circling the bases in fourteen seconds in 1891, he led the AA three times and the PL once in stolen bases. The solid home run hitter led or tied for most homers in a season five times and belted a career-high 19 in 1889. Stovey slugged three triples in games on August 18, 1884, and July 21, 1892. In 1888 he showed his strong arm in a distance-throwing contest sponsored by the Cincinnati *Enquirer*, finishing second to Ned Williamson with a throw of 123 yards, 2 inches. A premier performer of the pre–1900 era, Stovey became the first player to combine speed with both power and average. He batted .301 lifetime, hit 120 career home runs, and stole 441 bases (after 1887). In 1,488 games, he made 1,844 hits, 348 doubles, and 185 triples, and scored 1,494 runs. Stovey played on championship teams in three major leagues: the AA, PL, and NL.

BIBLIOGRAPHY: Gene Karst and Martin J. Jones, Jr., *Who's Who in Professional Baseball* (New Rochelle, NY, 1973); New Bedford (MA) *Standard-Times*, September 20, 1937, October 1, 1982; New York *Clipper*, August 7, 1880; Harold Seymour, *Baseball: The Early Years* (New York, 1960); George V. Tuohey, *A History of the Boston Base Ball Club* (Boston, 1897); David Quentin Voigt, *American Baseball*, vol. 1 (Norman, OK, 1966).

Ralph S. Graber

SUTTER, Howard Bruce (b. 8 January, 1953, Lancaster, PA), player, is the son of Howard Sutter, retired manager of a Farm Bureau warehouse in Mt. Joy, PA, and Thelma Sutter. Sutter is married and resides with his wife, Jamye, and their three sons in Kennesaw, GA. After graduation from Donegal High School in Mt. Joy in 1972, he entered organized baseball that year, pitching two games for Bradenton, FL (GCL). The 6 foot, 2 inch, 190 pound right-hander pitched for Quincy, IL (ML), in 1973, Key West (FSL) and Midland, TX (TL), in 1974, Midland in 1975, and Wichita (AA) in 1976 in the Chicago Cubs minor league system. The Chicago Cubs (NL), impressed with his strikeout-walk ratio, summoned him early in the 1976 season as a relief pitcher. He popularized a baffling "out" pitch, his split-finger fastball. Through 1986, Sutter has appeared in 623 major league games without making a start. During that span, he posted an NL record 286 saves and 67–67 won-lost record, struck out 821 batters in 995 1/3 innings pitched, and compiled a 2.75 ERA.

In December 1980 the St. Louis Cardinals (NL) obtained Sutter in a trade with the Cubs. The trade paid dividends for the Cardinals in 1982, when Sutter pitched in 70 games and led the NL with 36 saves. St. Louis won the NL and World Series titles, helped by Sutter's two saves and one win. Sutter, selected for the NL All-Star team five successive seasons and in 1984, won the 1978 and 1979 games and was credited with saves in 1980 and 1981. Besides leading the NL in saves four consecutive years through 1982, Sutter received the Rolaids Relief Pitcher of the Year Award for the NL and was selected All-Star Fireman of the Year by *The Sporting News* in 1979, 1981–1982, and 1984. In 1979 37 saves and 6 victories earned Sutter the Cy Young Award. On September 8, 1977, he struck out the side on nine pitches, tying the major league record. In 1984 he tied the then major league record for the most saves (45) in a season. Sutter, whose prospects for the National Baseball Hall of Fame are most promising, signed in December 1984 with the Atlanta Braves (NL) as a free agent. He underwent elbow surgery at the end of the 1985 season and spent much of the 1986 campaign on the disabled list.

BIBLIOGRAPHY: Chicago *Tribune*, 1976–1980; Joseph L. Reichler, ed., *The Baseball Encyclopedia*, 6th ed. (New York, 1985), p. 2,068; *St. Louis Cardinals Yearbook, 1984*; St. Louis *Post Dispatch*, 1980–1984; *TSN Official Baseball Register, 1984* (St. Louis, 1984); Don Weiskoff, "Keep 'Em Close," *Athletic Journal* 64 (January, 1984), pp. 40–47.

Emil H. Rothe

SUTTLES, George "Mule" (b. 31 March 1901, Brockton, LA; d. ca. 1968), player and manager, starred in black baseball during a career spanning over one-quarter of a century. The powerfully built right-hander stood 5 feet, 11 inches and weighed 195 pounds. Nicknamed "Mule," Suttles began his baseball career in 1918 as a first baseman with the Birmingham Black Barons and entered the top echelon of black baseball when the Barons joined the NNL in 1924. He spent 1926 through 1931 with the St. Louis Stars (NNL) and 1932 with the doomed EWL's Washington Pilots and Detroit Wolves. From 1933 through 1936, he performed in the NNL with the Chicago American Giants (1933–1935) and Newark Eagles (1936). Suttles also played with the Newark Eagles in the NNL from 1937 through 1940 and 1942 through 1944. He spent the 1941 NNL season with the New York Black Yankees and winters playing in California and Cuba.

Although not considered a talented defensive player or high-average hitter, Suttles ranked among the most feared black league sluggers. Available statistics also indicate that his career average ranged in the .330s and .340s for post-season championship play. A .325 batter in the 1933–1934 CWL, he paced the loop with 14 home runs in 42 games. In 27 contests against white major leaguers, he hit .350 with 7 home runs and a .670 slugging average. Suttles participated in five East-West (Negro league) All-Star games, starting for the West in 1933, 1934, 1935, and for the East in 1937 and 1939. His two All-Star homers included a game-winning blow off Hall of Famer Martin Dihigo* in 1935 with two on and two out in the bottom of the eleventh to produce a dramatic 11–8 West victory. He posted robust All-Star .412 batting and .882 slugging averages.

The 1928, 1930, and 1931 St. Louis Stars captured NNL titles, while the Chicago American Giants made disputed NNL title claims with the Pittsburgh Crawfords in 1933 and the Philadelphia Stars in 1934. Suttles managed the Newark Eagles to an 18–14 mark in a short 1943 NNL season. Teammates included Hall of Famers James "Cool Papa" Bell* and Monte Irvin*, Raymond Dandridge,* and stars Larry Doby,* Biz Mackey,* and Willie Wells.* Suttles reportedly died in 1968.

BIBLIOGRAPHY: Chicago *Defender*, September 29, October 6, 13, 1928, September 20, 27, 1930, September 15, 22, 1934; Robert W. Peterson, *Only the Ball Was White* (Englewood Cliffs, NJ, 1970); Philadelphia *Tribune*, October 4, 1934; Pittsburgh *Courier*, October 4, 1934; James A. Riley, *All-Time All Stars of Black Baseball* (Cocoa, FL, 1983); Art Rust, Jr., *Get That Nigger off the Field* (New York, 1976).

Merl F. Kleinknecht

SUTTON, Donald Howard "Don" (b. 2 April 1945, Clio, AL), player, pitched for the Los Angeles Dodgers (1966–1980) and Houston Astros (1981–1982) of the NL and for the Milwaukee Brewers (1982–1984), Oakland A's (1985), and California Angels (1985–1986) of the AL. After signing with the Dodgers on September 11, 1964, the right-handed Sutton began his professional baseball career with Santa Barbara (CaL) in 1965. He posted an 8–1 mark with a 1.50 ERA in 10 games there and quickly was promoted to Albuquerque, where he led the TL in winning percentage (.714) and was named its Player of the Year. Aside from two games at Spokane (PCL) in 1968, Sutton joined the Dodgers' starting rotation of Sandy Koufax,* Don Drysdale,* and Claude Osteen in 1966, compiled a 12–12 record, and struck out 209 batters in 225 2/3 innings. He was named *The Sporting News* Rookie Pitcher of the Year, helping the Dodgers win the NL pennant.

The 6 foot, 1 inch, 190 pound Sutton excelled as a Dodger. As of 1985, he ranked first on the all-time Dodger lists for regular season games pitched (534), innings pitched (3,728), strikeouts (2,652), shutouts (52), wins (230), and for Championship Series innings (32 2/3), strikeouts (17), and wins (3). In 1976, his only season as a 20-game winner, he compiled a 21–10 record and was named right-handed pitcher on *The Sporting News* NL All-Star team. Sutton led the NL in ERA (2.21) in 1980, games started (40) in 1974, shutouts (9) in 1972, earned runs allowed (118) in 1970, and balks (3) in 1968. From 1966 to 1969, he lost 13 consecutive games to the Chicago Cubs, a major league record for consecutive losses to a single opponent. Sutton struck out at least 100 batters in twenty-one seasons (1966–1986), establishing a major league record for most consecutive years accomplishing that feat. Although he never pitched a no-hitter, he hurled an NL record five career one-hit games. In a game against the Cincinnati Reds on May 27, 1980, Sutton surrendered a record three consecutive home runs in the third inning to Ken Griffey, George Foster,* and Dan Driessen. Sutton, high on the all-time strike-out-to-walk ratio list, never hit a major league home run. He was granted free agency on October 23, 1980, and joined the Houston Astros (NL) on December 4, 1980. During their successful AL pennant drive of 1982, the Milwaukee Brewers acquired Sutton on August 30 in a trade for three players.

In Championship Series play, Sutton won the first and deciding fourth game of Los Angeles' successful 1974 series against the Pittsburgh Pirates and pitched a complete-game victory in game two of the Dodgers' triumphant 1977 series against the Philadelphia Phillies. Sutton's only Championship Series loss came in game three of the 1978 series against the Phillies. Sutton's win in game three of the 1982 series helped the Brewers defeat the California Angels for the AL pennant. Sutton pitched well in relief in the 1986 AL Championship Series against the Boston Red Sox, but was not involved in any decision.

Sutton posted an overall record of 2–3 in World Series competition, winning game two of the 1974 Series against the Oakland A's and game five of the 1977 World Series for Los Angeles against the New York Yankees. His World Series losses came in games three and six of the 1978 Series against the New York Yankees and in game six of the 1982 Series against the St. Louis Cardinals. Sutton, who was eligible for but did not appear in the 1966 World Series, compiled a World Series 5.26 ERA. He pitched for the NL

All-Star team in 1972, 1973, 1975, and 1977. In his only All-Star Game decision, Sutton started and won the 1977 game at Yankee Stadium and considers this game the highlight of his career. Sutton struck out seven and did not allow a run in eight composite All-Star innings.

By the end of the 1986 season, Sutton had compiled a 310–239 win-loss record with a 3.20 ERA. He ranks sixth on the all-time strikeout list (3,431), eighth in shutouts (58), and near the top in games started (706) and innings pitched (5,002 2/3). Sutton was originally signed with the Dodgers in 1965 for $7,500 by scout Monte Basgall. As a free agent in 1980, Sutton received a $500,000 bonus to sign a $700,000 annual three-year contract with the Houston Astros (NL). His father Howard, a Florida tenant farmer, works as a construction company superintendent, while his mother, Lillian, is a postmistress. Sutton attended Gulf Coast Junior College, Mississippi College, Whittier College, and the University of Southern California, leaving thirty credits short of a degree. Sutton, who met his wife, Patti, an interior decorator, in 1967, has one son, Daron, and one daughter, Staci. In 1978 he was involved in a widely publicized clubhouse fight with teammate Steve Garvey.* On June 18, 1986, Sutton pitched a three hitter for his 300th career major league victory in a 5–1 triumph over the Texas Rangers at Anaheim, CA. The 41-year-old right-hander, in his twenty-first major league season, became the nineteenth pitcher in baseball history to win 300 major league games.

BIBLIOGRAPHY: Ron Bergman, "Don Sutton," *USA Today*, September 19, 1985, p. 9C; Ron Fimrite, "Blood on the Dodger Blue," *SI* 49 (September 4, 1978), pp. 24–25; Mickey Herskowitz, "Houston Bets a Fortune That Don Can Break the Jinx," *Sport* 72 (June, 1981), pp. 26–32; Tot Holmes, *Dodgers Blue Book, 1983*; Joseph L. Reichler, ed., *The Baseball Encyclopedia*, 6th ed. (New York, 1985), p. 2,069; Sue Reilly, "Don and Patti Sutton Were Striking Out Till They Got Help—And Now They're Safe at Home," *People Weekly* 17 (April 5, 1982), pp. 89–93; Don Sutton, "The Game I'll Never Forget," *Baseball Digest* 43 (November, 1984), pp. 25–27; *TSN Official Baseball Dope Book, 1983*; *TSN Official Baseball Guide, 1983* (St. Louis, 1983); *TSN Official World Series Records, 1982* (St. Louis, 1982).

Jack P. Lipton

T

TANNEHILL, Jesse Niles (b. 14 July 1874, Dayton, KY; d. 22 September 1956, Dayton, KY), player, manager, and umpire, spent most of his life in the Dayton area. His younger brother Lee played infield for ten seasons with the Chicago White Sox (AL). The 5 foot, 8 inch, 150 pound left-handed pitcher proved a steady performer and hurled a 6–0 no-hit victory for the Boston Red Sox (AL) over Chicago on August 17, 1904. After compiling a 1–0 mark with the Cincinnati Reds (NL) in 1894, Tannehill enjoyed outstanding seasons with Richmond, VA (VL), in 1895 and 1896 before joining the Pittsburgh Pirates (NL) in 1897. From 1898 to 1902, he won 25, 24, 20, 18, and 20 games, respectively, for the Pirates. Tannehill helped Pittsburgh win NL pennants in 1901 and 1902 with sparkling 2.18 and 1.95 ERAs and led the NL in winning percentage (1900) and ERA (1901). In 1903 he joined teammate John Chesbro* in jumping to New York (AL) for more money. Tannehill compiled a mediocre 15–15 record, while the Pirates won a third straight NL pennant.

After one season with the Highlanders, he was traded in December, 1903, to the Boston Red Sox (AL) for Thomas Hughes. At Boston, he won 21 games in 1904, 22 in 1905, and 13 in 1906. In July, 1908, he and Robert Unglaub were traded to the Washington Senators (AL) for Casey Patten. Tannehill compiled a 1–1 mark for Washington in 1909 and left the major leagues except for one appearance with Cincinnati (NL) in 1911. From 1910 to 1913, he journeyed around the minor leagues with Minneapolis (AA) in 1910, Birmingham, AL, and Montgomery, AL (SA), in 1911, South Bend, IN (CL), and Chillicothe, OH (OSL) in 1912, and St. Joseph, MO (WL) in 1913. In fifteen major league seasons, Tannehill garnered 197 wins (117 in the NL) and 116 losses, completed 263 of 318 starts, struck out 943 batters, walked only 478 hitters in 2,770 1/3 innings, hurled 34 shutouts, and compiled a 2.77 ERA. A lifetime .256 batter, he occasionally played the outfield early in his career. After his playing days, Tannehill managed at Portsmouth, VA (VL), in 1914 and Topeka (SWL) in 1923 and umpired in the OSL (1916), IL (1917), and WL (1920).

BIBLIOGRAPHY: Paul MacFarlane, ed., *TSN Daguerreotypes of Great Stars of Baseball* (St. Louis, 1968), p. 202; Joseph L. Reichler, ed., *The Baseball Encyclopedia*, 6th ed. (New York, 1985), p. 2,072.

David B. Merrell

TAYLOR, Benjamin H. "Ben" (1888, Anderson, SC), player and manager, was the youngest of four brothers significant in Negro league history. His oldest brother, Charles,* became one of the greatest black managers and a vice-president of the NNL. A second brother, John, pitched with a half dozen clubs before World War I, while his brother "Candy Jim" played third base and managed with sixteen different teams from 1904 through 1948. Ben began his professional baseball career with the St. Louis Giants in 1911 as a first baseman and reached his prime with the Indianapolis ABC's (NNL) from 1915 through 1922. The ABC's, sponsored by the American Brewing Company, ranked among the top teams of that era. The club featured Ben's brother Jim, Oscar Charleston,* and Dave Malarcher and was managed by Ben's oldest brother, Charles.

After Charles died in 1922, Ben joined the Chicago American Giants (NNL) powerhouse club, one of black baseball's most enduring franchises. Taylor's career spanned the entire period between World Wars I and II. Taylor also played for and/or managed the Atlantic City Bacharach Giants (ECL) in 1923, Washington Potomacs (ECL) in 1924, Harrisburg Giants (ECL) from 1925 through 1927, Baltimore Black Sox (ECL), Baltimore Stars in 1933, Brooklyn Eagles (NNL) in 1935, Washington Black Senators (NNL) in 1938, and New York Cubans (NNL) in 1940 before retiring. Taylor, who batted around .333 lifetime, already had reached the twilight of his career when the annual East-West Game became a feature of black baseball. Although he never played in the annual game, Taylor apparently umpired the first game in 1933. Contemporaries remember Taylor as a sterling fielder and excellent hitter who threw and batted left-handed. He was considered about the best first baseman in black baseball prior to Buck Leonard's* arrival. Taylor first managed Leonard with the Baltimore Stars and taught him how to play first base.

BIBLIOGRAPHY: William Brashler, *Josh Gibson* (New York, 1978); John Holway, *Voices from Great Black Baseball Leagues* (New York, 1975); Robert W. Peterson, *Only the Ball Was White* (Englewood Cliffs, NJ, 1970); Donn Rogosin, *Invisible Men: Life in Baseball's Negro Leagues* (New York, 1983).

Douglas D. Martin

TAYLOR, Charles I. "C. I." (b. ca. 1872, NC; d. 2 March 1922), player, manager, and executive, was the oldest of four baseball brothers, attended Clark College in Atlanta, GA, and served in the U.S. Army during the Spanish-American War. In 1904 Taylor became manager of the Birmingham,

AL, Giants and moved the team in 1910 to West Baden, IN, as the Sprudels. He shifted the franchise in 1914 to Indianapolis, where it was sponsored by the American Brewing Company and christened the ABC's. Under Taylor's tutelage, the Indianapolis ABC's ranked among the premier teams in black professional baseball. The club became financially sound and usually traveled by rail. In 1920 Taylor put the ABC's into the fledgling NNL, the first black major baseball circuit to survive its baptismal season. The NNL endured until the Depression ended it in 1932. Taylor served as NNL vice-president from its inception until his death and perhaps left his greatest legacy with his pioneering efforts for this league.

Taylor, of impeccable reputation and appearance, was considered gentlemanly, honest, fair, strict, and a good teacher. Players benefitting from his tutorship included Bingo De Moss,* Dave Malarcher, Dizzy Dismukes, National Baseball Hall of Famer Oscar Charleston,* and his brothers Ben,* James, and Johnny Taylor. The 1916 ABC's, probably his greatest team, defeated Rube Foster's* Chicago American Giants five games to four in the Negro World Series. Earlier that season, Indianapolis bested the top eastern club, the New York Lincoln Stars, in four of five games. Taylor is ranked as one of the three greatest black baseball managers.

BIBLIOGRAPHY: Chicago *Defender*, September 2, October 28, November 4, 1916; Leon Hardwick and Effa Manley, *Negro Baseball* (Chicago, 1976); Indianapolis *Freeman*, September 2, 16, October 28, November 4, 1916; Indianapolis *Star*, July 24–26, 28, August 28–31, October 23–25, 27, 30, 1916; Robert W. Peterson, *Only the Ball Was White* (Englewood Cliffs, NJ, 1970); James A. Riley, *The All-Time All-Stars of Black Baseball* (Cocoa, FL, 1983).

Merl F. Kleinknecht

TENER, John Kinley (b. 25 July 1863, County Tyrone, Ireland; d. 19 May 1946, Pittsburgh, PA), player and executive, was the son of George Evans and Susan (Wallis) Tener and had nine brothers and sisters. The Teners immigrated to the United States and settled in Pittsburgh, where John was orphaned at age 9. The 6 foot, 4 inch, 180 pound, right-handed Tener played amateur baseball from 1881 to 1885 and began his professional career the latter year with Baltimore (AA). After hurling with Haverhill, MA (NEL), in 1886, he was signed by Cap Anson* in 1887 and pitched the next two seasons for the Chicago White Stockings (NL). In 1888 he started 30 games, won 15 decisions, lost 15 contests, hurled 1 shutout, and batted .273. When the Brotherhood of Professional Baseball Players was organized in 1885, Tener became one of its most influential members. In 1890 he joined Pittsburgh (PL), but compiled a disappointing 3–11 mark in 14 starts and left baseball to pursue a banking career. As a major league pitcher, Tener finished 25–31, struck out 174 batters, walked 200, surrendered 552 hits in 506 innings pitched, and threw 2 shutouts.

A banker until his retirement in 1930, the Republican represented Pittsburgh in the U.S. Congress from 1909 to 1911 and served one term as governor of Pennsylvania from 1911 to 1915. Although chosen NL president in 1913, he served only part-time until his term as governor expired. He held the presidency until 1918, initiating the splitting of World Series receipts and handling the Scott Perry case. Tener proposed sharing World Series player receipts with the other first-division teams, thus averting a players' strike. In 1918 Philadelphia Athletics (AL) pitcher Perry was awarded by Tener and Garry Herrmann of the National Commission to the Boston Braves (NL), who originally had signed him. After the AL obtained an injunction against the Commission's action, Tener resigned in protest. As president, Tener also negotiated the breakup of the FL. After leaving baseball, he served on the boards of several Pittsburgh businesses and frequently attended Pittsburgh Pirates games. Tener married Harriet J. Day in 1889. One year after her death in 1935, he married Leone Evans and again became a widower the next year.

BIBLIOGRAPHY: *Biographical Dictionary of the American Congress* (Washington, DC, 1961); Glenn Dickey, *The History of National League Baseball* (New York, 1982); *NYT*, May 20, 1946; Joseph L. Reichler, ed., *The Baseball Encyclopedia*, 6th ed. (New York, 1985). p. 2,075.

                                                                                        Robert E. Jones

TENNEY, Frederick Clay "Fred" (b. 26 November 1871, Georgetown, MA; d. 3 July 1952, Boston, MA), player and manager, was among the first college graduates to enter major league baseball. After graduating from Brown University in June, 1894, the 5 foot, 9 inch, 155 pound Tenney was signed by the injury riddled Boston Beaneaters (NL) and became one of the few left-handed catchers in major league history. From 1894 through 1896, Tenney caught in 68 games and played the outfield in 94 contests for Boston. After shifting to first base in 1897, he joined Jimmy Collins,* Herman Long,* and Bobby Lowe to form one of baseball's most famous infields. Tenney performed for fourteen consecutive seasons, including the 1905–1907 campaigns as player-manager at Boston. On December 13, 1907, he was traded to the New York Giants (NL) in one of the biggest trades in major league baseball history. Tenney was released by the Giants in 1910 and completed the season with Lowell, MA (NEL), as player-manager. He returned to Boston in 1911 as their player-manager, compiling a .263 batting average in 102 games at age 39. He retired from baseball after managing Newark (IL) in 1916 and batting .318 in 16 games.

The intelligent, competitive Tenney was unrivaled at fielding a bunt and cutting the runner down at second base by perfecting the "first to second to first" double play. Tenney and Christy Mathewson* developed the "quick pitch" to hold runners close to first base, but the strategy was eliminated when the balk rule was initiated. Tenney, who threw and batted left-handed, batted .295 in 1,994 games with 2,239 hits, 1,278 runs scored, 270 doubles, 77 triples, 22 home runs, 688 RBIs, and 285 stolen bases. He hit above .300 six full seasons and made six hits in a May 31, 1897, contest. Tenney's best season came in 1899, when he batted a career-high .347, collected 209 base hits, made 17 triples, and scored 115 runs. He led the NL with 566 at bats (1897) and 101 runs scored (1908), paced in putouts (1905, 1907–1908), assists (1898, 1901–1907), and fielding average (1902) at first base. He holds the NL record for most assists (1,363) at first base and the major league mark for most years leading the league in assists (8). Tenney, who married Bessie Berry on October 21, 1895, enjoyed little success as Boston's manager (1905–1907, 1911). Under Tenney, Boston won only 202 of 616 games and finished in seventh and eighth place twice. After leaving baseball, Tenney wrote articles for a newspaper syndicate.

BIBLIOGRAPHY: Gene Karst and Martin J. Jones, Jr., *Who's Who in Professional Baseball* (New Rochelle, NY, 1973); Paul MacFarlane, ed., *TSN Daguerreotypes of Great Stars of Baseball* (St. Louis, 1971); Joseph L. Reichler, ed., *The Baseball Encyclopedia*, 6th ed. New York, 1985), pp. 1,452–1,453; Ira L. Smith, *Baseball's Famous First Basemen* (New York, 1956).

John L. Evers

TERRY, William Harold "Bill," "Memphis Bill" (b. 30 October 1898, Atlanta, GA), player, manager, and executive, attended grade school in Atlanta and left school at age 13 to support himself after his parents separated. He married Elvena Snead of Memphis in November, 1916, and has three sons and one daughter. After pitching for local Atlanta teams, Terry began his professional baseball career with Newnan (GAL) in 1915. He pitched for Newnan in 1915 and played with Shreveport, LA (TL), in 1916–1917. Terry left organized baseball in 1918 to work with the Standard Oil Company of Memphis, but pitched for the company's semi-pro team. He remained with Standard Oil until 1922, when owner Tom Watkins of Memphis (SA) recommended him to New York Giants manager John McGraw.* McGraw was more impressed with Terry's hitting than his left-handed pitching and assigned him to Toledo (AA). Now a full-time first baseman, the left-handed, 6 foot, 1 inch, 200 pound Terry hit .377 for Toledo in 1923 and joined the Giants (NL) that September.

Terry, a straightaway hitter, drove balls to all parts of the field rather than aiming for the nearby right field stands at the Polo Grounds. After hitting a mediocre .239 for the Giants in 1924, he batted .319 in 1925. In 1927 he compiled the first of six consecutive seasons with at least 100 runs scored and batted in and the first of ten straight seasons batting over .300. Nicknamed "Memphis Bill," he enjoyed his best year in 1930 by batting .401 and tying the NL record for hits with 254. No NL player has topped the 254 hits or .400 mark since. Terry won the NL's Most Valuable Player Award in 1930 despite the Giants' third place finish. Besides compiling an outstanding .341 lifetime batting average over fourteen major league seasons, he ranked among the all-time great fielding first basemen and was the premier NL first baseman most of his playing career. In 1,721 games, he compiled 2,193 hits, 373 doubles, 112 triples, 154 home runs, 1,120 runs scored, 1,078 RBIs, and 56 stolen bases.

Terry's brilliance as a player was complemented by his successful reign as Giants manager from June 1932 through the 1941 season. McGraw, although he had a personality conflict with Terry and was not on speaking terms with him for two years, recommended him as his managerial successor. Through several successful trades and clever defensive field strategy, Terry moved the Giants from a sixth place finish in 1932 to a surprise NL pennant and World Series victory over the Washington Senators in 1933. With superb pitching by Carl Hubbell* and powerful hitting by Mel Ott,* Terry's clubs won NL pennants again in 1936 and 1937. The Giants were defeated in the World Series both years by overpowering New York Yankee teams. The Giants finished third in 1938 and slipped to the second division from 1939 through 1941, after which Ott replaced Terry as manager. As Giants manager from 1932 to 1941, Terry compiled 823 wins, 661 losses, and a .555 winning percentage. Terry served one season as the Giants' farm system director and left the major leagues permanently. He became president of the SAL in 1955, but quit that post two years later for a full-time business career.

The very bright, purposeful Terry worked in the cotton business after leaving the Giants in 1942 and operated a profitable automobile agency in Memphis. Terry conducts a larger agency in Jacksonville, FL, and has participated in Jacksonville civic and religious affairs. Always blunt and businesslike, Terry clashed continually with sportswriters during his managerial career. After his belated election to the National Baseball Hall of Fame in 1954, he was asked for his reaction upon becoming a baseball immortal. Miffed over having waited so long for his election, Terry characteristically responded, "I have nothing to say."

BIBLIOGRAPHY: Martin Appel and Burt Goldblatt, *Baseball's Best: The Hall of Fame Gallery* (New York, 1977); Frank Graham, *McGraw of the Giants* (New York, 1944); Arnold Hano, *Greatest Giants of Them All* (New York, 1967); Fred Stein, *Under Coogan's Bluff* (Glyddon, MD, 1979); Fred Stein and Nick Peters, *Day by Day in Giants History* (New York, 1984).

Fred Stein

THOMAS, Clinton "Clint," "Hawk" (b. 25 November 1896, Greenup, KY), player, excelled as a left-handed power hitting outfielder in the Negro leagues. The son of janitor James and Lutie Thomas, he journeyed to Columbus, OH, in 1910 and played amateur ball there. Thomas, who did not attend high school, worked in a restaurant and grocery store and joined the U.S. Army in World War I. After his discharge, he returned to Columbus and played semi-pro ball with the Bowers Easters in 1919. Thomas began his professional career as a second baseman in 1920 with the Brooklyn Royal Giants and played in 1921 with the Columbus Buckeyes (NNL). After he joined the Detroit Stars (NNL) in 1922, manager Bruce Petway moved him to the outfield. Nicknamed "Hawk" because of his great range, he worked that winter at the Ford Plant in Detroit.

After jumping to the new ECL, Thomas played seven years with the Philadelphia Hilldale and hit an unconfirmed .286 in 1923, .407 in 1924, and .348 in 1925. He played in both the 1924 and 1925 Negro World Series, helping Hilldale win the 1925 ECL title with his excellent fielding. He batted an unconfirmed .328 in 1926 and barnstormed against the Philadelphia A's, reportedly slugging his twenty-eighth home run of the season off Eddie Rommel.* Thomas, an exceptional base stealer, batted .310 in six seasons in Cuba between 1923 and 1931. He hit .371 in the 1924–1925 season and .331 in the 1926–1927 season against Adolfo Luque, Fred Fitzsimmons,* Jesse Petty, and other major league pitchers. Thomas worked as a truck driver for Ballantine Scotch when not playing winter ball.

Thomas moved to the Atlantic City Bacharach Giants (NNL) in 1929 and jumped to the Lincoln Giants in 1930, hitting an unconfirmed .346 and playing in the NNL playoffs against the Homestead Grays. He played against major leaguers Tony Lazzeri,* Earl Averill,* and Lefty Gomez* in California in the 1932–1933 winter season and tripled and stole home in 1934 to beat Dizzy Dean* and his All Stars 1–0. Thomas later worked for the West Virginia Department of Mines and the state senate, where he became staff supervisor. He married Ellen Odell (Smith) Bland in 1963 and had no children. Called the black Joe DiMaggio* by Monte Irvin,* Thomas combined speed, power, and superb defensive skills. Thomas and others proved that black players could compete against major league baseball players, paving the way for the ensuing integration.

BIBLIOGRAPHY: Terry A. Baxter, correspondence with Jorge Figueroda, 1984 Cuban League statistics, Terry A. Baxter collection, Lee's Summit, MO; Terry A. Baxter, telephone interview with Monte Irvin, 1984; Terry A. Baxter, telephone interview with Clint Thomas, 1984; Pat Hemlepp, "Clint Thomas Was That Good," Ashland (KY) *Daily Independent*, July 5, 1979, p. 15; James Riley, *The All-Time All-Stars of Black Baseball* (Cocoa, FL, 1983); Donn Rogosin, *Invisible Men: Life in Baseball's Negro Leagues* (New York, 1983); *TSN*, February 8, 1978.

Terry A. Baxter

THOMPSON, Samuel "Sam," "Big Sam," "The Marvel" (b. 5 March 1860, Danville, IN; d. 7 November 1922, Detroit, MI), player, was scouted on Danville sandlots by Indianapolis minor league manager Dan O'Leary. O'Leary had heard about a Danville player who "never does anything but hit home runs." Thompson began his professional baseball career with Evansville, IN (NWL) in 1884 and starred the next year for Indianapolis (WL). Bill Watkins, manager of the 1884 Indianapolis (AA) entry, also saw Thompson play. After becoming manager of the 1885 Detroit Wolverines (NL), Watkins recommended that Detroit purchase Thompson's contract and kept him as a reserve. When regular left fielder Gene Moriarty sustained an injury, Watkins used Thompson. Since the 6 foot 2 inch, 210 pound Thompson was much larger than his contemporaries, Watkins could not find a uniform large enough to fit "Big Sam." Thompson, looking like a man in a boy's outfit, hit a triple his first time at bat. Thompson's trousers split in the seat as he rounded second base, while the cuffs came up to his knees. He combined color and skill, making him among the gaslight era's most popular players.

In his second year (1886), the left-handed Thompson became an NL star by hitting .310 and driving in 89 runs. Although hitting a career-high .404 in 1894, he enjoyed his best year in 1887, when he led the NL with a .372 batting average, 203 hits, 23 triples, and 166 RBIs. He and Detroit first baseman Dan Brouthers* comprised the best power tandem in baseball and spearheaded Detroit's 1887 championship season. A home run hitter in the deadball era, he was nicknamed "The Marvel" for his fielding and slugging skills. Thompson often crashed through the low white fence at Recreation Park to make one-handed catches after long runs, possessed a fine throwing arm, and became the first outfielder to throw to home plate on the bounce.

When the Detroit team dissolved in 1888, he was sold to the Philadelphia Phillies (NL). Thompson twice led the NL in homers, with 20 in 1889 and 18 in 1895, and finished his career in 1898 there. His 128 career home runs remained a major league record until Babe Ruth* broke it in 1921. Thompson also led the NL in hits three times (203 in 1887, 172 in 1890, 222 in 1893), RBIs twice (166 in 1887, 165 in 1895) and slugging average twice (.571 in 1884, .654 in 1895). Thompson, who settled in Detroit in 1899, became a real estate agent, dabbled in Republican party politics, and served as a trusted adviser and confidant to Detroit Tigers general manager and part-owner Frank Navin.* From 1900 to 1907, he starred as an outfielder for the Detroit Athletic Club. The great fan favorite, whose team occasionally outdrew the Detroit Tigers, retired in his prime.

During September, 1906, the injury-riddled Detroit Tigers persuaded Thompson to play the final eight games of the season. His appearance against the Chicago White Sox, then engaged in a close pennant race with the New York Highlanders, was criticized by New York manager Clark Griffith.* Griffith contended that the Tigers, by inserting a 46-year-old player into the lineup, were giving the AL championship to the White Sox. Although Chicago swept the Detroit series, Thompson patrolled the outfield with rookie Ty Cobb* and veteran Sam Crawford.* He experienced trouble hitting the spitter—a pitch not used in his day—but batted .226 and showed flashes of his old form at season's end. In Thompson's final appearance, fans packed

Bennett Park to see him play rather than the second division Tigers. Thompson, who treated them with a triple that drove in two runs, stated that baseball had not changed much from the 1880s to 1906. During fifteen seasons, Thompson compiled 1,986 hits, 340 doubles, 160 triples, 1,263 runs scored, 1,299 RBIs, 221 stolen bases, and a .331 batting and .505 slugging average.

Thompson regularly attended Tigers games and stayed close to his 1887 Detroit teammates, for whom he arranged a reunion in 1907. Despite being stronger and larger than most players, he did not bully them. The modest Thompson likened his home runs to bunts compared to Ruth's blasts. Thompson's contemporaries, however, claimed that he could have matched Ruth with a livelier ball. Thompson's self-deprecatory humor, colorful playing style, and immense skills made him Detroit's most popular nineteenth-century athlete.

BIBLIOGRAPHY: Detroit Baseball Club Letterbooks, vol. 1, Ernie Harwell Collection, Detroit Public Library; Detroit *News*, September, 1906; November 8, 1922; Frederick G. Lieb, *The Detroit Tigers* (New York, 1946); John Lodge, *I Remember Detroit* (Detroit, 1928).

Anthony J. Papalas

TIERNAN, Michael Joseph "Mike," "Silent Mike" (b. 21 January 1867, Trenton, NJ; d. 9 November 1918, New York, NY), player, was the son of an Irish laborer, grew up near the Trenton State Prison, and played for the Athletic Juniors. The renowned ice skater and trackman ran the 100 yard dash in slightly under ten seconds. He debuted as a pitcher at age 17 with Williamsport, PA, and struck out 15 batters in an exhibition game against the NL champion Providence club. Providence manager Frank Bancroft, impressed with Tiernan's performance, observed the teenager from the grandstand after the fourth inning. Nicknamed "Silent Mike," the 5 foot, 11 inch, 165 pound Tiernan disliked publicity and was reserved on the field even when disagreeing with the umpire.

Tiernan, who batted and threw left-handed, began his professional baseball career in 1885 with Trenton (EL) and led the EL in hitting with .390 at Jersey City in 1886. From 1887 to 1889, he played outfield for the New York Giants (NL) and batted .287 as a 20-year-old rookie. The versatile, durable Tiernan batted well, demonstrated power in the dead ball era, ran swiftly, and fielded well. In 1,476 career major league games, he batted .311, made 1,834 hits, slugged 255 doubles, 162 triples, and 108 home runs, scored 1,313 runs, knocked in 851 runs, stole 428 bases, and compiled a .463 slugging average. Tiernan surpassed the .300 mark at the plate seven times, including a stellar .361 performance in 1896.

Tiernan led the NL in home runs in 1891 (17) and led the NL in runs scored (147) in 1889 and in slugging percentage in 1890 (.495) and 1891 (.500). Besides pacing NL outfielders defensively in 1888 and 1889, he stole

428 bases during his career and recorded a season-high 56 stolen bases in 1890. On June 15, 1887, he made two triples, three singles, and walked once and tied an NL record by scoring six runs against the Philadelphia Phillies. Hall of Famers Amos Rusie* and Kid Nichols* were engaged in a scoreless duel in the bottom of the thirteenth inning on May 12, 1890, when Tiernan slammed a long home run off Nichols to end what news accounts termed the finest game ever played. After retiring from baseball, Tiernan operated a cafe in New York City. He died of tuberculosis.

BIBLIOGRAPHY: Gene Karst and Martin J. Jones, Jr., *Who's Who in Professional Baseball* (New Rochelle, NY, 1973); Randolph Linthurst, "Silent Mike Tiernan Belongs in the Hall of Fame," *Trenton Magazine* (April, 1975), pp. 30–31; Paul MacFarlane, ed., *TSN Daguerreotypes of Great Stars of Baseball* (St. Louis, 1968); Eugene C. Murdock, "The Pre–1900 Batting Stars," *Baseball Research Journal* 2 (1973), pp. 75–78.

B. Randolph Linthurst

TINKER, Joseph Bert, "Joe" (27 July 1880, Muscotah, KS; d. 27 July 1948, Orlando, FL), player, manager, and executive, was the son of Samuel and Elizabeth (Williams) Tinker, attended Kansas City, KS public schools, and played semi-pro baseball for the Coffeyville, KS, team in 1899. Tinker, who married Ruby Rose Menown and had three sons and one daughter, later wed Suzanne Chabot in 1942. He began his professional career as a shortstop with Denver (WL) and Great Falls-Helena, MT (MtSL), in 1900 and Portland, OR (PNL), in 1901. The next year he joined the Chicago Cubs (NL).

From 1902 to 1912, the 5 foot, 10 inch, 175 pound right-hander achieved fame with the Cubs as a member of the Tinker to John Evers* to Frank Chance* double play combination, immortalized in poetry by Franklin P. Adams. Although the trio actually executed relatively few double plays, Tinker played solidly on offense and defense and performed well on the 1906–1908 and 1910 NL championship teams. Despite his .263 career batting average, the aggressive, spirited Tinker excelled as a clutch hitter and batted exceptionally well against pitcher Christy Mathewson.* Tinker hit .350 in 1902 and over .400 in 1908 against the New York Giants hurler. On July 28, 1910, he tied a major league record by stealing home twice in one game. In 1,805 games, he made 1,695 hits, 264 doubles, 114 triples, 773 runs, 782 RBIs, 336 stolen bases, and a .354 slugging percentage.

Following the 1912 season, the Cubs traded Tinker to the Cincinnati Reds (NL). Tinker managed the Reds to a 64–89 record and seventh place finish and clashed with owner Garry Herrmann over his salary. He was sold to the Brooklyn Dodgers (NL) for $25,000 in December 1913 but demanded $10,000 of the sale price. Since neither club complied, Tinker became the first "name" player to join the newly formed FL in 1914. He served as player-manager of the Chicago Whales (FL) and led the team in 1915 to a first place finish. With the demise of the FL, the Cubs hired Tinker in 1916 as team manager. Tinker piloted the Cubs to a 67–86 mark and fifth place finish. As a major league manager, Tinker recorded 304 wins and 308 losses (.497).

In 1917 he joined Columbus (AA) as manager and president and left the field two years later exclusively for the front office. Tinker bought controlling interest in the Orlando Gulls (FSL) in 1921, managing the club that year and serving as its vice-president in 1923. He also briefly managed Buffalo and Jersey City (IL) and scouted several years for the Chicago Cubs. During the 1920s, he made and subsequently lost a fortune in Florida real estate. Tinker owned an Orlando billiard parlor and bar and invested in the stadium (Tinker Field) where the Cincinnati Reds trained. Although surviving a serious illness in 1936, he later developed diabetes and lost a leg. On his sixty-eighth birthday, he succumbed to respiratory complications. With Evers and Chance, he was elected to the National Baseball Hall of Fame in 1946.

Tinker, minimally involved in the "Merkle Boner" 1908 game against the New York Giants, hit a triple to decide the playoff game in October, 1908, for the NL pennant. Tinker belted the only home run of the 1908 World Series against the Detroit Tigers, the first fall classic round tripper in Cubs history. Although first acquired as a third baseman, Tinker was shifted against his will by Cubs manager Frank Selee* to shortstop. Baseball's first holdout, he demanded a $1,000 raise and sat out part of the 1909 season until settling for $200. Tinker's quarrel with second baseman Evers over the payment of a taxicab fare resulted in the two not speaking to each other for nearly three years. An advocate of the hit-and-run play, Tinker often supported progressive changes in baseball and proved instrumental in the abolition of the spitball from the AA and the major leagues.

BIBLIOGRAPHY: Alan R. Asnen, interview with Jeff Kernan, August 21, 1984, National Baseball Hall of Fame Library, Cooperstown, NY; Warren Brown, *The Chicago Cubs* (New York, 1946); Glenn Dickey, *History of National League Baseball* (New York, 1980); Jim Enright, *Chicago Cubs* (New York, 1975); Ralph Hickok, *Who Was Who in American Sports* (New York, 1971); Gene Karst and Martin J. Jones, Jr., *Who's Who in Professional Baseball* (New Rochelle, NY, 1973); Paul MacFarlane, ed., *TSN Daguerreotypes of Great Stars of Baseball* (St. Louis, 1981); National Biographical Society, *Who's Who in American Sports* (Washington, DC, 1928); *NYT*, July 17, 28, 31, 1948; Joseph L. Reichler, ed., *The Baseball Encyclopedia*, 6th ed. (New York, 1985), pp. 652, 1,463; Lowell Reidenbaugh, *Cooperstown: Where Baseball's Legends Live Forever* (St. Louis, 1983).

Alan R. Asnen and John E. Findling

TOBIN, John Thomas "Jack" (4 May 1892, St. Louis, MO; d. 10 December 1969, St. Louis, MO), player, manager, coach, and scout, attended St. Malachy's Elementary School for eight years. He signed a professional baseball contract with Houston (TL), but never reported and was released. After joining the St. Louis Terriers (FL) as an outfielder in 1914, he hit .270 that inaugural season and led the FL with 184 hits in 1915. Tobin played briefly with the St. Louis Browns (AL) in 1916, after Phil Ball, owner of the now defunct Terriers, purchased the club. At Salt Lake City (PCL), Tobin in 1917 paced the PCL in runs scored (149) and hits (265) and was reacquired before the 1918 season by the Browns. From 1919 through 1923, the 5 foot, 8 inch, 142 pound left-hander teamed with Ken Williams* and "Baby Doll" Jacobson* to form one of baseball's most prolific outfields. For those five seasons, the outfield trio each hit at least .300. The streak ended in 1924, when the right fielder Tobin slipped to .299.

An adroit bunter, Tobin in 1926 was traded with Joe Bush to the Washington Senators (AL) for Win Ballou and Tom Zachary. Later that same season, Tobin joined the Boston Red Sox (AL) and retired after the 1927 campaign. Tobin later managed Bloomington, IL (3IL) in 1930 and coached and scouted for the St. Louis Browns (AL) from 1944 through 1951. Tobin's career statistics included a .309 batting average, 1,906 hits, 936 runs scored, 294 doubles, 99 triples, 64 home runs, 581 RBIs, and 147 stolen bases in 1,619 games. He hit .300 or better seven times, his best mark being .352 in 1921. He made at least 200 hits four times and ranked among the AL leaders in runs scored and total bases. Tobin's two grand slam homers off Walter Johnson* gave him his greatest thrill. The best drag bunter in baseball history, he was elected to the All-Time St. Louis team in 1957. He married Loretta Sack on March 4, 1914, and had one daughter.

BIBLIOGRAPHY: Bill Borst, *Last in the American League* (St. Louis, 1976); Gene Karst and Martin J. Jones, Jr., *Who's Who in Professional Baseball* (New York, 1973); Paul MacFarlane, ed., *TSN Daguerreotypes of Great Stars of Baseball* (St. Louis, 1981).

William A. Borst

TOPPING, Daniel Reid, Sr., "Dan" (b. 11 June 1912, Greenwich, CT; d. 18 May 1974, Miami, FL), baseball and football executive, owned the New York Yankees (AL) baseball team for twenty-two years. The son of Henry J. and Rhea (Reid) Topping, he became heir to a family fortune made in the tin and steel industries. He attended the Hun School in Lawrenceville, NJ, and Wharton School of Finance at the University of Pennsylvania. Topping entered professional sports as a football executive, hiring Dr. Jock Sutherland* (FB) in 1940 for $17,500 to coach the Brooklyn Dodgers (NFL). After World War II, Topping shifted his interest to the All-America Football Conference New York Yankees, but concentrated on baseball when the league folded in 1949.

His association with the New York Yankees baseball club began in the U.S. Marines during World War II. In 1945 Leland S. (Larry) MacPhail, Sr.,* Del E. Webb,* and Topping purchased the Bronx Bombers from the heirs of Jacob Ruppert* for $2.8 million. Two years later, Topping joined Webb in buying out MacPhail and became president. Not a baseball expert,

Topping knew his limitations and let general manager George M. Weiss* and field manager Casey Stengel* conduct daily operations. Stengel won nine AL pennants and seven World Series before finishing third in 1959. After the Yankees lost a heartstopping Series to the Pittsburgh Pirates in 1960, Topping announced a new mandatory retirement policy and dismissed the 70-year-old Stengel and the 65-year-old Weiss.

The Yankees captured four straight AL championships under managers Ralph Houk* and Yogi Berra,* but the team's fortunes had begun to decline after the 1960 firings. Yankee superstars had aged, while the amateur draft and expansion cut into the club's domination of player development. During the 1964 season, Topping and Weiss sold 80 percent of the club's stock to CBS for $11.2 million. Topping later faced a congressional inquiry into a possible antitrust violation. Two years later, Topping severed his official connections with the Yankees and retired to a Florida yacht. The father of nine children, Topping was married six times—to Theodora Boettger in 1932, actress Arline Judge in 1937, Olympic gold medal figure skater Sonja Henie in 1940, actress Kay Sutton in 1946, Alice Lowther in 1952, and Charlotte Ann Lillard in 1957.

BIBLIOGRAPHY: Dave Anderson, Murray Chass, Robert Creamer, and Harold Rosenthal, *The Yankees* (New York, 1979); Frank Graham, *The New York Yankees* (New York, 1943); *NYT*, October 1960, February 19, 1965, May 20, 1974; *TSN*, January 3, 1962, pp. 4, 5, 16.

John David Healy

TORRE, Joseph Paul, Jr. "Joe" (b. 18 July 1940, Brooklyn, NY), player, manager, and broadcaster, is the youngest of five children born to Joseph Paul and Margaret Torre and grew up in a baseball family. His father scouted for the Milwaukee Braves and the Baltimore Orioles, while his older brother, Frank, played first base for Milwaukee (1956–1960) and Philadelphia (1962–1963).

A star third baseman at St. Francis Prep School, Torre began his professional baseball career as a catcher because of a tendency to put on weight. An all-star performance in his first season with Eau Claire, WI (NoL), led to his promotion to the Milwaukee Braves (NL) for the last two weeks of the 1960 season. He began the 1961 season at Louisville (AA), but hit .342 in the first 27 games and returned to the majors. He played for eighteen years with the NL Braves (Milwaukee, 1960–1965; Atlanta, 1966–1968), NL St. Louis Cardinals (1969–1974), and hometown NL New York Mets (1975–1977).

An excellent fielder who could hit for power and average, the 6 foot, 2 inch, 215 pound Torre also proved a versatile and consistent performer. Primarily a catcher with the Braves, he divided playing time after 1971 between first and third base. His best year was 1971, the only season he played exclusively at third. Named NL Most Valuable Player, he led the majors in batting average (.363), hits (230), RBIs (137), total bases (352), and putouts by a third baseman. Remarkably, he went hitless in only 28 of 161 games. Selected to the NL All-Star team nine times (1963–1967, 1970–1973), the right-handed Torre compiled career totals of 2,209 games played, 2,342 hits, 344 doubles, 252 home runs, 996 runs scored, 1,185 RBIs, .452 slugging percentage, and .297 batting average.

In May 1977 Torre became manager of the New York Mets. He was fired in October 1981 after five losing seasons (286–420, .405), which saw the team finish no higher than fifth place. He then was hired by the Atlanta Braves, which in 1982 won the Western Division title and lost to St. Louis in the NL Championship Series. Despite leading the Braves to second place finishes in 1983 and 1984, Torre was released as manager after the 1984 season. His managerial record for eight seasons included 543 wins, 649 losses, and .456 winning percentage.

Torre married Diane Romaine in 1968. They have three children: Christina Lynn, Loren from Diane's previous marriage, and Michael from his previous marriage to Jacqueline Ann Reed. In 1985 he became a television broadcaster with the California Angels (AL).

BIBLIOGRAPHY: *CB* (1972), pp. 430–433; Gene Karst and Martin J. Jones, Jr., *Who's Who in Professional Baseball* (New Rochelle, NY, 1973), pp. 867–868; *NYT*, June 3, 1976, June 1, 1977, October 5, 21, 1981, October 2, 1984; Joseph L. Reichler, ed., *The Baseball Encyclopedia*, 6th ed. (New York, 1985), pp. 652, 1,467; Barry Siegel, ed., *TSN Official Baseball Register, 1984* (St. Louis, 1984); *TSN*, November 7, 28, 1981, October 22, 1984.

Larry R. Gerlach

TRAUTMAN, George McNeal (b. 11 January 1890, Bucyrus, OH; d. 24 June 1963, Columbus, OH), player, coach, manager, club official, and administrator, served as president and treasurer of the National Association of Professional Baseball Leagues from 1947 through 1962. After pitching from 1905 to 1908 for Bucyrus High School, Trautman played varsity football, basketball, and baseball at Ohio State University from 1909 through 1913 and formed a battery with noted politician John W. Bricker.

Following graduation, the red-haired hurler studied at Harvard University Graduate School in physical education and served as athletic director at Camp Sheridan, AL, with the rank of army captain. He spent two years as coach and athletic director at Fostoria, OH, High School and served until 1929 in the Ohio State physical education department. Besides being head basketball coach, he was an assistant athletic director under longtime associate Lynn St. John* (IS) and joined the National Intercollegiate Wrestling Rules Committee. Trautman in 1929 became director of conventions and publicity for the Columbus Chamber of Commerce and helped bring the 1931 Ryder Cup golf matches to the Scioto Country Club. At Ohio State, he had directed the U.S. Open golf championship tournament at Scioto in 1926. He received a lifetime honorary membership from the American Bowling Congress for promoting its annual meet at Columbus in 1933.

In 1933 he succeeded Leland MacPhail, Sr.,* as president of the Columbus Red Birds (AA), then the top minor league baseball circuit. Under Trautman's direction, the St. Louis Cardinals farm club won AA pennants his first and second years and remained in contention with profitable attendance. He served as AA president from 1936 to 1944 and became general manager of the Detroit Tigers (AL) under owner Walter O. Briggs.* As executive vice-president, he was asked to fulfill only assignments strictly related to his job and disliked having visitors or callers.

In 1946 the minor leagues made Trautman a virtually unanimous choice to replace ailing Judge William Bramham of Durham, NC, as their president. Trautman promptly moved the league headquarters from Durham to Columbus, took along several key staffers, and presided over the greatest growth of professional baseball. By 1949, the minor leagues expanded to 59 leagues and 448 teams. The tremendous growth of major league farm systems and the mass signing of young players returning from World War II military service spurred the increase. Trautman, however, believed that much of the expansion was irresponsible and doomed to failure because television competed heavily with minor league baseball. Towns without strong financial structures for their teams and well-developed promotion programs lost their club franchises. The number of leagues and franchises steadily declined, causing detractors to predict doom for the minors.

Trautman in 1957 launched the strongest promotion program devised for pro-sports to that time. He organized a promotional staff, headed by former wire services sportswriter Carl Lundquist and including field representatives Eddie Stumpf, G. E. Gilliland, Warren LeTarte, and Bob Frietas. They traveled throughout the minor league empire, devising promotional projects to bring fans back to the ballparks. Despite a continuing reduction in leagues and clubs, Trautman's plan stabilized the minor league structure. Trautman had assured the future of the minors when illness forced him to resign as president in 1962.

BIBLIOGRAPHY: *American League 1946 Official Red Book* (Chicago, 1946); Columbus *Dispatch*, June 25, 1963; Columbus *Dispatch Sunday Magazine*, April 1, 1962; *TSN Official Baseball Guide, 1964* (St. Louis, 1964); *Seventy Nights in a Ball Park* (Columbus, 1958); George M. Trautman, *The Story of Minor League Baseball* (Columbus, 1952).

Carl Lundquist

TRAYNOR, Harold Joseph "Pie" (b. 11 November 1899, Framingham, MA; d. 16 March 1972, Pittsburgh, PA), player, manager, sportscaster, and scout, was one of eight children of an Irish printer and his English wife. He may have received his nickname, "Pie," for his favorite childhood food or when his father one day declared that the dirty boy resembled pied type. Traynor began working as an office boy at age 12 and tried to enlist during World War I, but was rejected and became a freight car checker. He started his professional baseball career as a shortstop with Portsmouth, VA (VL), in 1920 and then was purchased by the Pittsburgh Pirates (NL). After one minor league season at Birmingham, AL (SA), he joined the Pirates permanently in 1922.

Although originally a shortstop, Traynor the next twelve years became baseball's finest third baseman. The slightly over 6 foot, 170 pound right-hander lined many extra-base hits to right and right center field and made 2,416 hits, including 371 doubles, 164 triples, and 58 home runs. Traynor also batted .320 lifetime, drove in over 100 runs seven times, scored 1,183 runs, knocked in 1,273 career runs, and stole 158 bases. In the 1925 and 1927 World Series, he batted .293. Traynor used his speed in the field, where his range and throwing arm were legendary. It was often said that a player "doubled down the third base line, but Traynor threw him out." He exhibited daring base running and led the NL in triples (19) in 1923, but his aggressiveness shortened his career. While trying to score in a 1934 game against the Philadelphia Phillies, he slid and reached back for home plate. The catcher landed on Traynor's right arm, injuring it. Traynor played little more than a season after that.

In 1934 he became the Pirates' manager. His 1938 team narrowly lost the NL pennant to the Chicago Cubs on Gabby Hartnett's* famous "homer in the gloaming." He was asked to resign after the 1939 season, having posted a 457–406 (.530) career record. Traynor, who married Eva Helmer of Cincinnati in 1931 and had no children, moved to Cincinnati after leaving baseball. Although he never learned to drive, Traynor sold cars there. In 1944 he returned to Pittsburgh as a sports commentator for radio station WKQV and held that job for the next twenty-two years. He also became a part-time Pirates scout and instructor (1940–1972), frequently received speaking invitations, and did commercial endorsements. The elegant and articulate Traynor was beloved for his good humor and gentle disposition.

In the 1920s, John McGraw* termed Traynor "the greatest team player in baseball today." Upon Traynor's induction into the National Baseball Hall of Fame in 1948, Branch Rickey* lauded him as "a mechanically perfect third baseman, a man of intellectual worth on the field of play." During baseball's 1969 centennial celebration, he was named the greatest third baseman in baseball history. Traynor helped baseball's star shine brightly during sports' golden age between the world wars.

BIBLIOGRAPHY: Bob Broeg, *Super Stars of Baseball* (St. Louis, 1971); Lowell Reidenbaugh, *Cooperstown: Where Baseball's Legends Live Forever* (St. Louis, 1983).

                                                                        Luther W. Spoehr

TROSKY, Harold Arthur "Hal" (b. Harold Arthura Troyavesky, 11 November 1912, Norway, IA; d. 18 June 1979, Cedar Rapids, IA), player and coach, was of German ancestry. Trosky compiled excellent statistics as a Cleveland Indians (AL) first baseman during the 1930s and became one of the most emotionally enigmatic performers of his era. By mid-1939 Trosky, a hard-hitting, 6 foot, 2 inch, 207 pound left-handed slugger, was considered second only to Hank Greenberg* at his AL position. Cleveland scout Cy Slapnicka discovered him batting corncobs against the side of a barn. Trosky played outfield at Cedar Rapids-Dubuque (MOVL) in 1931 and at Quincy, IL (3IL), and Burlington, IA (MOVL), in 1932. After spending 1933 at Toledo (AA), he came to the Indians in September and hit .295 in 11 games. In 1934 the right-handed first baseman hit. .330 with 35 home runs and 142 RBIs for a spectacular rookie season. He fell victim to a sophomore slump with a .271 batting average, 26 homers, and 113 RBIs. In 1936 Trosky enjoyed a dream year with a .343 batting average, 42 home runs, and a major league leading 162 RBIs. He continued a first-rate performance in 1937 and 1938, improving his fielding, learning to hit to left field, and hitting 32 and 19 homers. In 1939, however, Trosky participated in a player rebellion against manager Ossie Vitt. In the "Cleveland Crybabies" incident, Trosky complained that the press singled him out as team captain and for his Russian-sounding name. A series of unexplained illnesses and migraine headaches forced him to drop out of baseball for various periods after the 1941 season. Trosky spent the World War II years in a factory and on a farm and attempted comebacks in 1944 and 1946 with the Chicago White Sox (AL). He left a solid eleven-year record of 1,561 hits, 331 doubles, 58 triples, a lifetime .302 batting average, and 1,012 RBIs. Trosky, who scouted for the White Sox in 1947 and 1948, married Lorraine Glenn in November, 1933, and had one son, Harold Jr., who played professional baseball.

BIBLIOGRAPHY: Franklin Lewis, *The Cleveland Indians* (New York, 1949); Hal Trosky file, National Baseball Hall of Fame Library, Cooperstown, NY.

Eric Solomon

U

UHLE, George Ernest "The Bull" (b. 18 September 1898, Cleveland, OH; d. 26 February 1985, Cleveland, OH), player, coach, and scout, grew up in Cleveland and attended Orchard Elementary School and then Cleveland West High School for two years. Uhle pitched for the Cleveland East Views, Dubsky Furnitures, and Standard Parts before the Cleveland Indians (AL) signed him to a $1,500 contract in 1919. During his rookie season, he compiled a 10–5 won-loss record with a 2.91 ERA. The 6 foot, 190 pound right-hander hurled for Cleveland from 1919 to 1928, the Detroit Tigers (AL) from 1929 to April 1933, New York Giants (NL) until July 1933, and New York Yankees (AL) from July in 1933 to 1934. Uhle pitched for Toledo (AA) in 1934, returned to Cleveland (AL) in 1936, and finished his career with Buffalo (IL) in 1938 and 1939.

In ten seasons with Cleveland, Uhle won 147 games and lost only 118 decisions. He led the AL in victories and innings pitched in 1923 and 1926, in games started three times, in games completed and hits surrendered twice, and in walks once. Three times Uhle won over 20 games. His best season came in 1926, when he compiled 27 victories, allowed only 2.83 earned runs per game, struck out 159 batters, and led the AL with a .711 winning percentage. In the 1920 World Series against the Brooklyn Dodgers, Uhle pitched in two games without a decision and allowed one hit and struck out three batters in three innings. Uhle claimed credit for developing the slider while throwing batting practice to Harry Heilmann* of the Detroit Tigers. In 1929 he hurled 20 innings of a 21-inning game and outdueled Ted Lyons* of the Chicago White Sox for the victory, but his arm never recovered from the strain.

In seventeen major league seasons, Uhle won 200 games, lost 166 contests, and compiled a 3.99 ERA. In 513 appearances, he won ten or more games ten times, allowed 3,417 hits and 1,635 runs in 3,119 2/3 innings pitched, issued 966 bases on balls, struck out 1,135 batters, and hurled 21 shutouts. New York Yankees slugger Babe Ruth* considered Uhle the most difficult pitcher to hit and slugged only two home runs off him. An excellent batter, he frequently pinch hit and belted nine career home runs. Uhle hit three doubles in one game and drove in six runs in another contest. He slugged a grand slam home run in 1921 and two years later became one of only seventeen AL pitchers ever to win 20 games and compile a batting average over .300. Uhle won 26 games that year and batted .361, third best ever for AL pitchers. His 52 hits in 1923 (equalled by Wes Ferrell* in 1935) were the most made by a pitcher in one season, while his 393 career hits rank him sixth on the all-time list. Uhle compiled a .288 career batting average, second only to Ruth's .304 career mark among pitchers.

Uhle served as coach for Cleveland (AL) in 1937, Buffalo (IL) in 1938 and 1939, Chicago (NL) in 1940, and Washington (AL) in 1944, and as scout for Brooklyn (NL) in 1941 and 1942. Uhle married Helen Schultz on October 20, 1920, and had two sons and one daughter. Following his retirement from baseball, he was employed as a manufacturer's representative for steel and aluminum companies in Bay Village, OH.

BIBLIOGRAPHY: Gene Karst and Martin J. Jones, Jr., *Who's Who in Professional Baseball* (New Rochelle, NY, 1973); Paul MacFarlane, ed., *TSN Daguerreotypes of Great Stars of Baseball* (St. Louis, 1971); Joseph L. Reichler, *The Great All-Time Baseball Record Book* (New York, 1981); Joseph L. Reichler, ed., *The Baseball Encyclopedia*, 6th ed. (New York, 1985); pp. 2,089–2,090; George Uhle file, National Baseball Hall of Fame Library, Cooperstown, NY.

John L. Evers and Harry A. Jebsen, Jr.

V

VANCE, Arthur Charles "Dazzy" (b. 4 March 1891, Orient, IA; d. 16 February 1961, Homosassa Springs, FL), player, was the son of A. T. and Sarah (Ritchie) Vance and grew up on farms in Iowa and Nebraska. His famous nickname derived from an often used childhood phrase, "Ain't that a daisy." Vance, however, pronounced the last word "dazzy." After graduating from rural Hastings (NE) High School, Vance played professionally for Red Cloud, NE (NeSL), in 1912, but did not reach the major leagues permanently until 1922. After pitching briefly for the Pittsburgh Pirates (NL) in 1915 and New York Yankees (AL) in 1915 and 1918, he won his first major league game at age 31. The 6 foot, 2 inch, 200 pound right-hander had developed an exaggerated leg kick, which caused him control problems throughout his minor league career. Upon finding his control, however, Vance became the premier NL pitcher.

In his rookie season with the second division Brooklyn Dodgers, Vance won 18 games and led the NL in strikeouts. He walked only 840 career batters and compiled 2,045 career strikeouts, pacing the NL in that category seven consecutive seasons. In addition, he topped the NL three times in ERA, four in shutouts and twice in victories and complete games. He threw a no-hit game against Philadelphia in 1925 as well as one-hit games in 1923 and 1925. Although pitching for a habitual second division club, he won 197 games and lost only 140 decisions with 30 shutouts and a 3.24 ERA. He hurled for the Dodgers from 1922 to 1932, performed with the St. Louis Cardinals (NL) in 1933 and until June 1934 and the Cincinnati Reds (NL) in 1934 and finished his career with Brooklyn in 1935. He appeared in the 1934 World Series with the triumphant Cardinals against the Detroit Tigers.

Vance won the initial NL MVP Award in 1924, leading the NL with 28 victories, 262 strikeouts, and a 2.16 ERA. He outpolled Rogers Hornsby,* who that year had set a major league record with a .424 batting average, because one voter failed to place the latter on the ballot. Vance used the award to negotiate a highly publicized three-year contract worth $47,500 from Brooklyn owner Charles Ebbets.* By the end of the 1920s, Vance became the highest paid major league pitcher and achieved spectacular success despite playing on the erratic Dodgers. Managed by Wilbert Robinson* and led by Babe Herman* and Vance, the Dodgers were known for bizarre behavior, eccentric plays, and inconsistent baseball. The fun-loving, gregarious Vance earned the respect of his fellow players. During the land boom of the 1920s, Vance invested in Florida real estate. Following retirement in 1935, he managed his extensive realty and business operations around Homosassa Springs, FL. In 1955 he was elected to the National Baseball Hall of Fame.

BIBLIOGRAPHY: *NYT*, February 17, 1961; Joseph L. Reichler, ed., *The Baseball Encyclopedia*, 6th ed. (New York, 1985), p. 2,042; Lowell Reidenbaugh, *100 Years of National League Baseball* (St. Louis, 1976); Harold Seymour, *Baseball: The Golden Age* (New York, 1971); Arthur Vance file, National Baseball Hall of Fame Library, Cooperstown, NY; Arthur Vance with Furman Bisher, "I'd Hate to Pitch Nowadays," *SEP* 228 (August 20, 1955), pp. 27-ff.

Harry A. Jebsen, Jr.

VAN HALTREN, George Edward Martin "Rip" (b. 30 March 1866, St. Louis, MO; d. 29 September 1945, Oakland, CA), player, manager, umpire, and scout, grew up in Oakland, CA, where his family had moved when he was three years old. Van Haltren gained prominence in the Bay area in 1886 while pitching and playing outfield for the amateur Greenhood and Morans, under the management of Colonel T. P. Robinson. He began his professional career the following year with the Chicago White Stockings (NL), managed by Cap Anson.* In his first season, the left-handed Van Haltren was used as a utility outfielder and spot starting pitcher. He compiled an 11–7 record with 18 complete games, sharing mound duties with the redoubtable John Clarkson* and Mark Baldwin.

In 1888 the 5 foot, 11 inch, 170 pound left-hander divided his time between the mound and the outfield, posting a mediocre 13–13 pitching record and batting a respectable .283. Given the regular left field position the next year, he hit .309 as part of a skillful outfield trio that included Jimmy Ryan* in center field and High Duffy* in right. In 1890 Van Haltren jumped to Brooklyn of the ill-fated PL, where he played the outfield and posted a 15–10 record in 28 games as a pitcher. He played with Baltimore (AA) in 1891, managing the team for the last week of the season. Van Haltren remained as player-manager when Baltimore shifted to the NL in 1892, but was relieved of managerial duties after the team opened with a dismal 1–14 record. In September 1892 he was traded to Pittsburgh (NL) for outfielder Joe Kelley* and hit .338 in 1893 as the team's starting center fielder.

In 1894 Van Haltren signed with the New York Giants (NL), where he became a fixture in center field. For eight seasons (1894–1901), Van Haltren averaged 185 hits, 115 runs scored, and a composite .327 batting mark. He led the NL in triples (21) in 1896, at bats (654) in 1898, and stolen bases (45) in 1900. Early in 1902, he broke his leg while sliding and missed the rest of the season. In 1903 he lost the starting center field job to Roger Bresnahan* and was sent to Seattle (PCL) at the end of the year by Giants manager John McGraw.* With Seattle in 1904, Van Haltren knocked out 253 hits and led the PCL with a robust 941 at bats.

In 1905 Oakland Oaks (PCL) owner Cal Ewing signed the 39-year-old Van Haltren as player-manager. As a regular Oaks outfielder for the next four years, he averaged 184 hits and 745 at bats in over 187 games per season. He was released by Ewing in June 1909 and finished the year as a PCL umpire. He scouted for Pittsburgh (NL) owner Barney Dreyfuss* for two years (1910–1911) and umpired in the NWL in 1912.

In seventeen major league seasons, Van Haltren played in 1,984 games, collected 2,536 hits, scored 1,639 runs, and batted .316. As a pitcher, he started 68 games, completed 65, and finished with a 40–31 record and 4.05 ERA. In 1887 he set a major league record as a rookie hurler by walking 16 batters in one game. The following season, he pitched a six-inning no-hitter to beat Pittsburgh 1–0. In 1901 Van Haltren roomed with Giants rookie Christy Mathewson* and helped the young hurler develop into one of the game's finest pitchers.

BIBLIOGRAPHY: Paul MacFarlane, ed., *TSN Daguerreotypes of Great Stars of Baseball* (St. Louis, 1981); Joseph L. Reichler, ed., *The Baseball Encyclopedia*, 6th ed. (New York, 1985), p. 1,480; San Francisco *Chronicle*, October 3, 1945; David Quentin Voigt, *American Baseball*, vol. 1 (Norman, OK, 1966).

Raymond D. Kush

VAUGHAN, Joseph Floyd "Arky" (b. 9 March 1912, Clifty, AR; d. 30 August 1952, Eagleville, CA), player, was the son of farmers who moved to California when Vaughan was small. He played baseball the year round with his brothers and performed for his high school and local teams. After being signed by the Pittsburgh Pirates (NL) in 1931, Vaughan hit .338 with 21 home runs and 81 RBIs for Wichita (WL). He married Margaret Allen in October 1931 and replaced an injured Pirates shortstop a month into the 1932 season. In 1932 he batted .318 in 129 games for Pittsburgh and led the NL in errors. For the next nine years, he remained Pittsburgh's regular shortstop. Although his fielding improved, he made the most impact at the plate. Honus Wagner,* Pirates coach and Vaughan's roommate on road trips, facilitated the latter's development. In his best season (1935), Vaughan led the NL with a .385 batting average, a .607 slugging average, and 97 walks and produced career highs in hits (192), home runs (19), and RBIs (99). *The Sporting News* named Vaughan to the NL All-Star team and as NL Most

Valuable Player. Overall, Vaughan hit .324 for a Pirates squad invariably finishing out of contention.

Vaughan batted .364 in seven All-Star games (1934–1935, 1937, 1939–1942) and enjoyed his finest performance in the 1941 classic, making three hits and becoming the first player to belt two homers in an All-Star game. Despite Vaughan's heroics and four RBIs, the NL lost the game on a widely publicized ninth-inning home run by Ted Williams.* In December, 1941, Vaughan was traded to the Brooklyn Dodgers, where he played third base and batted .277 in 1942. The following year, he divided his time between third base and shortstop, batted .305, and led the NL in stolen bases. The "Newsom Revolt," which involved a dispute over an alleged spitter, caused Vaughan and others to confront manager Leo Durocher.* Vaughan voluntarily retired at the end of the season, but returned in 1947 when Durocher was suspended from baseball. In 1947 Vaughan performed well as a part-time outfielder and pinch hitter, hitting .325 overall and .385 as a pinch hitter to help the Dodgers win the NL pennant. He doubled once in two at bats in the 1947 World Series loss to the New York Yankees. For the Dodgers in 1948, Vaughan batted a career low .244 and was released. He hit .288 as an outfielder for the San Francisco Seals (PCL) in 1949 and then retired from baseball to live with his family on their Surprise Valley ranch. Vaughan drowned in a sudden storm while fishing in August, 1952, and was survived by his wife and four children.

Vaughan ranked among the leading NL hitters in the 1930s and proved an adequate defensive player, pacing NL shortstops in putouts in 1936, 1938, and 1939. During fourteen NL seasons, he led the league in runs scored three times (1936, 1940, 1943), triples three times (1933, 1937, 1940), and stolen bases once (1943). During his career, Vaughan batted .318, produced 2,103 hits, 356 doubles, 128 triples, 926 RBIs, and 118 stolen bases, scored 1,173 runs, and struck out only 276 times. His performance faded into obscurity partly because his best years came with a non–pennant-winning team outside a major media center and because he was a quiet person. In 1985 the Veterans Committee belatedly elected Vaughan to the National Baseball Hall of Fame.

BIBLIOGRAPHY: Leo Durocher, *The Dodgers and Me: The Inside Story* (Chicago, 1948); Paul MacFarlane, ed., *TSN Daguerreotypes of Great Stars of Baseball* (St. Louis, 1971); *NYT*, August 31, 1952; Joseph L. Reichler, ed., *The Baseball Encyclopedia*, 6th ed. (New York, 1985), p. 1,481.

Douglas D. Martin

VAUGHN, James Leslie "Hippo" (b. 9 April 1888, Weatherford, TX; d. 29 May 1966, Chicago, IL), player, was one of eight children of stonemason Thomas H. and Josephine S. Vaughn. He completed elementary school in Weatherford and played his first professional baseball with Temple, TX

(TL), in 1906. In 1908 he shuttled among three teams and was sold by Macon, GA (SAL), to the New York Yankees (AL). He pitched only two innings for the Yankees and was optioned to Macon in 1909. After tossing no-hitters at Macon and Louisville (AA), he was recalled for the 1910 season by the Yankees. He contributed 13 wins and a 1.83 ERA in 1910 but slumped to an 8–10 mark and 4.39 ERA a year later. He was waived to the Washington Senators (AL) in June 1912 and traded two months later to Kansas City (AA). In August 1913 he was traded to the Chicago Cubs (NL) and won five of six decisions in seven starts.

In his first full NL season (1914), the 26-year-old, 6 foot, 4 inch, 215 pound Vaughn proved slow afoot (hence "Hippo") and a hard-throwing left-hander with solid pitching skills. He finished with a 21–13 in 293 2/3 innings pitched and compiled a 2.05 ERA. Vaughn, who won 20 and 17 games the next two years, married Edna Coburn DeBold on February 11, 1916, and had one son. In 1917 he registered the first of three consecutive 20-win seasons and hurled the most extraordinary game of his career. On a cold midweek May 2 afternoon at Chicago, he engaged in a nine-inning, double no-hit duel with Fred Toney of Cincinnati. In the tenth inning, the Reds scored on a single, an outfield error, and a topped hit down the third base line. With no play at first base, Vaughn tried unsuccessfully to scoop the ball to the catcher with his glove hand. Vaughn struck out ten, while Toney fanned only three, two in the bottom of the tenth to preserve the victory. For the year, Vaughn's record included 23 wins, 13 losses, 295 2/3 innings pitched, and 195 strikeouts.

Vaughn's peak season came in 1918, when his 22 victories helped the Cubs win their only NL pennant between 1910 and 1929. Aside from his games won, he led the NL in games started (33), innings pitched (290 1/3), strikeouts (148), shutouts (8), and ERA (1.74). Against the mostly right-handed Boston Red Sox in the World Series, the Cubs started only left-handers. Vaughn, who won one game and lost two by a run each, achieved four World Series records. Besides hurling three complete games in six days, he tied marks for most innings pitched in a six-game World Series (27), total chances (17), and putouts (6). His 1.00 ERA remains the sixth best in World Series history. In 1919 Vaughn won 21 games and again led the NL in innings pitched (306 2/3) and strikeouts (141). He also made a remarkable steal of home against the New York Giants. He won 19 decisions in 1920, but slumped to 3–11 in his final season (1921). His career totals included 178 wins, 136 losses, a respectable 41 shutouts, 1,416 strikeouts, and a 2.49 ERA. He played semi-pro baseball with a Fairbanks-Morse Company team at Beloit, WI, and with Chicago's Logan Squares and Mills until age 47. He contemplated a comeback with the Cubs, but only pitched batting practice. He also worked as an assembler for a refrigeration products company.

BIBLIOGRAPHY: Lee Allen, *The Cincinnati Reds* (New York, 1948); Chicago *Sun-Times*, May 30, 1966; Chicago *Tribune*, May 3, 1917, p. 13; May 30, 1966, pp. 1, 4; Leonard Gettelson, "Pitchers Stealing Home," *Baseball Research Journal* 5 (1976), pp. 12–14;

Paul MacFarlane, ed., *TSN Daguerreotypes of Great Stars of Baseball* (St. Louis, 1981); Joseph L. Reichler, ed., *The Baseball Encyclopedia*, 6th ed. (New York, 1985), pp. 2,094–2,095; Lawrence S. Ritter, *The Glory Of Their Times* (New York, 1966); James Vaughn file, National Baseball Hall of Fame Library, Cooperstown, NY.

A. D. Suehsdorf

VEACH, Robert Hayes "Bobby" (b. 29 June 1888, Island, KY; d. 7 August 1945, Detroit, MI), player, was one of three sons of coal miner Mark and Sally Veach, both of Irish descent. He moved to Herrin, IL, as a youth. Without graduating from high school, he entered professional baseball as a pitcher with Kankakee (NoA) in 1910. Since Veach lacked speed and base-running ability, he was not considered a major league prospect. At Peoria (3IL) in 1911, he batted .297 and was converted to an outfielder. St. Louis Browns (AL) scout Charlie Barrett, who had joined the Peoria club as fundamentals coach, gave Veach specialized instruction. In 1912 Veach batted .285 for Indianapolis (AA) and .342 in 23 games for the Detroit Tigers (AL) at the end of that season. Veach became a mainstay in left field for the Tigers from 1913 through 1923 and combined with center fielder Ty Cobb* and right fielders Sam Crawford* (until 1917) and Harry Heilmann* (1918–1923) to give Detroit one of the most potent outfields in AL history. He was sold on January 12, 1924, to the Boston Red Sox (AL) and was traded on May 9, 1925, to the New York Yankees (AL). Veach was sold to the Washington Senators (AL) on August 17, 1925, and pinch-hit in the 1925 World Series against the New York Giants. After playing from 1926 through 1929 for Toledo (AA), he ended his career with Jersey City (IL) in 1930.

Baseball historian Robert Creamer remarked that Veach is "surely one of the least remembered of the really fine hitters." Besides batting .310 lifetime, he led the AL twice in doubles (1915, 1919), once each in triples (1919) and hits (1919), and three times in RBIs (1915, 1917–1918). Veach enjoyed his best season in 1919, when his 191 hits, 45 doubles, and 17 triples paced the AL and his .355 batting average placed second to roommate Cobb's .384 mark. His 2,064 major league hits included 393 doubles, 147 triples, and 64 home runs. He also stole 195 bases and scored 953 runs, while driving in 1,166 tallies. In one 12-inning game in 1920, he batted six for six, including a double, triple, and home run.

The 5 foot, 11 inch, 160 pound Veach had gray eyes and dark hair, threw right-handed, and batted left-handed. Fred Lieb described him as "a phlegmatic chap who lacked Cobb's inspirational qualities, but packed a terrific punch for his size." In 1921 Tigers manager Cobb allegedly tried to "put more fire into Bobbie" by ordering Heilmann to "ride" Veach all season long. Veach hit .338 and developed a lasting resentment of Heilmann, but Cobb apparently never admitted his role in the scheme.

Veach married Ethel Clare Spiller on January 22, 1910, and had four sons. After leaving baseball, he became a coal dealer in Detroit and proved instrumental in persuading the Tigers to sign infielder Charlie Gehringer* of Fowlerville, MI. Veach brought Gehringer to Detroit for a tryout under the watchful eye of manager of Cobb, who signed him instantly. In 1945 Veach died after a long illness. Although overshadowed by Cobb, he proved a consistently outstanding performer and made substantial contributions to the Detroit teams of the World War I era.

BIBLIOGRAPHY: Robert W. Creamer, *Babe: The Legend Comes to Life* (New York, 1974); Detroit *Free Press*, December 30, 1943; August 7, 1945; Frederick G. Lieb, *The Detroit Tigers* (New York, 1946); Joseph L. Reichler, ed., *The Baseball Encyclopedia*, 6th ed. (New York, 1985), pp. 1,481–1,482; *TSN*, June, 1913.

David S. Matz and Luther W. Spoehr

VEECK, William Louis, Jr., "Bill" (b. 9 February 1914, Chicago, IL; d. 2 January 1986, Chicago, IL), college football player, sports executive, scout, and announcer, was the son of baseball executive William Louis and Grace (DeForest) Veeck. His father served as president of the Chicago Cubs (NL) from 1919 to 1933. Following grammar school, Veeck attended Phillips Academy in Andover, MA, Hinsdale, IL, High School (where he played blocking back on the football team), and Los Alamos, NM, Ranch School. Although he failed to graduate from high school, Veeck attended Kenyon College after passing entrance examinations. He played football for the Lords until his father's death in 1933, when he joined the Cubs as office boy and learned the complete operation of a baseball franchise. He worked in the Cubs' advertising agency, operated the commissary, handled ushers and ticket sellers, and conducted tryout schools for high school players. Veeck also worked in the concession stands, directed park maintenance, and in 1940 became club treasurer and assistant secretary. He attended night school at Northwestern University to study accounting and business law and Lewis Institute for designing and blueprint reading.

Veeck owned his first team at age 28 and brought fun and excitement into the game with innovative promotional gimmicks. He operated five clubs, including three major league and two minor league teams. In three cities, his teams won pennants and broke attendance records. In 1941 Veeck and Charlie Grimm* purchased the Milwaukee Brewers (AA) and made the team a highly successful franchise, winning three pennants (1943–1945). Veeck was named Minor League Executive of the Year by *The Sporting News* in 1942. After joining the U.S. Marine Corps in 1944, he was wounded and later had to have his leg amputated. Veeck sold the Brewers following the 1945 season and purchased the Cleveland Indians (AL) as part of a ten-man syndicate. Cleveland's attendance soared to a remarkable 2,620,627 in 1948, when the Indians won the AL flag and the World Series under player-manager Lou Boudreau.* The same year, Veeck was named Major League Executive of the Year. Veeck signed Larry Doby,* the first AL black player, in 1947 and recruited Satchel Paige* the next year to pitch for the Indians. After selling his interest in the Indians, Veeck purchased the St. Louis Browns (AL) in July, 1951. He could not advance the Browns financially and sold his interest in 1953, when the franchise was moved to Baltimore. His finest promotional stunt came on August 29, 1951, when he sent midget Eddie Gaedel to bat in a game against the Detroit Tigers (AL).

Baseball owners considered him a maverick and prevented Veeck from purchasing the Philadelphia (AL) franchise in 1954 and the Detroit club in 1956. He formed a public relations firm in Cleveland and scouted for the Indians before operating a minor league franchise in Miami (IL) for one season. After announcing sports for NBC-TV (1957–1958), Veeck in March 1959 purchased the Chicago White Sox (AL) club. Chicago won the AL pennant Veeck's first year and set another attendance record. The White Sox had not won a pennant since 1919, the year of the "Black Sox" scandal. Veeck helped design Comiskey Park for the comfort and convenience of the fans. His promotions included placing players' names on the backs of uniforms and installing exploding scoreboards, which were touched off by home runs hit by the home team. Veeck later sold his interest in the Chicago team and served as president of Boston's Suffolk Downs race track. Veeck again purchased the White Sox in 1976 and operated the franchise until 1980, when failing health forced him to sell the club. The co-author of *Veeck As In Wreck*, *The Hustler's Handbook* and *Thirty Tons a Day*, Veeck married Eleanor Raymond on December 8, 1935, and had three children. After their divorce in 1949, he married Mary Frances Ackerman on April 29, 1950; they had six children.

BIBLIOGRAPHY: *CB* (1948), pp. 645–647; Bill Veeck with Ed Linn, *Veeck As in Wreck* (New York, 1962); WWA, 43rd ed. (1984–1985).

John L. Evers

VERNON, James Barton "Mickey" (b. 22 April 1918, Marcus Hook, PA), player, coach, and manager, attended Villanova College for one year and married Elizabeth Firth on March 14, 1941. A 6 foot, 2 inch, 170 pound, left-handed batting and throwing first baseman, he ranked among the most productive, consistent major league players and in 1969 was voted the Washington Senators (AL) All-Time first baseman. Vernon began his professional career with Easton, MD (ESL) in 1937. After hitting .328 with Greenville (SAL) in 1938, he batted .343 for Springfield, MA (EL), in 1939 and finished that season with the Washington Senators (AL). He played most of the 1940 campaign at Jersey City (IL) before returning permanently to the major leagues in late September.

Vernon started at first base for the Washington Senators from 1941 through 1943, spent 1944 and 1945 in military service, and rejoined the Senators in 1946. After performing three years with Washington, he was traded in December 1948 to Cleveland (AL). Vernon played with the Indians in 1949 and 1950 and returned to the Senators in June 1950 for six more seasons. He spent the 1956 and 1957 campaigns with the Boston Red Sox (AL) as a part-time first baseman and rejoined Cleveland in 1958. Before retiring as a player, he performed briefly with the Milwaukee Braves (NL) in 1959 and the Pittsburgh Pirates (NL) in 1960.

Vernon twice led the AL in batting with .353 in 1946 and .337 in 1953, paced AL hitters in doubles in 1946 (51), 1953 (43), and 1954 (33), and batted over .300 in 1955 and 1956. In 2,409 major league games, he netted 2,495 hits, 1,196 runs scored, 490 doubles, 120 triples, 172 home runs, and 1,311 RBIs, batted .286, and compiled a .428 slugging percentage. A seven-time AL All Star, Vernon led AL first basemen in putouts three times, assists once, and fielding four times. He ranks second on the all-time major league list in games played by a first baseman (2,237), sixth in putouts (19,808); and chances (21,467); and first in double plays (2,044). Besides establishing a major league record for most assists by a first baseman in a season (155; since broken) in 1949, he holds AL records for most career games and putouts. He participated in ten double plays in an August 18, 1943, doubleheader, made two unassisted double plays in a game on May 29, 1946, and led AL first basemen in double plays in 1941, 1953, and 1954.

President Dwight D. Eisenhower's favorite player, Vernon remains one of the few major leaguers to perform in four different decades. Vernon managed the Washington Senators to a 61 win, 100 loss, ninth place finish in 1961 and 60–101 tenth place finish in 1962. The Senators stood in last place with a 14–26 mark in 1963 when he was replaced by Gil Hodges.* Vernon managed Vancouver (PCL) from 1966 through 1968, Richmond, VA (IL), in 1969 and 1970, and Manchester, NH (EL), in 1971. The Wallingford, PA, resident also coached for the Pittsburgh Pirates (NL) in 1960 and 1964, St. Louis Cardinals (NL) in 1965, and Montreal Expos (NL) in 1977 and 1978; worked as a minor league batting instructor for the Kansas City Royals (AL) in 1973 and 1974 and for the Los Angeles Dodgers (NL) in 1975 and 1976; and scouts for the New York Yankees (AL).

BIBLIOGRAPHY: Gene Karst and Martin J. Jones, Jr., *Who's Who in Professional Baseball* (New Rochelle, NY, 1983); Paul MacFarlane, ed., *TSN Daguerreotypes of Great Stars of Baseball* (St. Louis, 1981); Joseph L. Reichler, ed., *The Baseball Encyclopedia*, 6th ed. (New York, 1985), p. 1,483; *TSN Official Baseball Record Book, 1985* (St. Louis, 1985).

Jack R. Stanton

VON DER AHE, Christian Frederick Wilhelm "Der Poss Bresident" (b. 7 October 1851, Hille, Germany; d. 7 June 1913, St. Louis, MO), owner and manager, came to St. Louis in 1870 to make his fortune and opened a combination grocery and saloon on the corner of Grand and St. Louis Avenues. Although understanding very little about baseball, "der Poss Bresident" associated thirsty customers with the game. With John Peckington, Al Spink, and other area businessmen, Von der Ahe formed the Sportsman's Park Association. This group founded the AA, a new league in direct competition with the established NL. Its first game was played in 1882.

When Von der Ahe hired veteran Charles Comiskey* to manage his St. Louis Brown Stockings franchise in 1883, he started realizing his dreams. From 1885 through 1888, the Browns won four AA pennants and compiled a 1–2–1 record in the World Series against the NL. Von der Ahe, who thrived on ceremony, treated his players and fans with regal affection during prosperous times. He often transported his players to Sportsman's Park in open carriages pulled by white steads and spent a fortune taking his fans on the road during the World Series. He ceremoniously took the game's receipts each day to the bank in a wheelbarrow, flanked by armed guards.

When Comiskey left the team during the Brotherhood War in 1890 for a year and permanently to manage the Cincinnati Red Stockings (NL) in 1892, Von der Ahe's team started declining. Von der Ahe, an early-day Bill Veeck,* made the game more of a sideshow than the main attraction with merry-go-rounds, beer gardens, and artificial lakes. Baseball's P. T. Barnum wanted to make Sportsman's Park the "Coney Island of the West." In 1892 Von der Ahe managed his club to an eleventh place finish in the twelve-team NL with a 56–94 record. During the next few years, Von der Ahe suffered numerous personal and business reverses. He managed St. Louis in a few games from 1895 to 1897 to a 3–16 record. Two divorces, a terrible fire on April 16, 1898, unwise real estate deals, and his kidnapping by officials of the Pittsburgh club over his dispute with pitcher Mark Baldwin forced Von der Ahe out of baseball. He sold the team to attorney G. A. Gruner, who represented Frank and Stanley Robison. Von der Ahe slipped into obscurity and became a charity case for the St. Louis Cardinals (NL), who played a benefit in his honor in 1908. He married Emma Hoffmann on March 3, 1870 and had one son. He later wed Della Wells, who divorced him in 1898, and finally Anna Kaiser, who survived him.

BIBLIOGRAPHY: Bill Borst, *Last in the American League* (St. Louis, 1976); Bill Borst, *Baseball Through a Knothole* (St. Louis, 1980); Frederick G. Lieb, *The St. Louis Cardinals* (New York, 1945); *Missouri Republican*, January 19, 1913; St. Louis *Post Dispatch*, June 6, 1913.

William A. Borst

VOSMIK, Joseph Franklin "Joe" (b. 4 April 1910, Cleveland, OH; d. 27 January 1962, Cleveland, OH), player, manager, and scout, was the son of Joseph and Anna (Klecan) Vosmik, both of Bohemian ancestry. His father worked as a sawman for the Reliance Electric Company. After attending a local grade school, he played sandlot ball because his high school, Cleveland East Tech, fielded no baseball team. After playing for Rotbart Jewelers in

1928, the blond, stocky 6 foot, 185 pound right-hander signed a Cleveland Indians (AL) contract and joined their Class D Frederick, MD, farm team (BRL) in 1929. He batted .397 in Class B baseball at Terre Haute (3IL) his second year.

On the second day of the Indians' 1931 season, Vosmik became the starting left-fielder and batted five for five at Cleveland's League Park. The line drive hitter finished the year with a .320 average. For the next six seasons, he and Earl Averill* became one of the best outfield duos of all time. After hitting .341 in 1934, Vosmik led the AL in batting the next year until Buddy Myer* of Washington topped his .348 average by less than one-hundredth of a point in the last game. The same season, Vosmik led the AL in hits (216), doubles (47), and triples (20). At the 1935 All-Star Game in Cleveland, fans gave him a two-minute standing ovation when he came to the plate. Vosmik married Sally Joanne Okla in November 1936 and had three children, Joseph Robert, Larry Earl, and Karen.

After Vosmik experienced an off year in 1936, the Indians traded him to the St. Louis Browns (AL) in 1937. He hit .325 for St. Louis that year and .324 for the Boston Red Sox (AL) in 1938, when he paced the AL in hits (201). Plagued by chronic leg problems, he finished his major league career with the Brooklyn Dodgers (NL) in 1940–1941 and the Washington Senators (AL) in 1944. Vosmik, who played with Louisville (AA) in 1941 and Minneapolis (AA) from 1942 to 1944, retired in 1944 with a lifetime .307 batting average, 1,682 hits, 335 doubles, 92 triples, 65 home runs, 818 runs scored, and 874 RBIs.

Vosmik made his managerial debut with the Indians' team in Tucson (ArTL) in 1947. After some managerial success at Dayton, OH (CL), in 1948 and Oklahoma City (TL) in 1949 and 1950, he ended his career at Batavia, NY (Pol), in 1951 and as a Cleveland (AL) scout in 1951 and 1952 because of health problems. Never happy out of baseball, he spent his last years as a department store salesman and died after an operation for lung cancer. The quiet, easygoing Vosmik ranks among the most popular all-time Cleveland players.

BIBLIOGRAPHY: Cleveland *News*, March 20, 1935, January 18, 1937, February 17, 1940, July 5, 1941, March 9, 1943, January 1, 1948, January 16, 1956; Cleveland *Plain Dealer*, January 28, 1962; Cleveland *Press*, January 27, 1962; Franklin Lewis, *The Cleveland Indians* (New York, 1949); David S. Neft, Jordan A. Deutsch et al, *The Sports Encyclopedia: Baseball*, 1st ed. (New York, 1974); Emily Yusek to author, June 18, 1984.

James N. Giglio

W

WADDELL, George Edward "Rube" (b. 13 October 1876, Bradford, PA; d. 1 April 1914, San Antonio, TX), player, was born into a poor farm family and received little formal education. At age 18, he began pitching for the Butler, PA, town team and quickly achieved stardom. In 1896 he pitched semi-pro baseball for Franklin, PA, and won all four games for the Homestead Athletic Club in a series against Duquesne County. Waddell earned $100 for this feat and signed a $500 contract with the Louisville (NL) franchise. Waddell's first major league seasons proved eventful and erratic largely because he possessed little discipline. He participated in two games for Louisville before jumping the Colonels in 1898 to pitch for Detroit (WL) and then for semi-pro Chatham, Ontario, Canada. In 1899 he finished with a 26–8 mark for Columbus/Grand Rapids (WL) and won seven of nine decisions for Louisville at the season's end. Waddell pitched for Pittsburgh (NL) in 1900, when the Louisville and Pirates organizations merged. He compiled an impressive 2.37 ERA and 130 strikeouts before leaving the Pirates in July. Milwaukee skipper Connie Mack* acquired Waddell, but the latter pitched so well for the AL club that Pittsburgh demanded his return. After coming back to the Pirates in 1901, he was sold to the Chicago Cubs (NL) in May. The 1902 season began with Waddell at Los Angeles (PCL), where he pitched well and became very popular. He agreed to join the Philadelphia Athletics (AL), but it required two Pinkerton detectives to bring him eastward to Connie Mack's new club.

Waddell's years with Philadelphia marked the most stable period in his career. In four of six seasons with the Athletics, the 6 foot, 1 1/2 inch, 196 pound left-hander won over 20 games (24–7 in 1902, 21–16 in 1903, 25–19 in 1904, 26–11 in 1905). Waddell led the AL in strikeouts from 1902 through 1907 and paced the major leagues in that category all those years except 1907. In 1905 he combined with Eddie Plank,* Chief Bender,* and Andrew Coakley for 88 victories and led the AL with a superb 1.48 ERA as Philadelphia won the AL pennant. Waddell's 26 wins tied Plank for the club lead, even though the former missed the last four weeks of the season and the World Series. Waddell and Plank together won 267 games for Philadelphia from 1902 through 1907, accounting for 56 percent of the team's victories. Mack sold Waddell to the St. Louis Browns (AL) in October, 1907, for $5,000. When the teams met the next season, Waddell struck out a then record 16 Athletics. Waddell recorded 19 victories and a 1.89 ERA for the Browns that year, but his performance declined in 1909 and 1910. Waddell in 1910 joined Newark (EL), where he compiled a 5–3 record. In 1911 he finished with a 20–17 mark for Minneapolis (AA) and befriended club owner Joe Cantillon. The following year, Waddell compiled a 12–6 slate with Minneapolis and then stayed that winter at the Cantillon home near Hickman, KY. Floodwaters broke a nearby dike, threatening the community. Waddell stood shoulder deep in the swirling water for hours helping to repair the dike, but caught a severe cold from which he never recovered. A very sick Waddell slumped to 3–9 in 1913 with Virginia, MN (NoL). Cantillon paid for Waddell's admission to a tuberculosis sanitarium in San Antonio, where the latter died.

Nicknamed "Rube," Waddell became one of the greatest major league pitchers ever. He possessed an excellent fastball, a deep-biting curve, and superb control. In thirteen major league seasons, he won 191 games and lost 145 for a .568 percentage, compiled a 2.16 ERA, and struck out 2,316 batters and walked only 803 hitters in 2,961 1/3 innings. He never pitched a no-hitter, but defeated Cy Young* 4–2 in a 20-inning game on July 4, 1905. In a remarkable 1900 doubleheader, he won both the 17-inning first game and the second game 1–0. Waddell, remembered for his antics and carefree attitude toward discipline, missed games to go fishing, attend fires, play marbles, wrestle alligators, and tend bar. Married three times, he spent time in jail for missing alimony payments, drank too much, and could not manage money. Although the stories that he sat his outfielders down and then struck out the side in major league games are false, Waddell did this several times in exhibition contests. The legendary Waddell was admitted to the National Baseball Hall of Fame in 1946.

BIBLIOGRAPHY: Martin Appel and Burt Goldblatt, *Baseball's Best: The Hall of Fame Gallery* (New York, 1977); Donald Honig, *The American League: An Illustrated History* (New York, 1983); Paul MacFarlane, ed., *TSN Daguerreotypes of Great Stars of Baseball* (St. Louis, 1971); Connie Mack, *My Sixty-six Years in the Big Leagues* (Philadelphia, 1950); Tom Meany, *Baseball's Greatest Players* (New York, 1955); Joseph L. Reichler, *The Baseball Trade Register* (New York, 1984); Joseph L. Reichler, ed., *The Baseball Encyclopedia*, 6th ed. (New York, 1985) p. 2,098; Ken Smith, *Baseball's Hall of Fame* (New York, 1978).

Douglas D. Martin

WAGNER, John Peter "Honus," "Hans," "The Flying Dutchman" (b. 24 February 1874, Carnegie, PA; d. 6 December 1955, Carnegie, PA), player, manager, and coach, was elected to the National Baseball Hall of Fame in 1936. Although having a thick chest, huge shoulders, bowed legs, and long arms, the 5 foot, 11 inch, 200 pound Wagner exhibited great speed. His speed and German heritage resulted in his nickname "The Flying Dutchman." From 1895 at Steubenville, OH (ISL), Mansfield, OH (OSL), Adrian, MI (MISL), and Warren, OH (IOL), to 1913, Wagner never batted below .300. He entered the NL with Louisville in 1897 and played with the Colonels through the 1899 season. With the Pittsburgh Pirates (NL) from 1900 through 1917, the right-handed batting and throwing Wagner led the NL in batting average eight times (1900, 1903–1904, 1906–1909, 1911) and won successive titles from 1906 to 1909. Besides leading or tying twice for the NL lead in hits (1908, 1910) and runs scored (1902, 1906), he paced the NL four times in RBIs (1901–1902, 1908–1909). Wagner also led the NL eight times in doubles, three times in triples, five times in stolen bases, and six times in slugging percentage. With a .329 career batting average and .469 slugging average in 10,427 at bats (8th all-time), he compiled 1,740 runs scored, 3,430 hits (6th), 651 doubles (5th), 252 triples (3rd), 101 home runs, 1,732 RBIs, and 722 stolen bases (5th). Wagner, one of baseball's greatest shortstops, exhibited outstanding fielding ability and leadership.

In the winter of 1899–1900, the NL was reduced from twelve to eight teams. Louisville owner Barney Dreyfuss* became Pittsburgh club president and brought Wagner with him. With Wagner batting an NL leading .381 in 1900, Pittsburgh started dominating the league. The Pirates won NL pennants from 1901 to 1903 and in 1909, the year Forbes Field opened. In 1909 the Pirates defeated the Detroit Tigers in a seven-game World Series to atone for their 1903 Series loss to Boston. Wagner outhit Ty Cobb* .333 to .231 and stole four more bases than Cobb. During that Series, Cobb attempted to steal second base. Cobb allegedly yelled to Wagner, " 'Hey, Kraut Head, I'm comin' down on the next pitch.' I told him to come ahead. George Gibson, our catcher, laid the ball perfect, right in my glove and I stuck it on Ty as he came in. I guess I wasn't too easy about it, cause it took three stitches to sew up his lip."

When Dreyfuss fired manager Jimmy Callahan in 1917, Wagner directed the club to one win in five games in early July. Wagner resigned, stating, "I never was cut out to be a manager." Although finishing the year as a player, the 43-year-old Wagner then retired after twenty-one major league seasons. Subsequently, Wagner coached baseball and basketball at Carnegie Tech (now Carnegie-Mellon University) in Pittsburgh, not far from Forbes Field, and served as sergeant-at-arms for the Pennsylvania Legislature. Along with Pirates third baseman Pie Traynor,* he owned a sporting goods store in downtown Pittsburgh. From 1933 to 1951, Wagner served as a Pirates coach.

Wagner, one of five sons and four daughters of coal miner Peter and Katrina Wolf Wagner, began working at age 12 in the coal mines and steel mills of Western Pennsylvania and also was employed as a barber. He married Bessie Baine Smith on December 30, 1916, and had two daughters, Betty and Virginia (Jennie). He learned to play every position while performing on a sandlot team with his four brothers. New York Giants Manager John J. McGraw* remarked, "While Wagner was the greatest shortstop, I believe he could have been the number one player at any position he might have selected. That's why I vote him baseball's foremost all-time player."

BIBLIOGRAPHY: John P. Carmichael, *My Greatest Day in Baseball* (New York, 1946); Ed Fitzgerald, *The National League* (New York, 1952); David Neft, Jordan A. Deutsch, et al., *The Sports Encyclopedia: Baseball*, 1st ed. (New York, 1974); *NYT*, December 6, 1955; Jimmy Powers, *Baseball Personalities* (New York, 1949); *The Reach Official American League Baseball Guide, 1910* (Philadelphia, 1910); Lowell Reidenbaugh, *Cooperstown: Where Baseball's Legends Live Forever* (St. Louis, 1983).

Edward J. Walsh

WALKER, Fred "Dixie," "The People's Cherce" (b. 24 September 1910, Villa Rica, GA; d. 17 May 1982, Birmingham, AL), player, coach and manager, performed as an outfielder for the New York Yankees (1931–1936), Chicago White Sox (1936–1937), and Detroit Tigers (1938–July 1939) of the AL and for the Brooklyn Dodgers (July 1939–1947) and Pittsburgh Pirates (1948–1949) of the NL. Nicknamed "Dixie," he became one of the most popular players in Brooklyn history and earned the label "The People's Cherce" for his consistent clutch fielding and hitting. His father, Ewart Gladstone "Dixie"Walker, pitched for the Washington Senators (AL) from 1909 to 1912, while his uncle, Ernie Walker, played outfield for the St. Louis Browns (AL) from 1913 to 1915. The left-handed hitting and right-handed throwing Dixie and his brother Harry combined for a .303 career batting average and became one of only six brother combinations in baseball history to surpass the .300 lifetime level.

Walker, a .306 career batter and .270 lifetime pinchhitter, won the NL batting title in 1944 with a .357 average and led the NL with 124 RBIs in 1945. On April 30, 1939, he scored five runs in one game. He participated in .300-hitting outfields with Rip Radcliff and Mike Kreevich on the 1937 White Sox and with Pete Reiser and Joe Medwick* on the 1942 Dodgers. Not a power hitter, Walker slugged a career-high 15 home runs in 1933. Although he hit only nine homers in 1946, he drove in 116 runs. During his eighteen-year major league career, he compiled 2,064 hits, 376 doubles, 96 triples, 105 home runs, 1,037 runs scored, 1,023 RBIs, 817 walks, and 59 stolen bases.

Walker played in the 1941 and 1947 World Series for the Dodgers and in the 1943–1944 and 1946–1947 All-Star games. In 1943 and 1947, he joined his brother Harry on the NL All-Star team. In 1944 *The Sporting News* named him to its major league All-Star team. After retiring, Walker managed in the minor leagues at Atlanta (SA) in 1950–1952, Houston (TL) in 1953–1954, Rochester, NY (IL), in 1955–1956, and Toronto (IL) in 1957–1959, coached for the NL St. Louis Cardinals (1953, 1955) and NL Milwaukee Braves (1963–1965), scouted for the Milwaukee (1900–1962) and Atlanta Braves (1966–1968), and served as a batting instructor in the Los Angeles Dodgers organization (1968–1978).

At a Waldorf-Astoria luncheon in 1943, Walker, Carl Hubbell* of the New York Giants, and Joe Gordon of the New York Yankees were "auctioned off" for pledges toward War Bonds. Walker drew a $11,250,000 bid from a Brooklyn social club. In late 1943, Walker, Stan Musial,* and other major leaguers visited U.S. military troops in the Aleutian Islands.

Walker began his professional career at age 12, earning $5 a game by playing on a semi-pro Calvert, AL, team managed by his father. Walker batted .401 for Greenville, SC (SAL), in 1930, when the Yankees bought him in midseason for a then record $25,000. Unfortunately, he suffered serious injuries throughout his career. When the Dodgers purchased Walker from Detroit, many baseball followers considered his career finished. After home state Alabamans pressured him not to play with Jackie Robinson,* Walker wrote Dodgers' president W. Branch Rickey* asking to be traded. Walker, born in a log cabin, was a high school dropout. He married Estelle Shea in May 1936. Tragedy struck at the height of his career on May 23, 1940, when his daughter Mary Ann died from double pneumonia. The mild Walker, who spoke in a slow, high-pitched southern drawl, died of cancer.

BIBLIOGRAPHY: Craig Carter, *TSN Official Baseball Dope Book* (St. Louis, 1983); Stanley Frank, "Nobody Wanted Him but the Fans," *SEP* 214 (February 14, 1942), pp. 27ff; Sam Goldaper, "Dixie Walker, Dodger Star of the 1940s, Dead at 71," *NYT* May 18, 1982; Tot Holmes, *Dodgers Blue Book* (Los Angeles, 1983); William B. Mead, *Even the Browns* (Chicago, 1978); Joseph L. Reichler, ed., *Baseball Encyclopedia*, 6th ed. (New York, 1985), pp. 1,489–1,490; Larry Wigge, ed., *TSN Official Baseball Guide, 1983* (St. Louis, 1983).

Jack P. Lipton

WALKER, Gerald Holmes "Gee" (b. 19 March 1908, Gulfport, MS; d. 20 March 1981, Whitfield, MS), player, became a leading hitter in the 1930s and was a brother of major leaguer "Hub" Walker. After attending the University of Mississippi, the 5 foot, 11 inch, 188 pound right-hander entered organized baseball in 1928 with Fort Smith, AR (WA). He progressed rapidly through the minor leagues, joining the Detroit Tigers (AL) in 1931. He quickly developed into a hard hitter but proved an erratic outfielder and a reckless baserunner with an incorrigible tendency to be caught off base. Walker's flamboyant base running made him the despair of some managers but a great favorite of Tigers fans. When manager Mickey Cochrane* polled his players in 1934 whether Walker should be retained, the Tigers voted almost unanimously in the outfielder's favor. Walker enjoyed his finest years in Detroit, hitting .300 or more in five of seven seasons. He played on the Tigers' championship teams of 1934 and 1935 but was limited mainly to pinch hitting in the World Series. When Walker was traded to the Chicago White Sox (AL) in December, 1937, Tigers fans uttered the greatest protest the club had ever experienced.

Walker, mainly a singles hitter, was well suited to the spacious Comiskey Park. Although his performance in Chicago nearly equalled his play in Detroit, he never achieved his earlier popularity, partly because he had been traded for the well-liked Fred "Dixie" Walker.* Walker was traded to the Washington Senators (AL) in 1939, Cleveland Indians (AL) in 1940, and Cincinnati Reds (NL) in 1942. Despite arthritis, he played with the Reds throughout World War II and was released at the end of the 1945 season. In fifteen major league seasons, Walker played in 1,783 games, made 1,991 hits, 399 doubles, 76 triples, and 124 home runs, scored 954 runs, batted in 997 runs, and stole 223 bases. He achieved a lifetime .294 batting average. Walker, of English ancestry, married Grace McLain on November 14, 1930, and later sold real estate in Mississippi and Florida.

BIBLIOGRAPHY: Joseph L. Reichler, ed., *The Baseball Encyclopedia*, 6th ed. (New York, 1985), p. 1,490; *Who's Who in Baseball, 1945*, 30th ed. (New York, 1945).

George W. Hilton

WALKER, Moses Fleetwood "Fleet" (b. ca. 1856, Mt. Pleasant, OH; d. 11 May 1924, Cleveland OH), player, was the fourth of five children of minister or doctor Moses and Caroline Walker and became the major league's first black baseball performer. Between 1878 and 1882, Walker attended Oberlin College and the University of Michigan Law School. Although he caught for both baseball teams, he earned degrees from neither school. In the summer of 1883, "Fleet" joined Toledo (AA), ostensibly to earn money to complete his education. Walker, however, pursued a professional baseball career with Toledo (in 1884 the AA became a major league, making Walker the first black major leaguer), Cleveland (1885), Waterbury, CT (1885–1886), Newark (1887), Syracuse (1888–1889), and perhaps Terre Haute (1890). During these seven years, Walker compiled mediocre statistics, never hit above .263, and often had among the worst league fielding averages. The right-hander proved a strong-armed, erratic catcher in a bare-handed era and a fair hitter with good speed.

Walker's tenure in white leagues came in years of increasing separatist sentiment and was plagued by racial harassment. In both 1883 and 1887, Cap Anson* refused to allow his Chicago White Stockings (NL) to play against Walker. Baseball fans in the southern cities of Louisville, KY, and

Richmond, VA, occasionally threatened Walker, while the press in cities of opposition teams wrote negative, tauntingly racist accounts. Nevertheless, Walker rejected playing for all-Negro teams. Although involved in the Sunday baseball controversy and affected by the political vigilance his younger brother Welday brought to the black cause, Walker increased his political activity following his retirement from baseball.

In 1908 he and Welday edited a newspaper, *The Equator*, and opened a Steubenville, OH, office for Liberian emigration. Walker's treatise, *Our Home Colony*, comprised a bitter, oversimplified history of the Negro race, urging American blacks to return to Africa. Despite his baseball career, his ventures in hotel and theater ownership, and his sophisticated, articulate nature, Walker suffered from the myth of black incapability, the nearly systematic exclusion of blacks from the economic market, and the continuing futile preoccupation of some with the possibility for African colonization. Walker outlived both of his wives, Arabella Taylor and Edna Jane Mason, the first of whom bore him three sons.

BIBLIOGRAPHY: Ocania Chalk, *Pioneers of Black Sport* (New York, 1975); Robert W. Peterson, *Only the Ball Was White* (Englewood Cliffs, NJ, 1970); Moses Fleetwood Walker, *Our Home Colony: A Treatise on the Past, Present, and Future of the Negro Race in America* (Steubenville, OH, 1908); Moses Fleetwood Walker file, National Baseball Hall of Fame Library, Cooperstown, NY; Moses Fleetwood Walker papers, Oberlin College Archives, Oberlin, OH; Carl F. Wittke, "Oberlinian First Negro Player in Major Leagues," *Oberlin Alumni Bulletin*, 1946; David Zang, "Moses Fleetwood Walker: A Reaction to Baseball's Nineteeenth Century Color Line," paper presented at the Eleventh Annual Convention of the North American Society for Sport History (Mont Alto, PA, 1983).

David W. Zang

WALLACE, Roderick John "Bobby," "Rhody" (b. 4 November 1873 or 1874, Pittsburgh, PA; d. 3 November 1960, Torrance, CA), player, coach, manager, scout, and umpire, was the son of John Wallace of Scottish descent and attended the First Ward Elementary School in Millvale, PA. As a teenager, he worked in his brother-in-law's food store in Millvale and pitched for semi-pro baseball teams in western Pennsylvania. In 1894 the Franklin, PA, semi-pro team signed Wallace for $45 per month. Wallace then joined the Cleveland Spiders (NL). The 5 foot, 8 inch right-hander compiled 12–14 and 10–7 records with the Spiders in 1895 and 1896 before moving to third base and hitting .339 in 1897.

After the Spiders became the St. Louis Cardinals (NL) in 1899, Wallace moved to shortstop. From 1899 to 1901 with the Cardinals, he fielded well and twice hit over .300. In 1902 he jumped to the St. Louis Browns (AL), received a $6,500 advance, and signed a five-year, no-trade, $32,500 contract, making him the day's highest paid player. He married June Mann on August 8, 1906. From 1902 to 1910, Wallace ranked as the premier AL shortstop and often led in assists, putouts, and fielding average. He reluctantly became player-manager of the Browns in 1911, but quit after a last place finish that year and a 12–27 start in 1912. A broken hand in 1912 and severe burns in 1914 greatly limited his playing time.

Wallace became an AL umpire in June 1915 but rejoined the Browns in August 1916. He started the 1917 campaign managing Wichita (WL), signed with the Cardinals following his June release, and completed a twenty-five year major league career in 1918 by playing 32 games for the Redbirds. His career totals included 2,314 hits, 393 doubles, 153 triples, 35 home runs, 1,057 runs scored, 1,121 RBIs, 201 stolen bases, and a .267 batting average in 2,386 games. Although Wallace owns no single-season or career offensive records, he ranks in the top ten for career chances (11,130), assists (6,303), putouts (4,142), assists per game (3.5), and chances per game among short-stops (6.1). He compiled a 24–22 record and 3.89 ERA as a pitcher and a 62–154 mark as manager of the Browns and the 1937 Cincinnati Reds (NL). Wallace also managed Muskogee, OK (SWL), in 1921, scouted for the Chicago Cubs (NL) in 1924, coached with the Cincinnati Reds in 1926, and scouted for Cincinnati from 1927 until his death. Wallace, who enjoyed billiards and golf in his later years, was elected to the National Baseball Hall of Fame in 1953.

BIBLIOGRAPHY: Martin Appel and Burt Goldblatt, *Baseball's Best: The Hall of Fame Gallery* (New York, 1977); Bill Borst, *The Pride of St. Louis: A Cooperstown Gallery* (St. Louis, 1984); Lowell Reidenbaugh, *Cooperstown: Where Baseball's Legends Live Forever* (St. Louis, 1983); Ken Smith, *Baseball's Hall of Fame*, rev. ed. (New York, 1970); Roderick Wallace file, National Baseball Hall of Fame Library, Cooperstown, NY.

                                                                          Frank J. Olmsted

WALSH, Edward Augustine "Ed," "Big Ed" (b. 14 May 1881, Plains, PA; d. 26 May 1959, Pompano Beach, FL), player, manager, coach, and umpire, became the greatest practitioner of the legal spitball. Walsh was the youngest of thirteen children of Irish immigrant Michael Walsh, an anthracite miner in the Wilkes-Barre, PA, area. He attended parochial schools for five years and then worked in the mines, developing exceptional arm and shoulder muscles. After establishing a local reputation in amateur and semi-pro baseball, Walsh entered organized baseball with Wilkes-Barre (PSL) in 1902 and progressed to Meriden, CT (CtL). He met Rosemary Carney, an ice cream vendor at the ballpark there, and married her in 1904. His son Edward pitched for the Chicago White Sox (AL) from 1928 to 1932.

The 6 foot, 1 inch, 193 pound right-hander won 20 composite games at Meriden and Newark (EL) in 1903, but scouting reports indicated that he possessed little beyond a fastball. Consequently, Charles A. Comiskey* drafted him for the Chicago White Sox (AL) for only $750. At spring training in 1904, he learned the spitball from Elmer Striklett and encountered difficulty controlling the pitch for two years. He mastered the pitch by 1906 and compiled a 17–13 record to help the White Sox win the AL pennant in spite of the team's .230 batting average. When the White Sox upset the Chicago Cubs in the 1906 World Series, Walsh won two games.

In 1907 Walsh blossomed as one of baseball's leading pitchers, winning 24 of 42 decisions. Walsh, who threw four variants of the spitball and possessed an impressive fastball, later said, "I had such control of my spitter that I could hit a tack on a wall with it." In 1908 he pitched a modern record 464 innings, won 40 games (the second highest in modern baseball), lost 15 decisions, threw 42 complete games, and recorded 11 shutouts. In a futile effort to win the AL pennant, he pitched in the season's last seven games. On September 29 he won both complete games of a doubleheader for the second time in his career. He lost a four-hit shutout 1–0 on a passed ball, while his opponent Addie Joss* pitched a perfect game. Walsh won 15 games in 1909 and 18 contests in 1910, but returned to peak form with 27–18 in 1911 and 27–17 in 1912. He pitched his only no-hit game on August 27, 1911, defeating Boston 5–0. Walsh hurled his best in the 1912 City Series, recording four complete games, two relief appearances, and two of the White Sox' four victories.

At spring training in 1913, Walsh strained his arm throwing a medicine ball. After years of overwork, the arm remained weak and tired rather than sore. With the White Sox through 1916, he won only 13 more games and lost his effectiveness. Never paid more than $6,000 by the penurious Comiskey, Walsh refused a $75,000 offer for three seasons in the FL because he could not certify his arm as sound. He last appeared in four games for the Boston Braves (NL) in 1917, losing one decision. His lifetime record was 195–126 and a 1.82 ERA, the lowest in major league history. Walsh completed 250 of 315 starts, struck out 1,736 batters in 2,964 1/3 innings, and hurled 57 shutouts (9th best). He led the NL five times in games pitched, four times in innings pitched and saves, three times in games started and shutouts, twice in ERA, games completed, and strikeouts, and once in winning percentages.

Walsh's subsequent career proved mainly unsuccessful. He managed Bridgeport, CT (EL), in 1920, umpired for the AL in 1922, and coached for the White Sox from 1923 to 1925 and 1928 to 1930. In 1926 he served as baseball coach at Notre Dame University and used his sons Edward Arthur and Robert as pitchers. He left baseball and lived in Meriden, CT, until 1957, when an arthritic condition caused him to move to Florida. In 1946 Walsh was elected to the National Baseball Hall of Fame.

BIBLIOGRAPHY: Jerry Holtzman, "Big Ed Walsh, 77, Former White Sox Star, Gets Day to Remember at Comiskey Park," *TSN*, July 2, 1958; Frederick G. Lieb, "Hall of Famer Ed Walsh Dies," *TSN*, June 3, 1959; Paul MacFarlane, ed., *TSN Daguerreotypes of Great Stars of Baseball* (St. Louis, 1981); Joseph L. Reichler, ed., *The Baseball*

Encyclopedia, 6th ed. (New York, 1985), pp. 1,493–1,494, 2,102; *Spalding's Official Baseball Record, 1913* (New York, 1913).

George W. Hilton

WALTERS, William Henry, Jr., "Bucky" (b. 19 April 1909, Philadelphia, PA), player, coach, and manager, is the eldest of seven children of telephone employee William Henry and Mildred (Scheetz) Walters. Nicknamed "Bucky," like his father, young Walters left Germantown High School his sophomore year to become an electrician and entered professional baseball in 1929 with High Point, NC (Pil). He married June Caroline Yoast on December 21, 1931, and has three children.

During his nineteen-year major league career, the 6 foot, 1 inch, 180 pound Walters switched from journeyman third baseman (1931–1934) to become one of the era's premier right-handed pitchers. After playing for seven minor league teams and having indifferent seasons with Boston's Braves (NL) in 1931 and 1932 and Red Sox (AL) in 1933 and 1934, he was sold to the Philadelphia Phillies (NL) in 1934. Manager Jimmie Wilson, who had acquired Johnny Vergez to play third base, urged that Walters move to the mound. The quiet, adaptable Walters possessed a strong arm and a cool head and threw a sinking fastball and sharp-breaking, no-name curve (now called the slider) that he learned from Chief Bender.* A willing worker, he hurled 3,104 2/3 innings in fifteen NL seasons and completed 242 (61 percent) of 398 games started, the sixth best all-time record.

After being the NL's losingest pitcher in 1936 (21 games), he became an immediate winner at Cincinnati. The Reds traded catcher Virgil Davis, pitcher Al Hollingsworth, and $55,000 for him in 1938. In his best season (1939), he topped the NL in wins (27), innings pitched (319), and ERA (2.29), and tied for the lead in strikeouts (137). He completed 31 games in 36 starts, batted .325, and was voted the NL Most Valuable Player. Six times he made the NL All-Star team.

During his career, he won 198 games and lost 160 (.553), compiled a 3.30 ERA, hurled 42 shutouts, and struck out 1,107 batters. The adroit fielder ranks fourth in double plays for a pitcher (76) and is one of only fourteen NL pitchers to steal home. As a hitter, he compiled a .243 batting average, made 477 hits, 99 doubles, 16 triples, and 23 home runs, scored 227 runs, knocked in 234 runs, and stole 12 bases. He lost two games to the New York Yankees in the 1939 World Series, but won two contests in the 1940 triumph over the Detroit Tigers.

Walters managed the Reds for parts of the 1948 and 1949 seasons to a composite 81–123 record (.397) and ended his pitching career in 1950 with the Boston Braves (NL). He served as a pitching coach with the Braves from 1950 until 1955 and with the New York Giants (NL) in 1956 and 1957. After retiring from baseball, he worked several years as the public relations representative of a small Philadelphia metal-working company. His only regret is not having succeeded as a major league infielder: "I liked to play every day."

BIBLIOGRAPHY: Lee Allen, *The Cincinnati Reds* (New York, 1948); Leonard Gettelson, "Pitchers Stealing Home," *Baseball Research Journal* 5 (1976), pp. 12–14; Donald Honig, *Baseball When the Grass Was Real* (New York, 1977); Gene Karst and Martin J. Jones, Jr., *Who's Who in Professional Baseball* (New Rochelle, NY, 1973); Paul MacFarlane, ed., *TSN Daguerreotypes of Great Stars of Baseball* (St. Louis, 1981); Martin Quigley, *The Crooked Pitch* (Chapel Hill, NC, 1984); Joseph L. Reichler, ed., *The Baseball Encyclopedia*, 6th ed. (New York, 1985), pp. 1,494–1,495, 2,102–2,103; A. D. Suehsdorf, telephone interview, William Walters, Jr., August 18, 1983, July 9, 1984.

David L. Porter

WANER, Lloyd James "Little Poison" (b. 16 March 1906, Harrah, OK; d. 22 July 1982, Oklahoma City, OK), player and scout, was nicknamed "Little Poison" and began his career in a way similar to older brother Paul.* Lloyd attended the State Teachers' College (East Central Oklahoma State) in Ada, OK, for over two years while playing amateur and semi-pro baseball. He signed a professional contract with the San Francisco Seals (PCL) but became a free agent after the 1925 season, when the Seals failed to pay a $2,500 bonus within a ninety-day time limit. Upon the recommendation of his brother Paul, the Pittsburgh Pirates (NL) signed Lloyd and assigned him to Columbia, SC (SAL). At Columbia, Lloyd hit .345 and was named SAL Most Valuable Player in 1926.

The next year Lloyd started in center field for Pittsburgh and teamed with brother Paul to help lead the Pirates to the NL pennant. During the 1927 season, he finished third in the league with a .355 batting average and second to Paul in hits with 223. His 198 singles set a modern major league record, while his 133 runs scored paced the NL in scoring. During the 1927 World Series against the New York Yankees, Lloyd made six hits in fifteen at bats, for a .400 average and scored five runs. Like brother Paul, Lloyd never participated in another World Series.

Waner's greatest attributes were his exceptional speed and keen eye at the plate. Al Lopez,* Hall of Famer, manager, and Lloyd's former roommate, remarked, "Infielders would have to play him differently. He had unbelievable speed for those days. I don't know if he was the reason why, but soon after he came up, you started hearing about teams looking for fast ball players." According to former Pirate Frank Gustine, Lloyd claimed that "the ball looked bigger than it was." During Waner's eighteen-year major league career, he struck out only 173 times and ranked among the all-time best leadoff hitters.

Waner's career highlights, mostly from his fourteen seasons with the Pirates, included setting a major league record for putouts in a doubleheader by a center fielder (18, on August 25, 1935), being selected to the 1938 NL All-Star team, having a .316 career batting average, and being elected to the National Baseball Hall of Fame in 1967. His career totals included 2,459 hits, 281 doubles, 118 triples, 28 home runs, 1,201 runs scored, and 598 RBIs.

Lloyd, traded by the Pirates to the Boston Braves (NL) in 1941, also played with the Cincinnati Reds (NL), Philadelphia Phillies (NL), and Brooklyn Dodgers (NL). He returned in 1944 to the Pirates, where he finished his career the next year. Upon retirement, Lloyd scouted for the Pirates from 1946 to 1949 and for the Baltimore Orioles (AL) in 1955 and worked as a field clerk for Oklahoma City from 1950 through 1967. Waner, who married Frances Mae Snyder on September 17, 1929, had two children, Lloyd, Jr., and Lydia. He died after a long bout of emphysema.

BIBLIOGRAPHY: Dan Donovan, "Little Lloyd Waner, A Baseball Giant, Dies," Pittsburgh *Press*, July 23, 1982; Dan Donovan, "Lloyd Waner, Brother Paul Were Poison to Pitchers," Pittsburgh *Press*, June 19, 1981; Daniel Okrent and Harris Lewine, eds., *The Ultimate Baseball Book* (Boston, 1981); Joseph L. Reichler, *The Great All Time Baseball Record Book* (New York, 1981); Lawrence S. Ritter, *The Glory of Their Times* (New York, 1966); Regis M. Stefanik, "Little Poison," Pittsburgh *Post Gazette*, July 23, 1982.

William A. Sutton

WANER, Paul Glee "Big Poison" (b. 16 April 1903, Harrah, OK; d. 29 August 1965, Sarasota, FL), player, coach, and manager, was the brother of star major leaguer Lloyd Waner.* He spent the majority of his baseball career with the Pittsburgh Pirates (NL) and also played with the Boston Bees/Braves (NL), Brooklyn Dodgers (NL), and New York Yankees (AL). Nicknamed "Big Poison," Waner starred as a hard-hitting outfielder for the Pittsburgh Pirates. He began his professional baseball career at age 20 with the San Francisco Seals (PCL) in 1923. Previously, Waner had attended the State Teachers' College in Ada, OK, for two years in hopes of becoming a teacher and ultimately a lawyer. As a college student, he played baseball on various Oklahoma amateur and semi-pro teams. Waner began his professional career as a pitcher, but his hitting proficiency caused San Francisco manager Dots Miller to move him to the outfield. After finishing the 1923 season there with a .369 batting average, he impressed major league clubs by collecting 209 hits and 97 RBIs in 1924. San Francisco asked for $100,000, a price many clubs considered excessive for the small 5 foot, 8 inch, 153 pound Waner. When Waner batted .401 and collected 280 hits in 1925, the Pittsburgh Pirates (NL) purchased him.

During his rookie year (1926), he hit .336 and persuaded the Pirates to sign his younger brother Lloyd. Paul said of Lloyd, "He's a better player than me." Lloyd joined the Pirates the next season (1927) and teamed with

Paul to help lead the Pirates to the NL pennant. In 1927 Paul led the NL in batting with a .380 batting average and set Pirates club records with 237 hits and 131 RBIs. He also hit .333 and knocked in three runs that year in his only World Series appearance, but the Pirates were swept four games to zero by what many consider the greatest all-time team, the 1927 New York Yankees. Waner's forte remained hitting, as he again led the NL in 1934 and 1936, and compiled a lifetime .333 batting average over twenty major league seasons.

Despite his small stature, the speedy Waner collected 3,152 career hits, ranks in the top ten all-time players in career doubles (603) and triples (190), and made 200 or more hits eight seasons. Waner also scored 1,626 runs, knocked in 1,309 runs, walked 1,091 times, struck out only 376 times, and stole 104 bases. The 5,611 hits made by Paul and Lloyd Waner exceed the total collected by the five Delahanty brothers and three DiMaggio brothers. Waner also was selected a four-time NL All Star (1933–1935, 1937) and proved a talented and very colorful player. Although wearing glasses off the field, he was too vain to wear them on the field and admitted that he could not read the scoreboard from his right field position. Nevertheless, he maintained that "the baseball was as big as a grapefruit" when hitting. Waner also became a legendary drinker and apparently found drinking beneficial to his baseball career. According to his brother Lloyd, "Paul thought you played best when you relaxed and drinking was a good way to relax." When Pirates management asked Waner to give up drinking in 1938 because Pittsburgh considered themselves contenders for the pennant, he agreed and hit only .280. This marked the only year in his Pirates career that he failed to hit .300.

Waner was married twice, to Corrine Moore on June 10, 1927, and to Mildred Arnold Carroll on June 12, 1953. After retiring as an active player, he managed Miami (IL) in 1946, and served terms as a batting coach for the Milwaukee Braves in 1957, St. Louis Cardinals (NL) in 1958 and 1959, and for the Philadelphia Phillies (NL) in 1960 and from 1965 until his death. In 1952 Waner was elected to the National Baseball Hall of Fame.

BIBLIOGRAPHY: Dan Donovan, "Holdout Paul Waner Was Big Poison to N.L.," Pittsburgh *Press*, June 12, 1981; Daniel Okrent and Harris Lewine, eds., *The Ultimate Baseball Book* (Boston, 1981); Joseph L. Reichler, *All Time Baseball Record Book* (New York, 1981); Lawrence S. Ritter, *The Glory of Their Times* (New York, 1966).

William A. Sutton

WARD, John Montgomery "Monte" (b. 3 March 1860, Bellefonte, PA; d. 4 March 1925, Augusta, GA), player, manager, and executive, was the son of tobacconist James and Ruth (Hall) Ward. A gifted student and athlete, Ward attended Pennsylvania State College and in 1887 received both Bachelor's and law degrees from Columbia University. That year Ward married actress Helen Dauvray, but divorced her three years later. Neither this marriage nor a later one to Katharine Waas produced any offspring. At age 18, Ward joined the Providence Grays (NL) midway through the 1878 season, compiled a 22–13 record as a pitcher, and led the NL in ERA (1.51). The following year, his 47–17 pitching mark carried the Grays to the NL pennant. The 5 foot, 9 inch, 165 pound right-hander paced the NL in wins, pitching percentage (.734), and strikeouts (239). After Ward posted a 40–23 record in 1880, injuries shortened his pitching career. In seven NL seasons, Ward compiled a 161–101 record (.615), hurled 25 shutouts and a perfect game, and registered a 2.10 ERA (4th best). He completed 244 of 261 starts and struck out 920 batters.

After being sold to the New York Giants (NL) in the fall of 1882, Ward played infield and became a star shortstop. Ward, who retired in 1894, batted .278 lifetime with 2,123 hits, 232 doubles, 97 triples, 26 home runs, 1,408 runs scored, 686 RBIs, and 504 stolen bases after 1886. The left-handed batting Ward led the NL in stolen bases in 1887 (111) and 1892 (88) and in hits in 1890 (207). An able tactician and leader, he managed the Giants in 1884 and captained the team to world championships in 1888 and 1889. He served as player-manager of the Brooklyn team (PL) in 1890 and of the Brooklyn Nationals (NL) in 1891–1892. After returning to the Giants (NL) as player-manager (1893–1894), he led New York to a Temple Cup victory in 1894. As manager, he compiled a 394–307 record (.562) over six seasons.

The most memorable action of Ward's seventeen-year major league career came with his leadership in the cause of players' rights. His strong opposition to the reserve clause and other monopolistic practices of baseball club owners led Ward to organize and preside over the Brotherhood of Professional Base Ball Players. From 1886 to 1888, Ward's attacks on the reserve clause appeared in *Lippincott's*, *Cosmopolitan*, and other magazines and rallied major league players to the cause of reform. When the owners refused to deal with the Brotherhood and unilaterally imposed a salary limitation plan in 1889, Ward organized the PL in 1890 to challenge the established majors. The Brotherhood provided star players and planted teams in most NL cities. Ward consequently confronted the established majors with a formidable challenge. Although the PL outdrew its major league rivals, financial losses of $400,000 forced the PL financiers to surrender. The victory enabled owners to maintain control over major league players until the 1960s.

Retiring after the 1894 season, Ward became a leading corporate lawyer in New York City. He maintained an interest in baseball, representing players against owners and running unsuccessfully for the NL presidency in 1909. Ward served as president of the Boston Nationals in 1911 and 1912 and as business manager of the Brooklyn (FL) team in 1913. An expert golfer, Ward founded and was the first president of the Long Island Golf Association. He authored *Base Ball: How to Become a Player* and was elected to the National Baseball Hall of Fame in 1964.

BIBLIOGRAPHY: Cynthia Bass, "The Making of a Baseball Radical," *National Pastime: A Review of Baseball History* 2 (Fall, 1982), pp. 63–65; Lee Lowenfish, "The Later Years of John M. Ward," *National Pastime: A Review of Baseball History* 2 (Fall, 1982), pp. 66–69; Lee Lowenfish and Tony Lupien, *The Imperfect Diamond* (New York, 1980); Francis C. Richter, *A Brief History of Baseball* (Philadelphia, 1909); Albert G. Spalding, *America's National Game* (New York, 1911); David Quentin Voigt, *American Baseball*, vol. 1 (University Park, PA, 1983); David Quentin Voigt, *America Through Baseball* (Chicago, 1976); John M. Ward, *Base Ball: How to Become a Player* (Philadelphia, 1888); John M. Ward, "Is the Base Ball Player a Chattel?" *Lippincott's Magazine* 40 (August, 1887).

David Quentin Voigt

WARNEKE, Lonnie "Lon," "The Arkansas Hummingbird" (b. 28 March 1909, Mount Ida, AR; d. 23 June 1976, Hot Springs, AR), player and umpire, grew up in the small Mount Ida community not far from picturesque Lake Ouachita and fifty miles from Hot Springs. In 1928 the lean, lanky, 6 foot, 2 inch, 180 pound, right-handed pitcher traveled to Houston for his first professional baseball tryout with the St. Louis Cardinals' TL club. After an impressive showing, he joined Laurel, MS (CSL). Unsuccessful there, he left the Cardinals' organization and posted a 16–10 record in 1929 for Alexandria, LA (CSL).

In 1930 Alexandria sold Warneke for $100 to the Chicago Cubs (NL), where he made his major league debut early that season and joined Reading, PA (IL). He returned to the majors permanently in 1931 and proved a mainstay in the Cubs' starting rotation for the next five seasons, compiling a 98–55 record (.641 winning percentage). The most popular Cubs pitcher since Mordecai Brown,* Warneke appeared in the 1932 World Series against the New York Yankees and in the 1935 fall classic against the Detroit Tigers. In the 1935 World Series, he made three appearances, pitched a four-hit shutout in the opening game, and compiled a 0.54 ERA in 16 2/3 innings.

Despite his popularity with Cubs fans, Warneke was traded to the St. Louis Cardinals (NL) for Rip Collins and Roy Parmelee following the 1936 campaign. He spent the next five and one-half seasons with the Redbirds, posting a 83–52 record (.615 winning percentage). In 1941 he pitched the major leagues' only no-hitter, a 2–0 shutout over the Cincinnati Reds at Crosley Field. Warneke was nicknamed the "Arkansas Hummingbird" by a St. Louis *Post-Dispatch* writer, impressed with his lively fastball and darting form of delivery. The Cardinals in mid–1942 sold him back to the Cubs, where he played until entering military service after the 1943 season. Following World War II, he pitched in nine games for the 1945 NL pennant-bound Chicago Cubs and then retired.

After his playing career, the modest, taciturn Warneke rejected major league coaching and minor league managing offers for the more secure occupation of umpiring. With help from Cubs owner Philip K. Wrigley,* he began umpiring in 1946 with the PCL and joined the NL three years later. He spent the next seven seasons (1949–1955) as a NL arbiter, umpiring in the 1952 All-Star game and 1954 World Series.

Following the 1955 season, Warneke returned to his native Arkansas to pursue farming and politics. In 1962 he was elected a Garland County judge to mediate civil cases and served in that position until retiring for health reasons ten years later. He died of a heart attack in 1976, survived by his wife Erma Charlyne (Shannon) Warneke, whom he had married in February 1933, and one son and one daughter.

During his playing career, Warneke ranked among the game's best low-ball pitchers and most skilled fielders at his position. A three-time 20-game winner for the Cubs (1932, 1934, and 1935), he pitched four shutouts in five different seasons (1932, 1933, 1936, 1938, and 1941), averaged over 17 wins per season from 1932 through 1941, and handled his final 227 fielding chances without an error (1938–1945). He hurled four innings in the first major league All-Star Game at Comiskey Park in 1933, slugging a triple in his only at bat and scoring the first NL run in All-Star history. Warneke also appeared in the 1934 and 1936 All-Star games and remains the only major leaguer to have played and umpired in both an All-Star game and a World Series.

BIBLIOGRAPHY: Warren Brown, *The Chicago Cubs* (New York, 1946); Paul Mac-Farlane, ed., *TSN Daguerreotypes of Great Stars of Baseball* (St. Louis, 1981); Joseph L. Reichler, ed., *The Baseball Encyclopedia*, 6th ed. (New York, 1985), p. 2,104; St. Louis *Post-Dispatch*, June 24, 1976; *TSN*, July 10, 1976.

Raymond D. Kush

WATSON, Robert Jose "Bob," "Bull" (b. 10 April 1946, Los Angeles, CA), player and coach, grew up with his grandparents near the Watts district of Los Angeles. He attended the 28th Street Grade School and graduated in 1964 from Fremont High School in Los Angeles, where he played baseball with future major leaguers Bobby Tolan and Willie Crawford. He also attended Los Angeles Harbor College and attained sergeant rank in the U.S. Marine Corps. He and his wife, Carol, have two children, Keith and Kathy.

On January 31, 1965, Watson signed as a catcher with the Houston Astros (NL) and played with Salisbury, NC (WCL). He batted .302 at Cocoa, FL (FSL) in 1966. After trials with Houston in 1966, 1967, and 1968, Watson hit .408 in 61 games for Oklahoma City (AA) in 1969 and returned permanently to the major leagues. From 1970 through 1978, the 6 foot, 2 inch, 205 pound Watson proved the heart of the Astros offense at first base at the outfield. The right-handed slugger hit .312 or better four times from 1972 to 1976 and powered career highs in 1977 of 22 home runs and 110 RBIs.

On May 4, 1978, Watson scored the millionth run in major league history. After his slow start in 1979, Houston dealt him to the Boston Red Sox (AL) for pitchers Pete Ladd and Bob Sprowl. In 84 games at Boston, Watson batted .337 with 13 home runs. Granted free agency, he signed with the New York Yankees (AL) on November 8, 1979, and hit .307 as the regular first baseman in 1980. In his only World Series, Watson powered the 1981 Yankees with two home runs, seven RBIs, and a .318 batting average against the Los Angeles Dodgers. The Yankees traded Watson in April 1982 to the Atlanta Braves (NL) for pitcher Scott Patterson. From 1982 to 1984, he served as the Braves' main pinch hitter. Watson retired as a player on October 1, 1984, and is currently minor league batting instructor for the Oakland A's (AL). His career totals included 1,826 hits, 307 doubles, 184 home runs, 989 RBIs, and a .295 batting average. Watson hit for the cycle in both major leagues and played on the NL All-Star team in 1973 and 1975. Watson, active in a church started by former major league pitcher Dave Roberts, enjoys fishing and listening to music in his free time.

BIBLIOGRAPHY: Zander Hollander, *The Complete Handbook of Baseball, 1976* (New York, 1976); Zander Hollander, *The Complete Handbook of Baseball, 1977* (New York, 1977); Irv Kaze, "Bob Watson, N.L. Player of the Month," *National League Press-Radio-TV Information* (San Francisco, June 12, 1975); Harry Shattuck, " 'As You Were,' Virdon Tells Astro Infield," *TSN*, March 24, 1979, p. 38; Harry Shattuck, "Watson Asking Astros for Trade," *TSN*, October 21, 1978, p. 14; Bob Watson file, National Baseball Hall of Fame Library (Cooperstown, NY).

                                                              Frank J. Olmsted

WEAVER, Earl Sydney (b. 14 August 1930, St. Louis, MO), player, coach, manager, scout, and broadcaster, is the son of dry cleaning shop proprietor Earl Milton and Ethel Genieve (Wakefield) Weaver and played second base at Beaumont High School in St. Louis. Despite his small size and mediocre talents, the 5 foot, 7 inch, 160 pound, right-hander impressed five professional clubs and signed with the St. Louis Cardinals (NL) in 1948. He played second base with West Frankfort, IL (ISL), in 1948, St. Joseph, MO (WA), in 1949, Winston-Salem, NC (CrL), in 1950, Houston (TL) and Omaha (WL) in 1951 and 1952, Omaha (WL) in 1953, and Denver (WL) in 1954. In 1955 the Cardinals sold him to the Pittsburgh Pirates (NL) Class AA New Orleans (SA) farm club. Weaver began managing a year later while playing for Montgomery, AL Knoxville, TN (SAL). In 1957 he served as player-manager at Fitzgerald, GA (GFL), and then experienced a steady, methodical rise in the Orioles farm system. His clubs included Dublin, GA (GFL), in 1958, Aberdeen, SD (NoL), in 1959, Fox Cities, WI (3IL), in 1960 and 1961, Elmira, NY (EL), from 1962 through 1965, and Rochester, NY (IL), in 1966 and 1967.

Under Weaver, Rochester won the IL pennant in 1966 and tied for first place in 1967, when the Redwings lost a one-game playoff. In 1961 he directed the Orioles' minor league central spring training camp and designed an instructional program of techniques and fundamentals for every club in the

Baltimore organization below the Class AAA level. Harry Dalton, former director of player personnel and general manager with the Orioles, persuaded the Baltimore organization to hire and promote Weaver and refuted critics who claimed that Weaver was "a push-button manager." Dalton later stated, "Weaver set a plan of instruction in 1961 when he was 31 years old which we've barely changed to this day. [He is] the most knowledgeable, most methodical, most careful manager in baseball. Push button manager? He built the machine and installed all the buttons." In 1968 Weaver joined the Baltimore Orioles as a coach and replaced Hank Bauer later that season as manager.

From 1968 through 1982 and 1985 through 1986, Weaver guided the Orioles to a .583 winning percentage, a 1,480–1,060 win-loss mark (among the ten best in major league history), four AL pennants (1969–1971, 1979), one world championship (1970), and five 100-victory seasons (exceeded only by Joe McCarthy's* six). A brilliant, highly motivated, aggressive manager, Weaver made unprecedented use of computers and charts. He developed a system that combined scouting reports with data on how to pitch and defend against opposing batters and on the success of Orioles batters against opposing pitchers. The resulting information was employed in consultation with his coaches to best use all twenty-five players on his roster and only expect players to execute within their abilities and limitations, a lesson he learned early in his career. Weaver's other innovations, including the development of a training manual for the entire Orioles' organization, solid pitching staffs, and sound offensive philosophy, brought new life to the Baltimore organization. Weaver enjoyed the longest unbroken tenure (fifteen years) of any contemporary major league manager. His intense habit of winning, developed early in his minor league playing career, made him the most ejected manager in the majors with at least 91 dismissals from games and 4 suspensions. In 1985 he was ejected from both games of a doubleheader.

Weaver wed Marianna Osgood in 1964, a year after his fourteen-year marriage to Jane Johnston ended in divorce. By his first marriage, Weaver has three children, Michael, Rhonda, and Theresa. He also has a stepdaughter from his present wife's first marriage. Weaver retired from managing in 1982 and became a television analyst, Orioles consultant, and scout. In June 1985 he replaced Joe Altobelli as Baltimore manager and guided the Orioles to a 53–52 mark. The Orioles finished in last place with a 73–89 mark in 1986; Weaver had suffered his first losing season as a major league manager, and he resigned at the end of the season.

BIBLIOGRAPHY: Ed Linn, "Earl of Baltimore: He's a Mouthful," *Sport* 71 (July, 1980), pp. 32–36; Los Angeles *Times*, October 11, 1982, p. 13; Joseph L. Reichler, ed. *The Baseball Encyclopedia*, 6th ed. (New York 1985), p. 653; *TSN*, July 26, 1982, p. 2; Earl

Weaver and Terry Pluto, *The Earl of Baltimore* (New York, 1982); Earl Weaver and Berry Stainback, *It's What You Learn After You Know It All That Counts* (New York, 1982); Earl Weaver and Berry Stainback, *Winning* (New York, 1972).

Albert J. Figone

WEISS, George Martin (b. 23 June 1895, New Haven, CT; d. 13 August 1973, Greenwich, CT), executive, began a fifty-nine-year career in baseball administration managing his New Haven high school baseball team and then attended Yale University (1914–1916). Weiss, whose parents, Conrad and Anna Weiss, owned a grocery store, organized a semi-pro team that used Ty Cobb* and other major league stars on their days off. When his promotions overshadowed the local EL team, he bought the minor league franchise with borrowed money and at age 24 became the youngest owner in organized baseball. For nine years, his EL club played in Weiss Park, ranked among the best in the minors, and sent many players to the major leagues.

Weiss displayed his talents as general manager of the Baltimore Orioles (IL) from 1929 to 1931 by reviving the ailing team through player sales. His Baltimore success impressed New York Yankees (AL) owner Jacob Ruppert,* who hired Weiss in 1932. Weiss was instructed to develop a farm system modeled on clubs already organized by Branch Rickey* to train young baseball players for the St. Louis Cardinals (NL). A tireless worker, Weiss assembled a premier farm system that sent Joe DiMaggio,* Charlie Keller, and other stars to the Yankees. During the fifteen years Weiss directed the Yankees farm system, New York won nine AL pennants and eight world championships and sold an estimated $2 million worth of players to other teams. Weiss married Boston sculptor Hazel Wood in 1937 and brought up a foster son, Allen Wood III.

As Yankees general manager from 1948 through 1960, Weiss built a dynasty that won ten AL pennants and seven World Series in thirteen seasons, and a record five straight championships from 1949 to 1953. He hired Casey Stengel,* whom some regarded as a clown, to manage the "Bronx Bombers" from 1949 through 1960 and provided Stengel with Mickey Mantle,* Yogi Berra,* Whitey Ford,* and other stars. The coldly efficient Weiss kept the Yankees on top with a superior farm system and skillful trades. In a seventeen-player swap with the Baltimore Orioles (AL) in 1954, he acquired pitchers Bob Turley and Don Larsen. In 1960 he shrewdly engineered a deal with Kansas City (AL) for slugger Roger Maris.* With uncanny ability, the Yankees boss plucked veterans from NL rosters. Johnny Mize* came from the New York Giants in 1949 and Enos Slaughter* from the St. Louis Cardinals in 1954 to help in AL pennant drives. Many players resented Weiss' hard bargaining on salaries, while others criticized his reluctance to use black players. The shy, conservative Weiss won a record four Major League Executive of the Year awards and was elected to the National Baseball Hall of Fame in 1971.

After being retired by the Yankees in 1960, Weiss became president of the expansion New York Mets (NL) in 1961. Besides hiring Stengel to manage the Mets, he built an organization that in 1969 produced the first pennant and world championship for an expansion club. Weiss retired from the Mets in 1966 but remained an advisor for the club until 1971. Sportswriter Red Smith* (OS) rated Weiss the "greatest baseball executive who ever lived."

BIBLIOGRAPHY: Robert W. Creamer, *Stengel: His Life and Times* (New York, 1984); Peter Golenbock, *Dynasty: The New York Yankees, 1949–1964* (Englewood Cliffs, NJ, 1975); Leonard Koppett, *The New York Mets: The Whole Story* (New York, 1970); New York *Daily News*, August 14, 1972; *NYT*, August 14, 1972; Lowell Reidenbaugh, *Cooperstown: Where Baseball's Legends Live Forever* (St. Louis, 1983); David Quentin Voigt, *American Baseball*, vol. 3 (University Park, PA, 1983); George M. Weiss, "The Administration Man," in Harold Rosenthal, ed., *Baseball Is Their Business* (New York, 1952).

                                                                    Joseph E. King

WELCH, Michael Francis "Mickey," "Smiling Mickey" (b. 4 July 1859, Brooklyn, NY; d. 30 July 1941, Nashua, NH), player, learned the fundamentals of baseball on the streets and sandlots of Brooklyn. Welch, a 5 foot, 8 inch, 160 pound, right-handed pitcher, left home at age 18 to pitch for the Poughkeepsie, NY, Volunteers. Nicknamed "Smiling Mickey," Welch became the third of nineteen major league pitchers to attain 300 victories. Welch began his professional baseball career with Auburn, NY, (NA) and Holyoke, MA (NA), in 1878 and 1879. Upon joining the Troy, NY, Haymakers (NL) in 1880, Welch won 34 games and pitched 574 innings. He lacked tremendous speed, but utilized an effective curveball, change of pace, and screwball. The durable Welch pitched a double victory over Cleveland in 1881 and hurled complete games in his first 105 league starts. In 1883 the Troy franchise transferred to New York and became the Maroons. Welch hurled the first game at the original Polo Grounds on May 1 and pitched over 400 innings that season. The next year he completed 62 of 65 starts and struck out 345 batters. On August 28, 1884, Welch established a major league record by striking out the first nine Cleveland batters to face him.

In 1885 the New York club became the Giants. Between July 18 and September 4, Welch won 17 consecutive games and hurled 4 shutouts and 4 one-run games. The 44-game winner compiled a 1.66 ERA and led the NL with an .800 winning percentage. During the next two seasons, Welch won 56 games. Welch and Tim Keefe* in 1888 accounted for 61 of the team's 84 victories and pitched the Giants to their first NL pennant. In a postseason series against the St. Louis Browns (AA), the Giants won six of ten games and Welch split two decisions. By winning 17 of their last 20 games in 1889, the Giants repeated as NL champions and defeated Brooklyn (AA) in the post-season series. Welch won 24 games the next two seasons. After one game in 1892, he was sent to the Giants farm club at Troy and terminated his active career there. After retirement, Welch moved to Holyoke and served for a long time as steward of the Elks Club. He returned to New York in 1912, when John McGraw* offered him a job at the Polo Grounds.

Elected to the National Baseball Hall of Fame in 1973, Welch ranks high on the all-time major league lists for pitchers in several departments. In thirteen major league seasons, he posted 20 or more victories nine times (3rd) and at least 30 wins four times (4th), hurled 40 shutouts, and recorded a 2.71 lifetime ERA. He won 311 games (13th), lost 207 (31st), started 549 games (18th), completed 525 games (6th) and pitched 4,802 innings (12th). Welch surrendered 4,587 hits (11th) and 2,548 runs (4th), issued 1,297 bases on balls (25th), and struck out 1,850 batters.

BIBLIOGRAPHY: Gene Karst and Martin J. Jones, Jr., *Who's Who in Professional Baseball* (New Rochelle, NY, 1973); Paul MacFarlane, ed., *TSN Daguerreotypes of Great Stars of Baseball* (St. Louis, 1971); Lowell Reidenbaugh, *Cooperstown: Where Baseball's Legends Live Forever* (St. Louis, 1983).

John L. Evers

WELLS, Willie "El Diablo" (b. 10 October 1905, Austin, TX), player and manager, is the son of a delivery man. He graduated from Anderson High School and attended Sam Houston College. The premier Negro league short-stop from the late 1920s until the mid–1940s, Wells moved from the Texas sandlots to the Negro leagues and played winter ball in Mexico, Cuba, and Puerto Rico. After leading local all-star teams against barnstorming Negro league teams in Texas, Wells joined the St. Louis Stars in 1923. The slick-fielding shortstop overcame initial difficulties at the plate to lead the NNL in batting with .400 in 1929 and .409 in 1930. When the Stars disbanded after the 1931 season, Wells played with the Detroit Wolves, Homestead Grays (NNL), Kansas City Monarchs (NAL), Chicago American Giants (NAL), New York Black Yankees (NNL), Newark Eagles (NNL), Indianapolis Clowns (NAL), and Memphis Red Sox (NAL) until 1949.

In the late 1930s, Wells performed with the Newark Eagles' "million dollar infield." Wells, who played in eight East-West classics, compiled a career .332 batting average in the Negro leagues and hit .392 against major leaguers in exhibition games. In the 1940s, the 5 foot, 7 inch, 160 pound Wells played and managed in Mexico, where he was nicknamed "El Diablo." Wells also managed the Newark Eagles from 1936 to 1941 and in 1946, when the Eagles won the NNL pennant. He was ranked among the best managers the Negro leagues produced and is considered the first professional player to use a batting helmet, having fashioned one out of a hardhat after he was knocked unconscious in a 1942 game against the Baltimore Elite Giants.

The Austin, TX, resident, who has two children, Thelma and Willie Jr., spoke for many Negro leaguers when he wrote to the Pittsburgh *Courier* to explain why he had left the Newark Eagles to play for Vera Cruz (MEL):

Not only do I get more money playing here, but I live like a king. . . . I am not faced with the racial problem. . . . We live in the best hotels, we eat in the best restaurants. . . . We don't enjoy such privileges in the U.S. I didn't quit Newark and join some other team in the United States. I quit and left the country. . . . I've found freedom and democracy here, something I never found in the United States. . . . Here, in Mexico, I am a man.

BIBLIOGRAPHY: Robert Peterson, *Only the Ball Was White* (Englewood Cliffs, NJ, 1970); Donn Rogosin, *Invisible Man: Life in Baseball's Negro Leagues* (New York, 1983).
                                                                    Robert L. Ruck

WEYHING, August "Gus," "Cannonball" (b. 29 September 1866, Louisville, KY; d. 3 September 1955, Louisville, KY), player, manager, and umpire, grew up in the Louisville area and married Mamie J. Gehrig, cousin of Lou Gehrig,* on January 9, 1901. His younger brother John pitched briefly with Cincinnati (AA) and Columbus (AA) in 1888 and 1889. The 5 foot, 10 inch, 145 pound right-hander began his professional baseball career with a brilliant 19–3 won-lost record at Richmond, VA (VL), in 1885, striking out 187 batters and walking only 39. The following year, Weyhing slipped to a 12–17 mark with Charleston, SC (SL), but remained a control pitcher. In 1887 he reached the major leagues with Philadelphia (AA), won 26 games and lost 28, and allowed a remarkable 465 hits and 338 runs. The next year Weyhing posted a 28–18 record at Philadelphia and hurled a 4–0 no-hitter against Kansas City on July 31. In 1889 he compiled 30 wins, 4 shutouts, and 213 strikeouts in 449 innings.

In 1890 Weyhing won 30 games after jumping with second baseman Lou Bierbauer to Brooklyn of the new PL. When the PL folded, Weyhing rejoined Philadelphia and notched career highs of 31 victories and 219 strikeouts in 1891. He was left without a team after that season when the AA ceased operation. Weyhing and teammates Lave Cross* and Bill Hallman remained in Philadelphia in 1892 and signed with the Phillies (NL). Weyhing won 32, 23, and 16 games for the Phillies from 1892 to 1894 before the strain of over 3,200 innings in eight seasons and the increased pitching distance from 50 to 60 1/2 feet told on his performance. Weyhing struggled through an 8–21 season in 1895 with Philadelphia, Pittsburgh (NL), and Louisville (NL) and temporarily retired in 1896 after pitching poorly in five starts for Louisville.

In 1898 the Washington Senators (NL) lured Weyhing from retirement. In two seasons he compiled a 32–49 record and averaged nearly 350 innings per year. He finished his major league career with the Brooklyn Superbas (NL) and St. Louis Cardinals (NL) in 1900 and the Cleveland Broncos (NL) and Cincinnati Reds (NL) in 1901. Weyhing completed the 1901 season with a 14–6 record at Grand Rapids, MI (WL). In 1902 and 1903, he recorded a composite 29–29 mark with Memphis, Atlanta, and Little Rock (SL). Weyhing spent the 1910 season in the TL as manager of the Tulsa club and as an umpire. He pitched 4,324 1/3 innings, started 503 games, won 264 games, lost 236 decisions, and ranks eleventh in career major league complete games (448). Although walking nearly as many batters as he struck out and surrendering over one hit per inning, Weyhing won 23 or more games seven consecutive years and pitched over 400 innings five times. He compiled a career 3.89 ERA and struck out 1,665 batters. Weyhing, one of few ball players to perform in four major leagues, later operated a tavern and worked as a night watchman in Louisville.

BIBLIOGRAPHY: Gene Karst and Martin J. Jones, Jr., *Who's Who in Professional Baseball* (New Rochelle, NY, 1973); Paul MacFarlane, ed., *TSN Daguerreotypes of Great Stars of Baseball* (St. Louis, 1981); August Weyhing file, National Baseball Hall of Fame Library, Cooperstown, NY.

                                                              Frank J. Olmsted

WHEAT, Zachariah David "Zack," "Buck" (b. 23 May 1888, Hamilton, OH; d. 11 March 1972, Sedalia, MO), player, was the son of farmer Basil C. Wheat, grew up on a farm near Bonanza, OH, and moved with his family to Kansas City, MO, at age 14. After playing semi-pro baseball in Enterprise, KS, he performed at Shreveport (TL) in 1908 and Mobile (SL) in 1909. In 1909 a Brooklyn Dodgers (NL) scout signed him to a contract. From August, 1909, through 1926, the 5 foot, 10 inch, 170 pound, right-handed thrower served as a regular left fielder for the Dodgers. Since Wheat wore a 5 1/2 inch shoe, however, he frequently suffered ankle injuries.

Known for his line drives, the soft-spoken left-handed batter made 2,884 hits, compiled a lifetime .317 batting average, and was never ejected from a game. In 2,410 games, he made 476 doubles, 172 triples, and 132 home runs, scored 1,289 runs, knocked in 1,261 runs, and stole 205 bases. Although hitting .375 in both 1923 and 1924, he won only one NL batting title with a .335 mark in 1918. Wheat enjoyed above all playing in the 26-inning 1–1 tie between the Dodgers and the Boston Braves in 1920. After batting .324 in a part-time capacity for the Philadelphia Athletics (AL) in 1927, he ended his career the next year with the Minneapolis Millers (AA). Wheat three times made more than 200 hits in a season, played in more games (2,322) than any Dodger in history, and led the NL in slugging percentage (.461) in 1916.

Wheat spent off-seasons at his 162 acre farm near Polo, MO, until depression conditions forced him to sell the property. He also had owned a bowling and billiards parlor in Kansas City, and later served on the Kansas City police force. In April 1936 Wheat was seriously injured in a patrol car accident and left the police force. Upon doctors' orders, Wheat settled on the Lake of the

Ozarks at Sunrise Beach, near Versailles, MO. Except during World War II, Wheat resided at Sunrise Beach and he operated a fishing camp there until the 1950s. In 1959 Wheat was elected unanimously to the National Baseball Hall of Fame.

He married Daisy Forsman in 1912 and had one son, Zachary, and one daughter, Mary. His wife died in November 1959. Once described by Branch Rickey* as the best outfielder Brooklyn ever had, Wheat batted over .300 thirteen of his eighteen years with the Dodgers.

BIBLIOGRAPHY: *The Baseball Encyclopedia*, 3rd ed., (New York, 1976); Kansas City *Star*, March 13, 1972; Lowell Reidenbaugh, *Cooperstown: Where Baseball's Legends Live Forever* (St. Louis, 1983).

Arthur F. McClure

WHITE, Guy Harris "Doc" (b. 9 April 1879, Washington, DC; d. 17 February 1969, Silver Spring, MD), player and executive, was the seventh son of a seventh son in an affluent Washington, DC, family and a left-handed pitcher with outstanding control. He was the youngest of nine children of George White, who owned the only iron foundry in the nation's capital, and Marian Adelaide (Harris) White. White attended Georgetown University and earned a dental degree in 1902. After playing semi-pro baseball, he signed with the Philadelphia Phillies (NL) for $1,200 before the 1901 season. In the 1901 and 1902 NL seasons, White won 30 games and lost 33 contests.

White jumped to the Chicago White Sox (AL) in 1903 and quickly became the team's leading left-hander by relying on a fastball, sinker, and superb control. On September 6, 1903, the 6 foot, 1 inch, 150 pound White pitched a ten-inning one-hit game. During a pennant race with New York and Boston in September 1904 he hurled an AL record five consecutive shutouts. In 1906 he helped pitch the White Sox to the world championship, winning 18 games during the regular season as well as the final World Series game. White enjoyed his best season with a 27–13 mark in 1907, the only time he won 20 or more games. After White hurled 18 victories in 1908, his performance declined. He remained with the White Sox through 1913, winning 159 and losing 123, with 43 shutouts. During thirteen major league seasons, he compiled a 190–157 mark (.548), completed 262 of 363 starts, struck out 1,384 batters in 3,050 innings, hurled 46 shutouts, and had a 2.38 ERA. Although he never before pitched in the minor leagues, he ended his career with two seasons (1914–1915) at Venice and Vernon, CA (PCL).

White practiced dentistry in the off-season only until 1906. A favorite of the White Sox management, he once designed the team's home uniform, composed songs to lyrics by Ring Lardner* (OS), and performed them in vaudeville. After his active career, White owned TL franchises at Dallas in 1917–1918 and Waco in 1919. He returned to Washington, DC, to teach physical education at Central High School, from which he had graduated, and became baseball and basketball coach and athletic director at Wilson Teachers College. White's wife, Iva Josephine Martin, whom he had met in high school, died in 1955. The couple had one son, Martin, and one daughter, Marian Palmer White, with whom the pitcher lived in his final years.

BIBLIOGRAPHY: *The Evening Star* (Washington, DC), February 18, 1969; George W. Hilton, correspondence with Martin Harris White, August 25, September 14, 1984; Gene Karst and Martin J. Jones, Jr., *Who's Who in Professional Baseball* (New Rochelle, NY, 1973); Paul MacFarlane, ed., *TSN Daguerreotypes of Great Stars of Baseball* (St. Louis, 1981); *TSN*, March 8, 1969.

George W. Hilton

WHITE, James Laurie "Deacon" (b. 2 December 1847, Caton, NY; d. 7 July 1939, Aurora, IL), player, manager, and club owner, was the son of farmer James S. White and brother of major league pitcher William H. White* and attended Country Day School in Caton, NY. On April 24, 1871, he married Marium Van Arsdale of Caton. After her death, he wed Alice Force Thurber of Caton and was survived by a daughter, Grace Watkins of Aurora, IL. White, who learned baseball from a Civil War veteran, began to play amateur ball in 1866 with the Caton town team and in 1867 with the Monitor club of nearby Corning, NY. In 1868 he joined the semi-pro Forest City team of Cleveland as a catcher. The 5 foot, 11 inch, 175 pound White became a full-fledged professional in 1871, when the Forest Citys became a charter member of the NA baseball's first professional league. When the Forest Citys played the Kekiongas of Fort Wayne, IN, on May 4, 1871, White became the first player to bat in a recognized major league game. The left-handed batting and right-handed throwing White made the first hit and first extra-base hit, a double, and became the initial player extinguished in a double play.

After the 1872 season, he moved to the Boston Red Stockings (NA) and gained recognition there as a member of the famed Big Four, including Al Spalding,* Ross Barnes,* and Cal McVey.* From 1871 to 1875, he made 456 hits and batted .347 in 259 games in the NA. Boston won a fourth straight championship in 1875, but the Big Four shocked the baseball world by signing with the Chicago White Stockings (NL) for the 1876 season. As Spalding's battery mate in 1876, White helped lead the White Stockings to a championship by batting .343, catching all but three games, and pacing the NL with 60 RBIs. The versatile White returned to Boston for the 1877 season at first base, third base, outfield, and catcher, and led the NL with a .387 batting average, .545 slugging average, 11 triples, and 49 RBIs. After the 1877 season, White and his brother Will moved to Cincinnati (NL). White managed the club to an 8–8 record, but was replaced during the season by McVey and continued as a player there during the 1879 and 1880 seasons.

In 1881 he joined Buffalo (NL) and won greater fame as a third baseman, outfielder, and occasional catcher. At Buffalo, he played with baseball legends Jim Galvin,* Jim O'Rourke,* and Dan Brouthers,* and formed part of a second Big Four with Brouthers, Hardy Richardson, and Jack Rowe. Late in the 1885 season, all Buffalo players were sold to Detroit in baseball's first mass player sale. White led Detroit (NL) to a second place finish in 1886 and a pennant in 1887. After the 1888 season, 40-year-old White was sold to Boston (NL) and then shipped to Pittsburgh (NL). He and teammate Jack Rowe, meanwhile, had purchased the Buffalo franchise (IA). Pittsburgh, however, refused to release White and Rowe from their playing contracts and threatened to have the Buffalo club expelled if the pair attempted to play there. The stalemate continued until the middle of the 1889 season, when White and Rowe finally reported to Pittsburgh. When the PL was formed in 1890, Rowe and White surfaced as part-owners of the Buffalo club. At age 42, White batted .260 in 122 games for the Bisons. The PL collapsed after just one season, ending White's long baseball career. During fifteen NL seasons, he played in 1,299 games, batted .303, and compiled 1,619 hits, 217 doubles, 73 triples, 18 home runs, 849 runs scored, and 602 RBIs.

White continued to live in Buffalo, working for his brother Will as an optician and later operating a livery stable and garage. Around 1910 he moved to Aurora, IL, where he lived until his death. An anomaly in a hard-bitten era of baseball history, he never drank, smoked, or swore, carried his Bible with him on the road, and attended church regularly. To White's great distress, he was never elected to the National Baseball Hall of Fame.

BIBLIOGRAPHY: Lee Allen, *The Cincinnati Reds* (New York, 1948); Arthur Bartlett, *Baseball and Mr. Spalding* (New York, 1951); Paul MacFarlane, ed., *TSN Daguerreotypes of Great Stars of Baseball* (St. Louis, 1981); Joseph M. Overfield, "James 'Deacon' White," *Baseball Research Journal* 4 (1975), pp. 1–11; James L. White file, informal reminiscences, National Baseball Hall of Fame Library, Cooperstown, NY.

Joseph M. Overfield

WHITE, William Henry "Will," "Whoop-La" (b. 11 October 1854, Caton, NY; d. 30 August 1911, Port Carling, Ontario, Canada), player and manager, was the son of farmer James S. White and brother of baseball player James L. White.* After attending Country Day School in Caton, NY, he graduated in 1890 from the College of Ophthalmics in Corning, NY. White married Hattie L. Holmes in December, 1875, and had one daughter, Katherine (White) Shull. The 5 foot, 9 1/2 inch, 175 pound White learned to pitch from his brother Jim as a Caton teenager. By age 17, the right-hander had mastered the curveball and could curve a ball around a post in the ground. He began his professional baseball career in 1877 by joining brother Jim with the Boston Red Stockings (NL) and won two of three decisions. The next year he and his brother moved to Cincinnati (NL), where he became one of the NL's hardest working pitchers with 30 wins and 21 losses. In 1879 and 1880, he compiled 43–31 and 18–42 records, respectively. White led NL pitchers in games (76), games started (75), complete games (75), innings pitched (680), and hits surrendered (676) in 1879.

This hard work hurt his arm, as he pitched only two games with Detroit (NL) in 1881. Upon returning to Cincinnati (AA) in 1882, however, he resumed his almost daily mound trips. From 1882 to 1885, he recorded 40–12, 43–22, 34–18, and 18–15 marks. In 1882 he paced the AA in wins, winning percentage (.769), complete games (52), innings pitched (480), and shutouts (8). The next year, he led the AA in wins (43), ERA (2.09), and shutouts (6). In 1884 he also managed the Cincinnati club, but resigned at midseason with a 43–25 record. White claimed that he did not have the temperament or personality to be a baseball manager. After experiencing arm trouble again late in the 1885 season, White appeared in just three games the next season and retired. During ten major league seasons, he won 229 games and lost 166 contests for a remarkable .580 percentage, completed 394 of 401 starts, and recorded 36 shutouts. White struck out 1,041 batters and walked only 496 in 3,542.2 innings and compiled a 2.28 ERA (10th best). He made his final professional appearance in 1889 with Buffalo (IA), compiling a 6–12 record.

White grew up near the glassmaking center of Corning, NY, and became the first major league player to wear glasses on the field. He founded the Buffalo Optical Company in 1893. In August 1911, at his Port Carling summer home in the Lake Muskoka region of Ontario, White, a non-swimmer, was teaching a young niece to swim when he suffered a heart seizure in the water and drowned. The deeply religious White helped found and was chief benefactor of Christ Mission in his adopted city of Buffalo.

BIBLIOGRAPHY: Lee Allen, *The Cincinnati Reds* (New York, 1948); Buffalo *Courier*, August 31, September 1, 2, 1911; Buffalo *Evening News*, August 31, September 1, 2, 1911; Buffalo *Morning Express*, August 31, September 1, 2, 1911; Paul MacFarlane, ed., *TSN Daguerreotypes of Great Stars of Baseball* (St. Louis, 1981); Joseph L. Reichler, ed., *The Baseball Encyclopedia*, 6th ed. (New York, 1985), pp. 654, 2,113.

Joseph M. Overfield

WHITEHILL, Earl Oliver "The Earl" (b. 7 February 1899, Cedar Rapids, IA; d. 22 October 1954, Omaha, NE), player, coach, and executive, learned the sport on sandlots of Cedar Rapids. Cy Slapnicka, a Cedar Rapids native, NL pitcher, and scout who later discovered Bob Feller,* recommended Whitehill to the Detroit Tigers (AL). In 1919 Tigers manager Hugh Jennings* optioned Whitehill to Des Moines (WL). From 1920 through 1923, Whitehill hurled for Birmingham, AL (SA), and Columbia, SC (SAL). At the end of the 1923 season, new Tiger manager Ty Cobb* promoted Whitehill to the parent club. He created a sensation by winning his two decisions and posting a 2.73 ERA. In 1924 he led the Tigers with 17 wins and only 9 losses to help Detroit stay in or near first place in July and August and proved especially effective against the New York Yankees. Before a then-record 43,000 spectators at Navin Field in Detroit, he shut out the Yankees on August 4. Two days later, he defeated New York again to put the Tigers in first place.

In the spring of 1925, Whitehill experienced arm trouble and sought the services of Bonesetter Reese in Youngstown, OH. Due to Whitehill's slow start, Cobb wanted him to throw curves and trick pitches. On occasion Whitehill proved effective with his "junk" pitches. Umpire Pants Rowland repeatedly checked the ball for a foreign substance on June 11 when Whitehill defeated Walter Johnson* and the Washington Senators 7–2. Whitehill proved a disappointment in 1925, however, winning only 11 of 22 decisions. Cobb, who had promised Detroit fans an AL pennant in 1925, held Whitehill largely responsible for the club's lackluster showing and wanted him to rely on off-speed pitches. On several occasions, Cobb rushed in from center field to the mound and gave Whitehill a public scolding for throwing a fastball. The feisty, outspoken Whitehill once retorted, "I like my fastball." The enraged "Georgia Peach" did not speak to Whitehill for nearly two years, conveying messages through a coach and giving him only a few minutes' notice about pitching assignments.

Whitehill, who was delighted when Cobb was fired as Tigers manager after the 1926 season, did not fulfill his great potential. Under manager George Moriarty, he won 16, lost 14 and posted a 3.36 ERA in 1927 and won 11, lost 16, and compiled a 4.31 ERA in 1928. From 1929 to 1932, he won 60 and lost 56 for Tigers manager Bucky Harris.* Although Whitehill was not much better than a .500 pitcher for Detroit, Washington Senators (AL) owner Clark Griffith* considered him one of the game's best hurlers. Whitehill proved particularly adept at vanquishing the New York Yankees, a team Griffith needed to beat consistently to win the AL pennant. In 1933 Griffith made one of his best deals by trading veteran pitcher Fred Marberry and rookie Carl Fischer to Detroit for Whitehill. Whitehill led the Senators to the AL pennant in 1933 and enjoyed his best season with 22 wins, 8 losses, and a 3.33 ERA. He proved a formidable competitor, once challenging Yankees outfielder Ben Chapman* to a fight. Whitehill was suspended for five days for the altercation, but won the admiration and respect of the Washington fans and players. He pitched the third game and home opener of the 1933 World Series. Before President Franklin D. Roosevelt and a large congressional delegation, he shut out the New York Giants on five hits. The 4–0 victory was Washington's only Series win.

Whitehill slumped to a 14–11 record in 1934, as the Senators dropped into the second division. In four years with Washington, he won 64 decisions and lost 43. Since Whitehill's fastball was no longer effective, Griffith traded him to the Cleveland Indians (AL) in December 1936. Whitehill won 17 and lost 16 for Cleveland the next two years and ended his major league career in 1939 with a 4–7 record for the Chicago Cubs (NL). Altogether, Whitehill won 218 games, lost 185 decisions, walked 1,431 batters in 3,565 2/3 innings, hurled 17 shutouts, and boasted a 4.36 ERA. A workhorse, he averaged over 30 starts a year during the peak of his career. The 5 foot, 9 1/2 inch, 175 pound left-hander possessed an extraordinary fastball.

Whitehill, an extremely handsome player and elegant dresser possessing a lordly manner, was nicknamed "The Earl" and was a notorious lady's man until his marriage to Violet Linda Oliver on November 23, 1925. Mrs. Whitehill, a model, became famous as the Sun Maid and is pictured on that firm's package of raisins. After his playing career, he coached for the Cleveland Indians (AL) in 1941, Philadelphia Phillies (NL) in 1943, and Buffalo Bisons (IL) in 1944. Upon leaving baseball, Whitehill became a public relations director for the A. G. Spalding* Sporting Goods Company and was killed in an automobile accident while representing the company.

BIBLIOGRAPHY: Detroit *News*, 1923–1932; Frederick G. Lieb, *Detroit Tigers* (New York, 1946); Shirley Povich, *The Washington Senators* (New York, 1954); *TSN*, November 3, 1954.

Anthony J. Papalas

WILHELM, James Hoyt (b. 26 July 1923, Huntersville, NC), player, was an extremely durable relief pitcher and hurled effectively in the major leagues until age 49. One of eleven children in a family of tenant farmers, he attended high school in Cornelius, NC. Wilhelm learned to throw the knuckleball there, enabling him to enjoy a very long major league career. After reading about Emil "Dutch" Leonard's* knuckleball in a newspaper, he soon made it his most effective pitch. During his eighteenth major league season (1969), he said, "I don't even try to fool anybody. I just throw the knuckleball 85 to 90 percent of the time. You don't need variations, because the damn ball jumps around so crazily, it's like having a hundred pitches." After high school, he pitched three seasons for Mooresville, NC (NCSL), and then served three years in the armed forces during World War II. Four more minor league seasons followed, during which he was used primarily as a starting pitcher. He married Patti Reeves in September, 1951, and has three children, Patti, Pam, and Jim.

At the relatively advanced age of 28, Wilhelm made the New York Giants (NL) roster in the spring of 1952 and hit a home run in his first major league at bat. Converted by manager Leo Durocher* to relief pitching, Wilhelm in 1952 became the first rookie to lead the NL in both ERA (2.43) and winning percentage (.833). He also led the NL in game appearances in 1952 (71) and 1953 (68) and in relief wins in 1952 (15) and 1954 (12), helping the Giants win the NL pennant. When he paced the AL in ERA (2.19) in 1959 with the Baltimore Orioles, he became one of few pitchers to so lead both major leagues. On September 20, 1958, he hurled a no-hit, no-run game against the New York Yankees. During 1958, 1959 and 1960 with Baltimore, he made the majority of his 52 major league starts. His 1,070 pitching appearances comprised a major league record. During twenty-one major league seasons, he won 143 games and lost 122 (.540) for a 2.52 ERA. Wilhelm struck out 1,610 batters in 2,254 innings, won 123 games in relief, and compiled 227 saves.

Wilhelm pitched for nine major league teams. His clubs included the New York Giants (NL), 1952–1956; St. Louis Cardinals (NL), 1957; Cleveland Indians (AL), 1957–1958; Baltimore Orioles (AL), 1958–1962; Chicago White Sox (AL), 1963–1968; California Angels (AL), 1969; Atlanta Braves (NL), 1969–1971; Chicago Cubs (NL), 1970–1971; and Los Angeles Dodgers (NL), 1971–1972. Since his knuckleball proved even more difficult to catch than to hit, his catchers repeatedly led the league in passed balls. When Wilhelm pitched with Baltimore, manager Paul Richards developed a special large catcher's mitt, which reduced the number of passed balls considerably. A 1965 rule, however, limited the size of the mitt. Ted Williams* considered Wilhelm one of the five toughest pitchers he faced "strictly for his knuckleballs. Wilhelm has a sure-strike knuckler, then a real good knuckler, then with two strikes, an utterly unhittable knuckler, dancing in your face. The closest thing to an unhittable ball I ever saw." In 1985 he became the first relief pitcher elected the the National Baseball Hall of Fame.

BIBLIOGRAPHY: *CB* (1971), pp. 441–443; "King of the Flutter," *Newsweek* 73 (April 21, 1969), p. 127; Tom Meany and Tommy Holmes, *Baseball's Best* (New York, 1964); Martin Quigley, *The Crooked Pitch* (Chapel Hill, NC, 1984); Joseph L. Reichler, *Thirty Years of Baseball's Greatest Moments* (New York, 1974); Lou Sabin, *Record Breakers of the Major Leagues* (New York, 1974); Hoyt Wilhelm, "So I Escaped from the Bullpen," *SEP* 232 (August 1, 1959), pp. 25, 58, 60.

                                                                    Leverett T. Smith, Jr.

WILKINSON, James L. (b. 1874, Perry, IA; d. 21 August 1964, Kansas City, MO), executive, was a Negro league baseball pioneer and team owner from 1909 through 1948. Wilkinson, the son of the president of Algona Normal College, grew up in Des Moines and suffered an injury as a young man that ended his baseball playing career. He managed a team sponsored by a Des Moines firm and dubbed it "All Nations." Wilkinson's team, which included players of several nationalities and even a young woman, barnstormed through small towns of prairie America and big cities against top semi-pro and black clubs.

When the NNL was formed in 1920, the white Wilkinson assembled the Kansas City Monarchs. After the NNL collapsed in 1931, Wilkinson made the Monarchs a barnstorming club. He guided the Monarchs from 1937, when the NAL began, until 1948, two years before the league disbanded.

The powerful Monarchs captured ten Negro league pennants from 1920 through 1948, winning in 1923, 1925, 1929, 1937, 1939–1942, and 1946. Wilkinson initiated the first interleague Negro World Series with the ECL in 1924. Kansas City competed in four Negro World Series, defeating the Hilldale Club in 1924 and sweeping the Washington (Homestead) Grays in 1942. The Hilldale won a 1925 rematch, while the Newark Eagles triumphed in 1946.

Wilkinson helped pioneer night baseball, being among the first to use lights. As others installed permanent lights in scattered minor league parks, he first installed portable lighting on the beds of trucks in 1930. The initial $50,000 system proved so successful that it was paid for during the team's spring training tour of the Southwest. The Monarchs eventually sent more players (27) into the major leagues than any other black team. These stars included Jackie Robinson,* Satchel Paige,* Hank Thompson, Elston Howard, and Ernie Banks*.

Wilkinson traveled with the team, while his wife operated an antique shop in Kansas City. He loved baseball and treated his players well, with the Monarchs traveling by rail and bus and staying in the best available hotels. Bonuses were distributed liberally when available. Wilkinson, respected for his honesty, often conducted business with a handshake until selling his interest in the team in 1948.

BIBLIOGRAPHY: Janet Bruce, *The Kansas City Monarchs: Champions of Black Baseball* (Lawrence, KS, 1985); John Holway, "The Gift of Light: J. L. Wilkinson," John Holway Collection, Alexandria, VA.

                                                  John Holway and Merl F. Kleinknecht

WILLIAMS, Billy Leo "Sweet Swinging" (b. 15 June 1938, Whistler, AL), player and coach, is the son of Frank and Jesse Mary Williams. He was educated in Whistler public schools, married Shirley Ann Williams on February 25, 1960, and has four daughters. "Sweet Swinging" Williams broke into the Chicago Cubs (NL) lineup in 1961 with a .278 batting average and 25 home runs, and won NL Rookie of the Year honors. His illustrious career included 1,117 consecutive games, at the time an NL record.

Signed directly out of high school by Chicago, Williams performed briefly with the Cubs in 1959 and 1960. He played for Ponca City, OK (SSL), in 1956 and 1957, Pueblo, CO (WL), and Burlington, IA (3IL), in 1958, San Antonio (TL) and Fort Worth (AA) in 1959, and Houston (AA) in 1960. The modest and unassuming Williams, who batted left and threw right-handed, formed with Ernie Banks* and Ron Santo* the nucleus of Cubs power throughout the decade. Although playing on unsuccessful Chicago teams until the late 1960s, Williams enjoyed consecutive .300-plus batting seasons in 1964–1965 and contributed 33 and 34 home runs those seasons. The latter year, he topped the Cubs in every offensive category.

As the Cubs improved in the late 1960s, the 6 foot, 1 inch, 175 pound Williams spearheaded the offense. He tied a major league record by hitting five homers in two consecutive games in September, 1968, and collected ten hits in fourteen at bats. When the Cubs astonished fans by almost winning an NL pennant in 1969, Williams batted .293 and broke the NL record for consecutive games. The Cubs faltered that year and resumed their familiar lackluster performance as also-rans in the 1970s. Williams, however, responded with three consecutive .300 seasons and in 1972 won the batting (.333) and slugging (.606) championships. In 1970 Williams led the NL with 205 hits and 137 runs. An outfielder throughout his career, Williams also played first base during his last three seasons with the Cubs. In October, 1974, Williams was traded to the Oakland A's (AL) and spent two seasons there, mostly as a designated hitter.

A .290 batting average, 2,711 hits, 426 home runs, and 1,475 RBIs distinguish Williams' eighteen-year major league career. He also recorded 434 doubles, 88 triples, 1,410 runs, 1,045 walks, 1,046 strikeouts, and a .492 slugging percentage. Williams ranks in the top ten among all-time Cubs hitters in every category except batting average. The six-time NL All-Star also earned numerous other honors, including being named *The Sporting News* Major League Player of the Year in 1972. Following his retirement, he became a major league batting instructor for Chicago and Oakland. In 1986 Williams rejoined the Chicago Cubs as a coach. He was elected to the National Baseball Hall of Fame in January 1987.

BIBLIOGRAPHY: Art Ahrens and Eddie Gold, *Day by Day in Chicago Cubs History* (West Point, NY, 1982); *Chicago Cubs Media Guide, 1973, 1985*; Eddie Gold and Art Ahrens, *The New Era Cubs* (Chicago; 1985); Joseph L. Reichler, ed., *The Baseball Encyclopedia*, 6th ed. (New York, 1985), p. 1,519.

Duane A. Smith

WILLIAMS, Fred C. "Cy" (b. 21 December 1887, Wadena, IN; d. 23 April 1974, Eagle River, WI), player, was the son of farmer Oscar and Anna (Mead) Williams, both of Irish descent. Although a very small town, Wadena produced two well-known baseball figures born within a three-month period: Williams and pitcher-outfielder Otis "Doc" Crandall. A 6 foot, 2 inch, 180 pounder, Williams acquired the common nickname "Cy" and matriculated at the University of Notre Dame in 1908. He excelled as a track hurdler, vaulter, and sprinter, played for the football team, and won acclaim as a center fielder in baseball. Williams, who married Vaida Glenne Perkins on December 24, 1913, and had two sons and two daughters, impressed the Chicago Cubs' (NL) management in an exhibition game. Upon graduating from Notre Dame with a Bachelor's degree in architecture in 1912, the left-handed Williams immediately joined the Cubs as an outfielder. During 1915 he began playing regularly and slugged 13 home runs. He tied for the NL lead with 12 homers in 1916, but was traded to the Philadelphia Phillies (NL) after the 1917 season for Dode Paskert. Since Paskert already had reached the twilight of his career, this trade ranked among the worst in Cubs history.

In 1920 Williams hit .325 for Philadelphia and belted 15 home runs for the NL lead. He batted over .300 five of the next six seasons and slugged at least 12 home runs for nine consecutive campaigns, quite a feat considering that Babe Ruth* had just popularized the long ball. Williams enjoyed his best year in 1923 with 41 round trippers and 114 RBIs and tied Ruth for the major league home run title. In 1927, at age 38, he belted 30 home runs for his fourth NL title and produced 98 RBIs. The effective outfielder also led the NL with 29 assists in 1921.

Since Williams usually pulled the ball, NL managers defended him extremely deep and definitely toward right field to produce the first Williams shift. Over twenty years later, this term became a household word when Cleveland Indians manager Lou Boudreau* developed a similar maneuver for Boston Red Sox slugger Ted Williams.* Williams served under fourteen different managers, including the entire Joe Tinker* to John Evers* to Frank Chance* double play combination, in his first fourteen major league seasons. During his final three seasons, he excelled as one of the top major league pinch hitters.

Williams led the NL in career home runs with 251 until Rogers Hornsby* surpassed him. He also held the NL left-handed home run record until Mel Ott* broke it. His other records included most career pinch hit homers (11); most NL homers through May 31 (18, 1923); most homers during May (15, 1923); most years leading and sharing the lead in homers (6); and most years leading or sharing the lead in homers on the road (5). In 2,002 career games, he batted .292 with 1,981 hits, 306 doubles, 1,024 runs scored, 1,005 RBIs, and 115 stolen bases. After retiring to his several-hundred acre Wisconsin farm, he worked in the construction business. Some of the finest buildings in northeastern Wisconsin stand as a tribute to his architectural capabilities. Although a left-handed athlete, he was an accomplished right-handed artist.

BIBLIOGRAPHY: Stan Baumgartner and Frederick G. Lieb, *The Philadelphia Phillies* (Philadelphia, 1953); Frank Bilovsky and Richard Westcott, *The Phillies Encyclopedia* (Philadelphia, 1984); Warren Brown, *The Chicago Cubs* (New York, 1946).

Cappy Gagnon

WILLIAMS, Joe "Smoky Joe," "Cyclone" (b. 6 April 1886, Sequin, TX; d. 12 March 1946, New York, NY), player, was born to an Indian mother and black father and was a lanky, hawk-nosed, 6 foot, 5 inch, 200 pound right-hander. His fastball, which exploded out of an easy overhand motion, earned him the nicknames "Smoky Joe" and "Cyclone." Williams, whose heritage forced him to pitch under baseball's color ban, pitched two seasons with the black San Antonio Broncos and entered big time black baseball in 1910 with the Chicago Leland Giants. After leaving the Lelands in 1912, he pitched for the New York Lincoln Giants (ECL) through 1923, spent 1924 with Brooklyn's Royal Giants (ECL), and performed from 1925 through 1932 on Cum Posey's* Homestead Grays (ANL). He then retired to tend bar in Harlem until his death.

The 1913 Lincolns and the 1930 and 1932 Grays claimed the eastern championship of black baseball, but the ECL did not operate during these years. The 1930 titlist won a championship series over the Lincoln Giants six games to four. Although the aging Williams struggled throughout the series, he bested Bill Holland in game five 7–3 and allowed no runs over the final six innings. Best known for the fastball, he possessed a full repertoire of pitches and displayed pinpoint control. His low chuckle was the closest the even-tempered Williams ever came to questioning an umpire's call.

Limited published records attest to Williams' skills. He compiled a 12–2 mark against major black competition and a 41–3 record against all competition, including semi-pro teams in 1914. With Rube Foster's* American Giants on a western tour in the spring of 1912, he compiled a 9–1 mark and victories over every PCL team except Portland. In the CUWL for three seasons, he produced a 22–15 career log, including a 10–7 mark in 1911–1912 to pace the league in wins. He also spent winters in Florida waiting tables and pitching.

Williams made his biggest impression by compiling a 19–7 mark against white major league competition in scattered exhibitions throughout his career. Two losses came at age 45, while two others were by 1–0 margins. He hurled 10 shutouts against the white stars, including 2 against the 1912 NL champion New York Giants and another against the 1915 NL titlist Philadelphia Phillies. His other legendary games included two contests for which only eye-witness accounts are available: a no-hit, 20-strikeout contest against the 1917 New York Giants lost on a tenth-inning error, and a 1–0 conquest over Walter Johnson.* Sufficient published evidence supports his victories over the Giants, Phillies, New York Highlanders (now Yankees), Buffalo (FL), and various All-Star aggregations. National Baseball Hall of Famers Grover Cleveland Alexander,* Chief Bender,* Waite Hoyt,* and Rube Marquard* were outhurled by Williams. Usually at least ten batters were fanned by Williams in these games.

His masterpieces against major black competition included a 1909 shutout of the Leland Giants and a 1919 no-hit victory over Cannonball Redding.* During the twilight of his career, he struck out 27 Kansas City Monarchs and surrendered just one hit under the lights in a twelve-inning victory. The following year (1931) he hurled a two-hitter against the NNL champion St. Louis Stars, featuring James "Cool Papa" Bell,* "Mule" Suttles,* and Willie Wells.* In semi-pro competition, he struck out 21 hitters in Philadelphia in 1920 and 25 batters in a 1924 loss to the powerful Brooklyn Bushwicks in twelve innings and tossed another no-hitter in 1928 at Akron Tire. Williams became a "Stage Door Johnny" during his New York years. He married a pretty Broadway showgirl, Beatrice, in 1922 in New York. He proved popular with fans and drew large crowds, with his age often exaggerated to augment the mystique surrounding his legend. In 1952 the Pittsburgh *Courier* polled a panel of black veterans and sportswriters on black baseball's greatest pitcher. Williams won the honor by edging Satchel Paige* 20 votes to 19.

BIBLIOGRAPHY: John Holway, *Smoky Joe and the Cannonball* (Alexandria, VA, 1983); Robert W. Peterson, *Only the Ball Was White* (Englewood Cliffs, NJ, 1970).

Merl F. Kleinknecht and John Holway

WILLIAMS, Kenneth Roy "Ken" (b. 28 June 1890, Grants Pass, OR; d. 22 January 1959, Grants Pass, OR), player, began his professional career in 1913 as an outfielder–third baseman at Regina, Saskatchewan (WCaL), and played in Edmonton (WCaL) and Spokane (NWL). His contract was purchased by the Cincinnati Reds (NL) in 1915. After two seasons of part-time play, he was returned to the minors for 1916–1917 with Spokane (NWL) and Portland, OR (PCL). He reached the majors as an outfielder in 1918, when the St. Louis Browns (AL) purchased his contract. After spending most of that year in military service, he hit .300 for the Browns in 1919. He played regularly with St. Louis through the 1927 season, and then was sold to the Boston Red Sox (AL), where he spent his last two major league seasons. The New York Yankees (AL) signed Williams in 1930, perhaps because of a salary battle with Babe Ruth,* but he played that year and 1931 at Portland (PCL) to finish his organized baseball career.

Williams' best season came in 1922, when his 39 home runs and 155 RBIs topped the AL and the St. Louis Browns lost a close pennant race to New York. He finished second in the AL in home runs in 1921, 1923, and 1925, and surpassed the 100 RBI mark in 1921 and 1925. One of the earliest sluggers in the lively ball era, Williams averaged 24 home runs per season from 1921 to 1927. He hit below .300 only once from 1919 through 1929, peaking at .357 in 1923, and averaged .319 for his major league career. In 1,397 games, Williams made 1,552 hits, 285 doubles, 196 home runs, 860 runs, 913 RBIs, 154 stolen bases, and a .531 slugging percentage. In 1922 he hit three home runs in game one (April 22) and two home runs in one inning (August 7) and homered in six consecutive games (July 28-August 2). Williams suffered a severe beaning in a game against Cleveland in 1925, the same year he led the AL in slugging percentage. A left-handed hitting, right-handed throwing outfielder, the 6 foot, 170 pound Williams married Edith Wilerons in 1919. He suffered from a heart condition and died at his home.

BIBLIOGRAPHY: Paul MacFarlane, ed., *TSN Daguerreotypes of Great Stars of Baseball* (St. Louis, 1981); Joseph L. Reichler, ed., *The Baseball Encyclopedia*, 6th ed. (New York, 1985), p. 1,522; *TSN*, January 30, 1959.

Phillip P. Erwin

WILLIAMS, Richard Hirschfield "Dick" (b. 7 May 1929, St. Louis, MO), player and manager, has ranked among the most successful and controversial major league managers since 1967, when he led the Boston Red Sox to an AL pennant and a near victory in the World Series against the St. Louis Cardinals. (The Red Sox had finished ninth in the previous season.)

The son of Harvey and Kathryn Louise (Rohde) Williams, he grew up a rabid baseball fan. After his family moved to southern California in the early 1940s, he starred at Pasadena Junior College (high school division) in baseball, basketball, and football and made the 1947 All-California baseball team as an outfielder. Drafted by the Brooklyn Dodgers (NL) in 1947, Williams played in Santa Barbara (CaL) and Fort Worth (TL) before reaching the major leagues in 1951. Thereafter he played outfield for Brooklyn and its Montreal (IL) and St. Paul (AA) farms until 1956, when he was sold to the Baltimore Orioles (AL). After an injury to his throwing arm impaired his effectiveness, he spent the next eight seasons moving among the Orioles, Cleveland Indians (AL), Kansas City A's (AL), Houston Astros (NL), and Boston Red Sox (AL). His .260 major league batting average included 1,023 games, 768 hits, 70 home runs, and 331 RBIs.

As manager of the Red Sox' Toronto farm team, Williams quickly displayed his skills by taking the Maple Leafs to the IL-AA playoff championships in 1965 and 1966. He was promoted to pilot the Red Sox and won AL Manager of the Year laurels for his 1967 victory. Released after the fourth and third place finishes in 1968 and 1969, he was hired by Charles Finley* in 1971 to manage the Oakland A's (AL). In three seasons with the A's, he won the AL West title (1971) and two pennants and world championships (1972 and 1973). Oakland defeated the Cincinnati Reds and New York Mets in the 1972 and 1973 World Series, respectively. Williams resigned after 1973 to protest Finley's policies and managed the California Angels for the 1974–1976 seasons, finishing sixth twice and fourth once in the AL West. In 1977 he joined the Montreal Expos (NL) and piloted them to two second place finishes in the NL East (1979 and 1980) before being replaced by Jim Fanning late in 1981, the Expos' NL East championship year. In 1982 he joined San Diego as manager and recorded two fourth places, one third place, and one NL pennant (1984) with the Padres. After coming back from a two-game deficit to top the Chicago Cubs in the NL Championship Series, San Diego lost to Detroit 4–1 in the World Series.

Among active managers, Williams trails only Gene Mauch and Sparky Anderson* in career wins (1,470), and is the only manager other than Bill McKechnie* to win pennants with three different teams. He has lost 1,334 games as a manager and led the AL All Stars three times (1968, 1973–1974) and the NL team once (1985). Williams and his wife Norma (Musato) have two sons and one daughter and live in Florida and Coronado, CA. Williams resigned as San Diego manager before the 1986 season and became pilot of the Seattle Mariners (AL) during that campaign.

BIBLIOGRAPHY: *CB* (1973), pp. 437–439; San Diego Padres Public Relations Department.

Leonard Frey

WILLIAMS, Theodore Samuel "Ted," "The Splendid Splinter," "The Thumper," "The Kid," "The Big Guy," "Teddy Ballgame" (b. 30 August 1918, San Diego, CA), player, manager, and coach, is the eldest of two sons born to Samuel Steward and May (Venzer) Williams. His father, variously described as a photographer and a "wanderer," played no significant role in the household. Williams grew up under the influence of his mother, an imperious personality who spent more time promoting the Salvation Army than caring for the family. As he later recalled of his youth, "The thing a kid remembers is that he never saw his mother or father very much." Williams grew up on the playgrounds and graduated from Herbert Hoover High School in San Diego, where he excelled at baseball but not academics. In 1936, at age 17, he signed with the newly organized San Diego Padres (PCL) and was nicknamed "The Kid." The Boston Red Sox (AL) bought his contract from the Padres after the 1937 season and sent him to Minneapolis (AA), where he led the AA in 1938 in batting average (.366), home runs (43), runs scored (130), and RBIs (142).

Williams was promoted to the majors in 1939 and, in his first season, hit .327, led the AL in RBIs (145) and was named Outstanding Rookie of the Year. In 1941 he hit .406 to become the first player since 1930 to surpass .400, the youngest ever to break the mark, and the last player to achieve that feat. He hit .388 in 1957 at age 39 to become the oldest player to win a batting title, an achievement repeated the next year with a .328 average. With uncanny eyesight, exceptionally quick wrists, and an intelligent understanding of both hitting and pitching, the 6 foot, 3 inch, 180 pound Williams was the premier batter of his generation. When he retired in 1960 after nineteen seasons with Boston, he achieved career rankings that still stand—second in walks (2,019) and slugging percentage (.634) and sixth in batting average (.344). Other career totals include 2,292 games, 2,654 hits, 525 doubles, 521 home runs, 1,798 runs scored, 1,839 RBIs, and a mere 709 strikeouts. He led the AL nine times in slugging percentage, eight times in walks, six times in batting average and runs scored, four times in home runs and RBIs, and twice in doubles.

Selected the AL Most Valuable Player in 1946 and 1949, Williams, who hit left-handed but threw right-handed, was named to every All-Star team from 1940 to 1960 except for his years in military service. His most notable All-Star achievements came in 1941, when he hit a game-winning home run off Claude Passeau in the ninth inning, and in 1946, when he turned in the greatest offensive performance in All-Star history by scoring four runs and driving in five more on four hits in four at bats. Two of his hits were home runs, one being the first homer ever hit off Rip Sewell's famous "ephus"or "blooper" pitch. Williams was voted into the National Baseball Hall of Fame in 1966.

His relative greatness as a hitter is uncertain because he lost nearly five prime seasons as a pilot in the U.S. Marine Corps during World War II (1943–1945) and the Korean War (1952–1953). Nonetheless, his record clearly shows that he ranks second only to Babe Ruth* for a combination of power and average. His average probably would have been much higher had he hit to left field instead of stubbornly hitting into the strength of variations of the Williams shift. This defensive alignment, devised in 1946 by Cleveland Indians player-manager Lou Boudreau,* placed three infielders between first and second base.

Williams had a tempestuous relationship with Boston sportswriters and fans because of his candor, tactlessness, temper, and perfectionism. His stormy relations with the press probably cost him deserved recognition inasmuch as he was denied the MVP designation the year he hit .406 and the seasons he won the Triple Crown (1942 and 1947). Yet umpires universally regarded him as a gentleman on the field, and his fundraising efforts on behalf of the Children's Cancer Hospital in Boston (the Jimmy Fund) endeared him to millions off the field.

Upon retiring in 1960, appropriately after hitting a home run in Fenway Park in his last time at bat, he served as chairman of the Ted Williams Sports Advisory Staff endorsing outdoor and recreational equipment for Sears & Roebuck and pursued his hobbies of hunting and fishing. He briefly emerged from his baseball "exile" to manage the AL Washington Senators (1969–1971) and Texas Rangers (1972). His best and only winning season came in 1969, when the Senators compiled a 86–76 record to finish fourth in the AL. Unable to relate well to modern players who lacked his talent and determination, he concluded his managerial career with 273 wins and 364 losses for a .429 winning percentage.

Williams married and divorced Doris Soule, Lee Howard, and Dolores Wettach. He has two children, a daughter, Bobby Jo, and a son, John Henry. In recent years, Williams has served as batting instructor during spring training for the Red Sox and has achieved international acclaim as an expert fisherman.

BIBLIOGRAPHY: *CB* (1947), pp. 685–687; James S. Kunen, "Last of the .400 Hitters," *NYT Magazine*, May 12, 1974, pp. 22–25; Ed Linn, *Ted Williams* (Chicago, 1961); *NYT*, January 21, July 26, 1966, February 14, 22, 1969, October 1, 2, 1972, August

10, 1982; Joseph L. Reichler, ed., *The Baseball Encyclopedia*, 6th ed. (New York, 1985), pp. 1,522–1,523; *TSN Baseball Register, 1961* (St. Louis, 1961); John Underwood, "Ted Williams at Midstream," *SI 55* (June 29, 1981), pp. 66–82; John Updike, "Hub Fans Bid Kid Adieu," *New Yorker* (October 22, 1960), pp. 109ff; Ted Williams and John Underwood, *My Turn at Bat* (New York, 1969); Ted Williams and John Underwood, *The Science of Hitting* (New York, 1971).

Larry R. Gerlach

WILLIS, Victor Gazaway "Vic" (b. 12 April 1876, Wilmington, DE; d. 3 August 1947, Elkton, MD), player, completed high school in Wilmington, married Mary J. Minnis on February 8, 1900, and had two children, Victor, Jr., and Gertrude. In 1895 Willis entered professional baseball with Harrisburg, PA (PSL). After winning 10 games in 1896 and 21 contests in 1897 with Syracuse, NY (EL), he trained with the Boston Braves (NL) in the spring of 1898. From 1898 to 1905, Willis proved the mainstay of the Boston pitching staff with his excellent curveball. He won 51 games his first two seasons on strong Boston teams featuring Hugh Duffy,* Billy Hamilton,* and Kid Nichols.* On August 7, 1899, he hurled a 7–1 no-hitter against the Washington Senators. In 1899 and 1901, he paced the NL in shutouts with 5 and 6, respectively. After recording 27 wins, 45 complete games, and 410 innings in 1902, he experienced pitching problems. Willis led the NL in 1902 in losses (19), appearances (51), games started (46), games completed, innings pitched, hits surrendered (372), and strikeouts (225). In 1903 the contracts of Willis and fifteen other players were disputed between the NL and AL. Since Willis' contract was awarded to the NL, he remained with Boston, compiled a 12–18 record in 1903, and led the NL with 25 and 29 losses the next two seasons with the now dismal Braves. Willis paced the NL with 39 complete games in 1904 and 340 hits surrendered in 1905.

Before the 1906 season, Willis was traded to the Pittsburgh Pirates (NL) for infielder Dave Brain and two minor league players. The 6 foot, 2 inch, 185 pound right-hander rebounded with four outstanding years for the Pirates, winning 89 games, averaging over 300 innings per year, and compiling a sparkling 1.73 ERA in 1906. Willis hurled in the 1909 World Series, as the Pirates defeated the Detroit Tigers in seven games. He pitched 6 1/3 innings in relief in the second game and started the sixth game, but lasted just five innings and suffered the loss. Willis finished his career with the 1910 St. Louis Cardinals (NL), winning 9 of 21 decisions. His career totals included 247 victories, 206 defeats, 3,996 innings pitched, 388 complete games in 471 starts, 1,651 strikeouts, 50 shutouts, and a 2.63 ERA. After retiring from baseball, Willis operated a hotel in Newark, DE.

BIBLIOGRAPHY: Gene Karst and Martin J. Jones, Jr., *Who's Who in Professional Baseball* (New Rochelle, NY, 1973); Paul MacFarlane, ed., *TSN Daguerreotypes of Great Stars of Baseball* (St. Louis, 1968), *TSN Official World Series Records, 1903–1978* (St. Louis,

1903–1978); Victor Willis file, National Baseball Hall of Fame Library, Cooperstown, NY.

Frank J. Olmsted

WILLS, Maurice Morning "Maury," "The Mouse" (b. 2 October 1932, Washington, DC), player, coach, manager, and broadcaster, played in the minor leagues for nine years with stops at Hornell, NY (Pol), in 1951–1952, Pueblo (WL) in 1953–1954 and 1956, Miami (FIL) in 1953, Fort Worth (TL) in 1955, Seattle (PCL) in 1957, and Spokane (PCL) in 1958–1959. Although primarily a shortstop and third baseman, Wills actually played all nine positions. After an unsuccessful spring training tryout with the Detroit Tigers (AL) in 1951, the fleet-footed Wills played with the Los Angeles Dodgers (NL) from 1959 to 1966. On December 1, 1966, he was traded to the Pittsburgh Pirates (NL) for Gene Michael and Bob Bailey. Wills performed for two full seasons for the Pirates (1967–1968) before the Montreal Expos (NL) selected him in the expansion draft. In midseason 1969, the Expos traded Wills and Manny Mota to the Dodgers for Ron Fairly and Paul Popovich. Wills played with Los Angeles through the 1972 season and was released at age 40.

Wills stole 104 bases in 1962, breaking the major league record (96) established by Ty Cobb* in 1915. Wills' record subsequently was broken by Lou Brock* (118 in 1974) and Rickey Henderson* (130 in 1982). Wills, Brock, Henderson, and Vince Coleman remain the only players in major league history to steal over 100 bases in one season. Wills revolutionized baseball by reintroducing the stolen base as a major offensive weapon and refining the "science" of base stealing. Before Wills led the NL a record six consecutive seasons (1960–1965) in stolen bases, Willie Mays* had paced the NL in 1959 with only 27 steals. As Dodgers captain and leadoff hitter in the mid–1960s, Wills sparked a team that relied heavily upon speed and pitching. When he reached base during his prime, sellout crowds at Dodger Stadium often spontaneously chanted "Go, Maury, Go." Wills also established a major league record for leading the NL seven years (1961–1963, 1965–1966, 1968–1969) in being caught stealing. The 5 foot, 11 inch, 170 pound Wills, nicknamed "The Mouse," lacked power and hit only 20 career home runs. He led the NL in singles a record four years (1961, 1962, 1965, 1969), in at bats twice (1961–1962), and in triples (10) in 1962.

In 1962 Wills was named NL Most Valuable Player and Major League Co-Player of the Year with teammate Don Drysdale.* He was selected as shortstop on *The Sporting News* NL All-Star team in 1961, 1962, and 1965 and on *The Sporting News* NL All-Star fielding team in 1961 and 1962. Wills also won the Gold Glove Award in 1961 and 1962. When the Dodgers and San Francisco Giants ended the 162-game 1962 season in a tie and played a three-game playoff, he established a major league record by appearing in all

165 games. As of the end of the 1986 season, the switch-hitting, right-handed throwing Wills ranked among the top ten on the all-time Dodgers lists for career games (1,593), at bats (6,156), runs scored (876), and hits (1,732). Wills, the all-time Dodgers leader in stolen bases with 490, finished twelfth in the 1984 National Baseball Hall of Fame voting. Wills batted .281 lifetime with 2,134 hits, 177 doubles, 71 triples, 1,067 runs scored, 458 RBIs, and 586 stolen bases in 1,942 games.

Wills played in four World Series with the Dodgers (1959, 1963, 1965, 1966) and enjoyed his best performance in the 1965 Series, including four hits in game six. Wills also compiled a .357 batting average in six All-Star games and was named MVP of the 1961 games. Wills later worked as a commentator for NBC-TV and cable television, managed winter league teams in Mexico, and served as an instructor for the Dodgers (1977). In 1976 he published *How to Steal a Pennant*. Wills replaced Darrell Johnson as manager of the Seattle Mariners (AL) on August 4, 1980, making him the third black major league manager following Frank Robinson* and Larry Doby.* The Mariners compiled a 20–38 record under Wills to finish in last place, 38 games behind the Kansas City Royals. As Mariners' manager, Wills was fined $500 and suspended for two games in April, 1981, for ordering the batters' boxes lengthened illegally. Wills was fired on May 6, 1981, after the Mariners started the season with a 6–18 record.

In 1958 Spokane (PCL) manager Bobby Bragan encouraged Wills to become a switch-hitter. Dodgers manager Walter Alston* later considered him "an absolute marvel." Wills, the son of a minister, grew up in the slums of Washington, DC, with his twelve siblings. His main hobbies are playing the banjo and training bird dogs. His son, Elliott "Bump," played second base for the Texas Rangers (1977–1981), Chicago Cubs (1982), and Hankyu Braves (Japan). Wills works in public relations for the Los Angeles Dodgers Community Service Department.

BIBLIOGRAPHY: Walter Alston, *Alston and the Dodgers* (Garden City, NY, 1966); Craig Carter, *TSN Official World Series Records, 1982* (St. Louis, 1982); John Devaney, "Maury Wills: A Revealing Look at a Man on the Go," *Sport* 41 (May, 1966), pp. 72–77; John Duxbury, *TSN Baseball Register, 1969* (St. Louis, 1969); Tot Holmes, ed., *Dodgers Blue Book* (Los Angeles, 1983, 1985); William Leggett, "Stealing Onto the Air," *SI* 41 (August 19, 1974), p. 45; "Mariners Oust Wills" *NYT*, May 7, 1981, p. B15; Joseph L. Reichler, ed., *The Baseball Encyclopedia*, 6th ed. (New York, 1985), p. 1,524; Maury Wills, "The Great Stealer Tells Some Secrets," *Life* 53 (September 28, 1962), pp. 50–52; Maury Wills and Don Freeman, *How to Steal a Pennant* (New York, 1976).

Jack P. Lipton

WILSON, Ernest Judson "Jud" (b. 28 February 1899, Remington, VA; d. 27 June 1963, Washington, DC), player, performed in the Negro and Caribbean winter leagues. The powerful 5 foot, 8 inch, 195 pound Wilson had an unusual build; he had a Herculean torso tapering to a small waist and was slightly bowlegged and pidgeon-toed. The sincere, fearless Wilson exhibited a moody, ill-tempered nature. These traits resulted in frequent fights, sometimes involving the police and leading to occasional arrests. An unyielding desire to win earned him a reputation for being a mean, nasty, talented competitor. Wilson variously held contempt for umpires, opposing players, and teammates. Wilson's strength produced vicious line drives that jumped off his bat. The left-handed Wilson crowded the plate and regularly was hit by pitches. His limited defensive skills at third base caused numerous knots and bruises. He often smothered or blocked balls rather than catching them and used his strong arm to throw out runners.

After serving in the U.S. Army in 1918, he played sandlot ball in a Washington, DC, ghetto and with the Baltimore Black Sox (ECL, and later ANL) from 1922 through 1930. The Black Sox won the 1929 ANL title and featured stars Wilson at first base, manager Frank Warfield at second, Dick Lundy* at shortstop, and Oliver Marcelle* at third. Wilson in 1931 moved to the Homestead, PA, Grays (EWL) and split the next season between Homestead and the Pittsburgh Crawfords. From 1933 through 1939, he performed with the Philadelphia Stars (NNL). The 1934 unit won the second half of a split season and claimed the NNL crown after a disputed series with the first half titlist Chicago American Giants. In 1940 Wilson joined the Washington (Homestead) Grays (NNL) and played there until retiring in 1945. They captured the NNL championship each year, winning the 1943 and 1944 Black World Series and dropping the 1942 and 1945 classics.

Available statistics substantiate Wilson's awesome hitting skills and approximate .390 career batting average. His sparkling winter league career averages included .409 in Cuba and .412 in Puerto Rico. During his prime, Wilson led or ranked near the top of his leagues in most offensive categories. He competed in three East-West (Negro league) All-Star games, making 5 hits in 11 at bats and driving home the only run in the 1934 classic. In 26 games against white major leaguers, he posted a .360 batting mark. Subsequently, he worked for several years for a road crew building Washington DC's Whitehurst Freeway. Wilson, whose wife Betty came from rural Virginia, eventually suffered epileptic seizures and was institutionalized.

BIBLIOGRAPHY: John Holway, "Boojum, Jud Wilson," John Holway Collection, Alexandria, VA.

Merl F. Kleinknecht and John B. Holway

WILSON, Lewis Robert "Hack" (b. 26 April 1900, Ellwood City, PA; d. 23 November 1948, Baltimore, MD), player, grew up in Chester, PA, quit school at an early age, and worked for a print shop, railroad company and shipyard. His baseball career began in 1921 with Martinsburg, WV (BRL). In 1923 he played for Portsmouth, VA (VL), and at midseason joined the New York Giants (NL). In 1925 he was assigned to Toledo (AA) and was chosen by the Chicago Cubs (NL) in that year's post-season draft. The Cubs paid $5,000 for draft rights to Wilson, inspiring the phrase, "A Million Dollar Slugger from the Five and Ten Cent Store." Wilson played outfield for the Cubs from 1926 through 1931 and became one of the NL's top sluggers. Besides hitting an NL record 56 home runs in 1930, he paced the NL in home runs from 1926 to 1928. He drove in 190 runs in 1930 (a major league record that still stands), led the NL in RBIs with 159 in 1929, and remains the only NL player to have over 150 RBIs two consecutive seasons. In 1930 Wilson recorded a phenomenal .723 slugging percentage. Wilson, whose career batting average was a respectable .307, hit a career-high .356 in 1930 and led the NL five times in strikeouts and twice in walks.

During a twelve-year major league career, he compiled 1,461 hits, 266 doubles, 67 triples, 244 homers, 884 runs scored, 1,062 RBIs, 713 strikeouts, and a .545 slugging average. Although a good defensive player, Wilson became the goat of the 1929 World Series by losing a fly ball in the sun. This miscue enabled the Philadelphia A's to rally from an 8–0 deficit in the seventh inning of the fourth game and win 10–8. Philadelphia won the Series, despite Wilson's .471 batting average. After his spectacular 1930 season, Wilson signed a record $40,000 contract for the next season. Rogers Hornsby* became Cubs manager and clashed with Wilson frequently, causing the outfielder's production to plunge. From 1932 to August 1934, he played for the Brooklyn Dodgers (NL). Wilson was traded in August 1934 to the Philadelphia Phillies (NL), who released him following the season.

After playing with Albany (IL) in 1935 and Portland (PCL) in 1936, Wilson left baseball. He was divorced, lived in Martinsburg, WV, and operated a saloon in Chicago. Wilson finally settled in Baltimore, where he worked in a defense plant during World War II and later as a groundskeeper and swimming pool manager for the city parks system. In 1948 he quit that job and died of internal hemorrhaging complicated by influenza.

Wilson, resembling a veritable fire hydrant, stood only 5 feet, 6 inches, weighed about 210 pounds, and wore a size 18 collar and size 6 shoes. A notorious disciplinary problem off the field, he shortened both his baseball career and his life by excessive drinking. Nicknamed "Hack," he resembled Russian strongman and wrestler George Hackenschmidt, popular in Wilson's youth. Some compared Wilson to Hack Miller, a Cubs outfielder of the mid–1920s. After a long campaign by his supporters, Wilson was elected to the National Baseball Hall of Fame in 1979.

BIBLIOGRAPHY: Warren Brown, *The Chicago Cubs* (New York, 1946); Jim Enright, *Chicago Cubs* (New York, 1975); Ralph Hickok, *Who Was Who in American Sport* (New York, 1971); Gene Karst and Martin J. Jones, Jr., *Who's Who in Professional Baseball* (New Rochelle, NY, 1973); Mark Kram, "Why Ain't I in the Hall?" *SI* 46 (April 11, 1977), pp. 88ff.; *Macmillan Baseball Encyclopedia* (New York, 1969); *NYT*, November

24, 1948, March 8, 11, 1979; Lowell Reidenbaugh, *Cooperstown: Where Baseball's Legends Live Forever* (St. Louis, 1983).

John E. Findling

WILSON, Willie James (b. 9 July 1955, Montgomery, AL), player, graduated from Summit, NJ, High School in 1974 with 250 college football offers. When the Kansas City Royals (AL) baseball club offered him a reported $50,000 bonus and selected him in the first round of the draft, he signed a contract and actually received $90,000. Wilson played minor league ball for Sarasota (GCL) in 1974, Waterloo, IA (ML), in 1975, Jacksonville (SL) in 1976, and Omaha (AA) in 1977. In three of four seasons in the minors, he led his respective leagues in stolen bases.

The speedy 6 foot, 3 inch, 190 pounder, who throws and bats right-handed, joined the Kansas City Royals full-time in 1978 and began switch-hitting upon the request of manager Whitey Herzog. As a rookie, Wilson probably ranked as the fastest player in the major leagues. He sprinted from home plate to first base in 3.9 seconds, routinely took extra bases, and occasionally scored from second base on singles, but saw limited action. The regular left fielder in 1979, Wilson batted .315 and led the AL with 83 stolen bases. In 1980 he exploded with an all-time major league leading 705 plate appearances and paced the AL with 133 runs and 230 hits. Wilson's 15 triples tied the AL season record, while his 32 consecutive stolen bases equalled the all-time AL mark. Besides hitting .326, he placed among the top ten in at least seven offensive categories and won the Gold Glove for defensive excellence.

In 1982 Wilson's .332 batting average and 15 triples comprised AL season bests. For the first time since he became a Royals starter, his batting average in 1983 fell below .300. At the season's end, he was indicted on a misdemeanor cocaine charge and suspended from baseball. After returning to the Royals in May, 1984, Wilson became active in antidrug programs for youth and quickly regained his pre–1983 form. In 1985 he batted .278, made 168 hits, and stole 43 bases to help the Royals win the AL pennant.

Wilson has appeared in two All-Star games, the 1981 Western Division series, four Championship Series, and the 1980 and 1985 World Series. He hit only .154 and struck out a record twelve times in the 1980 World Series against the Philadelphia Phillies. In the 1985 World Series triumph over the St. Louis Cardinals, Wilson batted .367 and made eleven hits, three RBIs, and three stolen bases. He also batted over .300 in the AL Championship Series against New York in 1980 and Toronto in 1985 and in the 1981 divisional series.

After nine major league seasons, Wilson's career .297 batting average has included 765 runs scored and 1,457 hits. His speed has produced 470 stolen bases and the highest AL stolen base percentage (around .850). During his career, Wilson has also compiled 176 doubles, 97 triples, 30 home runs, and

357 RBIs. He seldom hits into double plays, setting an AL record by grounding into only one in 1979. Wilson, the established center fielder, always has played in the Royals organization and lives with his wife, Kathy, and two children in Blue Springs, MO.

BIBLIOGRAPHY: Joe Flaherty, "Wilson Making Every Hit Count," *NYT Biographical Service* (August, 1982), pp. 1,112–1,114; "Fleetest of the Royal Fleet," *SI* 48 (April 24, 1978), pp. 54–56; Jim Kaplan, "K.C. Takes Off on Willie's Wings," *SI*, 51 (September 10, 1979), pp. 26–27; Jim Kaplan, "Will He Be Willie Again?" *SI* 54 (February 9, 1981), pp. 78–79; Joseph L. Reichler, ed., *The Baseball Encyclopedia*, 6th ed. (New York, 1985), p. 1,527; *TSN Official Baseball Register, 1985* (St. Louis, 1985); "Two Rookies with a Royal Look," *NYT Biographical Service* (May, 1978), p. 602.

Gaymon L. Bennett

WINFIELD, David Mark "Dave" (b. 3 October 1951, St. Paul, MN), baseball player and all-around athlete, is the son of dining car waiter Frank and Arline (Allison) Winfield. After his father left the family in 1954, he grew up with his mother, a St. Paul schools employee, and his grandmother. At St. Paul Central High School, he did not play baseball until his junior year and yet made the All-City and All-State teams as a senior. Although drafted by the Baltimore Orioles (AL) in 1969, Winfield instead attended the University of Minnesota and made the baseball team his sophomore year as a right-handed pitcher. An arm injury forced Winfield off the mound as a junior, but he pitched again his senior year with a 13–1 record, batted .385, and slugged 9 home runs. He was named Most Valuable Player of the 1973 National Collegiate Athletic Association College World Series.

Drafted by four teams in three sports, the 6 foot, 6 inch, 220 pounder signed with the San Diego Padres (NL) for a bonus estimated at between $50,000 and $100,000. The Padres wanted him as an everyday player and immediately inserted him as a starting outfielder. (He remains one of only three current major leaguers without minor league experience.) The right-handed batting Winfield hit a respectable .277 in 1973 and belted 20 home runs in 1974. He raised his batting average to .308 in 1978 and 1979 and led the NL with 118 RBIs, 333 total bases, and 24 intentional walks the latter season. Always among defensive leaders, he led the NL in assists with 15 in 1976 and received the NL Gold Glove Award in 1979 and 1980.

Frustrated by playing on a losing team, Winfield signed as a free agent with the New York Yankees (AL) after the 1980 season. His ten-year contract, then the most lucrative in sports, is estimated to be worth up to $25 million. In his first six seasons in New York, Winfield has averaged 89 runs per season on 158 hits compared to 74 runs scored and 141 hits at San Diego. His average home run output has risen from 19 to 25, while his RBIs have increased from 78 to 101. In 1984 Winfield battled teammate Don Mattingly for the AL batting title until the last day of the season, finishing second with .340. The next year, he finished third in the AL in RBIs (114) and second in game-winning hits (19). He led the AL with 17 assists in 1982 and made only 2 errors in 1984 for a .994 fielding average to earn his third AL Gold Glove. Winfield often saves extra base hits and runs with his bullet-like throws from the outfield. In 1985 he earned another Gold Glove.

Winfield has appeared in every All-Star Game since becoming a Yankee, batting .384 in these games, and has played in the 1981 Eastern Division, AL championship, and World Series. Through the 1986 season, he has averaged .286 with 1,135 runs scored, 1,234 RBIs, 2,083 hits, and 195 stolen bases. His 729 extra-base hits include 353 doubles, 71 triples, and 305 homers. Through the Winfield Foundation, which he operates with his brother Steve, Winfield promotes several charities for underprivileged youth: free seats for ballgames, All-Star Game children's parties, and yearly scholarships to scholar-athletes in Minnesota. A bachelor, he maintains homes in Teaneck, New Jersey and St. Paul, Minnesota. Besides decorating both homes, he designs his own clothes and enjoys photography. On July 17, 1986, Winfield tripled for his 2,000th major league hit in a 14–3 victory over the Texas Rangers.

BIBLIOGRAPHY: Phil Berger, "The Yankees' $20 Million Gamble," *NYT Magazine* (March 29, 1981), pp. 26–40; Ira Berkow, "Winfield Looks Back on Satisfying Season," *NYT Biographical Service* (November, 1981), pp. 1,609–1,611; *CB* (1984), pp. 42–45; Joseph Durso, "All-round Athlete," *NYT Biographical Service* (December, 1980), pp. 1,832–1,833; Ron Fimrite, "Good Hit, Better Man," *SI* 51 (July 9, 1979), pp. 32–34; Ron Fimrite, "Richest Kid on the Block," *SI* 54 (January 5, 1981), pp. 22–26; William Oscar Johnson, "Al Gave It His All," *SI* 54 (January 5, 1981), pp. 26–35; Joseph L. Reichler, ed., *The Baseball Encyclopedia*, 6th ed. (New York, 1985), p. 1,528; Barry Siegel, ed., *TSN Official Baseball Register, 1985* (St. Louis, 1985); *WWA*, 43rd ed., (1984–1985), p. 3,523.

Gaymon L. Bennett

WOOD, Joe "Smoky Joe" (b. 25 October 1889, Kansas City, MO; d. 27 July 1985, West Haven, CT), player and coach, was the son of attorney John and homemaker Rebecca (Stephens) Wood and grew up in Ouray, CO, and Ness City, KS. He married Laura O'Shea on December 20, 1913, and had four children, Stephen, Robert K., Joseph P., and Virginia. In 1943 Joseph P. played 60 games with the Detroit Tigers (AL). A devoted family man, the modest, sincere, fair-minded, and friendly Wood signed a contract for $20 in 1906 to play baseball with the touring Kansas City Bloomer Girls. In 1907 he played briefly with Cedar Rapids, IA (3IL) and joined Hutchinson, KS (WA), where he struck out 224 batters in 196 innings. After being sold in 1908 to Kansas City, MO (AA), he was purchased that summer by the Boston Americans (AL) and signed for $2,600.

At Boston in 1911, he compiled a 23–17 mark, struck out a club-record 231 batters, and on July 29 pitched a no-hitter against the St. Louis Browns. In 1912 the 5 foot, 11 inch, 180 pound right-hander won 34 of 39 regular season decisions and three World Series contests to help Boston defeat the

New York Giants four games to three. During 1912 he tied the AL consecutive victory pitching record (16), struck out 258 batters, led the AL in shutouts (10), and compiled a sparkling 1.91 ERA. In early 1913, Wood fell on slippery grass while fielding a bunt and broke his pitching-hand thumb. Although pitching occasionally in 1913 and 1914 and leading the AL in 1915 with a 15–5 mark and 1.49 ERA, Wood hurled in almost continuous pain and never recovered his fastball. Pitching phenom Walter Johnson* in 1912 had commented, "No man alive can throw a baseball harder than Joe Wood."

Wood sat out the 1916 season, unable to raise his right arm. Ranked first in Red Sox career winning percentage (.674) and ERA (1.98), Wood in early 1917 was recommended by Tris Speaker* as an outfielder to Cleveland Indians (AL) manager Lee Fohl. On February 24, 1917, the Red Sox sold him to the Indians for $15,000. With Cleveland from 1917 through 1922, he batted .298 and proved that a forced retirement pitcher could stay in the major leagues as an outfielder. As a pitcher, he compiled 116 wins and 57 losses for a superb .671 record, 2.03 ERA, and 989 strikeouts in 1,434 1/3 innings. Wood completed 121 of 158 starts and hurled 28 career shutouts. A .283 lifetime batter, he compiled 553 hits, 118 doubles, 30 triples, 24 home runs, 267 runs scored, and 325 RBIs. He participated on world championship teams with the 1912 and 1915 Red Sox and 1920 Indians. From 1923 to 1942, Wood piloted Yale University to a composite 283–228–1 mark. In 1984 Yale awarded Wood an honorary Doctor of Humane Letters degree. Wood's main impact upon baseball was his courageous, successful decision to become an outfielder after an arm injury had ruined his brilliant pitching career.

BIBLIOGRAPHY: *Boston Red Sox, Media Guide, 1984*; Ellery H. Clark, Jr., *Boston Red Sox: 75th Anniversary History* (Hicksville, NY, 1975); Ellery H. Clark, Jr., [Red Sox Analytical Letter Collection], correspondence with Harry Hooper, "Duffy" Lewis, Joe Wood; Ellery H. Clark, Jr., *Red Sox Fever* (Hicksville, NY, 1979); Ellery H. Clark, Jr., *Red Sox Forever* (Hicksville, NY, 1977); Ellery H. Clark, Jr. Interviews, Everett Scott, September, 1924, Tris Speaker, June, 1926, June, 1927, Bill Carrigan, May, 1928, Buck O'Brien, July, 1950, Joe Wood, June, 1974, July, 1982, August, 1983, Larry Gardner, July, 1974, Robert K. Wood, July, 1983; Joseph L. Reichler, ed., *The Baseball Encyclopedia*, 6th ed. (New York, 1985), pp. 1,533, 2,128.

Ellery H. Clark, Jr.

WRIGHT, Forrest Glenn "Buckshot" (b. 6 February 1901, Archie, MO; d. 6 April 1984, Olathe, KS), player, manager, and coach, ranked among the finest shortstops of the 1920s and 1930s. He possessed great range and a rifle arm, earning him the nickname "Buckshot." Besides setting a still record 601 assists at shortstop in 1924, he executed an unassisted triple play on May 1, 1925. In 1925 he made both *The Sporting News* and *Baseball Magazine* All-Star teams. Wright's parents, Robert Lee and Alberta (Musick) Wright, operated a farm and hardware store. Wright wed Margaret Josephine Benn in 1929 and had one son and one daughter. Divorced in 1940, he later remarried. After completing high school in Archie, MO, in 1919, he attended the University of Missouri for two years and played football and basketball there. An outstanding sandlot baseball player, he left Missouri in the spring of 1921 and signed as a shortstop with the Kansas City Blues (AA). Wright played with Independence, MO (SWL), in 1921 and performed impressively in 1922 and 1923 at Kansas City.

The Pittsburgh Pirates (NL) purchased him before the 1924 season for $40,000. An instant star, the 5 foot, 11 inch, 170 pound, right-handed Wright hit .287 and drove in 111 runs in 1924 and batted .308 with 121 RBIs the following year. He and "Kiki" Cuyler* each slugged 18 home runs in 1925, which remained the Pittsburgh record for a decade. Wright, an important cog in the Pirates lineup for five years, starred on the 1925 and 1927 NL pennant-winning teams. After the 1928 season, Pittsburgh needed left-handed pitching help and peddled him to the Brooklyn Dodgers (NL) for Jesse Petty. In a handball game that winter, he crushed his right shoulder, damaging his throwing arm, and consequently missed much of the 1929 season. Shoulder surgery in August enabled him to throw again, but his arm no longer possessed "buckshot" velocity. Nevertheless, Wright enjoyed his best offensive year in 1930 by hitting .321, driving in 126 runs, and belting 22 homers. His home run output remained the NL record for shortstops until 1953. Wright captained the Dodgers for several years, but his play declined and Brooklyn released him in 1933. Wright, who played with Kansas City (AA) in 1934 and briefly with the Chicago White Sox (AL) in 1935, compiled an eleven-year career .294 batting average. In 1,119 games, he made 1,219 hits, 203 doubles, 76 triples, 93 home runs, 584 runs scored, 723 RBIs, and 38 stolen bases. Wright managed Wenatchee, WA (WeIL), from 1937 to 1939 and later coached for Hollywood (PCL).

BIBLIOGRAPHY: "Glenn Wright's Sensational Comeback," *Baseball Magazine* 46 (January, 1931), pp. 351–352; Harold "Speed" Johnson, *Who's Who in Major League Baseball* (Chicago, 1933); F. C. Lane, "The All-America Baseball Club of 1925," *Baseball Magazine* 36 (December, 1925), pp. 305–308, 331–334; Eugene Murdock, "Glenn Wright, Last of the 1925 All-Stars," *Baseball Research Journal* 8 (1979), pp. 109–113; Eugene Murdock interview, Glenn Wright, June 23, 1978, Fresno, CA; Joseph L. Reichler, ed., *The Baseball Encyclopedia*, 6th ed. (New York, 1985), p. 1,536; John J. Ward, "Has Pittsburgh Found a Worthy Successor to Hans Wagner?" *Baseball Magazine* 35 (November, 1925), pp. 538, 568.

Eugene C. Murdock

WRIGHT, George (b. 28 January 1847, New York, NY; d. 21 August 1937, Boston, MA), baseball and cricket player, golfer, and sporting goods entrepreneur, was the brother of **William Henry "Harry" Wright** (b. 10 January 1835, Sheffield, England; d. 3 October 1895, Atlantic City, NJ), baseball player and manager, cricket player, and bowler, who brought respectability to professional baseball and paved the way for the first pro league. In 1869

Harry transformed Cincinnati's Red Stockings into baseball's first openly pro team. With his younger brother George as their star player, the Red Stockings won 87 consecutive games over two seasons and showed that pro baseball could succeed.

Harry emigrated as an infant to New York with his parents, Samuel, a professional cricket player, and Ann (Tone) Wright. After attending New York schools to age 14, he worked for a jewelry manufacturer. In 1857 he joined Staten Island's St. George Cricket Club as a pro bowler and assistant to his father, who coached the club. Harry and George saw their first baseball game that same year at Elysian Fields, Hoboken, NJ, where cricket and baseball clubs played on adjacent grounds. Both brothers liked the new game. Harry joined the New York Knickerbockers as an outfielder, while George played with the junior club of New York's Gothams. At age 15 George was elevated to the Gotham seniors, where he played various positions before settling at shortstop. During this time, he was also named assistant pro of the St. George Cricket Club. He spent 1865 as a pro with the Philadelphia Cricket Club and also played baseball with Philadelphia's Olympics. He returned to the Gothams the following year, but in July joined another New York club, the Unions of Morrisania. In 1867 20-year-old George captained and played shortstop for the Washington, DC, Nationals, but returned to the Unions in 1868.

Harry, meanwhile, was hired by the Union Cricket Club of Cincinnati in August, 1865, as instructor and player. The following summer, he helped organize and captained the Cincinnati Base Ball Club (which became known as the Red Stockings after Harry added scarlet stockings to the uniform in 1867). When the Red Stockings in November, 1867, offered him a salary equal to that paid him by the Union Cricket Club, Harry quit cricket to concentrate on baseball. With Harry and several other pros on the club, the Red Stockings in 1868 won the championship of the Midwest.

In 1869 Harry brought George to Cincinnati, where he assembled for the Red Stockings baseball's first fully professional team. George's skillful and innovative fielding (he was the first shortstop to position himself out beyond the baseline) and astonishing hitting (49 home runs, .629 batting average) helped lead the team to an undefeated season in 57 games against challengers from Boston to San Francisco. Although the Red Stockings disbanded after a less successful 1870 season, their early success demolished long-held prejudices against pro baseball and led to the formation in 1871 of the National Association of Professional Base Ball Players.

George Wright was the first player signed by the Boston Red Stockings (NA), while Harry was hired soon after as team manager and center fielder. Boston finished third that year, but from 1872 through 1875 Harry piloted the club to four successive championships. In these five years, Boston compiled a 227–60 won-lost record for an impressive .791 winning percentage. George compiled a five-year .353 batting average, the NA's fourth highest.

In hits (494) and runs scored (399) he ranked second only to teammate Ross Barnes.*

When the NA folded after the 1875 season, the Wright brothers joined the Boston Red Stockings of the new NL. Harry concentrated on managing, but George played regularly for four more years. Although his batting average fell below .300, George continued to field skillfully (except for 1877, when he played second base and led the NL in errors), leading NL shortstops twice in putouts and assists and once in fielding average. Stung by the defection to the Chicago White Stockings of their "big four" (Barnes, Cal McVey,* Al Spalding,* and Deacon White*), Boston placed only fourth in its initial NL season. But manager Harry lured Hartford pitcher Tommy Bond,* who twice led the NL in wins and paced Boston to NL pennants in 1877 and 1878.

George managed and played shortstop for the Providence Grays (NL) in 1879. In his only year as a manager, he in 1879 led the Grays to the NL pennant by five games (59–25) over Harry's second place Red Stockings with a 59-25 mark. George founded a sporting goods firm when he first went to Boston in 1871. In 1879 Henry A. Ditson joined him to form Wright & Ditson. Although he played a few games for Harry's Red Stockings in 1880–1881 and half a season for Harry's Providence club in 1882, George concentrated on the sporting goods business. He supported the outlaw UA in its one year of existence (1884), investing in Boston's club and persuading the UA to use Wright & Ditson baseballs.

Harry managed Providence (NL) in 1882 and 1883 and the Philadelphia Phillies (NL) from 1884 through 1893. Although he won no championship after 1878, Harry guided Providence in 1882 and Philadelphia in 1887 to close second place finishes. In eighteen years of NL play, Harry's teams won 1,042 games, and lost 848 contests for a .551 winning percentage. Harry's integrity, sense of fair play, and gentle firmness in managing ballplayers were widely admired qualities. In 1890 a severe eye disorder left him nearly blind. His return to Philadelphia after several months' absence brought an outpouring of affection from players and fans. When he retired from managing after the 1893 season, the NL created for him the largely honorary post Chief of Umpires. He died of pneumonia in 1895. Married three times, Harry first wed Mary Fraser of New York, then Carrie Mulford of Cincinnati. His third wife, a sister of the first, survived him, as did seven of his eight children.

George lived to age 90, surviving his wife, Abbraria "Abbie" (Coleman) Wright. After retiring from baseball, he played cricket for many years and golf for over forty years. He introduced golf to Boston in 1890, importing equipment from England and setting up New England's first nine-hole golf course. He also figured prominently in introducing Canadian ice hockey to the United States and developing America's interest in tennis. (His two sons, Beals* (OS) and Irving, won national tennis championships). He died from myocarditis and pneumonia and was survived by his sons and two daughters.

George, through his sporting goods company and his promotion of sports other than baseball, probably had the greater impact on American sport in general, but Harry had a more profound influence on baseball. Although George surpassed Harry as a ballplayer, Harry gained acceptance for professional baseball and set the game on its present course. Harry's example of moral vigor in twenty-six years as manager helped establish the integrity and stability of the pro game. Both brothers are enshrined in the National Baseball Hall of Fame. George, elected in the year of his death, was among the earliest chosen. Harry, whose contribution to baseball was less visible, was elected belatedly in 1953.

BIBLIOGRAPHY: W. S. Barnes, Jr. "Grand Old Man of Baseball Set Notable Sports Record," Boston *Globe*, August 22, 1937; Boston *Globe*, August 23, 1937; Henry Chadwick Scrapbooks, Albert Spalding Collection, New York Public Library; Sam Crane, "George Wright," New York *Journal*, November 23, 1911; Sam Crane, "Harry Wright," New York *Journal*, March 27, 1915; *DAB* 20 (1936), p. 554; *DAB* 22, Supp. 6 (1956–1960), p. 737; "George Wright Recalls Triumphs of 'Red Stockings,' " New York *Sun*, November 14, 1915; Ernie Harwell, "Brilliant Career of Harry Wright Shows Greatness of Pro Ball's Dad," *TSN*, November 18, 1953; Harold Kaese, *The Boston Braves* (New York, 1948); Paul MacFarlane, ed., *TSN Daguerreotypes of Great Stars of Baseball* (St. Louis, 1981); Preston D. Orem, *Baseball 1845–1881* (Altadena, CA, 1961); Joseph L. Reichler, ed. *The Baseball Encyclopedia*, 6th ed. (New York, 1985), pp. 71, 655, 1,536; Harold Seymour, "Baseball's First Professional Manager," *Ohio Historical Quarterly* 64 (October, 1955), pp. 406–423; Harry Simmons, "100 Years Ago—Birth of First Baseball League," *TSN*, May 1, 1971; Albert G. Spalding, *America's National Game* (New York, 1911); George Wright file, National Baseball Hall of Fame Library, Cooperstown, NY; Harry Wright correspondence, Albert Spalding Collection, New York Public Library; Harry Wright file, National Baseball Hall of Fame Library, Cooperstown, NY.

Frederick Ivor-Campbell

WRIGHT, William Henry "Harry". See WRIGHT, George

WRIGLEY, Philip Knight "Phil" (b. 5 December 1894, Chicago, IL; d. 12 April 1977, Elkhart, WI), executive, was the longest active representative of a once flourishing but long anachronistic baseball practice, the family-owned team. He succeeded his father, William Wrigley, who founded a fortune on chewing gum and owned the Chicago Cubs (NL). Wrigley graduated from Phillips Academy, Andover, MA in 1914 and served at Great Lakes Naval Station in World War I. He married Helen Blanche Atwater on March 26, 1918, and had two daughters and one son, William, who succeeded Philip as Cubs owner on the latter's death. In 1981 William ended the sixty-year Wrigley ownership by selling the club to the Chicago Tribune Corporation.

Wrigley, who had varied interests and a complex personality, possessed remarkable mechanical aptitude. Innovative skill and business acumen enabled him to expand the chewing gum business into a worldwide enterprise. He served on or headed many boards, civic enterprises, and philanthropic organizations and served as NL vice-president from 1947 to 1956. In contrast to his gregarious father, Phil preferred privacy, a trait that many interpreted as indifference to baseball.

Wrigley's lengthy supervision of the Cubs spanned from his father's death in 1932 until his own death. His Cubs won NL pennants in 1932, 1935, 1938, and 1945, but captured no World Series. During his last thirty years, the Cubs produced no NL pennant winners. In later life, Wrigley lost the deep commitment to the team's fortunes that success in sports requires. His propensity for innovation proved fitful, diffuse, and impractical when applied to baseball. He inappropriately used the notorious college of coaches to replace the time-proved manager and employed a retired naval athletic director without baseball experience as superintendent. And yet, decades after all other teams had converted to night games, his Cubs continued to play only day baseball. The latter quaint practice and other fan-oriented gestures helped create an amazingly loyal fandom in the face of adversity, but did nothing to make the Cubs a contender. With the advent of corporation ownership, huge television contracts, and player free agency, the Wrigley family ownership could not cope with the many special interests comprising billion dollar baseball. Regrettably, Wrigley left a team that had not won in forty years.

BIBLIOGRAPHY: Chicago *Sun-Times*, April 12, 1977; Leo Durocher, *Nice Guys Finish Last* (New York, 1975); Jim Langford, *The Game Is Never Over* (South Bend, IN, 1980); *TSN*, February 4, 1932, January 12, 1956, February 12, 1966, July 4, 1981; Bill Veeck with Ed Linn, *Veeck-As In Wreck* (New York, 1962); *Who Was Who in America*, 7 (1977–1981), p. 630.

                                                        Lowell L. Blaisdell

WYNN, Early Jr., "Gus" (b. 6 January 1920, Hartford, AL), player, manager, coach, scout, and broadcaster, grew up in Hartford, AL, attended Geneva County High School, and excelled in football and baseball there. His father, Early, Sr., worked as an auto mechanic. At age 16, Wynn signed as a pitcher with the Washington Senators (AL). Although appearing in three games for the Senators in 1939, Wynn spent from 1937 to 1941 hurling for Sanford, FL (FSL), Charlotte, NC (Pil), and Springfield, MA (EL). The 6 foot, 190 pound right-hander returned to Washington late in 1941 and pitched the next seven seasons for the Senators, except for spending 1945 in the U.S. Army.

After enjoying only average success with Washington, Wynn was traded to the Cleveland Indians (AL) following the 1948 season. Cleveland coach Mel Harder* taught him the finer points of pitching. Wynn became one of the game's toughest competitors, as his brushback pitch was feared by every-one. He won at least 20 games four times for the Indians, leading Cleveland to the AL pennant in 1954. Following the 1957 season, Wynn was traded to Chicago (AL). At age 39, he won an AL-leading 22 games for the pennant-winning 1959 White Sox and captured the Cy Young Award. Wynn in 1962 triumphed in seven games, one victory short of the coveted 300 mark. Chicago released Wynn in November 1962, and Cleveland signed him in June 1963. On July 13, 1963, he became the fourteenth pitcher in major league history to win 300 or more games in recording his last victory.

Wynn, one of a few players whose major league career spanned four decades, established the AL record for most years pitched (23). He led the AL in strikeouts twice (1957–1958), innings pitched three times (1951, 1954, 1959), victories twice (1954, 1959), and ERA once (1950) and ranks high on the all-time major league lists in several departments. In 691 games (34th), he started 612 contests (10th), completed 290 (34th), won 300 (18th), and lost 244 (10th). Wynn hurled 4,564 innings (16th), allowing 2,037 runs (14th), 4,291 hits (21st), and 1,775 bases on balls (2nd). With a lifetime 3.54 ERA, he struck out 2,334 batters (25th), won at least 20 games five times, and pitched 49 shutouts (21st). In World Series competition, Wynn triumphed in one game and lost two. He pitched in seven All-Star games, earning the victory in 1958. As a batter, Wynn slugged 17 home runs to rank nineteenth on the all-time list for pitchers and made 365 career base hits for tenth best.

Wynn served as a pitching coach for Cleveland from 1964 to 1966 and for the Minnesota Twins (AL) from 1967 to 1969. He managed Evansville, IN (AA) in 1970, Wisconsin Rapids (ML) in 1971, and Orlando (FSL) in 1972 and broadcast for the Toronto Blue Jays (AL) in 1977 and later for the Chicago White Sox. Wynn also co-owns a Florida construction company and restau-rant-bowling alley. In 1939 he married Mabel Allman, who was killed two years later in an automobile accident. They had one son, Joe Early. Wynn married Lorraine Follin in 1944 and has a daughter, Shirley. In 1972 he was elected to the National Baseball Hall of Fame.

BIBLIOGRAPHY: Paul MacFarlane, ed., *TSN Daguerreotypes of Great Stars of Baseball* (St. Louis, 1971); Lowell Reidenbaugh, *Cooperstown: Where Baseball's Legends Live Forever* (St. Louis, 1983); *TSN*, July 25, 1981, pp. 30–31; *TSN Official Baseball Record Book, 1985* (St. Louis, 1985).

John L. Evers

Y

YASTRZEMSKI, Carl Michael "Yaz" (b. 22 August 1939, Southampton, NY), player, was one of the dominant AL hitters from 1961 until he retired in 1983. He followed Ted Williams* as left fielder for the Boston Red Sox and amassed one of the highest hit totals (3,419) in major league history. The son of Carl and Hattie Yastrzemski, he grew up in a farm environment and helped his father, a semi-professional baseball player and youth athletic coach. A devout Roman Catholic, Carl served as an altar boy and as a student body leader (twice class president) at Bridgehampton, NY, High School. An all-around athlete, he set a Long Island high school record in basketball by scoring 628 points in 1957. He caught, pitched, and played outfield in baseball and impressed major league scouts by batting .506 one season.

After his 1957 graduation from high school, Yastrzemski attended Notre Dame University for one year on a baseball scholarship. He tried out with the New York Yankees, but signed a contract with the Boston Red Sox for a $108,000 bonus. After batting .377 with the Boston farm club at Raleigh, NC (CrL), in 1959 and .339 for Minneapolis (AA) in 1960, he joined the Red Sox when Ted Williams retired. Under pressure from the inevitable comparison with Williams (Williams was a natural pull hitter, while Yastrzemski batted to all fields), he started slowly with a .266 batting average, only 11 home runs, and 80 RBIs his rookie year. During the next five seasons, he led the AL in hitting once (.321 in 1963) and averaged .299 at the plate with 84 home runs and 381 RBIs for a regular second division finisher.

After Dick Williams* was named manager in 1967, Yastrzemski enjoyed an extraordinary season and led the Red Sox to the AL pennant. In 1967 he won the AL Triple Crown with a .326 batting average, 121 RBIs, and 44 homers (tied with Harmon Killebrew*) and led the AL in base hits (189), total bases (360), and runs scored (112). In the final two decisive regular season games against the Minnesota Twins, he made seven hits in eight at bats. In the World Series against the St. Louis Cardinals, he batted .400 and fielded brilliantly in the Red Sox' seven-game losing effort. He was named the AL Most Valuable Player, *Sports Illustrated*'s Sportsman of 1967, and the Associated Press Male Athlete of the Year. He repeated as batting leader in 1968 with a .301 mark, the lowest such figure in major league history. After 1967, Yastrzemski achieved a career-high batting average of .329 in 1970 and 40 home runs in both 1969 and 1970. During his twenty-three major league seasons, Yastrzemski's production varied considerably, with six .300 or better seasons and nine seasons with .270 or less, home run totals ranging from 44 to 7, and RBI figures varying from 121 to 50.

In the Red Sox pennant year of 1975, he batted .455 in the team's stretch drive and compiled a .310 mark against the victorious Cincinnati Reds in the World Series. The seven-time Gold Glove winner played errorless outfield for 140 games in 1977. Defensively, he made 10,437 putouts, 775 assists, and 135 errors in twenty-three seasons. Yastrzemski batted .294 in 14 All-Star games (1963, 1967–1972, 1974–1977, 1979, 1982–1983). At 6 feet tall and 180 pounds, he ranked among the outstanding throwers and most feared designated hitters in modern AL history. Yastrzemski led the AL three times in batting average, doubles, runs scored, and slugging percentage, twice in hits and walks, and once in home runs and RBIs. His overall production put him among the all-time leaders in several categories. As of 1986, Yastrzemski ranked second in games played (3,308), third in at bats (11,988), fourth in walks (1,845), seventh in hits (3,419) and doubles (646), and ninth in RBIs (1,844). The Highland Beach, FL, resident married Carol Ann Casper in January, 1960, has two daughters, Mary and Ann and one son, Carl Michael, and graduated from Merrimack College in 1966. Mike is a designated hitter in the Chicago White Sox (AL) farm system.

BIBLIOGRAPHY: *CB* (1968); *The Lincoln Library of Sports Champions*, vol. 14 (Columbus, 1978); Joseph L. Reichler, ed., *The Baseball Encyclopedia*, 6th ed. (New York, 1985), p. 1,539.

Leonard Frey

YAWKEY, Thomas Austin "Tom" (b. Thomas Austin, 21 February 1903, Detroit, MI; d. 9 July 1976, Boston, MA), owner and sportsman, was the son of Thomas J. and Augusta L. Austin and the adopted son of uncle William H. Yawkey, who owned the Detroit Tigers (AL) and was a millionaire from timber and mining investments. Yawkey, who was educated in private academies and at Yale University, inherited a vast family fortune as a teenager and built its value to approximately $200 million at his death. His first marriage to Elsie Sparrow, in which they adopted a daughter, Julie, ended in divorce. In December 1944 he married Jean Hollander.

Yawkey purchased the struggling Boston Red Sox (AL) in 1933 and for the next forty-four years spent heavily to build winning teams. During the depressed 1930s, his wealth enabled the Red Sox to secure star players from poorer teams. Yawkey acquired Lefty Grove* and Jimmie Foxx* from the

Philadelphia A's (AL) and shortstop Joe Cronin for $250,000 from the Washington Senators (AL). In the 1950s, Yawkey tried to buy Cleveland pitcher Herb Score for $1 million. His large investments in the Boston farm system produced some exceptional players, including Ted Williams,* Carl Yastrzemski,* and Jim Rice.* Despite these efforts, Boston did not keep pace with the arch-rival New York Yankees. The Red Sox won only three pennants (1946, 1967, and 1975) and lost each World Series in seven games. The popular owner revived fan interest in the Red Sox and increased attendance at Fenway Park, which he rebuilt in 1934.

Critics claimed that Yawkey overpaid and pampered his players, diminishing his team's desire to win. A paternalistic employer, he paid high salaries even to mediocre players and exhibited personal interest in their welfare. His generosity also extended to numerous charities. Soon after World War II, Yawkey cooperated with attempts to resist racial integration of the big leagues. Boston did not add a black player to its roster until 1959, being the last major league team to integrate.

An avid sportsman and conservationist, he established the Tom Yawkey Wildlife Center in coastal South Carolina to protect migrating birds. He saved his deepest affection for the Red Sox, which he owned a record forty-four years and which remained one of the last individually owned major league franchises. Always protective of his privacy, Yawkey proved a strong voice in major league councils and served as AL vice-president from 1956 to 1973. He was elected to the National Baseball Hall of Fame in 1980.

BIBLIOGRAPHY: Al Hirshberg, "The Sad Case of the Red Sox," *SEP*, 232 (May 21, 1960), pp. 38–39, 87–88; James S. Kunen. "The Man with the Best Job in Boston," *Boston Magazine* (September, 1975), pp. 60–63, 97–102; Frederick G. Lieb, *The Boston Red Sox* (New York, 1947); *NYT*, July 10, 1976; *TSN*, July 24, 1976; Jules Tygiel, *Baseball's Great Experiment* (New York, 1983).

Joseph E. King

YOUNG, Denton True "Cy" (b. 29 March 1867, Gilmore, OH; d. 4 November 1955, Peoli, OH), player and manager, was the son of farmer McKenzie and Nancy Mot (Miller) Young. He grew up on a Gilmore, OH, farm, married neighboring farm daughter Robba Miller, and played third base in 1889 for the Tuscarawas County baseball team. In 1890 he began his professional career with Canton, OH (TSL), and compiled a 15–15 win-loss mark as a pitcher. The same season, he signed with the Cleveland Spiders (NL) for $300 and became the squad's only winning hurler with a 9–7 mark. Cleveland raised his salary to $1,400 for the 1891 season. Young, who worked vigorously on the farm when not playing baseball, credited much of his athletic success to his excellent physical condition. He demonstrated remarkable concentration on hitters and was admired as a gentleman by teammates, opponents, umpires, and fans.

With Cleveland from 1890 to 1898, Young compiled a 239–134 mark and hurled a September 18, 1897, no-hitter against Cincinnati. At St. Louis (NL) in 1899 and 1900, he finished with a 46–33 record and saw his annual salary increased to $2,400. After the 1900 season, Ban Johnson* persuaded him to jump to the Boston club of the new AL with a $3,000 salary. Young won 193 of 305 decisions for the Boston Americans from 1901 to 1908 and pitched a perfect game on May 5, 1904, against the Philadelphia Athletics. At age 41, he hurled a no-hitter on June 30, 1908, against the New York Highlanders. A member of championship Boston squads in 1903 and 1904, he won two of three decisions in the first modern World Series (1903) to help Boston defeat the Pittsburgh Pirates, five games to three. In early 1907, Young temporarily managed the Red Sox to a 3–4 mark.

During his final season with the Red Sox, the AL players and Boston fans honored Young in August, 1908, and presented him with a large silver cup, money, and other gifts. Young on September 15 gave his Boston teammates a complimentary dinner at Putnam's Hotel and had each course named for one of the athletes. Young already had won a record 19 games at the Huntington Avenue Grounds in 1901 and had pitched 45 2/3 consecutive scoreless innings in 1904. No other Red Sox pitcher has recorded more career total innings, games started, complete games, victories, strikeouts, and shutouts with the club. In February 1909 Cleveland (AL) purchased him for $12,500. After compiling a 29–29 record for Cleveland from 1909 to July, 1911, Young finished his career in 1911 with a 4–5 mark for the Boston Nationals (NL) and returned to his Ohio farm.

With five clubs spanning twenty-two years, Young holds the major league records for most wins (511), complete games (751), and innings pitched (7,356); ranks fourth in games appeared in (906) and in shutouts (77); and registered a strikeout-walk ratio of .697 percent to .303 percent. The right-hander started 815 games, struck out 2,799 batters, lost 313 games, and compiled a 2.63 ERA. Young led the NL in fewest walks per nine-inning game in 1890 and from 1893 to 1900. He achieved the same honor seven times, including the 1903–1907 seasons in the AL. Young reached the 20-game victory plateau sixteen seasons, 25 games twelve times, and 30 games five times (1892–1893, 1895, 1901–1902). Young paced his league in shutouts seven times; in most wins four times; in complete games three times; in games, win-loss percentage, ERA, innings, pitched, and strikeouts twice; and in losses, games started, and hits surrendered once.

Until his final years, Young remained strong and active on his Ohio farm. The much-honored hurler was elected to the National Baseball Hall of Fame in 1937. Since his death, the major leagues have given the Cy Young Award annually to the major league's top hurler. In 1982 Boston fans voted him to the first Red Sox "dream team" as right-handed pitcher. The 6 foot, 2 inch, 210 pound Young relished facing Rube Waddell* and other outstanding contemporary pitchers and used four effective pitches. Abbott Thayer's painting at Cooperstown shows him in his 1908 red stocking blouse, delivering an overhand fastball. The first Boston and AL pitching folk hero, Young became the city's best-liked player since King Kelly,* helped popularize the new AL, and became a gracious legend.

BIBLIOGRAPHY: *Boston Red Sox Media Guide, 1984*; Bob Broeg, "Durable Ace Cy Young—A 511 Game Winner," *TSN*, April 17, 1971; Ellery H. Clark, Jr., *Boston Red Sox: 75th Anniversary* (Hicksville, NY, 1975); Ellery H. Clark, Jr., correspondence with Norwood Gibson, Fred Parent, Cy Young, (Red Sox Analytical Letter Collection, Ellery H. Clark, Jr., Papers, Annapolis, MD; Ellery H. Clark, Jr. interviews, Lou Criger, June, 1928, Cy Young, July 1928, October, 1954, George La Chance, June, 1929, Kip Selbach, January, 1955, Norwood Gibson, June, 1955, Fred Parent, July, 1965; Ellery H. Clark, Jr., *Red Sox Fever* (Hicksville, NY, 1979); Ellery H. Clark, Jr., *Red Sox Forever* (Hicksville, NY, 1977); Joseph L. Reichler, ed., *The Baseball Encyclopedia*, 6th ed. (New York, 1985), p. 2,135.

Ellery H. Clark, Jr.

YOUNG, Nicholas Emanuel (b. 12 September 1840, Amsterdam, NY; d. 31 October 1916, Washington, DC), cricket player and baseball executive, was born in Johnson Hall, the colonial estate of Sir William Johnson. Young was the son of Almarian T. Young, a descendant of Dutch settlers and wealthy mill owner, and Mary (Miller) Young. After serving in the Union Army during the Civil War, Young became a clerk and later auditor in the U.S. Treasury Department. An outstanding cricket player in his youth, he performed for the Olympic Club of Washington and acted as secretary and business manager of the professional National Club. Young married Mary E. Cross of Washington in 1872 and had four children, Robert H., Ford E., Hulbert, and Lee. In March, 1871, he organized a meeting of professional baseball clubs. This group formed the first professional league, the National Association of Professional Base Ball Players, and selected Young as the league secretary. When the NL was formed in 1876, Young became its secretary-treasurer.

In 1885 Young succeeded his friend and Washington colleague A. G. Mills as NL president. Young's selection resulted from a split between club owners and the NL president, who took a hard line in treating the rival UA. The owners, anxious for accommodation, chose Young because he offered no objection to their desires. Young seldom attempted to influence events during his tumultuous years as NL president. Baseball historian David Quentin Voigt characterized Young's tenure thus: "Having neither the authority nor the *charisma* to be a policy-shaper, Young was the perfect figurehead." Since his job depended on the owners, Young tried to avoid disputes. When the NL owners split into two factions after the 1901 season, reformers attempted to replace Young with Albert G. Spalding.* The owners eventually reached a compromise requiring both Spalding and Young to withdraw their candidacies. Young dutifully stepped down and returned to his government job.

The well-liked Young, affectionately called "Uncle Nick" in his last years as NL president, served baseball for over thirty years but provided ineffective leadership.

BIBLIOGRAPHY: Lee Allen, *The National League Story* (New York, 1961); Arthur Bartlett, *Baseball and Mr. Spalding* (New York, 1951); Francis C. Richter, "Recalled by a Missive from 'Uncle Nick' Young," *Sporting Life* (February 31, 1906); Harold Seymour, *Baseball: The Early Years* (New York, 1960); David Quentin Voigt, *American Baseball: From Gentleman's Sport to the Commissioner System* (Norman, OK, 1966).

William E. Akin

YOUNGS, Ross Middlebrook "Pep" (b. 10 April 1897, Shiner, TX; d. 22 October 1927, San Antonio, TX), player, grew up in the semi-arid plains. At West Texas Military Academy, he starred in football and track and played baseball. Youngs sparkled in the infield for Sherman, TX (WA), in 1916, leading the WA in batting average (.362), hits (195), runs scored (103), and at bats (539). The New York Giants (NL) purchased him after that season. He played at Rochester, NY (IL), for most of the 1917 campaign learning the outfield, and batted .346 when brought up to the parent Giants at season's end. During eight full years with New York, Youngs invariably ranked among NL leaders in several offensive categories and led the NL in runs scored (121) in 1923 and in doubles (31) in 1919. The confident, husky, 5 foot, 8 inch, 162 pound right-hander batted .322 lifetime and became the first player in World Series history to make two hits in a single inning, slashing a double and triple against the New York Yankees in the seventh inning of the third game in 1921. In four consecutive fall classics (1921–1924), Youngs appeared in all 26 games and batted .286. A superb throwing arm and above average speed helped offset his often overly enthusiastic style of defensive play. Twice Youngs led the NL in both assists and errors.

Youngs' batting average fell below .300 for the first time in 1925, when the Giants slipped to second place following four consecutive pennants. Called by Giants manager John McGraw* "my greatest outfielder," Youngs tragically was struck down in his prime by Bright's disease. After Youngs' ailment was discovered during spring training in 1926, the Giants hired a full-time nurse to travel with him. Using every physical and emotional resource, Youngs managed a .306 batting average in 95 games and also helped teach 17-year-old Mel Ott* the subtleties of covering the outfield. In 1927 Youngs was bedridden the entire season and saw the Giants fall to fifth place in the standings before succumbing. McGraw hung a picture of Youngs alongside a photograph of Christy Mathewson* behind his desk. In 1,211 career games, Youngs compiled 1,491 hits, 236 doubles, 93 triples, 812 runs, 592 RBIs, 153 stolen bases, and a .441 slugging percentage. As baseball still trembled under the suspicions aired in the Chicago Black Sox scandal, claims were made in 1924 that Youngs was taking bribes from New York gambling concerns. His quick, direct denial of these charges, along with his well-respected abilities and overall character, led to his immediate exoneration. In 1972 he was inducted into the National Baseball Hall of Fame.

BIBLIOGRAPHY: Gene Karst and Martin J. Jones, Jr., *Who's Who in Professional Baseball* (New Rochelle, NY, 1973); Paul MacFarlane, ed., *TSN Daguerreotypes of Great Stars of Baseball* (St. Louis, 1981); *NYT*, October 23, 1927; Joseph L. Reichler, ed., *The Baseball Encyclopedia*, 6th ed. (New York, 1982), p. 1,544; Lowell Reidenbaugh, *Cooperstown: Where Baseball's Legends Live Forever* (St. Louis, 1983); *TSN*, October 27, 1927.

Alan R. Asnen

YOUNT, Robin R. (b. 16 September 1955, Danville, IL), player, is the son of engineer Philip and Marion Yount and moved when he was a year old to Woodland Hills, CA, where his father became an aerospace engineer with Rocketdyne. His older brother Larry pitched briefly with the Houston Astros (NL) in 1971. Yount graduated from Taft High School in Woodlawn, CA, and played football and baseball there. After being named City Baseball Player of the Year in 1973, he was selected by the Milwaukee Brewers (AL) in the first round of the free agent draft. The 6 foot, 170 pound, right-handed Yount played one year (1973) in the minor leagues with Newark, NY, where he was named All-Star shortstop in the NYPL. Upon joining the Brewers in 1974 at age 18, he became the youngest player in the major leagues and one of the youngest regulars in baseball history. The Brewers employed Yount as starting shortstop from 1974 to 1984, but an injured right shoulder forced him to play the outfield in 1985. Yount underwent surgery in September 1985 and made a fine comeback in 1986.

In 1982 he was named Major League Player of the Year and AL Most Valuable Player after leading the Brewers to the AL championship. Besides batting .331, he paced the AL in hits (210), doubles (46), and slugging percentage (.578). Yount also scored 129 runs, drove in 114 tallies, and hit 29 home runs. He batted .414 in the World Series and made 12 hits, 1 home run, and 6 RBIs, as the Brewers lost in seven games to the St. Louis Cardinals. He established a World Series record with two four-hit games in that series. Yount made the AL All-Star team that year, as well as in 1980 and 1983.

Consistency has characterized Yount's major league career. In his first thirteen major league seasons, he batted over .270 nine times, attained at least 150 hits eight times, and averaged over 80 runs scored and 63 RBIs per season. Yount led AL batters in doubles (49) in 1980 and in triples (10) in 1983 and paced AL shortstops in putouts (290), total chances (831), and double plays (104) in 1976. Yount also led AL shortstops in fielding average (.985) in 1981 and in assists (489) in 1982. He was named shortstop on *The Sporting News* AL All-Star teams in 1978, 1980, and 1982, named to *The*

Sporting News Silver Slugger team as the best hitting AL shortstop in 1980 and 1982, and chosen on the AL All-Star fielding team in 1982.

Yount signed a lucrative multi-year contract in 1978 after holding out and threatening to join the professional golf tour. He married high school sweetheart Michele Edelstein after the 1977 season and has three children, including daughters Melissa and Amy. In 1,811 games through the end of the 1986 season, he has made 2,019 hits, 380 doubles, 82 triples, 153 home runs, 1,043 runs scored, 827 RBIs, 167 stolen bases, and a .287 batting average.

BIBLIOGRAPHY: *Milwaukee Brewers Media Guide, 1975–1985*; Joseph L. Reichler, ed., *The Baseball Encyclopedia*, 6th ed. (New York, 1985), p. 1,544; *TSN Official Baseball Record Book, 1985* (St. Louis, 1985); *TSN Official Baseball Register, 1985* (St. Louis, 1985).

                                                                    Jack R. Stanton

Baseball Entries by Main Category

The following is an alphabetical list of the baseball entries profiled in the book by the main category for which they were selected. The four main categories are player, manager, umpire, and executive. Some baseball figures excelled in more than one category, but are listed below in the category which the editor deems most appropriate. Players whose names are followed by a dagger were also managers. Managers whose names are followed by a dagger were also major league players, and those followed by a double dagger were also Negro league players. Umpires and executives followed by daggers were also major league players, and those followed by a double dagger were also major league managers.

Players (433)

Henry Aaron
Charles Adams
Joseph Adcock†
Grover Cleveland Alexander
Newton Allen†
Richard Allen
Adrian Anson†
Luis Aparicio, Jr.†
Lucius Appling†
Don Richie Ashburn
Earl Averill
John Franklin Baker
David Bancroft†
Ernest Banks
Roscoe Barnes
Richard Bartell†
Clarence Beaumont
Jacob Beckley†
John Beckwith†
David Bell
James Bell†
Johnny Bench
Charles Bender†
Walter Berger†
Lawrence Berra†
Vida Blue
Thomas Bond†
Bobby Bonds
James Bottomley†
Louis Boudreau†
Lawrence Bowa†
Kenton Boyer†
Roger Bresnahan†
George Brett
Thomas Bridges
Louis Brock
Dennis Brouthers
Mordecai Brown†
Willard Brown
Louis Browning
William Buckner
Charles Buffinton†
James Bunning†
Selva Lewis Burdette

Jesse Burkett†

George H. Burns†

George J. Burns†

Roy Campanella

Rodney Carew

Max Carey†

Steven Carlton

Gary Carter

Robert Caruthers

Norman Cash

Philip Cavaretta†

Orlando Cepeda

Frank Chance†

Spurgeon Chandler

William Benjamin Chapman†

Oscar Charleston†

Harold Chase†

John Chesbro

Clarence Childs

Edward Cicotte

Fred Clarke†

John Clarkson

Roberto Clemente

Tyrus Cobb†

Gordon Cochrane†

Rocco Colavito

Edward Collins†

James Collins†

Earle Combs

Roger Connor†

John Coombs†

Arley Wilbur Cooper†

Cecil Cooper

Lawrence Corcoran

Thomas Corcoran

Stanley Coveleski

Roger Cramer

Clifford Cravath†

Samuel Crawford

James Creighton

Joseph Cronin†

Lafayette Cross†

John Crutchfield

William Cummings

Hazen Cuyler†

William Dahlen†

Raymond Dandridge†

Alvin Dark†

Jacob Daubert†

George Dauss

George Davis†

Herman Davis

Willie Davis

Andre Dawson

Leon Day

Jay Dean

Edward Delahanty

Elwood De Moss†

Paul Derringer

William Dickey†

Martin Dihigo†

Joseph DiMaggio

Herbert Dixon

Lawrence Doby†

Robert Doerr

Michael Donlin†

Patrick Donovan†

William Donovan†

Lawrence Doyle

Donald Drysdale

Hugh Duffy†

James Dykes†

Robert Elliott†

Delmer Ennis

John Evers†

William Ewing†

Urban Faber

ElRoy Face

Robert Feller

Richard Ferrell†

Wesley Ferrell†

Roland Fingers

Carlton Fisk

Frederick Fitzsimmons†

Elmer Flick

Curtis Flood

Edward Ford

Andrew Foster†

George Foster

Willie Foster†

John Fournier†

David Foutz†

John Fowler†

Nelson Fox

James Foxx†

Lawrence French

Frank Frisch†
James Galvin†
William Lawrence Gardner
Steve Garvey
Henry Louis Gehrig
Charles Gehringer
Joshua Gibson
Robert Gibson
John Glasscock†
Vernon Gomez†
Leon Goslin†
Richard Gossage
Frank Grant
Henry Greenberg
Michael Griffin
Burleigh Grimes†
Charles Grimm†
Henry Groh†
Robert Grove
Ronald Guidry
Stanley Hack†
Charles Hafey
Jesse Haines
William Hamilton†
Melvin Harder†
E. Victor Harris†
Charles Hartnett†
Harry Heilmann
Rickey Henderson
Floyd Herman
William Herman†
Keith Hernandez
Michael Higgins†
J. Preston Hill†
Paul Hines
Gilbert Hodges†
Thomas Holmes†
Harry Hooper†
Rogers Hornsby†
Willie Horton
Frank Howard†
William Hoy
Waite Hoyt
Carl Hubbell
Samuel Hughes
James Hunter
Monford Irvin
Joseph Jackson

Reginald Jackson
Travis Jackson†
William Jacobson
Charles Jamieson
Hugh Jennings†
Samuel Jethroe
Thomas John
Grant Johnson†
Robert Johnson†
Walter Johnson†
William Johnson
Samuel Jones
Adrian Joss
Joseph Judge
James Kaat
Albert Kaline
Timothy Keefe
William Keeler
George Kell
Joseph Kelley†
George Kelly
Michael Kelly†
Harmon Killebrew
Ralph Kiner
Charles King
Charles Klein
John Kling†
Theodore Kluszewski
Edward Konetchy†
Jerome Koosman
Sanford Koufax
Harvey Kuenn†
Joseph Kuhel†
Napoleon Lajoie†
William Lange
Anthony Lazzeri†
Thomas Leach†
Samuel Leever†
Robert Lemon†
Emil Leonard
Walter Leonard
Frederick Lindstrom†
John Lloyd†
Michael Lolich
Ernest Lombardi
Herman Long†
Richard Lundy†
Albert Lyle

Frederic Lynn
James Lyons†
Theodore Lyons†
Thomas McCarthy†
Frank McCormick†
James McCormick†
Willie McCovey
Lyndall McDaniel
Joseph McGinnity†
John McInnis†
Edward McKean†
John J. McMahon
David McNally
John McPhee†
Harold McRae
Calvin McVey†
Bill Madlock, Jr.
Sherwood Magee
Mickey Mantle
Henry Manush†
Walter Maranville†
Oliver Marcelle
Juan Marichal
Martin Marion†
Roger Maris
Richard Marquard†
Johnny Martin†
Edwin Mathews, Jr.†
Robert Mathews
Christopher Mathewson†
Lee May
Carl Mays
Willie Mays
William Mazeroski
Joseph Medwick†
Emil Meusel
Robert Meusel
Levi Meyerle
Jesse Clyde Milan†
Edmund Miller
John Mize
Joseph Morgan
Wallace Moses
Anthony Mullane
George Mullin
Dale Murphy
Eddie Murray
Stanley Musial

Charles Myer
Arthur Nehf
Donald Newcombe
Harold Newhouser
Charles Nichols†
Joseph Niekro
Philip Niekro
Albert Oliver
James O'Rourke†
David Orr†
Albert Orth
Amos Otis
Melvin Ott†
Leroy Paige
James Palmer
Milton Pappas
David Parker
Richard Pearce†
Herbert Pennock
Gaylord Perry
James Perry
John Pesky†
Charles Phillippe
Walter William Pierce
Vada Pinson
Edward Plank
Spottswood Poles
John Joseph Powell
John Wesley Powell
Derrill Pratt†
John Quinn
Daniel Quisenberry
Charles Radbourne
Richard Redding†
Harold Reese
Edward Reulbach
Allie Reynolds
Edgar Rice
James Rice
Eppa Rixey
Philip Rizzuto
Robin Roberts
Brooks Robinson
Frank Robinson†
Jack Robinson
Wilbur Rogan†
Edwin Rommel†
Charles Root†

Peter Rose†
Edd Roush
Charles Ruffing†
James Runnels†
Amos Rusie
George Herman Ruth
James Ryan†
Lynn Nolan Ryan
Ronald Santo
Louis Santop†
Raymond Schalk†
Michael Schmidt
Albert Schoendienst†
George Thomas Seaver
Joseph Sewell
James Seymour
James Robert Shawkey†
Samuel James Sheckard†
Aloysius Simmons
Ted Simmons
Kenneth Singleton
George Sisler†
Enos Slaughter†
Carl Reginald Smith
Charles Smith
Hilton Smith
Edwin Snider†
Lewis Sockalexis†
Warren Spahn†
Tristram Speaker†
Wilver Stargell
Joseph Start
Daniel Staub
Norman Stearns
Vernon Stephens
Jackson Riggs Stephenson†
John Stivetts
Harry Stovey
Howard Bruce Sutter
George Suttles†
Donald Sutton
Jesse Tannehill†
Benjamin Taylor†
Fred Tenney†
William Terry†
Clinton Thomas
Samuel Thompson
Michael Tiernan

Joseph Tinker†
John Tobin
Joseph Torre†
Harold Traynor†
Harold Trosky
George Uhle
Arthur Vance
George Van Haltren
Joseph Vaughan
James Vaughn
Robert Veach
James Vernon†
Joseph Vosmik†
George Waddell
John Wagner†
Fred Walker†
Gerald Walker
Moses Walker
Roderick Wallace†
Edward Walsh†
William Walters†
Lloyd Waner
Paul Waner†
John Ward†
Lonnie Warneke
Robert Watson
Michael Welch
Willie Wells†
August Weyhing†
Zachariah Wheat
Guy White
James White†
William White†
Earl Whitehill
James Hoyt Wilhelm
Billy Williams
Fred Williams
Joe Williams†
Kenneth Williams
Theodore Williams†
Victor Willis
Maurice Wills†
Ernest Judson Wilson†
Lewis Wilson
Willie Wilson
David Winfield
Joe Wood
Forrest Glenn Wright†

Early Wynn†
Carl Yastrzemski
Denton Young†
Ross Youngs
Robin Yount

Managers (22)

Walter Alston†
George Anderson†
Leo Durocher†
Edward Hanlon†
Stanley Harris†
Ralph Houk†
Miller Huggins†
Alfonso Lopez†
Joseph McCarthy
John McGraw†
Connie Mack†
William McKechnie†
Raleigh Mackey‡
Alfred Martin†
Cumberland Posey‡
Wilbert Robinson†
Frank Selee
William Southworth†
Charles Stengel†
Charles I. Taylor
Earl Weaver
Richard Williams†

Umpires (6)

Emmett Ashford
Albert Barlick
John Conlan†
Thomas Connolly
William Evans
William Klem

Executives (61)

Ernest Barnard
Edward Barrow‡
Sam Breadon
Walter Briggs
Robert Brown†
Morgan Bulkeley
August Busch, Jr.
Robert Carpenter, Jr.
Alexander Cartwright

Henry Chadwick
Albert Chandler
Charles Comiskey† ‡
Powel Crosley, Jr.
Barney Dreyfuss
Charles Ebbets
William Eckert
Charles Feeney
Charles Finley
Andrew Freedman
Ford Frick
John W. and Daniel Galbreath
Warren Giles
William A. Greenlee
Clark and Calvin Griffith†‡
William Harridge
John Heydler
William Hulbert
Byron Johnson
Bowie Kuhn
Kenesaw Mountain Landis
Thomas Lynch
John McHale†
Leland MacPhail, Sr.
Leland MacPhail, Jr.
Marvin Miller
Frank Navin
Walter O'Malley
Gabriel Paul
Harry Pulliam
Alfred Reach† ‡
Wesley Branch Rickey† ‡
Jacob Ruppert
Benjamin Shibe
Charles Somers
Albert Spalding† ‡
Charles and Horace Stoneham
John Tener†
Daniel Topping
George Trautman
William Veeck, Jr.
Christian Von der Ahe‡
George Weiss
James L. Wilkinson
George Wright† ‡
Harry Wright† ‡
Philip Wrigley
Thomas Yawkey
Nicholas Young‡

Baseball Players By Main Position Played

The following is a list of the major league players profiled in the book by the main position they played. Outfielders are listed as a group rather than as left, center, and right fielders. Players who performed at more than one position are listed at the position they played most frequently in the major leagues.

First Baseman (53)

Joseph Adcock
Richard Allen
Adrian Anson
Jacob Beckley
James Bottomley
Dennis Brouthers
William Buckner
George H. Burns
Rodney Carew
Norman Cash
Philip Cavaretta
Orlando Cepeda
Frank Chance
Harold Chase
Charles Comiskey
Roger Connor
Cecil Cooper
Jacob Daubert
John Fournier
James Foxx
Steve Garvey
Henry Louis Gehrig
Henry Greenberg
Charles Grimm
Keith Hernandez
Gilbert Hodges

Joseph Judge
George Kelly
Harmon Killebrew
Theodore Kluszewski
Edward Konetchy
Joseph Kuhel
Walter Leonard
Frank McCormick
Willie McCovey
John McHale
John McInnis
Calvin McVey
Lee May
John Mize
Eddie Murray
David Orr
John Wesley Powell
James Runnels
George Sisler
Joseph Start
George Suttles
Benjamin Taylor
Fred Tenney
William Terry
Harold Trosky
James Vernon
Robert Watson

Second Baseman (29)

Newton Allen
George Anderson
Roscoe Barnes
Clarence Childs
Edward Collins
Elwood De Moss
Robert Doerr
Lawrence Doyle
John Evers
John Fowler
Nelson Fox
Frank Frisch
Charles Gehringer
Frank Grant
Stanley Harris
William Herman
Rogers Hornsby
Miller Huggins
Samuel Hughes
Napoleon Lajoie
Anthony Lazzeri
John McPhee
Alfred Martin
William Mazeroski
Joseph Morgan
Charles Myer
Alfred Reach
Jack Robinson
Albert Schoendienst

Third Baseman (29)

John Franklin Baker
David Bell
Kenton Boyer
George Brett
Robert Brown
James Collins
Lafayette Cross
Raymond Dandridge
James Dykes
Robert Elliott
William Lawrence Gardner
Henry Groh
Stanley Hack
Michael Higgins
William Johnson

George Kell
Frederick Lindstrom
John McGraw
William McKechnie
Bill Madlock, Jr.
Oliver Marcelle
Edwin Mathews, Jr.
Levi Meyerle
Brooks Robinson
Ronald Santo
Michael Schmidt
Harold Traynor
James White
Ernest Judson Wilson

Shortstops (40)

Luis Aparicio, Jr.
Lucius Appling
David Bancroft
Ernest Banks
Richard Bartell
John Beckwith
Louis Boudreau
Lawrence Bowa
Thomas Corcoran
Joseph Cronin
William Dahlen
Alvin Dark
George Davis
Leo Durocher
John Glasscock
Travis Jackson
Hugh Jennings
Grant Johnson
Harvey Kuenn
John Lloyd
Herman Long
Richard Lundy
Edward McKean
Walter Maranville
Martin Marion
Richard Pearce
Harold Reese
Philip Rizzuto
Joseph Sewell
Vernon Stephens
Joseph Tinker
Joseph Vaughan

John Wagner
Roderick Wallace
John Ward
Willie Wells
Maurice Wills
Forrest Glenn Wright
George Wright
Robin Yount

Outfielders (145)

Henry Aaron
Don Richie Ashburn
Earl Averill
Clarence Beaumont
James Bell
Walter Berger
Bobby Bonds
Louis Brock
Willard Brown
Louis Browning
Jesse Burkett
George J. Burns
Max Carey
William Benjamin Chapman
Oscar Charleston
Fred Clarke
Roberto Clemente
Tyrus Cobb
Rocco Colavito
Earle Combs
John Conlan
Roger Cramer
Clifford Cravath
Samuel Crawford
John Crutchfield
Hazen Cuyler
Herman Davis
Willie Davis
Andre Dawson
Edward Delahanty
Joseph DiMaggio
Herbert Dixon
Lawrence Doby
Michael Donlin
Patrick Donovan
Hugh Duffy
Delmer Ennis
Elmer Flick

Curtis Flood
George Foster
Leon Goslin
Michael Griffin
Charles Hafey
William Hamilton
Edward Hanlon
E. Victor Harris
Harry Heilmann
Rickey Henderson
Floyd Herman
J. Preston Hill
Paul Hines
Thomas Holmes
Harry Hooper
Willie Horton
Frank Howard
William Hoy
Monford Irvin
Joseph Jackson
Reginald Jackson
William Jacobson
Charles Jamieson
Samuel Jethroe
Robert Johnson
Albert Kaline
William Keeler
Joseph Kelley
Michael Kelly
Ralph Kiner
Charles Klein
William Lange
Thomas Leach
Fredric Lynn
James Lyons
Thomas McCarthy
Harold McRae
Sherwood Magee
Mickey Mantle
Henry Manush
Roger Maris
Johnny Martin
Willie Mays
Joseph Medwick
Emil Meusel
Robert Meusel
Jesse Clyde Milan
Edmund Miller

Wallace Moses
Dale Murphy
Stanley Musial
Albert Oliver
James O'Rourke
Amos Otis
Melvin Ott
David Parker
Vada Pinson
Spottswood Poles
Cumberland Posey
Derrill Pratt
Edgar Rice
James Rice
Frank Robinson
Peter Rose
Edd Roush
George Herman Ruth
James Ryan
James Seymour
Samuel James Sheckard
Aloysius Simmons
Kenneth Singleton
Enos Slaughter
Carl Reginald Smith
Charles Smith
Edwin Snider
Lewis Sockalexis
William Southworth
Tristram Speaker
Wilver Stargell
Daniel Staub
Norman Stearns
Charles Stengel
Jackson Riggs Stephenson
Harry Stovey
Clinton Thomas
Samuel Thompson
Michael Tiernan
John Tobin
George Van Haltren
Robert Veach
Joseph Vosmik
Fred Walker
Gerald Walker
Lloyd Waner
Paul Waner
Zachariah Wheat

Billy Williams
Fred Williams
Kenneth Williams
Richard Williams
Theodore Williams
Lewis Wilson
Willie Wilson
David Winfield
Harry Wright
Carl Yastrzemski
Ross Youngs

Catchers (25)

Johnny Bench
Lawrence Berra
Roger Bresnahan
Roy Campanella
Gary Carter
Gordon Cochrane
William Dickey
William Ewing
Richard Ferrell
Carlton Fisk
Joshua Gibson
Charles Hartnett
Ralph Houk
John Kling
Ernest Lombardi
Alfonso Lopez
Connie Mack
Raleigh Mackey
Wesley Branch Rickey
Wilbert Robinson
Louis Santop
Raymond Schalk
Ted Simmons
Joseph Torre
Moses Walker

Pitchers (139)

Charles Adams
Grover Cleveland Alexander
Charles Bender
Vida Blue
Thomas Bond
Thomas Bridges
Mordecai Brown
Charles Buffinton

James Bunning
Selva Lewis Burdette
Steven Carlton
Robert Caruthers
Spurgeon Chandler
John Chesbro
Edward Cicotte
John Clarkson
John Coombs
Arley Wilbur Cooper
Lawrence Corcoran
Stanley Coveleski
James Creighton
William Cummings
George Dauss
Leon Day
Jay Dean
Paul Derringer
Martin Dihigo
William Donovan
Donald Drysdale
Urban Faber
ElRoy Face
Robert Feller
Wesley Ferrell
Roland Fingers
Frederick Fitzsimmons
Edward Ford
Andrew Foster
Willie Foster
David Foutz
Lawrence French
James Galvin
Robert Gibson
Vernon Gomez
Richard Gossage
Clark Griffith
Burleigh Grimes
Robert Grove
Ronald Guidry
Jesse Haines
Melvin Harder
Waite Hoyt
Carl Hubbell
James Hunter
Thomas John
Walter Johnson
Samuel Jones

Adrian Joss
James Kaat
Timothy Keefe
Charles King
Jerry Koosman
Sanford Koufax
Samuel Leever
Robert Lemon
Emil Leonard
Michael Lolich
Albert Lyle
Theodore Lyons
James McCormick
Lyndall McDaniel
Joseph McGinnity
John J. McMahon
David McNally
Juan Marichal
Richard Marquard
Robert Mathews
Christopher Mathewson
Carl Mays
Anthony Mullane
George Mullin
Arthur Nehf
Donald Newcombe
Harold Newhouser
Charles Nichols
Joseph Niekro
Philip Niekro
Albert Orth
Leroy Paige
James Palmer
Milton Pappas
Herbert Pennock
Gaylord Perry
James Perry
Charles Phillippe
Walter William Pierce
Edward Plank
John Joseph Powell
John Quinn
Daniel Quisenberry
Charles Radbourne
Richard Redding
Edward Reulbach
Allie Reynolds
Eppa Rixey

Robin Roberts
Wilbur Rogan
Edwin Rommel
Charles Root
Charles Ruffing
Amos Rusie
Lynn Nolan Ryan
George Thomas Seaver
James Robert Shawkey
Hilton Smith
Warren Spahn
Albert Spalding
John Stivetts
Howard Bruce Sutter
Donald Sutton
Jesse Tannehill
John Tener
George Uhle

Arthur Vance
James Vaughn
George Waddell
Edward Walsh
William Walters
Lonnie Warneke
Michael Welch
August Weyhing
Guy White
William White
Earl Whitehill
James Hoyt Wilhelm
Joe Williams
Victor Willis
Joe Wood
Early Wynn
Denton Young

APPENDIX 3

Baseball Entries by Place of Birth

The following is a list of nearly all of the baseball entries profiled in the book by state, territory, or foreign nation of birth.

United States

Alabama (16)

Henry Aaron
Charles Finley
George Foster
Monford Irvin
Willie McCovey
Henry Manush
Lee May
Willie Mays
Amos Otis
Leroy Paige
Joseph Sewell
Jackson Riggs Stephenson
Donald Sutton
Billy Williams
Willie Wilson
Early Wynn

Arkansas (8)

Louis Brock
Willie Davis
Jay Dean
Travis Jackson
George Kell
Brooks Robinson
Joseph Vaughan
Lonnie Warneke

California (35)

Emmett Ashford
Bobby Bonds
Lawrence Bowa
William Buckner
Gary Carter
Frank Chance
Harold Chase
Clifford Cravath
Joseph Cronin
Joseph DiMaggio
Robert Doerr
Donald Drysdale
Robert Elliott
Lawrence French
Vernon Gomez
Stanley Hack
Charles Hafey
Harry Heilmann
Keith Hernandez
Harry Hooper
George Kelly
William Lange
Anthony Lazzeri
Robert Lemon
Ernest Lombardi
Alfred Martin
Emil Meusel
Robert Meusel

Eddie Murray
Daniel Quisenberry
George Thomas Seaver
Edwin Snider
Robert Watson
Theodore Williams
Robin Yount

Colorado (1)

Richard Gossage

Connecticut (8)

Morgan Bulkeley
Roger Connor
Thomas Corcoran
Edward Hanlon
Thomas Lynch
James O'Rourke
Daniel Topping
George Weiss

Delaware (3)

Robert Carpenter, Jr.
John McMahon
Victor Willis

District of Columbia (3)

Paul Hines
Guy White
Maurice Wills

Florida (9)

Steven Carlton
Andre Dawson
Steve Garvey
E. Victor Harris
John Lloyd
Alfred Lopez
Richard Lundy
Harold McRae
John Wesley Powell

Georgia (10)

Spurgeon Chandler
Tyrus Cobb
Herbert Dixon
Joshua Gibson
John Mize

Wallace Moses
Richard Redding
Jack Robinson
William Terry
Fred Walker

Idaho (1)

Harmon Killebrew

Illinois (33)

Albert Barlick
Edward Barrow
Richard Bartell
Walter Berger
James Bottomley
Louis Boudreau
Philip Cavaretta
Charles Comiskey
John Conlan
Michael Donlin
Lawrence Doyle
William Eckert
William Evans
Warren Giles
William Harridge
Rickey Henderson
William Jacobson
Samuel Jethroe
Theodore Kluszewski
Emil Leonard
Frederick Lindstrom
Herman Long
Fredric Lynn
Joseph McGinnity
John Joseph Powell
Robin Roberts
Charles Ruffing
Raymond Schalk
Albert Schoendienst
Albert Spalding
William Veeck, Jr.
Philip Wrigley
Robin Yount

Indiana (17)

Charles Adams
Mordecai Brown
Max Carey

Oscar Charleston
George Dauss
Frederick Fitzsimmons
Ford Frick
William Herman
Gilbert Hodges
Thomas John
Charles Klein
Arthur Nehf
Edgar Rice
Edd Roush
Amos Rusie
Samuel Thompson
Fred Williams

Iowa (12)

Adrian Anson
David Bancroft
Fred Clarke
John Coombs
Urban Faber
Robert Feller
Calvin McVey
Edmund Miller
Harold Trosky
Arthur Vance
Earl Whitehill
James L. Wilkinson

Kansas (4)

Elwood De Moss
Ralph Houk
Walter Johnson
Joseph Tinker

Kentucky (15)

John Beckwith
Louis Browning
James Bunning
Albert Chandler
Earle Combs
Paul Derringer
Samuel Hughes
Carl Mays
Harry Pulliam
Harold Reese
Vernon Stephens
Jesse Tannehill

Clinton Thomas
Robert Veach
August Weyhing

Louisiana (11)

Joseph Adcock
Vida Blue
Willard Brown
William Dickey
Ronald Guidry
Theodore Lyons
Oliver Marcelle
Melvin Ott
Carl Reginald Smith
Daniel Staub
George Suttles

Maine (1)

Lewis Sockalexis

Maryland (11)

John Franklin Baker
Clarence Childs
David Foutz
James Foxx
Robert Grove
William Johnson
Albert Kaline
Bowie Kuhn
Robert Mathews
Edwin Rommel
George Herman Ruth

Massachusetts (18)

Charles Buffinton
John Chesbro
John Clarkson
Gordon Cochrane
William Cummings
William Donovan
Leo Durocher
Frank Grant
Timothy Keefe
Joseph Kelley
Thomas McCarthy
John McInnis
Connie Mack
Walter Maranville

Wilbert Robinson
James Ryan
Fred Tenney
Harold Traynor

Michigan (16)

Walter Briggs
Edward Cicotte
Hazen Cuyler
John Fournier
Charles Gehringer
James Kaat
John McHale
Leland MacPhail, Sr.
Charles Myer
Frank Navin
Harold Newhouser
Milton Pappas
Walter William Pierce
Edward Reulbach
Ted Simmons
Thomas Yawkey

Minnesota (4)

Charles Bender
Jerome Koosman
Roger Maris
David Winfield

Mississippi (3)

James Bell
David Parker
Gerald Walker

Missouri (19)

Jacob Beckley
Lawrence Berra
Kenton Boyer
August Busch, Jr.
John Crutchfield
James Galvin
Clark Griffith
Charles Grimm
Carl Hubbell
Charles King
John Kling
Albert Orth
Charles Stengel

John Tobin
George Van Haltren
Earl Weaver
Richard Williams
Joe Wood
Forrest Glenn Wright

Montana (1)

David McNally

Nebraska (6)

Grover Cleveland Alexander
Don Richie Ashburn
Samuel Crawford
Robert Gibson
Melvin Harder
William Southworth

New Hampshire (1)

Frank Selee

New Jersey (10)

Roger Cramer
Charles Feeney
Leon Goslin
William Hamilton
Charles Jamieson
Joseph Medwick
Donald Newcombe
Charles and Horace Stoneham
Michael Tiernan

New Mexico (2)

Ralph Kiner
Vernon Stephens

New York (59)

Roscoe Barnes
Sam Breadon
Dennis Brouthers
George J. Burns
Alexander Cartwright
Rocco Colavito
Edward Collins
James Collins
Lawrence Corcoran
James Creighton
William Dahlen

George Davis
Herman Davis
Charles Ebbets
John Evers
ElRoy Face
Edward Ford
John Fowler
Andrew Freedman
Frank Frisch
Henry Louis Gehrig
Henry Greenberg
Michael Griffin
Henry Groh
Stanley Harris
Floyd Herman
John Heydler
Thomas Holmes
Waite Hoyt
William Hulbert
Joseph Judge
William Keeler
Michael Kelly
William Klem
Sanford Koufax
Thomas Leach
Frank McCormick
John McGraw
John McPhee
Marvin Miller
Walter O'Malley
David Orr
James Palmer
Gabe Paul
Richard Pearce
Charles Radbourne
Philip Rizzuto
Jacob Ruppert
James Seymour
Kenneth Singleton
Warren Spahn
Joseph Start
Joseph Torre
Michael Welch
James White
William White
George Wright
Carl Yastrzemski
Nicholas Young

North Carolina (11)

Lucius Appling
Richard Ferrell
Wesley Ferrell
William A. Greenlee
James Hunter
Walter Leonard
Gaylord Perry
James Perry
Enos Slaughter
Charles I. Taylor
James Hoyt Wilhelm

Ohio (38)

Walter Alston
Roger Bresnahan
George H. Burns
Powel Crosley, Jr.
Edward Delahanty
William Ewing
Roland Fingers
Elmer Flick
John W. and Daniel Galbreath
Jesse Haines
Frank Howard
William Hoy
Miller Huggins
Byron Johnson
Grant Johnson
Samuel Jones
Joseph Kuhel
Kenesaw Mountain Landis
Samuel Leever
Edward McKean
Richard Marquard
George Mullin
Joseph Niekro
Philip Niekro
Albert Oliver
Wesley Branch Rickey
Charles Root
Peter Rose
Michael Schmidt
George Sisler
Charles Somers
George Trautman
George Uhle

Joseph Vosmik
Moses Walker
Zachariah Wheat
Denton Young

Oklahoma (11)

Johnny Bench
Alvin Dark
Robert Johnson
Lyndall McDaniel
Mickey Mantle
Johnny Martin
Allie Reynolds
Wilbur Rogan
Wilver Stargell
Lloyd Waner
Paul Waner

Oregon (4)

Michael Lolich
Dale Murphy
John Pesky
Kenneth Williams

Pennsylvania (35)

Richard Allen
David Bell
Roy Campanella
Stanley Coveleski
Jacob Daubert
James Dykes
Delmer Ennis
Nelson Fox
Reginald Jackson
Hugh Jennings
Albert Lyle
Joseph McCarthy
William McKechnie
Sherwood Magee
Christopher Mathewson
Levi Meyerle
Stanley Musial
Herbert Pennock
Edward Plank
Cumberland Posey
John Quinn
James Robert Shawkey
Samuel James Sheckard

Benjamin Shibe
John Stivetts
Harry Stovey
Howard Bruce Sutter
James Vernon
George Waddell
John Wagner
Roderick Wallace
Edward Walsh
William Walters
John Ward
Lewis Wilson

Rhode Island (3)

Hugh Duffy
Charles Hartnett
Napoleon Lajoie

South Carolina (7)

Lawrence Doby
Joseph Jackson
Martin Marion
Derrill Pratt
James Rice
Charles Smith
Benjamin Taylor

South Dakota (1)

George Anderson

Tennessee (8)

Thomas Bridges
Robert Caruthers
William Benjamin Chapman
Leland MacPhail, Jr.
Bill Madlock, Jr.
Jesse Clyde Milan
Vada Pinson
Norman Stearns

Texas (22)

Newton Allen
Ernest Banks
Norman Cash
Cecil Cooper
Curtis Flood
Andrew Foster
Willie Foster

Michael Higgins
Rogers Hornsby
Raleigh Mackey
Edwin Mathews, Jr.
Joseph Morgan
Frank Robinson
James Runnels
Lynn Nolan Ryan
Louis Santop
Hilton Smith
Tristram Speaker
James Vaughn
Willie Wells
Joe Williams
Ross Youngs

Vermont (2)

Carlton Fisk
William Lawrence Gardner

Virginia (7)

Raymond Dandridge
Leon Day
Willie Horton
Charles Phillippe
Spottswood Poles
Eppa Rixey
Ernest Judson Wilson

Washington (3)

Earl Averill
Robert Brown
Ronald Santo

West Virginia (7)

Ernest Barnard
George Brett
Selva Lewis Burdette
Jesse Burkett
Arley Wilbur Cooper
John Glasscock
William Mazeroski

Wisconsin (8)

Clarence Beaumont
Lafayette Cross

Burleigh Grimes
Adrian Joss
Edward Konetchy
Harvey Kuenn
Charles Nichols
Aloysius Simmons

Puerto Rico (2)

Orlando Cepeda
Roberto Clemente

FOREIGN NATIONS

Canada (1)

Calvin Griffith

Cuba (1)

Martin Dihigo

Dominican Republic (1)

Juan Marichal

England (4)

Henry Chadwick
Thomas Connolly
Alfred Reach
Harry Wright

Germany (2)

Barney Dreyfuss
Christian Von der Ahe

Ireland (4)

Thomas Bond
Patrick Donovan
Anthony Mullane
John Tener

Panama (1)

Rodney Carew

Scotland (1)

James McCormick

Venezuela (1)

Luis Aparicio, Jr.

APPENDIX 4

Negro League Baseball Entries

The following is a list of the baseball figures profiled in the book who spent all or most of their professional baseball careers in the Negro leagues.

Newton Allen
John Beckwith
James Bell
Willard Brown
Oscar Charleston
John Crutchfield
Raymond Dandridge
Leon Day
Elwood De Moss
Martin Dihigo
Herbert Dixon
Andrew Foster
Willie Foster
John Fowler
Joshua Gibson
Frank Grant
William A. Greenlee
E. Victor Harris
J. Preston Hill
Sammy Hughes
Grant Johnson
William Johson
Walter Leonard

John Lloyd
Richard Lundy
James Lyons
Raleigh Mackey
Oliver Marcelle
Leroy Paige
Spottswood Poles
Cumberland Posey
Richard Redding
Wilbur Rogan
Louis Santop
Charles Smith
Hilton Smith
Norman Stearns
George Suttles
Benjamin Taylor
Charles I. Taylor
Clinton Thomas
Willie Wells
James L. Wilkinson
Joe Williams
Ernest Judson Wilson

Major and Negro Leagues

The following is a list of the major leagues and Negro leagues in chronological order of their establishment, with the year(s) they were in operation. Major leagues have operated since 1871, while the Negro leagues existed approximately from 1920 to 1950. The National League and American League are the only professional major leagues still in operation.

Professional Major Leagues

National Association (1871–1875)
National League (1876-)
American Association (1882–1891)
Union Association (1884)
Players League (1890)
American League (1901-)
Federal League (1914–1915)

Negro Leagues

Negro National League (1920–1931,
  1933–1948)
Eastern Colored League (1923–1928)
American Negro League (1929)
Negro Southern League (1932)
East-West League (1932)
Negro American League (1937–1950)
Negro National League (1920–1931,
  1933–1948)

APPENDIX 6

National Baseball Hall of Fame Members

Many baseball figures included in this book have been elected to the National Baseball Hall of Fame in Cooperstown, New York. As of 1986, the National Baseball Hall of Fame consisted of 199 members, including 16 first basemen, 9 second basemen, 8 third basemen, 15 shortstops, 50 outfielders, 10 catchers, 46 pitchers, 10 Negro league players, 10 managers, 5 umpires, and 20 pioneers and executives. Through 1986, the National Baseball Hall of Fame members are:

Henry Aaron
Grover Cleveland Alexander
Walter Alston
Adrian Anson
Luis Aparicio, Jr.
Lucius Appling
H. Earl Averill
J. Franklin Baker
David Bancroft
Ernest Banks
Edward Barrow
Jacob Beckley
James Bell
Charles Bender
Lawrence Berra
James Bottomley
Louis Boudreau
Roger Bresnahan
Louis Brock
Dennis Brouthers
Mordecai Brown
Morgan Bulkeley
Jesse Burkett
Roy Campanella
Max Carey
Alexander Cartwright

Henry Chadwick
Frank Chance
Albert Chandler
Oscar Charleston
John Chesbro
Fred Clarke
John Clarkson
Roberto Clemente
Tyrus Cobb
Gordon Cochrane
Edward Collins
James Collins
Earle Combs
Charles Comiskey
John Conlan
Thomas Connolly
Roger Connor
Stanley Coveleski
Samuel Crawford
Joseph Cronin
William Cummings
Hazen Cuyler
Raymond Dandridge
Jay Dean
Edward Delahanty
William Dickey

Martin Dihigo
Joseph DiMaggio
Robert Doerr
Don Drysdale
Hugh Duffy
William Evans
John Evers
William Ewing
Urban Faber
Robert Feller
Richard Ferrell
Elmer Flick
Edward Ford
Andrew Foster
James Foxx
Ford Frick
Frank Frisch
James Galvin
Henry Louis Gehrig
Charles Gehringer
Joshua Gibson
Robert Gibson
Warren Giles
Vernon Gomez
Leon Goslin
Henry Greenberg
Clark Griffith
Burleigh Grimes
Robert Grove
Charles Hafey
Jesse Haines
William Hamilton
William Harridge
Stanley Harris
Charles Hartnett
Harry Heilmann
William Herman
Harry Hooper
Rogers Hornsby
Waite Hoyt
R. Cal Hubbard†
Carl Hubbell
Miller Huggins
James Hunter
Monford Irvin
Travis Jackson
Hugh Jennings
Byron Johnson

Walter Johnson
William Johnson
Adrian Joss
Albert Kaline
Timothy Keefe
William Keeler
George Kell
Joseph Kelley
George Kelly
Michael Kelly
Harmon Killebrew
Ralph Kiner
Charles Klein
William Klem
Sanford Koufax
Napoleon Lajoie
Kenesaw Mountain Landis
Robert Lemon
Walter Leonard
Frederick Lindstrom
John Lloyd
Ernest Lombardi
Alfonso Lopez
Theodore Lyons
Joseph McCarthy
Thomas McCarthy
Willie McCovey
Joseph McGinnity
John McGraw
Connie Mack
Leland MacPhail, Sr.
Mickey Mantle
Henry Manush
Walter Maranville
Juan Marichal
Richard Marquard
Edwin Mathews, Jr.
Christopher Mathewson
Willie Mays
Joseph Medwick
John Mize
Stanley Musial
Charles Nichols
James O'Rourke
Melvin Ott
Leroy Paige
Herbert Pennock
Edward Plank

Charles Radbourne
Harold Reese
Edgar Rice
Wesley Branch Rickey
Eppa Rixey
Robin Roberts
Brooks Robinson
Frank Robinson
Jack Robinson
Wilbert Robinson
Edd Roush
Charles Ruffing
Amos Rusie
George Herman Ruth
Raymond Schalk
Joseph Sewell
Aloysius Simmons
George Sisler
Enos Slaughter
Edwin Snider
Warren Spahn
Albert Spalding
Tristram Speaker
Charles Stengel
William Terry
Samuel Thompson

Joseph Tinker
Harold Traynor
Arthur Vance
Joseph Vaughan
George Waddell
John Wagner
Roderick Wallace
Edward Walsh
Lloyd Waner
Paul Waner
John Ward
George Weiss
Michael Welch
Zachariah Wheat
James Hoyt Wilhelm
Billy Williams
Theodore Williams
Lewis Wilson
George Wright
William H. Wright
Early Wynn
Thomas Yawkey
Denton Young
Ross Youngs

†Included in Football volume

Index

Note: The locations of main entries in the dictionary are indicated in the index by italic page numbers.

Greenlee, William, A., 88, *223–24*, 290, 436, 453

Greensboro, NC, baseball club (CrL, Pil), 179, 376, 403

Greensburg, PA, baseball club (PSA),. 114

Greenville, MI, baseball club (MISL), 195

Greenville, SC, baseball club (SAL, WCL), 115, 313, 497, 574, 583

Greenville, TX, baseball club (ETL), 387

Greenwade, Thomas, 374

Greenwood, SC, baseball club (EDL), 8

Greenwood, SC, baseball club (WCL), 409

Griffey, George Kenneth, 544

Griffin, Michael J., *224–25*

Griffith, Calvin R., Sr., 225, 227–28, 305

Griffith, Clark, 11, 91–92, 160–61, *225–28*, 245, 304, 321, 331, 400, 408, 430, 470, 524, 554, 606

Griffith Stadium, Washington, DC, 213, 318, 453–54

Grimes, Burleigh A., *228–29*

Grimm, Charles J., 29, 41, 114, *229–30*, 246, 573

Groh, Henry, 66, *230–31*, 302, 332

Groh, Lewis C., 231

Grove, Robert M., 101, *231–33*, 241, 359, 401, 437, 444, 453, 468, 634–35

Gruner, G. A., 576

Guidry, Ronald A., *233–34*

Guilford College, 177

Gustine, Frank W., 589

Haas, George W., 163

Haas, Walter J., 181

Hack, Stanley C., 49, *235–36*

Haddock, George S., 160

Hadley, Irving D., 101

Hadley, Kent W., 382

Hafey, Charles J., 40, *236–37*

Haines, Jesse J., 5, *237–38*

Hallman, William W., 600

Hamey, Roy, 75

Hamilton, William R., 143, *238–39*, 617

Hanlon, Edward H., 117, *239–41*, 281, 299, 301, 363, 481

Hannegan, Robert, 45

Hannibal, MO, baseball club (CA), 29

Hano, Arnold, 278

Hanover, PA, baseball club (BRL, CbL), 66, 326

Harder, Melvin L., *241–42*, 630

Harding, Hallie, 6

Harlan, KY, baseball club (ApL), 431

Harrelson, Kenneth S., 182

Harridge, William H., 110, 219, *242–43*

Harris, Chalmer Luman, 12

Harris, David S., 49

Harris, E. Victor, *243–44*, 453

Harris, Joseph, 65

Harris, Stanley R., 226, *244–45*, 469, 535, 606

Harrisburg, PA, baseball club (AtA, EIL, PSL, TSL), 221, 239, 509, 617

Harrisburg, PA, Colored Giants baseball club (ECL), 451, 548

Harrisburg, PA, Giants baseball club (ANL), 30, 150

Harrisburg, PA, Hilldale baseball club (ECL), 88

Harriss, William, J. B., 500

Hart, James, 11

Hartford, CT, baseball club (EL, NECS), 64, 160–61, 210, 222, 258, 266, 279, 358, 525

Hartford, CT, baseball club (NL), 38, 128, 271, 531, 628

Hartford, CT, Dark Blues baseball club (NA), 60, 128

Hartnett, Charles Leo, 146, 230, *245–46*, 562

Hartsel, Tully F., 255

Harvard University, 39, 161, 166, 298, 357, 560

Hastings, NE, baseball club (NSL), 94

Hattiesburg, MS, baseball club (CSL), 456

Hauser, Joseph J., 279

Contributors

William E. Akin, Professor of History and Dean, Ursinus College, Collegeville, PA.

Charles C. Alexander, Professor of History, Ohio University, Athens, OH.

Louis J. Andolino, Associate Professor of Political Science, Rochester Institute of Technology, Rochester, NY.

Sheldon L. Appleton, Professor of Political Science and Associate Dean of College of Arts and Sciences, Oakland University, Rochester, MI.

Alan R. Asnen, Freelance Writer, Columbia, SC.

Terry A. Baxter, Research Analyst, Missouri Public Service Company, lives in Lee's Summit, MO.

Gaymon L. Bennett, Professor of English and Chairman of the Department of English, Northwest Nazarene College, Nampa, ID.

Lowell L. Blaisdell, Professor of History, Texas Tech University, Lubbock, TX.

Stephen D. Bodayla, Head of Department of History and Pre-Law Coordinator, Marycrest College, Davenport, IA.

William A. Borst, Baseball Author and Television Host, resides in St. Louis, MO.

Robert T. Bowen, Jr., Retired Professor of Physical Education, University of Georgia, Athens, GA.

Frank P. Bowles, Associate Professor of English, University of Northern Colorado, Greeley, CO.

Gerald E. Brennan, Bookstore Manager, resides in Chicago, IL.

Robert J. Brown, Associate Professor of History and Political Science, Rochester Institute of Technology, Rochester, NY.

Dennis T. "Tom" Chase, Librarian, resides in Beamont, TX.

Ellery H. Clark, Jr., Baseball Author and Retired Professor of Naval History, U.S. Naval Academy, Annapolis, MD.

L. Robert Davids, Retired Federal Government Public Affairs Officer and Founder of Society for American Baseball Research, lives in Washington, DC.

John E. DiMeglio, Professor of History, Mankato State University, Mankato, MN.

Leslie Eldridge, Librarian, Boise Public Library, and Freelance Writer, resides in Boise, ID.

Bruce Erricson, Field Representative, Independent Research Firm, and Actor, lives in San Diego, CA.

Phillip P. Erwin, Editor-Publisher of *Baseball Insight* and Freelance Writer, lives in Portland, OR.

John L. Evers, Retired High School Teacher and Administrator, resides in Carmi, IL.

Albert J. Figone, Associate Professor and Graduate Coordinator, Department of Physical Education, Humboldt State University, Arcata, CA.

John E. Findling, Professor of History, Indiana University Southeast, New Albany, IN.

Leonard Frey, Professor, Department of Linguistics, San Diego State University, San Diego, CA.

Ronald L. Gabriel, Account Executive, U.S. Government, lives in Chevy Chase, MD.

Cappy Gagnon, Director of Special Programs, Los Angeles Sheriff's Department, and former President of Society for American Baseball Research, resides in Hollywood, CA.

Larry R. Gerlach, Professor of History, University of Utah, Salt Lake City, UT.

James N. Giglio, Professor of History, Southwest Missouri State University, Springfield, MO.

Horace R. Givens, Professor of Business Administration, University of Maine, Orono, ME.

Ralph S. Graber, Professor of English and Director of American Studies Program, Muhlenberg College, Allentown, PA.

Lloyd J. Graybar, Professor of History, Eastern Kentucky University, Richmond, KY.

John Hanners, Associate Professor of Drama and Chairperson, Communication Arts/Theatre Department, Allegheny College, Meadville, PA.

James W. Harper, Associate Professor of History, Texas Tech University, Lubbock, TX.

John David Healy resides in Washington, DC.

George W. Hilton, Professor of Economics, University of California at Los Angeles, CA.

John B. Holway, Writer and Baseball Author, lives in Alexandria, VA.

Allen E. Hye, Associate Professor of German, Wright State University, Dayton, OH.

Frederick Ivor-Campbell, Writer and former English Professor, University of Rhode Island and The King's College, resides in Warren, RI.

William Ivory, Writer and Baseball Coach at St. Albans, resides in Washington, DC.

Harry A. Jebsen, Jr., Dean, College of Arts and Sciences, Capital University, Columbus, OH.

Robert E. Jones, Research Analyst, lives in Aumsville, OR.

Thomas D. Jozwik, Insurance Inspector and a Director of the Society for American Baseball Research, resides in Milwaukee, WI.

Thomas L. Karnes, Professor of History and former Chairman, Department of History, Arizona State University, Tempe, AZ.

Gene Karst, Retired Baseball Publicity Director and Baseball Writer, lives in Branson, MO.

Brian R. Kelleher, Publicist in Press Relations, resides in Saratoga, NY.

Joseph E. King, Professor of History, Center for History of Engineering and Technology, Texas Tech University, Lubbock, TX.

Merl F. Kleinknecht works for the U.S. Postal Service and lives in Galion, OH.

Dan E. Krueckeberg, Writer and Consultant, resides in Webster Groves, MO.

Raymond D. Kush, Software Documentation Supervisor, lives in Minneapolis, MN.

Tony Ladd, Professor, Lifetime Fitness Center, Wheaton College, Wheaton, IL.

Joseph Lawler (Nicoteri), Librarian, University of Rhode Island, Kingston, RI.

Mary Lou LeCompte, Assistant Professor, Physical and Health Education, University of Texas, Austin, TX.

B. Randolph Linthurst, Public Information Director, State of New Jersey, and Baseball Author, resides in West Trenton, NJ.

Jack P. Lipton, Department of Psychology, University of Arizona, Tucson, AZ.

Carl Lundquist, Author, former Wire Services Sportswriter and Promoter for Minor League Baseball, lives in Westbury, NY.

Arthur F. McClure, Professor of History and Anthropology and Chairman, Department of History, Central Missouri State University, Warrensburg, MO.

Gordon B. McKinney, Professor of History, Western Carolina University, Cullowhee, NC.

Douglas D. Martin, Professor of History, Towson State University, Towson, MD.

David S. Matz, Professor, Department of Classical Languages, St. Bonaventure University, St. Bonaventure, NY.

David B. Merrell, Dean, College of Liberal and Fine Arts, and Chairman, Department of English, Abilene Christian University, Abilene, TX.

Charles R. Middleton, Associate Dean, College of Arts and Sciences, University of Colorado, Boulder, CO.

William J. Miller, Associate Professor of History, St. Louis University, St. Louis, MO.

Eugene C. Murdock, Baseball Author, Professor of History, Marietta College, Marietta, OH.

Clark Nardinelli, Assistant Professor of Economics, Clemson University, Clemson, SC.

John E. Neville, Instructor, Health and Physical Education Department, Youngstown State University, Youngstown, OH.

Douglas A. Noverr, Professor, Department of American Thought and Language, Michigan State University, East Lansing, MI.

Frank J. Olmsted, Theology Teacher, De Smet Jesuit High School, St. Louis, MO.

Joseph M. Overfield, Baseball Author, Vice-President of Monroe Abstract & Title, resides in Tonawanda, NY.

Anthony J. Papalas, Associate Professor of History, East Carolina University, Greenville, NC.

Robert W. Peterson, Freelance Writer and Editor, lives in Ramsey, NJ.

Frank V. Phelps, Retired Group Insurance Agent, resides in King of Prussia, PA.

David L. Porter, Louis Tuttle Shangle Professor of History and Political Science, William Penn College, Oskaloosa, IA.

Kevin R. Porter, Student, resides in Oskaloosa, IA.

Donald J. Proctor, Professor, University of Michigan-Dearborn, resides in Dearborn, MI.

Samuel John Regalado, Department of History, Washington State University, Pullman, WA.

Steven A. Riess, Associate Professor of History, Northeastern Illinois University, Chicago, IL, and Editor, *Journal of Sport History*.

James A. Riley, Teacher and Author, resides in Rockledge, FL.

John P. Rossi, Professor, Department of History, LaSalle University, Philadelphia, PA.

Emil H. Rothe, Retired Teacher and High School Administrator, Chicago, IL.

Robert L. Ruck, Assistant Professor of History, Chatham College, Pittsburgh, PA.

Mark D. Rucker, Artist, resides in Sarasota Springs, NY.

Steven P. Savage, Professor, Department of Anthropology and Sociology, Eastern Kentucky University, Richmond, KY.

Eric C. Schneider, Program Associate, Delaware Humanities Forum, Wilmington, DE.

William J. Serow, Professor, Department of Economics, Florida State University, Tallahassee, FL.

Fred M. Shelley, Assistant Professor of Geography, University of Southern California, Los Angeles, CA.

William M. Simons, Assistant Professor, SUNY College at Oneonta, Oneonta, NY.

Douglas G. Simpson, High School English and Journalism Teacher, Issaquah, WA.

James K. Skipper, Jr., Professor of Sociology, Virginia Polytechnic Institute and State University, Blacksburg, VA.

Duane A. Smith, Teacher, Historian, and Writer, Fort Lewis College, Durango, CO.

James D. Smith III, Pastor, Elim Baptist Church, Minneapolis, MN.

Leverett T. Smith, Jr., Jefferson-Pilot Professor of English, North Carolina Wesleyan College, Rocky Mount, NC.

Eric Solomon, Teacher, San Francisco State University, San Francisco, CA.

Luther W. Spoehr, Teacher and Writer, resides in Providence, RI.

Jack R. Stanton, Journalist, Broadcaster, and Freelance Writer, resides in Minneapolis, MN.

Fred Stein, Environmental Consultant and Baseball Author, lives in Springfield, VA.

A. D. Suehsdorf, Retired Writer and Editor, resides in Sonoma, CA.

William A. Sutton, Professor, Department of Sport Management, Ohio State University, Columbus, OH.

Robert B. Van Atta, Public Relations Management, resides in Greensburg, PA.

David Quentin Voigt, Baseball Author and Professor of Sociology, Albright College, Reading, PA.

Edward J. Walsh, Professor of English, Slippery Rock University, Slippery Rock, PA.

Robert G. Weaver, Professor of English, Pennsylvania State University, University Park, PA.

David W. Zang, Instructor, Department of Physical Education, University of Maryland, College Park, MD.

Lawrence E. Ziewacz, Assistant Professor, Department of American Thought and Language, Michigan State University, East Lansing, MI.

ABOUT THE EDITOR

DAVID L. PORTER is Louis Tuttle Shangle Professor of History and Political Science at William Penn College in Oskaloosa, Iowa. He is the author of *The Seventy-Sixth Congress and World War II, 1939–1940* and *Congress and the Waning of the New Deal*, as well as numerous articles. His articles have appeared in such journals as *The North American Society for Sport History Proceedings*, *The Society for American Baseball Research Review of Books*, *American Heritage*, *Senate History*, *The Palimpsest*, *American Historical Assocation Perspectives*, and *Midwest Review* and in such books as *The Book of Lists #3*, *The Hero in Transition*, and *Sport History*.